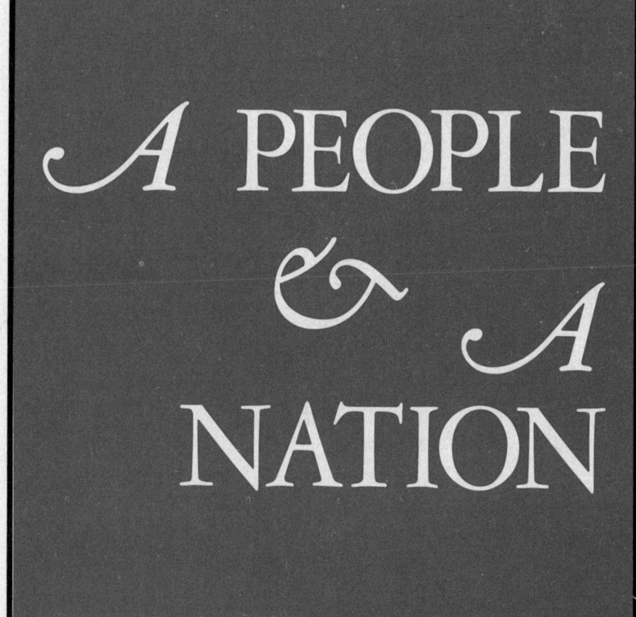
A PEOPLE
& A
NATION

MARY BETH NORTON
Cornell University
DAVID M. KATZMAN
University of Kansas
PAUL D. ESCOTT
University of North Carolina, Charlotte
HOWARD P. CHUDACOFF
Brown University
THOMAS G. PATERSON
University of Connecticut
WILLIAM M. TUTTLE, JR.
University of Kansas

HOUGHTON MIFFLIN COMPANY BOSTON

Dallas Geneva, Illinois Hopewell, New Jersey Palo Alto

A PEOPLE & A NATION

A HISTORY OF THE UNITED STATES

Complete Edition

Printed in the U.S.A.
Library of Congress Catalog Card Number: 81-81318
ISBN: 0-395-29090-2

Cover photo: *Stone City, Iowa.* Oil on masonite.
By Grant Wood (1892–1942).
Joslyn Art Museum, Omaha, Nebraska.

Chapter Openers

Chapter 1
Tenochtitlan. The American Museum of Natural History.

Chapter 2
Indigo culture. William R. Perkins Library, Duke University.

Chapter 3
"The Fishing Lady." Museum of Fine Arts, Boston, Seth K. Sweetser Fund.

Chapter 4
British troops on the Boston Common, 1768. Boston Athenaeum.

Chapter 5
The Battle of Lexington. The Connecticut Historical Society.

Chapter 6
Washington presiding over debate at the Constitutional Convention. The Library Company of Philadelphia.

Chapter 7
Salute to General Washington in New York Harbor. National Gallery of Art, Gift of Edgar William and Bernice Chrysler Garbisch.

Chapter 8
Washington, D.C., in 1800. Library of Congress.

Chapter 9
The Erie Canal. The New-York Historical Society.

Chapter 10
Slaves returning from the fields. The New-York Historical Society.

Chapter 11
Farmers at Dennison Hill, Southbridge, Massachusetts (artist unknown). National Gallery of Art, Gift of Edgar William and Bernice Chrysler Garbisch.

Chapter 12
Antislavery rally (1841). Library of Congress.

Chapter 13
"The Eagle's Nest." The Connecticut Historical Society.

Chapter 14
Army of the Potomac. National Archives.

Chapter 15
Richmond, Virginia, following the Civil War. National Archives.

Chapter 16
Chow hall in a Minnesota lumber camp, 1890s. State Historical Society of Wisconsin.

Chapter 17
National Cash Register Company. Library of Congress.

Chapter 18
Chicago. Chicago Historical Society.

Chapter 19
Main floor of the Pegues-Wright Department Store in Junction City, Kansas, 1906. Joseph J. Pennell Collection, Kansas Collection, University of Kansas Libraries.

Chapter 20
Republican National Convention, Chicago, 1880. From *Harper's Weekly,* June 19, 1880. Library of Congress.

Chapter 21
Visiting nurse making the rounds in New York City, about 1910. Brown Brothers.

Chapter 22
U.S. battleships return in triumph from the Spanish-American War. Painted by Fred Pansing. Museum of the City of New York.

Chapter 23
Makeshift orderly room on a battlefield in France, First World War. National Archives.

Chapter 24
Filling station in New York City. Brown Brothers.

Chapter 25
Depression era bread line. Margaret Bourke-White, *Life* Magazine © Time Inc.

Chapter 26
Migrant labor camp. Photographed by Dorothea Lange. The Oakland Museum.

Chapter 27
President Franklin D. Roosevelt reviewing the fleet, 1934. UPI (Acme).

Chapter 28
Atomic test on Bikini Island, July 1946. National Archives.

Chapter 29
Assembly line at Douglas Aircraft plant. National Archives.

Chapter 30
Senator Joseph McCarthy warning of Communist party strength. UPI.

Chapter 31
Middle-class family with its suburban house and custom Ford sedan. UPI.

Chapter 32
Mob threatens Vice President Nixon's car in Caracas, Venezuela, 1958. UPI.

Chapter 33
Police attack civil rights demonstrators in Birmingham, Alabama, 1963. Charles Moore / Black Star.

Chapter 34
The House Judiciary committee following their vote to recommend impeachment of President Nixon, July 1974. Photo J. P. Laffont / Sygma.

Map Credits

Page 62
Non-English White Settlements 1775, Black Population, c. 1775, in *Atlas of Early American History: The Revolutionary Era 1760–1790,* by Lester J. Cappon et al. (copyright © 1976 by Princeton University Press), published for the Newberry Library and the Institute of Early American History and Culture, pp. 24 and 25. Reprinted by permission of Princeton University Press.

Page 97
Stamp Act Crisis, in *Atlas of Early American History: The Revolutionary Era 1760–1790,* by Lester J. Cappon et al. (copyright © 1976 by Princeton University Press), published for the Newberry Library and the Institute of Early American History and Culture, p. 42. Reprinted by permission of Princeton University Press.

Page 147
Cession of Indian Lands to U.S., 1775–1790, in *Atlas of Early American History: The Revolutionary Era 1760–1790,* by Lester J. Cappon et al. (copyright © 1976 by Princeton University Press), published for the Newberry Library and the Institute of Early American History and Culture, p. 61. Reprinted by permission of Princeton University Press.

Page 188
1790 Black Population: Proportion of Total Population, in *Atlas of Early American History: The Revolutionary Era 1760–1790,* by Lester J. Cappon et al. (copyright © 1976 by Princeton University Press), published for the Newberry Library and the Institute of Early American History and Culture, p. 67. Reprinted by permission of Princeton University Press.

Page 371
The War in the West, 1861–July 1863, from *The Essentials of American History,* Second Edition, by Richard N. Current, T. Harry Williams and Frank Freidel. Copyright © 1976 by Alfred A. Knopf, Inc. Copyright © 1959, 1961, 1964, 1966, 1971, 1972 by Richard N. Current, T. Harry Williams and Frank Freidel. Reprinted by permission of Alfred A. Knopf, Inc.

CONTENTS

3 ~ COLONIAL SOCIETY AT MIDCENTURY

4 ~ SEVERING THE BONDS OF EMPIRE, 1754–1774

5 ~ A REVOLUTION, INDEED, 1775–1783

6 ☙ FORGING A NATIONAL REPUBLIC, 1776–1789

7 ☙ POLITICS AND SOCIETY IN THE EARLY REPUBLIC, 1790–1800

8 ☙ THE REPUBLIC ENDURES, 1801–1824

9 ~ THE ECONOMIC EVOLUTION OF THE NORTH AND WEST, 1800–1860

10 ~ SLAVERY AND THE GROWTH OF THE SOUTH, 1800–1860

11 ~ THE AMERICAN SCENE, 1800–1860

12 ~ REFORM, POLITICS, AND EXPANSION, 1824–1848

13 ~ THE UNION IN CRISIS: THE 1850s

14 ~ TRANSFORMING FIRE: THE CIVIL WAR, 1860–1865

15 ~ RECONSTRUCTION BY TRIAL AND ERROR, 1865–1877

16 ~ TRANSFORMATION OF THE WEST AND SOUTH, 1877–1892

17 ~ THE MACHINE AGE, 1877–1920

18 ~ THE FAME AND SHAME OF THE CITIES, 1877–1920

19 ~ EVERYDAY LIFE AND CULTURE, 1877–1920

20 ~ GILDED AGE POLITICS, 1877–1900

21 THE PROGRESSIVE ERA, 1895–1920

22 THE QUEST FOR EMPIRE, 1865–1914

23 AMERICA AT WAR, 1914–1920

27 DIPLOMACY IN A BROKEN WORLD, 1920–1941

28 GLOBAL WARS: SECOND, COLD, AND KOREAN, 1941–1953

29 THE SECOND WORLD WAR AT HOME, 1941–1945

30 COLD WAR POLITICS, 1945–1961

31 LIFE IN THE MIDDLE CLASS, 1945–1970

32 ~ AMERICA IN A REVOLUTIONARY WORLD: FOREIGN POLICY SINCE 1953

33 ~ REFORM, RADICALISM, AND DISAPPOINTED EXPECTATIONS, 1961–1973

34 A DISILLUSIONED PEOPLE: AMERICA SINCE 1973

APPENDIX

INDEX

Maps and Charts

PREFACE

We are always recreating our past, rediscovering the personalities and events that have shaped us, inspired us, or bedeviled us. When we are buffeted by the erratic winds of current affairs, we look back for reassuring precedents. But we do not always find that history is comforting. The past holds much that is disturbing, for the story of a people or a nation—like any story—is never one of unbroken progress. As with our own personal experience, it is both triumphant and tragic, filled with injury as well as healing.

This volume is our recreation of the American past: our rediscovery of its people and of the nation they founded and sustained. Drawing on recent research as well as on seasoned, authoritative works, we have sought to offer a comprehensive book that tells the whole story of American history. Presidential and party politics, congressional legislation, Supreme Court decisions, diplomacy and treaties, wars and foreign interventions, economic patterns, and state and local politics have been the stuff of American history for generations. Into this traditional fabric we have woven social history, broadly defined. We have investigated the history of the majority of Americans—women—and of minorities. And we have sought to illuminate the private side of the American story: work and play; dress and diet; entertainment; family and home life; relationships between men and women; and race, ethnicity, and religion. From the ordinary to the exceptional—the steelworker, the office secretary, the plantation owner, the slave, the ward politician, the president's wife, the actress, the canal builder—Americans have had personal stories that have intersected with the public policies of their government. Whether victors or victims, dominant or dominated, all have been actors in their own right, with feelings, ideas, and aspirations that have fortified them in good times and bad. All are part of the American story.

Several questions guided our telling of this intricate narrative. On the official, or public, side of

Major themes

American history, we have sought to identify Americans' expectations of their government, to show who governs and how power is exercised, to explain the origins of reform movements, and to compare the everyday practice of government and politics with the egalitarian principles to which Americans theoretically subscribe. We have looked at the domestic sources of foreign policy and at the reasons why the United States has chosen to intervene abroad or to wage war. We have sought as well to capture the mood or mentality of an era, in which Americans reveal what they think about themselves and their public officials through their letters, music, and literature, their rallies and riots.

In the social and economic spheres, we have emphasized technological development and its effects on the worker and the workplace. We have traced major economic trends. And because geographic mobility is such a striking part of American history, we have given considerable attention to the questions of why people migrate and how they adapt to new environments. The interactions of racially and ethnically diverse people, the social divisions that have resulted and the efforts that have been made to heal them, are also, it seems to us, central to the study of the American past.

In the private domain of the family and the home, we have examined sex roles, childbearing and childrearing, diet and dress. We have attempted to show how public policy and technological development—war and mass production, for example—have forced change on these most basic institutions. Finally, we have asked how Americans have chosen to entertain themselves, as participants or spectators, with sports, music, the graphic arts, reading, theater, film, and television.

Our experience as teachers of American history has shown us that students not only need to address these questions, but can and want to address them. Unfortunately, dull, abstract writing often kills their natural curiosity. Thus we have taken pains to write in clear, concrete language and to include wherever possible the stories of real people, as told in their letters and diaries and in oral histories. We have tried to stimulate readers to think about the meaning of American history—not just to memorize it.

In planning the book, we decided to open each chapter with the true story of an American, ordinary

Structure of the book

or exceptional, whose experience was representative of the times. Following the story we devote a few paragraphs to placing it in historical perspective and introducing the major themes and events of the chapter. Students should find these introductory sections, which in effect provide an overview of the chapters, useful study guides.

We have used boxed glosses to highlight key persons, events, concepts, and trends. Our illustrations, maps, tables, and graphs are closely related to important points in the text. Similarly, the four full-color photographic studies of changing patterns in work and leisure are specifically related to the chapters in which they appear.

Most chapters close with a chronological list of important events, and all chapters end with a bibliography for follow-up reading. In the Appendix we have provided a bibliography of general reference books by subject; important documents; tables of election results, administrations (including Cabinet members), party strength in Congress, justices of the Supreme Court, and territorial acquisitions; and a statistical profile of the American people.

During the long and painstaking course of writing and revision the six of us read and reread one another's work and debated one another across note-strewn tables. In our effort to produce a unified and spirited book, we became friends and better scholars. Though each of us feels answerable for the whole, we take primary responsibility for particular chapters as follows: Mary Beth Norton, Chapters 1–7; David M. Katzman, Chapters 8–9, 11–12; Paul D. Escott, Chapters 10, 13–15; Howard P. Chudacoff, Chapters 16–21, 24; Thomas G. Paterson, Chapters 22–23, 25, 27–28, 32; and William M. Tuttle, Jr., Chapters 26, 29–31, and 33–34.

Acknowledgments

We have been alert to the constructive suggestions of the many teachers and scholars who have read and criticized our manuscript in successive drafts. Their advice has been invaluable, and we are grateful for it:

Robert Abzug, *University of Texas, Austin*
Lois Banner, *George Washington University*
William Barney, *University of North Carolina, Chapel Hill*
Michael C. Batinski, *Southern Illinois University, Carbondale*
Susan Becker, *University of Tennessee, Knoxville*
Barton Bernstein, *Stanford University*
Stephen Botein, *Michigan State University*
Jonathan Chu, *University of Massachusetts, Boston*
Allen Davis, *Temple University*
Peter Filene, *University of North Carolina, Chapel Hill*
Lewis Gould, *University of Texas, Austin*
J. William Harris, *Committee on Degrees in History & Literature, Harvard University*
George Herring, *University of Kentucky, Lexington*
William Holmes, *University of Georgia, Athens*
Michael F. Holt, *University of Virginia, Charlottesville*
Nancy Jaffe, *Riverside City College, California*
Charles Johnson, *University of Tennessee, Knoxville*
Alice Kessler-Harris, *Hofstra University*
Richard Lowitt, *Iowa State University*
George Lubick, *Northern Arizona University*
John G. MacNaughton, *Monroe Community College, Rochester, New York*
Pauline Maier, *Massachusetts Institute of Technology*
Robert Martin, *St. Louis Community College at Florissant Valley*
Arthur F. McClure, *Central Missouri State University*
Russell Menard, *University of Minnesota, Minneapolis*
Eric Monkkonen, *University of California, Los Angeles*
Philip D. Morgan, *Institute of Early American History and Culture, Williamsburg, Virginia*
Jerome Mushkat, *University of Akron*
William O'Neill, *Rutgers The State University of New Jersey, New Brunswick*
George Pilcher, *University of Colorado, Boulder*
Jackson Putnam, *California State University, Fullerton*
Harvard Sitkoff, *University of New Hampshire, Durham*
James Smallwood, *Oklahoma State University*
Sue Taishoff, *University of South Florida, Tampa*
David Thelen, *University of Missouri, Columbia*
John Trickel, *Richland College, Dallas, Texas*
James Turner, *University of Massachusetts, Boston*
Ronald Walters, *Johns Hopkins University*
Darold Wax, *Oregon State University*
William Bruce Wheeler, *University of Tennessee, Knoxville*

We acknowledge with thanks the special contributions of Nancy Chudacoff, Warren I. Cohen, Jeffrey Crow, Gregory DeLapp, Paul Dest, John Emond, Shirley Harmon, Pam Harrison, Chico Herbison, Sharyn A. Katzman, Jean Manter, Sally McMillen, Paula Oliver, Holly Izard Paterson, Roberta Rudgate, and Mary Erickson Tuttle. We also appreciate the guidance and generous assistance of the many members of the staff of Houghton Mifflin Company who worked on the book.

T.G.P.

ABOUT THE AUTHORS

Mary Beth Norton

Now a professor of history at Cornell University, Mary Beth Norton was born in Ann Arbor, Michigan, and received her B.A. from the University of Michigan (1964). Harvard University awarded her the Ph.D. in 1969, the year her dissertation won the Allan Nevins Prize. Her writing includes two books, *The British-Americans: The Loyalist Exiles in England, 1774–1789* (1972) and *Liberty's Daughters: The Revolutionary Experience of American Women, 1750–1800* (1980). With Carol Berkin she has edited a book of original essays, *Women of America: A History* (1979). Mary Beth's articles have appeared in the *William and Mary Quarterly* and in *Signs.* She has been active in the Organization of American Historians' Committee on the Status of Women and the executive committee of the Society of American Historians, and has served on the National Council of the Humanities.

David M. Katzman

David M. Katzman is a professor of history at the University of Kansas, where he directs the college honors program. Born in New York City, he attended Queens College (B.A., 1963) and the University of Michigan (Ph.D., 1969). David won the Philip Taft Labor History Prize for his book *Seven Days a Week: Women and Domestic Service in Industrializing America* (1978) and has received awards from the Guggenheim Foundation, the National Endowment for the Humanities, and the Ford Foundation. He is known for his book *Before the Ghetto: Black Detroit in the Nineteenth Century* (1973) and for his contribution to *Three Generations in Twentieth-Century America: Family, Community and Nation* (Second edition, 1981). With William M. Tuttle, Jr., David has edited *Plain Folk: The Life Stories of Undistinguished Americans* (1981). He has written articles for the *Dictionary of American Biography* and serves as the associate editor of the journal *American Studies.*

Paul D. Escott

A native of St. Louis, Missouri, Paul D. Escott earned his B.A. from Harvard College (1969) and his Ph.D. from Duke University (1974). Now an associate professor of history at the University of North Carolina, Charlotte, he has written two books: *After Secession: Jefferson Davis and the Failure of Confederate Nationalism* (1978) and *Slavery Remembered: A Record of Twentieth-Century Slave Narratives* (1979). Paul's articles have appeared in the *Georgia Historical Quarterly, Civil War History,* and the *Encyclopedia of Southern History* (1979). He is a recipient of the Whitney M. Young, Jr., academic fellowship and the Rockefeller Foundation fellowship.

Howard P. Chudacoff

Born in Omaha, Nebraska, Howard P. Chudacoff received his degrees from the University of Chicago (A.B., 1965; Ph.D., 1969). He is now a professor of history at Brown University, where he has co-chaired the American civilization program. Howard's many articles have appeared in the *Journal of American History* and the *Journal of Family History,* among others. He has published *Mobile Americans: Residential and Social Mobility in Omaha, 1880–1920* (1972) and *The Evolution of American Urban Society* (Second edition, 1981), and has won many awards, including grants from Brown University for curriculum enrichment.

Thomas G. Paterson

Born in Oregon City, Oregon, Thomas G. Paterson graduated from the University of New Hampshire in 1963 and received his Ph.D. from the University of California, Berkeley, in 1968. He is now a professor of history at the University of Connecticut, where he has served as a coordinator of undergraduate studies. His many books include *Soviet-American Confrontation* (1973), *On Every Front: The Making of the Cold War* (1979), and the bestselling textbook *American Foreign Policy: A History* (1977); his articles have appeared in the *American Historical Review, The Nation,* and the *Journal of American History.* Tom has served on the editorial board of the journal *Diplomatic History* and has been elected to the council of the Society for Historians of American Foreign Relations. Recently he has spent his summers directing a National Endowment for the Humanities summer seminar for college teachers.

William M. Tuttle, Jr.

William M. Tuttle, Jr., received his B.A. from Denison University in 1959 and his doctorate from the University of Wisconsin, Madison, in 1967. A native of Detroit, Michigan, he is now a professor of history at the University of Kansas. Bill has written *Race Riot: Chicago in the Red Summer of 1919* (1970) and with David M. Katzman has edited *Plain Folk* (1981). His numerous articles have appeared in the *Journal of Negro History, Labor History, Journal of American History, Phylon,* and *Technology and Culture,* and he has received research assistance from the Guggenheim Foundation, the National Endowment for the Humanities, the Charles Warren Center, and the Harry S Truman Library Institute.

A PEOPLE
&
A
NATION

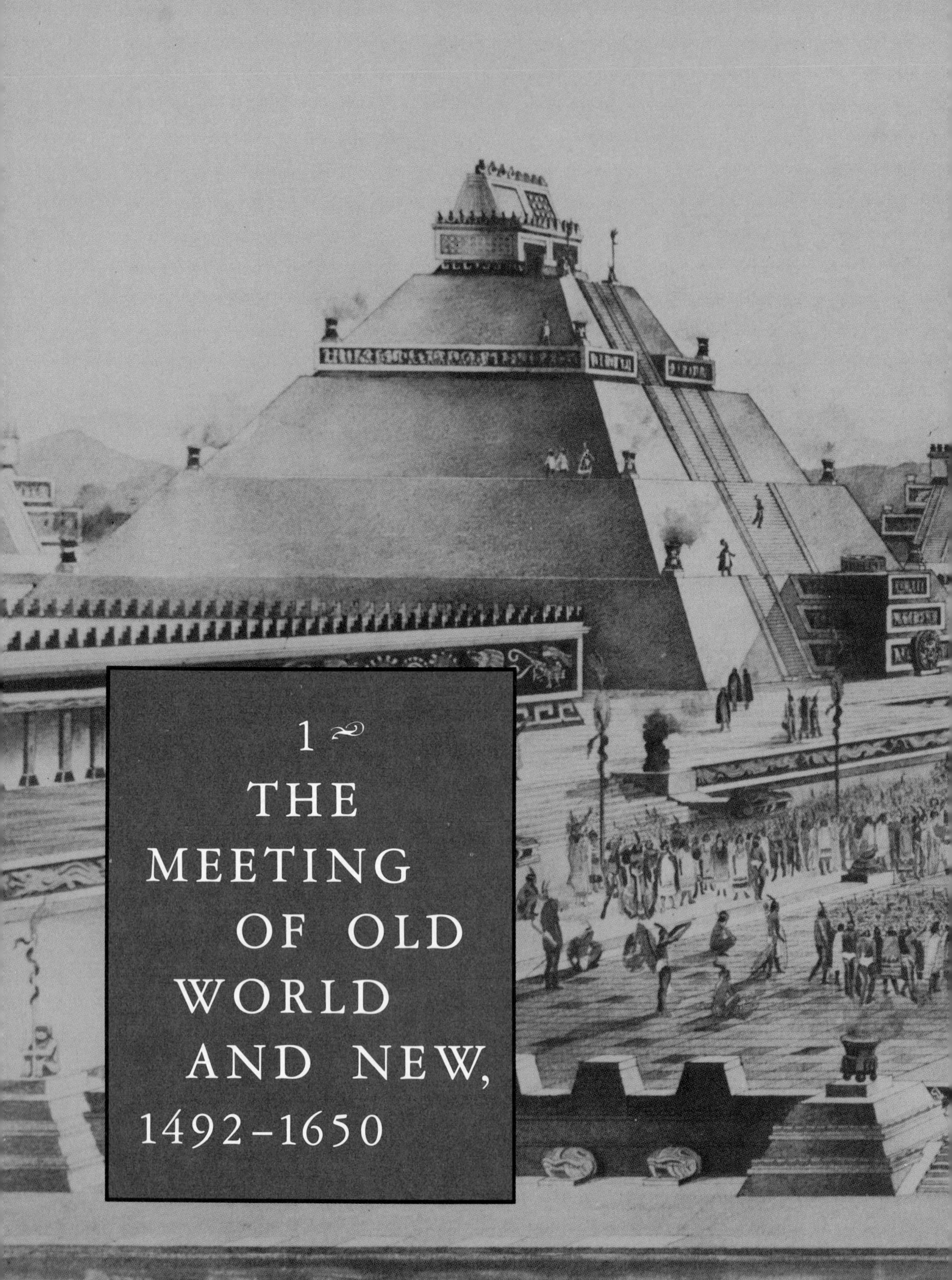

1 THE MEETING OF OLD WORLD AND NEW, 1492–1650

"It spread over the people as great destruction," the old man told the priest. "Some it quite covered [with pustules] on all parts—their faces, their heads, their breasts. . . . There was great havoc. Very many died of it. They could not stir; they could not change position, nor lie on one side, nor face down, nor on their backs. And if they stirred, much did they cry out. Great was its destruction. Covered, mantled with pustules, very many people died of them. And very many starved; there was death from hunger, [for] none could take care of [the sick]; nothing could be done for them."

It was, by European reckoning, September 1520. Spanish troops led by Hernando Cortés had abandoned the Aztec capital of Tenochtitlan after failing in their first attempt to gain control of the city. But they had unknowingly left behind the smallpox germs that would ensure their eventual triumph. By the time the Spaniards returned three months later, the great epidemic described above had fatally weakened Tenochtitlan's inhabitants. Even so, the city held out for months against the Spanish siege. But in the Aztec year Three House, on the day One Serpent (August 1521), Tenochtitlan finally surrendered. The Spaniards had conquered Mexico, and on the site of the Aztec capital they constructed what is now Mexico City.

After many millennia of separation, inhabitants of the Eastern Hemisphere—the so-called Old World—had encountered the residents of the Americas, with catastrophic results for the latter and untold benefits for the former. By the time Spanish troops occupied Tenochtitlan, the age of European expansion and colonization was already well under way. Over the next three hundred and fifty years, Europeans would spread their civilization across the globe. They would come to dominate native peoples in Asia and Africa as well as in the New World. The history of the thirteen tiny English colonies in North America that eventually became the United States must be seen in the broader context of worldwide exploration and exploitation.

Two themes pervade the early history of English settlement in America: the clash of divergent cultures—European and Indian—and the English settlers' adaptation to an alien environment. A latecomer to the New World, England hoped to copy Spanish successes and exploit the New World's rich resources of gold and silver. But the region colonized by the English, the North American coast, had few such resources. As a result, England soon shifted its focus and began to establish agricultural settlements. The colonists' attempts to transplant English ways of life to the New World led to repeated conflicts with the native peoples. For some years the Indians' determination to resist seizure of their lands, coupled with the Europeans' difficulties adjusting to the unfamiliar surroundings, called into question the ultimate survival of the settlements. But by the middle of the seventeenth century English colonies had taken firm root in American soil.

European exploration of America

Christopher Columbus

October 12, 1492, is one of those historical rarities: a well-known date that deserves the significance attributed to it. On that day Christopher Columbus, a forty-one-year-old Genoese sea captain sailing under the flag of the Spanish monarchs Ferdinand and Isabella, landed on a Caribbean island he named San Salvador (one of the Bahamas). He and the three ships under his command—the *Pinta,* the *Niña,* and the *Santa Maria*—had sailed west from Palos, Spain, on August 3, in hopes of reaching China and the East Indies. Until the day he died in 1506, Columbus evidently persisted in believing that he had discovered a new route to the fabled wealth of the Indies. Others knew better even before his death. Columbus did not accomplish his goal, but he changed the dimensions of the known world.

In his own day, Columbus was regarded as something of a crackpot. Like other well-informed men of his time, especially other experienced navigators, Columbus believed the world to be round. (Only ignorant folk still thought it was flat.) Where he differed with most of his contemporaries was in his estimate of its size. Columbus thought that the distance from Portugal to Japan was less than 3,000 miles (it is actually 12,000 miles), and that no land mass lay in his path. Experts scoffed at both assumptions. Thus when Columbus approached the monarchs of France, Portugal, and England in search of support for his planned expedition to China, his proposal was rejected out of hand. But Columbus was obsessed with his idea and persisted in his quest for financial backing for more than a decade. Finally, Queen Isabella of Spain—who rather liked him in spite of his eccentric views—agreed to fund the voyage.

Why was Columbus so intent on finding a route to the East by sailing west? Why was Queen Isabella willing to support him? Most Europeans had lived for centuries in ignorance of the land beyond the western ocean. Only the Norsemen had ventured past Ireland, reaching Iceland (870 A.D.) and Greenland (c. 985 A.D.) and finally, in 1001, under the leadership of Leif Ericsson, encountering a wooded land they called Markland (present-day Labrador). The Norse adventurers established a permanent camp in a region they named Vinland (now identified as L'anse aux Meadows, Newfoundland). But after several attempts to colonize the area, they retreated to Greenland, frightened off by hostile natives. Aside from that single flurry of interest, lasting no more than two decades nearly five hundred years earlier, Europeans had failed to investigate whether there was any truth to the rumors of wealthy lands beyond the seas.

Early Norse explorers

But in the fifteenth century four new developments combined to propel Europeans like Columbus out into the unknown oceans. The first development was purely technical: the invention and refinement of navigational instruments such as the quadrant, which enabled sailors to determine their latitude by measuring the height of the sun and stars above the horizon. The new instruments allowed mariners to spend weeks and months out of sight of land and still have some rough idea of their location. The other three factors—political changes in Europe, the quest for scarce trade goods, and a desire to convert heathen peoples to Christianity—were more complex.

Throughout Europe, the fifteenth century witnessed the consolidation of power and authority in the hands of kings. These political changes were important preconditions for exploration. In England, Henry VII founded the Tudor dynasty and began uniting a land divided for generations by the Wars of the Roses between the houses of York and Lancaster. In France, Francis I similarly established a claim to unchallenged authority. In Spain, Ferdinand and Isabella, rulers of the independent states of Aragon and Castile, married and combined their kingdoms. In 1492, the year Columbus sailed westward, they defeated the Moors and expelled the Jews from their domain, which was now unified under Christian rule for the first time. Only such powerful monarchies could muster the resources necessary to support large-scale colonial enterprises.

The third factor impelling the westward thrust was greed—the desire to find an easy trade route to the East. For centuries Europeans had traded with the Orient via the ports of the eastern Mediterranean (especially Venice and Constantinople) and the long land route across Asia known as the Silk Road. They treasured the valuable and expensive items they obtained from the East: dyes, silk, perfumes, drugs, gold, jewels, and spices, particularly pepper, cinnamon, nutmeg, and cloves. In 1477 the publication of Marco Polo's *Travels*—which had circulated in manuscript for nearly two centuries—stimulated Europeans' interest in China, where Polo had lived for twenty-four years. His report that China was bordered by an ocean on the east helped to convince many, including Christopher Columbus, that that land of fabulous wealth could be reached by ship. It was in hopes of establishing a shorter trade route to China, Japan, and the Spice Islands (the Moluccas) that Columbus chose to sail west from Spain.

Search for a trade route to the East

He was not the first to cherish thoughts of tapping the riches of the Indies directly. During the first half of the fifteenth century, Prince Henry the Navigator, son of King John I of Portugal, had dispatched ship after ship southward along the coast of Africa in an attempt to discover a passage to the East. In 1488, long after Prince Henry's death, Bartholomew Dias first rounded the Cape of Good Hope, and a decade later Vasco da Gama reached India by sailing south around Africa. The Portuguese, then, found what Columbus did not: a usable oceanic trade route to the East.

But Columbus did not realize he had failed, especially on his first voyage. In his logbook and official reports he described the extraordinary beauty and fertility of the islands he had discovered, and commented on the friendliness and gentleness of most of their inhabitants. He insisted that the islands lay close to the Asian mainland and that he could have found vast stores of gold and spices had he had more time to explore. Columbus also expressed his belief that the Indians (as he called the natives, thinking them residents

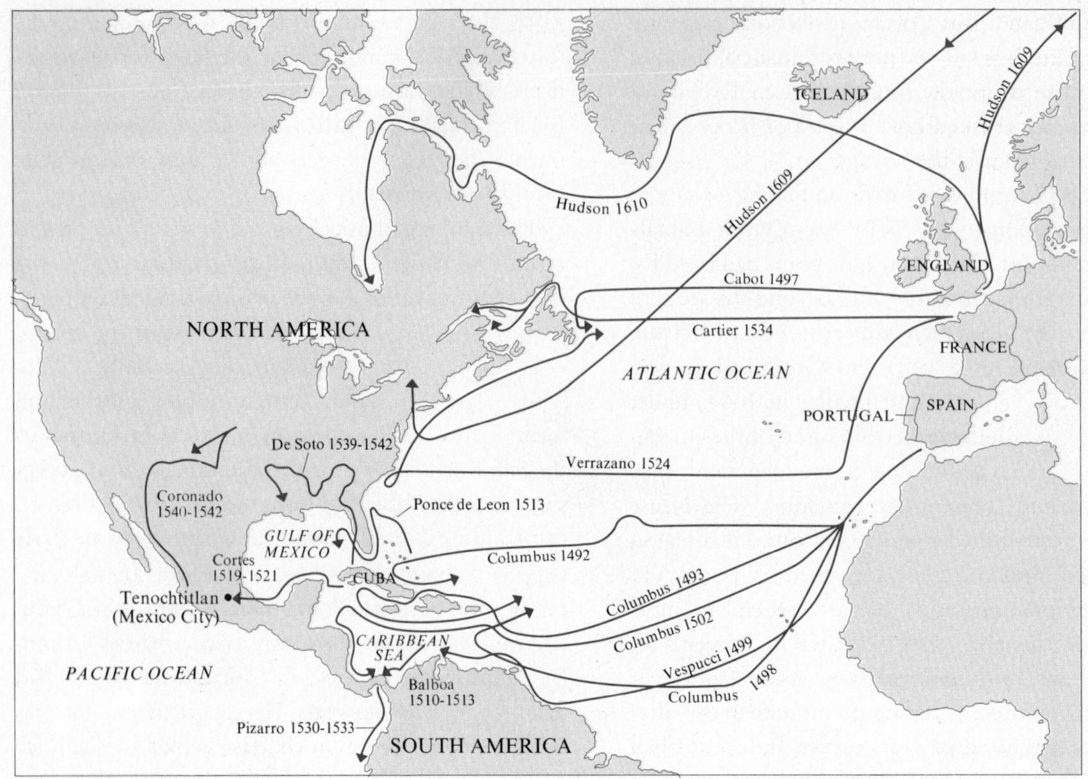

European explorations in America

of the Indies) could easily be converted to Christianity. They would, he predicted, readily become faithful subjects of the Spanish monarchs.

Columbus's prediction arose from the fourth major cause of the fifteenth-century impulse toward exploration: the desire to convert heathen peoples. This motive alone would not have impelled Europeans to sail in search of unknown lands, but it provided them with a spiritual justification for doing so. They were not necessarily being hypocritical. Fifteenth-century Europeans were convinced that Christianity was the only true religion and that it was their duty to spread Jesus Christ's message across the world. If they and their nations became wealthy in the process, so much the better. Most of them saw no conflict between their dual motives.

Columbus made four voyages to the Western Hemisphere, sailing along the coasts of Central and South America and further exploring the Caribbean (see map). In 1497 John Cabot, a Genoese backed by England, rediscovered Newfoundland, the Norse outpost of five centuries earlier. Giovanni da Verrazano, a Florentine dispatched by Francis I, explored the North American coast in 1524. A decade later Jacques Cartier, also sailing for France, found the mouth of the St. Lawrence River and ventured inland as far as the first rapids. By then, everyone realized that a new world had been discovered. Because the first to reach that conclusion in print was Amerigo Vespucci, who had sailed along the coast of the southern continent in 1499, a mapmaker in 1507 labelled the new land *America*.

Most Europeans saw the Americas as a barrier on the route to the Indies, rather than a region to be exploited and colonized. Indeed, both Verrazano and Cartier were looking for the fabled Northwest Passage through the North American continent when they made their voyages of exploration. Long after Ferdinand Magellan (1521–1522) and Francis Drake (1577–1580) circumnavigated the globe, Europeans were still exploring America chiefly in the hope of finding an easy route to China and India.

Only Spain, with its reinvigorated monarchy and belief in Columbus's prediction of vast wealth in the interior of the continent (even if the continent was America rather than Asia), immediately moved to take advantage of the discoveries. On his first voyage, Columbus had established a base on the island of Hispaniola. From there, Spanish explorers fanned out around the Caribbean basin: in 1513, Ponce de Leon reached Florida and Vasco Nuñez de Balboa crossed the Isthmus of Panama to find the Pacific Ocean. Less than ten years later, the Spaniards' dreams of wealth were realized when Cortés conquered the Aztec empire, killing its ruler, Moctezuma, and seizing a fabulous treasure of gold and silver. Venturing northward, conquistadores like Hernando de Soto (who discovered the Mississippi River) and Coronado (who explored the southwestern portion of what is now the United States) found little of value. By contrast, Francisco Pizarro, who explored south along the western coast of South America, conquered and enslaved the Incas in 1535, thus acquiring the richest silver mines in the world. Just half a century after Columbus's first voyage, the Spanish monarchs—who treated the American territories as their personal possessions—controlled the richest, most extensive empire Europe had known since ancient Rome.

Conquistadores

The costs to the New World were extraordinarily high. The conquistadores destroyed sophisticated Indian civilizations that had built huge urban centers, developed a calendar more accurate than the Europeans' own, invented systems of writing and mathematics, and constructed roads, bridges, and irrigation canals. The Spaniards deliberately leveled Indian cities, building cathedrals and monasteries on sites once occupied by Aztec, Incan, and Mayan temples. Just as deliberately, they attempted to erase all vestiges of the great Indian cultures by burning whatever written records they found. As a result, present-day knowledge of the Aztec, Maya, and Inca civilizations rests almost entirely on architectural remains, pottery artifacts, and records left by some of the priests who accompanied the colonizers.

But the greatest destruction wrought by the Europeans—English and French as well as Spanish—was unintended. Diseases carried from the Old World to the New by the alien invaders killed hundreds of thousands, even millions, of native Americans, who had no immunity to germs that had infested Europe, Asia, and Africa for centuries. The greatest killer was smallpox, which was spread by direct human contact. The epidemic that hit Tenochtitlan in 1520 had begun in Hispaniola two years earlier and subsequently spread through Mexico, Central America, and South America. Indeed, the reason Pizarro conquered the Incas so easily was that their society had been devastated by the epidemic shortly before his arrival. Smallpox was not the only villain; influenza, measles, and other diseases added to the destruction.

Effects of disease

The statistics are staggering. When Columbus landed on Hispaniola in 1492, about one million Indians resided there. Fifty years later, only five hundred were still alive. According to the best current estimates, five to ten million Indians inhabited central Mexico before Cortés's invasion. By the end of the century, fewer than one million remained.

Even in the north, where smaller Indian populations encountered only a few European explorers, traders, and fishermen, disease ravaged the countryside. A Frenchman commented early in the seventeenth century that the Canadian Indians were "astonished and often complain that, since the French mingle with them and carry on trade with them, they are dying fast and the population is thinning out." In 1616–1617, four years before the Pilgrims landed at Plymouth to begin the first English settlement north of Virginia, the local tribes suffered greatly from an unknown malady brought by fishermen. One of the English witnesses later wrote that the Indians had "died on heapes, as they lay in their houses. . . . And the bones and skulls upon the severall places of their habitations made such a spectacle upon my coming into those partes, that, as I travailed in the Forrest nere the Massachusetts, it seemed to me a new found Golgotha." As one historian has observed, America was more a widowed land than a virgin one when the English finally settled there.

The Americans, though, took a revenge of sorts. They gave the Europeans a disease previously unknown in the Old World: syphilis. The first recorded case of syphilis in Europe occurred in Barcelona, Spain, in 1493, shortly after Columbus's return from the Caribbean. Although less deadly than smallpox,

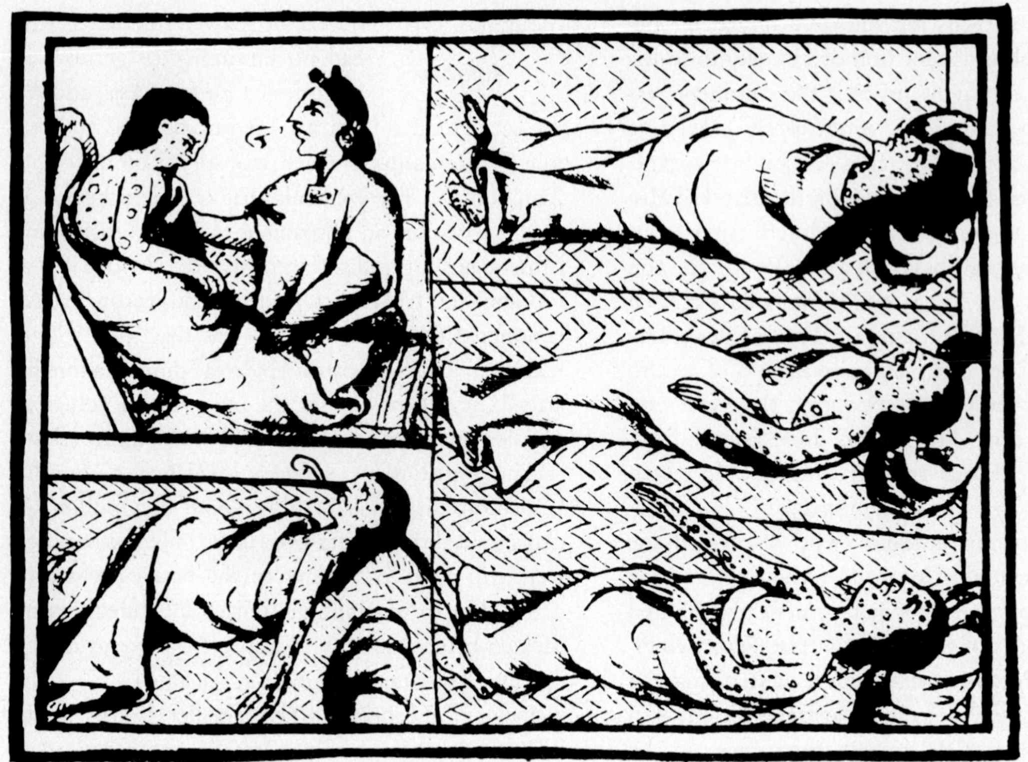

Aztec Indians suffering from smallpox during the Cortés invasion. From Fray Bernardo de Sahagun's *General History of the Things of New Spain (Historia de las Cosas de Nueva Espana),* published in the sixteenth century. Biblioteca Medices Laurenziana.

syphilis was more virulent in sixteenth-century Europe than it is today, and doctors did not know how to treat it. It spread quickly through the Mediterranean, carried by sailors and prostitutes, reaching England by 1496, Russia by 1499, and China by 1505. Syphilis caused considerable havoc among the ruling houses of Europe. Most royal families of the day were infected with the disease, which interfered with the normal biological processes of conception and childbirth, and as a result they could not produce legitimate heirs.

The exchange of diseases was only part of a broader mutual transfer of plants and animals that resulted directly from Columbus's voyages. The two hemispheres had evolved separately over millions of years, developing widely different forms of life. Many large mammals were native to the connected continents of Europe, Asia, and Africa, but the Americas contained no domesticated beasts larger than dogs and llamas. On the other hand, the vegetable crops of the New World—particularly corn, beans, squash, and potatoes—were more nutritious and produced higher yields than those of the Old, like wheat and rye. In time the Indians learned to raise and consume European domestic animals (cattle, pigs, and sheep) and the Europeans became accustomed to planting and eating American crops. As a result, the diets of both peoples were vastly enriched. One consequence was the doubling of the world's population over the next three hundred years, after centuries of stability.

Exchange of plants and animals

The exchange of two other commodities significantly influenced the two civilizations. In America the Europeans discovered tobacco, and smoking and chewing the "Indian weed" quickly became a fad in the Old World. Tobacco cultivation was later to form the basis for the prosperity of the first successful English colonies in North America. Despite the efforts of such skeptics as King James I of England, who in

1604 pronounced smoking to be "loathsome to the eye, hatefull to the Nose, harmfull to the brain, [and] dangerous to the Lungs," tobacco's popularity has continued almost undiminished to the present day.

But more important than tobacco's influence on Europe was the impact of horses on certain native American cultures. The conquistadores brought with them the first horses Americans had ever seen. Inevitably, some escaped or were stolen by the natives; such horses were traded north through Mexico into the Great Plains, where tribes like the Apache, Comanche, Sioux, and Blackfeet eventually made the horse the focal point of their existence. They used horses for hunting and warfare, measured a man's wealth and status by how many horses he owned, and moved their camps frequently because their horses continually needed fresh pastures.

Spaniards on horseback meet Aztec messengers. Although popular myth has it that the Indians were terrified by the strange four-legged creatures (and that that was a major reason for the Spanish triumph), these Aztec warriors do not seem overawed. Fray Bernardo de Sahagun, *Historia de las Cosas de Nueva Espana.*

The first English outposts in America

During the sixteenth century, while Spain was expanding and consolidating its empire in Mexico, the Caribbean, and Central and South America, other European nations had only sporadic contacts with the New World. Fishermen from a number of countries discovered that the Newfoundland Banks, off the north coast of North America, offered an abundant supply of cod and other fish. They set up temporary summer camps on the American shore, where they dried and salted their catch to preserve it on the long voyage home. But each autumn the fishermen returned to Europe; none of them seem to have contemplated living permanently in America.

Other Europeans who sailed along the coast soon found that the American natives, who still used stone implements, were eager to trade for steel knives, brass kettles, and other metal goods, along with beads and cloth. In exchange, the Indians offered the Europeans furs. As the trade developed and Europe began to demand more pelts (especially beaver, which was used for making felt hats), some nations began to establish permanent trading posts on North American soil. In 1608 the French, led by the explorer Samuel de Champlain, founded Quebec on the site of some abandoned Indian villages on the St. Lawrence River.

Early trading posts

Seventeen years later the Dutch built a trading post on Manhattan Island, at the mouth of the river Henry Hudson had discovered in 1609 and named for himself. And in 1638 Sweden sent a small number of traders to the Delaware River valley.

The French, Dutch, and Swedish settlements differed considerably from those of New Spain. The northern European colonists made no attempt to subject the Indians to European rule, although—particularly in New France—they did try to convert them to Christianity. Unlike the Spaniards, they viewed the Indians as trading partners rather than laborers, and did not try to enslave them or destroy their cultures. For the most part, they were also content to control only the land immediately surrounding their forts. The trading posts were permanent settlements, to be sure, but they were not intended as beachheads for large-scale European migration to the New World.

At first, English colonizers thought along the same lines as their northern European neighbors. In the

1580s, a group of West Countrymen, among them Sir Humphrey Gilbert and his younger half-brother Sir Walter Raleigh, hoped to establish American outposts that would trade with native peoples for gold and silver, serve as way-stations on the long sea routes to China and India, and bring the message of Christianity to heathen Americans. Their ambitions were fed by England's increasingly hostile relationship with Spain.

In 1533, when the English king Henry VIII divorced his Spanish queen Catherine of Aragon for failing to produce a male heir after twenty years of marriage, the once-cordial relationship between England and Spain had begun to crumble. The cracks widened when the pope refused to approve Henry's divorce. Henry left the Catholic Church, founded the Protestant Church of England, and proclaimed himself its head–a series of actions that appalled the orthodox Spanish Catholics. The marriage of Henry's Catholic daughter Mary (the child of Catherine) to Philip II of Spain was designed to cement the alliance once again. But when Queen Mary died childless in 1558, her Protestant half-sister Elizabeth I (Henry's daughter by his second marriage, to Anne Boleyn) ascended the throne. Thereafter England and Spain, though not always at war, were bitter enemies.

Accordingly, Gilbert and Raleigh pressed their case for English colonies in America by advancing a persuasive argument: such settlements would serve as excellent bases for attacks on New Spain, and especially on the Spanish treasure ships that carried the New World's wealth home to Europe. English "sea dogs" like John Hawkins and Francis Drake had proved in the 1560s and 1570s that well-executed raids on Spanish colonies and vessels could produce riches rarely dreamed of by previous English adventurers. Outposts in the New World appeared to hold enormous promise.

Queen Elizabeth agreed, and authorized Raleigh and Gilbert to colonize North America. Gilbert failed to plant a colony in Newfoundland, dying in the attempt, and Raleigh was only briefly more successful. After an exploring party reported favorably on the territory he named Virginia (for Elizabeth, the "Virgin Queen"), Raleigh in 1587 dispatched 117 colonists, including 17 women and 9 children, to Roanoke Island in what is now North Carolina. But tragedy struck. A supply ship destined for the colony was delayed by the Spanish Armada, Spain's aborted attempt to invade England in 1588. When the vessel finally arrived at Roanoke in 1590, the colonists had vanished without a trace. Among the missing were Eleanor Dare and her daughter Virginia, the first white child born in English America.

Founding of Roanoke

The failure of Raleigh's attempt to colonize Virginia ended English efforts at settlement for nearly two decades. Three years after Elizabeth's death in 1603, though, a group of West Countrymen interested in American ventures combined forces with a like-minded group of London merchants. Together they asked James I, Elizabeth's successor and the first Stuart monarch, to charter a joint-stock company that would again try to establish English colonies in the New World.

Joint-stock companies had been developed in England during the sixteenth century as a mechanism for pooling the resources of a large number of small investors. These forerunners of modern corporations were funded through the sale of stock. Since investors would receive returns only in proportion to their share of the whole enterprise, joint-stock companies did not hold forth the promise of immense wealth. But because they did not require individuals to put up large amounts of capital, they enabled merchants and members of the gentry to finance trading voyages without risking bankruptcy. Joint-stock companies thus had many benefits, but their drawbacks were to prove more decisive in the history of early colonization. Most investors wanted quick profits, which in the English colonies were rarely forthcoming. Many of the early colonization efforts thus suffered from a chronic lack of capital, causing dissent within the companies and conflicts with the settlers in America, who often accused the parent companies of failing to support them adequately.

Joint-stock companies

The charter James I granted the Virginia Company in 1606 gave it the right "to digg, mine, and searche for all manner of mines of goulde, silver, and copper." It also required the company to pay one-fifth of all proceeds to the king. The company's West Country investors (the Virginia Company of Plymouth) tried and failed to plant a colony at Sagadahoc, in what is now Maine. Meanwhile the merchant group (the Virginia Company of London) turned its attention southward. Although the settlers it sent to America at first searched for the precious metals named in the charter, they soon realized that Virginia was not another Mexico. Within twenty years the Virginia settlement had taken an entirely new form.

Pottery object created by the Mound Builders, Indian peoples who lived in the central and southeastern United States from around 1000 B.C. to 500 A.D. Unfortunately, we know little about the Mound Builders' civilization; they left no written records. But many of their huge mounds, some shaped like animals, still survive. Museum of the American Indian, Heye Foundation.

English and Indians encounter each other

Human beings were not native to the Americas. The "Indian" peoples who inhabited the Americas when the Europeans arrived were descended from Asians. Their forebears had migrated in waves across a now-vanished land bridge that joined the Asian and North American continents at the site of the Bering Strait. The first migrants may have arrived 75,000 years ago; others may have come as recently as 12,000 years ago. (There is conflicting evidence and considerable disagreement about when the migration occurred.) The migrants, who were nomadic hunters of game and gatherers of wild plants, spread slowly throughout North and South America.

Early Indian peoples

About 4000 B.C. Indians living in central Mexico learned how to cultivate food crops deliberately, instead of relying on foraging for their grain supply. As knowledge of agricultural techniques spread, many Indian groups started to live a more settled existence. Many became entirely settled or only seminomadic (moving only two or three times a year, among fixed sites). The development of agriculture brought about population increases by improving the food supply. It also allowed for more leisure: people no longer had to devote all their time to subsistence activities. That, in turn, made possible the production of ornamental objects, accumulation of wealth, and the creation of elaborate rituals and ceremonies.

In the fifteenth century, when Europeans first came to the New World in large numbers, the most sophisticated Indian civilizations in the Western Hemisphere were located in Central and South America. The Indian tribes living in what is now the United States varied dramatically in culture and lifestyle. The tribes along the Pacific coast lived largely by fishing, combined with some agriculture. While settled agriculture was the norm in the Southwest, tribes of nomadic hunters and gatherers roamed the Great Basin and the Great Plains. East of the Mississippi, most tribes lived a settled or seminomadic existence combining hunting, fishing, and agriculture. Their houses were made of bark, woven mats, or animal skins; they dressed largely in decorated skins and furs, and sometimes lived in extended family (or clan) groups. Most eastern coastal tribes spoke variants of Algonkian languages.

To an outside observer, had one existed, the cultures of seventeenth-century English and Algonkian peoples might have appeared similar at first glance. Both lived mainly in small villages, depending for subsistence chiefly on the cultivation of crops. Both supplemented a largely vegetable diet with meat and fish, although the Indians hunted meat and the English raised livestock. Both peoples were deeply religious, orienting their lives around festivals and rituals.

Both societies featured clear-cut social and political hierarchies; neither was egalitarian in the modern sense of the word. And finally, both cultures were characterized by sharply defined sex roles, with men and women occupying distinctly different spheres.

Such similarities were, however, outweighed by significant differences. The contrasts between the two ways of life were readily evident to both English and Indian witnesses. For example, Algonkian women bore the prime responsibility for cultivating crops.

Cultural differences between the Indians and the English

Once their husbands had felled trees and cleared the land, women handled the farming as well as cooking, making clothes, and raising children. In England, men worked in the fields while women cared for children and did the housework. Indian men thus regarded white males as effeminate because they did women's work, while white men described male Indians as lazy. Whites also considered Indian women oppressed, since they had to do heavy field labor.

Other differences between the two cultures caused serious misunderstandings. Although both societies were hierarchical, the nature of the hierarchies differed considerably. Among the east-coast Algonkian tribes, social and political standing were determined by a number of factors, including wealth, kinship, and talent. People were not born to automatic positions of leadership, nor were political power and social status necessarily inherited through the male line. A man's status might change several times, for better or worse, during the course of his life. English society was more rigid. A noticeable gap separated the gentry (who normally inherited their position from their fathers) from the common folk, even though successful individuals occasionally managed to rise into the gentry. English political and military leaders tended to rule autocratically; the authority of Indian leaders rested largely on a consensus they shared with their fellow tribesmen. Accustomed to the European concept of powerful kings, the English sought such figures within the tribes. If they found none, they created them. Often (for example, when negotiating treaties) they willfully overestimated the ability of chiefs to make independent decisions for their people.

Furthermore, the Indians and the English had very different notions of property ownership. In most eastern tribes, land was held communally by the entire group. The concept of absolute sale of property was utterly alien. The English, on the other hand, were accustomed to individual landholding. Perhaps more important, the English definition of entitlement to land excluded seminomadic tribes from consideration. Like other Europeans of the time, the English believed that nomadic peoples could not own land, properly speaking, since they had not placed it under intensive cultivation. They therefore paid little attention to tribal claims to traditional hunting territories and sites occupied only occasionally.

An aspect of the cultural clash that needs particular emphasis is the English settlers' unwavering belief in the superiority of their civilization. Although in the early years of colonization they often harbored thoughts of living peacefully alongside the Indians, they always assumed that they themselves would dictate the terms of such coexistence. They expected the Indians to adopt English customs and to convert to Christianity. When most tribes resisted, the English concluded that the Indians were irredeemable. Most colonists reached that conclusion quite early in the history of their settlements.

Ironically, the ethnocentric Englishmen dispatched by the Virginia Company settled in a region dominated by an equally ethnocentric coalition of Indian tribes, the so-called Powhatan Confederacy (see map, page 14).

Powhatan Confederacy

Powhatan, the chief of six allied tribes on the coast of what is now Virginia, was consolidating his control over about twenty-five other tribes in the area when the English colonists arrived. (His attempt to extend his power was unusual among Indians.) Fortunately for the Englishmen, Powhatan seems not to have viewed them as enemies but as potential allies in his struggle to establish uncontested authority over his Indian neighbors. Powhatan's confidence in his own strength apparently caused him to disregard the threat posed by the English colonists until it was too late.

Initially at least, Powhatan had good cause for self-assurance. The 104 men and boys who in May 1607 established the settlement called Jamestown, on a swampy peninsula in a river they also named for their

Founding of Jamestown

monarch, were indeed ill-equipped for survival. The colony was afflicted by dissension and disease; by January 1608 only 38 of the original colonists were

Secota, an unfortified Indian village on the Carolina coast, as drawn by John White, an artist with Raleigh's 1585 expedition. Letters A, B, C, D, and K identify ritual sites and show the dancing and feasting that were an important part of the Indians' religion. The picture also shows the Indians' chief crops–tobacco (E), corn in two stages of growth (G and H), and pumpkins (I). The hut labeled F housed a watchman assigned to keep animals and birds away from the fields. The river (L) was the village's source of water. Note the hunters shooting deer at top left. Rare Book Division, The New York Public Library, Astor, Lenox and Tilden Foundations.

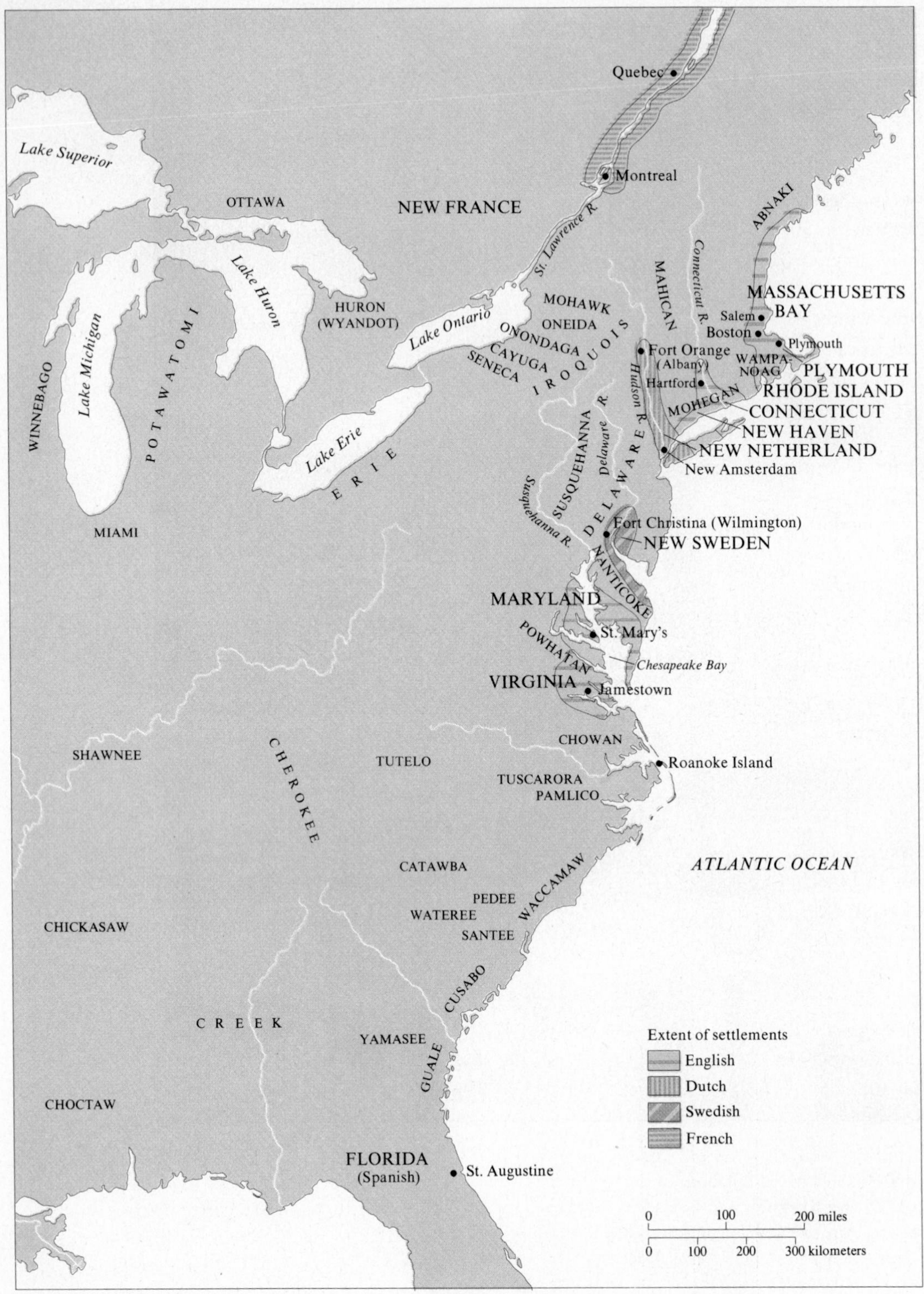

European settlements and Indian tribes in America, 1650. Source: Redrawn by permission of the Smithsonian Institution Press from B. A. E. Bulletin 145, *Indian Tribes of North America,* John Swanton, Smithsonian Institution, Washington, D.C., 1952.

still alive. Many of the first immigrants were gentlemen unaccustomed to working with their hands and artisans with irrelevant skills like glassmaking. Having come to Virginia expecting to make easy fortunes, most could not adjust to the conditions they encountered. They resisted living "like savages," retaining English dress and casual work habits despite their desperate circumstances. Such attitudes, combined with the effects of chronic malnutrition and epidemic disease, took a terrible toll. During the notorious "starving time," the winter of 1609–1610, some colonists even resorted to cannibalism. As late as 1624, fewer than 1,300 of the more than 8,000 immigrants to Virginia had survived.

The one Englishman who fully understood the necessity of adapting to the realities of life in Virginia was Captain John Smith, a daring soldier of fortune and former prisoner of war among the Turks. Smith, a member of the first group of settlers, took charge of the colony in September 1608, after its original leaders had died. The year in which he governed almost singlehandedly was, by nearly all accounts, the most successful in Jamestown's early history. Smith imposed military discipline on the settlers, requiring everyone to work. Recognizing the prevalence of disease at the Jamestown site, he copied the Indians' seminomadic lifestyle and dispersed the colonists during the summer, the most unhealthy season. And Smith's previous experience with alien peoples gave him an understanding of Powhatan lacking in his fellow colonists. Powhatan and Smith respected and sparred with each other as equals. Though their relationship was never cordial, it was founded upon a kind of reluctant mutual admiration.

The early Virginia settlers had frequent contacts with the Indians. Powhatan's people found the English settlers an infallible source of such desirable goods as steel knives, hatchets, and guns. In exchange, they traded their excess corn to the starving colonists—without which the settlement could not have survived, despite all Smith's efforts. Englishmen often wandered into Indian villages and vice versa; there were some violent clashes, but the two races were chiefly preoccupied with learning from each other. One of the most frequent visitors to Jamestown was Powhatan's favorite daughter, Pocahontas, who greatly admired Smith. She may never have saved him from execution at her father's hands (as Smith claimed in his memoirs), but on several occasions she warned Smith of Powhatan's plots against the colony.

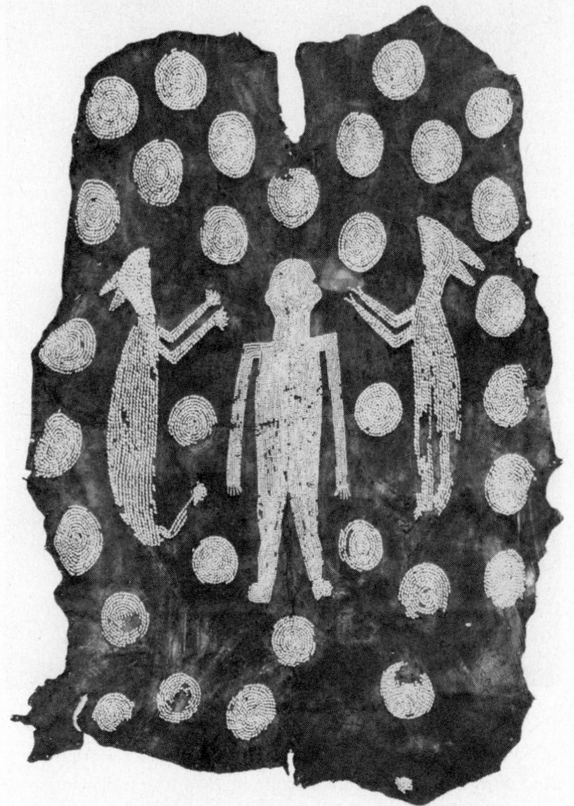

Powhatan's Mantle. This deerskin cloak, decorated with shells, may not have belonged to Powhatan, but it is one of the oldest known examples of North American Indian art. It was taken to England by early explorers returning from America. Ashmolean Museum, Oxford, England.

Smith left Virginia forever in 1609. But Pocahontas continued to visit Jamestown, and in 1613 the Englishmen seized her as a hostage. In captivity she fell in love with a widowed planter, John Rolfe, and married him the following year. Her father approved the match, agreeing as well to a formal treaty with the colonists. Pocahontas's marriage linked Powhatan with the whites; the treaty cemented the alliance, strengthening his position with respect to the thirty tribes he had subjected to his rule. Powhatan had cleverly used the presence of the Englishmen for his own purposes. It must have seemed to him that his strategy had worked.

Pocahontas (1595/96?–1617), here called Matoaka alias Rebecka, portrayed in Elizabethan dress. During her visit to England with her husband John Rolfe in 1616, the Indian princess became the toast of London society. She died the following year, just as she was leaving England to return to her homeland, and was buried in the parish church at Gravesend. National Portrait Gallery, Smithsonian Institution, Washington, D.C.

The peace established in 1614 lasted eight years, persisting beyond Pocahontas's death in 1617 and Powhatan's the next year. But even before 1614 the force that would eventually destroy the peace had been set in motion. That force was the spread of tobacco cultivation.

In tobacco the settlers and the Virginia Company found the saleable commodity for which they had been searching. The tobacco native to North America was harsh and unpleasant, but the climate was well suited to its cultivation. Thus John Rolfe imported the seeds of preferable varieties from South America, planting his first crop in 1611. By 1613 he shipped some home to England; in 1615 he and other Virginians exported 2,000 pounds of cured leaves. Just five years later their shipments reached 40,000 pounds, and by the end of the 1620s exports had jumped dramatically to 1.5 million pounds. The great tobacco boom had begun, fueled by high prices and substantial profits for planters. The price later fell almost as sharply as it had risen, and fluctuated wildly from year to year in response to increasing supply and international competition. Nevertheless, tobacco became the foundation of Virginia's prosperity.

Tobacco economy

Successful tobacco cultivation required abundant land, since the crop quickly drained soil of nutrients. Planters soon learned that a field could produce only about three satisfactory crops before it had to lie fallow for several years to regain its fertility. Thus the once small English settlements began to expand rapidly: eager planters applied to the Virginia Company for large land grants on both sides of the James and its tributary streams. Lulled into a false sense of security by years of peace, the planters established farms at some distance from one another along the river banks —a settlement pattern convenient for tobacco cultivation but poorly designed for defense.

Opechancanough, Powhatan's brother and successor, watched the English colonists steadily encroaching on Indian lands and attempting to convert members of the tribes to Christianity. He recognized the danger his brother had overlooked. On March 22 (Good Friday), 1622, under his leadership, the confederacy launched coordinated attacks all along the river. By the end of the day 347 colonists (about one-third of the total) lay dead, and only a timely warning from two Christianized Indians saved Jamestown itself from destruction.

Opechancanough's attack

The Virginia colony reeled from the blow but did not collapse. Reinforced by new shipments of men and arms from England, the settlers struck back. Over the next few years, they repeatedly attacked Opechancanough's villages, burning houses and crops. An uneasy peace returned in the 1630s, but in April 1644 Opechancanough tried one last time to repel the invaders. Perhaps 500 colonists were killed in a widespread attack on outlying settlements, but the English population of Virginia was by then over 8,000. In the ensuing war, Opechancanough himself was captured and killed.

In 1646, the survivors of the Powhatan Confederacy accepted a treaty formally subordinating them to English authority. They thus became official "friendly" Indians, their choice of chiefs subject to approval by the colonists. After 1646, the locus of conflict between Indians and the English intruders in the Chesapeake area moved westward. The Powhatan Confederacy's efforts to resist the spread of white settlement had ended.

Life in the Chesapeake

The 1622 massacre that failed to destroy the Virginia colony did succeed in killing its parent company, which had never made any profits from the enterprise. In 1624 James I revoked the company's charter and made Virginia a royal colony, ruled by the king through appointed officials. Significantly, though, two company policies remained in effect under royal authority. In an attempt to attract settlers, the company had in 1617 promised a land grant of fifty acres, called a headright, for every new arrival. Persons who financed the passage of others received a proportional number of headrights from the company. James continued that practice. He was more reluctant to retain the second company policy, implemented in 1619, which allowed the men of the major Virginia settlements to elect representatives to a legislative body called the House of Burgesses. At first, James abolished the legislature, but the settlers protested so vigorously that by 1629 the assembly was functioning once again. At the local level, Virginians adapted the forms of English county government to suit their needs. Only a few decades after the first permanent English settlement took root in the New World, the colonists had evolved a system of representative government with considerable local autonomy—a pattern that has continued in the United States to the present day.

By the 1630s, tobacco was firmly established in Virginia as the staple crop and chief source of revenue. It quickly became just as important in the second English colony planted on Chesapeake Bay: the proprietorship of Maryland, chartered by the king in 1632. The Calvert family, who founded Maryland, intended the colony to serve as a haven for their fellow Roman Catholics, who were being persecuted in England. Cecilius Calvert, second Lord Baltimore, became the first colonizer to offer prospective settlers freedom of religion, as long as they were practicing Christians. In that respect Maryland differed from Virginia, where the Church of England was the only officially recognized religion. In other ways, however, the two Chesapeake colonies resembled each other. In Maryland as in Virginia, tobacco planters spread out along the river banks, establishing isolated farms instead of towns. The region's deep, wide rivers offered dependable water transportation in an age of few and inadequate roads. Each farm or group of farms had its own wharf, where oceangoing vessels could take on or discharge cargo.

Founding of Maryland

Abundant land alone could not produce tobacco. As essential as acreage was labor, the second factor that shaped the Chesapeake. The planting, cultivation, and harvesting of tobacco had to be done by hand; these tasks did not take much skill, but they were repetitious and time-consuming. When the headright system was adopted in Maryland in 1640, a prospective tobacco planter anywhere in the Chesapeake could simultaneously obtain both land and the labor to work it. The more workers one brought into either colony, the more property one could acquire. Good management could make the process self-perpetuating: a planter could use his profits to pay for the passage of more workers, and thus gain title to more land. Under these circumstances, planters could accumulate substantial wealth rapidly.

There were two possible sources of laborers for the growing tobacco farms of the Chesapeake: Africa and England. In 1619, a Dutch privateer brought more than twenty blacks from the Spanish Caribbean islands to Virginia; they were the first known Negro inhabitants of the English colonies in North America. Nine years later, some natives of Africa were sold directly to Virginia settlers. Over the next few decades small numbers of blacks, mostly from the West Indies, were carried to the Chesapeake, but even as late as 1670 the black population of Virginia was at most 2,000 and probably no more than 1,500. Chesapeake tobacco planters first looked to England to supply their labor needs. And because they favored certain types of workers, the population of the Chesapeake soon became largely young and largely male. Such laborers migrated to America as indentured servants; that is, in return for their passage they contracted to work for planters for periods ranging from four to seven years.

Who were the thousands of English people who chose to emigrate to the Chesapeake as servants in the seventeenth century? Indentured servants accounted for 75 to 85 percent of the approximately 130,000 English immigrants to Virginia and Maryland during those years. Roughly three-quarters of them were men, mostly between the ages of fifteen and twenty-four. A majority had been farmers and laborers; though none were gentry, many had been skilled tradesmen and even clerks, teachers, and accountants. In other words, the servants did not represent the dregs of society. They were instead what their contemporaries called the "common" or "middling" sort. Judging by their youth, though, most had probably not yet established a firm foothold for themselves in England.

Immigrants to the Chesapeake

What motivated the servants to leave their homeland? Like later immigrants to America, they were probably influenced by a combination of push-and-pull factors. Many of the servants came from areas of England that were experiencing severe economic disruption. Some had already moved from their home districts to London or Bristol in search of work months or years before they decided to migrate to America. For such people the Chesapeake appeared to offer good prospects. Once they had fulfilled the terms of their indentures, servants were promised "freedom dues" consisting of clothes, tools, livestock, casks of corn and tobacco, and sometimes even land. From a distance at least, America seemed to hold out chances for advancement unavailable in England.

What did indentured servants actually find in Virginia and Maryland? Their lives were not easy. Servants typically worked six days a week, ten to fourteen hours a day, in a climate much warmer than they were accustomed to. Their masters could discipline or sell them, and they faced severe penalties for running away. Even so, they did have some rights enforceable in the courts. Their masters had to supply them with sufficient food, clothing, and shelter; they had to be allowed to rest on Sundays; and they could not be physically abused. Yet few seem to have been happy with their lot. Richard Frethorne, a Virginia servant, begged his parents in 1623 to purchase the time remaining on his indenture. Describing the hard work and poor food to which he was subjected, Frethorne pleaded, "Good father, do not forget me, but have mercy and pity my miserable case. I know if you did but see me, you would weep."

Conditions of servitude

Servants also had to contend with epidemic disease. Although the extremely high mortality rates characteristic of the Jamestown colony had fallen as the Chesapeake population dispersed, death rates remained high in comparison to seventeenth-century England. Immigrants had first to survive the process the colonists called "seasoning"–a bout with disease (probably malaria) that usually occurred during a servant's initial summer in the Chesapeake. They then had to endure recurrences of malaria, along with dysentery, influenza, typhoid fever, and other diseases. As a result, approximately 40 percent of male servants did not survive long enough to become freedmen. Even young men of twenty-two who had successfully weathered their "seasoning" could expect to live only another twenty years at best.

For those who survived the term of their indentures, however, the opportunities for advancement were real. Until the last decades of the century, former servants were usually able to become independent planters ("freeholders") and to live a modest but comfortable existence. Some even assumed such positions of political prominence as justice of the peace, sheriff, militia officer, and member of the assembly. But in the 1670s tobacco prices entered a thirty-year period of stagnation and decline. At the same time, good land grew increasingly scarce and expensive. In 1681 Maryland dropped its legal requirement that servants receive land as part of their freedom dues, forcing large numbers of freed servants to live as wage laborers or tenant farmers instead of acquiring freeholder status. By 1700 the Chesapeake was no longer the land of opportunity it had once been.

Life in the seventeenth-century Chesapeake was hard for everyone, regardless of sex or status. Farmers (and sometimes their wives) toiled in the fields alongside the servants, laboriously clearing the land of trees, then planting and harvesting not only tobacco but also corn, wheat, and vegetables. Chesapeake households subsisted mainly on pork and corn, a filling but monotonous and not particularly nutritious diet. Thus the health problems caused by epidemic disease were magnified by diet deficiencies and the near-impossibility of preserving food for safe winter consumption. (Salting, drying, and smoking, the only methods the colonists knew, did not always prevent spoilage.) Few farm households had many material possessions. Among the settlers' most valuable property was their clothing, since cloth usually had to be imported from England. (Spinning and weaving were traditionally done by women, and the few women in the Chesapeake could not supply the needs of the entire colony.) Linen clothing was especially prized because of its fine quality and thinness. But woolen cloth was easier to make and thus used more widely, despite its unsuitability for the hot, humid summer climate.

The predominance of males, called a high sex ratio,[1] and the high mortality rates combined to produce unusual patterns of family life. Because there were so few women, many men were never able to marry. Meanwhile, nearly every adult free woman in the Chesapeake married, and widows remarried quickly. Servant women, though, usually remained single during their term of indenture, since most masters denied them permission to marry, fearing pregnancy would make them unable to work. The high death rates also produced many widows, widowers, and orphans. In one Maryland county, for example, only one-third of marriages lasted as long as a decade. In a Virginia county, more than three-quarters of the children had lost at least one parent by the time they married or reached the age of twenty-one. As a result, both Maryland and Virginia developed elaborate laws and systems of orphans' courts designed to protect children from greedy step-parents and distant relatives.

Family life in the Chesapeake

Family life in the seventeenth-century Chesapeake therefore differed considerably from family life at home in England. There, powerful husbands and fathers had controlled the lives of their wives and children (called a *patriarchal* system of family governance). In the early Chesapeake, few fathers—or mothers, for that matter—lived long enough to have much say in their children's lives. Thus Chesapeake youths, who in England would have needed their parents' approval of an intended spouse, typically chose their own mates. Moreover, few social norms restricted people's behavior in the fluid Chesapeake society. More than a third of immigrant brides in Somerset County, Maryland, were already pregnant at the time of their weddings.

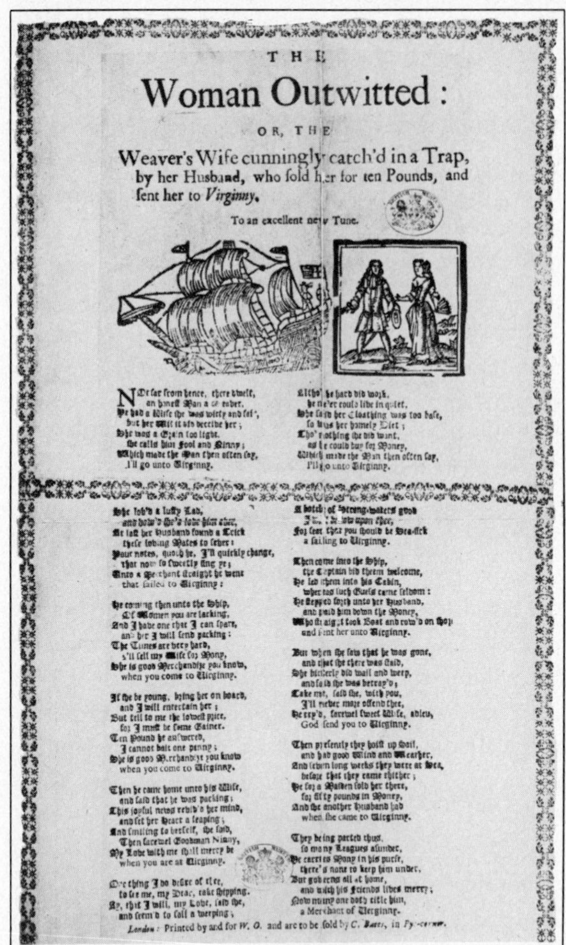
THE
Woman Outwitted:
OR, THE
Weaver's Wife cunningly catch'd in a Trap, by her Husband, who sold her for ten Pounds, and sent her to *Virginny*.
To an excellent new Tune.

London: Printed by and for *W. O.* and are to be sold by *C. Bates*, in *Py-corner*.

This popular English ballad drew its theme from the shortage of women in the Chesapeake. Contrary to its story, few white people seem to have been carried to the colonies against their will, except for convicted felons. And few married people of either sex immigrated to Virginia. Rare Book Division, New York Public Library, Astor, Lenox, and Tilden Foundations.

Seventeenth-century Chesapeake families were relatively few, small, and short-lived. Servant status prevented most immigrant women from marrying until their mid-to-late twenties. They probably bore only one or two children who survived to maturity. By contrast, their American-born daughters tended, because of the scarcity of women, to marry shortly after puberty. In Somerset County, amazingly, the mean age of marriage for girls born in America before 1670

[1] When men are in the majority, a society is said to have a high sex ratio; when women outnumber men, a society has a low sex ratio.

was sixteen-and-a-half. In the Chesapeake as a whole, most native-born women married before age twenty-one. They consequently bore more children than had their immigrant mothers—who had begun childbearing later—and the Chesapeake population slowly began to grow by natural increase as well as immigration. Even so, not until after 1700 did native-born residents of the Chesapeake outnumber their immigrant compatriots.

The fact that the Chesapeake population was primarily immigrant until 1700, if not longer, had important implications for politics in Maryland and Virginia. Both Virginia's House of Burgesses and Maryland's House of Delegates (established in 1635) were composed almost entirely of immigrants until late in the seventeenth century. The same was true of the governors' councils in both colonies. (The councils acted in two capacities: as the upper house of the legislature and as executive advisor to the governor.) Such immigrants came from different parts of England and had few ties to each other or to their new colonial homes. They tended to look to England for solutions to their problems. Moreover, most of the elected representatives felt little need to be responsive to their constituents, about whom they knew very little. Their bitter and prolonged struggles for power and personal economic advantage often thwarted the colonial governments' ability to function effectively. As a result, the existence of representative institutions failed to lead to political stability—the people's willingness to work out disagreements within an agreed-upon framework, instead of resorting to plotting and violence. The Chesapeake paid a high political price for its unusual population patterns.

Political instability

It is sometimes argued that the Chesapeake population's high sex ratio improved the status of women. Since men had to compete for the few available women, it is said, women were able to make better marital bargains. Yet it is difficult to see how conditions in the early Chesapeake worked to the benefit of women. Immigrant female servants could not marry until their mid-to-late twenties, and the fact that about one-third of them were pregnant at marriage does not suggest that they "shopped around" carefully for desirable husbands. Likewise, the fact that their daughters married very young does not seem to indicate the exercise of great care in the choice of a spouse. In short, although the lives of women in the seventeenth-century Chesapeake certainly contrasted sharply with those of their English counterparts, there is little evidence that they were on the whole any better off. Indeed, since colonial women were probably at greater risk of death, they might even be said to have worsened their condition through immigration.

The pattern of life prevalent in the Chesapeake was not, however, characteristic of all the English settlements in North America. In New England, immigrants seeking freedom of worship established a very different society.

The founding of New England

England's Protestant Reformation, mentioned earlier in the chapter, began the chain of events that eventually brought thousands of English men and women to the northern portion of Virginia, otherwise known as New England. When in the 1530s Henry VIII rejected Roman Catholicism and established the Church of England in its place, he set in motion forces he and his successors on the throne could not entirely control. Under Henry and his daughter Elizabeth, the Anglican Church reformed both theology and church structure. But by the early seventeenth century many people in England believed that Henry's reformation had not gone far enough. Instead of merely simplifying the church hierarchy, they wanted to abolish it altogether. Instead of a church subordinated to the interests of the state, they wanted a church free from political interference. And instead of a church composed automatically of all members of society, they wanted church membership to be more restricted. Because such people hoped above all to *purify* the church of corrupt influences, they were called Puritans.

The Puritans were followers of John Calvin, a Swiss cleric who had revised and enlarged on the Protestant doctrines originally outlined by Martin Luther. Calvin stressed the omnipotence of God and people's powerlessness to affect their ultimate fate. Reacting against the notion

Puritanism

(common in the medieval Catholic Church) that people could, in effect, ensure their spiritual salvation by donating money to the Church or doing good works, Calvin declared that God predestines souls to heaven or hell before their births. Christians could consequently do nothing to change their destiny.

Within that doctrine lay the Calvinists' major conceptual problem. If people's fates were determined by God before they were born, why should they behave well on earth? Members of the elect would be saved regardless of their actions, and those who were damned to hell would continue to be damned no matter how many good works they performed. The Calvinists resolved this dilemma ingeniously. God, they reasoned, did not just save the elect. He also gave them the ability to accept their salvation and to lead a good life during their stay on earth. Therefore, although good works could not earn one a place in heaven, a person might take his or her ability to live according to God's commandments as an indication of salvation. The reward for good works, in other words, was not guaranteed entrance into heaven; it was the likelihood that one's good works were evidence of elect status.

Conscientious Puritans devoted themselves to self-examination and Bible study, since it was considered each person's solemn duty to attempt to determine the state of his or her soul. (One result of that doctrine was the spread of literacy: to understand the Bible, Puritans obviously had to know how to read.) Despite their emphasis on self-study, though, Puritans believed that even the most pious could never be absolutely certain they were numbered among the elect. Mortals simply could not comprehend God's mind, motives, or behavior. Thus devout Puritans were often filled with anxiety about their spiritual state, and they felt deeply their inability to affect their own ultimate fate. For example, one man declared that he "had no power to think one good thought [or] speak one good word." His only hope for salvation, he realized, came "from the Lord out of his free and abundant grace and mercy to me," for God alone could "pardon my sins, subdue my lusts, remove my temptations."

Some Puritans (called Congregationalists) wanted to reform the Anglican Church rather than abandon it. Another group, known as Separatists, believed the Church of England to be so corrupt it could not be salvaged. They wanted to establish their own religious bodies, with membership restricted to the elect (as nearly as they could be identified).

In 1609 a group of about 125 Separatists migrated from the village of Scrooby, Nottinghamshire, to Leyden, Holland. The Netherlands' tolerant attitude enabled them to practice their religion openly, as they could not do in England. But ironically, the same relaxed atmosphere posed a serious threat to their little congregation. As William Bradford, one of the Separatists' leaders, later wrote in his *Of Plymouth Plantation,* the adults discovered that their children were "drawn away by evil examples into extravagant and dangerous courses, getting the reins off their necks and departing from their parents." Consequently, Bradford recounted, the members of the congregation began to think about moving to America, where they could practice their religion without such worries.

In early 1620 the Separatists obtained permission to settle in the northern part of the territory controlled by the Virginia Company of Plymouth. A total of 101 men and women, some of them "strangers" (non-Separatists), set sail in September on the aged, crowded *Mayflower.* Two months later they sighted land—the tip of Cape Cod, which was outside the northern boundary of the company's territory. But by then it was too late in the fall to go elsewhere. The Pilgrims located their settlement, named Plymouth after the English city from which they had sailed, on a fine harbor that had once been the site of an Indian village.

Founding of Plymouth

Though the weather that year was quite mild, the Pilgrims were ill prepared to survive the rigors of a New England winter. They were racked by disease and suffered seriously from malnutrition. When spring arrived, only half the *Mayflower*'s passengers were still alive. But spring also brought what Bradford termed "a special instrument sent of God for their good beyond their expectation" in the person of Squanto, a friendly Indian. Squanto had been kidnapped and carried to Europe in 1614 by an English sea captain who had hoped to sell him as a slave. Four years later he had escaped and made his way back to America, only to discover that his tribe had been wiped out in the great epidemic of 1616–1617. Squanto spoke good English and served as the Pilgrims' interpreter. In addition, Bradford noted, "he directed them how to set their corn, where to take fish, and to procure other commodities, and was also their pilot to bring them to unknown places for their profit, and never left them till he died."

Although the Pilgrims had to endure one year of a "starving time," they were far more fortunate than the Jamestown settlers. The northern climate was healthier than that of the Chesapeake, and the Pilgrims displayed a willingness to work uncharacteristic of the early Virginians. They also benefited from the seriously weakening effect the great epidemic had had on the tribes of the Cape Cod region. Massasoit, the chief of the Wampanoags, the strongest tribe in the immediate area, agreed to a peace with the Pilgrims during their first spring in America, and the treaty was observed by both sides for more than half a century.

The Pilgrim colony at Plymouth grew slowly, and was completely absorbed into the larger and more prosperous Massachusetts Bay colony in 1691. It is nonetheless famous for the so-called First Thanksgiving—when the settlers gave thanks to God for their first harvest in their new home—and for the Mayflower Compact. Because the Pilgrims landed outside the jurisdiction of the Virginia Company, some of the "strangers" questioned the authority of the colony's leaders. In response, the Compact, signed in November 1620 while everyone was still on board the *Mayflower,* established a "Civil Body Politic" and a rudimentary legal authority for the colony. The settlers elected a governor and at first made all decisions for the colony at town meetings. Later, after more towns had been founded and the population had increased, Plymouth, like Virginia and Maryland, created an assembly to which the male settlers elected representatives.

Before the 1620s had ended, another group of Puritans—this time Congregationalists, not Separatists—launched the colonial enterprise that would come to dominate New England. When Charles I, who was hostile to Puritan beliefs, succeeded his father James I in 1625, some non-Separatists began to think about settling in America. Under the auspices of the New England Company, which held a land grant from the Council for New England (the successor to the Virginia Company of Plymouth), a group of Congregationalist merchants sent out a body of settlers to Cape Ann, north of Cape Cod, in 1628. The following year the merchants obtained a royal charter, constituting themselves as the Massachusetts Bay Company.

Founding of Massachusetts Bay

The new company quickly attracted the attention of other Puritans of the "middling sort" who were becoming increasingly convinced that they would no longer be able to practice their religion freely in England. The Congregationalists who now looked to the Massachusetts Bay Company for a solution to their problems remained committed to the goal of reforming the Church of England. But prudence seemed to dictate that they pursue that aim in America rather than at home. In a dramatic move designed to further their purposes, the Congregationalist merchants boldly decided to transfer the headquarters of the Massachusetts Bay Company to New England. The settlers would then be answerable to no one in the mother country, and would be able to handle their affairs, secular and religious, as they pleased.

The most important recruit to the new venture was John Winthrop, a pious but practical landed gentleman from Suffolk and a justice of the peace. In October 1629, the members of the Massachusetts Bay Company elected the forty-one-year-old Winthrop as their governor. With the exception of only isolated years in the mid-1630s and early 1640s, he served in that post until his death in 1649. It thus fell to Winthrop to organize the initial segment of the great Puritan migration to America. In 1630 more than 1,000 English men and women were transported to Massachusetts—most of them to Boston, which soon became the largest town in North America. By 1643 nearly 20,000 compatriots had followed them.

Governor John Winthrop

On board the *Arbella,* en route to New England in 1630, John Winthrop preached a sermon, "A Modell of Christian Charity," laying out his expectations for the new colony. Above all, he stressed the communal nature of the endeavor on which he and his fellow settlers had embarked. God, he explained, "hath so disposed of the condition of mankind as in all times some must be rich, some poor, some high and eminent in power and dignity, others mean and in subjection." But differences in status did not imply differences in worth. On the contrary: God had planned the world so that "every man might have need of other, and from hence they might be all knit more nearly together in the bond of brotherly affection." The Puritans faced a "community of perils"; thus "the care of the public must oversway all private respects." In America, Winthrop asserted, "we shall be as a city upon a hill, the eyes of all people are upon us." If the Puritans failed to carry out their "special commission" from God, "the Lord will surely break out in wrath against us. . . . [and] we shall surely perish out of the good land whither we pass over this vast sea to possess it."

Winthrop's was a transcendent vision. The society he foresaw in Puritan America was a commonwealth in the true meaning of the word, a community in which each person put the good of the whole ahead of his or her private concerns. It was, furthermore, to be a society whose members all lived according to the precepts of Christian charity, loving and aiding friends and enemies alike. Of course, such an ideal was beyond human reach. Early New England had its share of bitter quarrels and unchristian behavior. What is remarkable is how long the ideal prevailed as a goal to be sought, if seldom or never attained.

The Puritans' communal ideal was expressed chiefly in the doctrine of the covenant. As Winthrop's words indicated, they believed God had made a covenant—that is, an agreement or contract—with them when He chose them for the special mission to America. In turn they convenanted with each other, promising to work together toward their goals. The founders of churches and towns in the new land often drafted formal documents setting forth the principles on which such institutions would be based. The same thing was true of the colonial governments of New England. The Pilgrims' Mayflower Compact was a covenant; so too was the Fundamental Orders of Connecticut (1639), which laid down the basic law for the settlements established along the Connecticut River valley in 1636 and thereafter. The leaders of Massachusetts Bay likewise interpreted their original joint-stock company charter in ways that enabled them to establish a covenanted community based on mutual consent. They gradually transformed the General Court, officially merely the company's governing body, into a colonial legislature, and opened the status of "freeman," or voting member of the company, to

Ideal of the covenant

John Winthrop (1588–1649). His strength and determination are clearly shown in this portrait, painted before he immigrated to America. Massachusetts Historial Society.

all adult male church members resident in Massachusetts. Less than two decades after the first large group of Puritans had arrived in Massachusetts Bay, the colony had a functioning system of self-government composed of a governor and a two-house legislature. The General Court also established a judicial system modeled on England's and in 1641 adopted a legal code, *The Laws and Liberties of Massachusetts,* spelling out crimes and their proper punishments.

The colony's method of distributing land helped to further the communal ideal. Unlike Virginia and Maryland, where individual applicants sought headrights for themselves and their servants, in Massachusetts groups of families—often from the same region of England—applied together to the General Court for grants of land on which to establish towns. The founders of Dedham in 1636 came largely from Yorkshire and East Anglia; the town fathers of Sudbury were from Hampshire, Essex, and Suffolk; and

Town land grants

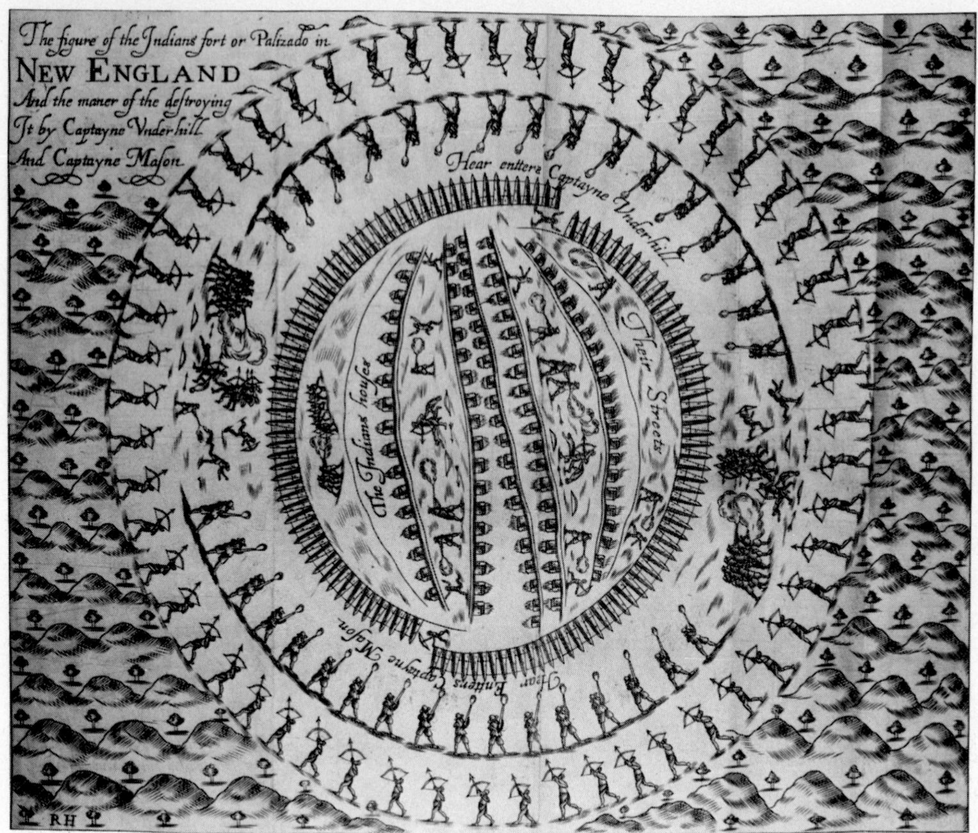

Diagram of the attack on the Pequot fort at Mystic. The Puritans and their Narragansett allies surround the fort, shooting everyone who tries to escape the flames. Drawn by Captain John Underhill, who participated in the attack. The Library Company of Philadelphia.

those who moved to Andover in 1646 came from Wiltshire, Hampshire, and Lincolnshire.

The men who received the original town grant had the sole authority to determine how the land would be distributed. Understandably, they copied the villages from which they came. First they laid out town lots for houses and a church. Then they gave each family parcels of land scattered around the town center: pasture here, a woodlot there, an arable field elsewhere. They also reserved the best and largest plots for the most distinguished among them (usually including the minister); people who had been low on the social scale in England received far smaller allotments. In Sudbury, for example, the clergyman was granted 112 acres in the original distribution, but the poorest of the settlers received just 7½ acres. Indentured servants commonly received nothing.

In their new towns, the Puritans quickly established diversified farming as the chief means of subsistence. The first settlements in New England thus bore little resemblance to those in the Chesapeake. The Puritans attempted to create in the New World an idealized version of the village life they had known in the Old. As more immigrants poured into Massachusetts than could be housed in the earliest towns, the process repeated itself. First the General Court and then the founders of each town kept a tight communal grip on the colony's land. The settlement of Massachusetts was orderly and controlled. Even when immigrants began to move beyond the territorial limits of the Bay Colony into Connecticut (1636), New Haven (1638), and New Hampshire (1638), the same pattern of town land grants was maintained in these areas as well.

The migration to Connecticut ended the Puritans' relative freedom from clashes with neighboring Indian tribes. The first English settlers in the Connecticut River valley moved there from Newtown (Cambridge), under the direction of their minister, Thomas Hooker. Connecticut was fertile, though remote from the other English towns, and the wide river promised easy access to the ocean for purposes of trade. The site had just one problem: it fell within the territory controlled by the Pequot tribe.

The strong Pequots, themselves recent migrants from the upper Hudson valley, dominated the weaker tribes native to the region. The Puritans and the Pequots had concluded a peace treaty in 1634, but that was before English families began to move into northern Connecticut lands occupied by the Pequots' tributaries. (Some of the weaker tribes invited the Puritans into the area, hoping to counterbalance Pequot power.) After two incidents in which Indians (probably not Pequots) brutally killed white men, a Massachusetts force in 1636 burned some Pequot villages and crops. The raid provoked the Pequots to attack the new English town of Wethersfield, on the Connecticut River. Nine settlers, six men and three women, were killed and two others captured in that attack in April 1637.

Pequot War

In retaliation, Massachusetts sent a force of about ninety Englishmen, accompanied by some Narragansett Indians, to attack one of the main Pequot villages on the Mystic River. The Puritans and their allies surrounded the fortified village at dawn on May 26, 1637, set it on fire, and slaughtered at least four hundred Pequots, many of them women and children. Of the English, only two were killed and twenty wounded. The power of the Pequots was broken. The few surviving members of the tribe, dispirited and despairing, were captured and enslaved by the colonists and their Indian allies. (Slavery was often the fate of Indians captured by the English colonists—see Chapter 2.)

In *Of Plymouth Plantation,* William Bradford described the Puritans' pleasure at their conquest. "It was a fearful sight to see them thus frying in the fire and the streams of blood quenching the same," he commented, adding that the settlers praised God for giving them "so speedy a victory over so proud and insulting an enemy." The Puritans had good reason to be thankful, for the Pequots had been the only tribe strong enough to oppose their rapid migration into the New England interior. Their victory in the short but bloody Pequot War had won the colonists forty years of peace in which to expand the area of English settlement.

Life in New England

Colonists in New England led lives dramatically different from those of their contemporaries in the Chesapeake. The chief differences lay in their patterns of settlement, in the relative importance of religion in the settlers' daily lives, and in their family organization and behavior.

Although religion seems to have played a minor role in the lives of seventeenth-century Chesapeake settlers (largely because it proved difficult to transfer the Church of England as an institution to the colonies), it was ever-present in the lives of New Englanders, even those who were not Puritans. The governments of Massachusetts Bay, Plymouth, Connecticut, and the other northern colonies were all controlled by Puritans. Congregationalism was the only officially recognized religion; members of other sects had no freedom of worship except in Rhode Island. Only male church members could legally vote in colony elections, although some non-Puritans appear to have voted in town meetings. All households were taxed to build meetinghouses and pay ministers' salaries. Massachusetts' *Body of Laws and Liberties* incorporated regulations drawn from Old Testament scriptures into the legal code of the colony. Moreover, penalties were prescribed for expressing contempt for ministers or their preaching, and for failing to attend church services regularly.

In the New England colonies, church and state were intertwined. Puritans objected to secular interference in religious affairs, but at the same time expected the church to influence the conduct of politics. They also believed that the state had an obligation to support and protect the one true church—theirs. As a result, though they came to America seeking freedom of worship, they saw no contradiction in their refusal to grant that freedom to others. Indeed, the two most significant divisions in early Massachusetts were caused by religious disputes, and by Massachusetts Bay's unwillingness to tolerate dissent.

Roger Williams

Roger Williams, a Separatist, immigrated to Massachusetts Bay in 1631 and became assistant pastor at Salem. Williams was well liked but soon began to express eccentric opinions. Among them was the notion that the Massachusetts and Plymouth charters were both defective because the king of England had no right to give away land belonging to the Indians. Another was his insistence that church and state should be kept entirely separate. Furthermore, Williams argued, if Puritans could not be certain of their own salvation, they could hardly require others to conform to their religious beliefs. Banished from Massachusetts in 1635, Williams founded the town of Providence on Narragansett Bay. Because of his beliefs, Providence and other towns in what became the colony of Rhode Island adopted a policy of tolerating all religions, including Judaism.

Anne Hutchinson

The other dissenter, and an even greater challenge to Massachusetts Bay orthodoxy, was Anne Marbury Hutchinson, the pious daughter of an Anglican clergyman with Puritan leanings. Anne Hutchinson had immigrated to Boston with her husband and family in 1634 in order to follow her pastor, John Cotton, who had moved to New England the previous year. Cotton's preaching particularly stressed God's free gift of salvation to unworthy human beings (the covenant of grace), whereas most Massachusetts clerics emphasized preparing oneself to receive God's grace through good works, study, and reflection. As a disciple of Cotton, Hutchinson too stressed the covenant of grace.

Anne Hutchinson quickly became well known in Boston as a skilled midwife. In 1636 she began to hold women's meetings in her home to discuss Cotton's sermons. Soon men started to attend as well. At first Hutchinson simply summarized Cotton's sermons, but eventually she began to express her own interpretations of his statements. In so doing, she emphasized the covenant of grace more heavily than did Cotton himself. Indeed, she went so far as to adopt the so-called Antinomian heresy–the belief that the elect can communicate directly with God and be assured of salvation. Such ideas had an immense intrinsic appeal for Puritans. Anne Hutchinson offered them certainty of salvation in exchange for the state of constant tension in which they otherwise had to live, never knowing whether they would be saved or damned for eternity.

Hutchinson's ideas were a dangerous challenge to Puritan orthodoxy, so in November 1637 she was brought before the General Court of Massachusetts. She was charged with having libeled the colony's clergymen by claiming that they preached salvation through works. For two days she defended herself cleverly against her accusers, matching scriptural references and wits with John Winthrop himself. Finally, in an unguarded moment late in the second day, Hutchinson declared that God had spoken to her "by an immediate revelation." That heretical assertion assured her banishment; she and her family, along with some faithful followers, were exiled to Rhode Island.

The authorities in Massachusetts Bay perceived Anne Hutchinson as doubly dangerous to the existing order: she threatened not only religious orthodoxy but also traditional sex roles. Puritans believed in the equality before God of all souls, including women, but they also considered women inferior to men, forever tainted by Eve's guilt. Christians had long followed St. Paul's dictum that women should keep silent in church and be submissive to their husbands. Anne Hutchinson did neither. The magistrates' comments during her trial make it clear that they were almost as outraged by her "masculine" behavior as by her religious beliefs. Winthrop charged her with having set wife against husband, since so many of her followers were women. Another of her judges told her bluntly: "You have stept out of your place, you have rather bine a Husband than a Wife and a preacher than a Hearer; and a Magistrate than a Subject."

The vehemence with which the General Court reacted to Anne Hutchinson's implicit challenge to customary gender roles indicates the extent to which traditional English family patterns had been duplicated in New England. The northern environment and the characteristics of the migrant population combined to make the familial experiences of Puritan New Englanders very different from those of residents of the Chesapeake.

In the first place, Puritans commonly migrated as families–sometimes even three-generation families–

Important events

1001	Norse explorers reach Labrador
1477	Marco Polo's *Travels* published
1488	Bartholomew Dias rounds Cape of Good Hope
1492	Christopher Columbus discovers Bahama Islands
1493	Syphilis first recorded in Europe
1497	John Cabot charts coast of Newfoundland
1498	Vasco da Gama reaches India
1507	Western Hemisphere first called America
1513	Ponce de Leon explores Florida Vasco Nuñez de Balboa crosses Isthmus of Panama; discovers Pacific Ocean
1518–30	Smallpox pandemic decimates Indian population of New World
1521	Tenochtitlan surrenders to Cortés; Aztec empire falls to Spaniards
1521–22	Ferdinand Magellan circumnavigates the globe
1524	Giovanni da Verrazano explores North American coast
1533	Henry VIII divorces Catherine of Aragon
1535	Francisco Pizarro conquers Inca empire
1539–42	Hernando de Soto explores southeastern United States
1540–42	Francisco Vásquez de Coronado explores southwestern United States
1558	Elizabeth I becomes queen
1577–80	Sir Francis Drake circumnavigates the globe
1587–90	Sir Walter Raleigh's Roanoke colony fails
1603	James I becomes king
1606	Virginia Company chartered
1607	Jamestown founded
1608	Samuel de Champlain founds Quebec
1609	Henry Hudson explores Hudson River
1611	First Virginia tobacco crop
1619	First blacks arrive in Virginia
1620	Plymouth Colony founded
1622	Powhatan Confederacy attacks Virginia colony
1624	Dutch settlement on Manhattan Island Virginia Company charter revoked; Virginia becomes royal colony
1625	Charles I becomes king
1629	Massachusetts Bay Company chartered
1630	Massachusetts Bay Colony founded
1634	Maryland founded
1635	Roger Williams expelled from Massachusetts Bay; founds Providence, Rhode Island
1636	Connecticut founded
1637	Pequot War Anne Hutchinson expelled from Massachusetts Bay
1638	New Haven Colony founded New Hampshire founded Swedish outpost on Delaware River established
1640	Great Migration to New England ends

rather than as individuals. That meant that the age range of the immigrants was wider and the sex ratio more balanced, so that the population could immediately begin to reproduce itself. Second, New England's climate was much healthier than that of the Chesapeake. Once Puritan settlements had survived the difficult first two or three years and established self-sufficiency in foodstuffs, New England proved to be even healthier than the mother country. Though adult male migrants to the Chesapeake lost about ten years from their English life expectancy of fifty to fifty-five years, their Massachusetts counterparts gained about ten years.

Consequently, although Chesapeake population patterns made for families that were few in number, small in size, and transitory, the demographic characteristics of New England made families there numerous, large, and long-lived. In New England more men were able to marry, since there were more female migrants; immigrant women married earlier (at twenty, on the average); and marriages lasted longer and produced more children, who were more likely to live to maturity. If seventeenth-century Chesapeake women could expect to rear three healthy children, New England women could anticipate raising six to eight. Households were thus very crowded, since New England dwellings usually contained only four small rooms.

Family life in New England

The nature of the population had other major implications for family life. New England in effect created grandparents, since in England people rarely lived long enough to know their children's children. And while seventeenth-century southern parents normally died before their children married, northern parents exercised a good deal of control even over their adult children. Young men could not marry without acreage to cultivate, and because of the communal land-grant system they were dependent on their fathers to supply them with that land. Daughters, too, needed the dowry of household goods their parents would give them when they married. Yet parents needed their children's labor on their farms, and were often reluctant to see them marry and start their own households. That at times led to considerable conflict between the generations. On the whole, though, children seem to have obeyed their parents' wishes. They had few alternatives. One indication of tighter parental control there than in the Chesapeake was New England's lower premarital pregnancy rate. Fewer than 20 percent of northern brides in one town were pregnant when they married, as opposed to more than 33 percent in a southern county.

In 1630 John Winthrop wrote to his wife Margaret, who was still in England, "my deare wife, we are heer in a paradise." He was, of course, exaggerating. In another letter he admitted that "our fare be but coarse in respect of what we formerly had (pease, pudding, & fishe, being our ordinary diet)" and detailed the many difficulties that beset the Puritan settlers, along with numerous deaths. Yet even though America was not a paradise, it was a place where English men and women could worship as they wished or attempt to better their economic circumstances. Many died, but those who lived laid the foundation for subsequent colonial prosperity. That they did so by dispossessing the Indians bothered few besides Roger Williams. By the middle of the seventeenth century, one fact was indisputable: English people had come to the New World to stay.

Suggestions for further reading

General

Charles M. Andrews, *The Colonial Period of American History: The Settlements,* 3 vols. (1934–1937); John E. Pomfret, *Founding the American Colonies, 1583–1660* (1970).

Indians

Harold E. Driver, *Indians of North America,* 2nd ed. (1969); George E. Hyde, *Indians of the Woodlands: From Prehistoric Times to 1725* (1962); Alvin Josephy, Jr., *The Indian Heritage of America* (1968); Smithsonian Institution, *Handbook of North American Indians,* 15: *The Northeast* (1978); Robert F. Spencer, Jesse D. Jennings, *et al., The Native Americans: Ethnology and Backgrounds of the North American Indians,* 2nd ed. (1977).

England

Carl Bridenbaugh, *Vexed and Troubled Englishmen, 1590–1642* (1967); Mildred Campbell, *The English Yeoman under Elizabeth and the Early Stuarts* (1942); G. R. Elton,

England under the Tudors (1955); Peter Laslett, *The World We Have Lost* (1965); Wallace Notestein, *The English People on the Eve of Colonization 1603–1630* (1954); Lawrence Stone, *The Crisis of the Aristocracy, 1558–1641* (1965); Michael Walzer, *The Revolution of the Saints* (1965).

Exploration and Discovery

Fredi Chiapelli, *et al.*, eds., *First Images of America: The Impact of the New World on the Old,* 2 vols. (1976); Alfred W. Crosby, Jr., *The Columbian Exchange: Biological and Cultural Consequences of 1492* (1972); J.H. Elliott, *The Old World and the New, 1492–1650* (1970); Charles Gibson, *Spain in America* (1966); James Lang, *Conquest and Commerce: Spain and England in the Americas* (1975); Samuel Eliot Morison, *Admiral of the Ocean Sea* (1942); Samuel Eliot Morison, *The European Discovery of America: The Northern Voyages, A.D. 1500–1600* (1971), *The Southern Voyages, A.D. 1492–1616* (1974); J.H. Parry, *The Age of Reconaissance* (1963); David B. Quinn, *North America from Earliest Discovery to First Settlements* (1977).

Early contact between whites and Indians

Wilbur R. Jacobs, *Dispossessing the American Indian: Indians and Whites on the Colonial Frontier* (1972); Francis Jennings, *The Invasion of America: Indians, Colonialism, and the Cant of Conquest* (1975); Nancy O. Lurie, "Indian Cultural Adjustment to European Civilization," in *Seventeenth-Century America: Essays in Colonial History,* ed. James M. Smith (1959); Calvin Martin, *Keepers of the Game: Indian-Animal Relationships and the Fur Trade* (1978); Frances Mossiker, *Pocahontas: The Life and the Legend* (1976); Alden T. Vaughan, *American Genesis: Captain John Smith and the Founding of Virginia* (1975); Alden T. Vaughan, *The New England Frontier: Puritans and Indians 1620–1675,* rev. ed. (1979).

New England

Ben Barker-Benfield, "Anne Hutchinson and the Puritan Attitude toward Women," *Feminist Studies,* I (1972), 65–96; Charles E. Clark, *The Eastern Frontier: The Settlement of Northern New England, 1610–1763* (1970); John Demos, *A Little Commonwealth: Family Life in Plymouth Colony* (1970); John Faragher, "Old Women and Old Men in Seventeenth-Century Wethersfield, Connecticut," *Women's Studies,* 4, No. 1 (Jan. 1976), 11–31; Philip J. Greven, Jr., *Four Generations: Population, Land, and Family in Colonial Andover, Massachusetts* (1970); Sydney V. James, *Colonial Rhode Island* (1975); Lyle Koehler, *A Search for Power: The 'Weaker Sex' in Seventeenth-Century New England* (1980); George Langdon, *Pilgrim Colony: A History of New Plymouth, 1620–1691* (1966); Kenneth A. Lockridge, *A New England Town: The First Hundred Years (Dedham, Massachusetts, 1636–1736)* (1970); Edmund S. Morgan, *The Puritan Dilemma: The Story of John Winthrop* (1958); Edmund S. Morgan, *The Puritan Family: Religion and Domestic Relations in Seventeenth-Century New England,* rev. ed. (1966); Edmund S. Morgan, *Visible Saints: The History of a Puritan Idea* (1963); Samuel Eliot Morison, *Builders of the Bay Colony* (1930); Sumner Chilton Powell, *Puritan Village: The Formation of a New England Town* (1963); Darrett Rutman, *American Puritanism: Faith and Practice* (1970); Darrett Rutman, *Winthrop's Boston: A Portrait of a Puritan Town, 1630–1649* (1965); Alan Simpson, *Puritanism in Old and New England* (1955).

Chesapeake

Lois Green Carr and Lorena Walsh, "The Planter's Wife: The Experience of White Women in Seventeenth-Century Maryland," *William and Mary Quarterly,* 3rd ser., 34 (1977), 542–571; Wesley Frank Craven, *The Southern Colonies in the Seventeenth Century, 1607–1689* (1949); Wesley Frank Craven, *White, Red, and Black: The Seventeenth Century Virginian* (1971); Karen O. Kupperman, "Apathy and Death in Early Jamestown," *Journal of American History,* 66 (1979), 24–40; Aubrey C. Land, Lois Green Carr, and Edward C. Papenfuse, eds., *Law, Society, and Politics in Early Maryland* (1977); Edmund S. Morgan, *American Slavery, American Freedom: The Ordeal of Colonial Virginia* (1975); Darrett Rutman and Anita Rutman, "Of Agues and Fevers: Malaria in the Early Chesapeake," *William and Mary Quarterly,* 3rd ser., 33 (1976), 31–60; Abbot E. Smith, *Colonists in Bondage: White Servitude and Convict Labor in America, 1607–1776* (1947); Thad W. Tate and David L. Ammerman, eds., *The Chesapeake in the Seventeenth Century: Essays on Anglo-American Society & Politics* (1979); *William and Mary Quarterly,* 3rd ser., 30, No. 1 (Jan. 1973): *Chesapeake Society.*

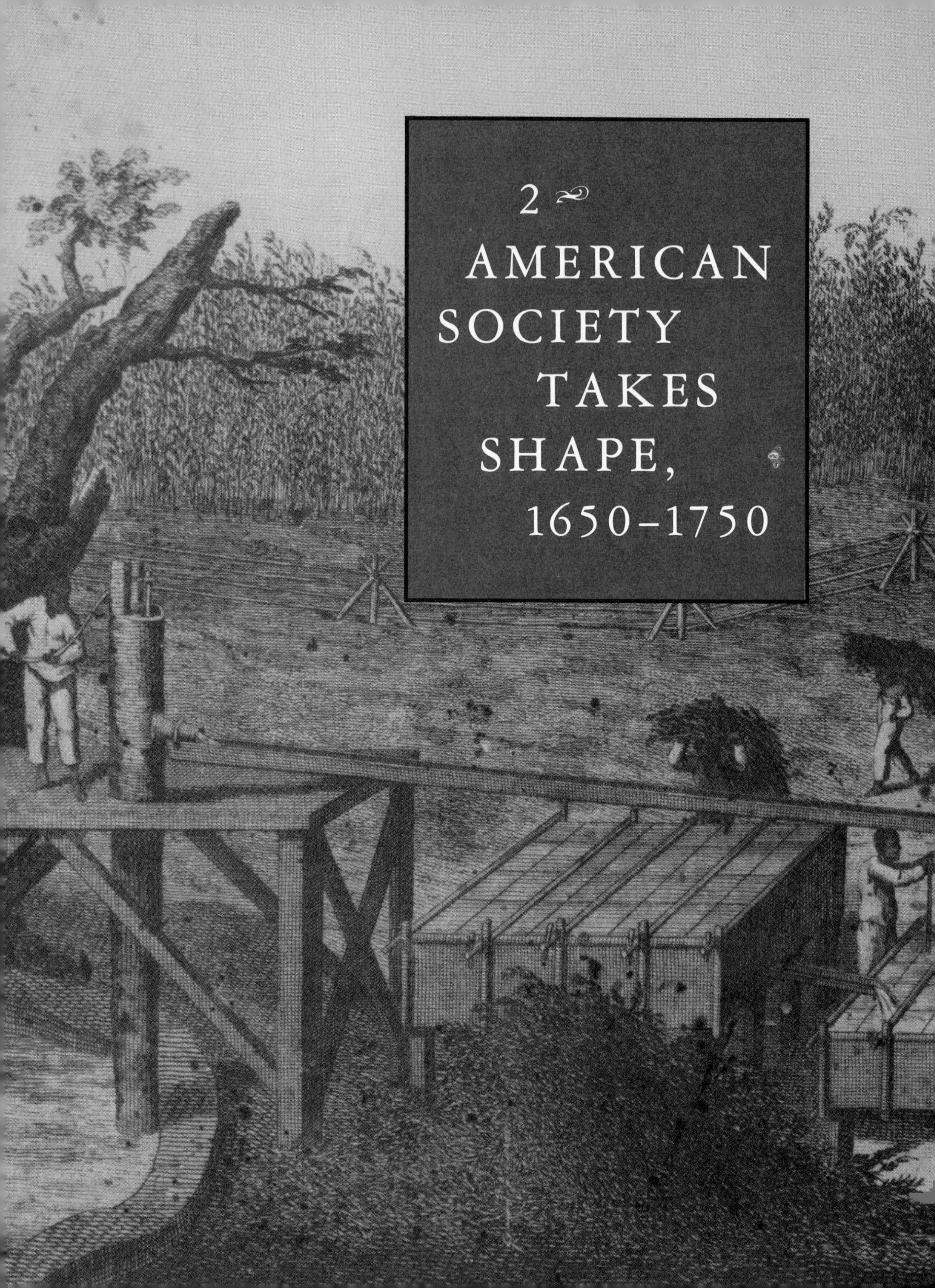

2 AMERICAN SOCIETY TAKES SHAPE, 1650–1750

Olaudah Equiano was eleven years old in 1756 when black raiders in search of slaves kidnapped him and his younger sister from their village in what is now Nigeria. Until then, he had lived peacefully with his father and mother, his father's other wives, and his seven siblings and half-siblings in a mud-walled compound that itself resembled a small village. Equiano and other members of the Ibo tribe were, he later observed, "habituated to labour from our earliest years." Men, women, and children worked together to cultivate corn, yams, beans, cotton, tobacco, and plantains (a type of banana). They also raised cattle, poultry, and goats. Equiano's family, like others in the region, held prisoners of war as slaves. With what may have been idealized hindsight, he later recalled that the slaves did "no more work than other members of the community, even their master; their food, clothing, and lodging were nearly the same. . . . There was scarce any other difference between [masters and slaves] than a superior degree of importance which the head of a family possesses . . . and that authority which, as such, he exercises over every part of his household."

Equiano's experiences as a captive differed sharply from the life he had led as a child in his father's house. For months he was passed from master to master, finally arriving at the coast, where an English slave ship lay at anchor. Terrified by the light complexions, long hair, and strange language of the sailors, he was afraid that "I had gotten into a world of bad spirits and that they were going to kill me." Equiano was placed below decks, where "with the loathsomeness of the stench and crying together, I became so sick and low that I was not able to eat, nor had I the least desire to taste anything." The whites flogged him to make him eat, and he thought about jumping overboard but was so closely watched that his plan was foiled. At last some other Ibos told him that they were being taken to the whites' country to work. "I then was a little revived," Equiano remembered, "and thought if it were no worse than working, my situation was not so desperate."

After a long voyage during which many of the Africans died of disease caused by the cramped, unsanitary conditions and poor food, the ship arrived at Barbados, a British island in the West Indies. Equiano and his shipmates feared that "these ugly men" they saw there were cannibals, but experienced slaves were brought on board to assure them that they would not be eaten and that many blacks like themselves lived on the islands. "This report eased us much," Equiano recalled, "and sure enough soon after we landed there came to us Africans of all languages." Everything in Barbados was new and surprising, but Equiano later remarked particularly on two-storied buildings and horses, neither of which he had ever seen.

Because of his youth, Equiano was not purchased in the West Indies, and was instead carried to Virginia along with the other less-desirable slaves. There, on the plantation of his new owner, he was separated from the other Africans and put to work weeding and clearing rocks from the fields. "I was now exceedingly miserable and thought myself worse off than any of the rest of my companions," Equiano reported, "for they could talk to each other, but I had no person to speak to that I could understand. In this state I was constantly grieving and pining and wishing for death rather than anything else."

But Equiano did not remain in Virginia for long. Bought by a sea captain, Olaudah Equiano eventually became an experienced sailor. He learned to read and write English, purchased his freedom at the age of twenty-one, and later actively supported the English antislavery movement. In 1789 Equiano published *The Interesting Narrative of the Life of Olaudah Equiano . . . Written by Himself,* from which this account of his captivity is drawn. Until he was purchased by the sailor, Equiano's experiences differed very little from those of other Africans who were forced into slavery in the English colonies of the New World. Like him, many were kidnapped by black slavers and taken first to the West Indies, then to North America. His *Interesting Narrative,* one of a number of memoirs by former slaves, depicts the captives' terror powerfully and convincingly.

If the most important aspect of the first fifty years of English colonization was the meeting of European and Indian, the key occurrence of the next century was the importation of more than two hundred thousand Africans into North America. That massive influx of black slaves, and the geographic patterns it took, has dramatically influenced the shaping of American society ever since.

Many other major events also marked the years between 1650 and 1750. New colonies were founded, populating the gap between the widely separated

New England and Chesapeake settlements. England also took over the coastal outposts established by other European nations. As English settlements spread to the north, west, and south, they moved onto territory controlled by the powerful Indian tribes of the interior. After many years of peace, colonists and native Americans once again went to war. Furthermore, internal disputes within the colonies often resulted in open rebellions against established governments. Yet by the middle of the eighteenth century, stable political and social structures had evolved in all the colonies. After a century and a half of English colonization, the American provinces assumed a mature form.

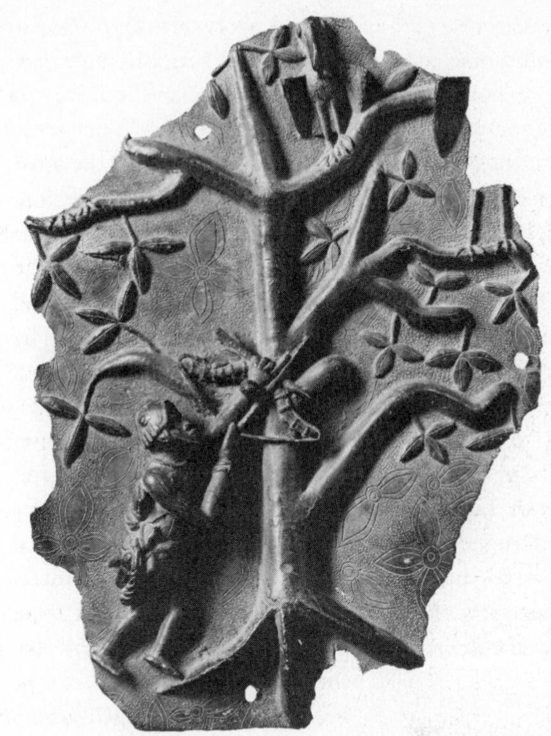

This bronze plaque from Benin, Nigeria, demonstrates the artistry of that sophisticated African civilization, and suggests the cultural loss Africans must have suffered when they were enslaved and carried to the Americas. Museum für Völkerkunde, Staatliche Museen Preubischer Kulturbesitz, Berlin (West).

The forced migration of Africans

Few Africans were imported into the English mainland colonies before the last quarter of the seventeenth century. This pattern was in sharp contrast to that of Britain's Caribbean colonies. The Caribbean islands were first settled in the 1620s and 1630s, and by the 1640s the white colonists had already begun to purchase large numbers of slaves to work in the production of sugar cane. As early as 1655, enslaved blacks nearly equalled whites in numbers on the island of Barbados, and by 1680 blacks outnumbered their white masters two-to-one. In the Leeward Islands (Nevis, St. Christopher, Antigua, and Montserrat), whites still made up a small majority in 1680, but thirty years later they comprised only one-quarter of the total population. What accounted for the difference between the island and mainland colonies with respect to black slavery? More important, since England itself had no tradition of slavery, why did English settlers in the New World begin to enslave Africans at all? The answers to both questions lie in the combined effects of economics and racial attitudes.

The English were an ethnocentric people. They believed firmly in the superiority of their values and civilization, especially when compared to the native cultures of Africa and North America. Furthermore, they believed that fair-skinned peoples like themselves were superior to the darker-skinned races. Those beliefs alone did not cause them to enslave Indians and Africans, but the idea that other races were inferior to whites helped to justify slavery.

Moreover, although the English had not previously practiced slavery, other Europeans had. English people knew that Spanish and Portuguese Christians had enslaved Moorish prisoners of war (who were black and Moslem), and that Christian doctrine allowed the enslavement of heathen peoples. Thus when the English settlers in the New World needed laborers, almost without thinking they looked to dark-skinned non-Christians to supply those needs. In the Spanish colonies, the Catholic Church discouraged Indian slavery because it wanted to convert the native peoples rather than subjugate them. No such religious motive worked against Indian slavery in the English settlements, but there as elsewhere the native peoples' familiarity with the environment made them difficult to enslave. Often Indian captives were able to escape from their white masters.

Africans were a different story. Transported far from home and set down in alien surroundings, they were frequently unable–like Olaudah Equiano–to communicate with their fellow workers. They were also the darkest (and thus, to European eyes, the most inferior) of all peoples. Black Africans therefore seemed to be ideal candidates for perpetual servitude. By the time the English established settlements in the Caribbean and North America, Spanish colonists had already held Africans in slavery for over a century. The English newcomers to the New World, in other words, had a ready-made model to copy.

Nevertheless, a fully developed system of lifelong slavery did not emerge immediately in the English colonies. Lack of historical evidence makes it difficult to determine the legal status of blacks during the first two or three decades of English settlement, but at least a few of them seem to have been free. After 1640, on the other hand, some blacks were being permanently enslaved in each of the English colonies. Colonial assemblies started to pass laws specifically governing the behavior of blacks. Also, black servants began to command higher sale prices than their white counterparts, suggesting service for life rather than a fixed term of years. By the end of the century, the blacks' status was fixed. Barbados adopted a comprehensive slave code as early as 1661, and the mainland provinces soon did the same. In short, even before the extension of the direct African slave trade to North America, the English settlements there had established a clear legal basis for a slave system.

Emergence of slavery

The question still remains: why did Chesapeake and Caribbean colonists differ at first in their choice of laborers, and why did the Chesapeake tobacco planters turn increasingly to blacks after 1675? Both supply and demand factors were influential.

In the West Indies, the environment was decisive. English people did not adapt easily to life in the tropics; they died in droves from epidemic diseases their doctors did not know how to treat. Potential servant migrants to the Caribbean may well have learned of the area's dangers and decided to go elsewhere. In any event, sugar planters soon came to prefer African laborers, who were accustomed to the tropical climate and resistant to the most serious of the diseases that killed whites. (The inherited sickle-cell blood trait carried by many blacks helped to combat malaria, and exposure to yellow fever in Africa had immunized black immigrants to that disease.) Thus the black population of the Caribbean islands grew rapidly due to continuing importation.

The Chesapeake environment, though dangerous, was measurably less deadly to whites than the Caribbean, and tobacco planters relied almost exclusively on white indentured servants for fully half a century. But after about 1675 they could no longer obtain an adequate supply of white workers. A falling birth rate and improved economic conditions in England combined to decrease the number of possible migrants to the colonies. And by the end of the century many other English settlements in North America were competing with the Chesapeake for newcomers, both indentured and free. As a result, the number of servant migrants to the Chesapeake levelled off after 1665 and fell in the 1680s. After 1674, when the shortage of servants became acute, imports of Africans increased dramatically. As early as 1690, the Chesapeake colonies contained more black slaves than white indentured servants, and by 1710 one-fifth of the region's population was black. Slaves usually cost about two-and-a-half times as much as servants, but they repaid the greater investment by their lifetime of service.

Decline in white immigration

Yet not all white planters could afford to devote so much money to purchasing workers. Accordingly, the transition from indentured to enslaved labor increased the social and economic distance between richer and poorer planters. Whites with enough money could acquire slaves and accumulate greater wealth, while less affluent whites could not even buy indentured servants, whose price had been driven up by scarcity. As time passed, white Chesapeake society thus became more and more stratified; that is, the gap between rich and poor steadily widened. The introduction of large numbers of Africans into the Chesapeake, in other words, had a significant impact on white society, in addition to reshaping the population as a whole.

The other southern colony founded in the seventeenth century was also dramatically affected by the institution of slavery and the presence of blacks. In 1669 King Charles II, grandson of James I, granted a

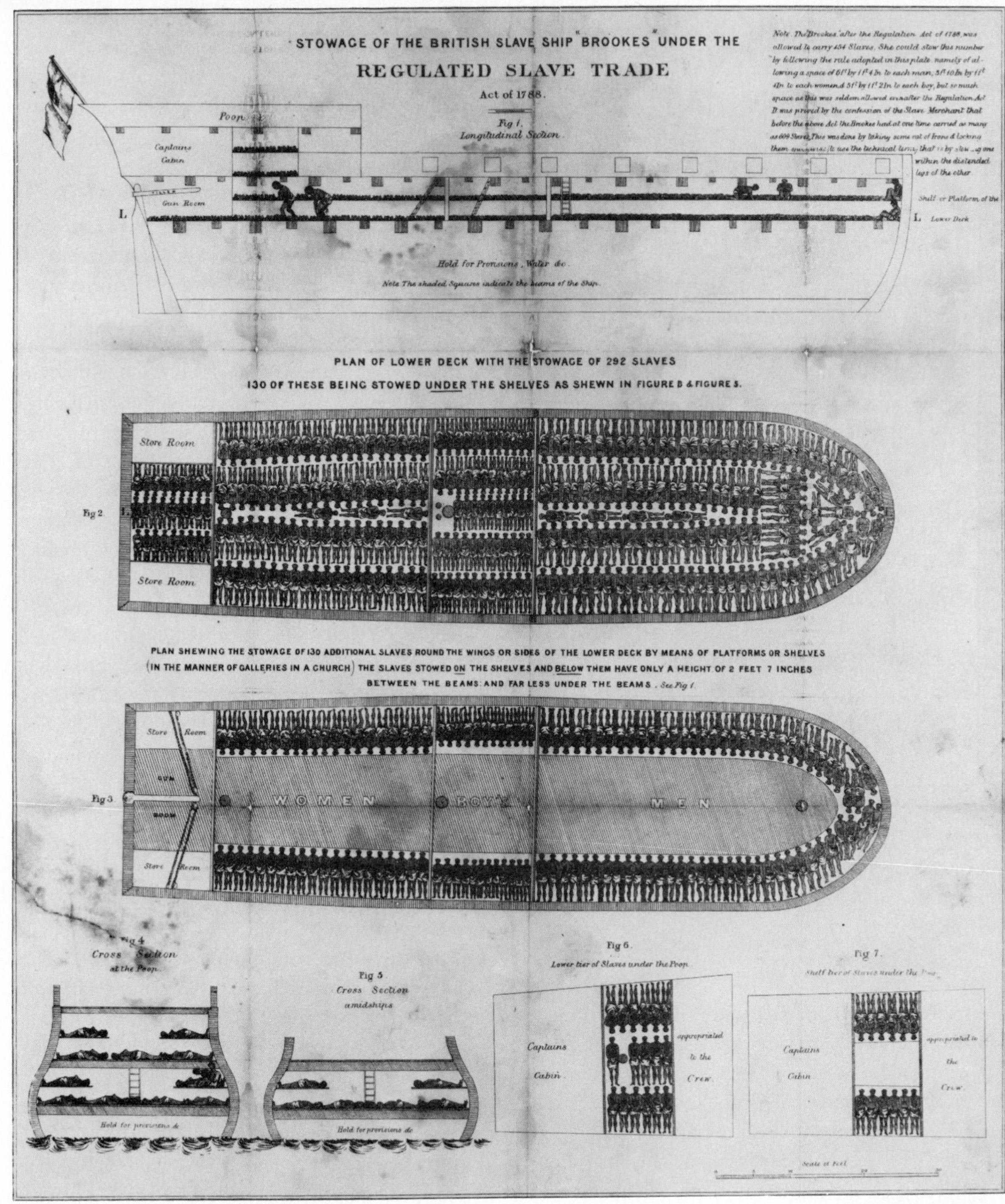

Eighteenth-century diagram of a slave ship, with its human cargo stowed according to British regulations. Many captains did not give slaves even this much room. On the assumption that a large number of Africans would die en route, shipmasters packed as many slaves as possible into the hold to increase their profit. Library of Congress.

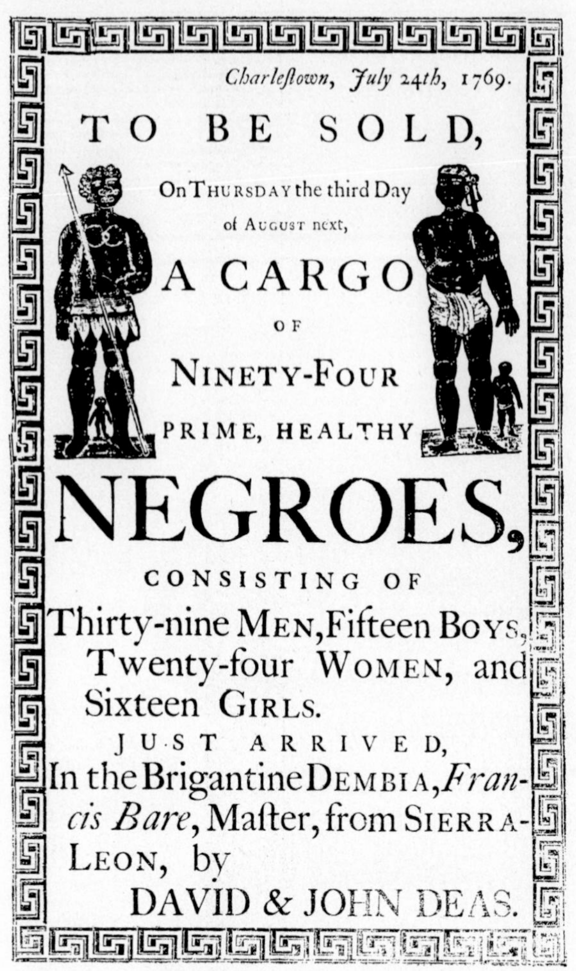

Slave traders announced their sales in newspaper advertisements and broadsides like this one, from South Carolina. Note the imbalanced sex ratio among the slaves in the cargo. American Antiquarian Society.

group of his friends a tract of land stretching from the southern boundary of Virginia to Spanish Florida. The proprietors named their new province Carolina in honor of their king (whose name in Latin was Carolus), and planned to establish a colony governed by an elaborate hierarchy of landholding aristocrats. The "Fundamental Constitutions of Carolina," written by the political philosopher John Locke, amounted to a blueprint for a utopian society with a carefully structured distribution of political and economic power. But Carolina failed to follow the course Locke had outlined for it. Instead it quickly developed two distinct population centers, which in 1730 split into separate colonies.

Founding of the Carolinas

The Albemarle region that became North Carolina was first settled by Virginians. They established a society much like their own, with an economy based on tobacco cultivation and the export of such forest products as pitch, tar, and timber. Because North Carolina lacked a satisfactory harbor, its planters continued to rely on Virginia's ports and merchants to conduct their trade, and the two colonies remained tightly linked.

South Carolina developed quite differently. Its first settlers—who founded Charleston in 1670—came from Barbados, which was already overcrowded. With them they brought their slaves; perhaps one-quarter to one-third of the first residents of South Carolina were black, and of those three-fourths were male. The high proportion of Africans and Caribbean-born blacks in South Carolina's population from the very beginning inexorably shaped the colony's early history.

The Africans' familiarity with a semitropical environment was useful to white South Carolinians, who found the region alien and threatening. African-style dugout canoes became the chief means of transportation in the colony, which was crisscrossed by innumerable rivers. Fishing nets copied from African models proved to be more efficient than those of English origin. The baskets slaves wove and the gourds they hollowed out came into general use as containers for food and drink. Africans' skill at killing crocodiles equipped them to handle alligators as well. And, finally, slaves adapted African techniques of cattleherding for use in the American context. Since meat and hides were the colony's chief exports in its earliest years, blacks obviously contributed significantly to South Carolina's prosperity.

Their central position in the colony's economy was not established, however, until almost the end of the century. In the 1670s and 1680s, white Carolinians, like other English people in the New World, employed white indentured servants and Indian slaves as well as blacks. But in the last decade of the century South Carolinians developed a new staple crop: rice. Europeans knew little about techniques of cultivating and processing rice, but slaves from Africa's

Introduction of rice and indigo

so-called Rice Coast (present-day Ghana and Sierra Leone) had spent their lives working in the rice fields. It may well have been their expertise that enabled their English masters to grow rice successfully. As the colony's commitment to rice cultivation grew, so did the demand for African workers (as opposed to workers of English or American origin). The Africans' relative immunity to malaria and yellow fever also prompted Carolina planters, like those in the West Indies, to prefer them to other laborers. As a result, by 1710 a majority of South Carolina's residents were black.

South Carolina developed a second staple crop in the 1740s, and it too made use of blacks' special skills. The crop was indigo, much prized in Europe as a blue dye for clothing. Carolinians had first tried unsuccessfully to grow indigo in the late seventeenth century. Then, in the early 1740s, Eliza Lucas, a young Antigua woman who was managing her father's South Carolina plantations, began to experiment with indigo cultivation. Drawing on the knowledge of an overseer from Montserrat and the experience of some West Indian blacks familiar with the crop, she developed the planting and processing techniques later adopted throughout the colony. Indigo was grown on high ground, and rice was planted in low-lying swampy areas; rice and indigo also had opposite growing seasons. Thus the two crops complemented each other perfectly. Although South Carolina indigo never matched the quality of that raised in the West Indies, the indigo industry flourished because Parliament offered Carolinians a bounty on every pound they exported to Great Britain.

After 1700 white southerners were irrevocably committed to Negro slavery as their chief source of labor. The same was not true of white northerners. Only a small proportion of the slaves brought to the English colonies in America went to the northern mainland provinces, and most of those who did worked as domestic servants. Lacking large-scale agricultural enterprises, the rural North did not demand many enslaved laborers. In northern urban areas, though, white domestic servants were hard to find and harder to keep (because higher wages were paid for other jobs in the labor-scarce economy), and blacks there filled an identifiable need. In some northern colonial cities (notably Newport, Rhode Island, and New York City), black slaves accounted for more than 10 percent of the population.

Slave importation, 1492–1770

Between 1492 and 1770 more Africans than Europeans came to the New World. But just 4.5 percent of them (345,000 persons by 1861, or 275,000 during the eighteenth century) were imported into the region that later became the United States. By contrast, 42 percent of the approximately 9.5 million enslaved blacks were carried to the Caribbean, and 49 percent went to South America, mainly to the Portuguese colony of Brazil. At first, most of the slaves brought to the English mainland colonies arrived via the West Indies, but as time passed direct traffic from Africa increased. Overall, about 80 percent of the slaves imported into the colonies before the American Revolution had been born in Africa. Early in the century South Carolina and the Chesapeake imported roughly equal numbers of slaves, but by the 1760s the southern colony dominated the trade. Carolinians by then purchased three times as many blacks each year as did Virginians and Marylanders together.

When Africans arrived in the English colonies, what kind of life did they find? The conditions under which they labored varied considerably from place to place. In the West Indies, the unhealthy environment and rigorous work schedules on sugar plantations combined to produce appallingly high mortality rates. Also, planters there preferred male laborers, and bought few female slaves. Thus the black population could not reproduce itself, and planters had to continue to import large numbers of slaves from Africa simply to maintain their labor force at a constant level.

Among the mainland colonies, South Carolina most closely resembled the West Indies. Rice cultivation was difficult and unhealthful, partly because the rice swamps were ideal breeding-grounds for malaria-carrying mosquitoes. Furthermore, Carolina planters, like those of the islands, maintained a slave population with a high proportion of males to females (about two-to-one). During the mid-eighteenth century, therefore, South Carolina slaves barely managed to reproduce themselves, and the black population increased in size only because of massive imports of slaves from Africa.

In the Chesapeake, by contrast, imports accounted for black population growth only until about 1720. From 1740 on, the black population of Maryland and Virginia grew chiefly through natural increase. This significant change indicates that—against all the odds—Africans had been able to create families in the Chesapeake. Precisely how and why such a transition occurred is not yet clear. The more moderate climate and less demanding work routines in the Chesapeake probably contributed to greater survival rates among the immigrants. Moreover, by the middle of the eighteenth century some whites had begun to recognize the advantages of encouraging their slaves to marry and have children. As the Virginia slaveholder Thomas Jefferson put it some years later: "I consider a woman who brings a child every two years more profitable than the best man of the farm. What she produces is an addition to the capital, while his labors disappear in mere consumption."

Natural increase of the slave population

Jefferson thus correctly identified one of the most important consequences of the fact that the black population of the Chesapeake had started to rise through natural increase. A planter who began with only a few slave families could watch the size of his labor force increase steadily over the years without making additional major investments in workers. It was no coincidence that the first truly large Chesapeake plantations appeared in the 1740s, when natural increase became the dominant factor in the growing slave population. The two developments went hand in hand. Greater concentrations of slaves and more balanced sex ratios (due to natural increase) meant a greater likelihood of marriage and childbearing among blacks. This in turn meant greater wealth for their owners. These changes affected the nature of both the plantations and the slave society in the Chesapeake.

By midcentury, then, the vast majority of slaves in the Chesapeake and a substantial proportion of those in South Carolina had formed persistent marital unions and had American-born children. A distinctive Afro-American society had begun to emerge out of the forced migration of thousands of blacks from different tribes and regions of Africa. That society will be described further in Chapter 3.

The secularization and commercialization of New England

In 1642 civil war broke out in England between Puritans led by Oliver Cromwell and Anglicans supporting Charles I, who in 1625 had succeeded his father James I. Charles not only persecuted Puritans but also ruled autocratically. The Puritans, who dominated Parliament, successfully overthrew him after several years of war and executed him in 1649. Cromwell then controlled the government (taking the title of Protector) until his own death in 1658. Two years later the Stuart family was peacefully restored to the throne in the person of Charles II, son of Charles I. Thus ended the tumultuous chapter in English history known as the Interregnum (Latin for "between reigns").

These events had profound consequences for the American colonies, especially New England. The Puritans' triumph at home eliminated their major incentive for immigration to America. The Puritan migration largely ceased, and some colonists even packed up and returned to the mother country. New England's population growth in the seventeenth century, therefore, resulted almost entirely from natural increase. The first settlers' many children also produced many children, who tended to live longer, on the average, than their Chesapeake contemporaries. In 1700, therefore, when the Chesapeake population totaled no more than the number of immigrants to the region (perhaps 100,000), New England's population had already quadrupled its total immigration and had also reached approximately 100,000.

Population growth and land use

In New England, the area of settlement and the number of towns constantly expanded as members of each subsequent generation sought land on which to establish and support their families. This process was not always smooth, nor was there an infinite amount of land available for farming. As noted in Chapter 1, fathers often resisted giving sons their own independent allotments of land. Since sons (and occasionally daughters) usually shared equally in their father's property, the size of landholdings tended to decrease with each generation. The earliest settlers of some of the first Massachusetts towns, for example, eventually received land grants averaging about 150 acres during their lifetimes. By the third quarter of the eighteenth century, the average landholding in the same towns was only 30 to 50 acres.

Many of the acres in those first large farms went unused because the New Englanders did not have the manpower to cultivate them, nor would they have had a market for surplus crops in any case. The smaller eighteenth-century farms were still adequate to support a family, which was all that was necessary. But the comparison illustrates the pressures that the ever-increasing population placed on the supply of arable land. Members of the first American-born generation could usually farm in their home towns. But their children and grandchildren often had to migrate—north into New Hampshire or Maine, south to New York, westward beyond the Connecticut River valley—to find sufficient farm land. Alternatively, they could learn artisanal skills such as blacksmithing or carpentry and ply their trades in their home towns or in such seaports as Boston, Salem, New Haven, Newport, or Providence.

As the population increased, New England towns changed in shape and character. The settlement patterns established by the town founders, in which each family lived on a village lot and cultivated small scattered pieces of land, soon gave way to consolidated farms situated at some distance from the town center. When the population in an outlying area had reached a sufficient number, the farmers there commonly asked the town for permission to construct their own church, so they would not have to travel so far on Sundays. Often the next step was a formal division of the town.

The history of Dedham, Massachusetts, will serve to illustrate the process. The first settlers (about thirty families) received title in 1637 to more than 200 square miles of territory. Over the course of the next century, five more towns were carved out of the original grant. (Eventually another seven towns were created). Medfield (1651), Wrentham (1671), and Bellingham (1719), whose centers of settlement were located more than ten miles from Dedham village, seceded from Dedham with little difficulty. But Dedham strongly resisted the loss of the nearby areas that became Needham (1711) and Walpole (1724). The struggle went on for years, causing angry disputes between townspeople eager to maintain Dedham's traditional character and outlying farmers who sought greater local control over churches, roads, schools, and other matters.

Just as inevitable as changes in the land-population ratio and alterations in town boundaries was the major religious crisis caused by a conflict between two basic tenets of New England Puritanism. The first was a belief in infant baptism for the children of all church members. The second was the requirement that potential church members prove to the congregation that they had experienced the gift of God's grace, or "saving faith," before they could be admitted to full membership. (That usually involved a searching examination into the state of their souls. It did not mean that applicants had to identify a single moment of conversion.)

The passage of time alone brought the requirements for church membership into conflict with the practice of infant baptism. By the 1650s, baptized American-born children of immigrant church members were themselves marrying and having children. But many of them had not applied for full church membership, since they had not experienced saving faith. What was to be done when such families presented their infants for baptism? A synod of Massachusetts ministers, convened in 1662 to consider the problem, responded by establishing a category of "halfway" membership in the church. In a statement that has become known as the Halfway Covenant, the clergymen declared that adults who had been baptized as children but were not full church members could have their children baptized. In return, such parents would have to acknowledge the authority of the church and live according to moral precepts. They would not be allowed to vote in church affairs or take communion.

Halfway Covenant

Local churches at first resisted the change, but were eventually forced to accept it in order to maintain adequate levels of membership. Understandably, American-born Puritans did not display the same religious fervor that had prompted their ancestors to cross the Atlantic. Their piety had not been strengthened by persecution; they were not dissenters but adherents of an orthodox religion. Though Puritan divines repeatedly scolded their congregations for lack of piety, using a standard sermon form known as the jeremiad, church records for the period show no decline in the total number of members. On the contrary, the Halfway Covenant brought into the church people who would otherwise have been outside its bounds, most notably third-generation Puritans who had had no direct experience of saving faith.

Studies of patterns of membership in Puritan churches after 1660 have yielded an important finding: ever-larger proportions of church members were women. In New England's early days men and women had joined the church in approximately equal numbers, but by the end of the seventeenth century women were in the majority in many congregations. It was probably in response to their increasingly female audiences that clerics such as Cotton Mather, the most prominent member of a family of distinguished ministers, began to preach sermons outlining woman's proper role in church and society. Mather's sermons were the first formal examination of that theme in American history. In "Ornaments for the Daughters of Zion," Mather instructed women to be submissive to their husbands, watchful of their children, and attentive to religious duty. The evidence from church membership rolls suggests a growing division between pious women and their more worldly husbands, a split that was to be enshrined in the ideology of "woman's place" in nineteenth-century America. It also reflects the significant economic changes occurring in New England during the latter half of the seventeenth century, which originated in the impact of the English Civil War.

Before 1640 the northern colonies had developed only one dependable export–furs–which they obtained by trading such items as knives, combs, scissors, and mirrors to local Indian tribes. Beaver pelts in particular commanded a premium price in Europe, and the New England colonies competed with each other for control of the major sources of supply. One measure of the importance of the fur trade to New England's economy was the colonies' adoption of wampum, the Indians' currency, as legal tender for payment of debts and taxes. Strings of wampum (polished beads made from seashells by the Narragansett tribe) were routinely used as money by both whites and Indians. The colonists began to produce their own coins in 1652, and though wampum ceased to be legal tender in the 1660s, it continued to be used in private transactions until the early eighteenth century.

Proceeds from furs alone were insufficient to purchase all the manufactured goods the settlers required. For one thing, New England's supply of pelts was limited because the region lacked rivers giving ready access to the interior of the continent. Furthermore, when the outbreak of the English Civil War virtually ended the flow of immigrants, it became apparent that the colonies' economy had depended heavily on a continuing influx of new settlers. New England farmers had been producing surplus crops–such as seed grains and cattle–which they sold to the newcomers, who in return supplied them with clothing, plows, and other such items. When there were no longer many newcomers, New England's first economic system collapsed.

The Puritans then began a search for new saleable crops and markets. They found such crops in the waters off the coast–fish–and on their own land–grain and wood products. By 1643 they had also found the necessary markets: first the Wine Islands (the Azores and Canaries) in the Atlantic, and then the new English colonies in the Caribbean, which were beginning to cultivate sugar intensively and to invest heavily in slaves. The islands lacked precisely the goods New England could produce in abundance: cheap food (corn and salted fish) to feed the slaves, and wood for barrels to transport wine (the Atlantic islands) and molasses (the Caribbean colonies).

Rise of a mercantile economy

Thus developed the series of transactions that has become known, inaccurately, as the triangular trade. Since New England's products duplicated England's, the northern colonists sold their goods in the West Indies and elsewhere to earn the money with which to purchase English products. (Southerners did not have the same problem. Their crops–tobacco, rice, and indigo–could be sold directly to England.) There soon grew up in New England's ports a cadre of merchants who acquired–usually through barter–cargoes of timber and foodstuffs, which they then dispatched to the West Indies for sale. In the Caribbean the ships sailed from island to island, exchanging fish, barrel staves, and grains for molasses, fruit, spices, and slaves.

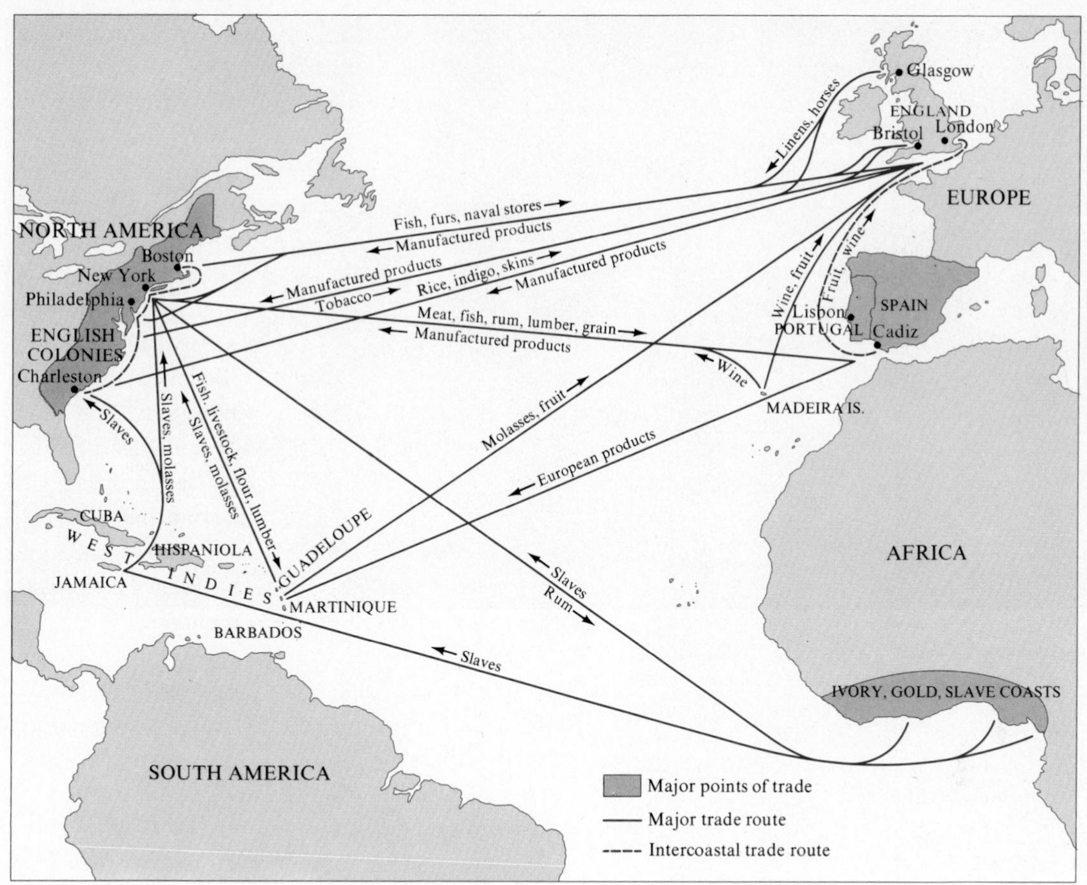

Atlantic trade routes

Sometimes they would then sail to England, and occasionally to Africa for slaves to sell in South Carolina or the Chesapeake. Most often, though, they returned to Boston, Newport, or New Haven to dispose of their cargoes. Thus the trading pattern was not a neat triangle but a shifting set of irregular polygons (see map). Its sole constant was uncertainty, due to the weather, rapid changes of supply and demand in the small island markets, and the delicate system of credit on which the entire structure depended.

The network of seventeenth-century trade, which had achieved mature form by the 1660s, was fueled not by cash (no one had much of that) but by credit in the form of bills of exchange. These were, in effect, promissory notes in which one merchant pledged to pay another a certain sum on demand. Bills of exchange passed from hand to hand, circulating much as currency does today. Ultimately, though, their value rested on trust and the credit standing of the first merchant in the chain. That was one of the major reasons why the seventeenth-century mercantile community was composed chiefly of men related to each other by blood or marriage. A Bostonian who needed a reliable representative in Barbados would send his brother-in-law, son, or cousin to handle his interests; a London merchant might dispatch a relative to Boston for the same reason.

The Puritan New Englanders who ventured into commerce were soon differentiated from their rural counterparts by their ties to a wider trans-Atlantic world and by their preoccupation with material endeavors. Moreover, as time passed, increasing numbers of Puritans became involved in trade. Small investors who owned shares of voyages soon dominated the field numerically if not monetarily. The gulf between commercial and farming interests widened after 1660, when—with the end of the Interregnum and the restoration of the Stuarts to the English throne—

Sea Captains Carousing in Surinam, a scene that could have occurred in any tavern in any Caribbean port. Several recognizable Rhode Island merchants are included among the merrymakers. Painted by John Greenwood (1758), a Bostonian who lived in Surinam (Dutch Guiana), on the northern coast of South America. The St. Louis Art Museum.

Anglican merchants began to migrate to New England. Such men had little stake in the survival of Massachusetts Bay and Connecticut in their original form, and some were openly antagonistic to Puritan traditions. As non-Congregationalists they were denied the vote, and they could not freely practice their religion. They resented their exclusion from the governing elite, believing that their wealth and social status entitled them to political power. Congregationalist clergymen returned their hostility in full measure, and the jeremiads lamenting New England's fall from pristine piety also criticized its new commercial orientation. The Reverend Increase Mather (Cotton Mather's father) reminded his congregation in 1676 that "*Religion and not the World* was that which our Fathers came hither for."

A clash between the commercial community and Puritan political leaders was inevitable. In 1684, encouraged by the merchants and their allies, England revoked the Massachusetts Bay Colony's charter. After several years of experimentation with a combined government for all of the New England provinces (see page 54), a new charter making Massachusetts a royal colony was issued in 1691. Henceforth, its governors were to be appointed by the king, and church membership could no longer be a condition for voting. An Anglican parish was even established in the heart of Boston. It seemed that the "city upon a hill," at least as John Winthrop had envisioned it, was no more.

The extreme stress New England was undergoing as a result of upheavals in its religious life, social organization, and economic system gave rise in 1692 to accusations of witchcraft in Salem Village (now Danvers), Massachusetts. Like their contemporaries elsewhere, seventeenth-century New Englanders believed in and greatly feared witches, who appeared human but whose power, they thought, came from the devil. If New Englanders could not find rational explanations for their troubles, they tended to suspect they were being bewitched. Although such accusations occurred elsewhere, the tensions resulting from New England's commercialization and secularization exploded most dramatically in a little rural community adjoining the bustling port of Salem.

Witchcraft in Salem Village

The crisis began when a group of adolescent girls accused a number of older women–mostly outsiders of one sort or another–of having bewitched them. Before the hysteria spent itself ten months later, nineteen people (including several men, most of them related to accused female witches) had been hanged, another pressed to death by heavy stones, and more than one hundred others jailed. Historians have puzzled ever since about the origins of the witchcraft episode. It has been variously attributed to tension between mothers and daughters (with the witches serving as surrogate mothers), persistent antagonisms among the town's leading families, and even hallucinations arising from a form of food poisoning.

But the most plausible explanation may lie in the uncertainty of life in late seventeenth-century New England. Salem Village, a farming town on the edge of a commercial center, was torn between old and new styles of life. Some families were abandoning agriculture for trade, while others were struggling to maintain traditional ways. The villagers who exploited the new economic opportunities were improving their status relative to their neighbors. Most people were uncertain about their destiny, but none more so than adolescent girls. As children their fate lay in the hands of their parents, yet their ultimate destiny would depend on their husbands. But would their husbands be farmers or artisans or merchants? What would their future lives be like? No one knew. By lashing out and in effect seizing command of the entire town, the girls gave their lives a certainty previously lacking. At the same time, they afforded their fellow townspeople an opportunity to vent their frustrations at the unsettling changes in their lives. The accused witches were scapegoats for the shattered dream of an isolated Bible Commonwealth.

The founding of the middle colonies

New Netherland, founded in 1624, remained small in comparison to its English neighbors to the north and south. A trading outpost of the Dutch West India Company, New Netherland was neglected because the company's economic interests lay chiefly in Africa and Brazil. And because the Dutch were not afflicted by the economic and religious pressures that caused English people to migrate to the New World, immigration remained sparse. Even a 1629 company policy promising a large land grant, or patroonship, to anyone who would bring fifty settlers to the province failed to attract takers. (Only one such tract–Rensselaerswyck, near today's Albany–was ever established.) In the 1660s, New Netherland still had only about 5,000 white and black inhabitants. Virginia's population had by then reached 40,000, and New England's 50,000.

Founding of New Netherland

New Netherland's chief export was furs, which the settlers obtained by trading with the Indians at Fort Orange (Albany) on the upper Hudson River. The Dutch presence at Fort Orange exerted a decisive influence on the balance of power among tribes in the area. Lured by European trade goods, the Mohawks, whose territory lay to the west, attacked the Mahicans, who lived in the vicinity of the fort, driving them east of the Hudson. By 1629 the Mohawks were the chief suppliers of furs to Dutch traders.

The powerful Mohawk tribe was the easternmost component of the Iroquois Confederacy, which also included the Seneca, Cayuga, Onondaga, and Oneida tribes. Under the terms of a defensive alliance forged in the sixteenth century, the key decisions of war and peace for the entire confederacy were made by a council composed of tribal representatives, although each tribe retained some autonomy. The Five Nations vigorously protected their territory against encroachments by whites and other Indians alike, and sought to destroy or subjugate potential rivals. Thus in the 1640s the Iroquois went to war against the Hurons, their major competitor for control of the European trade. Using guns supplied by their Dutch allies, the Iroquois practically exterminated the Huron tribe, forcing its tiny remnant to migrate south and west beyond the confederacy's reach. After the defeat of the Hurons, the Iroquois reigned supreme from the Great Lakes to the Hudson.

Iroquois Confederacy

Because the Dutch traders and the Iroquois needed each other, their relationship was–if sometimes uneasy–generally cordial. But this was a matter of circumstance rather than principle. When Dutch colonists wanted land, not pelts, like the English they paid

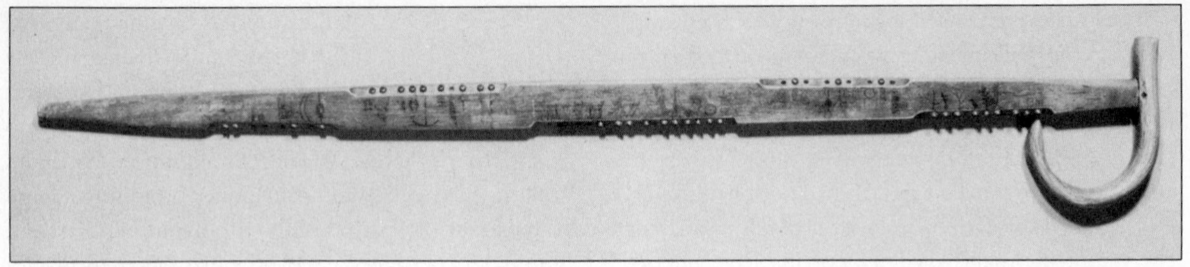

This notched staff recorded attendance at the Great Council of the Iroquois. Each row of notches corresponded to a particular tribe. The number of tribal representatives was indicated by the holes, and the pegs recorded which of them actually attended the meetings. Cranbrook Institute of Science.

little attention to Indian concepts of land ownership. The farmers of New Amsterdam, at the mouth of the Hudson, clashed repeatedly with neighboring tribes as they sought to expand their territory. (Among the dead in the bloody and costly warfare between 1641 and 1646 were Anne Hutchinson and her family, who had moved to New Netherland after seven years in Rhode Island.) In 1655, the Indians attacked New Amsterdam itself as a last gesture of defiance, but could not dislodge the Dutch.

The English were more successful in achieving that goal. As early as the 1640s Puritan New Englanders had begun to settle on Long Island, and New Netherland thus contained an appreciable English minority. Then in March 1664, in total disregard of Dutch claims to the area, Charles II gave the entire region between the Connecticut and Delaware rivers, including the Hudson valley, to his brother James, Duke of York. James immediately organized an invasion fleet. In late August the vessels anchored off the coast of New Netherland and demanded the colony's surrender. The Dutch complied without firing a shot. Although the Netherlands regained control of the colony in 1672, it permanently ceded the province two years later.

English conquest of New Netherland

Thus James (and—after he became king in 1685—the English nation) acquired a tiny but heterogeneous possession. Together, the Dutch and the English accounted for the majority of the population. But New York, as it was now called, also included sizable numbers of Germans, French-speaking Walloons, Scandinavians (New Netherland had swallowed up Swedish settlements on the Delaware River in 1655), and Africans, as well as a smattering of other European peoples. Because the Dutch West India Company actively imported slaves into the colony after its efforts to attract white settlers had failed, almost one-fifth of New York City's approximately 1,500 inhabitants were black. Slaves thus comprised a higher proportion of New York's urban population than of the Chesapeake's in the early 1670s. One observer commented—probably exaggerating only slightly—that eighteen different languages could be heard in the colony.

Recognizing the diversity of the population, the Duke of York's representatives moved slowly and cautiously in their efforts to establish English authority. The Duke's Laws, a legal code proclaimed in March 1665, at first applied only to the Puritan settlements on Long Island; they were later extended to the rest of the colony. Dutch forms of local government were maintained and Dutch land titles confirmed. Religious toleration was guaranteed through a sort of multiple establishment: each town was permitted to decide which church to support with its tax revenues. Furthermore, the Dutch were allowed to maintain their customary legal practices. Until the 1690s, for example, many Dutch couples wrote joint wills, which were enforced in New York courts even though under English law married women could not draft wills. Much to the chagrin of English residents of the colony, the Duke's Laws made no provision for a representative assembly. Not until 1683 did the duke agree to the colonists' requests for an elected legislature. Before then, New York was ruled by an autocratic governor, as it had been under the Dutch.

The English takeover thus had little immediate effect on the colony. Its population grew slowly, barely reaching 18,000 by the time of the first English census in 1698. Until the second decade of the eighteenth century, New York City remained a commercial backwater within the orbit of Boston. The English renamed Fort Orange "Albany," but did not alter Dutch-Indian trade policies. Pelts obtained from the Mohawks continued to be the province's major export.

One of the chief reasons why the English conquest brought so little change to New York was that the Duke of York quickly regranted the land between the Hudson and Delaware rivers—New Jersey—to his friends Sir George Carteret and John Lord Berkeley.

Founding of New Jersey

That left his own colony confined between Connecticut to the east and New Jersey to the west, depriving it of much fertile land and hindering its economic growth. He also failed to promote immigration. Meanwhile the New Jersey proprietors acted rapidly to attract settlers, promising generous land grants, freedom of religion, and—without authorization from the crown—a representative assembly. In response, large numbers of Puritan New Englanders migrated southward to New Jersey, along with some Dutch New Yorkers and a contingent of families from Barbados.

Within twenty years, Berkeley and Carteret sold their interests in New Jersey to separate groups of investors. Because of the resulting large number of individual proprietary shares, and because the governor of New York had granted lands in New Jersey before learning that the duke had given it away, land titles in northern New Jersey were clouded for many years to come. Nevertheless, New Jersey grew quickly; at the time of its first census in 1726, it had 32,500 inhabitants, only 8,000 fewer than New York.

The purchasers of all of Carteret's share (West Jersey) and portions of Berkeley's East Jersey were Quakers seeking a refuge from persecution in England. The Quakers, formally known as the Society of Friends, denied the need for an intermediary between the individual and God. Anyone, they believed, could receive the "inner light" and be saved, and all were equal in God's sight. They had no formally trained clergy; any Quaker, male or female, who felt the call could become a "public Friend" and travel from meeting to meeting to discuss God's word. Moreover, any member of the Society could speak in meetings if he or she desired. In short, the Quakers were true religious radicals, Antinomians in the mold of Anne Hutchinson. (Indeed, Mary Dyer, who followed Hutchinson into exile, became a Quaker, returned to Boston as a missionary, and was hanged for her beliefs.)

In Quaker meetinghouses men and women sat separately, with their heads covered unless they were speaking. Note that among the meeting's leaders, seated on the raised platform, are two women. Museum of Fine Arts, Boston, M. and M. Karolik Collection.

The Quakers obtained a colony of their own in 1681, when Charles II granted the region between Maryland and New York to William Penn, one of the sect's most prominent members. The pious yet fun-loving Penn was then thirty-seven years old. Penn's

Pennsylvania, a Quaker haven

father, Admiral William Penn, had originally served Oliver Cromwell, but later joined forces with Charles II and even loaned the monarch a substantial sum of money. The younger Penn became a Quaker in the mid-1660s, much to his father's dismay. But despite Penn's radical political and religious beliefs, he and Charles II were close personal friends. Were it not for their friendship, the despised Quakers would never have won a charter for an American settlement. As it was, the publicly

Penn's Treaty with the Indians, by Benjamin West (1771), one of the first great American-born artists. A Pennsylvanian, West had been raised on stories of Penn's benevolent Indian policies. His painting of Penn's negotiations with the Delawares captured the spirit of the colony's founder. Joseph and Sarah Harrison Collection, Pennsylvania Academy of the Fine Arts.

stated reason for the grant–repayment of the loan from Penn's father–was just that, a public rationalization for a private act.

William Penn held the colony as a personal proprietorship, and the vast property holdings earned profits for his descendants until the American Revolution. Even so, Penn, like the Roman Catholic Calverts of Maryland before him, saw the province not merely as a source of revenue but also as a haven for his persecuted co-religionists. Penn offered land to all comers on liberal terms, promised toleration for all religions (though only Christians were given the right to vote), guaranteed such English liberties as the right to bail and trial by jury, and pledged to establish a representative assembly. He also publicized the ready availability of land in Pennsylvania through promotional tracts published in German, French, and Dutch.

Penn's activities and the natural attraction of his lands for Quakers gave rise to a migration whose magnitude was equalled only by the Puritan exodus to New England in the 1630s. By mid-1683, over 3,000 people–among them Welsh, Irish, Dutch, and Germans–had already moved to Pennsylvania, and within five years the population had reached 12,000. (By contrast, it took Virginia more than thirty years to achieve a comparable population.) Philadelphia, carefully planned to be the major city in the province, drew merchants and artisans from throughout the English-speaking world. From mainland and West Indian colonies alike came Quakers seeking religious freedom; they brought with them years of experience on American soil and well-established trading connections. Pennsylvania's lands were both plentiful and fertile, and the colony soon began exporting flour and other foodstuffs to the West Indies. Practically overnight Philadelphia acquired more than 2,000 citizens and began to challenge Boston's commercial preeminence.

A pacifist with egalitarian principles, Penn was determined to treat the Indians of Pennsylvania fairly. He carefully purchased tracts of land from the Delawares (or Lenni Lenape), the dominant tribe in the region, before selling them to settlers. Penn also established strict regulations for the Indian trade and forbade the sale of alcohol to tribesmen. In 1682 he visited a number of Lenni Lenape villages, after taking pains to learn the language. "I must say," Penn commented, "that I know not a language spoken in Europe that hath words of more sweetness in Accent and Emphasis, than theirs."

News of the Quakers' exemplary Indian policies spread to other tribes, some of whom decided to move to Pennsylvania. Several tribes from western Maryland, Virginia, and North Carolina came northward near the end of the seventeenth century to escape repeated clashes with white settlers. The most important of these were the Tuscaroras, whose experiences will be described later in this chapter. Likewise, the Shawnees and Miamis chose to move eastward from the Ohio valley. By a supreme irony, however, the same toleration that attracted Indians to Penn's domains also brought non-Quaker Europeans who showed little respect for Indian claims to the soil. In effect, Penn's policy was so successful that it caused its own downfall. The Scotch-Irish, Palatine Germans, and Swiss emigrants who settled in Pennsylvania in the first half of the eighteenth century clashed repeatedly over land with tribes that had also recently migrated to the colony.

Relations between whites and Indians

As the area of English settlement expanded after 1650, white colonists came into contact with increasing numbers of Indian tribes. By no means all of these contacts were peaceful; as will be seen, the years from 1670 to 1730 witnessed some of the fiercest Indian-white conflicts of the entire colonial period. But warfare was not the only way whites and Indians interacted.

Two circumstances helped to bring the races together. First, there was no clearly defined frontier: white settlements and Indian villages were often located near each other, and in many cases tribal lands were surrounded, rather than overrun, by whites. As a result, Indians were a common sight in many English towns, and white merchants frequently visited Indian villages. Second, the Indian trade contributed significantly to the colonial economies, especially in the earliest years of each settlement. Some time usually elapsed before English settlers were themselves able to produce surplus goods for sale elsewhere. In the meantime, they relied on trade with nearby tribes for saleable items to send to Europe in exchange for manufactured goods.

South Carolina is a case in point. The Barbadians who founded the colony were fortunate that the Carolina coast was inhabited by weak tribes who tended to welcome, rather than oppose, the newcomers. The whites quickly realized that they could reap substantial profits from trade with the coastal Indians and the stronger tribes of the interior (Cherokees, Creeks, and Choctaws). At first, the chief commodity obtained in trade was deerskins, which were almost as valuable as beaver pelts in European markets. During the first decade of the eighteenth century, South Carolina exported an average of 54,000 skins annually, and deerskin exports later reached a peak of 160,000.

Indian slave trade

A traffic in Indian slaves also enriched the pockets of white Carolina traders. The many local tribes were frequently at war, a fact that white Carolinians exploited by urging victorious tribes to sell their captives into slavery and even by fomenting wars. Initially the whites kept many such enslaved Indians within the colony; in 1708, for example, 14 percent of South Carolina's population was Indian slaves. But the Indians' ability to escape, coupled with fears of a general Indian uprising, soon caused the whites to export most enslaved Indians to the West Indies and New England. There are no reliable statistics on the extent of the trade in Indian slaves. Certainly, though, thousands of southern Indians and at least hundreds of northern ones (captured in such conflicts as the Pequot War) were sold into slavery, mostly far from their ancestral homes.

By contrast, whites captured by Indians were often adopted into the tribes as full members of Indian families. A number of such people (especially women captured when young) refused to return to white society when offered the chance to do so. One such captive was Mary Jemison, taken by the Senecas when she was only twelve. She married, bore children, and became a respected matron among the Iroquois. In her memoirs, written late in life, Jemison explained that she had stayed with the Indians not only because of her ties to her husband and children, but also because she preferred the work life of an Iroquois. Seneca women's work was "probably not harder than that of white women," she wrote, and their cares were "certainly . . . not half as numerous, nor as great." Women labored in the fields together, keeping their children with them, and, as Jemison remarked, "[we] had no master to oversee or drive us, so that we could work as leisurely as we pleased." Though the lives led by white captives of the Indians should not be romanticized, it is clear that some of them found a "savage" existence preferable to a "civilized" one. (To the colonists' dismay, few Indians were similarly attracted to white society.) The mere existence of such captives indicated, of course, that relations between Indians and whites were not always cordial. And after 1670, a new cycle of hostilities began as English colonists gradually moved beyond the territory of the coastal tribes they had already defeated.

The Spanish and the French also encountered serious difficulties in their efforts to expand their control into the American interior. The experience of the French resembled that of the Dutch in New Netherland. The French outposts along the St. Lawrence River valley (notably Montreal and Quebec) were primarily fur-trading centers rather than permanent agricultural settlements. Few French men and fewer women emigrated to the colonies; many of the fur traders (called *coureurs de bois*—literally, "woods runners") took Indian wives and lived among the tribes.

French-Indian relations

After the Iroquois victory over the Hurons, France's chief trading partner, in the 1640s, coureurs de bois ranged westward in search of new sources of pelts. Frenchmen like Louis Jolliet, Father Jacques Marquette, and the Chevalier de la Salle explored the Great Lakes and the Mississippi valley in the 1670s and 1680s, but not until the eighteenth century did France try to establish some control over that region. France then planned to construct a series of forts along the western rivers in order to surround the English settlements, a scheme vigorously resisted by the Natchez tribe of the lower Mississippi. Only when the French enlisted the aid of the Choctaws in 1730 did they defeat the Natchez in a bloody conflict and finally implement their strategy.

The Spaniards also met with resistance from the local tribes as they spread northward from Mexico into what is now Texas, Arizona, and New Mexico, establishing a capital at Santa Fe. The Pueblo Indians, forced to pay heavy taxes and cultivate the land for their conquerors, grew restless under the heavy-handed rule of the autocratic Spanish governor. In August 1680, led by Popé, a respected medicine man, they rebelled and drove the Spaniards south to El Paso. For a time New Mexico remained solely in Indian hands, but after Popé's death in 1692 the Spaniards returned to re-establish their authority.

Just five years before Popé's uprising forced Europeans to leave New Mexico (if only temporarily), Metacomet—known to the English as King Philip—had set out to achieve a similar goal in New England. The son of Massasoit, who had signed the treaty with the Pilgrims in 1621, Metacomet was chief of the Wampanoags, whose lands on Narragansett Bay were now entirely surrounded by white settlements. Metacomet was concerned not only about white encroachments on his lands but also about the impact of European culture on his people. When a Plymouth

King Philip's War

colony court presumed to apply English law to three Wampanoags accused of killing another Wampanoag (they were hanged), Metacomet and his warriors took the act as a grievous insult. In late June 1675, they began to attack nearby white communities.

Soon two other local tribes, the Nipmucs and the Narragansetts, joined Metacomet's forces. In the fall, the three tribes jointly attacked settlements in the northern Connecticut River valley; in the winter and spring of 1676, they devastated such well-established villages as Sudbury and Andover and even attacked Plymouth and Providence. Altogether, the alliance totally destroyed twelve of the ninety Puritan towns and attacked forty others. A tenth of the able-bodied adult males in Massachusetts were captured or killed; proportional to population, it was the most costly war in American history. New England's very survival seemed to be at stake.

But the tide turned in the summer of 1676. The Indian coalition ran short of food and ammunition, and

Captives of the Tuscaroras at a tribal dance in 1711. After their ransom, Count Christopher von Graffenried, founder of the Swiss-German settlement in North Carolina, sketched this picture showing himself, his surveyor, and his black servant being tortured. Burgerbibliothek, Bern.

whites began to use Christianized tribesmen as guides and scouts. After Metacomet was killed in an ambush in August, the alliance crumbled. Many surviving Wampanoags, Nipmucs, and Narragansetts, including Metacomet's wife and son, were captured and sold into slavery in the West Indies. The power of New England's coastal tribes was broken.

It was more than coincidence that Virginia, the other original English mainland colony, was wracked by conflict with Indians at precisely the same time. In both areas the whites' earlier accommodation with the tribes—reached after the defeat of the Pequots in the north and the Powhatan Confederacy in the south—no longer satisfied both parties. In Virginia, though, it was the whites, rather than the Indians, who felt aggrieved.

By the early 1670s, whites were hungrily eyeing the rich lands north of the York River that had been reserved for the Indians under earlier treaties. Using as a pretext the July 1675 killing of a white servant by some Doeg Indians, they attacked not only the Doegs but also the Susquehannocks, a more important tribe. In retaliation, the Susquehannocks began to raid frontier plantations in the winter of 1676. The land-hungry whites rallied behind the leadership of Nathaniel Bacon, a planter who had arrived in the colony only two years before. Bacon and his followers wanted, in his words, "to ruine and extirpate all Indians in generall." Governor William Berkeley, however, hoped to avoid setting off a major war like that raging in New England.

Berkeley and Bacon soon clashed. After Bacon forced the House of Burgesses to authorize him to attack the Indians, Berkeley declared Bacon and his men to be in rebellion. As the chaotic summer of 1676 wore on, Bacon alternately pursued Indians and battled with the governor's supporters. In September he marched on Jamestown itself and burned the capital to the ground. But after Bacon died of dysentery the following month, the rebellion collapsed. A new Indian treaty signed in 1677 opened much of the disputed territory to whites, and thereafter only the Iroquois Confederacy stood in the path of English expansion north of the Carolinas.

Bacon's Rebellion

In the Carolinas, on the other hand, whites were just beginning to gain a foothold along the coast. In 1709, a group of Swiss and German settlers expropriated without payment lands belonging to the Tuscarora tribe, an Iroquoian people who had migrated southward many years earlier. In 1711, the Tuscaroras and their allies struck back, initially killing more than

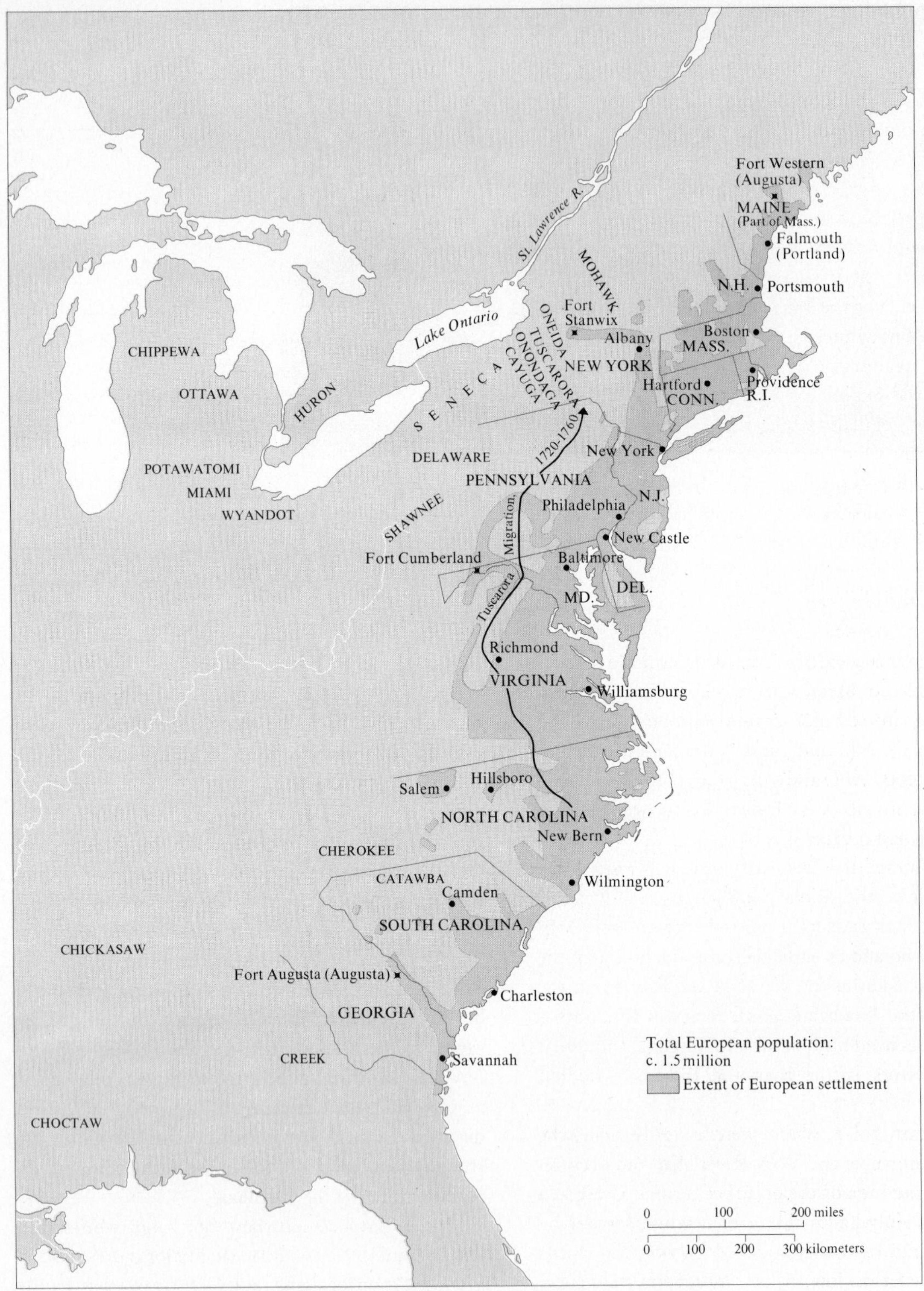

European settlements and Indian tribes, 1750

one hundred whites, then conducting further raids along the frontier. Since thinly populated North Carolina was incapable of raising a force large enough to oppose the Indians, South Carolina came to its aid in 1712 and again in 1713 with armies composed largely of tribesmen. The Tuscaroras, badly defeated in the second campaign, gradually began drifting northward to New York, where they became the sixth nation in the Iroquois Confederacy (see map).

Tuscarora and Yamasee wars

Two years later the Yamasees, who had helped the South Carolina whites subdue the Tuscaroras, themselves rose against the English colonists. Their chief grievance was exploitation at the hands of Carolina traders, who regularly engaged in corrupt and deceptive practices. One contemporary observer reported that the traders "go to any of [the Yamasees'] plantations take what they pleas'd without Leave . . . and if the Indians grumbled or Seem Discontented threaten to beat them and very often did beat them Cruelly." He noted that the traders bragged openly about raping Yamasee women, and that he had himself witnessed such an incident. Furthermore, the traders overcharged the Yamasees, and then seized women and children to sell as slaves in payment of the Indians' "debts."

With the aid of the Creeks, the Yamasees began coordinated attacks on outlying white settlements on April 15 (Good Friday), 1715. As the raids continued through the summer, white refugees streamed into Charleston by the hundreds. At times the Creek-Yamasee offensive came close to driving the whites from the mainland altogether. (At Port Royal, for example, three hundred people were saved only because they crowded aboard a ship in the harbor while the Yamasees set fire to the town.) But the key to victory lay in the hands of the Cherokees. Wooed by both sides, they finally decided to align themselves with the whites against their ancient enemies, the Creeks. Their cause lost, the Yamasees moved south into Florida to seek the protection of the Spanish, and the Creeks retreated to their villages in the western highlands.

By the end of the first quarter of the eighteenth century, therefore, the colonists had effectively destroyed the power of all the Indian tribes east of the Appalachian mountains. The entire eastern seaboard, extending inland for over a hundred miles, was safe for settlement. The one dangerous gap—between the southern border of South Carolina and Spanish Florida—was plugged in 1732 with the chartering of Georgia, the last of the colonies that would become part of the United States. Intended as a haven for debtors by its founder James Oglethorpe, Georgia was specifically designed as a garrison province. Since all its landholders were expected to serve as militiamen to defend English settlements against the Spanish, the charter prohibited women from inheriting or purchasing land in the colony. That clause was soon altered, but it, and a similarly short-lived injunction against the introduction of slavery, revealed the founders' intention that Georgia should be peopled by sturdy yeoman farmers who could take up their weapons at a moment's notice.

Colonial political development and imperial reorganization

From the mid-1630s to the restoration of the Stuarts in 1660, England was too concerned with its own internal disputes to pay much attention to its New World possessions. The American provinces were thus left to develop political structures and practices largely on their own. The New England Puritans worked out their own governmental forms without outside interference, and in the Chesapeake neither the king (Virginia) nor the proprietor (Maryland) exercised heavy-handed executive authority.

In the absence of direct intervention from England, the colonists gradually evolved governments composed of a governor and a two-house legislature. In New England, the governors were elected by the people or the legislature; in the Chesapeake, they were appointed by the king or the proprietor. A council, elected in some colonies and appointed in others, advised the governor on matters of policy and sometimes served as the province's highest court. The council also had a legislative function: initially its members met jointly with representatives elected by their districts to debate and vote on laws affecting the colony. But as time passed, the fundamental differences between the two legislative groups'

Colonial political structures

purposes and constituencies led them to separate into two distinct houses. In Virginia, that important event occurred in 1663; in Massachusetts Bay it had happened earlier, in 1644. Thus developed the two-house legislature still used in almost all American states.

While provincial governments were taking shape, so too were local political institutions. In New England, elected selectmen governed the towns at first, but by the end of the century the town meeting, held at least annually and attended by most adult white townsmen, handled most matters of local concern. In the Chesapeake the same function was performed by the judges of the county court and by the parish vestry, a group of laymen charged with overseeing church affairs, whose power also encompassed secular concerns.

The English colonies established later in the century adopted similar political structures. Charles II, who authorized the new settlements, included in each charter (except that of New York) a provision requiring the inhabitants' consent to governmental measures. None of the charters specified the form such consent should take or defined the voting population; such questions were left in the hands of the proprietors. In the Carolinas, Pennsylvania, and even New Jersey (where the New York charter was at first the controlling document), representative assemblies were established as the means of obtaining consent. Pennsylvania's legislature had only one house, but the other colonies followed the two-house pattern. As already noted, an assembly was formed in New York in 1683 at the urging of the people.

By late in the seventeenth century, therefore, the American colonists were accustomed to exercising a considerable degree of local political autonomy. The tradition of consent was especially firmly established in New England. Massachusetts, Connecticut, and Rhode Island were, in effect, independent entities, subject neither to the direct authority of the king nor to a proprietor. In 1662 and 1663 respectively, Charles II confirmed the status of Connecticut and Rhode Island by granting them charters legitimizing the political systems evolved since their founding. In the colonies to the south, political structures were somewhat less stable and assemblies less powerful because the largely immigrant population prevented the development of coherent colonial interests and consistent leadership. The desire for local control was basically identical in north and south, but greater continuity of officeholding in New England made for more political coherence and less instability throughout most of the seventeenth century. For example, at the end of the century all the major officeholders in Windsor, Connecticut, were descendants of leading early settlers; in Maryland in the same period, fewer than one-quarter of the officeholders had even been born in the province. Terms of service differed as well. Once elected, New Englanders usually continued to serve in some capacity for most of their lives. In Maryland, though, more than three-quarters of assembly members before 1715 served fewer than three terms in office.

The Stuart restoration ended England's neglect of its American colonies, and clashes between the mother country and its possessions became practically inevitable. Charles II (who reigned from 1660 to 1685) and his brother James II (1685 to 1688) both concerned themselves with colonial administration more directly than had any of their predecessors, including Oliver Cromwell. The trend continued even after the Catholic James II was ousted by Parliament in the bloodless rebellion known as the Glorious Revolution. His Protestant successors, the Dutch Prince William of Orange and his wife Mary (a Stuart), oversaw a major reorganization of colonial administration at the end of the century.

The chief reason for the unprecedented interest in America was economic. By 1660, it had become evident that the American colonies could make important contributions to England's economic well-being. Tobacco from the Chesapeake and sugar from the West Indies had obvious value, but other colonial products also had profitable potential. The new policies thus had two related goals. First, the Stuart monarchs wanted to ensure that colonial commerce would benefit England rather than competing with the mother country or aiding other nations. Second, as a means of achieving that end, they (particularly James II) wanted to tighten England's administrative controls over the colonies. England's pursuit of those goals aroused considerable opposition from the Americans, who had long been accustomed to substantial independence of action.

English administrators in the late seventeenth century based their commercial policy on a series of assumptions about the operations of the world's economic system. Collectively, these assumptions are usually called *mercantilism,* though neither the term itself nor a unified mercantilist theory was formulated until a century later. The economic world was seen as a collection of national states, each competing for shares of a finite amount of wealth. What one nation gained was automatically another nation's loss. Each nation's goal was to become as economically self-sufficient as possible while maintaining a favorable balance of trade with other countries (that is, exporting more than it imported). Colonies had an important role to play in such a scheme. They could supply the mother country with valuable raw materials to be consumed at home or sent abroad, and they could serve as a market for the mother country's manufactured goods.

Parliament applied that mercantilist theory to the American colonies in a series of laws known as the Navigation Acts. The major acts—passed in 1660, 1663, and 1673—established three main principles. First, only English or colonial merchants and ships could engage in trade in the colonies. Second, certain valuable American products could be sold only in the mother country. At first these "enumerated" goods were wool, sugar, tobacco, indigo, ginger, and dyes; later acts added rice, naval stores (masts, spars, pitch, tar, and turpentine), copper, and furs to the list. Third, all foreign goods destined for sale in the colonies had to be shipped via England and pay English import duties. Some years later, a new series of laws declared a fourth principle: the colonies could not make or export items that competed with English products (such as wool clothing, hats, and iron).

Navigation Acts

The intention of the Navigation Acts was clear: American trade was to center on England. The mother country was to benefit from colonial imports and exports both. England had first claim on the most valuable colonial exports, and all foreign imports into the colonies had to pass through England first, enriching its customs revenues in the process. Furthermore, English and colonial shippers were given a monopoly of the American trade. (It is important to note that the American provinces, especially those in the north, produced many goods that were not enumerated—such as fish, flour, and barrel staves. These products could be traded directly to foreign purchasers as long as they were carried in English or American ships.)

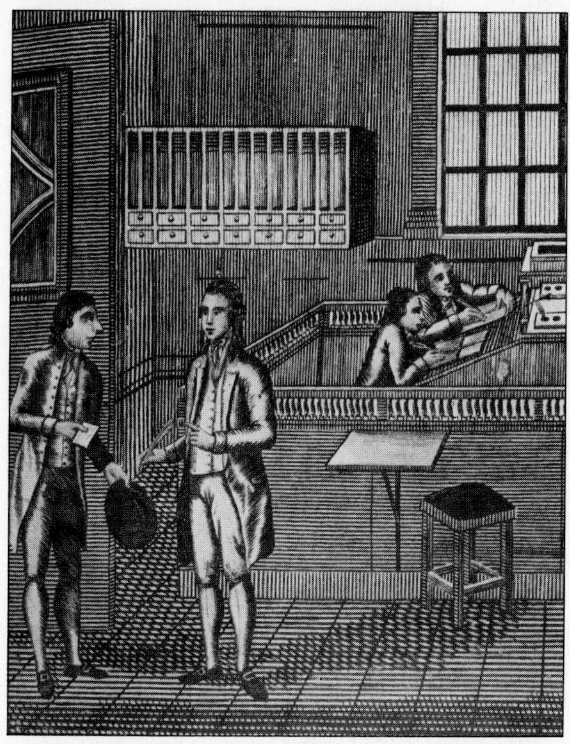

Northern merchants conducting business at their city offices, or counting houses. In the background, their clerks copy letters to overseas traders and maintain the elaborate credit accounts that underlay the merchants' transactions. The Library Company of Philadelphia.

The English authorities soon learned that it was easier to write mercantilist legislation than to enforce it. The many harbors of the American coast provided ready havens for smugglers, and colonial officials often looked the other way when illegally imported goods were offered for sale. In ports such as Curaçao in the Dutch West Indies, American merchants could easily dispose of enumerated goods and purchase foreign items on which duty had not been paid. Consequently, Parliament in 1696 enacted another Navigation Act designed to strengthen enforcement of the first three. This law established in America a number of vice-admiralty courts, which operated without juries. In England such courts dealt only with cases involving piracy, vessels taken as wartime prizes, and the like. But since American juries had already demonstrated a tendency to favor local smugglers over customs officers (a colonial customs service had been started in 1671), Parliament decided to remove Navigation Act cases from the regular colonial courts.

England took another major step in colonial administration in 1696 by creating the Board of Trade and Plantations to replace the loosely structured standing committee of the Privy Council that had handled colonial affairs since 1675. The fifteen-member Board of Trade thereafter served as the chief organ of government concerned with the American colonies. It gathered information, reviewed Crown appointments in America, scrutinized legislation passed by colonial assemblies, supervised trade policies, and advised successive ministries on colonial issues. Still, the Board of Trade did not have any direct powers of enforcement. Furthermore, it shared jurisdiction over American affairs not only with the customs service and the navy but also with the secretary of state for the southern department (the member of the ministry responsible for the colonies). In short, although the Stuart monarchs' reforms considerably improved the quality of colonial administration, supervision of the American provinces remained decentralized and haphazard.

As part of the same campaign to bring more order into the administration of the colonies, successive kings began to chip away at the privileges granted in colonial charters and to reclaim proprietorships for the Crown. New Hampshire (1679), its parent colony Massachusetts (1691), New Jersey (1702), and the Carolinas (1729) all became royal colonies. The charters of Rhode Island, Connecticut, Maryland, and Pennsylvania were temporarily suspended as well, but were ultimately restored to their original status.

The most drastic reordering of colonial administration was attempted in 1686 through 1689, and its chief target was Puritan New England. Reports from America had convinced English officials that New England was a hotbed of smuggling. Moreover, the Puritans refused to allow freedom of religion and insisted on maintaining laws that often ran counter to English practice. New England thus seemed an appropriate place to exert English authority with greater vigor. The charters of all the colonies from New Jersey to Maine (part of Massachusetts) were revoked, and a Dominion of New England established in 1686.

Dominion of New England

Sir Edmund Andros, the governor, was given immense power: all the assemblies were dissolved, and he needed only the consent of an appointed council to make laws and levy taxes. New Englanders endured Andros's autocratic rule for more than two years. Then, after hearing that William and Mary had assumed the throne in England, they overthrew Andros and resumed their customary form of government.

In other American colonies too, the Glorious Revolution proved to be a signal for revolt. In Maryland the Protestant Association overturned the government of the Catholic proprietor, and in New York Jacob Leisler, a militia officer of German origin, assumed control of the province. When these three uprisings are seen in conjunction with those of the previous decade–Bacon's Rebellion in Virginia (1676) and Culpeper's Rebellion in North Carolina (1677)–it is clear that the late seventeenth century was a time of turmoil for the American colonies.

What had caused the rash of rebellions? Certainly the Stuart monarchs' attempts to tighten England's control over the colonies were a major contributing factor. The new class of alien officials who arrived in America determined to implement the policies of king and Parliament owed nothing to the colonists. By distributing patronage in the form of offices and land grants, they tried to create "court parties" that would support their claims to expanded power. In the process they won the gratitude of those they favored and the hostility of those they did not. Many members of the developing colonial social and economic elites–whose wealth derived from staple-crop production in the south and commerce in the north–resented their exclusion from political power and opposed the new regimes.

The difficulties resulting from imperial reorganization were compounded by political instability in most of the colonies. Only in New England was a majority of the population native-born in the latter decades of the seventeenth century. Continuing immigation in the South and ethnic diversity in the recently settled middle colonies heightened the disorders that would have existed in any event. Not until the end of the first quarter of the eighteenth century did native-born Americans predominate in all the colonies. It was then that American-born elite families consolidated their hold on economic power and social status. And it is no coincidence that at the same time the colonial political systems outside New England assumed more mature form.

In eighteenth-century American politics, the representative assembly became the chief vehicle through

Important events

1642	English Civil War begins
1649	Charles I executed
1655	Dutch conquer Swedish settlements on Delaware River
1656	Iroquois-Huron Wars end with defeat of Hurons
1658	Oliver Cromwell dies
1660	Stuarts restored to throne; Charles II becomes king First Navigation Act passed
1662	Halfway Covenant drafted Connecticut granted charter
1663	Rhode Island granted charter
1664	English conquer New Netherland; New York founded New Jersey established
1669	Carolina chartered
1670	Charleston founded
1673	Jacques Marquette and Louis Jolliet explore Great Lakes and Mississippi Valley
1674	Netherlands permanently cede New York to England
1675–76	King Philip's (Metacomet's) War (New England)
1676	Bacon's Rebellion (Virginia)
1677	Culpeper's Rebellion (North Carolina)
1679	New Hampshire becomes royal colony
1670s	Imports of African slaves to southern colonies increase dramatically
1680	Pueblo revolt (New Mexico)
1681	Pennsylvania chartered
1682	Sieur de La Salle reaches mouth of Mississippi River
1684	Massachusetts Bay charter revoked
1685	James II becomes king
1686–89	Dominion of New England
1688–89	James II deposed in Glorious Revolution; William and Mary ascend throne
1689	Protestant Association Rebellion (Maryland) Leisler's Rebellion (New York)
1691	Massachusetts Bay and Plymouth colonies combined under one royal charter
1692	Witchcraft outbreak in Salem Village
1696	Board of Trade and Plantations established
1690s	Rice cultivation begins in South Carolina
1702	New Jersey becomes royal colony
1710	Blacks become a majority in South Carolina
1711–13	Tuscarora War (North Carolina)
1715	Yamasee War (South Carolina)
1720s	Native-born Americans become a majority in Chesapeake
1729	North and South Carolina become separate royal colonies
1732	Georgia chartered
1740s	Indigo cultivation begins in South Carolina Black population of Chesapeake begins to grow chiefly through natural increase

which politically talented Americans expressed their opinions on colonial policy. Denied access to top appointive posts (which were usually filled with the friends and relatives of English politicians), such men sought to increase their power by expanding the role of the assembly. Colonial assemblies began to claim privileges associated with the House of Commons, such as the right to initiate all tax legislation and to control the militia. The assemblies also developed effective ways of influencing governors, judges, customs officers, and other appointed officials (including threats to withhold their salaries). Colonial assemblies were often wracked by internal disputes among competing factions; though Virginia and South Carolina elite families usually presented a united front to royal officials, New Yorkers fought with each other so long and so bitterly that the provincial government was at times virtually paralyzed. Nevertheless, Americans agreed on one point: members of the assembly represented the people in a way that appointed English officials did not.

Rise of the representative assembly

By the middle of the eighteenth century, the colonists had developed a standard way of thinking about their political system. They believed that their governments mimicked the balance between king, lords, and commons found in Great Britain–a combination that was thought to produce a stable polity. Although the analogy was not exact, the colonists equated their governors with the monarch, their councils with the aristocracy, and their assemblies with the House of Commons. All three were thought essential to good government, but the colonists did not regard them with the same degrees of approval. They saw the governors and appointed councils as aliens who posed a potential threat to colonial freedoms and customary ways of life. As representatives of England rather than America, the governors and councils were to be feared and guarded against rather than trusted. The colonists saw the assemblies, on the other hand, as the people's protectors. Elected in most colonies by men who met minimal property-holding requirements, the assemblies regarded themselves as representatives of the people. Their constituents shared the same view; in some colonies, notably Massachusetts, towns even began to instruct their representatives how to vote on some controversial issues.

That vision of politics, which emerged slowly over the first half of the eighteenth century, was to be of immense importance in the revolutionary crisis that developed in the years following 1763. The notions of government's proper role expounded then in innumerable pamphlets did not appear out of thin air, but rather rested on generations of political experience. The colonists had become accustomed to a political structure in which the executive was feared and the legislature trusted, in which authority was widely dispersed and decentralized, and in which the supreme power (England, in this case) had little direct effect on most people. What they were familiar with, in other words, was a *limited* government–though limited more by circumstances than by design. When Americans had to create governmental structures for themselves after 1775, they incorporated all those elements of their past experience into a formal political theory.

Suggestions for further reading

General

Charles M. Andrews, *The Colonial Period of American History,* vol. 4 (1938); George Louis Beer, *The Old Colonial System, 1660–1754,* 2 vols. (1912); Carl Bridenbaugh, *Cities in the Wilderness: The First Century of Urban Life in America, 1625–1742* (1938); Stuart Bruchey, *Roots of American Economic Growth, 1607–1861* (1965); Wesley Frank Craven, *The Colonies in Transition, 1660–1713* (1968); George M. Wrong, *The Rise and Fall of New France,* 2 vols. (1928).

Africa and the slave trade

Philip D. Curtin, *The Atlantic Slave Trade: A Census* (1969); Basil Davidson, *The Africans: An Entry to Cultural History* (1969); Basil Davidson, *Black Mother* (1969); David B. Davis, *The Problem of Slavery in Western Culture* (1966); Herbert S. Klein, "Slaves and Shipping in Eighteenth-Century Virginia," *Journal of Interdisciplinary History,* 5 (1974–1975), 383–412.

Blacks in Anglo-America

Richard S. Dunn, *Sugar and Slaves: The Rise of the Planter Class in the English West Indies, 1624–1713* (1972); Lorenzo

Johnson Greene, *The Negro in Colonial New England* (1942); Allan Kulikoff, "A 'Prolifick' People: Black Population Growth in the Chesapeake Colonies, 1700–1790," *Southern Studies,* 16 (1977), 391–428; Edgar J. McManus, *Black Bondage in the North* (1973); Russell Menard, "From Servants to Slaves: The Transformation of the Chesapeake Labor System," *Southern Studies,* 16 (1977), 355–390; Edmund S. Morgan, *American Slavery, American Freedom: The Ordeal of Colonial Virginia* (1975); Peter H. Wood, *Black Majority: Negroes in Colonial South Carolina from 1670 through the Stono Rebellion* (1974).

Indian-white relations

James Axtell, "The White Indians of Colonial America," *William and Mary Quarterly,* 3rd ser., 32 (1975), 55–88; Judith K. Brown, "Economic Organization and the Position of Women among the Iroquois," *Ethnohistory,* 17 (1970), 151–167; David H. Corkran, *The Creek Frontier, 1540–1783* (1967); Verner W. Crane, *The Southern Frontier, 1670–1732* (1929); George T. Hunt, *The Wars of the Iroquois: A Study in Intertribal Relations* (1940); Douglas Leach, *Flintlock and Tomahawk: New England in King Philip's War* (1958); Allen W. Trelease, *Indian Affairs in Colonial New York: The Seventeenth Century* (1960); Alden T. Vaughan and Daniel K. Richter, "Crossing the Cultural Divide: Indians and New Englanders, 1605–1763," *Proceedings of the American Antiquarian Society,* 90, 1 (1980), 23–99; C.A. Weslager, *The Delaware Indians: A History* (1972).

New England

Bernard Bailyn, *The New England Merchants in the Seventeenth Century* (1955); Paul Boyer and Stephen Nissenbaum, *Salem Possessed: The Social Origins of Witchcraft* (1974); Richard Bushman, *From Puritan to Yankee: Character and the Social Order in Connecticut, 1690–1765* (1967); John Demos, "Underlying Themes in the Witchcraft of Seventeenth-Century New England," *American Historical Review,* 75 (1970), 1311–1326; Mary Maples Dunn, "Saints and Sisters: Congregational and Quaker Women in the Early Colonial Period," *American Quarterly,* 30 (1978), 582–601; Kenneth A. Lockridge, "Land, Population, and the Evolution of New England Society, 1630–1790," *Past and Present,* 39 (1968), 62–80; Perry Miller, *The New England Mind: From Colony to Province* (1953); Robert G. Pope, *The Half-Way Covenant: Church Membership in Puritan New England* (1969); Richard Pares, *Yankees and Creoles: The Trade Between North America and the West Indies before the American Revolution* (1956); Laurel Thatcher Ulrich, "Virtuous Women Found: New England Ministerial Literature 1668–1735," *American Quarterly,* 28 (1976), 20–40.

New Netherland and the Restoration colonies

Edwin B. Bronner, *William Penn's "Holy Experiment": The Founding of Pennsylvania 1681–1701* (1962); Thomas J. Condon, *New York Beginnings: The Commercial Origins of New Netherland* (1968); Wesley Frank Craven, *New Jersey and the English Colonization of North America* (1964); Mary Maples Dunn, *William Penn: Politics and Conscience* (1967); Michael Kammen, *Colonial New York: A History* (1975); Lawrence Lee, *The Lower Cape Fear in Colonial Days* (1965); Robert C. Ritchie, *The Duke's Province: A Study of Politics and Society in Colonial New York, 1660–1691* (1977); M. Eugene Sirmans, *Colonial South Carolina: A Political History, 1663–1763* (1966).

Colonial politics

Bernard Bailyn, *The Origins of American Politics* (1968); Bernard Bailyn, "Politics and Social Structure in Virginia," in *Seventeenth-Century America: Essays in Colonial History,* ed. James M. Smith (1959), 90–115; Lois Green Carr and David W. Jordan, *Maryland's Revolution of Government 1689–1692* (1974); Jack P. Greene, *The Quest for Power: The Lower Houses of Assembly in the Southern Royal Colonies, 1689–1776* (1963); Kenneth A. Lockridge and Alan Kreider, "The Evolution of Massachusetts Town Government, 1640–1740," *William and Mary Quarterly,* 3rd ser., 23 (1966), 549–574; David S. Lovejoy, *The Glorious Revolution in America* (1972); Charles S. Sydnor, *"Gentlemen Freeholders": Political Practices in Washington's Virginia* (1952).

Imperial administration

Viola F. Barnes, *The Dominion of New England: A Study in British Colonial Policy* (1923); Thomas C. Barrow, *Trade and Empire: The British Customs Service in Colonial America 1660–1775* (1967); Lawrence A. Harper, *The English Navigation Laws: A Seventeenth-Century Experiment in Social Engineering* (1939); Michael Kammen, *Empire and Interest: The American Colonies and the Politics of Mercantilism* (1970); I.K. Steele, *Politics of Colonial Policy: The Board of Trade in Colonial Administration* (1968); Stephen Saunders Webb, *The Governors-General: The English Army and the Definition of the Empire, 1569–1681* (1979).

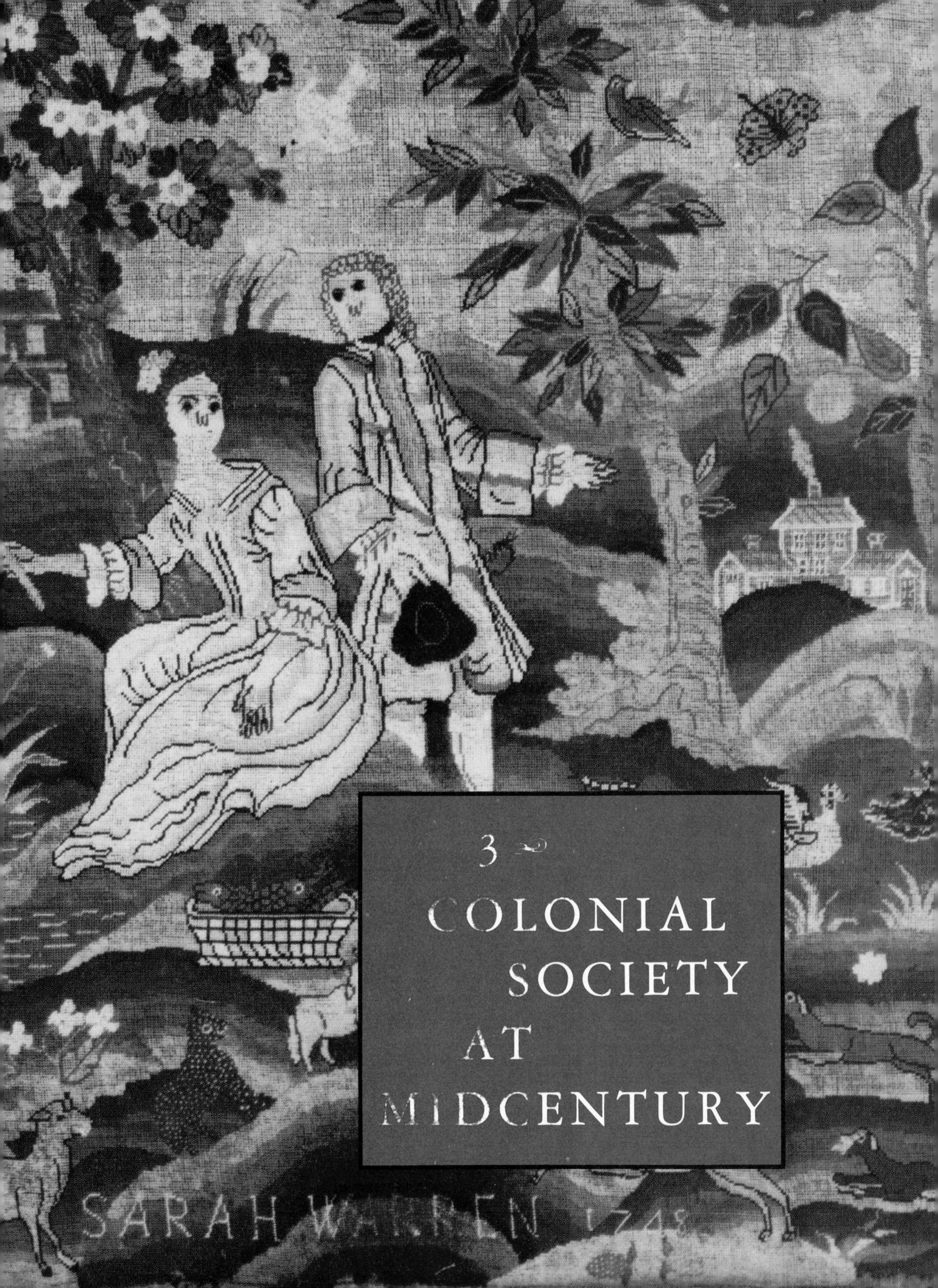

3

COLONIAL SOCIETY AT MIDCENTURY

Around the middle of the eighteenth century, the immigrant Alexander McAllister received a letter from a cousin in Scotland asking whether he too should consider moving to the American colonies. McAllister, who had settled in North Carolina along with many fellow Scotsmen, responded encouragingly. "As for the country it is a very good one a poor man that will incline to work may have the value of his labour for ther is nothing that he puts in the ground but what yealds beyount any Idea that a Strenger can conceive," he told his cousin. Indeed, he continued, "you would do well to advise all poor people whom you wish well to take curradge and com to this Country it will be of Benefite to ther riseing generation."

A few years later Martha McClouting, a Scotch-Irish woman living in Charleston, expressed the same attitude to her mother in Derry: "I am marred Now and fowlos the Stoar Ceping I have got three Cheldren two Sons and wan Dauther. . . . I have got Sex Negros wich keps me Easey From hard Lebar and I wish that meney moor of you had the good fortun to Cum to this Contry with me. . . . Many days have I worked hard in Ireland but many days her I Live at Ease–this Country very few works hard in it."

McAllister and McClouting were two among the hundreds of thousands of European immigrants who flooded into England's mainland colonies during the years from 1715 to 1775. Their attitude was representative. Migrants from overpopulated and distressed areas of Europe, especially Scotland, northern Ireland (Ulster), and Germany, found opportunities in America undreamed of in their homelands. That these opportunities were more restricted than they had been in the previous century meant little to men and women who had owned almost nothing in the Old World and could acquire property in the New. The arrival of these immigrants was one of the most important occurrences in eighteenth-century America.

The life they found in the colonies was less primitive and precarious than it had been during the first century of settlement. The entire coastal plain was free of any threat of Indian attack; representative politics allowed colonists a voice in their own government; and the economy was flourishing, despite occasional wild fluctuations. A majority of colonists, black and white, were now native-born, and the colonies were beginning to develop a distinctive identity of their own. Colleges had been founded, newspapers established, social clubs and literary societies formed, a regular postal service begun, roads built, laws codified, and histories of the colonies written. Life in America, in short, had started to fall into set, predictable, and distinctive patterns. The provinces could no longer be seen as extensions of England. Individually and collectively, they had become quite different.

Population growth

One of the most striking characteristics of the mainland colonies in the eighteenth century was their rapid population growth. Only about 250,000 people (excluding Indians) resided in the colonies in 1700; thirty years later that number had more than doubled, and by 1775 it had become 2.5 million. Although immigration accounted for a considerable share of the growth, most of it resulted from natural increase. By 1750 the sex ratio among both whites and blacks was approximately equal throughout the mainland colonies; thus almost all Americans could marry and have children. Most white women married in their early twenties, most black women in their late teens. Their husbands were usually a few years older. Most women bore between five and eight children, becoming pregnant every two or three years throughout their fertile years, and a large proportion of their children survived to maturity. In 1775 about half the American population, white and black, was under sixteen years of age. (In 1980, by contrast, only about one-third of the American population was under sixteen.)

Such a dramatic phenomenon did not escape the attention of contemporaries. As early as the 1720s, Americans began to point with pride to their fertility, citing population growth as evidence of the advantages of living in the colonies. In 1755 Benjamin Franklin published his *Observations Concerning the Increase of Mankind,* which attributed America's striking population growth to early marriages made possible by the availability of land. (Franklin was partly right, but he did not realize that the greater length of marriages and the high proportion of American women who married and bore children also contributed to the rate of increase.) Franklin estimated that the Ameri-

This portrait of an eighteenth-century family shows the typical colonial childbearing pattern in the large number of "stairstep" children, born at approximately two-year-intervals. National Gallery of Art, Gift of Edgar William and Bernice Chrysler Garbisch.

can population would double every twenty years, and he predicted that in another century "the greatest Number of Englishmen will be on this Side the Water. What an Accession of Power to the British Empire by Sea as well as Land!" he rhapsodized. "What Increase of Trade and Navigation!"

Interestingly enough, Franklin's purpose in writing his *Observations* was to argue that Britain should stop allowing Germans to emigrate to Pennsylvania. Since the English population in America was increasing so rapidly, he asked, "why should the Palatine Boors be suffered to swarm into our Settlements? . . . Why should Pennsylvania, founded by the English, become a Colony of *Aliens,* who will shortly be so numerous as to Germanize us instead of Anglifying them, and will never adopt our Language or Customs?" Franklin was exaggerating the potential effects of German immigration, but his fears were not wholly misplaced. By the late eighteenth century, emigrants from the Rhineland—known as "Pennsylvania Dutch," a corruption of *Deutsch*—comprised one-third of the colony's residents.

Not all the approximately 100,000 Germans who emigrated to Pennsylvania, mainly between 1730 and 1755, stayed in that colony. Some who landed at Philadelphia moved west and then south along the eastern slope of the Appalachian mountains, eventually finding homes in western Maryland and Virginia. Others sailed first to Charleston or Savannah and settled in the interior of South Carolina or Georgia. The German immigrants belonged to a wide variety of Protestant sects—primarily Lutheran, German Reformed, and Moravian—and therefore added to the already substantial religious diversity of the middle colonies.

German immigration

Many Germans arrived in America as redemptioners. Under that variant form of indentured servitude,

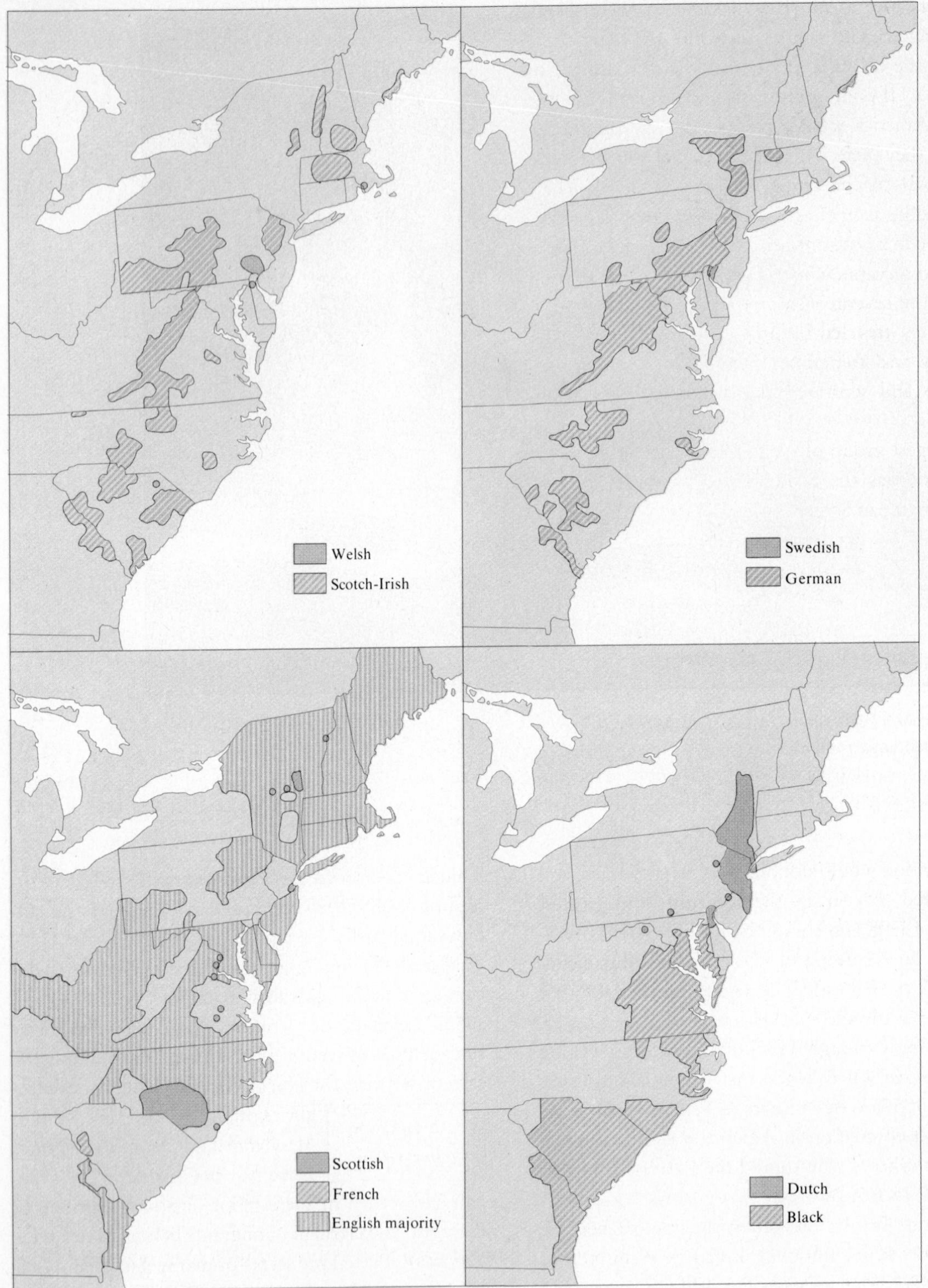

Non-English white settlements 1775, black population, c. 1775.
Source: Reprinted by permission of Princeton University Press.

immigrants paid as much as possible of the cost of their passage before sailing from Europe. After they landed in the colonies, the rest of the fare had to be "redeemed." If poor immigrants had no friends or relatives in America willing to take on the burden of payment, they were indentured for a term of service proportional to the amount they still owed. That term could be as brief as a year or two, but was more likely to be four. In contrast to the unmarried English indentured servants who had migrated to the Chesapeake in the seventeenth century, German redemptioners often traveled in family groups. In America, the family was sometimes divided among different purchasers and separated for the term of their indentures.

Scotch-Irish and Scottish immigration

The largest group of white non-English emigrants to America was the Scotch-Irish, chiefly descended from Presbyterian Scots who had settled in Protestant portions of Ireland during the seventeenth century. Perhaps as many as 250,000 Scotch-Irish people moved to the colonies. Fleeing economic distress and religious discrimination–Irish law favored Anglicans over Presbyterians and other dissenters–at home, they were lured as well by hopes of obtaining land in America. Like the Germans, the Scotch-Irish often landed in Philadelphia. They also moved west and south from that city, settling chiefly in the western portions of Pennsylvania, Maryland, Virginia, and the Carolinas. Frequently unable to afford any acreage, they simply squatted where they wished, building crude houses and carving fields out of the wilderness. Such squatters simply ignored the Indian tribes, land speculators, or colonial governments that nominally owned the land.

The more than 25,000 Scots who came directly to America from Scotland should not be confused with the Scotch-Irish. Many Scottish immigrants were Jacobites–supporters of Stuart claimants to the throne of England. After the death of William and Mary's successor Queen Anne in 1714, the British throne had passed to the German house of Hanover, in the person of King George I. In 1715 and again in 1745, Jacobite rebels attempted unsuccessfully to capture the crown for the Stuart pretender, and many were exiled to America as punishment for their treason. (The British also imposed the same punishment on some ordinary criminals.) Most of the Jacobites settled in North Carolina. Ironically, they tended to become loyalists during the Revolutionary War because of their strong commitment to monarchy. Another wave of Scottish immigration began in the 1760s and flowed mainly into northern New York; most of these new arrivals settled as tenants on large tracts of land in the Mohawk River valley.

A ceramic pie plate manufactured in southeastern Pennsylvania in 1786 shows the continuing use of German by Pennsylvania Dutch immigrants. Philadelphia Museum of Art.

Due to these migration patterns and the concentration of slaveholding in the South, half the colonial population south of New England was of non-English origin by 1775 (see map). Yet, with the exception of certain religious sects like the Mennonites, Amish, and Dunkards (all of whom preserved their traditional lifestyles), most immigrants assimilated fairly readily into Anglo-American culture. In Germantown, Pennsylvania, for example, German continued to be spoken in churches and within families. But English soon became the language of public communication. Although the immigrant generation used both German and English, their children and grandchildren spoke English almost exclusively. Instruction in the town's first school was conducted in English (classes in German were later added). People baptized "Maria Holtz" and "Jacob Zimmermann" changed their names to "Mary Wood" and "James Carpenter." It was chiefly the continuing influx of new settlers from Germany and the retention of German for religious purposes that kept some of the old ways alive in Germantown.

Social stratification

The vast majority of eighteenth-century immigrants entered white society at the bottom of the social scale and on the geographic fringes of settlement. By the time they arrived, American society was dominated by wealthy, native-born elite families. Furthermore, the social and economic structure was more rigid than it had been before 1700. Unlike their seventeenth-century predecessors, the new non-English immigrants had little opportunity to improve their circumstances dramatically. The most they could realistically hope for was to accumulate a modest amount of property over a lifetime of hard work. Even that limited goal appears to have become more difficult to attain as the century progressed, but—considering the poverty they had left behind in Europe—it is unlikely that many regretted their decision to emigrate.

Distribution of wealth

Increasing social stratification—a widening gap between rich and poor—was most noticeable in the cities, which contained less than 10 percent of the population but displayed greater extremes of wealth and poverty than did rural areas outside the plantation South. There were few large cities in mid-eighteenth-century America. The biggest—as it had been since 1630—was Boston, with about 17,000 residents. Next came Philadelphia (approximately 13,000), closely followed by New York (about 11,000). Charleston, South Carolina, the only city of appreciable size in the South, had approximately 7,000 inhabitants, about half of whom were black. Smaller but still important were Newport, New Haven, Salem, and Hartford in the North and Norfolk, Annapolis, and Savannah in the South. In such cities lived the wealthy merchants who dominated the Atlantic trade, and the impoverished sailors employed on their ships; well-paid skilled artisans who made furniture, silver, fancy clothing, and carriages for the rich, and common laborers who had trouble making ends meet; well-to-do appointed officials who supervised colonial governments, and hundreds, if not thousands, of poor folk who owned little more than the clothes on their backs.

In late seventeenth- and early eighteenth-century America, there was little dire poverty and little ostentatious wealth. Surviving city tax records show that at the turn of the century the bottom half of the population possessed about one-tenth of the property, and the richest 10 percent owned perhaps 40 percent. By contrast to European cities of the same period, this division of wealth was relatively equitable. Sixty to seventy years later, conditions had changed significantly, although American society was still far less stratified than Europe's. The poor relief systems of all the northern cities—especially Boston—were overwhelmed with applicants for assistance. Meanwhile, families with large fortunes were building luxurious mansions and filling them with imported furniture. By 1774, the most prosperous tenth of Philadelphia's population possessed 55 percent of the wealth, while the poorest third owned less than 2 percent.

What had happened? In the cities, obviously, the rich had gotten significantly richer and the poor had gotten poorer. But who were the rich? And who were the poor? The first question is easier to answer than the second. The rich were those American families who had begun the century with sufficient capital to take advantage of changes in the colonial economy. The rapidly increasing population had added both consumers and producers to the economy. Exports of raw materials skyrocketed and so did purchases of imported goods; the colonies developed into a major market for British manufactures. Controlling much of this expanded commerce, and earning sizable profits from it, were the merchants of urban America. (British merchants, their chief competitors, dominated only the tobacco and sugar trades.) In contrast to the late seventeenth century, when most voyages were joint ventures by a large number of small investors, mid-eighteenth-century voyages were funded by fewer merchants with larger amounts of capital. That meant greater individual risk (making marine insurance a thriving field) but also potentially greater individual profits.

Merchants and professionals

In addition to the merchants, the cities contained a growing well-to-do professional class composed of doctors, lawyers, and government officials. Many appointive colonial offices carried substantial salaries;

Work and Leisure in the Mature Colonies, 1750–1775

Colonial women combined work with leisure by using their sewing skills, essential for making the family's clothing, to create fancy needlework. Often they devoted their few leisure hours to the art, stitching samplers and pictures or embellishing clothing.

These needlework pictures, both from the mid-eighteenth century, show two of colonial women's most time-consuming tasks, spinning and dairying. The spinner is using a hand-held drop spindle rather than a wheel, which was easier to use but more expensive and cumbersome. The picture of the milker is probably of Pennsylvania Dutch Origin. The Henry Francis du Pont Winterthur Museum, Winterthur, Delaware.

Mercy Otis Warren, who was to become a leading intellectual and author of the Revolutionary era, embroidered the top of this card table sometime before 1770. She and her husband James, like other genteel eighteenth-century Americans, probably spent many leisure hours playing cards. The Pilgrim Society, Plymouth, Massachusetts.

Weddings provided an opportunity for colonists to relax and socialize. The Massachusetts couple whose 1756 wedding is shown in the needlework picture at left was well-to-do, as is indicated by the carriage, the uniformed footmen, and the elaborate clothing of the guests. American Antiquarian Society, Worcester, Mass.

Those colonists who could afford instruments and music lessons could spend their leisure hours like this family, painted late in the century but typical of earlier Americans in their entertainment. The daughter probably learned to play the piano at a school for well-to-do young ladies like herself. The Corcoran Gallery of Art, Washington, D.C.

Africans did not leave their cultural heritage behind when they were forced into slavery. This unique painting, done in 1775 or after, shows slaves passing their few hours of leisure on a Sunday or holiday with a dance. Several identifiably African elements appear in the picture. The drum and banjo-like instrument are both of African origin, as are the scarves and cane used in the tribal dance. The blue-and-white bandannas worn by two of the women are similar to Yoruba cloth (from West Africa). Abby Aldrich Rockefeller Folk Art Collection, Williamsburg, Virginia.

judges, members of governors' councils, customs officers, and the like were amply rewarded for their labors on behalf of the crown. Prominent families thus often sought political alliances with colonial governors or English administrators, for it was through such connections that coveted positions could be won. As the economy became more complex, the legal system also grew more elaborate. In the seventeenth century, America had had few formally trained lawyers. By the 1750s, lawyers who had studied in London were practicing in all the major cities. They were needed to deal with the intricacies of commerce, property transfers, and all the other legal transactions that undergirded economic development. Successful lawyers could earn sizable incomes, as could the doctors educated in England or Scotland who had begun to practice medicine in Boston, Philadelphia, and smaller colonial cities. (In medicine as in law, the second quarter of the eighteenth century witnessed the shift from amateur to professional practitioner, and men with formal training could command high fees.)

The urban poor are more difficult to identify. Recent immigrants must have been among the poor; whether indentured or not, they often hired themselves out as live-in servants so as at least to have food and lodging, however low their wages. The elderly and disabled—who would have found it hard to obtain work—were another component of the urban poor. Women, mostly widows, also accounted for a large proportion of the urban poor. In the eighteenth century, like today, women were paid less than men for comparable work. (Female servants, for example, earned about half the salary of male servants.) And, though opportunities for employment were better in the city than in the countryside, a woman's chances of finding well-paid work were considerably more limited than a man's. Sewing and nursing commanded far lower fees than did blacksmithing, shipbuilding, and other male occupations.

Poor relief

The effects of increasing poverty can be seen in city records. Philadelphia is a case in point. From the 1730s on, city taxpayers were assessed a three-penny annual fee to supply the needy with food and firewood (distributed to applicants by city officials). A private Hospital for the Sick Poor was founded in 1751 under the leadership of Benjamin Franklin. But in the 1760s, in the aftermath of the French and Indian War and the subsequent depression (see pages 88–90 and 92–93), such arrangements proved inadequate. The poor tax was raised to five pennies, then to six; a Bettering House—a combined almshouse and workhouse—was founded to shelter the growing number of poor people and to give employment to the able-bodied among them. The problem, however, was insoluble. No matter what method they tried, eighteenth-century Philadelphians were unable to reduce the incidence of poverty in their midst.

Mary and Elizabeth Royall, painted by the Boston artist John Singleton Copley in 1758. The thirteen- and eleven-year-old daughters of the wealthy Medford merchant Isaac Royall wear elaborate gowns that display the Royall family's elite status. The sumptuous setting mimics portraits of the English nobility. Museum of Fine Arts, Boston, Julia Knight Knox Fund.

Circumstances were still worse in Boston, which suffered serious losses of manpower during the colonial wars (see pages 86–87). The city's economy began to stagnate at midcentury. Boston's merchants had built their fortunes on exporting fish to the West Indies and southern Europe; when England and Spain went to war in 1739, that trade collapsed. (Trading with the enemy was illegal, and the Spanish navy also harassed colonial shipping.) At the same time, a series of poor grain harvests in Europe caused flour prices to rise rapidly. Philadelphia and New York, which could draw on large fertile grain- and livestock-producing areas, thus gained the lead in the foodstuffs trade. Boston never fully recovered, partly because its hinterland was limited in both size and fertility, and partly because of the competition from such nearby ports as Salem, New Haven, and Newport. As one indication of Boston's economic problems, the records of an overseer of the poor in the late 1760s show that about 15 percent of the people in his district were receiving some form of relief—a sizable proportion indeed. In 1790 Boston had only 1,000 more inhabitants than it had had in 1750 (for a total of 18,000), while Philadelphia already boasted over 42,000 residents and New York more than 33,000.

Stratification was increasing in the countryside as well. In the Chesapeake, the fact that the slave population had begun to grow through natural increase spurred the development of very large plantations and helped to create an aristocracy of wealthy planters. Such planters increased their wealth still further by serving as middlemen in the tobacco trade. They loaned less well-to-do planters money, marketed their crops, sold them imported goods, and enriched themselves in the process. In New England, meanwhile, the continuing population growth and the relatively static amount of land under cultivation forced more and more men either to migrate or accept landless status. The same trend appeared even in such fertile areas as Chester County, Pennsylvania, which participated in and contributed to Philadelphia's prosperity. In the late seventeenth century the bottom third of Chester County's residents had owned 17 percent of the wealth, and the top tenth just 24 percent. By 1760 the poorest third possessed only 6 percent of the property, and the top tenth had increased its share to 30 percent.

The trend seems clear, but interpreting it is difficult. Certain families were indeed growing richer, but were other families growing poorer? That is, had individual members of the urban poor (or their parents) once been better off? Or were those increasing numbers of applicants for relief either the victims of unusual circumstances (such as war widows) or recently arrived immigrants who would eventually be self-supporting? It is impossible to tell from the available evidence whether a class of permanently impoverished people was forming in eighteenth-century America, or whether poverty was a phase many people passed through (usually during youth or old age). But this much can be said: the gap between rich and poor was widening, and it had become more difficult for a person starting out at the bottom of the economic ladder to reach its upper rungs.

The transition to a more rigid social and economic structure did not occur without conflict. People who had trouble earning a living wage occasionally exploded into violence when goaded by particularly blatant examples of profiteering.

Social conflict

Such riots were not unique to colonial cities; for centuries, European crowds had taken to the streets to protest unpopular measures. Urban crowds tended to direct their hostility at merchants suspected of monopolizing or hoarding necessary commodities in hopes of driving up prices. In Boston in both 1710 and 1713, for example, rioters prevented a wealthy merchant from exporting large quantities of grain at a time of severe bread shortages. (On the second occasion they cleaned out his warehouse.) Forty years later New York workers took to the streets to protest a devaluation of coinage that, in effect, reduced their meager wages still further. And city dwellers throughout the colonies resisted collectively when the British navy attempted to press them into service. Navy press gangs would roam the streets of colonial cities, gathering up all the able-bodied men they found. The poor had less chance of escaping their clutches than the rich, and frequently had to fight for their freedom.

Rural riots frequently erupted over land titles—a matter of much concern to farmers, regardless of their relative prosperity. In the 1740s, for example, New Jersey farmers holding land under grants from the governor of New York (dating from the brief period when both provinces were owned by the Duke of York) clashed repeatedly with agents of the East Jersey proprietors. The proprietors claimed the land as theirs and demanded annual payments, called quitrents, for the use of the property. Similar violence occurred in the 1760s in the region that later became Vermont. There, farmers (many of them migrants from eastern New England) holding land grants issued by New Hampshire battled with speculators claiming title to the area through grants from New York authorities. In both cases the rioters saw themselves as virtuous yeomen defending their way of life against monied interlopers.

The same theme can be detected in the most serious land riots of the period, which took place along the Hudson River in 1765 and 1766. Late in the seventeenth century, Governor Benjamin Fletcher of New York had granted several huge tracts in the lower Hudson valley to prominent colonial families. The proprietors in turn divided these estates into small farms, which they rented chiefly to poor Dutch and German immigrants, who evidently regarded tenancy as a way station on the road to independent freeholder status. By the 1750s, some proprietors were earning as much as £1,000 to £2,000 annually from quitrents and other fees.

After 1740, though, increasing migration from New England brought conflict to the great New York estates. The mobile New Englanders, who had moved in search of land, did not want to become tenants. Many squatted on vacant portions of the manors and resisted all attempts to evict them. In the mid-1760s, the Philipse family brought suit against the New Englanders, some of whom had lived on Philipse land for twenty or thirty years. New York courts upheld the Philipse claim and ordered the squatters to make way for tenants with valid leases. Instead of complying, the farmers organized a rebellion against the proprietors. For nearly a year the insurgent farmers controlled much of the Hudson valley. They terrorized proprietors and loyal tenants, freed their friends from jail, and on one occasion fought a pitched battle with a county sheriff and his posse. The rebellion was put down only after British troops dispatched from New York City captured its most important leaders.

The land riots in New York, New Jersey, and Vermont revealed the tenacity with which eighteenth-century Americans would defend their cherished positions as independent yeomen farmers. That status played a major part in colonial Americans' perceptions of themselves and their culture.

Colonial culture

From 1754 to 1756, John Dickinson, a Pennsylvanian who would later become a somewhat reluctant revolutionary, studied law at the Middle Temple in London in preparation for a legal career in Philadelphia. Dickinson's letters to his parents provided a running commentary on British politics, the many attractions of the mother country, his studies, and—perhaps most interestingly—his attitudes toward what he was seeing. The young American described England unhesitatingly as a land of "luxury & corruption," observing that "it is grown a vice here to be virtuous."

Dickinson saw his own country as quite different. "Notwithstanding all the diversions of England," he told his parents, "I shall return to America with rapture. . . . Tis rude, but it's innocent. Tis wild, but its private. There life is a stream pure & unruffled, here an ocean briny & tempestuous. There we enjoy life, here we spend it."

John Dickinson was expressing what had become the prevailing view among the colonists: life in America was simpler, purer, and less corrupt than life in England. If America could not boast of a literary culture equal to London's, it could at least point to publications displaying good common sense. If the colonists lacked polish, they nevertheless had unaffected manners. If residence in the colonies meant remoteness from centers of power and influence, it also conveyed immunity to the vice that automatically accompanied the exercise of power. Dickinson and his fellow Americans were, in other words, making a virtue out of a necessity. By no stretch of the imagination could their culture be considered comparable to England's. Instead of trying to compete with their undeniable superior, they changed the terms of the contest: they glorified their lack of the attributes usually considered essential to a proper, civilized existence.

But it was not quite that easy. Fifty years later Americans developed an ideology of republicanism (see Chapter 6) that affirmed and solidified their image of themselves as simple, virtuous yeomen. But while they were still part of the British Empire, they could not reject categorically the standards by which English people were commonly judged. In mid-eighteenth-century America, two opposing tendencies prevailed in the thinking of the colonial cultural, political, and economic elite. One—reflected in John Dickinson's letters—celebrated the simple virtues of life in the colonies and openly criticized England's failings. The other stressed the links between European and American culture. Colonial intellectuals prided themselves on reading the latest English books and corresponding with leading thinkers in the mother country and on the Continent. Wealthy colonists imitated as best they could the manners, dress, and behavior of English aristocrats, and professionals introduced English practices into the conduct of their daily business. (Judges and some lawyers, for example, adopted the English custom of wearing long white wigs and black robes in courtrooms.)

The most important aspect of the transatlantic cultural connection was Americans' participation in the European intellectual movement known as the Enlightenment. Since the sixteenth century, some continental thinkers had been analyzing nature in an effort to determine the laws that govern the universe. They employed experimentation and abstract reasoning to discover general principles behind such everyday phenomena as the motions of the planets and stars, the behavior of falling objects, and the characteristics of light and sound. Above all, Enlightenment philosophers emphasized acquiring knowledge through reason, rather than intuition and revelation. Many European Enlightenment thinkers, like John Locke—whose *Essay on Human Understanding* disputed the Calvinist notion that human beings were innately depraved—wrote abstract analytical philosophy. Colonial participants in the Enlightenment, meanwhile, oriented their studies toward the concrete and particular.

American Enlightenment

For example, Americans were intensely interested in their natural surroundings. The Western Hemisphere housed many plants and animals unknown in the Old World. Naturalists like John Bartram of Pennsylvania and Cadwallader Colden of New York eagerly assisted a trans-Atlantic attempt to identify and classify plant species. Bartram traveled widely through the South, gathering specimens and sending reports of his findings to the Swedish naturalist Linnaeas, whose *Systema Naturae* (1735) had advanced the idea that all plants could be fitted into a universal classification system. American naturalists also sought evidence to disprove the claim that the American environment was unhealthy. Some Enlightenment natural scientists had written that life forms native to the Western Hemisphere were inferior to those found in Europe, and that human beings who emigrated to the Americas would degenerate into savagery and sterility within a few generations.

The American Philosophical Society epitomized the colonists' participation in the Enlightenment. The society was founded in Philadelphia in 1769 as the result of a merger of two rival groups, one of which had focused on natural history and the other on basic science, especially astronomy. Among its first members were political leaders, educators, physicians, and skilled artisans (notably the clockmaker David Rittenhouse, who was constructing an orrery, a mechanical model of the solar system). Benjamin Franklin, the best-known American scientist, was selected as the organization's president even though he was living in London. Over the next few years the society elected new members from other colonies and published a volume of its *Transactions*—a sure sign of scientific prestige and respectability. (Not until after the Revolution did additional volumes appear.)

It was in the realm of medicine that Enlightenment activity had the greatest impact on the lives of ordinary colonists. The key figure in the drama was the Reverend Cotton Mather, the Puritan divine, who was a member of England's Royal Society (the model for the American Philosophical Society). In a Royal Society publication Mather read about the benefits of inoculation (deliberately infecting a person with a mild case of a disease) as a protection against the dreaded smallpox. In 1720 and 1721, when Boston suffered a major smallpox epidemic, Mather and a doctor ally urged people to be inoculated; there was fervent opposition, including that of Boston's leading physician. When the epidemic had ended, the statistics bore out Mather's opinion: of those inoculated, fewer than 3 percent died; of those who became ill without inoculation, nearly 15 percent perished. Though it was midcentury before inoculation was generally accepted as a preventive procedure, enlightened methods had provided colonial Americans protection from the greatest killer disease of all.

Smallpox inoculations

On the whole, though, few Americans were affected by the transatlantic intellectual currents of the day. Only a limited number of well-to-do colonists saw Shakespeare's "Romeo and Juliet," the most popular play in America, or more modern productions such as Richard Cumberland's "The Fashionable Lover." Only a well-educated minority could appreciate the carefully constructed phrases of the great English essayist Joseph Addison or enjoy reading that daring new literary form, the novel. (Samuel Richardson's novels *Pamela, Clarissa,* and *Sir Charles Grandison* were practically required reading for genteel colonial young people.)

Indeed, of all the arts, music alone had a significant effect on the general public. And the roots of American music were less European than local. The music of the common people was vocal and chiefly religious, for communal singing was an important part of both Congregational and Presbyterian church ritual. It was no accident that the first book printed in the colonies was *The Bay Psalm Book* (1640), consisting of Old Testament psalms recast in metrical prose so they could be sung during worship services. The participation of the entire congregation was considered more important than the quality of the music they produced. Such questions as which version of the psalms to use and whether instruments should accompany the singing were resolved by majority vote. Seating in church was assigned by the church leaders: each family had its own pew, whose location at the front, back, or sides depended on the family's relative wealth and social prominence. But communal singing reduced the significance of such hierarchical arrangements, adding an egalitarian element to American religion and bringing a kind of crude democracy into Presbyterian and Congregational churches.

One of the chief reasons why music was the only art that had a broad impact in America was its adaptability for use in a society filled with people who could neither read nor write. Colonial hymns were written in short, rhyming, metrical lines that were easy to learn and remember. Many churches also aided singing by "lining-out"—that is, having a leader read each line aloud before the congregation sang it.

The shortcomings of colonial education ensured that there would be many illiterate Americans who needed such assistance. In New England, which probably had the highest literacy rates in the colonies, 80 to 90 percent of adult men but only about 50 percent of adult women could sign their names at the time of the Revolution. Why did so many people never learn to read and write? Literacy was certainly less essential in eighteenth-century America than it is today. People—especially women—could live their entire lives without ever being called upon to read a book or write a letter. Important information tended to be transmitted orally rather than in writing. Thus education—especially education beyond the rudiments of reading, writing, and "figuring"—was usually regarded as a frill for either sex. Massachusetts Bay alone among the colonies attempted (in a law passed in 1647) to require its towns to maintain public schools, but that law was widely ignored.

Dr. William Glysson (1740–1793) treating a smallpox patient. Painted by his brother-in-law Winthrop Chandler in the early 1780s. Campus Martius Museum.

Whether colonial children learned to read and write thus depended largely on their parents. Most youngsters learned their ABCs at home, often using the Bible or an almanac—the most commonly owned books—as a text. Their first teachers were their parents or older siblings. Later, if their parents were willing and able to pay for further education, they might attend a private "dame school" run by a local widow, where they would learn more of the basics. A few fortunate boys might then go on to a grammar school, to study with a minister and prepare to enter college at age fourteen or fifteen.

Primary education

Girls were usually not educated beyond the rudiments. One Harvard graduate declared, for example, that his daughters "knew quite enough if they could make a shirt and a pudding." Only a very few daughters of elite families received any advanced intellectual training. One such girl was Eliza Lucas, whose father,

Benjamin Franklin (1706–1789), painted by the itinerant artist Robert Feke in 1746, when Franklin was forty. The portrait shows Franklin at the height of his business career, a prosperous Philadelphian. Harvard University Portrait Collection, Bequest, Dr. John C. Warren in 1856.

a West Indian planter, sent her to school in England because he did not want her mind to be "vacant and uninformed." Just before she married Charles Pinckney in 1745, Eliza thanked her father "[for] the pains and mony you laid out in my Education which I esteem a more valuable fortune than any you could now have given me." Eliza Lucas Pinckney was to demonstrate the value of her education by helping to develop a successful means of cultivating indigo (see Chapter 2) and by giving her sons, Thomas and Charles Cotesworth, the rigorous training that enabled them to become national leaders in the 1790s (see Chapter 7).

Ironically, the colonial system of higher education for males was more fully developed than was basic instruction for either sex. In part, the disparity resulted from the large number of university graduates who participated in the Puritan migration; by the mid-1640s, 130 graduates of Oxford and Cambridge had moved to America. (In its early days, therefore, Massachusetts Bay had a higher proportion of learned men in its population than did England.) New England's founders placed heavy emphasis on the need for an institution of higher learning to train young men for the ministry. In 1636 the General Court of Massachusetts voted to set up a college, and two years later instruction began in Newtown, renamed Cambridge. The college itself was named for John Harvard, a minister who died in the fall of 1638, leaving the college his library and half his estate. Throughout the seventeenth and much of the eighteenth century, Harvard College primarily trained clergymen; lawyers and doctors usually received their education through formal or informal apprenticeships. Its curriculum stressed Greek and Hebrew (a thorough knowledge of Latin was required for admission), logic, theology, rhetoric, and metaphysics.

Founding of Harvard

The other early colonial colleges were also designed to educate clerics. The College of William and Mary in Williamsburg, Virginia, chartered in 1693 but not a regularly functioning entity until 1726, prepared Anglican ministers to serve in parishes throughout the Chesapeake region. Yale College was founded in New Haven, Connecticut, in 1701 by a group of ministers who thought Harvard's theological teachings had become too liberal. The College of New Jersey (Princeton, 1747), King's College (Columbia, 1754), the College of Rhode Island (Brown, 1756), and Queen's College (Rutgers, 1766), were begun by Presbyterians, Anglicans, Baptists, and Dutch Reformed clergy, respectively. All wanted to ensure adequate supplies of ministers to fill the pulpits of their churches. Dartmouth College (1769), though not explicitly aimed at educating clerics, also had a religious purpose: Christianizing the Indians. Of all the major colonial colleges, only the College of Philadelphia (later the University of Pennsylvania, 1755), had nonsectarian origins, and it too eventually fell under the domination of the Anglican Church.

The College of Philadelphia was largely the creation of two men: Benjamin Franklin, who first outlined its purposes and curriculum, and William Smith, a Scots emigrant who became its first provost. Franklin, born in Boston in 1706, was the perfect example of a self-made, self-educated man. Indentured at an early age to his older brother James, a Boston printer and newspaper publisher, Franklin ran away to

Philadelphia in 1723. There he worked as a printer and eventually started his own publishing business, printing the *Pennsylvania Gazette* and *Poor Richard's Almanack* among other books. The business was so successful that Franklin was able to retire from active control in 1748, at forty-two. He thereafter devoted himself to intellectual endeavors and public service (as deputy postmaster general for the colonies, as an agent representing colonial interests in London, and eventually as a diplomat during the Revolution). Franklin's *Experiments and Observations on Electricity* (1751) was the most important scientific work by a colonial American; it established the terminology and basic theory of electricity still in use today.

In 1749 and 1751 Franklin published pamphlets proposing the establishment of a new educational institution in Pennsylvania. The purpose of Franklin's "English School" was not to produce clerics or scholars but to prepare young men "for learning any business, calling or profession, except such wherein languages are required." He wanted to enable them "to pass through and execute the several offices of civil life, with advantage and reputation to themselves and country." The College of Philadelphia, in other words, was intended to graduate youths who would resemble Franklin himself—talented, practical men of affairs competent in a number of different fields.

Benjamin Franklin on education

Franklin and the student he envisioned were perfect representatives of colonial culture. Free of the Old World's traditions and corruptions, the ideal American would achieve distinction through hard work and the application of common-sense principles. He would be unlettered but not unlearned, simple but not ignorant, virtuous but not priggish. The American would be a true child of the Enlightenment, knowledgeable about European culture yet not bound by its fetters, advancing through reason and talent alone. To him all things would be possible, all doors open.

The contrast with the original communal ideals of the early New England settlements could not have been sharper. Franklin's American was an individual, free to make choices about his future, able to contemplate a variety of possible careers. John Winthrop's American, outlined in his "Modell of Christian Charity" (see pages 22–23), had been a component of a greater whole that required his unhesitating, unquestioning submission. But the two visions had one point in common: both described only white males. Neither blacks—nearly one-fifth of the total population—nor females—about half of the population—played any part in them. Yet both groups were of crucial importance in American society.

Life on farms and in towns

The basic unit of colonial society was the household. Headed by a white male (or perhaps his widow), the household was the chief mechanism of production and consumption in the colonial economy. Its members—bound by ties of blood or servitude—worked together to produce goods for consumption or sale. The white male head of the household represented it to the outside world, serving in the militia or political posts, casting the household's sole vote in elections. He managed the finances and held legal authority over the rest of the family—his wife, his children, and his servants or slaves. (Eighteenth-century Americans used the word *family* for people who lived together in one house, whether or not they were blood kin.) Such households were considerably larger than American families today; in 1790, the average home contained seven people, one of whom was black.

The vast majority of eighteenth-century American families—more than 90 percent of them—lived in rural areas. The unique qualities of large southern plantations will be discussed in the next section. But other farm households, whether in the North or the South, had many characteristics in common, as did rural people throughout the colonies. Nearly all adult men were farmers and all adult women farm wives. Though men might work as millers, blacksmiths, or carpenters, and women might sell surplus farm produce to neighbors, they typically did so in addition to their primary agricultural tasks. The tasks different members of the household performed were clearly differentiated by sex. Servants, slaves, and children aided either the master or the mistress of the household, laboring under his or her supervision. Thus the following summary describes the work of all members of a farm family above the age of eight.

"Who shall write the history of the American revolution?" John Adams wrote to Thomas Jefferson in 1815. "Who can write it? Who will ever be able to write it?" Adams and Jefferson were by this time old men, recently reconciled to their former friendship after decades of hostility caused by their political disagreements in the 1790s and early 1800s. The correspondence they had begun in 1812 ranged widely over a variety of topics, but repeatedly returned to the great events in which both had participated, the events that had led to the establishment of American independence. Adams took up the same theme three weeks later, asking Jefferson, "What do We Mean by the Revolution?" His own response to that question, Adams remarked, might be thought "peculiar, perhaps singular." To him, "the Revolution was in the Minds of the people, and this was effected, from 1760 to 1775, in the course of fifteen Years before a drop of blood was drawn at Lexington."

At first glance, Adams's statement does indeed seem peculiar. His view of what constituted the Revolution certainly differs from that held by most Americans today. To us, the Revolution was the war for independence fought from 1775 to 1783—a military, political, and constitutional struggle. To Adams, the Revolution was quite a different thing: it was the American colonists' change of heart about their traditional loyalty to the mother country. Adams's opinion has much to recommend it. In 1750 white colonists gloried in their identity as Britons. Just twenty-five years later, they were engaged in open revolt. What had caused the dramatic shift, a change so startling that it can be termed revolutionary?

The answer lies largely in the events of the two decades preceding the outbreak of war. To be sure, some friction had always marred the relationship between colonies and mother country. Disputes over charters, unpopular royal and proprietary policies, problems with the enforcement of customs regulations, and other such matters had frequently caused difficulties in the imperial relationship. Yet none of these disputes had involved more than one or two colonies, and few had lasted long.

Accordingly, no one on either side of the Atlantic was prepared for the explosive protests against parliamentary acts that began in the mid-1760s. Crisis followed crisis as the British government adopted, then repealed, a stamp tax and new trade duties; as Americans clashed with British soldiers in the streets of Boston; as the colonists gradually became convinced that Britain intended to oppress them. Finally a decisive confrontation developed over the seemingly minor issue of a tea tax. To the Americans, that levy on tea had come to symbolize British tyranny. To officials in London, it was a sign of imperial authority. Neither side was willing to compromise, and so the final crisis developed.

Ironically, the event that may be said to have started the movement toward revolution was England's overwhelming victory in the worldwide war that ended in 1763. That victory altered the balance of power in America and fundamentally changed the nature of the British Empire. As a result, Parliament and successive ministries adopted a new approach to Britain's colonial possessions. It was in response to those measures that the North American colonists eventually turned to revolution.

1763: a turning point

Pontiac, the war chief of an Ottawa village near Detroit, was one of the first Americans to understand the changes wrought by the British triumph. A man of vision and commanding bearing, Pontiac had dedicated himself to promoting the welfare of his people. His reaction to Britain's victory was unhesitating. Using all his powers of persuasion, he forged an unprecedented alliance among the Ottawas and their neighbors. Then, in May and June 1763, combined bands of Hurons, Chippewas, Potawatomis, Iroquois, Delawares, and Shawnees launched devastating attacks on settlements and forts on the frontier. But why did the British triumph motivate Pontiac and his allies to take such a drastic step?

For hundreds of years Britain and France had fought each other in Europe. After they established outposts in North America, the continuing warfare enveloped their colonial possessions as well. The two countries were formally at war for nearly half of the three-quarters of a century between 1689 and 1763. Inhabitants of the colonies—white, black, and red alike—thus found themselves in-

Anglo-French warfare in the colonies

volved in armed struggles that had begun in Europe over such issues as France's attempts to expand its territory and the succession to the throne of Austria. These questions mattered little to Americans, but because they did care which nation controlled the chief portion of their continent, they fought willingly on England's side. In the colonies, the War of the League of Augsberg (1689–1697) was called King William's War, the War of the Spanish Succession (1702–1713) was Queen Anne's War, and the War of the Austrian Succession (1740–1748) was King George's War. All three conflicts were inconclusive; neither side was ever able to achieve an unqualified success in America or Europe.

In the colonies, most of the fighting took place along the coast and on the fringes of settlement, where the subjects of the two nations had the easiest access to each other. Since large-scale inland attacks were impractical in a wilderness with few roads, colonial militia and their Indian allies instead conducted swift raids on frontier settlements. In 1689, during King William's War, Iroquois warriors allied with the British destroyed a French village near Montreal. A year later a force of French and Indians retaliated by nearly wiping out the isolated community of Schenectady, New York; and in the winter of 1704, during Queen Anne's War, raiders devastated the Massachusetts town of Deerfield.

The major attacks launched during the three wars were seaborne, since both sides could transport men and weapons more easily on shipboard than by wagon or horseback. Accordingly, the English settlers obtained their most important victories through assaults from the sea. In 1690 they captured Port Royal in Nova Scotia. In 1745 they seized the fortress of Louisbourg on Cape Breton Island, particularly important because of its strategic position at the entrance to the St. Lawrence River, the lifeline of French settlement. (Both prizes were eventually returned to France in treaty negotiations.)

If the European disputes that started the three wars seemed irrelevant to white colonists, they were even less meaningful to American Indians. But the tribes reaped many advantages from the whites' quarrels. Above all, the Indians of the interior wanted to protect their territory from white settlement and to avoid the fate already suffered by their seacoast counterparts. Most of the tribes concluded that their goals could best be achieved by maintaining outward neutrality and playing off the European powers against one another. Their strategy proved resoundingly successful—as long as the Europeans were evenly matched.

Therefore, after a brief alliance with the British during King William's War, the Iroquois Confederacy signed neutrality treaties with both sides (1701) and persisted in that neutrality for over fifty years. Two Iroquois tribes, though, did take sides: the Mohawks usually supported the British, while the Senecas favored the French. In the South the Creeks adopted a similar policy, maintaining formal nonalignment and placing some of their villages under the protection of the British, others under the Spanish. Since the English were the stronger threat, however, the Creeks commonly aided Britain's Indian enemies, such as the Yamasees, and attacked its Indian allies, especially the Cherokees.

The conditions that allowed the tribes to preserve the balance of power in the American interior ended forever with the close of the conflict known in Europe as the Seven Years' War, in America as the French and Indian War. What distinguished this war from its three predecessors was not only its decisive outcome, but also the fact that it began on the North American continent. For the first time a war spread to Europe from America rather than vice versa. Specifically, the war arose from the clash between England and France over which nation would dominate the land west of the Appalachian Mountains (see map, page 88). Because that land was the home of the interior tribes, they necessarily became involved in the struggle.

In 1753 the French began to push southward from Lake Erie into the Ohio country, building fortified outposts in a region previously inhabited only by Indians and occasional white traders. The French threat stimulated an intercolonial conference in June 1754. Encouraged by authorities in London, delegates from seven northern and middle colonies met with representatives of the Iroquois at Albany, New York, in an attempt to persuade the confederated Indian nations to ally themselves with the British. But the Albany Congress failed to convince the Iroquois tribes to abandon their traditional neutrality.

Albany Congress

The delegates at Albany also adopted a Plan of Union designed to coordinate the defenses of the colonies. They proposed the establishment of an elected

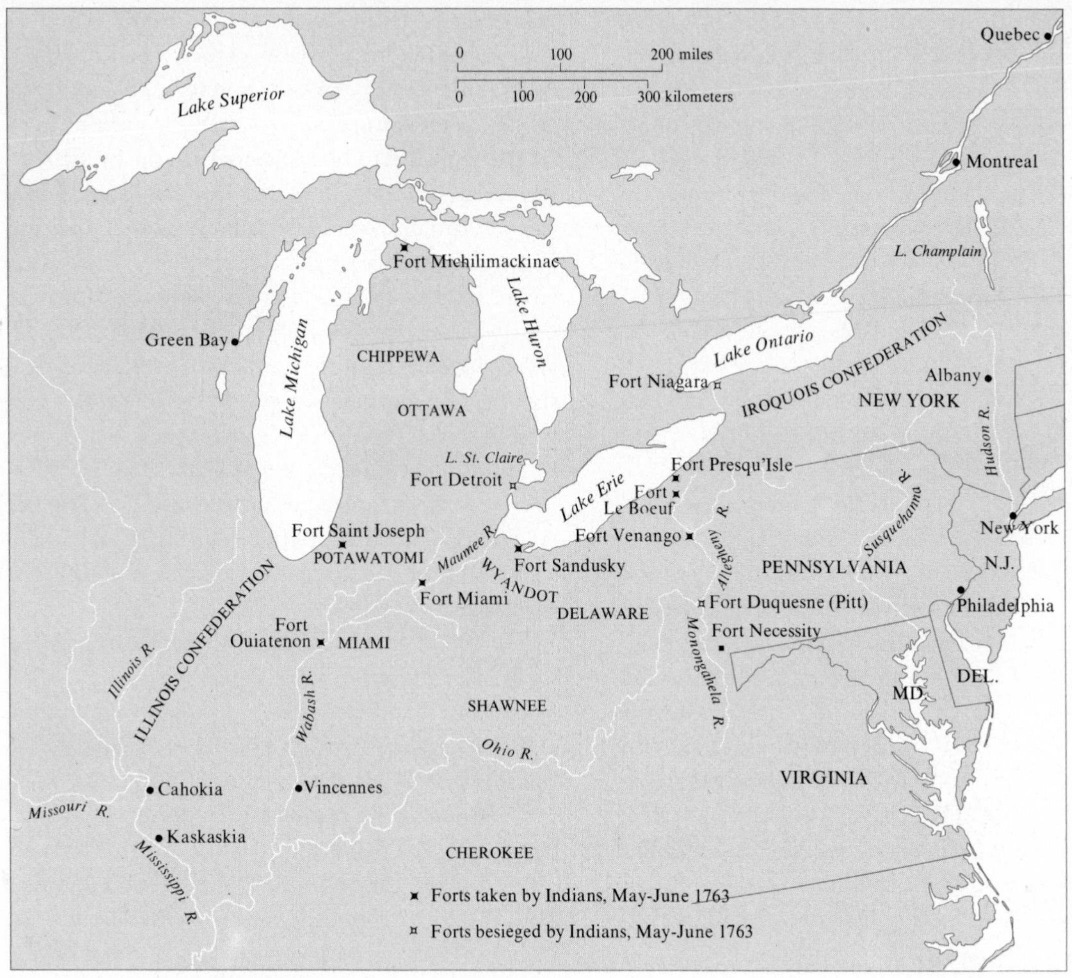

The Northwest, 1754–1763

intercolonial legislature with the power to tax, headed by a president-general appointed by the king. But their home governments, fearing the resulting loss of autonomy, uniformly rejected the idea. The Congress thus failed to achieve its major objectives, but it did produce an enduring symbol of union. Benjamin Franklin, the delegate who wrote the first draft of the Plan of Union, published in his *Pennsylvania Gazette* the famous cartoon of a segmented snake captioned "Join, or Die." It was later to be reprinted many times by supporters of unified colonial resistance to Britain.

The delegates to the Congress did not know that, while they deliberated, the war they sought to prepare for was already beginning. Governor Robert Dinwiddie of Virginia had sent a small militia force westward to counter the French moves. Virginia claimed ownership of the region that is now western Pennsylvania, and Dinwiddie was eager to prevent the French from establishing a permanent post there. But the Virginia militiamen arrived too late. The French had already taken possession of the strategic point—now Pittsburgh—where the Allegheny and Monongahela rivers meet to form the Ohio, and they were busily engaged in constructing Fort Duquesne. The foolhardy and inexperienced young colonel who commanded the Virginians allowed himself to be trapped by the French in his crudely built Fort Necessity at Great Meadows, Pennsylvania. After a day-long battle in which more

Beginning of the Seven Years' War

than one-third of his men were killed or wounded, the twenty-two-year-old George Washington surrendered. He signed a document of capitulation, and he and his men were allowed to return to Virginia.

Washington had blundered grievously. He had started a war that would eventually encompass nearly the entire world. He had also ensured that the Indians of the Ohio Valley would for the most part support France in the coming conflict. The Indians took Washington's mistakes as an indication of Britain's inability to win the war, and nothing that occurred in the next four years made them change their minds. In 1755 a combined force of French and Indians ambushed General Edward Braddock, two regiments of British regulars, and some colonial troops a few miles south of Fort Duquesne. Braddock was killed and his men demoralized by their complete defeat. For three more years one disaster followed another for Great Britain. Everywhere the two sides clashed, the French were consistently victorious.

Finally, under the leadership of William Pitt, who was named secretary of state in 1757, the British mounted the effort that won them the war in North America. In July 1758 they recaptured the fortress at Louisbourg. In a surprise night attack in September 1759 they broke down the defenses of Quebec, a victory that gained them the Iroquois as allies. A year later the British took Montreal, the last French stronghold. The war in America ended then, though fighting continued for three more years in the Caribbean, India, and Europe. When the Treaty of Paris was finally signed in 1763, France ceded its major North American holdings to Britain. Spain, an ally of France toward the end of the war, gave Florida to the victorious English. And since Britain feared the presence of France in Louisiana, it forced the cession of that region to Spain, a weaker power. No longer would the English seacoast colonies have to worry about the threat to their existence posed by France's extensive North American territories.

In order to achieve this stunning victory, Pitt had had to alter many of the policies his predecessors had pursued in their dealings with the colonies. When the war began, the British intended to rely heavily on American enlistments. But Braddock's fate and later British defeats raised serious questions in the colonists' minds about London's ability to conduct the war. Enlistments lagged, and British officers adopted coercive techniques to fill the ranks. In 1757, American crowds resisted forced recruitment in New York City and elsewhere. Other clashes developed over the army's heavy-handed attempts to commandeer wagons and supplies from American farmers and merchants and to house troops in private homes wherever public accommodations were inadequate. Over the objections of local authorities, for example, householders in Albany, New York, were required to take in an average of seven soldiers each during the winter of 1756.

Anglo-American tensions

Franklin's Join, or Die cartoon, produced at the beginning of the French and Indian War, was used during the Revolution as a symbol of America's need to unite. The Library Company of Philadelphia.

In 1758, Pitt acted to ease the strains that were threatening to disrupt the Anglo-American war effort. He agreed to reimburse the colonies for their military expenditures, and placed the recruitment of American troops in their hands. Each province could control both the number of soldiers to be recruited and the methods used to do so. The result was an immediate increase in the number and enthusiasm of colonial volunteers. The colonial governments, assured of financial aid from the mother country, began to devote more of their resources to the task of winning the war. At the same time, Pitt dispatched a large number of British regulars to the colonies. The well-trained redcoats did most of the actual fighting, with colonial militia relegated to support roles.

Pitt's measures won the war, but they also caused discord within the Anglo-American ranks. British commanders could not understand why the colonies seemed so reluctant to contribute to the war effort; they were especially angry at the merchants who continued to trade with the French West Indies and accused them of prolonging the conflict by supplying the enemy with food. Redcoat officers and enlisted men alike looked down on their American counterparts as undisciplined and ignorant of military procedures. As one arrogant colonel declared, "The Provincials [are] sufficient to work our Boats, drive our Waggons, and fell our Trees, and do the Work that in inhabited Countrys are performed by Peasants." For their part, the Americans resented the Britons' condescension, and soldiers and civilians both chafed at the restrictions imposed on their behavior by military regulations. In sum, even though the combined efforts of colonies and mother country resulted in victory, the first large-scale encounter between British regulars and American colonists was less than satisfactory to both sides.

Over the decade and a half following 1760, as the colonies and Great Britain moved slowly toward a confrontation, each drew on impressions of the other gained during the French and Indian War. The British dismissed any suggestion of American military prowess with a laugh, recalling the colonists' evident lack of fighting ability. The Americans, meanwhile, remembered the threat of arbitrary military power embodied in coercive recruiting, the seizure of supplies, and the quartering of troops in private homes. Nor had they forgotten the British officers' arrogance and their own wounded pride. In both cases the victorious alliance of colonies and mother country had done nothing to dispel—and possibly much to promote—the gathering clouds of disagreement.

It was several years before white colonists felt the full impact of the British victory in the French and Indian War. The Indians, however, felt it almost immediately. After 1760 they could no longer pursue their traditional balancing strategy, for France had been ousted from North America and Spain was too weak to pose a serious threat to British power. The Ottawas and their neighbors, the Chippewas and the Potawatomis, became angry when Britain, lacking competition, raised the price of trade goods and ended the French custom of giving them ammunition for hunting. Even more significantly, the British refused to pay the customary rent for forts established within tribal territory. They also permitted white settlers to move into the Monongahela and Susquehanna valleys, which belonged to the Iroquois and Delawares. Thus the British signalled their disregard for Indian claims to sovereignty over the interior.

Pontiac, the Ottawa chief who realized the meaning of the British victory, had been a loyal ally of the French since the 1740s. When he organized the Indian alliance in the spring of 1763, he was probably in his midforties and at the height of his power and prestige. Pontiac planned to seize the fort at Detroit through a ruse, but failed when an informer betrayed his plot. In early May, he laid siege to the fort while his war parties attacked the other British outposts in the Great Lakes region. Detroit withstood the siege, but by the end of June all the other forts west of Niagara and north of Fort Pitt (old Fort Duquesne) had fallen to the Indian alliance.

Pontiac's uprising

That was the high point of the uprising. The tribes raided the Virginia and Pennsylvania frontiers at will throughout the summer, killing at least two thousand whites. But they could not take the strongholds of Niagara, Fort Pitt, or Detroit. In early August, a combined force of Delawares, Shawnees, Hurons, and Mingoes (Pennsylvania Iroquois) was soundly defeated at Bushy Run, Pennsylvania, by troops sent from the coast. Conflict ceased when Pontiac broke off the siege of Detroit in late October, after most of his warriors had returned to their villages. A formal treaty ending the war was finally negotiated in 1766.

In the aftermath of the bloody summer of 1763, white frontiersmen from Paxton Township, Pennsylvania, sought revenge on the only Indians within reach, a peaceful band of Christian converts living at Conestoga. In December the whites raided the Indian village twice, killing twenty people. Two months later hundreds of frontier dwellers known to history as the Paxton Boys marched on Philadelphia to demand military protection against future Indian attacks. City officials feared violence and mustered the militia to repel the westerners, but the protesters presented their request in an orderly fashion and returned home.

Pontiac's uprising and the march of the Paxton Boys showed that Great Britain would not find it easy to govern the huge territory it had just acquired from

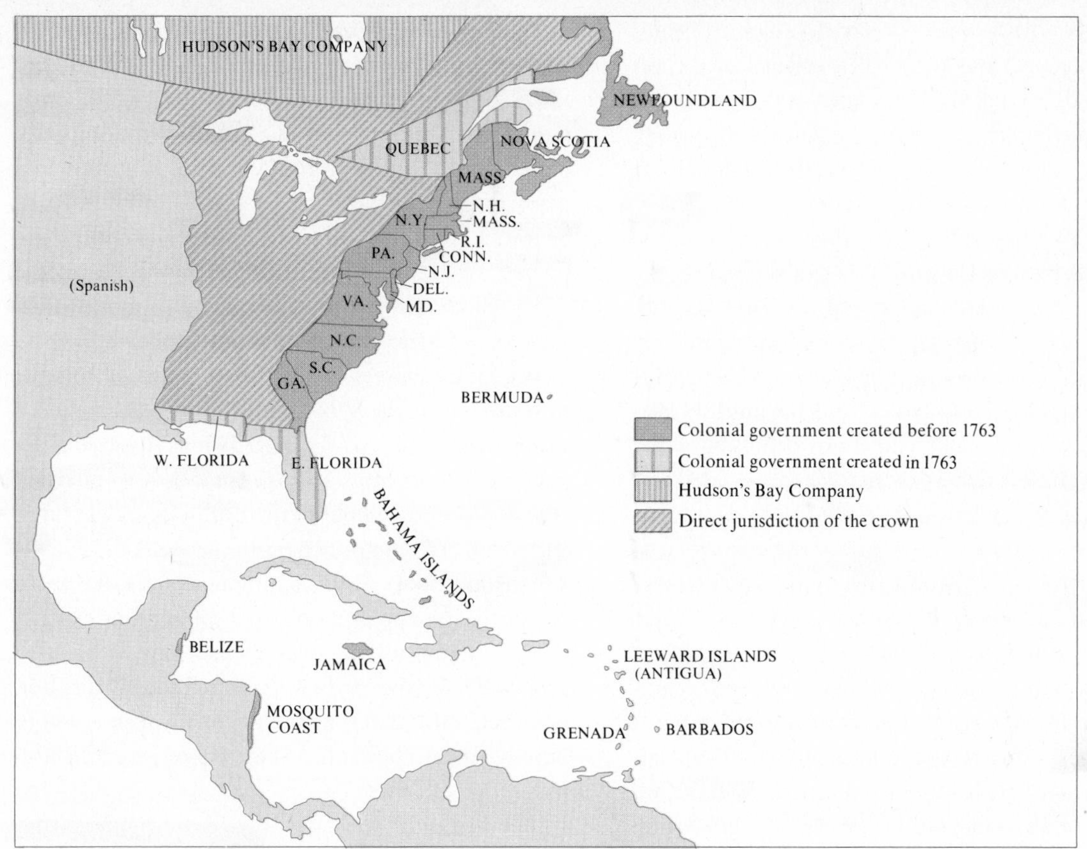

Britain's American empire after the Proclamation of 1763

France. The central administration in London had had no prior experience in managing such a vast tract of land, particularly one inhabited by two hostile peoples–the remaining French settlers along the St. Lawrence and the many Indian tribes. In October, in a futile attempt to assert control over the interior, the ministry issued the Proclamation of 1763, which declared the headwaters of rivers flowing into the Atlantic from the Appalachian Mountains to be the temporary western boundary for colonial settlement (see map). The proclamation was intended to prevent future clashes between Indians and colonists by forbidding whites to move onto Indian lands until the tribes had given up their land by treaty. But many whites had already established farms west of the proclamation line, and the policy was doomed to failure from its outset.

Proclamation of 1763

The beginnings of colonial protest

At the close of the war George Grenville, who had been named prime minister, and George III, who became king in 1760, faced an immediate problem: Britain's immense war debt. The figures were staggering. England's burden of indebtedness had nearly doubled since 1754, from £73 million to £137 million. Annual expenditures before the war had amounted to no more than £8 million; now the yearly interest on the debt alone came to £5 million. Clearly Grenville's ministry had to find new sources of funds, and the English people themselves were already heavily taxed. Since the colonists had been major beneficiaries of the wartime expenditures, Grenville concluded that the Americans should be asked to pay a greater share of the cost of running the empire.

When Grenville decided to tax the colonies, he did not stop to consider whether Parliament had the authority to do so. Like all his countrymen, he believed that the government's legitimacy derived ultimately from the consent of the people, but he defined consent far more loosely than did the colonists. Americans had come to believe that they could be represented only by men for whom they or their property-holding neighbors had actually voted; otherwise they could not count on legislators to be faithful to their interests. To Grenville and his English contemporaries, however, Parliament by definition represented all English subjects, wherever they resided and whether or not they could vote. According to this theory of government, called *virtual representation,* the colonists were said to be virtually, if not actually, represented in Parliament. Thus their consent to acts of Parliament could be presumed.

Theories of representation

With regard to the basis for a government's legitimacy, in other words, the Americans and the English began at the same theoretical starting-point, but arrived at different conclusions in practice. In England, members of Parliament were viewed as representing the entire nation, whatever constituency elected them. (Indeed, some districts had few or no inhabitants; holders of those seats in the House of Commons were hand-picked by the king or local nobles.) In the colonies, by contrast, members of the lower houses of the assemblies were expected to speak for the particular voters who had chosen them. Before Grenville proposed to tax the colonists, the two notions existed side by side without apparent contradiction. But the events of the 1760s pointed up the difference between the English and colonial definitions of representation.

The same events threw into sharp relief Americans' attitudes toward political power. The colonists had become accustomed to a government that wielded only limited authority over them and affected their daily lives very little. In consequence, they believed that a good government was one that largely left them alone, a view in keeping with the theories of a group of British writers known as the Real Whigs. Drawing on a tradition of English dissenting thought that reached back to the days of the Civil War in the mid-seventeenth century, the Real Whigs stressed the dangers inherent in a powerful government, particularly one headed by a monarch. They warned that the people had to guard constantly against the government's attempts to encroach on their liberties. Political power, wrote John Trenchard and Thomas Gordon in their essay series *Cato's Letters* (originally published in England in 1720–1723 and reprinted many times thereafter in the colonies), was always to be feared. Rulers would try to corrupt and oppress the people. Only the perpetual vigilance of the people and their elected representatives could possibly preserve their fragile yet very precious freedoms.

Britain's attempts to tighten the reins of colonial government in the 1760s and early 1770s convinced many Americans that the Real Whigs' reasoning applied to their circumstances. They began to interpret British measures in light of the Real Whigs' warnings, and to see evil designs behind the actions of Grenville and his successors. Historians disagree over the extent to which those perceptions were correct, but by 1775 a large number of colonists unquestionably believed they were. In the mid-1760s, the colonists did not, however, immediately accuse Grenville of an intent to oppress them. They at first simply questioned the utility of the new laws.

The first such measures, the Sugar and Currency Acts, were passed by Parliament in 1764. The Sugar Act revised the existing system of customs regulations; laid new duties on certain foreign imports into the colonies; established a vice-admiralty court at Halifax, Nova Scotia; and included special provisions aimed at stopping the widespread smuggling of molasses, one of the chief commodities in American trade. The Currency Act in effect outlawed colonial issues of paper money. (For years, the colonies had printed their own money to supplement the private bills of exchange that circulated chiefly among merchants.) Americans could accumulate little hard cash, since they imported more than they exported; thus the act seemed to the colonists to deprive them of the means of doing business.

Sugar and Currency Acts

The Sugar and Currency Acts were visited upon an economy already in the midst of depression. A business boom had accompanied the French and Indian War, but the brief spell of prosperity had ended abruptly in 1760, when the war shifted overseas. Urban merchants could not sell all their imported goods to colonial customers alone, and without the military's demand for foodstuffs, American farmers found fewer buyers for their products. The bottom dropped out of the European tobacco market, threatening the livelihood of Chesapeake planters. Sailors were thrown out of work and onto the streets of port cities, and artisans found few employers to hire them. In such circumstances, the prospect of increased customs duties and inadequate supplies of currency naturally aroused merchants' hostility.

It is not surprising that both individual colonists and colonial governments decided to protest the new policies. But, lacking any precedent for a united campaign against acts of Parliament, Americans in 1764 took only hesitant and uncoordinated steps. Eight colonial legislatures sent separate petitions to Parliament requesting repeal of the Sugar Act. They argued that the act placed severe restrictions on their commerce (and would therefore hurt Britain as well), and that they had not consented to its passage. They also instructed their agents in London to lobby against another proposed levy, the stamp tax.

That tax was modeled on a law that had been in effect in England for nearly a century. It would touch nearly every colonist by requiring tax stamps on most printed materials. Anyone who purchased a newspaper or pamphlet, made a will, transferred land, bought dice or playing cards, needed a liquor license, accepted a government appointment, or borrowed money would have to pay the tax. Never before had a revenue measure of such scope been proposed for the colonies. The act would also require that tax stamps be paid for with hard money and that violators be tried in vice-admiralty courts, without juries. Finally, such a law would break decisively with the colonial tradition of self-imposed taxation.

Stamp Act

The most important colonial pamphlet protesting the Sugar Act and the proposed stamp act was *The Rights of the British Colonies Asserted and Proved,* by James Otis, Jr., a brilliant young Massachusetts attorney who later went insane. Otis starkly exposed the ideological dilemma that was to confound the colonists for the next decade. How could they justify their opposition to certain acts of Parliament without questioning Parliament's authority over them? On the one hand, Otis asserted that Americans were "entitled to all the natural, essential, inherent, and inseparable rights" of Britons, including the right not to be taxed without their consent. "No man or body of men, not

Test impressions of one of the tax stamps intended for use in America. Inland Review Library.

excepting the parliament . . . can take [those rights] away," he declared. On the other hand, Otis was forced to admit that, under the British system, "the power of parliament is uncontroulable, but by themselves, and we must obey. . . . Let the parliament lay what burthens they please on us, we must, it is our duty to submit and patiently bear them, till they will be pleased to relieve us."

Otis's first contention, drawing on colonial notions of representation, implied that Parliament could not constitutionally tax the colonies because Americans were not represented in its ranks. Yet his second point both acknowledged political reality and accepted the prevailing theory of British government—that Parliament was the sole, supreme authority in the empire. Even unconstitutional laws enacted by Parliament had to be obeyed until Parliament decided to repeal them. According to orthodox British political theory, there could be no middle ground between absolute submission to Parliament and a frontal challenge to its authority. Otis tried to find such a middle ground by proposing colonial representation in Parliament, but his idea was never taken seriously on either side of the Atlantic. The British believed that the colonists were already virtually represented in Parliament, and the Americans quickly realized that a handful of colonial delegates to London would simply be outvoted.

The Stamp Act crisis

When Americans learned of the passage of the Stamp Act in the spring of 1765, they did not at first know how to proceed. Few colonists publicly favored the law; opposition to it was nearly universal, even among government officials. But the colonists had already failed to prevent its adoption, and further lobbying appeared futile. Perhaps Otis was right, and the only course open to them was to pay the stamp tax, reluctantly but loyally. Acting on that assumption, colonial agents in London sought the appointment of their American friends as stamp distributors, so that the law would at least be enforced equitably.

Not all the colonists were resigned, however, to paying the new tax without a fight. One who was not was a twenty-nine-year-old lawyer serving his first term as a member of the Virginia House of Burgesses. Patrick Henry later recalled that he was at the time "young, inexperienced, unacquainted with the forms of the House and the members that composed it," and appalled by his fellow legislators' unwillingness to oppose the Stamp Act openly. Henry decided to act. "Alone, unadvised, and unassisted, on a blank leaf of an old law book," he wrote the Virginia Stamp Act Resolves.

Patrick Henry

Little in Henry's earlier life foreshadowed his success in the political arena he entered so dramatically. The son of a prosperous Scottish immigrant to western Virginia, Henry had had little formal education. After marrying at eighteen, he failed at both farming and storekeeping before turning to the law as a means of supporting his wife and their six children. Henry lacked legal training, but his oratorical skills made him an effective advocate, first for his clients and later for his political beliefs. As a prominent Virginia lawyer wrote in 1774, "He is by far the most powerful speaker I ever heard. Every word he says not only engages, but commands the attention; and your passions are no longer your own when he addresses them."

Patrick Henry introduced his proposals in late May, near the end of the legislative session; many members of the House of Burgesses had already departed for home. Henry's fiery speech in support of his resolutions led the Speaker of the House to accuse him of treason. (Henry quickly denied the charge, contrary to the nineteenth-century myth that had him exclaiming in reply, "If this be treason, make the most of it!") The small number of burgesses remaining in Williamsburg formally adopted five of Henry's resolutions by a bare majority. Though they repealed the most radical resolution the next day, their action had far-reaching effects. Some colonial newspapers printed Henry's seven original resolutions as if they had been uniformly passed by the House, even though one had been rescinded and two others were evidently never debated or voted on at all.

The four propositions adopted by the burgesses resembled the arguments James Otis had advanced the previous year. The colonists had never forfeited the rights of British subjects, they declared, and consent to taxation was one of the most important of those rights. The other three resolutions went much further. The one that was repealed claimed for the burgesses "the only exclusive right" to tax Virginians. The final two asserted that residents of the colony did not have to obey tax laws passed by other legislative bodies (namely Parliament) and termed any opponent of that opinion "an Enemy to this his Majesty's Colony."

The burgesses' decision to accept only the first four of Henry's resolutions was a clear expression of the position most Americans took throughout the following decade. Though willing to contend for their rights, the colonists did not seek independence. They merely wanted some measure of self-government. Accordingly they backed away from the dangerous assertions that they owed Parliament no obedience and that their own assemblies alone could tax them. Indeed, declared the Maryland lawyer Daniel Dulany, whose *Considerations on the Propriety of Imposing Taxes*

on the British Colonies was the most widely read pamphlet of 1765, "The colonies are dependent upon Great Britain, and the supreme authority vested in the king, lords, and commons, may justly be exercised to secure, or preserve their dependence." But, warned Dulany, a superior did not have the right "to seize the property of his inferior when he pleases"; there was a crucial distinction between a condition of "dependence and *inferiority*" and one of "absolute *vassalage* and *slavery*."

Over the course of the next ten years, Americans searched for a political formula that would enable them to control their internal affairs, especially taxation, but remain within the British Empire. The chief difficulty lay in British officials' inability to compromise on the issue of parliamentary power. The notion that Parliament could exercise absolute authority over all colonial possessions was basic to the orthodox British theory of government. Even the harshest British critics of the ministry's colonial policy questioned only the wisdom of that policy, not the principles on which it was based. In effect, the Americans wanted British leaders to revise their fundamental understanding of the workings of their government. That was simply too much to expect, given the circumstances.

The ultimate effectiveness of Americans' opposition to the Stamp Act did not rest on ideological arguments over parliamentary power. What gave the resistance its primary force were the decisive and inventive actions of the colonists during the late summer and fall of 1765.

Loyal Nine

In August the Loyal Nine, a Boston social club of printers, distillers, and other artisans, organized a demonstration against the Stamp Act. Hoping to show that people of all social and economic ranks opposed the act, they approached the leaders of the city's rival laborers' associations, the North End and South End mobs. The two mobs, composed of unskilled workers and poor tradesmen, often fought pitched battles with each other, but the Loyal Nine convinced them to lay aside their differences and participate in the demonstration. After all, the stamp taxes would have to be paid by all colonists, not just affluent ones.

Early in the morning of August 14, the demonstrators hung an effigy of Andrew Oliver, the province's stamp distributor, from a tree on Boston Common. That night a large crowd led by a group of about fifty well-dressed tradesmen paraded the effigy around the city. The crowd tore down a small building they thought was intended as the stamp office and built a bonfire with the wood near Oliver's house. They then beheaded the effigy and added it to the flames. Members of the crowd broke most of Oliver's windows—an apparently unplanned gesture—and threw stones at officials who tried to disperse them. In the midst of the melee, the North End and South End leaders drank a toast to their successful union. The Loyal Nine's demonstration achieved its objective when Oliver publicly promised not to fulfill the duties of his office. One Bostonian jubilantly told a relative, "I believe people never was more Universally pleased not so much as one could I hear say he was sorry, but a smile sat on almost every ones countinance."

But another crowd action twelve days later, aimed this time at Oliver's brother-in-law Lieutenant Governor Thomas Hutchinson, drew no praise from the respectable citizens of Boston. On the night of August 26, a mob reportedly led by the South End leader, Ebenezer MacIntosh, attacked the homes of several customs officers. The crowd then completely destroyed Hutchinson's elaborately furnished townhouse in one of Boston's most fashionable districts. The lieutenant governor reported that by the next morning "one of the best finished houses in the Province had nothing remaining but the bare walls and floors." His trees and garden were ruined as well, and the mob had "emptied the house of every thing whatsoever except a part of the kitchen furniture." But Hutchinson took some comfort in the fact that "the encouragers of the first mob never intended matters should go this length and the people in general express the utmost detestation of this unparalleled outrage."

Thoughtful residents of other colonies drew two important conclusions from the Boston mob actions of August 14 and 26. First, they realized that they could prevent enforcement of the Stamp Act simply by imitating the Bostonians and forcing the stamp distributors (one for each colony) to resign. Second, they recognized the danger of inciting mob action to achieve their goals. Although mobs could be useful, they would have to be carefully controlled to avoid the kind of excessive violence that had destroyed Hutchinson's house.

This woodcut, produced half a century after the event, shows a crowd parading the effigy of the New Hampshire stamp distributor through the streets of Portsmouth in 1765. The procession is led, as it was in many cities, by men carrying a coffin to symbolize the death and burial of the Stamp Act. The Metropolitan Museum of Art, Bequest of Charles Allen Munn.

The Stamp Act controversy drew disfranchised Americans into the vortex of imperial politics for the first time. Lower-class whites, blacks, and even women began to participate in public discussions and demonstrations. Such people had long expressed their opinions on local issues, often through crowd action, but never before had they been aroused by broad questions of imperial policy. In 1765, though, as Sally Franklin wrote to her father Benjamin, then serving as a colonial agent in London, "nothing else is talked of, the Dutch [Germans] talk of the stompt act the Negroes of the tamp, in short every body has something to say."

The aims of such newly politicized Americans were often quite different from those of resistance leaders. The Loyal Nine had accomplished their end when Oliver agreed not to distribute stamps, but the Boston crowd had its own goals. Chief among them seems to have been a desire to punish the haughty Hutchinson for his ostentatious display of wealth, in a city whose average citizen's share of the economic pie had steadily decreased since about 1750. Hutchinson's losses that night amounted to more than £900 sterling; most personal estates in Boston at the time were worth less than £30. Although Hutchinson was erroneously believed to be a supporter of the Stamp Act, his self-advertised wealth probably contributed significantly to motivating the crowd's "hellish Fury."

The Loyal Nine's tactics were immediately imitated elsewhere in the colonies. The organizers of subsequent anti-Stamp Act demonstrations made certain, however, that crowds remained orderly. They were so successful that by November 1, when the law was scheduled to go into effect, not a single stamp distributor was willing to carry out the duties of his office. To coordinate their efforts at directing opposition into acceptable channels, resistance leaders throughout the colonies formed an association known as the Sons of

Liberty. The first such group was created in New York City in early November, and branches spread rapidly through the colonies. Largely composed of merchants, lawyers, prosperous tradesmen, and the like, the Sons of Liberty linked resistance leaders in cities from Charleston, South Carolina, to Portsmouth, New Hampshire, by early 1766 (see map).

Sons of Liberty

But not even the Sons of Liberty could control all reactions in the new climate of protest. In Charleston in late October 1765 an organized crowd shouting "Liberty Liberty and stamp'd paper" forced the resignation of the South Carolina stamp distributor. The event was celebrated a few days later in the largest demonstration the city had ever known, at which was displayed a British flag with the word LIBERTY written across it. But white resistance leaders were horrified when in January 1766 local slaves paraded through the streets similarly crying "Liberty." The local militia was mustered, messengers were sent to outlying areas with warnings of a possible plot, and one black was banished from the colony.

In Philadelphia, resistance leaders were dismayed when an angry mob threatened to attack Benjamin Franklin's house. The city's laborers believed Franklin to be partly responsible for the Stamp Act, since he had obtained the post of stamp distributor for a close friend. But Philadelphia's artisans–the backbone of the opposition movement there and elsewhere–were fiercely loyal to Franklin, one of their own who had made good. They gathered to protect his home and family from the crowd. The house was saved, but the resulting split between the better-off tradesmen and the common laborers prevented Philadelphians from establishing a successful workingmen's alliance like that of Boston.

During the fall and winter of 1765 and 1766, opposition to the Stamp Act proceeded on three separate fronts. The colonial legislatures petitioned Parliament to repeal the hated law and sent delegates to an intercolonial congress, the first since 1754. In October the Stamp Act Congress met in New York to draft a unified but relatively conservative statement of protest. At the same time, the Sons of Liberty held mass meetings in an effort to win public support for the resistance movement. Finally, American merchants organized nonimportation associations to put economic pressure on British exporters. Recognizing that the

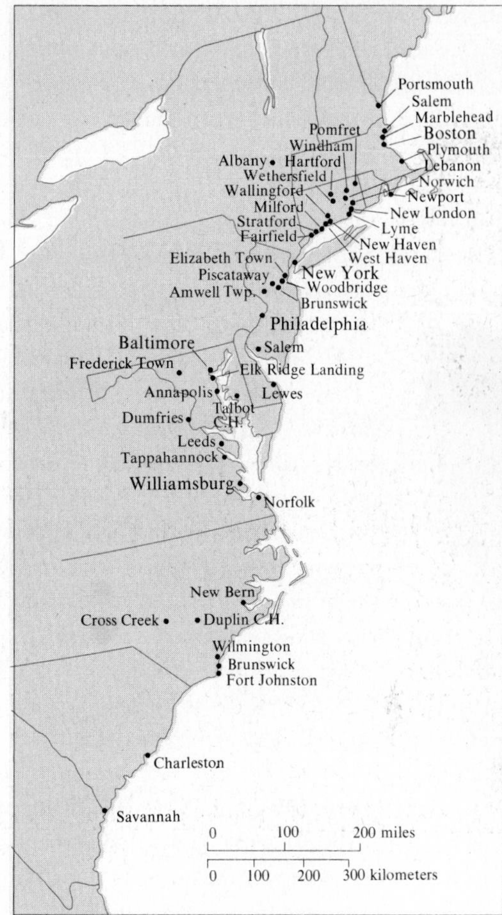

Stamp Act crisis. Source: Reprinted by permission of Princeton University Press.

colonial market contributed greatly to the exporters' profits, they reasoned that London merchants whose sales suffered would lobby for repeal. Since times were bad and American merchants were finding few customers for imported goods in any case, a general moratorium on future purchases would also help to reduce their bloated inventories.

In March 1766, Parliament repealed the Stamp Act. The nonimportation agreements had had the anticipated effect, creating allies within the powerful circle of wealthy London merchants. But boycotts, formal protests, and crowd actions were less important in winning repeal than was Grenville's replacement as prime minister in summer 1765. Lord Rockingham, the new minister, had opposed the Stamp Act, not because Parliament lacked power to tax the colonies but because he thought the law unwise and divisive. Thus, although Rockingham proposed repeal, he linked it to passage of the Declaratory Act, which asserted Parliament's ability to tax and legislate for Britain's American possessions "in all cases whatsoever."

Repeal of the Stamp Act

News of the repeal arrived in Newport, Rhode Island, in May, and the Sons of Liberty quickly transmitted the welcome tidings to all parts of the colonies. They also organized many celebrations commemorating the glorious event, all of which stressed the Americans' unwavering loyalty to Great Britain. Their goal achieved, the Sons of Liberty dissolved. Few colonists recognized the ominous implications of the Declaratory Act.

Resistance to the Townshend Acts

The colonists had accomplished their aim, but they had not developed a consistent ideological defense against parliamentary taxation. Some had raised the basic question of consent, others had objected primarily to the amount of taxation, and still others had criticized the type of tax chosen. Yet Benjamin Franklin confidently assured a parliamentary committee that Americans uniformly acknowledged Parliament's unlimited right to regulate their trade, even while they rejected internal taxes. Charles Townshend, a Grenvillite who became chancellor of the exchequer in the coalition ministry that succeeded Rockingham's in the summer of 1766, decided to use Franklin's erroneous statement as a means of obtaining additional funds from the colonies.

The new taxes Townshend proposed in 1767 were levied on trade goods like paper, glass, and tea, and thus seemed on the surface to be nothing more than extensions of the existing Navigation Acts. But the Townshend duties differed from previous customs taxes in two ways. First, they were levied on items imported into the colonies from Britain, not from foreign countries. Thus they were at odds with mercantilist theory. Second, they were designed to raise money, not to regulate the availability and use of certain commodities in America. The receipts, moreover, would pay the salaries of royal officials in the colonies. That posed a direct challenge to the colonial assemblies, which derived considerable power from threatening to withhold officials' salaries. In addition, Townshend's scheme provided for the establishment of an American Board of Customs Commissioners and for the creation of vice-admiralty courts at Boston, Philadelphia, and Charleston. Both moves angered merchants, whose profits would be threatened by more vigorous enforcement of the Navigation Acts. Lastly, Townshend proposed the appointment of a secretary of state for American affairs and the suspension of the New York legislature for refusal to comply with an act requiring colonial governments to supply certain items (like firewood and candles) to British troops stationed permanently in America.

Townshend Acts

Unlike 1765, when months passed before the colonists began to protest the Stamp Act, the Townshend Acts drew a quick response. One series of essays in particular, *Letters from a Farmer in Pennsylvania* by the prominent lawyer John Dickinson, expressed a consensus that had not existed two years earlier. Eventually all but four colonial newspapers printed Dickinson's essays; in pamphlet form they went through at least seven American editions. Dickinson contended that Parliament could regulate colonial trade, but could not exercise that power for the purpose of raising revenues. He thus avoided the complicated question of colonial consent to parliamentary legislation. But his argument had another flaw: it was clearly unworkable for Americans to assess Parliament's motives

Silver bowl crafted for the Sons of Liberty by Paul Revere in 1768 to commemorate the ninety-two members of the Massachusetts House of Representatives who refused to rescind the circular letter. Museum of Fine Arts, Boston, Gift by Subscription and Francis Bartlett Fund.

for passing a trade law before deciding whether to obey it.

The Massachusetts assembly responded to the acts by drafting a circular letter to the other colonial legislatures, calling for unity and suggesting a joint petition of protest to the king. It was less the letter itself than the ministry's reaction to it that united the colonies. When Lord Hillsborough, the first secretary of state for America, learned of the circular letter, he ordered Governor Francis Bernard of Massachusetts to insist that the assembly recall it. He also directed other governors to prevent their assemblies from discussing the letter. Hillsborough's order gave the colonial assemblies the incentive they needed to forget their differences and join forces to meet the new threat to their prerogatives. In late 1768 the Massachusetts legislature met, debated, and resoundingly rejected recall by a vote of 92 to 17. Bernard immediately dissolved the assembly, and other governors followed suit when their legislatures debated the circular letter.

Massachusetts assembly dissolved

The figure 45 had become a symbol of resistance to Great Britain when John Wilkes, a radical Englishman sympathetic to the American cause, had been jailed for libel because of his publication of the essay *The North Briton No. 45.* Now 92, the number of votes cast against recalling the circular letter, assumed ritual significance as well. In Charleston, the city's tradesmen decorated a tree with 45 lights and set off 45 rockets. Carrying 45 candles, they adjourned to a tavern whose tables were set with 45 bowls of wine, 45 bowls of punch, and 92 glasses. In Newport, 45 members of the revived Sons of Liberty dined on 45 dishes and drank 92 toasts. And in Boston, the silversmith Paul Revere made a punchbowl weighing 45 ounces, which held 45 gills (half-cups) and was engraved with the names of the 92 legislators; James Otis, John Adams, and others drank 45 toasts from it. (Not surprisingly, newspapers often described these affairs as having been full of "mirth and jollity.")

Pleasant social occasions though they were, such public rituals served an important educational function. Many colonists–especially men in the lower

A Society of Patriotic Ladies, painted by Philip Dawes(?) in 1775. A disapproving Briton produced this grotesque caricature of female patriots. At left the women empty their tea canisters into a chamber pot. The cartoon bears no resemblance to the actual event, the signing of an anti-British petition by female residents of Edenton, North Carolina. Library of Congress.

ranks of society and most women—could neither read nor write, and they learned about political issues not by reading closely reasoned pamphlets but by watching and participating in public activities. When Boston's Sons of Liberty invited hundreds of the city's residents to dine with them each August 14 to commemorate the first Stamp Act uprising, and the Charleston Sons of Liberty held their meetings in public, crowds gathered to watch and listen. The participants in such events were openly expressing their commitment to the cause of resistance and encouraging others to join them.

During the two-year campaign against the Townshend duties, the Sons of Liberty and other American leaders made a deliberate effort to broaden the base of the resistance movement. In addition to asking merchants not to import British products, they urged ordinary citizens not to buy them. In June 1769, for example, a Maryland nonimportation agreement identified its signers as "Merchants, Traders, Freeholders, Mechanics [artisans], and other Inhabitants" of the colony, all of whom agreed not to import or consume certain British goods. As a result of these tactics, an increasing number of Americans found themselves aligned in a united cause.

Even women, who had previously regarded politics as outside their proper sphere, joined in the formal resistance movement. In towns throughout America, young women calling themselves Daughters of Liberty met to spin in public, in an effort to spur other women to make homespun and end the colonies' dependence on English cloth. These symbolic displays of patriotism, often held in the minister's house, served the same purpose as the male rituals involving the numbers 45 and 92. When young ladies from well-to-do families sat publicly at spinning wheels all day, eating only American food and drinking herbal tea, and afterwards listening to patriotic sermons, they were serving as political instructors. Many women took great satisfaction in their new-found role. When a New England satirist hinted that women discussed only "such triffling subjects as Dress, Scandal and Detraction" during their spinning bees, three Boston women replied angrily: "Inferior in abusive sarcasm, in personal invective, in low wit, we glory to be, but inferior in veracity, sincerity, love of virtue, of liberty and of our country, we would not willingly be to any."

Daughters of Liberty

Women also took the lead in promoting nonconsumption of tea. In Boston more than three hundred matrons publicly promised not to drink tea, "Sickness excepted." The women of Wilmington, North Carolina, burned their tea after walking through town in a solemn procession. Housewives throughout the colonies exchanged recipes for tea substitutes or drank coffee instead. The best known of the protests (because it was satirized by a British cartoonist), the so-called Edenton Ladies Tea Party, actually had little to do with tea; it was a meeting of prominent North Carolina women who pledged formally to work for the public good and to support resistance to British measures.

Not all Americans acquiesced in nonimportation. Many merchants continued to import British goods, some as a matter of principle and others for economic reasons. The earlier boycotts of 1765 and 1766 had helped to revive a depressed economy; but in 1768 and 1769 merchants were enjoying boom times and had no financial incentive to support a boycott. In the commercial cities of the North and in Charleston in the South, merchants signed the agreements only reluctantly. Artisans, on the other hand, supported nonimportation enthusiastically, recognizing that the absence of British goods would create a ready market for their own manufactures. Thus tradesmen formed the core of the crowds that coerced both importers and their customers by picketing stores, publicizing offenders' names, and sometimes destroying property.

Such tactics were effective: colonial imports from England dropped dramatically in 1769 (see figure), especially in New York, New England, and Pennsylvania. But they also aroused significant opposition. Some Americans who supported resistance to British measures began to question the use of violence to force others to join the boycott. The wealthier and more conservative colonists were frightened by the threat to private property inherent in the campaign. Moreover, political activism on the part of colonists who had once deferred to the judgment of their superiors posed a threat to the local ruling classes. In 1769 a Charleston essayist warned that "the industrious mechanic [is] a useful and essential part of society . . . in his own sphere," but "when he steps out of it, and sets up for a statesman! believe me he is in a fair way to expose himself to ridicule, and his family to distress, by neglecting his private business." Pretending concern for tradesmen's welfare, the author obviously feared for his own position in society.

All Americans were relieved when the news arrived in April 1770 that a new prime minister, Lord North, had persuaded Parliament to repeal the Townshend duties, except the tea tax, on the grounds that duties on trade within the empire were bad policy. Although the more radical Americans argued that nonimportation should be maintained until even the tea tax was repealed, merchants quickly resumed importing. The rest of the Townshend Acts remained in force, but repeal of the taxes made the other laws appear less objectionable to the colonists.

Repeal of the Townshend duties

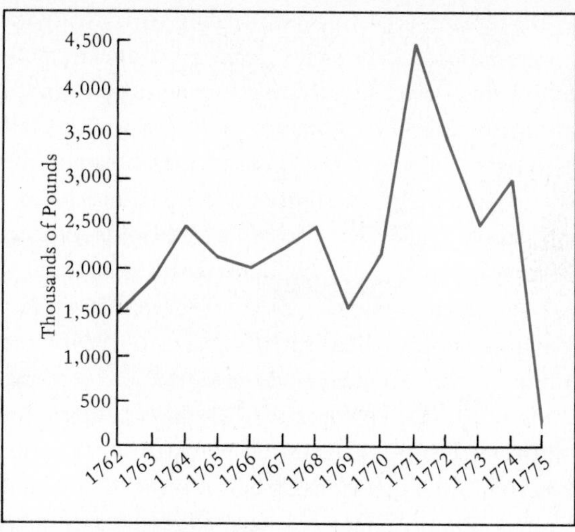

Goods exported to the thirteen colonies, 1762–1775. Source: Adapted from John J. McCusker, "The Current Value of English Exports, 1677 to 1800," *William and Mary Quarterly, 28* (October 1971), Table IIIc, pp. 625–626.

Growing rifts

At first the new ministry did nothing to antagonize the colonists. Yet on the very day Lord North proposed repeal of the Townshend duties, a clash between civilians and soldiers in Boston led to the death of five Americans. The origins of the event patriots called the Boston Massacre lay in repeated clashes between customs officers and the people of Massachusetts. The Townshend Acts' creation of an American Board of Customs Commissioners had been error enough, but basing it in Boston severely compounded the mistake.

From the day of their arrival in November 1767, the customs commissioners were frequent targets of mob action. In June 1768, their seizure of the patriot leader John Hancock's sloop *Liberty* on suspicion of smuggling caused a violent riot in which prominent customs officers' property was destroyed. The riot in turn helped to convince the ministry in London that troops were needed to maintain order in the unruly port. The assignment of two regiments of regulars to their city confirmed Bostonians' worst fears; the redcoats were a constant reminder of the oppressive potential of British power.

Bostonians, accustomed to leading their lives with a minimum of interference from government, now found themselves hemmed in at every turn. Guards on Boston Neck, the entrance to the city, checked all travelers and their goods. Redcoat patrols roamed the city day and night, questioning and sometimes harassing passers-by. Military parades were held on Boston Common, accompanied by loud martial music and often the brutal public whipping of deserters and other violators of army rules. Parents began to fear for the safety of their daughters, who were subjected to the soldiers' coarse sexual insults when they ventured out on the streets. But the greatest potential for violence lay in the uneasy relationship between the soldiers and Boston laborers. Many redcoats sought employment in their off-duty hours, competing for unskilled jobs with the city's ordinary workingmen, and members of the two groups brawled repeatedly in taverns and on the streets.

On March 2, 1770, workers at a ropewalk (a ship-rigging factory) attacked some redcoats seeking jobs; a pitched battle resulted when both groups acquired reinforcements. Three days later, the tension exploded. Early on the evening of March 5, a crowd began throwing hard-packed snowballs at sentries guarding the Customs House. Goaded beyond endurance, the sentries fired on the crowd against express orders to the contrary, killing four and wounding eight, one of whom died a few days later. Among the dead were Samuel Maverick, Ebenezer MacIntosh's brother-in-law, and a mulatto sailor, Crispus Attucks. Resistance leaders idealized the dead rioters as martyrs for the cause of liberty, holding a solemn funeral three days later and commemorating March 5 annually with patriotic orations. The best-known engraving of the massacre, by Paul Revere, was itself a part of the propaganda campaign. It depicts a peaceful crowd, an officer ordering the soldiers to fire, and shots coming from the window of the Customs House.

Boston Massacre

The leading patriots wanted to make certain the soldiers did not become martyrs as well. Furthermore, despite the political benefits the patriots derived from the massacre, it is unlikely that they approved of the crowd action that provoked it. Ever since August 1765 the men allied with the Sons of Liberty had supported orderly demonstrations and expressed distaste for uncontrolled riots, of which the Boston Massacre was a prime example. Thus when the soldiers were tried for the killings in November, they were defended by John Adams and Josiah Quincy, Jr., both unwavering patriots. All but two of the accused men were acquitted, and those convicted were released after having been branded on the thumb. Undoubtedly the favorable outcome of the trials prevented London officials from taking further steps against the city.

For more than two years after the Boston Massacre and the repeal of the Townshend duties, a superficial calm descended on the colonies. Local incidents, like the burning of the customs vessel *Gaspée* in 1772 by Rhode Islanders, marred the relationship of individual colonies and the mother country, but nothing caused Americans to join in a unified protest. Even so, the resistance movement continued to gather momentum. The most radical colonial newspapers, such as the *Boston Gazette,* the *Pennsylvania Journal,* and the *South Carolina Gazette,* published essays drawing on Real Whig ideology and accusing Great Britain of a deliberate plan to oppress America. After repeal of the Stamp Act, the patriots had praised Parliament; following repeal of the Townshend duties, they warned of impending tyranny. What had seemed to be an isolated mistake, a single ill-chosen tax, now appeared to be part of a plot against American liberties. Among other things, essayists pointed to Parliament's persecution of the English radical John Wilkes, the stationing of troops in Boston, the growing number of vice-admiralty courts, and a host of other matters (including England's policies toward Ireland and Corsica) as evidence of a plan to enslave the colonists. Indeed, patriot writers played repeatedly on the word *enslavement.* Most white colonists had direct knowledge of slavery (either being slaveholders themselves or having slave-owning neighbors), and the threat of enslavement by Britain must have hit them with peculiar force.

Still, no one yet advocated complete independence from the mother country. Though the patriots were becoming increasingly convinced that they should seek freedom from parliamentary authority, they continued to acknowledge their British identity and to pledge their allegiance to George III. Indeed, they hoped to ally themselves with English radicals in working for imperial reform. They began, therefore, to try to envision a system that would enable them to

Paul Revere's engraving of the Boston Massacre, a masterful piece of propaganda. At right the British officer seems to be ordering the soldiers to fire on a peaceful, unresisting crowd. The Customs House has been labeled Butcher's Hall, and smoke drifts up from a gun barrel sticking out the window. American Antiquarian Society.

be ruled largely by their own elected legislatures while remaining loyal to the king. But any such scheme was totally alien to Britons' conception of the nature of their government, which was that Parliament held sole undivided sovereignty over the empire. Conservative colonists recognized the dangers inherent in the patriots' new mode of thinking. The former stamp distributor Andrew Oliver, for example, predicted in 1771 that "serious consequences" would follow from the fact that "the leaders of the people were never [before] so open in asserting our independence of the British Legislature," even though "there is an intermission of Acts of violence at present."

Oliver's prediction proved correct when, in the fall of 1772, the North ministry began to implement the portion of the Townshend Acts that provided for governors and judges to be paid from customs revenues. In early November, voters at a Boston town meeting established a Committee of Correspondence to publicize the decision by exchanging letters with other Massachusetts towns. Heading the committee was the man who had proposed its formation, Samuel Adams. As much as a year earlier, Adams had described in a letter to a Virginia friend the benefits of organizing an official communications network

Committees of correspondence

Samuel Adams (1722–1803), painted by John Singleton Copley. Copley's famous portrait, painted two years before Adams headed the Boston Committee of Correspondence, shows the patriot leader at his most determined. Adams points a finger at the Massachusetts Charter, the symbol of the traditional liberties he sought to protect. Museum of Fine Arts, Boston, Deposited by the city of Boston.

within and among the separate colonies. "If conducted with a proper spirit," Adams had asked, "would it not afford reason for the Enemies of our common Liberty, to tremble?"

Samuel Adams was fifty-one years old in 1772, thirteen years the senior of his distant cousin John and a decade older than most other leaders of American resistance. He had been a Boston tax collector, a member and clerk of the Massachusetts Assembly, and an ally of the Loyal Nine (though evidently not a member). Unswerving in his devotion to the American cause, Adams drew a sharp contrast between a corrupt Britain and the virtuous colonies. His primary forum was the Boston town meeting. An experienced political organizer, Adams continually stressed the necessity of prudent collective action. His Committee of Correspondence thus undertook to create an informed consensus among all the citizens of Massachusetts, including residents of rural areas. The formal resistance movement had until then been largely confined to cities and towns.

The Boston town meeting directed the Committee of Correspondence "to state the Rights of the Colonists and of this Province in particular," to list "the Infringements and Violations thereof that have been, or from time to time may be made," and to send copies to the other towns in the province. In return, Boston requested "a free communication of their Sentiments on this Subject."

Samuel Adams, James Otis, Jr., and Josiah Quincy, Jr., prepared the statement of the colonists' rights. Declaring that Americans had absolute rights to life, liberty, and property, the committee asserted that the idea that "a British house of commons, should have a right, at pleasure, to give and grant the property of the colonists" was "irreconcileable" with "the first principles of natural law and Justice . . . and of the British Constitution in particular." The list of grievances, drafted by another group of prominent patriots, was similarly sweeping. It complained of taxation without representation, the presence of unnecessary troops and customs officers on American soil, the use of imperial revenues to pay colonial officials, the expanded jurisdiction of vice-admiralty courts, and even the nature of the instructions given to American governors by their superiors in London.

The entire document, which was printed as a pamphlet for distribution to the towns, exhibited none of the hesitation that had characterized colonial claims against Parliament in the 1760s. That body had become nothing more than "a British house of commons." No longer were patriots—at least in Boston—concerned about defining the precise limits of parliamentary authority. No longer did they mention the necessity of obedience to Parliament. Clearly, they were committed to a course that placed American rights first, loyalty to Great Britain a distant second.

The response of the Massachusetts towns to the committee's pamphlet must have caused Samuel Adams to rejoice. Some towns disagreed with Boston's assessment of the state of affairs, but most aligned themselves with the city. From Braintree came the assertion that "all civil officers are or ought to be Servants to the people and dependent upon them for their official Support, and every instance to the Contrary from the Governor downwards tends to crush and destroy civil liberty." The town of Holden declared that "the People of New England have never given the People of Britain any Right of Jurisdiction over us." The citizens of Petersham commented that resistance to tyranny was "the first and highest social Duty of this people." And Pownallborough warned, "allegiance is a relative Term and like Kingdoms and commonwealths is local and has its bounds." It was beliefs like these that made the next crisis in Anglo-American affairs the final one.

The Boston Tea Party

The only one of the Townshend duties still in effect by 1773 was the tax on tea. In the years since 1770 some Americans had continued to boycott English tea, while others had resumed drinking it either openly or in secret. At one inn, John Adams requested tea "provided it has been honestly smuggled," but found that the landlady had on principle banished all tea from the premises. Less scrupulous colonists purchased smuggled Dutch tea, drank tea from coffeepots, or hid when they consumed it.

Even though the boycott was less than fully effective, tea retained its explosive symbolic character. When in May 1773 Parliament passed an act designed to save the East India Company from bankruptcy, which changed the way British tea was sold in the colonies, resistance leaders were immediately suspicious. Under the Tea Act, certain duties paid on tea were to be returned to the company. Furthermore, tea was to be sold only by designated agents, which would enable the East India Company to control the price and undersell any competitors, even smugglers. The net result would be cheaper tea for American consumers. But many colonists interpreted the new measure as a pernicious device to make them admit Parliament's right to tax them, since the less expensive tea would still be taxed under the Townshend law. Others saw the Tea Act as the first step in the establishment of an East India Company monopoly of all colonial trade. Residents of the four cities singled out to receive the first shipments of tea prepared to respond to what they perceived as a new threat to their freedom.

Tea Act

A 1789 engraving of the Boston Tea Party. A large crowd of bystanders looks on as colonists disguised as Indians break open the tea chests and empty them into the harbor. Library of Congress.

In New York City, the tea ships failed to arrive on schedule. In Philadelphia, the captain was persuaded to turn around and sail back to England. In Charleston, the tea was unloaded, stored under the direction of local tradesmen, and later destroyed. The only confrontation occurred in Boston, where both sides–the town meeting, joined by participants from nearby towns, and Governor Thomas Hutchinson, two of whose sons were tea agents–rejected compromise.

The first of three tea ships, the *Dartmouth,* entered Boston Harbor on November 28. Under the customs laws, duty had to be paid within twenty days of a ship's arrival or its cargo would be seized by customs officers. After a series of mass meetings, Bostonians voted to prevent the tea from being unloaded and to post guards on the wharf. Hutchinson, for his part, refused to permit the vessels to leave the harbor, since that too would violate the law.

On December 16, 1773, one day before the cargo would have to be confiscated, more than five thousand people (nearly a third of the city's population) crowded into Old South Church. The meeting, chaired by Samuel Adams, made a final attempt to persuade Hutchinson to send the tea back to England. But Hutchinson remained adamant. At about 6 p.m., Adams reportedly announced "that he could think of nothing further to be done–that they had now done all they could for the Salvation of their Country." As if his statement were a signal, cries rang out from the back of the crowd: "Boston harbor a tea-pot night! The Mohawks are come!" Small groups pushed their way out of the meeting. Within a few minutes, about sixty men crudely disguised as Indians assembled at the wharf, boarded the three ships, and dumped the cargo into the harbor. By 9 p.m. their work was done: 342 chests of tea worth approximately £10,000 floated in splinters on the ebbing tide.

Boston Tea Party

Among the "Indians" were many representatives of Boston's artisans. Five masons, eleven carpenters and builders, three leatherworkers, a blacksmith, a hatter,

Important events

1689–98	War of League of Augsberg (King William's War)
1701	Iroquois neutrality treaties
1702–13	War of Spanish Succession (Queen Anne's War)
1740–48	War of Austrian Succession (King George's War)
1754	Albany Congress George Washington's defeat
1755	Braddock's defeat
1756	Seven Years' War formally declared
1757	William Pitt becomes secretary of state
1759	Quebec falls to British
1760	Montreal falls to British; American phase of war ends George III becomes king
1763	Treaty of Paris George Grenville becomes prime minister Pontiac's uprising Proclamation of 1763
1764	Sugar Act Currency Act James Otis, Jr., *Rights of the British Colonies Asserted and Proved* March of Paxton Boys
1765	Stamp Act Sons of Liberty formed
1766	Repeal of Stamp Act Hostilities between British and Ottawas end
1767	Townshend Acts John Dickinson, *Letters of a Pennsylvania Farmer*
1768	*Liberty* riot British troops stationed in Boston
1770	Lord North becomes prime minister Repeal of Townshend duties except tea tax Boston Massacre
1772	*Gaspée* incident
1773	Tea Act Boston Tea Party
1774	Coercive Acts First Continental Congress

three coopers, two barbers, a coachmaker, a silversmith, and twelve apprentices have been identified as participants. Their ranks also included four farmers from outside Boston, ten merchants, two doctors, a teacher, and a bookseller. The next day John Adams exulted in his diary that the Tea Party was "so bold, so daring, so firm, intrepid and inflexible" that "I can't but consider it as an epocha in history."

The North administration reacted with considerably less enthusiasm when it learned of the Tea Party. In March, after failing in an attempt to charge the Boston resistance leaders with high treason, the ministry proposed a bill closing the port of Boston until the tea was paid for, and prohibiting all but

Coercive and Quebec Acts

coastal trade in food and firewood. Colonial sympathizers in Parliament were easily outvoted by those who wished to punish the city that had been the center of opposition to British policies, and American hopes for an alliance with English radicals collapsed. Later in the spring, Parliament passed three further punitive measures. The Massachusetts Government Act altered the province's charter, substituting an appointed council for an elected one, increasing the powers of the governor, and forbidding special town meetings. The Justice Act provided that a person accused of committing murder in the course of suppressing a riot or enforcing the laws could be tried outside the colony where the incident had occurred. Finally, the Quartering Act gave broad authority to military commanders seeking to house their troops in private dwellings.

After passing the last of what became known as the Coercive Acts in early June, Parliament turned its attention to much-needed reforms in the government of Quebec. The Quebec Act, though unrelated to the Coercive Acts, thus became linked with them in the minds of the patriots. Intended to ease the strains that had arisen since the British conquest of the formerly French colony, the Quebec Act granted greater religious freedom to Catholics–alarming the Protestant colonists, who regarded Roman Catholicism as a mainstay of religious and political despotism. It also reinstated French civil law, which had been replaced by British procedures in 1763, and established an appointed council (rather than an elected legislature) as the governing body of the colony. Finally, in an attempt to provide the northern Indian tribes some protection against white settlement, the act annexed to Quebec the area east of the Mississippi River and north of the Ohio River. Thus that region, parts of which were claimed by individual seacoast colonies, was removed from their jurisdiction.

The members of Parliament who had voted for the punitive legislation believed that the acts would be obeyed, that at long last they had solved the problem posed by the troublesome Americans. But the patriots showed little inclination to bow to the wishes of Parliament. In their eyes, the Coercive Acts and the Quebec Act proved what they had feared since 1768: that Great Britain had embarked on a deliberate plan to oppress them. If the port of Boston could be closed, why not those of Philadelphia or New York? If the royal charter of Massachusetts could be changed, why not that of South Carolina? If certain people could be removed from their home colonies for trial, why not all violators of all laws? If troops could be forcibly quartered in private houses, did not that pave the way for the occupation of all of America? If the Roman Catholic Church could receive favored status in Quebec, why not everywhere? It seemed as though the full dimensions of the plot against American rights and liberties had at last been revealed.

The Boston Committee of Correspondence urged all the colonies to join in an immediate boycott of British goods. But the other provinces were not yet ready to take such a drastic step. Instead, they suggested that another intercolonial congress be convened to consider an appropriate response to the Coercive Acts. Few people wanted to take hasty action; even the most ardent patriots still hoped for reconciliation with Great Britain. Despite their objections to British policy, they continued to see themselves as part of the empire. Americans were approaching the brink of confrontation, but they had not committed themselves to an irrevocable break. And so the colonies agreed to send delegates to Philadelphia in September.

Over the preceding decade, momentous changes had occurred in the ways the colonists thought about themselves and their allegiance. Once linked unquestioningly to Great Britain, they had begun to develop a sense of their own identity as Americans. Though they had not yet taken the final step, they had started to sever the bonds of empire. During the next decade, they would forge the bonds of a new American nationality to replace those rejected Anglo-American ties.

Suggestions for further reading

General

Charles M. Andrews, *The Colonial Background of the American Revolution* (1924); Ian R. Christie, *Crisis of Empire: Great Britain and the American Colonies 1754–1783* (1966); Ian R. Christie and Benjamin W. Labaree, *Empire or Independence, 1760–1776: A British-American Dialogue on the Coming of the American Revolution* (1976); Lawrence Henry Gipson, *The Coming of the Revolution 1763–1775* (1954); Merrill Jensen, *The Founding of a Nation: A History of the American Revolution, 1763–1776* (1968); Edmund S. Morgan, *The Birth of the Republic, 1763–1789* (1956).

Colonial warfare and the British Empire

Lawrence Henry Gipson, *The British Empire Before the American Revolution,* 15 vols. (1936–1970); Robert C. Newbold, *The Albany Congress and Plan of Union of 1754* (1955); Richard Pares, *War and Trade in the West Indies, 1739–1763* (1936); Howard H. Peckham, *The Colonial Wars, 1689–1762* (1963); Alan Rogers, *Empire and Liberty: American Resistance to British Authority, 1755–1763* (1974); Neil R.

Stout, *The Royal Navy in America, 1760–1775* (1973); John Shy, *Toward Lexington: The Role of the British Army in the Coming of the American Revolution* (1965).

British politics and policy

George L. Beer, *British Colonial Policy 1754–1765* (1907); John Brewer, *Party Ideology and Popular Politics at the Accession of George III* (1976); John Brooke, *King George III* (1972); Bernard Donoughue, *British Politics and the American Revolution: The Path to War, 1773–1775* (1965); Michael Kammen, *A Rope of Sand: The Colonial Agents, British Politics, and the American Revolution* (1968); Lewis B. Namier, *England in the Age of the American Revolution,* 2nd ed. (1961); Lewis B. Namier, *The Structure of Politics at the Accession of George III,* 2nd ed. (1957); P.D.G. Thomas, *British Politics and the Stamp Act Crisis* (1975); Carl Ubbelohde, *The Vice-Admiralty Courts and the American Revolution* (1960); Franklin B. Wickwire, *British Subministers and Colonial America, 1763–1783* (1966).

Indians and the West

Thomas P. Abernethy, *Western Lands and the American Revolution* (1959); John R. Alden, *John Stuart and the Southern Colonial Frontier: A Study of Indian Relations, War, Trade, and Land Problems in the Southern Wilderness, 1754–1775* (1944); David H. Corkran, *The Cherokee Frontier: Conflict and Survival, 1740–1762* (1962); R.S. Cotterill, *The Southern Indians: The Story of the Civilized Tribes Before Removal* (1954); James T. Flexner, *Mohawk Baronet: Sir William Johnson of New York* (1959); Georgiana C. Nammack, *Fraud, Politics, and the Dispossession of the Indians: The Iroquois Land Frontier in the Colonial Period* (1969); Howard H. Peckham, *Pontiac and the Indian Uprising* (1947); Jack M. Sosin, *Whitehall and the Wilderness: The Middle West in British Colonial Policy, 1760–1775* (1961).

Revolutionary ideology

Bernard Bailyn, *The Ideological Origins of the American Revolution* (1967); Edwin G. Burrows and Michael Wallace, "The American Revolution: The Ideology and Psychology of National Liberation," *Perspectives in American History,* 6 (1972), 167–302; H. Trevor Colbourn, *The Lamp of Experience: Whig History and the Intellectual Origins of the American Revolution* (1965): Isaac Kramnick, *Bolingbroke and His Circle: The Politics of Nostalgia in the Age of Walpole* (1968); J.G.A. Pocock, "Machiavelli, Harrington, and English Political Ideologies in the Eighteenth Century," *William and Mary Quarterly,* 3rd ser., 22 (1965), 547–583; Caroline Robbins, *The Eighteenth-Century Commonwealthman: Studies in the Transmission, Development, and Circumstance of English Liberal Thought from the Restoration of Charles II until the War with the Thirteen Colonies* (1959); Clinton Rossiter, *Seedtime of the Republic: The Origin of the American Tradition of Political Liberty* (1953).

American resistance

David Ammerman, *In the Common Cause: American Response to the Coercive Acts of 1774* (1974); Richard Beeman, *Patrick Henry: A Biography* (1974); Richard D. Brown, *Revolutionary Politics in Massachusetts: The Boston Committee of Correspondence and the Towns, 1772–1774* (1970); Joseph Albert Ernst, *Money and Politics in America, 1755–1775: A Study in the Currency Act of 1764 and the Political Economy of Revolution* (1973): Dirk Hoerder, *Crowd Action in Revolutionary Massachusetts, 1765–1780* (1977); Benjamin W. Labaree, *The Boston Tea Party* (1964); Jesse Lemisch, "Jack Tar in the Streets: Merchant Seamen in the Politics of Revolutionary America," *William and Mary Quarterly,* 3rd ser., 25 (1968), 371–407; Pauline R. Maier, *From Resistance to Revolution: Colonial Radicals and the Development of American Opposition to Britain, 1765–1776* (1972); Pauline R. Maier, *The Old Revolutionaries: Political Lives in the Age of Samuel Adams* (1980); Edmund S. Morgan and Helen M. Morgan, *The Stamp Act Crisis: Prologue to Revolution* (1953); Gary B. Nash, *The Urban Crucible: Social Change, Political Consciousness, and the Origins of the American Revolution* (1979); Richard Ryerson, *The Revolution is Now Begun: The Radical Committees of Philadelphia, 1765–1776* (1978); Arthur M. Schlesinger, *The Colonial Merchants and the American Revolution 1763–1776* (1918); Richard Walsh, *Charleston's Sons of Liberty: A Study of the Artisans, 1763–1789* (1959); John J. Waters, Jr. *The Otis Family in Provincial and Revolutionary Massachusetts* (1968); Alfred H. Young, ed. *The American Revolution: Explorations in the History of American Radicalism* (1976); Hiller B. Zobel, *The Boston Massacre* (1970).

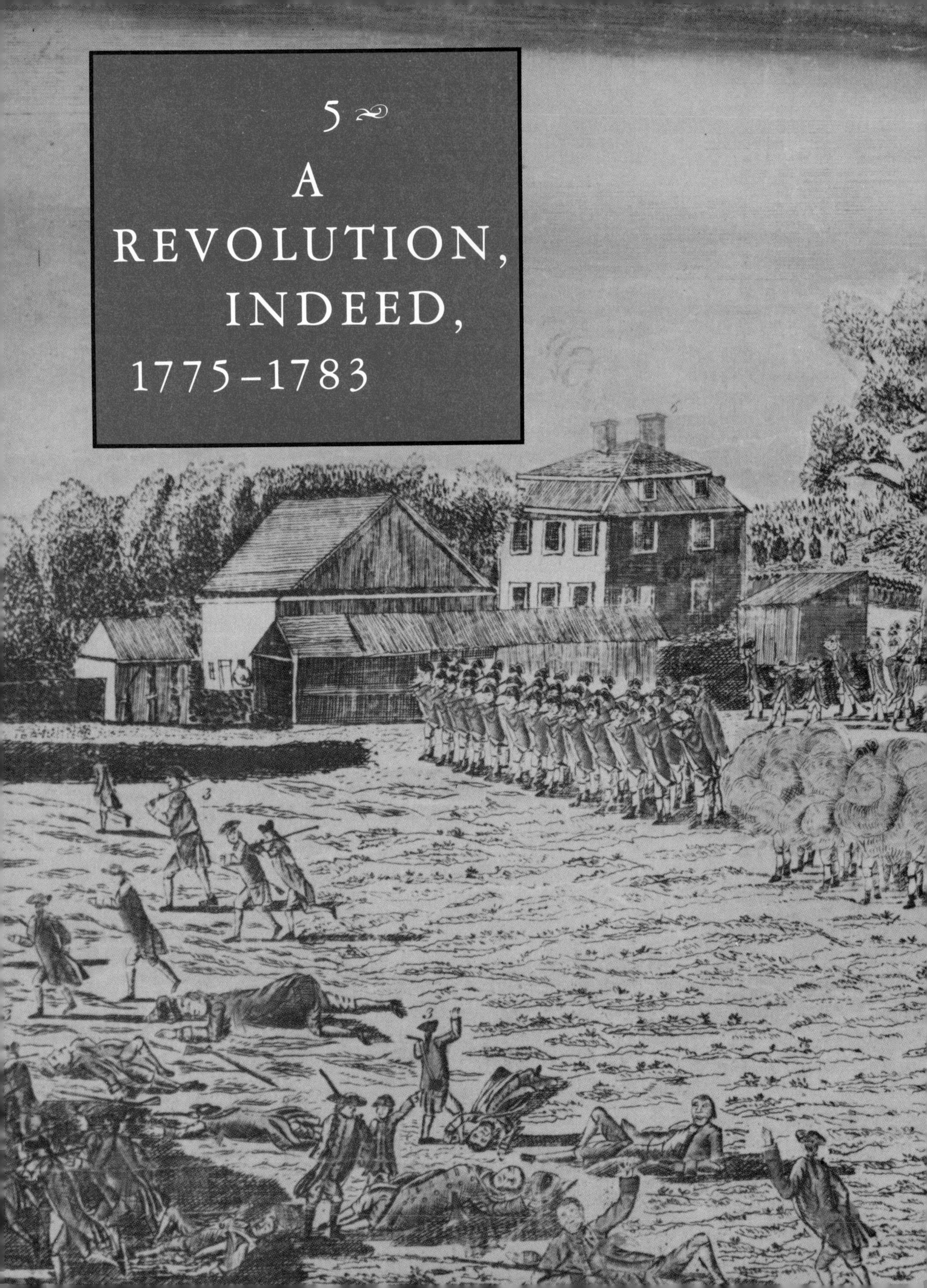

5

A REVOLUTION, INDEED, 1775–1783

One April morning in 1775, Hannah Winthrop awoke with a start to drumbeats, bells, and the continuous clang of the Cambridge fire alarm. She and her husband, a professor at Harvard, soon learned that redcoat troops had left Boston late the evening before, bound for Concord. A few hours later they watched British soldiers march through Cambridge to reinforce the first group. The Winthrops quickly decided to leave home and seek shelter elsewhere. Along with seventy or eighty other refugees, mostly wives and children of patriot militiamen, they made their way to an isolated farmhouse near Fresh Pond. But it was no secure haven. They were, Mrs. Winthrop later wrote, "for some time in sight of the Battle, the glistening instruments of death proclaiming by an incessant fire that much blood must be shed, that many widowd and orphand ones be left as monuments of that persecuting Barbarity of British Tyranny."

Afraid to abandon their refuge even after the sounds of battle ceased, the Winthrops and their companions remained in the farmhouse overnight, sleeping in chairs and on the floor. The next morning, warned that Cambridge was still unsafe, the couple headed west toward Andover. The roads were filled with other frightened families, some carrying all their belongings. Their route took them through Menotomy (now Arlington), scene of some of the bloodiest fighting the day before. The battlefield, Mrs. Winthrop recorded, was "strewd with the mangled bodies." Along the way they encountered a farmer gathering the corpses of his neighbors and searching for the body of his son, who had reportedly been killed in battle. As she walked toward Andover, Hannah Winthrop mentally compared herself with Eve expelled from the Garden of Eden; lines from John Milton's *Paradise Lost,* she later told a friend, had echoed repeatedly in her mind. She was convinced that nothing would be the same again.

In that expectation, Hannah Winthrop was wrong. She and her husband soon returned to their Cambridge home and resumed their normal lives. But their experience in 1775 was typical of that of thousands of other Americans over the next eight years. The Revolution, one of only two major conflicts ever fought on American soil—the other was to be the Civil War—was more than just a series of clashes between British and patriot armies. It also uprooted thousands of civilian families, disrupted the economy, reshaped society by forcing many colonists into permanent exile, and led Americans to develop new conceptions of politics. Indeed, even before the shooting began the patriots had established functioning revolutionary governments throughout the colonies.

In the war itself, the Americans were on the defensive most of the time. British ministers and army officers persisted in comparing the conflict to wars they had fought in Europe, and consequently made numerous errors in strategy and tactics. They also failed to realize that winning a few battles would not achieve their goal of retaining the colonies' allegiance. The patriots, meanwhile, had to worry not only about the redcoat army but also about the blacks, Indians, and loyalists who constituted potentially subversive elements within their own society. That the patriots eventually triumphed over all their foes was more a tribute to their endurance than to their military prowess.

Government by congress and committee

First Continental Congress

When the fifty-five delegates to the First Continental Congress convened in Philadelphia in September 1774, they knew that any measures they adopted were likely to enjoy strong support among their fellow countrymen and women. During the summer of 1774, open meetings held in towns, cities, and counties throughout the colonies had endorsed the idea of another nonimportation pact. Participants in such meetings had promised (in the words of the freeholders of Johnston County, North Carolina) to "strictly adhere to, and abide by, such Regulations and Restrictions as the Members of the said General Congress shall agree to, and judge most convenient." The committees of correspondence that had been established in many communities publicized these popular meetings so effectively that Americans everywhere knew about them. Most of the congressional delegates were selected by extralegal provincial conventions whose members were chosen at such local gatherings, since the royal governors had forbidden the regular assemblies to conduct formal elections. Thus the very act of designating delegates to attend the congress involved Americans in open defiance of British authority.

The colonies' leading political figures–most of them lawyers, merchants, or planters–were sent to the Philadelphia congress. The Massachusetts delegation included both Samuel Adams, the experienced organizer of the Boston resistance, and his younger cousin John, an ambitious lawyer. Among others New York sent John Jay, a talented young attorney. From Pennsylvania came the conservative Joseph Galloway, speaker of the assembly, and his long-time rival John Dickinson. Virginia elected Richard Henry Lee and Patrick Henry, both noted for their patriotic zeal, as well as the stolid and reserved George Washington. Most of these men had never met, but in the weeks, months, and years that followed they were to become the chief architects of the new nation.

The congressmen faced three tasks when they convened at Carpenters Hall on September 5, 1774. The first two were explicit: defining American grievances and developing a plan for resistance. The third was implicit–outlining a theory of their constitutional relationship with England–and proved troublesome. The delegates readily agreed on a list of the laws they wanted repealed (notably the Coercive Acts) and chose as their method of resistance an economic boycott coupled with petitions for relief. But they could not reach a consensus on the constitutional issue. Their discussion of this crucial question was rendered all the more intense by events in Massachusetts.

On the second day of the meeting, word arrived that the British had attacked the Massachusetts countryside and were bombarding Boston from land and sea. This rumor was proven false two days later, but it nevertheless lent a sense of urgency to the congressmen's discussions. That thousands of militiamen had gathered in Cambridge to repel the rumored attack demonstrated how close to the brink of war Great Britain and the colonies had already come. The congressmen accordingly set about their work with particular fervor and commitment.

Since the colonists' resistance was based on the claim that their constitutional rights had been violated, it seemed necessary to define what the colonies' constitutional relationship with England was. But the delegates held widely differing views on that subject. The most radical congressmen, like Lee of Virginia and Roger Sherman of Connecticut, agreed with the position published a few weeks earlier by Thomas Jefferson–who was not a delegate–in his *Summary View of the Rights of British America.* Jefferson argued that the colonists owed allegiance only to George III, and that Parliament was nothing more than "the legislature of one part of the empire." As such, he declared, it could not exercise legitimate authority over the American provinces, which had historically been governed by their own assemblies.

Meanwhile the conservative Joseph Galloway and his ally James Duane of New York insisted that the congress should acknowledge Parliament's supremacy over the empire and its right to regulate American trade. Galloway embodied these ideas in a formal plan of union, like the one his friend Benjamin Franklin had presented at the Albany Congress in 1754. His plan proposed the establishment of an American legislature, its members chosen by individual colonial assemblies, which would have to consent to laws pertaining to America. The delegates rejected Galloway's proposal, though, eventually accepting instead a position outlined by John Adams.

Declaration of Rights and Grievances

The clause Adams drafted in the congress's Declaration of Rights and Grievances read in part: "From the necessity of the case, and a regard to the mutual interest of both countries, we cheerfully consent to the operation of such acts of the British parliament, as are bona fide, restrained to the regulation of our external commerce." Note the key phrases. "From the necessity of the case" indicated Americans' abandonment, once and for all, of the unquestioning loyalty to the mother country that had so bedeviled James Otis, Jr., just a decade earlier. The colonists were now declaring that they owed obedience to Parliament only because they had decided it was in the best interest of both countries. "Bona fide, restrained to the regulation of our external commerce" resonated with overtones of the Stamp Act controversy and Dickinson's arguments in his *Farmer's Letters.* The delegates intended to make clear to Lord North that they would continue to resist taxes in disguise, like the Townshend duties. Most striking of all was that such language, which only a few years before would have been regarded as irredeemably radical, could be presented and accepted as a compromise in the fall of 1774. The Americans had come a long way since their first hesitant protests against the Sugar Act.

Once the delegates had resolved the constitutional issue, they discussed the tactics by which to force another British retreat. They quickly agreed on nonimportation of all goods from Great Britain and Ireland, as well as tea and molasses from other British possessions and slaves from any source, effective December 1. An end to the consumption of British products was also readily accepted as part of the agreement that became known as the Continental Association; it would become effective on March 1, 1775. Nonexportation, on the other hand, generated considerable debate. The Virginia delegation adamantly refused to accept a ban on exports to England until after its planters had had a chance to market their 1774 tobacco crop. As a result, the congress provided that nonexportation would not begin until September 10, 1775.

More influential than the details of the Continental Association was the method the congress recommended for its enforcement: the election of committees of observation and inspection in every county, city, and town in America. Such committees were officially charged only with overseeing enforcement of the association, but over the next six months they became de facto governments. Since the congress specified that committee members be chosen by all persons qualified to vote for members of the lower house of the colonial legislatures, the committees were guaranteed a broad popular base. Furthermore, their large size ensured that many new men would be incorporated into the resistance movement. In some places the committeemen were former local officeholders; in other places they were obscure men who had never before held office. Everywhere, however, these committeemen—perhaps seven to eight thousand of them in the colonies as a whole—found themselves increasingly linked to the cause of American resistance.

Committees of observation

At first the committees confined themselves to enforcing the nonimportation clause—examining merchants' records and publishing the names of those who continued to import or sell British goods. But the Continental Association also promoted home manufactures and encouraged Americans to adopt simple modes of dress and behavior. Wearing homespun garments became a sign of patriotism, just as it had been in the late 1760s. Since expensive leisure-time activities were symbols of vice and corruption (characteristic of England, not the virtuous colonies), the congress urged Americans to forgo dancing, gambling, horse racing, cock fighting, and other forms of "extravagance and dissipation." In enforcing these injunctions, the committees gradually extended their authority over nearly all aspects of American life.

Committees forbade public and private dancing, extracted apologies from people caught gambling or racing, prohibited the slaughter of lambs (due to the need for wool), and offered prizes for the best locally made cloth. The Baltimore County committee even advised citizens not to attend the upcoming town fair, which they described as nothing more than an occasion for "riots, drunkenness, gaming, and the vilest immoralities."

The committees also attempted to identify opponents of American resistance. Although seeking to protect American rights—which presumably included freedom of speech and thought—the patriots saw no reason to grant those rights to people who disagreed with them. They viewed the resistance movement as a collective endeavor that would succeed only if all colonists supported it. Consequently, the committees developed elaborate spy networks, circulated copies of the association for signatures, and investigated reports of dissident remarks and activities. Suspected dissenters were first urged to convert to the colonial cause; if that failed, the committees had them watched or restricted their movements. Sometimes people engaging in casual political exchanges with friends one day found themselves charged with "treasonable conversation" the next. Committees cooperated with each other, too. In 1775, for example, the Northampton, Massachusetts, committee told its counterpart in nearby Hadley that a townsman had been heard to call the congress "a Pack or Parcell of Fools" that was "as tyrannical as Lord North and ought to be opposed & resisted." The Hadley committee examined the accused man, who admitted his statements and refused to recant. The committee thereafter had him watched.

What is striking about such incidents is not that there were so many but that there were so few. The committees were extralegal bodies, drawing on no source of authority other than popular election. They had no connection–except in some cases overlapping membership–with the ordinary organs of government Americans were accustomed to obeying. Furthermore, they assumed unprecedented powers of supervision over the daily lives, actions, and even thoughts of the citizenry. That most colonists apparently submitted to their rule without overt complaint certainly suggests, if it does not altogether prove, broad public support for resistance to Great Britain. As the patriots were to discover, however, this did not necessarily mean that independence would later have the same broad support. Many people who were willing to work for reform within the empire by means of boycotts and petitions were unwilling to seek independence by force of arms.

While the committees were expanding their power during the winter and early spring of 1775, the established governments of the colonies were collapsing. Only in Connecticut, Rhode Island, Delaware, and Pennsylvania did regular assemblies continue to meet without encountering patriot challenges to their authority. In every other colony, popularly elected provincial conventions took over the task of running the government, sometimes entirely replacing the legislatures and at other times holding concurrent sessions. In late 1774 and early 1775, these conventions approved the Continental Association, elected delegates to the Second Continental Congress (scheduled for May), organized militia units, and gathered arms and ammunition. The British-appointed governors and councils, unable to stem the tide of resistance, watched helplessly as their authority crumbled.

Provincial conventions

The frustrating experience of Governor Josiah Martin of North Carolina is a case in point. When a provincial convention was called to meet at New Bern on April 4, 1775–the same day the legislature was to convene–Martin proclaimed that "the Assembly of this province duly elected is the only true and lawful representation of the people." He asked all citizens to "renounce disclaim and discourage all such meetings cabals and illegal proceedings . . . which can only tend to introduce disorder and anarchy." Martin's proclamation had no visible effect, and when the convention met at New Bern its membership proved to be virtually identical to that of the colonial legislature. The delegates proceeded to act alternately in both capacities and even passed some joint resolves. Continuing the farce, the exasperated Martin delivered a speech to the assembly denouncing the election of the convention. On April 7, Martin admitted to Lord Dartmouth, the American Secretary in North's ministry, that his government was "absolutely prostrate, impotent, and that nothing but the shadow of it is left."

Royal officials in the other colonies suffered the same frustrations. Courts were prevented from holding sessions; taxes were paid to agents of the conventions rather than provincial tax collectors; sheriffs' powers were questioned; and militiamen refused to muster except by order of the local committees. In short, during the six months preceding the battles at Lexington and Concord, independence was being won at the local level, but without formal acknowledgment and for the most part without shooting or bloodshed. Not many Americans fully realized what was happening. Most were carried along by events, unaware of the ultimate implications of their acts and arguments. The vast majority of colonists still proclaimed their loyalty to Great Britain and denied that they sought to leave the empire. Among the few Americans who did recognize the trend toward independence were those who opposed it.

Internal enemies

The first protests against British measures, in the mid-1760s, had won the support of most colonists. Only in the late 1760s and early 1770s did a significant number of Americans begin to question both the aims and the tactics of the resistance movement. In 1774 and 1775 such people found themselves in a difficult position. Like their more radical counterparts, most of them objected to parliamentary policies and wanted some kind of constitutional reform. (Joseph Galloway, for instance, was a conservative by American standards, but his plan for restructuring the empire was too novel for Britain to accept.) Nevertheless, if forced to a choice, these colonists sympathized with Great Britain rather than with an independent America. The events of the crucial year between the passage of the Coercive Acts and the outbreak of fighting in Massachusetts had crystallized their thinking. Their doubts about violent protest, their desire to uphold the legally constituted colonial governments, and their fears of anarchy combined to make them especially sensitive to the dangers of resistance.

In 1774 and 1775 some conservatives began to publish essays and pamphlets critical of the congress and its allied committees. In New York City, a group of Anglican clergymen jointly wrote seven pamphlets, as well as numerous shorter essays, arguing the importance of maintaining a cordial connection between England and America. In Pennsylvania, Joseph Galloway published *A Candid Examination of the Mutual Claims of Great Britain and the Colonies,* attacking the Continental Congress for rejecting his plan of union. In Massachusetts, the young attorney Daniel Leonard, writing under the pseudonym Massachusettensis, engaged in a prolonged newspaper debate with Novanglus (John Adams). All the conservative authors stressed the point that Leonard put so well in his sixth essay in January 1775: "There is no possible medium between absolute independence and subjection to the authority of parliament." Leonard and his fellows realized that what had begun as a dispute over the extent of American subordination within the empire had now raised the question of whether the colonies would remain linked to Great Britain at all. "Rouse up at last from your slumber!" the Reverend Thomas Bradbury Chandler of New Jersey cried out to Americans. "There is a set of people among us . . . who have formed a scheme for establishing an independent government or empire in America."

Some colonists heeded the conservative pamphleteers' warnings. About one-fifth of the white American population remained loyal to Great Britain, actively opposing independence. With notable exceptions, most people of the following types became loyalists: British-appointed government officials; merchants whose trade depended on imperial connections; Anglican clergy everywhere and lay Anglicans in the North–where their denomination was in the minority–since the king was the head of their church as well as the state; former officers and enlisted men from the British army, many of whom had settled in America after 1763; non-English ethnic minorities, especially Scots; tenant farmers, particularly those whose landlords sided with the patriots; members of persecuted religious sects; and many of the backcountry southerners who had rebelled against eastern rule in the 1760s and early 1770s. All these people had one thing in common: the patriot leaders were their long-standing enemies, though for different reasons. Local and provincial disputes thus helped to determine which side a person chose in the imperial conflict.

Loyalists, patriots, and neutrals

The active patriots, who accounted for about two-fifths of the population, came chiefly from the groups that had dominated colonial society, either numerically or politically. Among them were yeoman farmers, members of dominant Protestant sects (both Old and New Lights), Chesapeake gentry, merchants dealing mainly in American commodities, city artisans, elected officeholders, and people of English descent. Wives usually but not always adopted their husbands' political beliefs.

There remained in the middle perhaps two-fifths of the white population. Some of those who tried to avoid taking sides were sincere pacifists, such as Pennsylvania Quakers. Others opportunistically shifted their allegiance depending on which side happened to be winning at the time. Still others simply wanted to be left alone to lead their lives; they cared little about politics and normally obeyed whichever side controlled their area. But such colonists also resisted the British and the Americans alike when the demands made on them seemed too heavy–when taxes became too high, for example, or when calls for militia service came too often. Their attitude might best be summed up in the phrase "a plague on both your houses." Such persons made up an especially large proportion of the population in the southern backcountry, where the Scots-Irish settlers had little love for either the patriot gentry or the English authorities.

To American patriots, that sort of apathy or neutrality was a crime as heinous as loyalism. Those who were not for them were against them; in their minds, there could be no conscientious objectors. By the winter of 1775 and 1776, less than a year after Lexington and Concord, the Continental Congress was recommending to the states that all "disaffected" or "inimical" persons be disarmed and arrested. The state legislatures quickly passed laws prescribing severe penalties for suspected loyalists. Many began to require all voters (or, in some cases, all free adult males) to take oaths of allegiance; the punishment for refusal was usually banishment or extra taxes. In 1778 and thereafter, many states formally confiscated the property of

Connecticut imprisoned many of its loyalists in notorious Newgate prison, a converted copper mine. The offenders were housed in caverns below the large structure left of center. Some prominent loyalists (like Benjamin Franklin's son William, the last royal governor of New Jersey) were held in private homes. The Connecticut Historical Society.

banished loyalists. At the end of the war, perhaps as many as 100,000 white Americans were exiled to England, Canada, or the West Indies because of their loyalism.

The patriots' policies helped to ensure that the weak, scattered, and persecuted loyalists could not band together to threaten the revolutionary cause. But loyalists were not the only internal enemies the resistance leaders had to contend with. As they embarked on war against the crown, they also had to fear potential subversion by blacks and Indians.

Slave conspiracies

In late 1774 and early 1775 news of slave conspiracies surfaced in different parts of the colonies. All shared a common element: a plan to assist the British in return for freedom. A group of black Bostonians petitioned General Thomas Gage, who had replaced Thomas Hutchinson as governor of Massachusetts, promising to fight for the redcoats if he would liberate them. In Virginia, whites learned that a number of blacks were preparing to join the British. The governor of Maryland authorized the issuance of extra guns to militiamen in four counties where slave uprisings were expected. The most serious incident occurred during the summer of 1775 in Charleston, where Thomas Jeremiah, a free black harbor pilot, was brutally executed after being convicted of attempting to foment a slave revolt.

RUN away from *Hampton*, on *Sunday* laſt, a luſty Mulatto Fellow named ARGYLE, well known about the Country, has a Scar on one of his Wriſts, and has loſt one or more of his fore Teeth; he is a very handy Fellow by Water, or about the Houſe, *&c.* loves Drink, and is very bold in his Cups, but daſtardly when ſober. Whether he will go for a Man of War's Man, or not, I cannot ſay; but I will give 40s. to have him brought to me. He can read and write.

NOVEMBER 2, 1775. JACOB WRAY.

An advertisement for a runaway slave suspected of joining Lord Dunmore—a common sight in Virginia and Maryland newspapers during the fall and winter of 1775 to 1776. Virginia State Library.

It was fear of acts such as these that made white residents of the British West Indian colonies far more cautious in their opposition to parliamentary policies than their counterparts on the mainland. On most of the Caribbean islands, blacks outnumbered whites by six or seven to one. The planters simply could not afford to risk opposing Britain, their chief protector, with the ever-present threat of black revolt hanging over their heads. The Jamaica assembly agreed with the mainland colonial legislatures that citizens should not be bound by laws to which they had not consented. Nevertheless its members assured the king in 1774 that "it cannot be supposed, that we now intend, or ever could have intended Resistance to Great Britain." They cited as reasons Jamaica's "weak and feeble" condition, "its very small number of white inhabitants, and . . . the incumbrance of more than Two hundred thousand Slaves."

Racial composition affected politics in the continental colonies as well. In the North, where whites greatly outnumbered blacks, revolutionary fervor was at its height. In Virginia and Maryland, where whites constituted a safe majority of the population, there was occasional alarm over potential slave revolts but no disabling fear. But in South Carolina, which was over 60 percent black, and Georgia, where the racial balance was nearly even, whites were noticeably less enthusiastic about resistance. Georgia, in fact, sent no delegates to the First Continental Congress, and reminded its representatives at the Second Continental Congress to consider its circumstances, "with our blacks and tories within us," when voting on the question of independence.

The whites' worst fears were realized in November 1775, when Lord Dunmore, the governor of Virginia, offered to free any slaves and indentured servants who would leave their patriot masters to join the British forces. Dunmore hoped to use black manpower in his fight against the revolutionaries, and to disrupt the economy by depriving white Americans of their labor force. But fewer blacks than expected rallied to the British standard in 1775 and 1776 (there were at most two thousand). Many of those who did perished in a smallpox epidemic that raged through the naval vessels housing them in Norfolk harbor.

Though black Americans did not pose a serious threat to the revolutionary cause in its early years, the patriots managed to turn rumors of slave uprisings to their own advantage. In South Carolina in particular, they won adherents by promoting white unity under the revolutionary banner. The Continental Association was needed, they argued, to protect whites from blacks at a time when the royal government was unable to muster adequate defense forces. Undoubtedly many wavering Carolinians were drawn into the revolutionary camp by fear that an overt division among the colony's whites would encourage a slave revolt.

A similar factor—the threat of Indian attacks—helped to persuade some reluctant westerners to support the struggle against Great Britain. In the years since the Proclamation of 1763, British officials had won the trust and respect of the interior tribes by attempting to protect them from land-hungry whites.

Indian neutrality

The British-appointed superintendents of Indian affairs, John Stuart in the South and Sir William Johnson in the North, lived among and sympathized with the Indians. In 1768, Stuart and Johnson negotiated separate agreements modifying the proclamation line and attempting to draw realistic defensible boundaries between tribal holdings and white settlements. The two treaties–signed respectively at Hard Labor Creek, South Carolina, in October and at Fort Stanwix, New York, in November–supposedly established permanent borders for the colonies. But just a few years later, in the treaties of Lochaber (1770) and Augusta (1773), the British pushed the southern boundary even farther west to accommodate the demands of whites in western Georgia and the "overmountain" region known as Kentucky.

By the time of the Revolution, the Indians were impatient with the Americans' aggressive pressure on their lands. They also recognized the colonists' contempt for the Indians' way of life and resented the whites' unwillingness to prosecute frontiersmen who wantonly killed innocent natives. In combination with the tribes' confidence in Stuart and Johnson, these grievances predisposed most Indians toward an alliance with the British. Only two tribes favored the colonists: the northern Oneidas, who had been converted to Christianity by Boston-based missionaries, and the southern Catawbas, who were heavily dependent on American traders. Even so, the British hesitated to make full and immediate use of their potential Indian allies. The superintendents were well aware that the tribes might prove a liability, since their aims and style of fighting were not necessarily compatible with those of the British. Accordingly, John Stuart and Guy Johnson (who became northern superintendent following his uncle's death) sought nothing more from the tribes than a promise of neutrality. The superintendents even helped to prevent a general Indian uprising in the summer of 1774. Because of the royal officials' clever maneuvering, the Shawnees found no allies when they decided to attack frontier villages in Kentucky. They were defeated by the Virginia militia in Lord Dunmore's War and consequently withdrew north and west of the Ohio, leaving Kentucky open to white settlement.

John Murray, Lord Dunmore (1730–1809), the last royal governor of Virginia. Dunmore tried in vain to raise a black army to combat the Revolution. Virginia Historical Society.

The patriots, recognizing that their standing with the tribes was poor, also sought the Indians' neutrality. In 1775 the Second Continental Congress sent a general message to the tribes describing the war as "a family quarrel between us and Old England" and requesting that they "not join on either side," since "you Indians are not concerned in it." The Overhill Cherokees, led by Chief Dragging Canoe, nevertheless decided that the whites' "family quarrel" would allow them to settle some old scores. They attacked white settlements along the western borders of the Carolinas and Virginia in the summer of 1776. But a coordinated campaign by Carolina and Virginia militia destroyed many of their towns, along with crops and large quantities of supplies. Dragging Canoe and his diehard followers fled west to the Tennessee River,

In Provincial Congreſs,

New-York, Auguſt 8th, 1775.

RESOLVED,

THAT the ſeveral Committees and Sub-Committees of the different Counties within this Colony, be directed immediately to purchaſe or hire all the ARMS, with or without Bayonets, that are fit for preſent Service (on the Credit of this Colony) and to deliver them to the reſpective Colonels in this Colony employed in the Continental Service, or their Order, for the Uſe of the Continental Army.

A true Copy from the Minutes,

Robert Benson, Secry.

Broadside authorizing the purchase of muskets for the Continental troops beseiging Boston. Published by the New York Provincial Congress in August 1775. John Carter Brown Library.

where they established new outposts, while the rest of the Cherokees agreed to a treaty that ceded more of their land to the whites.

The other major southern tribe–the Creeks–failed to come to the Cherokees' aid in the 1776 war. The Creeks were preoccupied by a long-standing feud with the Choctaws, and resentful that both the British and the Americans had devoted most of their attention (and gifts) to wooing the Cherokees. This sort of factionalism was the Indians' chief problem during the Revolutionary War. Had the tribes ever arrived at a unified position–whether an alliance with the British, with the Americans, or even a consistently independent role–they could have protected their common interests better. But they had distrusted each other too long to set aside their differences for the sake of a common goal.

Thus, although the patriots could never completely ignore the threats posed by loyalists, blacks, neutrals, and Indians, only rarely did fear of these groups seriously hamper the revolutionary movement. Occasionally frontier militia refused to turn out for duty on the seaboard because they feared Indians would attack in their absence. Sometimes southern troops refused to serve in the North because they (and their political leaders) were unwilling to leave the South unprotected against a slave insurrection. But the practical impossibility of a large-scale slave revolt, coupled with tribal feuds and the patriots' successful campaign to disarm and neutralize loyalists, ensured that the revolutionaries would remain firmly in control as they fought for independence.

War begins

On January 27, 1775, the secretary of state for America, Lord Dartmouth, addressed a fateful letter to General Thomas Gage, the British commander-in-chief at Boston. Expressing his belief that American resistance was nothing more than the response of a "rude rabble without plan," Dartmouth ordered Gage to arrest "the principal actors and abettors in the provincial congress." If such a step were taken swiftly and silently, Dartmouth observed, no bloodshed need occur. Opposition could not be "very formidable," Dartmouth wrote, and even if it were, "it will surely be better that the Conflict should be brought on, upon such ground, than in a riper state of Rebellion."

Because of poor sailing weather, Dartmouth's letter did not reach Gage until April 14. The major patriot leaders had by then already left Boston, and in any event Gage did not believe that arresting them would serve a useful purpose. The order nevertheless spurred him to action: he decided to send an expedition to confiscate provincial military supplies stockpiled at Concord. Bostonians dispatched two messengers, William Dawes and Paul Revere (later joined by a third, Dr. Samuel Prescott), to rouse the countryside. Thus when the British vanguard approached Lexington at dawn on April 19, they found a straggling group of 70 militiamen–approximately half the adult male population of the town–drawn up before them on the town common. The Americans' commander, Captain John Parker, ordered his men to withdraw, realizing that they were too few to halt the redcoat advance. But as

Battles of Lexington and Concord

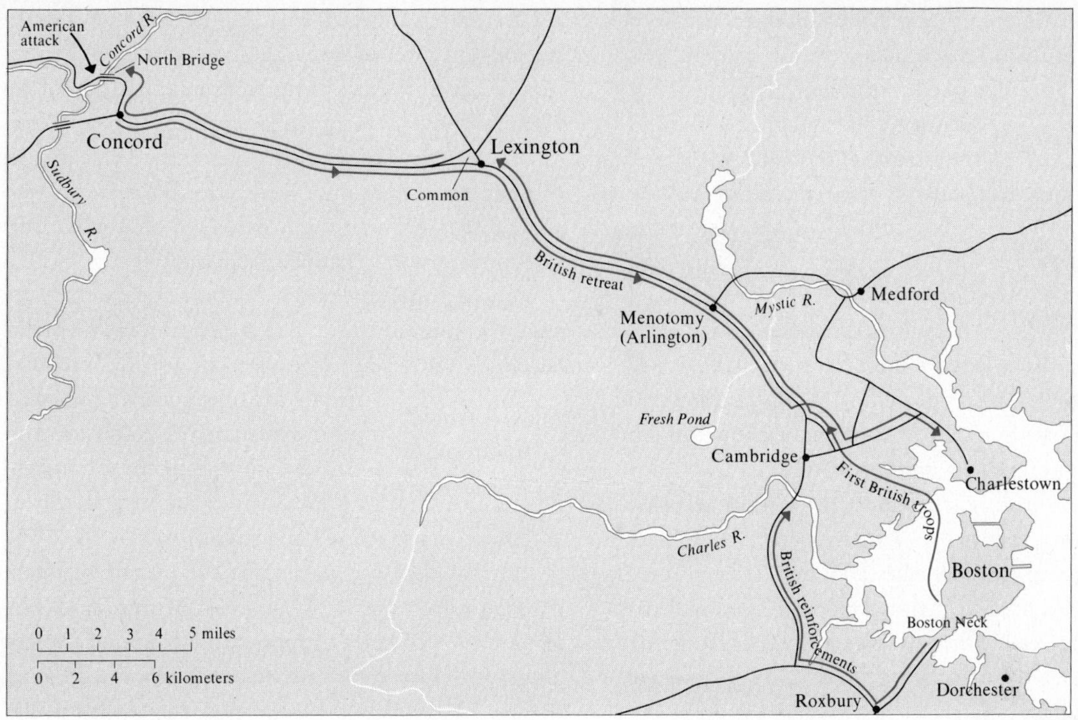

Lexington and Concord, April 19, 1775

they began to disperse, a shot rang out; the British soldiers then fired several volleys. When they stopped, 8 Americans lay dead and another 10 had been wounded. The British moved on to Concord, five miles away (see map).

There the contingents of militia were larger; the men of Concord had been joined by groups from Lincoln, Acton, and other nearby towns. The Americans allowed the British to enter Concord unopposed, but later in the morning they attacked the British infantry companies guarding the North Bridge. The brief exchange of gunfire there spilled the first British blood of the Revolution: 3 men were killed and 9 (including 4 officers) wounded. On their march back to Boston, the British were attacked by thousands of militiamen, firing from behind trees, bushes, and houses along the road. By the end of the day, the redcoats had suffered 272 casualties, 70 of whom were dead. Only the arrival of reinforcements from the city and the militia's lack of coordination prevented much heavier British losses. The patriots suffered just 93 casualties.

By the evening of April 20, perhaps as many as twenty thousand American militiamen had gathered around Boston, summoned by local committees that spread the alarm across the New England countryside. Many did not stay long, since they were needed at home for spring planting, but those who remained dug in along siege lines encircling the city. For nearly a year the two armies sat and stared at each other across those lines. During that period the redcoats attacked their besiegers only once, on June 17, when they drove the Americans from trenches atop Breed's Hill in Charlestown. In that misnamed Battle of Bunker Hill, the British incurred their greatest losses of the entire war: over 800 wounded and 228 killed. The Americans, though forced to abandon their position, lost fewer than half that number. During the same eleven-month period, the patriots captured Fort Ticonderoga, a British post on Lake Champlain, acquiring much-needed cannon. In the hope of bringing Canada into the war on the American side, they also mounted an uncoordinated northern campaign that ended in disaster at Quebec in early 1776. But the chief significance of the first year of the war lay in the long lull in fighting between the main armies at Boston. The delay gave both sides a chance to regroup, organize, and plan their strategies.

Lord North and his new American secretary, Lord George Germain, made three major assumptions about the war they faced. First, they concluded that

British strategy

patriot forces could not withstand the assaults of trained British regulars. They and their generals were convinced that the campaign of 1776 would be the first and last of the war. Accordingly, they dispatched to America the largest single force Great Britain had ever assembled anywhere: 370 transport ships carrying 32,000 troops (including thousands of German mercenaries) and tons of supplies, accompanied by 73 naval vessels and 13,000 sailors. Such an extraordinary effort would, they thought, ensure a quick victory.

Second, British officials and army officers persisted in comparing this war to wars they had fought successfully in Europe. Thus they adopted a conventional strategy of capturing major American cities and defeating the rebel army decisively without suffering serious casualties themselves. Third, they assumed that a clear-cut military victory would automatically bring about their goal of retaining the colonies' allegiance.

All these assumptions proved false. North and Germain, like Lord Dartmouth before them, vastly underestimated the Americans' commitment to armed resistance. Defeats on the battlefield did not lead the patriots to abandon their political aims and sue for peace. The ministers also failed to recognize the significance of the American population's dispersal over an area 1,500 miles long and more than 100 miles wide. Although at one time or another during the war the British would control each of the most important American ports, less than 5 percent of the population lived in those cities. And the coast offered so many excellent harbors that essential commerce was easily rerouted. In other words, the loss of the cities did little to damage the American cause, while the desire for such ports repeatedly led redcoat generals astray.

Most of all, the British did not at first understand that a military victory would not necessarily bring about a political victory. Securing the colonies permanently would require hundreds of thousands of Americans to return to their original allegiance. The conquest of America was thus a far more complicated task than the defeat of France twelve years earlier. The British needed not only to overpower the patriots, but also to convert them. After 1778, they adopted a strategy designed to achieve that goal through the expanded use of loyalist forces and the restoration of civilian authority in occupied areas. But the new policy came too late. The British never fully realized that they were not fighting a conventional European war at all, but rather an entirely new kind of conflict: the first modern war of national liberation.

Yet the British at least had a bureaucracy ready to supervise the war effort. The Americans had only the Second Continental Congress, originally intended

Second Continental Congress

merely as a brief gathering of colonial representatives to consider the British response to the Continental Association. Instead, the delegates who convened in Philadelphia on May 10, 1775, found that they had to assume the mantle of intercolonial government. "Such a vast Multitude of objects, civil, political, commercial and military, press and crowd upon us so fast, that we know not what to do first," John Adams wrote a close friend early in the session. Yet as the summer passed the congress slowly organized the colonies for war. It authorized the printing of money with which to purchase necessary goods, modified the Continental Association to allow trade in needed military supplies with friendly European nations, and took steps to strengthen the militia. Most important of all, the congress created the Continental Army and appointed its generals.

Until the congress met, the Massachusetts provincial congress had taken responsibility for organizing the massive army of militia encamped at Boston. But that army, composed of men from all the New England states, was proving to be a heavy drain on limited local resources. Consequently, on May 16 Massachusetts asked the Continental Congress to assume the task of directing the army. One of the first decisions the congress had to make was to choose a commander-in-chief. Since the war had thus far been a wholly northern affair, many delegates recognized the importance of naming a non-New Englander to command the army in order to ensure colonial unity in the struggle. There seemed only one obvious candidate. The delegates unanimously selected their fellow delegate, the Virginian George Washington.

Washington was no fiery radical, nor was he a reflective political thinker. He had not played a promi-

George Washington (1732–1799), painted in his uniform as commander-in-chief. His stalwart bearing, so vividly conveyed in this portrait, was one of his prime assets as a leader. Washington and Lee University, Washington-Custis-Lee Collection.

nent role in the prerevolutionary agitation, but his devotion to the American cause was unquestioned. He was dignified, conservative, respectable, and a man of unimpeachable integrity. The younger son of a Virginia planter, Washington had not expected to inherit substantial property and had planned to make his living as a surveyor. But the early death of his older brother and his marriage to the wealthy widow Martha Custis had made him a rich man. Though unmistakably an aristocrat, Washington was unswervingly committed to representative government. And he had other desirable traits as well.

George Washington: his traits

His stamina was remarkable: in more than eight years of war Washington never had a serious illness and took only one brief leave of absence. Moreover, he both looked and acted like a leader. Six feet tall in an era when most men were five inches shorter, his presence was stately and commanding. Other patriots praised his judgment, steadiness, and discretion, and even a loyalist admitted that Washington could "atone for many demerits by the extraordinary coolness and caution which distinguish his character."

Washington needed all the coolness and caution he could muster when he took command of the army outside Boston in July 1775. It took him months to impose hierarchy and discipline on the unruly troops and to bring order to the supply system. But by March 1776, when the arrival of cannon from Ticonderoga enabled him at last to put direct pressure on the red-coats in the city, the army was prepared to act. As it happened, an assault on Boston proved unnecessary. Sir William Howe, who had replaced Gage as the British commander-in-chief, had been considering an evacuation for some time; he wanted to move his troops to a more central location, New York City. The patriots' bombardment of Boston early in the month decided the matter. On March 17, the British and more than a thousand of their loyalist allies abandoned Boston forever.

That spring of 1776, as the British fleet left Boston for the temporary haven of Halifax, Nova Scotia, the colonies were moving inexorably toward the act the Massachusetts loyalists on board the ships feared most: a declaration of independence. Even months after fighting had begun, American leaders still denied they sought a break with the empire. Then in January 1776 there appeared a pamphlet by a man who not only thought the unthinkable but advocated it.

Thomas Paine's Common Sense

Thomas Paine's *Common Sense* exploded on the American scene like a bombshell. Within three months of publication, it sold 120,000 copies. The author, a radical English printer who had lived in America only since 1774, called stridently and stirringly for independence. More than that: Paine challenged many common American assumptions about government and the colonies' relationship to England. Rejecting the notion that a balance of monarchy, aristocracy, and democracy was necessary to preserve freedom, he advocated the establishment of a republic. Instead of acknowledging the benefits of a connection with the mother country, Paine insisted that Britain had exploited the colonies unmercifully. In place of the frequent assertion that an independent America would be weak and divided, he substituted an unlimited confidence in America's strength when freed from European control. These striking statements were clothed in equally striking prose. Scorning the polite, rational style of his classically educated predecessors, Paine adopted a furious, raging tone. His work was couched in the language of the common people and relied heavily on the Bible—the only book familiar to most Americans—as his primary source of authority. No wonder the pamphlet had a wider distribution than any other political publication of its day.

There is no way of knowing how many people were converted to the cause of independence by reading *Common Sense.* But by late spring 1776 independence had clearly become inevitable. On May 10, the Second Continental Congress formally recommended that individual colonies "adopt such governments as shall, in the opinion of the representatives of the people, best conduce to the happiness and safety of their constituents in particular, and America in general." From that source flowed the first state constitutions. Perceiving the trend of events, the few loyalists still connected with the congress severed their ties to that body.

Then on June 7 came the confirmation of the movement toward independence. Richard Henry Lee of Virginia, seconded by John Adams of Massachusetts, introduced the crucial resolution: "that these United Colonies are, and of right ought to be, free and independent States, that they are absolved of all allegiance to the British Crown, and that all political connection between them and the State of Great Britain is, and ought to be, totally dissolved." The congress debated but did not immediately adopt Lee's resolution. Instead, consideration was postponed until early July, to allow time for consultation and public reaction. In the meantime, a committee composed of Thomas Jefferson, John Adams, Benjamin Franklin, Robert R. Livingston of New York, and Roger Sherman of Connecticut was directed to draft a declaration of independence.

Declaration of Independence

The committee in turn assigned primary responsibility for writing the declaration to Jefferson, who was well known for his apt and eloquent style. Years later John Adams recalled that Jefferson had modestly protested his selection, suggesting that Adams prepare the initial draft. The Massachusetts revolutionary recorded his frank response: "You can write ten times better than I can."

Thomas Jefferson was at the time thirty-four years old, a Virginia lawyer educated at the College of William and Mary and in the law offices of the prominent attorney George Wythe. He had also read widely in history and political theory, especially after his election to the House of Burgesses. His broad knowledge

Edward Savage never completed this engraving of the July 2 vote in the Second Continental Congress, but the likenesses of the members of the committee that drafted the Declaration of Independence dominate the center. Thomas Jefferson places a draft of the document on the table. Grouped around Jefferson are the other members of the drafting committee: John Adams, Roger Sherman, Robert R. Livingston, and Benjamin Franklin (seated). American Antiquarian Society.

was evident not only in the declaration but also in his draft of the Virginia state constitution, completed just a few days before his appointment to the committee. Jefferson, an intensely private man, loved his home and family deeply. This early stage of his political career was marked by his beloved wife Martha's repeated difficulties in childbearing. While he wrote and debated in Philadelphia during the summer of 1776, she suffered a miscarriage at their home, Monticello. Only after her death in 1782, from complications following the birth of their sixth (but only third surviving) child in ten years of marriage, did Jefferson fully commit himself to a career of public service.

The draft of the declaration was laid before congress on June 28. The delegates officially voted for independence four days later, then debated the wording of the declaration for two more days, adopting it with some changes on July 4. Since Americans had long since ceased to see themselves as legitimate subjects of Parliament, the Declaration of Independence concentrated on George III. It accused the king of attempting to destroy representative government in the colonies and of oppressing Americans through the unjustified use of excessive force. But the declaration's chief importance did not lie in its lengthy catalogue of grievances against the king (including, in a section omitted by congress, Jefferson's charge that George III had introduced slavery into America). It lay instead in the ringing statements of principle that have served ever since as the ideal to which Americans adhere, nominally at least. "We hold these truths to be self evident, that all men are created equal; that they are endowed by their creator with certain inalienable rights; that among these are life, liberty and the pursuit of happiness; that, to secure these rights, governments are instituted among men, deriving their just powers from the consent of the governed, that whenever any form of government becomes destructive of these ends, it is the right of the people to alter or abolish it, and to institute new government." These phrases have echoed down through American history like no others.

The delegates in Philadelphia who voted to accept the Declaration of Independence did not have the advantage of our two hundred years of hindsight. When they adopted the declaration, they risked their necks; they were unequivocally committing treason against the crown. Thus when they concluded the declaration with the assertion that they "mutually pledge[d] to each other our lives, our fortunes, and our sacred honor," they spoke no less than the truth. The real struggle still lay before them, and few of them had Thomas Paine's boundless confidence in success.

The long struggle in the North

In late June 1776, the first of the ships carrying Sir William Howe's troops from Halifax appeared off the coast of New York. On July 2, the day the congress voted for independence, the redcoats landed on Staten Island. But Howe waited until mid-August, after the arrival of troop transports from England, to begin his attack on the city. The delay gave Washington sufficient time to march his army south to meet the threat. To defend New York, Washington had approximately 17,000 soldiers: 10,000 Continentals who had promised to serve until the end of the year, and 7,000 militiamen who had enlisted for shorter terms. Neither he nor most of his men had ever fought a major battle against the British, and their lack of experience led to disastrous mistakes. The difficulty of defending New York City only compounded the errors.

Battle for New York City

Washington's problem was as simple as the geography of the region was complex. To protect the city adequately, he would have to divide his forces among Long Island, Manhattan Island, and the mainland. But the British fleet under Admiral Lord Richard Howe, Sir William's brother, controlled the harbors and rivers that separated the American forces. The patriots thus constantly courted catastrophe, for swift action by the British navy could cut off the possibility of retreat and perhaps even communication. But despite these dangers, Washington could not afford to surrender New York to the Howes without a fight. Not only did the city occupy a strategic location, but the region that surrounded it was known to contain many loyalist sympathizers. A show of force was essential if the revolutionaries were to retain any hope of persuading waverers to join them.

Washington fortified strong entrenchments atop Brooklyn Heights, overlooking lower Manhattan, and awaited the British attack. It came on August 27. Sir William Howe brilliantly outflanked the untried American troops posted in poorly designed forward positions, forcing them back into the Brooklyn trenches with heavy losses. But instead of pressing his advantage by making a frontal assault on the Americans, Howe delayed. Perhaps the memory of Bunker Hill casualties was still fresh in his mind. Nor did he order his brother's ships to sail into the East River to prevent the Americans from retreating. As a result, the patriots escaped. On the night of August 29, a troop of Marblehead, Massachusetts, fishermen ferried the entire Brooklyn contingent of 9,000 men to Manhattan in less than nine hours.

But Washington was not safe. Indeed, he still faced possible defeat, for the British could easily trap him and his men on the southern tip of Manhattan by means of combined sea and land movements. The Howe brothers again let their quarry escape, maneuvering their huge force so slowly that Washington was able to retreat northward onto the mainland. Once more the American commander-in-chief erred, leaving nearly 3,000 men in the supposedly impregnable Fort Washington on the west shore of Manhattan. When Sir William Howe finally decided to stop chasing Washington through Westchester County

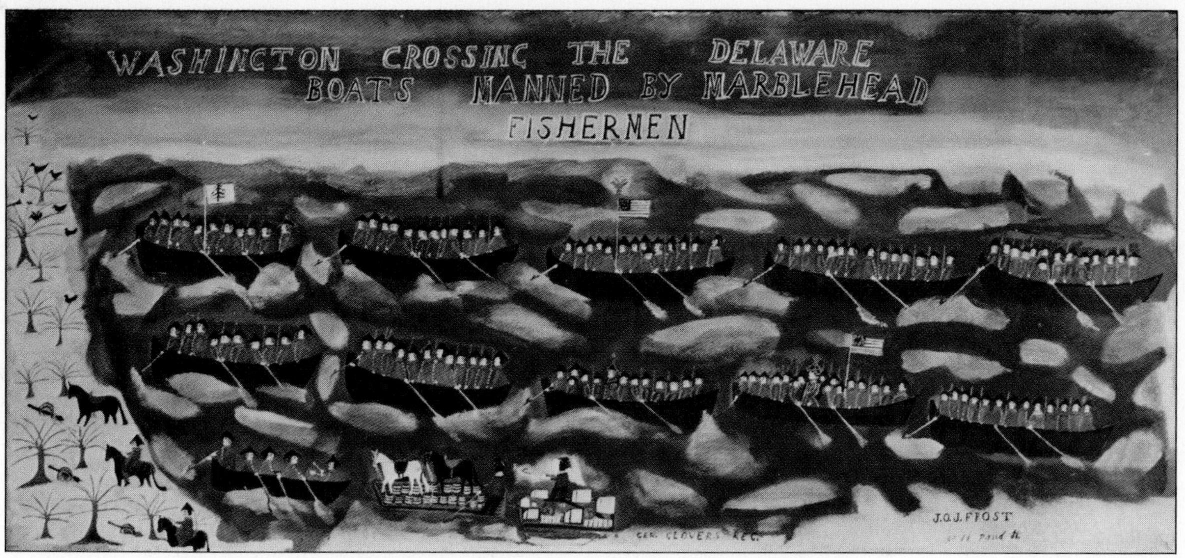

Years after Marblehead fishermen ferried Washington's troops across the Delaware to attack the Hessians at Trenton, J.O.J. Frost, an untrained artist, celebrated his townsmen's heroism. Private Collection.

and turned his attention back to the fort, its defenses quickly collapsed. The large garrison surrendered in early November. Only when Charleston fell to the British in May 1780 did the Americans lose more men on a single occasion.

George Washington had defended New York, but he had done a bad job of it. He had repeatedly broken a primary rule of military strategy: never divide your force in the face of a superior enemy. In the end, though, the Howe brothers' failure to move quickly prevented a decisive defeat of the Americans. Although Washington's army had been seriously reduced by battlefield casualties, the surrender of Fort Washington, and the loss of most of the militiamen (who had headed home for the harvest), its core remained. Through November and December, Washington led his men in a retreat across New Jersey. Howe followed at a leisurely pace, setting up a string of outposts manned mostly by Hessian mercenaries. After Washington crossed the Delaware River into Pennsylvania, the British commander turned back and settled into comfortable winter quarters in New York City.

The British now controlled most of New Jersey. Hundreds of Americans accepted the pardons offered by the Howes. Among them were Joseph Galloway, the one-time delegate to the First Continental Congress, and Richard Stockton, a signer of the Declaration of Independence. The occupying troops met with little opposition, and the revolutionary cause appeared to be in disarray. "These are the times that try men's souls," wrote Thomas Paine in his pamphlet *The Crisis.* "The summer soldier and the sunshine patriot will, in this crisis, shrink from the service of his country; . . . yet we have this consolation with us, that the harder the conflict, the more glorious the triumph."

In the aftermath of battle, as at its height, the British generals let their advantage slip away. The redcoats stationed in New Jersey went on a rampage of rape and plunder. Because loyalists and patriots were indistinguishable to the British and Hessian troops, families on both sides suffered equally. Livestock, crops, and firewood were seized for use by the army. Houses were looted and burned, churches and public buildings desecrated. But nothing was better calculated to rally doubtful Americans to the cause of independence than the wanton murder of innocent civilians and the epidemic of rape inflicted on the women of New Jersey. Sixteen girls from Hopewell were held captive for days in the British camp and repeatedly molested; a thirteen-year-old was raped by six soldiers;

Jean Baptiste Antoine de Verger, a sublieutenant in the French army in America, painted this watercolor of revolutionary soldiers in his journal. They are, from left to right, a black light infantryman, a musketman, a rifleman, and an artilleryman. The Anne S. K. Brown Military Collection.

another thirteen-year-old, two of her friends, and her aunt were similarly attacked. A resident of Princeton, in his eyewitness account of the occupation of the state, lamented that "against both justice and reason we despise these poor innocent sufferers." Consequently, he observed, "many honest virtuous women have suffered in this manner and kept it secret for fear of making their lives misserable."

The soldiers' marauding alienated potentially loyal New Jerseyites and Pennsylvanians whose allegiance the British could ill afford to lose. It also spurred Washington's determination to strike back. The enlistments of most of the Continental troops were to expire on December 31, and Washington also wanted to take advantage of short-term Pennsylvania militia who had recently joined him. Thus he had to move quickly. And he did, attacking the Hessian encampment at Trenton early in the morning of December 26, while the redcoats were still reeling from their Christmas celebration. The patriots captured more than 900 Hessians and killed another 30; only 3 Americans were wounded. A few days later, after persuading many of his men to stay on beyond the term of their enlistments, Washington attacked again at Princeton. Having gained command of the field and buoyed American spirits with the two swift victories, Washington set up winter quarters at Morristown, New Jersey.

Battle of Trenton

The campaign of 1776 established patterns that were to persist throughout much of the war, despite changes in British leadership and strategy. British forces were usually more numerous and often better led than the Americans. But their ponderous style of maneuvering, lack of familiarity with the terrain, and inability to live off the land without antagonizing the populace helped to offset those advantages. Furthermore, although Washington always seemed to lack regular troops – the Continental Army never numbered more than 18,500 men – he could usually count on the militia to join him at crucial points. American militiamen did not like to sign up for long terms of service or to fight far from home, but when their homes were threatened they would rally to the cause. Washington and his officers frequently complained about the militia's habit of disappearing during planting or harvesting. But time and again their presence, however brief, enabled the Americans to launch an attack or counter an important British thrust.

As the war dragged on, the Continental Army and the militia took on decidedly different characters. State governments, responsible for filling military quotas, discovered that most men willing to enlist for long periods in the regular army were young, single, and footloose. Farmers with families tended to prefer short-term militia duty. As the supply of whites willing to sign up for the Continentals diminished, recruiters in the northern states turned increasingly to blacks, both slave and free. (White southerners continued to resist this approach.) Perhaps as many as 5,000 blacks eventually served in the Revolutionary army, and most of them won their freedom as a result. Also attached to the American forces were a number of women, mostly wives and widows of poor soldiers. Such camp followers worked as cooks, nurses, and launderers, performing vital services for the army in return for rations and extremely low wages. The presence of the women, as well as the militiamen who floated in and out of the American camp at irregular intervals, made for an unwieldy army its officers found difficult to manage. Yet the army's shapelessness also reflected its greatest strength: an almost unlimited reservoir of man and woman power.

In 1777, the chief British effort was planned by the flashy "Gentleman Johnny" Burgoyne, a playboy general as much at home at the gaming tables of London as on the battlefield. Burgoyne, a subordinate of Howe, had spent the winter of 1776 and 1777 in London, where he gained the ear of Lord George Germain. Burgoyne convinced Germain that he could lead an invading force of redcoats and Indians down the Hudson River from Canada, cutting off New England from the rest of the states. He proposed to rendezvous near Albany with a similar force that would move east from Niagara along the Mohawk River valley. The combined force would then presumably link up with that of Sir William Howe in New York City.

Deborah Sampson (1760–1827), a patriot who disguised herself as a man and enlisted in the Continental Army under the name Robert Shurtleff. She served from May 1782 to October 1783, when her sex was discovered and she was discharged. In later years she made a living by giving public lectures describing her wartime experiences. After her death her husband became the only man to receive a pension as the "widow" of a revolutionary soldier. Rhode Island Historical Society.

That Burgoyne's scheme would give "Gentleman Johnny" all the glory and relegate Howe to a supporting role did not escape Howe's notice. In fact, while Burgoyne was plotting in London, Howe was laying his own plans in New York City. Joseph Galloway and other Pennsylvania loyalists persuaded Howe that Philadelphia could be taken easily and that his troops would be welcomed by many residents of the region.

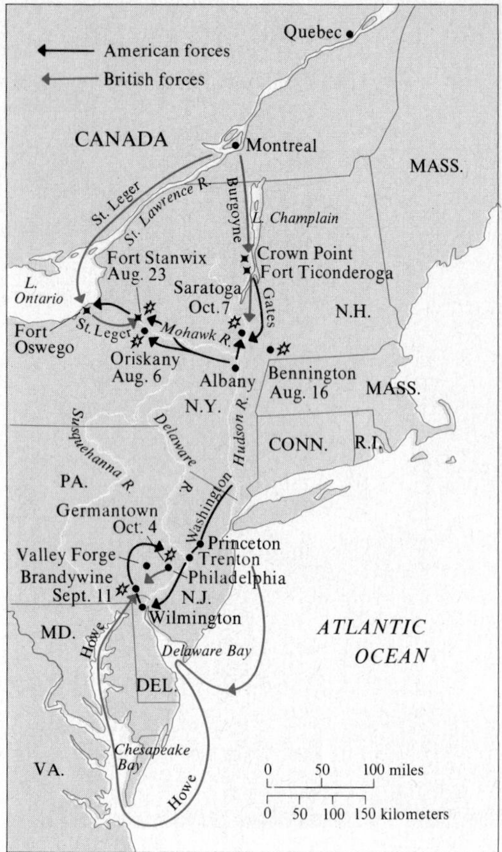

Campaign of 1777

Just as Burgoyne left Howe out of his plans, Howe left Burgoyne out of his. Thus the two major British armies in America would operate independently in 1777, and the result would be a disaster (see map).

Howe takes Philadelphia

Howe accomplished his objective: he captured Philadelphia. But he did so in an inexplicable fashion, delaying for months before beginning the campaign, then taking six weeks to transport his troops by sea to the head of Chesapeake Bay instead of marching them overland. That maneuver cost him at least a month, debilitated his men, and depleted his supplies. Incredibly, due to contrary winds and a change of destination, he was only forty miles closer to Philadelphia at the end of the lengthy voyage than when he had begun. Two years later, when Parliament formally inquired into the conduct of the war, Howe's critics charged that his errors were so extraordinary he must have deliberately committed treason. Even today, historians have not been able to explain his motives adequately. In any event, by the time Howe was ready to move on Philadelphia, Washington had had time to prepare its defenses. Twice, at Brandywine Creek and again at Germantown, the two armies clashed near the rebel capital. Though the British won both engagements, the Americans handled themselves well. The redcoats took control of Philadelphia in late September, but to little effect. The campaign season was nearly over; the Revolutionary army had gained confidence in itself and its leaders; few welcoming loyalists had materialized; and, far to the north, Burgoyne was going down to defeat.

Burgoyne's campaign in New York

Burgoyne and his men had set out from Montreal in mid-June, floating down Lake Champlain into New York in canoes and flat-bottomed boats. In early June they had easily taken Fort Ticonderoga from its outnumbered and outgunned defenders. But trouble began as Burgoyne started his overland march. His clumsy artillery carriages and baggage wagons foundered in the heavy forests and ravines. Progress was further slowed by patriot militia, who felled giant trees across the army's path. As a result, Burgoyne's troops took 24 days to travel the 23 miles to Fort Edward, on the Hudson River. Short of supplies, the general dispatched 800 German mercenaries into Vermont to forage the countryside. On August 16 American militia companies nearly wiped out the Germans at Bennington, a severe blow to the redcoats. Yet Burgoyne failed to recognize the seriousness of his predicament and continued to dawdle, giving the Americans more than enough time to prepare for his coming. By the time he finally crossed the Hudson in mid-September, bound for Albany, Burgoyne's fate was sealed. After several bloody clashes with the American force commanded by Horatio Gates, Burgoyne was surrounded near Saratoga, New York. On October 17, 1777, he surrendered his entire force of more than 6,000 men.

Long before, the 1,400 redcoats and Indians marching along the Mohawk River toward Albany had also been turned back. Under the command of Colonel Barry St. Leger, they had advanced easily until they reached the isolated American outpost at Fort Stanwix in early August. After they had laid siege to the well-fortified structure, they learned that a patriot relief column was en route to the fort. Leaving only a

The Mohawk chief Joseph Brant (1742–1807), painted in London in 1786 by Gilbert Stuart. New York State Historical Association, Cooperstown.

small detachment at Fort Stanwix, the British ambushed the Americans at Oriskany on August 6. The British claimed victory in the ensuing battle, one of the bloodiest of the war, but they and their Indian allies lost their taste for further fighting. The Americans tricked them into believing that another large patriot force was on the way, and in late August the British abandoned the siege and returned to Niagara.

The battle of Oriskany marked the division of the Iroquois Confederacy. In 1776 the Six Nations had formally pledged to remain neutral in the Anglo-American struggle. But two influential Mohawk leaders, Joseph and Mary Brant, worked tirelessly to persuade their fellow Iroquois to join the British. Mary Brant, a powerful tribal matron in her own right, was also the widow (in fact if not in law) of the respected Indian superintendent Sir William Johnson. Her younger brother Joseph, a renowned warrior who visited London early in the war, was convinced that the Six Nations should ally themselves with the British in order to prevent American encroachment on their lands. As an observer said of Mary, "one word from her goes farther with them [the Iroquois] than a thousand from any white man without exception." The Brants won over to the British the Senecas, Cayugas, and Mohawks, all of whom contributed warriors to St. Leger's expedition. But the Oneidas persisted in their traditional preference for the Americans, bringing the Tuscaroras with them. (The remaining Iroquois tribe, the Onondagas, split into three factions, one on each side and

Crumbling of the Iroquois Confederacy

one supporting neutrality.) At Oriskany, the Oneidas and the Tuscaroras joined the patriot militia to fight their Iroquois brethren; thus a league of friendship that had survived for more than three hundred years was torn apart by the whites' family quarrel.

For the Indians, Oriskany was the most significant battle of the northern campaign; for the whites, it was Saratoga. The news of Burgoyne's surrender brought joy to patriots, discouragement to loyalists and Britons. In exile in London, Thomas Hutchinson wrote of the "universal dejection" among loyalists there. "Everybody in a gloom," he commented; "most of us expect to lay our bones here." The disaster prompted Lord North to authorize a peace commission to offer the Americans everything they had requested in 1774—in effect, a return to the imperial system of 1763. It was, of course, far too late for that: the patriots rejected the overture and the peace commission sailed back to England empty-handed in mid-1778.

French entry into the war

Most important of all, the American victory at Saratoga drew France into the war. Ever since 1763, the French had been seeking ways to avenge their defeat in the Seven Years' War, and the American Revolution was the perfect opportunity to do so. King Louis XVI and his ministers had covertly aided the revolutionaries with money and supplies since 1776, and American emissaries in France (notably the clever Benjamin Franklin) had worked tirelessly to strengthen those ties. Not until Saratoga, though, did France agree to a formal alliance with the patriots. After 1778, the British could no longer focus their attention on the American mainland alone, for they had to fight the French in the West Indies and elsewhere. Spain's entry into the war in 1779 as an ally of France (but not the United States) further magnified Britain's problems. In the last years of the war, French assistance was to prove vital to the Americans.

The long struggle in the South

In the aftermath of the Saratoga disaster, Lord George Germain and the military officials in London reassessed their strategy. Maneuvering in the North had done them little good; perhaps shifting the field of battle southward would bring success. The many loyalist exiles in England encouraged this line of thinking. They argued that loyal southerners would welcome the redcoat army as liberators, and that once the region had been pacified and returned to civilian control it could serve as a base for attacking the North.

By early 1778 Sir William Howe had resigned and been replaced by Sir Henry Clinton, a former subordinate who had sharply criticized Howe in 1776 for failure to act decisively. But as commander-in-chief Clinton too was afflicted with sluggishness and lack of resolution. Clinton oversaw the regrouping of British forces in America, ordering the evacuation of Philadelphia in June 1778 and dispatching a small expedition to Georgia at the end of the year. When Savannah and then Augusta fell easily into British hands, Clinton became convinced that a southern strategy would work. In late 1779 he sailed down the coast with an invasion force of 8,500 troops to attack Charleston, the most important American city in the South.

Fall of Charleston

Although the Americans worked hard to bolster Charleston's defenses, the city fell to the British on May 12, 1780. General Benjamin Lincoln surrendered the entire southern army—5,500 men—to the invaders. In the weeks that followed, the redcoats spread throughout South Carolina, establishing garrisons at key points in the interior. As in New Jersey in 1776, hundreds of South Carolinians renounced allegiance to the United States and proclaimed their loyalty to the crown. Clinton organized loyalist regiments and the process of pacification began.

Yet the British triumph was less complete and secure than it appeared. The success of the southern campaign depended on British control of the seas, for only by sea could the widely dispersed British armies remain in communication with one another. For the moment the Royal Navy safely dominated the American coastline, but French naval power posed a threat to the entire southern enterprise. Moreover, the redcoats never managed to establish full control of the areas they seized. As a result, patriot bands operated freely throughout the state, and loyalists could not be guaranteed protection against their enemies. Last but not least, the fall of Charleston did not dishearten the patriots; instead, it spurred them to greater exertions.

As one Marylander declared confidently, "The Fate of America is not to be decided by the Loss of a Town or Two." Patriot women in four states formed the Ladies Association, which collected money to purchase shirts for needy soldiers. Recruiting efforts were stepped up.

Throughout most of 1780, though, the war in South Carolina went badly for the patriots. In August, a reorganized southern army under the command of Horatio Gates was crushingly defeated at Camden by the forces of Lord Cornwallis, who had been placed in charge of the southern campaign. The British army was joined wherever it went by hundreds, even thousands, of blacks seeking freedom with the redcoats on the basis of Lord Dunmore's proclamation. Slaves ran away from their patriot masters individually and as families, in such numbers that they seriously disrupted planting and harvesting in 1780 and 1781. More than 55,000 blacks were lost to their owners as a result of the war. Not all of them joined the British or won their freedom if they did, but their flight had just the effect Dunmore wanted. And a good many served the British as scouts, guides, and laborers.

Esther DeBerdt Reed (1746–1780), founder of the Ladies Association of 1780. Reed coordinated fund raising for the war effort until her untimely death from dysentery in the fall of 1780. Reed Collection.

After the defeat at Camden, Washington (who had to remain in the North to oppose the British army occupying New York) gave command of the southern campaign to General Nathanael Greene of Rhode Island. Greene was appalled by what he found in South Carolina. As he wrote to a friend, "the word difficulty when applied to the state of things here . . . is almost without meaning, it falls so far short" of reality. His troops needed clothing, blankets, and food, but "a great part of this country is already laid waste and in the utmost danger of becoming a desert." The constant guerrilla warfare had, he commented, "so corrupted the principles of the people that they think of nothing but plundering one another." Under such circumstances, Greene had to move cautiously. He adopted a conciliatory policy toward loyalists and neutrals, persuading the governor of South Carolina to offer complete pardons to those who had fought for the British if they would join the patriot militia. He also ordered his troops not to loot loyalist property and to treat captives fairly. Greene recognized that the patriots could win only by convincing the people that they could bring stability to the region. He thus helped the shattered provincial congresses of Georgia and South Carolina to begin reestablishing civilian authority in the interior—a goal the British were never able to accomplish, even along the coast.

Greene rallies South Carolina

Greene also took a conciliatory approach to the southern Indians, in contrast to the policy adopted in the North. After Iroquois bands allied with the British made bloody raids on the New York frontier settlements of Wyoming and Cherry Valley in 1778, the whites had retaliated by burning Iroquois crops and villages in 1779. The following years were filled with even more bloodshed as both sides sought revenge for past wrongs. But Greene, with his desperate need for soldiers, could not afford to have frontier militia companies occupied in defending their homes against Indian attacks. Since he had so few regulars (only 1,600 when he took command), Greene had to rely on western volunteers. Thus he negotiated with the Indians.

His policy eventually met with success, although at first royal officials cooperating with the British invasion forces won allies among the Creeks, Choctaws,

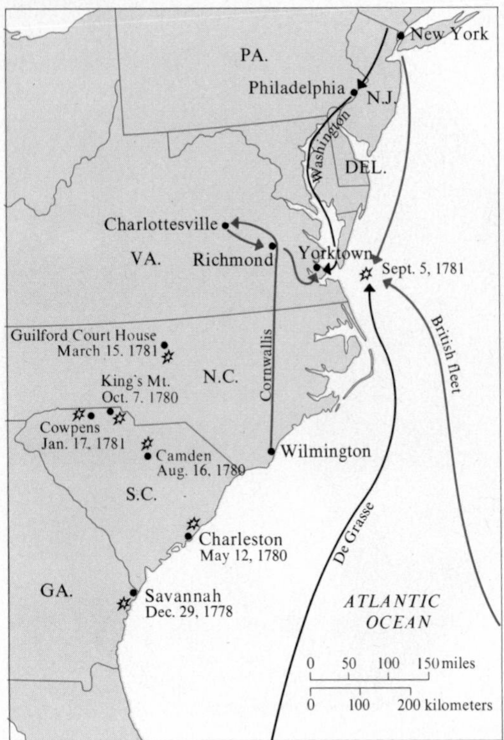

The war in the South

Chickasaws, and especially Dragging Canoe's Cherokees. But these southern tribes, recalling the disastrous defeat the Cherokees had suffered in 1776, never committed themselves wholeheartedly to the British. In 1781 the Cherokees began negotiations with the patriots, and the next year the other tribes too sued for peace. By the end of the war only the Creeks remained allied to the redcoats. A group of Chickasaw chiefs explained their reasoning to American agents in July 1782, after Greene's battlefield successes had forced the British to withdraw into Savannah and Charleston: "The English put the Bloody Tomahawk into our hands, telling us that we should have no Goods if we did not Exert ourselves to the greatest point of Resentment against you, but now we find our mistake and Distresses. The English have done their utmost and left us in our adversity. We find them full of Deceit and Dissimulation."

Even before Greene took command of the southern army in December 1780, the tide had begun to turn. At King's Mountain in October, a force of "overmountain men" from the settlements west of the Appalachians had defeated a large party of redcoats and loyalists. Then in January 1781 Greene's trusted aide, Brigadier General Daniel Morgan, brilliantly defeated the crack British regiment Tarleton's Legion at Cowpens, near the border between North and South Carolina. Greene himself confronted the main body of British troops under Lord Cornwallis at Guilford Court House, North Carolina, in March. Cornwallis controlled the field at the end of the day, but his army had been largely destroyed. He had to retreat to Wilmington, on the coast, to receive supplies and fresh troops from New York by sea. In the meantime Greene returned to South Carolina, where, in a series of swift strikes, he forced the redcoats to abandon their posts in the interior and retire to Charleston.

Cornwallis had already ignored explicit orders not to leave South Carolina unless the state was safely in British hands. Evidently bent on his own destruction, he now headed north into Virginia, where he joined forces with a detachment of redcoats commanded by the American traitor Benedict Arnold. (Arnold had fought heroically with the patriots early in the war, but defected to the British in 1780 in the belief that the Americans did not fully appreciate him.) Instead of acting decisively with his new army of 7,200 men, Cornwallis withdrew to the tip of the peninsula between the York and James rivers, where he fortified Yorktown and in effect waited for the end. Seizing the opportunity, Washington quickly moved over 7,000 troops south from New York City. When a French fleet under the Comte de Grasse arrived from the West Indies to cut the Britons' vital sea supply line, Cornwallis was trapped (see map). On October 19, 1781, four years and two days after Burgoyne's defeat at Saratoga, Cornwallis surrendered to the combined American and French forces while his military band played "The World Turned Upside Down."

Surrender at Yorktown

When news of the surrender reached England, Lord North's ministry fell. Parliament voted to cease offensive operations in America and authorized peace negotiations. But guerrilla warfare between patriots and loyalists continued to ravage the Carolinas and Georgia for more than a year, and in the North vicious retaliatory raids by Indians and whites kept the frontier aflame. Indeed, the single most brutal massacre of the war occurred in March 1782, at Gnadenhuetten, Pennsylvania. There a group of white militia-

GREAT JOY
TO THE
DAY.

WASHINGTON
AND
COUNT DE GRASSE:
A NEW SONG,

Deſigned to add Mirth to the Day of General Thankſgiving, Rejoicing and Illumination, on Account of the late great and glorious News of the taking York-Town, in Virginia, in which were Lord Cornwallis and a large Knot of Britiſh troops, &c. ſaid to be 9000 in the whole; with a 40 gun ſhip, a frigate, an arm'd ſloop and 100 tranſports.

[☞ Tune of WASHINGTON, or any one of the merrieſt Tunes you can find.]

COME jolly brave AMERICANS, and toſs the glaſs around,
Unto thoſe worthy PATRIOTS who rule in Camp or Town;
Unto our Great Commander brave glorious WASHINGTON,
To COUNT DE GRASSE and General GREENE and ev'ry Patriot Son.

GOD bleſs our valiant WASHINGTON! and may he long ſurvive,
'Till he compleats a victory o'er all his foes alive;
May Heaven's bleſſings each deſcend, unitedly engage
To crown his life with happineſs unto a good old age.

Let all who love AMERICA, in all their ſonnets ſing
The late exploits of COUNT DE GRASSE and warlike General GREENE!
And may each true AMERICAN thoſe valiant SONS adore,
For all their brave heroic deeds 'till time ſhall be no more.

Part of a broadside ballad celebrating the American victory at Yorktown. Published in Boston, probably in early 1782. The Henry Francis du Pont Winterthur Museum.

men, seeking the Indians who had killed a frontier family, encountered a peaceful band of Delawares. The Indians, who had been converted to both Christianity and pacifism by Moravian missionaries, were slaughtered unmercifully. Ninety-six men, women, and children died that day, some burned at the stake, others tomahawked. Two months later, hostile members of the Delaware tribe captured three white militiamen and subjected them to gruesome tortures in reprisal. The persistence of this sort of warfare after Yorktown, all too often overlooked in accounts of the Revolution, should serve to underline that the British and American armies were not the only combatants in the conflict.

The fighting finally ended when Americans and Britons learned of the signing of a preliminary peace treaty at Paris in November 1782. The American negotiators–Benjamin Franklin, John Jay, and John Adams–ignored their instructions to be guided by France and instead struck a separate agreement with Great Britain. Their instincts were sound: the French government was more an enemy to Britain than a friend to the United States. In fact, French ministers worked secretly behind the scenes to try to prevent the establishment of a strong, unified, independent republic in America. The new British ministry, headed by Lord Shelburne (formerly a persistent critic of Lord

Treaty of Paris

Important events	
1768	Treaty of Hard Labor Treaty of Fort Stanwix
1770	Treaty of Lochaber
1773	Treaty of Augusta
1774	Lord Dunmore's War First Continental Congress Continental Association; committees of observation formed
1775	Battles of Lexington and Concord Battle of Bunker Hill Lord Dunmore's Proclamation Second Continental Congress American invasion of Canada
1776	Thomas Paine, *Common Sense* British evacuate Boston Declaration of Independence New York campaign Battle of Trenton Cherokee War
1777	Battle of Princeton British take Philadelphia Battle of Oriskany Burgoyne surrenders at Saratoga
1778	British Peace Commission French alliance British evacuate Philadelphia British take Savannah
1779	Sullivan expedition against Iroquois villages
1780	British take Charleston Battle of Camden Battle of King's Mountain
1781	Battle of Guilford Court House Cornwallis surrenders at Yorktown
1782	North's ministry falls Gnadenhuetten massacre British evacuate Savannah Preliminary peace treaty British evacuate Charleston
1783	Treaty of Paris British evacuate New York City

North's harsh American policies), was weary of war and made numerous concessions–so many, in fact, that Parliament ousted the ministry shortly after the peace terms were approved.

Under the treaty, finalized on September 3, 1783, the Americans were granted unconditional independence and unlimited fishing rights off Newfoundland. The boundaries of the new nation were generous: to the north, approximately the current boundary with Canada; to the south, the thirty-first parallel; to the west, the Mississippi River. The British conveniently overlooked the fact that their Indian allies, particularly the Iroquois and the Creeks, had joined them precisely because of their promise to protect Indian lands from white encroachment. Thus the tribes found themselves and their interests sacrificed to European power politics. Loyalists were also poorly served by the British negotiators. In effect the treaty legalized the wartime confiscation of loyalist property and forced people like Joseph Galloway into permanent exile.

The long war finally over, the victorious Americans could look back on their achievement with satisfaction and awe. In 1775, with an inexperienced ragtag army, they had taken on the greatest military power in the world–and eight years later they had won. They had accomplished their goal more through persistence and commitment than through brilliance on the battlefield. Actual victories had been few, but their army had always survived defeat and stand-offs to fight again. Ultimately, the Americans had simply worn their enemy down.

Suggestions for further reading

Essay collections

Larry Gerlach, ed., *Legacies of the American Revolution* (1978); *Journal of Interdisciplinary History,* 6, No. 4 (spring 1976), *Interdisciplinary Studies of the American Revolution;* Stephen G. Kurtz and James H. Hutson, eds., *Essays on the American Revolution* (1973); Library of Congress, *Symposia on the American Revolution,* 5 vols. (1972–1976); Edmund S. Morgan, *The Challenge of the American Revolution* (1976); *William and Mary Quarterly,* 3rd ser., 33, No. 3 (July 1976), *The American Revolution;* Alfred Young, ed., *The American Revolution: Explorations in the History of American Radicalism* (1976).

Military

John Richard Alden, *The American Revolution 1775–1783* (1964); Ira Gruber, *The Howe Brothers and the American Revolution* (1972); Don Higginbotham, *The War of American Independence: Military Attitudes, Policies, and Practice, 1763–1789* (1971); Piers Mackesy, *The War for America, 1775–1783* (1964); Charles Royster, *A Revolutionary People at War: The Continental Army and American Character, 1775–1783* (1980); John Shy, *A People Numerous & Armed: Reflections on the Military Struggle for American Independence* (1976); Marshall Smelser, *The Winning of Independence* (1972); Herbert T. Wade and Robert A. Lively, *This Glorious Cause: The Adventures of Two Company Officers in Washington's Army* (1958); Willard M. Wallace, *Appeal to Arms: A Military History of the American Revolution* (1950); William Willcox, *Portrait of a General: Sir Henry Clinton in the War of Independence* (1964).

Local and regional

Jeffrey Crow and Larry Tise, eds., *The Southern Experience in the American Revolution* (1978); Robert A. Gross, *The Minutemen and Their World* (1976); Ronald Hoffman, *A Spirit of Dissension: Economics, Politics, and the Revolution in Maryland* (1973); Robert J. Taylor, *Western Massachusetts in the Revolution* (1954).

Indians and blacks

Barbara Graymont, *The Iroquois in the American Revolution* (1972); Winthrop Jordan, *White Over Black: American Attitudes toward the Negro 1550–1812* (1968); Duncan J. MacLeod, *Slavery, Race, and the American Revolution* (1974); James H. O'Donnell, III, *Southern Indians in the American Revolution* (1973); Benjamin Quarles, *The Negro in the American Revolution* (1961); Anthony F.C. Wallace, *The Death and Rebirth of the Seneca* (1969).

Loyalists

Bernard Bailyn, *The Ordeal of Thomas Hutchinson* (1974); Robert McCluer Calhoon, *The Loyalists in Revolutionary America 1760–1781* (1973); William H. Nelson, *The American Tory* (1961); Mary Beth Norton, *The British-Americans: The Loyalist Exiles in England, 1774–1789* (1972); Mary Beth Norton, "Eighteenth-Century American Women in Peace and War: The Case of the Loyalists," *William and Mary Quarterly,* 3rd ser., 33 (1976), 486–409; Paul H. Smith, *Loyalists and Redcoats: A Study in British Revolutionary Policy* (1964); James W. St. G. Walker, *The Black Loyalists: The Search for a Promised Land in Nova Scotia and Sierra Leone 1783–1870* (1976).

Women

Linda Grant DePauw, *Founding Mothers: Women of America in the Revolutionary Era* (1975); Linda Grant DePauw and Conover Hunt, *"Remember the Ladies": Women in America 1750–1815* (1976); Linda K. Kerber, *Women of the Republic: Intellect & Ideology in Revolutionary America* (1980); Mary Beth Norton, *Liberty's Daughters: The Revolutionary Experience of American Women, 1750–1800* (1980).

Diplomacy

Samuel F. Bemis, *The Diplomacy of the American Revolution* (1935); Richard B. Morris, *The Peacemakers: The Great Powers and American Independence* (1965); Gerald Stourzh, *Benjamin Franklin and American Foreign Policy,* 2nd ed. (1969); Richard W. Van Alstyne, *Empire and Independence: The International History of the American Revolution* (1965).

Patriot leaders

Fawn M. Brodie, *Thomas Jefferson: An Intimate History* (1974); Verner W. Crane, *Benjamin Franklin and a Rising People* (1954); Marcus Cunliffe, *George Washington: Man and Monument* (1958); James T. Flexner, *George Washington,* 4 vols. (1965–1972); Eric Foner, *Tom Paine and Revolutionary America* (1976); Claude A. Lopez and Eugenia Herbert, *The Private Franklin: The Man and His Family* (1975); Dumas Malone, *Jefferson and His Time,* 5 vols. (1948–1974); Peter Shaw, *The Character of John Adams* (1976).

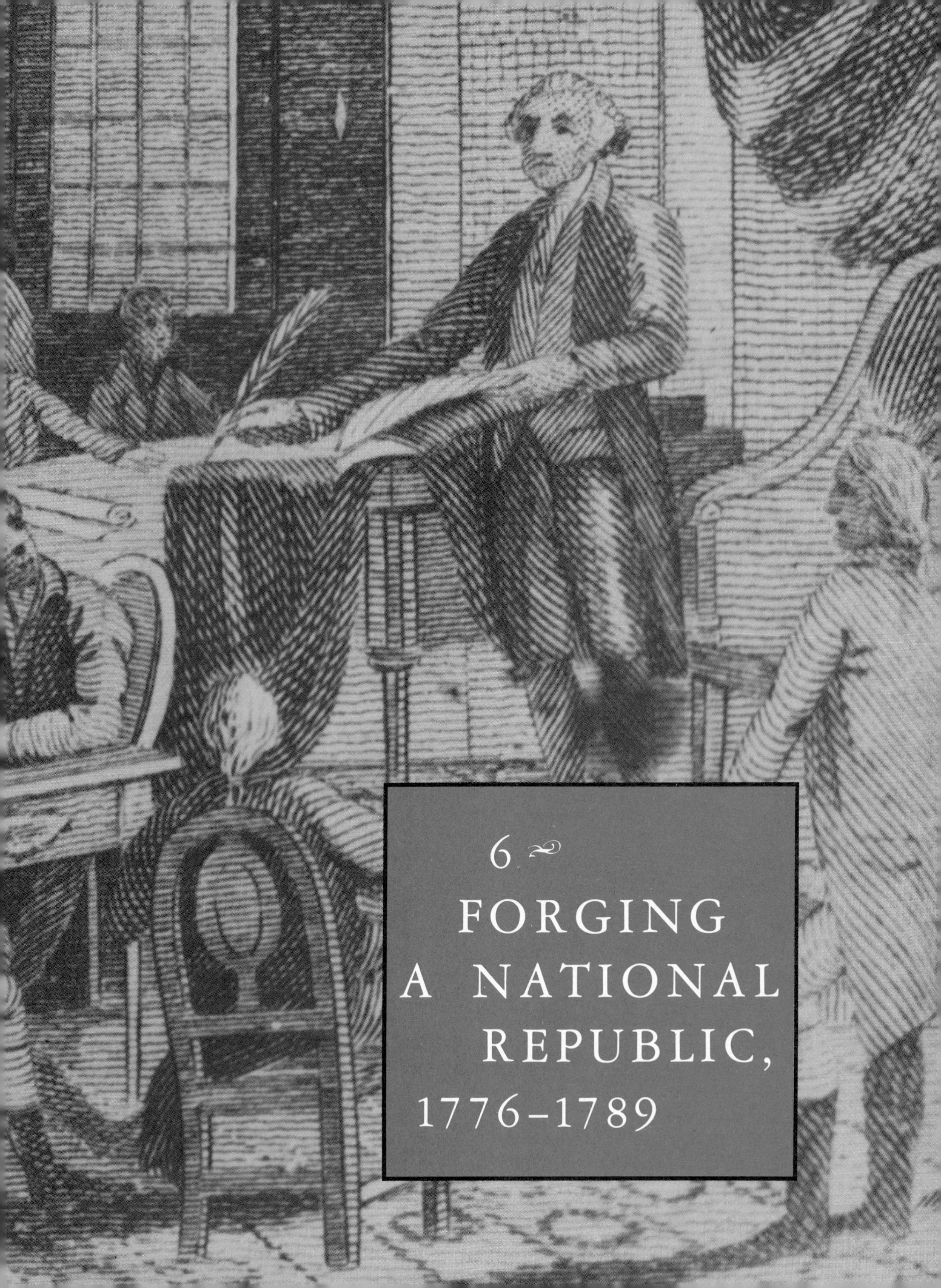

6
FORGING A NATIONAL REPUBLIC, 1776–1789

"In the new Code of Laws which I suppose it will be necessary for you to make I desire you would Remember the Ladies," Abigail Adams wrote her congressman husband John on March 31, 1776. "Remember all Men would be tyrants if they could," she continued. "If perticuliar care and attention is not paid to the Laidies we are determined to foment a Rebelion, and will not hold ourselves bound by any Laws in which we have no voice, or Representation."

With these words, Abigail Adams took a step that was soon to be duplicated by other disfranchised Americans. She was deliberately employing the ideology that had been developed to combat Great Britain's claims to political supremacy, but applying it to the legal status of women. Since men were "Naturally Tyrannical," she argued, America's new legal code should "put it out of the power of the vicious and the Lawless to use us with cruelty and indignity."

John Adams failed to take his wife's suggestion seriously. Two weeks later he replied, "As to your extraordinary Code of Laws, I cannot but Laugh. We have been told that our Struggle has loosened the bands of Government every where"–that children, apprentices, slaves, Indians, and college students had all become "disobedient" and "insolent." Her letter was the first indication that "another Tribe more numerous and powerfull than all the rest were grown discontented." But women, he insisted, had little reason for complaint. "In Practice you know We are subjects. We have only the Name of Masters, and rather than give up this, which would compleatly subject Us to the Despotism of the Peticoat, I hope General Washington and all our brave Heroes would fight."

Abigail Adams's famous words have often been cited as the first stirrings of feminism in America. Whether or not such an interpretation is accurate, her comments were, as John Adams recognized, a sign of the impact the Revolution and its ideology had had on American society. The colonists had ventured into revolution to protect their rights as English people, especially their right of consent to taxation. Gradually they had developed broader definitions of those rights and rejected monarchy once and for all. The accompanying abandonment of some political commonplaces, like the notion of absolute parliamentary supremacy, had called others into question. For example, the Americans' prolonged effort to define the relationship between the British government and their own local political institutions led them to question the traditional notion that sovereignty–the ultimate authority in any political unit–was indivisible. As a result, they created a federal system, in which the states and the central government shared political authority.

The experience of revolution prompted Americans to rethink their assumptions on nonpolitical matters as well. In the years before the Revolution, members of dissenting religious sects had protested their unequal status in colonies with a state-supported, or established, church. In those colonies (all but Rhode Island, Pennsylvania, New Jersey, and Delaware, which guaranteed complete religious freedom), dissenters could be taxed to support the established church. They also had to have the permission of the legislature to hold their own worship services. Revolutionary ideology helped dissenters combat such policies. Isaac Backus, a New England Baptist, observed forcefully that "many, who are filling the nation with the cry of LIBERTY and against *oppressors* are at the same time themselves violating that dearest of all rights, LIBERTY of CONSCIENCE." Legislators could not resist the logic of these arguments. Many states dissolved their ties to churches during the war; others vastly reduced state support for established denominations.

It was not just in the realms of religion and women's rights that revolutionary ideology had unexpected consequences. Propertyless men, who had always been denied the vote, began to claim that they too should have access to the ballot box. Other men argued that representation in state and national governments should be proportional to population, rather than allotted equally to governmental units (towns, counties, and states) of varying sizes. Some questioned the institution of slavery. Still others asked why one American citizen should be expected to defer automatically to the judgment of another, no matter how wealthy or well educated. Veterans returned home with a new sense of national pride, and with political loyalties that transcended state boundaries. They accordingly viewed politics differently than they had before the war. The cultural climate had changed: an independent America would be something more than a collection of former colonies.

In redefining their politics and society between 1775, when the war began, and 1787, when the new

Constitution was drafted, Americans drew their ideas from the ideology of resistance and from their own experiences. They designed state and national governments incorporating the features they had decided would best protect their rights: weak executives and powerful legislatures, separation of powers among branches of government, and division of sovereignty between national and state governments. Over time they modified their ideas somewhat, but these basic elements remained intact. The Articles of Confederation and the Constitution, which historians have often seen as reflecting opposing political philosophies (the "democratic" Articles versus the "aristocratic" Constitution), should instead be viewed as separate and successive attempts to solve the same problems. Both represented Americans' efforts to apply the lessons of the Revolution to their form of government.

Learning the lessons of the Revolution

Abigail Adams seems an unlikely revolutionary. In 1776 she was thirty-one years old, daughter of a minister, wife of a lawyer, and mother of four growing children. Throughout her life she emphasized the "Relative Duties" of her roles as wife, mother, and mistress of a household. She believed that women were more tender and delicate than men, that each sex had its distinct role to fulfill, and that ladies like herself should avoid the rough-and-tumble world of politics and public affairs. She had little formal education (as is apparent in her spelling and punctuation), but she read widely and thoughtfully. More important still, she had the intelligence to perceive the incongruities in her society and the initiative to point them out.

Abigail Adams

Yet not until the American Revolution began did Abigail Adams think to question the assumptions that had previously defined her world. Her husband, like many other leaders of the Revolution, was away from home for long periods of time. John Adams served first in congress and then in the fledgling diplomatic corps; other male patriots enlisted in the Continental Army or the militia. In their absence their wives, who had previously handled only the "indoor affairs" of the household, had to shoulder the responsibility for "outdoor affairs" as well. As the wife of a Connecticut militiaman later recalled, her husband "was out more or less during the remainder of the war [after 1777], so much so as to be unable to do anything on our farm. What was done, was done by myself."

In the Adams household and many others, the necessary shift of responsibilities that occurred during the war taught men and women that their traditional notions of proper sex roles had to be rethought. Both Adamses took great pride in Abigail's developing skills as a "farmeress," and John praised her courage repeatedly. "You are really brave, my dear, you are an Heroine," he told her in 1775. Abigail Adams, like her female contemporaries, stopped calling the farm "yours" in letters to her husband, and began referring to it as "ours." (This simple change of pronoun spoke volumes.) Both men and women realized that female patriots had made a vital contribution to winning the war through their work at home. Thus, in the years after the Revolution, Americans began to develop new ideas about the role women should play in a republican society.

Only a very few thought that role should include the right to vote. Abigail Adams called women's patriotism "the most disinterested of all virtues" because women were "excluded from honours and from offices" and "deprived of a voice in Legislation, obliged to submit to those Laws which are imposed upon us." Nevertheless, she did not press for female suffrage, believing that women's influence was best exerted in private. But some women thought differently, as events in New Jersey proved. The men who drafted the state constitution in 1776 had defined voters loosely as "all free inhabitants" who met certain property qualifications. They thereby unintentionally gave the vote to property-holding white spinsters and widows, as well as free black men. In the 1780s and 1790s women successfully claimed the right to vote in New Jersey's local and congressional elections. They continued to exercise that right until 1807, when women and blacks were disfranchised by the state legislature on the grounds that their votes could be easily manipulated. Yet the fact that they had voted at all was evidence of their altered perception of their place in political life.

Such dramatic episodes were unusual. On the whole the re-evaluation of women's position had its

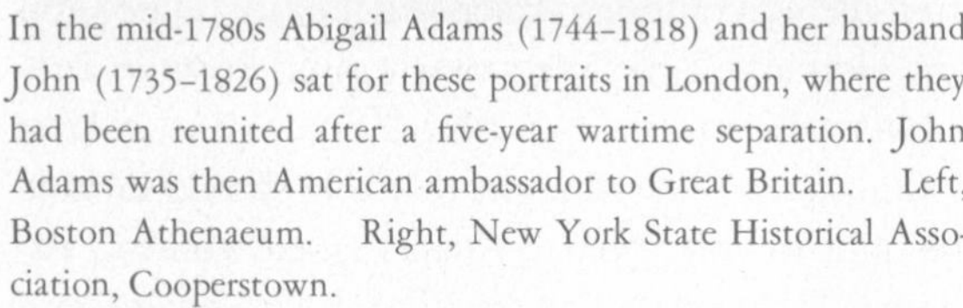

In the mid-1780s Abigail Adams (1744–1818) and her husband John (1735–1826) sat for these portraits in London, where they had been reunited after a five-year wartime separation. John Adams was then American ambassador to Great Britain. Left, Boston Athenaeum. Right, New York State Historical Association, Cooperstown.

greatest impact on private life. For instance, the traditional colonial view of marriage had stressed the subordination of wife to husband. But in 1790 a female "Matrimonial Republican" asserted that "marriage ought never to be considered as a contract between a superior and an inferior, but a reciprocal union of interest. . . . The obedience between man and wife is, or ought to be mutual." This new understanding of the marital relationship seems to have contributed to a rising divorce rate after the war. Dissatisfied wives proved less willing to remain in unhappy marriages than they had been previously. At the same time, state judges became more sympathetic to women's desires to be freed from abusive or unfaithful husbands.

Revolutionary ideal of womanhood

Furthermore, though the father had previously been seen as the most influential parent, the republican decades witnessed an ever-increasing emphasis on the importance of mothers. A list of "Maxims for Republics" first published in 1779 and reprinted in 1788 declared that "it is of the utmost importance, that the women should be well instructed in the principles of liberty in a republic. Some of the first patriots of antient times, were formed by their mothers." In 1790 one woman even argued publicly for female superiority, resting her claim on woman's maternal role. Men, she said, had assumed primacy in the past "on the vain presumption of their being assigned the most important duties of life." But God had clearly intended otherwise, since to women He had "assigned the care of making the first impressions on the infant minds of the whole human race, a trust of more importance than the government of provinces, and the marshalling of armies."

Other Americans did not go that far. To be sure, they were more willing than before to expand the meaning of the phrase "all men are created equal" to apply to women, but they still viewed woman's role in traditional terms. Like Abigail Adams, eighteenth-century Americans assumed that women's place was in the home, and that their primary function was to be good wives and mothers. They accepted the notion of equality, but within the context of men's and women's separate spheres. Whereas their forebears had seen women as inferior and subordinate to men, members of the revolutionary generation regarded the sexes and their roles as more nearly equal in importance. However, equality did not mean sameness. Despite the shift in opinion, it would be more than half a century before some Americans began to argue formally for women's rights.

To white men, too, the Revolution brought change. It is estimated that 40 percent of adult white male patriots served six months or more in the Revolutionary armies. (The total number of deaths in battle and from disease, approximately 25,000, seems small until one realizes that the proportional equivalent today would be two million.) In the ranks, American men learned four new political lessons. The first was nationalism. According to David Ramsay, a South Carolina physician and Continental Army veteran who was an early historian of the Revolution, the war "set them on thinking, speaking and acting in a line far beyond that to which they had been accustomed." The army and the congress, by "freely mixing together" men from all the states, "assimilated [them] into one mass." Thus, concluded Ramsay, "a foundation was laid for the establishment of a nation out of discordant materials."

Beginnings of nationalism

Ramsay's statement was too sweeping, but he had correctly recognized that the experience of fighting, sacrificing, and working together for a common goal had given men from different regions a new notion of where their loyalties lay. At the First Continental Congress in 1774, John Adams made no secret of his preference for New England and its inhabitants, openly criticizing the beliefs and behavior of fellow congressmen from the southern and middle states. Yet within only a few years Adams had reordered his loyalties, putting primary emphasis not on his birthplace but on the nation as a whole.

Soldiers' letters confirm that Adams's change of heart was typical. In March 1776 a Massachusetts shoemaker in the Continental Army told his wife that "I am willing to serve my contery in the Best way & manner that I am Capeble of." Reporting to her the likelihood that his regiment would be moved south to New York City, he commented, "I would not Be understood that I should Chuse to March But as I am ingaged in this glories Cause I am will[ing] to go whare I am Called." Similarly, a surgeon assigned to Valley Forge during the difficult winter of 1777 and 1778 observed that "nothing tends to the establishment of the firmest Friendship like Mutual Sufferings." When such men returned to their homes after the war, they retained their patriotism and pride in their accomplishments. They had also acquired a knowledge of other parts of the country that few earlier Americans had possessed.

The second and third lessons concerned the theory and practice of republicanism. As John Dickinson later recalled, "there was no question concerning forms of Government, no enquiry whether a Republic or a limited Monarchy was best. . . . We knew that the people of this country must unite themselves under some form of Government and that this could be no other than the Republican form." To Dickinson and other Americans, a republican government had to rest directly and solely on the consent of the people. By definition it did not contain the balance of monarchical and aristocratic elements Europeans believed necessary for political stability. Members of the revolutionary generation therefore devoted much time and attention to molding state governments into proper republican shapes. They also attempted to order their lives in accordance with republican principles.

Nowhere was this more true than in the ranks of the Revolutionary army and navy, where enlisted men repeatedly revealed their commitment to the concept of government by mutual consent. Captured American sailors on British prison hulks lived by mutually agreed-upon rules formalized in written "constitutions." One such group of more than 100 seamen imprisoned in Plymouth, England, declared that "we are determined to stand, and so remain as long as we live, true and loyal to our Congress, our country, our wives, children and friends." When a thousand Pennsylvania soldiers mutinied at the American army's

Republican soldiers

main winter encampment at Morristown, New Jersey, on January 2, 1781, their chief complaint was not poor food and clothing but that their rights had been violated. They had enlisted for three years, they argued, and their term of service was up; Pennsylvania contended that they had signed on for the duration of the war. The disgruntled soldiers chose a proper republican solution to their problem, leaving camp peacefully en masse to lay their case before Pennsylvania's civilian leaders. The military authorities agreed to a compromise that discharged most of the men.

Another republican lesson soldiers learned had to do with status and its prerequisites. Before the war, only men of distinguished social and economic standing had held political or military office in the colonies. But the unwieldy Revolutionary army required numerous officers (perhaps 15,000 to 20,000 in all). Consequently, men with no pretenses to gentlemanly status achieved posts of prestige and responsibility. At the same time, close contact with genteel officers gave many common soldiers a more realistic view of their betters. Privates who saw inexperienced officers make mistakes that cost both battles and men–there were many such mistakes during the long years of war–became less inclined to defer automatically to the gentry's judgment. Furthermore, military service at any rank brought honor to veterans in their home towns. After the war, former soldiers and sailors commanded the sort of respect from their fellow townsmen previously accorded only to clergymen and some secular leaders. Veterans accounted for a very high proportion of postwar officeholders, both elected and appointed. And since many states paid their soldiers in land grants rather than cash, propertyless young men could become independent yeoman farmers after they were mustered out of the service.

The fourth lesson of the Revolution was less heartening. In the heady days of 1775 and early 1776, before the British victories around New York City, the patriots had been convinced of their invincibility and of the willingness of the people to make necessary wartime sacrifices. But as the war dragged on and patriotic fervor subsided, the men serving their country grew bitter. The Valley Forge surgeon complained that those who sat comfortably at home around a warm fire "enjoying their wives & families" wanted the soldiers to "suffer everything for their Benefit & advantage, and yet are the first to Condemn us for not doing more!" Soldiers were often underfed and underclothed, short of guns and ammunition, and unpaid–all because state legislatures failed to support the war with adequate appropriations and because war profiteers sold the army shoddy merchandise and spoiled food. For many soldiers, military salaries were the sole source of income. When skyrocketing inflation destroyed the value of the currency in 1779 and 1780, they had nothing to show for their years of service. Thus once-optimistic patriots learned that many Americans were unwilling to sacrifice personal gain for public good, and that it would be unwise to put too much confidence in their new governments.

Ironies of the Revolution

For white Americans, male and female, the war did more than change the way they thought about themselves. It also exposed them to one of the primary contradictions in their society. Just as Abigail Adams pointed out to her husband his failure to apply revolutionary doctrines to the status of women, both blacks and whites recognized the irony of slaveholding Americans claiming they wanted to prevent Britain from enslaving them.

As early as 1764, James Otis, Jr., had identified the basic problem in his pamphlet *The Rights of the British Colonies Asserted and Proved* (see pages 93–94). If according to natural law all people were born free and equal, that meant *all* humankind, black and white. "Does it follow that 'tis right to enslave a man because he is black?" Otis asked. "Can any logical inference in favor of slavery be drawn from a flat nose, a long or short face?" The same theme was later voiced by other revolutionary leaders. In 1773 the Philadelphia doctor Benjamin Rush called slavery "a vice which degrades human nature," warning ominously that "the plant of liberty is of so tender a nature that it cannot thrive long in the neighborhood of slavery." Common folk too saw the contradiction. When Josiah Atkins, a Connecticut soldier marching south, saw George Washington's plantation, he observed in his journal: "Alas! That persons who pretend to stand for the *rights of mankind* for the *liberties of society,* can delight in oppression, & that even of the worst kind!"

Elizabeth Freeman, known as Mumbet, whose suit for freedom in the mid-1780s prompted Massachusetts courts to outlaw slavery. The portrait was painted by Susan Sedgwick, daughter of Theodore Sedgwick, the Federalist lawyer who presented Mumbet's case in court. Mumbet later worked for Sedgwick as a paid servant. Massachusetts Historical Society.

Blacks themselves were quick to recognize the implications of revolutionary ideology. In 1779 a group of slaves from Portsmouth, New Hampshire, asked the state legislature "from what authority [our masters] assume to dispose of our lives, freedom and property," and pleaded "that the name of slave may not more be heard in a land gloriously contending for the sweets of freedom." That same year several black residents of Fairfield, Connecticut, petitioned the legislature for their freedom, characterizing slavery as a "dreadful Evil" and "flagrant Injustice." Surely, they declared pointedly, "your Honours who are nobly contending in the Cause of Liberty, whose Conduct excited the Admiration, and Reverence, of all the great Empires of the World; will not resent, our thus freely animadverting, on this detestable Practice."

Both legislatures responded negatively. But the postwar years did witness the gradual abolition of slavery in the North. Massachusetts courts decided in the 1780s that the clause in the state constitution declaring that "all men are born free and equal, and have certain natural, essential, and unalienable rights" had abolished slavery in the state. Pennsylvania passed an abolition law in 1780; four years later Rhode Island and Connecticut provided for gradual emancipation, followed by New York (1799) and New Jersey (1804). Although New Hampshire did

Gradual emancipation

The Reverend Richard Allen (1760–1831) of Philadelphia, founder of the African Methodist Episcopal Church. Allen was attracted to Methodism because "the Methodists were the first people that brought glad tidings to the colored people." Later elected bishop of the AME Church, he was the first black bishop in the United States. Moorland-Spingarn Research Center, Howard University.

not formally abolish slavery, only eight slaves were reported on the 1800 state census and none remained a decade later.

In the South the pattern differed. Antislavery impulses prompted the state legislatures of Virginia (1782), Delaware (1787), and Maryland (1790 and 1796) to pass laws allowing masters to free their slaves without legal restrictions. But South Carolina and Georgia never considered adopting such acts, and North Carolina decided to insist that all manumissions–emancipations of individual slaves–be approved by county courts. None of the southern states came close to adopting general emancipation laws.

Thus revolutionary ideology had limited impact on the well-entrenched economic interests of large slaveholders. Only in the North, where there were few slaves and where little money was invested in human capital, could state legislatures vote to abolish slavery with relative ease. Even there, legislators' concern for property rights–the Revolution was, after all, fought for property as well as life and liberty–led them to favor gradual emancipation over immediate abolition. Most states provided only for the freeing of children born after passage of the law, not for the emancipation of adults. And even those children were to remain slaves until age twenty-one or twenty-eight. As a result, some northern states still had a few legally held slaves at the time of the Civil War.

Despite the slow progress of abolition, the free black population of the United States grew dramatically in the first years after the Revolution. Before the war there had been few free blacks in America. (According to a 1755 Maryland census, for example, only 4 percent of the blacks in the colony were free.) Most prewar free blacks were mulattoes, born of unions between white masters and enslaved black women. But wartime disruptions radically changed the size and composition of the free black population. Slaves who had escaped from plantations during the war, others who had served in the American army, and still others who had been emancipated by their owners or by state laws were now free. Because most of them were not mulattoes, dark skin was no longer an automatic sign of slave status. By 1790 there were nearly 60,000 free people of color in the United States; ten years later they numbered more than 108,000 and represented nearly 11 percent of the total black population. The effects of postwar manumissions were felt most sharply in the upper South, where they were fostered by such economic changes as declining soil fertility and a shift from tobacco to grain production. The free Negro population of Virginia more than doubled between 1790 and 1810, and by the latter year nearly a quarter of Maryland's black population was no longer in legal bondage.

Growth of the free black population

But the trend toward abolition of slavery was not a trend toward racial equality. Even whites who recognized blacks' right to freedom were unwilling to accept them as equals. Laws discriminated against emancipated blacks as they had against slaves–South Carolina, for example, did not permit free blacks to testify against whites in court. Public schools often refused to educate the children of free black parents. Freedmen found it difficult to purchase property and find good jobs. And though in many areas blacks were accepted as members–even ministers–of evangelical churches, whites rarely allowed them an equal voice in church affairs.

Gradually free blacks developed their own separate institutions, sometimes by choice, sometimes because whites imposed segregation on them. In Charleston, mulattoes formed the Brown Fellowship Society, which provided insurance coverage for its members, financed a school for free children, and helped to support black orphans. In 1787 blacks in Philadelphia and Baltimore founded churches that eventually became the African Methodist Episcopal (AME) denomination. AME churches later sponsored schools in a number of cities and often became cultural centers of the free black community.

Development of black institutions

For freed blacks, then, the lesson of the Revolution was that freedom from bondage did not necessarily mean freedom from discrimination. If they were to survive and prosper, they would have to rely on their own efforts rather than the benevolence or goodwill of their white compatriots.

American Indians had long since learned the same lesson. Even so, the Revolution meant the end of an independent tribal existence for most of those who lived east of the Mississippi River. They tried to resist the whites' westward thrust, but to no avail. Though tribal claims were not discussed by British and American diplomats at the end of the war, the United States assumed that the Treaty of Paris (1783) cleared its title to all land east of the Mississippi except the areas still held by Spain. But recognizing that some sort of land cession should be obtained from the major tribes, Congress initiated negotiations with both northern and southern Indians. At Fort Stanwix, New York, in 1784, and at Hopewell, South Carolina, in late 1785 and early 1786, American representatives signed treaties of questionable legality with the Iroquois and with Choctaw, Chickasaw, and Cherokee chiefs respectively (see map). The United States took the treaties as final confirmation of its sovereignty over the Indian territories, and authorized white settlers to move onto the land. Whites soon poured over the southern Appalachians, provoking the Creeks–who were receiving supplies from the Spanish and who had not agreed to the Hopewell treaties–to defend their territory by declaring war. Only in 1790, when the Creek chief Alexander McGillivray traveled to New York to negotiate a treaty, did the Creeks finally come to terms with the United States.

Encroachment on Indian lands

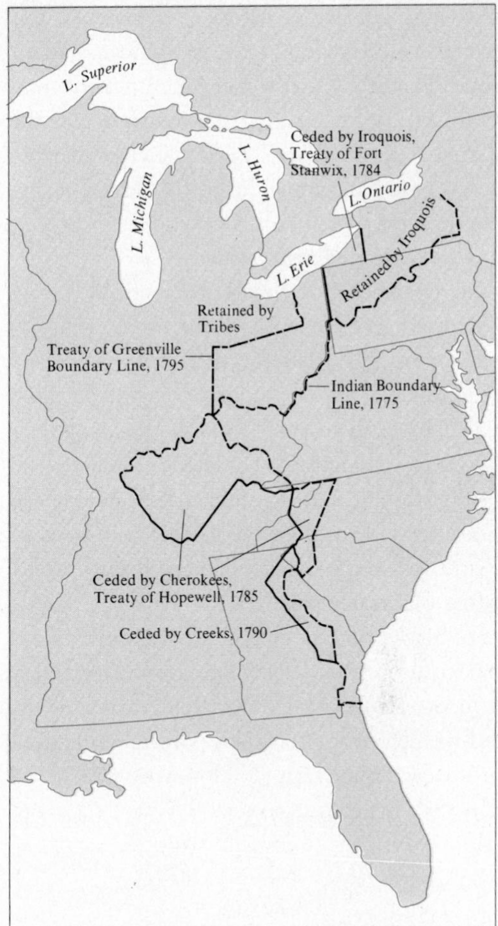

Cession of Indian lands to U.S., 1775–1790. Source: Reprinted by permission of Princeton University Press.

In the North, meanwhile, the Iroquois Confederacy was in disarray. The retaliatory raids Americans launched against their villages in 1779 had forced many tribesmen to flee to Canada. Most of them, including the Mohawk leaders Joseph and Mary Brant, never returned to live within the borders of the United States. Instead they established villages on lands set aside for them by the British north of the St. Lawrence River. The Iroquois who did remain soon found that they had little bargaining power. In 1786 they formally repudiated the Fort Stanwix treaty and warned of new attacks on frontier settlements, but both whites and Indians knew the threat was an empty one. The flawed treaty was permitted to stand by default. At intervals during the remainder of the decade the state of New York purchased large amounts of land from individual Iroquois tribes. By 1790 the once-proud Iroquois Confederacy was confined to a few scattered reservations.

It is one of the crueler ironies of American history that a revolution fought in the name of personal liberty and property rights failed to deliver those benefits to large segments of the population. The loyalists were exiled from their homes and deprived of their property for exercising what could have been seen as their right to dissent. Indians and blacks suffered even more grievously. Because of the Revolution the eastern Indian tribes lost much of their traditional homeland. Most blacks remained slaves. And the sizable number of blacks who did acquire freedom discovered that emancipation from slavery did not bring equality of treatment. However, the war had caused white men and women to look at their political and social roles in a new light. That development was to influence Americans' efforts to establish new state and national governments during and after the war.

Designing republican governments

About two months after his wife urged him to "Remember the Ladies," John Adams received a letter from a friend requesting advice on drafting the suffrage provisions of a new Massachusetts constitution and proposing that propertyless men be given the vote. It is clear from Adams's reply that he had begun to think seriously about the issues raised by his wife and by the changing circumstances in America. Government must be founded on the consent of the people, Adams observed, but what precisely did that mean? "How then does the right arise in the majority to govern the minority against their will? Whence arises the right of the men to govern the women without their consent? whence the right of the old to bind the young without theirs?"

In response to his own questions, Adams drew a parallel between disfranchised groups. "Very few men who have no property, have any judgment of their own," he asserted. Therefore, if the franchise was to be broadened to include men without property, "the same reasoning . . . will prove that you ought to admit women and children: for, generally speaking, women and children have as good judgment, and as independent minds, as those who are wholly destitute of property." Thus Adams used the specter of women and children at the polls to argue for maintaining traditional property requirements for voting. "Depend upon it, sir," he declared, "it is dangerous to open so fruitful a source of controversy and altercation, as would be opened by attempting to alter the qualifications of voters. There will be no end of it. . . . It tends to confound and destroy all distinctions, and prostrate all ranks to one common level."

Clearly, although Adams was a revolutionary and a republican, he was not a democrat by today's standards. Neither he nor the other leaders of the Revolution wanted to establish a democracy in the twentieth-century meaning of the term. They believed that government had to be based on the consent of the people, and that republics, with elected rather than hereditary rulers, were preferable to monarchies and aristocracies. But they still wanted to define the electorate—those who had a direct voice in the government—as white male property-holders.

Politically aware Americans believed that republics were especially fragile forms of government that risked chronic instability. A study of the histories of popular governments in such places as Greece and Rome convinced Americans that republics could succeed only if they were small in size and homogeneous in population. Furthermore, unless the citizens of a republic were especially virtuous, willing to sacrifice their own private interests for the good of the whole, the government would inevitably collapse. In return for sacrifices, though, a republic offered its citizens equality of opportunity. Under such a government, rank would be based on merit rather than inherited wealth and status. Society would be ruled by members of a "natural aristocracy," men of talent who had risen from what might have been humble beginnings to positions of power and privilege. As John Adams had indicated, rank would not be abolished but instead placed on a different footing.

Designing governments that put such precepts into effect proved difficult. On May 10, 1776, even before passage of the Declaration of Independence, the Continental Congress directed the states to devise new republican governments to replace the provincial congresses and committees that had met since 1774. Thus Americans initially concentrated on drafting state constitutions and devoted little attention to their national government–an oversight they were later forced to remedy. At the state level, they immediately faced the problem of defining just what a constitution was. The British constitution could not serve as a model because it was an unwritten mixture of law and custom; Americans wanted tangible documents specifying the fundamental structures of government. Several years passed before the states agreed that their constitutions could not be drafted by regular legislative bodies, like ordinary laws. Following the lead established by Massachusetts in 1780, they began to call conventions for the sole purpose of drafting constitutions. Thus the states sought direct authorization from the people–the theoretical sovereigns in a republic–before establishing new governments. After the new constitutions had been drawn up, delegates submitted them to the people for ratification.

Drafting of state constitutions

Those who wrote the state constitutions concerned themselves primarily with outlining the distribution of and limitations on governmental power. Both questions were crucial to the survival of republics. If authority was improperly distributed among the branches of government or not confined within reasonable limits, the states might become tyrannical, as Britain had. Indeed, Americans' experience with British rule affected every provision of their new constitutions.

Under their colonial charters, Americans had learned to fear the power of the governor–in most cases the appointed agent of the king or the proprietor–and to look on the legislature as their defender. Accordingly, the first state constitutions typically provided for the governor to be elected annually (usually by the legislature), limited the number of terms any one governor could serve, and gave him little independent authority. At the same time the constitutions expanded the powers of the legislature. They redrew the lines of electoral districts to reflect population patterns more accurately and increased the number of members in both the upper and lower houses. Finally, despite John Adams's dire predictions, most states lowered property qualifications for voting. As a result the legislatures came to include some men who before the war would not even have been eligible to vote. Thus the revolutionary era witnessed the first deliberate attempt to broaden the base of American government, a process that has continued into our own day.

But the authors of the state constitutions knew that governments designed to be responsive to the people would not necessarily provide sufficient protection should tyrants be elected to office. Consequently, they included limitations on governmental authority in the documents they composed. Seven of the constitutions contained formal bills of rights, and the others had similar clauses. Most of them guaranteed citizens freedom of the press and of religion, the right to a fair trial, the right of consent to taxation, and protection against general search warrants. An independent judiciary was charged with upholding such rights.

In sum, the constitution-makers put far greater emphasis on preventing state governments from becoming tyrannical than on making them effective wielders of political authority. Their approach to the process of shaping governments was understandable, given the American experience with Great Britain. But establishing such weak political units, especially in wartime, practically ensured that the constitutions would soon need revision. As early as the 1780s some states began to rewrite the constitutions they had drafted in 1776 and 1777. Invariably, the revised versions increased the powers of the governor and reduced the scope of the legislature's authority. Only then, a decade after the Declaration, did Americans start to develop a formal theory of checks and balances as the primary means of controlling governmental power. Once they realized that legislative supremacy did not in itself guarantee good government, Americans attempted to achieve their goal by balancing the powers of the legislative, executive, and judicial branches against one another. The national constitution they drafted in 1787 would embody that principle.

The constitutional theories that Americans applied at the state level did not at first influence their conception of the nature of a national government. The powers and structure of the Continental Congress evolved by default early in the war, since Americans had little time to devote to legitimizing their de facto government while organizing the military struggle against Britain. Not until late 1777, after Burgoyne's defeat at Saratoga, did Congress send the Articles of Confederation to the states for ratification.

The articles by and large wrote into law the arrangements that had developed, unplanned and largely unheeded, in the Continental Congress. The chief organ of national government was a unicameral legislature in which each state had one vote. Its powers included the conduct of foreign relations, the settlement of disputes between states, control over maritime affairs, the regulation of Indian trade, and the valuation of state and national money. The articles did not give the national government the ability to tax effectively or to enforce a uniform commercial policy. The United States of America was described as "a firm league of friendship" in which each state "retains its sovereignty, freedom and independence, and every Power, Jurisdiction and right, which is not by this confederation expressly delegated to the United States, in Congress assembled."

Articles of Confederation

The articles required the unanimous consent of the state legislatures for ratification or amendment, and a clause concerning western lands turned out to be troublesome. The draft accepted by Congress allowed the states to retain all land claims derived from their original colonial charters. But states with definite western boundaries in their charters (like Maryland, Delaware, and New Jersey) wanted the other states to cede the lands west of the Appalachian Mountains to the national government. Otherwise, they feared, states with large claims could expand and overpower their smaller neighbors. Maryland absolutely refused to accept the articles until 1781, when Virginia finally promised to surrender its western holdings to national jurisdiction (see map).

The fact that a single state could delay ratification for three years was a portent of the fate of American government under the Articles of Confederation. The unicameral legislature, whether it was called the Second Continental Congress (until 1781) or the Confederation Congress (thereafter), was too inefficient and unwieldy to govern effectively. The authors of the articles had not given adequate thought to the distribution of power within the national government or to the relationship between the Confederation and the states. The congress they created was simultaneously a legislative body and a collective executive, but it had no independent income and no authority to compel the states to accept its rulings. What is surprising, in other words, is not how poorly the Confederation functioned in following years, but rather how much the government was able to accomplish.

Trials of the confederation

During and after the war the most persistent problem faced by the American governments, state and national, was finance. Because legislators at all levels were understandably reluctant to levy taxes on their fellow countrymen, both Congress and the states tried to finance the war by simply printing currency. Even though the money was backed by nothing but good faith, it circulated freely and without excessive depreciation during 1775 and most of 1776. Demand for military supplies and civilian goods was high, stimulating trade (especially with France) and local production. Indeed, the amount of money issued in those years was probably no more than what a healthy economy required as a medium of exchange.

But in late 1776, as the American army suffered major battlefield reverses in New York and New Jersey, prices began to rise and inflation set in. The value of the currency rested on Americans' faith in their government, a faith that was sorely tested in the years that followed, especially during the dark days of the early British triumphs in the South (1779 and 1780). Some state governments fought inflation by controlling wages and prices, requiring acceptance of paper currency on an equal footing with hard money, borrowing, and even levying taxes. Their efforts were futile. So too was Congress's attempt to stop printing currency altogether and to rely solely on state contributions. By early 1780 it took forty paper dollars to purchase one in silver. A year later Continental currency was worthless.

Monetary problems

The severe wartime inflation seriously affected people on fixed incomes–including many soldiers and civilian leaders of the Revolution. Abigail Adams managed to keep her family solvent during the war primarily by selling small luxury items her husband

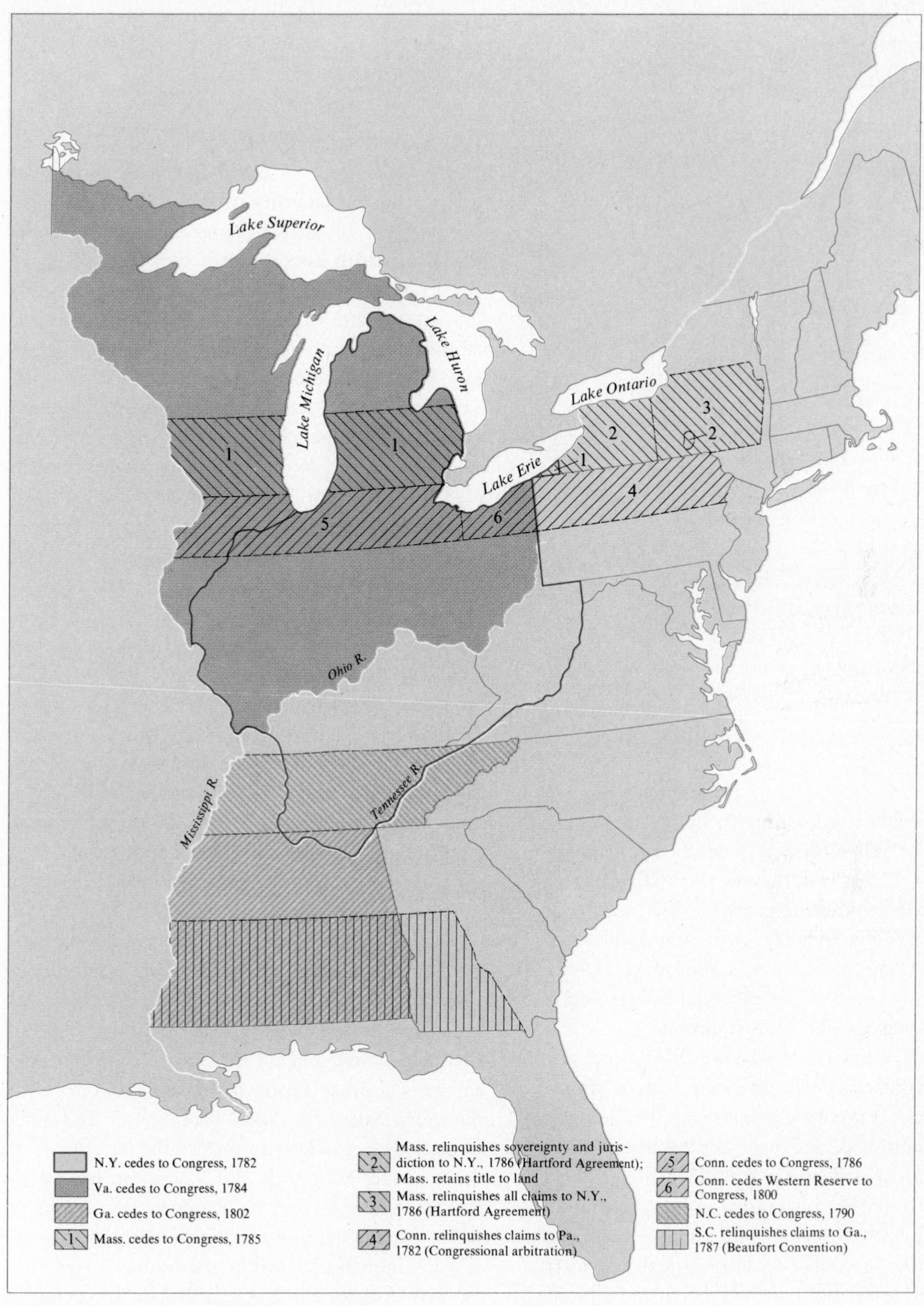

Western land claims and cessions, 1782–1802

Privateers—privately owned warships licensed by Congress or the states—recruited sailors with promises of quick wealth. Captured enemy ships were sold and the proceeds divided among the crew and owners. American Antiquarian Society.

John sent at her request from his diplomatic posts in Europe. The prices of such goods as fine handkerchiefs, gloves, fans, and ribbons climbed so precipitously that she was able to keep pace with rising food costs. Most people in similar circumstances were less fortunate. Common laborers, small farmers, clergymen, and poor folk in general could do nothing to stop the declining value of their incomes.

Yet there were people who benefited from such economic conditions. Military contractors could make sizable profits. Large-scale farmers who produced surpluses of meat, milk, and grains could sell their goods at high prices to the army or to civilian merchants. People with money could invest in lucrative trading voyages. If Abigail Adams could profit by occasional sales, much more could be gained through systematic effort. More risky, but potentially even more profitable, was privateering against enemy shipping—an enterprise that attracted venturesome sailors and wealthy merchants alike. Indeed, as a Nantucket, Massachusetts, mother wrote her son in early 1778, urging him to take advantage of the new opportunities, "it was Never better times here for Seamen then it is Now."

But accumulations of private wealth did not help Congress with its financial problems. In 1781, faced with the total collapse of the monetary system, the delegates undertook major reforms. After establishing a department of finance under the wealthy Philadelphia merchant Robert Morris, they asked the states to amend the Articles of Confederation to allow Congress to levy a duty on imported goods. Morris put national finances on a solid footing, but the customs duty was never adopted. First Rhode Island, then New York refused to agree to the tax. The states' resistance reflected genuine fear of a too-powerful central government. As one worried citizen wrote in 1783, "If permanent Funds are given to Congress, the aristocratical Influence, which predominates in more than a major part of the United States, will fully establish an arbitrary Government."

Failure to enforce the Treaty of Paris

Congress also faced major diplomatic problems at the close of the war. Chief among them were issues involving the peace treaty itself. Article 4, which promised the repayment of prewar debts (most of them owed by Americans to British merchants), and Article 5, which suggested that loyalists might recover their confiscated property, aroused considerable opposition. States passed laws denying British subjects the right to sue for recovery of debts or property in American courts, and town meetings decried the loyalists' return. As residents of Norwalk, Connecticut, put it, few Americans wanted to permit the "Tory Villains" to return "while filial Tears are fresh upon our Cheeks and our Murdered Brethren scarcely cold in their Graves." The state governments also had reason to oppose enforcement of the treaty. Sales of loyalists' land, houses, and other possessions had helped to finance the later stages of the war; since most of the purchasers were prominent patriots, the states had no desire to raise questions about the legitimacy of their property titles.

The failure of state and local governments to comply with Articles 4 and 5 gave Britain an excuse to maintain posts on the Great Lakes long after its troops were supposed to be withdrawn. Furthermore, Congress's inability to convince the states to implement the treaty pointed up its lack of power, even in an area–foreign affairs–in which it had been granted specific authority by the Articles of Confederation. Concerned nationalists argued publicly that enforcement of the treaty, however unpopular, was a crucial test for the republic. "Will foreign nations be willing to undertake anything with us or for us," asked Alexander Hamilton, "when they find that the nature of our governments will allow no dependence to be placed on our engagements?"

Congress's weakness was especially evident in the realm of trade, because the Articles of Confederation specifically denied it the power to establish a national commercial policy. Immediately following the war, both Britain and France restricted American trade with their colonies. Americans, who had hoped independence would bring about free trade with all nations, were outraged but could do little to change matters. Members of Congress watched helplessly as British and French manufactured goods flooded the United States while American produce could no longer be sold in the British West Indies, once its prime market, or even the French islands. The South Carolina indigo industry, deprived of the British bounty that had supported it, suffered a setback after the war. Though Americans opened a profitable trade with China in 1784, it was no substitute for access to closer and larger markets.

Congress also had difficulty dealing with the threat posed by Spain's presence on the southern and western borders of the United States. Determined to prevent the new nation's expansion, Spain in 1784 closed the Mississippi River to American navigation. It thus deprived the growing settlements west of the Appalachians of their major access route to the rest of the nation and the world. If Spain's policy were not reversed, westerners might have to accept Spanish sovereignty as the necessary price for survival. Congress opened negotiations with Spain in 1785, but even John Jay, one of the nation's most experienced diplomats, could not win the necessary concessions on navigation. The talks collapsed the following year after Congress divided sharply on the question of whether agreement should be sought on other issues. Southerners, voting as a bloc, insisted on navigation rights on the Mississippi, while northerners were willing to abandon that claim in order to win commercial concessions. The impasse raised questions about the possibility of a national consensus on foreign affairs.

Diplomatic problems of another sort confronted the congressmen when they considered the status of the territory north of the Ohio River. The United States had nominally acquired that land from Great Britain by the Treaty of Paris, and state land cessions had then placed the domain directly under congressional jurisdiction. But in actuality the land was still occupied by Indians–and by tribes, moreover, that had not participated in the negotiations at Fort Stanwix in 1784. The Shawnee, Chippewa, Ottawa, Potawatomi, and other western tribes had once allowed the Iroquois to speak for them. In the aftermath of the Revolution, though, they formed their own confederacy and demanded direct negotiations with the United States. Their aim was to present a united front, so as to avoid the piecemeal surrender of land by individual tribes.

At first the national government ignored the western Indian confederacy. Shortly after the state land cessions were completed, Congress began to organize the Northwest Territory, bounded by the Mississippi River, the Great Lakes, and the Ohio River. Ordinances passed in 1784, 1785, and 1787 outlined the process through which the land could be sold to settlers and formal governments organized. To ensure orderly development, Congress directed that the land be surveyed into townships six miles square, each divided into thirty-six sections of 640 acres (one square mile). Revenue from the sale of the sixteenth section of each township was to be reserved for the support of public schools–the first instance of federal aid to education in American history. The minimum price per acre was set at one dollar, and the minimum sale was to be 640 acres. Congress was clearly not especially concerned about helping the small farmer: the minimum outlay of $640 was beyond the reach of most Americans (except, of course, veterans who had received part of their army pay in land warrants). The proceeds from the land sales were the first independent revenues available to the national government.

Northwest Ordinances

The most important ordinance was the third, passed in 1787. The Northwest Ordinance contained a bill of rights guaranteeing settlers in the territory freedom of religion and the right to a jury trial, prohibiting cruel and unusual punishments, and abolishing slavery. It also specified the process by which residents of the territory could eventually organize state

The town of Marietta being laid out by the Ohio Company in the midst of earthworks left by the Mound Builders. Ohio Historical Society.

governments and seek admission to the union "on an equal footing with the original States." Early in the nation's history, therefore, Congress laid down a policy of admitting new states on the same basis as the old and assuring residents of the territories the same rights as citizens of the original states. Both provisions stemmed from the congressmen's experience as colonists resentful of their inferior status. Having suffered under the rule of a colonial power, they understood the importance of preparing the United States' first "colony" for eventual self-government. Nineteenth- and twentieth-century Americans were to be less generous in their attitudes toward residents of later territories, many of whom were nonwhite or non-Protestant. But the nation never fully lost sight of the egalitarian principles of the Northwest Ordinance.

In a sense, though, the ordinance was purely theoretical at the time it was passed. The Indians in the region refused to acknowledge American sovereignty and insisted on their right to the land. They opposed white settlement violently, attacking unwary pioneers who ventured too far north of the Ohio River. In 1788 the Ohio Company, to which Congress had sold a large tract of land at reduced rates, established the town of Marietta at the juncture of the Ohio and Muskingum rivers. But the Indians prevented the company from extending settlement very far into the interior. It was soon apparent that the United States would have to negotiate with the western confederacy.

In January 1789 General Arthur St. Clair, the first governor of the Northwest Territory, asked the tribes to come to a council at Fort Harmar, on the Muskingum. Only a few Indians attended, none of them ma-

General Anthony Wayne accepting the surrender of the Indian leader Little Turtle after the United States Army's victory in the Battle of Fallen Timbers, August 1794. Chicago Historical Society.

jor chiefs. According to one of the Americans present, the negotiations were conducted in French, which St. Clair did not speak, through a Canadian interpreter who had to "guess at" St. Clair's meaning "for he can neither write nor speak the [English] language so as to make himself understood in any matter of importance." The treaty signed by St. Clair and the Indians was utterly meaningless.

After that fiasco, war was inevitable. General Josiah Harmar (1790) and then St. Clair himself (1791) were defeated in major battles near the present border between Indiana and Ohio. More than six hundred of St. Clair's men were killed and scores more wounded; it was the whites' worst defeat in the entire history of the American frontier. In 1793 the tribal confederacy declared that peace could be achieved only if the United States recognized the Ohio River as the boundary between white and Indian lands. But the national government refused to relinquish its claim to the Northwest Territory. A new army under the command of General Anthony Wayne, a Revolutionary War hero, attacked and defeated the tribesmen in August 1794, at the Battle of Fallen Timbers (near Toledo, Ohio). This victory made it possible for serious negotiations to begin.

War in the Northwest

By the summer of 1795, Wayne had reached agreement with delegates from the western tribes. The Treaty of Greenville gave each side a portion of what it wanted. The United States gained the right to settle much of what was to become the state of Ohio, the tribes retaining only the northwest corner of the region. The Indians received the acknowledgment they had long sought: American recognition of their rights to the soil. At Greenville, the United States formally accepted the principle of Indian sovereignty, by virtue of residence, over all lands the tribes had not yet ceded. Never again would the United States government claim that it had acquired Indian territory solely through negotiation with a European or American country.

The problems the United States encountered in ensuring safe settlement of the Northwest Territory pointed up, once again, the basic weakness of the Confederation government. Not until after the Articles of Confederation were replaced with a new Constitution could the United States muster sufficient force to implement all the provisions of the Northwest Ordinance. Thus, although the ordinance is often viewed as one of the few major accomplishments of the Confederation Congress, it must be seen within a context of political impotence.

From crisis to a constitution

The Americans most deeply concerned about the inadequacies of the Articles of Confederation were those involved in overseas trade and foreign affairs. It was in those areas that the articles were most obviously deficient: Congress could not impose its will on the states to establish a uniform commercial policy or to ensure the enforcement of treaties. The problems involving trade were particularly serious. Less than a year after the end of the war, the American economy slid into a depression; both exporters of staple crops and importers of manufactured goods were adversely affected by the postwar restrictions on American commerce imposed by European powers. Although recovery had begun by 1786, the war's effects proved impossible to erase entirely.

Indeed, the economy was significantly changed by the Revolution. Whereas the thirteen colonies had sold their goods primarily to foreign markets, the domestic market began to assume greater overall importance in the independent United States. As the nation was winning political independence, in other words, it was also beginning to gain economic independence. Americans lost access to their traditional markets, but steady population growth and the spread of settlement helped to create new internal ones. In addition, freed from the mercantilist restrictions of the British Empire and drawing on European technological innovations, Americans began to establish manufacturing enterprises. The first American textile mill opened in Pawtucket, Rhode Island in 1793; later, in the early nineteenth century, textile manufacturing would come to play a major role in the American economy.

Recognizing the Confederation Congress's inability to deal with the nation's trade problems, Virginia invited the other states to a conference at Annapolis, Maryland, to discuss commercial policy. Although eight states named representatives to the meeting in September 1786, only five delegations attended. Those present realized that they were too few in number to have any real impact on the political system. They issued a call for another convention, to be held in Philadelphia in nine months, "to devise such further provisions as shall . . . appear necessary to render the constitution of the federal government adequate to the exigencies of the Union."

That fall an incident occurred in western Massachusetts that helped to convince other Americans that broad changes were necessary in their national government. Crowds of farmers angered by high taxes and the low supply of money halted court proceedings in which the state was trying to seize property for nonpayment of taxes. The insurgents were led by Daniel Shays, a farmer who had risen to the rank of captain in the American army; many of them were respected war veterans, described as gentlemen in contemporary accounts of the riots. Clearly the incident could not be dismissed as the work of an unruly rabble. What did the uprising mean for the future of the republic? Was it a sign of impending anarchy? Those were the questions that worried the nation's political leaders.

Shays' Rebellion

The protesters explained their position in an address to the governor and council of Massachusetts. They "were not induced to rise from a disaffection to the Commonwealth, or instigated by British Emissaries but from those sufferings which dissenabled them to provide for their Wives and Children or to Discharge their honest debts though in possession of the lands of their Country." Referring to their experience as revolutionary soldiers, they asserted that they "es-

A woodcut of Daniel Shays and one of his chief officers, Job Shattuck, in 1787. National Portrait Gallery, Smithsonian Institution, Washington, D.C.

teem[ed] one moment of Liberty to be worth an eternity of Bondage."

To residents of eastern Massachusetts and other citizens of the United States, the most frightening aspect of the uprising was the rebels' attempt to forge direct links between themselves and the earlier struggle for independence. The state legislature issued an address to the people, asking and replying to a rhetorical question: "Because they could not have everything as they wished, could they be justified in resorting to force? . . . In a republican government the majority must govern. If the minor part governs it becomes aristocracy, if every one opposed at his pleasure, it is no government, it is anarchy and confusion." Thus Massachusetts officials asserted that the formation of the republic had narrowed the range of acceptable political alternatives. The crowd actions that had once been a justifiable response to British tyranny were no longer legitimate. In a republic, reform had to come about through the ballot box rather than by force. If the nation's citizens refused to submit to legitimate authority, the result would be chaos and collapse of the government.

It was this issue that made Shays' Rebellion seem to challenge the existence of the entire United States, though it never seriously threatened even the state of Massachusetts. The rebels were easily dispersed by militia early in 1787. Shays and some of his followers fled to Vermont; many others were quickly caught and jailed. The reality of the threat the insurgents posed was never at issue: the importance of the uprising lay in its symbolic meaning. Of the major American political thinkers, only Thomas Jefferson could view the Massachusetts incidents without alarm. "What country can preserve its liberties, if its rulers are not warned from time to time that their people preserve the spirit of resistance?" Jefferson wrote from Paris, where he was serving as American ambassador. "What signify a few lives lost in a century or two? The tree of liberty must be refreshed from time to time, with the blood of patriots and tyrants. It is its natural manure."

But Jefferson was clearly exceptional. Shays' Rebellion unquestionably accelerated the movement toward comprehensive revision of the Articles of Confederation.

Calling of the Constitutional Convention

In February 1787, after most of the states had already appointed delegates, the Confederation Congress belatedly en-

James Madison (1751–1836), the youthful scholar and skilled politician who earned the title Father of the Constitution. Mr. Albert Errol Leeds, Philadelphia.

dorsed the convention. In mid-May, fifty-five men, representing all the states but Rhode Island, assembled in Philadelphia to begin their deliberations.

The vast majority of the delegates were men of property and substance. Among their number were merchants, planters, physicians, generals, governors, and especially lawyers–twenty-three had studied the law. Most had been born in America, and many came from families that had immigrated in the seventeenth century. In an era when only a tiny proportion of the population had any advanced education, more than half had attended college. A few had been educated in Britain, but most were graduates of American institutions: Princeton (ten), William and Mary (four), Yale (three), Harvard and Columbia (two each). The youngest delegate was twenty-six, the oldest–Benjamin Franklin–eighty-one. Like George Washington, whom they elected chairman, most were in their vigorous middle years. A dozen men did the bulk of the convention's work: Oliver Ellsworth and Roger Sherman of Connecticut; Elbridge Gerry and Rufus King of Massachusetts; William Paterson of New Jersey; Gouverneur Morris of New York; James Wilson of Pennsylvania; John Rutledge and Charles Pinckney of South Carolina; and Edmund Randolph, George Mason, and James Madison of Virginia. Of those leaders, Madison was by far the most important; he truly deserves the title Father of the Constitution.

James Madison: his early life

The frail, shy, slightly built James Madison was thirty-six years old in 1787. Raised in the Piedmont country of Virginia, he had attended Princeton, served on the local committee of safety, and been elected successively to the Virginia provincial convention, the state's lower and upper houses, and finally the Continental Congress (1780–1783). Although Madison returned to Virginia to serve in the state legislature in 1784, he remained in touch with national politics, partly through his continuing correspondence with his close friend Thomas Jefferson. A promotor of the Annapolis convention, he strongly supported its call for further reform.

Madison was unique among the delegates in his systematic preparation for the Philadelphia meeting. Through Jefferson in Paris he bought more than two hundred books on history and government, and carefully analyzed their accounts of past confederacies and republics. In April 1787, a month before the convention began, he summed up the results of his research in a lengthy paper entitled "Vices of the Political System of the United States." After listing the eleven major flaws he perceived in the current structure of the government (among them "encroachments by the states on the federal authority" and "want of concert in matters where common interest requires it"), Madison revealed the conclusion that would guide his actions over the next few months. "The great desideratum [desire] in Government is such a modification of the sovereignty as will render it sufficiently neutral between the different interests and factions, to controul one part of the society from invading the rights of another, and at the same time sufficiently controuled itself, from setting up an interest adverse to that of the whole Society."

Thus Madison set forth the principle of checks and balances. The government, he believed, had to be constructed in such a way that it could not become tyrannical or fall wholly under the influence of a particular interest group. He regarded the large size of a potential national republic as an advantage in that respect. Rejecting the common assertion that republics had to be small to survive, Madison argued that a large, diverse republic was in fact to be preferred. Because the nation would include many different interest groups, no one of them would be able to control the government. Political stability, he declared, would result from compromises among the contending parties.

Madison's conception of national government was embodied in the so-called Virginia plan, introduced on May 29 by his colleague Edmund Randolph. The plan provided for a two-house legislature with proportional representation in both houses, an executive and a judiciary (both of which the Confederation government lacked), and congressional veto over state laws. It gave Congress the broad power to legislate "in all cases to which the separate states are incompetent." Had the Virginia plan been adopted intact, it would have created a government in which national authority reigned unchallenged and state power was greatly diminished.

Virginia and New Jersey plans

But the convention included many delegates who, while recognizing the need for change, believed that the Virginians had gone too far in the direction of national consolidation. After Randolph's proposal had been debated for several weeks, the disaffected delegates united under the leadership of William Paterson. On June 15 Paterson presented an alternative scheme, the New Jersey plan, calling for modifications in the Articles of Confederation rather than a complete overhaul of the government. Even before introducing his proposals, Paterson had made his position clear in debate. On June 9 he had asserted that the articles were "the proper basis of all the proceedings of the convention," and warned that if the delegates did not confine themselves to amending the articles they would be charged with "usurpation" by their constituents. All that was needed, Paterson contended, was "to mark the orbits of the states with due precision and provide for the use of coercion" by the national government. Although the delegates rejected Paterson's narrow interpretation of their task, he and his allies won a number of major victories in the months that followed.

Debate quickly focused on three key questions involving representation. Should there be proportional representation in both houses of the national legislature? (Paterson's group readily agreed to replace Congress with a bicameral body.) What should the representation in either or both houses be proportional *to*—people, property, or a combination of the two? And, finally, how should the representatives to the two houses be elected? The three questions were intertwined, since a decision on one could determine the answers to the others; yet each had to be considered on its own merits. Matters were further complicated by the existence of more than two opinions on each issue.

The easiest question to resolve was the mode of electing representatives. The Virginia plan suggested that the lower house be elected at large by the people, and that the upper house be elected by the lower. The latter proposal was quickly discarded, and a compromise was reached as early as June 21. John Dickinson best expressed the somewhat reluctant consensus. It was, he declared, "essential that one branch of the legislature should be drawn immediately from the people and expedient that the other should be chosen by the legislatures of the states." The delegates, in other words, agreed that the people should have a direct say in the choice of some national legislators (thus the House of Representatives). They also knew that the state governments, which had named delegates to the Confederation Congress, would insist on a similar privilege in the new government. In providing for senators to be selected by state legislatures, they thus adhered to republican principles but recognized political reality.

The most difficult problem was the issue of proportional representation in the Senate. On June 11 the convention accepted the principle of proportional representation in the lower house, reaffirming its vote on June 29. The Senate was quite another matter. Speaking for the states with large populations, the democratically minded James Wilson inquired, "Can we forget for whom we are forming a government? Is it for *men,* or for the imaginary beings called *states?*" But Luther Martin of Maryland, the major spokesman for the smaller states, argued that "an equal vote in each state was essential to the federal idea and was founded in justice and freedom, not merely in policy; . . . the states, like individuals, were in a state of nature equally sovereign and free."

Debate over representation

For weeks both sides remained adamant. An impasse was reached on July 2 when a motion to give each state one vote in the Senate failed on a tie vote of five states in favor, five against. (Three states were absent at the time.) In desperation, the convention appointed a committee to work out a compromise. Three days later the committee recommended equal representation for states in the Senate, coupled with a proviso that all appropriation bills must originate in the lower house. The large states were still dissatisfied, but fears that the meeting would collapse led delegates to urge reconciliation. On July 16, by a vote of 5 to 4 with one state (Massachusetts) divided, the convention at last agreed to the small states' demand for equal representation in the Senate. But not until a week later, when the convention adopted Roger Sherman's suggestion that the two senators from each state vote as individuals rather than as a bloc, was a breakdown averted.

One potentially divisive question remained unresolved: how was representation in the lower house to be apportioned among the states? Aside from the few who wanted representation distributed according to wealth, most delegates fell into one of three groups: those who wanted representation proportional to total population; those who wanted to count only the free population; and those who proposed counting three-fifths of the slaves as well. (The three-fifths formula for counting slaves was not original to the convention; it had been developed by the Confederation Congress in 1783 as a means of allocating taxation.) Delegates from Georgia and South Carolina wanted to count the entire population, slave and free alike, because doing so would increase their total number of representatives. New Englanders wanted to count only free people, fearing that their representatives would be outvoted in the lower house by southern slaveholders. Delegates from the middle states and the upper South insisted on compromise. After the three-fifths formula was linked to a clause allowing Congress to stop the slave trade after twenty years (thus preventing the slave population from increasing indefinitely), it was unanimously accepted. Only two delegates, Gouverneur Morris and George Mason, spoke out strongly against the institution of slavery.

Three-fifths compromise

Once agreement was reached on the knotty problem of representation, the delegates had little difficulty achieving consensus on the other major issues confronting them. Instead of giving Congress the nearly unlimited scope proposed in the Virginia plan, the delegates enumerated congressional powers and then provided for flexibility by granting all authority "necessary and proper" to carry out those powers. Discarding the legislative veto contained in the Virginia plan, the convention implied a judicial veto instead. The Constitution plus national laws and treaties would constitute "the supreme law of the land; and the judges in every state shall be bound thereby." The convention placed primary responsibility for the conduct of foreign affairs in the hands of the president, who was also designated commander-in-chief of the armed forces. The delegates established an elaborate independent mechanism, the electoral college, to select the president, and agreed that the chief executive should serve a short term but be eligible for re-election.

The final document still showed signs of its origins in the Virginia plan, but compromises had created a system of government less powerful at the national level than Madison and Randolph had envisioned. The key to the Constitution was the distribution of political authority–separation of powers among the executive, legislative, and judicial branches of the national government, and division of powers between states and nation. The branches were balanced against one another, their powers deliberately entwined to prevent them from acting independently. The president was given a veto over congressional legislation, but his treaties and major appointments required the consent of the Senate. Congress could impeach the president and the federal judges, but the courts appeared to have the final say on interpretation of the Constitution. The system of checks and balances would make it difficult for the government to become tyrannical, as Madison had intended. At the same time, though, the elaborate system would sometimes prevent the government from acting quickly and decisively. Finally, the line between state and national powers was so ambiguously and vaguely drawn that the United States was to fight a civil war in the next century before the issue was fully resolved.

Separation of powers

The convention held its last session on September 17, 1787. Of the forty-two delegates present, only three refused to sign the Constitution. (Two of the three, George Mason and Elbridge Gerry, declined because of the lack of a bill of rights.) Benjamin Franklin had written a speech calling for unity; because his voice was too weak to be heard, James Wilson read it for him. "I confess that there are several parts of this constitution which I do not at present approve," Franklin admitted. Yet he urged its acceptance "because I expect no better, and because I am not sure, that it is not the best." Only then was the Constitution made public. The convention's proceedings had been entirely secret—and remained so until the delegates' private notes were published in the nineteenth century.

Opposition and ratification

Later that same month the Confederation Congress submitted the Constitution to the states but did not formally recommend approval. The ratification clause of the Constitution provided for the new system to take effect once it was approved by special conventions in at least nine states. The delegates to each state convention were to be elected by the people. Thus the national constitution, unlike the Articles of Confederation, would rest directly on popular authority (and the presumably hostile state legislatures would be circumvented).

As the states began to elect delegates to the special conventions, debate over the proposed government grew more heated. It quickly became apparent that the disputes within the Constitutional Convention had been minor compared to the divisions of opinion within the country as a whole. After all, the delegates at Philadelphia had agreed on the need for basic reforms in the American political system. Many citizens, though, not only rejected that conclusion but believed that the proposed government, despite its built-in safeguards, held the potential for tyranny.

Critics of the Constitution, who became known as Antifederalists, fell into two main groups: those who emphasized the threat to the states embodied in the

Antifederalists

new national government, and those who stressed the dangers to individuals posed by the lack of a bill of rights. Ultimately, though, the two positions were one. The Antifederalists saw the states as the chief protectors of individual rights, and their weakening as the onset of arbitrary power.

Fundamentally the Antifederalists were traditionalists, steeped in the notion that a republican form of government could succeed only in a small geographical area. James Madison had concluded from his study of ancient republics that increasing the size of the political unit might help to reduce destructive factionalism. But the Antifederalists regarded Madison's argument as heretical nonsense. "It is the opinion of the most celebrated writers on government, and confirmed by uniform experience," the Antifederalist delegates to the Pennsylvania convention pointed out, "that a very extensive territory cannot be governed on the principles of freedom, otherwise than by confederation of republics." The same men went on to charge that "the powers vested on Congress by this constitution, must necessarily annihilate and absorb the legislative, executive, and judicial powers of the several States." The result, they predicted, would be "*an iron handed despotism,* as nothing short of the supremacy of despotic sway could connect and govern these United States under one government."

As the months passed and public debate continued, the Antifederalists focused more sharply on the Constitution's lack of a bill of rights. Even if the states were weakened by the new system, they believed, the people could still be protected from tyranny if their rights were specifically guaranteed. The Constitution did contain some prohibitions on congressional power—for example, the writ of habeas corpus, which prevented arbitrary imprisonment, could not be suspended except in dire emergencies—but the Antifederalists found these provisions inadequate. Nor were they reassured by the Federalists' assertion that, since the new government was one of limited powers, it had no authority to violate the people's rights. *Letters of a Federal Farmer,* perhaps the most widely read Antifederalist pamphlet, listed the rights that should be protected: freedom of the press and of religion, the right to trial by jury, and guarantees against unreasonable search warrants.

From Paris, Thomas Jefferson added his voice to the chorus. Replying to Madison's letter conveying a copy of the Constitution, Jefferson wrote: "I like much the general idea of framing a government which should go on of itself peaceably, without needing continual recurrence to the state legislatures." He

Important events

1776	Second Continental Congress directs states to draft constitutions
1777	Articles of Confederation sent to states for ratification
1780	Pennsylvania becomes first state to abolish slavery Massachusetts becomes first state to call constitutional convention
1781	Articles of Confederation ratified
1782	Virginia becomes first southern state to allow individual manumissions without legal restrictions
1784	Treaty of Fort Stanwix Spain closes Mississippi River to American navigation
1785–86	Treaty of Hopewell
1786	Iroquois repudiate Treaty of Fort Stanwix Annapolis Convention
1786–87	Shays' Rebellion (Mass.)
1787	Northwest Ordinance Constitutional Convention
1788	Hamilton, Jay, and Madison, *The Federalist* Constitution ratified
1789	Treaty of Fort Hamar
1791	St. Clair's defeat
1794	Battle of Fallen Timbers
1795	Treaty of Greenville

also approved of the separation of powers among the three branches of government and declared himself "captivated" by the compromise between the large and small states. Nevertheless, he added, he did not like "the omission of a bill of rights. . . . A bill of rights is what the people are entitled to against every government on earth, general or particular, and what no just government should refuse, or rest on inference."

As the state conventions met to consider ratification, the lack of a bill of rights loomed larger and larger as a flaw in the new form of government. Four of the first five states to ratify did so unanimously, but serious disagreements then began to surface. Massachusetts ratified by a majority of only 19 votes out of 355 cast; in New Hampshire the Federalists won by a majority of 57 to 47. When New Hampshire ratified, in June 1788, the requirement of nine states had been satisfied. But New York and Virginia had not yet voted, and everyone realized the new constitution could not succeed unless those key states accepted it. In Virginia, despite a valiant effort by the Antifederalist Patrick Henry, the pro-Constitution forces won 89 to 79. In New York James Madison, John Jay, and Alexander Hamilton campaigned for ratification by publishing *The Federalist,* one of the most important political tracts in American history. Their reasoned arguments, coupled with the promise that a bill of rights would be added to the Constitution, helped carry the day. On July 26, 1788, New York ratified the Constitution by the slim margin of 3 votes. The new government was a reality, even though the last state (Rhode Island, which had not participated in the convention) did not formally join the union until 1790.

Ratification of the Constitution

In the years since 1776, Americans had altered their political ideas and their social practices. Once wedded to a conception of politics and government drawn almost entirely from traditional definitions of republicanism, they had gradually forged their national government out of a combination of direct experience and political theory. They had begun to think more deeply than ever before about themselves and their society, raising questions about the institution of slavery, the position of women, and the role of the citizen in a republic. Still the question remained: could they successfully implement the new system?

Suggestions for further reading

General

Stuart Bruchey, *The Roots of American Economic Growth, 1607–1861* (1965); Staughton Lynd, *Class Conflict, Slavery, & the United States Constitution: Ten Essays* (1967); Forrest McDonald, *E Pluribus Unum: The Formation of the American Republic 1776–1790* (1965); Jackson Turner Main, *The Social Structure of Revolutionary America* (1965); Curtis P. Nettels, *The Emergence of a National Economy, 1775–1815* (1962); Robert R. Palmer, *The Age of the Democratic Revolution: A Political History of Europe and America 1760–1800,* 2 vols. (1959, 1964); Morton White, *The Philosophy of the American Revolution* (1978); Chilton Williamson, *American Suffrage from Property to Democracy 1760–1860* (1960); Garry Wills, *Inventing America: Jefferson's Declaration of Independence* (1978); Benjamin F. Wright, Jr., *Consensus and Continuity, 1776–1787* (1958); Gordon S. Wood, *The Creation of the American Republic, 1776–1787* (1969).

Continental Congress and Articles of Confederation

Jack Eblen, *The First and Second United States Empires: Governors and Territorial Government, 1784–1912* (1968); E. James Ferguson, *The Power of the Purse: A History of American Public Finance, 1776–1790* (1961); H. James Henderson, *Party Politics in the Continental Congress* (1974); Merrill Jensen, *The Articles of Confederation: An Interpretation of the Social-Constitutional History of the American Revolution, 1774–1781,* 2nd ed. (1959); Merrill Jensen, *The New Nation: A History of the United States during the Confederation, 1781–1789* (1950); Jack N. Rakove, *The Beginnings of National Politics: An Interpretive History of the Continental Congress* (1979); Clarence L. VerSteeg, *Robert Morris, Revolutionary Financier* (1954).

State politics

Willi Paul Adams, *The First American Constitutions: Republican Ideology and the Making of the State Constitutions in the Revolutionary Era* (1980); Elisha P. Douglass, *Rebels & Democrats: The Struggle for Equal Political Rights & Majority Rule During the American Revolution* (1955); Richard T. McCormick, *Experiment in Independence: New Jersey in the Critical Period 1781–1789* (1950); Jackson Turner Main, "Government by the People: The American Revolution and the Democratization of the Legislatures," *William and Mary Quarterly,* 3rd ser., 23 (1966), 391–407; Jackson Turner Main, *Political Parties Before the Constitution* (1973); Jackson Turner Main, *The Sovereign States, 1775–1783* (1973); Jackson Turner Main, *The Upper House in Revolutionary America, 1763–1788* (1967); Allan Nevins, *The American States during and after the Revolution, 1775–1789* (1924); Stephen E. Patterson, *Political Parties in Revolutionary Massachusetts* (1973); J.R. Pole, *Political Representation in England and the Origins of the American Republic* (1966); Irwin H. Polishook, *Rhode Island and the Union, 1774–1795* (1969); Marion L. Starkey, *A Little Rebellion* (1955); Robert J. Taylor, *Western Massachusetts in the Revolution* (1954).

The Constitution

Douglass Adair, *Fame and the Founding Fathers* (1974); Charles A. Beard, *An Economic Interpretation of the Constitution of the United States* (1913); Irving Brant, *James Madison,* 6 vols. (1941–1961); Linda Grant DePauw, *The Eleventh Pillar: New York State and the Federal Constitution* (1966); Max Farrand, *The Framing of the Constitution of the United States* (1913); Forrest McDonald, *We the People: The Economic Origins of the Constitution* (1958); Jackson Turner Main, *The Anti-Federalists: Critics of the Constitution, 1781–1788* (1961); Frederick W. Marks, III, *Independence on Trial: Foreign Affairs and the Making of the Constitution* (1973); Clinton Rossiter, *1787: The Grand Convention* (1973); Robert A. Rutland, *The Ordeal of the Constitution* (1966); Gerald Stourzh, *Alexander Hamilton and the Ideal of Republican Government* (1970); Carl Van Doren, *The Great Rehearsal: The Story of the Making and Ratifying of the Constitution of the United States* (1948).

Women

Charles Akers, *Abigail Adams: An American Woman* (1980); Ruth Bloch, "American Feminine Ideals in Transition: The Rise of the Moral Mother, 1785–1815," *Feminist Studies,* 4, No. 2 (June 1978), 100–126; Nancy F. Cott, "Divorce and the Changing Status of Women in Massachusetts," *William and Mary Quarterly,* 3rd ser., 33 (1976), 586–614; Linda K. Kerber, *Women of the Republic: Intellect & Ideology in Revolutionary America* (1980); Mary Beth Norton, *Liberty's Daughters: The Revolutionary Experience of American Women, 1750–1800* (1980).

Blacks and Indians

Ira Berlin, *Slaves without Masters: The Free Negro in the Antebellum South* (1974); David Brion Davis, *The Problem of Slavery in the Age of Revolution, 1770–1823* (1975); Winthrop D. Jordan, *White Over Black: American Attitudes Toward the Negro, 1550–1812* (1968); Duncan J. MacLeod, *Slavery, Race, and the American Revolution* (1974); Bernard Sheehan, *Seeds of Extinction: Jeffersonian Philanthropy and the American Indian* (1973); Anthony F.C. Wallace, *The Death and Rebirth of the Seneca* (1969); Arthur Zilversmit, *The First Emancipation: The Abolition of Slavery in the North* (1967).

THE
PSALM SINGER'S AMUSEMENT
CONTAINING
A Number of Fuging pieces and Anthems
composed by
William Billings: Author of the Singing Master's Assistant
Printed and sold by the Author at his House near the white Horse
BOSTON 1781
J Norman sculp.

The title page of William Billings's *Psalm-Singers' Amusement* (1781) illustrates the new musical trends opposed by traditionalists. In the upper left and lower right corners choirs of women and men practice fuguing pieces and anthems. In the other corners musicians play stringed instruments, and above the title a soloist plays an oboe.

American composer, published such works as *The New-England Psalm-Singer* (1770) and *The Psalm-Singers' Amusement* (1781) for use in the special singing schools that instructed choir members. Traditionalists resisted the trend, partly because it required altering the standard hierarchical seating patterns in the church, but also because it excluded most of the congregation from music-making.

Music was not the only realm in which disturbing tendencies occurred. By the mid-1780s, some Americans were beginning to detect signs of luxury and corruption all around them. The end of the war and resumption of European trade brought a return to fashionable clothing styles for both men and women, and abandonment of the simpler homespun garments patriots had once worn with such pride. Balls and concerts resumed in the cities and were attended by well-dressed elite families. Parties no longer seemed complete without gambling and card-playing. Social clubs for young people multiplied; Samuel Adams worried in print about the possibilities for corruption lurking behind innocent plans for tea drinking and genteel conversation among Boston youths. Especially alarming to fervent republicans was the establishment of the Society of the Cincinnati, a hereditary organization of Revolutionary War officers and their descendants. Many feared that the group would become the nucleus of a native-born aristocracy. All these developments directly challenged the United States's image as a virtuous, self-sacrificing republic.

Their deep-seated concern for the future of the infant republic focused Americans' attention on their children, the "rising generation." Education acquired new significance in the context of the republic. Since

Educational reform

the early days of the colonies, education had been seen chiefly as a private means to personal advancement, and thus a matter of concern only to individual families. Now, though, it would serve a public purpose. If young people were to resist the temptation of vice, they would have to learn the lessons of virtue at home and at school. In fact, the very survival of the nation depended on it. The early republican period was thus a time of major educational reform.

The 1780s and 1790s brought three significant changes in American educational practice. First, the states began to be willing to use tax money to support public elementary schools. Until that time nearly all education in the colonies had been privately financed. Parents who wanted their children taught any subject, from the rudiments of reading and writing to advanced Latin and Greek, had to pay individually for the privilege. But the provision in the Northwest Ordinance of 1787 setting aside land to support public education reflected Americans' new attitude toward schooling. In the republic, schools had a claim on tax dollars. Consequently, the Massachusetts legislature in 1789 adopted a law requiring towns to supply their citizens with free public elementary education.

Second, the college curriculum was reformed. Since their founding, American colleges—with the notable exception of Franklin's College of Philadelphia, later the University of Pennsylvania—had offered students a classical education aimed primarily at producing well-trained clerics. But the end of the eighteenth century brought major changes in the traditional course of study. Although colleges like Harvard, Yale, and William and Mary continued to instruct their students in classical languages and theology, they added classes in history, geography, modern languages, and "natural philosophy" (science). At its highest level, then, American education broadened its scope and focused on producing well-informed republican citizens rather than future clergymen.

Third, schooling for girls was vastly improved. Because the colonists placed little emphasis on formal education for girls, at least half the American female population was illiterate at the time of the Revolution. But Americans' new recognition of the importance of the rising generation led to the realization that mothers would have to be properly educated if their children were to be educated. Therefore Massachusetts insisted in its 1789 law that town elementary schools be open to girls as well as boys. Throughout the United States, private academies were founded to give teenage girls from well-to-do families an opportunity for advanced schooling. No one yet proposed opening colleges to women, but a few fortunate girls could now study history, geography, rhetoric, and mathematics. The academies also trained female students in fancy needlework—the only artistic endeavor open to women.

Judith Sargent Murray (1751–1820), painted by John Singleton Copley about the time of her marriage to the sea captain John Stevens. Although her steady gaze suggests clear-headed intelligence, there is little in the stylized portrait—typical of Copley's work at the time—to suggest her later emergence as the first notable American feminist theorist. Frick Art Reference Library.

The chief theorist of women's education in the early republic was Judith Sargent Murray, of Gloucester, Massachusetts. Born in 1751, Murray married a sea captain at age eighteen. Widowed in 1786, she took as her second husband John Murray, the founder of the Universalist sect. Though she began to think and write about woman's status during the American Revolution, her first published essay did not appear until 1784. Murray argued that women and men had equal intellectual capacities, though women's inadequate education might make them seem to be less intelligent. "We can only reason

Judith Sargent Murray on education

from what we know," she declared, "and if an opportunity of acquiring knowledge hath been denied us, the inferiority of our sex cannot fairly be deduced from thence." Therefore, concluded Murray, boys and girls should be offered equivalent scholastic training. She further contended that girls should be taught to support themselves by their own efforts: "Independence should be placed within their grasp." Because she rejected the prevailing notion that a young woman's chief goal in life should be finding a husband, Judith Sargent Murray deserves the title of the first American feminist. (That distinction is usually accorded to better-known nineteenth-century women like Margaret Fuller or Sarah Grimké.)

By 1800, therefore, the struggle for political independence had prompted Americans to think about their society and culture in new ways. The process of breaking away from their colonial origins had already had a profound influence on the arts. Americans were also attempting to ensure their nation's future by instructing their children–and themselves–in the principles of virtue and morality. All their efforts would prove useless, though, if the new federal government was not placed on a sound footing.

Building a workable government

In 1788 Americans celebrated the ratification of the Constitution with a series of parades, held in many cities on the Fourth of July. The processions were carefully planned to symbolize the unity of the new nation and to recall its history to the minds of the watching throngs. The Philadelphia parade, planned largely by Charles Willson Peale, was more or less typical.

About 5,000 people participated in the procession, which stretched for a mile and a half and lasted three hours. Twelve costumed "axe-men" representing the first pioneers were followed by a mounted military troop and a group of men with flags symbolizing independence, the peace treaty, the French alliance, and other revolutionary events. A band played a "Federal March" composed for the occasion. There followed a Constitution float, displaying a large framed copy of the Constitution and a thirteen-foot-high eagle. A number of local dignitaries marched in front of the next float, "The Grand Federal Edifice," a domed structure supported by thirteen columns (three of which were left unfinished to signify the states that had not yet ratified).

The remainder of the parade consisted of groups of artisans and professionals marching together and dramatizing their work. One of the farmers scattered seed in the streets; on the manufacturers' float, cloth was being made; the printers operated a press, distributing copies of a poem written to honor the Constitution. More than forty other groups of tradesmen, such as barbers, hatters, and clockmakers, sponsored similar floats. The artisans were followed by lawyers, doctors, clergymen of all denominations, and congressmen. Bringing up the rear was a symbol of the nation's future, a contingent of students from the University of Pennsylvania and other city schools. Marching with their teachers, they carried a flag labelled "The Rising Generation."

The nationalistic spirit expressed in the ratification processions carried over into the first session of Congress. In the congressional elections, held late in 1788, only a few Antifederalists had run or been elected to office. Thus the First Congress was composed chiefly of men who were considerably more inclined toward a strong national government than had been the delegates to the Constitutional Convention. Since the Constitution had deliberately left many key issues undecided, the nationalists' domination of Congress meant that their views on those points quickly prevailed.

First Congress

Congress faced four immediate problems when it convened in April 1789: raising revenue to support the new government, responding to the state ratification conventions' calls for amendments to the Constitution, establishing executive departments, and organizing the federal judiciary. The latter task was especially important. The Constitution declared only that there should be a Supreme Court and other lower federal courts, leaving it to Congress to work out not just the details of the national judiciary but also its basic structure.

The Virginian James Madison, who had been elected to the House of Representatives, soon became as influential in Congress as he had been at the Philadelphia convention. Only a few months into the session, he persuaded Congress to impose a tariff on certain imported goods. Consequently, the First Congress quickly achieved what the Confederation Congress never had: an effective national tax law. The new government was to have its problems, but lack of sufficient revenue was not one of them.

Madison also took the lead on the issue of constitutional amendments. At the convention and thereafter, he had consistently opposed additional limitations on the national government on the grounds that it was unnecessary to guarantee the people's rights when the government was one of limited, delegated powers. But Madison recognized that public opinion, as expressed by the state ratifying conventions, was against him, and accordingly placed nineteen proposed amendments before the House. Congress eventually sent twelve amendments to the states for ratification. Two, having to do with the number of congressmen and their salaries, were not accepted by a sufficient number of states. The other ten amendments officially became part of the Constitution on December 15, 1791. Not for many years, though, did they become known collectively as the Bill of Rights.

Bill of Rights

The first amendment specifically prohibited Congress from passing any law restricting the people's right to freedom of religion, speech, press, peaceable assembly, or petition. The next two arose directly from the former colonists' fear of standing armies as a threat to freedom. The second guaranteed the people's right "to keep and bear arms" because of the need for a "well regulated Militia"; the third defined the circumstances in which troops could be quartered in private homes. The next five amendments pertained to judicial procedures. The fourth amendment prohibited "unreasonable searches and seizures"; the fifth and sixth established the rights of accused persons; the seventh specified the conditions for jury trials in civil, as opposed to criminal, cases; and the eighth forbade "cruel and unusual punishments." Finally, the ninth and tenth amendments reserved to the people and the states other unspecified rights and powers. In short, the authors of the amendments made clear that in listing some rights explicitly they did not mean to preclude the exercise of others.

While debating the proposed amendments, Congress also concerned itself with the organization of the executive branch. It was readily agreed to continue the three administrative departments established under the Articles of Confederation: War, Foreign Affairs (renamed State), and Treasury. Congress also instituted two lesser posts: the attorney general–the nation's official lawyer–and the postmaster general, who would oversee the Post Office. The only serious controversy was whether the president alone could dismiss officials whom he had originally appointed with the consent of the Senate. After some debate, the House and Senate agreed that he had such authority. Thus was established the important principle that the heads of the executive departments are responsible solely to the president. Though it could not have been foreseen at the time, this precedent paved the way for the development of the president's cabinet.

Aside from the constitutional amendments, the most far-reaching piece of legislation enacted by the First Congress was the Judiciary Act of 1789. That act was largely the work of Senator Oliver Ellsworth of Connecticut, a veteran of the Constitutional Convention who in 1796 would become the third chief justice of the United States. The Judiciary Act provided for the Supreme Court to have six members: a chief justice and five associate justices. It also defined the jurisdiction of the federal judiciary and established thirteen district courts and three circuit courts of appeal.

Judiciary Act of 1789

The act's most important provision may have been its section 25, which allowed appeals from state courts to the federal court system when certain types of constitutional issues were raised. This section was intended to implement Article VI of the Constitution, which stated that federal laws and treaties were to be considered "the supreme Law of the Land." If Article VI was to be enforced uniformly, the national judiciary clearly had to be able to overturn state court decisions in cases involving the Constitution, federal laws, or treaties. Yet nowhere did the Constitution explicitly permit such action by federal courts. The nationalistic First Congress accepted Ellsworth's argument that the right of appeal from state to federal courts was implied in the wording of Article VI. Eventually, however, judges and legislators committed to the ideal of states' rights were to challenge that interpretation.

During the first decade of its existence, the Supreme Court handled few cases of any importance. Indeed, for its first three years it heard no cases at all.

The first political buttons in the United States were just that—buttons sewn on clothing. These proclaimed the wearer's support of George Washington during his first term in office. Edmund B. Sullivan Collection, University of Hartford.

John Jay, the first chief justice, served only until 1795, and only one of the first five associate justices remained on the bench in 1799. But in a significant 1796 decision, *Ware* v. *Hylton,* the Court—acting on the basis of section 25 of the Judiciary Act of 1789—for the first time declared a state law unconstitutional. That same year it also reviewed the constitutionality of an act of Congress, upholding its validity in the case of *Hylton* v. *US.* The most important case of the decade, *Chisholm* v. *Georgia* (1793), established that states could be freely sued in federal courts by citizens of other states; this decision, unpopular with the states, was overruled five years later by the eleventh amendment to the Constitution.

Domestic policy under Washington and Hamilton

George Washington did not seek the presidency. When he returned to Mount Vernon in 1783, he was eager for the peaceful life of a Virginia planter. He rebuilt his house, redesigned his gardens, experimented with new agricultural techniques, improved the breeding of his livestock, and speculated in western lands. Yet his fellow countrymen never regarded Washington as just another private citizen. Although he took little part in the political maneuverings that preceded the Constitutional Convention, he was unanimously elected its presiding officer. As a result, he did not participate in debates, but he consistently voted for nationalistic positions. Once the proposed structure of the government was presented to the public, Americans concurred that only George Washington had sufficient prestige to serve as the republic's first president. The vote of the electoral college was just a formality.

Election of the first president

Washington was reluctant to return to public life, but knew he could not resist his country's call. Awaiting the summons to New York, he wrote to an old friend, "My movements to the chair of Government will be accompanied by feelings not unlike those of a culprit who is going to the place of his execution. . . . I am sensible, that I am embarking the voice of my Countrymen and a good name of my own, on this voyage, but what returns will be made for them, Heaven alone can foretell."

During his first months in office Washington acted cautiously, knowing that whatever he did would set precedents for the future. He held weekly receptions at which callers could pay their respects, and toured different areas of the country in turn. When the title by which he should be addressed aroused a good deal of controversy (John Adams favored "His Highness, the President of the United States of America, and Protector of their Liberties"), Washington said nothing; the accepted title soon became a plain "Mr. President." Washington also concluded that he should exercise his veto power over congressional legislation very sparingly—only, indeed, if he was convinced a bill was unconstitutional.

Washington's first major task as president was to choose the men who would head the executive departments. For the War Department he selected an old comrade-in-arms, Henry Knox, who had been his reliable general of artillery during much of the Revolution. His choice for the State Department was his fellow Virginian Thomas Jefferson, who had just returned to the United States from his post as ambassador to France. Finally, for the crucial position of secretary of the treasury, the president chose the brilliant, intensely ambitious Alexander Hamilton.

The illegitimate son of a Scottish aristocrat and a woman divorced by her husband for adultery and desertion, Hamilton was born on the British West Indian island of Nevis in 1757. His early years were spent in poverty; after his mother's death when he was eleven, he worked as a clerk for a mercantile firm. In 1773 Hamilton enrolled in King's College (later Columbia University) in New York City; only eighteen months later the precocious seventeen-year-old contributed a major pamphlet to the prerevolutionary publication wars of late 1774. Devoted to the patriot cause, Hamilton volunteered for service in the American army, where he came to the attention of George Washington. In 1777 Washington appointed the young man as one of his aides-de-camp, and the two developed great affection for one another. Indeed, in some respects Hamilton became the son Washington never had.

Alexander Hamilton: his early life

The general's patronage enabled the poor youth of dubious background to marry well. At twenty-three he took as his wife Elizabeth Schuyler, the daughter of a wealthy New York family. After the war, Hamilton practiced law in New York City and served as a delegate first to the Annapolis Convention in 1786 and the following year to the Constitutional Convention. Though he exerted little influence at either convention, his contributions to *The Federalist* in 1788 revealed him to be one of the chief political thinkers in the republic.

In his dual role as secretary of the treasury and one of Washington's major advisors, two traits distinguished Hamilton from most of his contemporaries. First, he displayed an undivided, unquestioning loyalty to the nation as a whole. As a West Indian who had lived on the mainland only briefly before the war, Hamilton had no ties to an individual state. He showed little sympathy for, or understanding of, demands for local autonomy. Thus his fiscal policies aimed always at consolidation of power at the national level. Furthermore, he never feared the exercise of centralized executive authority, as did his older counterparts who had clashed repeatedly with colonial governors.

Second, he regarded his fellow human beings with unvarnished cynicism. Perhaps because of his difficult early life and his own overriding ambition, Hamilton believed people to be motivated primarily, if not entirely, by self-interest—particularly economic self-interest. He placed absolutely no reliance on people's capacity for virtuous and self-sacrificing behavior. That outlook immediately set him apart from other republicans who foresaw a rosy future in which public-spirited citizens would pursue the common good rather than their own private advantage. More important, his beliefs significantly influenced the way in which he tackled the monumental task before him: straightening out the new nation's tangled finances.

In 1789 Congress ordered the new secretary of the treasury to study the state of the public debt and to submit recommendations for supporting the government's credit. Hamilton discovered that the country's remaining war debts fell into three categories: those owed by the United States to foreign governments and investors, mostly to France (about $11 million); those owed by the national government to merchants, former soldiers, holders of revolutionary bonds, and the like (about $27 million); and, finally, similar debts owed by state governments (roughly estimated at $25 million). With respect to the national debt, there was little disagreement: Americans uniformly recognized that if their new government was to succeed it would have to pay the obligations the nation incurred while winning independence.

Alexander Hamilton (1737–1804), painted by John Trumbull in 1792. Hamilton was then at the height of his influence as secretary of the treasury, and his haughty, serene expression reveals his supreme self-confidence. Trumbull, an American student of the English artist Benjamin West, painted the portrait at the request of John Jay. National Gallery of Art, Gift of the Avalon Foundation.

The state debts were quite another matter. Some states–notably Virginia, Maryland, North Carolina, and Georgia–had already paid off most of their war debts. They would oppose the national government's assumption of responsibility for other states' debts, since their citizens would be taxed to pay such obligations in addition to their own. Massachusetts, Connecticut, and South Carolina, on the other hand, still had sizable unpaid debts, and would welcome a system of national assumption. The possible assumption of state debts also had political implications. Consolidation of the debt in the hands of the national government would unquestionably help to concentrate both economic and political power at the national level. A contrary policy would reserve greater independence of action for the states.

Hamilton's "Report on Public Credit," sent to Congress in January 1790, reflected both his national loyalty and his cynicism. It proposed that Congress assume outstanding state debts, combine them with national obligations, and issue new securities covering both principal and accumulated unpaid interest. Current holders of state or national debt certificates would have the option of taking a portion of their payment in western lands.

Hamilton's "Report on Public Credit"

Hamilton's aims were clear: he wanted to expand the financial reach of the United States government and reduce the economic power of the states. He also wanted to ensure that the holders of public securities–many of them wealthy merchants and speculators–would have a significant financial stake in the survival of the national government.

Hamilton's plan stimulated lively debate in Congress. The opposition coalesced around his former ally James Madison. Madison opposed the assumption of state debts, since his own state of Virginia had already paid off most of its obligations. As a congressman tied to agrarian rather than moneyed interests, he opposed the notion that only current holders of public securities should receive payments. Believing with some reason that speculators had purchased large quantities of debt certificates at a small fraction of their face value, Madison proposed that the original holders of the debt also be compensated by the government. But Madison's plan, though probably more just than Hamilton's–in that it would have directly rewarded those people who had actually supplied the revolutionary governments with goods or services–was exceedingly complex and perhaps impossible to administer. The House of Representatives accordingly rejected it.

At first, however, the House also rejected the assumption of state debts. Since the Senate, by contrast, adopted Hamilton's plan largely intact, a series of compromises followed. Hamilton agreed to changes in the assumption plan that would benefit Virginia in particular. The assumption bill also became linked in a complex way to the other major controversial issue of that congressional session: the location of the permanent national capital. Northerners and southerners both wanted the capital in their region. The traditional story that Hamilton and Madison agreed over Jefferson's dinner table to exchange assumption of state debts for a southern site is distorted and simplistic, but in the end the Potomac River was designated as the site for the capital. Simultaneously, the four congressmen from Maryland and Virginia whose districts contained the most likely locations for the new city switched from opposition to support for assumption. As a result, the first part of Hamilton's financial program became law in August 1790.

Four months later Hamilton submitted to Congress a second report on public credit, recommending the chartering of a national bank. Like his proposal for assumption of the debt, this recommendation too aroused considerable opposition. Unlike the earlier debate, which involved matters of policy, this one focused on constitutional issues. It also arose primarily after Congress had already passed the law.

First Bank of the United States

Hamilton modeled his proposed bank on the Bank of England. The Bank of the United States was to be capitalized at $10 million, with only $2 million coming from public funds. The rest would be supplied by private investors. Its charter was to run for twenty years, and one-fifth of its directors were to be named by the government. Its bank notes would circulate as the nation's currency; it would also act as the collecting and disbursing agent for the treasury, and lend money to the government. Most people recognized that such an institution would benefit the country, especially because it would solve the problem of America's perpetual shortage of an acceptable medium of exchange. But there was another issue: did the Constitution give Congress the power to establish such a bank?

James Madison, for one, answered that question with a resounding no. He pointed out that the delegates at the Philadelphia convention had specifically rejected a clause authorizing Congress to issue corporate charters. Consequently, he argued, that power could not be inferred from other parts of the Constitution.

Washington was sufficiently disturbed by Madison's contention that he decided to request other opinions before signing the bill. Edmund Randolph, the attorney general, and Thomas Jefferson, the secretary of state, agreed with Madison that the bank was unconstitutional. Jefferson referred to Article I, section 8 of the Constitution, which gave Congress the power "to make all Laws which shall be necessary and proper for carrying into Execution the foregoing Powers." *Necessary* was the key word, Jefferson argued: Congress could do what was needed but it could not do what was merely desirable without specific constitutional authorization.

Washington asked Hamilton to reply to these negative assessments of his proposal. Hamilton's "Defense of the Constitutionality of the Bank," presented to Washington in February 1791, was a brilliant exposition of what has become known as the broad-con-

Washington's strong response to the Whiskey Rebellion inspired artists to commemorate the event in pictures. Here a soldier says good-bye to his girlfriend before leaving to help put down the rebellion. Historical Society of Pennsylvania.

structionist view of the Constitution. Hamilton argued forcefully that Congress could choose any means not specifically prohibited by the Constitution to achieve a constitutional end. In short, he said, if the end was constitutional and the means was not *un*constitutional, then the means was also constitutional.

Washington was convinced. The bill became law; the bank proved successful. So did the scheme for funding and assumption: the new nation's securities became desirable investments for its own citizens and for wealthy foreigners. But two other aspects of Alexander Hamilton's wide-ranging financial scheme did not fare so well.

In December, Hamilton presented to Congress his "Report on Manufactures," the third and last of his prescriptions for the American economy. In it he outlined an ambitious plan for encouraging and protecting the United States's infant industries, like shoemaking and textile manufacturing. Hamilton argued that the nation could never be truly independent as long as it had to rely heavily on Europe for its manufactured goods. He thus urged Congress to promote the immigration of technicians and laborers, enact protective tariffs, and support industrial development. Although many of Hamilton's ideas were implemented in later decades, few congressmen in 1791 could see much merit in his proposal. They firmly believed that America's future was agrarian. The mainstay of the republic was, after all, the virtuous yeoman farmer. Therefore, Congress rejected the report.

That same year Congress did accept the other part of Hamilton's financial program, an excise tax on whiskey, because of the need for additional government revenues. The tax fell most heavily on New England, where most of the nation's large distilleries were located, and on western farmers. Because transportation over the mountains was difficult and expensive, the frontier-dwellers' most salable "crop" was whiskey made from the corn they raised. Jugs of spirits were, after all, much more easily handled than wagonloads of bulky corn. Whiskey was also much in demand; the citizens of the new nation were already notorious for their heavy consumption of alcohol.

News of the excise law set off immediate protests in frontier areas of Pennsylvania and the Carolinas. But matters did not come to a head until the summer of

Whiskey Rebellion

1794, when western Pennsylvania farmers tried to stop a federal marshal from arresting some men charged with violating the law. The only person killed in the disturbances was a leader of the rioters, but President Washington was determined to prevent a recurrence of Shays' Rebellion. On August 7, he issued a proclamation calling on the insurgents to disperse by September 1, and he summoned more than 12,000 militia from Pennsylvania and neighboring states. By the time the federal forces marched westward in October and November (headed some of the time by Washington himself), the riots had long since ended. The troops, who met with no resistance, arrested a number of suspects. Only two were ever convicted of treason, and Washington pardoned both. The rebellion, such as it was, ended almost without bloodshed.

The chief importance of the Whiskey Rebellion was not military victory over the rebels–for there was none–but rather the message it forcefully conveyed to the American public. The national government, Washington had demonstrated, would not allow violent organized resistance to its laws. In the new republic, change would be effected peacefully, by legal means. Those who were dissatisfied with the law should try to amend or repeal it, not take extralegal action.

By 1794, a group of Americans had already begun to seek change systematically within the confines of electoral politics, even though traditional political theory regarded organized opposition–especially in a republic–as illegitimate. The leaders of the opposition were Thomas Jefferson and James Madison, who became convinced as early as 1792 that Hamilton and his supporters intended to impose a corrupt, aristocratic government on the United States. Jefferson and Madison justified their opposition to Hamilton and his policies by contending that they were the true heirs of the revolution, whereas Hamilton was actually plotting to subvert republican principles. To emphasize their point, they and their followers in Congress began calling themselves *Republicans.* Hamilton in turn accused Jefferson and Madison of the same crime: attempting to destroy the republic. To legitimize their claim to being the rightful interpreters of the Constitution, Hamilton and his supporters called themselves *Federalists.* In short, each group accused the other of being an illicit faction. (A faction was, in the traditional sense of the term, by definition opposed to the public good.)

At first, President Washington tried to remain aloof from the political dispute that divided his chief advisors, Hamilton and Jefferson. Even so, the controversy helped to persuade him to seek a second term of office in 1792 in hopes of promoting political unity. But in 1793 and thereafter, a series of developments in foreign affairs magnified the disagreements.

The beginnings of partisan politics

The first years under the Constitution were blessed by international peace. Eventually, however, the French Revolution, which began in 1789, brought about the resumption of hostilities between France, America's wartime ally, and Great Britain, America's most important trading partner.

At first, Americans welcomed the news that France was turning toward republicanism. The French people's success in limiting, then overthrowing, the monarchy seemed to vindicate the United States revolution. Now more than ever, Americans could see themselves as being in the vanguard of an inevitable historical trend that would reshape the world for the better. But by the early 1790s the reports from France were disquieting. Outbreaks of violence continued, ministries succeeded each other with bewildering rapidity, and executions were commonplace. The king himself was beheaded in early 1793. Although many Americans, including Jefferson and Madison, retained their sympathy for the French revolutionaries, others began to view France as a prime example of the perversion of republicanism. As might be expected, Alexander Hamilton fell into the latter group.

At that juncture, France declared war on Britain, Spain, and Holland. The Americans thus faced a dilemma. The 1778 treaty with France bound them to that nation "forever," and a mutual commitment to republicanism created ideological bonds. Yet the United States was connected to Great Britain as well. Aside from sharing a common history and language, America and England were economic partners. Americans still purchased most of their manufactured goods from Great Britain and sold their own produce chiefly in British and British colonial markets. Indeed, since the Hamiltonian financial system depended heavily on import tariffs as a source of revenue, and America's imports came primarily from Britain, the nation's economic health in effect required uninterrupted trade with the former mother country.

The political and diplomatic climate was further complicated in April 1793, when Citizen Edmond Genet, a representative of the French government, landed in Charleston. As Genet made his leisurely way northward toward New York City, he was wildly cheered and lavishly entertained at every stop. En route, he recruited Americans for expeditions against British and Spanish possessions in the Western Hemisphere and distributed privateering commissions with a generous hand. Genet's arrival raised a series of key questions for President Washington. Should he receive Genet, thus officially recognizing the French revolutionary government? Should he acknowledge the United States obligation to aid France under the terms of the 1778 treaty? Or should he proclaim American neutrality in the conflict?

Citizen Genet

For once, Hamilton and Jefferson saw eye to eye. Both told Washington that the United States could not afford to ally itself firmly with either side. Washington agreed; thus he received Genet officially, but also issued a proclamation informing the world that the United States would adopt "a conduct friendly and impartial toward the belligerent powers." In deference to Jefferson's continued support for France, the word *neutrality* did not appear in the declaration—but its meaning was nevertheless clear.

Genet himself was removed as a factor in Franco-American relations at the end of the summer. His faction, the Girondists, fell from power in Paris, and instead of returning home to face almost-certain execution he sought political asylum in the United States. But his disappearance from the diplomatic scene did not lessen the continuing impact of the French Revolution in America. The domestic divisions Genet helped to widen were perpetuated by clubs called Democratic-Republican societies, formed by Americans sympathetic to the French Revolution and worried about trends in the Washington administration. The societies thus expressed grass-roots concern about the same developments that troubled Jefferson and Madison.

Democratic-Republican societies

More than forty Democratic-Republican societies were organized between 1793 and 1800, in both rural and urban areas. Their members saw themselves as heirs of the Sons of Liberty, seeking the same goal as their predecessors: protection of the people's liberties against encroachments by corrupt and evil rulers. To that end, they publicly protested government policies and published "addresses to the people" warning of impending tyranny. The societies repeatedly proclaimed their belief in "the equal rights of man," stressing in particular the rights to free speech, free press, and assembly. Like the Sons of Liberty, the Democratic-Republican societies were composed chiefly of artisans and craftsmen of various kinds, although professionals, farmers, and merchants also joined.

The rapid growth of such groups, outspoken in their criticism of the Washington administration for its failure to come to the aid of France and for its domestic economic policies, deeply disturbed Hamilton and eventually Washington himself. Newspapers sympathetic to the Federalists charged that the societies were subversive agents of a foreign power. Their "real design," one asserted, was "to involve the country in war, to assume the reins of government and tyrannize over the people." The climax of the attack came in the fall of 1794, when Washington accused the societies of having fomented the Whiskey Rebellion.

In retrospect, Washington's and Hamilton's reaction to the Democratic-Republican societies seems hysterical, overwrought, and entirely out of proportion to whatever challenge they may have posed to the administration. But it must be kept in mind that "faction" was believed to be dangerous to the survival of a republic. In a monarchy, opposition groups were to be expected, even encouraged. In a government of the people, though, serious and sustained disagreement was taken as a sign of corruption and subversion. The Democratic-Republican societies were the first formally organized political dissenters in the United States. As such, they aroused the fear and suspicion of elected officials who had not yet accepted the idea that one component of a free government was an organized loyal opposition.

That same year George Washington decided to send Chief Justice John Jay to England to try to reach agreement on four major unresolved questions affecting Anglo-American affairs. Jay's diplomatic mission had important domestic consequences. The first point at issue was recent British seizures of American merchant ships trading in the French West Indies. The United States wanted to establish the principle of freedom of the seas and to assert its right, as a neutral nation, to trade freely with both sides. Second, Great Britain had not yet carried out its promise in the Treaty of Paris (1783) to evacuate its posts in the American Northwest. Western settlers believed that the British were responsible for the renewed Indian warfare in the region (see pages 154–156), and they wanted that threat removed. Third and fourth, the Americans hoped for a commercial treaty and sought compensation for the slaves who had left with the British army at the end of the war.

Jay Treaty

The negotiations in London proved difficult, since Jay had little to offer Britain in exchange for the concessions he wanted. In the end, Britain did agree to evacuate the western forts and ease the restrictions on American trade to England and the West Indies. (Some limitations were retained, however, violating the Americans' stated commitment to open commerce.) No compensation for lost slaves was agreed to, but Jay accepted a provision establishing an arbitration commission to deal with the matter of prewar debts owed to British creditors. A similar commission was to handle the question of compensation for the seizures of American merchant ships. Under the circumstances, Jay had done remarkably well: the treaty averted war with England at a time when the United States, which lacked an effective navy, could not have hoped to win a conflict with its former mother country. Nevertheless, most Americans, including the president, were dissatisfied with at least some parts of the treaty.

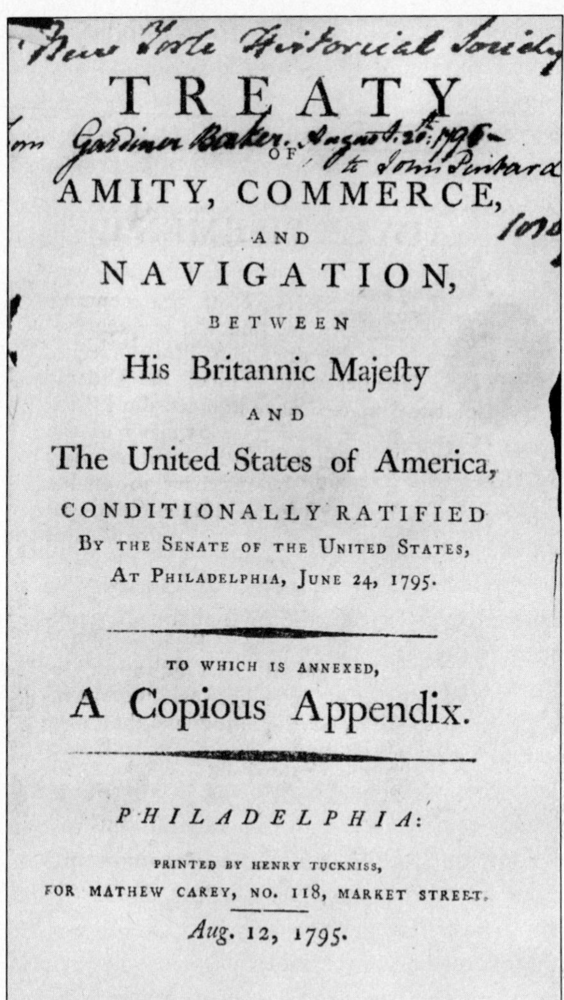
TREATY
OF
AMITY, COMMERCE,
AND
NAVIGATION,
BETWEEN
His Britannic Majesty
AND
The United States of America,
CONDITIONALLY RATIFIED
BY THE SENATE OF THE UNITED STATES,
AT PHILADELPHIA, JUNE 24, 1795.

TO WHICH IS ANNEXED,
A Copious Appendix.

PHILADELPHIA:
PRINTED BY HENRY TUCKNISS,
FOR MATHEW CAREY, NO. 118, MARKET STREET.
Aug. 12, 1795.

Title page of the Jay Treaty. Publication of the document after its secret ratification by the Senate aroused widespread protest against its terms. The House of Representatives tried but failed to halt its implementation. The New-York Historical Society.

At first, however, potential opposition was blunted, because the Senate debated and ratified the treaty in secret. Not until after it was formally approved on June 24, 1795, was the public informed of its provisions. The Democratic-Republican societies led protests against the treaty, which were especially intense in the South. Planters criticized Jay's failure to obtain compensation for runaway slaves as well as the commitment to repay prewar debts. Once President Washington had reluctantly signed the treaty, though, there seemed to be little the Republicans could do to prevent it from taking effect. Just one opportunity remained: Congress had to appropriate funds to carry out the treaty provisions, and according to the Constitution money bills had to originate in the House of Representatives.

When the House took up the issue in March 1796, opponents of the treaty tried to prevent approval of the appropriations. To that end, they called on Washington to submit to the House all documents pertinent to the negotiations. In successfully resisting the House's request, Washington developed the doctrine of executive privilege—that is, the power of the president to withhold information from Congress if he believes circumstances warrant doing so. Although the treaty's opponents initially appeared to be in the majority, pressure for approval built as time passed. Frontier residents were eager for evacuation of the British posts, fearing a new outbreak of Indian war despite the signing of the Treaty of Greenville the previous year (see page 155). Merchants wanted to reap the benefits of widened trade with the British Empire. Furthermore, Thomas Pinckney of South Carolina had negotiated a popular treaty with Spain giving the United States navigation privileges on the Mississippi, which would be an economic boost to the West and South. Federalist senators threatened not to ratify Pinckney's Treaty if the Jay Treaty appropriations were defeated. For all these reasons the House on April 30, 1795, voted the necessary funds by the narrow margin of 51 to 48.

Analysis of the vote reveals both the regional nature of the division and the growing cohesion of the Republican and Federalist factions in Congress. Voting in favor of the appropriations were 44 Federalists and 7 Republicans; voting against were 45 Republicans and 3 Federalists. The final tally was also split by region. The vast majority of votes against the bill were cast by southerners (including the three Federalists, who were Virginians). The bill's supporters were largely from New England and the middle states, with the exception of two South Carolina Federalists. The seven Republicans who broke ranks with their faction to vote for the appropriations were from commercial areas in New York, Pennsylvania, and Maryland.

Republicans and Federalists

The small number of defectors revealed a new force at work in American politics: partisanship. Voting statistics from the first four congresses show the ever-increasing tendency of members of the House of Representatives to vote as coherent groups, rather than as individuals. If factional loyalty is defined as voting together at least two-thirds of the time on national issues, the percentage of nonaligned congressmen dropped from 42 percent in 1790 to just 7 percent in 1796. Also, the majority slowly shifted from Federalist to Republican. Federalists controlled the first three congresses, through spring 1795; Republicans gained the ascendancy in the Fourth Congress; Federalists returned to power with slight majorities in the Fifth and Sixth Congresses; and the Republicans took over in the Seventh Congress in 1801.

To describe these shifts is easier than to explain them. The growing division cannot be accurately explained in the terms used by Jefferson and Madison (aristocrats versus the people) or by Hamilton and Washington (true patriots versus subversive rabble). Simple economic differences between agrarian and commercial interests do not provide the answer either, since more than 90 percent of Americans in the 1790s lived in rural areas. Yet certain distinctions can be made. Republicans tended to be self-assured, confident, and optimistic about both politics and the economy. They did not fear instability, at least among the white population, and they sought to widen the people's participation in government. They foresaw a prosperous future, and looked first to the United States's own resources, second to her position in the world. Republicans also remained sympathetic to France in international affairs.

Federalists, on the other hand, were insecure, uncertain of the future. They stressed the need for order, authority, and regularity in the political world. Unlike Republicans, they had no grass-roots political organization and put little emphasis on involving ordinary people in government. The nation was, in their eyes, perpetually threatened by potential enemies, both internal and external, and best protected by a continuing alliance with Great Britain. Their vision of international affairs may have been more accurate, given the warfare in Europe, but it was also narrow and unattractive. Since it held out little hope of a better future to the voters of any region, it is not surprising that the Republicans eventually became dominant.

If the factions' respective attitudes are translated into economic and regional affiliations, the pattern is clear. Northern merchants and commercially oriented farmers, well aware of the uncertainties of international trade, tended to be Federalists. Since New England's soil was poor and agricultural production could not be expanded, northern subsistence farmers also gravitated toward the more conservative party, which wanted to preserve the present (and past) rather than look to the future.

Republican southern planters, on the other hand, firmly in control of their region and of a class of enslaved laborers, could anticipate unlimited westward expansion. Many Tidewater planters successfully shifted from cultivating soil-draining tobacco to grains and other foodstuffs. The invention of the cotton gin in 1793 allowed them to plant many more acres of cotton (see Chapter 10). For their part, small farmers in the South found the Republicans' democratic rhetoric (despite aristocratic leadership) more congenial than the approach of the Federalists, who said and did little to attract the allegiance of such folk.

Finally, the two sides drew supporters from different ethnic groups. Americans of English stock tended to be Federalists, while those of Celtic origin (Welsh, Irish, Scots) were more likely to be Republicans. The third largest group, the Germans, were split fairly evenly at first but eventually moved into the Republican camp. To what degree traditional antagonisms between English and Celts in particular contributed to the growing political split is impossible to say. But since patterns of migration to and within America (see pages 61–64) rendered regional and ethnic lines largely parallel, it is conceivable that ethnicity was as important as other factors in determining eventual political alignments.

The presence of the two organized groups, not yet parties in the modern sense but nonetheless active contenders for office, made the presidential election of 1796 the first that was seriously contested. George Washington, tired of the criticism to which he had been subjected, decided to retire from office. (Presidents had not yet been limited to two terms by constitutional amendment.) In September Washington published his famous "Farewell Address," most of which was written by Hamilton. Washington outlined two principles that guided American foreign policy at least until the late 1940s: maintain commercial but not political ties to other nations and enter no permanent alliances. He also drew a sharp distinction between the United States and Europe, stressing America's uniqueness and the need for independent action.

Domestically, Washington lamented the existence of factional divisions among his fellow countrymen. His call for an end to partisan strife has often been interpreted by historians as the statement of a man who could see beyond political affiliations to the good of the whole. But it is more accurately read in the context of its day as an attack on the legitimacy of the Republican opposition. What Washington wanted was unity behind the Federalist banner, which he saw as the only proper political stance. The Federalists (like the Republicans) continued to see themselves as the sole guardians of the truth, the only true heirs of the Revolution, and they perceived their opponents as misguided, unpatriotic troublemakers.

Election of 1796

To succeed Washington, the Federalists put forward the candidacy of Vice President John Adams, with the diplomat Thomas Pinckney of South Carolina as his vice-presidential running mate. The Republicans in Congress chose Thomas Jefferson as their candidate; the lawyer, revolutionary war veteran, and active Republican politician Aaron Burr of New York agreed to run for vice president.

That the election was contested did not mean that its outcome was decided by the people. Voters could cast their ballots only for electors, not for the candidates themselves. Many voters did not even have that opportunity, since more than 40 percent of the members of the electoral college that year were chosen by state legislatures, some even before the candidates had been selected. Furthermore, the method of voting prescribed for the electoral college by the Constitution tended to work against the new factions,

This Federalist political cartoon was probably drawn shortly after the presidential election of 1796. Jefferson kneels in front of the altar of French despotism, kindling a fire from the controversial writings of radicals. He is stopped from adding the Constitution to the flames by an American eagle—meant to symbolize John Adams, whose election has saved the nation from disorder. The Library Company of Philadelphia.

which was not surprising, since the authors of the Constitution had not foreseen the development of opposing national political organizations. Members of the electoral college were required to vote for two persons, without specifying the office. The man with the highest total became president; the second highest became vice president. In other words, there was no way an elector could explicitly support one person for president and another for vice president.

This procedure proved to be the Federalists' undoing. Adams won the presidency with 71 votes, but a number of Federalist electors (especially those from New England) failed to cast ballots for Pinckney. Thomas Jefferson won 68 votes, 9 more than Pinckney, and became vice president. The incoming administration was thus politically divided. The next four years were to see the new president and vice president, once allies and close friends, become bitter enemies.

John Adams and political dissent

John Adams took over the presidency peculiarly blind to the partisan developments of the past four years. As president he never abandoned the outdated notion George Washington had discarded as early as 1794: that the president should be above politics, an independent and dignified figure who did not seek petty factional advantage. Thus Adams kept Washington's cabinet intact, despite its key members' allegiance to his chief rival, Alexander Hamilton. He often adopted a passive posture, letting others (usually Hamilton) take the lead, when he should have acted decisively. As a result his administration gained a reputation for inconsistency. When Adams's term ended, the Federalists were severely divided and the Republicans had won the presidency. But at the same time Adams's detachment from Hamilton's maneuverings enabled him to weather the greatest international crisis the republic had yet faced: the so-called Quasi-War with France.

The Jay Treaty improved America's relationship with England, but it provoked retaliation from France. Angry that the United States had, in effect, abandoned the 1778 French-American treaty, the Directory (the coalition then in power in Paris) ordered French vessels to seize American ships carrying British goods. In response, Adams appointed three special commissioners to try to reach a settlement with France: Elbridge Gerry, an old friend from Massachusetts; John Marshall, a Virginia Federalist; and Charles Cotesworth Pinckney of South Carolina, Thomas's older brother. At the same time Congress increased military spending, authorizing the building of ships and the stockpiling of weapons and ammunition.

XYZ Affair

For months, the American commissioners futilely sought to open negotiations with Talleyrand, the French foreign minister. But Talleyrand's agents demanded a bribe of $250,000 before talks could begin. The Americans retorted, "No, no; not a sixpence," and reported the incident in dispatches that President Adams received in early March 1798. Adams informed Congress of the impasse and recommended increased appropriations for defense.

Convinced that Adams had deliberately sabotaged the negotiations, congressional Republicans insisted that the dispatches be turned over to Congress. Aware that releasing the reports would work to his advantage, Adams complied. He withheld only the names of the French agents, referring to them as X, Y, and Z. The revelation that the Americans had been treated with utter contempt by the Directory stimulated a wave of anti-French sentiment in the United States. A journalist's version of the commissioners' reply, "Millions for defense, but not a cent for tribute," became the national slogan. Cries for war filled the air. Congress formally abrogated the 1778 treaty and authorized American ships to seize French vessels.

The Republicans, who opposed war and continued to sympathize with France, could do little to stem the tide. Since Agent Y had boasted of the existence of a "French party in America," Federalists flatly accused the Republicans of traitorous designs. A New York newspaper declared that anyone who remained "lukewarm" after reading the XYZ dispatches was a "criminal—and the man who does not warmly reprobate the conduct of the French must have a soul black enough to be *fit* for *treason Strategems* and *spoils.*" John Adams wavered between calling the Republicans traitors and acknowledging their right to oppose administration measures. His wife was less tolerant: "Those whom the French boast of as their Partizans," Abigail Adams told her older sister, deserved to be "adjudged traitors to their country." If Jefferson had been president, she observed, "we should all have been sold to the French."

The Federalists saw this climate of opinion as an opportunity to deal a death blow to their Republican opponents. Now that the country seemed to see the truth of what they had been saying ever since the Whiskey Rebellion in 1794—that the Republicans were subversive foreign agents—the Federalists sought to codify that belief into law. In the spring and summer of 1798, the Federalist-controlled Congress adopted a set of four laws known as the Alien and Sedition Acts, intended to suppress dissent and prevent further growth of the Republican party.

Three of the acts were aimed at immigrants, whom the Federalists quite correctly suspected of being Republican in their sympathies. The Naturalization Act lengthened the residency period required for citizenship from five to fourteen years and ordered all resident aliens to register with the federal government. The Alien Enemies Act provided for the detention of enemy aliens in time of war. The Alien Friends Act, which was to be in effect for only two years, gave the president almost unlimited authority to deport any alien he deemed dangerous to the nation's security. (Adams never used that authority. The Alien Enemies Act was not implemented either, since war was never formally declared.)

Alien and Sedition Acts

The fourth law, the Sedition Act, sought to control both citizens and aliens. It outlawed conspiracies to prevent the enforcement of federal laws and set the maximum punishment for such offenses at five years in prison and a $5,000 fine. The act also tried to control speech. Writing, printing, or uttering "false, scandalous and malicious" statements "against the government of the United States, or the President of the United States, with intent to defame . . . or to bring them or either of them, into contempt or disrepute" became a crime punishable by as much as two years imprisonment and a fine of $2,000. Today the Supreme Court would declare unconstitutional any such law punishing speech alone. But in the eighteenth century, when organized political opposition was regarded with suspicion, the Sedition Act was legally acceptable.

In all, there were fifteen indictments and ten convictions under the Sedition Act. Most of the accused were outspoken Republican newspaper editors who failed to mute their criticism of the administration in response to the law. But the first victim—whose story may serve as an example of the rest—was a Republican congressman from Vermont, Matthew Lyon. The Irish-born Lyon, a former indentured servant who had purchased his freedom and fought in the Revolution, was indicted for declaring in print that John Adams had displayed "a continual grasp for power" and "an unbounded thirst for ridiculous pomp, foolish adulation, and selfish avarice." Though convicted, fined $1,000, and sent to prison for four months, Lyon was not silenced. He conducted his re-election campaign from jail, winning an overwhelming majority. The fine, which he could not afford, was ceremoniously paid by contributions from leading Republicans around the country.

Faced with the prosecutions of their major supporters, Jefferson and Madison sought an effective means of combating the Alien and Sedition Acts. Petitioning the Federalist-controlled Congress to repeal the laws

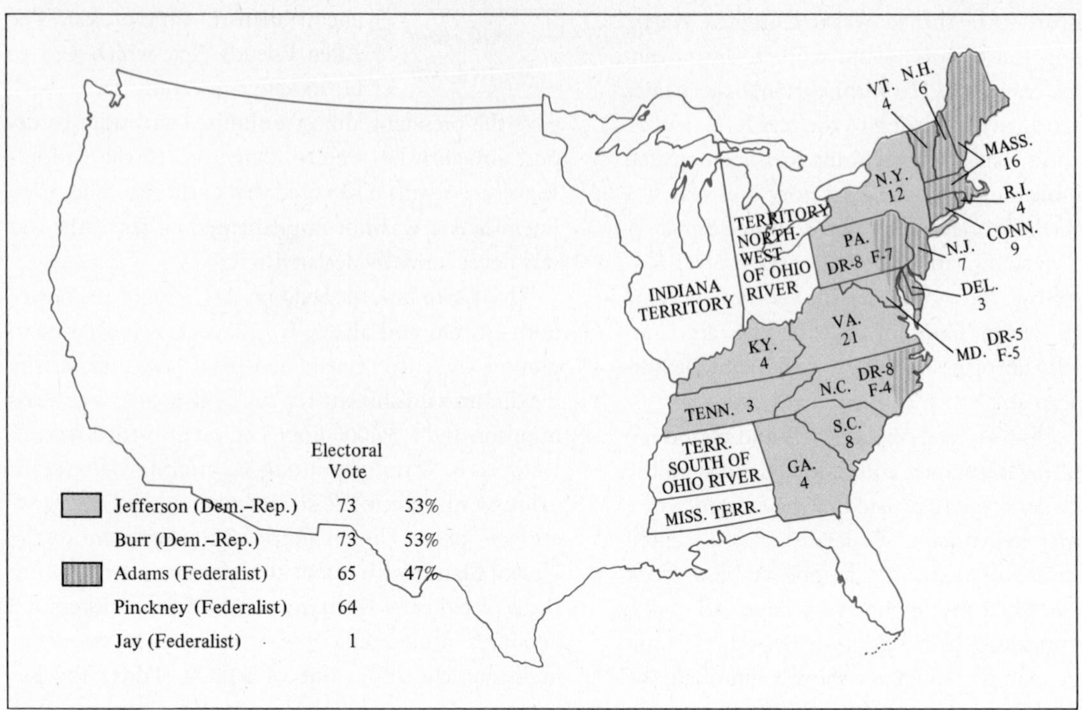

Presidential election, 1800

would clearly do no good. Furthermore, Federalist judges refused to allow accused persons to question the Sedition Act's constitutionality. Accordingly, the Republican leaders turned to the only other possible mechanism for protest: the state legislatures. Carefully concealing their own role (it would hardly have been desirable for the vice president to be indicted for sedition), Jefferson and Madison each drafted a set of resolutions. Introduced into the Kentucky and Virginia legislatures respectively in the fall of 1798, the resolutions differed somewhat but their import was the same. Since the Constitution was created by a compact among the states, they contended, the people speaking through their states had a legitimate right to judge the constitutionality of actions by the federal government. Both sets of resolutions pronounced the Alien and Sedition Acts unconstitutional and asked other states to join in the protest.

Although no other state replied positively to the Virginia and Kentucky resolutions, they nevertheless had major significance. In the first place, they were superb political propaganda, rallying Republican opinion throughout the country. They placed the opposition party squarely in the revolutionary tradition of resistance to tyrannical authority. Second, the theory of union they proposed was expanded on by southern states'-rights advocates in the 1830s and thereafter. Jefferson and Madison had identified a key constitutional issue: how far could the states go in opposing the national government? How could a conflict between the two be resolved? These questions were not to be finally answered until 1865.

Ironically, just as the Sedition Act was being implemented and northern state legislatures were rejecting the Virginia and Kentucky resolutions, Federalists split badly over the course of action the United States should take toward France. Hamilton and his supporters still called for a declaration legitimizing the undeclared naval war the two nations had been waging for months. But Adams had received a number of private signals that the Directory now regretted its treatment of the three American commissioners. Acting on these assurances, he dispatched the envoy William Vans Murray to Paris. In September 1800 Murray reached agreement with Napoleon Bonaparte, who had seized power in France, thus ending the threat of war. The results of the negotiations were not known in the United States until after the presidential election of

Although the camp meeting shown here occurred in the later years of the Second Great Awakening, the scene was typical of the period. Note the preponderance of women in the crowd. The New-York Historical Society.

1800. Even so, Adams's decision to seek a peaceful settlement probably cost him re-election because of the divisions it caused in Federalist ranks.

Election of 1800

In sharp contrast, the Republicans entered the 1800 presidential race firmly united behind the Jefferson-Burr ticket. Though they won the election, their lack of foresight almost cost them dearly. The problem was caused by the system of voting in the electoral college, which the Federalists understood more clearly than the Republicans. The Federalists arranged in advance for one of their electors to fail to vote for Charles Cotesworth Pinckney, their vice-presidential candidate. John Adams thus received the highest number of Federalist votes (65 to Pinckney's 64). The Republicans failed to make the same distinction between their candidates, and all 73 cast ballots for both Jefferson and Burr (see map). Because neither Republican had a plurality, the Constitution required that the contest be decided in the House of Representatives, with each state's congressmen voting as a unit. Since the new House, dominated by Republicans, would not take office for some months, Federalist congressmen decided the election. It took them thirty-five ballots to decide that Jefferson would be a lesser evil than Burr. As a result of the tangle, the twelfth amendment to the Constitution (1804) changed the method of voting in the electoral college to allow for a party ticket.

Religious dissent and racial ferment

Ever since the fervor of the Great Awakening (see pages 80–82) had burned itself out in the 1760s, America's churches had been largely quiescent. Clergymen, like their congregations, had become preoccupied with secular issues—the Revolution, the Constitution, foreign threats. But in the late 1790s a few revivals began to occur in New England, and in 1800 a full-fledged Second Awakening broke

Second Great Awakening

Mourning scenes like this one were common in women's art during the late eighteenth and early nineteenth centuries. The concern for grieving widows and orphans revealed in such works also found expression in church-sponsored female charitable associations. Museum of Fine Arts, Boston, M. and M. Karolik Collection.

out in Kentucky and Tennessee. Itinerant Presbyterian and Methodist ministers spread over the countryside, carrying the word of salvation to all who would listen.

Frontier folk, for the most part poor, uneducated, and rootless, were particularly receptive to the enthusiastic preachers. At camp meetings, sometimes attended by thousands of people and usually lasting from three days to a week, clergymen exhorted their audiences to repent their sins and become genuine Christians. They stressed that salvation was open to all, downplaying the doctrine of predestination that had characterized orthodox colonial Protestantism. The emotional nature of the conversion experience was emphasized far more than the need for careful study and preparation. Such preachers thus brought the message of religion to the people in more ways than one. They were in effect "democratizing" American religion, making it available to all rather than to a preselected and educated elite.

The most famous camp meeting took place at Cane Ridge, Kentucky, in 1801. At a time when the largest settlement in the state had no more than 2,000 inhabitants, attendance at Cane Ridge was estimated at from 10,000 to 25,000. One witness, a Presbyterian cleric, marvelled that "no sex nor color, class nor description, were exempted from the pervading influence of the spirit; even from the age of eight months to sixty years, there were evident subjects of this marvellous operation." He went on to recount how people responded to the preaching with "loud ejaculations of prayer, . . . some struck with terror, . . . others, trembling, weeping and crying out . . . fainting and swooning away, . . . others surrounding them with melodious songs, or fervent prayers for their happy resurrection, in the love of Christ." Such scenes

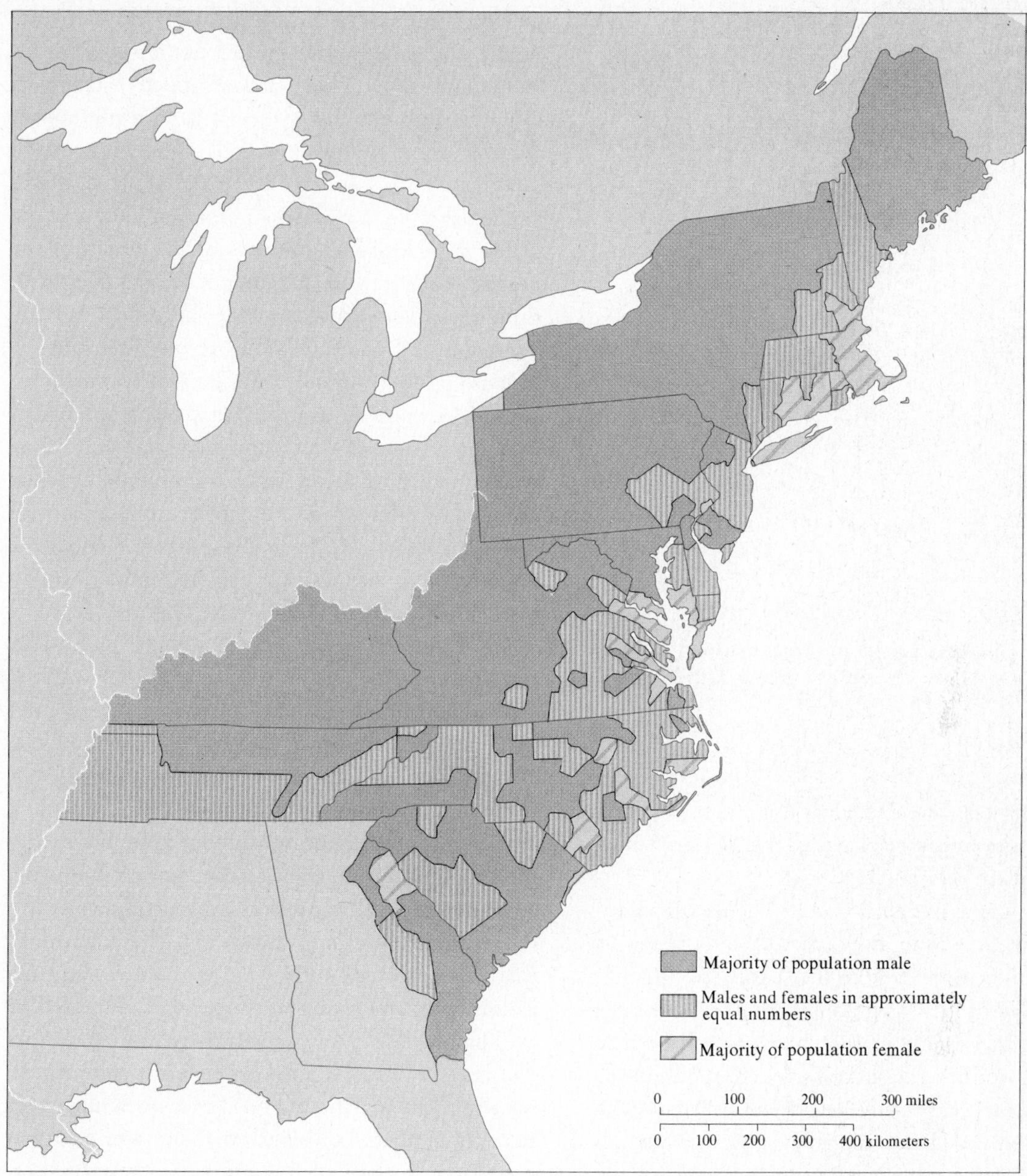

Sex ratio of white population, 1790

were to be repeated many times in the decades that followed. Revivals swept across different regions of the country until nearly the middle of the century, leaving an indelible legacy of evangelism to American Protestant churches.

The revivals also led to increasingly female church congregations. Unlike the First Great Awakening, when converts were evenly divided by sex, more women than men–particularly young women–answered the call of Christianity during the Second Awakening. The increase in female converts seems to have been directly related to major changes in women's circumstances at the end of the eighteenth century. In some areas of the country, especially New England (where the revival movement flourished), women outnumbered men after 1790, since many men had migrated westward in search of land (see map). Thus girls could no longer count on finding

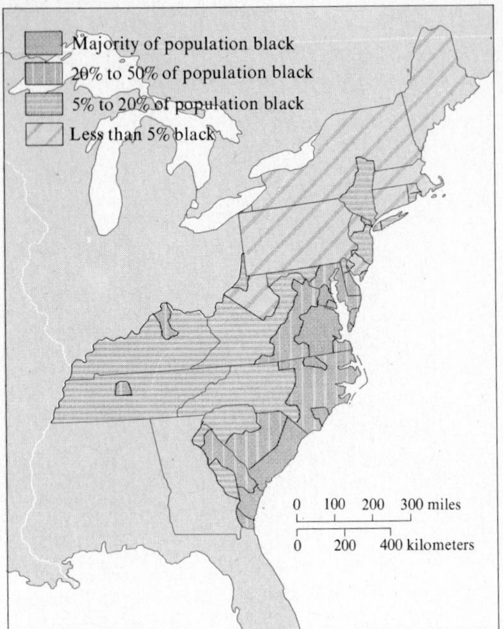

1790 black population: proportion of total population. Source: Reprinted by permission of Princeton University Press.

marital partners. The uncertainty of their social and familial position may well have led them to seek spiritual certainty in the church.

Young women's domestic roles changed dramatically at the same time, as cloth production began to move from the household to the factory (see Chapter 9). Deprived of their chief household role, New England daughters found in the church a realm where they could continue to make useful contributions to society. Church missionary societies and charitable associations provided an acceptable outlet for their talents. One of the most striking developments of the early nineteenth century was the creation of thousands of female associations to aid widows and orphans, collect money for foreign missions, or improve the quality of maternal care.

The religious ferment among both blacks and whites in frontier regions of the upper South contributed to racial ferment as well. People of both races attended the camp meetings, and sometimes black preachers exhorted whites in addition to members of their own race. When revivals spread eastward into more heavily slaveholding areas, white planters became fearful of the egalitarianism implied in the evangelical message of universal salvation and harmony. At the same time, revivals created a group of respected black leaders—preachers—and provided them with a ready audience for a potentially revolutionary doctrine.

Recent events in the West Indies gave whites ample reason for apprehension. In the 1790s, over the course of several years, mulattoes and blacks in the French colony of Saint Domingue (Haiti) overthrew European rule under the leadership of a mulatto, Toussaint L'Ouverture. The revolt was bloody, vicious, prolonged, and characterized by numerous atrocities committed by both sides. In an attempt to prevent the spread of such unrest to their own slaves, southern state legislators passed laws forbidding white Haitian refugees from bringing their slaves with them. But North American blacks learned about the revolt anyway. Furthermore, the preconditions for racial upheaval did not have to be imported into the South from the West Indies: they already existed on the spot.

The Revolution had caused immense destruction in the South, especially in the states south of Virginia. The heavy losses of slaves and constant guerrilla warfare, not to mention the changes in American trading patterns brought about by withdrawal from the British Empire, wreaked havoc on the southern economy. Also, the vast postwar increase in the number of free blacks severely strained the system of race relations that had evolved during the eighteenth century. Color, caste, and slave status no longer coincided, as they had when the few free blacks were all mulattoes (see map). Furthermore, like their white compatriots, blacks (both slave and free) had become familiar with notions of liberty and equality. They had also witnessed the benefits of fighting collectively for freedom, rather than resisting individually or running away. The circumstances were ripe for an explosion, and the Second Awakening was the match that lit the fuse in both Virginia and North Carolina.

Gabriel's Rebellion

The Virginia revolt was planned by Gabriel Prosser, a blacksmith who argued that blacks should fight to obtain the same rights as whites, and who explicitly placed himself in the tradition of the French and Haitian revolutions. At revival meetings led by his brother, Martin, a preacher, Gabriel recruited other blacks like himself—artisans who moved easily in both black and white circles and who lived in semifreedom under minimal white supervision. The artisan leaders then enlisted rural blacks in the cause. The conspirators planned to attack Richmond on the night of August 30, 1800, setting fire to the city, seizing the state capital, and capturing the governor. Their plan showed considerable political sophistication, but heavy rain made it impossible to execute the plot as scheduled. Several whites then learned of the plan from their slaves and spread the alarm. Gabriel avoided capture for some weeks, but most of the other leaders of the rebellion were quickly arrested and interrogated. The major conspirators, including Prosser himself, were hanged, but in the months that followed other insurrectionary scares continued to frighten Virginia slaveowners.

Two years later a similar wave of fear swept North Carolina and the bordering counties of Virginia. A slave conspiracy to attack planters' homes, kill all whites except small children, and seize the land was uncovered in Bertie County. Similar plots were rumored elsewhere. Again, slave artisans and preachers played prominent roles in the planned uprisings. Nearly fifty blacks were executed as a result of the whites' investigations of the rumors. Some were certainly innocent victims of the planters' hysteria, but there can be no doubt about the existence of most of the plots.

As the eighteenth century ended, then, white and black inhabitants of the United States were moving toward an accommodation to their new circumstances. The United States was starting to take shape as an independent nation no longer dependent on England. In domestic politics, the Jeffersonian interpretation of republicanism had prevailed over the Hamiltonian approach. The country would be characterized by a decentralized economy, minimal government (especially at the national level), and maximum freedom of action and mobility for individual white males.

But that freedom would be purchased at the expense of white females and black men, women, and children. In the decades to come, both groups would be subject to further control. To prevent a recurrence of outbreaks of violence like those of 1800 through 1802, slaveholders increased the severity of the slave codes, further restricting their human property. Before long, all talk of emancipation (gradual or other-

Important events

1789	George Washington inaugurated Judiciary Act of 1789 French Revolution
1790	Alexander Hamilton's first "Report on Public Credit"
1791	First National Bank chartered Hamilton's "Report on Manufactures" First ten amendments (Bill of Rights) ratified Haitian revolt begins
1793	France declares war on Britain, Spain, and Holland Neutrality Proclamation Democratic-Republican societies founded Invention of cotton gin *Chisholm* v. *Georgia*
1794	Whiskey Rebellion (Pennsylvania)
1795	Jay Treaty
1796	First contested presidential election: John Adams elected president, Thomas Jefferson vice president *Ware* v. *Hylton*
1798	XYZ affair Alien and Sedition Acts Virginia and Kentucky resolutions Eleventh amendment
1798–99	"Quasi-War" with France
1800	United States and France reach peace agreement Jefferson elected president, Aaron Burr vice president Second Great Awakening begins Gabriel's Rebellion (Virginia) Mason Locke Weems, *Life of Washington*
1804	Twelfth amendment Haiti becomes independent republic

wise) ceased, and slavery became even more firmly entrenched as an economic institution and way of life. Likewise, the Revolution's implicit promise for women was never fully realized. Woman's place was still in the home; in the first half of the nineteenth century an unprecedented outpouring of books and magazine articles asserted that conclusion with ever greater force and fervor. Jeffersonian Republicans, like almost all Americans before them, failed to extend to women the freedom and individuality they recognized as essential for men.

Among Indians as well, the end of the eighteenth century marked an important turning point. The United States had unquestionably established its independence; henceforth, the influence of European powers in the American interior would be negligible. The tribes accordingly had no alternative but to confront directly the problems posed by land-hungry white Americans. West of the Appalachians, the Indians had yet to feel the full force of the whites' westward thrust. East of the mountains, though, the Iroquois–who well knew the difficulty of trying to stop the white flood–were experiencing their own religious awakening on their small, scattered reservations. Led by their prophet, Handsome Lake, they embraced the traditional values of their culture and renounced such destructive white customs as drinking alcohol and playing cards. At the same time, though, they began abandoning their ancient way of life. The traditional economic system based on male hunters and female cultivators gave way to one, like that of the whites, founded on male farming and female housekeeping. The Indians too had come to the end of one path and the beginning of another that would affect their lives, individually and collectively.

Suggestions for further reading

National government and administration

Ralph Adams Brown, *The Presidency of John Adams* (1975); John R. Howe, *The Changing Political Thought of John Adams* (1966); Richard H. Kohn, *Eagle and Sword: The Federalists and the Creation of the Military Establishment in America, 1783–1802* (1975); Stephen G. Kurtz, *The Presidency of John Adams: The Collapse of Federalism, 1795–1800* (1957); Forrest McDonald, *Alexander Hamilton: A Biography* (1979); Forrest McDonald, *The Presidency of George Washington* (1974); John C. Miller, *Alexander Hamilton, Portrait in Paradox* (1959); John C. Miller, *The Federalist Era, 1789–1801* (1960); Merrill D. Peterson, *Thomas Jefferson & The New Nation: A Biography* (1970); Carl E. Prince, *The Federalists and the Origins of the U.S. Civil Service* (1978); Leonard D. White, *The Federalists: A Study in Administrative History* (1948).

Partisan politics

Leland D. Baldwin, *The Whiskey Rebels* (1939); Lance Banning, *The Jeffersonian Persuasion: Evolution of a Party Ideology* (1978); Richard Beeman, *The Old Dominion and the New Nation, 1788–1801* (1972); Richard W. Buel, Jr., *Securing the Revolution: Ideology in American Politics, 1789–1815* (1972); William Nisbet Chambers, *Political Parties in a New Nation: The American Experience, 1776–1809* (1963); Joseph Charles, *The Origins of the American Party System* (1956); Noble E. Cunningham, *The Jeffersonian Republicans: The Formation of Party Organization, 1789–1801* (1957); Manning J. Dauer, *The Adams Federalists* (1953); Paul Goodman, *The Democratic Republicans of Massachusetts* (1964); Richard Hofstadter, *The Idea of a Party System: The Rise of Legitimate Opposition in the United States, 1780–1840* (1970); Adrienne Koch, *Jefferson and Madison: The Great Collaboration* (1950); Eugene P. Link, *Democratic-Republican Societies, 1790–1800* (1942); Norman K. Risjord, *Chesapeake Politics, 1781–1800* (1978); Patricia Watlington, *The Partisan Spirit: Kentucky Politics, 1779–1792* (1972); Alfred F. Young, *The Democratic-Republicans of New York: The Origins, 1763–1797* (1967); John Zvesper, *Political Philosophy and Rhetoric: A Study of the Origins of American Party Politics* (1977).

Diplomacy

Harry Ammon, *The Genet Mission* (1973); Samuel F. Bemis, *Jay's Treaty,* 2nd ed. (1962); Samuel F. Bemis, *Pinckney's Treaty,* 2nd ed. (1960); Jerald A. Combs, *The Jay Treaty* (1970); Alexander DeConde, *Entangling Alliance: Politics and Diplomacy under George Washington* (1958); Alexander DeConde, *The Quasi-War: Politics and Diplomacy of the Undeclared War with France, 1797–1801* (1966); Felix Gilbert, *To the Farewell Address: Ideas of Early American Foreign Policy* (1961); Bradford Perkins, *The First Rapprochement: England and the United States, 1795–1805* (1967); Charles Ritcheson, *Aftermath of Revolution: British Policy Toward the United States, 1783–1795* (1969); Paul A. Varg, *Foreign Policies of the Founding Fathers* (1963).

Civil liberties

Leonard W. Levy, *Legacy of Suppression: Freedom of Speech and Press in Early American History* (1960); Leonard W. Levy, *Origins of the Fifth Amendment* (1968); Robert A. Rutland, *The Birth of the Bill of Rights, 1776–1791* (1955); James Morton Smith, *Freedom's Fetters: The Alien and Sedition Laws and American Civil Liberties* (1956).

Education and culture

Lawrence A. Cremin, *American Education: The National Experience, 1783–1876* (1981); Joseph J. Ellis, *After the Revolution: Profiles of Early American Culture* (1979); Carl F. Kaestle, *The Evolution of an Urban School System: New York City, 1750–1850* (1973); David P. McKay and Richard Crawford, *William Billings of Boston: Eighteenth-Century Composer* (1975); Russel B. Nye, *The Cultural Life of the New Nation: 1776–1803* (1960); Kenneth Silverman, *A Cultural History of the American Revolution* (1976).

Women and blacks

Nancy F. Cott, *The Bonds of Womanhood: "Woman's Sphere" in New England, 1780–1835* (1977); Nancy F. Cott, "Young Women in the Second Great Awakening in New England," *Feminist Studies,* 3, No. 1/2 (1975), 15–29; Jeffrey J. Crow, "Slave Rebelliousness and Social Conflict in North Carolina, 1775 to 1802," *William and Mary Quarterly,* 3rd ser., 37 (1980), 79–102; Gerald W. Mullin, *Flight and Rebellion: Slave Resistance in Eighteenth-Century Virginia* (1972).

the continent, and prevented the United States from being drawn into European politics. The acquisition was the boldest of federal actions and the single most popular achievement of Jefferson's presidency. Yet for Jefferson, the purchase presented a dilemma. It offered fulfillment of the dream of an empire of liberty reaching to the Pacific Coast, "with room enough for our descendants to the hundredth and thousandth generation," as he put it in his second inaugural address. But its legality was questionable. The Constitution gave him no clear authority to acquire new territory and incorporate it into the nation. Jefferson considered requesting a constitutional amendment to allow the purchase, but in the end he justified it on the grounds that it was part of the president's implied powers to protect the nation. The people, he knew, would accept or reject the purchase on election day.

In 1804 the voters expressed their overwhelming approval of Jefferson's action; he and his running mate, George Clinton, rode the wave of popularity to a second term. Charles C. Pinckney and Rufus King, their Federalist opponents, carried only Connecticut and Delaware.

Republicans versus Federalists

Jefferson's re-election was both a personal and a party triumph. The political dissenters of the 1790s had turned their Democratic-Republican societies into a political party–an organization for the purpose of winning elections. More than anything else, opposition to the Federalists had molded and unified them. Indeed, it was where the Federalists were strongest–in New York and Pennsylvania in the 1790s and in New England in the 1800s–that the Republicans had organized most effectively.

Until the Republican successes in 1800 and 1804, Federalists had disdained widespread electioneering. They believed in government by the "best" people–those whose education, wealth, and experience marked them as leaders. For candidates to debate their qualifications before their inferiors–the voters–was unnecessary and undignified. The direct appeals of the Republicans therefore struck them as a subversion of the natural political order.

But after their resounding defeat in 1800, a younger generation of Federalists began to imitate the Republicans. They organized statewide, and led by men like Josiah Quincy, a young congressman from Massachusetts, they began to campaign for popular support. Quincy cleverly identified the Federalists as the people's party, attacking Republicans as autocratic planters. "Jeffersonian Democracy," Quincy satirized in 1804, was "an indian word, signifying '*a great tobacco planter who had herds of black slaves.*' " The self-styled Younger Federalists also exploited westerners' concern about Indians, New Englanders' concern about commerce, and everyone's concern about national strength.

Younger Federalists

In the states where both parties organized and ran candidates, participation in elections increased markedly. In some states more than 90 percent of the eligible voters–nearly all of whom were white males–cast ballots between 1804 and 1816. People became more interested in politics generally, especially at the local level; and as participation in elections increased, the states expanded suffrage.

In response to the new competition, the Republicans introduced the political barbecue, which became the symbol of grassroots campaigning. In New York they roasted oxen; on the New England coast they fried fish and baked clams; in Maryland they served turtles and oysters. The guests washed down their meals with beer and punch and sometimes competed in corn shuckings or horse pulls. Throughout the barbecue, candidates and party leaders spoke from the stump. Oratory was a popular form of entertainment, and the speakers delivered lengthy and uninhibited speeches. They often made wild accusations, which–given the slow speed of communications–might not be answered until after the election. In 1808, for example, a New England Republican accused the Federalists of causing the Boston Massacre.

Soon both parties were using barbecues to appeal directly to voters. Holidays became occasions for partying and electioneering, a practice that helped to make the Fourth of July a day of national celebration and local oratory. But although the Younger Federalists adopted the political barbecue, the Federalist party never fully mastered the art of wooing voters. Older Federalists still opposed such blatant campaigns. And although they were strong in a few states

Citizens gather at the State House in Philadelphia to whip up support for their candidates and parties. This picture, drawn on Election Day in 1816, suggests the overwhelmingly white, exclusively male composition of the electorate. Historical Society of Pennsylvania.

like Connecticut and Delaware, the Federalists never offered the Republicans sustained competition. Divisions between Older and Younger Federalists often hindered them, and the extremism of some Older Federalists tended to discredit the party. A case in point was Timothy Pickering, a Massachusetts congressman and former secretary of state who opposed the Louisiana Purchase, feared Jefferson's re-election, and urged the secession of New England in 1803 and 1804. Pickering won some support among the few Federalists in Congress, but others opposed his plan for a northern confederacy. When Vice President Burr lost his bid to become governor of New York in 1804, the plan collapsed. (Burr, more an opportunist than a loyal Republican, was to have led New York into secession, with the other states to follow.)

Both political parties suffered from factionalism. In 1804, for instance, the Federalist Alexander Hamilton backed a rival Republican faction against Burr in his race for the governorship of New York; Hamilton had caught wind of the Pickering-Burr conspiracy. Burr, his political career in ruins, turned his resentment on Hamilton and challenged him to a duel. The specific insult was Hamilton's description of Burr as dangerous and unfit to hold office. Three years before, Hamilton's son Philip had been killed in a duel when he refused to fire at his opponent. Now, with his own honor at stake, Hamilton accepted Burr's challenge, although he found duelling repugnant. He faced Aaron Burr on July 11, 1804, at Weehawken, New Jersey, and followed his son's lead: he did not fire. Hamilton paid for that decision with his life.

Hamilton-Burr duel

The Burr-Hamilton duel reflected the intensity of party factionalism, which combined with the personal nature of political conflict to keep both Republicans and Federalists from becoming full-blown parties in the modern sense. Where Federalists were too weak to

John Marshall (1755–1835), chief justice of the Supreme Court from 1801 to 1835. This portrait shows the strength of personality that enabled Marshall to make the Court into a Federalist stronghold. Note the head of Solon, an Athenian lawgiver of the sixth century B.C., at the top of the portrait. Supreme Court of the United States.

be a threat, Republicans succumbed to the temptation to fight among themselves. Even Jefferson's congressional leader, John Randolph, abandoned the president in 1806 to start a third party.

Parties also had shallow roots; they tended to organize from the top down, with control resting in a legislative caucus. In Virginia, the Carolinas, and Georgia, there were no statewide elections and hence no statewide parties. Governors were chosen by the legislature, and members of the electoral college and congressmen were elected in districts. Candidates in these states nominated themselves, since party committees and caucuses did not exist. Congressional representatives joined party caucuses in Washington but had no party ties at home.

Thus, although this period is commonly called the era of the first party system, parties as such never fully developed. Competition encouraged party organization, but personal ambition, personality clashes, and local, state, and regional loyalties worked against it. And as the election of 1804 revealed, the Federalists could offer only weak competition at the national level. Indeed, after the death of Alexander Hamilton, only one Federalist played a strong and sustained role in national politics: Chief Justice John Marshall.

John Marshall

Marshall was an astute lawyer who was always to be found on the winning side. A Virginia Federalist who had served under George Washington in the Revolutionary War, he had been minister to France and then secretary of state under President Adams before being named chief justice in the midnight appointments. An autocrat by nature, Marshall nevertheless possessed a grace and openness of manner well suited to the new Republican political style. Under Marshall's domination from 1801 until 1835, the Supreme Court remained a Federalist stronghold even after Republican justices achieved a majority in 1811. Throughout his tenure the Court upheld federal supremacy over the states and protected the interests of commerce and capital.

More important, Marshall made the Court the equal of the other branches of government in practice as well as theory. First, he made a place on the Court a coveted honor. Prior to Marshall it had been difficult to keep the Court filled. Fifteen justices had served on the six-member Court during its first twelve years; after Marshall's appointment it would take 40 years for fifteen new members to be appointed. Marshall's presence had made the Court worthy of ambitious and talented men. Second, he built a unified Court, influencing the justices to issue a single majority opinion rather than individual concurring judgments. Marshall himself became the voice of the majority. From 1801 through 1805 he wrote 24 of the Court's 26 decisions; through 1810 he wrote 85 percent of the 171 opinions, including every important decision.

Finally, Marshall increased the Court's power. Ironically *Marbury* v. *Madison* (1803), the landmark case that enabled Marshall to strengthen the Courts, involved another of Adams's midnight appointees. William Marbury, whom Adams had designated a justice of the peace in the District of Columbia, sued the new secretary of state, James Madison, for canceling Marbury's appointment so Jefferson could appoint a Republican. In his suit Marbury requested a writ of mandamus, or a court order compelling Madison to appoint him.

Marbury *v.* Madison

At first glance, the case presented a political dilemma. It was highly possible that even if the Supreme Court ruled in favor of Marbury and issued a writ of mandamus, the president would not comply. After all, why should the president, sworn to uphold the Constitution, allow the Court to decide for him what was constitutional? But if, on the other hand, the Court refused to issue the writ, it would be handing the Republicans a victory. Marshall avoided both alternatives and turned what seemed like a no-win situation into a Federalist triumph. Speaking for the Court, he ruled that Marbury had a right to his commission but that the Court could not compel Madison to honor it, because the Constitution did not grant the Court power to issue a writ of mandamus. Thus Marshall declared unconstitutional section 13 of the Judiciary Act of 1789, which authorized the Court to issue such writs. Marbury lost his job and the justices denied themselves the power to issue writs of mandamus, but the Supreme Court claimed its great power of judicial review.

In succeeding years Marshall fashioned the theory of judicial review. Since the Constitution was the supreme law, he reasoned, any act of Congress contrary to the Constitution must be null and void. And since the Supreme Court was responsible for upholding the law, it had a duty to decide whether a conflict existed between a legislative act and the Constitution. If such a conflict did indeed exist, the Court would declare the congressional act unconstitutional.

Marshall's decision rebuffed Republican attacks on the Court's independence. He avoided a confrontation with the Republican-dominated Congress by not ruling on their repeal of the Judiciary Act of 1801, which had created positions for the midnight appointees. And he enhanced the Court's independence.

Under Marshall, the Supreme Court also became the bulwark of a nationalist point of view. In *McCulloch* v. *Maryland* (1819), the Court struck down a Maryland law taxing the federally chartered Second Bank of the United States. Maryland had adopted the tax in an effort to destroy the bank's Baltimore branch. The issue was thus one of state versus federal power. Speaking for a unanimous Court, Marshall asserted the supremacy of the federal government over the states. "The Constitution and the laws thereof are supreme," he declared; "they control the constitution and laws of the respective states and cannot be controlled by them."

McCulloch *v.* Maryland

Having established federal supremacy, the Court went on to consider whether Congress could issue a bank charter. No such power was specified in the Constitution. But Marshall noted that Congress had the authority to pass "all laws which shall be necessary and proper for carrying into execution" the enumerated powers of the government (Article I, Section 8). Therefore Congress could legally exercise "those great powers on which the welfare of the nation essentially depends." If the ends were legitimate and the means were not prohibited, Marshall ruled, a law was constitutional. The Constitution was in Marshall's words, "intended to endure for ages to come, and consequently, to be adapted to the various causes of human affairs." The bank charter was declared legal.

In *McCulloch* v. *Maryland* Marshall combined Federalist nationalism with Federalist economic views. By asserting federal supremacy he was protecting the commercial and industrial interests that favored a national bank. This was Federalism in the tradition of Alexander Hamilton. The decision was only one in a series. In *Fletcher* v. *Peck* (1810) the Court voided a Georgia law that violated individuals' right of contract. Similarly, in the famous *Dartmouth College* v. *Woodward* (1819), the Court nullified a New Hampshire act altering the charter of Dartmouth College, which Marshall ruled constituted a contract. In protecting such contracts, Marshall thwarted state interference in commerce and business.

The struggle for power between Marshall's Federalist court and Republican legislatures, though fierce, proved benign. A certain amount of sparring was to be expected in the process of hammering out governmental relationships in a new republic. If the nation were to be threatened in these times, it would be not from within, but from without.

Preserving American neutrality

"Peace, commerce, and honest friendship with all nations, entangling alliance with none," President Jefferson had sensibly proclaimed in his first inaugural address. And Jefferson's efforts to stand clear of European conflict worked until 1805. Thereafter he found peace and undisturbed commerce an elusive goal, though pursuit of it occupied nearly his entire second administration.

After the Senate ratified Jay's Treaty in 1795 (see pages 179–180), the United States and Great Britain had appeared to reconcile their differences. Britain withdrew from its western forts and interfered less in American trade with France. More importantly, trade between the United States and Britain increased: the republic became Britain's best customer, and the British Empire in turn bought the bulk of American exports.

But renewal of the Napoleonic wars in May 1803–two weeks after Napoleon sold Louisiana to the United States–again trapped the nation between the two unfriendly superpowers. For two years American commerce actually benefited from the conflict. As the world's largest neutral carrier, the United States became the chief supplier of food to Europe. American merchants also gained control of most of the West Indian trade, which was often transshipped through American ports to Europe.

Meanwhile, the United States victory over Tripolitan pirates on the north coast of Africa provided Jefferson with his one clear success in protecting American trading rights. In 1801 Jefferson had refused the demands of the Sultan of Tripoli for payment of tribute. Instead he sent a naval squadron to the Mediterranean to protect American merchant ships from Barbary Coast pirates. In 1803 and 1804, under Lieutenant Stephen Decatur, the navy blockaded Tripoli Harbor while seven marines marched overland from Egypt to seize the port of Derna. The United States signed a peace treaty with Tripoli in 1805, but continued to pay tribute to other Barbary states.

That same year American merchants became victims of Anglo-French enmity. First Britain tightened its control over the high seas with its victory over the French and Spanish fleets at the Battle of Trafalgar in October 1805. Two months later Napoleon defeated the Russian and Austrian armies at Austerlitz. Stalemated, the two powers waged commercial war, blockading and counterblockading each other's trade. As a trading partner of both countries, the United States paid a high price.

At the same time the British navy stepped up impressments of American sailors. Britain, whose navy was the world's largest, was suffering a severe shortage

Impressment of American sailors

of sailors. Few enlisted, and those already in service frequently deserted, discouraged by poor food and living conditions and brutal discipline. The Royal Navy resorted to stopping American ships and forcibly removing British deserters, British-born naturalized American seamen, and other unlucky sailors mistakenly suspected of being British. About six to eight thousand Americans were drafted in this manner between 1803 and 1812.

Americans saw impressment as a direct assault on their new republic. It violated America's rights as a neutral nation, and the British principle of "once a British subject, always a British subject" ignored American citizenship and sovereignty. Moreover, the practice exposed the weakness of the new nation; the United States was in effect unable to protect its citizens from impressment.

In February 1806 the Senate denounced British impressment as aggression and a violation of neutral rights. To protest the insult Congress passed the Non-Importation Act, prohibiting importation from Great Britain of a long list of cloth and metal articles. In November Jefferson suspended the act temporarily while William Pinckney joined James Monroe in London in an attempt to negotiate a settlement. But the treaty Monroe and Pinckney carried home violated their instructions–it did not mention impressment–and Jefferson never submitted it to the Senate for ratification.

Less than a year later the *Chesapeake* Affair exposed American military weakness and revealed the emotional impact of impressment on the public. In June 1807 the forty-gun frigate U.S.S. *Chesapeake* left Norfolk, Virginia, on a mission to protect American ships trading in the Mediterranean. About ten miles out, still inside American territorial waters, it met the fifty-gun British frigate *Leopard.* When the *Chesapeake* refused to be searched for deserters, the *Leopard* repeatedly emptied its guns broadside into the American ship. Three Americans were killed and eighteen wounded, including the ship's captain, Commodore James Barron. Four sailors were impressed–three of them American citizens, all of them deserters from the Royal Navy. Wounded and humiliated, the *Chesapeake* crept back into port.

Chesapeake *Affair*

THE MPRESSMENT OF AN

American Sailor Boy,

SUNG ON BOARD THE BRITISH PRISON SHIP CROWN PRINCE, THE FOURTH OF JULY, 1814
BY A NUMBER OF THE AMERICAN PRISONERS.

THE youthful sailor mounts the bark,
And bids each weeping friend adieu :
Fair blows the gale, the canvass swells :
Slow sinks the uplands from his view.

Three mornings, from his ocean bed,
Resplendent beams the God of day :
The fourth. high looming in the mist,
A war-ship's floating banners play.

Her yawl is launch'd ; light o'er the deep,
Too kind, she wafts a ruffian band :
Her blue track lengthens to the bark,
And soon on deck the miscreants stand.

Around they throw the baleful glance :
Suspense holds mute the anxious crew—
Who is their prey ? poor sailor boy !
The baleful glance is fix'd on you.

Nay, why that useless scrip unfold ?
They damn'd the " lying yankee scrawl,"
Torn from thine hand, it strews the wave—
They force thee trembling to the yawl.

Sick was thine heart as from the deck,
The hand of friendship wav d farewell ;
Mad was thy brain, as far behind,
In the grey mist thy vessel fell.

One hope, yet, to thy bosom clung,
The captain mercy might impart ;
Vain was that hope, which bade thee look,
For mercy in a Pirate's heart.

What woes can man on man inflict,
When malice joins with uncheck'd power ;
Such woes, unpitied and unknown,
For many a month the sailor bore !

Oft gem'd his eye the bursting tear,
As mem'ry linger'd on past joy ;
As oft they flung the cruel jeer,
And damn'd the " chicken liver'd boy."

When sick at heart, with " hope defer'd."
Kind sleep his wasting form embrac'd,
Some ready minion ply'd the lash,
And the lov'd dream of freedom chas'd.

Fast to an end his miseries drew :
The deadly hectic flush'd his cheek :
On his pale brow the cold dew hung,
He sigh'd, and sunk upon the deck !

The sailor's woes drew forth no sigh ;
No hand would close the sailor's eye :
Remorseless, his pale corse they gave,
Unshrouded to the friendly wave.

And as he sunk beneath the tide,
A hellish shout arose ;
Exultingly the demons cried,
" So fare all Albion's Rebel Foes !"

Ballad of an American sailor impressed by the British during the War of 1812. References to the British captain as a "Pirate" and the British crew as "demons" reveal the intense indignation felt by the American public. The New-York Historical Society.

Had the United States been better prepared for war, the howl of public indignation that resulted might have brought about a declaration of war. But the United States was ill equipped to defend its neutral rights with force; it was no match for the British navy. Fortunately, Congress was not in session at the time of the *Chesapeake* Affair, and Jefferson was able to avoid hostilities. The president responded instead by strengthening the military and putting economic pressure on Great Britain: in July Jefferson closed American waters to British warships to prevent similar incidents and soon thereafter he increased military and naval expenditures. On December 14, 1807, Jefferson again invoked the Non-Importation Act, followed eight days later by a new measure, the Embargo Act.

Embargo Act

Intended as a short-term measure, the Embargo Act forbade virtually all exports from the United States to any country. Imports came to a halt as well, since foreign ships delivering goods would have to leave American ports with empty holds. Smuggling blossomed overnight.

Few American policies have been as unsuccessful as Jefferson's embargo. The lucrative American merchant trade collapsed; exports fell 80 percent from 1807 to 1808. New England, the heart of Federalist opposition to the Virginia dynasty, felt the brunt of the depression. Ships rotted in harbors and grass grew on wharves; unemployment soared. In the winter of 1808 and 1809, talk of secession spread through New England port cities. Great Britain, in contrast, was only mildly affected by the embargo. Those English citizens who were hurt most–West Indians and English factory workers–had no voice in policy. English merchants actually gained, since they took over the Atlantic carrying trade from the stalled American merchant marine. Moreover, because the British blockade of Europe had already ended most trade with France, the embargo had little practical effect on the French. Indeed, it gave France an excuse to privateer against American ships that had managed to escape the embargo by avoiding American ports. The French argued that such ships must be British ships in disguise, since the embargo barred American ships from the seas.

In the election of 1808, the Republicans faced the Federalists, the embargo, and factional dissent in their own party. Jefferson followed Washington's example, renouncing a third term and supporting James Madison, his secretary of state, as the Republican standard-bearer. Madison won the endorsement of the congressional caucus, but Virginia Republicans put forth James Monroe (who later withdrew), and some eastern Republicans supported Vice President George Clinton. This was the first time the Republican nomination had been contested.

Charles C. Pinckney and Rufus King again headed the Federalist ticket, but with new vigor. The Younger Federalists pounded away at the widespread disaffection with Republican policy, especially the embargo. Although Pinckney received only 47 electoral votes to Madison's 122, the Federalists did manage to make the election a race. Pinckney carried all of New England except Vermont, and won Delaware and some electoral votes in two other states as well. Federalists also gained seats in Congress and captured the New York state legislature. For the Younger Federalists, the future looked bright.

Non-Intercourse Act

As for the embargo, it eventually collapsed under the weight of domestic opposition. Jefferson withdrew it in his last days in office, replacing it with the Non-Intercourse Act of 1809. The act reopened trade with all nations except Britain and France, and authorized the president to resume trade with either country if it ceased to violate neutral rights. But the new act solved only the problems that had been created by the embargo; it did not convince Britain and France to change their policies. For one brief moment it appeared to work: President Madison reopened trade with England in June 1809 after the British minister to the United States assured him that Britain would offer the concessions he sought. His Majesty's government in London, however, repudiated the minister's assurances, and Madison renewed nonintercourse.

When the Non-Intercourse Act expired in spring 1810, the United States tried to sell old wine in a new bottle, relabeled Macon's Bill Number 2. A congressional invention, the bill reopened trade with both Great Britain and France, but provided that if either nation ceased to violate American rights, the president could shut down American commerce with the other. Madison, eager to use the bill rather than go to war, was tricked at his own game. When Napoleon declared that French edicts against United States shipping would be lifted, Madison declared nonintercourse against Great Britain in March 1811. But Napoleon did not keep his word. The French continued to seize American ships, and nonintercourse failed a second time.

Because the British navy controlled the Atlantic, Britain was the main target of American hostility, not France. New York harbor was virtually blockaded by the Royal Navy, so reopening trade with any nation had little practical effect. Angry American leaders tended to blame even Indian resistance in the West on British agitation, ignoring the Indians' legitimate protests against white encroachment and treaty violations. Frustrated and having exhausted all efforts to alter British policy, the United States in 1811 and 1812 drifted into war with Great Britain.

Meanwhile, unknown to the president and Congress, Great Britain was changing its policy. The Anglo-French conflict had ended much of British commerce with the European continent, and exports to the United States had fallen 80 percent. Depression had hit the British Isles. On June 16, 1812, Britain opened the seas to American shipping. But two days later, before word had crossed the Atlantic, Congress declared war.

The War of 1812 was the logical outcome of United States policy since the renewal of war in Europe in 1803. The grievances enumerated in President Madison's message to Congress on June 1, 1812, were old ones: impressment, interference with neutral commerce, and the stirring-up of western Indians. Unmentioned was the resolve to defend American independence and honor—and the thirst of expansionists for British Canada. Yet Congress and the country were divided. Much of the sentiment for war came from the War Hawks, land-hungry southerners and westerners led by Henry Clay of Kentucky and John C. Calhoun of South Carolina. Most representatives from the coastal states opposed war, since armed conflict with the great naval power threatened to close down all American shipping. The vote for war—79 to 49 in the House, 19 to 13 in the Senate—was close and reflected these sharp regional differences. The split would also be reflected in the way Americans fought the war.

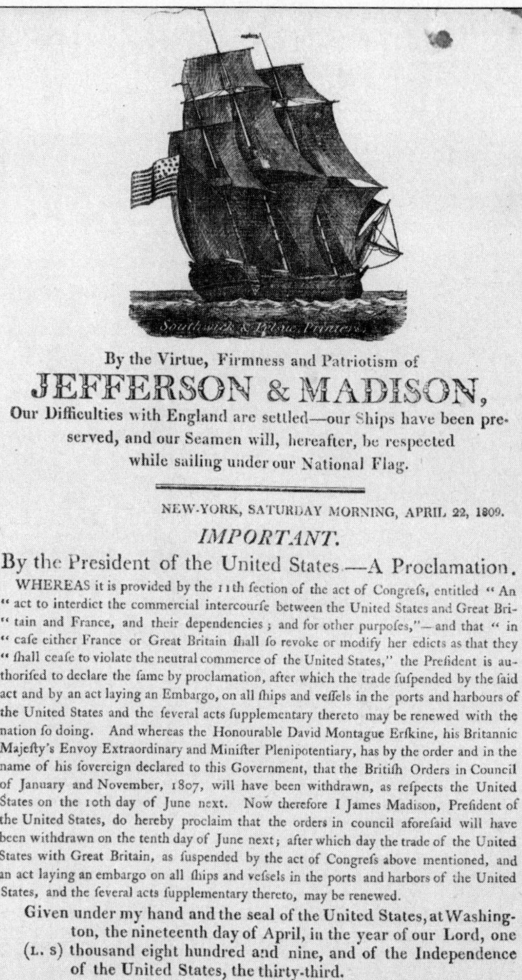

By the Virtue, Firmness and Patriotism of

JEFFERSON & MADISON,

Our Difficulties with England are settled—our Ships have been preserved, and our Seamen will, hereafter, be respected while sailing under our National Flag.

NEW-YORK, SATURDAY MORNING, APRIL 22, 1809.

IMPORTANT.

By the President of the United States—A Proclamation.

WHEREAS it is provided by the 11th ſection of the act of Congreſs, entitled "An "act to interdict the commercial intercourſe between the United States and Great Bri-"tain and France, and their dependencies; and for other purpoſes,"—and that "in "caſe either France or Great Britain ſhall ſo revoke or modify her edicts as that they "ſhall ceaſe to violate the neutral commerce of the United States," the Preſident is authoriſed to declare the ſame by proclamation, after which the trade ſuſpended by the ſaid act and by an act laying an Embargo, on all ſhips and veſſels in the ports and harbours of the United States and the ſeveral acts ſupplementary thereto may be renewed with the nation ſo doing. And whereas the Honourable David Montague Erſkine, his Britannic Majeſty's Envoy Extraordinary and Miniſter Plenipotentiary, has by the order and in the name of his ſovereign declared to this Government, that the Britiſh Orders in Council of January and November, 1807, will have been withdrawn, as reſpects the United States on the 10th day of June next. Now therefore I James Madiſon, Preſident of the United States, do hereby proclaim that the orders in council aforeſaid will have been withdrawn on the tenth day of June next; after which day the trade of the United States with Great Britain, as ſuſpended by the act of Congreſs above mentioned, and an act laying an embargo on all ſhips and veſsels in the ports and harbors of the United States, and the ſeveral acts ſupplementary thereto, may be renewed.

Given under my hand and the seal of the United States, at Washington, the nineteenth day of April, in the year of our Lord, one (L. S) thousand eight hundred and nine, and of the Independence of the United States, the thirty-third.

JAMES MADISON.

By the President,
RT. SMITH, *Secretary of State.*

A broadside celebrating the brief reopening of trade with Britain in 1809. This Republican propaganda made the most of a small victory resulting from the generally unsuccessful and highly unpopular policy of nonintercourse. The New-York Historical Society.

The War of 1812

Militarily, war was a foolish adventure for the United States in 1812; despite six months of preparation, American forces were still ill equipped. Because the army had neither an able staff nor an adequate force of enlisted men, the burden of fighting fell on the state militia—and not all the states cooperated. The navy did have a corps of well-trained, experienced

Major campaigns of the War of 1812

officers who had proven their mettle in protecting American merchantmen from Mediterranean pirates. But next to the Royal Navy, the ruler of the seas, the U.S. Navy was minuscule. Jefferson's warning that "our constitution is a peace establishment–it is not calculated for war" proved a wise one.

For the United States, the only readily available battlefront on which to confront Great Britain was Canada. The mighty Royal Navy was useless on the waters separating the United States and Canada, since no river afforded it access from the sea. Invasion of Canada, thousands of miles from British supply sources, therefore would give the United States an edge. And England, preoccupied with fighting Napoleon on the European continent, was unlikely to reduce its continental forces to defend Canada.

Invasion of Canada

Begun with high hopes, the invasion of Canada proved disastrous. The American strategy was to concentrate on the West, splitting Canadian forces and isolating the Indians who supported the British. General William Hull marched his troops into lower Canada, near Detroit. But the British anticipated the invasion, moved troops into the area, and demanded

Cameo portraits of the naval heroes of the War of 1812 surround a lithograph of the Battle of Put-in-Bay (1813), in which the United States gained control of Lake Erie. Clockwise from top center: Oliver H. Perry, Stephen Decatur, Johnston Blakeley, William Bainbridge, David Porter, and James Lawrence. Drawn and published by Currier in 1846. The New-York Historical Society.

Hull's surrender. When pro-British Indians captured Fort Dearborn, near Detroit, Hull capitulated (see map). Farther to the west, other American forts surrendered. By the winter of 1812 and 1813, the British controlled about half the Old Northwest (Ohio, Indiana, Illinois, Michigan, and Wisconsin).

The United States had no greater success on the Niagara front, where New York borders Canada. At the Battle of Queenstown, north of Niagara, the United States regular army met defeat because the New York state militia refused to leave the state. This scene was repeated near Lake Champlain, where American plans to attack Montreal were foiled when the militia declined to cross the border.

The navy provided the only bright note in the first year of the war: the U.S.S. *Constitution,* the U.S.S. *Wasp,* and the U.S.S. *United States* all bested British warships on the Atlantic. But their victories gave the United States only a brief advantage. In defeat the British lost just 1 percent of their strength; in victory the Americans lost 20 percent. The British admiralty simply shifted its fleet away from the American ships, and by 1813 the Royal Navy again dominated the seas.

Great Lakes campaign

In 1813 the two sides also vied over control of the Great Lakes, the key to the war in the Northwest. The contest was largely a ship-building race. Under Master Commandant Oliver Hazard Perry and shipbuilder Noah Brown, the United States outbuilt the British on Lake Erie and defeated them at the bloody Battle of Put-in-Bay on September 10. The ships fought fiercely and at close range; of 103 men on duty on the U.S.S. *Lawrence,* 21 were killed and 63 wounded. With this costly victory, the Americans gained control of Lake Erie.

Silk bandanna glorifying Andrew Jackson (1767–1845), hero of the Battle of New Orleans. Edmund B. Sullivan Collection, University of Hartford.

General William Henry Harrison then began the campaign that would prove to be the United States' brightest moment in the war. Harrison's 4,500-man force, mostly Kentucky volunteers, crossed Lake Erie and pursued the British and their Indian allies into Canada, defeating them at the Battle of the Thames on October 5. The great Shawnee Chief Tecumseh died in that battle, and with him, the Indian confederacy he had formed to resist American expansion (see Chapter 11). Once again the United States controlled the Old Northwest.

The American success on Lake Erie could not be repeated on Lake Ontario. After the Battle of the Thames, both sides seemed to favor petty victories over strategic goals in the Northwest. The Americans raided York (now Toronto), the Canadian capital, and looted and burned the Parliament before withdrawing, too few in number to hold the city.

British naval blockade

Outside the Old Northwest the British dominated the war. In December 1812 the Royal Navy blockaded the Chesapeake and Delaware bays. By May 1813 the blockade had closed nearly all southern and Gulf of Mexico ports, and by November it had reached north to Long Island Sound. By 1814 all New England ports were closed. American trade had declined nearly 90 percent since 1811, and the decline in revenues from customs duties threatened to bankrupt the federal government.

Following their overthrow of Napoleon in April 1814, the British stepped up the land campaign against the United States, concentrating their efforts in the Chesapeake. In retaliation for the burning of York—and to divert American troops from Lake Champlain, where the British planned a new offensive—royal troops occupied Washington and set it to the torch. The attack on the capital was, however, only a raid. The major battle occurred at Baltimore, where the Americans held firm. Although the British inflicted heavy damages both materially and psychologically, they achieved no more than a stalemate.

The last campaign of the war was waged in the South, along the Gulf of Mexico. It began when Tennessee militia general Andrew Jackson defeated the Creeks and Cherokees at the Battle of Horseshoe Bend in March 1814. The battle ended the year-long Creek War, which had begun after a series of skirmishes between Indians and settlers. As a result, the Creeks ceded two-thirds of their land and withdrew to southern and western Alabama. Jackson became a major general in the regular army and continued south toward the Gulf. To forestall a British invasion at Pensacola Bay, which provided an overland route to New Orleans, Jackson seized Pensacola—in Spanish Florida—on November 7, 1814. After securing Mobile, he marched on to New Orleans and prepared for a British attempt to capture the city.

Battle of New Orleans

The Battle of New Orleans was the final engagement of the war. Early in December the British fleet had landed east of New Orleans, 1,500 strong, hoping to gain control of the Mississippi River. They faced an American force of regular army troops, plus a larger contingent of Tennessee and Kentucky frontiersmen and two companies of free black volunteers from New Orleans. For three weeks the British under Sir Edward Pakenham and the Americans under Jackson played cat-and-mouse, each trying to gain a major strategic position. Finally, on January 8, 1815, the two forces met head on. Jackson and his mostly untrained army held their ground against two frontal assaults. It was a massacre. More than 2,000 British soldiers lay dead or wounded at the day's end; the Americans suffered only 21 casualties. Andrew Jackson was a national hero. Ironically, the Battle of New Orleans was fought two weeks after the end of the war; unknown to Jackson, a treaty had been signed in Ghent, Belgium, on December 24, 1814.

The United States government had gone to war only reluctantly, and during the conflict had continued to probe for a diplomatic end to hostilities. In 1813, for instance, President Madison had eagerly accepted a Russian offer to mediate, but Great Britain had refused to participate. Then in November, three months after the Russian offer failed, British Foreign Minister Lord Castlereagh had suggested opening peace talks. It took over ten months to arrange for meetings, but in August 1814 a team of American negotiators, including John Quincy Adams and Henry Clay, began talks with the British in Ghent.

Treaty of Ghent

The Ghent treaty made no mention of the issues that had led to war. The United States received no satisfaction on impressment, blockades, or other maritime rights. Likewise, British demands for a neutral Indian buffer state in the Northwest and territorial cessions from Maine to Minnesota went unmet. Essentially, the Treaty of Ghent restored the prewar status quo. It provided for an end to hostilities, release of prisoners, restoration of conquered territory, and arbitration of boundary disputes. Other questions—notably compensation for losses and fishing rights—would be negotiated by joint commissions.

Why did the negotiators settle for so little? Events in Europe had made peace and the status quo acceptable at the end of 1814, as they had not been in 1812. Napoleon's fall from power allowed the United States to abandon its demands, since peace in Europe made impressment and interference with American commerce moot questions. Similarly, war-weary Britain, its treasury nearly depleted, gave up pressing for a military victory.

The war did reinforce the independence of the young American republic. Although conflict with Great Britain continued, it never again led to war. The experience strengthened America's resolve to steer clear of European politics, for it had been the British-French conflict that had drawn the United States into war. For the rest of the century the nation would shun involvement with Europe.

Domestically, the war prompted recognition of the need for better transportation and an efficient army. American generals had found American roads inadequate to move an army and its supplies among widely scattered fronts. In the Northwest, General Harrison's troops had depended on homemade cartridges and gifts of clothing from Ohio residents. In Maine, troops had melted down spoons to make bullets. Clearly, improved transportation and a well-equipped army were major priorities. In 1815 President Madison made a beginning by centralizing control of the army. And Congress voted a standing army of 10,000 men, one-third of the army's wartime strength but three times its size during Jefferson's administration.

The war also sealed the fate of the Federalist party. Realizing that their chances of winning a presidential election in wartime were slight, the Federalists had joined dissatisfied Republicans in supporting De Witt Clinton of New York in 1812. This was the high point of Federalist organization at the state level, and the Younger Federalists campaigned hard. Clinton nevertheless lost to President Madison by 128 to 89 electoral votes; areas that favored the war (the South and West) voted solidly Republican. The Federalists did, however, gain some congressional seats, and they carried many local elections.

Hartford Convention

But once again extremism was the Federalists' undoing. During the war Older Federalists had revived talk of secession, and from December 15, 1814, to January 5, 1815, Federalist delegates from New England met in Hartford, Connecticut, to take action. With the war in a stalemate and trade in ruins, they planned to revise the national compact or pull out of the republic. Moderates prevented a resolution of secession, but convention members continued to call for radical changes in the Constitution. In particular, they wanted constitutional amendments restricting the presidency to one term and requiring a two-thirds congressional vote to admit new states. They also hoped to abolish the three-fifths compromise, whereby slaves were counted in the apportionment of congressional representatives, and to forbid naturalized citizens from holding office. These proposals were aimed at the growing West and South—the heart of Republican electoral strength—and at Irish immigrants.

If nothing else, the timing of the Hartford Convention proved fatal. The victory at New Orleans and news of the peace treaty made the Hartford Convention, with its talk of secession and proposed constitutional amendments, look ridiculous. Rather than harassing a beleaguered wartime administration, the Federalists now retreated before a rising tide of nationalism. Though it remained strong in a handful of states until the 1820s, the Federalist party began to dissolve. The war, at first a source of revival as opponents of war flocked to the Federalist banner, had killed the party.

Possibly most important of all, the war stimulated economic change. The embargo, the Non-Importation and Non-Intercourse acts, and the war itself had spurred the production of manufactured goods—cloth and metal—to replace banned imports. And in the absence of commercial opportunities abroad, New England capitalists had begun to invest in manufactures. The effects of these changes were to be far reaching (see Chapter 9).

Postwar nationalism

With peace came a new sense of American nationalism. Five new states joined the union: Indiana (1816), Mississippi (1817), Illinois (1818), and Alabama (1819). (Louisiana had been admitted in 1812.) Self-confidently, the nation asserted itself at home and abroad as Republicans aped Federalists in encouraging economic development and commerce. In his last message to Congress in December 1815, President Madison embraced Federalist doctrine by recommending military expansion and a program to stimulate development and growth. Wartime experiences had, he said, demonstrated the need for a national bank (the first bank had expired) and for better transportation. To raise government revenues and perpetuate the wartime growth in manufacturing, Madison called for a protective tariff—a tax on imported goods. Yet in straying from Jeffersonian Republicanism, Madison did so within limits. Only a constitutional amendment, he argued, could give the federal government authority to build roads and canals that were less than national in scope.

The congressional leadership pushed Madison's nationalist program energetically. Representative John C. Calhoun and Speaker of the House Henry Clay, who named the program the American System, believed it would unify the country. They looked to the tariff on imported goods to stimulate industry. New mills would purchase raw materials; new millworkers would buy food from the agricultural South and West. New roads would make possible the flow of produce and goods, and tariff revenues would provide the money to build them. Finally, the national bank would facilitate all these transactions.

American System

Indeed, Hamilton's original plan for a Bank of the United States became fundamental to the new Republican policy. Fearing the concentration of economic power in a central bank, the Republicans had allowed the charter of the first Bank of the United States to expire in 1811. State banks, however, proved inadequate to the nation's needs. Their resources had been insufficient to assist the government in financing the War of 1812. Moreover, people distrusted currency issued by banks in distant localities. Because many banks issued notes without gold to back them up, and counterfeit notes were common, merchants hesitated to accept strange currency. Republicans therefore came to favor a national bank. In 1816 Congress chartered for twenty years the Second Bank of the United States, to be headquartered in Philadelphia. The government provided $7 million of the $35 million capital and appointed one-fifth of the directors, and the bank opened its doors on January 1, 1817.

Congress did not share Madison's reservations about the constitutionality of using federal funds to build local roads. "Let us, then, bind the republic together," Calhoun declared, "with a perfect system of roads and canals." But Madison vetoed Calhoun's internal improvements bill, which provided for the construction of roads of mostly local benefit, adamantly insisting that it was unconstitutional. Internal improvements were the province of the states and of private enterprise. (Madison did, however, approve funds for the continuation of the National Road, on the grounds that it was a military necessity.)

Protective tariffs completed Madison's nationalist program. Though the embargo and the war had stimulated domestic industry, especially cloth and iron manufacturing, resumption of trade after the war brought competition from abroad. Americans

This watercolor by George Tattersall shows the primitive state of American roads in the early nineteenth century. Museum of Fine Arts, Boston, M. and M. Karolik Collection.

charged that British firms were dumping their goods on the American market at below cost to stifle American manufacturing. To aid the new industries, Madison recommended and Congress passed the Tariff of 1816, the first protective tariff in American history. The act levied taxes on imported woolens and cottons, especially inexpensive ones, and on iron, leather, hats, paper, and sugar. In effect it raised the cost of these imported goods. Some New England representatives viewed the tariff as interference in free trade, and southern representatives (except Calhoun and a few others) opposed it because it raised the cost of imported goods to southern farmers with no interest in industry. But the western and Middle Atlantic states backed it, and the tariff passed.

James Monroe, Madison's successor as president, retained Madison's domestic program, supporting the bank and tariffs and vetoing internal improvements on constitutional grounds. Monroe, Madison's secretary of state, was nominated by the Republican congressional caucus in 1816. Later that year he easily defeated Rufus King, the last Federalist nominee, sweeping all the states except the Federalist strongholds of Massachusetts, Connecticut, and Delaware. Monroe optimistically declared that "discord does not belong to our system." The American people were, he said, "one great family with a common interest." And for his first term that was true.

Monroe's secretary of state, John Quincy Adams, managed the nation's foreign policy brilliantly from 1817 to 1825. An experienced diplomat who had served in the Netherlands, Prussia, Russia, and Great Britain and negotiated the Treaty of Ghent, Adams stubbornly pushed for expansion, political distance from

John Quincy Adams as secretary of state

John Quincy Adams (1767–1848), secretary of state from 1817 to 1825, in an early daguerreotype taken by Southworth and Hawes shortly before his death. This famous photograph suggests Adams's bulldog tenacity. The Metropolitan Museum of Art, Gift of I. N. Phelps Stokes, Edward S. Hawes, Alice Mary Hawes, Marion Augusta Hawes, 1937.

the Old World, and peace. Party politics, he firmly believed, had no place in foreign relations; the national interest, not loyalty or good intentions, should guide American policy. A small, austere man who described himself as a bulldog, Adams was a giant as a diplomat.

Adams's first step was to strengthen the peace with Great Britain. In April 1817 the two nations agreed to the Rush-Bagot Treaty, which grew out of negotiations Adams had begun the previous year in his capacity as diplomatic minister in London. Britain and the United States agreed in this pact to limit their Great Lakes naval forces to one ship each on Lake Ontario and Lake Champlain and two vessels each on the other lakes. This first disarmament treaty of modern times began the process that led to demilitarization of the United States–Canadian border.

Adams then pushed for the Convention of 1818—also a sequel to the Treaty of Ghent—which fixed the United States–Canadian border from Lake of the Woods west to the Rockies. When agreement could not be reached on the territory west of the mountains, the two nations settled on joint occupation of Oregon for ten years. Adams, who wanted to fix the border at the 49th parallel, hoped for a better negotiating position at the end of that period.

Adams moved next to settle long-term disputes with Spain. During the War of 1812, the United States had seized Mobile and West Florida. Afterward it took advantage of Spain's preoccupation with domestic and colonial troubles to negotiate for the purchase of Florida. Talks took place in 1818, while General Andrew Jackson's troops occupied much of Florida on the pretext of suppressing Seminole raids against American settlements across the border. The following year, under dictated terms, Spain agreed to cede Florida to the United States without payment. In this Transcontinental, or Adams-Onís Treaty, the United States also defined the southern boundary of the Louisiana Purchase from the Gulf of Mexico to the Pacific Ocean. In return, the United States government assumed $5 million worth of claims by American citizens against Spain and gave up its dubious claim to Texas. Expansion had thus been achieved at little cost and without bloodshed, and American claims now stretched from the Atlantic to the Pacific.

The Panic of 1819 and renewed sectionalism

Monroe's domestic achievements could not match his diplomatic successes. The period of harmony that began his presidency–dubbed the Era of Good Feelings by a Boston newspaper–was short-lived. By 1819 postwar nationalism and confidence had eroded, and financial panic darkened the land. (Neither panic nor the resurgence of sectionalism hurt Monroe politically; without a rival political party to rally opposition, he won a second term unopposed.)

But hard times spread. The postwar expansion had been built on loose money and widespread speculation. When it slowed, the manufacturing depression that had begun in 1818 deepened, and prices spiraled downward. Distressed urban workers lobbied for relief and began to take a more active role in politics. Manufacturers demanded greater tariff protection–and eventually got it in the Tariff of 1824. Farmers, on the other hand, wanted lower tariffs. Hurt by a sharp decline in the price of cotton, southern planters railed at the protective Tariff of 1816, which had raised prices at the same time their incomes were falling sharply. The Virginia Agricultural Society of Fredericksburg, for example, argued that the tariff violated the very principles on which the nation had been founded. In a protest to Congress in January 1820, the society called the tariff an unequal tax that awarded exclusive privileges to "oppressive monopolies, which are ultimately to grind both us and our children after us 'into dust and ashes.' "

Western farmers suffered too. Those who had purchased public land on credit could not repay their loans. To avoid mass bankruptcy, Congress delayed payment of the money, and western state legislatures passed "stay laws" restricting mortgage foreclosures. Many westerners blamed the panic on the Second Bank of the United States, which in self-protection had cut off loans it had issued in the previous three years. Having fueled the boom with credit, the bank now sped the contraction by tightening the money supply. Many state banks, in debt to the national bank, folded, and westerners bitterly accused the bank of saving itself while the nation went to ruin. Although the economy recovered in the mid-1820s, the seeds of the Jacksonian movement (see Chapter 12) had been sown.

Even more divisive was the question of slavery. Ever since the drafting of the Constitution, political leaders had avoided the issue. In February 1819, however, slavery finally crept into the political agenda when Missouri residents petitioned Congress for admission to the Union as a slave state. For the next two-and-one-half years the issue dominated all congressional action. "This momentous question," Thomas Jefferson wrote, fearful for the life of the Union, "like a fire bell in the night, awakened and filled me with terror."

The debate transcended slavery in Missouri. At stake was the undoing of the compromises that had kept the issue quarantined since the Constitutional Convention. Missouri was on the same latitude as free Illinois, Indiana, and Ohio, and its admission as a slave state would thus thrust slavery further northward. It would also tilt the political balance toward the states

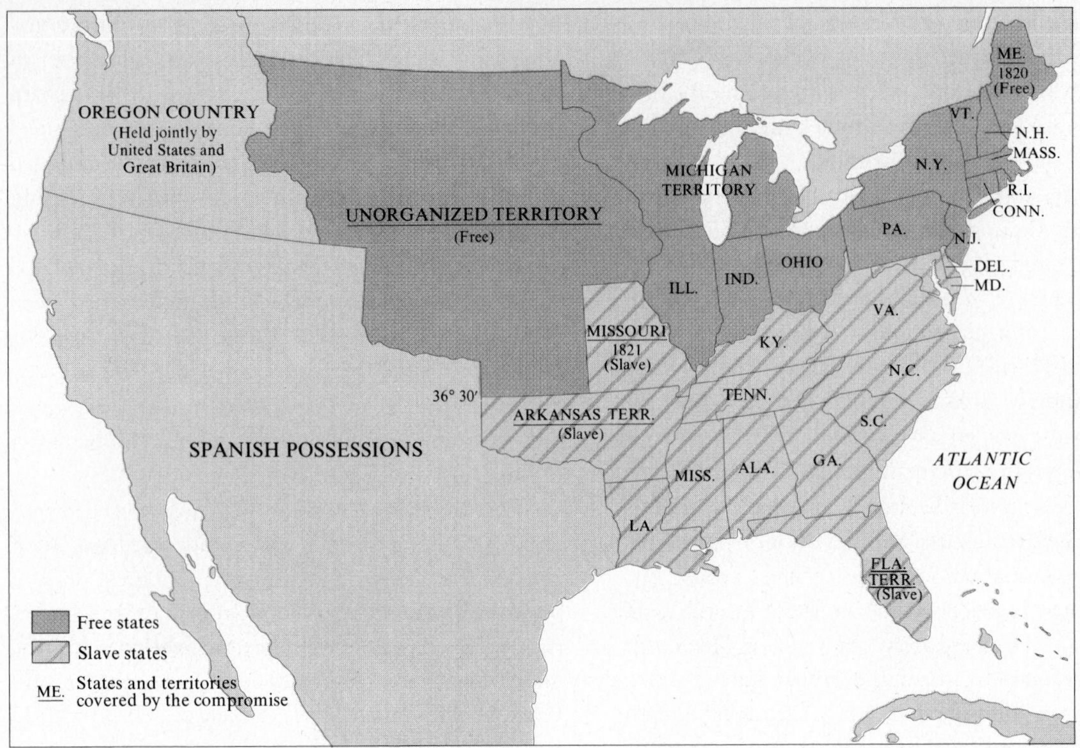

The Missouri Compromise of 1820

committed to slavery. In 1819 the Union consisted of an uneasy balance of eleven slave and eleven free states. (Of the five new states admitted since 1812, three–Louisiana, Mississippi, and Alabama–were slave states.) If Missouri entered as a slave state, the slave states would have a two-vote edge in the Senate.

But what made the issue so divisive was not the politics of admission to statehood, but people's emotional attitudes toward slavery. The settlers of Missouri were mostly Kentuckians and Tennesseeans who had grown up with slavery. But in the North, slavery was slowly dying out, and many northerners had come to the conclusion that it was evil. Thus when Representative James Tallmadge, Jr., of New York introduced an amendment providing for gradual emancipation in Missouri, it led to passionate and sometimes violent debate on moral grounds. The House, which had a northern majority, passed the Tallmadge amendment, but the Senate rejected it. The two sides were deadlocked.

A compromise emerged in 1820 under pressure from House Speaker Henry Clay: the admission of free Maine, carved out of Massachusetts, was linked with that of slave Missouri. In the rest of the Louisiana Territory north of 36°30′ (Missouri's southern boundary), slavery was prohibited forever (see map). The compromise carried, but the agreement almost came apart in November when Missouri submitted a constitution barring free blacks from settling in the state. Opponents contended that the proposed state constitution violated the federal Constitution's provision that "the Citizens of each state shall be entitled to all privileges and immunities of Citizens in the several States." Advocates argued that restrictions on free blacks were common in state law both North and South. In 1821 Clay produced a second compromise: Missouri guaranteed that none of its laws would discriminate against citizens of other states. (Once admitted to the Union, however, Missouri twice adopted laws banning free blacks from entering the state.)

Missouri Compromise

Although political leaders had successfully removed slavery from the congressional agenda, the issue ultimately destroyed Republican unity and ended the reign of the Virginia dynasty. The Republican party would come apart in 1824 as presidential candidates from different sections of the country scrambled for caucus support (see Chapter 12).

In foreign policy, one thorny issue remained to be resolved: recognition of revolutionary forces in Latin America. The United Provinces of the Rio de la Plata (Argentina), Chile, Peru, Colombia, and Mexico had broken free of Spain between 1808 and 1822, and Americans clamored to recognize them officially. But Monroe and Adams moved slowly in acknowledging Latin American independence. They sought to avoid conflict with European powers and to assure themselves of the stability of the revolutionary regimes. Shortly after the Adams-Onís Treaty with Spain was safely signed and ratified, in 1823, however, the United States became the first nation outside Latin America to recognize the new states.

We Owe Allegiance to No Crown, painted by John A. Woodside, shows the self-confident nationalism that prevailed at the time of the Monroe Doctrine. Liberty crowns an American sailor with a laurel wreath as he tramples on the symbols of British tyranny. Collection of Davenport West, Jr.

Later the same year, events in Europe again threatened the stability of the New World. Spain experienced a domestic revolt, and France occupied Spain in an attempt to bolster the weak monarchy against the rebels. The United States feared that France and its allies might also seek to overturn the new Latin American states and restore them to Spanish rule. Great Britain, which shared this concern, proposed joint United States–British protection of South America. But Adams rejected the British overture, fearing any European intervention in the New World. He insisted that the United States act independently and on its own initiative; action in concert with Britain would violate the long-standing principle of avoiding foreign entanglements.

To thwart an alliance with Great Britain, the bulldog Adams tenaciously outargued other Cabinet members. Those who favored joint action believed that Britain alone had the power to prevent French or Russian intervention. They were supported by former President Jefferson, then in retirement at Monticello. Adams, however, won out. "It would be more candid, as well as more dignified," he argued, "to avow our principles explicitly to Russia and France, than to come in as a cock-boat in the wake of the British man-of-war."

The result was the Monroe Doctrine, a unilateral declaration against European interference in the New World. The president enunciated the famous doctrine in his last message to Congress on December 2, 1823. Monroe called for, first, *noncolonization* of the Western Hemisphere by European nations, a principle that expressed American anxiety not only about Latin America but also about Russian expansion in Alaska. Second, he demanded *nonintervention* by Europe in the affairs of independent New World nations. Finally, Monroe pledged *noninterference* by the United States in European affairs, including those of Europe's existing New World colonies.

Monroe Doctrine

The Monroe Doctrine proved popular at home as an anti-British, anti-European assertion of American nationalism, and it eventually became the foundation of American policy in the Western Hemisphere. Monroe's words, however, had no force behind them. Indeed, the policy could not have succeeded without the support of the British, who were already committed to keeping other European nations out of the New

Important events

1801	John Marshall becomes Chief Justice Jefferson inaugurated
1801–05	Tripoli War
1803	*Marbury* v. *Madison* Louisiana Purchase
1803–12	British impressment of American seamen
1804	Jefferson re-elected
1806	Non-Importation Act
1807	*Chesapeake* Affair Embargo Act
1808	James Madison elected president
1809–10	Non-Intercourse Acts
1810	Macon's Bill No. 2
1812–15	War of 1812
1814	Treaty of Ghent
1814–15	Hartford Convention
1815	Battle of New Orleans
1816	James Monroe elected; last Federalist presidential candidate
1817	Second Bank of the United States Rush-Bagot Treaty
1819	*McCulloch* v. *Maryland* Adams-Onís Treaty
1819–23	Financial panic; depression
1820	Missouri Compromise
1821	Missouri admitted as state
1823	Monroe Doctrine

World. Europeans ignored the doctrine; it was the Royal Navy they respected, not American policy.

The foreign-policy problems confronting the infant republic from the turn of the century through the mid-1820s strikingly resembled those faced today by the newly established nations of the Third World. The mother country often treated its former colony as if it had not won its independence. A second war—the War of 1812—had to be fought to reiterate American independence; thereafter the nation was able to settle most disputes at the bargaining table. And like Third World nations today, the young United States steered clear of alliances with superpowers, preferring neutrality and unilateralism.

At home the United States worked to establish an enduring central government. As a union of states whose boundaries were an inheritance from the colonial past, the republic was no more than a shaky federation. And although Federalist talk of secession never led to action, sectional differences ran deep. Some issues, like slavery, seemed beyond resolution, though compromise did succeed in delaying the judgment day. Political division in itself proved benign, and the young country established a tradition of peaceful transition of power through presidential elections. It was the Supreme Court that made the first advances toward national unity, establishing federal power over the states and encouraging commerce. After the war all branches of the government, responding to the popular mood, pursued a more vigorous national policy. Their efforts would help to transform the nation and its economy.

Suggestions for further reading

General

Henry Adams, *History of the United States of America During the Administration of Thomas Jefferson and of James Madison*, 9 vols. (1889–1891); Marcus Cunliffe, *The Nation Takes Shape, 1789–1837* (1959); Marshall Smelser, *The Democratic Republic, 1801–1815* (1968); Charles M. Wiltse, *The New Nation, 1800–1845* (1961).

Party politics

James M. Banner, *To The Hartford Convention: The Federalists and the Origins of Party Politics in the Early Republic, 1789–1815* (1967); Noble E. Cunningham, Jr., *The Jeffersonian Republicans in Power: Party Operations, 1801–1809* (1963); David Hackett Fischer, *The Revolution of American Conservatism: The Federalist Party in the Era of Jeffersonian De-*

mocracy (1965); Richard Hofstadter, *The Idea of a Party System* (1969); Linda K. Kerber, *Federalists in Dissent* (1970); James S. Young, *The Washington Community, 1800–1828* (1966).

The Virginia presidents

Harry Ammon, *James Monroe: The Quest for National Identity* (1971); Irving Brant, *The Fourth President: A Life of James Madison* (1970); Irving Brant, *James Madison,* 6 vols. (1941–1961); Noble E. Cunningham, Jr., *The Process of Government Under Jefferson* (1978); Alexander De Conde, *The Affair of Louisiana* (1976); James Ketcham, *James Madison* (1970); Forrest McDonald, *The Presidency of Thomas Jefferson* (1976); Dumas Malone, *Jefferson and His Time,* 5 vols. (1948–1974); Merrill D. Peterson, *The Jefferson Image in the American Mind* (1960); Merrill D. Peterson, *Thomas Jefferson and the New Nation* (1970).

The Supreme Court and the law

Leonard Baker, *John Marshall: A Life in Law* (1974); Albert Beveridge, *The Life of John Marshall,* 4 vols. (1916–1919); Richard E. Ellis, *The Jeffersonian Crisis: Courts and Politics in the Young Republic* (1971); Charles G. Haines, *The Role of the Supreme Court in American Government and Politics, 1789–1835* (1944); Morton J. Horowitz, *The Transformation of American Law, 1780–1860* (1977); R. Kent Newmyer, *The Supreme Court under Marshall and Taney* (1968).

The War of 1812

Roger H. Brown, *The Republic in Peril: 1812* (1964); A. L. Burt, *The United States, Great Britain, and British North America* (1940); Harry L. Coles, *The War of 1812* (1965); Reginald Horsman, *The Causes of the War of 1812* (1962); Reginald Horsman, *The War of 1812* (1969); Bradford Perkins, *Prologue to War: England and the United States, 1805–1812* (1961); Julius W. Pratt, *Expansionists of 1812* (1925).

Nationalism and sectionalism

George Dangerfield, *The Awakening of American Nationalism, 1815–1828* (1965); George Dangerfield, *The Era of Good Feelings* (1952); Shaw Livermore, *Twilight of Federalism: The Disintegration of the Federalist Party, 1815–1830* (1962); Glover Moore, *The Missouri Compromise 1819–1821* (1953); Murray N. Rothbard, *The Panic of 1819* (1962).

The Monroe Doctrine

Samuel F. Bemis, *John Quincy Adams and the Foundations of American Foreign Policy* (1949); Walter LaFeber, ed., *John Quincy Adams and American Continental Empire* (1965): Ernest R. May, *The Making of the Monroe Doctrine* (1976); Dexter Perkins, *Hands Off: A History of the Monroe Doctrine* (1941); Dexter Perkins, *The Monroe Doctrine 1823–1826* (1927).

9
THE
ECONOMIC
EVOLUTION
OF THE
NORTH
AND WEST,
1800–1860

John Jervis suffered from canal fever and railroad fever nearly all his life. He first contracted the obsession in 1817, when at age twenty-two he left his father's upstate New York farm to clear a cedar swamp for the Erie Canal. Like the other laborers, as well as the men directing the project, Jervis had had no experience in canal construction. Indeed, he had never built anything according to a plan or diagram.

Together the directors and workers learned enough on the job to construct 363 well-engineered miles of canal. Jervis's education began his first day. Though he was an expert axeman, he had never had to down a line of trees along a precise path. With "a little trouble" he learned to hew with precision. Jervis learned new skills each year, advancing from axeman to surveyor to engineer to superintendent of a division.

When the Erie Canal was completed in 1825, Jervis moved on to become second-in-command of the Delaware and Hudson Canal project. To reduce costs, he substituted a railroad line for the last seventeen miles of the canal. Since there was not a single locomotive in the United States in 1828, Jervis had one sent from England. The engine that was delivered, however, was heavier than the one he had ordered, and on both tests it crushed the hemlock rails.

Undaunted, the self-trained engineer left the Delaware canal company to supervise construction of another early rail experiment, the Mohawk and Hudson Railroad from Albany to Schenectady. In building the railroad Jervis redesigned the locomotive's wheel assembly, and his design became standard throughout America.

Jervis spent the next two decades building the 98-mile Chenango Canal and the fresh-water supply—Croton Reservoir, 33-mile aqueduct, and pumping system—for New York City. Later he built other railroads, including the Michigan Southern, the Rock Island, and the Nickel Platte. In 1864, at age sixty-nine, Jervis returned home to Rome, New York, and organized an iron mill. He had spent his life constructing the mechanisms—canals and railroads—that would change America.

John Jervis's life bridged the old and the new. His roots lay in the rural farm country that was typical of the United States at the beginning of the nineteenth century. He had learned to read and write during occasional attendance at common school, and to farm and handle an axe from his father. But in 1817 he left behind much of that tradition and became involved in undertakings that would lead to a new, far different nation. He had to acquire skills not used on the farm: the ability to follow and create construction plans, to calculate weight stresses, and to work precisely in tandem with others.

The canals and railroads John Jervis helped build were the most visible signs of the evolution of the American economy from 1800 through 1860. The canal boat, the steamboat, the locomotive, and the telegraph were all agents of change and economic growth. They helped to open up the frontier and brought mostly self-sufficient farmers into the market economy. They made it profitable to manufacture cloth in New England and ship the finished goods to retail outlets in New Orleans or St. Louis or even, by the 1850s, San Francisco. They forged the beginnings of a national, capitalist economy.

Public and private investment and a growing population stimulated economic growth during these years. Government, especially state government, promoted an environment in which farming and industry could blossom, however unevenly and unsteadily. Banks, insurance companies, and corporations amassed the capital for large-scale enterprises like factories and railroads. Meanwhile, farming and manufacturing methods became more complex. Factories and precision-made machinery began to replace home workshops and hand-made goods, and mechanized reapers and sowers revolutionized the farming industry.

But for Americans living in this era of rapid economic growth, the rewards of economic improvement were accompanied by problems and tensions. Not everyone profited, as John Jervis did, in wealth and opportunity. The journeyman cobbler who had to abandon his tools for a machine had a far different experience from the master shoemaker who became a factory owner. As traditional ways began to give way to the demands of a market economy, survival required that most free Americans sell their labor for wages. By the second half of the nineteenth century, the engine of economic change and growth roared ahead full-steam; economic growth would not be derailed.

The transition to a market economy

The base of the old economy had been staple exports–grain, tobacco, and other crops grown by free farmers and slaves for overseas markets. Farmers who did not cultivate for export tended to be self-sufficient, producing nearly everything they needed–clothing, candles, soap, and the like–and bartering for the few items they could not produce, such as cooking pots and horseshoes. By the Civil War, however, the United States had an industrializing economy in which an increasing number of men and women worked in factories or offices for a wage, and in which most citizens–farmers and workers–had become dependent on store-bought necessities. The export of agricultural products was still important to the economy, but the revenues it brought in were increasingly used to finance industrial growth.

In the new economy crops were grown and goods were produced for sale in the marketplace, at home or abroad. The money received in market transactions, whether from the sale of goods or of a person's labor, was used to purchase items produced by other people–such as the candles and soap no longer made at home. Such a system encouraged specialization. Formerly self-sufficient farmers, for example, began to grow just one or two crops, or to concentrate on raising only cows, pigs, or sheep for market. Farm women gave up spinning and weaving at home and purchased fabric produced by wage-earning farm girls in Massachusetts textile mills.

Definition of a market economy

Sustained growth was the result of this economic evolution. Improvements in transportation and technology, the division of labor, and new methods of financing all fueled expansion of the economy–that is, the multiplication of goods and services. In turn, this growth prompted new improvements. The effect was cumulative; by the 1840s the economy was growing more rapidly than in the previous four decades. Per-capita income doubled between 1800 and 1860.

The Ohio dairy industry illustrated this process. In the first decades of the century, Ohio farmers made whatever cheese they needed for their own tables. Some made cheese to sell elsewhere, but only because they had a surplus of milk. However, the development of canals and railroads in the 1830s and 1840s changed Ohio farming. Farmers began to specialize, finding it more profitable to invest in better tools and spend all their time on one product. Some chose to grow wheat or tobacco for market, and to purchase whatever dairy products they needed. Other Ohioans, especially in the Western Reserve, decided to devote full time to dairy farming. Beginning in 1847, entrepreneurs built cheese factories in rural towns and contracted to buy curd from these local dairy farmers. In 1851 one such factory in Gustavus, Ohio, produced a daily average of 5,000 pounds of cheese from the milk of 2,500 cows. The cheese was shipped by canal and railroad to cities and eastern ports. In Boston and New York, some merchants turned to handling cheese and other dairy products exclusively, selling to consumers as far away as California, England, and China. By 1860 Ohio dairymen were producing 21.6 million pounds of cheese a year for market–a huge leap in production over the early 1800s.

Though such economic growth was sustained, it was not even. Prosperity reigned during two long periods, from 1823 to 1835 and from 1843 to 1857. But there were long stretches of economic contraction as well. During the time from Jefferson's 1807 embargo through 1815, in fact, upheaval was so great that the growth rate was actually negative–that is, fewer goods and services were produced. Contraction and deflation occurred again during the depressions of 1819 through 1823, 1839 through 1843, and 1857. These periods were characterized by the collapse of banks, business bankruptcies, and a decline in wages and prices. Workers faced increasing insecurity as a result of these cycles; on the down side, they suffered not only lower incomes but also unemployment.

Boom-and-bust cycles

Working people, a Baltimore physician noted during the depression of 1819, felt hard times "a thousand fold more than the merchants." Yet even during good times wage earners could not build up sufficient financial reserves to get them through the next depression; often they could not make it through the winter without drawing on charity for food, clothing, and firewood. In the 1820s and 1830s, free laborers in Baltimore found steady work from March through October and unemployment and hunger from November through February.

If good times were hard on workers and their families, depressions devastated them. In 1839 in Baltimore, all small manufacturers for the local market closed their doors; tailors, shoemakers, milliners, and shipyard and construction workers lost their jobs. Ninety miles to the north, Philadelphia took on an eerie aura. "The streets seemed deserted," Sidney George Fisher observed in 1842; "the largest [merchant] houses are shut up and to rent, there is no business . . . no money, no confidence." Only auctions boomed, as the sheriff sold off seized property at a quarter of predepression prices. Elsewhere in the city, soup societies fed the hungry. In New York, breadlines and beggars crowded the sidewalks. In smaller cities like Lynn, Massachusetts, those who did not leave became scavengers, digging for clams and harvesting dandelions.

In 1857 hard times struck again. The Mercantile Agency recorded 5,123 bankruptcies in 1857—nearly double the number in the previous year. The bankrupt firms had a total debt of $300 million, only half of which would be paid off. Contemporary reports estimated 20,000 to 30,000 unemployed in Philadelphia, and 30,000 to 40,000 in New York City. Benevolent societies expanded their soup kitchens and distributed free firewood to the needy. In Chicago, charities reorganized to meet the needs of the poor; in New York, the city hired the unemployed to fix streets and develop Central Park. And in Fall River, Massachusetts, a citizens' committee disbursed public funds on a weekly basis to nine hundred families. The soup kitchen, the breadline, and public aid had become permanent fixtures in urban America.

What caused the cycles of boom and bust that brought about such suffering? In general, they were a direct result of the new market economy. Prosperity inevitably stimulated greater demand for staples and finished goods. Increased demand led in turn to higher prices and still higher production, to speculation in land, and to the flow of foreign currency into the country. Eventually production surpassed demand, leading to lower prices and wages; and speculation outstripped the true value of land and stocks. The inflow of foreign money led first to easy credit and then to collapse when unhappy investors withdrew their funds.

Cause of boom-and-bust cycles

Some economists considered this process healthy—a self-adjusting cycle in which unprofitable economic ventures were eliminated. In theory, people concentrated on the activities they did best, and the economy as a whole became more efficient. Advocates of the system argued also that it furthered individual freedom, since ideally each seller, whether of goods or labor, was free to determine the conditions of the sale. But in fact the system put workers on a perpetual rollercoaster; they had become dependent on wages—and the availability of jobs—for their very existence.

Many also felt a distinct loss of status. For Joseph T. Buckingham, foreman of the Boston printing shop of West & Richardson, wage labor represented failure. Buckingham had been a master printer, running the shop of Thomas & Andrews on commission and doing some publishing of his own. In 1814 he purchased the shop, but did not get enough work to pay his debts. Without the capital to sustain his losses or to compete with larger shops, Buckingham had to sell his presses at auction. He became a wage earner, albeit a foreman. Though his wages were about the equal of an ordinary printer's income, Buckingham was unhappy. In his own words, he was "nothing more than a journeyman, except in responsibility."

Government promotion of the economy

To stimulate economic growth, the federal and state governments intervened actively during these years in the economy. Beginning with the purchase of Louisiana in 1803, the nation embarked on a deliberate program of westward expansion, western settlement, and promotion of agriculture. In 1803 President Jefferson dispatched Meriwether Lewis and William Clark to explore the new territory and report on its flora, fauna, minerals, and metals. The Lewis and Clark expedition was the beginning of a continuing federal interest in geographic and geologic surveying, which were the first steps in opening western land to exploitation and settlement.

Survey and sale of land

New steps followed quickly. In 1817 and 1818 Henry Rowe Schoolcraft explored the Missouri and Arkansas region, reporting on its geologic features and mineral resources. In 1819 and 1820 Major Stephen Long explored the Great Plains, mapping the area between the Platte and Canadian rivers. Between 1827 and 1840 the government surveyed about fifty railroad routes. The final door to western settlement was opened in 1843 and 1844 by John C. Frémont's expedition, which followed the Oregon Trail to the Pacific, then traveled south to California and returned east by way of the Great Salt Lake. An officer in the U.S. Topological Corps, Frémont published a report of his journey dispelling a long-standing myth that the center of the continent was a desert.

To encourage western agriculture, the federal government offered public lands for sale at reasonable prices (see page 153) and evicted Indian tribes from their traditional lands. And because transportation was crucial to development of the frontier, the government financed roads and subsidized railroad construction through land grants. Even the State Department aided agriculture: its consular offices overseas collected horticultural information, seeds, and cuttings and published technical reports in an effort to improve American farming.

The federal government also played a key role in technological and industrial growth. Federal arsenals pioneered new manufacturing techniques and helped to develop the machine-tool industry. The United States Military Academy at West Point, founded in 1802, emphasized technical and scientific subjects in its curriculum. And the U.S. Post Office stimulated interregional trade and played a brief but crucial role in the development of the telegraph: the first telegraph line, from Washington to Baltimore, was constructed under a government grant, and during 1845 the Post Office ran it, employing inventor Samuel F. B. Morse as superintendent. Finally, to create an atmosphere conducive to economic growth, the government protected inventions and domestic industries. Patent laws gave inventors a seventeen-year monopoly on their inventions, and tariffs protected American industry from foreign competition.

Legal foundations of commerce

The federal judiciary also promoted business enterprise. In *Gibbons* v. *Ogden* (1824), the Supreme Court overturned a New York state law that had given Robert Fulton and Robert Livingston a monopoly on the New York–New Jersey steamboat trade. Ogden, their successor, lost his monopoly when Chief Justice Marshall ruled that the trade fell under the sway of the commerce clause of the Constitution. Thus Congress, not New York, had the controlling power. Since the federal government issued such licenses on a nonexclusive basis, the decision ended monopolies on waterways throughout the nation. Within a year, 43 steamboats were plying Ogden's route.

In defining interstate commerce broadly, the Marshall Court expanded federal powers over the economy while limiting the ability of states to control economic activity within their borders. Its action was consistent with its earlier decision in *Dartmouth College* v. *Woodward* (1819), which protected the sanctity of contracts against interference by the states (see page 201). "If business is to prosper," Marshall wrote, "men must have assurance that contracts will be enforced."

Federal and state courts, in conjunction with state legislatures, also encouraged the proliferation of corporations–groups of investors that could hold property and transact business as one person. In 1800 the United States had about 300 incorporated firms; in 1817 about 2,000. By 1830 the New England states alone had issued 1,900 charters, one-third to manufacturing and mining firms. At first each firm needed a special legislative act to incorporate, but after the 1830s applications became so numerous that incorporation was authorized by general state laws. Though legislative action created corporations, the courts played a crucial role in defining their status, extending their powers, and protecting them.

State promotion of the economy

State governments far surpassed the federal government in promoting economic growth. From 1815 through 1860, for example, 73 percent of the $135 million invested in canals was government money, mostly from the states. In the 1830s the states shifted their investments to rail construction. Even though the federal government played a larger role in building railroads than canals, state and local governments provided more than half of southern rail capital. Overall, railroads received 131 million acres in land subsidies, 48 million of which was provided by the states. State governments also invested in corporation and bank stocks, providing those institutions with much-needed capital. Pennsylvania, probably the most active of the states in promoting its economy, invested a total of $100 million in canals, railroads, banks, and manufacturing firms; its appointees sat on more than 150 corporate boards of directors.

States actually equaled or surpassed private enterprise in their investments. But they did more than invest in industry. By establishing bounties for agricultural prizes, they stimulated commercial agriculture, especially sheep raising and wool manufacture (see page 232). Through special acts and general incorporation laws, states regulated the nature and activities of both corporations and banks. They also used their licensing capacity to regulate industry; in Georgia, for example, grading and marketing of tobacco was state-regulated.

From the end of the War of 1812 until 1860 the United States experienced uneven but sustained economic growth largely as a result of these government efforts. Though political controversy raged over questions of state versus federal activity—especially with regard to internal improvements and banking—all parties agreed on the general goal of economic expansion (see Chapters 8 and 12). Indeed, the major restraint on government action during these years was not philosophical but financial: both the government and the public purse were small.

Transportation and regionalization

From 1800 through 1860 the North, South, and West followed distinctly different paths economically. Everywhere agriculture remained the foundation of the American economy. Nevertheless, factories and merchant houses came to characterize the North, plantations the South, and frontier farms the West. Paradoxically, this tendency toward regional specialization made the sections at once more different and more dependent on each other.

The revolution in transportation and communications was probably the single most important cause of these changes. It was the North's heavy investment in canals and railroads that made it the center of American commerce; its growing seaboard cities distributed western produce and New England textiles. New York financial and commercial houses linked even the southern cotton-exporting economy to the North. The South, with most of its capital invested in slave labor, built fewer canals, railroads, and factories and remained largely rural and undeveloped (see Chapter 10).

Before the canal fever of the 1820s and 1830s and the railroad fever of the 1830s and after became epidemic, it was by no means self-evident that New England and the Middle Atlantic states would dominate American economic life. In fact, the natural orientation of the 1800 frontier—Tennessee, Kentucky, and

Change in trade routes

Ohio—was to the South. The southward-flowing Ohio and Mississippi rivers were the lifelines of early western settlement. Flatboats transported western grain and hogs southward for consumption or transfer to oceangoing vessels at New Orleans. Southern products—first tobacco, then lumber and cotton—flowed directly to Europe. Settlement of southern Illinois and Indiana and the appearance of steamboats on western rivers only intensified this pattern.

But the pattern changed in the 1820s and 1830s. New roads and turnpikes opened up east-west travel. The National Road, a stone-based, gravel-topped highway beginning in Cumberland, Maryland, reached Wheeling (then in Virginia) in 1818 and Columbus, Ohio, in 1833. More important, the Erie Canal, completed in 1825, forged an east-west axis from the Hudson River to Lake Erie, linking the Great Lakes with New York City and the Atlantic Ocean. The canal carried easterners and then immigrants to settle the Old Northwest and the frontier beyond; in the opposite direction, it bore western grain to the large and growing eastern markets. Railroads and later the telegraph would solidify these east-west links. By contrast, only at one place—Bowling Green, Kentucky—did a northern railroad actually connect with a southern one. Although trade still continued southward along the Ohio and Mississippi rivers, the bulk of western trade flowed eastward by 1850. Thus, by the eve of the Civil War, the northern and Middle Atlantic states were closely tied to the former frontier of the Old Northwest.

Construction of the 363-mile-long Erie Canal was a visionary enterprise. When the state of New York authorized it in 1817, the longest existing American

Canals

canal was only 28 miles long. Vigorously promoted by Governor De Witt Clinton, the Erie cost $7 million, much of it

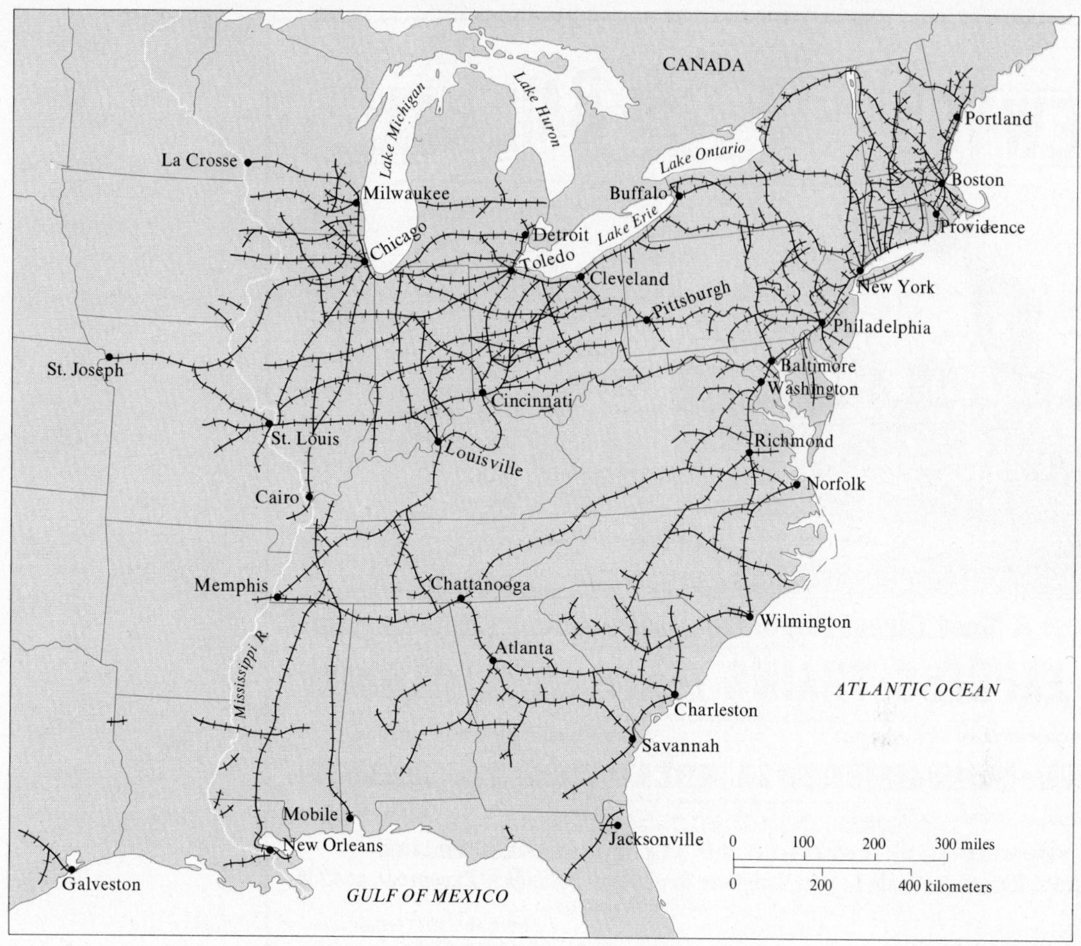

Major railroads in 1860

raised by loans from British investors. The canal shortened the journey between Buffalo and New York City from twenty to six days and reduced freight charges from $100 to $5 a ton. By 1835 traffic was so heavy that the Erie had to be widened from forty to seventy feet and deepened from four to seven feet. The skeptics who had called the canal "Clinton's big ditch" had long since been silenced.

The Erie triggered an explosion of canal building. Other states and cities, fearing the advantage New York had gained, rushed to follow suit. By 1840 canals crisscrossed the Northeast and Midwest, and canal mileage in the United States had reached 3,300—an increase of more than 2,000 miles in a single decade. Unfortunately for investors, none of these canals enjoyed the financial success achieved by the Erie. The high cost of construction, lack of federal financing, and economic contraction after 1837 all lowered profitability. As a result, investment in canals began to slump in the 1830s. By 1850 more miles were being abandoned than built, and the canal era had ended.

Railroads

Meanwhile, railroad construction was on the upswing. The railroad era began in 1830 when Peter Cooper's locomotive *Tom Thumb* first steamed along 13 miles of track constructed by the Baltimore and Ohio Railroad. In 1833 a second railroad ran 136 miles from Charleston to Hamburg, South Carolina. By 1850 the United States had nearly 9,000 miles of railroad; by 1860, roughly 31,000 (see map). Canal fever stimulated this early railroad construction. Promoters of the Baltimore and Ohio had turned to the railroad in an effort to compete with the Canal. Similarly, the line between Boston and Worcester, Massachusetts, was

BAGGAGE CHECKED THRO' FROM NEW-YORK or BOSTON

TO ALL POINTS WEST, NORTHWEST AND SOUTHWEST.

Shortest & Most Direct Route from all Points in New England.

FIVE EXPRESS TRAINS LEAVE ALBANY DAILY,

(SUNDAYS EXCEPTED,)

CONNECTING AT BUFFALO WITH THE	CONNECTING AT SUSP. BRIDGE, WITH THE
LAKE SHORE AND BUFFALO & LAKE HURON R.R.	**GREAT WESTERN RAILWAY.**

Well Ventilated SLEEPING CARS commodiously fitted up with every necessary requisite for comfort, are attached to the Night Trains thereby affording Travelers the luxury of a Nights Sleep, without the necessity of laying over on their route.

SMOKING CARS ATTACHED TO ALL PASSENGER TRAINS

An Emigrant Passenger Train Leaves Emigrant Depot Daily (Sundays Excepted), at 12 M.

FOR FURTHER PARTICULARS SEE SMALL BILLS.

E. CORNING, President. GERSH BANKER, Chief Clerk. C. VIBBARD, Gen'l Supt. S. DRULLARD, Gen'l Freight Agent. JOHN S. DALEY, Eastern Traveling Agent.

A mid-nineteenth-century poster boasts of the superior services of the New York Central Railroad. American Antiquarian Society.

intended as the first link in a line to Albany, at the eastern end of the Erie Canal.

The earliest railroads connected two cities or one city and its surrounding area. Not until the 1850s would railroads offer long-distance service at reasonable rates. And the early lines also had technical problems to contend with. As John Jervis had discovered, locomotives heavy enough to climb steep grades and pull long trains required strong rails and resilient roadbeds. Engineers met those needs by replacing wooden track with iron rails and by supporting the rails with ties embedded in gravel. John Jervis's wheel alignment–called the swivel truck–removed another major obstacle by enabling engines to hold the track on sharp curves. Other problems persisted, though: notably the continued use of hand brakes, which severely restricted speed, and the lack of a standard gauge for track. The Pennsylvania and Ohio railroads, for instance, had no fewer than seven different track widths. Thus a journey from Philadelphia to Charleston involved eight changes in gauge.

In the 1850s technological improvements, competition, and economic recovery prompted the development of regional and later national rail networks. The West experienced a railroad boom. By 1853 rail lines linked New York to Chicago, and a year later track had reached the Mississippi River. By 1860 rails stretched as far west as St. Joseph, Missouri–the edge of the frontier. In that year the railroad network east of the Mississippi approximated its physical pattern for the next century, but the process of corporate integration had only begun. In 1853 seven short lines combined to form the New York Central system, and the Pennsylvania Railroad was unified from Philadelphia to Pittsburgh. Most lines, however, were still independently run, separated by gauge, scheduling, differences in car design, and a commitment to serve their home towns first and foremost.

Railroads did not completely replace water transportation. Steamboats, first introduced in 1807 when Robert Fulton's *Clermont* paddled up the Hudson from New York City, still plied the rivers. They had proven their value on western rivers in 1815 when the *Enterprise* first carried cargo upstream on the Mississippi and Ohio rivers. Until the 1850s, when western rail development blossomed, steamboats outdid railroads in carrying freight. Great Lakes steamers managed to hold their own even into the fifties, for the sea-like lakes permitted the construction of giant ships and the widespread adoption of propellers in place of paddle wheels. These unique ships, lying as whales in the water, were especially well suited to carrying heavy bulk cargoes like lumber, grain, and ore.

Steamboats

Gradually steamboats began to replace sailing vessels on the high seas. In days gone by, sailing ships—whalers, sleek clippers, and square-rigged packets—had been the pride of American commerce. But sailing ships were dependent on prevailing winds and weather, and thus could not schedule regular crossings. In 1818 packets began making four round trips a year between New York and Liverpool, sailing on schedule rather than waiting for a full cargo as had ships before then. The breakthrough came in 1848, though, when steamship owner Samuel Cunard began the Atlantic Shuttle, which reduced travel time between Liverpool and New York from 25 days eastbound and 49 days westbound to 10–14 days each way. Sailing ships quickly lost their first-class passengers and light cargo to these swift new ocean steamships. For the next decade they continued to carry immigrants and bulk cargo, but by 1860 only the freight trade remained to them.

By far the fastest spreading technological advance of the era was the magnetic telegraph. Samuel F. B. Morse's invention freed messages from the restraint of traveling no faster than the messenger; instantaneous communication became possible even over long distances. By 1853, only nine years after construction of the first experimental line, 23,000 miles of telegraph wire spread across the United States; by 1860, 50,000. The first transatlantic cable was laid in 1858, and by 1861 the telegraph bridged the continent, connecting the east and west coasts. The new invention revolutionized news gathering, provided advance information for railroads and steamships, and altered patterns of business and finance. Rarely has innovation had so great an impact so quickly.

Telegraph

The changes in transportation and communications from 1800 to 1860 were revolutionary. Railroads reduced the number of loadings and unloadings, were cheap to build over difficult terrain, and remained in use all year. But time was the key. In 1800 it took four days to travel from New York City to Baltimore, and nearly four weeks to reach Detroit. By 1830 Baltimore was only a day-and-a-half away and Detroit only a two-week journey. By 1857 Detroit was but an overnight trip; in a week one could reach Texas, Kansas, or Nebraska. This reduced travel time saved money and facilitated commerce. During the first two decades of the century, wagon transportation cost 30 to 70 cents per ton per mile. By 1860, railroads in New York state carried freight at an average charge of 2.2 cents per ton per mile; wheat moved from Chicago to New York for 1.2 cents a ton-mile. In sum, the transportation revolution had transformed the economy—and with it the relationships of the North, West, and South.

The North: merchants and farmers

The development of the North as the nation's clearing-house was hastened by its rapid population growth. Between 1800 and 1860, the number of Americans increased sixfold to 31.4 million. As the population grew, the frontier receded, and rural settlements became towns and cities (see figure). In 1800 the nation had only 33 towns with 2,500 or more people and only 3 with more than 25,000. By 1860, 392 towns exceeded 2,500 in population and 35 had more than 25,000.

In the Northeast, the percentage of people living in

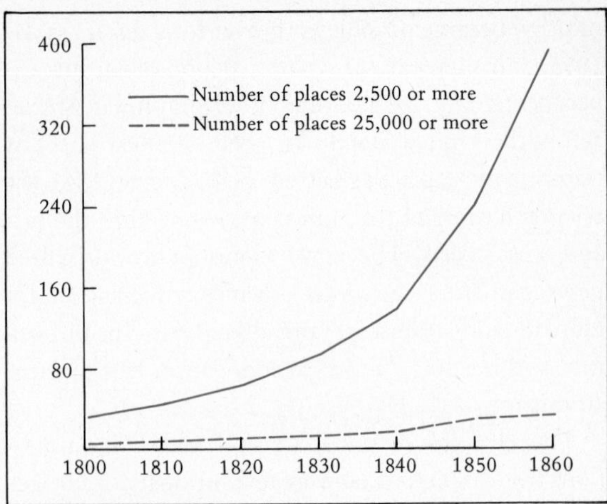

Number of urban areas, 1800–1860

urban areas grew from 9.3 to 35.7 from 1800 to 1860. Significantly, most of this growth occurred in northern and western communities located along the new transportation routes, where increased commerce created new jobs and opportunities. Kingston, New York, 90 miles north of New York City on the Hudson River, was one example. The Delaware and Hudson Canal, which extended from the Hudson Valley to the coalfields of Pennsylvania, rapidly transformed Kingston from a sleepy farm village of 1,000 in the 1820s to an urban community of more than 10,000 in 1850.

Growth of cities

The hundreds of small new cities like Kingston were surpassed by stars of even greater magnitude: the great metropolitan cities. In 1860 21 cities exceeded 40,000 in population and 9 exceeded 100,000 (see maps). By 1810 New York City had overtaken Philadelphia as the nation's most populous city; its population soared thereafter, reaching 1,174,779 in 1860. Baltimore and New Orleans dominated the South, and San Francisco became the leading West Coast city. In the Midwest the new lake cities (Chicago, Detroit, Milwaukee, and Cleveland) began to surpass the frontier river cities (Cincinnati, Louisville, and Pittsburgh) founded a generation earlier. These cities formed a nationwide urban network whose center was the great metropolises of the North.

Rapid urban growth in turn brought about a radical change in American commerce and trade. In 1800 most merchants performed the functions of retailer, wholesaler, importer and exporter, shipper, banker, and insurer. Some even engaged in manufacturing, as master craftsmen. But in New York and Philadelphia in the 1790s, and increasingly in all large cities after the War of 1812, the general merchant gave way to the specialist. As a result, the distribution of goods became more systematic. By the 1830s and 1840s, urban centers had been transformed into a pattern we would recognize today: retail shops featured such specialized lines as shoes, wines and spirits, dry goods, groceries, and hardware. Within the downtown area importers and exporters, wholesalers, jobbers, bankers, and insurance brokers clustered on particular streets, near transportation and the merchant exchanges that made it convenient to carry on their businesses more efficiently.

Specialization of commerce

Thus Kingston in the 1850s differed from Kingston in the 1820s not just in size and population density but also in the complexity of its institutions. In the small rural village of the 1820s, homes and workplaces were often combined; thirty years later Kingston had separate commercial and residential districts. By 1858 Kingston's downtown boasted six china and glassware shops, ten clothing stores, two fancy-goods outlets, and ten dry-goods stores, as well as other retail shops, doctors' and lawyers' offices, and financial firms. Beyond the commercial center, two small industrial zones housed nearly all of the city's manufacturing.

On a personal level the specialization of commerce was illustrated by the cotton trader. Cotton had become a staple export following the invention of the cotton gin in 1793; exports rose from half a million pounds in that year to 83 million pounds in 1815. At first northern cotton traders sold the crop abroad or in New England; in turn they bought household goods, supplies, and equipment for southern plantations, extending credit to the purchasers. Gradually some agents came to specialize in finance alone: cotton brokers appeared, men who brought together buyers and sellers for a commission. Similarly, wheat and hog brokers sprang up in the West–in Cincinnati, Louisville, and St. Louis. The supply of finished goods also became more specialized. Wholesalers bought large quantities of a particular item from manufacturers, and jobbers broke down the wholesale lots for retail stores and county merchants.

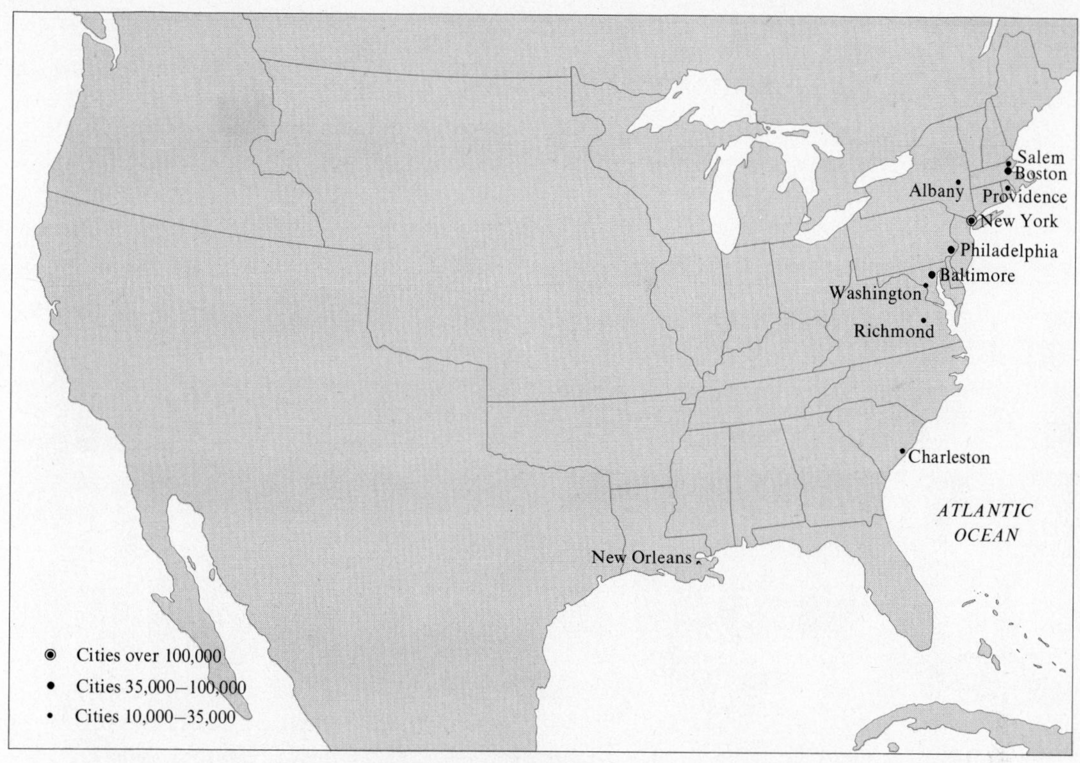

Major American cities, 1820

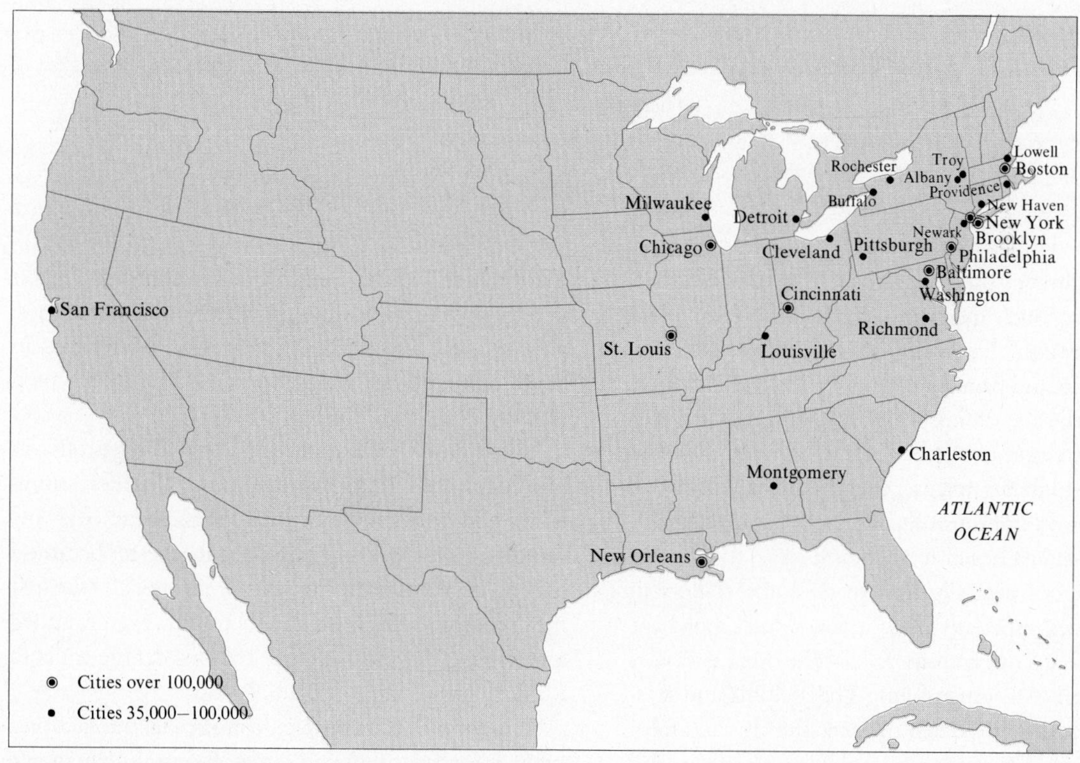

Major American cities, 1860

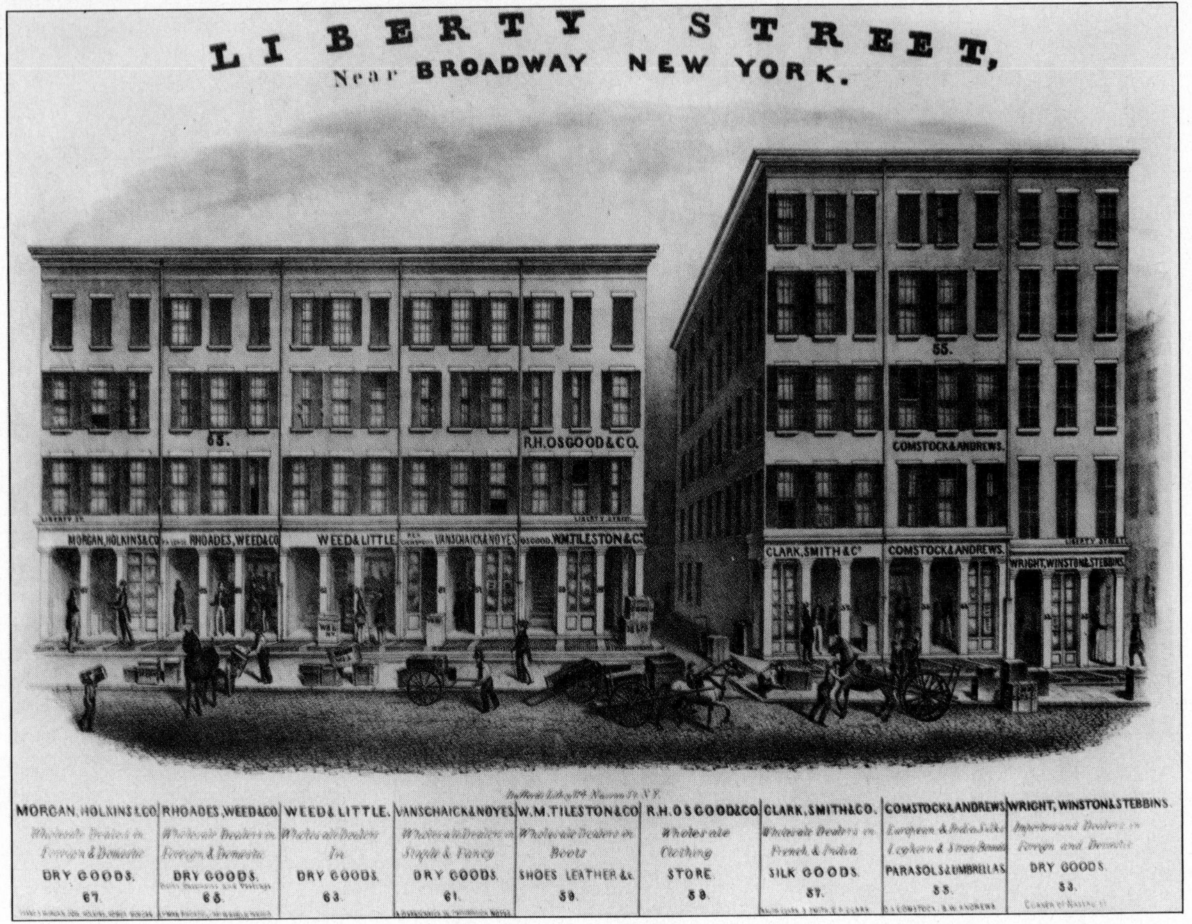

A dry goods center on Liberty Street in New York City. The key below the picture identifies most of the proprietors as wholesale dealers. Museum of the City of New York.

In small towns the general merchant persisted for a longer time. Such merchants continued to sell some goods through barter–exchanging, for example, flour or pots and pans for eggs or other local produce. They left the sale of finished goods, such as shoes and clothing, to local craftsmen. In rural areas and on the frontier, peddlers acted as general merchants. But as transportation improved and towns grew, even small-town merchants began to specialize.

Commercial specialization made some traders in the big cities, especially New York, virtual merchant princes. New York had emerged as the dominant port in the late 1790s, outstripping Philadelphia and Boston. When the Erie Canal opened, the city became a standard stop on every major trade route–from Europe, the ports of the South, and the West. New York traders were the middlemen in southern cotton and western grain trading; in fact, New York was the nation's major cotton-exporting city. Merchants in other cities played a similar role within their own regions.

These newly rich traders invested their profits in processing and then manufacturing, further stimulating the growth of northern cities. Some cities became leaders in specific industries: Rochester became a milling center and Cincinnati–"Porkopolis"–the first meat-packing center. Boston merchants even founded a new city, Lowell, to house the first textile mills in Massachusetts.

To support their complex commercial transactions, many merchants required large office staffs. In an age before typewriters and carbon paper, much of the

Counting house and credit systems

office staff—all male—worked on high stools laboriously copying business forms and correspondence. The scratch of their pens was the early nineteenth-century equivalent of the typewriter's clatter. At the bottom of the office hierarchy were messenger boys, often pre-teenagers, who delivered documents. Above them were the ordinary copyists, who hand-copied documents in ink as many times as needed. Clerks handled such assignments as customs-house clearances and duties, shipping papers, and translations. Above them were the bookkeeper and the confidential chief clerk. Those seeking employment in such an office, called a counting house, could take a course from a writing master to acquire a "good hand." All hoped to rise to the status of partner.

Because the entire trading system was built on credit, it was extremely susceptible to the boom-and-bust cycles that characterized the era. In boom times credit was easy to come by and merchants flourished. During slumps and depressions—1819 through 1823, 1837 through 1843, and 1857—bank credit and investment loans contracted sharply and many merchant houses collapsed. Merchants learned to evaluate their customers carefully before shipping them goods on credit. One response to the need to minimize risk was Lewis Tappan's mercantile agency, founded in 1841. The forerunner of Dun and Bradstreet, Tappan furnished his subscribers with confidential credit reports on country merchants. One such report read:

> James Samson is a peddler, aged 30; he comes to Albany to buy his goods, and then peddles them out along the canal from Albany to Buffalo. He is worth $2,000; owns a wooden house at Lockport . . . has a wife and three children . . . drinks two glasses cider brandy, plain, morning and evening—never more; drinks water after each; chews fine cut; never smokes; good teeth generally; has lost a large double tooth on lower jaw, back, second from throat on left . . . purchases principally jewelry and fancy articles.

Beyond the town and city limits, agriculture remained the backbone of the New England economy. For although urban areas were growing quickly, America was still overwhelmingly rural; even in 1860 rural residents far outnumbered urban dwellers (see figure). Indeed, it was rural population growth that transformed so many farm villages into bustling small cities. And it was the ability of northeastern farmers to feed the growing town and village populations that made possible the concentration of population and the resulting development of commerce and industry.

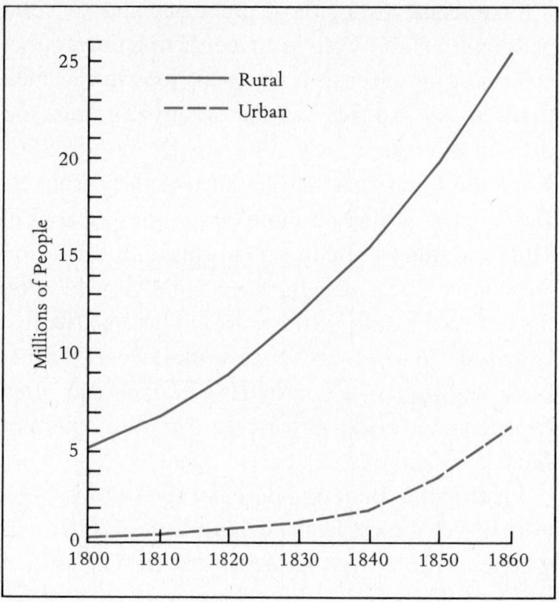

Urban-rural population, 1800–1860

In the early part of the century New England and Middle Atlantic farmers supplied their own needs and produced a surplus of crops for sale to the growing towns. Farmers achieved their surpluses by using homemade goods and implements—wooden plows, rakes, shovels, and yokes—as their fathers had done. For iron parts, they turned to the local blacksmith.

But then canals and railroads began transporting grains, especially wheat, eastward from the fertile Old Northwest. And at the same time, northeastern agriculture developed some serious problems. Northeastern farmers had already cultivated all the land they could; expansion was impossible. Moreover, these small New England farms with their uneven terrain did not lend themselves to the new labor-saving farm implements introduced in the 1830s—mechanical sowers, reapers, threshers, and balers. Many northeastern farms also suffered from soil exhaustion: the worn-out land produced lower yields while requiring a greater investment in seed.

Northeastern agriculture

In response to all these problems, and to competition from the West, many northern farmers either went west or gave up farming for jobs in the merchant houses and factories. For eastern farm sons and daughters, western New York was the first frontier. After the Erie Canal was completed, these Yankees and Yorkers settled on more fertile, cheaper land in Ohio and Illinois, and then in Michigan, Indiana, and Wisconsin. Farm daughters who did not go west flocked to the early textile mills and became the first large-scale American industrial work force. Still other New Englanders–urban, better educated, and often experienced in trade–entered the counting houses of New York and other cities.

Neither the counting house nor the factory, however, depleted New England agriculture. The farmers who remained proved as adaptable at farming as their children did at copy desks and water-powered looms. By the 1850s New England and Middle Atlantic farmers were successfully adjusting to competition from western agricultural products. They abandoned commercial production of wheat and corn and stopped tilling poor land. Instead they improved their livestock, especially cattle, and specialized in vegetable and fruit production and dairy farming. They financed these changes through land sales or borrowing. In fact, their greatest profit was made from increasing land values, not from farming itself.

State governments promoted commercial agriculture in order to spur economic growth and sustain the values of an agrarian-based republic. Massachusetts in 1817 and New York in 1819 subsidized agricultural prizes and county fairs. New York required contestants to submit written descriptions of how they grew their prize crops; the state then published the best essays to encourage the use of new methods and to promote specialization. Farm journals also helped to familiarize farmers with developments in agriculture. By 1860 there were nearly sixty journals with a combined circulation of from 250,000 to 300,000.

Even so, the Old Northwest gradually and inevitably replaced the northeastern states as the center of American agriculture. Farms in the Old Northwest were much larger than northeastern ones, and better suited to the new mechanized farming implements.

Mechanization of agriculture

The farmers of the region bought machines such as the McCormick reaper on credit and paid for them with the profits from their high yields. By 1847 Cyrus McCormick was selling a thousand reapers a year. Using interchangeable parts, he expanded production to five thousand a year, but still demand outstripped supply. Similarly, John Deere's steel plow, invented in 1837, replaced the inadequate iron plow; steel blades kept the soil from sticking and were tough enough to break the roots of prairie grass. By 1856, Deere's sixty-five employees were making 13,500 plows a year.

These machines eased the problem of scarce farm labor and permitted a 70-percent surge in wheat production in the 1850s alone. By that time the area that had been the western wilderness in 1800 had become one of the world's leading agricultural regions. Midwestern farmers fed an entire nation and a generation of immigrants, and had food left over to export.

The western frontier

Between 1800 and 1860 the frontier moved westward at an incredible pace (see map). In 1800 the edge of settlement formed an arc from western New York through the new states of Kentucky and Tennessee,

Movement of the frontier

south to Georgia. Twenty years later it had shifted to Ohio, Indiana, and Illinois in the North and Louisiana, Alabama, and Mississippi in the South. By 1860 settlement had reached the West Coast; the 1800 frontier was long-settled, and once-unexplored regions were dotted with farms and mines, towns and villages. Unsettled land remained–mostly between the Mississippi River and the Sierra Nevadas–but essentially the frontier and its native inhabitants, the Indians, had given way to white settlement (see Chapter 11). All that remained for whites was to people the plains and mountain territories.

The legal boundaries of the country also changed rapidly during this period. Between 1803 and 1857 the United States pushed its original boundaries to their present continental limits (except for Alaska). The Louisiana Purchase roughly doubled the nation's size, and the War of 1812 and acquisition of Florida from Spain in 1819 secured the Southeast. In the 1840s the United States annexed the Republic of Texas, defined its northern border with Canada, and purchased Cali-

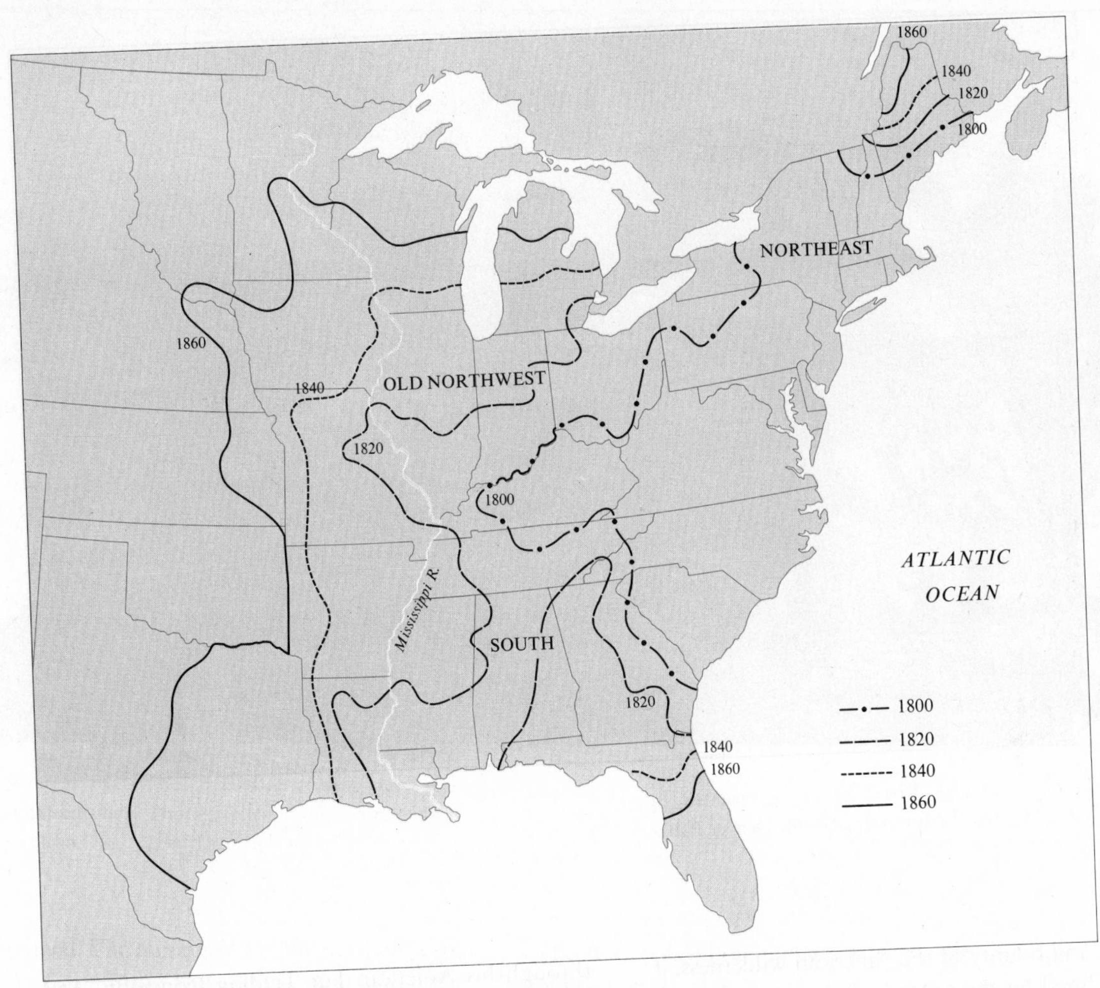

The moving frontier: the edge of settlement, 1800–1860. Source: From Ross M. Robertson, *History of the American Economy,* 2nd edition. N.Y.: Harcourt Brace & World, 1964.

fornia, Nevada, Utah, and most of Arizona from Mexico (see Chapter 12). In the 1850s the Gadsden Purchase added southern Arizona and New Mexico (see Chapter 13).

The lore of the vanishing frontier forms part of the mythology of America: fur trappers, explorers, and pioneers braving an unknown environment and hostile Indians; settlers crossing the arid plains and snow-covered Rockies by Conestoga wagon to bring civilization to the wilderness; Mormons finding Zion in the Great American Desert; forty-niners sailing on clipper ships to California in search of gold.

Americans have only recently come to recognize that there are other sides to these familiar stories. Women as well as men were pioneers. The fur trappers, explorers, and pioneers did not discover North America by themselves, nor did the wagon trains fight their way across the plains–Indians guided them along traditional paths and led them to food and water. And rather than civilizing the frontier, settlers at first brought a rather primitive economy and society, which did not compare favorably with the well-ordered Indian civilizations. In the South, frontier settlement carried with it slavery. The Mormons who sought a new Jerusalem by Salt Lake were fleeing the gehenna (hell) imposed on them by intolerant, violent frontier folk farther east (see Chapter 12). And all those who sought furs, gold, and lumber spoiled the virgin landscape in the name of progress and development.

This was the ironic contrast between the ideal and the reality of the frontier. If pioneers were attracted by

wheat. In its growing cities, merchant princes arose to supply, feed, and clothe the new settlers. One such merchant was Levi Strauss, whose tough mining pants eventually became synonymous with American jeans.

Gold altered the pattern of settlement along the entire Pacific Coast. Before 1848 most overland traffic flowed north over the Oregon Trail; few pioneers turned south to California. But by 1849 a pioneer observed that the Oregon Trail "bore no evidence of having been much traveled this year." Traffic was instead flowing south, and California was becoming the new population center of the Pacific Slope. One measure of the shift was the overland mail routes. In the 1840s the Oregon Trail had been the major communications link between the Pacific and the Midwest. But the Post Office officials who organized mail routes in the 1850s terminated them in California; there was no route farther north than Sacramento.

By 1860 California, like the Great Plains and prairies farther east, had become a farmers' and merchants' frontier. Though the story of these settlers is less dramatic than that of the trappers and forty-niners, it is nevertheless the story of the overwhelming majority of westerners before 1860. The farming frontier started first on the western fringes of

Farming frontier

the eastern seaboard states and in the Old Northwest, then moved to the edge of the Great Plains and California. Pioneer families cleared the land of trees or prairie grass, hoed in corn and wheat, fenced in animals, and constructed cabins of logs or sod. If they were successful–and many were not–they slowly cleared more land. As settled areas expanded, farmers built roads to carry their stock and produce to market and bring back supplies they could not produce themselves. Growth brought specialization; as western farmers shifted from self-sufficiency to commercial farming, they too tended to concentrate on one crop. By this time the area was no longer a frontier, and families seeking new land had to go farther west. In John Jervis's time a farmer from Rome, New York, might have gone to Michigan via the Erie Canal and Lake Erie. A later generation would go farther west to Iowa, Nebraska, or even California.

What made farm settlement possible was the availability of land and credit. Some public lands were granted as a reward for military service: veterans of the

Land grants and sales

War of 1812 received 160 acres; veterans of the Mexican War (see Chapter 12) could purchase land at reduced prices. And until 1820, civilians could buy government land at $2 an acre (a relatively high price) on a liberal four-year payment plan. More important, from 1804 to 1817 the government successively reduced the minimum purchase from 320 to 80 acres. However, when the availability of land prompted a flurry of land speculation that ended in the Panic of 1819, the government discontinued credit sales. Instead it reduced the price further, to $1.25 an acre.

Some eager pioneers settled land before it had been surveyed and put up for sale. Such illegal settlers, or squatters, then had to buy the land they lived on at auction, and faced the risk of being unable to purchase it. In 1841, to facilitate settlement, simplify land sales, and end property disputes, Congress passed the Preemption Act, which legalized settlement prior to surveying.

Since most settlers, squatters or not, needed to borrow money, private credit systems arose. Banks, private investors, country storekeepers, and speculators all extended credit to farmers. Railroads also sold land on credit–land they had received from the government as construction subsidies. (The Illinois Central, for example, received 2.6 million acres in 1850.) Indeed, nearly all economic activity in the West involved credit, from land sales to the shipping of produce to railroad construction. And again in 1836, 1855, and 1856 the credit system helped to fuel land prices. Much land fell into the hands of speculators, and as a result tenancy became more common in the West than it had been in New England.

Towns and cities were the lifelines of the agricultural West. Cities along the Ohio and Mississippi rivers–Pittsburgh, Louisville, Cincinnati, and St. Louis–

Frontier cities

preceded most of the settlement of the early frontier. A generation later the lake cities of Cleveland, Detroit, and Chicago spearheaded settlement farther west. Steamboats connected farms with these river and lake cities, carrying grain east to market and bringing back finished goods in return. As in the Northeast, these western cities eventually developed into manufacturing centers when merchants shifted their investments from commerce to industry. Chicago became a center for the

Cincinnati in 1800 (above) and 1848 (below). These two pictures show the rapid growth of the city from a frontier hamlet to a major urban center. The steamboats lined up along the riverfront in the bottom picture helped to link the frontier to southern and eastern cities. Above: The Cincinnati Historical Society; below: Rare Book Room, Cincinnati Public Library.

manufacture of farm implements, Louisville of textiles, and Cleveland of iron. Smaller cities specialized in flour mills, and all produced consumer goods for the hinterlands.

Urban growth in the West was so spectacular that by 1860 Cincinnati, St. Louis, and Chicago had populations exceeding 100,000, and Buffalo, Louisville, San Francisco, Pittsburgh, Detroit, Milwaukee, and Cleveland had surpassed 40,000. Thus commerce, urbanization, and industrialization eventually overtook the farmers' frontier, wedding the Old Northwest and areas beyond to the Northeast.

The rise of manufacturing

The McCormick reaper, ridiculed the London *Times,* looked like "a cross between a flying-machine, a wheelbarrow, and an Astley chariot." Put to a competitive test through rain-soaked wheat, however, the Chicago-made reaper alone passed, to the spontaneous cheers of the skeptical English spectators. The reaper and hundreds of other American products made their international debut at the 1851 London Crystal Palace Exhibition, the first modern world's fair. There the design and quality of American machines and wares–from familiar farm tools to such exotic devices as an ice-cream freezer and the reaper–astonished observers. American manufacturers returned home with dozens of medals, including all three prizes for piano making. But more impressive to the Europeans were three simple machines: Alfred C. Hobb's unpickable padlocks, Samuel Colt's revolvers, and Robbins and Lawrence's six rifles with completely interchangeable parts. All were machine-made rather than hand-tooled, products of what the British called the American system of manufacturing.

So impressed were the British–the leading industrial nation of the time–that in 1853 they sent a parliamentary commission to study the American system. A year later a second committee returned to examine the firearms industry in detail. In their report to the British government, the committee described an astonishing experiment performed at the federal armory in Springfield, Massachusetts. To test the interchangeability of machine-made muskets, they selected rifles made in each of the previous ten years. While the committee watched, the guns were dismantled "and the parts placed in a row of boxes, mixed up together." The Englishmen "then requested the workman, whose duty it is to 'assemble' the arms, to put them together, which he did–the Committee handing him the parts, taken at hazard–with the use of a turnscrew only, and as quickly as though they had been English muskets, whose parts had carefully been kept separate." Britain's Enfield arsenal subsequently converted to American equipment. Within the next few years other nations followed Great Britain's lead, sending delegations across the Atlantic to bring back American machines.

The American system of manufacturing used precision machinery to produce interchangeable parts that needed no filing or fitting. In 1798 Eli Whitney had used a primitive system of interchangeable parts when he contracted with the federal government to make ten thousand rifles in twenty-eight months. By the 1820s the Connecticut manufacturer Simeon North, the Springfield, Massachusetts, Arsenal, and the Harpers Ferry, Virginia, Armory were all producing machine-made interchangeable parts for firearms. From the arsenals the American system spread, giving birth to the machine-tool industry–the mass manufacture of specialized machines for other industries. One by-product was an explosion in consumer goods: since the time and skill involved in manufacturing had been greatly reduced, the new system permitted mass production at low cost. Waltham watches, Yale locks, Singer sewing machines, and Colt revolvers became household items, inexpensive yet of uniformly high quality.

American system of manufacturing

Interchangeable parts and the machine-tool industry were uniquely American contributions to the industrial revolution. Both paved the way for America's swift industrialization following the Civil War. The process of industrialization began, however, in a simple and traditional way, not unlike that of other nations. In 1800 manufacturing was relatively unimportant to the American economy. What manufacturing there was took place mostly in small workshops and homes, where journeymen and apprentices worked with and under master craftsmen. These tailors, shoemakers, and blacksmiths made articles by hand for a specific customer.

It was the rise of merchant-investors, wholesalers, and retailers, in combination with the transportation revolution, that transformed this system. First the "putting-out" system of home manufacture established the merchant as a middleman between the worker and the customer. In the shoe industry, for instance, shoemakers worked in their homes from 1800 until about 1840, receiving the materials—leather, thread, and so on—from a merchant or master cordwainer and delivering the finished product to him. Then in the 1820s, entrepreneurs set up central shops where leather was cut into soles and uppers before being put out. The upper parts were then sent to one group of workers and the soles and finished uppers to another group. This system introduced a division of labor, in which workers performed specialized tasks—cutting leather, shaping and sewing uppers, or finishing the shoe. By the 1840s, machinery had begun to replace the traditional tools, and by the 1850s steam-powered factory production had become widespread. In the process the master craftsman had disappeared, the journeyman had become a factory worker, and shoes were produced impersonally for distant markets.

Putting-out system

Even more dramatic and influential was the development of the New England textile industry. The first American textile mill, built in Pawtucket, Rhode Island, in 1790, used water-powered spinning machines constructed by the English immigrant Samuel Slater. By 1800 the mill employed one hundred people, and its cloth was sold from Maine to Maryland. Soon other mills sprang up, stimulated by the embargo on English imports from 1807 through 1815.

These early mills also used the putting-out system. Traditionally women had spun their own yarn and woven it into cloth for their own families; now many women received yarn from the mills and returned finished cloth. The change was subtle but significant: although the work itself was familiar, women now operated their looms for piece-rate wages and produced cloth for the market, not for their own use.

Textile manufacturing was radically transformed in 1813 by the construction of the first American power loom and the chartering of the Boston Manufacturing Company. The corporation was capitalized at $400,000—ten times the amount behind the Rhode Island mills—by Francis Cabot Lowell and other Boston merchants. Its goal was to eliminate problems of timing, shipping, coordination, and quality control inherent in the putting-out system. The owners erected their factories in Waltham, Massachusetts, combining all the manufacturing processes at a single location. They also employed a resident manager to run the mill, thus separating ownership from management. The company produced cheap, coarse cloth suitable for the mass market.

Waltham (Lowell) system

In the rural setting of Waltham not enough hands could be found to staff the mill, so the managers recruited New England farm daughters, accepting responsibility for their living conditions and their virtue. To persuade young women to come, they offered high wages, company-run boarding houses, and such cultural events as evening lectures—none of which were available on the farm. This paternalistic approach, called the Waltham or Lowell system, was adopted in other mills erected alongside New England rivers. The Hamilton Corporation (1825), the Appleton and Lowell corporations (1828), and the Suffolk, Tremont, and Lawrence firms (1831) all followed suit. By the 1850s, though, another work force had entered the mills—Irish immigrants. With a surplus of cheap labor available, Lowell and other mill towns abandoned their model systems. By 1860 a cotton mill had become a modern factory, and work relationships in American society had been radically altered.

Textile manufacturing changed New England. Lowell, the famous "city of spindles" that came to symbolize early American industrialization, grew from 2,500 people in 1826 to 33,000 in 1850. The industry became the most important in the nation before the Civil War, employing 115,000 workers in 1860, more than half of whom were women. The key to its success was that the machines, not the women, spun the cloth. The workers watched the machines and intervened to maintain smooth operation. When a thread broke, for instance, the machine stopped automatically; the worker would find the break, piece the ends together, and restart the machine. The mills used increasingly specialized machines, relying heavily on advances in the machine-tool industry. Here was the American system of manufacturing applied.

Though shoe factories and textile mills were in the

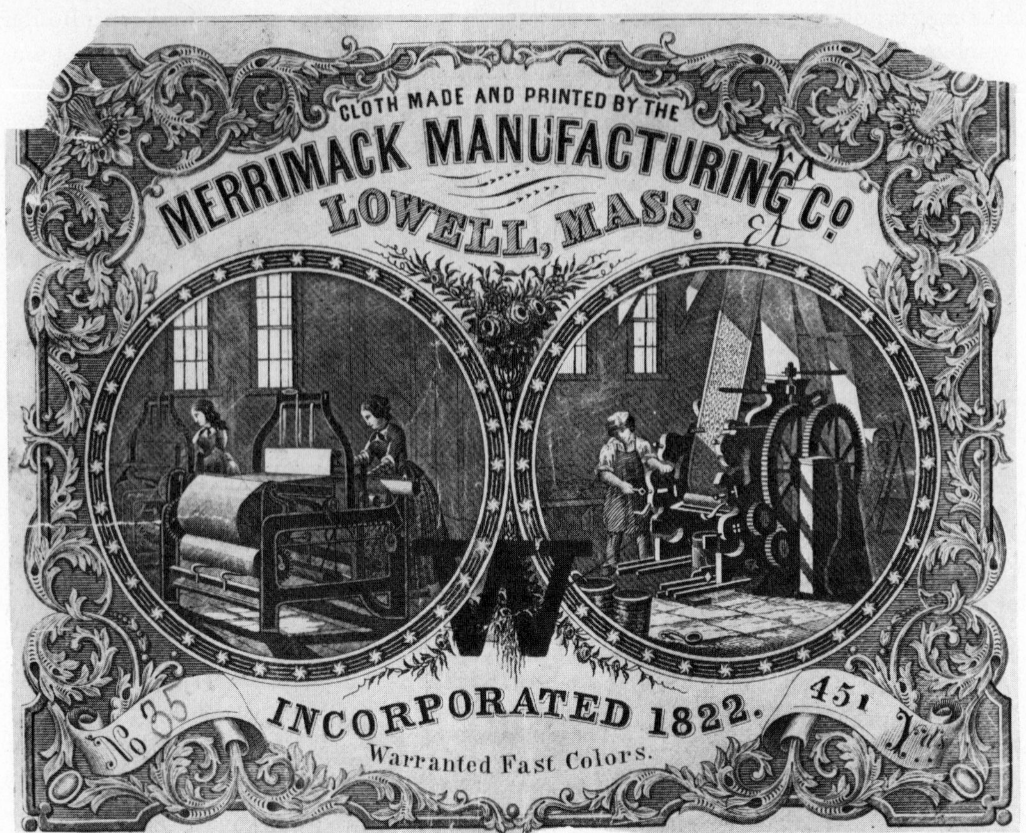

A Merrimack Manufacturing Company label shows the mill girls who came from rural areas to work at the looms in Lowell, Massachusetts. Merrimack Valley Textile Museum.

vanguard of industrialization, the United States experienced broad-based growth in many kinds of manufacturing. Woolen textiles, farm implements, machine tools, iron, glass, and finished consumer goods all became major industries. "White coal"—water power—was widely used to run the machines. Yet by 1860, the United States was still predominantly an agricultural nation; just over one-half of the work force was engaged in agriculture. Manufacturing accounted for only a third of total production, even though that percentage had doubled in twenty years.

To a great extent, industrialization in this period must be seen as the result of other changes in American life rather than the agent of change. Ever since Alexander Hamilton's report on manufactures, national self-consciousness and pride had led to emphasis on the development of home industry. Contrary to Hamilton's hopes, however, more money flowed into the merchant marine than into industry between 1789 and 1808. In the early republic, greater profits could be made by transporting British products to the United States than by producing the same items at home. But the embargo and the War of 1812 reversed the situation, and merchants began to shift their capital from shipping to manufacturing (see pages 210–211). It was in this new economic environment that the Waltham system took root.

Other factors also helped to stimulate industry. Population growth, especially in urban areas and the Old Northwest, created a large domestic market for finished goods (see maps). The rise of commercial agriculture further increased demand by replacing self-sufficient farming. Specialty merchants and new modes of transportation speeded up the development of these new markets. And the relative scarcity of skilled craftsmen encouraged mechanization—as more workers moved westward than entered the factories, merchants had to find some way to produce more

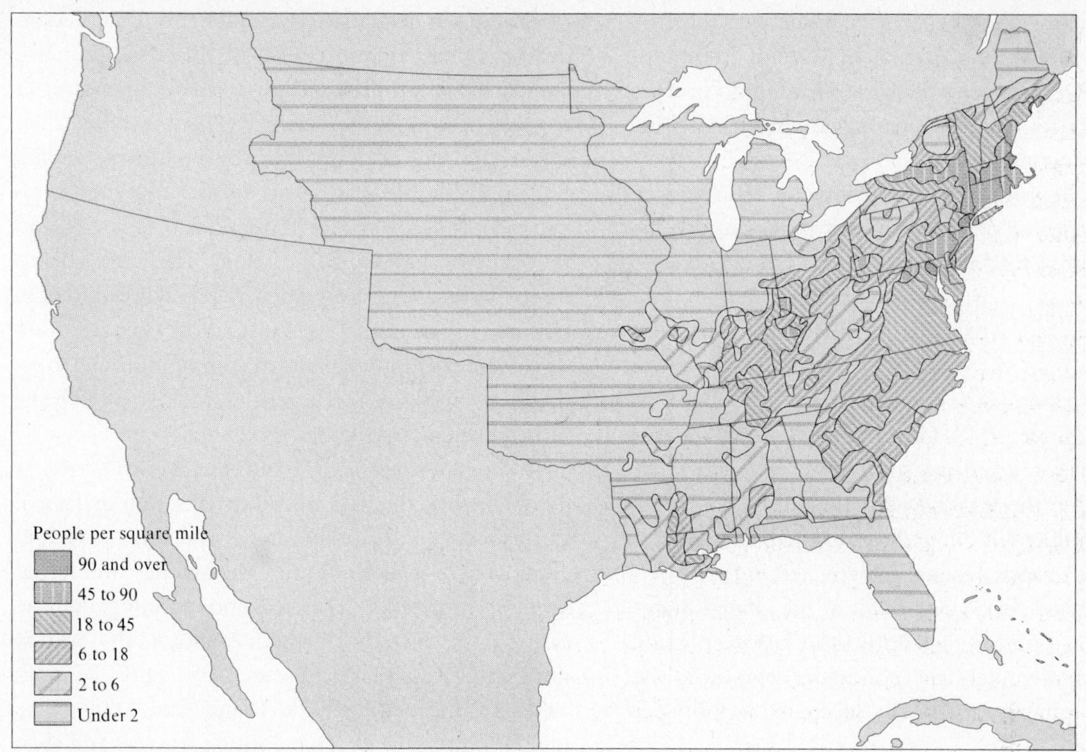

United States population, 1820

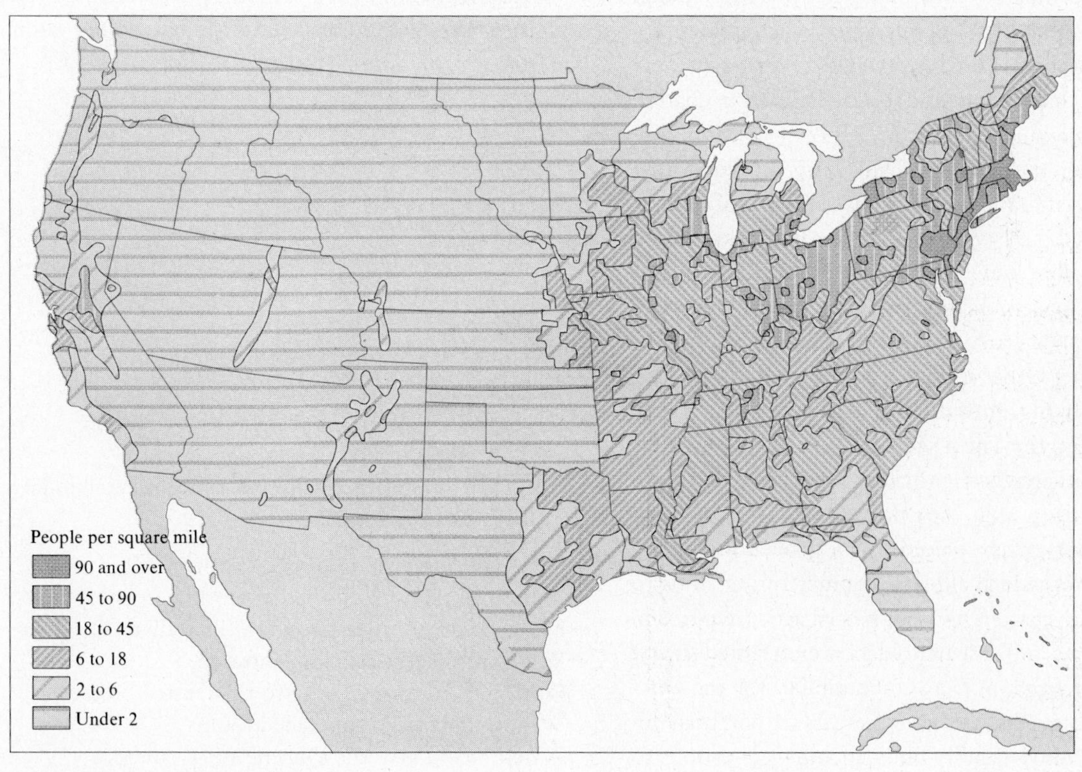

United States population, 1860

goods with less labor. Finally, beginning with the Tariff of 1816 and culminating in the Tariff of Abominations of 1828, Congress passed tariffs more to protect the market for domestic manufacturers than to increase the treasury.

Equally important to the rise of manufacturing was the development of financial institutions (banks, insurance companies, and corporations) linking savers–those who put money in the bank–with producers or speculators–those who wished to borrow money for equipment. The expiration of the Bank of the United States in 1811 after Congress refused to renew its charter, acted as a stimulus to state-chartered banks, and in the next five years the number of banks more than doubled. Nonetheless, state banks proved inadequate to spur national growth, and in 1816 Congress chartered the Second Bank of the United States (see page 210). From then until 1832, however, many farmers, local bankers, and politicians denounced the bank as a monster, and finally succeeded in killing it (see Chapter 12).

Banking and credit systems

The closing of the Second Bank in 1836 caused a nationwide credit shortage that, along with the Panic of 1837, stimulated some major reforms in banking. Michigan and New York introduced charter laws promoting what was called *free banking.* Previously every new bank had required a special legislative charter, which made each bank incorporation a political decision. Under the new laws, any proposed bank that met certain minimum conditions–amount of money, notes issued, and types of loans to be made–would automatically receive a state charter. Although banks were thus freer to incorporate, more restrictions were placed on their practices, slightly reducing the risk of bank failure. Other states soon followed suit.

Free banking proved a significant stimulus to the economy in the late 1840s and 1850s. New banks sprang up everywhere, providing merchants and manufacturers the credit they needed. The free banking laws also served as a precedent for general incorporation statutes, which allowed manufacturing firms to receive state charters without special acts. Investors in corporations, called shareholders, were granted *limited liability,* or freedom from responsibility for the company's debts. An attractive feature to potential investors, limited liability thus encouraged people to back new business ventures.

Changes in insurance companies also promoted industrialization. In the course of business, insurance companies accumulated large amounts of money as reserves against future claims. Then as now, their greatest profits came from investing those reserves. Beginning in the 1840s and 1850s, insurance companies lent money for longer periods than banks, and they bought shares in corporations. They were able to do so by persuading customers to buy whole-life policies rather than annual term insurance. They also took advantage of improvements in communications to establish networks of local agencies, thus expanding the number of customers they served.

In the 1850s, with credit and capital both more easily obtainable, the pace of industrialization increased. In the North, industry began to rival agriculture and commerce in dollar volume. Meanwhile commercial farming, financed by the credit boom, integrated the early frontier into the northern economy. By 1860 six northern states–Massachusetts, New York, Pennsylvania, Connecticut, Rhode Island, and Ohio–were highly industrialized. The clothing, textile, and shoe industries employed more than 100,000 workers each, lumber 75,000, iron 65,000, and woolens and leather 50,000. Although agriculture still predominated even in these states, industrial employment would soon surpass it.

Mill girls and mechanics

Oh, sing me the song of the Factory Girl!
So merry and glad and free!
The bloom in her cheeks, of health how it speaks,
Oh! a happy creature is she!
She tends the loom, she watches the spindle,
And cheerfully toileth away,
Amid the din of wheels, how her bright eyes kindle,
And her bosom is ever gay.

Oh, sing me the song of the Factory Girl!
Whose fabric doth clothe the world.
From the king and his peers to the jolly tars
With our flag o'er all seas unfurled.
From the California's seas, to the tainted breeze
Which sweeps the smokened rooms,
Where "God save the Queen" to cry are seen
The slaves of the British looms.

This idyllic portrait of factory work was an anachronism when it appeared in the Chicopee, Massachusetts, *Telegraph* in 1850. But it was a fitting song for the first women who entered the New England textile mills: young women, mostly single and between fifteen and thirty years old, who left the villages and farms of New England to work in the mills. They went on their own, lured by the chance to be independent and self-supporting, to get away from home, to save for a trousseau, and to enjoy city life. The mill owners, believing that the degradation of English factory workers arose from their living conditions and not from the work itself, designed a model community offering airy courtyards and river views, secure dormitories, prepared meals, and cultural activities. Housekeepers enforced strict curfews, banned alcohol, and reported to the corporations on workers' behavior and church attendance.

Some workers saw factory life as an escape from the drudgery of farming and home manufacture. At home, farm daughters spent their extra time spinning wool by hand and weaving it into cloth. One sixteen-year-old, after weaving steadily for three months and producing 176 yards of cloth, recorded in her diary: "Welcome Sweet Liberty, once more to me. How I have longed to meet again with thee." Her freedom would soon be lost when the annual cycle of spinning and weaving resumed. Factory workers were guaranteed leisure time—not much, but enough to tempt a farm girl. Eventually the New England textile mills replaced home manufacture of cloth altogether.

By the 1840s the songs of the factory girls had become rebellious. "The Factory Girl's Come-All-Ye" (about 1850) expressed the workers' desire to leave the oppressive mill:

No more I'll take my bobbins out,
No more I'll put them in,
No more the overseer will say
"You're weaving your cloth too thin!"

No more will I eat cold pudding,
No more will I eat hard bread,
No more will I eat those half-baked beans,
For I vow! They're killing me dead!

I'm going back to Boston town
And live on Tremont Street;
And I want all you fact'ry girls
To come to my house and eat!

What had happened to dash the hopes of these young women? The corporation's goal of building an industrial empire had taken precedence over its concern for workers' living conditions. In the race for profits, owners had lengthened hours, cut wages, and tightened discipline. Eliza R. Hemingway, a six-year veteran of the Massachusetts mills, told a state House of Representatives committee that the worker's hours were too long, "her time for meals too limited. In the summer season, the work is commenced at 5 o'clock, A.M., and continued 'til 7 o'clock, P.M., with half an hour for breakfast and three quarters of an hour for dinner." When Hemingway worked evenings—which was compulsory—293 small lamps and 61 large ones lit the room. There was no bloom of health in her cheeks.

Mill girl protests

New England mill workers responded to their deteriorating working conditions by organizing and striking. In 1834, in reaction to a 25-percent wage cut, they unsuccessfully "turned out" (struck) against the Lowell mills. Two years later, when boarding-house rates were raised, they turned out again. Following the period from 1837 to 1842, when most mills ran only part-time because of a decline in demand for cloth, managers applied still greater pressures on workers. The speedup, the stretch-out, and the premium system became common methods of increasing production. The speedup increased the speed of the machines; the stretch-out increased the number of machines each worker had to operate. Premiums were paid to overseers whose departments produced the most cloth. The result was that in Lowell between 1836 and 1850, the number of spindles and looms increased 150 and 140 percent respectively, while the number of workers increased by only 50 percent. Mill workers began to think of themselves as slaves.

As conditions worsened, workers changed their methods of resistance. By the 1850s strikes had given way to a concerted effort to shorten the workday. Massachusetts mill women joined forces with other workers to press for legislation mandating a ten-hour day. They aired their complaints in worker-run newspapers—the *Factory Girl* appeared in New Hampshire and the *Wampanoag and Operatives' Journal* in Massachusetts, both in 1842. Two years later the *Factory Girl's Garland* and the *Voice of Industry,* nicknamed "the factory girl's voice," were founded. Even the

TIME TABLE OF THE LOWELL MILLS,

Arranged to make the working time throughout the year average 11 hours per day.

TO TAKE EFFECT SEPTEMBER 21st., 1853.

The Standard time being that of the meridian of Lowell, as shown by the Regulator Clock of AMOS SANBORN, Post Office Corner, Central Street.

From March 20th to September 19th, inclusive.

COMMENCE WORK, at 6.30 A. M. LEAVE OFF WORK, at 6.30 P. M., except on Saturday Evenings.
BREAKFAST at 6 A. M. DINNER, at 12 M. Commence Work, after dinner, 12.45 P. M.

From September 20th to March 19th, inclusive.

COMMENCE WORK at 7.00 A. M. LEAVE OFF WORK, at 7.00 P. M., except on Saturday Evenings.
BREAKFAST at 6.30 A. M. DINNER, at 12.30 P.M. Commence Work, after dinner, 1.15 P. M.

BELLS.

From March 20th to September 19th, inclusive.

Morning Bells.	*Dinner Bells.*	*Evening Bells.*
First bell,...........4.30 A. M.	Ring out,...............12.00 M.	Ring out,.............6.30 P. M.
Second, 5.30 A. M.; Third, 6.20.	Ring in,............12.35 P. M.	Except on Saturday Evenings.

From September 20th to March 19th, inclusive.

Morning Bells.	*Dinner Bells.*	*Evening Bells.*
First bell,...........5.00 A. M.	Ring out,..........12.30 P. M.	Ring out at..........7.00 P. M.
Second, 6.00 A. M.; Third, 6.50.	Ring in,.............1.05 P. M.	Except on Saturday Evenings.

SATURDAY EVENING BELLS.

During APRIL, MAY, JUNE, JULY, and AUGUST, Ring Out, at 6.00 P. M.
The remaining Saturday Evenings in the year, ring out as follows:

SEPTEMBER.

First Saturday,	ring out	6.00	P. M.
Second	"	5.45	"
Third	"	5.30	"
Fourth	"	5.20	"

OCTOBER.

First Saturday,	ring out	5.05	P. M.
Second	"	4.55	"
Third	"	4.45	"
Fourth	"	4.35	"
Fifth	"	4.25	"

NOVEMBER.

First Saturday,	ring out	4.15	P. M.
Second	"	4.05	"

NOVEMBER.

Third Saturday	ring out	4.00	P. M.
Fourth	"	3.55	"

DECEMBER.

First Saturday,	ring out	3.50	P. M.
Second	"	3.55	"
Third	"	3.55	"
Fourth	"	4.00	"
Fifth	"	4.00	"

JANUARY.

First Saturday,	ring out	4.10	P. M.
Second	"	4.15	"

JANUARY.

Third Saturday,	ring out	4.25	P. M.
Fourth	"	4.35	"

FEBRUARY.

First Saturday,	ring out	4.45	P. M.
Second	"	4.55	"
Third	"	5.00	"
Fourth	"	5.10	"

MARCH.

First Saturday,	ring out	5.25	P. M.
Second	"	5.30	"
Third	"	5.35	"
Fourth	"	5.45	"

YARD GATES will be opened at the first stroke of the bells for entering or leaving the Mills.

SPEED GATES commence hoisting three minutes before commencing work.

This 1853 timetable from the Lowell Mills illustrates the regimentation workers had to submit to in the new environment of the factory. Note that workers frequently began before daylight, finished after sunset, and were given only half an hour for meals. Merrimack Valley Textile Museum.

Lowell Offering, the owner-sponsored paper that was the pride of mill workers and managers alike, became embroiled in controversy when some workers charged that articles critical of working conditions had been suppressed.

But not all the militant native-born mill workers stayed on to fight the managers and owners, and gradually fewer New England daughters entered the mills. The immigrant women, mostly Irish, who constituted a majority of mill workers by the end of the 1850s were driven to the mills by the need to support their families. Most could not afford to complain about their working conditions.

What happened in the New England mills occurred in less dramatic fashion throughout the nation. Workers experienced undesirable changes in their tasks and in their relationships with their employers.

Changes in the workplace

In the old journeyman-apprentice system that skilled workers had known for centuries, the master had worked alongside his employees, often living in the same household. Work relationships were intensely personal, and there was little social distance between master and journeyman–after all, the journeymen and apprentices expected to become masters themselves someday. All had an interest in the standards of their craft, and they made their finished goods to order and with pride.

But textile mills, shoe factories, insurance companies, wholesale stores, canals and railroads were the antithesis of the old master-journeyman tradition. Supervisors separated the workers from the owners. The division of labor and the use of machines reduced the skills required of workers. And the coming and going of the large work forces was governed by the bell, the steam whistle, or the clock. In 1844 the *Factory Girl's Garland* published a poem describing how the ringing of the factory bell controlled when the workers awoke, ate, began and ended work, and went to sleep. The central problem, of course, was the quickening of the work between the bells. Since owners and managers no longer shared the workers' tasks, it was easy for them to expect faster and faster performance.

Like the mill women, most workers at first welcomed the new manufacturing methods; new jobs and higher wages seemed adequate compensation. But later wage reductions, speed-ups, and stretch-outs changed their minds. Other adjustments were difficult too. Young women in the mills had to become used to the roar of the looms, and all workers on power machines risked accidents that could kill or maim. Most demoralizing of all, they had to accept that their future was relatively fixed. Opportunities to become an owner or manager in the new system were virtually nil.

The growing division between worker and owner was mirrored in commercial agriculture by the gap between hired hands or tenants and farm owners. Though the United States was still primarily an agricultural nation–and many saw the frontier farm as the antidote to commerce and industrialization–not all farmers were yeomen. Farm laborers, once scarce in the United States, had become commonplace. In the North in 1860 there was one hired hand for every 2.3 farms. Given the high cost of land and of farming by that time, hired hands had little opportunity to acquire farms of their own. By the 1850s it took from ten to twenty years for a rural laborer to save enough money to farm for himself. For the same reason, the number of tenant farmers increased.

One response to increasing economic insecurity and social rigidity was the active participation of workers in reform politics. In the 1820s labor parties

Emergence of a labor movement

arose in Pennsylvania, New York, and Massachusetts; they eventually spread to a dozen states. These parties advocated free public education, abolition of imprisonment for debt, revision of the militia system (in which workers bore the greatest burden) and opposed banks and monopolies. Workers' reform often crossed paths with middle-class benevolent movements, since the two groups shared a concern not only for public education but also for public morals: temperance, observance of the Sabbath, and suppression of vice (see Chapter 12). Ironically, however, reform politics tended to divide workers. Many of the reforms–moral education, temperance, Sabbath closings–served merchants and industrialists seeking a more disciplined work force. Others broadened the divisions between native-born and immigrant workers. Anti-immigrant and anti-Catholic movements spread.

Due both to these divisions and to economic upheaval, organized labor was not a strong force during this period. Labor unions tended to be local in nature; the strongest resembled medieval guilds. The first

Women shoe workers strike for higher wages at Lynn, Massachusetts, in 1860. Culver.

unions arose among urban journeymen in printing, woodworking, shoemaking, and tailoring. These craftsmen sought to protect themselves against the competition of inferior workmen by regulating apprenticeship and establishing minimum wages. In the 1820s and 1830s craft unions–unions organized by occupation–forged larger umbrella organizations in the cities, including the National Trades Union (1834). But in the depression of 1839 through 1843, the movement fell apart amidst wage reductions and unemployment. In the 1850s the deterioration of working conditions strengthened the labor movement again. Workers won a reduction in hours, and the ten-hour day became standard. Though the Panic of 1857 wiped out the umbrella organizations, some of the new national unions for specific trade groups–notably printers, hat finishers, and stonecutters–survived. By 1860 five more national unions had been organized by the painters, cordwainers, cotton spinners, iron molders, and machinists.

Organized labor's greatest achievement during this period was in gaining recognition of its right to exist. When journeymen shoemakers organized in the first decade of the century, employers turned to the courts, charging criminal conspiracy. The cordwainers' conspiracy cases, which involved six trials from 1806 through 1815, left labor organizations in a tenuous position. Although the journeymen's right to organize was recognized, the courts ruled unlawful any coercive action that harmed other businesses or the public. In effect, therefore, strikes were unlawful. Eventually a Massachusetts case, *Commonwealth* v.

Hunt (1842), effectively reversed the decision when Chief Justice Lemuel Shaw ruled that Boston journeymen bootmakers had a right to combine and strike "in such manner as best to subserve their own interests."

Right to strike

The impact of economic and technological change, however, fell more heavily on individual workers than on their organizations. As a group, the workers' share of the national wealth declined after the 1830s. Individual producers–craftsmen, factory workers, and farmers–had less economic power than they had had a generation or two before. And workers were increasingly losing control over their own work.

For the nation as a whole, the period from 1800 through 1860 was one of sustained growth. The population grew from 5.3 to 31.5 million. Settlement, once restricted to the Atlantic seaboard and the eastern rivers, extended more than a thousand miles inland by 1860 and was spreading east from the Pacific Ocean as well. Whereas agriculture had completely dominated the nation at the turn of the century–in 1800 nearly every American not engaged in farming either processed food or provided services for farmers–by mid-century farming was being challenged by a booming manufacturing sector. And agriculture itself was becoming mechanized.

Still, traditional work persisted. Every town had its blacksmith and tailor, stablehands and day laborers, seamstresses and domestic servants. And in the South, although some black slaves worked in the new factories and mills, the overwhelming majority of slaves still performed traditional agricultural work.

Important events

1803–06	Lewis and Clark expedition
1807	Fulton's steamboat, *Clermont*
1810	New York becomes the most populous city
1813	Boston Manufacturing Company founded
1817–30	Canal era
1818	National Road reaches Wheeling, Virginia
1819	*Dartmouth College* v. *Woodward*
1819–23	Depression
1820s	New England textile mills expand
1824	*Gibbons* v. *Ogden*
1825	Erie Canal completed
1830	Baltimore and Ohio Railroad begins operation *Tom Thumb*
1830–86	Railroad era
1831	McCormick invents the reaper
1834	Mill women strike at Lowell
1837	Financial panic
1839–43	Depression
1841	Tappan's mercantile agency
1844	Baltimore-Washington telegraph line
1848	Cunard's Atlantic shuttle
1849	Gold rush
1853	British study of American system of manufacturing
1854	Railroad reaches the Mississippi
1857	Depression
1858	Transatlantic cable

Suggestions for further reading

General

W. Elliot Brownlee, *Dynamics of Ascent: A History of the American Economy* (1979); Stuart Bruchey, *The Roots of American Economic Growth, 1607–1861: An Essay in Social Causation* (1965); North Douglass, *Economic Growth of the United States, 1790–1860* (1961); David Klingaman and Richard Vedder, eds., *Essays in 19th Century History* (1975); Susan Previant Lee and Peter Passell, *A New Economic View of American History* (1979); Nathan Rosenberg, *Technology and American Economic Growth* (1972).

Transportation

Robert G. Albion, *The Rise of New York Port, 1815–1860* (1939); Albert Fishlow, *American Railroads and the Transformation of the Ante-Bellum Economy* (1965); Carter Goodrich, *Government Promotion of American Canals and Railroads, 1800–1890* (1960); Erik E. Haites, *et al., Western River Transportation: The Era of Internal Development, 1810–1860* (1975); Louis C. Hunter, *Steamboats on the Western Rivers* (1949); Samuel E. Morison, *Maritime History of Massachusetts, 1789–1860* (1921); Harry N. Scheiber, *Ohio Canal Era: A Case Study of Government and the Economy, 1820–1861* (1969); Ronald E. Shaw, *Erie Water West: Erie Canal, 1797–1854* (1966); George R. Taylor, *The Transportation Revolution, 1815–1860* (1951).

Commerce and manufacturing

Alfred D. Chandler, Jr., *The Visible Hand: Managerial Revolution in American Business* (1977); Victor Clark, *History of Manufactures in the United States,* 3 vols. (1929); Arthur H. Cole, *The American Wool Manufacture,* 2 vols. (1926); H. J. Habakkuk, *American and British Technology in the Nineteenth Century* (1962); Diane Lindstrom, *Economic Development in the Philadelphia Region, 1810–1850* (1978); Louis Hartz, *Economic Policy and Democratic Thought: Pennsylvania, 1776–1860* (1954); James D. Norris, *R. G. Dun & Co. 1841–1900* (1978); Merritt Roe Smith, *Harpers Ferry Armory and the New Technology* (1977); Peter Temin, *Iron and Steel in Nineteenth-Century America* (1964); Joseph E. Walker, *Hopewell Village: A Social and Economic History of an Ironmaking Community* (1966); Caroline F. Ware, *Early New England Cotton Manufacturing* (1931).

Agriculture

Percy Bidwell and John Falconer, *History of Agriculture in the Northern United States 1620–1860* (1925): Allan G. Bogue, *From Prairie to Corn Belt: Farming on the Illinois and Iowa Prairies in the Nineteenth Century* (1963); Clarence Danhof, *Change in Agriculture: The Northern United States, 1820–1870* (1969); Paul W. Gates, *The Farmer's Age: Agriculture, 1815–1860* (1962); Paul W. Gates, *The Illinois Central and Its Colonization Work* (1934); Benjamin H. Hibbard, *A History of Public Land Policies* (1939); Julie Roy Jeffrey, *Frontier Women: The Trans-Mississippi West 1840–1880* (1979); Edward C. Kendall, *John Deere's Steel Plow* (1959); William T. Hutchinson, *Cyrus Hall McCormick,* 2 vols. (1930–1935).

The western frontier

Ray A. Billington, *The Far Western Frontier, 1830–1860* (1956); Ray A. Billington, *Westward Expansion* (1974); Hiram M. Chittenden, *The American Fur Trade of the Far West,* 3 vols. (1935); Gloria G. Cline, *Exploring the Great Basin* (1963); John Mack Faragher, *Women and Men on the Overland Trail* (1979); William H. Goetzmann, *Exploration and Empire: The Explorer and the Scientist in the Winning of the American West* (1966); John A. Hawgood, *America's Western Frontier: The Exploration and Settlement of the Trans-Mississippi West* (1967); Rodman W. Paul, *California Gold: The Beginning of Mining in the Far West* (1974); John D. Unruh, Jr., *The Overland Emigrants and the Trans-Mississippi West, 1840–1860* (1979); David J. Wishart, *The Fur Trade of the American West, 1807–1840* (1979).

Workers

Alan Dawley, *Class and Community: The Industrial Revolution in Lynn* (1977); Thomas Dublin, *Women at Work: The Transformation of Work and Community in Lowell, Massachusetts, 1826–1860* (1979); Philip S. Foner, ed., *The Factory Girls* (1977); Susan E. Hirsch, *Roots of the American Working Class: The Industrialization of Crafts in Newark, 1800–1860* (1978); Hannah Josephson, *The Gold Threads: New England's Mill Girls and Magnates* (1949); Bruce Laurie, *Working People of Philadelphia, 1800–1850* (1980); Norman Ware, *The Industrial Worker, 1840–1860* (1924).

10 SLAVERY AND THE GROWTH OF THE SOUTH, 1800–1860

He was weeping, sobbing. In a humble voice he had begged his master not to give him to Mr. King, who was going away to Alabama, but it had done no good. Now his voice rose and he uttered "an absolute cry of despair." Raving and "almost in a state of frenzy," he declared that he would never leave the Georgia plantation that was home to his father, mother, wife, and children. He twisted his hat between clenched fists and flung it to the ground; he would kill himself, he said, before he lost his family and all that made life worth living.

To Fanny Kemble, watching from the doorway, it was a horrifying and disorienting scene. One of the most famous British actresses ever to tour America, Fanny had grown up breathing England's antislavery tradition as naturally as the air. In New England she had become friends with such enlightened antislavery thinkers as William Ellery Channing, the liberal Boston minister who founded Unitarianism; Catharine Maria Sedgwick, America's foremost woman novelist; and Elizabeth Dwight Sedgwick, an educator and Catharine's sister-in-law. Amid such company, Fanny understandably assumed that attitudes in America were advanced and civilized. Then the man she married took her away from New England to a Georgia rice plantation, where hundreds of dark-skinned slaves produced the white grain that was his source of wealth.

Pierce Butler, Fanny's husband, was all that a cultured Philadelphia gentleman should be. He had lived all his life in the North, though part of his family's fortune had always sprung from southern slavery. When Fanny chose him from dozens of suitors, he had seemed an attractive exemplar of American culture. Yet now he shattered his slave's hopes without hesitation. Quietly "leaning against a table with his arms folded," Butler advised the distraught black man not to "make a fuss about what there was no help for."

Fanny wondered what America was really like. In the South, the northerner she thought she knew seemed a different man. Only with tears and vehement pleas was she able to convince Butler to keep the slave family together. He finally agreed as a favor to her, not as an act of principle.

This incident, which occurred in 1839, illustrates both the similarities between South and North and the differences that were beginning to emerge. Though racism existed in the North, its influence was far more visible on southern society. And though some northerners, like Pierce Butler, were undisturbed by the idea of human bondage, a growing number considered it shocking and backward. In the years after the Revolution, these northerners, possessing few slaves and influenced by the revolutionary ideal of natural rights, had adopted gradual emancipation laws (see Chapter 11). At the same time they had embarked on an industrial revolution that transformed their economy, gradually mechanizing their farms and rendering forced labor obsolete.

In the South too, the years from 1800 to 1860 were a time of growth and prosperity; new lands were settled and new states peopled. But as the North grew and changed, economically the South merely grew; change there only reinforced existing economic patterns. Steadily the South emerged as the world's most extensive and vigorous slave economy. Its people were slaves, slaveholders, and nonslaveholders rather than farmers, merchants, mechanics, and manufacturers. Its well-being depended on agriculture alone, rather than agriculture plus commerce and manufacturing. Its population was almost wholly rural rather than rural and urban.

These facts meant that the social lives of southerners were unavoidably distinct from those of northerners. Nonslaveholders operated their family farms in a society dominated by slaveholding planters. A handful of planters developed an aristocratic lifestyle, while slaves—one-third of the South's people—lived without freedom, struggling to develop a culture that sustained hope. The influence of slavery spread throughout the social system, affecting not just southern economics but southern values, customs, and laws. It created a society that was noticeably different.

The South remains rural

The South in the early 1800s was the product of precisely the kind of resource-exploiting commercial agriculture that most of the early colonies had aspired to develop. Only there, nonmechanized agriculture remained highly profitable, as it did not in the Northeast. Southern planters were not sentimentalists who held onto their slaves for noneconomic reasons even in the face of the industrial revolution. Like other Americans, they were profit-oriented. Circumstances dictated that the most profitable investment lay in the continuation of a plantation economy.

At the time of the Revolution, slave-based agriculture was not exceedingly lucrative. Debt hung heavily over most of Virginia's extravagant and aristocratic tobacco growers, prodding them to consider the disadvantages of slavery. Cotton was a lucrative export crop only for sea-island planters, who grew the luxurious long-staple variety. The short-staple cotton that grew readily in the interior was unmarketable because its sticky seeds lay tangled in the fibers. But in spite of the limited usefulness of slavery, social inertia and fear of slave revolts prevented its abolition.

Then England's burgeoning textile industry changed the southern economy. English mills needed more and more cotton. Sea-island cotton was so profitable between 1785 and 1795 that thousands of farmers in the interior experimented with the short-staple variety; by the early 1790s southern farmers were planting 2 to 3 million pounds of it each year. Some of this cotton was meant for domestic use, but most was grown in the hope that some innovation would make the crop salable to the English. In such circumstances the invention of a cotton gin was almost inevitable, and Eli Whitney responded in 1793 with a simple machine that removed the seeds from the fibers. By 1800 cotton was spreading rapidly westward from the seaboard states.

Rise of the Cotton South

So the antebellum South, or Old South, became primarily a cotton South. Tobacco continued to be grown in Virginia and North Carolina, and rice and sugar were still very important in certain coastal areas, especially in South Carolina, Georgia, and Louisiana. But cotton was the largest crop, the most widespread, and the force behind the South's hunger for new territory. Ambitious cotton growers poured into the West, pushing the Indians off their fabulously fertile Gulf lands and across the Appalachians (see Chapter 11). The boom in the cotton economy came in the 1830s in Alabama and Mississippi. But not until the 1850s did the wave of cotton expansion cross Louisiana and pour into Texas (see maps page 254). Migration into Texas was still strong in 1860.

Thus the Old South was not old at all; in 1860 it was still growing. For although prices plunged sharply at least once a decade after 1820, overall demand for cotton soared. Since English mills would buy virtually all the cotton a planter could grow, eager southerners bought more slaves and more land. Soon they were exporting more than three-quarters of their crop and supplying almost the same proportion of England's purchases. In just a few decades some of these planters amassed great personal fortunes and rose to an aristocratic position in society. Though some old Virginia and South Carolina families were represented among the proud new "cotton snobs," most of the wealthy were newly rich.

Jefferson Davis: his early life

To the hard-working and lucky, riches came quickly. A good example is the family of Jefferson Davis. Like Abraham Lincoln, Davis was born in humble circumstances. His father was one of the thousands of American farmers on the frontier who moved frequently, unwisely buying land when prices were high and selling when they were low, never making his fortune. Luckily for Davis, his older brother migrated to Mississippi and became successful. Settling on rich bottomlands next to the Mississippi River, Joseph Davis made profits, expanded his holdings of land and slaves, and made more profits. Soon he was an established figure in society, and he used his position to arrange an education at West Point for his younger brother. A large plantation awaited Jefferson's retirement from the army. Thus the Davis family became aristocrats in one generation.

A less fortunate consequence of the cotton boom was the relative indifference of farmers to the long-term fertility of the soil. In an expanding economy, with cheap and superior land available farther west, most people preferred to exhaust the land and move on rather than invest heavily in preserving it. Only in the older states of the upper South, where the major landholders stayed behind, and where the cotton boom had less impact, did serious interest in diversified farming develop.

An even more important consequence of the boom was thin population distribution. Producers spread

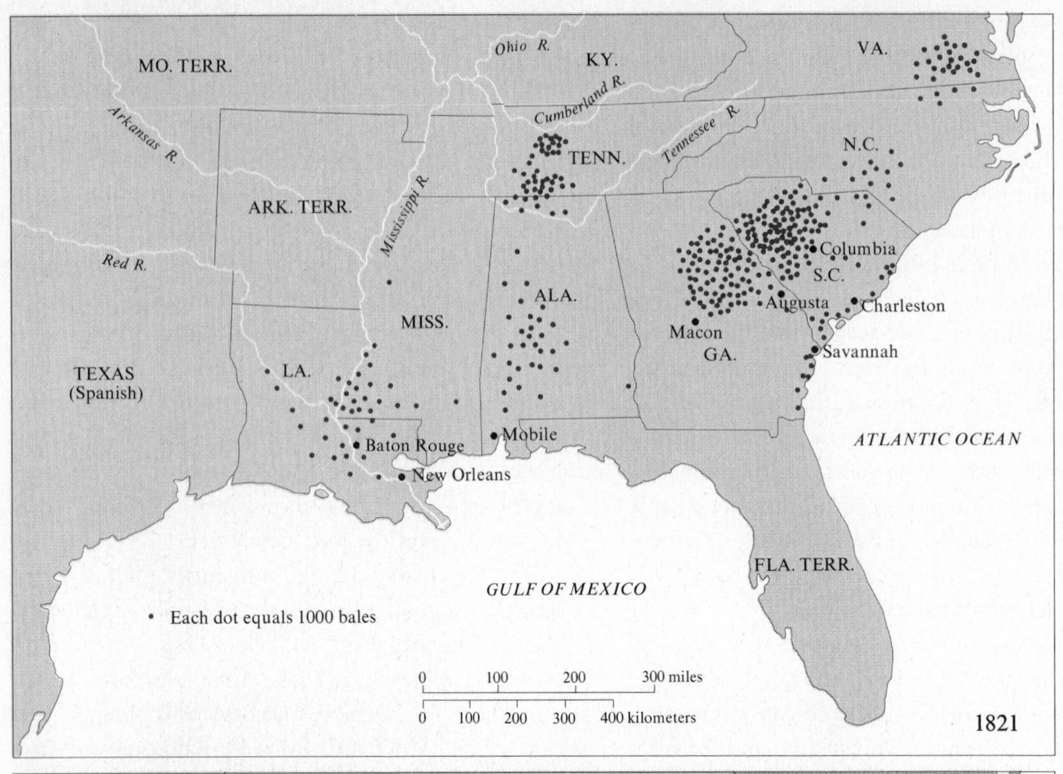

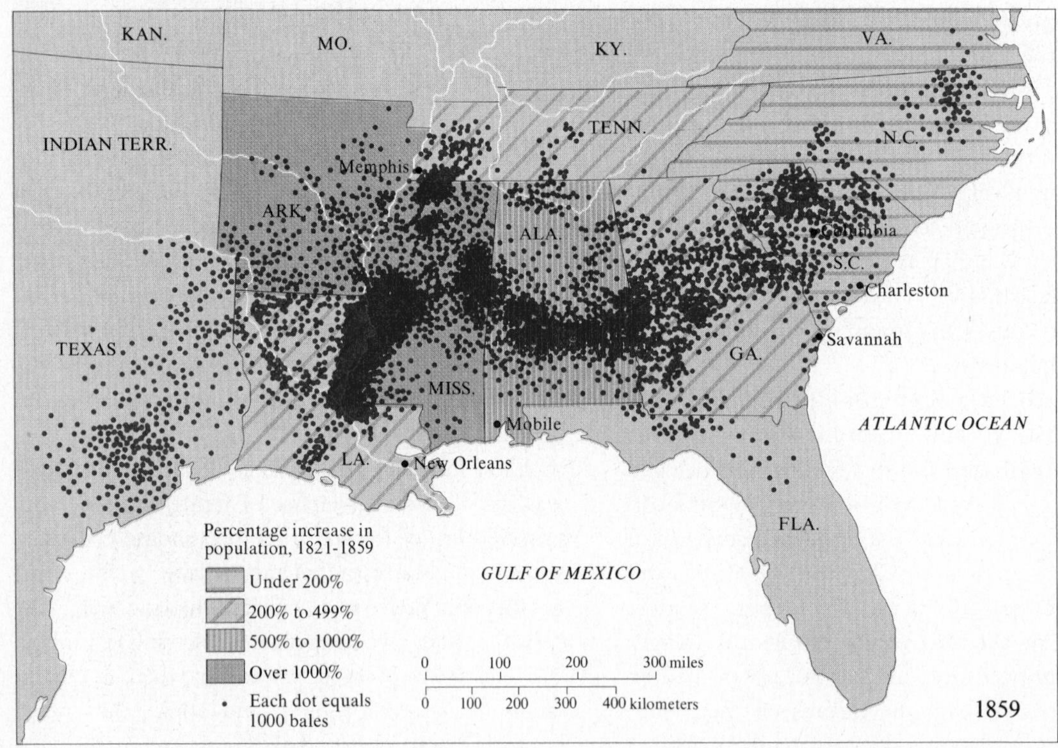

Cotton production in the South

Charleston, one of the South's larger cities, remained small compared to many urban centers in the industrializing North. Painted in 1831 by S. Barnard. The Yale University Art Gallery, Mabel Brady Garvan Collection.

out over as large an area as possible in order to maximize production and income. Because farms were far apart, southern society remained predominantly rural. Population density, low even in the older plantation states, was especially so in the frontier areas being brought under cultivation. In 1860 there were only 2.3 people per square mile in Texas, 15.6 in Louisiana, and 18.0 in Georgia. By contrast, population density in the nonslaveholding states east of the Mississippi River was almost three times higher. The northeast had an average of 65.4 persons per square mile, and in some places the density was much higher. Massachusetts had 153.1 people per square mile, and New York City, where overcrowding reached epic proportions, compressed 86,400 people into each square mile.

Population distribution

Even in the 1850s, much of the South seemed almost uninhabited, a virtual wilderness. Frederick Law Olmsted, a northerner who later became famous as a landscape architect, made several trips through the South in the 1850s as a reporter. He found that the few trains and stagecoaches available to travelers offered only rough accommodations and kept their schedules poorly. Indeed, he had to do most of his traveling on horseback along primitive trails. Passing from Columbus, Georgia, to Montgomery, Alabama, Olmsted observed "a hilly wilderness, with a few dreary villages, and many isolated cotton farms." Alabama was, of course, on the frontier in 1800, but Olmsted encountered the same conditions in parts of eastern Virginia: "For hours and hours one has to ride through the unlimited, continual, all-shadowing, all-embracing forest, following roads in the making of which no more labor has been given than was necessary to remove the timber which would obstruct the passage of wagons; and even for days and days he may sometimes travel and see never two dwellings of mankind within sight of each other."

Society in such rural areas was characterized by relatively weak institutions, for it takes people to create and support organized activity. Where the concentration of people was low, it was difficult to finance and operate schools, churches, libraries, or even hotels, restaurants, and other urban amenities. Southerners were strongly committed to their churches, and some believed in the importance of universities, but all such institutions were far less developed than those in the North.

The few southern cities were likewise smaller and less developed than those in the North. As exporters, southerners did not need large cities; a small group of merchants working in connection with northern brokers sufficed to ship their cotton overseas and to import necessary supplies and luxuries. As planters, southerners invested most of their capital in slaves; they had little money left to build factories—another source of urban growth. A few southerners did invest in iron or textiles on a small scale. But the largest southern industrial plants were cigar factories, where slaves finished tobacco products. As a result, in 1860 only 49,000 out of 704,000 South Carolinians lived in towns with 2,500 or more residents. Less than 3 percent of Mississippi's population lived in places of comparable size. In 1860 the population of Charleston was only 41,000, Richmond 38,000, and Mobile 29,000. New Orleans, by far the largest southern city, had only 169,000 residents.

Economic development

Thus, although it was economically attuned to an international market, the South was only semi-developed in comparison with other sections of the country. Its people prospered, but neither as rapidly nor as independently as residents of the North. There commerce and industry brought unprecedented advances in productivity, widening the range of affordable goods and services and raising the average person's standard of living. In the South, change was quantitative rather than qualitative; farming techniques remained essentially the same. To prosper, southerners increased their acreage and hoped for continued high demand from foreign customers—decisions that worked to the ultimate disadvantage of the region.

The society that developed in this largely agrarian economy was a society of extremes. The social distance between a wealthy planter and a small slaveholder was as great as the distance between a slaveholder and a nonslaveholder (to say nothing of the distance between whites and slaves). And, contrary to popular belief, planters were neither the most numerous nor the most typical group. The typical white southerner was a yeoman farmer.

Yeoman farmers

More than two-thirds of white southern families owned no slaves. Some of them lived in towns and ran stores or businesses, but most were farmers who owned their own land and grew their own food. Independent and self-respecting, with a hearty share of frontier individualism, they settled the southern wilderness, first by herding livestock and then by planting crops.

Successive waves of these herdsmen and farmers moved down the southern Appalachians into the new regions of the Southwest following the War of 1812. The herdsmen grazed their cattle and pigs on the abundant natural vegetation in the woods. Before long, however, the next wave of settlers arrived and broke ground for crops. These yeomen farmers forced the herdsmen farther and farther west, and eventually across the Mississippi. Some yeomen acquired large tracts of level land and became wealthy planters. Others clung to the beautiful mountainous areas they loved, or pressed farther into the wilds because they "couldn't stand the sound of another man's axe." As they moved, they tended to stick to the climate and soils they knew best. Yeomen could not afford the richest bottomlands, which were swampy and required expensive draining, but they owned land almost everywhere else.

Observers sometimes concluded that these people were poor and idle, especially the herdsmen who sat on their cabin porches while their stock foraged in the woods. It would be more accurate to say that they were frontiersmen and farmers who did not manage to become rich. They worked hard, as farmers do everywhere, and enjoyed a folk culture based on fam-

Many southern yeomen led an almost frontier style of life, farming and raising livestock in sparsely populated areas. Culver.

ily, church, and community. They spoke with a drawl and their inflections were reminiscent of their Scottish and Irish backgrounds. Once a year they flocked to religious revivals called protracted meetings or camp meetings, and in between they enjoyed house raisings, log rollings, corn shuckings, and the ancient Scottish habit of burning the woods (to remove underbrush or clear land). The men did most of the farming; though the women occasionally helped in the fields, they commonly spent their time preserving and preparing food, making clothes, blankets, and candles, and tending to household matters.

Folk culture of the yeoman

Beyond these basic facts, historians know little about the yeomen. Because their means were modest, they did not generate the voluminous legal papers, such as contracts, wills, and inventories of estates, that document the activities of the rich. Only a few letters have found their way into libraries and archives. It is reasonable to suppose, though, that yeomen held a variety of opinions and pursued individual goals. Some envied the planters and strove to be rich; others were content with their independence, recreation, family life, and religion.

At the first extreme was a North Carolinian named John F. Flintoff, whose rare diary records the ambitions of a nonslaveholder who hungered to be rich. Flintoff was born in 1823 and at age eighteen went to Mississippi to seek his fortune. Like other aspiring yeomen, he worked as an overseer, but often found it impossible to please his employers. At one time he gave up and returned to North Carolina, where he married and lived in his parents' house. But Flintoff was "impatient to get along in the world," so he tried Louisiana next and then Mississippi again.

For Flintoff, the fertile Gulf region had its disadvantages. "My health has been very bad here," he noted; "chills and fever occasionally has hold of me."

"First rate employment" alternated with "very low wages." Moreover, as a young man working on isolated plantations, Flintoff often felt "all alone." Even a revival meeting in 1844 proved "an extremely cold time" with "but little warm feeling." His uncle and other employers found fault with his work, and in 1846 Flintoff concluded in despair that "managing negroes and large farms is soul destroying."

Still, a desire to succeed kept him going. At twenty-six, before he owned a foot of land, Flintoff bought his first slave, "a negro boy 7 years old." Soon he had purchased two more children, the cheapest slaves available. Conscious of his status as a slaveowner, Flintoff resented the low wages he was paid and complained that his uncle offered him "*hand pay*," the wages of a day laborer rather than a slaveowner and manager. In 1853, with nine young slaves and a growing family, Flintoff faced "the most unhappy time of my life." He was fired by his uncle, "treated shamefully." Finally he said, "I will have to sell some of my negroes to buy land. This I must have. I want *a home*."

Returning to North Carolina, Flintoff purchased 124 acres with help from his in-laws. He grew corn, wheat, and tobacco and earned extra cash hauling wood in his wagon. By 1860 he owned 3 horses, 26 hogs, 10 cattle, and several slaves, and was paying off his debts. Eventually Flintoff owned 217 acres and became a fairly prosperous tobacco and grain farmer. He was able to send his sons to college, and prided himself that his wife "has lived a *Lady*." But the struggle upward had not been easy, and Flintoff never became the cotton planter he had aspired to be.

Probably more typical of the southern yeoman was Ferdinand L. Steel. As a young man Steel moved from North Carolina to Tennessee to work as a hatter and river boatman, but he eventually settled down to farming in Mississippi. He rose every day at five and worked until sundown. With the help of his family he raised corn, wheat, pork, and vegetables for the family table. Cotton was his cash crop: like other yeomen he sold five or six bales a year to obtain money for sugar, coffee, salt, calico, gunpowder, and a few other store-bought goods.

Steel picked his cotton himself (never exceeding 120 pounds per day—less than many slaves averaged) and regretted that cotton cultivation was so arduous and time-consuming. He was not tempted to grow more of it. The market fluctuated, and if cotton prices fell, a small grower like himself could be driven into debt and lose his farm. Steel, in fact, wanted to grow less cotton. "We are too weak handed" to manage it, he noted in his diary. "We had better raise small grain and corn and let cotton alone, raise corn and keep out of debt and we will have no necessity of raising cotton."

Steel's life in Mississippi in the 1840s retained much of the flavor of the frontier. He made all the family's shoes; his wife and sister sewed dresses, shirts, and "pantiloons." The Steels also rendered their own soap, spun and wove cotton into cloth, and hunted for game. House raisings and corn shuckings provided entertainment, and Steel doctored his illnesses with boneset tea and other herbs.

The focus of Steel's life was his family and his religion. The family prayed together every morning and night, and he prayed and studied Scripture for an hour after lunch. Steel joined a temperance society and looked forward to church and camp meetings. "My Faith increases, & I enjoy much of that peace which the world cannot give," he wrote in 1841. Seeking to improve himself and be "ready" for judgment, Steel borrowed histories, Latin and Greek grammars, and religious books from his church. Eventually he became a traveling Methodist minister. "My life is one of toil," he reflected, "but blessed be God that it is as well with me as it is."

Toil was also the lot of another group of free southerners: free blacks. In 1860 nearly a quarter million of them faced conditions that were worse than the yeoman's, and often little better than the slave's. The free blacks of the upper South were descendants of men and women emancipated by their owners in the 1780s and 1790s, a period of post-Revolutionary idealism that coincided with a decline in tobacco prices. They had few material advantages; most did not own land and had to labor in someone else's field, frequently beside slaves. By law they could not own a gun or liquor, violate curfew, assemble except in church, testify in court, or (everywhere after 1835) vote. Despite these obstacles, a minority bought land, and others found jobs as artisans, draymen, boatmen, and fishermen. A few owned slaves, who were almost always their wives and children, purchased from bondage.

Free blacks

Farther south, in the cotton and Gulf regions, a large proportion of free blacks were mulattoes, the privileged offspring of wealthy planters. Some received good educations and financial backing from their fathers, who recognized a moral obligation to them. In a few cities such as New Orleans and Mobile, extensive interracial sex had produced a mulatto population that was recognized as a distinct class. Mulattoes formed a society of their own and sought a status above slaves and other freedmen, if not equal to planters. But outside New Orleans and Mobile such groups were rare, and most mulattoes encountered disadvantages more frequently than they enjoyed benefits from their light skin tone. (For a more detailed discussion of free blacks, see Chapter 11.)

Slaveholding planters

At the opposite end of the spectrum from free blacks were the slaveholders. As a group slaveowners lived well, on incomes that enabled them to enjoy superior housing, food, clothing, and luxuries. But most did not live on the opulent scale that legend suggests. A few statistics tell the story: 88 percent of southern slaveholders had fewer than twenty slaves; 72 percent had fewer than ten; 50 percent had fewer than five. Thus the average slaveholder was not a man of great wealth but an aspiring farmer. Nor was he a polished aristocrat, but more usually a person of humble origins, with little formal education and many rough edges to his manner. In fact, he probably had little beyond a degree of wealth and a growing ambition to distinguish him from a nonslaveholder.

Even wealthy slaveowners often lacked the refined manner of aristocrats. A Louisiana planter named Bennet Barrow, for example, was neither especially polished nor unusually coarse. Barrow's plantation lay in a wealthy parish in Louisiana, but his wealth was new and Barrow was preoccupied with moneymaking. He worried constantly over his cotton crop, filling his diary with tedious weather reports and gloomy predictions of his yields. Yet Barrow also strove to appear above such worries, and in boom times he grandly endorsed notes for men who left him saddled with debt.

Barrow hunted frequently, and he had a passion for racing horses and raising hounds. Each year he set aside several weeks to attend the races in New Orleans, where he entered stallions brought from as far away as Tennessee. Barrow could report the loss of a slave without feeling, but emotion shattered his laconic manner when misfortune struck his sporting animals. "Never was a person more unlucky than I am," he complained; "My favorite pup never lives." His strongest feelings surfaced when his horse Jos Bell—equal to "the best Horse in the South"—"broke down in running a mile . . . ruined for Ever." That same day the distraught Barrow gave his field hands a "general Whipping." Barrow was rich, but his wealth had not softened his rough, direct style of life.

The wealth of the greatest planters gave ambitious men like Barrow something to aspire to. If most planters lived in spacious, comfortable farmhouses, some did live in mansions. If most slaveowners sat down at mealtimes to an abundance of tempting country foods—pork and ham, beef and game, fresh vegetables and fruits, tasty breads and biscuits, cakes and jams—the sophisticated elite consumed such delights as "gumbo, ducks and olives, *supreme de volaille,* chickens in jelly, oysters, lettuce salad, chocolate cream, jelly cake, claret cup, etc." On formal and business occasions such as county court days, a traveler in Mississippi would see gentlemen decked out in "black cloth coats, black cravats and satin or embroidered silk waistcoats; all, too, sleek as if just from a barber's hands, and redolent of perfumes." The ladies wore the latest fashions to parties and balls.

Among the wealthiest and oldest families, a paternalistic ideology prevailed. Instead of stressing the acquisitive aspects of commercial agriculture, these people focused on *noblesse oblige.* They saw themselves as custodians of the welfare of society as a whole and of the black families who depended on them. The paternalistic planter saw himself not as an oppressor but as the benevolent guardian of an inferior race. He developed affectionate feelings toward his slaves (as long as they kept in their place) and was genuinely shocked at outside criticism of his behavior.

Southern paternalism

A few words from the letters of Paul Carrington Cameron, North Carolina's largest slaveholder, illustrate this mentality. After a period of sickness among

The North Carolina planter Duncan Cameron (1776–1853) built this spacious and comfortable farmhouse for his bride, Rebecca Bennehan, in 1804. The house, called Fairntosh, is more typical of the average planter's home than the elaborate Greek-revival-style mansions of popular legend. Courtesy of the North Carolina Division of Archives and History, Raleigh.

his approximately one thousand North Carolina slaves (he owned hundreds more in Alabama and Mississippi), Cameron wrote, "I fear the Negroes have suffered much from the want of proper attention and kindness under this late distemper . . . no love of lucre shall ever induce me to be cruel, or even to make or permit to be made any great exposure of their persons at inclement seasons." On another occasion he described to his sister the sense of responsibility he felt: "I cannot better follow the example of our venerated Mother than in doing my duty to her faithful old slaves and their desendants. Do you remember a cold & frosty morning, during her illness, when she said to me 'Paul my son the people ought to be shod' this is ever in my ears, whenever I see any ones shoes in bad order; and in my ears it will be, so long as I am master."

There is no doubt that the richest southern planters saw themselves in this way. It was comforting to do so, and slaves, accommodating themselves to the realities of power, encouraged their masters to think their benevolence was appreciated. Paternalism also provided a welcome defense against abolitionist criticism. Still, for most planters, paternalism affected the manner and not the substance of their behavior. It was a matter of style. Its softness and warmth covered harsher assumptions: Negroes were inferior; planters should make money.

Southern women and their servants, photographed in 1860. The Western Reserve Historical Society.

Even Paul Cameron's concern vanished with changed circumstances. Following the Civil War he bristled at their efforts to be free and made sweeping economic decisions without regard to their welfare. Writing on Christmas Day 1865, Cameron showed little Christian charity (but a healthy profit motive) when he expressed his desire to get "free . . . of the negro. I am convinced that the people who gets rid of the free negro first will be the first to advance in improved agriculture. Have made no effort to retain any of mine [and] will not attempt a crop beyond the capacity of 30 hands." With that he turned out nearly a thousand black agriculturalists, rented his lands to several white farmers, and invested in industry.

Relations between men and women in the planter class were similarly paternalistic. The southern woman was raised and educated to be a companion and helpmate to men. At an age when her brothers were studying science, law, or medicine, the wealthy young woman was expected to devote herself to drawing, music, literature, and social life. Her proper responsibility was home management. She was not to venture into politics and other worldly affairs. If she did, she met universal condemnation. Within the domestic circle, furthermore, the husband reigned supreme. "He is master of the house," wrote South Carolina diarist Mary Boykin Chesnut. "To hear is to obey . . . all the

Woman's role

comfort of my life depends upon his being in a good humor." In a darker mood Chesnut once observed that "there is no slave . . . like a wife." Unquestionably there were some, possibly many, close and satisfying relationships between men and women in the planter class. But it is clear that many women were oppressed.

Childbearing brought grief and sickness as well as joy to southern women. In 1840 the birthrate for southern women in their fertile years was almost 20 percent higher than the national average. At the beginning of the nineteenth century, the average southern woman could expect to bear eight children; by 1860 the figure had decreased only to six, and a miscarriage was likely among so many pregnancies. The high birthrate took a toll on women's health, for complications of childbirth were a major cause of death. Moreover, a mother had to endure the loss of many of the infants she bore. Infant mortality in the first year of life exceeded 10 percent. In the South in 1860 almost five out of ten children died before age five, and among all South Carolinians younger than twenty, fewer than four in ten survived to reach the 20-to-60-year-old category. For those women who wanted to plan their families, methods of contraception were not always reliable. And doctors had few remedies for infection or irritation of the reproductive tract.

Slavery was another source of trouble, a nasty sore that women sometimes had to bandage but were not supposed to notice. "Violations of the moral law . . . made mulattoes as common as blackberries," protested a woman in Georgia, but wives had to play "the ostrich game." "A magnate who runs a hideous black harem," wrote Mrs. Chesnut, "under the same roof with his lovely white wife, and his beautiful accomplished daughters . . . poses as the model of all human virtues to these poor women whom God and the laws have given him. From the height of his awful majesty, he scolds and thunders at them, as if he never did wrong in his life."

In the early 1800s, some southern women, especially Quakers, had spoken out against slavery. But in the 1840s and 1850s, as national and international criticism of slavery increased, southern men published a barrage of articles stressing that women should restrict their concerns to the home. A writer in the *Southern Literary Messenger* bemoaned "these days of Women's Rights." Perhaps in fear of women's political opinions, the *Southern Quarterly Review* declared, "The proper place for a woman is at home. One of her highest privileges, to be politically merged in the existence of her husband." Thomas Dew, one of the nineteenth century's first proslavery theorists, advised that "women are precisely what the men make them," and another writer promoted "affection, reverence, and duty" as a woman's proper attitudes.

But southern women were beginning to chafe at their customary exclusion from financial matters. Education was another sore spot. Some of the most privileged women were acquiring a taste for knowledge, and schools for women were multiplying. These academies emphasized domestic skills, but their students nevertheless picked up some knowledge of the world's affairs that they were not, after graduation, permitted to use.

For another large category of southern men and women, education in any form was not allowed. Male or female, slaves were expected to accept ignorance as part of their condition.

Slaves and the conditions of their servitude

For Afro-Americans, slavery was a curse that brought no blessings other than the strengths they developed to survive it. Slaves knew a life of poverty, coercion, toil, heartbreak, and resentment. They had few hopes that were not denied; often they had to bear separation from their loved ones; and they were despised as an inferior race. That they endured and found loyalty and strength among themselves is a tribute to their courage, but it could not make up for a life without freedom or opportunity.

Slave diet, clothing, and housing

Southern slaves enjoyed few material comforts beyond the bare necessities. Their diet was plain and limited, though generally they had enough to eat. The basic ration was cornmeal, fat pork, molasses, and occasionally coffee. Many masters allowed slaves to tend gardens, which provided the variety and extra nutrition of greens and sweet potatoes. Fishing and hunting benefited some

Most slave families lived in crude and crowded quarters, but the five generations pictured here drew strength from their close family ties. Photographed in Beaufort, South Carolina, in 1862. Library of Congress.

slaves. "It warn't nothin' fine," recalled one woman, "but it was good plain eatin' what filled you up." Most slaveowners were innocent of the charge that they starved their slaves, but there is considerable evidence that slaves often suffered the effects of beriberi, pellagra, and other dietary-deficiency diseases.

Clothing too was plain, coarse, and inexpensive. Children of both sexes ran naked in hot weather and wore long cotton shirts in cool. When they were big enough to go to the fields, the boys received a work shirt and a pair of britches and the girls a simple dress. On many plantations slave women made their own clothing of cheap osnaburg, or "nigger cloth." Probably few received more than one or two changes of clothing for hot and cold seasons and one blanket each winter. Those who could earn a little money by doing extra work often bought additional clothing. Many slaves had to go without shoes until December, even as far north as Virginia. The shoes they received were frequent objects of complaint–uncomfortable brass-toed brogans or stiff wraparounds made from leather tanned on the plantation.

Summer and winter, slaves lived in small one-room cabins with a door and possibly a window opening, but no glass. Logs chinked with mud formed the walls, dirt was the only floor, and a wattle or stone chimney vented the fireplace that provided heat and light. Bedding consisted of straw, straw mattresses, or wooden bedframes lashed to the walls with rope. A few crude pieces of furniture and cooking utensils completed the furnishings of most cabins. More substantial houses survive today from some of the richer plantations, but the average slave lived in crude accommodations. The gravest drawback of slave cabins was not their appearance and lack of comfort but their unhealthfulness. In each small cabin lived one or two whole families. Crowding and lack of sanitation fostered the spread of infection and contagious diseases. Many slaves (and whites) carried worms and intestinal parasites picked up from fecal matter or the soil. Lice were widespread among both races, and flies and other insects spread such virulent diseases as typhoid fever, malaria, and dysentery.

Hard work was the central fact of the slaves' existence. Overseers rang the morning bell before dawn, so early that some slaves remembered being in the fields "before it was light enough to see clearly . . . holding their hoes and other implements–afraid to start work for fear that they would cover the cotton plants with dirt because they couldn't see clearly." And, as one woman testified, when interviewed by workers in the Federal Writers' Project of the 1930s, "it was way after sundown 'fore dey could stop dat field wuk. Den dey had to hustle to finish deir night wuk in time for supper, or go to bed widout it." Except on some rice plantations, where slaves were assigned daily tasks to complete at their own pace, working from "sun to sun" became universal in the South. These long hours and hard work were at the heart of the advantage of slave labor. As one planter put it, slaves were the best labor because "you could command them and *make* them do what was right." White workers, by contrast, were few and couldn't be *driven;* "they wouldn't stand it."

Slave work routines

Planters aimed to keep all their laborers busy all the time. Slave women did heavy field work, often as much as the men and even during pregnancy. Old people–of whom there were few–were kept busy caring for young children, doing light chores, or carding, ginning, or spinning cotton. Children had to gather kindling for the fire, carry water to the fields, or sweep the yard. But slaves had a variety of ways to keep from being worked to death. It was impossible for the master to supervise every slave every minute, and slaves slacked off when they were not being watched. Thus travelers frequently described lackadaisical slaves who seemed "to go through the motions of labor without putting strength into them," and owners complained that slaves "never would lay out their strength freely . . . it was impossible to make them do it." Stubborn misunderstanding and literal-mindedness was another defense. One exasperated Virginia planter exclaimed, "You can make a nigger work, *but you cannot make him think.*"

Of course the slave could not cheat too much, because the owner enjoyed a monopoly on force and violence. Whites throughout the South believed that Negroes "can't be governed except with the whip." One South Carolinian frankly explained to a northern journalist that he had whipped his slaves occasionally, "say once a fortnight; . . . the Negroes knew they would be whipped if they didn't behave themselves, and the fear of the lash kept them in good order." Evidence suggests that whippings were less frequent on small farms than on large plantations, but the reports of former slaves show that a large majority even of small farmers plied the lash. These beatings symbolized authority to the master and tyranny to the slaves, who made them a benchmark for evaluating a master. In the words of former slaves, a good owner was one who did not "whip too much," whereas a bad owner "whipped till he'd bloodied you and blistered you."

Physical and mental abuse of slaves

As this testimony suggests, terrible abuses could and did occur. The master wielded virtually absolute authority on his plantation; courts did not recognize the word of chattel, and southern society was slow to put pressure on all but the most debased and vicious slaveowners. One slave told of a sadistic owner who several times opened a jug of whiskey, tied up some slaves, and staged a "whippin' frolic" that lasted for hours. Other owners refined the cruelty of whipping by cutting open the blisters on a slave's back and dripping sealing wax into them, or throwing salt or pepper water onto the sores. Sometimes, pregnant women received terrible lashings after their master

In some parts of the South slaves and even free blacks had to wear demeaning identification tags like these, issued in Charleston. The Charleston Museum.

had dug a hole in the ground in which to lay their bellies. There were burnings, mutilations, tortures, and murders.

Slavery in the United States was physically cruel, but less so than elsewhere in the New World. In some parts of the Western Hemisphere in the 1800s, slaves were regarded as an expendable resource and scheduled for replacement after seven years. Treatment was so poor and families so uncommon that death rates were high and the heavily male slave population did not replace itself, and rapidly shrank in size. In the United States, by contrast, the slave population showed a steady natural increase, births exceeded deaths, and each generation grew larger.

The worst evil of American slavery was not its physical cruelty but the fact of slavery itself: coercion, loss of freedom, belonging to another person. Recalling their days in bondage, some former slaves emphasized the physical abuse–those were "bullwhip days" to one woman; another said, "W'at I t'ink 'bout slabery? Huh–nigger get back cut in slabery time, enty [didn't he]?" But their comments focused on the tyranny of whipping as much as the pain. A woman named Delia Garlic cut to the core when she said, "It's bad to belong to folks dat own you soul an' body. I could tell you 'bout it all day, but even den you couldn't guess de awfulness of it." And a man named Thomas Lewis put it this way: "There was no such thing as being good to slaves. Many people were better than others, but a slave belonged to his master and there was no way to get out of it."

As these comments show, American slaves retained their mental independence and self-respect despite their bondage. They hated their oppression, and contrary to some whites' perceptions, they were not grateful to their oppressors. Although they had to be subservient and speak honeyed words in the presence of their masters, they talked quite differently later on among themselves. The evidence of their resistant attitudes comes from their actions and from their own life stories.

Former slaves reported some kind feelings between masters and slaves, but the overwhelming picture was one of antagonism and resistance. Slaves mistrusted kindness from whites and suspected self-interest in their owners. A woman whose mistress "was good to us Niggers" said her owner was kind " 'cause she was raisin' us to wuk for her." A man recalled that his owners "allus thunk lots of their niggers and Grandma Maria say, 'Why shouldn't they–it was their money.' " Christmas presents of clothing from the master did not mean anything, observed another, " 'cause he goin' to [buy] that anyhow."

Slaves' attitudes toward whites

Slaves also saw their owners as people who used human beings as beasts of burden. "Massa was purty good," said one man. "He treated us jus' 'bout like you would a good mule." Another said that his master "fed us reg'lar on good, 'stantial food, jus' like you'd tend to you hoss, if you had a real good one." A third recalled his master saying, " 'A well-fed, healthy nigger, next to a mule, is de bes' propersition a man kin' ves' his money in.' "

Slaves were sensitive to the thousand daily signs of their degraded status. One man recalled the general rule that slaves ate cornbread and owners ate biscuits. If blacks did get biscuits, "de flour dat we made de biscuits out of wus de third-grade shorts." A woman reported that on her plantation "Ol' Marster hunted a heap, but us never did get none of what he brought in." "Us cotch lots of 'possums, but mighty few of 'em us Niggers ever got a chance to eat or rabbits neither," said another. "Dey made Niggers go out and hunt 'em and de white folks et 'em." If the owner took slaves' garden produce to town and sold it for them, the slaves suspected him of pocketing part of the profits.

Suspicion and resentment often grew into hatred. According to a former slave from Virginia, "the white folks treated the nigger so mean that all the slaves prayed God to punish their cruel masters." When a yellow fever epidemic struck in 1852, many slaves saw it as God's retribution. As late as the 1930s an elderly woman named Minnie Fulkes cherished the conviction that God was going to punish white people for their cruelty to blacks. She described the whippings that her mother had had to endure and then exclaimed, "Lord, Lord, I hate white people and de flood waters gwine drown some mo." A young slave girl who had suffered abuse as a house servant admitted that she took cruel advantage of her mistress when the woman had a stroke. Instead of fanning the mistress to keep flies away, the young slave struck her in the face with the fan whenever they were alone. "I done that woman bad," the slave confessed, but "she was so mean to me."

The bitterness between blacks and whites was vividly expressed by a former slave named Savilla Burrell, who visited her former master on his deathbed long after the Civil War. Sitting beside him, she reflected on the lines that "sorrow had plowed on dat old face and I 'membered he'd been a captain on hoss back in dat war. It come into my 'membrance de song of Moses: 'de Lord had triumphed glorily and de hoss and his rider have been throwed into de sea.' " She felt sympathy for a dying man, but she also felt satisfaction at God's revenge.

On the plantation, of course, slaves had to keep such thoughts to themselves. Often they expressed one feeling to whites, another to their own race. When one mistress died, "all the slaves come in the house just a hollering and crying and holding their hands over their eyes, just hollering for all they could. Soon as they got outside of the house they would say, 'Old Goddamn son-of-a-bitch, she gone on down to hell.' " A young girl who appeared overcome with tears of emotion when her newly married young mistress chose her as a servant was in reality only glad her new owner "didn't beat." And filing solemnly by the coffin of her cruel and much-hated master, one girl recounted, "I jist happened to look up and caught my sister's eye and we both jist natchelly laughed–Why shouldn't we? We was glad he was dead."

Slave culture and everyday life

The force that helped slaves to maintain such defiance was their culture. They had their own view of the world, a body of beliefs and values born of both their past and their present, as well as the fellowship

The Old Plantation. Slaves do the Juba, a dance of Yoruba origin, to the music of a stringed *molo* and a *gudugudu* (drum). The women's colorful headscarves recall African styles and customs, as does the man's use of a cane in his dance. Drawn in the late eighteenth century on a plantation between Charleston and Orangeburg. The Abby Aldridge Rockefeller Folk Art Center, Williamsburg, Virginia.

and support of their own community. With power overwhelmingly in the hands of whites, it was not possible for slaves to change their world. But drawing strength from their culture, they could refuse to accept their condition or to give up the struggle against it.

Slave culture changed significantly after the turn of the century. Between 1790 and 1808, when Congress banned further importation of slaves, there was a rush to import Africans. After that the proportion of native-born blacks rose steadily, reaching 96 percent in 1840 and almost 100 percent in 1860. (For this reason blacks can trace their American ancestry back further than many white Americans.) Meanwhile, more and more slaves adopted Christianity. With time the old African culture faded further into memory, though it did not disappear. Differences among slaves from various tribes became less noticeable. An Afro-American culture was emerging.

In many ways African influences remained primary. For African practices and beliefs reminded the slaves that they were and ought to be different from their oppressors, and thus encouraged them to resist. The most visible aspects of African culture were the slaves' dress and recreation. Some slave men plaited their hair into rows and fancy designs; slave women often wore their hair "in string"–tied in small bunches with a string or piece of cloth. A few men and many women wrapped their heads in kerchiefs following the styles and colors of West Africa.

Remnants of African culture

For entertainment slaves made musical instruments with carved motifs that resembled some African stringed instruments. Their drumming and dancing clearly followed African patterns; whites marveled at them. One visitor to Georgia in the 1860s described a ritual dance of African origin: "A ring of singers is formed . . . and they . . . walk slowly around and around in a circle. . . . They then utter a kind of melodious chant, which gradually increases in strength, and in noise, until it fairly shakes the house, and it can be heard for a long distance. This chant is responded to at intervals. . . . The dancers usually bend their bodies into an angle of about forty-five degrees, and thus bent, march around, accompanying their steps, every second or so, with a quick, jerking motion, or jump, which I can compare to nothing else than the brisk jumping of a frog. . . . The songs are . . . handed down by tradition from their ancestors."

Many slaves continued to see and believe in spirits. Some whites believed in ghosts, but the belief was more widespread among slaves. It closely resembled the African concept of the living dead—the idea that deceased relatives visited the earth for many years until the process of dying was complete. Slaves also practiced conjuration, voodoo, and quasi-magical root medicine. By 1860 the most notable conjurers and root doctors were reputed to live in South Carolina, Georgia, Louisiana, and other isolated coastal areas of heavy slave importation.

These cultural survivals provided slaves with a sense of their separate past. Black achievement in music and dance was so exceptional that whites felt entirely cut off from it; in this one area some whites became aware that they stood completely outside the slave community. Conjuration and folklore also directly fed resistance; slaves could cast a spell or direct the power of a hand (a bag of articles belonging to the person to be conjured) against the master. Not all masters felt confident enough to dismiss such a a threat.

In adopting Christianity, slaves fashioned it too into an instrument of support and resistance. Theirs was a religion of justice quite unlike that of the propaganda their masters pushed at them. Former slaves scorned the preaching arranged by their masters. "You ought to heared that preachin'," said one man. " 'Obey your massa and missy, don't steal chickens and eggs and meat,' but nary a word 'bout havin' a soul to save." To the slaves, Jesus cared about their souls and their present plight. They rejected the idea that in heaven whites would have "de colored folks . . . dar to wait on em." Instead, when God's justice came, the slaveholders would be "brillin' in hell fur dey sin." "God is punishin' some of dem ol' suckers an' their chillun right now fer de way dey use to treat us poor colored folks," said one woman.

Slave religion

For slaves Christianity was a religion of personal and group salvation. Devout men and women worshipped and prayed every day, "in de field or by de side of de road," or in special "prayer grounds" such as a "twisted thick-rooted muscadine bush" that afforded privacy. Beyond seeking personal guidance, these worshippers prayed "for deliverance of de slaves." Some waited "until the overseer got behind a hill" and then laid down their hoes and called on God to free them. Others held fervent secret prayer meetings that lasted far into the night. From such activities many slaves gained the unshakeable belief that God would end their bondage. As one man asserted, "hit was de plans of God to free us niggers." This faith and the joy and emotional release that accompanied their worship sustained blacks.

Slaves also developed a sense of racial identity. The whole experience of southern blacks taught them that whites despised their race. White people, as one ex-slave put it, "have been and are now and always will be against the Negro." Even "the best white woman that ever broke bread wasn't much," said another, " 'cause they all hated the po' nigger." Blacks naturally drew together, helping each other in danger, need, and resistance. "We never tole on each other," one woman declared. Former slaves were virtually unanimous in denouncing those who betrayed the group or sought personal advantage through allegiance to whites.

Of course, different jobs and circumstances created natural variations in attitude among slaves. But for most slaves, there was no overriding class system within the black community. Only one-quarter of all slaves lived on plantations of fifty blacks or more, so few knew a wide chasm between exalted house servants and lowly field hands. In fact, many slaves did both housework and field work, depending on their age and the season. Their primary loyalty was to each other.

Hundreds of thousands of slaves were forced to move west as the South expanded. Almost always they traveled on foot, either with their masters or as shown here, under the supervision of slave traders. The Virginia State Library, Richmond.

Slave family life

The main source of support was the family. Slave families faced severe dangers. At any moment the master could sell a husband or wife, give a slave child away as a wedding present, or die in debt, forcing a division of his property. Many families were broken in such ways. Others were uprooted in the trans-Appalachian expansion of the South, which caused a large interregional movement of the black population. Between 1810 and 1820 alone, 137,000 slaves were forced to move from North Carolina and the Chesapeake states to Alabama, Mississippi, and other western regions. An estimated 2 million persons were sold between 1820 and 1860. When the Union Army registered thousands of black marriages in Mississippi and Louisiana in 1864 and 1865, 25 percent of the men over forty reported that they had been forcibly separated from a previous wife. A similar proportion of former slaves later recalled that slavery had destroyed one of their marriages. Probably a substantial minority of slave families suffered disruption of one kind or another.

But this did not mean that slave families could not exist. American slaves clung tenaciously to the personal relationships that gave meaning to life. For although American law did not protect slave families, masters permitted them. In fact, slave owners expected slaves to form families and have children. As a result, even along the rapidly expanding edge of the cotton kingdom, where the effects of the slave trade would have been most visible, there remained a normal ratio of men to women, young to old.

Following African kinship taboos, Afro-Americans avoided marriage among cousins (a frequent occurrence among aristocratic slaveowners). Adapting to the circumstances of their captivity, they did not condemn unwed mothers, although they did expect a young girl to form a stable marriage after one preg-

These examples of slave craftsmanship show some African influences, as well as the painstaking skill invested in the manufacture of even the most common objects. Left to right: a diamond-pattern quilt; a hand-carved cane with African motifs; and hand-made egg and vegetable baskets. Cane from the National Gallery of Art, Washington, D.C., Index of American Design. Quilt and baskets from the Old Slave Mart.

nancy, if not before. By naming their children after relatives of past generations, Afro-Americans emphasized their family histories. If they chose to bear the surname of a white slaveowner, it was often not their current master's but that of the owner under whom their family had begun.

Slaves abhorred interference in their family lives. Some of their strongest protests sought to prevent the break-up of a family. Indeed, some individuals refused to accept such separations and struggled for years to maintain or re-establish contact. Rape was a horror for both men and women. Some husbands faced death rather than permit their wives to be sexually abused; and women sometimes fought back. In other cases slaves seethed with anger at the injustice but could do nothing except to soothe each other with human sympathy and understanding. Significantly, blacks condemned the guilty party, not the victim.

Because of the pressures of bondage, black couples had more equal relationships than their white owners. Each member of the immediate family, as well as grandparents, uncles, and aunts, had to take on extra duties as the need arose; thus there was no opportunity to restrict women to narrow responsibilities. Women often worked in the fields with men, but they still cooked the meals and performed traditional household chores. The men cared for the livestock in the evening or fished and hunted on the weekends. Female house servants attained a high level of skill in sewing, weaving, embroidery, and cooking, but only on the largest plantations did male slaves have the chance to develop skill in a craft. Even so, the slave husband and father held a respected place in his home. And though the marriage ceremony consisted only of jumping over a broomstick, partners "stuck lots closer den," in one woman's words. "[When] they married they stayed married," said another. When husbands and wives lived on neighboring plantations, visits on Wednesday and Saturday nights included big dinners of welcome and celebration. Christmas was a similarly joyous time " 'cause husbands is comin' home an' families is gittin' 'nited again."

Slaves brought to their efforts at resistance the same common sense, determination, and practicality that characterized their family lives. American slavery produced some fearless and implacable revolutionaries. Gabriel's conspiracy apparently was known to more than a thousand slaves when it was discovered in 1800, just before it was put into motion (see Chapter 7). A similar conspiracy in Charleston in 1822, headed by a free black named Denmark Vesey, involved many of the most trusted slaves of leading families. But the most famous rebel of all, Nat Turner, rose in violence in Southampton County, Virginia, in 1831.

Resistance to slavery

The son of an African woman who passionately hated her enslavement, Nat was a precocious child who learned to read very young. Encouraged by his first owner to study the Bible, he enjoyed some special privileges but also knew changes of masters and hard work. His father, who successfully ran away to freedom, stood always before him as an example of defiance. In time young Nat became a preacher, an impressive orator with a reputation among whites as well as blacks. He also developed a tendency toward mysticism, and he became increasily withdrawn. After nurturing his plan for several years, Turner led a band of rebels from house to house in the predawn darkness of August 22, 1831. The group severed limbs and crushed skulls with axes or killed their victims with guns. Before they were stopped, Nat Turner and his followers had slaughtered sixty whites of both sexes and all ages. Nat and as many as two hundred blacks lost their lives as a result of the rebellion.

But most slave resistance was not violent, for the odds against revolution were especially poor in North America. The South had the highest ratio of whites to blacks in the hemisphere; at the same time plantations were relatively small, which meant that whites had ample opportunity to supervise the slaves' activities. There was thus literal truth to one slave's remark that "the white man was the slave's jail." Moreover, the South lacked vital geographic and demographic features that had aided revolution elsewhere. The land offered relatively few jungles and mountain fastnesses to which rebels could flee. And compared to South America, southern slave importations were neither large nor prolonged. The South therefore lacked a preponderance of young male slaves. Nor were its military forces weak and overtaxed, like those of many South American colonies.

Thus the scales weighed heavily against revolution, and the slaves knew it. Consequently they directed

The most famous of all slave rebels, Nat Turner, led an uprising that took the lives of sixty whites and spread fear throughout the South. Library of Congress.

their energies toward improving their lot as slaves. A desperate slave could run away for good, but as often or probably more often slaves simply ran off temporarily to hide in the woods. There they were close to friends and allies who could help them escape capture in an area they knew well. Every day that a slave "lay out" in this way the master lost a day's labor. Most owners chose not to mount an exhaustive search and sent word instead that the slave's grievances would be redressed. The runaway would then return to bargain with the master. Most owners would let the matter pass, for, like the owner of a valuable cook, they were "glad to get her back."

Other modes of resistance had the same object: to better the conditions of slavery. Appropriating food (stealing, in the master's eyes) was so common that even whites sang humorous songs about it. Blacks were also alert to the attitudes of individual whites, and learned to ingratiate themselves or play off one white person against another. Field hands frequently tested a new overseer to intimidate him or win more favorable working conditions. Other blacks fought with patrollers. Some slaves engaged in verbal arguments and even physical violence to deter or resist beatings. The harshest masters were the most strongly resisted. "Good masters had good slaves 'cause they treated 'em good," but "whar the ole master was mean an' ornery," his slaves were ornery too.

Harmony and tension in a slave society

Not only for blacks but for whites too, slave labor stood at the heart of the South's social system. A host of consequences flowed from its existence, from the organization of society to an individual's personal values.

For blacks, the nineteenth century brought a strengthening and expansion of the legal restrictions of slavery. In all things, from their workaday movements to Sunday worship, slaves fell under the supervision of whites. Courts held that a slave "has no civil right" and could not even hold property "except at the will and pleasure of his master." When slaves revolted, legislators tightened the legal straitjacket: after the Nat Turner insurrection in 1832, for example, they prohibited owners from teaching their slaves to read.

The weight of this legal and social framework fell on nonblacks as well. All white male citizens bore an obligation to ride in patrols to discourage slave movements at night. Whites in strategic positions, such as ship captains and harbor masters, were required to scrutinize the papers of blacks who might be attempting to escape bondage. White southerners who criticized the slave system out of moral conviction or class resentment were intimidated, attacked, or legally prosecuted. (Some, like James Birney, went north to join the antislavery movement.) Urban residents who did not supervise their domestic slaves as closely as planters found themselves subject to criticism. And the South's few manufacturers felt pressure to use slave rather than free labor.

Small wonder, for slavery was the main determinant of wealth in the South. Ownership of slaves guaranteed the labor to produce cotton and other crops on a large scale—labor otherwise unavailable in a rural society. Slaves were therefore vital to the acquisition of a fortune. Beyond that, slaves were a commodity and an investment, much like gold; people bought them on speculation, hoping for a steady rise in their value. In fact, for southern society as a whole, slaves equaled wealth almost completely. Important economic enterprises not based on slavery were so rare that the correspondence between geographic variations in wealth and variations in slaveholding was nearly one-to-one.

Slavery as the basis of wealth and social standing

It was therefore natural that slaveholding should be the main determinant of a person's social position. Wealth in slaves was the foundation on which the ambitious built their reputations. Ownership of slaves also brought political power: a solid majority of political officeholders were slaveholders, and the most powerful of them were generally large slaveholders. Though lawyers and newspaper editors were sometimes influential, they did not hold independent positions in the economy or society. Dependent on the planters for business and support, they served planters' interests and reflected their outlook.

As slavery became entrenched, its influence spread throughout the social system until even the values and mores of nonslaveholders bore its imprint. For one thing, the availability of slave labor tended to devalue free labor. Where strenuous work under another was reserved for an enslaved race, few free people relished working "like a nigger." Nonslaveholders therefore preferred to work for themselves rather than to hire out. This kind of thinking engendered an aristocratic value system ill-suited to a newly established democracy.

In modified form, the attitudes characteristic of the planter elite gained a considerable foothold among the masses. The ideal of the aristocrat emphasized lineage, privilege, power, pride, and refinement of person and manner. Some of those qualities were necessarily in short supply in an expanding economy, however; they mingled with and were modified by the tradition of the frontier. In particular, masculinity and defense of one's honor were highly valued by planter and frontier farmer alike.

Aristocratic values and frontier individualism

Fights and even duels over personal slights were not uncommon in southern communities. This custom sprang from both frontier lawlessness and aristocratic tradition. Throughout the sparsely settled regions of America in the early nineteenth century, pugnacious people took the law into their own hands. Thus it was not unusual for a southern slaveowner who had warned patrollers to stay off his property to shoot at the next group of trespassers. But instead of gradually disappearing, as it did in the North, the code duello, which required men to defend their honor through the rituals of a duel, hung on in the South and gained an acceptance that spread throughout the society.

An incident that occurred in North Carolina in 1851 will illustrate. There a wealthy planter named Samuel Fleming responded to a series of disputes with the rising lawyer William Waightstill Avery by cowhiding him on a public street. According to the code, Avery had two choices: to redeem his honor through violence or to brand himself a coward through inaction. Three weeks later Avery shot Fleming dead at point-blank range during a session of Burke County Superior Court, with Judge William Battle and numerous spectators looking on. A jury took just ten minutes to find Avery not guilty, and the spectators gave him a standing ovation. Some people, including Judge Battle, were troubled by the victory of the unwritten code over the law, but most white males seemed satisfied.

Other aristocratic values that marked the planters as a class were less acceptable to the average citizen. Simply put, planters believed they were better than other people. In their pride, they expected not only to wield power but to receive special treatment. By the 1850s, some planters openly rejected the democratic creed, vilifying Jefferson for his statement that all men were equal.

These ideas, which shaped the outlook of the southern elite for generations, were inappropriate to a democratic political system. Throughout America democratic ideals were gaining strength; even in the South the majority of voters rejected the principle of the superiority of a few. Thus there were frequent conflicts between aristocratic pretensions and democratic zeal. As Mary Boykin Chesnut pointed out, a wealthy planter who sought public office could not announce his status too haughtily. She described the plight of Colonel John S. Preston, a South Carolinian with great ambitions. Preston, a perfect aristocrat, carried his high-flown manners too far; he refused to make the necessary gestures of respect toward the average voter–mingling with the crowd, exchanging jokes and compliments. Thus his highest aspiration, political leadership, could never be fulfilled. The voters would not accept him.

Such tensions found significant expression in the western parts of the seaboard states during the 1820s and 1830s. There yeomen farmers and citizens resented their underrepresentation in state legislatures, corruption in government, and undemocratic control over local government. After vigorous debate, the reformers won most of their battles. Five states–Alabama, Mississippi, Tennessee, Arkansas, and Texas–adopted what was for that time a thoroughly democratic system: popular election of governors; white manhood suffrage; legislative apportionment based on the white population; and locally chosen county government. Georgia, Florida, and Louisiana were not far behind, and reformers won significant concessions in North Carolina and Maryland. Kentucky was democratically governed except in its counties. Only South Carolina and Virginia effectively defended property qualifications for office, legislative malapportionment, appointment of county officials, and selection of the governor by the lawmakers. Democracy had expanded with the cotton kingdom.

Democratic reform movements

Even in Virginia, nonslaveholding westerners raised a basic challenge to the slave system. Following the Nat Turner rebellion, advocates of gradual abolition forced a two-week legislative debate on slavery, arguing that it was injurious to the state and inherently dangerous. When the House of Delegates finally voted, the motion favoring abolition lost by just 73 to 58. This was the last major debate on slavery in the antebellum South.

With such tensions in evidence, it was perhaps remarkable that slaveholders and nonslaveholders did not experience frequent and serious conflict. Why were class confrontations among whites so infrequent? Historians who have considered this question have given many answers. In a rural society, family bonds and kinship ties are valued, and some of the poor nonslaveholding whites were related to the rich new planters. The experience of frontier living must also have created a relatively informal, egalitarian atmosphere. And there is no doubt that the South's racial ideology, which stressed whites' superiority to blacks and race, not class, as the social dividing line, tended to reduce conflict among whites.

Finally, it is important to remember that the South was a new and mobile society. Many people had risen in status, and far more were moving away geographically. Yeomen often moved several times during a lifetime of farming, and many slaveowners did too. Even in cotton-rich Alabama in the 1850s, fewer than half the richest families in a county belonged to its elite category ten years later. Most had not died or lost their wealth; they had merely moved on to some new state. This constant mobility meant that southern society had not settled into a rigid, unchanging pattern.

But two other factors, social and economic, were probably more important. First, the South was rural and uncrowded. Travel was difficult, and people stayed much to themselves. Consequently slaveowners and nonslaveowners rarely collided. Where there is little contact, there can be little conflict. Second, the two groups were economically independent. The yeomen farmed for themselves; planters farmed for themselves and for the market. The complementary growing patterns of corn and cotton allowed planters to raise food for their animals and laborers without lowering cotton production: from spring through December, cotton and corn needed attention alternately, but never at the same time. Thus the planter did not need to depend on the nonslaveholder, and yeomen needed nothing from the planters.

There were signs, however, that the relative lack of conflict between slaveholders and nonslaveholders was coming to an end. As the region grew older, nonslaveholders saw their opportunities beginning to narrow; meanwhile wealthy planters enjoyed an expanding horizon. In effect, the risk involved in substantial cotton production was becoming too great for most nonslaveholders. Thus from 1830 to 1860 the percentage of white southern families holding slaves declined steadily from 36 percent to 25 percent. At the same time, the monetary gap between the classes was widening. Though nonslaveholders were becoming more prosperous, slaveowners' wealth was increasing much faster. And though slaveowners made up a smaller portion of the population in 1860, their share of the South's agricultural wealth remained between 90 and 95 percent. In fact, the average slaveholder was almost 14 times as rich as the average nonslaveholder.

Hardening of class lines

Pre-Civil War politics reflected these realities. Facing the prospect of a war to defend slavery, slaveowners expressed growing fear for the loyalty of nonslaveholders and discussed schemes to widen slave ownership. In North Carolina, a prolonged and increasingly bitter controversy over the combination of high taxes on land and low taxes on slaves erupted under the influence of a class-conscious nonslaveholder named Hinton R. Helper. Convinced that slavery had impoverished many whites and retarded the whole region, Helper attacked the institution in his book *The Impending Crisis,* published in New York in 1857. Discerning planters knew that such fiery controversies lay close at hand in every southern state.

But for the moment slaveowners stood secure. They held from 50 to 85 percent of the seats in state legislatures and a similarly high percentage of the South's congressional seats. In addition to their near-monopoly on political office, they had established their point of view in all the other major social institutions. Professors who criticized slavery had been dismissed from colleges and universities; schoolbooks that contained "unsound" ideas had been replaced. And almost all the Methodist and Baptist clergy, some of whom had criticized slavery in the 1790s, had given up preaching against the institution. In fact, except for a few obscure persons of conscience, southern clergy had become the most vocal defenders of the institution. Society as southerners knew it seemed stable, if not unthreatened.

Elsewhere in the nation, however, society was anything but stable. Social diversity was becoming one of the major characteristics of northern society, and social conflict an increasingly common phenomenon.

Suggestions for further reading

Southern society

W. J. Cash, *The Mind of the South* (1941); Avery O. Craven, *The Growth of Southern Nationalism, 1848–1861* (1953); Clement Eaton, *Freedom of Thought in the Old South* (1940); Clement Eaton, *The Growth of Southern Civilization, 1790–1860* (1961); William W. Freehling, *Prelude to Civil War* (1965); W. Conard Gass, " 'The Misfortune of a High Minded and Honorable Gentleman': W. W. Avery and the Southern Code of Honor," *North Carolina Historical Review,* LVI (Summer 1979), 278–297; Eugene D. Genovese, *The*

World the Slaveholders Made (1964); Eugene D. Genovese, "Yeoman Farmers in a Slaveholders' Democracy," *Agricultural History,* 49 (April 1975), 331–342; William Sumner Jenkins, *Pro-Slavery Thought in the Old South* (1935); Robert McColley, *Slavery and Jeffersonian Virginia* (1964); Frederick Law Olmsted, *The Slave States,* ed. Harvey Wish (1959); Edward Phifer, "Slavery in Microcosm: Burke County, North Carolina," *The Journal of Southern History,* XXVIII (May 1962), 137–165; Charles S. Sydnor, *The Development of Southern Sectionalism, 1819–1848* (1948); Ralph A. Wooster, *The People in Power* (1969); Ralph A. Wooster, *Politicians, Planters, and Plain Folk* (1975); Gavin Wright, *The Political Economy of the Cotton South* (1978).

Slaveholders and nonslaveholders

Bennet H. Barrow, *Plantation Life in the Florida Parishes of Louisiana, as Reflected in the Diary of Bennet H. Barrow,* ed. Edwin Adams Davis (1943); Ira Berlin, *Slaves Without Masters* (1974); Mary Boykin Chesnut, *A Diary from Dixie,* ed. Ben Ames Williams (1949); William J. Cooper, *The South and the Politics of Slavery, 1828–1856* (1978); Everett Dick, *The Dixie Frontier* (1948); Clement Eaton, *The Mind of the Old South* (1967); Drew Faust, *A Sacred Circle: The Dilemma of the Intellectual in the Old South* (1977); John Hope Franklin, *The Militant South, 1800–1861* (1956); John Hope Franklin, *The Free Negro in North Carolina, 1790–1860* (1943); Luther P. Jackson, *Free Negro Labor and Property Holding in Virginia, 1830–1860* (1942); Frances Anne Kemble, *Journal of a Residence on a Georgian Plantation in 1838–1839* (1863); Donald G. Mathews, *Religion in the Old South* (1977); Robert Manson Myers, ed., *The Children of Pride* (1972); Frank L. Owsley, *Plain Folk of the Old South* (1949); Mary D. Robertson, ed., *Lucy Breckinridge of Grove Hill* (1979); Anne Firor Scott, *The Southern Lady* (1970); J. Mills Thornton, III, *Politics and Power in a Slave Society* (1978).

Conditions of slavery

Kenneth F. Kiple and Virginia H. Kiple, "Black Tongue and Black Men," *The Journal of Southern History,* XLIII (August 1977), 411–428; Ronald L. Lewis, *Coal, Iron, and Slaves* (1979); Richard G. Lowe and Randolph B. Campbell, "The Slave Breeding Hypothesis," *The Journal of Southern History,* XLII (August 1976), 400–412; Leslie Howard Owens, *This Species of Property* (1976); Willie Lee Rose, ed., *A Documentary History of Slavery in North America* (1976); Todd L. Savitt, *Medicine and Slavery* (1978); Kenneth M. Stampp, *The Peculiar Institution* (1956); Robert S. Starobin, *Industrial Slavery in the Old South* (1970).

Slave culture and resistance

Herbert Aptheker, *American Negro Slave Revolts* (1943); John W. Blassingame, *The Slave Community* (1972); Judith Wragg Chase, *Afro-American Art and Craft* (1971); Jeffrey J. Crow, *The Black Experience in Revolutionary North Carolina* (1977); Dena J. Epstein, *Sinful Tunes and Spirituals* (1977); Paul D. Escott, *Slavery Remembered* (1979); Eric Foner, ed. *Nat Turner* (1971); Eugene D. Genovese, *From Rebellion to Revolution* (1979); Eugene D. Genovese, *Roll, Jordan, Roll* (1974); Herbert G. Gutman, *The Black Family in Slavery and Freedom, 1750–1925* (1976); Vincent Harding, *There is a River* (1981); Lawrence W. Levine, *Black Culture and Black Consciousness* (1977); Gerald W. Mullin, *Flight and Rebellion* (1972); Stephen B. Oates, *The Fires of Jubilee* (1975); Albert J. Raboteau, *Slave Religion* (1978); Robert S. Starobin, *Denmark Vesey* (1970); Peter H. Wood, *Black Majority* (1974).

For twenty years Edwin Forrest and his English rival William Charles Macready had vied for the favor of American audiences. Literary and intellectual circles lionized Macready; artisans and mechanics preferred Forrest, an American who stressed his love of flag, country, and democracy. When the two actors appeared simultaneously in New York City in May 1849, posters went up challenging Macready:

WORKING MEN,
shall
AMERICANS OR ENGLISH RULE
in this city?

Macready's opening night was ruined by noise and a barrage of objects, including four chairs, thrown from the gallery. Later in his run a crowd gathered outside the theater, protesting Macready's appearance as a symbol of "English ARISTOCRATS!! and Foreign Rule!" Adding to the fray were Anglophobic Irish immigrants, recently escaped from the bootheel of English rule. As Macready left the theater under police protection, the mob surged. The militia, on guard to maintain order, fired above the heads of the crowd, missing the rioters but felling dozens of bystanders. Twenty-two people were killed, thirty-six injured.

This incident was an extreme version of the chaos typical of theaters. The Englishwoman Frances Trollope, in her *Domestic Manners of the Americans* (1832), described the audience at a Cincinnati theater: "The spitting was incessant," accompanied by "the mixed smell of onions and whiskey. . . . The noises, too, were perpetual, and of the most unpleasant kind." An 1830 theater poster forbade "personal altercations in any part of the house," "the uncourteous habit of throwing nut shells, apples, etc., into the Pit," and "clambering over the balustrade into the Boxes, either during or at the end of the Performance." Indeed, theater regularly evoked the strongest of passions among Americans. "When a patriotic fit seized them, and 'Yankee Doodle' was called for," Trollope observed, "every man seemed to think his reputation as a citizen depended on the noise he made."

That the theater could elicit such emotions, and that class, ethnic, and patriotic conflicts spilled into its arena, reflected its pre-eminent role in American life. Theater was an early development in the rise of mass popular culture in the United States. It was also a mirror of American social life. Like society itself, theater audiences were divided by occupation, wealth, status, sex, and race. On the floor of the theater were the benches of the pit, where the mass of mechanics and artisans sat. In the tiers of boxes beyond the pit were the most expensive seats, where merchants, professionals, and ladies gathered. The third tier of boxes was generally reserved for less respectable women—boarding-house keepers and other gainfully employed women. Above these boxes, farthest from the stage, was the gallery (balcony). If the theater permitted blacks, they sat in the gallery, along with prostitutes and those of the working class unable to afford a seat in the pit.

As the American scene changed, so did the theater. As cities and towns grew larger, they boasted more than one or two theaters, and different houses began to cater to different classes. In New York, the Park Theater enjoyed the patronage of the carriage trade, the Bowery drew the middle class, and the Chatham attacted workers. The opera house generally became the upper-class playhouse. Again, the theater mirrored society, for with the increasing pace of urbanization and industrialization, the gap between the classes yawned wider. It was economic hardship as much as patriotism that sent Edwin Forrest's admirers into the streets of New York in 1849. The theater was the stage for their much larger drama.

Indeed, as the United States grew, its society became at once more diverse and more turbulent. More and more people lived in cities, where poverty, overcrowding, and crime set them against each other. Opulent mansions existed within sight of notorious slums, and both wealth and poverty reached extremes unknown in traditional agrarian America.

Immigration further increased social diversity. Within large cities and in the countryside, whole districts became European enclaves. The immigrants helped to build transportation and industry, in the process reshaping American culture.

The position of free blacks and Indians within this society was uncertain. Their very presence disturbed many Americans. Free people of color were second-class citizens at best, struggling to better their lot against overwhelming legal and racial barriers. Eastern Indians, forced to abandon their lands for resettlement beyond the Mississippi River, fared no better.

Private life changed too during these years. With increasing industrialization, the home began to lose its

A performance of an English farce at the fashionable Park Street Theatre in 1822. Faces in the audience are portraits of upper-class New Yorkers known to the artist, John Searle. The New-York Historical Society.

function as a workplace. Especially among the middle and upper classes, it became woman's domain, a refuge from the jungle of a man's world. At the same time birth control was more widely practiced and families became smaller.

To a great degree, many Americans were uncomfortable with the new direction of American life. Antipathy toward immigrants was common among native-born Americans, who feared competition for jobs. Blacks fought unceasingly for equality, and Indians tried unsuccessfully to resist forced removal. And some women began to raise their voices against the restrictions they faced. In a diverse and complex society, conflict became common.

Country life, city life

Surprisingly, it was the isolated pioneer—the frontier hunter, the fur trapper, the lonesome farm family—who came to symbolize the United States in the decades before the Civil War. These were the legendary Americans, as Frances Trollope observed, who were as independent as Robinson Crusoe. In the late 1820s Mrs. Trollope visited a self-sufficient farm family living near Cincinnati. The family grew or produced all their necessities except for coffee, tea, and whiskey, which they got by sending butter or chickens to market. But until other settlers came to live near them, they lacked the human contact that a community offered. For their inexpensive land and self-sufficiency they paid the price of isolation and loneliness. " 'Tis strange to us to see company," lamented the mother. "I expect the sun may rise and set a hundred times before I shall see another *human* that does not belong to the family."

It was, however, the farm community rather than the isolated family that dominated rural America. The farm village was the center of rural life—the farmers' link with religion, politics, and the outside world. But rural social life was not limited to trips to the village; families gathered on each other's farms to do as a community what they could not do individually. Barn-raising was among the activities that regularly brought people together. In preparation for the event, the farmer and an itinerant carpenter built a platform and cut beams, posts, and joists. When the neighbors arrived by buggy and wagon, they put together the sides and raised them into position. After the roof was up, everyone celebrated with a communal meal, and perhaps with singing and dancing. Similar gatherings took place at harvest time and on other special occasions.

Farm communities

Rural women met more formally than did men. Farm men had frequent opportunities to gather informally at general stores, markets, and taverns. Women, though, had to prearrange their regular work and social gatherings: weekly after-church dinners; sewing, quilting, and husking bees; and preparations for marriages and baptisms. These were times to exchange experiences and thoughts, offer each other support, and swap letters, books, and news.

Irene Hardy, who spent her childhood in rural southwestern Ohio in the 1840s, left a record of the gatherings she attended as a girl. Most vivid in her memory fifty years later were the apple bees. Since canning was unknown at the time, neighbors gathered to make apple butter, preserves, or dried apples. "Usually invitations were sent about by word of mouth," she recalled. " 'Married folks' came and worked all day or afternoon, peeling by hand and with peelers, coring and quartering, and spreading out . . . in the sun to dry." A dinner feast followed, for which the visiting women made biscuits, vegetables, and coffee. After cleaning up, "the old folks went home to send their young ones for their share of work and fun." The elders had gossiped to pass the time; the youngsters played tricks, joked, and teased each other in a comic-serious precourting ritual. "Then came supper, apple and pumpkin pies, cider, doughnuts, cakes, cold chicken and turkey," Hardy wrote, "after which games, 'Forfeits,' 'Building a Bridge,' 'Snatchability,' even 'Blind Man's Buff' and 'Pussy Wants a Corner.' "

Traditional country bees had their town counterparts. Fredrika Bremer, a Swedish visitor to the United States, described a sewing bee in 1849 in Cambridge, Massachusetts, at which neighborhood women made clothes for "a family who had lost all their clothing by fire." Yet these town bees were not the all-day family affairs typical of the countryside, and when the Hardy family moved to the town of Eaton in 1851, young Irene missed the country gatherings. The families of Eaton seldom held bees; they purchased their goods at the store.

City people had more formal amusements. As work and family life grew apart, there were fewer opportunities to turn work into festivals or family gatherings. Entertainment became a separate activity for which one purchased a ticket—to the theater, the circus, or P. T. Barnum's American Museum; or in the 1840s, to the race track; or a decade later, to the baseball park. The concentration of population in cities supported this diversity of activities, a luxury unknown in the countryside.

City life

Though population density and cultural diversity animated city life, they also became problems in themselves. Sporting events became so crowded that one New Yorker doubted whether it was worth battling the mobs of people to attend the racetrack. The

Country people looked forward to combining work and play in communal bees. Here Pennsylvanians scutch flax, beating the stalks to separate the linen fibers from the woody ones. National Gallery of Art, Gift of Edgar William and Bernice Chrysler Garbisch.

"crowd and the dust and the danger and the difficulty of getting on and off the course with a carriage," Philip Hone wrote in 1842, "are scarcely compensated by any pleasure to be derived from the amusement." Everywhere there seemed to be mobs of people. When P. T. Barnum brought Jenny Lind, the famous Swedish soprano, to New York in September 1850, twenty thousand people mobbed the hotel entrance for a glimpse of her.

As cities grew in size, public transportation made it easier to get around. Horse-drawn omnibuses appeared in New York in 1827, and horse-drawn streetcars soon followed. The Harlem Railroad, completed in 1832, ran the length of Manhattan. By the 1850s all big cities had streetcars. And they needed them. Cities grew so fast, they seemed to leap overnight into the countryside. George Templeton Strong, a New York lawyer and devoted diarist, recorded in 1856 that he had attended a party at a Judge Hoffman's "in thirty-seventh!!!–it seems but the other day that thirty-seventh Street was an imaginary line running through a rural district and grazed over by cows."

Strong and other upper-class New Yorkers found the density and diversity of the city repugnant. His diary is filled with his distaste for mixing with the masses. He especially disliked riding the city railroad or the omnibus. One day in 1852, suffering from a "splitting headache," Strong vented his rage at the immigrant population that crowded the city's public transportation. In "the choky, hot railroad car," he gagged on the "stale, sickly odors from sweaty Irishmen in their shirt sleeves." The other people repelled him as well: "German Jew shop-boys in white coats, pink faces, and waistcoats that looked like virulent prickly heat; fat old women, with dirty-nosed babies; one sporting man with black whiskers, miraculously crisp and curly, and a shirt collar insulting stiff, who contributed a reminiscence of tobacco smoke–the spiritual body of ten thousand bad cigars." Even tragedy provoked Strong's distaste: passing by a fire on Elizabeth Street in 1854, he observed "two or three wooden shanties blazing and disgorging an incredible number of cubic feet of Irish humanity and filthy feather beds."

Leaving aside Strong's ugly prejudices, his picture of city life was an accurate one. By twentieth-century standards, early nineteenth-century cities were disorderly, unsafe, and unhealthy. Expansion occurred so suddenly and swiftly that few cities could handle the problems it brought. For example, migrants from rural areas were used to relieving themselves and throwing refuse in any vacant area. But in the city waste spread disease, polluted wells, and gave off obnoxious smells. New York City solved part of the problem in the 1840s by abandoning wells in favor of reservoir water piped into buildings and outdoor fountains. In some districts scavengers and refuse collectors carted away garbage and human waste, but in much of the city it just rotted.

Crime was another problem. To keep order and provide for public safety, Boston supplemented (1837) and New York replaced (1845) its colonial watchmen and constables with paid policemen. Nonetheless, middle-class men and women did not venture out alone at night, and during the day stayed clear of many city districts. And the influx of immigrants to the cities compounded social tensions by pitting people of different backgrounds against each other in the contest for jobs and housing. Ironically, in the midst of the dirt, the noise, the crime, and the conflict, as if to tempt those who struggled to survive, rose the opulent residences of the very rich.

Extremes of wealth

Some observers, notably the young French visitor Alexis de Tocqueville, saw the United States before the Civil War as a place of equality and opportunity. Over a nine-month period in 1831 and 1832, Tocqueville and his companion Gustave de Beaumont traveled four thousand miles and visited all twenty-four states. He later introduced *Democracy in America,* his classic analysis of the American people and nation, with the statement: "No novelty in the United States struck me more vividly during my stay there than the equality of conditions."

Tocqueville saw American equality–the relative fluidity of the United States' social order–as the result of its citizens' geographic mobility. Migration offered people opportunities to start anew regardless of where they came from or who they were. Prior wealth or family or education mattered little; a person could be known by deeds alone. And indeed, ambition for security and success drove Americans on; sometimes they seemed unable to stop. "An American will build a house in which to pass his old age," Tocqueville wrote, "and sell it before the roof is on; he will plant a garden and rent it just as the trees are coming into bearing; he will clear a field and leave others to reap the harvest; he will take up a profession and leave it, settle in one place and soon go off elsewhere with his changing desires."

Talent and hard work, many Americans and Europeans believed, found their just reward in such an atmosphere. It was common advice that anyone could advance by working hard and saving money. A local legend from Newburyport, Massachusetts, sounded this popular theme. Tristram Dalton, a Federalist lawyer, wanted his carriage repaired. Moses Brown, an energetic mechanic, refused to wait for Dalton's servants to tow the carriage to his shop; he sought out the vehicle and fixed it on the spot. After Dalton's death his heirs squandered the family fortune, but Brown's industriousness paid off. Through hard work the humble carriage craftsman became one of Massachusetts' richest men. Eventually he bought the Dalton homestead and lived out his life there. The message was clear: "Men succeed or fail . . . not from accident or external surroundings," as the Newburyport *Herald* put it in 1856, but from "possessing or wanting the elements of success in themselves."

But other observers recorded the rise of a new aristocracy based on wealth and power, and a growing gap between the upper and working classes. Among those who disagreed with the egalitarian view of American life was *New York Sun* publisher Moses Yale Beach, author of twelve editions of *Wealth and Biography of the Wealthy Citizens of New York City.* In 1845 Beach listed a thousand New Yorkers with

Distribution of wealth

assets of $100,000 or more. (John Jacob Astor led with a $25 million fortune.) Combining gossip-column tidbits with often erroneous guesses at people's wealth, Beach's book nevertheless provided some idea of the enormous wealth of New York's upper class. Tocqueville himself, ever sensitive to the conflicting trends in American life, had described the growth of an American aristocracy based on industrial wealth. The rich and well educated "come forward to exploit industries," Tocqueville wrote, and become "more and more like the administrator of a huge empire. . . . What is this if not an aristocracy?"

Throughout the United States, wealth was becoming concentrated in the hands of a relatively small number of people. In Brooklyn in 1810 two-thirds of the families owned only 10 percent of the wealth; by 1841 their share had decreased to almost nothing. In New York City between 1828 and 1845, the wealthiest 4 percent of the city's population increased its holdings from an estimated 63 percent to 80 percent of all individual wealth. That slaves accounted for 15 percent of the population in 1840, and that relatively large-scale immigration began in the 1840s, contributed further to the growing disparity. By 1860 the top 5 percent of families owned more than half the nation's wealth; the top tenth owned over 70 percent.

Inequality of wealth prevailed in rural areas as well. The combined income of just 1,000 southern planters nearly equaled that of the remaining 660,000 white families. In southern cotton counties, 10 percent of the landholders owned 40 percent of the taxable assets; wealth was even more concentrated in the sugar-producing parishes of Louisiana. In the Old Northwest—the frontier of the first four decades of the nineteenth century—the richest 10 percent owned nearly 40 percent of taxable wealth. Farther west there was great disparity between the owners of large tracts of unmortgaged land and the easterners and immigrants who bought parcels of it on credit. During economic downturns large numbers of these small farmers abandoned their land or lost it to foreclosures; the number of hired hands, both men and women, grew.

Another manifestation of the growing inequality and insecurity in American society was the frequency of rioting and sporadic incidents of violence. In the 1830s riots became commonplace as skilled workers

Urban riots

vented their rage against new migrants to the city and other symbols of the new industrial order. In Philadelphia, for instance, native-born workers fought Irish weavers in 1828; whites and blacks rioted on the docks in 1834 and 1835. In 1835 and 1838 antiabolitionist riots broke out. And in North Philadelphia from 1840 to 1842, residents took to the streets continuously until the construction of a railroad through their neighborhood was abandoned. These disturbances climaxed in the great riots of 1844, in which mostly Protestant skilled workers fought Irish Catholics. Nationwide between 1828 and 1833 there were twenty major riots; in the year 1834 alone there were sixteen; in 1835, thirty-seven. By 1840 more than 125 people had died in urban riots, and by 1860 more than a thousand.

A cloud of uncertainty hung over working men and women. Many were afraid that in periods of economic depression they would become part of the urban flotsam and jetsam of able-bodied men and women, white and black, who could not find steady work. They feared the competition of immigrant and slave labor. They feared the insecurities and indignities of poverty, chronic illness, disability, old age, widowhood, and desertion. And they had good reason.

Indeed, poverty and squalor stalked the urban working class. Cities were notorious for the dilapidated districts where newly arrived immigrants, in-

Urban slums

digent blacks, working poor and thieves, beggars, and prostitutes lived. Five Points in New York City's Sixth Ward was probably the worst slum in pre-Civil War America. Dominated by the Old Brewery, which in 1837 had been privately converted to housing for hundreds of adults and children, the neighborhood was equally divided between Irish and blacks. Ill-suited to human habitation and lacking such amenities as running water and sewers, it exemplified all that was worst in American society.

In New York and other large cities lived street rats, children and young men who earned their living off the streets—by boot blacking or petty thievery—and slept on boats, in hay lofts, or in warehouses. Charles Loring Brace, a founder of the Children's Aid Society (1853), described the street rats in his *Dangerous Classes of New York* (1872): "Like the rats, they were too quick and cunning to be often caught in their petty plunderings, so they gnawed away at the foundations of society undisturbed." To Brace and others,

The infamous Five Points section of New York City's Sixth Ward, probably the worst slum in pre-Civil War America. Immodestly dressed prostitutes cruise the streets or gaze from windows, while a pig roots for garbage in their midst. Brown Brothers.

the street rats threatened American society. "They will vote–they will have the same rights as we ourselves," warned the first report of the Children's Aid Society in 1854, "though they have grown up ignorant of moral principle, as any savage or Indian." Moreover, "they will perhaps be embittered at the wealth and luxuries they never share. Then let society beware, when the vicious, reckless multitude of New York boys, swarming now in every foul alley and low street, come to know their power and *use it!*"

A world apart from Five Points and street rats was the upper-class elite society of Philip Hone, one-time mayor of New York. Hone's diary, meticulously kept from 1826 until his death in 1851, records the activities of an American aristocrat. On February 28, 1840, for instance, Hone attended a masked ball at the Fifth Avenue mansion of Henry Breevoort, Jr., and Laura Carson Breevoort. The ball began at the fashionable hour of 10 P.M., and the five hundred ladies and gentlemen who filled the five rooms of the mansion's first floor wore costumes adorned with ermine, gold, and silver. For more than a week, Hone believed, the affair "occupied the minds of the people of all stations, ranks, and employments. . . . " Few balls attained such grandeur, but at one time or another similar parties were held in Boston, Philadelphia, Baltimore, Charleston, and New Orleans.

At a less rarefied level, Hone's social calendar was filled with elegant dinner parties featuring fine cuisine and imported wines. The New York elite who filled the pages of Hone's diary–the 1 percent of the population who owned 50 percent of the city's wealth–lived in large townhouses and mansions, with corps of servants to tend to their elaborate furniture and fine

Immigration to the United States, 1821–1860

COUNTRY OF ORIGIN	1821–1830	1831–1840	1841–1850	1851–1860
Ireland	51,000	207,000	781,000	914,000
German states	6,800	152,000	435,000	952,000
Great Britain (excluding Ireland)	25,000	76,000	267,000	424,000
British North America	2,300	14,000	42,000	59,000
China	2	8	35	41,000

wine cellars. In the summer, country estates, ocean resorts, mineral spas, and grand tours of Europe afforded them relief from the winter and spring social seasons.

By and large the elite were not idle, although their fortunes were often built on inherited wealth. Nearly all received sizable inheritances, and their inbred marriage patterns enhanced their inherited possessions. Yet as a group they devoted at least some of their energies to increasing their fortunes and their power. Philip Hone, like other urban capitalists and southern planters, was actively engaged in transportation and manufacturing ventures. Wealth begat wealth.

New lives in America

Though they did not bring much wealth with them, immigrants contributed in other ways to the changing American scene. In numbers alone they drastically altered the United States. The 5 million immigrants who settled in the states between 1820 and 1860 outnumbered the entire population of the country at the first census in 1790. They came from all over the world—from North America, the Caribbean, Latin America, Asia, and Africa, though Europeans made up the vast majority (see table). The peak period of pre–Civil War immigration was from 1847 through 1857; in that eleven-year period, 3.3 million immigrants entered the United States, 1.3 million from Ireland and 1.1 million from the German states. By 1860, 15 percent of the white population was foreign-born.

This massive migration had been set in motion decades earlier. In Europe around the turn of the nineteenth century, the Napoleonic wars had begun one of the greatest population shifts in history, which was to last more than a century. One part of the movement, increasingly significant as time went on, was emigration of Europeans to the United States. War and revolution, crop failure and famine, industrialization and economic displacement, political and religious persecution dogged weary Europeans. Meanwhile, the United States beckoned. Millions of unplowed acres awaited Europeans, offering them not only economic opportunity but also the chance to

Background of immigration

found new communities. Large construction projects needed strong young laborers, as did the expanding mills and mines. Europeans' awareness of the United States heightened as employers, states, and shipping companies advertised the opportunities to be found across the Atlantic. Often the message was stark: work and prosper in America or starve in Europe. With regularly scheduled sailing ships commuting across the ocean, the cost of transatlantic travel was within easy reach of millions of Europeans.

So they came, enduring the hardships of travel and of settling in a strange land. The journey was difficult. The average crossing took six weeks; in bad weather it could take three months. Disease spread unchecked among people huddled together like cattle in steerage. More than 17,000 immigrants, mostly Irish, died from "ship fever" in 1847. On disembarking, immigrants became fair game for the con artists and swindlers who worked the docks. Runners and agents greeted them and tried to lure them from their chosen destinations. In 1855, in response to the immigrants' plight, New York state's commissioners of emigration established Castle Garden as an immigrant center. There, at the tip of Manhattan Island, the major port of entry, immigrants were sheltered from fraud. Authorized transportation companies maintained offices in the large rotunda and assisted immigrants with their travel plans.

Most immigrants gravitated toward the cities, since only a minority had farming experience or the means to purchase land and equipment. Many stayed in New York. By 1845, 35 percent of the city's 371,000 people were of foreign birth. Ten years later 52 percent of its 623,000 inhabitants were immigrants, 28 percent from Ireland and 16 percent from Germany. In the Sixth Ward, home of Five Points, no fewer than 70 percent of the residents were immigrants. Boston, an important entry point for the Irish, took on a European tone. Throughout the 1850s the city was about 35 percent foreign-born, of whom more than two-thirds were Irish. In the South, too, major cities had large immigrant populations. In 1860 New Orleans was 44 percent foreign-born, Savannah 33 percent, Charleston 26 percent, and the border city of St. Louis, 61 percent. On the West Coast, San Francisco had a foreign-born majority.

Some immigrants, however, did settle in rural areas. In particular, German, Dutch, and Scandinavian farmers gravitated toward the Midwest. Greater percentages of Scandinavians and Netherlanders became farmers than other nationalities; both groups came mostly as religious dissenters and migrated in family units. The Dutch who founded the American Holland in Michigan and Wisconsin, for instance, had seceded from the official Reformed Church of the Netherlands. Under such leaders as Albertus C. Van Raalte, they fled persecution in their native land to establish new and more pious communities—Holland, New Groningen, and Zeeland, Michigan, among them.

Promotion of immigration

Success in America bred further emigration. "I wish, and do often say that we wish you were all in this happy land," wrote shoemaker John West of Germantown, Pennsylvania, to his kin in Corsley, England, in 1831. "A man nor woman need not stay out of employment one hour here," he advised. "No war nor insurrection here. *But all is plenty and peace.*" John Down, a weaver from Frome, England, settled in New York City without his family. Writing to his wife in August, 1830, he described the bountiful meal he had shared with a farmer's family: "They had on the table puddings, pyes, and fruit of all kind that was in season, and preserves, pickles, vegetables, meats, and everything that a person would wish, and the servants [farm hands] set down at the same table with their masters." Though Down missed his family dearly, he wrote, "I do not repent of coming, for you know that there was nothing but poverty before me, and to see you and the dear children want was what I could not bear. *I would rather cross the Atlantic ten times than hear my children cry for victuals once.*" To those skeptics who claimed the United States was filling up, he advised, "There is plenty of room yet, and will be for a thousand years to come." These letters and others were widely circulated in England to advertise the success of pauper immigrants in America.

American institutions, both public and private, actively recruited European immigrants. Western states lured potential settlers in the interest of promoting their economies. In the 1850s, for instance, Wisconsin appointed a commissioner of emigration, who advertised the state's advantages in American and European newspapers. Wisconsin also opened a New York office and hired European agents to compete with other states and with firms like the Illinois Central Railroad for immigrants' attention.

Before the potato blight hit Ireland, tens of thousands of Irish were lured to America by recruiters. They came to swing picks and shovels on American canals and railroads, to dig the foundations of mills and factories. The popular folksong known variously as "Poor Paddy Works on the Erie" and "Working on the Railroad" records their story:

Oh in eighteen hundred and forty-three
I sailed away across the sea,
I sailed away across the sea,
To work upon the railway, the railway.
I'm weary of the railway;
Oh poor Paddy works on the railway!

. . .

Oh in eighteen hundred and forty-five
When Daniel O'Connell he was alive,
When Daniel O'Connell he was alive,
To work upon the railway, the railway . . .

Oh in eighteen hundred and forty-six
I changed my trade to carrying bricks,
I changed my trade to carrying bricks,
From working on the railway, the railway . . .

Oh in eighteen hundred and forty-seven
Poor Paddy was thinking of going to Heaven,
Poor Paddy was thinking of going to Heaven,
After working on the railway, the railway,
He was weary of the railway;
Oh poor Paddy worked on the railway![1]

Immigrant disenchantment

But as other verses reveal, not all the Irish immigrants were successful; tens of thousands of them returned to their homeland. Among them was Michael Gaugin, who had the misfortune of arriving in New York City during the financial panic of 1837. Gaugin, an assistant engineer in the construction of the Ballinasloe Canal in Dublin, had been attracted to the states by the promise that "he should soon become a wealthy man." The Dublin agent for a New York firm had convinced Gaugin to quit his job, which he had held for thirteen years and which included a house and an acre of ground, in order to immigrate to the United States. Within two months of arriving in the United States, Gaugin had become a pauper. In August 1837 he declared he was "now without means for the support of himself and his family, and has no employment, and has already suffered great deprivation since he arrived in this country; and is now soliciting means to enable him to return with his family home to Ireland." Many of those who had come with the Gaugins had already returned home.

Irish immigration

Such experiences did not deter Irish men and women from coming to the United States. Ireland was the most densely populated European country, and among the most impoverished. From 1815 on, small harvests prompted a steady stream of Irish to immigrate to America. Then in 1845 and 1846 potatoes—the basic Irish food—rotted in the fields. From 1845 to 1849, death in the form of starvation, malnutrition, and typhus stalked the island. In all, 1 million died and about 1.5 million fled, two-thirds of them to the United States. People became Ireland's major export.

In the 1840s and 1850s a total of 1.7 million Irish men and women entered the United States. At the peak of Irish immigration, from 1847 to 1854, 1.2 million came. By the end of the century there would be more Irish in the United States than in Ireland. The immigrants clustered in poverty in the cities, where they met growing anti-immigrant, anti-Catholic sentiment. Everywhere "No Irish Need Apply" signs appeared.

Anti-Catholicism

Anti-Catholicism had erupted in the American revolutionary movement when Quebec spurned the Continental Congress's invitation to join the Revolution. Later, though, French support of the colonists and the staunch patriotism of American Catholics had soothed such feelings. As the states freed themselves from established churches and abolished religious tests for office following the Revolution, anti-Catholicism receded. But in the 1830s the trend reversed, and anti-Catholicism appeared wherever the Irish did. Attacks on the papacy and the church circulated widely in the form of libelous texts like *The Awful Disclosures of Maria Monk* (1836), which alleged sexual orgies among priests and nuns. Nowhere was anti-Catholicism more open and nasty than in Boston, though such sentiments were widespread.

[1]Quoted in Carl Sandburg, *The American Songbag* (New York: Harcourt Brace Jovanovich, 1927), p. 357. Reprinted with permission.

Anti-Catholic riots were almost commonplace. In Charlestown, Massachusetts, a mob burned a convent (1834); a Philadelphia crowd attacked priests and nuns and vandalized churches (1844); and in Lawrence, Massachusetts, a mob leveled the Irish neighborhood (1854).

The native-born who embraced anti-Catholicism were motivated largely by anxiety. They feared that a militant Roman church would subvert American society, that unskilled Irish workers would displace American craftsmen, and that the slums inhabited in part by the Irish were undermining the nation's values. Every American problem from immorality and the evils of alcohol to poverty and economic upheaval was blamed on immigrant Irish Catholics. Impoverished workers complained to the Massachusetts legislature that the Irish displaced "the honest and respectable laborers of the State . . . and from their manner of living . . . work for much less per day . . . being satisfied with food to support the animal existence alone." American workers, on the other hand, "not only labor for the body but for the mind, the soul, and the State." Friction increased as Irish-Americans fought back against anti-Irish and anti-Catholic prejudice; in the 1850s they began to vote and to become active in politics.

German immigration

Though potato blight also sent many Germans to the United States in the 1840s, other hardships contributed to the steady stream of German immigrants. Many came from areas where small landholdings made it hard to eke out a living and to pass on land to their sons. Others were craftsmen displaced by the industrial revolution. These refugees were joined by middle-class Germans who had sought to unify the three dozen or so German states in a liberal republic. Frustration with abortive revolutions like one that occurred in 1848 led them to immigrate to the United States. For some, the only other choice was jail.

Unlike the Irish, who tended to congregate in towns and cities, Germans settled everywhere. Many came on German cotton boats, disembarked at New Orleans, and traveled up the Mississippi. In the South they became peddlers, traders, and merchants; in the North they worked as farmers, urban laborers, and businessmen. Also unlike the Irish, they tended to migrate in families. A strong desire to maintain the German language and culture prompted them to colonize areas as a group.

German immigrants transplanted their Old World institutions in the New World, creating New Germanies in rural areas and transforming the tone and culture of established cities like Cincinnati and Milwaukee. *Turnvereine*—German physical-culture clubs—sprouted in villages and cities; by 1853 sixty such societies were hosting exercise groups and German-language lectures.

In adhering to German traditions, German-Americans also met with antiforeign attitudes. More than half the German immigrants were Catholic, and their Sabbath practices were different from the Protestants'. On Sundays German families typically gathered at beer gardens to eat and drink beer, to dance, sing, and listen to band music, and sometimes to play cards. Protestants were outraged by such violations of the Lord's day. In Chicago riots broke out when Protestants enforced the Sunday prohibition laws.

In rural areas Germans were resented for their success as farmers. Familiar with scientific agriculture, German-Americans dominated farming in Ohio, Wisconsin, and Missouri. Their persistence in using the German language and their different religious beliefs also set them apart. Besides the Catholic majority, a significant number of German immigrants were Jewish. And even the Protestants—mostly Lutherans—founded their own churches and often educated their children in German-language schools. Not all Germans, however, were religious. The failure of the revolution of 1848 had sent to the United States a whole generation of liberals and free thinkers, some of whom were socialists, communists, and anarchists. The free thinkers entered politics with a loud voice, embracing abolitionism and the Republican party.

The conflict between the immigrants and the society they joined was paralleled by the inner tensions most immigrants experienced. On the one hand they felt impelled to commit themselves wholeheartedly to their new country, to learn the language and adapt themselves to American ways. On the other hand they were rooted in their own cultural traditions—the comfortable, tried, and tested customs of the country of their birth, the familiar ways and words that came intuitively and required no education.

The German Turnvereine, or physical-culture club, of Cincinnati, 1850. The Cincinnati Historical Society.

Nearly all found themselves altered in significant ways, even as they successfully resisted other changes. In the process American customs and society changed as well.

Free people of color

No black person was safe, wrote the abolitionist and former slave Frederick Douglass following the Philadelphia riot of 1849. "His life–his property–and all that he holds dear are in the hands of a mob, which may come upon him at any moment–at midnight or mid-day, and deprive him of his all." Between 1832 and 1849 five major antiblack riots occurred in Philadelphia. Mobs stormed black dwellings and churches, set them to the torch, and killed the people inside. For free people of color, mobs could take many forms. They could come in the shape of slave hunters, seeking fugitive slaves but as likely to kidnap a free black as a slave. Or they could take the form of civil authority, as in Cincinnati in 1829, when city officials, frightened by the growing black population, drove one-to-two thousand blacks from the city by enforcing a law requiring cash bonds for good behavior. In whatever form, free blacks faced insecurity daily.

Under federal law, blacks held an uncertain position. The Bill of Rights seemed to apply to free blacks; the Fifth Amendment specified that "no person shall . . . be deprived of life, liberty, or property, without due process of law." Nevertheless, early federal legislation discriminated against free people of color. In 1790 naturalization was limited to white aliens; in 1792 the militia was limited to white male citizens; and in 1810 blacks were barred from carrying the mails. Moreover, Congress approved the admission to the Union of states whose constitutions restricted the rights of blacks. Following the admission of Missouri in 1821, every new state admitted until the Civil War banned blacks from voting. And when the Oregon and New Mexico territories were organized, public land grants were limited to whites.

Dred Scott v. *Sanford* (1857) made the de facto position of free blacks official. Scott, a Missouri slave, had accompanied his master to the free state of Illinois and the free territory of Wisconsin. Once back in Missouri, he sued for his freedom on the grounds that his presence in areas where there was no slavery had made him free. After a ten-year battle, the Supreme Court ruled against Scott. Speaking for the majority, Chief Justice Roger Taney ruled that blacks "were not intended to be included, under the word 'citizens' in the Constitution, and can therefore claim none of the rights and privileges which that instrument provides for and secures to citizens of the United States." As George Fitzhugh, a defender of slavery, exclaimed in 1854, "A free Negro! Why, the very term seems an absurdity."

Dred Scott *v.* Sanford

The Dred Scott decision affirmed what had already become practice: each state decided the legal condition of blacks within its borders. In the North blacks faced legal restrictions nearly everywhere; Massachusetts was the major exception. Many states barred entry to free blacks or required bonds of $500 to $1,000 to guarantee their good behavior, as in Ohio (1804), Illinois (1819), Michigan (1827), Indiana (1831), Iowa (1839), and Oregon (1849). Although seldom enforced, these laws clearly indicated the less-than-free status of blacks. Only in Massachusetts, New Hampshire, Vermont, and Maine could blacks vote on an equal basis with whites throughout the pre–Civil War period. Blacks gained the right to vote in Rhode Island in 1842, but they had lost it earlier in Pennsylvania and Connecticut. No state but Massachusetts permitted blacks to serve on juries; four midwestern states and California did not allow blacks to testify against whites. In Oregon blacks could not own real estate, make contracts, or sue in court.

Legal status was important, but practice and custom were crucial. Although Ohio repealed its law barring black testimony against whites in 1849, the exclusion persisted as custom in southern Ohio counties. Throughout the North free people of color were either excluded from or segregated in public places. Abolitionist Frederick Douglass was repeatedly turned away from public facilities during a speaking tour of the North in 1844. A doorkeeper refused him admission to a circus in Boston, saying "We don't allow niggers in here." He met the same reply when he tried to attend a revival meeting in New Bedford. At a restaurant in Boston and on an omnibus in Weymouth, Massachusetts, he heard the familiar words. Hotels and restaurants were closed to blacks, as were most theaters and churches. But probably no practice inflicted greater injury than the general discrimination in hiring. Factory and skilled work were virtually closed to northern blacks.

Exclusion and segregation of blacks

Free people of color faced still severer legal and social barriers in the southern slave states, where their presence was often viewed as an incentive to insurrection. Indeed, southern states responded to fear of mass rebellion by tightening the restrictions on free blacks and forcing them to leave small towns and interior counties. After a successful slave rebellion in Haiti in the 1790s, southern states barred the entry of free blacks for two decades. And in 1806 Virginia required newly freed blacks to leave the state. Following Nat Turner's slave uprising in Southampton County in 1831, the position of free blacks weakened further. Within five years nearly all the southern states prohibited the freeing of any slaves without legislative or court approval, and by the 1850s Texas, Mississippi, and Georgia had banned manumission altogether.

To restrict free blacks and encourage them to migrate north, southern states adopted elaborate "black codes." Blacks were required to have licenses for certain occupations and were barred from others (for example, Virginia and Georgia banned black river captains and pilots). Some states forbade blacks to assemble without a license; some prohibited blacks from being taught to read and write. All the slave states except Delaware barred blacks from testifying against whites. In the late 1830s, when these black codes were enforced with vigor for the first time, free blacks increasingly moved northward, even though northern states discouraged the migration.

Black codes

A free black man being expelled from a whites-only railway car in Philadelphia. Prior to the Civil War blacks were commonly segregated or excluded from public places in the North. Library of Congress.

In spite of these obstacles, the free black population rose dramatically in the first part of the nineteenth century, from 108,000 in 1800 to almost 500,000 in 1860 (see table, page 294). Nearly half lived in the North, occasionally in rural settlements like Hammond County, Indiana, but more often in cities like Philadelphia, New York, or Cincinnati. Baltimore had the largest free black community; sizable free black populations also existed in New Orleans, Charleston, and Mobile (see Chapter 10).

The ranks of free blacks were constantly increased by ex-slaves. Some, like Frederick Douglass and Harriet Tubman, were fugitives. Douglass had hired himself out as a ship caulker in Baltimore, paying $3 monthly to his owner. Living among free workers made him yearn to escape slavery. By masquerading as a free black with the help of borrowed seaman's papers, he bluffed his way to Philadelphia and freedom. Tubman, a slave on the eastern shore of Maryland, escaped

Fugitive slaves

Black Population of the United States, 1800–1860

	TOTAL BLACK POPULATION	PERCENTAGE OF TOTAL U.S. POPULATION	FREE PEOPLE OF COLOR	FREE BLACKS AS A PERCENTAGE OF BLACK POPULATION
1800	1,002,000	18.9	108,000	10.8
1810	1,378,000	19.0	186,000	13.5
1820	1,772,000	18.4	234,000	13.2
1830	2,329,000	18.1	320,000	13.7
1840	2,874,000	16.8	386,000	13.4
1850	3,639,000	15.7	435,000	11.9
1860	4,442,000	14.1	488,000	11.0

to Philadelphia in 1849 when her master's death led to rumors that she would be sold out of the state. Within the next two years she returned twice to free her two children, her sister, her mother, and her brother and his family. Other slaves were voluntarily freed by their owners. Some, like a Virginia planter named Sanders who settled his slaves as freedmen in Michigan, sought to cleanse their souls by freeing their slaves in their wills. Others freed elderly slaves after a lifetime of service rather than support them in old age. The parents of the slave Isabella (Sojourner Truth) were freed when whites who inherited the family would not support the father, who was too old to work.

Sojourner Truth's experience reveals that the gradual emancipation laws of northern states had little effect as long as slavery existed elsewhere. In 1817 New York state adopted an emancipation plan whereby all slaves over forty years old were freed, and young slaves would serve ten more years. But owners tried to thwart the law by selling their slaves into other states. In 1826, fearing sale to the South, Sojourner Truth found refuge with a nearby abolitionist couple. With their help she sued successfully for the freedom of her son Peter, who had been sold unlawfully to an Alabaman. One can only guess how many blacks did not receive such help and were permanently deprived of their freedom.

Founding of black institutions

In response to their oppression, free blacks founded strong, independent self-help societies to meet their unique needs and fight their less-than-equal status. In every black community there appeared black churches, fraternal and benevolent associations, literary societies, and schools. The black Masons (affiliated with London because American Masons refused to accept blacks) grew from a single Boston lodge in 1784 to more than fifty lodges in seventeen states by 1860. Many black leaders believed that these mutual aid societies would encourage thrift,

Sojourner Truth (about 1797–1883), the spellbinding preacher, abolitionist, and crusader for women's rights. Sophia Smith Collection, Smith College.

industry, and morality, thus equipping their members to improve their lot. But no amount of effort could counteract white prejudice. Blacks remained second-class in status.

The black convention movement, which originated in the 1830s, also promoted education and industriousness. But under the leadership of the small black middle class, which included the Philadelphia sail manufacturer James Forten and the orator Reverend Henry Highland Garnet, the convention movement quickly turned into a protest movement. Increasingly the conventions served as a forum to attack slavery and agitate for equal rights (see Chapter 12). The struggle was also joined by militant new black publications. *Freedom's Journal,* the first black weekly, appeared in March 1827; in 1837 the *Weekly Advocate* began publication in New York City. Both papers circulated throughout the North, spreading black thought and activism.

Although abolitionism and civil rights remained at the top of the blacks' agenda, the mood of free blacks began to shift in the late 1840s and 1850s. Many were frustrated by the failure of the abolitionist movement and by the passage of the Fugitive Slave Law of 1850 (see Chapter 13). Some black leaders became more militant, and a few joined John Brown in his plans for rebellion. But many more were swept up in the tide of black nationalism, which stressed racial solidarity and unity, self-help, and a growing interest in Africa. Before this time, efforts to send Afro-Americans "back to Africa" had originated with whites seeking to solve racial problems by ridding the United States of blacks. But in the 1850s blacks held emigrationist conventions of their own under the leadership of Henry Bibb and Martin Delany. In 1859 Delany led a Niger Valley exploration party as the emissary of a black convention. He signed a treaty with Yoruba rulers allowing him to settle American blacks in that African kingdom (the plan was never carried out). With the coming of the Civil War and emancipation, however, the status of free blacks would move back onto the national political agenda, and Afro-Americans would focus with renewed intensity on their position at home.

Black nationalism

The Trail of Tears

Indians faced problems similar to blacks'. They too faced massive hostility. Midwesterners and southerners sought their land, and soldiers marched them off it. Missionaries tried to Christianize them. And like blacks, their troubles involved the law, for Indians too were directly dependent on government policy—or the lack of it.

Under the Constitution, Indians had a more clearly defined status than blacks. For all practical purposes they were not part of the American nation. They were not taxed, not counted in apportioning state representation, not citizens. Congress was given the power "to regulate Commerce with foreign Nations, and among the several States, and with the Indian Tribes." In exercising this mandate and its treaty-making and war powers, the federal government had come to treat Indian tribes as separate nations.

Legal status of Indians

The basis of Indian-white relations was the treaty. For its own convenience, the United States government demanded that one person or group have the power to obligate a tribe to a treaty's provisions. But like European nations in colonial times, government officials had difficulty applying this principle. Many tribes' traditions simply did not permit it. The Cherokees, for instance, were a common lingual group rather than a confederation of independent villages. No majority or unanimous leadership could sell the birthrights of all tribal members. Some frustrated United States officials simply designated a tribal leader. During the negotiations leading to the Treaty of Butte des Morts in 1827, for example, Governor Lewis Cass of the Michigan Territory named one Indian leader principal chief of the Menomonies. (The Menomonies, Cass confessed, "appear to us like a flock of geese without a leader.") Chiefs who worked closely with the government were well rewarded with gifts and honors.

Other circumstances made the treaty process less than the bargaining of two equal nations. Treaties were often made between victors and vanquished. In a context of coercion, old treaties often gave way to new ones in which the Indians ceded their traditional holdings in return for different lands in the West. Beginning with President Jefferson, the government withheld payments due to tribes for previous land cessions to pressure them to sign new treaties.

The Shawnee Chief Tecumseh led by far the most significant campaign of resistance to these federal tactics. Convinced that only a federation of nations and tribes could stop the advance of white society, Tecumseh sought in the first decade of the century to unify northern and southern Indians. His brother Laulewasika (the Prophet), like Tecumseh a powerful orator, spread the word of unity as well. Laulewasika, who had undergone a mystical conversion in overcoming alcoholism, contrasted the dignity and salvation of Indian ways with the corrupting influence of white culture.

Tecumseh

Under Tecumseh, the Indians refused to cede more land to the whites. In repudiating an Indian land sale, Tecumseh told Indiana's Governor William Henry Harrison at Vincennes in 1810 that "the only way to check and stop this evil is, for all the red men to unite in claiming a common and equal right in the land, as it was at first, and should be yet; for it never was divided, but belongs to all, for the use of each. . . . No part has a right to sell, even to each other, much less to strangers." Tecumseh then warned that the Indians would resist white occupation of the 2.5 million acres on the Wabash they had ceded to the United States in the Treaty of Fort Wayne the year before.

A year later, using a Potawatomi raid on an Illinois settlement as an excuse, Harrison attacked Prophet's Town, Tecumseh's headquarters on Tippecanoe Creek. Losses on both sides were heavy. Indian warriors throughout the Midwest came to Tecumseh's side; Harrison appealed for help to President Madison. When the War of 1812 started, Tecumseh joined the British in return for a promise of an Indian country in the Great Lakes region. But he was killed in the Battle of the Thames in October 1813, and with him died the dream of Indian unity.

By 1820 Indians in Ohio, southern Indiana and Illinois, southwestern Michigan, most of Missouri, central Alabama, and southern Mississippi had been forced to cede their lands. They had given up nearly 200 million acres for pennies an acre. But white settlers' appetites were insatiable; the demand for tribal lands east of the Great Plains continued until nearly all the Indians had been forced out. For this land Indians were paid rations, supplies, and annuities. Because forced migration had destroyed their economic base, the tribes became dependent on these government payments—a dependence that only made them more susceptible to government pressure.

In the 1820s the Cherokees, Creeks, Choctaws, Chickasaws, and Seminoles attempted to resist the whites' tactics and defend their ancestral lands. In 1825 President Monroe proposed that these tribes, the last of the large Indian nations east of the Mississippi, sign new treaties and resettle between the Missouri and Red rivers. The conflict had focused on northwestern Georgia, where lay the Cherokee lands and a small portion of the Creek lands. Georgia had accused the federal government of not fulfilling its 1802 promise to remove the Indians in return for the state's renunciation of its claim to western lands. Although in 1826 the Creeks, under federal pressure, ceded all but a small strip of their Georgia lands, Governor George M. Troup was not satisfied. Troup sent surveyors to the one remaining strip; President John Quincy Adams then threatened to send the army to protect the Indians' claims, and Troup countered with his own threats. Only the eventual removal of the Georgia Creeks to the West in 1826 prevented a clash between the state and the federal government.

In 1827 the Cherokees attempted to resist forced removal by adopting a written constitution and organizing themselves officially as an independent nation. But in 1828 the Georgia legislature annulled the constitution, extended state sovereignty over the Cherokees, and ordered the seizure of tribal lands. Under the new law a Cherokee named Corn Tassel was tried and convicted of murder in a state court. Though the Supreme Court issued a writ of error on appeal, Georgia refused to recognize it and executed Corn Tassel. He was only the first of thousands of victims in the conflict between Georgia and the Cherokees.

In 1829 the Cherokees, with the support of sympathetic whites but without the support of the new president, Andrew Jackson, turned to the federal courts to defend their treaty with the United States and prevent Georgia's seizure of their land. In *Cherokee Nation* v. *Georgia* (1831), Chief Justice John Marshall ruled that under the federal Constitution an Indian tribe was neither a foreign nation nor a state, and therefore had no standing in federal courts. Marshall referred to the Indians as "domestic dependent nations . . . their relation to the United States resembles that of a ward to his guardian." Nonetheless, said Marshall, the Indians had an unquestioned right to their lands; they could lose title only by voluntarily giving it up. A year later, in *Worcester* v. *Georgia,* Marshall defined the Cherokees' position more clearly. The Indian nation was, he declared, a distinct political community in which "the laws of Georgia can have no force," and into which Georgians could not enter without permission or treaty privilege.

Cherokee Nation *v.* Georgia

"John Marshall has made his decision," President Jackson is reported to have said; "now let him enforce it." Jackson, who as a general had led the expedition against the Seminoles in Spanish Florida in 1818, had little sympathy for the Indians. Concerned with opening up new lands for settlement, he was determined to remove the Cherokees at all costs. (His failure to carry out the Supreme Court decision served his states' rights position as well—see Chapter 12). In the Removal Act of 1830 Congress provided Jackson the funds he needed to negotiate new treaties and resettle the resistant tribes west of the Mississippi. The Choctaw were the first to go; in the winter of 1831 and 1832, they made the forced journey from Mississippi

ᏣᎳᎩ ᏧᎴᏫᏍᏓᏁᎯ.
CHEROKEE PHŒNIX.

VOL. I. NEW ECHOTA, WEDNESDAY JUNE 4, 1828. NO. 15.

EDITED BY ELIAS BOUDINOTT
PRINTED WEEKLY BY
ISAACH. HARRIS,
FOR THE CHEROKEE NATION.

At $2 50 if paid in advance, $3 in six months, or $3 50 if paid at the end of the year.

To subscribers who can read only the Cherokee language the price will be $2,00 in advance, or $2,50 to be paid within the year.

Every subscription will be considered as continued unless subscribers give notice to the contrary before the commencement of a new year.

of said river opposite to Fort Strother, on said river; all north of said line is the Cherokee lands, all south of said line is the Creek lands.

ARTICLE 2. WE THE COMMISSIONERS, do further agree that all the Creeks that are north of the said line above mentioned shall become subjects to the Cherokee nation.

ARTICLE 3. All Cherokees that are south of the said line shall become subjects of the Creek nation.

William Hambly, (Seal)
his
Big ⋊ Warrior, (Seal)
mark.
WITNESSES.
Major Ridge,
Dan'l. Griffin.
A. M'COY, Clerk N. Com.
JOS. VANN, Cl'k. to the Commissioners.

Be it remembered, This day, that I have approved of the treaty of boundary, concluded on by the Cherokees,

mitting murder on the subjects of the other, is approved and adopted; but respecting thefts, it is hereby agreed that the following rule be substituted, and adopted; viz: Should the subjects of either nation go over the line and commit theft, and he, she or they be bpprehended, they shall be tried and dealt with as the laws of that nation direct, but should the person or persons so offending, make their escape and return to his, her or their nation, then, the person or persons so aggrieved, shall make application to the proper authorities of that nation for redress, and justice shall be rendered as far as practicable, agreeably to proof and law, but in no case shall either nation be accountable.

The 10th article is approved and adopted, and all claims for thefts considered closed by the treaty as stipulated in that article.

The 11th article is approved and adopted, and it is agreed further, the contracting nations will extend their respective laws with equal justice towards the citizens of the other in regard to collecting debts due by the individuals of their nation to those of the other.

The 12th article is fully approved and confirmed. We do hereby further agree to allow those individuals who have fell within the limits of the other, twelve months from the date hereof, to determine whether they will remove into their respective nations, or continue and become subjects

CONSTITUTION

OF THE

CHEROKEE NATION,

MADE AND ESTABLISHED

AT A

GENERAL CONVENTION OF DELEGATES,

DULY AUTHORISED FOR THAT PURPOSE,

AT

NEW ECHOTA,

JULY 26, 1827.

PRINTED FOR THE CHEROKEE NATION,
AT THE OFFICE OF THE STATESMAN AND PATRIOT,
GEORGIA.

The *Cherokee Phoenix,* a bilingual newspaper published by the Cherokee nation (top) and the title page of the Cherokee constitution (bottom). This issue of the newspaper details the provisions of a recent treaty with the Creeks. Rare Book Division, The New York Public Library, Astor, Lenox and Tilden Foundations.

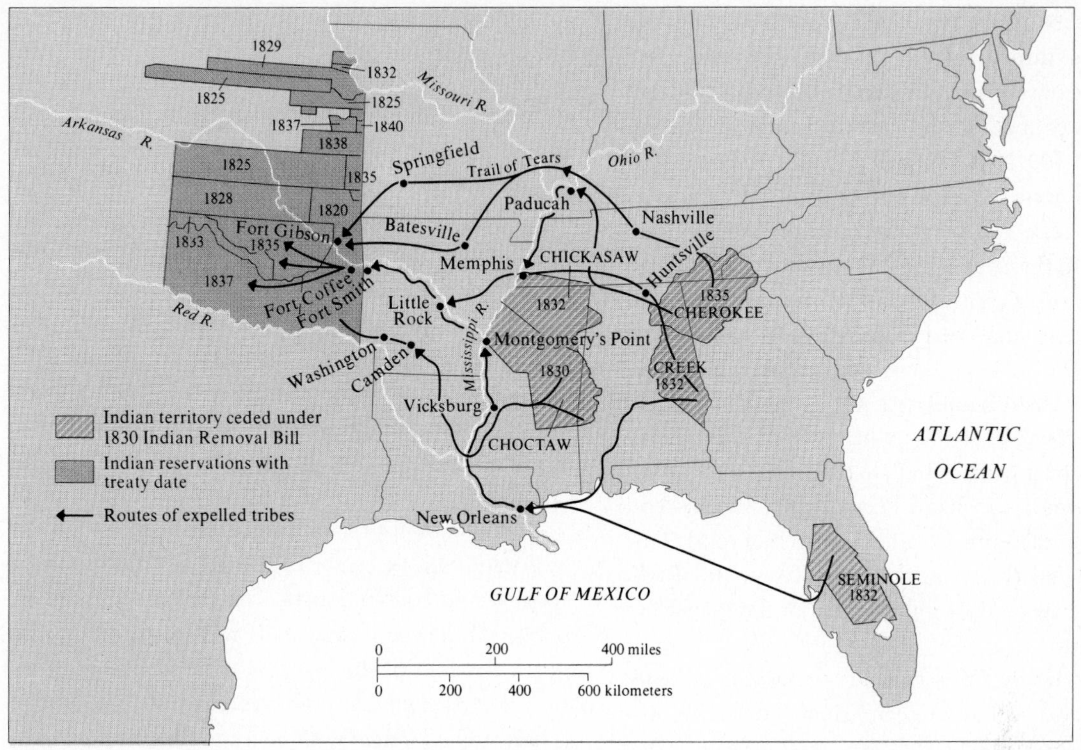

Removal of the Indians from the South, 1820–1840. Source: Redrawn by permission of Macmillan Publishing Company, Inc. From *American History Atlas* by Martin Gilbert, cartography by Peter Kingsland. Copyright © 1968 by Martin Gilbert.

Trail of Tears

and Alabama to the West (see map). Alexis de Tocqueville was visiting Memphis when they arrived there, "the wounded, the sick, newborn babies, and the old men on the point of death. . . . I saw them embark to cross the great river," he wrote, "and the sight will never fade from my memory. Neither sob nor complaint rose from that silent assembly. Their afflictions were of long standing, and they felt them to be irremediable."

Soon other tribes were forced west. The Creeks in Alabama delayed removal until 1836, when the army pushed them westward. A year later the Chickasaws followed. The Cherokees, having fought to stay through the courts, found themselves divided. Some recognized the hopelessness of further resistance and accepted removal as the only chance to preserve their civilization. The leaders of this minority signed a treaty in 1835 in which they agreed to exchange their southern home for western land. But when the time for evacuation came in 1838, most Cherokees refused to move. President Martin Van Buren then sent federal troops to round up the Indians. About twenty thousand Cherokees were evicted, held in detention camps, and marched to Oklahoma under military escort. Nearly one-quarter died of disease and exhaustion on the famous Trail of Tears. When it was all over, the Indians had traded about 100 million acres of land east of the Mississippi for 32 million acres west of the river plus $68 million. Only a few scattered remnants of the tribes, among them the Seminoles, remained in the East and South.

A small band of Seminoles successfully resisted removal and remained in Florida. In the 1832 Treaty of Payne's Landing, tribal chiefs agreed to relocate to the

Seminole War

West within three years. Under Osceola, however, a minority refused to vacate their homes, and from 1835 on they waged a fierce guerrilla war against the United States. The army in turn attempted, ruthlessly but unsuccessfully, to exterminate the Seminoles. In 1842 the United States finally abandoned the Seminole War; it had cost 1,500 soldiers' lives and $20 million. Osceola's followers remained in Florida.

Later that decade, when the United States frontier expanded to the Southwest, Indians again fought valiantly to protect their homelands. The annexation of Texas in 1846 and the United States victory in the Mexican War in 1848 led to new Indian-white confrontations (see Chapter 12). Other conflicts developed over the food supply: when white hunters decimated the great herds of buffalo that were the primary source of meat for many Plains tribes, Indians encroached on each other's lands in search of food. The Sioux violated the territory of the Crows and Pawnees, the Crows and Assiniboins that of the Blackfeet, and so forth.

To open up the West to white settlement and end the intertribal warfare, Commissioner of Indian Affairs William Medill in 1848 proposed gathering the western Indians into two great reservations, one northern and one southern. Between the two, in the Kansas and Platte valleys, would be a wide corridor for white settlers to cross on their way westward. In 1853, however, the government took back most of the northern lands in a new round of treaties, and Kansas and Nebraska were opened to white settlement.

Among whites, the forced Indian removals were motivated by a complex set of attitudes. Most whites merely wanted Indian lands; they had little or no respect for the rights or culture of the Indians. Others were aware of the injustice, but believed the Indians must inevitably give way to white settlement. Some, like John Quincy Adams, believed the only way to preserve Indian civilization was to remove the tribes and establish a buffer zone between Indians and whites. Others, including Thomas Jefferson, doubted that white civilization and Indian "savagery" could coexist. Supported by missionaries and educators, they hoped to "civilize" the Indians and assimilate them slowly into American culture. But however the motivation of whites might have varied, the result was the same: the destruction of an American people and their culture.

Woman's sphere

American democracy, Alexis de Tocqueville believed, was built on the foundation of family stability. "In Europe almost all the disorders of society are born around the domestic hearth," he wrote in *Democracy in America,* "and not far from the nuptial bed." By contrast, "when the American returns from the turmoil of politics to the bosom of the family, he immediately finds a perfect picture of order and peace." This regularity of family life was reflected in public affairs, Tocqueville wrote. Religion, too, influenced the family, "and by regulating domestic life it helps to regulate the state."

Whether or not the differences between the United States and Europe can be explained in terms of family stability and contentedness, Tocqueville's distinction between public and private life was an important one in the America of the first half of the nineteenth century. For the middle class and the elite, the public sphere was associated with men and the private, or domestic, sphere with women. The public sphere was the world of business and politics, of conflict and selfishness—a jungle where men fought for economic survival. The private sphere, the home, was a refuge from that jungle. Governed by women, it was the fount of spirituality and purity, a religious and moral institution where selflessness and cooperation ruled.

Changing role of women

The development of separate spheres for men and women reflected, in part, the changing economic and social roles of the family. Once a cradle of production and economic activity, the family was now losing that function to shops and factories outside the home. It became instead a service unit for the domestic needs of its members. Education, religion, morality, domestic arts, and culture were its new concerns.

The development of public and private spheres also reflected the growing class distinctions in American society. Those who could concentrate on developing the home as a spiritual and cultural sanctuary were elite and middle-class women who led lives of material ease and comfort. They employed other women's daughters to free themselves from menial tasks. Yet, paradoxically, the new ideal of womanhood gave

A watercolor and ink portrait of a scrubwoman, made in 1807. Domestic work was still the most common job held by women working outside the home in the early nineteenth century. The New-York Historical Society.

middle-class and elite women less status rather than more; it represented an extremely narrow definition of a woman's proper sphere. Though they were dominant within the home, women were expected to be passive and submissive to men in public. Many women fought and shed this role as active leaders in reform movements (see Chapter 12), but the overall effect was a constriction of women's options and independence.

The range of paying jobs a woman could hold was narrow; most of the crafts and professions were closed to females. Moreover, work outside the home was viewed with disapproval. After all, it conflicted with the ideal of female domesticity. But whether or not society approved of work outside the home, unmarried daughters of laborers and immigrants, mothers without husbands, widows, black women both slave and free, and rural pioneers had no choice: economic necessity required them to work. Gradually work outside the home became associated with the lower classes, and the work women performed—mill work, domestic service—fell in esteem. Lowell and other New England mill towns experienced this transformation. Originally the mills had attracted genteel farm daughters who worked a relatively short time before returning home to be married. But by the 1840s

Pen-and-watercolor drawing of a middle-class family in 1832. The picture suggests the growing emphasis on the home as a spiritual refuge rather than a center of production. Museum of Fine Arts, Boston.

Irish immigrant women had replaced most of the native-born workers, and wage levels and working conditions had deteriorated. Employment in the mills had been devalued and was shunned by respectable women.

Only two occupations were open to genteel women: nursing and teaching. Both were consistent with the new notion of womanhood, since they represented professional extensions of woman's domestic sphere. And since both nursing and teaching required education and training, they were closed to the daughters of workers and immigrants.

Decline in the birth rate

While woman's sphere was narrowing, family size was shrinking. In 1800 an American woman bore, on the average, six children; in 1860 she would bear five, and by 1900 four. This decline occurred even while many immigrants with large-family traditions were settling in the United States; thus the birth rate for native-born women declined more sharply than the average. Although rural families were larger than urban ones, birth rates in both areas declined to the same degree.

A number of factors lowered the birth rate. For many people, family life became less important as migration loosened family bonds. In cities, where there was less social pressure to marry than in rural areas, more people remained single. And increasingly, small families were viewed as desirable. Fewer children, it was believed, would enjoy greater opportunities. Parents could pay more attention to them, and would be better able to educate them and help them financially. Finally, contemporary marriage manuals stressed the harmful effects of too many births on a woman's health; too many children weakened women physically and overworked them as mothers.

All this evidence suggests that the decline in family size was the result of deliberate decisions. In rural areas with little cheap land, families were smaller than in other agricultural districts. It appears that parents who foresaw difficulty setting up their children as independent farmers chose to have fewer children. Similarly, in urban areas children were more and more an economic burden than an asset. As the family lost its role as a producer of goods, the length of time during which children were only consumers grew, as did the economic costs to parents.

How did men and women limit their families in the early nineteenth century? Many married later, thus shortening the period of childbearing. More important, however, was the widespread use of birth control. The first American book on birth control, *Moral Physiology; or, A Brief and Plain Treatise on the Population Question* (1831), as well as the popular marriage guide by the physician Charles Knowlton, *Fruits of Philosophy; or, the Private Companion of Young Married People* (1832), provide us with a glimpse of contemporary birth control methods. Probably the most widespread practice was *coitus interruptus,* or withdrawal of the male before completion of the sexual act. But mechanical devices were beginning to compete with this ancient folk practice. Although animal-skin condoms imported from France were too expensive for popular use, cheap rubber condoms were widely adopted when they became available in the 1850s. Dr. Knowlton advocated the dubious practice of douching with a chemical solution immediately after intercourse. And some couples used the rhythm method–attempting to confine intercourse to a woman's infertile periods. Knowledge of the "safe period" was so uncertain even among physicians, however, that the directions for avoiding conception were similar to today's advice to couples who want children! Another method was abstinence, or less frequent sexual intercourse. Frequently women abstained and men visited prostitutes.

Birth control

If all else failed, abortion was widely available, especially after 1830. Ineffective folk remedies for self-induced abortion had been around for centuries, but in the 1830s surgical abortions became common. Abortionists advertised their services in large cities, and middle-class and elite women boldly asked their doctors to perform abortions. One sign of the upswing in abortions was the increase in legislation against it. Between 1821 and 1841, ten states and one territory prohibited abortions; by 1860, twenty states had outlawed it. Only three of those twenty punished the mother, however, and the laws were rarely enforced.

Significantly, the birth control methods women themselves controlled–douching, the rhythm method, abstinence, and abortion–were the ones that were increasing in popularity. For the new emphasis on women's domesticity encouraged women's autonomy in the home and gave them greater control over their own bodies. According to the cult of true womanhood, the refinement and purity of women ruled the family, including the nuptial bed; as one woman put it, "woman's duty was to subdue male passions, not to kindle them."

In turn, smaller families and fewer births changed the position and living conditions of women. At one time birth and infant care had occupied the entire span of women's adult lives, and few mothers had lived to see their youngest child reach maturity. But after the 1830s many women had time for other activities. Smaller families also allowed women to devote more time to their older children, and slowly childhood came to be perceived as a distinct part of the life span. The beginnings of public education in the 1830s (see Chapter 12) and the policy of grouping school children by age tended to reinforce this trend.

Marriage patterns changed as well. Only among elite families did the pattern of marrying kin persist. And among all but the highest classes, young people married spouses of their own choosing, not their parents'. In the new social climate marriages were made between individuals, not families, and romantic love was the yardstick by which proposals were measured.

Change in marriage patterns

The experiences of Mollie Dorsey Sandford, a young schoolteacher who came of age in Indiana and Nebraska in the 1850s and kept a careful diary of her adventures, illustrated the new marriage patterns. To Mollie marriage was an uncertainty. "If I live to be an *old maid,*" Mollie wrote, "I will be one of the good kind that is a friend to everybody and that everyone loves. If I *do* ever marry," she promised herself, "it will be someone I love *very, very, very,* much." When finally, after courting, Byron Sandford proposed to marry her, she wrote in her diary that night: "He loves me tenderly, truly, and . . . I know now that I can place my hand in his and go with him this life, be path smooth or stormy." Mollie's aunt Eliza had tried to encourage her "to captivate Mr. Rucker, as he is rich . . . [and] *owns a farm.*" Byron, on the other hand, owned only a few lots. Eliza herself, however, "likes money, but *she* married for love" when she wed a poor itinerant minister.

Not all women accepted or could fulfill the domestic ideal. Mollie Dorsey Sandford was prepared if necessary for the life of a single schoolteacher, boarding out without a home of her own. And mill girls, especially by the 1840s when they organized and resisted wage reductions, were forging new roles for women in the public sphere. So too were the women who assembled at Seneca Falls, New York, in 1848. Modeling their protest on the Declaration of Independence, they called for political, social, and economic equality for women (see Chapter 12).

The United States in 1860 was a far more diverse and divided society than it had been in 1800. Industrialization, urbanization, and immigration had altered the ways people lived and worked. Communities had become larger and more varied, and differences in wealth, ethnicity, religion, race, and sex separated individuals and groups.

As American society changed during these years, conflict became commonplace. Riots, crime, and anti-Catholicism were just a few of the many manifestations of social division in America. But conflict took other forms as well. In reform movements and religious revivals, Americans attempted to deal constructively with social change. In future years the 1820s, 1830s, and 1840s would be known as an age of reform.

Suggestions for further reading

Communities

Stuart M. Blumin, *The Urban Threshold: Growth and Change in a Nineteenth-Century American Community* (1976); Robert Doherty, *Society and Power: Five New England Towns, 1800–1860* (1977); Don H. Doyle, *The Social Order of a Frontier Community: Jacksonville, Illinois, 1825–1870* (1978); Peter R. Knights, *The Plain People of Boston, 1830–1860* (1971); Roger W. Lotchin, *San Francisco, 1846–1856: From Hamlet to City* (1974); Raymond A. Mohl, *Poverty in New York, 1783–1825* (1971); Edward Pessen, *Riches, Class and Power Before the Civil War* (1973); Stephan Thernstrom, *Poverty and Progress: Social Mobility in a Nineteenth Century City* (1964); Alexis de Tocqueville, *Democracy in America,* 2 vols. (1835–1840); Richard C. Wade, *The Urban Frontier: 1790–1830* (1957); Anthony F. C. Wallace, *Rockdale: The Growth of an American Village in the Early Industrial Revolution* (1978).

Immigrants

Rowland Berthoff, *British Immigrants in Industrial America* (1953); Theodore C. Blegen, *Norwegian Migration to America, 1825–1860* (1931); Kathleen Neils Conzen, *Immigrant Milwaukee: 1836–1860* (1976); Jay P. Dolan, *The Immigrant Church: New York's Irish and German Catholics, 1815–1865* (1975); Charlotte Erickson, *Invisible Immigrants* (1972); Robert Ernst, *Immigrant Life in New York City, 1825–1863* (1949); Oscar Handlin, *Boston's Immigrants: A Study in Acculturation,* rev. ed. (1959); Marcus L. Hansen, *The Atlantic Migration, 1607–1860* (1940); Stuart Creighton Miller, *The Unwelcome Immigrant: The American Image of the Chinese 1785–1882* (1969); Harold Runblom and Hans Norman, *From Sweden to America* (1976); Philip Taylor, *The Distant Magnet: European Emigration to the United States of America* (1971); Carl Wittke, *The Irish in America* (1956).

Free people of color

Ira Berlin, *Slaves Without Masters: The Free Negro in the Antebellum South* (1974); Letitia Woods Brown, *Free Negroes in the District of Columbia, 1790–1846* (1972); James Horton and Lois Horton, *Black Bostonians: Family Life and Community Struggle in the Antebellum North* (1979); Luther Porter Jackson, *Free Negro Labor and Property Holding in Virginia, 1830–1860* (1942); David M. Katzman, *Before the Ghetto: Black Detroit in the Nineteenth Century* (1973); Rudolph M. Lapp, *Blacks in Gold Rush California* (1977); Leon Litwack, *North of Slavery: The Negro in the Free States, 1790–1860* (1961); Floyd J. Miller, *The Search for a Black Nationality: Black Colonization and Emigration 1787–1863* (1975); Emma Lou Thornbrough, *The Negro in Indiana* (1957); Arthur Zilversmit, *The First Emancipation: The Abolition of Slavery in the North* (1967).

Native Americans

Robert F. Berkhofer, Jr., *The White Man's Indian* (1978); Arthur De Rosier, *Removal of the Choctaw Indians* (1970); Grant Foreman, *Indian Removal: The Emigration of the Five Civilized Tribes of Indians,* rev. ed. (1953); Charles Hudson, *The Southeastern Indians* (1976); Alvin M. Josephy, Jr., *The Patriot Chiefs: a Chronicle of American Indian Resistance*

Work and Leisure in the Early Nineteenth Century, 1800–1860

Nineteenth-century American farmers made annual fairs an occasion for demonstrating their agricultural skills. The competition to select the finest cattle, sheep, horses, or pigs not only gave farmers a reason for pride in their work, but provided an opportunity for socializing. As in the colonial period, rural Americans continued to combine work with leisure. Collection of H. T. Peters, Jr.

Some traditional leisure activities took on new, more organized forms in the mid-nineteenth century. Colonial Americans had enjoyed skating on crude, home-made skates and had attended horse races on one another's farms. By mid-century, machine-made ice skates were readily available, and the New Yorkers shown at top right went skating in the newly completed Central Park. At the same time, formally designed race courses like the one in Louisville (bottom right) attracted spectators from miles around to carefully planned and publicized contests. Thus Americans engaged in both participatory and spectator sports early in the nation's history. Top: The St. Louis Art Museum, Eliza McMillan Fund; bottom: Collection of the J. B. Speed Art Museum, Louisville, Kentucky.

Like livestock competitions, quilting bees allowed Americans to socialize while working. The women at this bee have just completed a quilt, and one of them is removing it from its frame. As another clears leftover scraps from the floor, a black fiddler strikes up a dance tune. The Henry Francis du Pont Winterthur Museum, Winterthur, Delaware.

Until the 1850s, northern farm daughters like the girl at left made up most of the work force in the cotton mills: they were the nation's first factory workers. But although they were operating machines and working outside their homes, the mill girls still performed the same tasks their mothers had–spinning and weaving. Though women's work had in one sense changed dramatically, then, in another sense it had remained much the same. Slater Mill Historic Site, Pawtucket, Rhode Island.

OAKLAND
HOUSE

Despite the introduction of factories and farm machinery in the North and West, the use of manual labor persisted in the South. This mid-nineteenth-century painting shows the old-fashioned sugar-harvesting methods used by slaves in Texas and Louisiana cane fields. Perhaps because planters gained little by creating extra leisure time for their enslaved work force, old ways died slowly. The Glenbow-Alberta Institute, Canada.

(1961); John K. Mahon, *History of the Second Seminole War, 1835–1842* (1967); Francis P. Prucha, *American Indian Policy in the Formative Years* (1962); Ronald N. Satz, *American Indian Policy in the Jacksonian Era* (1975); Glen Tucker, *Tecumseh: Vision of Glory* (1956); Wilcomb E. Washburn, *The Indian in America* (1975); Thurman Wilkin, *Cherokee Tragedy* (1970).

Women and the family

Nancy F. Cott, *The Bonds of Womanhood: "Woman's Sphere" in New England, 1780–1835* (1977); Carl N. Degler, *At Odds: Women and the Family in America from the Revolution to the Present* (1980); Linda Gordon, *Woman's Body, Woman's Rights: A Social History of Birth Control in America* (1976); Gerda Lerner, "The Lady and the Mill Girl," *Mid-Continent American Studies Journal,* 10 (Spring 1969), 5–15; James C. Mohr, *Abortion in America: The Origins and Evolution of National Policy, 1800–1900* (1978); James Reed, *From Private Vice to Public Virtue: The Birth Control Movement and American Society Since 1830* (1978); Kathryn Kish Sklar, *Catherine Beecher: A Study in American Domesticity* (1973); Barbara Welter, "The Cult of True Womanhood, 1820–1860," *American Quarterly,* 18 (Summer 1966), 151–174.

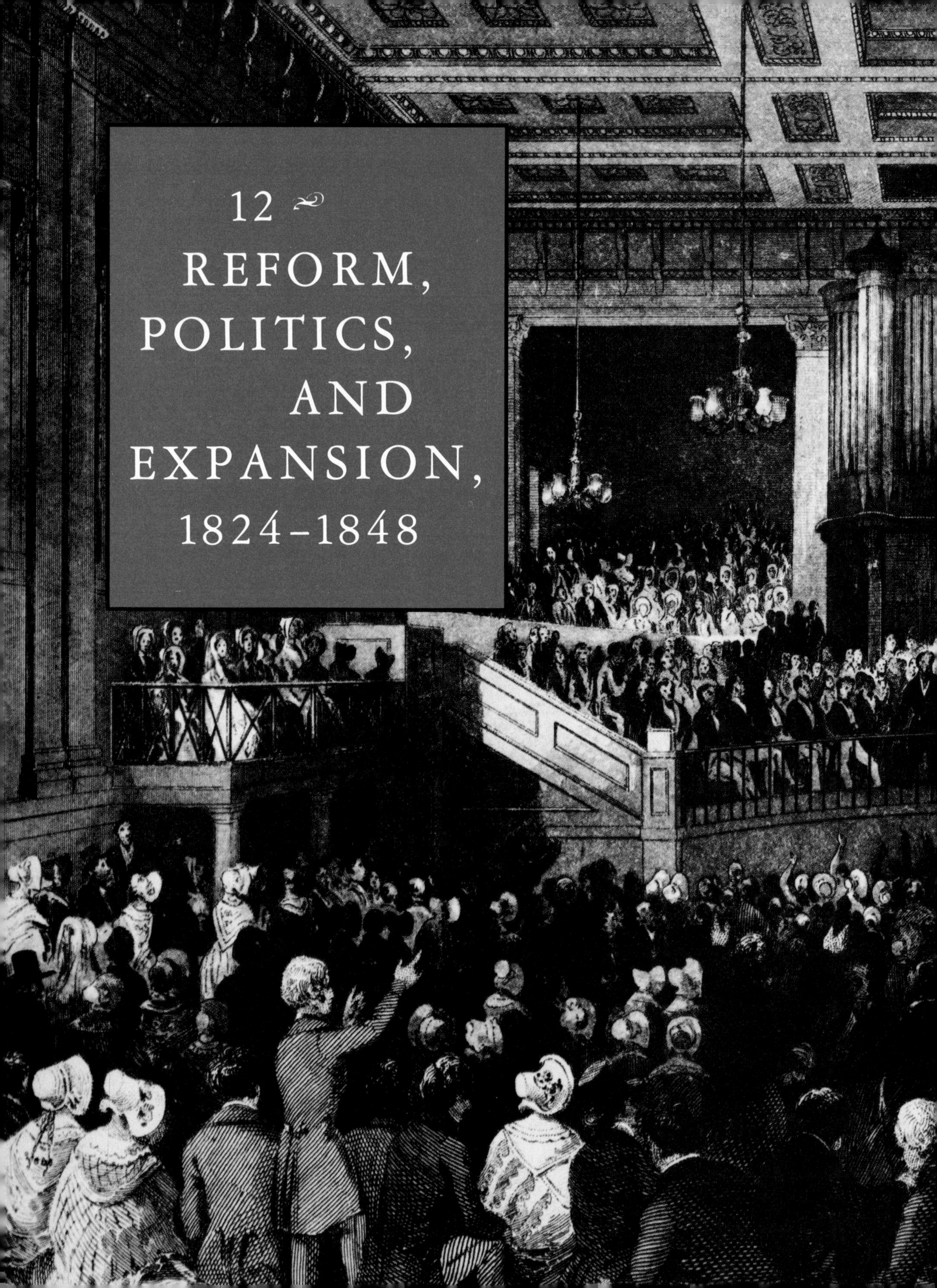

12 REFORM, POLITICS, AND EXPANSION, 1824–1848

Men sowing seed at the Bishop Hill Colony (1846–1862), a utopian farm community founded in Illinois by Swedish religious dissenters. At its peak in 1855 the colony had five hundred members. Bishop Hill State Historical Site.

mitted graduates out into the world to spread the gospel of reform. Evangelists also organized grassroots political movements. In the late 1830s and 1840s they rallied around the Whig party in an attempt to use government as an instrument of reform. Their efforts galvanized nonevangelical Protestants, Catholics, and Jews as well as evangelical Christians.

Other people, especially middle-class businessmen and their families, were drawn to revivalism for its efforts to restore traditional communal and familial values. Change had eroded the old ways of neighborliness and kinship. The new market economy tended to separate people from each other by emphasizing self above communal interest. Revivalism brought people back together and promised to restore the old order of things. It was an anchor in a sea of change.

Some of these seekers of a sense of community turned away from the larger society to establish utopian towns and farms. Such settlements offered an antidote to the untamed growth of large urban communities. Whatever their particular philosophy, utopians attempted to establish order and regularity in their daily lives and to build a cooperative rather than competitive environment. Some experimented with communal living and nontraditional work, family, and sex roles.

America's earliest utopian experiments were organized by the Shakers, who derived their name from the way they danced and swayed at worship services. An offshoot of the Quakers, their sect was established in America in 1774 by the English Shaker Ann Lee. Shakers believed that the end of the world was near, and that sin entered the world through sexual intercourse. They regarded existing churches as too worldly, and considered the Shaker family the instrument of salvation.

Shakers

After the death of Mother Ann Lee in 1784, the Shakers turned to communal living to fulfill their mission. In 1787 they "gathered in" at New Lebanon, New York, to live, worship, and work communally.

Other colonies soon followed. At its peak, between 1820 and 1860, the sect had about six thousand members in twenty settlements in eight states. Shaker communities emphasized agriculture and crafts; most managed to become self-sufficient, profitable enterprises. Shaker furniture became famous for its excellent construction, utility, and beauty of design.

Though economically conservative, the Shakers were social radicals. They abolished individual families, practiced celibacy, and made no distinction between the sexes in their government, economy, or society. Each colony was one large family, with religious authority vested in elders and eldresses and economic leadership in deacons and deaconesses. The Shaker ministry was headed by a woman, Lucy Wright, during its period of greatest growth.

The Shaker experiment in communal living proved both economically rewarding and emotionally satisfying to its members. It was the communities' celibacy that proved to be their eventual downfall. Unable to reproduce naturally, the colonies succumbed to death by attrition in the twentieth century.

Not all utopian communities were founded by religious groups. Robert Owen's New Harmony was a short-lived attempt to found a socialist utopia in Indiana. A wealthy Scottish industrialist, Owen established the cooperative community in 1825. According to his plan, its nine hundred members were to exchange their labor for goods at a communal store. Handicrafts (hat and boot making) flourished at New Harmony. But the economic base of the community, its textile mill, failed after Owen gave it to the community to run. Turnover in membership was too great for the community to develop any cohesion, and by 1827 the experiment had ended.

Brook Farm

More successful were the New England transcendentalists who lived and worked at the Brook Farm cooperative in West Roxbury, Massachusetts. Inspired by the philosophy that the spiritual transcends the worldly, members rejected materialism and sought satisfaction in a communal life combining spirituality, work, and play. Founded in 1841 by the Unitarian minister George Ripley, Brook Farm attracted not only farmers and skilled craftsmen but teachers and writers, among them Nathaniel Hawthorne. Indeed, the fame of Brook Farm rested on the intellectual achievements of its members. Its school attracted students from outside the community, and its residents contributed heavily to the *Dial,* the leading transcendentalist journal. In 1845 Brook Farm's hundred members organized themselves into model phalanxes (work-living units) in keeping with the philosophy of the French utopian Charles Fourier. Rigid regimentation replaced individualism, and membership dropped. Following a disastrous fire in 1846, the experiment collapsed.

Though short-lived, Brook Farm played a significant part in the Romantic movement. During these years Hawthorne, Emerson, and the *Dial*'s editor Margaret Fuller joined Thoreau, James Fenimore Cooper, Herman Melville, and others in creating what is known today as the American Renaissance–the flowering of a national literature. In poetry and prose these Romanticists praised individualism and intuition, rejecting or modifying the ordered world of the Enlightenment in favor of the mysteries of nature. Rebelling against convention, both social and literary, they probed and celebrated the American character and the American experience. Cooper, for instance, wrote of the frontier in the Leatherstocking Tales, and Melville wrote of great spiritual quests in the guise of seafaring adventures.

Mormon community of Saints

Far and away the most successful communitarians were the Mormons, who originated in the burned-over district of western New York. Fleeing persecution in Illinois because of their newly adopted practice of polygamy, the Mormons trekked across the continent in 1846 and 1847 to found a New Zion in the Great Salt Lake Valley. There, under Brigham Young, head of the Twelve Apostles, they established a cohesive community of Saints–a heaven on earth. The Mormons created agricultural settlements and distributed land according to family size. An extensive irrigation system, constructed by men who contributed their labor according to the quantity of land they received and the amount of water they expected to use, transformed the arid valley into a rich oasis. As the colony developed, its cooperative principles gradually gave way to benevolent corporate authority, and the church elders came to control water, trade, industry, and even the territorial government of Utah.

Revivalism encompassed the absurd as well as the sublime. Some naive revivalists, like the followers of Baptist minister William Miller, believed in the literal return of Jesus. Awaiting His appearance in 1843, the "year of the time," the Millerites prepared by holding camp meetings in locations as widely separated as Massachusetts, Iowa, and Kentucky and giving away all their earthly goods. But they did so in vain. Quick recalculations postponed the coming to October 1844. When the End of Days again failed to occur, the Second Coming was indefinitely postponed and most of the faithful abandoned the vigil. Presumably they turned to more earthly concerns, like the evils of alcohol.

Temperance, public education, and feminism

As a group, American men liked to drink alcoholic spirits–whiskey, rum, and hard cider. They gathered in public houses, saloons, taverns, and rural inns to socialize, gossip, discuss politics, play cards, and drink. Men drank on all occasions, social and business: contracts were sealed with a drink; celebrations were toasted with spirits; barn raisings and harvests ended with liquor. And though respectable women did not drink in public, many regularly tippled alcohol-based elixirs, patent medicines promoted as cure-alls.

There were economic and environmental reasons for the popularity of liquor. Spirits were more easily transported than grain; as a result, by 1810 they were surpassed only by cloth and tanned hides in total value of output. And in areas where clean water was either expensive or unobtainable, whiskey was not only cheaper but safer than water. Not until the Croton Reservoir brought clean water to New York City in 1842 did New Yorkers switch from spirits to water.

Why then was temperance such a vital issue? And why were women specially active in the movement? As with all reform, temperance had a strong religious base. "The Holy Spirit," a temperance pamphlet proclaimed, "will not visit, much less dwell with him who is under the polluting, debasing effects of intoxicating drink." To evangelicals, the selling of whiskey was a chronic symbol of Sabbath violation, for workers commonly labored six days a week, then spent Sunday at the public house drinking and socializing. Alcohol was seen as a destroyer of families as well, since men who drank heavily either neglected their families or could not adequately support them. Indeed, though craftsmen who worked for themselves could mix drink with work, the habit of drinking was not tolerated in the new world of the factory. Timothy Arthur Shay dramatized all these evils in *Ten Nights in a Barroom* (1853), a classic American melodrama.

Demon rum thus became the target of the most widespread and successful of the antebellum reform movements. As the reformers gained momentum, they shifted their emphasis from temperate use of spirits to voluntary abstinence and finally to a crusade to prohibit the manufacture and sale of spirits. The American Society for the Promotion of Temperance, organized in 1826 to urge drinkers to sign a pledge of abstinence, shortly thereafter became a pressure group for state prohibition legislation. By the mid-1830s there were some five thousand state and local temperance societies, and more than a million people had taken the pledge. By the 1840s the movement's success was reflected in a sharp decline in alcohol consumption in the United States. Between 1800 and 1830, annual per capita consumption of alcohol had risen from three to more than five gallons; by the mid-1840s, however, it had dropped below two gallons. Success bred more victories. In 1851 Maine prohibited the manufacture and sale of alcohol except for medicinal purposes, and by 1855 similar laws had been enacted throughout New England and in New York, Delaware, Indiana, Iowa, Michigan, Ohio, and Pennsylvania.

Temperance societies

Even though consumption of alcohol was declining, opposition to it did not weaken. Many reformers believed that alcohol was an evil introduced and perpetuated by Catholic immigrants. From the 1820s on, antiliquor reformers based much of their argument on this false prejudice. The Irish and Germans, the *American Protestant Magazine* complained in 1849, "bring the grog shops like the frogs of Egypt upon us." Rum and immigrants defiled the Sabbath; rum and immigrants brought poverty and pauperism; rum and immigrants supported the feared papacy. Some Catholics did join with nonevangelical Protestant sects like the Lutherans to oppose temperance legislation. But

"The Drunkard's Family," a Currier and Ives print that dramatized the evils of alcohol. With their pockets empty, their children shoeless and exposed to the elements, the drunkard and his long-suffering wife wander an unmarked trail. Edmund B. Sullivan Collection, Hartford University.

other Catholics took the pledge of abstinence and formed their own temperance organizations, such as the St. Mary's Mutual Benevolent Total Abstinence Society in Boston. Even nondrinking Catholics tended to oppose state regulation of drinking, however; temperance seemed to them a question of individual choice, not state coercion.

Another important part of the reform impulse was the development of new institutions to meet the social needs of citizens. The list of organizations founded during this era is a long one—Protestant denominations, Catholic orders, reform Judaism; schools and colleges, hospitals, asylums, orphanages, and penitentiaries; new political parties; and myriad reform societies. Many of these institutions experimented with new techniques for handling old problems. New York state's penitentiary at Auburn, for example, placed prisoners in rehabilitative cooperative labor programs during the day, confining them only at night. Other states soon followed New York's lead.

Public education was one of the more lasting results of the age of institution building. In 1800 there were no public schools outside New England; by 1860 every state had some public education, although southern states lagged far behind the North and West. Massachusetts took the lead, especially under Horace Mann, secretary of the state board of education from 1837 to 1848. Under Mann, Massachusetts established a minimum school year of six months, increased the number of high schools, formalized the training of teachers, and emphasized secular subjects and applied skills rather than religion.

Horace Mann on education

Horace Mann was an evangelist of public education and school reform; his preaching on behalf of free state education changed schooling not only in Massachusetts but also throughout the nation. "If we do not prepare children to become good citizens," Mann prophesied, "if we do not develop their capacities, . . . imbue their hearts with the love of truth and

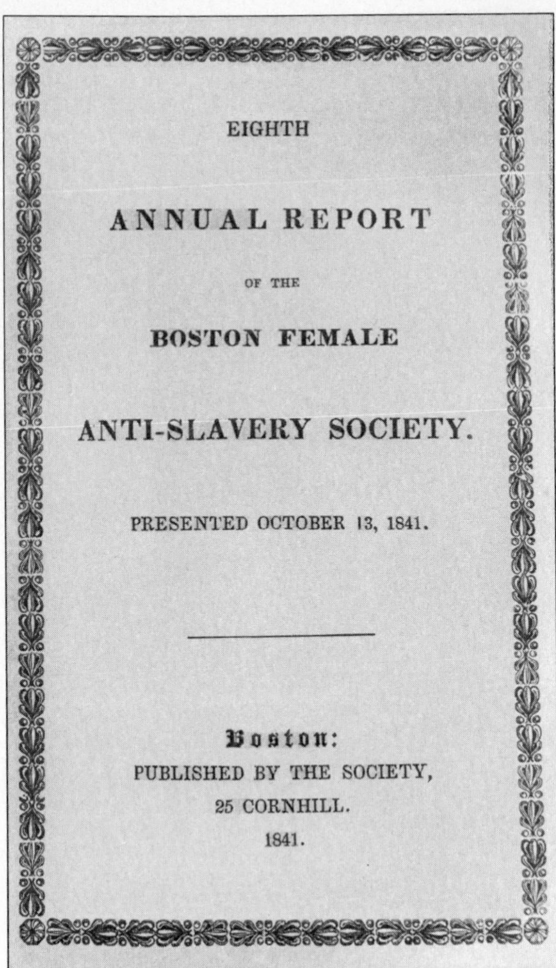
EIGHTH

ANNUAL REPORT

OF THE

BOSTON FEMALE

ANTI-SLAVERY SOCIETY.

PRESENTED OCTOBER 13, 1841.

Boston:

PUBLISHED BY THE SOCIETY,

25 CORNHILL.

1841.

Women organized in Boston in 1833 to fight the evils of slavery. This annual report of their society was published in 1841. Sophia Smith Collection, Smith College.

duty, and a reverence for all things sacred and holy, then our republic must go down to destruction." The abolition of ignorance, Mann claimed, would end misery, crime, and suffering. "The only sphere . . . left open for our patriotism," he wrote, "is the improvement of our chidren,—not the few, but the many; not a part of them but all."

In laying the basis of free public schools, Mann also broadened the scope of education. Previously, education had had little practical benefit, other than the discipline fostered by rote reading of the Bible; thus most parents were indifferent to whether or not their children attended school. Under Mann's leadership, the school curriculum became more appropriate for future clerks, farmers, and workers. Geography, American history, arithmetic, and science replaced many of the classics; teachers were trained in the new subjects at normal schools. Moral education was retained, but direct religious indoctrination was dropped.

Many traditionalists, including New England Congregationalists, fought to maintain the old ties between education and religion. Some feared secular public education was a sign of the decline of American morality and virtue. But others, including many deeply religious people reborn in the Second Great Awakening, believed that public education would strengthen religious values. Mann's ideals and motives—the general betterment of society—were similar to theirs, and they saw merit in a democratic school system available to all, rich and poor. They noted, furthermore, that the Bible remained the centerpiece of elementary school education. And free public education would enable Sunday schools to devote full time to their students' religious needs without having to teach reading and writing as well. Thus Sunday-school teachers became Mann's allies.

A more controversial reform movement was the rise of American feminism in the 1840s. Ironically, it was women's traditional image as pious and spiritual that brought them into the public sphere. The Second Great Awakening, with its emphasis on conversion through the heart, had served to elevate women; women were thought to be more emotional than men, and emotion was the most important element in being reborn. In the 1820s and 1830s, using their churches as a base, women began to play a prominent activist role in temperance, antislavery, and other reform movements. Organized into women's groups like the Boston Female Anti-Slavery Society, they slowly entered the public arena.

Reaction to the growing involvement of women in reform movements led many women to re-examine their position in society. In 1837 two antislavery lecturers, Angelina and Sarah Grimké, became objects of controversy when they were attacked for speaking before mixed groups of men and women. Some New England Congregationalists and even abolitionists joined in the criticism; as one pastoral letter put it, women should obey, not lecture, men. This hostile reception turned the Grimkés' attention from slavery to women's condition. The two attacked the concept of

Angelina and Sarah Grimké

"subordination to man," insisting that both men and women had the "same rights and same duties." Sarah Grimké's *Letters on the Condition of Women and the Equality of the Sexes* (1838) and her sister's *Letters to Catherine E. Beecher,* published the same year, were the opening volleys in the war against the legal and social inequality of women.

In arguing against slavery, some women noticed the similarities between their own position and that of slaves. They saw parallels in their legal disabilities—inability to vote or control their property, except in widowhood—and their social restrictions—exclusion from advanced schooling and from most occupations. "The investigation of the rights of the slave," Angelina Grimké confessed, "has led me to a better understanding of my own." The women who worked in the Lowell mills came to the same conclusion in the 1840s.

Unlike other reform movements, which succeeded in building a broad base of individual and organizational support, the movement for women's rights was confined mostly to women. Some men joined the ranks, notably abolitionist William Lloyd Garrison and ex-slave Frederick Douglass, but most actively opposed the movement. In the 1840s the question of women's rights split the antislavery movement, the majority declaring themselves opposed. Though the Seneca Falls Convention, led by Elizabeth Cady Stanton and Lucretia Mott, issued a much-published indictment of women's disabilities in 1848, it had little effect. By the 1850s feminists were focusing more and more on the single issue of suffrage. If women had the vote, these reformers argued, they would be able both to protect themselves and to realize their potential as moral and spiritual leaders. Their argument fell on deaf ears. Another cause would eclipse their movement, at least for a time.

The antislavery movement

Antislavery began as one among many reform movements. But, sparked by territorial expansion, the issue of slavery eventually became so overpowering that it consumed all other reforms. Passions would become so heated that they would threaten the nation itself. Above all else, those opposed to slavery saw it as a moral issue, evidence of the sinfulness of the American nation. When territorial questions in the 1850s forced the issue of slavery to center stage, the antislavery forces were well prepared (see Chapter 13).

Prior to the 1820s antislavery had played on the conscience of the individual slaveholder. Quakers had led the first antislavery movement in the eighteenth century, freeing their slaves and preaching that it was a sin for Christians to hold people in bondage. But in the North, where most states had abolished slavery by 1800, whites took little interest in an issue that did not concern them directly. It was in the upper South that antislavery sentiment was strongest, at least until the 1820s. But the movement there seemed to be as much concerned with preparing society for the natural death of slavery as with the plight of the slaves themselves. The American Colonization Society, founded in 1816 and supported by slaveholders and white abolitionists alike, worked to rid the nation of blacks by gradually settling them in Africa.

Black antislavery movement

Through the 1820s only free people of color demanded an immediate end to slavery. By 1830 there were at least fifty black antislavery societies in major black communities. These societies assisted fugitive slaves, attacked slavery at every turn, and reminded the nation that its mission as defined in the Declaration of Independence remained unfulfilled. A free black press helped to spread their word. When the climate of opinion changed and whites became more committed to antislavery, black abolitionists like Frederick Douglass, Sojourner Truth, and Harriet Tubman worked with white reformers in the American Anti-Slavery Society. These crusaders also stirred European support for their militant and unrelenting campaign. "Brethren, arise, arise, arise!" Henry Highland Garnet commanded the 1843 national colored convention. "Strike for your lives and liberties. Now is the day and hour. Let every slave in the land do this and the days of slavery are numbered. Rather die freemen than live to be slaves."

In the 1830s a full-fledged abolitionist crusade was ushered in by a small minority of white reformers who made antislavery their primary commitment. The most prominent and uncompromising abolitionist, though clearly not the most representative, was William Lloyd Garrison, who demanded "immediate and

VOL. I. No. 1.

THE
AMERICAN
ANTI-SLAVERY
ALMANAC,
FOR
1836,

Being Bissextile or Leap-Year, and the 60th of American Independence. Calculated for Boston, New York and Pittsburgh, and adapted to most parts of the United States.

An emancipated family.

"We are verily guilty concerning our brother."

BOSTON:
PUBLISHED BY WEBSTER & SOUTHARD,
No. 9, Cornhill.

The Anti-Slavery Almanac, propaganda of the American Anti-Slavery Society. Beneath the picture of an emancipated family is the motto "We are verily guilty concerning our brother." Sophia Smith Collection, Smith College.

William Lloyd Garrison

complete emancipation." Garrison had begun his career in the late 1820s editing the *National Philanthropist,* a weekly paper devoted to general reform, but especially to prohibition. It was in 1828, when Benjamin Lundy recruited him to *The Genius of Universal Emancipation,* that Garrison entered the ranks of the abolitionists. But Lundy favored colonization and sought to end slavery through persuasion, a position Garrison rejected. In January 1831 Garrison broke with gradualists like Lundy and published the first issue of the *Liberator,* which was to be his major weapon against slavery for thirty-five years. "I am in earnest–I will not equivocate–I will not excuse–I will not retreat a single inch–and *I will be heard,*" he wrote in the first issue.

Garrison's refusal to work with anyone who even indirectly delayed emancipation left him isolated. He even forswore political action, on the grounds that it was governments that permitted slavery. (On July 4, 1854, Garrison burned a copy of the Constitution, proclaiming, "So perish all compromises with tyranny.") Though not a great organizer, Garrison helped to make antislavery the prevailing issue through sheer force of rhetoric. His "immediatism" is probably best defined as tolerating no delay in ending slavery; he had no specific plan for abolishing it. In essence, Garrison called for an antislavery revival–all those who held slaves or cooperated with institutions supporting slavery should cast off their sins, repent, and join the battle against evil.

Garrison alone could not have made antislavery a central issue. By the 1830s many northern reformers were recognizing the evils of slavery and preparing to act. Moral and religious ferment in the burned-over district and the Old Northwest had primed evangelists to enter the fray. And the reform activities of the 1820s, including antislavery, had built a network of interrelated organizations. A state society in Michigan, for example, met one day as a temperance convention and reconvened the next day as an antislavery society.

Ironically, it was in defense of the constitutional rights of abolitionists, not slaves, that many whites entered the struggle. Wherever they went, abolitionists found their civil rights in danger, especially their right of free speech. Using the new steam press, the American Anti-Slavery Society had increased its distribution of antislavery propaganda tenfold between 1834 and 1835, sending out 1.1 million pieces in 1835. But southern mobs seized and destroyed much of the mail, and South Carolina intercepted and burned abolitionist literature that entered the state (with the approval of the postmaster general). President Andrew Jackson even proposed a law prohibiting the mailing of antislavery tracts.

Another civil rights confrontation developed in Congress. Exercising their constitutional right to petition Congress, abolitionists had mounted a campaign to abolish slavery and the slave trade in the District of Columbia. (Since the district was under federal rule, states' rights arguments against interfering with slavery did not apply there.) But Congress responded in 1836 by adopting the so-called gag rule, which automatically tabled abolitionist petitions, effectively preventing debate on them. In a dramatic defense of the right of petition, ex-president John Quincy Adams, then a Massachusetts representative, took to the floor repeatedly to defy the gag rule and eventually succeeded in getting it repealed (1844).

Gag rule

Antislavery speakers often faced hostile crowds, and their presses were under constant threat of attack. The martyrdom of Elijah P. Lovejoy at the hands of a mob in Alton, Illinois, in 1837, drew attention to proslavery violence. Lovejoy, who had been driven out of slaveholding Missouri, had re-established his printing plant just across the river in Illinois. He was killed by a mob that had come to sack his office, with the cooperation of local authorities. Public outrage at Lovejoy's murder, as with the gag rule and censorship of the mails, only served to broaden the base of antislavery support in the North.

Frustration with the federal government also fed northern support for antislavery. By and large, politicians and government officials sought to avoid the question of slavery. The Missouri Compromise of 1820 had been an effort to quarantine the issue by adopting a simple formula–banning slavery north of 36°30′, Missouri's southern boundary–that would make debate on the slave or free status of new states unnecessary. Censorship of the mails and the gag rule were similar attempts to keep the issue out of the political arena. Yet the more national leaders, especially Democrats, sought to avoid the matter, the more they hardened the resolve of the antislavery forces.

The effect of the unlawful, violent, and obstructionist tactics used by proslavery advocates cannot be overestimated. Antislavery was not at the outset a unified movement. It was splintered and factionalized, and its adherents fought each other as often as they fought the defenders of slavery. They were divided over Garrison's emphasis on "moral suasion" versus the more practical political approach of James G. Birney, the Liberty party's candidate for president in 1840 (see page 332). They were split over support of other reforms, especially the rights of women. And they disagreed over the place of black people in American society. Even so, abolitionists would eventually manage to unify and make antislavery a major issue in the politics of the 1850s.

Jacksonianism and the beginnings of modern party politics

Reformers were not the only Americans working to create or restore order in the 1820s and 1830s. Though their means differed, political leaders were also seeking to deal with the problems created by an expanding, urbanizing, market-oriented nation. John Quincy Adams advocated a nationalist program and an activist federal government; Andrew Jackson and his followers adhered to the Jeffersonian ideal of a limited federal government, with the primary power vested in the states.

The election of 1824, in which Adams and Jackson faced each other for the first time, signaled the beginning of a new, more open political system. From 1800 through 1820 a congressional caucus had chosen the Republican presidential nominees: Jefferson, Madison, and Monroe. Jefferson and Madison had both indicated to the caucus that their secretaries of state should succeed them, and the system had worked efficiently. Of course, such a system restricted voter involvement–but this was not a real drawback at first, since in 1800 only five of sixteen states selected presidential electors by popular vote. (In ten states, legislators designated the electors.) In 1816, however, ten out of nineteen states chose electors by popular vote, and in 1824, eighteen out of twenty-four did so.

End of the caucus system

Moreover, President Monroe never designated an heir apparent. Without direction from the president, therefore, the caucus in 1824 chose William H. Crawford, secretary of the treasury. But others, encouraged by the opportunity to appeal directly to the voters in most states, challenged Crawford. Secretary of State John Quincy Adams drew support from New England, and westerners backed Speaker of the House

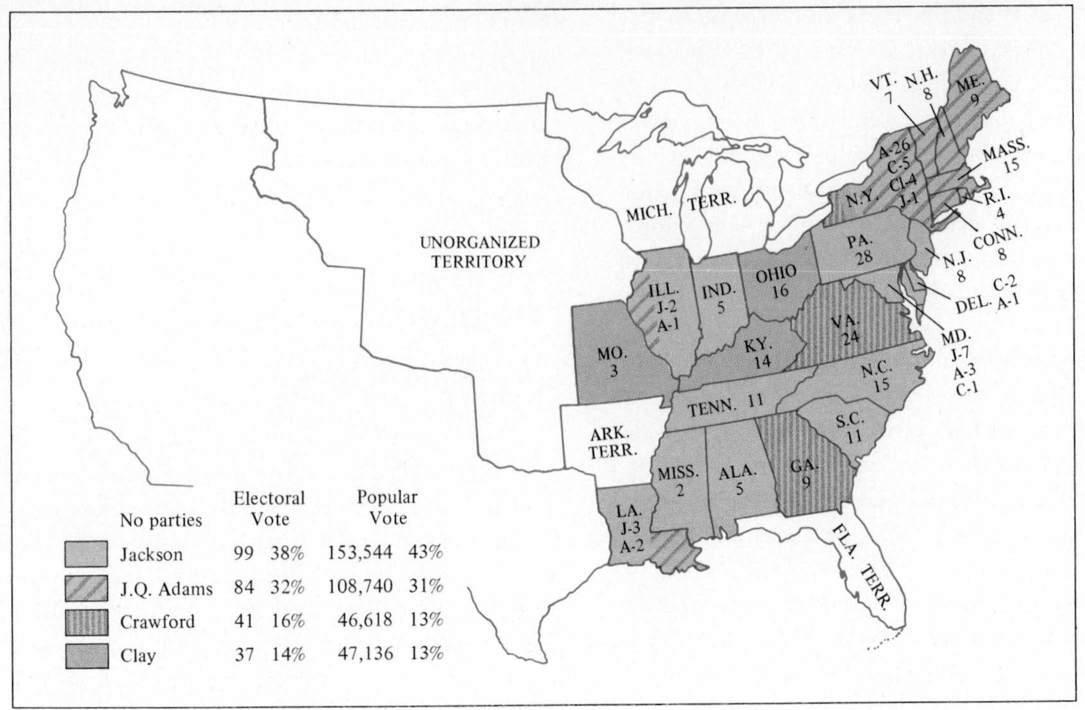

Presidential election, 1824

Henry Clay of Kentucky. Secretary of War John C. Calhoun looked to the South for support, and hoped to win Pennsylvania as well. Andrew Jackson, a popular military hero whose political views were unknown, was nominated by resolution of the Tennessee legislature and won support everywhere. But Crawford, who had declined to oppose Monroe in 1816 and 1820, had the most widespread support in Washington. Since his choice by the caucus was a foregone conclusion, the other four candidates joined in attacking the caucus system as undemocratic. When their supporters boycotted the deliberations, Crawford's victory became a hollow one, based on a minority vote. The role of the congressional caucus in nominating presidents was over.

Though Andrew Jackson led in both popular and electoral votes in the four-way presidential election of 1824, no one received a majority. Adams finished second, and Clay and Crawford trailed far behind. (Calhoun dropped out of the race before the election.) Under the Constitution, the selection of a president in such circumstances fell to the House of Representatives, which would vote by state delegation, one vote to a state. Crawford, a stroke victim, never received serious consideration; Clay, who had received the fewest votes, was dropped. But Clay, as Speaker of the House and leader of the Ohio Valley states, was in a position to influence the House vote for either Adams or Jackson. He backed Adams, who received the votes of thirteen out of twenty-four state delegations (see map). Clay was rewarded with the position of secretary of state in the Adams administration—the traditional stepping-stone to the presidency. Angry Jacksonians denounced the arrangement as a "corrupt bargain" that had stolen the office from the clear frontrunner.

As president, John Quincy Adams took a strong nationalist position emphasizing Henry Clay's American System of protective tariffs, a national bank, and internal improvements (see page 210). Adams believed the federal government should take an activist role not only in the economy but in education, science, and the arts; accordingly, he proposed a national university in Washington, D.C.

Tragically, Adams was as inept a president as he was brilliant as a diplomat and secretary of state. He un-

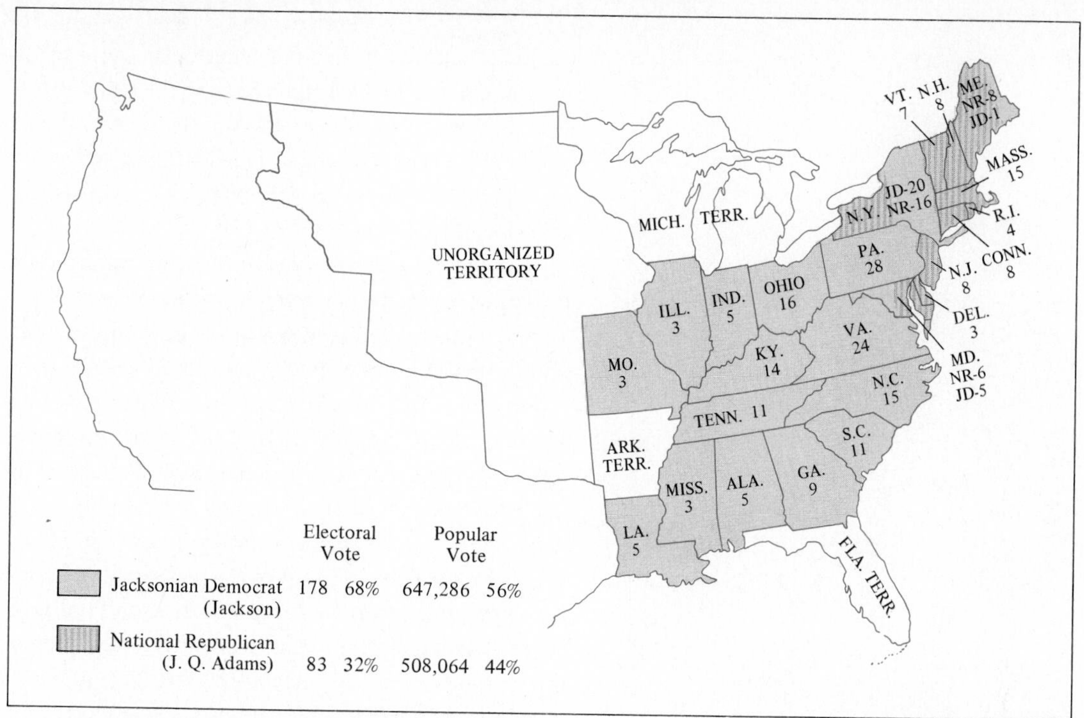

Presidential election, 1828

derestimated the lingering effects of the Panic of 1819 and the resulting bitter opposition to a national bank and protective tariffs. Distrustful of party organization, Adams failed to build a coalition to support his programs. Meanwhile, supporters of Andrew Jackson sabotaged Adams's administration at every opportunity. They even turned Adams's one success to their advantage: by supporting the extremely high Tariff of Abominations (1828), the Jacksonians won the support of eastern protectionists. "The bill referred to manufactures of no sort or kind," John Randolph observed in noting its effect on Jackson's candidacy, "but the manufacture of a President of the United States."

The 1828 campaign between Adams and Jackson was an intensely personal conflict. Whatever principles the two men stood for were obscured by the mudslinging both sides indulged in. Though Adams won the same states as in 1824, his opposition rallied around one candidate–Jackson–and swamped him. Jackson polled 56 percent of the popular vote and won in the electoral college, 178 to 83 (see map). For him and his supporters, the election of 1828 was the culmination of a long-fought, well-organized campaign based on party organization. Through a lavishly financed coalition of state parties, political leaders, and newspaper editors, a popular movement had elected a president.

Andrew Jackson

Andrew Jackson was nicknamed "Old Hickory," after the toughest American hardwood. A rough-and-tumble, ambitious man, he rose from humble birth to become a wealthy planter and slaveholder. Jackson was the first American president not born into comfortable circumstances, a self-made man at ease among both frontiersmen and southern planters.

Few Americans have been celebrated in myth and legend as has Andrew Jackson. As a general in the Tennessee militia, Jackson had led the battle against the Creeks on the Alabama frontier, forcing them from 22 million acres of land in Georgia and Alabama. He burst onto the national scene as the great hero of the War of 1812, and in 1818 enhanced his glory in an expedition against the Seminoles in Spanish Florida. Jackson also served as a congressional representative and senator from Tennessee, as a judge in his home state, and as the first territorial governor of

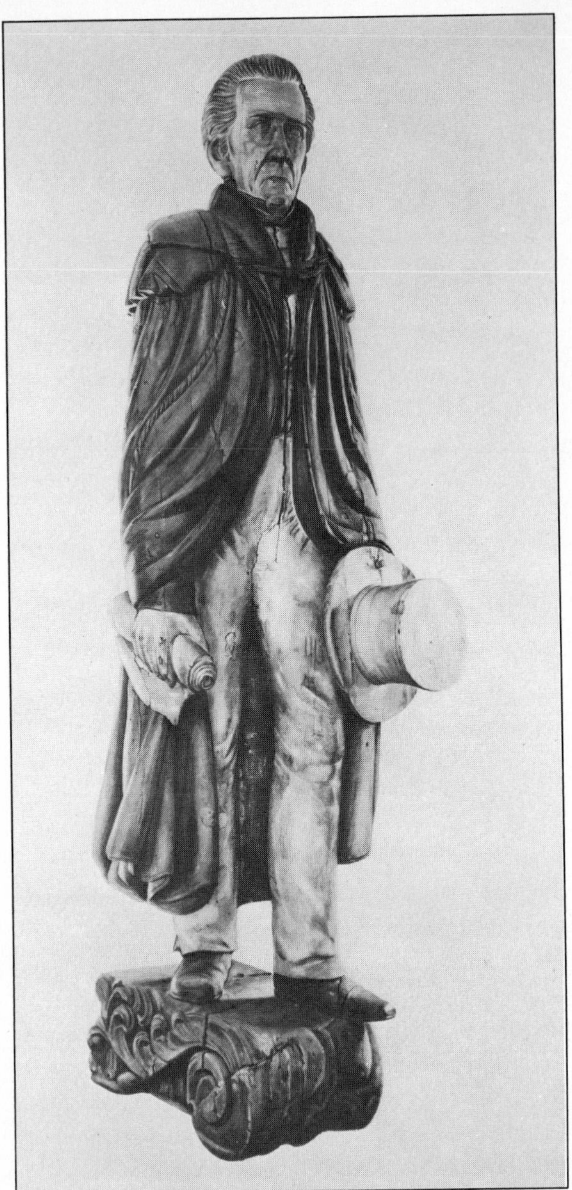

Wooden figurehead of "Old Hickory," Andrew Jackson, carved for the prow of the U.S.S. *Constitution* in 1834. Shortly after it was mounted, an enemy of Jackson sawed the head off. Museum of the City of New York.

Florida (1821) before being nominated for the presidency in 1824. He was an active presidential aspirant until he won the office in 1828.

Jackson and his supporters offered a distinct alternative to the activist federal government Adams had advocated. They and their party, the Democratic-Republicans (shortened to Democrats), represented a wide range of beliefs but shared some common ideals.

Democrats

Fundamentally, they sought to foster the Jeffersonian concept of an agrarian society, harkening back to the belief that a strong central government was the enemy of individual liberty, a tyranny to be feared. Thus, like Jefferson, they favored limited government and emphasized state sovereignty.

Jacksonians were as fearful of the concentration of economic power as they were of political power. They saw government intervention in the economy as benefiting special-interest groups and creating corporate monopolies, and thus rejected an activist economic program as favoring the rich. Jacksonians sought to restore the independence of the individual–the artisan and the yeoman farmer–by ending federal support of banks and corporations and restricting the use of paper currency. Their concept of the proper role of government tended to be negative, and Jackson's political power was largely expressed in negative acts; he used the veto more than all previous presidents combined.

Finally, Jackson and his supporters were hostile to reform as a movement and an ideology. Reformers were increasingly calling for an activist and interventionist government as they organized to turn their programs into legislation. But Democrats tended to oppose programs like educational reform and the establishment of public education. They believed, for instance, that public schools restricted individual liberty by interfering with parental responsibility, and undermined freedom of religion by replacing church schools. Nor did Jackson share reformers' humanitarian concerns. He showed little sympathy for the Indians, ordering their removal from the Southeast to make way for white agricultural settlement (see page 297).

Like Jefferson, Jackson strengthened the executive branch of government at the same time he weakened the federal role. Given his popularity and the strength of his personality, this concentration of power in the presidency was perhaps inevitable; but his deliberate policy of combining the roles of party leader and chief of state did centralize even greater power in the White House. Invoking the principle that rotating officeholders would make government more responsive to the public will, Jackson used the spoils system to reward loyal Democrats with appointments to office. Though he removed fewer than one-quarter of federal officeholders in his two terms, his use of patronage nevertheless strengthened party organization and loyalty.

In office Jackson invigorated the philosophy of limited government. In 1830 he vetoed the Maysville Road bill, which would have provided a federal subsidy to construct a sixty-mile turnpike from Maysville to Lexington, Kentucky. Jackson insisted that an internal improvement confined to one state was unconstitutional, and that such projects were properly a state responsibility. The veto undermined Henry Clay's American System and personally embarrassed Clay, since the project was in his home district.

The nullification and bank controversies

Jackson had to face more directly the question of the proper division of sovereignty between state and federal government. The growing reform crusades, especially antislavery, had made the southern states fearful of federal power–and none more so than South Carolina, where the planter class was strongest and slavery most concentrated. Having watched the growth of abolitionist sentiment in Great Britain, which resulted in 1833 in emancipation in the West Indies, South Carolinians feared the same thing would happen at home. Hard hit by the Panic of 1819, from which they never fully recovered, they also resented the high prices of imported goods created by protectionist tariffs.

To protect their interests, South Carolinian political leaders developed the doctrine of *nullification,* according to which a state had the right to overrule, or nullify, federal legislation that conflicted with its own. The act that directly inspired this doctrine was the passage in 1828 of the Tariff of Abominations. In his unsigned *Exposition and Protest,* John C. Calhoun argued that in any disagreement between the federal government and a state, a special state convention–like those called to ratify the Constitution–would decide the conflict by either nullifying or accepting the federal law. Only the power of nullification could protect the minority against the tyranny of the majority, Calhoun asserted.

South Carolina first invoked its theory of nullification against the tariff of 1832. Though this tariff had the effect of reducing some duties, it retained high taxes on imported iron, cottons, and woolens. A majority of southern representatives supported the new tariff, but South Carolinians refused to go along. In their view, their constitutional right to control their own destiny had been sacrificed to the demands of northern industrialists. They feared the consequences of accepting such an act; it could set a precedent for congressional legislation on slavery. In November 1832 a South Carolina state convention nullified the tariff, making it unlawful for officials to collect duties in the state after February 1, 1833. Immediately recruiters began to organize a volunteer army to ensure nonenforcement of the tariff.

Nullification crisis

President Jackson responded with the toughness that had earned him the nickname "Old Hickory." Privately, he threatened to invade South Carolina and hang Calhoun; publicly, he sought to avoid the use of force. On December 10, 1832, Jackson issued his own proclamation nullifying nullification. He moved troops to federal forts in South Carolina and prepared United States marshals to collect the required duties. At Jackson's request, Congress passed the Force Act, which supposedly renewed Jackson's authority to call up troops; it was actually a scheme to avoid the use of force by collecting duties before ships reached South Carolina. At the same time, Jackson extended the olive branch by recommending tariff reductions. Calhoun, disturbed by South Carolina's drift toward separatism, worked with Henry Clay to draw up the compromise tariff of 1833. Quickly passed by Congress and signed by the president, the revision lengthened the list of duty-free items and reduced duties over the next nine years. Satisfied, South Carolina's convention repealed its nullification law, and in a final salvo nullified Jackson's Force Act. Jackson ignored the gesture.

Although fought over the practical issue of tariffs (and the unspoken issue of slavery), the nullification controversy did represent a genuine debate on the true nature and principles of the republic. Each side believed it was upholding the Constitution. Both felt they were fighting special privilege and subversion of republican values. South Carolina was fighting the tyranny of the federal government and the manufacturers who sought tariff protection; Jackson was

When New York state banks stopped redeeming bank notes for gold or silver during the Panic of 1837, Whigs blamed the crisis on Jackson's opposition to the Second Bank of the United States. This satirical six-cent note drawn on the Humbug Glory Bank ridicules Jackson and Van Buren. Notice the Democratic donkey and the hickory leaf on the face of the paper. The New-York Historical Society.

fighting the tyranny of South Carolina, whose refusal to bow to federal authority threatened to split the republic. Neither side won a clear victory. Another issue, that of a central bank, would define the powers of the federal government more clearly.

At stake was the rechartering of the Second Bank of the United States, whose twenty-year charter expired in 1836. Like its predecessor, the bank served as a depository for federal funds, on which it paid no interest; and it served the republic in many other ways. Its bank notes circulated as currency throughout the country; they could be readily exchanged for gold, and the federal government accepted them as payment in all transactions. Through its twenty-five branch offices, the bank acted as a clearing-house for state banks, keeping them honest by refusing to accept their notes if they had insufficient gold in reserve.

Second Bank of the United States

But the bank had enemies. Many state banks resented the central bank's police role; by presenting state bank notes for redemption all at once, the Second Bank could easily ruin a state bank. Moreover, state banks, with less money in reserve, found themselves unable to compete on an equal footing with the Second Bank. And many state governments regarded the national bank, with its headquarters in Philadelphia, as unresponsive to local needs. Finally, westerners and urban workers remembered with bitterness the bank's conservative credit policies during the Panic of 1819. And there was some truth to their complaints. Though the Second Bank served some of the functions of a central bank, it was still a private profit-making institution, and its policies reflected the self-interest of its owners. Its president, Nicholas Biddle, controlled the bank completely. Conservative and anti-Jacksonian, Biddle symbolized all that westerners found wrong with the bank.

Although the bank's charter would not expire until 1836, Biddle, aware of Jackson's hostility, sought to make it an issue in the presidential campaign of 1832. His strategy backfired. In July 1832 Jackson vetoed the rechartering bill, and the Senate failed to override the veto. Jackson's veto message was an emotional attack on the undemocratic nature of the bank. "It is to be regretted," he said, "that the rich and powerful too often bend the acts of government to their selfish purposes." Rechartering would grant "exclusive privileges, to make the rich richer and the potent more powerful."

The bank became the major symbol and issue in the presidential campaign of 1832. Jackson did not debate its constitutionality or its functions; instead he denounced special privilege and economic power. The Jacksonians had organized a highly effective party, and they used it in the election. Operating in a system in which all the states but South Carolina now chose electors by popular vote, the Jacksonians mobilized voters by advertising the presidential election as the focal point of the political system.

But the most dramatic institutional change that accompanied the rise of parties–the convention system of nominating presidential candidates–did not originate with the Jacksonians. It was the Anti-Masonic party that in 1831 met in a national convention, named William Wirt their standard-bearer for 1832, and adopted a party platform, the first in the nation's history. The Democrats and the major opposition party, the National Republicans, quickly followed suit. Jackson and Martin Van Buren were nominated at the Democratic convention, Clay and John Sergeant at the National Republican. John Floyd ran as South Carolina's candidate. Jackson was re-elected easily in a Democratic party triumph.

After his victory and second inauguration in 1833, Jackson moved not only to dismantle the Second Bank of the United States but to ensure that it would not be resurrected. He deposited federal funds in favored state-chartered ("pet") banks; without federal money, the bank shriveled. When its federal charter expired in 1836, it became just another Pennsylvania-chartered private bank. In 1841 it went bankrupt.

The Whig challenge and the second party system

Once historians described the period from 1834 through the 1840s as the Age of Jackson, and the personalities of the leading political figures dominated history books. Increasingly, however, historians have viewed these years as an age dominated by popularly based political parties and reformers. For it was only when the passionate concerns of evangelicals and reformers spilled into politics that party differences became important and party loyalties solidified. For the first time grassroots political groups organized from the bottom up set the tone of political life.

In the 1830s the Democrats' opponents found shelter under a common umbrella, the Whig party. Resentful of Jackson's domination of Congress, the Whigs borrowed their name from the British party that had opposed the tyranny of the Stuart kings and George III in the previous century. From the congressional elections of 1834 through the 1840s, they and the Democrats competed nearly equally; only a few percentage points separated the two parties in national elections. They fought at every level–city, county, and state–and achieved a stability previously unknown in American politics. Both parties built strong organizations, commanded the loyalty of legislators, and attracted mass popular followings.

The two parties emphasized responsiveness to their supporters, a priority that reflected significant changes in the electoral process. At the local level, direct voting had replaced nomination and election by legislator's and electors. And though many states still permitted only taxpayers to vote in local elections, by the 1830s only a handful significantly restricted adult white male suffrage in nonlocal elections. Some even allowed immigrants who had taken out their first citizenship papers to vote. The effect of these changes was a sharp increase in the number of votes cast in presidential elections. Between 1824 and 1828 the number of votes cast for president increased threefold, from 360,000 to over 1.1 million. In 1840, 2.4 million men cast votes. The proportion of eligible voters who cast ballots also increased. In 1824 an estimated 27 percent of those eligible voted; from 1828 through 1836, about 55 percent; in 1840, more than 80 percent.

On the political agenda during these years were numerous fundamental issues. At the national level, officials struggled with the question of the proper constitutional roles of the federal and state governments, national expansion, and Indian policy. Also during this period, many state conventions were drafting new constitutions and deliberating over such basic issues as the rights of individuals and corporations; the rights of labor and capital; government aid to business; cur-

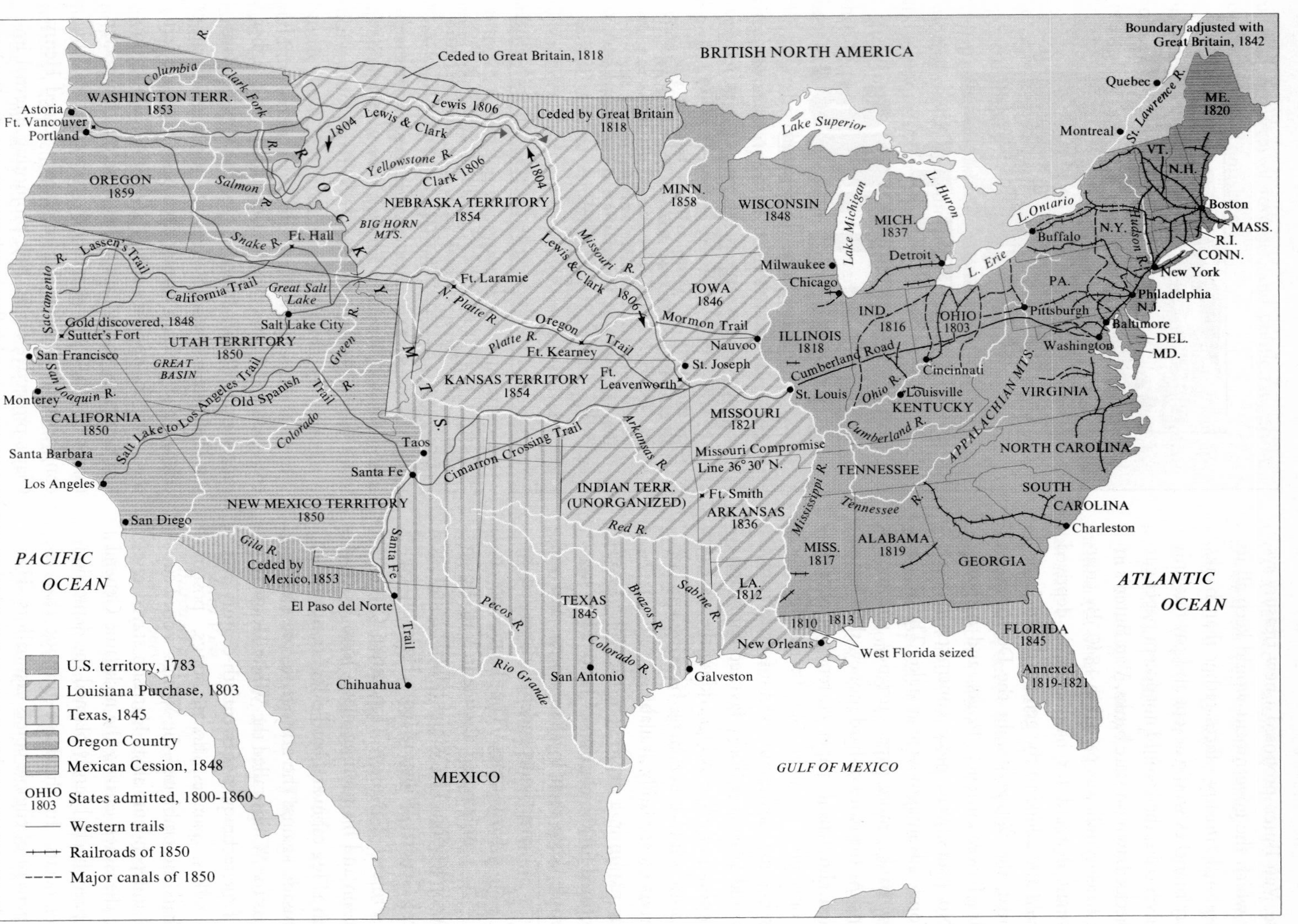

Westward expansion, 1800–1860

cabinet except Secretary of State Daniel Webster resigned. Webster, involved in negotiating a new treaty with Great Britain, left shortly thereafter. Tyler became a president without a party, and the Whigs lost the presidency without an election.

Virtually expelled from the Whig party and at war with them over domestic policy, Tyler turned his attention to territorial questions. During the late 1830s, Anglo-American relations, which had been friendly since the War of 1812, had again become tense. Southern alarm over West Indian emancipation; northern commercial rivalry with Britain; the default of state governments and corporations on British-held debts during the Panic of 1837; rebellion in Canada; boundary disputes; and American expansionism all fueled Anglo-American tensions.

Anglo-American tensions

Among the most troublesome of these disputes was the quarrel resulting from the *Caroline* affair, in which a United States citizen, Amos Durfee, had been killed when Canadian militia set the privately owned steamer *Caroline* afire in the Niagara River. (The *Caroline* had supported an unsuccessful uprising against Great Britain in Upper Canada in 1837.) Britain refused to apologize for its revenge, and patriotic Americans seethed with rage. Fearing that popular support for the Canadian rebels would ignite war, President Van Buren posted troops at the border to discourage border raids. Tensions subsided in November 1840 when Alexander McLeod, a Canadian deputy sheriff, was arrested in New York for the murder of Durfee. Fortunately McLeod was eventually acquitted; had he been found guilty and executed, Lord Palmerston, the British foreign minister, would surely have sought vengeance in war.

At about the same time another quarrel threatened Anglo-American relations. The peace of Ghent that ended the War of 1812 had not solved the boundary dispute between Maine and New Brunswick. Moreover, although Great Britain had accepted an 1831 arbitration decision fixing a new boundary, the United States Senate had rejected it in 1832. Thus when Canadians began to log the disputed region in the winter of 1838 and 1839, Maine attempted to expel them. Soon the lumbermen had captured the Maine land agent and posse; both sides had mobilized their militia; and Congress had authorized a call-up of fifty thousand men. No blood was spilled, though. General Winfield Scott, who had patrolled the border during the *Caroline* affair, was dispatched to Aroostook, Maine. Scott arranged a truce between the warring state and province, and the two sides compromised on their conflicting claims in the Webster-Ashburton Treaty (1842).

These border disputes with Great Britain prefigured an issue that became prominent in national politics in the mid- to late 1840s: the westward expansion of the United States. Tyler's succession to power in 1841 and a Democratic victory in the presidential election of 1844 ended activist, energetic government on the federal level for the rest of the decade. Meanwhile economic issues were eclipsed by debate over the nation's destiny to stretch from coast to coast. Reform, however, was not dead. Its passions would resurface in the 1850s in the debate over slavery in the territories.

Manifest destiny

The belief that American expansion westward was inevitable, divinely ordained, and just was first called *manifest destiny* by a Democrat, the newspaperman John L. O'Sullivan. The annexation of Texas, O'Sullivan wrote in 1845, was "the fulfillment of our manifest destiny to overspread the continent allotted by Providence for the free development of our yearly multiplying millions." Americans used the concept loosely during the 1840s to justify war and threats of war, and at the end of the century they would use it to justify imperialistic adventures beyond the nation's continental limits.

Americans had been hungry for western land ever since the colonists first turned their eyes westward. There lay virgin soil, valuable mineral resources, and the chance for a better life or a new beginning. Agrarian Democrats saw the West as an antidote to urbanization and industrialization. Enterprising Whigs looked to the new commercial opportunities the West offered. No wonder that between 1833 and 1860 the proportion of Americans living west of the Appalachians grew from one-quarter to one-half (see map).

German settlers in Texas. This watercolor must have been done in 1845 or after, since the title refers to Texas as a state. San Antonio Museum Association.

Equally important in the quest for western land was a fierce national pride. Dampened during times of depression, it reasserted itself during recoveries and booms, as in the 1840s. North or South, Whig or Democrat, Americans were convinced that theirs was the greatest country on earth, with a special role to play in the world. What better evidence of such a role could there be than expansion from coast to coast?

Americans also idealistically believed that westward expansion would extend American freedom and democracy. The acquisition of new territory would, they reasoned, bring the benefits of America's republican system of government to less fortunate people. Of course such idealism was self-serving, and contained an undercurrent of racism as well. Indians were perceived as savages best removed from their homes east of the Mississippi and confined to small areas in the West. Mexicans and Central and South Americans were also seen as inferior peoples, fit to be controlled or conquered. Thus the same racism that justified slavery in the South and discrimination in the North prompted expansion in the West.

Finally, the expansionist fever of the 1840s was fed by the desire to secure the nation from external enemies. The internal enemies of the 1830s—a monster bank, corporations, paper currency, alcohol, Sabbath violation—seemed to pale before the threats Americans found on their borders in the 1840s. Expansion, some believed, was necessary to preserve American independence.

Republic of Texas

Among the long-standing objectives of expansionists was the Republic of Texas, which included parts of present-day Oklahoma, Kansas, Colorado, and New Mexico as well as all of Texas. This entire territory was originally a part of Mexico. After winning its independence from Spain in 1821, Mexico encouraged the development of these rich but remote northern provinces, offering large tracts of land to settlers who agreed to bring two hundred or more families into the area. Americans like Moses and Stephen Austin, who had helped to formulate the policy, responded eagerly, for Mexico was offering rich land virtually free in return for settlers' promises to become Mexican citizens and adopt the Catholic religion.

By 1835, 35,000 Americans, including many slaveholders, lived in Texas. These new settlers ignored local laws and oppressed native Mexicans, and when the Mexican government attempted to tighten its control over the region, it stimulated a rebellion instead. At the Alamo in San Antonio in 1836, 200 Americans made a heroic stand against 3,000 Mexicans under General Santa Anna. All the defenders, including Davy Crockett and Colonel James Bowie, died in the battle, and "Remember the Alamo" became the Texans' rallying cry. By the end of the year the Texans had won their independence, to the delight of most Americans, some of whom saw the victory as a triumph of white Protestantism over Catholic Mexico.

Although they established an independent republic, Texans still sought annexation to the United States. Immediately after independence was declared, President Sam Houston opened negotiations. But the issue was politically explosive. Southerners favored annexing the proslavery territory; antislavery forces, Northerners, and most Whigs opposed it. Abolitionists saw the proposal as a southern plot to enlarge the area of slavery. In view of the political dangers, President Jackson delayed recognition of Texas until after the election of 1836, and President Van Buren ignored annexation altogether.

Rebuffed by the United States, Texans talked about developing close ties with the British and extending their republic all the way to the Pacific Coast. Faced with the specter of a rival republic to the south, and with British colonies already entrenched to the north, Americans feared encirclement. If Texas reached the ocean and became an English ally, would not American independence be threatened?

Now President Tyler—committed to expansion, fearful of the British presence, and hoping to build political support in the South—pushed for annexation. But in April 1844 the Senate rejected a treaty of annexation. A letter from Secretary of State Calhoun to the British minister justifying annexation as a step in protecting slavery so outraged senators that the treaty was defeated 16 to 35. Seven northern Democrats joined the Whigs in opposition to it.

Just as southerners sought expansion to the Southwest, northerners looked to the Northwest. In 1841 "Oregon fever" struck thousands. Lured by the glowing reports of missionaries, who showed as much interest in the Northwest's richness and beauty as in the conversion of the Indians, emigrants organized hundreds of wagon trains and embarked on the Oregon Trail. The two-thousand-mile journey took six months or more, but within a few years five thousand settlers had arrived in the fertile Willamette Valley south of the Columbia River. However, the organization of a provisional government in 1843 placed the United States and Britain on a collision course.

Oregon fever

Since the Anglo-American convention of 1818, Britain and the United States had jointly occupied the disputed Oregon territory (see page 213). Beginning with the administration of President John Quincy Adams, the United States had tried to fix the boundary at the 49th parallel, but Britain had refused, anxious to maintain access to the Puget Sound and the Columbia River. Time only increased the American appetite. In 1843 a Cincinnati convention called to consider the question demanded that the United States obtain the entire Oregon territory, up to its northernmost border of 54°40′. Soon "Fifty-four Forty or Fight" had become the rallying cry of American expansionists.

The presidential campaign of 1844 was the first to be dominated by foreign-policy issues. At the Democratic convention, southerners blocked Van Buren's nomination because of his opposition to the annexation of Texas. (Van Buren feared annexation would lead to war with Mexico.) Instead the party chose House Speaker James K. Polk, a hard-money Jacksonian and avid expansionist. The Whig leader Henry Clay, who opposed annexation, won his party's unanimous nomination. The main plank of the Democratic platform called for occupation of the entire Oregon territory and annexation of Texas. The

Election of 1844

Travelers on the Oregon Trail encamped at Independence Rock in Wyoming. Denver Public Library, Western History Department.

Whigs, though they favored expansion, argued that the Democrats' belligerent nationalism would lead the nation to war with Great Britain or Mexico or both. Clay favored expansion through negotiation, not force.

But few militant expansionists supported Clay, and Polk and the Democrats captured the White House by 170 electoral votes to 105 (they won the popular vote by just 38,000 out of 2.7 million). Polk carried New York's 36 electoral votes by just 6,000 votes; abolitionist James G. Birney, the Liberty party candidate, drew almost 16,000 votes away from Clay, handing the state and the election to Polk. Thus abolitionist forces had influenced the choice of a president.

Interpreting Polk's victory as a mandate for annexation, President Tyler proposed in his last days in office that Texas be admitted by joint resolution of Congress. (The usual method of admission, by treaty negotiation, required a two-thirds vote in the Senate—which expansionists clearly did not have. Joint resolution required only a simple majority in both houses.) Proslavery and antislavery congressmen debated the extension of slavery into the territory, and the resolution passed the House 120 to 98 and the Senate 27 to 25. Three days before leaving office, Tyler signed the measure. Mexico immediately broke relations with the United States.

Faced with the prospect of war in the Southwest, President Polk sought to avoid conflict with Great Britain in the Northwest. Thus he dropped the demand for a 54°40′ boundary in favor of the 49th parallel. But the United States was still demanding the lion's share of Oregon, and Britain rejected the offer. In April 1846 the United States therefore gave the required one-year notice for ending the 1818 joint-occupation agreement. Faced with what amounted to a threat of war, the British accepted the 49th parallel in the Oregon Treaty of 1846 (see map). The United

States gained all of present-day Oregon, Washington, and Idaho and parts of Wyoming and Montana.

Meanwhile, the crisis over Texas was worsening as a direct result of the president's expansionist aims. Polk was determined to have California and New Mexico as well as all of Texas; he intended to fulfill the nation's destiny and expand to the Pacific. After an attempt to buy the tremendous expanse of land failed, Polk resolved to ask Congress for a declaration of war, and set to work compiling a list of grievances. This task became unnecessary when word arrived that Mexican forces had engaged a body of American troops whom Polk had sent to guard the Texas border. American blood had been shed. Polk eagerly declared that "war exists by the act of Mexico itself" and summoned the nation to arms.

Although Congress voted overwhelmingly in May 1846 to recognize a state of war between Mexico and the United States, public opinion was sharply divided. Southwesterners anticipated war with enthusiasm; New Englanders strenuously opposed it. Antislavery Whigs charged that Polk had manipulated the United States into war; abolitionists regarded the war as no less than a plot to extend slavery and proslavery influence. But Whig congressmen remembered the fate of the Federalists, who had been driven into oblivion because of their opposition to the War of 1812. When the test came, they voted for war.

As in previous wars, the United States depended on volunteers raised by the states to augment its small standing army. Nationalist and expansionist fervor generated adequate forces, however, and American troops quickly established their superiority over the Mexicans. General Zachary Taylor attacked and occupied Monterrey, securing northeastern Mexico (see map). Polk then ordered Colonel Stephen Kearney and a small detachment of troops to invade the remote and relatively unpopulated provinces of New Mexico and California. Taking Santa Fe without opposition, Kearney pushed into California, where he joined forces with rebellious American settlers, commanded by Captain John C. Frémont, and a couple of United States naval units. Together they wrested control of California from Mexico with ease.

Mexican War

Meanwhile, General Winfield Scott led an army of fourteen thousand men from Vera Cruz, on the Gulf of Mexico, into Mexico City itself. The daring invasion brought the war to an end, and on February 2, 1848, representatives signed the Treaty of Guadalupe Hidalgo. The United States gained California and New Mexico (including present-day Nevada, Utah, and Arizona) and recognition of the Rio Grande as the southern boundary of Texas. In return, the American government agreed to settle the claims of its citizens against Mexico and to pay Mexico a mere $15 million for the new territory. The nation's manifest destiny had been achieved: the American flag waved on Atlantic and Pacific shores. The cost was thirteen thousand Americans and fifty thousand Mexicans dead, and Mexican-American enmity lasting into the twentieth century.

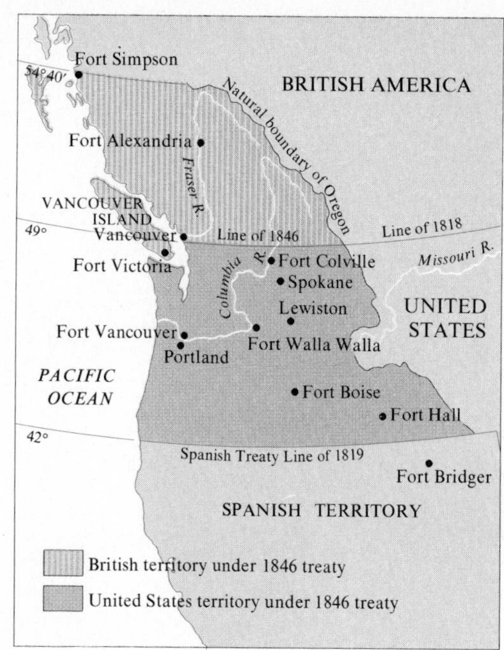

American expansion in Oregon

Ironically enough, instead of unifying the nation, the territorial expansion of the 1840s sparked sectional conflict. The debate over whether Oregon would be slave or free (Polk had recommended excluding slavery) revived old southern fears of congressional power. Northern expansionists, meanwhile, felt abandoned on the Oregon question by a South that

Sectional conflict over slavery in the territories

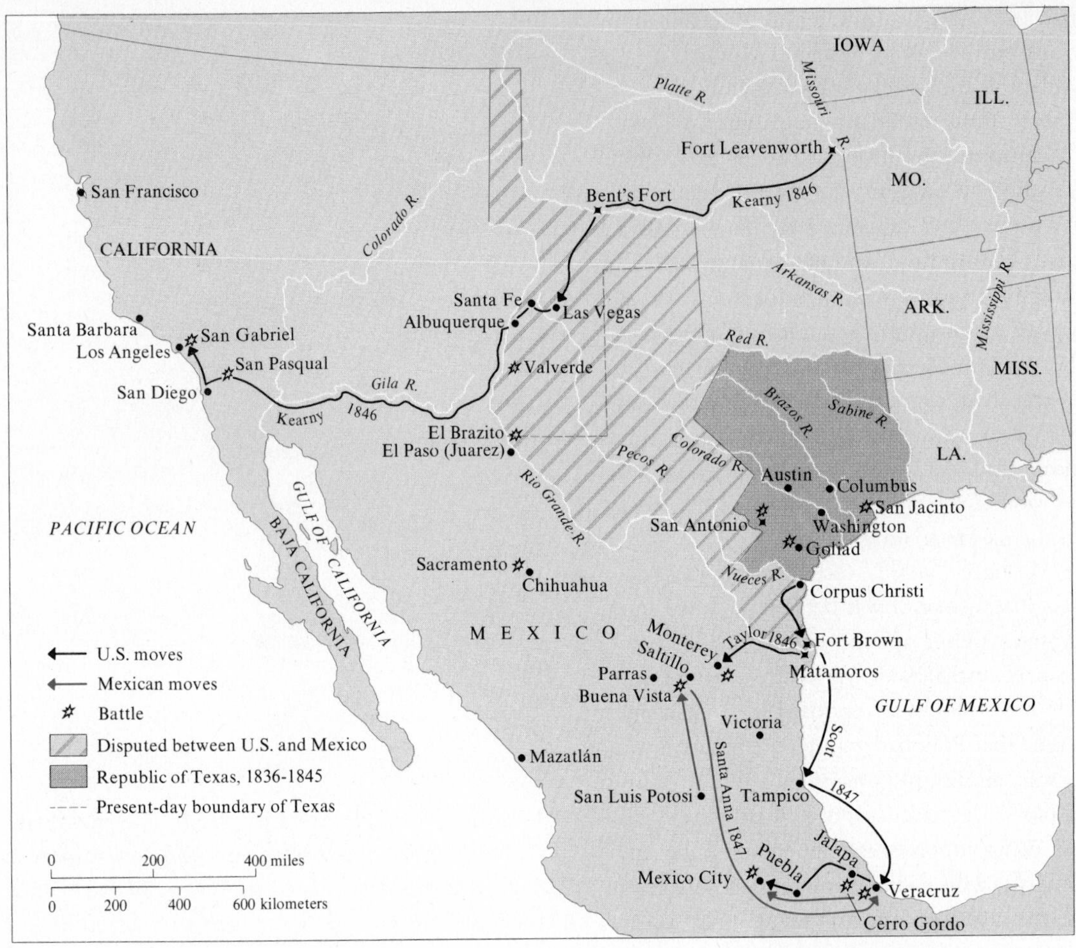

Texas independence and the Mexican War

had already won its plum–Texas. Reformers, charging that expansion was a Slave Power conspiracy, began to find a receptive audience in the North. Under the pressure of these sectional issues, the party unity of both Democrats and Whigs began to loosen. A Democratic faction in New York, for instance, opposed both the annexation of Texas and the war with Mexico.

Early in his administration Polk had renounced a second term, hoping to stem growing factionalism among Democrats. As president, Polk had offered regular Democrats nearly all they could ask–territorial expansion combined with traditional Jacksonian economic policy. He persuaded Congress to reinstitute the independent treasury system and remove protectionist features from the tariff, and he vetoed internal improvements. But one issue was beyond solution by him or anyone else: slavery in the territories. No position could have avoided splintering the Democratic party.

Election of 1848

In the presidental election of 1848, the political agenda changed radically. Prohibition of slavery in the territories was the one overriding issue; it dominated the conventions, the campaign, and the election. The Democrats tried to avoid sectional conflict by nominating General Lewis Cass of Michigan for president and General William O. Butler of Kentucky for vice president. Cass personally favored "squatter sovereignty"–letting the inhabitants of a territory decide the question of slavery themselves. The party platform in turn declared that Congress did

A sailor serving under Commodore Robert F. Stockton sketched this picture of Mexican and American troops clashing in southern California. The battle, a United States victory, brought California under American control. Franklin D. Roosevelt Library.

not have the power to interfere with slavery, and criticized those who pressed the question. Some Democrats broke with the party and nominated former President Van Buren. Also backed by members of the Liberty party and abolitionist Whigs, Van Buren became the Free-Soil candidate. The party slogan was "Free soil, free speech, free labor, and free men."

The regular Whigs nominated General Zachary Taylor, the military hero of the Mexican War and a slaveholding southerner, along with Millard Fillmore for vice president. Though the Whig convention refused to assert congressional power over slavery in the territories, its attempt to avoid the issue proved futile. Van Buren divided the Democratic vote, allowing Taylor to carry states he might not otherwise have won. The former president even outpolled Cass in his home state of Michigan. Again New York, Van Buren's home state, provided the crucial marginal votes–enough to put Taylor in the White House. Antislavery crusaders had influenced the outcome of the election.

The election of 1848 and the conflict over slavery in the territories shaped politics in the 1850s. At the national level, all issues would be seen through the prism of sectional conflict over slavery in the territories. The nation's uncertain attempts to deal with economic and social change would give way to more pressing questions about the nature of the Union itself. And the second party system developed in the 1830s and 1840s would itself succumb to crisis.

Important events

1790s–1840s	Second Great Awakening
1820s	Hudson River School
1824	House of Representatives elects John Quincy Adams president
1825–27	New Harmony, Indiana, experiment
1826	American Society for the Promotion of Temperance founded
1828	Tariff of Abominations Andrew Jackson elected president
1830s–40s	Second party system
1830	Maysville Road bill veto
1831	*Liberator* begins publication
1832	Veto of Second Bank of the United States recharter Jackson re-elected
1832–33	Nullification crisis
1836	Republic of Texas established Martin Van Buren elected president
1837	Financial panic
1837–39	U.S.–Canada border tensions
1837–48	Horace Mann heads Massachusetts Board of Education
1838	Sarah Grimké, *Letters on the Condition of Women and the Equality of the Sexes*
1839–43	Depression
1840	Whigs under William Henry Harrison win presidency
1841–47	Brook Farm
1841	John Tyler assumes the presidency
1844	James K. Polk elected president
1845	Texas admitted to the Union
1846–47	Mormon trek to the Great Salt Lake Valley
1846–48	Mexican War
1846	Oregon Treaty
1848	Treaty of Guadalupe Hidalgo Seneca Falls Convention General Zachary Taylor elected president
1851	Maine Temperance law

Suggestions for further reading

General

Marvin Myers, *The Jacksonian Persuasion: Politics and Belief* (1960); Russel B. Nye, *Society and Culture in America, 1830–1860* (1974); Edward Pessen, *Jacksonian America: Society, Personality, and Politics,* rev. ed. (1979); Arthur M. Schlesinger, Jr., *The Age of Jackson* (1945); John William Ward, *Andrew Jackson: Symbol for an Age* (1955).

Religion and revivalism

Whitney R. Cross, *The Burned-Over District* (1950); Leon A. Jick, *The Americanization of the Synagogue, 1820–1870* (1976); Charles A. Johnson, *The Frontier Camp Meeting* (1955); Paul E. Johnson, *A Shopkeeper's Millennium: Society and Revivals in Rochester, New York, 1815–1837* (1978); William G. McLoughlin, *Revivals, Awakenings, and Reform: An Essay on Religion and Social Change in America, 1607–1977* (1978); Perry Miller, *The Life of the Mind in America: From the Revolution to the Civil War* (1966); Timothy L. Smith, *Revivalism and Social Reform in Mid-Nineteenth Century America* (1957); William W. Sweet, *Revivalism in America* (1949).

Reform

Ray Allen Billington, *The Protestant Crusade, 1800–1860: A Study of the Origins of American Nativism* (1938); Henri Desroche, *The American Shakers from Neo-Christianity to Pre-Socialism* (1971); Clifford S. Griffin, *The Ferment of Reform,*

1830–1860 (1967); Clifford S. Griffin, *Their Brother's Keepers: Moral Stewardship in the United States, 1800–1865* (1960); Gerald N. Grob, *Mental Institutions in America: Social Policy to 1875* (1973); Raymond Muncy, *Sex and Marriage in Utopian Communities: 19th Century America* (1973); David J. Rothman, *The Discovery of the Asylum: Social Order and Disorder in the New Republic* (1971); Wallace Stegner, *The Gathering of Zion: The Story of the Mormon Trail* (1964); Alice Felt Tyler, *Freedom's Ferment* (1944); Ronald G. Walter, *American Reformers, 1815–1860* (1978).

Temperance, education, and feminism

Barbara J. Berg, *The Remembered Gate: Origins of American Feminism. The Woman and the City, 1800–1860* (1977); Lawrence A. Cremin, *American Education: The National Experience, 1783–1876* (1980); Ellen C. Du Bois, *Feminism and Suffrage: The Emergence of an Independent Woman's Movement in America 1848–1869* (1978); Michael Katz, *The Irony of Early School Reform* (1968); Jonathan Messerli, *Horace Mann* (1972); W. J. Rorabaugh, *The Alcoholic Republic: An American Tradition* (1979); Stanley K. Schultz, *The Culture Factory: Boston Public Schools, 1789–1860* (1973); Ian R. Tyrrell, *Sobering Up: From Temperance to Prohibition in Antebellum America, 1800–1860* (1979).

Antislavery and abolitionism

Frederick Douglass, *Life and Times of Frederick Douglass* (1881); Martin Duberman, ed., *The Anti-Slavery Vanguard: New Essays on the Abolitionists* (1965); Aileen S. Kraditor, *Means and Ends in American Abolitionism: Garrison and His Critics on Strategy and Tactics* (1967); Gerda Lerner, *The Grimké Sisters of South Carolina: Rebels Against Slavery* (1967); William H. Pease and Jane H. Pease, *They Would Be Free: Blacks' Search for Freedom, 1830–1861* (1974); Lewis Perry and Michael Fellman, eds., *Antislavery Reconsidered: New Perspectives on the Abolitionists* (1979); Benjamin Quarles, *Black Abolitionists* (1969); Leonard L. Richards, *"Gentlemen of Property and Standing": Anti-Abolition Mobs in Jacksonian America* (1970); John L. Thomas, *The Liberator: William Lloyd Garrison* (1963); Ronald G. Walter, *The Antislavery Appeal: American Abolitionism After 1830* (1976); Bertram Wyatt-Brown, *Lewis Tappan and the Evangelical War Against Slavery* (1969).

Democrats and Whigs

Lee Benson, *The Concept of Jacksonian Democracy: New York as a Test Case* (1964); William R. Brock, *Parties and Political Conscience: American Dilemmas, 1840–1850* (1979); James C. Curtis, *The Fox at Bay: Martin Van Buren and the Presidency, 1837–1841* (1970); Ronald P. Formisano, *The Birth of Mass Political Parties: Michigan, 1827–1861* (1971); William W. Freehling, *Prelude to Civil War: The Nullification Controversy in South Carolina* (1966); Daniel Walker Howe, *The Political Culture of the American Whigs* (1979); Richard B. Latner, *The Presidency of Andrew Jackson: White House Politics, 1829–1837* (1979); Richard P. McCormick, *The Second American Party System: Party Formation in the Jacksonian Era* (1966); Robert V. Remini, *Andrew Jackson* (1966); Robert V. Remini, *Andrew Jackson and the Bank War* (1967); William G. Shade, *Banks or No Banks: The Money Issue in Western Politics, 1832–1865* (1972).

Manifest destiny

K. Jack Bauer, *The Mexican-American War, 1846–1848* (1974); Bernard De Voto, *The Year of Decision, 1846* (1943); Frederick Merk, *Manifest Destiny and Mission in American History: A Reinterpretation* (1963); David M. Pletcher, *The Diplomacy of Annexation: Texas, Oregon, and the Mexican War* (1973); John H. Schroeder, *Mr. Polk's War: American Opposition and Dissent, 1846–1848* (1973); Charles G. Sellers, Jr., *James K. Polk: Continentalist, 1843–1846* (1966); Otis A. Singletary, *The Mexican War* (1960); Albert K. Weinberg, *Manifest Destiny* (1935).

MINNE-
SOTA
OREGON
IOWA
ILLINOIS
INDIA
CALIFORNIA
MISSOURI
KENTUCKY
Addled
KANSAS
ARKANSAS
Sebastian
TEXAS
Houston
Repudiated
Bonds
Jeff. Davis
Beauregard
LOUISIANA
FLORIDA
Mallory

13

THE UNION IN CRISIS: THE 1850s

"This great country will continue united," declared the senator from Mississippi. "Trifling politicians in the South, or in the North, or in the West, may continue to talk otherwise, but it will be of no avail. They are like the mosquitoes around the ox; they annoy, but they cannot wound, and never kill." So spoke Jefferson Davis, the future president of the Confederacy, while traveling through New England in the summer of 1858. Like millions of his fellow citizens, North and South, Davis was intensely proud of America and passionate in his nationalism. The United States "is my country," he said, "and to the innermost fibers of my heart I love it all, and every part." Davis was determined, he said, not to "dwarf myself to mere sectionality."

A more pessimistic statement came from Abraham Lincoln in the winter of 1860. An old friend, Alexander Stephens of Georgia, had written to the president-elect. Fearful that the growing momentum of sectional conflict would soon shatter the Union, Stephens appealed to Lincoln to make some gesture to reassure the South. But Lincoln refused to budge from his party's platform; he was unalterably opposed to the extension of slavery to the territories, though he readily acknowledged its right to exist in the southern states. Replying to Stephens, Lincoln wrote, "You think slavery is *right* and ought to be extended; while we think it is *wrong* and ought to be restricted. That I suppose is the rub." To Lincoln the conflict was fundamental.

Was compromise possible? Throughout the 1850s many Americans, North and South, worked for that end. One school of historians has blamed the outbreak of the Civil War on the failure of a blundering generation of politicians who let the possibilities for peace slip through their fingers. Others, like Lincoln, have argued that the split over slavery was deep-seated and unavoidable. In the words of Republican William H. Seward, it was an "irrepressible conflict" that had to lead to war.

There is evidence to support both interpretations. The politicians made mistakes. They passed laws that sparked unexpected controversy, and they seriously misunderstood each other. Their most critical decisions were often based on miscalculations. But there were also fundamental sectional issues that cropped up repeatedly. Some opinions could not have been compromised by even the wisest of leaders.

Circumstances worked against the peacemakers. Though northerners and southerners strove to avoid conflict over slavery, westward expansion continually injected their disagreement into politics by raising the question of whether slavery would be allowed in the territories. This recurring crisis eventually convinced each side that its very way of life was jeopardized. Northerners envisioned a Slave Power intent on trampling basic liberties; southerners imagined that northerners would not stop until they had abolished slavery everywhere. Finally, changes in the political party system magnified sectional divisions. These forces jointly caused far more damage to the Union than they could have separately.

In the 1850s sectional pressures built until they eventually overwhelmed the capacity of the changing political system to deal with them. The result was a tragedy–civil war–that most American voters in 1860 clearly did not want.

The sources of conflict

The bitter debate over the morality of slavery was one cause of sectional strife. Profound questions of morality, social responsibility, and national purpose were at issue. At times the debate was explosive.

In the 1830s and 1840s, a growing body of northern abolitionists–male and female, black and white–had preached against slavery, condemning it as a sin. "There is but one remedy for sin," the mathematician and reformer Elizur Wright, Jr., had warned slaveholders, "and that is available only by a repentance, evidenced by reformation." These missionaries spoke in thousands of churches and public halls, slowly winning converts, indicting slavery as a moral wrong that brutalized all who came in contact with it.

Debate over the morality of slavery

Stung by such criticism, southern slaveowners denied any wrongdoing, asserting that their slaves were well cared-for and protected. Some even argued that slavery was a social good. One of South Carolina's governors declared servitude to be an "essential constituent" of "all political communities." Senator John C. Calhoun agreed, calling slavery "a universal condition," and jurist William Harper wrote in 1837 that "the exclusive owners of property . . . ought to be the virtual rulers of mankind." Added Harper, "It is as much the order of nature that men should enslave each other as that animals should prey upon each other." Even more extreme were the pronouncements of a Virginian named George Fitzhugh, who analyzed relations between management and labor in both the North and the South and concluded that wage labor in industry was more inhumane than slavery. Fitzhugh went so far as to claim that slavery ought to be practiced in all societies, whatever their racial composition.

These arguments generated strong emotions, but they were not central to the conflict that eventually divided the Union. The abolitionists were significant because they were a growing minority opposed in principle to the status quo. Proslavery advocates also wanted change: greater security and acceptance of their institution. Both constituted a threat to political stability. But their argument was only one cause of sectional strife, and a small one at that. Most northerners were racists, not abolitionists, and most southerners paid scant attention to proslavery theories. The issue that ultimately led to disunion was more obscure and complicated than the morality of slavery. That issue was slavery in the territories.

Throughout the 1850s quarrels over the territories cropped up repeatedly. Abolitionists and proslavery advocates were too weak to impose their views on each other in the states, but the territories provided them a ready battleground. Americans kept moving west, prompting Congress to create new territories. Thus westward expansion guaranteed that controversy would arise over and over again. The prizes in these contests were both tangible and intangible. On achieving statehood, each territory elected two senators who would support either slavery or freedom in Washington. This gain directly affected sectional power. Indirectly, there was the prestige of victory, of extending influence. Some slaveowners dreamed of a West built on slave-based agriculture and mining; northerners envisioned a frontier of free-labor farms.

Debate over slavery in the territories

Ironically, the territorial question had only limited practical significance. Few slaves entered any territory during the 1850s, and many areas had few white settlers. Thus the territorial issue in itself was probably manageable. Its explosive power lay in its capacity to stir up other issues and arouse other fears.

The prospect of slaves in the territories broadened the dispute over slavery to matters of basic American liberties. It brought the conflict home to northerners who had little interest in abolition or westward migration. And it spread fear of an aggressive Slave Power. Abolitionists constantly warned of a threatening Slave Power; issues like slavery in the territories made the threat credible.

The Slave Power idea postulated a slaveholding oligarchy in control of the South and intent on controlling the nation. The evidence for such domination lay in the persecution of southern dissenters and the suppression of their ideas. Evidence for the oligarchy's desire to extend its control could be found in efforts to reopen the African slave trade and to acquire territory in the Caribbean, as well as in extreme proslavery arguments. A few slaveowners who wanted more slaves were saying that if Africans were unavailable, whites would do. Eventually, warned abolitionists, these southern oligarchs would consolidate their power, take over the government, deprive the middle and lower classes of their rights, and extend slavery nationwide.

Fear of a Slave Power

The Slave Power's assault on northern liberties was said to have begun in 1836, when Congress passed the gag rule (see page 319). White northerners, even those who saw nothing wrong with slavery, interpreted John Quincy Adams's stand against the rule as a defense of their rights. Each subsequent demand for slave territory or protection of slaveholders' interests was seen in light of the Slave Power thesis.

Fear of the sinister Slave Power transformed the abolitionist impulse into a broader and more influential antislavery movement. It turned people who were not abolitionists—who were in fact often racists—into opponents of slavery. These northern whites were seeking to protect themselves, not southern blacks, from the Slave Power. As the prevailing issues shifted away from the morality of slavery, they excited larger numbers of people: more northerners cared about the Slave Power than about the extension of slavery, and more cared about slavery extension than about abolition. In the form of territorial controversies, issues that had at first alarmed only a few claimed the attention of many.

Meanwhile, northerners and southerners were developing ideologies—ways of viewing the world—that hardened the lines of conflict. Northerners looked at their own growing population, booming industries, and increasing prosperity and thought they saw an explanation for it: the free labor system. Free labor and a free society seemed to be the key to progress. By contrast, the slave South appeared retrograde. Responding to this northern insult and a worldwide trend of opinion against slavery, southerners sprang to the defense of their society. They praised its traditions and stability, its order, and its devotion to the Constitution. The South, many of its leaders believed, was the true defender of constitutional principles, which runaway change in the North was subverting. On both sides, these increasingly influential ideologies lessened the possibility for compromise.

Conflicting ideologies

On top of all these conflicts came the unsettling impact of structural change in the political system. At a time when the nation most needed political institutions capable of handling a crisis, these institutions were themselves undergoing change. The second party system, which had blunted conflict successfully in the past, fell to pieces during the 1850s. Its collapse was only a symptom of the sectional crisis, but the system that replaced it made the crisis worse. Americans scrambled to form and adjust to new institutions, only to end up with a system that failed to promote unity. Indeed, the new system overstated sectional divisions and added momentum to the crisis.

Demise of the second party system

This political restructuring was forced by the demise of the Whig party. Though blessed with influential congressional representatives, the Whigs had lacked commanding presidents in an era of strong leaders like Jackson and Polk. The deaths of President Taylor (1850), Webster (1852), and Clay (1852) deprived them of their most renowned figures just as sectional discord split the party into southern and northern wings. Unable to recover from these blows, the Whig party fell apart, never to field a national candidate after 1852. A variety of new parties—Free-Soilers, Know-Nothings, and then Republicans—vied to replace them.

Although the Whig party disappeared, former Whigs accounted for approximately half the electorate, a magnificent prize for competing political organizations. The Whigs were emotionally unable to join the Democrats after fighting them vigorously for two decades, but they had to go somewhere. Thus the new parties stressed a variety of issues chosen to appeal to homeless Whigs. Immigration, temperance, homestead bills, the tariff, internal improvements—all played an important role in attracting voters during the 1850s. For many Americans it was these issues, not the controversy over slavery, that were the real stuff of politics.

But this process of party building had one crucial implication: if voters joined organizations that took strong sectional stands, they added to the sectional confrontation whether the issue of slavery seemed important to them or not. And that is exactly what happened. In the North, appeals to economic individualism and nativism brought into the Republican party many people who did not regard slavery as a primary issue. Nevertheless, they swelled the ranks of an organization whose stand was antislavery. In the South, Democratic leaders made a successful appeal to states' rights slaveholders, and the Democrats emerged as the only viable party in the region. The development of a one-party system in the South also magnified sectional divisions and obscured southern support for the Union.

Thus the interrelated problems of the 1850s reinforced each other and grew more dangerous and difficult. An examination of the decade's events will reveal how the issues shifted, intensified, and intertwined as the conflict escalated.

Sectional problems are compromised but re-emerge

The first sectional battle of the decade involved the territory of California. More than eighty thousand Americans flooded into California in 1849. President Taylor, seeing a simple solution to the challenge of governing lands acquired from Mexico, urged the settlers to apply for admission to the Union. They promptly did so, submitting a proposed state constitution that did not allow for slavery. But southern politicians wanted to make California slave territory, or at least to extend the Missouri Compromise line west through California. Representatives from nine southern states met in an unofficial convention in Nashville to assert the South's right to part of the territory.

Wilmot Proviso

Fourteen northern legislatures, on the other hand, were equally determined to keep slavery out of the new territories. They had endorsed the Wilmot Proviso, an amendment to a military appropriations bill proposed by Representative David Wilmot of Pennsylvania in 1846. Wilmot's proviso stated simply that slavery should be prohibited from any territory won from Mexico. Though it did not pass Congress, it became the rallying cry for free-soilers and attracted considerable support in the North. Thus the issue was joined.

Sensing that the Union was in peril, the venerable Whig leader Henry Clay marshalled his energies once more. Twice before, in 1820 and 1833, the "Great Pacificator" had taken the lead in shaping sectional compromise; now he labored one last time to preserve the nation. To hushed Senate galleries Clay presented a series of compromise measures, balancing the issues of California and nearby territories, the Texan boundary claim, runaway slaves, and the slave trade in the District of Columbia. Over the weeks that followed, Clay and Senator Stephen A. Douglas of Illinois steered the proposals through debate and amendment, persisting despite serious reverses. Line by line, concerned and angry senators hammered out the final language of the bills.

The problems to be solved were thorny indeed. Would California or a part of it become a free state? How should the land acquired from Mexico be organized? Texas, which allowed slavery, claimed large portions of the new land as far west as Santa Fe, so that too had to be settled. And in addition to southern complaints about fugitive slaves and northern objections to the sale of human beings in the nation's capital, the lawmakers had to deal with competing theories of settlers' rights in the territories. It was these theories that proved most troublesome in the continuing debate over the territories.

Popular sovereignty

In 1847 Lewis Cass (the Democratic candidate for president the following year) had introduced the idea of popular sovereignty. Though Congress had to approve statehood for a territory, it should "in the meantime," Cass said, allow the people living there "to regulate their own concerns in their own way." These few words, seemingly clear, proved highly ambiguous, disagreement centering on the meaning of "meantime."

When could settlers bar slavery? Southerners claimed equal rights in the territories; therefore neither Congress nor a territorial legislature could bar slavery. Only when settlers framed a state constitution could they take that step. Northerners, meanwhile, argued that Americans living in a territory were entitled to local self-government, and thus could outlaw slavery at any time, if they allowed it at all. To avoid dissension within their party, northern and southern Democrats had explained Cass's statement to their constituents in these two incompatible ways. Their conflicting interpretations caused strong disagreement in the debate on Clay's proposals.

Compromise of 1850

Despite bitter debate, the Compromise of 1850 finally passed (see map, 344). California was admitted as a free state, and the Texan boundary was set at its present limits. The United States paid Texas $10 million in consideration of the boundary agreement. And the territories of New Mexico and Utah were organized with power to legislate on "all rightful subjects ... consistent with the Constitution." A stronger fugitive slave law and an act to suppress the slave trade in the District of Columbia completed the compromise.

Jubilation greeted passage of the Compromise of 1850; in Washington, crowds celebrated the happy news. "On one glorious night," records a contemporary historian, "the word went abroad that it was the duty of every patriot to get drunk. Before the next morning many a citizen had proved his patriotism," and several prominent senators "were reported stricken with a variety of implausible maladies–headaches, heat prostration, or overindulgence in fruit."

In reality, there was less cause for celebration than citizens thought. Fundamentally, the Compromise of 1850 was not a settlement of sectional disputes. It was at best an artful evasion. Though the compromise bought time for the nation, it did not create guidelines for the settlement of subsequent territorial questions. It merely put them off.

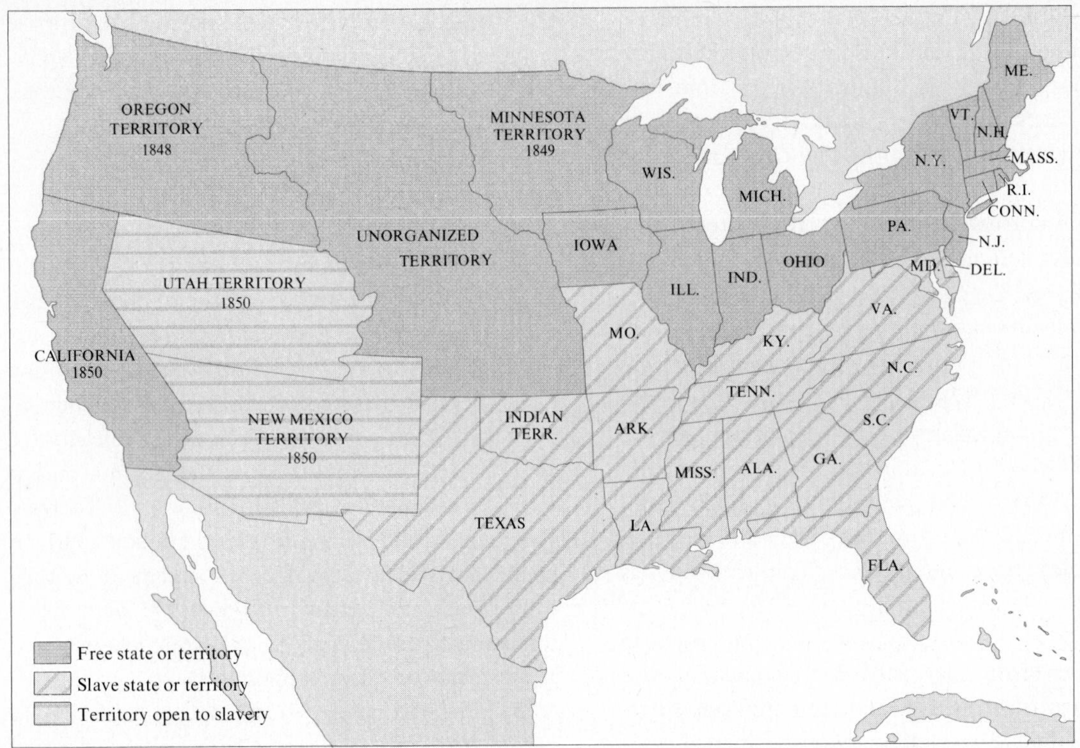

The Compromise of 1850

Furthermore, the compromise had two basic flaws. The first pertained to popular sovereignty. What were "rightful subjects of legislation, consistent with the Constitution"? During debate, southerners had defined them one way, northerners another. After passage of the compromise, legislators from the two sections went home and continued to define these words in two different ways, as if there were two different compromises. (In fact, the compromise admitted the disagreement by providing for the appeal of a territorial legislature's action to the Supreme Court. But no such case ever arose.) Thus, in the controversy over popular sovereignty, nothing had been settled. In one politician's words, the legislators seemed to have enacted a lawsuit instead of a law.

Fugitive Slave Act

The second flaw lay in the Fugitive Slave Act, which stirred up controversy instead of laying it to rest. The new law empowered slaveowners to go into court in their own states and present evidence that a slave who owed them service had escaped. The transcript of such a proceeding, including a description of the fugitive, was to be taken as conclusive proof of a person's slave status, even in free states and territories. Legal authorities had to decide only whether the black person brought before them was the person described, not whether he or she was indeed a slave. Fines and penalties encouraged U.S. marshals to assist in apprehending fugitives and discouraged citizens from harboring them. (Authorities were paid $10 if the alleged fugitive was turned over to the slaveowner, $5 if he was not.)

Abolitionist newspapers quickly attacked the fugitive slave law as a violation of the Bill of Rights. Why were alleged fugitives denied a trial by jury before being sent to bondage in a slave state? Why did suspected fugitives have no right to present evidence or cross-examine witnesses? Did not the law give authorities a financial incentive to turn prisoners over to slaveowners? These arguments convinced some northerners that free blacks could be sent into slavery, mistakenly or otherwise, with no means to defend themselves. Protest meetings were held in Massachusetts, New York, Pennsylvania, northern Ohio, northern Illinois, and elsewhere. In Boston in 1851, a mob grabbed a runaway slave from a U.S. marshal and sent him to safety in Canada.

At this point a novice writer dramatized the plight of the slave in a way that captured the sympathies of millions of northerners. Harriet Beecher Stowe, daughter of a religious New England family that had produced many prominent ministers, wrote *Uncle Tom's Cabin* out of deep moral conviction. Her book,

Uncle Tom's Cabin

published in March 1852, showed how slavery brutalized the men and women who suffered under it. Stowe also portrayed slavery's evil effects on slaveholders, indicting the institution itself more harshly than the southerners caught in its web. In nine months the book sold over 300,000 copies; by mid-1853, over a million. Countless people saw *Uncle Tom's Cabin* performed as a stage play or read similar novels inspired by it. Stowe had brought the issue of slavery home to many who had never before given it much thought.

At the same time, the policies of the newly elected Pierce administration revived sectional disputes. In 1852 Franklin Pierce, a Democrat from New Hampshire, won a smashing victory over the Whig presidential nominee, General Winfield Scott. Pierce backed the Compromise of 1850, believing that the defense of each section's rights was essential to the nation's unity. Scott was remembered as the conqueror of Mexico City but his views were unknown, and the Free-Soil candidate, John P. Hale of New Hampshire, openly repudiated the compromise. Thus Pierce's victory seemed to confirm most Americans' support for the Compromise of 1850.

But Pierce did not seem able to avoid sectional conflict. His proposal for a transcontinental railroad ran into congressional dispute over where it should be built, North or South. His attempts to acquire foreign territory stirred up more trouble. An annexation treaty with Hawaii failed because southern senators would not vote for another free state, and Pierce's efforts to annex Cuba angered antislavery northerners. Pierce tried to purchase Cuba from Spain in 1854. When publication of a government document revealed that three administration officials had rashly talked of "wresting" Cuba from Spain, some northerners concluded that Pierce was determined to acquire more slave territory.

CAUTION!!

COLORED PEOPLE

OF BOSTON, ONE & ALL,

You are hereby respectfully CAUTIONED and advised, to avoid conversing with the

Watchmen and Police Officers of Boston,

For since the recent ORDER OF THE MAYOR & ALDERMEN, they are empowered to act as

KIDNAPPERS

AND

Slave Catchers,

And they have already been actually employed in KIDNAPPING, CATCHING, AND KEEPING SLAVES. Therefore, if you value your LIBERTY, and the *Welfare of the Fugitives* among you, *Shun* them in every possible manner, as so many *HOUNDS* on the track of the most unfortunate of your race.

Keep a Sharp Look Out for KIDNAPPERS, and have TOP EYE open.

***APRIL* 24, 1851.**

This broadside reveals northern outrage over the Fugitive Slave Act. The reference to kidnappers stems from the fear that free blacks would be transported into slavery under the law. Library of Congress.

But the shattering blow to sectional harmony originated in Congress, when Senator Stephen Douglas introduced a bill to organize the Kansas and Nebraska territories. Douglas, a rising Illinois Democrat and

Kansas-Nebraska Act

potential presidential candidate, hoped for a midwestern transcontinental railroad to boost Chicago's economy and encourage settlement on the Great Plains. A necessary precondition for a railroad was the organization of the territory it would cross. Thus it was probably in the interest of building such a railroad that Douglas introduced a bill that inflamed sectional passions, completed the destruction of the Whig party, damaged the northern wing of the Democratic party, gave birth to the Republican party, and injured his own national ambitions.

The Kansas-Nebraska bill exposed the first flaw of the Compromise of 1850, and conflict over popular

An advertisement for *Uncle Tom's Cabin* indicates the tremendous effect of the book on the general public. The New-York Historical Society.

sovereignty erupted once more. Douglas's bill clearly left "all questions pertaining to slavery in the Territories . . . to the people residing therein," but northerners and southerners still disagreed violently over what territorial settlers could constitutionally do. Moreover, the Kansas-Nebraska bill opened a new Pandora's box by explicitly repealing the Missouri Compromise. The new territories lay within the Louisiana Purchase, and under the compromise of 1820 all that land from 36°30′ north to the Canadian border was off-limits to slavery. Douglas believed that conditions of climate and soil would effectively keep slavery out of Kansas and Nebraska. But from a legal point of view his bill threw land open to slavery where it had been prohibited before.

Even Douglas sensed that his measure would raise "a hell of a storm," but he was able to obtain the endorsement of a careless President Pierce. After a titanic struggle lasting almost six months, the bill passed both houses and was signed into law in May 1854 (see map).

Unfortunately the storm—far more violent than Douglas had imagined—was only beginning. The Kansas-Nebraska Act inflamed fears and angers that had only simmered before. Abolitionists charged that the act was sinister aggression by the Slave Power, its

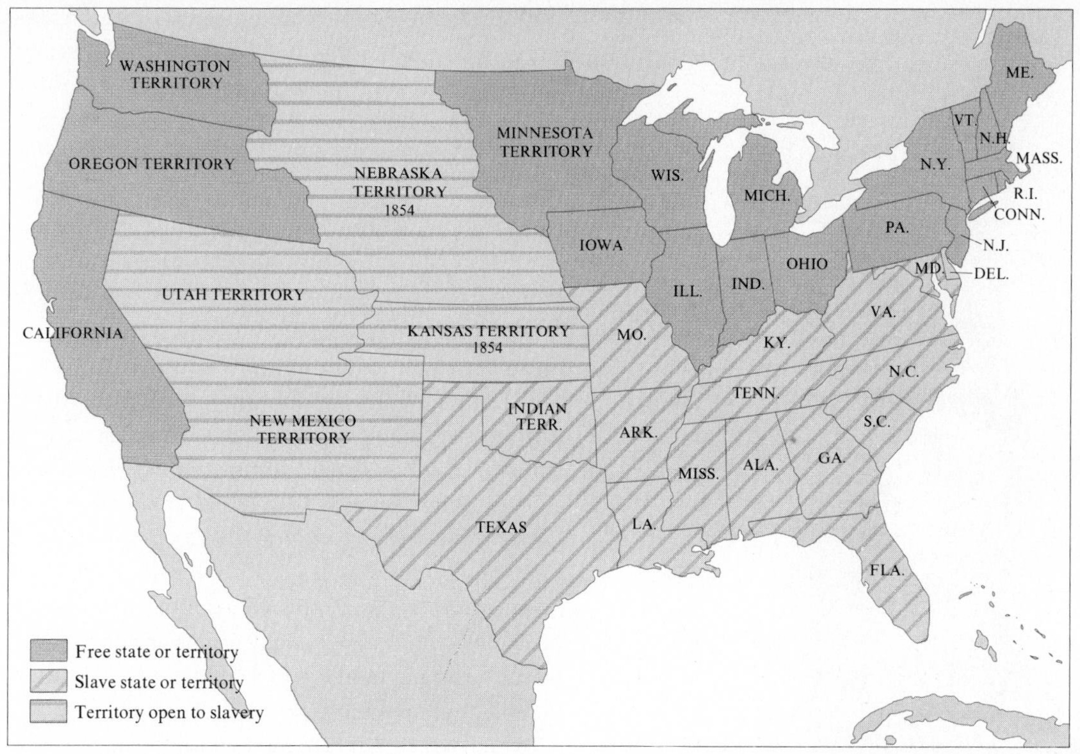

The Kansas-Nebraska Act, 1854

most brazen yet. Concern over the fugitive slave law deepened: between 1855 and 1859 Connecticut, Rhode Island, Massachusetts, Michigan, Maine, Ohio, and Wisconsin passed personal liberty laws designed to interfere with the swift action of the Fugitive Slave Act. These laws, which provided counsel for alleged fugitives and sought to guarantee trial by jury, revealed the strength of northern fear of the Slave Power. To the South, they were outrageous signs of bad faith. Even more important, however, was the devastating impact of the Kansas-Nebraska Act on political parties.

Political realignment

The Kansas-Nebraska Act divided the Whig party's northern and southern wings so irrevocably that it fell apart shortly thereafter. The Democrats survived, but they suffered at the polls in 1854 for their role in the legislation. Although southern Democrats retained most of the offices they held, northern Democrats lost sixty-six of the ninety-one congressional seats they had won in free states in 1852. A Democrat, James Buchanan, was elected president in 1856, but he owed his victory to southern support. Eleven of sixteen free states voted against him, and Democrats did not regain power in those states for decades.

Moreover, anger over the territorial issue created a new political party. During debate on the Kansas-Nebraska bill, six congressmen had published an "Appeal of the Independent Democrats" attacking Douglas's legislation as "a gross violation of a sacred pledge" (the Missouri Compromise) and a "criminal betrayal of precious rights" that would make free territory a "dreary region of despotism." This appeal sparked other protests. In the summer and fall of 1854, antislavery Whigs and Democrats, free-soilers, and other reformers throughout the Northwest met to form a new Republican party, dedicated to keeping slavery out of the territories. The Republicans' influence rapidly spread to the East, and they won a stunning victory in the 1854 elections. In the party's

A Know-Nothing campaign ribbon. Note the pictures of Washington and the American eagle, references to the early days of the republic. The eagle holds a banner reading "Beware of foreign influence." Edmund B. Sullivan Collection, University of Hartford.

first appearance on the ballot, Republicans captured a majority of House seats in the North.

For the first time, a sectional party based on a sectional issue had gained significant power in the political system. In the second party system, the national base of support enjoyed by both Whigs and Democrats had moderated sectional conflict. The two parties had always patched up sectional differences in order to compete more effectively for national office. But the Whigs were gone, and politics in the 1850s would never be the same.

Nor were Republicans the only new party. An anti-immigrant organization, the American party, seemed likely for a few years to replace the Whigs. This party, also known as the Know-Nothings (because its members at first kept their purposes secret, answering all queries with the words "I know nothing"), exploited nativist fear of foreigners. Between 1848 and 1860, nearly 3.5 million immigrants came to the United States—proportionally the heaviest influx of foreigners in American history (see pages 287–291). The Democratic party diligently ministered to the needs of these new citizens and relied on their votes in elections. But native Americans harbored serious misgivings about them. The temperance movement gained new strength early in these years, promising to stamp out the evils associated with liquor and immigrants. It was in this context that the Know-Nothings became prominent, campaigning to reinforce Protestant morality and restrict voting and officeholding to the native-born.

Know-Nothings

By the mid-1850s the American party was powerful and growing; in 1854 so many new congressmen won office with anti-immigrant as well as antislavery support that Know-Nothings could claim they outnumbered Republicans. In 1856 the Know-Nothing candidate for president, Millard Fillmore, won almost a million votes and ran a close third behind the Republican candidate, John C. Frémont, who garnered 1.3 million. The winner, Democrat James Buchanan, who benefited from superior party organization and a diplomatic assignment that had removed him from domestic controversy, captured fewer than 2 million votes. But like the Whigs, the Know-Nothings could not keep their northern and southern wings together, and they melted away after 1856. That left the field to the Republicans, who wooed nativists and in several states passed temperance ordinances and laws postponing suffrage for naturalized citizens (see table).

The Republicans also appealed to groups interested in the economic development of the West. Commercial agriculture was booming in the Ohio-Mississippi-Great Lakes area, but residents of that region needed more canals, roads, and river and harbor improvements to reap the full benefit of their labors. There was also widespread interest in a federal land-grant program: credit was

Republicans

Political Successors to the Whig Party

PARTY	PERIOD OF INFLUENCE	AREA OF INFLUENCE	OUTCOME
Free-Soil party	1848–1854	North	Merged with Republican party
Know-Nothings (American party)	1853–1856	Nationwide	Disappeared, freeing some northern voters to join Republican party
Republican party	1854–present	North (later nationwide)	Became rival of Democratic party in third party system

scarce, and proponents argued that western land should be made available free to whoever would use it. The Whigs had favored all these things before their party collapsed, but the Democrats resolutely opposed them. Following long-standing Democratic principles, presidents Pierce and Buchanan vetoed internal improvements bills, and Buchanan vetoed a homestead bill passed by Congress in 1859. Seizing their opportunity, the Republicans added internal-improvements and land-grant planks to their platform. They also backed higher tariffs as an enticement to industrialists and businessmen, whose interest in tariffs was quickened by a panic, or recession, in 1857.

Thus the Republican party picked up support from a variety of sources. Opposition to the extension of slavery had brought the party together, but party members carefully broadened their appeal by adopting the causes of other groups, whether or not those groups were alarmed by slavery. They were wise to do so. As the newspaper editor Horace Greeley wrote in 1856, "It is beaten into my bones that the American people are not yet anti-slavery." In 1860 Greeley observed again, "An Anti-Slavery man *per se* cannot be elected." But, he added, "a Tariff, River-and-Harbor, Pacific Railroad, Free Homestead man, *may* succeed *although* he is Anti-Slavery."

Greeley's last remark was insightful. The Republican party was an amalgam of many interests, but functionally it had only one stand in the North-South controversy. Since a high proportion of the original activist Republicans were strongly opposed to slavery, the party's position on slavery and the territories was immune to change. Thus all Republicans, whatever their reasons for joining the coalition, weighed as antislavery voters in the minds of nervous southerners. Republican strength was antislavery strength.

A similar process was under way in the South. The disintegration of the Whig party had left many southerners at loose ends politically. Much of the support for Whigs had come from wealthy planters and small-town businessmen and slaveholders. Some of these people gravitated to the American party, but not for long. In the increasingly tense atmosphere of sectional crisis, they were highly susceptible to strong states' rights positions, which provided a handy defense for slavery. Democratic leaders markedly increased their

This Republican banner shows the party's effort to broaden its appeal through issues like the tariff and fear of the Slave Power. The man in the picture is the Republican presidential candidate of 1856, John C. Frémont. Ontario County Historical Society.

Southern Democrats

use of such appeals during the 1850s, and managed to convert most of the formerly Whig slaveholders. Democrats spoke to the class interests of slaveholders, and the slaveholders responded.

Most Democrats south of the Mason-Dixon line, however, were not slaveholders. Yeomen had been the heart of the party since Andrew Jackson's day, and Democratic politicians, though often slaveowners themselves, had lauded the common man and appeared to champion his interests. Now the entry into the party of large numbers of anxious slaveholders threatened to change its character. But the yeomen did not immediately object to their strange bedfellows. Republican stands did not appeal to them. Their party loyalties were strong, and as long as political issues were not posed in a class-conscious way, they did not become restive.

Slaveholding Democrats were careful not to pursue their interests as class interests. On the contrary, they portrayed the sectional controversies as matters involving insult and injustice to all southerners. Their ultimate weapon—one they had been using in moments of danger for three decades—was the appeal to race prejudice. For years they had argued, as Jefferson Davis put it in 1851, that slavery elevated the status of the nonslaveholder and enabled the poor man to "*stand upon the broad-level of equality with the rich man.*" Now, as the sectional crisis heated up, slaveholders warned that the overriding issue was "shall negroes govern white men, or white men govern negroes?" The Montgomery *Mail* blatantly claimed that the aim of the Republicans was "to free the negroes and force amalgamation between them and the children of the poor men of the South. The rich will be able to keep out of the way of the contamination."

These arguments had some effect, at least as long as nonslaveholders perceived outside forces as their greatest threat. The result was a one-party system in the South that emphasized sectional issues. Racial fears and traditional political loyalties kept this political alliance between yeomen and planters intact through the 1850s. The latent question–would nonslaveholders be willing to fight to protect slaveholders' property–was not openly expressed during the decade. Instead, in the South as in the North, political realignment obscured support for the Union and made sectional divisions seem sharper and deeper than they really were.

Free labor versus proslavery theory

While the new political parties were emerging, northerners and southerners were also developing opposing ideologies. The Republicans spoke to the image northerners had of themselves, their society, and their future when they preached "Free Soil, Free Labor, Free Men." These ideas resonated with the traditional American ideals of freedom, opportunity, and individualism, undercutting charges that the Republican party was radical and unreliable.

The Republican emphasis on individualism took root easily because in the 1850s the northern economy was energetic, expanding, and prosperous. Untold thousands of farmers had moved west to establish productive farms and growing communities. Midwestern farmers were using machines that multiplied their yields. Railroads were carrying their crops to market. And industry was beginning to perform wonders of production, making available goods that had hitherto been beyond the reach of the average person. To most northerners, the economic system seemed to be working spendidly.

The key element in this successful economy seemed, in the eyes of many, to be free labor. People believed in the dignity of labor. Any hard-working,

Free labor

virtuous person, it was thought, could improve his condition and gain economic independence by applying himself to any of the numerous opportunities the country had to offer. And to a great extent popular opinion was correct. The scale of most business operations was small, and abundant fertile land lay to the west. Monopolies and mammoth industrial firms were still things of the future. Economically it was a good age for the individual, and those who labored generally did make progress.

Republicans took advantage of this boom and formulated an ideology that captured much of the spirit of the age. They praised workers and encouraged their ambitions, holding up Abraham Lincoln as an example of a person of humble origins who had improved his lot. They portrayed their party as the guardian of economic opportunity, working to ensure that individuals could continue to apply their energies to the land's resources and attain success. In the words of an Iowa Republican, the United States was thriving because its "door is thrown open to all, and even the poorest and humblest in the land, may, by industry and application, gain a position which will entitle him to the respect and confidence of his fellow-men."

Republicans who declared their determination to help the independent entrepreneur saw no conflict between the interests of labor and capital. They relied on an old Whig idea, the harmony of economic interests, to justify the capitalistic system. According to this theory, farms and factories benefited each other, and the tariff safeguarded the jobs of American workers. "I rise to advocate the rights of labor," said a Pennsylvania representative speaking for the tariff in 1860, and his words were not wholly insincere. If free labor, economic individualism, and opportunity were protected, even propertyless workers could save money, buy property, and command the means of production.

Thus the fate of the territories was crucial to the nation's future. The North's free-labor economic system had to be extended to the territories if coming generations were to prosper. After all, the territories were the great reservoir of opportunity for decent people without means. To allow an aristocratic system of bondage and forced labor to enter the territories would be to poison the reservoir.

Thus Republican ideology encompassed an image of the South as well as the North. In fact, Republicans clarified their image of themselves by comparing their society to the slaveholding regions. For what they saw in the South was often the antithesis of what they valued in the North. The southern aristocracy, they felt,

An illustration from the *American Anti-Slavery Almanac* showing southern society as an unrelieved succession of slave torture, duels, lynchings, gambling, and cockfighting. Such blatant propaganda reinforced Republican fearmongering in the North. Library of Congress.

defied equality and denied opportunity; proslavery theories posited a static, oppressive society rather than a developing and open one.

Southerners, meanwhile, had their own views. Abraham Lincoln clipped this description of northern society from a southern newspaper and put it into his political scrapbook:

> Free society! We sicken of the name! What is it but a conglomeration of greasy mechanics, filthy operatives, small-fisted farmers, and moon-struck theorists? All the Northern and especially the New England states are devoid of society fitted for well bred gentlemen. The prevailing class one meets is that of mechanics struggling to be genteel, and small farmers who do their own drudgery; and yet are hardly fit for association with a southern gentleman's body servant.

Influential southerners were, in fact, developing an ideology of their own. At its heart this ideology did not depend on proslavery theories, though southerners often invoked such theories to defend their region. Nor did it arise from territorial aspirations, though southerners insisted that they needed to expand west. Behind their ideology lay a deep fear that their way of life was about to collapse. Among southern representatives, state officials, and slaveholders generally, the feeling was growing that slavery was in jeopardy. The need to defend the institution became an obsession.

Slaveholders tended to see the world from the perspective of their plantations. Human bondage was so central to their world that life without slavery was almost unimaginable to them. They had built their fortunes and their society on the institution of slavery, and they wanted to keep the world they knew. But as intelligent men, southern leaders could not help but be aware of the worldwide movement away from slavery and the powerful forces gathering against it within the United States. Accordingly, they fought every battle in the sectional crisis with a white-hot intensity, for they knew what was ultimately at stake. In so doing they defended a whole range of propositions they did not truly believe in, all to protect the vital institution that supported their world.

By the 1850s virtually all southern representatives were familiar with the latest arguments in proslavery theory. At a moment's notice they could discuss the

Proslavery theory

anthropological evidence for the separate origin of the races; physicians' views on the inferiority of the black body; and sociological arguments for the superiority of the slave-labor system. But in private and in their hearts, most of these men fell back on two rationales: a belief that blacks were inferior and biblical accounts of slaveholding. Among friends, Jefferson Davis ignored all the latest racist theories and reverted to the eighteenth-century argument that southerners were doing the best they could with a situation they had inherited. "Is it well to denounce an evil for which there is no cure?" he asked. On another occasion, repeating the widespread belief that living with a sizeable free black population was impossible, he protested to a friend that Congress never discussed "any thing but that over which we have no control, slavery of the negro."

The South's defenders also developed a set of arguments to prove the necessity of expanding slavery into the territories. Expansion was essential to the welfare of the Negro, they declared, for prejudice lessened where the concentration of blacks decreased. It was necessary to the prosperity of the South, they argued, for rich opportunities lay waiting in the territories, while older areas of declining fertility had surplus slave populations. Yet there was a noticeable absence of huge migrations of slaveholders into the territories. A more likely cause of southern concern over the territories was the fear that if areas like Kansas became free soil, they would be used as a base from which to spread abolitionism into the slave states. Jefferson Davis voiced such a concern when he wrote in 1855 that "abolitionism would gain but little in excluding slavery from the territories, if it were never to disturb that institution in the States."

Southern leaders also spent a great deal of time commenting on the superior social values and practices of their region. Whereas the North was cold, materialistic, unstable, and polluted with radicalism and intellectual fads, the South was warm, caring (thanks to its practice of paternalism), and solidly devoted to home, family, and Christianity. The turmoil and change of northern life had evidently unhinged northern minds, these critics said. Even so, their arguments were primarily rebuttals of northern criticism. And many aspects of their thought—as well as the growing southern emphasis on woman's place in the home—were intended not so much to celebrate southern virtues as to suppress potential criticism from within.

But southern leaders' chief tool in defending slavery was constitutional theory. They developed an interpretation of the Constitution and the principles of American government that linked them to the founding fathers and the original purposes of the nation. Drawing on Thomas Jefferson's concept of strict construction, they emphasized that the nation arose from a compact among sovereign states; that the states were primary and the central government secondary; that the states retained all powers not expressly granted to the central government; and that the states were to be treated equally, and the rights of their citizens respected equally. Along with these theories went the philosophy that the power of the federal government should be kept to a minimum. By keeping government close to home, southerners hoped to keep slavery safe.

But as the 1850s advanced, a growing portion of slaveholders became convinced that slavery could not be protected within the Union. Such concern was not new. As early as 1838, the Louisiana planter Bennet Barrow had written in his diary, "Northern States medling with slavery . . . openly speaking of the sin of Slavery in the southern states . . . must eventually cause a separation of the Union." And in 1856, a calmer, more polished Georgian named Charles Colcock Jones, Jr., rejoiced at the Democrat James Buchanan's defeat of Republican John C. Frémont for the presidency. The result guaranteed four more years of peace and prosperity, wrote Jones, but "beyond that period . . . we scarce dare expect a continuance of our present relations." Increasingly slaveowners agreed with Jones and Barrow, accurately sensing that opposition to slavery was spreading in the North. Although Republicans disavowed any intention of disturbing slavery where it already existed, their ideology did portray slavery as a danger to the nation. Indeed, Jefferson Davis was not far wrong that hostility to slavery was the "vital element" in Republican strength.

Political impasse: slavery in the territories

Like successive hammer blows, events reinforced these sectional differences, driving North and South further apart. Controversy over Kansas did not subside; it grew. For among the settlers in the territory were partisans of both sides, each determined to make Kansas free or slave. Abolitionists and religious groups sent free-soil settlers to save the territory from slavery; southerners sent their own reinforcements, fearing that "northern hordes" were about to steal Kansas away. Clashes between the two groups led to violence, and soon the whole nation was talking about "Bleeding Kansas."

Indeed, political processes in the territory resembled war more than democracy. When elections for a territorial legislature were held in 1855, thousands of

Bleeding Kansas

proslavery Missourians invaded the polls and ran up a large but unlawful majority for slavery candidates. The legislature that resulted promptly legalized slavery, and in response free-soilers called an unauthorized convention and created their own government and constitution. A proslavery posse sent to arrest the free-soil leaders sacked the town of Lawrence; in revenge, John Brown, a fanatic who saw himself as God's instrument to destroy slavery, murdered five proslavery settlers. Soon armed bands of guerrillas roamed the state, battling over land claims as well as slavery.

The passion generated by this conflict erupted in the chamber of the United States Senate in May 1856, when Charles Sumner of Massachusetts denounced "the Crime against Kansas." Idealistic and radical in his antislavery views, Sumner attacked the president, the South, and Senator Andrew P. Butler of South Carolina. Soon thereafter Butler's nephew, Congressman Preston Brooks, approached Sumner at his Senate desk and beat him brutally with a cane. Voters in Massachusetts and South Carolina seethed; the country was becoming polarized.

But the agony of personal confrontation paled beside the consitutional issues raised by the Supreme Court's decision in *Dred Scott* v. *Sanford.* Scott, a Mis-

Dred Scott *v.* Sanford

souri slave, had sued his owner for his freedom, charging that he was free because he had resided in free territory (see page 292). After winding through the courts for eleven years, the case was decided in 1857, and the question of slavery in the territories was settled for good. Chief Justice Roger B. Taney wrote that Scott was not a citizen either of the United States or Missouri; that residence in free territory did not make Scott free; and most importantly, that Congress lacked the power to bar slavery from a territory, as it had done in the Missouri Compromise. This decision was not only controversial in content; it also had been reached in a manner that aroused sectional suspicions. The majority of the justices were southern; only one northerner had agreed with them. Three northern justices actively dissented or refused to concur in crucial parts of the decision.

A storm of angry reaction broke in the North. The decision alarmed a wide variety of northerners–abolitionists, would-be settlers in the West, even those who hated black people but feared the influence of the South. Every charge against the aggressive Slave Power seemed now to be confirmed. "There is such a thing as THE SLAVE POWER," warned the *Cincinnati Daily Commercial.* "It has marched over and annihilated the boundaries of the states. We are now one great homogenous slaveholding community." And the Cincinnati *Freeman* asked, "What security have the Germans and Irish that their children will not, within a hundred years, be reduced to slavery in this land of their adoption?" Echoed the *Atlantic Monthly,* "Where will it end? Is the success of this conspiracy to be final and eternal?" The poet James Russell Lowell both stimulated and expressed the anxieties of poor northern whites when he had his Yankee narrator, Ezekiel Biglow, say,

Wy, it's jest ez clear ez figgers,
    Clear ez one an' one make two,
Chaps thet make black slaves o' niggers,
    Want to make wite slaves o' you.

Republican politicians capitalized on these fears, using the threat of the Slave Power to build a coalition of abolitionists, who opposed slavery on moral grounds, and racists, who feared that slavery jeopardized their interests. Indeed, Abraham Lincoln's great-

Guerrilla warfare in Bleeding Kansas. Free staters fire on a proslavery settlement near Leavenworth (1856). Kansas State Historical Society.

est achievement in the 1850s, one historian has pointed out, was as a Republican political propagandist against slavery. Lincoln cloaked the crudest charges against the Slave Power in language of biblical majesty, chilling thousands of voters. The South threatened democracy, he argued, and slavery threatened all whites.

Abraham Lincoln on the Slave Power

At the crux of the matter was the self-interest of whites. Pointing to the southern obsession with the territories, Lincoln had declared as early as 1854 that "the whole nation is interested that the best use shall be made of these Territories. We want them for homes of free white people. This they cannot be, to any considerable extent, if slavery shall be planted within them." The territories must be reserved, he now insisted, "as an outlet for *free white people everywhere*" so that immigrants could come to America and "find new homes and better their condition in life." After the Dred Scott decision, Lincoln charged that the next step in the unfolding Slave Power conspiracy would be a Supreme Court decision "declaring that the Constitution does not permit a State to exclude slavery from its limits. . . . We shall lie down pleasantly, dreaming that the people of Missouri are on the verge of making their State free; and we shall awake to the reality instead, that the Supreme Court has made Illinois a slave State." The proslavery argument's denigration of freedom and southerners' harping on the inferiority of blacks, Lincoln warned, were signs of a desire "to make *things* out of poor white men."

Lincoln's most eloquent statement against the Slave Power was his famous House Divided speech. In it Lincoln declared: "I do not expect the Union to be dissolved–I do not expect the House to fall–but I do expect it to cease to be divided. It will become all one thing or all the other. Either the opponents of slavery will arrest the further spread of it, and place it where the public mind shall rest in the belief that it is in the course of ultimate extinction; or its advocates will push it forward, till it shall become alike lawful in all the States, old as well as new, North as well as South. Have we no tendency to the latter condition?" The concluding question was the key element of the passage, for it drove home the idea that slaveholders were trying to extend bondage over the entire nation.

The brilliance of Republican tactics offset the difficulties the Dred Scott decision posed for them. By endorsing southern constitutional arguments, the Court had invalidated the central position of the Republican party: no extension of slavery. Republicans could only repudiate the decision, appealing to a "higher law," or hope to change the personnel of the Court.

Campaign medallions of Abraham Lincoln and Stephen Douglas, done two years after the famous Lincoln-Douglas debates. Edmund B. Sullivan Collection, University of Hartford.

For northern Democrats like Stephen Douglas, meanwhile, there was no escape. Douglas faced an awful dilemma. Northerners were alarmed by the prospect that the territories would be opened up to slavery. To retain support in the North, therefore, Douglas had to find some way to hedge, to reassure voters. Yet he had to do so without alienating southern Democrats. Douglas's task was problematic even at best; given the emotions of the time, it proved impossible.

Douglas chose to stand by his principle of popular sovereignty, which encountered a second test in Kansas in 1857. There, after free-soil settlers boycotted an election, proslavery forces met at Lecompton and wrote a constitution that permitted slavery. New elections to the territorial legislature, however, returned an antislavery majority, and the legislature promptly called for a popular vote on the new constitution, which was defeated by more than ten thousand votes. Despite this overwhelming evidence that Kansans did not want slavery, President Buchanan tried to force the Lecompton constitution through Congress. Douglas threw his weight against a document the people had rejected; he gauged their feelings correctly, and in 1858 Kansas voters rejected the constitution a third time. But his action infuriated southern Democrats.

In his well-publicized debates with Abraham Lincoln in 1858, Douglas further alienated the southern wing of his party. Speaking at Freeport, Illinois, he attempted to revive the notion of popular sovereignty with some tortured extensions of his old arguments. Asserting that the Court had not ruled on the powers of a *territorial* legislature, Douglas claimed that a territorial legislature could bar slavery either by passing a law against it or by doing nothing. Without the patrol laws and police regulations that support slavery, he reasoned, the institution could not exist. This argument, called the Freeport Doctrine, temporarily shored up Douglas's crumbling position

Stephen Douglas proposes the Freeport Doctrine

in the North. But it gave southern Democrats further evidence that Douglas was unreliable, and some turned viciously against him. A few southerners, like William L. Yancey of Alabama, studied the trend in northern opinion and concluded that southern rights would be safe only in a separate southern nation.

Thus the territorial issue continued to generate wider and more dangerous conflict. In itself it had diminishing practical significance. By 1858 even Jefferson Davis had given up on agricultural development in the Southwest and admitted his uncertainty that slavery could succeed in Kansas. In territories outside Kansas the number of settlers was small, and everywhere the number of blacks was negligible—less than 1 percent of the population in Kansas and New Mexico. Nevertheless, men like Davis and Douglas spent many hours attacking each other's theories on the floor of the Senate. And the general public, both North and South, moved from anxiety to alarm and anger. The situation had become explosive.

Violence inflamed passions further in October 1859, when John Brown led a small band in an attack on Harpers Ferry, Virginia, hoping to trigger a slave rebellion. Brown failed miserably, and was quickly captured, tried, and executed. It came to light, however, that Brown had had the financial backing of several prominent abolitionists, and northern intellectuals such as Emerson and Thoreau praised him as a hero and a martyr. Since slave rebellion excited the deepest fears in the white South, these disclosures multiplied southerners' fear and anger many times over. The unity of the nation was now in peril.

The election of 1860 and secession

Many observers feared that the election of 1860 would decide the fate of the Union. An ominous occurrence at the beginning of the campaign did nothing to reassure them. For several years, the Democratic party had been the only remaining organization that was truly national in scope. Even religious denominations had split into northern and southern wings during the 1840s and 1850s. "One after another," wrote a Mississippi newspaper editor, "the links which have bound the North and the South together, have been severed . . . [but] the Democratic party looms gradually up, its nationality intact, and waves the olive branch over the troubled waters of politics." At the 1860 convention, however, the Democratic party broke in two.

Splintering of the Democratic party

Stephen A. Douglas wanted the party's presidential nomination, but could not afford to alienate northern opinion by accepting a strongly southern position on the territories. Southern Democrats like William L. Yancey, on the other hand, were determined to have their rights recognized, and they moved to block Douglas's nomination. When Douglas nevertheless marshalled a majority for his version of the platform, delegates from the five Gulf states plus South Carolina, Georgia, and Arkansas walked out of the convention hall in Charleston. Efforts at compromise failed, so the Democrats presented two nominees: Douglas for the northern wing, John C. Breckinridge for the southern. The Republicans nominated Abraham Lincoln; a Constitutional Union party, formed to preserve the nation but strong only in Virginia and the upper South, nominated John Bell of Tennessee.

Bell and Douglas clearly preferred saving the Union to endangering it, and Breckinridge quickly backed away from any appearance of extremism; his supporters in several states declared that he was not a threat to the Union. But the New Orleans *Bee* charged that every disunionist in the land was enthusiastic for Breckinridge, and a Texas paper made an earthy reference to his association with radicals: "Mr. Breckinridge claims that he isn't a disunionist. An animal not willing to pass for a pig shouldn't stay in the stye." Frightened by such criticism, Breckinridge altered his plan to do no speaking during the campaign and delivered one address in which he flatly denied that his aim was secession. Thereafter his supporters stressed his loyalty and even went so far as to ridicule the possibility of secession in case of a Republican victory.

Election of 1860

The results of the balloting were sectional in character, but they indicated clearly that most voters were satisfied in the Union. Breckinridge carried nine southern states, with his strength concentrated in the Deep South. Bell won pluralities in Virginia, Kentucky, and Tennessee. Lincoln defeated Douglas

Presidential Vote in 1860

	LINCOLN	OTHER CANDIDATES
Entire United States	1,866,452	2,815,617
North plus border and southern states that rejected secession prior to war[1]	1,866,452	2,421,752
North plus border states that fought for union[2]	1,864,523	1,960,842

Note the large vote for other candidates in the righthand column.
[1] Kentucky, Missouri, Maryland, Delaware, Virginia, North Carolina, Tennessee, Arkansas
[2] Kentucky, Missouri, Maryland, Delaware

Source: David Potter, *Lincoln and his Party in the Secession Crisis* (New Haven and London: Yale University Press, 1942, 1967), p. 189.

in the North, but in the states that ultimately remained loyal to the Union he won only a plurality, not a majority (see table). Lincoln's victory was won in the electoral college.

Thus the majority of voters cast their ballots against the extreme choices. And, given the heterogeneous nature of Republican voters, it is likely that most of even Lincoln's supporters did not view the issue of slavery in the territories as paramount. In such circumstances, partisan leaders had an opportunity either to work for compromise or to accentuate the conflict.

As it happened, Lincoln decided not to soften his party's position on the territories. In his inaugural address he spoke of the necessity of maintaining the bond of faith between voter and candidate, of declining to set "the minority over the majority." But Lincoln's party was *not* the majority. His refusal to compromise probably had more to do with the unity of the Republican party than with the integrity of the democratic process. For though many conservative Republicans–eastern businessmen and former Whigs who did not feel strongly about slavery–hoped for a compromise, the original and strongest Republicans–antislavery voters and "conscience Whigs"–would not back away from the platform. To preserve the unity of his party, then, Lincoln had to take a position that endangered the Union.

Furthermore, political leaders in the North and the South tragically misjudged each other. As the historian David Potter has shown, Lincoln and other prominent Republicans believed that southerners were bluffing when they threatened secession; they expected a pro-Union majority in the South to assert itself. Therefore Lincoln determined not to yield to threats, but to call the southerners' bluff. On their side, southern leaders had become convinced that northerners were not taking them seriously, and that a posture of strength was necessary to win respect for their position. "To rally the men of the North, who would preserve the government as our fathers found it, we . . . should offer no doubtful or divided front," wrote Jefferson Davis. Thus southern leaders who hoped to avert disaster did not offer compromise, for fear of inviting aggression. Nor did northern leaders who loved the Union, believing it unnecessary and unwise. The misunderstanding was complete; the communication between the two groups nil.

Meanwhile the Union was being destroyed. On December 20, 1860, South Carolina passed an ordinance of secession amid jubilation and cheering. This step marked the inauguration of a strategy known as separate-state secession. Despairing of persuading all the southern states to challenge the federal government simultaneously, foes of the Union had concentrated their hopes on the most extreme proslavery state. With South Carolina out of the Union, they hoped other states would follow suit and momentum would build toward disunion.

Secession of South Carolina

The strategy proved effective. By reclaiming its independence, South Carolina had raised the stakes in the sectional confrontation. No longer was secession an unthinkable step; the Union was broken. Now, argued extremists, other states should secede to support South Carolina. Those who wanted to compromise would surely be able to make a better deal outside the Union than in it. Moderates found it difficult to dismiss such arguments, since most of them—even those who felt deep affection for the Union—were committed to defending southern rights and the southern way of life.

Congress made last-minute efforts to save the Union. Both the Senate and the House established special committees to search for a satisfactory compromise. Their efforts focused on a series of proposals offered by Senator John J. Crittenden of Kentucky, who hoped to don the mantle of Henry Clay and avert disaster. Crittenden suggested that the two sections divide the territories between them at 36°30′. But his efforts came to grief when Lincoln indicated that Republicans would not make concessions on the territorial issue. Virginians called for a special convention in Washington, to which several states sent representatives. But this gathering, too, failed to find a magical formula or to reach unanimity on disputed questions.

In these circumstances, southern extremists soon got their way. Overwhelming their opposition, they quickly called conventions and passed secession ordinances in six other states: Mississippi, Florida, Alabama, Georgia, Louisiana, and Texas. By February 1861 these states had joined with South Carolina to form a new government in Montgomery, Alabama: the Confederate States of America. Choosing Jefferson Davis as their president, they began to function independently of the United States.

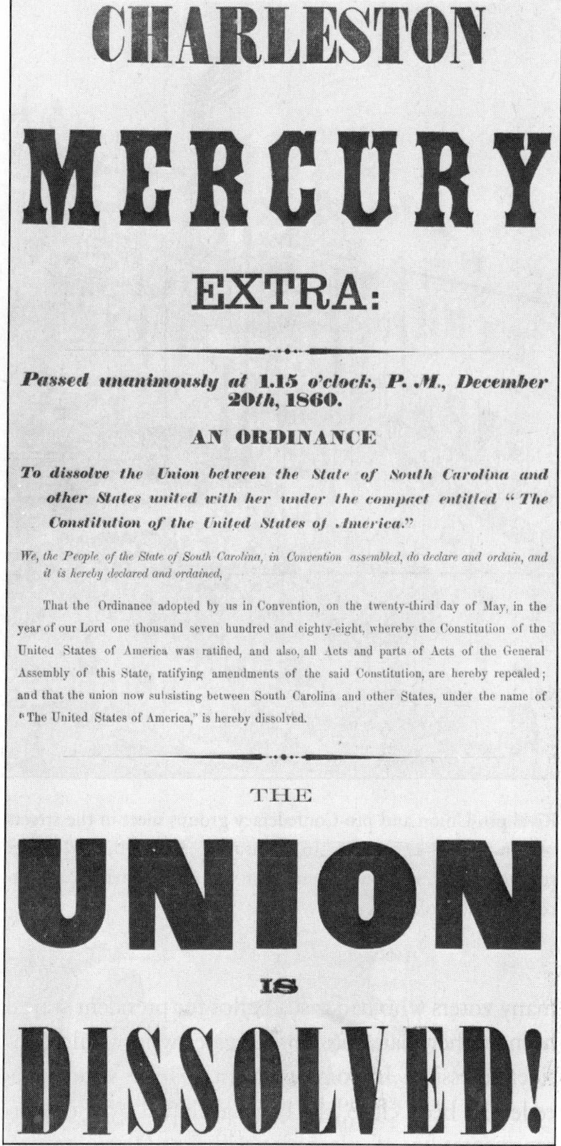

CHARLESTON

MERCURY

EXTRA:

Passed unanimously at 1.15 o'clock, P. M., December 20th, 1860.

AN ORDINANCE

To dissolve the Union between the State of South Carolina and other States united with her under the compact entitled "The Constitution of the United States of America."

We, the People of the State of South Carolina, in Convention assembled, do declare and ordain, and it is hereby declared and ordained,

That the Ordinance adopted by us in Convention, on the twenty-third day of May, in the year of our Lord one thousand seven hundred and eighty-eight, whereby the Constitution of the United States of America was ratified, and also, all Acts and parts of Acts of the General Assembly of this State, ratifying amendments of the said Constitution, are hereby repealed; and that the union now subsisting between South Carolina and other States, under the name of "The United States of America," is hereby dissolved.

THE

UNION

IS

DISSOLVED!

A handbill announcing passage of South Carolina's ordinance of secession. Rare Book Division, The New York Public Library, Astor, Lenox and Tilden Foundations.

Yet this apparent unanimity of action was deceiving. Confused and dissatisfied with the alternatives,

Voting Returns of Counties with Few Slaveholders, Eight Southern States, 1860 and 1861

STATE	MEDIAN % OF ELIGIBLE VOTERS FOR BRECKINRIDGE, 1860	MEDIAN % OF ELIGIBLE VOTERS FOR SECESSION, 1861	% CHANGE
Alabama	42.0	28.3	-13.7
Georgia	44.8	34.1	-10.7
Louisiana	35.3	28.1	-7.2
Mississippi	50.3	26.8	-23.5
North Carolina	29.6	22.0	-7.6
Tennessee	34.7	11.1	-23.6
Texas	43.7	33.0	-10.7
Virginia	27.2	6.5	-20.7

been the pride of millions of Americans and the boast of freemen the wide world over." Such sentiments presented problems for the Confederacy, though they were not sufficiently developed to prevent secession.

The dilemma facing President Lincoln on inauguration day in March 1861 was how to maintain the authority of the federal government without provoking war in the states that had left the Union. He decided to proceed cautiously; by holding onto federal fortifications, he reasoned, he could assert federal sovereignty while waiting for a restoration of relations. But Jefferson Davis, who could not claim to lead a sovereign nation if its ports and military facilities were under foreign control, would not cooperate. A collision was inevitable.

Attack on Fort Sumter

It came in the early morning hours of April 12, 1861, at Fort Sumter in Charleston harbor. A federal garrison there was running low on food. Lincoln had decided to send a supply ship and had notified the South Carolinians of his intention. For the Montgomery government, the only alternative to an attack on the fort was submission to Lincoln's authority. Accordingly, orders were sent to obtain surrender or attack the fort. Under heavy bombardment for two days, the federal garrison finally surrendered. The Confederates permitted the soldiers to sail away on unarmed vessels while the residents of Charleston celebrated. Thus the bloodiest war in the nation's history began in a deceptively gala and gentlemanly spirit.

Blacks, who would play a crucial role in the Civil War, were involved in preparations for the first battle. In this contemporary drawing they mount cannon for the Confederate attack on Fort Sumter. Library of Congress.

The war also began with its central issue shrouded in complexity and confusion. In the profoundest sense, slavery was tied up with the war. It had not been the single or direct cause of battle; the disagreement over the institution was complicated and unfocused. But indisputably the Civil War was, at bottom, about slavery. It arose from slavery in a multitude of ways, and it could hardly be conducted without affecting slavery. It addressed the questions of slavery's place in the law and black peoples' place in society. The answers to those questions, and the degree to which answers were sought, would be matters of fateful import.

Suggestions for further reading

Sources of conflict

Eugene H. Berwanger, *The Frontier Against Slavery* (1967); Ray Allen Billington, *The Protestant Crusade, 1800–1860* (1938 and 1964); Richard H. Brown, "The Missouri Crisis, Slavery, and the Politics of Jacksonianism," *South Atlantic Quarterly*, LXV (Winter 1966), 55–72; Louis Filler, *The Crusade Against Slavery, 1830–1860* (1960); Eric Foner, *Free Soil, Free Labor, Free Men* (1970); George M. Fredrickson, *The Black Image in the White Mind* (1971); Eugene D. Genovese, *The World the Slaveholders Made* (1969); Michael F.

Important events

1846	Wilmot Proviso
1847	Lewis Cass proposes idea of popular sovereignty
1848	Zachary Taylor elected president
1849	California applies for admission to Union as free state
1850	Nashville Convention Compromise of 1850 Vermont enacts personal liberty law
1851	Mob rescues fugitive slave in Boston
1852	Harriet Beecher Stowe, *Uncle Tom's Cabin* Franklin Pierce elected president
1854	Kansas-Nebraska bill "Appeal of the Independent Democrats" Free-Soil party promotes settlement of Kansas Republican party formed Pierce's effort to purchase Cuba fails Democrats lose ground in congressional elections
1856	Preston Brooks attacks Charles Sumner in Senate chamber Bleeding Kansas James Buchanan elected president
1857	*Dred Scott* v. *Sanford* Economic recession Lecompton Constitution
1858	Voters reject Lecompton Constitution Lincoln-Douglas debates Freeport Doctrine
1859	Buchanan vetoes homestead bill John Brown raids Harpers Ferry
1860	Democratic party splits in half Abraham Lincoln elected president Crittenden Compromise fails South Carolina secedes from Union
1861	Six more southern states secede Confederacy established Attack on Fort Sumter

Holt, *The Political Crisis of the 1850s* (1978); William Sumner Jenkins, *Pro-Slavery Thought in the Old South* (1935); Aileen S. Kraditor, *Means and Ends in American Abolitionism* (1969); Robert E. May, *The Southern Dream of a Caribbean Empire, 1854–1861* (1973); Roy F. Nichols, *The Disruption of American Democracy* (1948); Russell B. Nye, *Fettered Freedom* (1949); Lewis Perry and Michael Fellman, eds., *Antislavery Reconsidered* (1979); Joel H. Silbey, *The Transformation of American Politics, 1840–1860* (1967); Henry H. Simms, *A Decade of Sectional Controversy, 1851–1861* (1942); William R. Stanton, *The Leopard's Spots* (1960); Ronald G. Walters, *American Reformers, 1815–1860* (1978).

Political crises

Thomas B. Alexander, *Sectional Stress and Party Strength* (1967); William L. Barney, *The Secessionist Impulse* (1974); Stanley W. Campbell, *The Slave Catchers* (1968); Avery O. Craven, *The Coming of the Civil War* (1942); Don E. Fehrenbacher, *The Dred Scott Case* (1978); J. C. Furnas, *The Road to Harpers Ferry* (1959); Holman Hamilton, *Prologue to Conflict* (1964); Cleo Hearon, *Mississippi and the Compromise of 1850* (1913); Henry V. Jaffa, *Crisis of the House Divided* (1959); Paul D. Nagle, *One Nation Indivisible* (1964); Allan Nevins, *The Emergence of Lincoln,* 2 vols. (1950); Stephen B. Oates, *To Purge the Land with Blood* (1970); David M. Potter, *The Impending Crisis, 1848–1861* (1976); David M. Potter, *The South and the Sectional Conflict* (1968); Percy Lee Rainwater, *Mississippi: Storm Center of Secession, 1856–1861* (1938); James A. Rawley, *Race and Politics* (1969); Kenneth M. Stampp, *And the War Came* (1950); J. Mills Thornton III, *Politics and Power in a Slave Society* (1978); Alice Felt Tyler, *Freedom's Ferment* (1944); Gerald W. Wolff, *The Kansas-Nebraska Bill* (1977).

Secession and war

Steven A. Channing, *Crisis of Fear* (1970); Robert Gray Gunderson, *Old Gentlemen's Convention* (1961); Michael P. Johnson, *Toward a Patriarchal Republic* (1977); Seymour Martin Lipset, *Political Man* (1960); David M. Potter, *Lincoln and His Party in the Secession Crisis* (1942); Henry T. Shanks, *The Secession Movement in Virginia, 1847–1861* (1934); Joseph Carlyle Sitterson, *The Secession Movement in North Carolina* (1939); Ralph A. Wooster, *The Secession Conventions of the South* (1962).

Political leaders

Richard N. Current, *The Lincoln Nobody Knows* (1958); David Donald, *Charles Sumner and the Coming of the Civil War* (1960); David Donald, *Lincoln Reconsidered* (1956); Paul D. Escott, "Jefferson Davis and Slavery in the Territories," *Journal of Mississippi History*, 39 (May 1977), 97–116; Don E. Fehrenbacher, *Prelude to Greatness* (1962); George B. Forgie, *Patricide in the House Divided* (1979); Robert W. Johannsen, *Stephen A. Douglas* (1973); Roy F. Nichols, *Franklin Pierce* (1958); Philip Shriver Klein, *President James Buchanan* (1962).

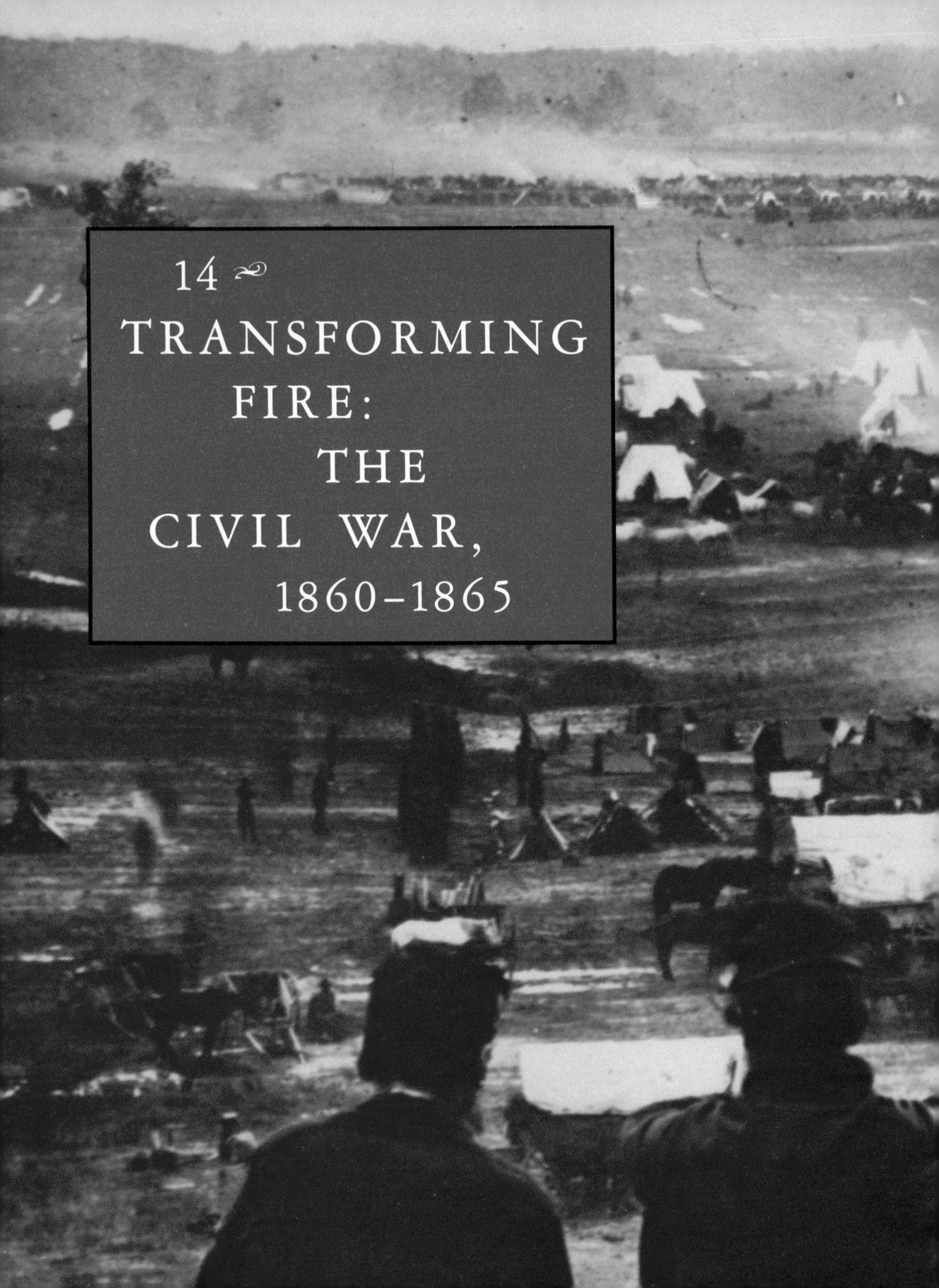

14
TRANSFORMING FIRE: THE CIVIL WAR, 1860–1865

They came from many different places. They held many different points of view. Perhaps the only thing that united them was the fact that they were caught in a gigantic struggle. Each felt dwarfed by the immense force of the Civil War, a vast and complex event beyond any individual's control.

Moncure Conway, a Virginian who had converted to abolitionism and settled in New England, saw the Civil War as a momentous opportunity to bring justice to human affairs. The progress of reform in the North, Conway wrote in an earnest pamphlet, heralded the dawn of "Humanity's advancing day." Before this dawn, "Slavery, hoary tyrant of the ages," cried out " 'Back! back . . . into the chambers of Night!' " Conway urged northerners to accept slavery's challenge and defeat it, so that "the rays of Freedom and Justice" could shine throughout America. Then the United States would stand as a beacon not only of commercial power but of moral righteousness.

Conway's lofty idealism was far removed from the motives that drove most federal soldiers to march grimly to their death. Though slaves believed they were witnessing God's "Holy War for de liberation of de poor African slave people," Union troops took a different perspective. When a Yankee soldier ransacked a slave family's cabin and stole their best quilts, the mother exclaimed, "Why you nasty, stinkin' rascal. You say you come down here to fight for the niggers, and now you're stealin' from em." The soldier replied, "You're a G-- D--- liar, I'm fightin for $14 a month and the Union."

Southerners too acted on limited and pragmatic motives, fighting in self-defense or out of regional loyalty. A Union officer interrogating Confederate prisoners noticed the poverty of one captive. Clearly the man was no slaveholder, so the officer asked him why he was fighting. "Because y'all are down here," replied the Confederate.

The great suffering and frustration of the war were apparent in the bitter words of another southerner, a civilian. Impoverished by the conflict, this farmer had endured inflation, taxes, and shortages to support the Confederacy. Then an impressment agent arrived to take from him still more–grain and meat, horses and mules and wagons. In return the agent offered only a certificate promising repayment sometime in the future. Angry and fed up, the farmer bluntly declared, "the sooner this damned Government falls to pieces, the better it will be for us."

In contrast, many northern businessmen looked to the economic effects of the war with optimism and anticipation. The conflict ensured vast government expenditures, a heavy demand for products, and lucrative government contracts. *Harper's Monthly* reported that an eminent financier expected a long war, the kind of war that would mean huge purchases, paper money, active speculation, and rising prices. "The battle of Bull Run," predicted the financier, "makes the fortune of every man in Wall Street who is not a natural idiot."

For each of these people and millions of others, the Civil War was a life-changing event. It obliterated the normal circumstances of life, sweeping millions of men into training camps and battle units. Armies numbering in the hundreds of thousands marched over the South, devastating once-peaceful countrysides. Families struggled to survive without their men; businesses tried to cope with the loss of workers. Women, North and South, faced added responsibilities in the home and moved into new jobs in the work force. Nothing seemed untouched.

Change was most drastic in the South, where the leaders of the secession movement had launched a revolution for the purpose of keeping things unchanged. Never were men more mistaken: their revolutionary means were fundamentally incompatible with their conservative purpose. Southerners had feared that a peacetime government of Republicans would interfere with slavery and upset the routine of plantation life. Instead their own actions led to a war that turned southern life upside down and imperiled the very existence of slavery. The Civil War forced drastic changes in every phase of southern society, and the leadership of Jefferson Davis resulted in policies more objectionable to the elite than any proposed by Lincoln. The Confederacy proved to be a shockingly unsouthern experience.

War altered the North as well, but not as deeply. Since the bulk of the fighting took place on southern soil, most northern farms and factories remained physically unscathed. The drafting of workers and the changing needs for products slowed the pace of industrialization somewhat, but factories and businesses remained busy. Though workers lost ground to inflation, the economy hummed. And a new probusiness

Optimistic and confident, these soldiers from a Virginia regiment vied for a place in the photographer's lens shortly before the war began. Valentine Museum, Richmond, Virginia.

atmosphere dominated Congress, where southern representatives no longer filled their seats. To the discomfort of some, the powers of the federal government and the president increased during the emergency.

The war strained society, both North and South. Disaffection was strongest in the Confederacy, where the sufferings of ordinary citizens were greatest. There poverty and class resentment fed a lower-class antagonism to the war that threatened the Confederacy from within as federal armies assailed it from without. But dissent also flourished in the North, where antiwar sentiment occasionally erupted into violence.

Ultimately, the Civil War forced new social and racial arrangements on the nation. Its greatest effect was to compel leaders and citizens to deal with an issue they had often tried to avoid: slavery. This issue had, in complex and indirect ways, given rise to the war; now the scope and demands of the war forced reluctant Americans to deal with it.

The South goes to war

In the first bright days of the southern nation, few foresaw the changes that were in store. Lincoln's call for troops to put down the Confederate insurrection stimulated an outpouring of regional loyalty that unified the classes. Though four border slave states–Missouri, Kentucky, Maryland, and Delaware–and western Virginia refused to secede, the rest of the upper South promptly joined the Confederacy. From every quarter southerners flocked to defend their region against Yankee aggression. In the first few months of the war half a million men volunteered to fight; there were so many would-be soldiers that the government could not arm them all.

This groundswell of popular support for the Confederacy generated a mood of optimism and gaiety. Women sewed dashing, colorful uniforms for men who would before long be lucky to wear drab gray or butternut homespun. Confident recruits boasted of whipping the Yankees and returning home in time for dinner. And the first major battle of the war only increased such cockiness. On July 21, 1861, General Irvin McDowell and thirty thousand federal troops attacked General P. G. T. Beauregard's twenty-two thousand southerners at a stream called Bull Run, near Manassas Junction, Virginia. Both armies were ill-trained, and confusion reigned on the battlefield. But nine thousand Confederate reinforcements and a timely stand by General Thomas Jackson (thereafter known as "Stonewall" Jackson) won the day for the South. Union troops fled back to Washington in disarray, and shocked northern picnickers who had expected to witness a victory suddenly feared their capital would be taken.

Battle of Bull Run

As 1861 faded into 1862, however, the North undertook a massive buildup of troops in northern Virginia. In the wake of Bull Run, Lincoln had given command of the army to General George B. McClellan, an officer who had always been better at organization and training than at fighting. McClellan devoted the fall and winter to readying a formidable force of a quarter-million men. "The vast preparation of the enemy," wrote one Confederate soldier, produced a "feeling of despondency" among southerners.

The North also moved to blockade southern ports in order to choke off the Confederacy's avenues of commerce and supply. At first the handful of available steamers proved woefully inadequate to the task of patrolling 3,550 miles of coastline. But the Union navy substantially reduced southern maritime traffic in the first year of the war and eventually imposed a near-total blockade.

Union naval campaign

In the fall of 1861 Union naval power came ashore in the South. Federal squadrons captured Cape Hatteras and Hilton Head, part of the Sea Islands off Port Royal, South Carolina. A few months later, similar operations secured Albemarle and Pamlico sounds, Roanoke Island, and New Bern in North Carolina, as well as Fort Pulaski, which defended Savannah. Then in April 1862 ships commanded by Admiral David Farragut smashed through log booms on the Mississippi and fought their way upstream to capture New Orleans (see map).

The coastal victories off South Carolina foreshadowed another major development in the unraveling of the southern status quo. At the gunboats' approach, frightened planters abandoned their lands and fled. Their slaves, who thus became the first to escape slavery through military action, greeted what they hoped to be freedom with rejoicing and destruction of the cotton gins, symbols of their travail. Their jubilation and the constantly growing stream of runaways who poured into the Union lines removed any doubt about which side the slaves would support, given the opportunity. Ironically the federal government, unwilling at first to wage a war against slavery, did not acknowledge the slaves' freedom—though it did set to work finding ways to use them in the national cause.

With the approach of spring 1862, the military outlook for the Confederacy darkened again, this time in northern Tennessee. There a hard-drinking, hitherto unsuccessful general named Ulysses S. Grant recognized the strategic importance of forts Henry and Donelson, the Confederate outposts guarding the Tennessee and Cumberland rivers. Grant saw that if federal troops could capture these forts, two prime routes into the heartland of the Confederacy would lie open. In the space of ten days he seized the forts, using his forces so well that he was able to demand unconditional surrender of Fort Donelson's defenders. A path into Tennessee, Alabama, and Mississippi now lay open before the Union army.

Grant's campaign in Tennessee

But orders from General Henry Halleck, who coordinated federal operations from Washington, kept Grant from pressing the southern commander, Albert Sidney Johnston. On April 6, Johnston caught Grant's army in an undesirable position at Pittsburg Landing in southern Tennessee. The Confederates inflicted heavy damage in fierce fighting. Close to victory, however, General Johnston was struck by a ball that severed an artery in his thigh; within minutes he was dead. Deprived of their leader, southern troops faced a reinforced Union army the next day, and the tide of battle turned. After ten hours of heavy combat, Grant's men forced the Confederates to withdraw to Corinth, Mississippi. Though the Battle of Shiloh was a Union victory, it was hideously destructive on both sides. Northern troops lost 13,000 of 63,000 men; southerners sacrificed 11,000 out of 40,000.

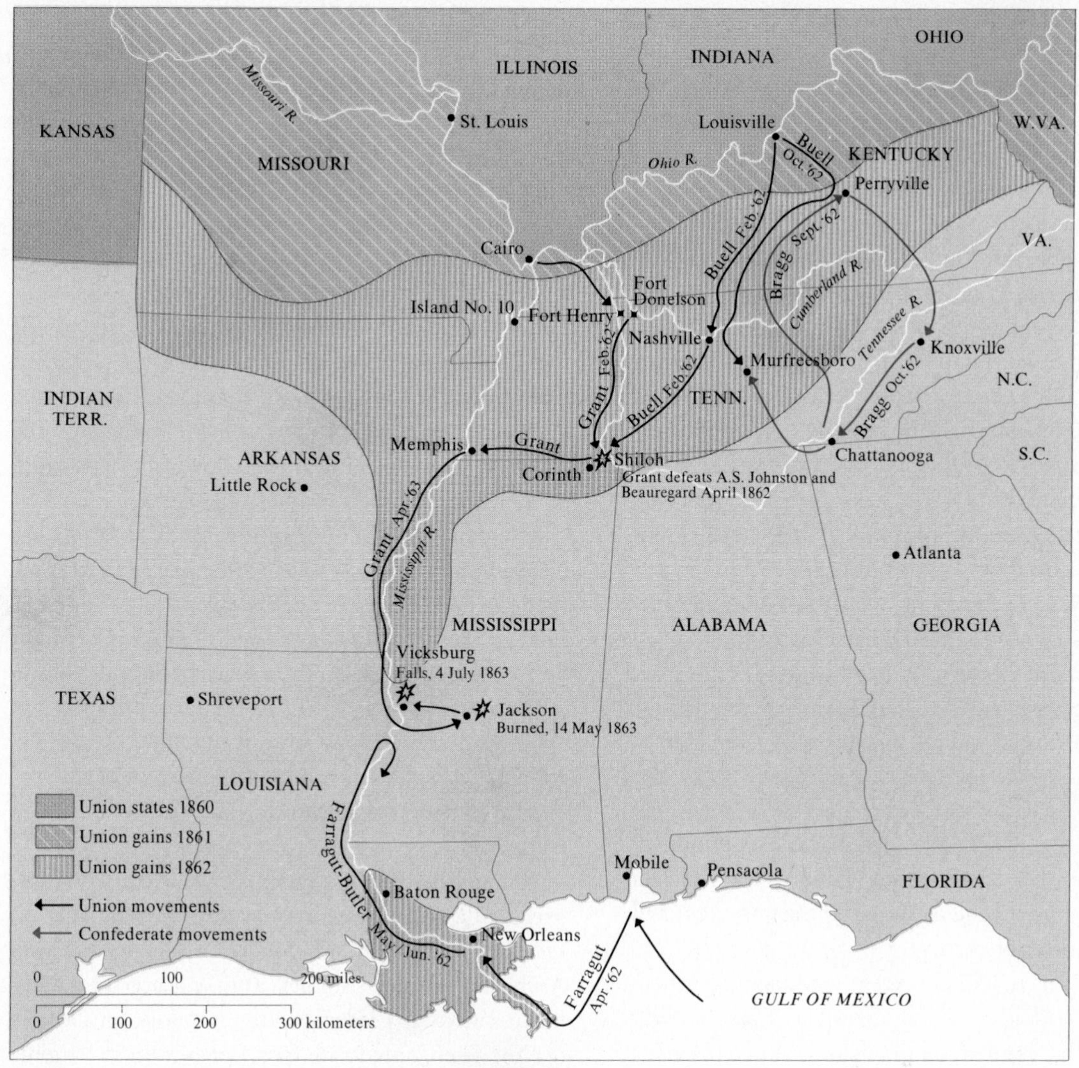

The war in the West, 1861–July 1863. Source: Reprinted by permission of Alfred A. Knopf, Inc.

Both soldiers and civilians were beginning to recognize the enormous costs of this war. Never before in Europe or America had such massive forces pummeled each other with weapons of such destructive power. Many citizens, like soldier–later Supreme Court Justice–Oliver Wendell Holmes, wondered at "the butcher's bill." The improved range of modern rifles multiplied casualties; and, since medical knowledge was rudimentary, even minor wounds often led to death through infection. The slaughter was most vivid, of course, to the soldiers themselves, who saw the blasted bodies of their friends and comrades. "Any one who goes over a battlefield after a battle," wrote one Confederate, "never cares to go over another. . . . I for one don't care if I am never near another fight again. . . . It is a sad sight to see the dead, and if possible more sad to see the wounded–shot in every possible way you can imagine."

Troops learned the hard way that soldiering was far from glorious. "The dirt of a camp life knocks all its poetry into a cocked hat," wrote a North Carolina volunteer in 1862. One year later he marveled at his earlier innocence. Fighting had taught him "the realities of a soldier's life. We had no tents after the 6th August, but slept on the ground, in the woods or open fields, without regard to the weather. ... I learned to eat fat bacon raw, and to like it. . . . Without time to wash our clothes or our persons, and sleeping on the ground all huddled together, the whole army became lousy more or less with body lice. It was a necessary and unavoidable incident to our arduous campaign."

The scope and duration of the conflict had begun to have a visible effect on Confederate morale. As the spring of 1862 approached, southern officials worried about the strength of their armies. Tens of thousands of Confederate soldiers had volunteered for just one year's service, planning to return home in the spring to plant their crops. To keep southern armies in the field, the War Department offered bounties and furloughs to all who would re-enlist. Officials then called for new volunteers; but, as one admitted, "the spirit of volunteering had died out." Three states threatened or instituted a draft. Finally, still faced with a critical shortage of troops, the Confederate government enacted the first national conscription law in American history. The war had forced an unprecedented change on the states that had seceded for fear of change.

Confederacy resorts to a draft

With their ranks swelled by conscripts, southern armies moved into heavier fighting. Early in 1862 most of the combat centered in Virginia. General McClellan sailed his troops to the York peninsula and advanced on Richmond from the east. By May and June the sheer size of the federal armies outside the South's capital was highly threatening. But when McClellan sent his legions into combat, generals Jackson and Lee managed to stave off his attacks. First Jackson maneuvered into the Shenandoah Valley, behind Union forces, and threatened Washington, drawing some of the federals away from Richmond to protect their own capital. Then, in a series of engagements culminating in the Seven Days' battles, Lee held McClellan off. On August 3 McClellan withdrew to the Potomac, and Richmond was safe for almost two more years.

Buoyed by these results, Jefferson Davis conceived an ambitious plan to turn the tide of the war and compel the United States to recognize the Confederacy. He ordered a general offensive, sending Lee north to Maryland and generals Kirby Smith and Braxton Bragg to Kentucky. The South would abandon the defensive and take the war north. Davis and his commanders issued a proclamation to the people of Maryland and Kentucky asserting that the Confederates sought only the right of self-government. Lincoln's refusal to grant them independence forced them to attack "those who persist in their refusal to make peace." Davis urged the invaded states to make a separate peace with his government and invited the Northwest, whose trade flowed down the Mississippi to New Orleans, to break with the Union.

Davis orders an offensive

The plan was promising, and Davis rejoiced that his outnumbered forces were at length ready to take the initiative. Every part of the offensive failed, however. In the bloodiest single day of fighting, September 17, 1862, McClellan turned Lee back in the Battle of Antietam near Sharpsburg, Maryland. Smith and Bragg had to withdraw from Kentucky just one day after Bragg had attended the inauguration of a provisional Confederate governor. The entire effort had collapsed.

But southern arms were not exhausted. Jeb Stuart executed a daring cavalry raid into Pennsylvania on October 10 through 12, and Lee decimated General Ambrose Burnside's soldiers as they charged his fortified positions at Fredericksburg, Virginia, on December 13. The Confederate Army of Northern Virginia performed so bravely and controlled the engagement so thoroughly that Lee, a restrained and humane man, was moved to say, "It is well that war is so terrible. We should grow too fond of it."

Nevertheless, the Confederacy had marshalled all its strength for a breakthrough and failed utterly. Outnumbered and disadvantaged in resources (see figure), the South could not continue its offensive. Meanwhile the North still had reserves of every kind on which to draw. Profoundly disappointed, Davis admitted to a committee of Confederate representatives that southerners had entered "the darkest and most dangerous period we have yet had." Tenacious defense and stoical endurance now seemed the South's only long-range hope. Perceptive southerners shared their president's despair.

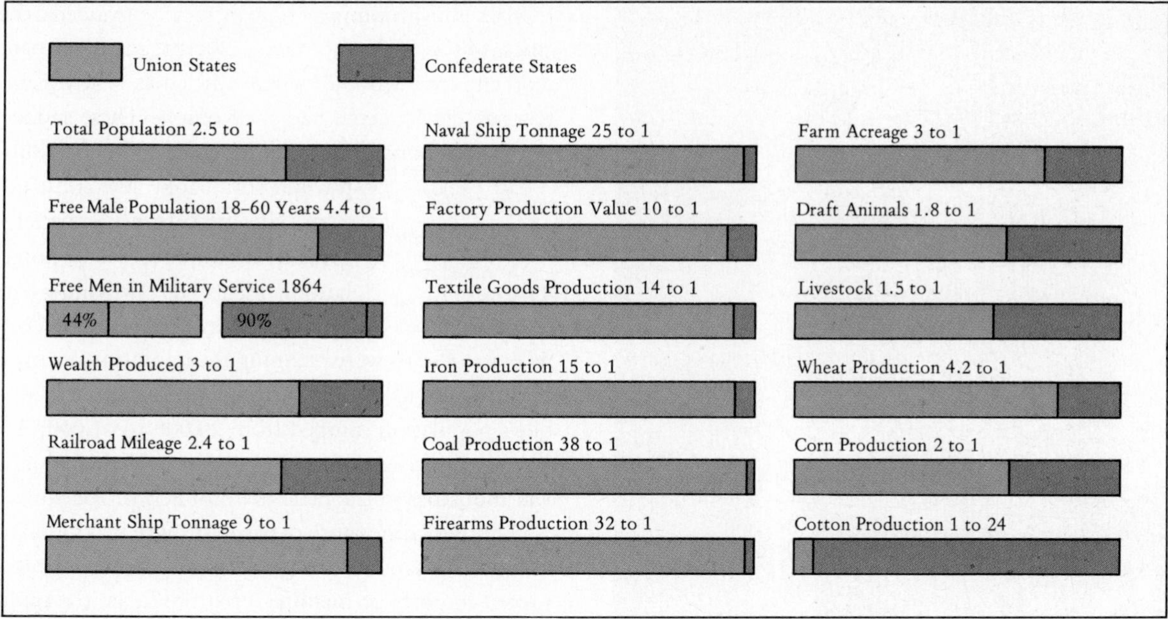

Comparative resources, Union and Confederate states, 1861
Source: *Times Atlas of World History*. Times Books, London, 1978.

War transforms the South

Even more than the fighting itself, changes in civilian life robbed southerners of their gaiety and nonchalance. The war altered southern society beyond all expectations and with astonishing speed. One of the first traditions to fall was the southern preference for local government.

The South had been an area of little government. States' rights had been its motto, but even the state governments were weak and sketchy affairs by modern standards. To withstand the massive power of the North, however, the South had to centralize; like the colonial revolutionaries, southerners faced a choice of join or die. No one saw the necessity of centralization more clearly than Jefferson Davis. If the states insisted on fighting separately, said Davis, "we had better make terms as soon as we can."

Centralization of power in the South

From the outset, Davis pressed to bring all arms, supplies, and troops under his control. He advocated conscription when the states failed to enroll enough new soldiers. And he took a strong leadership role toward the Confederate congress, which raised taxes and later passed a tax-in-kind—a levy not on money but on wheat, corn, oats, rye, cotton, peas, and other farm products. Almost three thousand agents dispersed to collect the tax, assisted by almost fifteen hundred appraisers. Where opposition arose, the government suspended the writ of habeas corpus and imposed martial law. In the face of a political opposition that cherished states' rights, Davis proved unyielding.

To replace the food that soldiers would have grown, Davis exhorted farmers to switch from cash crops to food crops; he encouraged the states to require that they do so. But the army was still short of food and labor. In emergencies the War Department resorted to impressing slaves for labor on fortifications, or took meat and grain in lieu of forced labor. After 1861, the government relied heavily on food impressment to feed the armies. Officers swooped down on farms in the line of march and carted away grain, meat, and other food, plus wagons and draft animals to carry it.

For her work in nursing the Confederate wounded, Sally Tompkins received a commission as a captain in the Confederate Army. Valentine Museum, Richmond, Virginia.

Soon the Richmond administration was taking virtually complete direction of the southern economy. Because it controlled the supply of labor through conscription, the administration could regulate industry, compelling factories to work on government contracts to supply government needs. In addition, the Confederate congress passed laws giving the central government almost full control of the railroads; and later shipping, too, came under extensive regulation. New statutes even limited corporate profits and dividends. A large bureaucracy sprang up to administer these operations: over seventy thousand civilians were needed to run the Confederate war machine. By the war's end the southern bureaucracy was proportionally larger than its northern counterpart.

The mushrooming bureaucracy expanded the cities. Clerks and subordinate officials, many of them women, crowded the towns and cities where Confederate departments had their offices. These sudden population booms stretched the existing housing supply and stimulated new construction. The pressure was especially great in Richmond, whose population increased two-and-a-half times. Before the war's end Confederate officials were planning the relocation of entire departments to diminish crowding in that city. Mobile's population jumped from 29,000 to 41,000; Atlanta began to grow; and 10,000 people poured into war industries in the little town of Selma, Alabama.

Effects of war on southern cities and industry

Another prime cause of urban growth was industrialization. Because of the Union blockade, which interrupted imports of manufactured products, the traditionally agricultural South became interested in industry. Davis exulted that southerners were manufacturing their own goods, thus "becoming more and more independent of the rest of the world." Many planters shared his expectations, remembering their battles against tariffs and hoping that their agrarian nation would industrialize enough to win "deliverance, full and unrestricted, from all commercial dependence" on the North. And indeed, though the Confederacy started from scratch, it achieved tremendous feats of industrial development. Chief of Ordnance Josiah Gorgas was able to increase the capacity of the Tredegar Iron Works and other factories to the point that his Ordnance Bureau was supplying all Confederate small arms and ammunition by 1865.

As a result of these changes southerners adopted new values. Women, sheltered in the patriarchal antebellum society, gained substantial new responsibilities. The wives and mothers of soldiers became heads of households and undertook what had previously been considered men's work. To them fell the added tasks of raising crops and tending animals. Though wives of nonslaveowners had a harder time cultivating their fields than women whose families owned slaves, the latter had to struggle with the management of field hands unused to feminine oversight. Only among the very rich were there enough servants to take up the slack and leave a woman's routine undisturbed. In the cities

Change in the southern woman's role

women found new and respectable roles (and paying jobs) in the workforce. "Government girls" who staffed the Confederate bureaucracy and female schoolteachers became a familiar sight. Such experiences undermined the image of the omnipotent male and gave thousands of women new confidence in their abilities.

One of those who acquired such confidence as a result of the war was a young North Carolinian named Janie Smith. Raised in a rural area by prosperous parents, she had faced few challenges or grim realities. Then suddenly the war reached her farm, and the troops turned her home into a hospital. "It makes me shudder when I think of the awful sights I witnessed that morning," she wrote to a friend. "Ambulance after ambulance drove up with our wounded. . . . Under every shed and tree, the tables were carried for amputating the limbs. . . . The blood lay in puddles in the grove; the groans of the dying and complaints of those undergoing amputation were horrible." But Janie Smith learned to cope with crisis. She helped to nurse the wounded and ended her account with the proud words "I can dress amputated limbs now and do most anything in the way of nursing wounded soldiers."

The Confederate experience introduced and sustained many other new values. Legislative bodies yielded power to the executive branch of government, which could act more decisively in time of war. The traditional emphasis on aristocratic lineage gave way to respect for achievement and bravery under fire. Thus many men of ordinary background, such as Josiah Gorgas, Stonewall Jackson, and General Nathan Bedford Forrest, gained distinction in industry and on the battlefield that would have been beyond their grasp in time of peace. Finally, sacrifice for the cause discouraged the pursuit of pleasure; hostesses gave "cold water parties" (at which water was the only refreshment) to demonstrate their patriotism.

For the elite such sacrifice was symbolic, but for millions of ordinary southerners it was terrifyingly real. Mass poverty descended on the South, afflicting for the first time a large minority of the white population. The crux of the problem was that many yeoman families had lost their breadwinners to the army. As a South Carolina newspaper put it, "The duties of war have called away from home the sole supports of many, many families. . . . Help must be given, or the poor will suffer." The poor sought such help from relatives, neighbors, friends, anyone. Sometimes they took their cases to the Confederate government, as did an elderly Virginian who pleaded, "If you dount send [my son] home I am bound to louse my crop and cum to suffer. I am eaighty one years of adge." One woman wrote: "I ask in the name of humanity to discharge my husband he is not able to do your government much good and he might do his children some good and thare is no use in keeping a man thare to kill and leave widows and poor little orphen children to suffer . . . my poor children have no home nor no Father."

Human suffering in the South

Other factors aggravated the effect of the labor shortage. The South was in many places so sparsely populated that the conscription of one skilled craftsman could work a hardship on the people of an entire county. Often they begged in unison for the exemption or discharge of the local miller or the neighborhood tanner, wheelwright, or potter. Physicians were also in short supply. Most serious, however, was the loss of a blacksmith. As a petition from Alabama explained, "our Section of County [is] left entirely Destitute of any man that is able to keep in order any kind of Farming Tules, Such as the few aged Farmers and families of Those that is gone to defend there rites is Compeled to have to make a Support With."

The blockade created further shortages of common but important items–salt, sugar, coffee, nails–and speculation and hoarding made them worse. Avaricious businessmen moved to corner the supply of some commodities; prosperous citizens tried to stock up on food. The Richmond *Enquirer* criticized one man for hoarding seven hundred barrels of flour; another man, a planter, purchased so many wagonloads of supplies that his "lawn and paths looked like a wharf covered with a ship's loads." Some people bought up the entire stock of a store and held the goods to sell later at higher prices. "This disposition to speculate upon the yeomanry of the country," lamented the Richmond *Examiner,* "is the most mortifying feature of the war." North Carolina's Governor Zebulon Vance asked where it would all stop: "the cry of distress comes up from the poor wives and children of our soldiers. . . . What will become of them?"

Hoarding and runaway inflation in the South

Many prosperous southerners avoided military service by hiring a substitute. This advertisement for a substitute is graphic evidence of the lack of enthusiasm for the draft. Library of Congress.

Indeed, inflation raged out of control until prices had increased almost 7,000 percent. As early as 1861 and 1862, newspapers were reporting that "the poor of our . . . country will be unable to live at all" and that "want and starvation are staring thousands in the face." Officials warned of "great suffering next year," predicting that "women and children are bound to come to suffering if not starvation."

Some concerned citizens tried to help. "Free markets," which dispersed goods as charity, sprang up in various cities; some families came to the aid of their neighbors. But there were other citizens who would not cooperate: "It is folly for a poor mother to call on the rich people about here," raged one woman. "Their hearts are of steel they would sooner throw what they have to spare to their dogs than give it to a starving child." The need was so vast that it overwhelmed private charity. A rudimentary relief program organized by the Confederacy offered some hope, but was soon curtailed to avoid conflict with the task of supplying the armies. Millions of southern yeomen sank into poverty and suffering.

As their fortunes declined, these people of once-modest means looked around them and found abundant evidence that all classes were not sacrificing equally. They saw that the wealthy curtailed only their luxuries, while many poor families went without necessities. They saw that the government contributed to these inequities through policies that favored the upper class. Until the last year of the war, for example, prosperous southerners could avoid military service by furnishing a hired substitute. Prices for substitutes skyrocketed, until it was common for a man of means to pay $5,000 or $6,000 to send someone to the front. Well over fifty thousand upper-class southerners purchased such substitutes; Mary Boykin Chesnut knew of one young aristocrat who had "spent a fortune in substitutes. Two have been taken from him [when *they* were conscripted], and two he paid to change with him when he was ordered to the front. He is at the end of his row now, for all able-bodied men are ordered to the front. I hear he is going as some general's courier."

Inequities of the Confederate draft

As Chesnut's last remark indicates, the rich also traded on their social connections to avoid danger. "It's a notorious fact," complained an angry Georgian, that "if a man has influential friends–or a little money to spare he will never be enrolled." The Confederate senator from Mississippi James Phelan informed Jefferson Davis that apparently "nine tenths of the youngsters of the land whose relatives are conspicuous in society, wealthy, or influential obtain some safe perch where they can doze with their heads under their wings."

Anger at such discrimination exploded when in October 1862 the Confederate congress exempted from military duty anyone who was supervising at least twenty slaves. The "twenty nigger law" became notorious. "Never did a law meet with more universal odium," observed one representative. "Its influence upon the poor is most calamitous." Immediately protests arose from every corner of the Confederacy, and North Carolina's legislators formally condemned the law. Its defenders argued, however, that the exemption preserved order and aided food production, and the statute remained on the books.

Dissension spread as growing numbers of citizens concluded that the struggle was "a rich man's war and a poor man's fight." Alert politicians and newspaper editors warned that class resentment was building to a dangerous level; letters to Confederate officials during this period contained a bitterness that suggested the depth of the people's anger. "If I and my little children suffer [and] die while there Father is in service," threatened one woman, "I invoke God Almighty that our blood rest upon the South." Another woman swore to the Secretary of War that

> an allwise god . . . will send down his fury and judgment in a very grate manar [on] all those our leading men and those that are in power if thare is no more favors shone to . . . the wives and mothers of those who in poverty has with patrootism stood the fence Battles. . . . I tell you that with out some grate and speadly alterating in the conduckting of afares in this our little nation god will frown on it.

Trouble was brewing in the Confederacy.

The northern economy copes with war

With the onset of war, a tidal wave of change rolled over the North, just as it had over the South. Factories and citizens' associations geared up to support the war, and the federal government and its executive branch gained power they had never had before. Civil liberties were restricted, and social values were influenced by both personal sacrifice and wartime riches. Idealism and greed flourished side by side.

But there was an important difference between North and South: the war did not destroy the North's prosperity. Northern factories ran overtime, and unemployment was low. Furthermore, northern farms and factories came through the war unscathed, whereas most areas of the South suffered extensive destruction. To Union soldiers on the battlefield, sacrifice was a grim reality; but northern civilians experienced only the bustle and energy of wartime production.

Initially, the war was a shock to business. With the sudden closing of the southern market, firms could no longer predict the demand for their goods; many companies had to redirect their activities in order to remain open. And southern debts became uncollectible, jeopardizing not only merchants but many western banks. In farming regions, families struggled with an aggravated shortage of labor. For reasons such as these, the war initially caused an economic slump.

Initial slump in northern business

A few enterprises never pulled out of the tailspin: cotton mills lacked cotton; construction declined; shoe manufacturers sold fewer of the cheap shoes planters had bought for their slaves. Overall the war slowed industrialization in the North. But historians have shown that the war's economic impact was not all negative. Certain entrepreneurs, such as wool producers, benefited from shortages of competing products, and soaring demand for war-related goods swept some businesses to new heights of production. To feed the voracious war machine the federal government pumped unprecedented amounts of money into the economy. The Treasury issued $3.2 billion in bonds and paper money called greenbacks, while the War Department spent over $360 million in tax revenues. Government contracts soon totaled more than $1 billion.

Secretary of War Edwin M. Stanton's list of supplies for the Ordnance Department indicates the scope of government demand: "7,892 cannon, 11,787 artillery carriages, 4,022,130 small-arms . . . 1,022,176,474 cartridges for small-arms, 1,220,555,435 percussion caps . . . 14,507,682 cannon primers and fuses, 12,875,294 pounds of artillery projectiles, 26,440,054 pounds of gunpowder, 6,395,152 pounds of niter, and 90,416,295 pounds of lead." Stanton's list covered only weapons; the government also purchased innumerable quantities of uniforms, boots, food, camp equipment, saddles, ships, and other necessaries.

War-related spending revived business in many northern states. In 1863, a merchants' magazine examined the effects of the war in Massachusetts: "Seldom, if ever, has the business of Massachusetts been more active or profitable than during the past year. . . . Labor has been in great demand . . . trade is again in a high state of prosperity. Wealth has flowed into the State in no stinted measure, despite war and heavy taxes. In every department of labor the government has been, directly or indirectly, the chief employer and paymaster." Government contracts had a particularly beneficial impact on the state's wool, metal, and shipbuilding industries, and saved shoe manufacturers there from ruin.

Effects of war on northern industry and agriculture

War production also promoted the development of heavy industry in the North. The output of coal rose substantially. Iron makers improved the quality of their product while boosting the production of pig iron from 920,000 tons in 1860 to 1,136,000 tons in 1864. And although new railroad construction slowed, the manufacture of rails increased. Of considerable significance for the future were the railroad industry's adoption of a standard gauge for track, and foundries' development of new and less expensive ways to make steel.

Another strength of the northern economy was the complementary relationship between agriculture and industry. The mechanization of agriculture had begun well before the war. Now, though, wartime recruitment and conscription gave western farmers an added incentive to purchase labor-saving machinery. This shift from human labor to machines had a doubly beneficial effect, creating new markets for industry and expanding the food supply for the urban industrial workforce.

The boom in the sale of agricultural tools was tremendous. Cyrus and William McCormick built an industrial empire in Chicago from their sale of reapers. Between 1862 and 1864 the manufacture of mowers and reapers doubled to 70,000 yearly; manufacturers could not supply the demand. By the end of the war, there were 375,000 reapers in use, triple the number in 1861. Large-scale commercial agriculture had become a reality. As a result, farm families whose breadwinners had gone to war did not suffer as they did in the South. "We have seen," one magazine observed, "a stout matron whose sons are in the army, cutting hay with her team . . . and she cut seven acres with ease in a day, riding leisurely upon her cutter."

The northern workers who suffered most during the war were wage earners, particularly industrial and urban workers. Though jobs were plentiful following the initial slump, inflation took much of a worker's paycheck. By 1863 nine-cent-a-pound beef was selling for eighteen cents. The price of coffee had tripled; rice and sugar had doubled; and clothing, fuel, and rent had all climbed. Studies of the cost of living indicate that between 1860 and 1864 consumer prices rose at least 76 percent; meanwhile daily wages rose only 42 percent. To make up the difference, workers' families had to do without.

As their real wages shrank, industrial workers also lost job security. To increase production, some employers were replacing workers with labor-saving machines. Other employers urged the government to liberalize immigration procedures so they could import cheap labor. Workers responded by forming unions

HARPER'S WEEKLY
A JOURNAL OF CIVILIZATION.

Vol. V.—No. 238.] NEW YORK, SATURDAY, JULY 20, 1861. [SINGLE COPIES SIX CENTS. $2 50 PER YEAR IN ADVANCE.

Entered according to Act of Congress, in the Year 1861, by Harper & Brothers, in the Clerk's Office of the District Court for the Southern District of New York.

FILLING CARTRIDGES AT THE UNITED STATES ARSENAL AT WATERTOWN, MASSACHUSETTS.—[See next Page.]

In both North and South women entered the factories to boost wartime production. This *Harper's Weekly* cover shows women filling cartridges in the United States arsenal at Watertown, Massachusetts. Library of Congress.

and sometimes by striking. Skilled craftsmen organized to combat the loss of their jobs and status to machines; women and unskilled workers, excluded by the craftsmen, formed their own unions. And in recognition of the increasingly national scope of business activity, thirteen occupational groups–including tailors, coalminers, and railway engineers–formed national unions during the Civil War. Because of the tight labor market, unions were able to win many of their demands without striking; but still the number of strikes rose steadily.

New militancy among northern workers

Employers reacted negatively to this new spirit among workers–a spirit that William H. Sylvis, leader of the iron molders, called a "feeling of manly independence." Manufacturers viewed labor activism as a threat to their property rights and freedom of action, and accordingly they too formed statewide or craft-based associations to cooperate and pool information. These employers compiled blacklists of union members and required new workers to sign "yellow dog" contracts, or promises not to join a union. To put down strikes, they hired strikebreakers from the ranks of the poor and desperate–blacks, immigrants, and women–and sometimes received additional help from federal troops.

Troublesome as unions were, they did not prevent many employers from making a profit. The biggest fortunes were made in profiteering on government contracts. Unscrupulous businessmen took advantage of the sudden immense demand for goods for the army by selling clothing and blankets made of "shoddy"–wool fibers reclaimed from rags or worn cloth. The goods often came apart in the rain; most of the shoes purchased in the early months of the war were worthless too. Contractors sold inferior guns for double the usual price and tainted meat for the price of good. Corruption was so widespread that it led to a year-long investigation by the House of Representatives. One group of contractors that had demanded $50 million for their products had to reduce their claims to $17 million as a result of the findings of the investigation.

Legitimate enterprises also turned a neat profit. The output of woolen mills increased so dramatically that dividends in the industry nearly tripled. Some cotton mills, though they reduced their output, made record profits on what they sold. Brokerage houses worked until midnight and earned unheard-of commissions. And railroads carried immense quantities of freight and passengers, increasing their business to the point that railroad stocks doubled or even tripled. Erie Railroad stock skyrocketed from $17 to $126 a share.

Wartime benefits to northern business

In fact, railroads were a leading beneficiary of government largesse. Congress had failed in the 1850s to resolve the question of a northern versus a southern route for the first transcontinental railroad. But with the South out of Congress, the northern route quickly prevailed. In 1862 and 1864 Congress chartered two corporations, the Union Pacific Railroad and the Central Pacific Railroad, and assisted them handsomely in connecting Omaha, Nebraska, with Sacramento, California. For each mile of track laid, the railroads received a loan of $16,000 to $48,000 plus twenty square miles of land along a free four-hundred-foot-wide right of way. Overall, the two corporations gained approximately 20 million acres of land and nearly $60 million in loans.

Other businessmen benefited handsomely from the Morrill Land Grant Act (1862). To promote public education in agriculture, engineering, and military science, Congress granted each state 30,000 acres of public land for each of its congressional representatives. The states were free to sell the land as they saw fit, as long as they used the income for the purposes Congress had intended. Though the law eventually fostered sixty-nine colleges and universities, one of its immediate effects was to enrich a few prominent speculators. Hard-pressed to meet wartime expenses, some states sold their land cheaply to wealthy entrepreneurs. Ezra Cornell, for example, purchased 500,000 acres in the Midwest.

Another measure that brought joy to the business community was the tariff. Northern businesses did not uniformly favor high import duties; some manufacturers desired cheap imported raw materials more than they feared foreign competition. But northeastern congressmen traditionally supported higher tariffs, and after southern lawmakers left Washington, they had their way: the tariff act of 1864 raised tariffs generously. According to one scholar, manufacturers had only to mention the rate they considered necessary and that rate was declared. And, as one would expect, some healthy industries made artificially high profits by raising their prices to a level just below that of the foreign competition. By the end of the war, tariff rates averaged 47 percent, more than double the rates of 1857.

The frantic wartime activity, the booming economy, and the Republican alliance with business combined to create a new atmosphere in Washington. The balance of opinion shifted against consumers and wage earners and toward large corporations; the notion spread that government should aid businessmen but not interfere with them. This was the golden hour of untrammeled capitalism, and railroad builders and industrialists–men such as Leland Stanford, Collis P. Huntington, John D. Rockefeller, John M. Forbes, and Jay Gould–took advantage of it. Their enterprises grew with the aid of government loans, grants, and tariffs.

Wartime powers of the U.S. executive

As long as the war lasted, the powers of the federal government and the president continued to grow. Abraham Lincoln found, as had Jefferson Davis, that war required active presidential leadership. At the beginning of the conflict, Lincoln launched a major ship-building program without waiting for Congress to assemble. The lawmakers later approved his decision, and Lincoln continued to act in advance of Congress when he deemed it necessary. In one striking exercise of executive power, Lincoln suspended the writ of habeas corpus for all people living between Washington and Philadelphia. The justification for this action was practical rather than legal; Lincoln was ensuring the loyalty of Maryland. Later in the war, with congressional approval, Lincoln repeatedly suspended the writ and invoked martial law. Roughly ten to twenty thousand United States citizens were arrested on suspicion of disloyal acts.

On occasion Lincoln used his wartime authority to bolster his political power. He and his generals proved adept at arranging furloughs for soldiers who could vote in close elections. Needless to say, the citizens in arms whom Lincoln helped to vote usually voted Republican. In another instance, when the Republican governor of Indiana found himself short of funds because of Democratic opposition, Lincoln generously supplied eight times the amount of money the governor needed to get through the emergency.

Among the clearest examples of the wartime expansion of federal authority were the National Banking Acts of 1863, 1864, and 1865. Prior to the Civil War the nation did not have a uniform currency. Banks operating under a variety of state charters issued no fewer than seven thousand different kinds of notes, which had to be distinguished from a variety of forgeries. Now, acting on the recommendations of Secretary of the Treasury Salmon Chase, Congress established a national banking system empowered to issue a maximum number of national bank notes. At the close of the war in 1865, Congress laid a prohibitive tax on state bank notes and forced most major institutions to join the system. This process led to a sounder currency and a simpler monetary system, but also to an inflexibility in the money supply and an eastern-oriented financial structure.

Soldiers may have sensed the increasing scale of things better than anyone else. Most federal troops were young; eighteen was the most common age, followed by twenty-one. Many soldiers went straight from small towns and farms into large armies supplied by extensive bureaucracies. By December 1861 there were 640,000 volunteers in arms, a stupendous increase over the regular army of 20,000 men. The increase occurred so rapidly that it is remarkable the troops were supplied and organized as well as they were. But many soldiers' first experiences with large organizations were unfortunate.

Blankets, clothing, and arms were often inferior. Vermin were commonplace. Hospitals were badly managed at first. Rules of hygiene in large camps were badly written or unenforced; latrines were poorly made or carelessly used. One investigation turned up "an area of over three acres, encircling the camp as a broad belt, on which is deposited an almost perfect layer of human excrement." Water supplies were unsafe and typhoid fever epidemics common. About 57,000 army men died from dysentery and diarrhea.

The situation would have been much worse but for the U.S. Sanitary Commission. A voluntary civilian organization, the commission worked to improve conditions in camps and to aid sick and wounded soldiers. Still, 224,000 Union troops died from disease or

The U.S. Sanitary Commission, a voluntary civilian organization, did much to improve conditions in military camps. Here some of its members pose at Fredericksburg, Virginia, in 1864. Library of Congress.

accidents, far more than the 140,000 who died in battle.

Such conditions would hardly have predisposed the soldier to sympathize with changing social attitudes on the home front. Amid the excitement of moneymaking, a gaudy culture of vulgar display flourished in the largest cities. A visitor to Chicago commented that "so far as lavish display is concerned, the South Side in some portions has no rival in Chicago, and perhaps not outside New York." Its new residences boasted "marble fronts and expensive ornamentation" that created "a glittering, heartless appearance." As William Cullen Bryant, the distinguished editor of the New York *Evening Post,* observed sadly, "Extravagance, luxury, these are the signs of the times. . . . What business have Americans at any time with such vain show, with such useless magnificence? But especially how can they justify it . . . in this time of war?"

Self-indulgence versus sacrifice in the North

The newly rich did not bother to justify it. *Harper's Monthly* reported that "the suddenly enriched contractors, speculators, and stock-jobbers . . . are spending money with a profusion never before witnessed in our country, at no time remarkable for its frugality. . . . The ordinary sources of expenditure seem to have been exhausted, and these ingenious prodigals have invented new ones. The men button their waistcoats with diamonds . . . and the women powder their hair with gold and silver dust." The New York *Herald* summarized that city's atmosphere:

> All our theatres are open . . . and they are all crowded nightly. . . . the most costly accommodations, in both hotels and theatres, are the first and most eagerly taken. . . . The richest silks, laces

and jewelry are the soonest sold. . . . Not to keep a carriage, not to wear diamonds, not to be attired in a robe which cost a small fortune, is now equivalent to being a nobody. This war has entirely changed the American character. . . . The individual who makes the most money—no matter how—and spends the most—no matter for what—is considered the greatest man. . . .

The world has seen its iron age, its silver age, its golden age, and its brazen age. This is the age of shoddy.

Yet strong elements of idealism coexisted with ostentation. Abolitionists, after initial uncertainty over whether to fight the South or allow division of the Union to separate the North from slavery, campaigned to turn the war into a war against slavery. Free black communities and churches both black and white responded to the needs of slaves who flocked to the Union lines. They sent clothing, ministers, and teachers in generous measure to aid the runaways.

Northern women, like their southern counterparts, took on new roles. Those who stayed home organized over ten thousand soldiers' aid societies, rolled innumerable bandages, and raised $3 million. Thousands served as nurses in front-line hospitals, where they pressed for better care of the wounded. The professionalization of medicine since the Revolution had created a medical system dominated by men; thus dedicated and able female nurses had to fight both military regulations and professional hostility to win the chance to make their contribution. In the hospitals they quickly proved their worth, but only the wounded welcomed them. Even Clara Barton, the most famous female nurse, was ousted from her post during the winter of 1863.

The poet Walt Whitman, who became a daily visitor to wounded soldiers in Washington, D.C., left a record of his experiences as a volunteer nurse. As he dressed wounds and tried to comfort suffering and lonely men, Whitman found "the marrow of the tragedy concentrated in those Army Hospitals." But despite "indescribably horrid wounds . . . the groan that could not be repress'd . . . [the] emaciated face and glassy eye," he also found in the hospitals inspiration and a deepening faith in American democracy. Whitman admired the "incredible dauntlessness" and sacrifice of the common soldier who fought for the Union. "The genius of the United States is not best or most in its executives or legislatures," he had written in the Preface to his great work *Leaves of Grass* (1855), "but always most in the common people." Whitman worked this idealization of the common man into his poetry, rejecting the lofty meter and rhyme characteristic of European verse and striving instead for a "genuineness" that would appeal to the masses.

Thus northern society embraced strangely contradictory tendencies. Materialism and greed flourished alongside idealism, religious conviction, and self-sacrifice. While wealthy men purchased 118,000 substitutes and almost 87,000 commutations at $300 each to avoid service in the Union army, other soldiers risked their lives out of a desire to preserve the Union or extend freedom. It was as if there were several different wars under way, serving several different motives.

The strange advent of emancipation

At the very highest levels of government there was a similar lack of clarity about the purpose of the war. Through the first several months of the struggle, both Davis and Lincoln studiously avoided references to slavery, the crux of the matter. For his part, Davis was intelligent enough to realize that emphasis on the issue might increase class conflict in the South. Earlier in his career he had struggled on occasion to convince nonslaveholders that defense of the planters' slaves was in their interest. Rather than face that challenge again, Davis articulated a conservative ideology. He told southerners they were fighting for constitutional liberty: northern betrayal of the founding fathers' legacy had necessitated secession. As long as Lincoln also avoided making slavery an issue, Davis's line seemed to work.

Lincoln had his own reasons for refraining from mention of slavery. For some time he clung to the hopeful but mistaken idea that a pro-Union majority would assert itself in the South. Perhaps it would be possible, he thought, to coax the South back into the Union and end the fighting. Raising the slavery issue would effectively end any such possibility of compromise.

Powerful political considerations also dictated that Lincoln remain silent. The Republican party was a young and unwieldy coalition. Some Republicans burned with moral outrage over slavery, while others were frankly racist, dedicated to protecting free whites from the Slave Power and the competition of cheap slave labor. Still others saw the tariff or immigration or some other issue as paramount. A forthright stand by Lincoln on the subject of slavery could split the party, pleasing some groups and alienating others. Until a consensus developed among the party's various wings, or until Lincoln found a way to appeal to all the elements of the party, silence was the best approach.

The president's hesitancy ran counter to some of his personal feelings. Lincoln was a sensitive and compassionate man whose self-awareness, humility, and moral anguish during the war were evident in his speeches and writings. But as a politician, Lincoln kept his moral convictions to himself. He distinguished between the personal and the official; he would not let his feelings determine his political acts. As a result, his political positions were studied and complex, calculated for maximum advantage. Frederick Douglass, the astute and courageous black protest leader, sensed that Lincoln the man was without prejudice toward black people. Yet Douglass judged him "preeminently the white man's president."

Lincoln first broached the subject of slavery in a major way in March 1862, when he proposed that the states consider emancipation on their own. He asked Congress to pass a resolution promising aid to any state that decided to emancipate, and he appealed to border-state representatives to give the idea of emancipation serious consideration. What Lincoln was talking about was gradual emancipation, with compensation for slaveholders and colonization of the freed slaves outside the United States. To a delegation of free Negroes he explained that "it is better for us both . . . to be separated." Until well into 1864 Lincoln steadfastly promoted an unpromising and in national terms wholly impractical scheme to colonize blacks in some region like Central America. Despite Secretary of State William H. Seward's care to insert phrases such as "with their consent," the word *deportation* crept into one of Lincoln's speeches in place of *colonization*. Thus his was as conservative a scheme as could be devised. Moreover, since the states would make the decision voluntarily, no responsibility for it would attach to Lincoln.

Lincoln's plan for gradual emancipation

But others wanted to go much further. A group of congressional Republicans known as the Radicals had dedicated themselves to seeing that the war was prosecuted vigorously. They had been instrumental in creating a joint committee on the conduct of the war, which investigated Union reverses, sought to increase the efficiency of the war effort, and prodded the executive to take stronger measures. Early in the war these Radicals, with support from other representatives, turned their attention to slavery.

In August 1861, at the Radicals' instigation, Congress passed its first confiscation act. Designed to punish the Confederate rebels, the law confiscated all property used for "insurrectionary purposes." That is, if the South used slaves in a hostile action, those slaves were declared seized and liberated from their owners' possession. A second confiscation act (July 1862) was much more drastic: it confiscated the property of all those who supported the rebellion, even those who merely resided in the South and paid Confederate taxes. Their slaves were "forever free of their servitude, and not again [to be] held as slaves." The logic behind these acts was that the insurrection—as Lincoln always termed it—was a serious revolution requiring strong measures. Let the government use its full powers, free the slaves, and crush the revolution, urged the Radicals.

Confiscation Acts

Lincoln chose not to go that far. He stood by his proposal of voluntary gradual emancipation by the states and made no effort to enforce the second confiscation act. His stance brought a public protest from Horace Greeley, editor of the powerful *New York Tribune*. In an open letter to the president entitled "The Prayer of Twenty Millions," Greeley wrote, "We require of you . . . that you execute the laws. . . . We think you are strangely and disastrously remiss . . . with regard to the emancipating provisions of the new Confiscation Act. . . . We complain that the Union cause has suffered from mistaken deference to Rebel Slavery." Reaching the nub of the issue, the influential editor went on, "On the face of this wide earth, Mr. President, there is not one disinterested, determined, intelligent champion of the Union cause who does not feel that all attempts to put down the

This photograph, taken four days before Lincoln's assassination, shows the effect of the burdens of war on the president. McLellan Lincoln Collection, Brown University Library.

Rebellion and at the same time uphold its inciting cause are preposterous and futile."

Lincoln's reply was an explicit statement of his complex and calculated approach to the question. He disagreed, he said, with all those who would make the saving or destroying of slavery the paramount issue of the war. "I would save the Union," announced Lincoln. "If I could save the Union without freeing *any* slave I would do it, and if I could save it by freeing *all* the slaves I would do it; and if I could save it by freeing some and leaving others alone I would also do that. What I do about slavery, and the colored race, I do because I believe it helps to save the Union." Lincoln closed with a personal disclaimer: "I have here stated my purpose according to my view of *official* duty; and I intend no modification of my oft-expressed *personal* wish that all men every where could be free."

When he wrote those words, Lincoln had already decided to take a new step: issuance of the Emancipation Proclamation. On the advice of the cabinet, however, he was waiting for a major Union victory before announcing it, so the proclamation would not appear to be an act of desperation. Yet the letter to Greeley was not an effort to stall; it was an integral part of Lincoln's approach to the future of slavery, as the text of the Emancipation Proclamation would show.

On September 22, 1862, shortly after the Battle of Antietam, Lincoln issued the first part of his two-part proclamation. Invoking his powers as commander-in-chief of the armed forces, he announced that on January 1 he would emancipate the slaves in states whose people "shall then be in rebellion against the United States." The January proclamation would designate the areas in rebellion based on the presence or absence of bona fide representatives in Congress.

Emancipation proclamations

The September proclamation was not a declaration of the right of slaves to be free, but a threat to southerners to lay down their arms. "Knowing the value that was set on the slaves by the rebels," said Garrison Frazier, a black Georgian, "the President thought that his proclamation would stimulate them to lay down their arms . . . and their not doing so has now made the freedom of the slaves a part of the war." Lincoln may not actually have expected southerners to give up their effort, but he was careful to offer them the option, thus putting the onus of emancipation on them.

Lincoln's designation of the areas in rebellion on January 1 is worth noting. He excepted from his list every Confederate county or city that had fallen under Union control. Those areas, he declared, "are, for the present, left precisely as if this proclamation were not issued." And in a telling omission, Lincoln neglected to liberate slaves in the border slave states that remained in the Union.

"The President has purposely made the proclamation inoperative in all places where . . . the slaves [are] accessible," complained the anti-administration New York *World*. "He has proclaimed emancipation only where he has notoriously no power to execute it." The exceptions, said the paper, "render the proclamation not merely futile, but ridiculous." Partisanship aside, even Secretary of State Seward, a moderate Republican, said sarcastically that, "we show our sympathy with slavery by emancipating slaves where we cannot reach them and holding them in bondage where we can set them free." A British official, Lord Russell, commented on the "very strange nature" of the document, noting that it did not declare "a principle adverse to slavery."

Furthermore, by making the liberation of the slaves "a fit and necessary war measure," Lincoln raised a variety of legal questions. How long did a war measure have force? Did its power cease with the suppression of a rebellion? The proclamation did little to clarify the status or citizenship of the freed slaves. And a reference to garrison duty in one of the closing paragraphs suggested that slaves would have inferior duties and rank in the army. (For many months, in fact, their pay and treatment were inferior.)

Thus the Emancipation Proclamation was a puzzling and ambiguous document that said less than it seemed to say. Physically it freed no bondsmen, and major limitations were embedded in its language. But if as a moral and legal document it was wanting, as a political document it was nearly flawless. Because the proclamation defined the war as a war against slavery, liberals could applaud it. Yet at the same time it protected Lincoln's position with conservatives, leaving him room to retreat if he chose and forcing no immediate changes on the border slave states. The president had not gone as far as Congress had, and he had taken no position he could not change.

Lincoln seemed to take a stronger stand in June 1864. On the eve of the Republican national convention, he called the party's chairman to the White House and issued these instructions: "Mention in your speech, when you call the convention to order . . . to put into the platform as the keystone, the amendment of the Constitution abolishing and prohibiting slavery forever." It was done; the party called for a new constitutional amendment, the thirteenth. And though Republican delegates would probably have adopted such a plank without Lincoln's urging, still Lincoln worked diligently to win approval for the measure in Congress. He succeeded, and the proposed amendment went to the states for ratification.

But even this was not Lincoln's last word on the matter. In 1865 the newly re-elected president considered allowing the defeated southern states to re-enter the Union and delay or defeat the amendment. In February he and Secretary of State Seward met with three Confederate commissioners at Hampton Roads, Virginia. The end of the war was clearly in sight, and southern representatives angled vainly for an armistice that would allow southern independence. But Lincoln was doing some political maneuvering of his own, apparently contemplat-

Hampton Roads Conference

Black troops, many of whom had been slaves, infused vital strength into the Union armies. The men above, members of Company E, Fourth U.S. Colored Infantry, were photographed at Fort Lincoln, Virginia. Chicago Historical Society.

ing the creation of a new and broader party based on a postwar alliance with southern Whigs and moderates. The cement for the coalition would be concessions on the status of blacks.

Pointing out that the Emancipation Proclamation was only a war measure, Lincoln predicted that the courts would decide whether it had granted all, some, or none of the slaves their freedom. Seward observed that the Thirteenth Amendment, which constitutionally and definitively abolished slavery, was not yet ratified; re-entry into the Union would allow the southern states to vote against it and block it. Lincoln did not contradict him, but spoke in favor of "prospective" ratification—ratification with a five-year delay. He also promised to seek $400 million in compensation for slaveholders and to consider their position on such related questions as confiscation. Such financial aid would provide an economic incentive for planters to rejoin the Union, and capital to ease the transition to freedom for both races.

These were startling propositions from a president who was on the verge of military victory. Most northerners opposed them, and only the opposition of Jefferson Davis, who set himself against anything short of independence, prevented discussion of the proposals in the South. They indicated that even at the end of the war, Lincoln was keeping his options open, maintaining the line he had drawn between "*official* duty" and "*personal* wish." Contrary to legend, then, Lincoln did not attempt to lead public opinion on race, as did advocates of equality in one direction and racist Democrats in the other. Instead he moved cautiously, constructing complex and ambiguous positions. He avoided the great risks inherent in challenging, educating, or inspiring national conscience.

Before the war was over, the Confederacy too addressed the issue of emancipation. Ironically, a strong proposal in favor of liberation came from Jefferson Davis. Though emancipation was far less popular in

Davis's plan for emancipation

the South than in the North, Davis did not flinch or conceal his purpose. He was dedicated to independence, and he was willing to sacrifice slavery to achieve that goal. After considering the alternatives for some time, Davis concluded in the fall of 1864 that it was necessary to act.

Reasoning that the military situation of the Confederacy was desperate, and that independence with emancipation was preferable to defeat with emancipation, Davis proposed that the central government purchase and train forty thousand male Negro laborers. The men would work for the army under a promise of emancipation and future residence in the South. Later Davis upgraded his proposal, calling for the recruitment and arming of slave soldiers. The wives and children of these soldiers, he made plain, must also receive freedom from the states. Bitter debate resounded through the South, but Davis stood his ground. When the Confederate congress approved enlistments without the promise of freedom, Davis insisted on more. He issued an executive order to guarantee that owners would cooperate with the emancipation of slave soldiers, and his allies in the states started to work for emancipation of the soldiers' families.

Confederate emancipation began too late to revive southern armies or win diplomatic advantages with antislavery Europeans. But Lincoln's Emancipation Proclamation stimulated a vital infusion of manpower into the Union armies. Beginning in 1863 slaves shouldered arms for the North. Before the war was over, 150,000 of them had fought for freedom and the Union. Their participation was crucial to northern victory, and it discouraged recognition of the Confederacy by foreign governments. Lincoln's policy, despite its limitations and its lack of clarity, had much greater practical effect.

The disintegration of the Confederacy

During the final two years of fighting, both northern and southern governments waged the war in the face of increasing opposition at home. Dissatisfaction that had surfaced earlier grew more intense and sometimes even violent. The unrest was connected to the military stalemate: neither side was close to victory in 1863, though the war had become gigantic in scope and costly in lives. But protest also arose from fundamental stresses in the social structures of the North and the South.

The Confederacy's problems were both more serious and more deeply rooted than the North's. Vastly disadvantaged in terms of industrial capacity, natural resources, and labor, southerners felt the cost of the war more quickly, more directly, and more painfully than northerners. But even more fundamental were the Confederacy's internal problems; crises that were integrally connected with the southern class system threatened the Confederate cause.

Planters' opposition to the Confederacy

One ominous development was the increasing opposition of planters to their own government, whose actions had had a negative effect on them. As a diplomatic weapon the South had withheld most of its cotton from world markets, hurting the planters' profits. Confederate military authorities had also impressed slaves to build fortifications. And when Union forces advanced on plantation areas, Confederate commanders had sent detachments through the countryside to burn stores of cotton that lay in the enemy's path. Such interference with plantation routines and financial interests was not what planters had expected of their government.

Nor were the centralizing policies of the Davis administration popular. Many planters agreed with the Charleston *Mercury* that the southern states had seceded because the federal government had grown and "usurped powers not granted–progressively trenched upon State Rights." The increasing size and power of the Richmond administration therefore startled and alarmed them.

The Confederate constitution, drawn up by the leading political thinkers of the South, had in fact granted substantial powers to the central government, especially in time of war. But for many planters, states' rights had become virtually synonymous with complete state sovereignty. R. B. Rhett, editor of the Charleston *Mercury,* wishfully (and inaccurately) described the Confederate constitution: "[It] leaves the States untouched in their Sovereignty, and commits to the Confederate Government only a few simple objects, and a few simple powers to enforce them." Governor Joseph E. Brown of Georgia took a similarly exalted view of the importance of the states. During the brief interval between Georgia's secession from the Union and its admission to the Confederacy, Brown sent an ambassador to Europe to seek recognition for the sovereign republic of Georgia from Queen Victoria, Napoleon III, and the King of Belgium. His mentality harkened back to the 1770s and the Articles of Confederation, not to the Constitution of 1789 or the Confederate constitution.

In effect, years of opposition to the federal government within the Union had frozen southerners in a defensive posture. Now they erected the barrier of states' rights as a defense against change, hiding behind it while their capacity for creative statesmanship atrophied. Planters sought a guarantee that their plantations and their lives would remain untouched; they were deeply committed neither to building a southern nation nor to winning independence. If the Confederacy had been allowed to depart from the Union in peace and continue as a semideveloped cotton-growing region, they would have been content. When secession revolutionized their world, they could not or would not adjust to it.

Confused and embittered, southerners struck out instead at Jefferson Davis. Conscription, thundered Governor Brown, was "subversive of [Georgia's] sovereignty, and at war with all the principles for the support of which Georgia entered into this revolution." Searching for ways to frustrate the law, Brown bickered over draft exemptions and ordered local enrollment officials not to cooperate with the Confederacy. The Charleston *Mercury* told readers that "conscription . . . is . . . the very embodiment of Lincolnism, which our gallant armies are today fighting." And in a gesture of stubborn selfishness, planter Robert Toombs of Georgia, a former U.S. Senator, defied the government, the newspapers, and his neighbors' petitions by continuing to grow large amounts of cotton. His action bespoke the inflexibility and frustration of the southern elite at a crucial point in the Confederacy's struggle to survive.

The southern courts ultimately upheld Davis's power to conscript. He continued to provide strong leadership and drove through the legislature measures that gave the Confederacy a fighting chance. Despite his cold formality and inability to disarm critics, Davis possessed two important virtues: iron determination and total dedication to independence. These qualities kept the Confederacy afloat, for he implemented his measures and enforced them. But his actions earned him the hatred of most influential and elite citizens.

Meanwhile, at the bottom of southern society, there were other difficulties. Food riots occurred in the spring of 1863 in Atlanta, Macon, Columbus, and Augusta, Georgia; and in Salisbury and High Point, North Carolina. On April 2, a crowd assembled in the Confederate capital of Richmond to demand relief from Governor Letcher. A passerby, noticing the excitement, asked a young girl, "Is there some celebration?" "There is," replied the girl. "We celebrate our right to live. We are starving. As soon as enough of us get together we are going to the bakeries and each of us will take a loaf of bread." Soon they did just that, sparking a riot that Davis himself had to quell at gunpoint. Later that fall, another group of angry rioters ransacked a street in Mobile, Alabama.

Food riots in southern cities

Throughout the rural South, ordinary people resisted more quietly—by refusing to cooperate with impressments of food, conscription, or tax collection. "In all the States impressments are evaded by every means which ingenuity can suggest, and in some openly resisted," wrote a high-ranking commissary officer. Farmers who did provide food refused to accept certificates of credit or government bonds in lieu of cash, as required by law. And conscription officers increasingly found no one to draft—men of draft age were hiding out in the forests. "The disposition to avoid military service," observed one of Georgia's senators in 1864, "is general." In some areas tax agents were killed in the line of duty.

Davis was ill-equipped to deal with such discontent. Austere and private by nature, he failed to communicate with the masses. For long stretches of time he buried himself in military affairs or administrative details, until a crisis forced him to rush off on a speaking tour to revive the spirit of resistance. His class perspective also distanced him from the sufferings of the common people. While his social circle in Richmond dined on duck and oysters, ordinary southerners leached salt from the smokehouse floor and went hungry. State governors who saw to the common people's needs won the public's loyalty, but Davis failed to reach out to them and thus lost the support of the plain folk.

Such civil discontent was certain to affect the Confederate armies. "What man is there that would stay in the army and no that his family is sufring at home?" an angry citizen wrote anonymously to the secretary of war. An upcountry South Carolina newspaper

A southern family flees its home as the battle lines draw near. Photographed by Matthew Brady. The Bettmann Archive.

agreed, asking, "What would sooner make our soldiers falter than the cry from their families?" Spurred by concern for their loved ones and resentment of the rich man's war, large numbers of men did indeed leave the armies, supported by their friends and neighbors.

Desertions from the Confederate army

Mary Boykin Chesnut observed a man being dragged back to the army as his wife looked on. "Desert agin, Jake!" she cried openly. "You desert agin, quick as you kin. Come back to your wife and children."

Desertion did not become a serious problem for the Confederacy until the summer of 1862, and stiffer policing solved the problem that year. But from 1863 on, the number of men on duty fell rapidly as desertions soared. By the summer of 1863, John A. Campbell, a former justice of the Supreme Court, wondered whether "so general a habit" as desertion could be considered a crime. Campbell estimated that 40,000 to 50,000 troops were absent without leave and that 100,000 were evading duty in some way. Liberal furloughs, amnesty proclamations, and appeals to return had little effect; by November 1863, Secretary of War James Seddon admitted that one-third of the army could not be accounted for. And the situation was to worsen.

The gallantry of those who stayed on in Lee's army and the daring of their commander made for a deceptively positive start to the 1863 campaign. On May 2 and 3 at Chancellorsville, Virginia, 130,000 members of the Union Army of the Potomac bore down on fewer than 60,000 Confederates. Acting as if they enjoyed being outnumbered, Lee and Stonewall Jackson boldly divided their forces, ordering 30,000 men under Jackson on a day-long march west-

Battle of Chancellorsville

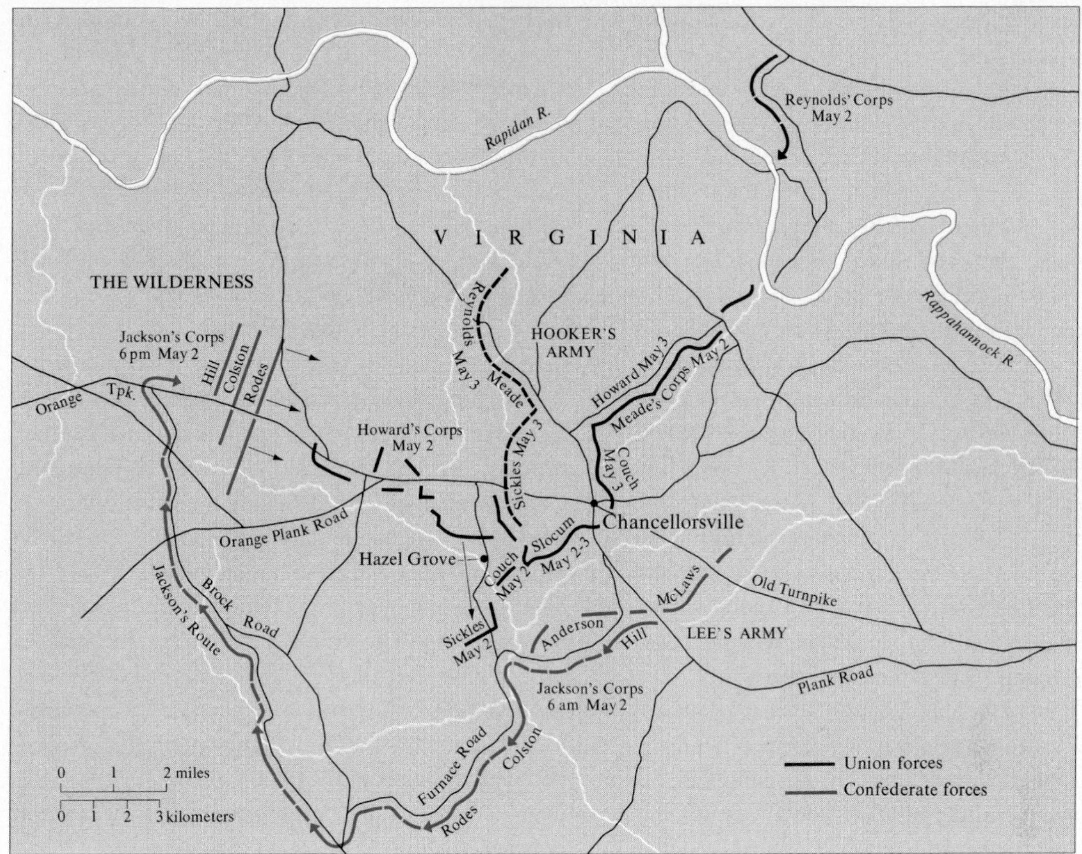

The Battle of Chancellorsville, May 2–3, 1863

ward and to the rear for a flank attack (see map). Jackson arrived at his position late in the afternoon to witness unprepared Union troops "laughing, smoking," playing cards, and waiting for dinner. "Push right ahead," Jackson said, and his weary but excited corps swooped down on the Federals and drove their right wing back in confusion. The Union forces left Chancellorsville the next day defeated. Though Stonewall Jackson had been fatally wounded, it was a remarkable southern victory.

But two critical battles in July 1863 brought crushing defeats to the Confederacy. General Ulysses S. Grant, after months of searching through swamps and bayous, had succeeded in finding an advantageous approach to Vicksburg, and promptly laid siege to that vital western fortification. If Vicksburg fell, U.S. forces would control the Mississippi, cutting the Confederacy in half and gaining an open path into the interior. Meanwhile, with no serious threat to Richmond, General Robert E. Lee proposed a Confederate invasion of the North, to turn the tables on the Union and divert attention from Vicksburg. Both movements drew toward conclusion early in July.

In the North, Lee's troops streamed through Maryland and into Pennsylvania, where they threatened both Washington and Baltimore. The possibility of a major victory before the Union capital became more and more likely. But along the Mississippi, Confederate prospects darkened. Davis and Secretary of War Seddon repeatedly wired General Joseph E. Johnston to concentrate his forces and attack Grant's army. "Vicksburg must not be lost, at least without a struggle," they insisted. Johnston, however, either failed in imagination or did not understand the possibilities of his command. "I consider saving Vicksburg hopeless," he telegraphed at one point, and despite prodding he did nothing to relieve the garrison. In the meantime, Grant's men were supplying themselves by drawing on the agricultural riches of the Mississippi River valley. With such provisions, they could continue their siege indefinitely. In fact, their rich meat-and-vegetables diet had become so tiresome to them that one day, as Grant rode by, a private looked up and muttered, "Hardtack" (pilot biscuit). Soon a line of soldiers was shouting "Hardtack! Hardtack!" demanding respite from turkey and sweet potatoes.

In such circumstances the fall of Vicksburg was inevitable, and on July 4, 1863, its commander surrendered. That same day a battle that had been raging since July 1 concluded at Gettysburg, Pennsylvania.

Battle of Gettysburg

On July 1 and 2, the Union and Confederate forces had both made gains in furious fighting. Then on July 3 Lee ordered a direct assault on Union fortifications atop Cemetery Ridge. Full of foreboding, General James Longstreet warned Lee that "no 15,000 men ever arrayed for battle can take that position." But Lee, hoping success might force the Union to accept peace with independence, stuck to his plan. His brave troops rushed the position, and a hundred momentarily breached the enemy's line. But most fell in heavy slaughter. On July 4 Lee had to withdraw, having suffered almost 4,000 killed and approximately 24,000 missing and wounded. The Confederate general reported to Jefferson Davis that "I am alone to blame," and tendered his resignation. Davis replied that to find a more capable commander was "an impossibility."

Though southern troops had displayed a courage and dedication that would never be forgotten, the results had been disastrous. Intelligent southerners could no longer deny that defeat lay ahead. Josiah Gorgas, the genius of Confederate ordnance operations, confided to his diary, "Today absolute ruin seems our portion. The Confederacy totters to its destruction." In desperation President Davis and several state governors resorted to threats and racial scare tactics to drive southern whites to further sacrifice. Defeat, Davis warned, would mean "extermination of yourselves, your wives, and children." Governor Charles Clark of Mississippi predicted "elevation of the black race to a position of equality–aye, of superiority, that will make them your masters and rulers." Abroad, English officials held back the delivery of badly needed warships, and diplomats postponed any thought of recognizing the Confederate government.

From this point on, the internal disintegration of the Confederacy quickened. A few newspapers and a few bold politicians began to call openly for peace. "We are for peace," admitted the Raleigh, North Carolina, *Daily Progress,* "because there has been enough of blood and carnage, enough of widows and orphans." A neighboring journal, the North Carolina *Standard,* vowed to "tell the truth," tacitly admitted that defeat was inevitable, and called for negotiations. Similar proposals were made in several state legislatures, though they were presented as plans for independence on honorable terms. But more important, Confederate leaders had begun to realize that they were losing the support of the common people. A prominent Texan noted in his diary that secession had been the work of political leaders operating without the firm support of "the mass of the people without property." Governor Zebulon Vance of North Carolina, who agreed, wrote privately that independence would require more "blood and misery . . . and our people will not pay this price I am satisfied for their independence. . . . The great popular heart is not now & never has been in this war."

In North Carolina a peace movement grew under the leadership of William W. Holden, a popular Democratic politician and editor. In the summer of 1863 over one hundred public meetings took place in

Southern peace movements

support of peace negotiations; many established figures believed that Holden had the majority of the people behind him. In Georgia early in 1864, Governor Brown and Alexander H. Stephens, vice president of the Confederacy, led a similar effort. Ultimately, however, these movements came to naught. The lack of a two-party system threw into question the legitimacy of any criticism of the government; even Holden and Brown could not entirely escape the taint of dishonor and disloyalty. That the movement existed despite the risks suggested deep disaffection.

The results of the 1863 congressional elections continued the tendency toward dissent. Everywhere secessionists and supporters of the administration lost seats to men who were not identified with the government. Many of the new representatives, who were often former Whigs, openly opposed the administration or publicly favored peace. In the last years of the war,

Davis depended heavily on support from Union-occupied districts to maintain a majority in the congress. Having secured the legislation he needed, he used the bureaucracy and the army to enforce his unpopular policies. Ironically, as the South's situation grew desperate, former critics such as the Charleston *Mercury* became supporters of the administration. They and a solid core of courageous and determined soldiers kept the Confederacy alive in the face of disintegrating popular support.

By 1864 much of the opposition to the war had moved entirely outside politics. Southerners were simply giving up the struggle, withdrawing their cooperation from the government, and forming a sort of counter-society. Deserters joined with ordinary citizens who were sick of the war to dominate whole towns and counties. Secret societies dedicated to reunion, such as the Heroes of America and the Red Strings, sprang up. Active dissent spread throughout the South but was particularly common in upland and mountain regions. "The condition of things in the mountain districts of North Carolina, South Carolina, Georgia, and Alabama," admitted Assistant Secretary of War John A. Campbell, "menaces the existence of the Confederacy as fatally as either of the armies of the United States." Confederate officials tried using the army to round up deserters and compel obedience, but this approach was only temporarily effective. The government was losing the support of its citizens.

Antiwar sentiment in the North

In the North opposition to the war was similar in many ways, but not as severe. There was concern over the growing centralization of government, and war-weariness was a frequent complaint. Discrimination and injustice in the draft sparked protest among poor citizens, just as they had in the South. But the Union was so much richer than the South in human resources that none of these problems ever threatened the stability of the government. Fresh recruits were always available, and food and other necessaries were not subject to severe shortages.

What was more, Lincoln possessed a talent that Davis lacked: he knew how to stay in touch with the ordinary citizen. Through letters to newspapers and to soldiers' families, he reached the common people and demonstrated that he had not forgotten them. Their grief was his also, for the war was his personal tragedy. After scrambling to the summit of political ambition, Lincoln had seen the glory of the presidency turn to horror. The daily carnage, the tortuous political problems, and the ceaseless criticism weighed heavily on him. In moving language, this president, with the demeanor of a self-educated man of humble origins was able to communicate his suffering. His words helped to contain northern discontent, though they could not remove it.

Much of this wartime protest sprang from politics. The Democratic party, though nudged from its dominant position by the Republican surge of the late 1850s, remained strong. Its leaders were determined to regain power, and they found much to criticize in Lincoln's policies: the carnage and length of the war, the expansion of federal powers, inflation and the high tariff, and the improved status of blacks. Accordingly, they attacked the continuation of the war, calling for reunion on the basis of "the Constitution as it is and the Union as it was." The Democrats denounced conscription and martial law, and defended states' rights and the interests of agriculture. They charged repeatedly that Republican policies were designed to flood the North with blacks, depriving white males of their status, jobs, and women. Their stand appealed to southerners who had settled north of the Ohio River, to conservatives, to many poor people, and to some eastern merchants who had lost profitable southern trade. In the 1862 elections, the Democrats made a strong comeback. And during the war, peace Democrats influenced New York state and won majorities in the legislatures of Illinois and Indiana.

Peace Democrats

Led by outspoken men like Clement L. Vallandigham of Ohio, the peace Democrats were highly visible. Vallandigham criticized Lincoln as a dictator who had suspended the writ of habeas corpus without congressional authority and arrested thousands of innocent citizens. Like other Democrats, he condemned both conscription and emancipation and urged voters to use their power at the polling place to depose "King Abraham." Vallandigham stayed carefully within legal bounds, but his attacks were so damaging

The New York City draft riot (July 1863), by far the most serious of northern riots against conscription. Library of Congress.

to the war effort that military authorities arrested him after Lincoln suspended habeas corpus. Fearing that Vallandigham might gain the stature of a martyr, the president decided against a jail term and exiled him to the Confederacy. Thus Lincoln rid himself of a troublesome critic, in the process saddling puzzled Confederates with a man who insisted on talking about "our country." Eventually Vallandigham returned to the North through Canada.

Lincoln believed that antiwar Democrats were linked to secret organizations, such as the Knights of the Golden Circle and the Order of American Knights, that harbored traitorous ideas. These societies, he feared, stimulated draft resistance, discouraged enlistment, sabotaged communications, and plotted to aid the Confederacy. Likening such groups to a poisonous snake striking at the government, Republicans sometimes branded them—and by extension the peace Democrats—as Copperheads. Though Democrats were connected with these organizations, most engaged in politics rather than treason. And though some saboteurs and Confederate agents were active in the North, they never effected any major demonstration of support for the Confederacy. Whether Lincoln overreacted in arresting his critics and suppressing opposition is still a matter of debate, but it is certain that he acted with a heavier hand and with less provocation than Jefferson Davis.

More violent opposition to the government came from ordinary citizens facing the draft, especially the urban poor. Conscription was a massive but poorly organized affair. Federal enrolling officers made up the list of eligibles, a procedure open to personal favoritism and ethnic or class prejudice. Lists of those conscripted reveal that poor men were called more often than rich, and that disproportionate numbers of immigrants were called. (Approximately 200,000 men born in Germany and 150,000 born in Ireland served in the Union army.) And rich men could furnish substitutes or pay a commutation to avoid service.

As a result, there were scores of disturbances and melees. Enrolling officers received rough treatment in many parts of the North, and riots occurred in Ohio, Indiana, Pennsylvania, Illinois, and Wisconsin, and in such cities as Troy, Albany, and Newark. By far the most serious outbreak of violence, however, occurred in New York City in July 1863. The war was unpopular in that Democratic stronghold, and ethnic and class tensions ran high. Shippers had recently broken a longshoremen's strike by hiring black strikebreakers who worked under police protection. Working-class New Yorkers feared an influx of such black labor from the South and regarded blacks as the cause of an unpopular war. Irish workers, often recently arrived and poor themselves, resented being forced to serve in the place of others. And indeed, local draft lists certified that the poor foreign-born were going to have to bear the burden of service.

New York City draft riot

The provost marshal's office came under attack first. Then mobs crying "Down with the rich" looted wealthy homes and stores. But blacks proved to be the rioters' special target. Luckless blacks who happened to be in the rioters' path were beaten; soon the mob rampaged through black neighborhoods, destroying an orphans' asylum. At least seventy-four people died during the violence, which raged out of control for three days. Only the dispatch of army units fresh from Gettysburg ended the episode.

Once inducted, northern soldiers felt many of the same anxieties and grievances as their southern counterparts. Federal troops too had to cope with loneliness and concern for their loved ones, disease, and the tedium of camp life. Thousands of men slipped away from authorities. Given the problems plaguing the draft and the discouragement in the North over lack of progress in the war, it is not surprising that the Union army struggled with a desertion rate as high as the Confederates'.

Discouragement and war-weariness neared their peak during the summer of 1864. At that point the Democratic party nominated the popular General George B. McClellan for president and put a qualified peace plank into its platform. The plank, written by Vallandigham, condemned "four years of failure to restore the Union by the experiment of war" and called for an armistice. Lincoln concluded that it was "exceedingly probable that this Administration will not be re-elected."

Then, during a publicized interchange with Confederate emissaries in Canada, Lincoln insisted that the terms for peace include reunion and "the abandonment of slavery." A wave of protest rose in the North, for many voters were weary of war and unready to demand terms beyond preservation of the Union. Lincoln quickly backtracked, denying that his offer meant "that nothing *else* or *less* would be considered, if offered." He would insist on freedom only for those slaves (about 150,000) who had joined the Union cause under his promise of emancipation. Thus Lincoln in effect acknowledged the danger that he would not be re-elected. The fortunes of war, however, soon changed the electoral situation.

The northern vise closes

The year 1864 brought to fruition the North's long-term diplomatic strategy. From the outset, the North had pursued one paramount diplomatic goal: to prevent recognition of the Confederacy by European nations. Foreign recognition would damage the North's claim that it was fighting an illegal rebellion, not a separate nation. But more important, recognition would open the way to the foreign military and financial aid that could assure Confederate victory. Among the British elite, there was considerable sympathy for southern planters, whose aristocratic values were similar to their own. And in terms of power politics, both England and France stood to benefit from a divided America, which would necessarily be a weaker rival. Thus Lincoln and Secretary of State Seward faced a difficult task. To achieve their goal, they needed to avoid both major military defeats and unnecessary controversies with the European powers.

Northern diplomatic strategy

Some southerners were supremely confident that England would recognize the Confederacy, in order to obtain cotton for its mills. But though cotton was a good card to play, it was not a trump. At the beginning of the war British mills had a 50-percent surplus of cotton on hand, and new sources of supply in India, Egypt, and Brazil helped to fill their needs later on. So the British government refused to be stampeded into recognition and kept its eye on the battlefield. France, though sympathetic to the South, was unwilling to act without the British. Confederate agents were able to purchase valuable arms and supplies in Europe and obtained some loans from continental financiers, but they never achieved a diplomatic breakthrough.

On three occasions the Union strategy nearly broke down. A major crisis occurred in 1861 when the overzealous commander of an American frigate stopped the British steamer *Trent* and abducted two Confederate ambassadors. The British reacted strongly, but Lincoln and Seward were able to delay until public opinion allowed them to back down and return the ambassadors. In another lengthy crisis, the United States protested but could not stop the sale of six warships to the Confederacy by British shipbuilders. And in the third crisis, the victories at Gettysburg and Vicksburg helped northern officials to block delivery to the Confederacy of British warships—the formidable Laird rams, whose pointed prows were designed to break the Union blockade.

The year 1864 also brought the military success the Union sought—a breakthrough in the West. After General George H. Thomas's inspired troops won the Battle of Chattanooga in November 1863 by ignoring orders and charging up Missionary Ridge, the heartland of the Confederacy lay open. In May Grant

"Our all depends on that army at Atlanta," wrote the southerner Mary Boykin Chesnut. But General Sherman's army occupied Atlanta on September 2, 1864, and demolished the railroad depot shown above. Library of Congress.

Union breakthrough in the West

moved to the Virginia theater, and General William Tecumseh Sherman, in command of 100,000 men, began an advance toward Atlanta. In Sherman's path the Confederacy placed the army of General Johnston. Popular with his men and a master of tactics, Johnston slowed Sherman down as he withdrew skillfully and with minimal losses toward Atlanta. From a purely military point of view, Johnston was conducting the defense shrewdly, if not with clear success.

But Jefferson Davis could not afford to take a purely military point of view. His entire political strategy for 1864 depended on the demonstration of Confederate military strength and a successful defense of Atlanta. With the federal elections of 1864 approaching, Davis hoped that a display of strength and resolution by the South would defeat Lincoln and elect a president who would sue for peace. Anxiously Davis pressed Johnston for news of his movements and assurances that Atlanta would be held. But the southern general was uninformative and continued to fall back. Finally Davis removed Johnston and replaced him with the one-legged General John Hood, who was ready to fight. "Our all depends on that army at Atlanta," wrote Mary Boykin Chesnut. "If that fails us, the game is up."

And the game was up. Hood attacked but was

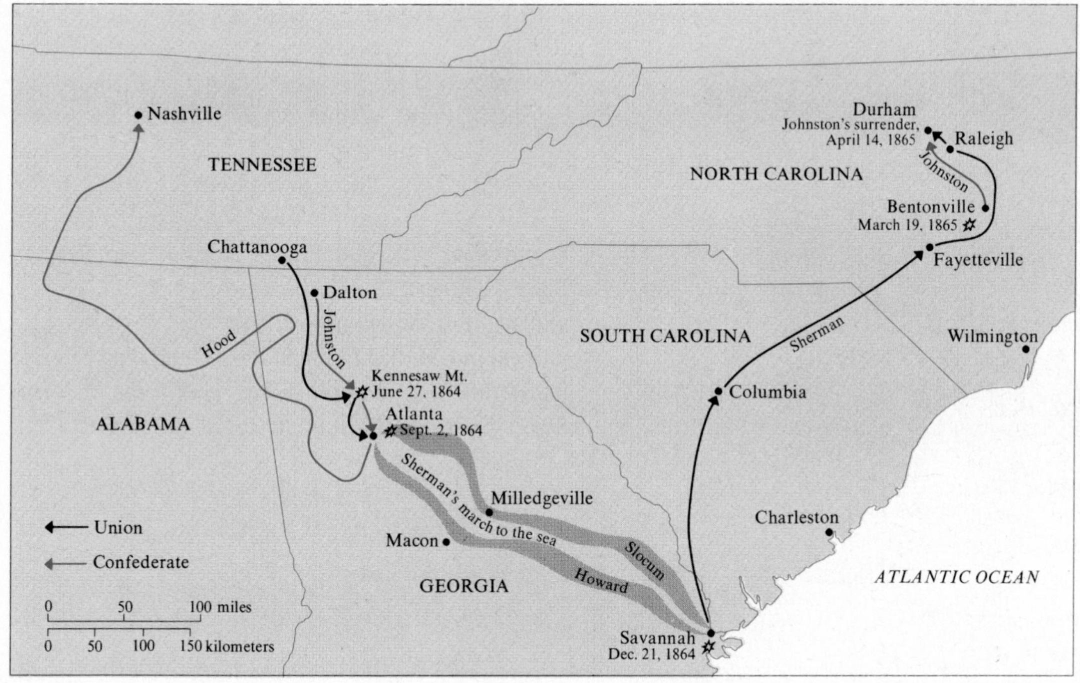

Sherman's march to the sea

beaten, and Sherman's army occupied Atlanta on September 2, 1864. The victory buoyed northern spirits and assured Lincoln's re-election. Mary Chesnut moaned, "There is no hope," and a government clerk in Richmond wrote, "Our fondly-cherished visions of peace have vanished like a mirage of the desert." Though Davis exhorted southerners to fight on and win new victories before the federal elections, he had to admit that "two-thirds of our men are absent . . . most of them absent without leave." Hood's army marched north to cut Sherman's supply lines and force him to retreat, but Sherman elected to live off the land and marched the greater part of his army straight to the sea, destroying Confederate resources as he went (see map).

Sherman's march through Georgia

The path Sherman cut across Georgia was fifty to sixty miles wide; the totality of the destruction was awesome. A Georgia woman described the "Burnt Country" this way: "The fields were trampled down and the road was lined with carcasses of horses, hogs, and cattle that the invaders, unable either to consume or to carry away with them, had wantonly shot down to starve our people and prevent them from making their crops. The stench in some places was unbearable." As many as nineteen thousand slaves gladly took the opportunity to escape bondage and join the Union army as it passed through the countryside. Others held back to await the end of the war on the plantations, either from an ingrained wariness of whites or from negative experiences with the soldiers. The destruction of food harmed them as well as white rebels; many blacks lost blankets, shoes, and other valuables to their liberators. In fact, the brutality of Sherman's troops shocked these veterans of the whip. "I'se seed dem cut de hams off 'n a live pig or ox and go off leavin' de animal groanin'," recalled one man. "De massa had 'em kilt den, but it wuz awful." Sherman reached Savannah in December, his mission accomplished.

In Virginia the preliminaries to victory were protracted and ghastly. Throughout the spring and summer Grant hurled his troops at Lee's army and suffered appalling losses: almost 18,000 casualties in the Battle of the Wilderness, more than 8,000 at Spotsylvania, and 12,000 in the space of a few hours at Cold

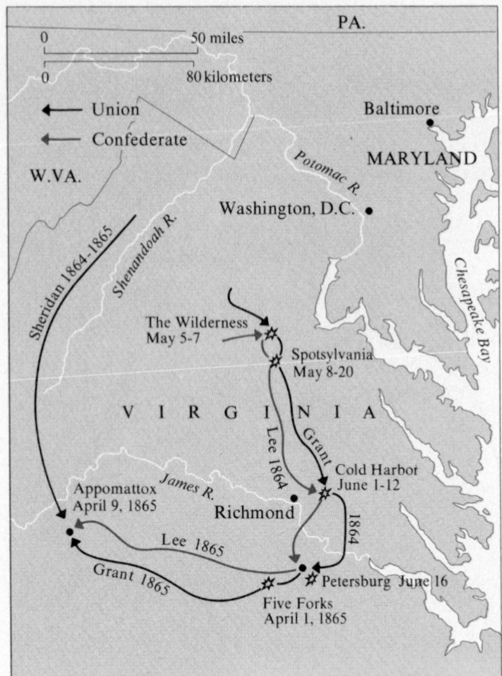

The war in Virginia, 1864–1865

Harbor (see map). Before the last battle, Union troops pinned scraps of paper bearing their names and addresses to their backs, certain that they would be mowed down as they rushed Lee's trenches. In four weeks in May and June, Grant lost as many men as were enrolled in Lee's entire army. Undaunted, Grant remarked, "I propose to fight it out along this line if it takes all summer." And the heavy fighting did prepare the way for eventual victory: Lee's army shrank to the point that offensive action was no longer possible, while the Union army kept replenishing its forces with new recruits.

The end finally came in 1865. Sherman marched north, wreaking great destruction on South Carolina, and into North Carolina, where he moved against a small army commanded by General Johnston. In Virginia Grant kept battering at Lee, who tried but failed to break through the federal line east of Petersburg on March 25. With the numerical superiority of Grant's army now upwards of two-to-one, Confederate defeat was inevitable. On April 2 Lee abandoned Richmond and Petersburg. On April 9, hemmed in by federal troops, short of rations, and with fewer than 30,000 men left, Lee surrendered to Grant. At Appomattox Courthouse the Union general treated his rival with respect and paroled the defeated troops. Within weeks Jefferson Davis was captured, and the remaining Confederate forces laid down their arms. The war was over.

Heavy losses force Lee's surrender

Lincoln did not live to see the last surrenders. On the evening of Good Friday, April 17, he went to Ford's Theatre in Washington, where an assassin named John Wilkes Booth shot him at point-blank range. Lincoln died the next day. The Union had lost its wartime leader, and to many, relief at the war's end was tempered by uncertainty about the future.

Costs and effects

The costs of the Civil War were enormous. Although precise figures on enlistments are impossible to obtain, it appears that during the course of the conflict the Confederate armies claimed the services of 700,000 to 800,000 men. Far more, possibly 2.3 million, served in the Union armies. Northern reserves were so great that more men were legally subject to the draft at the end of the war than at the beginning.

Statistics on casualties are more precise and more appalling. Approximately 364,222 federal soldiers died, 140,070 of them from wounds suffered in battle. Another 275,175 Union soldiers were wounded but survived. On the Confederate side, an estimated 258,000 lost their lives, and even a conservative estimate of Confederate wounded brings the total number of casualties on both sides to more than 1 million—a frightful toll for a nation of 31 million people. More men died in the Civil War than in all other American wars before Vietnam combined.

Casualties

Such carnage compels one to reflect on the choices that led to war. It is tempting to think of the Civil War as an unavoidable conflict, a necessary step in the elimination of an unjust and inhumane institution. But prewar election results clearly indicate that the majority in both North and South wanted peace. Their political system failed them, and other possibilities for compromise—such as a national convention—were never tried.

Important events

1861	Four more southern states secede from Union Battle of Bull Run General McClellan organizes Union army Union blockade begins First Confiscation Act
1862	Capture of Forts Henry and Donelson Capture of New Orleans Battle of Shiloh Confederacy adopts conscription McClellan attacks Virginia Seven Days' Battles Second Confiscation Act Confederacy mounts offensive Battle of Antietam Battle of Fredericksburg
1863	Emancipation Proclamation National Banking Act Union adopts conscription Black soldiers join Union army Food riots in southern cities Battle of Chancellorsville Battle of Gettysburg and surrender of Vicksburg Draft riots in New York City Battle of Chattanooga
1864	Battle of the Wilderness Battle of Spotsylvania Battle of Cold Harbor Battle of Petersburg President Lincoln requests party plank abolishing slavery McClellan nominated for presidency by northern Democrats General Sherman enters Atlanta Lincoln re-elected Jefferson Davis proposes Confederate emancipation Sherman marches through Georgia
1865	Sherman drives north through Carolinas Congress approves Thirteenth Amendment Hampton Roads Conference Lee surrenders at Appomattox Lincoln assassinated

Property damage and financial costs were also enormous, though difficult to tally. Federal loans and taxes during the conflict totaled almost $3 billion, and interest on the war debt was $2.8 billion. The Confederacy borrowed over $2 billion but lost far more in the destruction of homes, fences, crops, livestock, and other property. To give just one example of the wreckage that attended four years of conflict on southern soil, the number of hogs in South Carolina plummeted from 965,000 in 1860 to approximately 150,000 in 1865. Thoughtful scholars have noted that small farmers lost just as much, proportionally, as planters whose slaves were emancipated.

Financial cost of the war

Estimates of the total cost of the war exceed $20 billion–five times the total expenditure of the federal government from its creation to 1865. The northern government increased its spending by a factor of seven in the first full year of the war; by the last year its spending had soared to twenty times the prewar level. By 1865 the federal government accounted for over 26 percent of the gross national product.

These changes were more or less permanent. In the 1880s, interest on the war debt still accounted for approximately 40 percent of the federal budget, and soldiers' pensions for as much as 20 percent. Thus, although many southerners had hoped to separate government from the economy, the war made such separation an impossibility. And although federal expenditures shrank after the war, they stabilized at twice the prewar level, or 4 percent of the gross national product. Wartime emergency measures had brought the banking and transportation systems under federal control, and the government had put its power behind manufacturing and business interests through tariffs, loans, and subsidies. In political terms too, national power increased. Extreme forms of the states' rights controversy were dead, though Americans continued to favor a state-centered federalism.

Yet despite all these changes, one crucial question remained unanswered: what was the place of black men and women in American life? The Union victory provided a partial answer: slavery as it had existed before the war could not persist. But what would replace it? About 186,000 black soldiers had rallied to the Union cause, infusing it with new strength. Did their sacrifice entitle them to full citizenship? They and other former slaves eagerly awaited an answer, which would have to be found during Reconstruction.

Suggestions for further reading

Effects of the war on the South

Mary Boykin Chesnut, *A Diary from Dixie,* ed. Ben Ames Williams (1949); Beth G. Crabtree and James W. Patton, eds., *"Journal of a Secesh Lady": The Diary of Catherine Ann Devereux Edmondston, 1860–1866* (1979); Robert F. Durden, *The Gray and the Black* (1972); Clement Eaton, *A History of the Southern Confederacy* (1954); Paul D. Escott, *After Secession* (1978); Paul D. Escott, " 'The Cry of the Sufferers': The Problem of Poverty in the Confederacy," *Civil War History,* XXIII (September 1977), 228–240; Paul D. Escott, *Slavery Remembered* (1979); J. B. Jones, *A Rebel War Clerk's Diary,* 2 vols., ed. Howard Swiggett (1935); Ella Lonn, *Desertion During the Civil War* (1928); Charles W. Ramsdell, *Behind the Lines in the Southern Confederacy,* ed. Wendell H. Stephenson (1944); James L. Roark, *Masters Without Slaves* (1977); Georgia Lee Tatum, *Disloyalty in the Confederacy* (1934); Emory M. Thomas, *The Confederacy as a Revolutionary Experience* (1971); Emory M. Thomas, *The Confederate Nation* (1979); Emory M. Thomas, *The Confederate State of Richmond* (1971); Paul P. Van Riper and Harry N. Scheiber, "The Confederate Civil Service," *Journal of Southern History,* XXV (1959), 448–470; Bell Irvin Wiley, *The Life of Johnny Reb* (1943); Bell Irvin Wiley, *The Plain People of the Confederacy* (1943); W. Buck Yearns and John G. Barrett, *North Carolina Civil War Documentary* (1980).

Effects of the war on the North

Ralph Andreano, ed., *The Economic Impact of the American Civil War* (1962); Robert Cruden, *The War That Never Ended* (1973); Wood Gray, *The Hidden Civil War* (1942); Frank L. Klement, *The Copperheads in the Middle West* (1960); Susan Previant Lee and Peter Passell, *A New Economic View of American History* (1979); Benjamin Quarles, *The Negro in the Civil War* (1953); George Winston Smith and Charles Burnet Judah, *Life in the North during the Civil War* (1966); George Templeton Strong, *Diary,* 4 vols., ed. Allan Nevins and Milton Halsey Thomas (1952); Paul Studenski, *Financial History of the United States* (1952); Bell Irvin Wiley, *The Life of Billy Yank* (1952).

Military history

Bern Anderson, *By Sea and By River* (1962); Bruce Catton, *Grant Moves South* (1960); Bruce Catton, *Grant Takes Command* (1969); Bruce Catton, *This Hallowed Ground* (1956); Thomas L. Connelly and Archer Jones, *The Politics of Command* (1973); Burke Davis, *Sherman's March* (1980); Shelby Foote, *The Civil War, a Narrative,* 3 vols. (1958–1974); Douglas Southall Freeman, *R. E. Lee,* 4 vols. (1934–1935); Douglas Southall Freeman, *Lee's Lieutenants,* 3 vols. (1942–1944); Archer Jones, *Confederate Strategy from Shiloh to Vicksburg* (1961); J. B. Mitchell, *Decisive Battles of the Civil War* (1955); Thomas L. Livermore, *Numbers and Losses in the Civil War in America* (1957); Allan Nevins, *The War for the Union,* 4 vols. (1959–1972); Frank E. Vandiver, *Rebel Brass* (1956); T. Harry Williams, *Lincoln and His Generals* (1952).

Governmental policies during the war

Thomas B. Alexander and Richard E. Beringer, *The Anatomy of the Confederate Congress* (1972); Fawn Brodie, *Thaddeus Stevens* (1959); Dudley Cornish, *The Sable Arm* (1956); Richard N. Current, *The Lincoln Nobody Knows* (1958); David Donald, *Charles Sumner and the Rights of Man* (1970); Ludwell H. Johnson, "Lincoln's Solution to the Problem of Peace Terms, 1864–1865," *Journal of Southern History,* XXXIV (November 1968), 441–447; Peyton McCrary, *Abraham Lincoln and Reconstruction* (1978); James M. McPherson, *The Negro's Civil War* (1965); James M. McPherson, *The Struggle for Equality* (1964); Larry E. Nelson, *Bullets, Ballots, and Rhetoric* (1980); Frank L. Owsley, *State Rights in the Confederacy* (1925); James G. Randall, *Mr. Lincoln* (1957); Benjamin F. Thomas, *Abraham Lincoln* (1952); Hans L. Trefousse, *The Radical Republicans* (1969); Glyndon G. Van Deusen, *William Henry Seward* (1967); T. Harry Williams, *Lincoln and the Radicals* (1941).

15
RECONSTRUCTION BY TRIAL AND ERROR, 1865–1877

Reconstruction of the Union held many promises. For Senator Benjamin Wade of Ohio, it began in a reassuring way. As a radical Republican who had demanded confiscation and emancipation early in the war, Wade had worried about the new president Andrew Johnson. How would he, a southerner and a former Democrat, deal with the planters and their newly freed slaves? Could he be relied on to check the aristocrats and promote equality? An interview at the White House in April 1865 seemed to suggest a favorable answer.

After speaking of the enormous costs of the war and the need to secure the Union victory, Wade suggested the exile or execution of ten or twelve leading traitors to set an example. President Johnson did not blanch at the idea. Instead he replied, "How are you going to pick out so small a number? Robbery is a crime; rape is a crime; murder is a crime; *treason* is a crime; and *crime* must be punished."

At the same time, black men and women in the South were preparing to seize the advantages of freedom. Their first opportunity came in the sea islands. During his last campaign, General Sherman had issued Special Field Order No. 15, which set aside for exclusive Negro settlement the sea islands and all abandoned coastal lands thirty miles to the interior, from Charleston to the Saint John's River in northern Florida. Negro refugees quickly poured into these lands; by the middle of 1865, forty thousand freedmen were living in their new home. One former slaveowner who visited his old plantation in Beaufort, South Carolina, received friendly and courteous treatment. His ex-slaves "firmly and respectfully" informed him, however, that "we own this land now. Put it out of your head that it will ever be yours again."

But neither Sherman's promise nor Johnson's was fulfilled. Although Jefferson Davis was imprisoned for two years, no Confederate leaders were executed. In fact, within a year southern aristocrats had come to view Johnson not as their enemy but as their friend and protector. And in the fall of 1865, the federal government began to confiscate the freedmen's land and return it to its original owners. "Why do you take away our lands?" the blacks protested. "You take them from us who have always been true, always true to the Government! You give them to our all-time enemies! That is not right!"

The cries of the freedmen did not go completely unheard. The unexpected turn of events led Congress to examine the president's policies and design new plans for Reconstruction. Out of negotiations in Congress and clashes between the president and the legislators, there emerged first one and then two new plans for Reconstruction. Before the process was over the nation had adopted the Fourteenth and Fifteenth amendments and impeached its president. But racism continued to thrive.

The nation's reluctance to treat the freedmen as equal citizens had first become evident during the war, when black volunteers and runaways from the Confederacy were discouraged from helping the Union. Even after black troops had entered federal service, they had faced persistent and galling discrimination. Eventually the Union's need for troops and the ideal of equality had made some headway against these attitudes, but differences over the proper status of blacks remained.

In Congress now politicians debated the future of black people. Democrats opposed efforts to defend the rights of freedmen, and Republicans were often divided among themselves. But a mixture of idealism and party purposes drove the Republicans forward. Ultimately, fear of losing the peace proved decisive with northern voters. The United States enfranchised the freedmen and gave them a role in reconstructing the South. The nation would force change on that recalcitrant section.

For black people themselves the benefits of freedom were often practical and ordinary. They moved out of slave quarters and built cabins of their own; they worked together in family units and worshipped in their own churches without white supervision. Blacks also took the risk of political participation, voting in large numbers and gaining some offices. But they knew their political success depended on the determination and support of the North.

In the South, opposition to Reconstruction grew steadily. By 1869 the Ku Klux Klan had added organized violence to southern whites' repertoire of resistance. Despite federal efforts to protect them, black people were intimidated at the polls, robbed of their earnings, beaten, or murdered. Prosecution of Klansmen rarely succeeded, and Republicans lost their offices in an increasing number of southern states. By the early 1870s the failure of Reconstruction was apparent; Republican leaders and northern voters had to decide how far they would persist in their efforts to reform the South.

As the 1870s advanced, other issues drew attention away from Reconstruction. Industrial growth accelerated, creating new opportunities and raising new problems. Political corruption became a nationwide scandal and bribery a way of doing business. North Carolina's Jonathan Worth, an old-line Whig who had opposed secession as strongly as he now fought Reconstruction, deplored the atmosphere of greed. "Money has become the God of this country," he wrote in disgust, "and men, otherwise good men, are almost compelled to worship at her shrine." Eventually these other forces triumphed, politics moved on to new concerns, and the courts turned their attention away from civil rights. Even northern Republicans gave up on racial reform in 1877. Reconstruction was over, and the position of black people remained inferior, North and South.

Equality: the unresolved issue

For America's former slaves, Reconstruction had one paramount meaning: a chance to explore freedom. A southern white woman admitted in her diary that the black people "showed a natural and exultant joy at being free." Former slaves remembered rejoicing and singing far into the night after federal troops reached their plantations. In Virginia one elderly woman spoke of freedom in an impromptu song:

Tain't no mo' sellin' today,
Tain't no mo' hirin' today,
Tain't no mo' pullin' off shirts today,
It's stomp down freedom today.
Stomp it down.

The slaves on one Texas plantation jumped up and down and clapped their hands as one man shouted, "We is free—no more whippings and beatings."

A few blacks gave in to the natural desire to do what had been impossible before. One grandmother who had long resented her treatment "dropped her hoe" and ran to confront the mistress. "I'se free!" she yelled at her. "Yes, I'se free! Ain't got to work fo' you no mo! You can't put me in yo' pocket [sell me] now!" Another man recalled that he and others "started on the move" and left the plantation, either to search for family members or just to exercise their new-found freedom of movement. As he traveled, one man sang about being free as a frog, " 'cause a frog had freedom to git on a log and jump off when he pleases."

Most freedmen reacted more cautiously and shrewdly, taking care to test the boundaries of their new condition. "After the war was over," explained one man, "we was afraid to move. Jes' like tarpins or turtles after 'mancipation. Jes' stick our heads out to see how the land lay." As slaves they had learned to expect hostility from white people, and they did not presume it would instantly disappear. Life in freedom, they knew, might still be a matter of what was allowed, not what was right. " 'You got to say master?' " asked a freedman in Georgia. " 'Naw,' " answered his fellows, but "they said it all the same. They said it for a long time."

One sign of this shrewd caution was the way freedmen evaluated potential employers. "Most all de niggers dat had good owners stayed wid 'em, but de others lef'. Some of 'em come back an' some didn'," explained one man. If a white person had been relatively considerate to blacks in bondage, blacks reasoned that he might prove a desirable employer in freedom. Other blacks left their plantation all at once, for, as one put it, "that massa am sho' mean and if we doesn't have to stay we shouldn't, not with that massa."

Even more urgently than a fair employer, the freedmen wanted land of their own. Land represented their chance to farm for themselves, to have an independent life. It represented compensation for their generations of travail in bondage. A northern observer noted that freedmen made "plain, straight-forward" inquiries as they settled the land set aside for them by Sherman. They wanted to be sure the land "would be theirs after they had improved it." Not just in the sea island region but everywhere, blacks young and old thirsted for homes of their own. One southerner noted with surprise in her diary that

Blacks' desire for land

> Uncle Lewis, the pious, the honored, the venerated, gets his poor old head turned with false notions of freedom and independence, runs off to the

Yankees with a pack of lies against his mistress, and sets up a claim to part of her land!

Lewis simply wanted a new beginning. Like millions of other freedmen, he hoped to leave slavery behind.

But no one could say how much of a chance the whites, who were in power, would give to blacks. During the war there had been much hesitation before black people were allowed to aid and defend the Union. As soon as the fighting began, black men volunteered as soldiers. But the government and the people of the North refused their offers, saying that the conflict was "a white man's war." "What upon earth is the matter with the American Government and people?" asked Frederick Douglass. "Colored men were good enough to fight under Washington," he pointed out, and "they were good enough to fight under Andrew Jackson." Denying them the chance to fight was like "fighting rebels with only one hand."

But many whites agreed with Corporal Felix Brannigan of the Seventy-fourth New York Regiment. "We don't want to fight side and side with the nigger," he said. "We think we are a too superior race for that." Other northerners believed that black people lacked the courage and will to fight. In September 1862 Abraham Lincoln said, "If we were to arm [the Negroes], I fear that in a few weeks the arms would be in the hands of the rebels." When a few Union generals raised companies of blacks, the War Department refused to accept them.

Necessity forced the United States to change its policy in the fall of 1862. Because the war was going badly, the administration authorized black enlistments. By spring 1863 black troops were proving their value. General David Hunter, Commander of the Department of the South, reported that his "colored regiments" possessed "remarkable aptitude for military training" and were "imbued with a burning faith that now is the time appointed by God . . . for the deliverance of their race." "They fight like fiends," said another observer, and Lincoln now looked to "the colored population" as "the great *available* and yet *unavailed of* force for restoring the Union." Recruitment of blacks proceeded rapidly.

Black service in the military

Black leaders hoped that military service would secure equal rights for their people. As Frederick Douglass put it, "Once let the black man get upon his person the brass letter, U.S., let him get an eagle on his button, and a musket on his shoulder and bullets in his pocket, and there is no power on earth which can deny that he has earned the right of citizenship in the United States." If black soldiers turned the tide, asked another man, "Would the nation refuse us our rights . . . ? Would it refuse us our vote?"

Wartime experience seemed to prove it would. Despite their valor, black soldiers faced persistent discrimination. In Ohio, for example, a mob shouting "Kill the nigger" attacked an off-duty soldier; on duty, blacks did most of the necessary manual labor. One Union general objected that black troops were used only as "diggers and drudges," and pointed out that "their equipments have been of the poorest kind." In June 1864, the War Department finally ordered that "colored troops . . . will only be required to take their fair share of fatigue duty [heavy labor]. . . ." But five months later General Lorenzo Thomas reported that "where white and black troops come together in the same command, the latter have to do all the work."

Most objectionable was the fact that black soldiers were expected to accept inferior pay as they risked their lives. The government paid white privates $13 per month plus a clothing allowance of $3.50. Black troops earned $10 per month less $3 deducted for clothing. Blacks resented this injustice so deeply that in protest two regiments in South Carolina refused to accept any pay. In June 1864 Congress finally made equal pay retroactive to the date of enlistment for those who had been free on April 19, 1861. Even this law was unfair to thousands of runaway slaves who had joined the army before 1864, and many commanders allowed such men to swear that they "owed no man unrequited labor" in order to receive full pay. When the paymaster visited black regiments following the legislation, "songs burst out everywhere" to celebrate the victory of principle.

Still, this was only a small victory over prejudice; the general attitude of northerners on racial questions was mixed. On the one hand, wartime idealism had promoted equality and weakened discrimination. Many abolitionists had worked vigorously to extend equal rights to black Americans, and a powerful element in the Republican party had committed itself to fighting racism. In 1864 their efforts brought about the acceptance of black testimony in federal courts and the desegregation of New York City's streetcars. Segregation on streetcars in the District of Columbia ended in 1865, and one state, Massachusetts, enacted a comprehensive public accommodations law.

On the other hand, there were many more signs of resistance to racial equality. The Democratic party adopted an explicit and vociferous stand against blacks, charging that Republicans favored race-mixing and were undermining the status of the white worker. Moreover, voters in three states–Connecticut, Minnesota, and Wisconsin–rejected black suffrage in 1865. The racial attitudes of northerners seemed to be in flux, the outcome uncertain.

Nowhere was the fundamental ambiguity of northern attitudes clearer than in the sea islands. Even before Sherman's special field order, these islands–which had a large slave population and had been captured early in the war–had become a kind of national laboratory of freedom. Abolitionists and missionaries had arrived to help the blacks, businessmen had investigated what the area could produce, and Union army recruiters had sought enlistments there. Free blacks had organized committees and Union Relief Associations to send clothes and blankets, ministers and teachers. Northerners of a variety of opinions had watched to see what former slaves could do.

Sea-island blacks

The missionaries were delighted with the blacks' enthusiasm for education. Believing that "it was education which made us free [and] progressive," northern schoolteachers dispensed learning as the key to uplifting the slave. Along with literacy they stressed "industry and cleanliness" and the importance of work. The visiting businessmen believed that "the laws of labor, wages, competition, etc." would develop "habits of responsibility, industry, self-dependence, and manliness." Accordingly, they disapproved of charity and emphasized the values of competitive capitalism. "The danger to the Negro," wrote one worker in the sea islands, was "too high wages." It would be "most unwise and injurious," declared another, to give former slaves free land.

Sea-island blacks welcomed many of the missionaries' efforts, but they had some reservations. "The Yankees preach nothing but cotton, cotton!" complained one elderly man; most could not understand the capitalists' objection to free land. "We wants land," wrote one man, "dis bery land dat is rich wid de sweat ob we face and de blood ob we back." Asking only for a chance to buy land, this man complained that "dey make de lots too big, and cut we out." Indeed, the government did sell thousands of acres in the sea islands for nonpayment of taxes, but when blacks pooled their earnings to buy almost 2,000 of the 16,749 acres sold in March 1863, 90 percent of the land went to wealthy investors from the North. Thus even among their northern supporters, the former slaves received only partial support. How much opportunity would freedom bring? That was a major question to be answered during Reconstruction, and the answer depended on the evolution of policy in Washington.

Johnson's reconstruction plan

Throughout 1865 the formation of reconstruction policy rested solely with Andrew Johnson, for shortly before he became president Congress recessed and did not reconvene until December. Thus Johnson had almost eight months to design and execute a plan of reconstruction on his own, unhindered by legislative suggestions. The new president undertook to restore the seceded states to the Union under his power to grant pardons.

Johnson had a few precedents to follow in Lincoln's wartime plans for Reconstruction. In December 1863 Lincoln had proposed a "10-percent" plan for a government being organized in captured portions of Louisiana. According to this plan, a state government could be established as soon as 10 percent of those who had voted in 1860 took an oath of future loyalty. Only high-ranking Confederate officials would be denied a chance to take the oath, and Lincoln urged that at least a few well-qualified blacks be given the ballot. Radicals bristled, however, at such a mild plan, and a majority of Congress (in the Wade-Davis bill, which Lincoln vetoed) favored stiffer requirements and stronger proof of loyalty.

Lincoln's reconstruction plan

Later, in 1865, Lincoln suggested but then abandoned more lenient terms. At Hampton Roads, where he raised questions about the extent of emancipation (see page 386), Lincoln discussed restoration to

Andrew Johnson, a southern Unionist and an old foe of the planters. Library of Congress.

the Union, with full rights, of the very state governments that had tried to leave it. Then in April he considered allowing the Virginia legislature to convene in order to withdraw its support from the Confederate war effort. Faced with strong opposition in his cabinet, however, Lincoln reversed himself, denying that he had intended to confer legitimacy on a rebel government. At the time of his death, Lincoln had given general approval to a plan drafted by Secretary of War Stanton that would have imposed military authority and provisional governors as steps toward new state governments. Beyond these general outlines, it is impossible to say what Lincoln would have done had he survived.

Johnson began with the plan Stanton had drafted for consideration by the cabinet. At a cabinet meeting on May 9, 1865, Johnson's advisors split evenly on the question of voting rights for freedmen in the South. Johnson said that he favored black suffrage, but only if the southern states adopted it voluntarily. A champion of states' rights, he regarded this decision as too important to be taken out of the hands of the states. Such views were a long-established part of the president's philosophy. Just as his past opinions on states' rights shaped this initial act, so Johnson's personal history influenced the rest of his program.

Johnson was not the average southern politician. He had built his entire career on championing the cause of ordinary whites and attacking privileged planters. Born in humble circumstances, he started life as a tailor, uneducated and unable to read until taught by his wife. As he rose in Tennessee politics, he voiced his resentment of the pride and advantages of haughty aristocrats, who monopolized power and held the little man down. An outspoken Unionist, he refused to leave the Senate when Tennessee seceded, an action that commended him to Lincoln as a vice-presidential candidate in 1864.

Andrew Johnson: his early life

Now as president, Johnson was able to define the terms on which southern states and rebellious planters would re-enter the Union. He laid out his program in a series of proclamations, beginning with two proclamations on North Carolina in May 1865. The first decreed amnesty for most southerners who would take an oath of loyalty to the United States. The second established a provisional military government and prescribed steps for the creation of new civilian governments. The key aspects of both proclamations lay in the details.

Certain classes of southerners were barred from taking the oath and gaining amnesty. Federal officials, elected or appointed, who had violated their oaths to support the United States and aided the Confederacy could not take the oath. Nor could graduates of West Point or Annapolis who had resigned their commissions to fight for the South. The same was true for Confederate officers at the rank of colonel or above and for Confederate political leaders. Thus leaders of the rebellion and federal officeholders who had proved disloyal fell into an excepted category. To this category Johnson added southerners whose taxable property was worth more than $20,000. All such individuals had to apply personally to the president for pardon and restoration of political rights, or risk legal penalties, including confiscation of their land.

Oaths of amnesty and new state governments

Under an appointed provisional governor, elections

would be held for a state constitutional convention. The delegates chosen for the convention would draft a new constitution eliminating slavery and invalidating secession. After ratification of the constitution, new governments could be elected, and the state would be restored to the Union with full congressional representation. No southerner could participate in this process who had not taken the oath of amnesty or who had been ineligible to vote on the day the state seceded.

Thus freedmen could not participate in the new government, for although it was theoretically possible for the white constitutional conventions to enfranchise them, such action was at best unlikely. Nor could much of the former white leadership class, for the rich and powerful of prewar days needed Johnson's pardon first. To many observers, South and North, it appeared that the president meant to take his revenge on the haughty aristocrats whom he had always denounced, and to raise up a new leadership of deserving yeomen.

But the plan did not work as Johnson had hoped. The old white leadership proved resilient and influential; despite Johnson's regulations, prominent Confederates won election and turned up in appointive office. Moreover, Johnson himself had a hand in subverting his own plan. He pardoned first one and then another of the aristocrats and chief rebels. By fall 1865 the clerks at the pardon office were straining under the burden, and additional staff had to be hired to churn out the necessary documents.

Confederates regain power

Perhaps Johnson's vanity betrayed his judgment. Scores of gentlemen of the type who had previously scorned him now waited on him for an appointment. Too long a lonely outsider, Johnson may have succumbed to the attention and flattery of these pardon-seekers. Or perhaps he simply allowed himself too little time. It took months for the constitution-making and elections to run their course; by the time the process was complete and Confederate leaders had emerged in powerful positions, the reconvening of Congress was near. Johnson may have faced a choice between admitting failure and scrapping his entire effort or swallowing hard and supporting what had resulted. In either case, the president decided to stand behind his new governments and declare Reconstruction completed. Thus in December 1865 many Confederate congressmen traveled to Washington to claim seats in the United States Congress, and Alexander Stephens, vice-president of the Confederacy, returned to the capital as a senator.

The election of such prominent rebels was not the only result of Johnson's program that sparked negative comment in the North. Some of the state conventions were slow to repudiate secession; others only grudgingly admitted that slavery was dead. Two refused to take any action to repudiate the large Confederate debt. Northerners interpreted these actions as signs of defiance; subsequent legislation defining the status of freedmen confirmed their worst fears. Some legislatures merely revised large sections of the slave codes by substituting the word *freedman* for *slave.* In these black codes, former slaves who were supposed to be free were compelled to carry passes, observe a curfew, live in housing provided by a landowner, and give up hope of entering many desirable occupations. Finally, observers noted that the practice in state-supported institutions, such as schools and orphanages, was to exclude blacks altogether. To northerners, the South seemed intent on returning black people to a position of servility.

Black codes

Thus it was not surprising that a majority of northern congressmen decided to take a close look at the results of Johnson's plan. On reconvening, they voted not to admit the newly elected southern representatives, whose credentials were subject under the Constitution to congressional scrutiny. The House and Senate established a joint committee to examine Johnson's policies and advise on new ones. Reconstruction had entered a second phase, one in which Congress would play a strong role.

The congressional reconstruction plan

Northern congressmen disagreed on what to do, but they did not doubt their right to play a role in Reconstruction. The Constitution mentioned neither secession nor reunion, but it did assign a great many major responsibilities to Congress. Among them was the injunction to guarantee to each state a republican government. Under this provision, the legislators thought, they could devise policies for Reconstruction, just as Johnson had used his power to pardon for the same purpose.

They soon found that other constitutional questions had a direct bearing on the policies they followed. What, for example, had the fact of rebellion done to the relationship between southern states and the Union? Lincoln had always insisted that the Union remained unbroken; and not even Andrew Johnson could accept the southern view that the wartime state governments of the South could merely reenter the nation. Johnson argued that the Union had endured, though individuals had erred; thus the use of his power to grant or withhold pardons. But congressmen who favored vigorous reconstruction measures tended to argue that war *had* broken the Union. The southern states had committed legal suicide and reverted to the status of territories, they argued, or the South was a conquered nation subject to the victor's will. Moderate congressmen held that the states had forfeited their rights through rebellion, and had thus come under congressional supervision.

These diverse theories mirrored the diversity of Congress itself. Northern legislators fell into four major categories, no one of which held a majority: Democrats, conservative Republicans, moderate Republicans, and Radical Republicans. Overall, the Republican party had a majority, but there was considerable distance between conservative Republicans, who desired a limited federal role in Reconstruction and were fairly happy with Johnson's actions, and the Radicals. These men, led by Thaddeus Stevens, Charles Sumner, and George Julian, were a minority within their party, but they had the advantage of a clearly defined goal. They believed that it was essential to democratize the South, establish public education, and ensure the rights of freedmen. They favored black suffrage, often supported land confiscation and redistribution, and were willing to exclude the South from the Union for several years if necessary to achieve their goals. Between these two factions lay the moderates, who held the balance of power.

One overwhelming political reality forced these groups to unify: congressional elections were scheduled for the fall. Since Congress had questioned Johnson's program, they had to develop some modification or alternative program before the elections; as politicians they knew better than to go before their constituents empty-handed. Thus they had to form a coalition among the various party factions.

What determined the kind of coalition that was formed and the direction of policy thereafter was the fact that Johnson and the Democrats refused to cooperate with conservative or moderate Republicans. The president and northern Democrats insisted, despite evidence of widespread concern, that Reconstruction was over, that the new state governments were legitimate, and that southern representatives should be admitted to Congress. This unrealistic, intransigent position blasted any possibility of bipartisan compromise. Republicans found themselves all lumped together by Democrats, and thus bargaining over changes in the Johnson program went on almost entirely within the party.

This development and subsequent events enhanced the influence of the Radicals. But in 1865, Republican congressmen were loath to break with the president; he was, for better or worse, the titular head of their party, so they tried to work with him. Early in 1866 many lawmakers thought a compromise had been reached. Under its terms Johnson would agree to two modifications of his program. The life of the Freedmen's Bureau, which fed the hungry, negotiated labor contracts, and started schools, would be extended; and a civil rights bill would be passed to counteract the black codes. This bill, drawn up by a conservative Republican, was designed to force southern courts to recognize equality before the law by giving federal judges the power to remove cases in which blacks were treated unfairly.

Congress struggles for a compromise

But in spring 1866, Johnson destroyed the compromise by vetoing both bills (they were later repassed). Denouncing any change in his program, the president condemned Congress's action in inflammatory language. In so doing he questioned the legitimacy of congressional involvement in policy making and revealed his own racism. Because the Civil Rights Bill defined United States citizens as native-born persons who were taxed, Johnson pronounced it discriminatory toward "large numbers of intelligent, worthy, and patriotic foreigners . . . in favor of the negro." The bill, he said, would "operate in favor of the colored and against the white race."

All hope of working with the president was now gone. But Republican congressmen sensed that their constituents remained dissatisfied with the results of Reconstruction. They therefore pushed on, and from bargaining among their various factions there emerged a plan. It took the form of a proposed amendment to the Constitution–the fourteenth–and it represented a compromise between radical and conservative elements of the party.

Of four points in the amendment, there was nearly universal agreement on one: the Confederate debt was declared null and void, the war debt of the United States guaranteed. Northerners uniformly rejected the notion of paying taxes to reimburse those who had financed a rebellion; and business groups agreed on the necessity of upholding the credit of the United States government. There was also fairly general support for altering the personnel of southern governments. In language that harkened back to Johnson's Amnesty Proclamation, the Fourteenth Amendment prohibited political power for prominent Confederates. Only at the discretion of Congress, by a two-thirds vote of each house, could these political penalties be removed.

Fourteenth Amendment

The section of the Fourteenth Amendment that would have the greatest legal significance in later years was the first (see Appendix). On its face, this section was an effort to strike down the black codes and guarantee basic rights to freedmen. It conferred citizenship on freedmen and prohibited states from abridging their constitutional "privileges and immunities." Similarly, the amendment barred any state from taking a person's life, liberty, or property "without due process of law" and from denying "equal protection of the laws." These clauses were phrased broadly enough to become powerful guarantees of black Americans' civil rights. In later decades they would take on added meaning with court rulings that corporations were legally "persons" (see page 476).

The second section of the amendment clearly revealed the compromises and political motives that had produced the document. Though many idealistic northerners favored voting rights for blacks, large portions of the electorate were just as adamantly opposed. Commenting on the ambivalent nature of northern opinion, a citizen of Indiana wrote that there was strong feeling in favor of "humane and liberal laws for the government and protection of the colored population." But he admitted to a southern relative that there was prejudice, too. "Although there is a great deal [of] profession among us for the relief of the darkey yet I think much of it is far from being cincere. I guess we want to compell you to do right by them while we are not willing ourselves to do so."

Republican congressmen shied away from confronting this ambivalence, but political reality required them to do something. Under the constitution, representation was based on population. During slavery each black slave had counted as three-fifths of a person for purposes of congressional representation. Republicans feared that emancipation, which made every former slave five-fifths of a person, might increase the South's power in Congress. If it did, and if blacks were not allowed to vote, the former secessionists would gain seats in Congress.

Republicans were determined not to hand over power to their political enemies, so they offered the South a choice. According to the second section of the Fourteenth Amendment, states did not have to give black men the right to vote. But if they did not do so, their representation would be reduced proportionally. If they did, it would be increased proportionally–but Republicans would be able to appeal to the new black voters.

The Fourteenth Amendment dealt with the voting rights of black men and ignored female citizens, black and white. Its proposal elicited a strong reaction from the women's rights movement. For decades advocates of equal rights for women had worked with abolitionists, often subordinating their cause to that of the slaves. During the drafting of the Fourteenth Amendment, however, female activists demanded to be heard. When legislators defined them as nonvoting citizens, prominent women's leaders such as Elizabeth Cady Stanton and Susan B. Anthony decided that it was time to end their alliance with abolitionists. Thus the independent women's rights movement grew.

In 1866, however, the major question in Reconstruction politics was how the public would respond to the amendment. Johnson did his best to see that the public would reject it. Condemning Congress's plan and its refusal to seat southern representatives, the president convinced state legislatures in the South

Southern rejection of the Fourteenth Amendment

to vote against ratification. Every southern legislature except Tennessee's rejected the amendment by a large margin. It did best in Alabama, where it failed by a vote of 69 to 8 in the assembly and 27 to 2 in the senate. In three states the amendment received no support at all.

To present his case to northerners, Johnson arranged a National Union convention to publicize his program. The chief executive also took to the stump himself. In an age when active personal campaigning was rare for a president, Johnson boarded a special train for a "swing around the circle" that carried his message far into the Midwest and then back to Washington. In cities such as Cleveland and St. Louis, Johnson castigated the Republicans in his old stump-speaker style. But increasingly audiences rejected his views and hooted and jeered at him.

The election was a resounding victory for Republicans in Congress. Men whom Johnson had denounced won re-election by large margins, and the Republican majority increased as some new candidates defeated incumbent Democrats. Everywhere Radical and moderate Republicans gained strength. The section of the country that had won the war had spoken clearly: Johnson's policies, people feared, were giving the advantage to rebels and traitors. Thus Republican congressional leaders received a mandate to continue with their reconstruction plan.

Congress, however, had reached an impasse. All but one of the southern governments created by Johnson had turned their backs on the Fourteenth Amendment, determined to resist. Nothing could be accomplished as long as those governments existed, and as long as the southern electorate was constituted as it was. To break the deadlock, Republicans had little choice but to form new governments and enfranchise the freedmen. They therefore decided to do both. The unavoidable logic of the situation had forced the majority toward the Radical plan.

The Radicals hoped Congress would do much more. Thaddeus Stevens, for example, argued that economic opportunity was essential to the freedmen. "If we do not furnish them with homesteads from forfeited and rebel property, and hedge them around with protective laws; if we leave them to the legislation of their late masters, we had better left them in bondage," Stevens declared. To provide that opportunity, Stevens drew up a plan for extensive confiscation and redistribution of land. Significantly, only one-tenth of the land affected by his plan was earmarked for freedmen, in 40-acre plots. All the rest was to be sold, to generate money for veterans' pensions, compensation for damaged property, and payment of the federal debt. By these means Stevens hoped to win support for a basically unpopular measure. But he failed; and in general the Radicals were not able to command the support of the majority of the public.

Instead, the Military Reconstruction Act of 1867 incorporated only the bare bones of the Radical program. The act called for new governments in the

Military Reconstruction Act of 1867

South, with a return to military authority in the interim. It barred from political office those Confederate leaders listed in the Fourteenth Amendment. It guaranteed freedmen the right to vote in elections for state constitutional conventions and for subsequent state governments. In addition, each southern state was required to ratify the Fourteenth Amendment; to ratify its new constitution; and to submit the new constitution to Congress for approval. Thus black people gained an opportunity to fight for a better life through the political process. The only weapon put into their hands was the ballot, however. The law required no redistribution of land and guaranteed no basic changes in southern social structure. It did permit an early return to the Union.

Congress's role as the architect of Reconstruction was not quite over, for its quarrels with Andrew Johnson grew more bitter. To restrict Johnson's influence and safeguard its plan, Congress passed a number of controversial laws. First it set the date for its own reconvening—an unprecedented act, since the president had traditionally summoned the legislature to Washington. Then it limited Johnson's power over the army by requiring the president to issue military orders through the General of the Army, Ulysses S. Grant, who could not be sent from Washington without the Senate's consent. Finally, Congress passed the Tenure of Office Act, which gave the Senate power to interfere with changes in the president's cabinet. Designed to protect Secretary of War Stanton, who sympathized with the Radicals, this law violated the tradition that a president controlled his own cabinet.

The confrontation between Congress and Andrew Johnson culminated in the president's impeachment. Here the Senate sits in trial of Johnson, who ultimately escaped conviction and removal from office by a margin of one vote. Library of Congress.

Johnson took several belligerent steps of his own. He issued orders to military commanders in the South limiting their powers and increasing the powers of the civil governments he had created in 1865. Then he removed army officers who conscientiously enforced Congress's new law, preferring commanders who allowed disqualified Confederates to vote. Finally, in August 1867 he tried to remove Secretary of War Stanton. The confrontation had reached its climax.

Twice before, the House Judiciary Committee had considered impeachment, rejecting the idea once and then recommending it by only a five-to-four vote.

Impeachment of President Johnson

That recommendation had been decisively defeated by the House. After Johnson's last action, however, a third attempt to impeach the president carried easily. In 1868, the House was so determined to indict Johnson that it voted before drawing up specific charges. The indictment concentrated on Johnson's violation of the Tenure of Office Act, though modern scholars regard his systematic efforts to impede enforcement of the Military Reconstruction Act as a far more serious offense.

Johnson's trial in the Senate lasted more than three months. The prosecution, led by such Radicals as Thaddeus Stevens and Benjamin Butler, argued that Johnson was guilty of "high crimes and misdemeanors." But they also advanced the novel idea that impeachment was a political matter, not a judicial trial of guilt or innocence. The Senate ultimately rejected such reasoning, which would have transformed impeachment into a political weapon against any chief executive who disagreed with Congress. Though a majority of senators voted to convict Johnson, the prosecution fell one vote short of the necessary two-thirds majority. Johnson remained in office for the few months left in his term, and his acquittal established the precedent that only serious misdeeds merited removal from office.

In 1869, in an effort to write democratic principles and color-blindness into the Constitution, the Radicals succeeded in presenting the Fifteenth Amendment for ratification. The measure forbade states to deny the right to vote "on account of race, color, or previous condition of servitude." Ironically, the votes of four uncooperative southern states—required by Congress to approve the amendment as an added condition to rejoining the Union—proved necessary to impose this principle on parts of the North. Although several states outside the South refused to ratify, the Fifteenth Amendment became law in 1870.

Fifteenth Amendment

Thus Congress first tried to revise Johnson's program and then had to overturn it and start anew. And for black people in the South, the opportunities offered by Reconstruction did not fully come to pass until 1868. That year most of the state conventions met, and blacks participated in the democratic process for the first time. Blacks hoped to make a new life for themselves, but their task was formidable. According to Albion Tourgée, a northern soldier who became a Republican leader in postwar North Carolina, Congress had behaved toward the freedmen like a farmer who turns his livestock out in the middle of winter. The ex-slave had to fend for himself.

The response of the freedmen

Overjoyed as they were to be free, the freedmen also knew that their new status placed them in danger, for it infuriated some whites. When a Georgia planter heard a black woman singing about emancipation, he angrily knocked her down; another master threatened to "free" his servants with a shotgun. After announcing the end of the war, one slaveowner bitterly told his slaves, " 'you is free to live and free to die and free to go to de devil,' " as one of them later recalled. The idea of a freed slave wearing a starched shirt was intolerable to one planter, and a few southerners actually emigrated from the United States rather than stay, as one put it, "in a country with so many free Negroes."

Violence was directed at blacks from the first days of freedom. People took out their frustration on unlucky blacks, and often community mores did not challenge such abuses of the freedmen. In one North Carolina town a local magistrate clubbed a black man on a public street, and bands of "Regulators" terrorized blacks in parts of that state and Kentucky. Such incidents were predictable in a society in which many planters believed, as a South Carolinian put it, that blacks "can't be governed except with the whip."

The Union victory and emancipation changed this situation in principle but not always in reality. For the South remained a vast and sparsely settled region. Federal troops could not be everywhere at all times, even though they were theoretically in control. Sometimes racist northern troops and officials sided with local whites. Thus federal power often remained a distant or potential force, whereas the influence of local white people, who owned the land and controlled the jobs, was immediate and continuous.

Nevertheless, blacks took risks and reached out enthusiastically, hopefully, and prayerfully for freedom. As soon as Congress introduced black suffrage, freedmen seized the opportunity to participate in politics. They flocked to the polls and voted solidly Republican, for most agreed with one man who felt that he should "stick to de end wid de party dat freed me." Moreover, the freedmen had a shrewd sense of which party advocated their advancement. Although William Henry could read only "a little," he testified that he and his friends had no difficulty selecting the Republican ballot. "We stood around and watched," he explained. "We saw D. Sledge vote; he owned half the county. We knowed he voted Democratic so we voted the other ticket so it would be Republican."

Black suffrage

The zeal for voting spread through the entire black community. Women, who could not vote, encouraged their husbands and sons, and preachers exhorted their congregations to use the franchise. Such urging could be an effective counter to white pressure tactics. Some preachers advised black women "to have nothin' to do wid deir husbands" if they gave in to white

Freed from slavery, blacks of all ages filled the schools to seek the education that had been denied them in bondage. Valentine Museum, Richmond, Virginia.

intimidation. One man who had succumbed to coercion lamented that "my wife wouldn't sleep wid me for six months."

Black education

Former slaves also hungered for education. Throughout bondage the knowledge that was in books had been denied them, but with freedom they filled the schools–young and old, day and night. On "log seats" or "a dirt flo'," many freedmen studied their letters in old almanacs, discarded dictionaries, or whatever was available. Young children brought infants to school with them, and adults attended at night or after "de crops was laid by." Many a teacher had "to make herself heard over three other classes reciting in concert" in a small room, but the scholars kept coming. The desire to escape slavery's ignorance was so great that many blacks paid tuition, typically $1.00 or $1.50 a month, despite their poverty. This seemingly small amount constituted one-tenth of many peoples' agricultural wage.

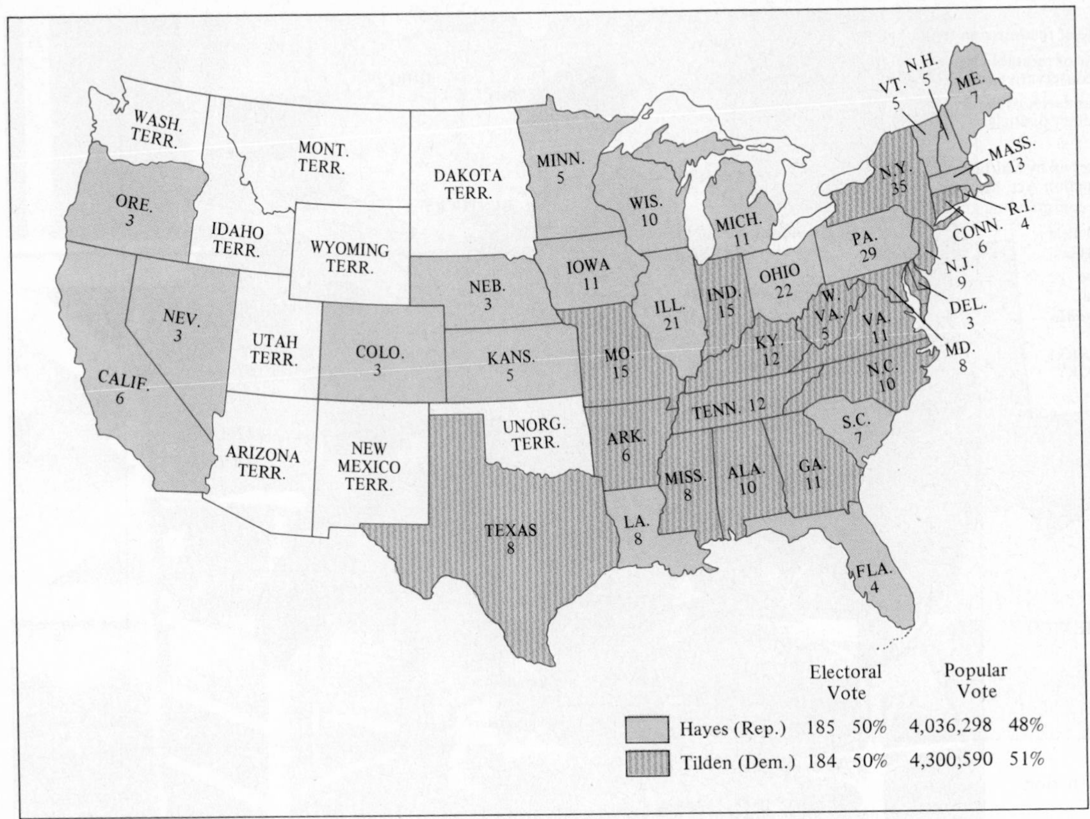

Presidential election, 1876

limited the inflationary impact of the greenbacks and aided creditors, not debtors.

Indeed, the government's financial policies were almost perfectly tailored to revive and support industrial growth. Soon after the war Congress had shifted some of the government's tax revenues to pay off the interest-bearing war debt. The debt fell from $2.33 billion in 1866 to only $587 million in 1893, and every dollar repaid was a dollar injected into the economy for potential investment. Thus approximately 1 percent of the gross national product was pumped back into the economy from 1866 to 1872, and only slightly less than that during the rest of the 1870s. Low taxes on investment and high tariffs on manufactured goods also aided industrialists. With such help the northern economy quickly recovered the rate of growth it had enjoyed just before the war.

Another issue that claimed new attention in the 1870s was immigration. After the war the number of immigrants entering the United States began to rise again, along with the ingrained suspicions and hostilities of native Americans. The Mormon question too—how Utah's growing Mormon community, which practiced polygamy, could be reconciled to American law—became prominent (see page 440).

Renewed pressure for expansion revived interest in international affairs. Secretary of State William H. Seward accomplished the only major addition of territory during these years in 1867. Through negotiation with the Russian government, he arranged the purchase of Alaska for $7.2 million dollars. Opponents ridiculed Seward's venture, calling Alaska Frigidia, the Polar Bear Garden, or Walrussia. But Seward convinced important congressmen of Alaska's economic potential, and other lawmakers favored the dawning of friendship with Russia. In the same year the United States took control of the Midway Islands, a thousand miles from Hawaii, which were scarcely mentioned again until the Second World War. Though in 1870 President Grant tried to annex the Dominican Republic, Senator Charles Sumner managed to block the attempt. Seward and his successor, Hamilton Fish,

All Colored People

THAT WANT TO

GO TO KANSAS,

On September 5th, 1877,

Can do so for $5.00

IMMIGRATION.

WHEREAS, We, the colored people of Lexington, Ky., knowing that there is an abundance of choice lands now belonging to the Government, have assembled ourselves together for the purpose of locating on said lands. Therefore,

BE IT RESOLVED, That we do now organize ourselves into a Colony, as follows:—Any person wishing to become a member of this Colony can do so by paying the sum of one dollar ($1.00), and this money is to be paid by the first of September, 1877, in instalments of twenty-five cents at a time, or otherwise as may be desired.

RESOLVED, That this Colony has agreed to consolidate itself with the Nicodemus Towns, Solomon Valley, Graham County, Kansas, and can only do so by entering the vacant lands now in their midst, which costs $5.00.

RESOLVED, That this Colony shall consist of seven officers—President, Vice-President, Secretary, Treasurer, and three Trustees. President—M. M. Bell; Vice-President—Isaac Talbott; Secretary—W. J. Niles; Treasurer—Daniel Clarke; Trustees—Jerry Lee, William Jones, and Abner Webster.

RESOLVED, That this Colony shall have from one to two hundred militia, more or less, as the case may require, to keep peace and order, and any member failing to pay in his dues, as aforesaid, or failing to comply with the above rules in any particular, will not be recognized or protected by the Colony.

Exodusters, southern blacks dismayed by the failure of Reconstruction, left the South by the thousands for Kansas in 1877. This handbill advertised the establishment of a black colony in Graham County, Kansas. Kansas State Historical Society.

successfully used diplomacy to arrange a financial settlement of claims against Britain for permitting the sale of the *Alabama* and other Confederate cruisers.

By 1876 it was obvious to most political observers that the North was no longer willing to pursue the goals of Reconstruction. The results of a disputed presidential election confirmed this fact. Samuel J. Tilden, Democratic governor of New York, ran strongly in the South and took a commanding lead in both the popular vote and the electoral college over Rutherford B. Hayes, the Republican nominee. Tilden won 184 electoral votes and needed only one more for a majority. Nineteen votes from Louisiana, South Carolina, and Florida were disputed; both Democrats and Republicans claimed to have won in those states despite fraud on the part of their opponents. One vote from Oregon was undecided due to a technicality (see map).

Election of 1876

To resolve this unprecedented situation, on which the Constitution gave no guidance, Congress established a fifteen-member electoral commission. In the

Important events

1865	Freedmen's Bureau established President Andrew Johnson organizes new southern governments Johnson permits election of prominent Confederates and passage of Black Codes Congress refuses to seat southern representatives Thirteenth Amendment ratified
1866	Congress passes Civil Rights Act over Johnson's veto Congress approves Fourteenth Amendment Freedmen's Bureau renewed by Congress over Johnson's veto Most southern states reject Fourteenth Amendment Tennessee readmitted to Union *Ex parte Milligan*
1867	Military Reconstruction Act; Command of the Army Act; Tenure of Office Act Purchase of Alaska Constitutional conventions called in southern states
1868	Johnson impeached by House of Representatives, tried by Senate, and acquitted Seven more southern states readmitted Fourteenth Amendment ratified Ulysses S. Grant elected president
1869	Congress approves Fifteenth Amendment
1870	Force Acts Four more southern states readmitted Attempt to annex Dominican Republic fails
1871	Ku Klux Klan Act Treaty with England settles *Alabama* claims
1872	Amnesty Act Liberal Republicans challenge party leadership Debtors urge government to keep greenbacks in circulation Grant re-elected
1873	*Slaughter-House* cases Economic recession
1874	Grant vetoes increase in paper money Democrats win control of House of Representatives
1875	Several Grant appointees indicted for corruption Civil Rights Act
1876	Grant's secretary of war indicted for receiving bribes, resigns Congress requires that after 1878 greenbacks be convertible into gold *U.S.* v. *Cruikshank* *U.S.* v. *Reese* Results of presidential election disputed; Congress establishes commission to examine returns
1877	Congressional Democrats acquiesce in election of Rutherford B. Hayes President Hayes withdraws troops from South; end of Reconstruction Black Exodusters migrate to Kansas

interest of impartiality, membership on the commission was to be balanced between Democrats and Republicans. But one independent Republican, Supreme Court Justice David Davis, refused appointment in order to accept his election as a senator. A regular Republican took his place, and the Republican party prevailed 8-to-7 on every decision, a strict party vote. Hayes would then become the winner if Congress accepted the commission's findings.

Congressional acceptance, however, was not sure. Democrats controlled the House and had the power to filibuster to block action on the vote. Many citizens worried that the nation had entered a major constitutional crisis and was slipping once again into civil war. But the crisis was resolved when Democrats acquiesced in the election of Hayes. Scholars have found that negotiations went on between some of Hayes's supporters and southerners who were interested in federal aid to railroads, internal improvements, federal patronage, and removal of troops from southern states. But the most recent studies suggest that these negotiations did not have a deciding effect on the outcome. Neither party was well enough organized to implement and enforce a bargain between the sections. Northern and southern Democrats simply yielded to the pressure of events and failed to contest the election. Thus Hayes became president, and southerners looked forward to the withdrawal of federal troops from the South. Reconstruction was unmistakably over.

Southern Democrats rejoiced, but black Americans grieved over the betrayal of their hopes for equality. Tens of thousands of blacks pondered leaving the South, where freedom was no longer a real possibility.

Black Exodusters

"[We asked] whether it was possible we could stay under a people who had held us in bondage," said Henry Adams, who led a migration to Kansas. "[We] appealed to the President . . . and to Congress . . . to protect us in our rights and privileges," but "in 1877 we lost all hopes." Thereafter many southern blacks "wanted to go to a territory by ourselves." In South Carolina, Louisiana, Mississippi, and other southern states, thousands gathered up their possessions and migrated to Kansas. They were known as Exodusters, disappointed people still searching for their share in the American dream.

Thus the nation ended over fifteen years of bloody civil war and controversial reconstruction without establishing full freedom for black Americans. Their status would continue to be one of the major issues facing the nation. A host of other issues would arise from industrialization. How would the country develop its immense resources in a growing and increasingly integrated national economy? How would farmers, industrial workers, immigrants, and capitalists fit into the new social system? Industrialization promised not just a higher standard of living but also a different life style in both urban and rural areas. Moreover, it augmented the nation's power and laid the foundation for an increased American role in international affairs. As the United States entered its second hundred years of existence, it confronted these serious challenges. The experience of the 1860s and 1870s suggested that the solutions, if any, might not be clear or complete.

Suggestions for further reading

National policy and politics

Herman Belz, *A New Birth of Freedom* (1976); Herman Belz, *Emancipation and Equal Rights* (1978); Herman Belz, *Reconstructing the Union* (1969); Michael Les Benedict, *A Compromise of Principle* (1974); Michael Les Benedict, *The Impeachment and Trial of Andrew Johnson* (1973); Ellen Carol Dubois, *Feminism and Suffrage* (1978); W. E. B. Du Bois, *Black Reconstruction* (1935); John Hope Franklin, *Reconstruction* (1965); Harold M. Hyman, *A More Perfect Union* (1973); Eric L. McKitrick, *Andrew Johnson and Reconstruction* (1966); James M. McPherson, *The Abolitionist Legacy* (1975); William S. McFeely, *Grant* (1981); William S. McFeely, *Yankee Stepfather: General O. O. Howard and the Freedmen* (1968); Kenneth M. Stampp, *Era of Reconstruction* (1965).

Freedmen and Reconstruction in the South

Jonathan Daniels, *Prince of Carpetbaggers* (1958); Paul D. Escott, *Slavery Remembered* (1979); W. McKee Evans, *Ballots and Fence Rails* (1966); Eric Foner, "Reconstruction and the Crisis of Free Labor," in *Politics and Ideology in the Age of the Civil War*, ed. Eric Foner (1980); Herbert G. Gutman, *The Black Family in Slavery & Freedom, 1750–1925* (1976);

William C. Harris, *Day of the Carpetbagger* (1979); Thomas Holt, *Black Over White* (1977); Elizabeth Jacoway, *Yankee Missionaries in the South* (1979); Jacqueline Jones, *Soldiers of Light and Love* (1980); Peter Kolchin, *First Freedom* (1972); Leon Litwack, *Been In The Storm So Long* (1979); Robert Manson Myers, ed., *The Children of Pride* (1972); Lillian A. Pereyra, *James Lusk Alcorn* (1966); Michael Perman, *Reunion Without Compromise* (1973); Lawrence N. Powell, *New Masters* (1980); James Roark, *Masters Without Slaves* (1977); C. Peter Ripley, *Slaves and Freedmen in Civil War Louisiana* (1976); Willie Lee Rose, *Rehearsal for Reconstruction* (1964); Rebecca Scott, "The Battle Over the Child," *Prologue,* 10, No. 2 (Summer 1978), 101–113; James Sefton, *The United States Army and Reconstruction, 1865–1877* (1967); Emma Lou Thornbrough, ed., *Black Reconstructionists* (1972); Albion W. Tourgée, *A Fool's Errand by One of the Fools* (1879); Allen Trelease, *White Terror* (1967); Okon Uya, *From Slavery to Public Service* (1971); Sarah Woolfolk Wiggins, *The Scalawag in Alabama Politics, 1865–1881* (1977).

The end of Reconstruction

Robert G. Athearn, *In Search of Canaan* (1978); Michael Les Benedict, "Southern Democrats in the Crisis of 1876–1877," *Journal of Southern History,* XLVI, No. 4 (November 1980), 489–524; Norman L. Crockett, *The Black Towns* (1979); Stephen J. DeCanio, *Agriculture in the Postbellum South* (1974); William Gillette, *Retreat from Reconstruction, 1869–1879* (1980); William Gillette, *The Right to Vote* (1969); Susan Previant Lee and Peter Passell, *A New Economic View of American History* (1979); Jay R. Mandle, *The Roots of Black Poverty* (1978); Nell Irvin Painter, *Exodusters* (1977); Keith Ian Polakoff, *The Politics of Inertia* (1973); Howard Rabinowitz, *Race Relations in the Urban South, 1865–1890* (1978); Roger L. Ransom and Richard Sutch, *One Kind of Freedom* (1977); Jonathan M. Wiener, *Social Origins of the New South* (1978); C. Vann Woodward, *Origins of the New South* (1951); C. Vann Woodward, *Reunion and Reaction* (1951); Joel Williamson, *After Slavery* (1966).

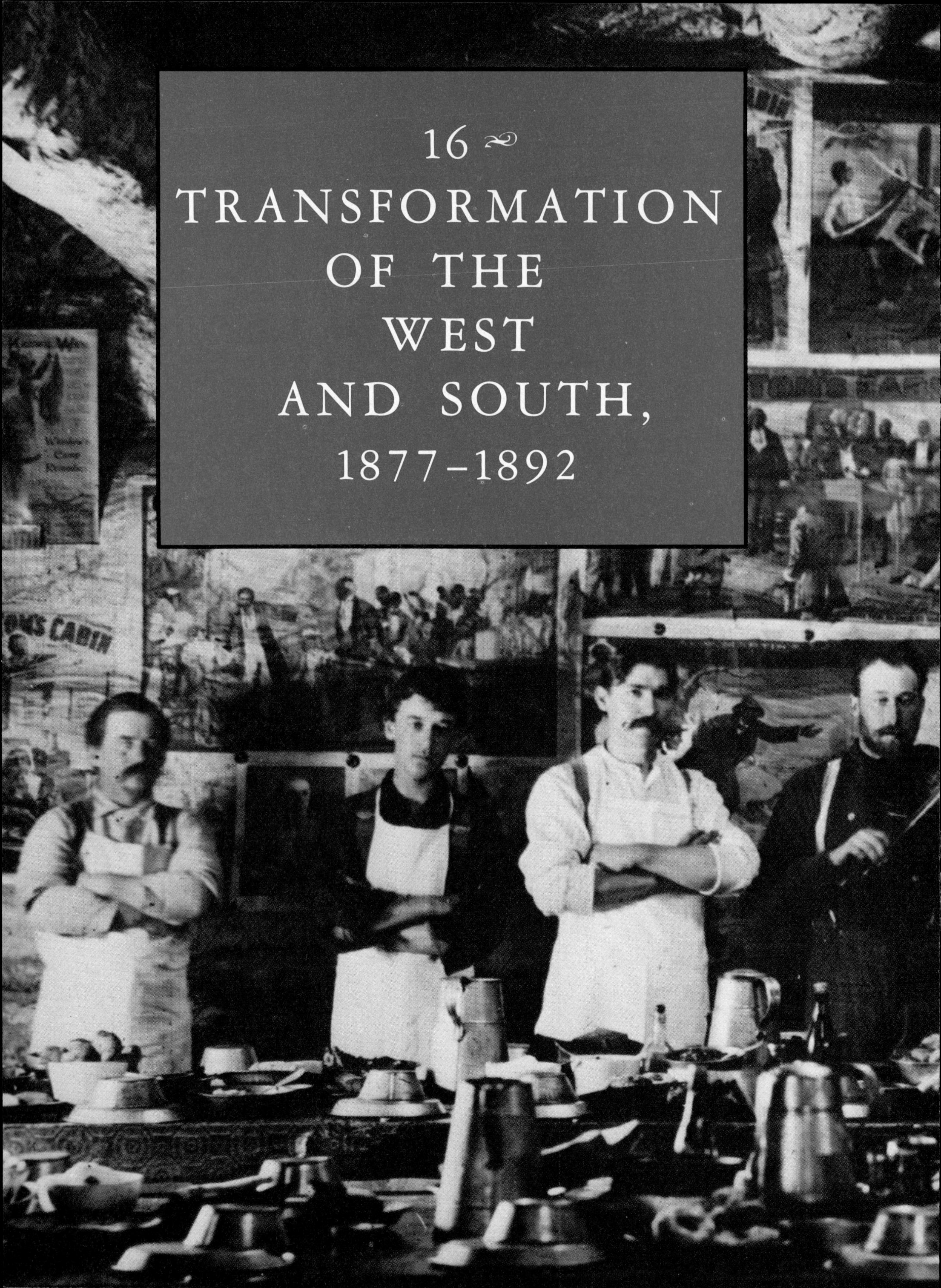

16 TRANSFORMATION OF THE WEST AND SOUTH, 1877–1892

"RIALTA"
VAUDEVILLE STAGE
DEATH OF UNCLE TOM
UNCLE TOM'S CABIN
PROPRIETOR
TOM'S CA
GEORGIA MI

On October 5, 1877, Chief Joseph of the Nez Perce decided he could hold out no longer. For fourteen years he had resisted the federal government's attempt to force his tribe onto a reservation in Idaho. When the army came to subdue them, the chief and eight hundred of his people fled. For four months the Nez Perce retreated through parts of Idaho, Montana, and Wyoming, outwitting hundreds of pursuing troops. Finally the army caught up with the starved and exhausted tribe thirty miles from the Canadian border. After five days of bitter resistance, Chief Joseph surrendered and reportedly said, "I am tired of fighting. . . . It is cold and we have no blankets. The little children are freezing to death. My people, some of them have run away to the hills and have no blankets, no food. . . . I want to look for my children and see how many of them I can find. . . . Hear me, my chiefs. My heart is sick and sad. I am tired."

Chief Joseph's capture marked the end of an era. Men and women who called themselves Americans had displaced and scattered the original Americans, and the West had become the scene of one of the greatest migrations in human history. By 1890 farms, ranches, mines, towns, and cities could be found in almost every region of what was to become the continental United States. That year, the superintendent of the census acknowledged that

> up to and including 1880, the country had a frontier of settlement, but at present the unsettled area has been so broken into by isolated bodies of settlement that there can hardly be said to be a frontier line. In the discussion of its extent and its westward movement, etc., it can not therefore, any longer have a place in the census reports.

What had happened to the frontier and what effect did its disappearance have on the nation?

Settlement of the American West proceeded at a furious pace. Between 1870 and 1890 the population living between the Mississippi River and the Pacific Ocean swelled from 7 million to nearly 17 million. The population of California doubled, and would have risen even more had not thousands of people moved eastward from the West Coast to settle the Rocky Mountain states. In those years the population of Texas tripled, and the Plains states–Kansas, Nebraska, and the Dakotas–grew even more rapidly.

Frontiers vanished in the South as well as the West. By the late 1870s cotton production had again reached prewar levels, and people were taking advantage of new opportunities afforded by the region's abundant natural resources. The agrarian economy revived as farmers and planters (many of them from the North) began to cultivate land left fallow in the wake of the Civil War and to extend cotton and tobacco cultivation into new areas. Meanwhile, timber and mining companies moved into unsettled areas.

In popular American thought, the frontier–which has been defined as "the edge of the unused"–has represented the birthplace of American self-confidence and individualism. Taming the continent's vast wilderness and bringing forth foodstuffs and raw materials from it, not to mention building cities in a single generation, filled Americans with a consciousness of power and a belief that anyone eager and persistent enough could succeed. Yet that very self-confidence was easily transformed into an arrogant attitude that Americans were somehow unique and special, and individualism often exerted itself at the expense of racial minorities and the propertyless.

As the continent filled in and the edge of the unused shifted and then faded in the late nineteenth century, Americans exhibited both their best and their worst characteristics. Development of the West was accomplished with courage, creativity, and a go-getter spirit that amazed the rest of the world. The optimistic conquerors, however, also displayed a wastefulness, violence, and greed that tarnished the American image. Recovery and growth in the South kindled new optimism, but careless exploitation exhausted the soil and left the lives of poor blacks and whites as downtrodden as ever. Industrialization failed to lessen the dominance of southern staple-crop agriculture, and by 1900 the section was more dependent economically on the North than it had been before the Civil War.

Americans rarely thought about conserving resources because there always seemed to be more territory to exploit. Thus the fading of the frontier, though of great symbolic importance, had little direct impact on people's behavior. Because vast stretches of land remained unsettled, millions of people continued to stream into the West, and more land in the South fell under cultivation. Compared with undeveloped regions in such other parts of the world as Siberia, South America, Africa, and Canada, the American West and South were relatively tame. If American settlers failed in one region, they did not usually perish; they could simply try again somewhere else. The West in particular offered an infinity of second chances. Moreover, new frontiers of different types emerged as Americans explored opportunities in industry, trade, services, transportation, and science.

Yet in spite of endless second chances, life in the West was less romantic and comfortable than settlers might have anticipated, and the reconstructed South failed to fulfill its potential. Hopeful western settlers often had to contend with barren land where water, trees, and contacts with the outside world were scarce and the weather was fickle and often cruel. Southerners found that the plantation and slave systems had been replaced by oppressive debt and vicious racial discrimination. Moreover, farming in the West and South expanded so rapidly that the impossible abruptly became a reality: productivity outstripped the nation's and the world's capacities to consume. As crop output and foreign competition increased in the 1880s, prices fell. Farmers' goals of wealth and comfort gave way to the necessity of producing more just to make ends meet.

Thus the passing of the frontier and the accompanying agricultural transformation created social and economic problems that would plague the nation for several decades. Just one month before Chief Joseph gave up his heroic retreat, a group of suffering farmers met in Lampassas County, Texas, and founded an organization to help solve their mounting problems. This organization, soon named the Farmers' Alliance, was to be the vanguard in a spreading movement of agrarian unrest that stirred the nation in the last two decades of the nineteenth century. Farmers, buffeted by forces beyond their control, strove to create the society of justice and opportunity that the American dream had promised. Their efforts gave rise to a mass movement called populism that remains today an important historical legacy.

Exploitation of natural resources

John D. Archbold, an officer of the Standard Oil Corporation, once allegedly offered to drink all the oil ever found outside the state of Pennsylvania. Luckily for him, no one ever challenged him to make good on his bravado; little did Archbold and others like him dream what vast natural resources lay waiting in the undeveloped regions of the United States. Discovery and use of these resources not only advanced settlement but also primed the revolutions in transportation, agriculture, and industry that swept the United States in the late nineteenth century. At the same time, the search for these resources produced a restless, get-rich-quick mentality and fed habits of racial oppression.

In the years just before the Civil War, eager prospectors began to comb little-known forests and mountains looking for iron, coal, timber, oil, and copper. By 1900, active exploitation of the land's riches, once confined to the Northeast and Appalachian regions, had spread across the continent. Timberlands in the Midwest, South, and Northwest were matching the outputs of those in Pennsylvania and surpassing those of New York and Maine. Alabama, Michigan, and Minnesota had become leading sources of iron ore. Montana and Arizona had taken the lead in copper and silver production. Coal mines in Illinois and West Virginia were challenging those of Pennsylvania for primacy. And discoveries of oil fields in California and Texas gave the lie to Archbold's faith that Pennsylvania was the only oil-rich state. In each instance, miners, lumbermen, and oilmen added their own distinctive flavors to regional culture.

Mining and lumbering

The mining frontier advanced rapidly, drawing thousands of people to California, Nevada, Idaho, Montana, and Colorado in the 1850s and 1860s. Prospectors tended to be restless optimists, willing to tramp mountains and deserts, searching icy streams for a telltale glint of precious metal. They shot game for food and financed their explorations by convincing merchants to advance credit for equipment in return for a share of the lode yet to be discovered. When their credit ran out, unlucky prospectors took jobs and saved up for another search for riches.

Extracting minerals from the ground involved high expenses for excavation and transportation. Thus individual prospectors who did discover veins of metal seldom mined them. Instead they sold their claims to mining syndicates, lived it up off their new wealth, and then set off on another quest. The mining companies, often financed by eastern investors, had ample capital to bring in engineers, heavy machinery, railroad lines, and work crews. Although discoveries of gold and silver first drew attention to the West and its resources, such companies usually moved into the Rocky Mountain states to exploit less romantic but equally lucrative bonanzas of lead, zinc, tin, quartz, and copper. In Montana, for example, speculator William Clark's Anaconda Mine, opened in 1881, yielded more than $2 billion worth of copper over the next fifty years. In the late 1870s, investors began financing the extraction of copper in Arizona, and by the early 1900s copper mines near Tucson were yielding higher profits than local gold and silver mines combined.

Mineral extraction concentrated intensively on a particular area or mine, but lumber production–another large-scale extractive industry–required vast stretches of land. As lumber companies moved into the thick forests of the Northwest, some not only stripped the land without regard for the future but also grabbed millions of acres fraudulently. To stimulate western settlement, Congress in 1878 passed the Timber and Stone Act; this measure, which applied to land in California, Nevada, Oregon, and Washington, allowed private citizens to buy at the low price of $2.50 per acre 160-acre plots "unfit for cultivation" and "valuable chiefly for timber." Taking advantage of the act, lumber companies hired thousands of seamen from waterfront boarding houses to register claims to timberland and turn them over to the companies. By 1900, claimants had bought over 3.5 million acres under Timber and Stone Act provisions, and most of that land belonged to corporations.

While lumbermen were acquiring claims to timberlands in the Northwest, oilmen were beginning to sink wells in the Southwest. In 1900 most of the nation's petroleum still came from fields in the Appalachians and the Midwest, but promising developments were under way in southern California and eastern Texas. The most spectacular strike occurred in 1901 at Spindletop, Texas, where a well shot a stream of oil 160 feet into the air. Although most oil and kerosene were still used for lubrication and lighting, discoveries in the Southwest were to become a vital new source of fuel in the twentieth century.

Much of the natural-resource frontier was a man's world. Mining, general labor, and some farming were

Frontier society

the predominant occupations. In 1880, men outnumbered women by more than two to one in Colorado, Nevada, and Arizona. Among twenty-to-forty-year-olds, men had a three-to-one majority. In the nation as a whole, by contrast, there were about 97 women for every 100 men; and in the older eastern states, women frequently outnumbered men.

Yet many western communities had substantial numbers of women. Most women who went to the mining frontier did so for the same reasons men went: to find a fortune. They usually accompanied a husband or father and seldom prospected themselves. Even so, many women realized their own opportunities in the towns, where they provided cooking, laundering, and, in some cases, sexual services for the miners. Some became the family's main breadwinner when their husbands failed to strike it rich. As one wife recalled, "I began at once to figure in my mind how many men I could cook for, if there should be no better way of making money." Women's presence had a settling influence on mining communities. While they pursued new opportunities and freedoms, women also helped to bolster family life and to combat raw materialism and vice by campaigning against drinking, gambling, and whoring. According to one resident of the mining frontier, women of "honest hearts have fallen victim to the peculiar seductions [of] the place," yet "paradoxicaly as the statement may sound, it is rigorously true that these women have improved the morals of the community."

Many of the mining and lumber communities were genuinely heterogeneous, containing Mexicans and Chinese as well as some Indians and blacks. Chinese and blacks were employed in the camps to do cooking and cleaning. Mexicans and Indians often had been the original settlers of land coveted by whites. Each of these minority groups met with white prejudice, especially when it became evident that the forests and mines would not make everyone rich. California imposed a tax on foreign miners and denied blacks, Indians, and Chinese the right to testify or submit evidence in court. Throughout the West any claims Indians or Mexicans might have had to land sought by white miners were ignored or simply stolen. Blacks and Chinese who worked in mining camps often suffered threats and violence. Nonwhites defended themselves as best they could against such intimidation, but their most common tactic was to pack up and seek jobs and homes in another town or mining camp.

Two women stand on a hill overlooking Helena, Montana, a typical mining town of the 1870s. In spite of their small numbers, women exerted a settling influence on frontier towns. Montana Historical Society, Helena.

Use of public lands

Development of the nation's oil, mineral, and timber resources raised serious questions about what belonged to all the people, as represented by the federal government, and what belonged to private interests whose motive was profit. Two factors worked at cross-purposes. First, most land west of the Mississippi was public domain, and many people believed the federal government, as owner of the land, should receive some return from exploitation of the land. But the government lacked both the motivation and the means to dig mines, sink wells, and cut forests, and thus sold land to private interests who would take the initiative to find and extract resources.

Inevitably, developers of natural resources were more interested in what the land yielded than in the land itself. They wanted trees, not forest land that would become useless once the trees were stripped away. They wanted oil, not the scrubby plain that would be doubly worthless if–as often happened–wells were dug but no oil was found. Thus, to many companies involved in resource production, land purchased at market price was an unnecessary and sometimes prohibitive expense.

To avoid such costs, developers used several ploys, some legal and some not. One method was to purchase or rent limited rights to extract resources. Lumbermen would buy permits to fell a certain number of trees on a given forest tract and share the profits with the landowner. Oilmen and iron miners often leased property from private owners or the government and paid royalties on the minerals extracted. Other practices were frankly corrupt or fraudulent. As they had done since colonial times, some lumbermen simply cut trees on public lands without paying a cent. And, as already noted, lumber companies used trickery to

Chinese gold miners at Auburn Ravine, California, in 1852. Chinese first came to California in the 1850s and 1860s to escape social and economic upheaval at home. They often paid for their transportation by working under a Chinese-operated contract-labor system. California State Library.

buy land cheaply under the Timber and Stone Act. Mining companies bribed and manipulated state and federal legislators for advantages in mineral extraction. Even when Congress and the U.S. Land Office tried to prevent fraud by passing tighter legislation and sending out more investigators, many communities resisted in the fear that such crackdowns would slow local economic growth.

Questions about natural resources thus caught Americans between the urge for progress and fear of spoiling the land. By the late 1870s and early 1880s, people concerned about the natural landscape began to coalesce into a conservation movement. The few scientists, educators, artists, and government officials involved in this movement worked chiefly to preserve forests, probably because logging so visibly altered the environment. With New York in the lead, a few states established public forests, and in 1891 Congress authorized the president to create forest reserves on public land, protected from cutting by private interests. Such policies met with strong objections. Lumber companies, lumber dealers, and railroads were joined in their opposition by private householders accustomed to cutting timber freely for fuel and building material. Public opinion on conservation also split along sectional lines. Most supporters came from the eastern states, where resources had become less plentiful; opposition was loudest in the West, where people were still eager to take advantage of nature's bounty.

Conquest of the mining and forest frontiers left legacies to the entire nation as well as the West. Development of new areas–first by miners, then by railroads and farmers–brought western territories to the threshold of statehood. Between 1876 and 1889, jockeying between Democrats and Republicans in Congress prevented the admission of any new states. But in 1889 Republicans seeking to solidify their control of Congress pushed through the Omnibus Bill, granting statehood to North Dakota, South Dakota, Washington, and Montana. Wyoming and Idaho were admitted in 1890, the same year the Census Bureau announced the disappearance of the frontier. Congress balked at granting statehood to Utah because the Mormons, who comprised a majority of the state's population and controlled its government, practiced polygamy. But the territory's prosperity could not be denied, and when the Mormons agreed to abandon polygamy, Congress relented, voting Utah into the Union in 1896.

Admission of new states

The mining towns and lumber camps in these states spiced American folk culture and fostered the go-getter optimism that distinguished the American spirit. The lawlessness and hedonism of places like Deadwood, in Dakota Territory, and Tombstone, in Arizona Territory, gave the West notoriety and romance. Legends grew up about inhabitants of these towns whose lives both typified and magnified western experience. One such character was Martha Jane Canary, known as Calamity Jane, who in the 1870s worked in eastern Wyoming and the western Dakotas as a scout and teamster, freighting supplies to mining camps. Skilled with a rifle and dressed in men's clothes, Calamity Jane acquired a reputation for wild behavior that fiction writers later glorified. Yet she appears simply to have been seeking a place in a hard world. According to an army captain who employed her, Jane was "eccentric and wayward rather than bad and had adopted male attire more to aid her in getting a living than for any improper purpose."

Arizona mining towns, with their free-flowing cash and loose law enforcement, attracted numerous gamblers, thieves, and opportunists whose names stood for the Wild West. Near Tombstone, the infamous Clanton family and their partner John Ringgold, called Johnny Ringo, engaged in smuggling and cattle rustling to supply materials and food to mining camps. Inside the town, the legendary Earp brothers–Wyatt, Jim, Morgan, Virgil, and Warren–and their friends William Barclay "Bat" Masterson and John Henry "Doc" Holliday operated on both sides of the law as lawmen, gunmen, gamblers, and politicians. A feud between Clanton and Earp factions climaxed on October 26, 1881, in the famous shoot-out at the OK Corral, where three Clantons were killed and Virgil and Morgan Earp were seriously wounded.

Characters like Wild Bill Hickok, Poker Alice, and Bedrock Tom became western folk heroes, and fiction writers like Mark Twain and Bret Harte captured for posterity some of the flavor of mining life. But violence and eccentricity were far from common. Most miners and lumbermen worked seventy hours a week and had neither time nor money for drinking and gambling, let alone gunfights. Women worked as long or longer as teachers, cooks, laundresses, storekeepers, and housewives; only a very few were gunslingers or dance-hall queens. For most westerners, life was a matter of adapting and surviving.

The age of railroad expansion

On May 10, 1869, the whole country knew what was happening at Promontory Point in the mountains of Utah. There, the Central Pacific Railroad, built 689 miles eastward from Sacramento, California, was to meet the Union Pacific Railroad, built 1,086 miles westward from Omaha, Nebraska, to form the nation's first transcontinental route. Work crews of six hundred Irish, Chinese, Mexicans, and white and black Americans participated in the ceremony. As the famous last spike, the golden one, was pounded into place, the hammer blows triggered telegraph impulses that set off bells in scores of cities from Boston to San Francisco. From coast to coast, shouting multitudes celebrated the event.

Discovery and development of natural riches provided the base on which the nation's economy expanded. But raw wealth would have been of limited use without means of carrying it to factories, storehouses, marketplaces, and ports. In today's world of trailer trucks, cargo planes, containerized shipping, and supertankers, a railway train, puffing steam and rattling across the countryside, seems almost an anachronism, a relic. But in the half-century following the Civil War, railroads refashioned the American economy, stitching together the nation, supporting new industries, and generating their own romance.

Growth of the national rail network

A web of railroad track spread across the country during these years. Between 1865 and 1890, total track in the United States grew from 35,000 to 200,000 miles; west of the Mississippi, it rose from 3,300 to 72,000 miles (see map). Construction in the South topped 25,000 miles. By 1910 the United States had a third of all railroad track in the world. In 1890 total railroad revenues topped $1 billion–two-and-one-half times the total revenues of the federal government. After 1880, when more durable steel rails began to replace iron rails, railroad demand helped to boost the nation's steel industry to international leadership. Finally, railroad expansion spawned a number of related activities, including coal production, passenger and freight-car manufacture, and depot construction.

Though the most awe-inspiring routes were those of the transcontinental lines, construction of feeder lines in the South, Midwest, and West and consolidation of northeastern trunk lines were equally important. Construction proceeded erratically, often tainted by stock fraud and fiscal mismanagement. But by the turn of the century, the country's railroad network was virtually complete. A few major lines had achieved dominance: the New York Central and the Pennsylvania lines in the Northeast; the Louisville and Nashville in the South; the Burlington in the Midwest; and the Southern Pacific, Santa Fe, Union Pacific, Northern Pacific, and Great Northern transcontinentals that ran to the West Coast. These lines linked major American cities and completed formation of a national market system. Henceforth the

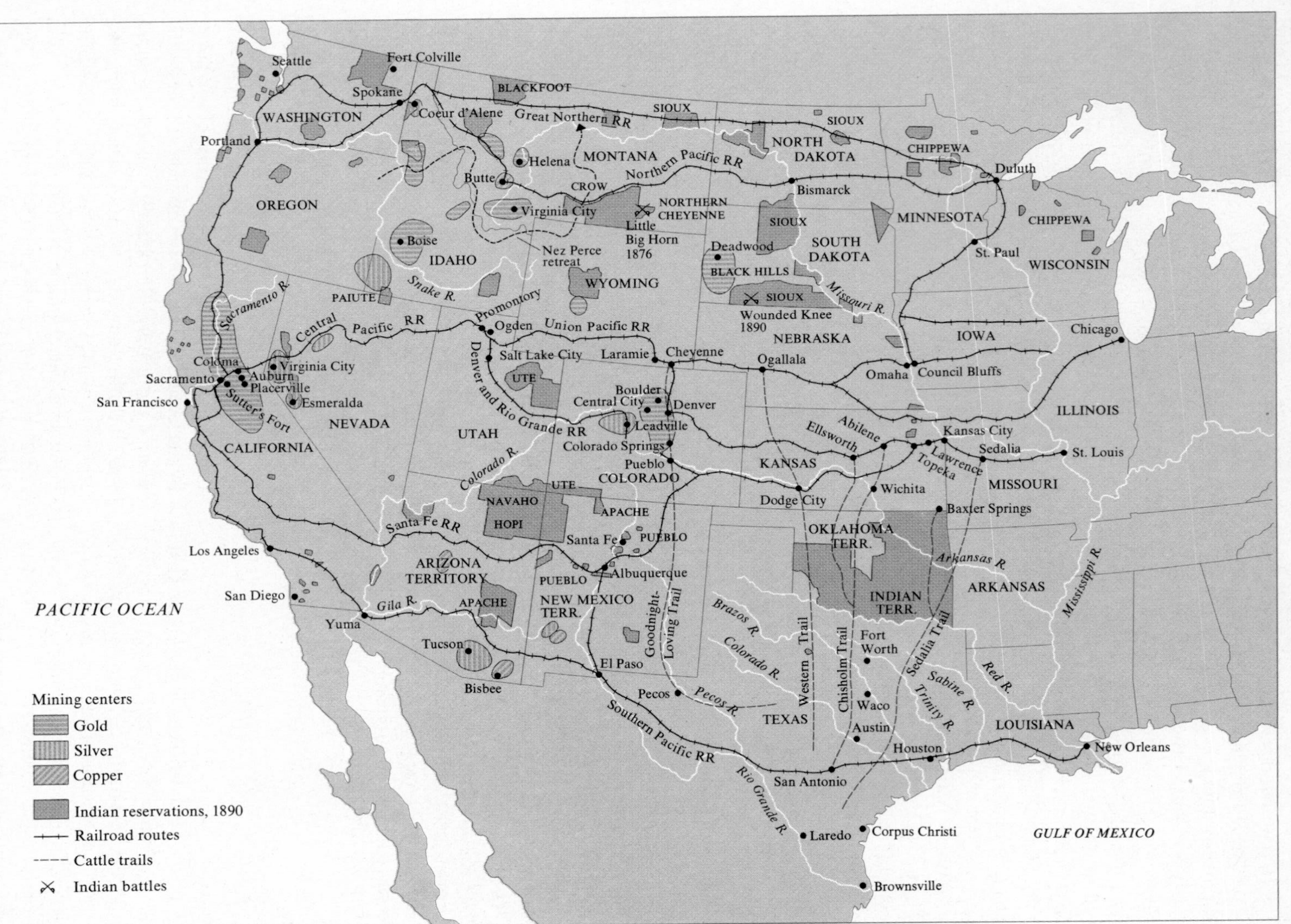

The American West, 1860–1890

The Promontory Point Grand Trestle, built in Utah by engineers of the Union Pacific Railroad. This photograph was taken in 1869, the day before workers drove down the golden spike that joined the Union Pacific with the Central Pacific. The Oakland Museum.

goods and raw materials of one section would be available in all other sections of the country.

Railroad construction provided employment for tens of thousands of laborers. In their haste to obtain government grants (see below) by laying track, railroad managers recruited workers wherever they could find them. Work crews, especially on the transcontinentals, were large and assorted. The Central Pacific imported seven thousand Chinese coolies to work in the western mountains, while the Union Pacific used Irish construction gangs. Both also hired former Civil War soldiers. The workers were housed in shacks and tents that could be dismantled, loaded on flatcars, and relocated at intervals of sixty or seventy miles. At one time, the Union Pacific needed forty rail cars to supply its crews with rails, ties, bridge materials, and food.

Besides its direct economic impact, the age of railroad construction brought about important technological and organizational reforms. By the late 1880s, almost all lines had adopted standard narrow-gauge rails so that their tracks could connect with one another. Such devices as the Westinghouse air brake, an automatic car coupler, and standardized handholds on freight cars made rail transportation safer and more efficient. Needs for gradings, tunnels, and bridges helped the American engineering profession to grow. Organizational advances included systems for coordinating complex passenger and freight schedules, the adoption of uniform freight-classification systems, and in 1883 consolidation of the nation's fifty-four different time zones into four standardized time zones.

From other perspectives, however, the effects of railroads were less favorable. First, the mania for railroad construction diverted attention and resources from other modes of transportation such as canals and highways. And returns on railroad investments, in the form of interest and dividends, were relatively low and uncertain. Between 1869 and 1897, average yields on railroad bonds fell from about 6 percent to just over 3 percent. Moreover, the high cost of construction and equipment demanded that new railroads begin operation as soon as possible in order to generate revenues to pay back accumulated debts and maintain investors' confidence. As a result, many miles of track were laid hastily, without regard for safety or durability.

Nevertheless, railroads became extremely influential and acquired a uniquely American function. European railroads were usually built to link established market centers and to improve or replace existing routes of traffic. In this country, however, railroads often created the very communities they were meant to serve and carried traffic that had never before existed. Particularly in the West and South, railroads accelerated the growth of regional centers such as Omaha, Kansas City, Cheyenne, Los Angeles, Portland, Seattle, Atlanta, and Nashville.

Government subsidy of railroads

Railroads accomplished these feats with the help of some of the largest government subsidies in American history. Railroad executives argued that their activities were benefiting the public interest and that the government should aid them by giving them land from the public domain. Congress, dominated by railroad enthusiasts and investors, was sympathetic. In order to encourage railroad construction, the government gave away over 180 million acres, mostly to interstate routes chartered between 1850 and 1871. These grants usually consisted of a right of way plus alternate sections of land in a strip twenty to eighty miles wide along the right of way. Railroad corporations financed construction by using this land as security for bonds or by selling it for cash.

States and localities heaped further subsidies on new routes. State land was frequently offered to railroads by legislators eager for the advantages railroads could bring—to them personally as well as to the state. Total state grants amounted to about 50 million acres. Counties, cities, and towns petitioned state legislatures for permission to assist railroads, usually by offering them loans or by purchasing railroad bonds or stocks.

Government subsidies had mixed effects. In an age dominated by the doctrine of laissez faire—the belief that government should not interfere in commerce—the huge grants laid bare the hypocrisy inherent in the American business system. Capitalists argued against government interference in one breath and accepted government aid in the next. They also pressured public agencies into meeting their needs. The Southern Pacific, for example, threatened to bypass Los Angeles unless the city came up with a bonus and built a depot. Without government help, few railroads could have established themselves sufficiently to attract private investment. Yet public aid was not always certain or salutary. Some laborers and farmers fought subsidies, arguing that companies like the Southern Pacific would become too powerful. During the 1880s, the policy of assistance haunted some communities whose zeal for railroads had prompted them to commit too much to shaky lines that were never built or that defaulted on repayment of loans. On the other hand, many communities boomed because they had linked their fortunes to the iron horse.

Competition and discriminatory rate setting

As the nation's rail network expanded, so did competition and duplication. One investigator reported in 1884 that there was "hardly a town or city of any magnitude in the United States which has not two or more tributary railroads." Shippers sending raw materials or finished products across the country now had several routes to choose from, and railroad operators scrambled for new customers. Local lines as well as trunk lines cut rates to attract more traffic and outmaneuver competitors. In the twenty-five years after the Civil War, freight and passenger rates between New York and Chicago fell by nearly two-thirds. But rate wars soon cut into profits, and several railroads had to reduce or omit dividends to stockholders. Moreover, wild vacillations in rates angered shippers and farmers who missed out on a saving by shipping goods just before a rate reduction or were caught awaiting a reduction when rates were raised. Some kind of stability was clearly desirable.

Ironically, while railroad rates generally were falling, complaints about excessively high rates were increasing. Railroads often boosted rates as high as possible on noncompetitive routes in order to compensate for unprofitably low rates on competitive routes. Thus pricing was not proportionate to distance: rates on short-distance hauls served by only one line could be far higher than those on long-distance hauls served by competing lines. For example, it cost twice as much to send a bushel of wheat from Fargo, North Dakota, to Duluth, Minnesota, than from Minneapolis to Chicago, even though the latter distance was twice as long. Pittsburgh, a large city served by only one railroad, paid 60 percent more for grain from Chicago than did New York, which was twice as far away. Railroad managers argued that small quantities shipped over short distances involved proportionately higher transportation costs than did bulk goods carried over long distances. But farmers and other shippers continued to believe such rates were illogical and unfair. A spokesman for Michigan farmers in 1886 said he could "hardly imagine a case where it would be right or proper for a railroad to charge more for a shorter than for a longer distance for freight [similar] in kind and quantity and over the same road or roads."

Railroads also devised other forms of discrimination. To increase traffic they made special contracts with large shippers, offering rebates and reductions of up to 50 percent of published freight rates. They courted the favor of important shippers and politicians by offering free passenger passes. And to reduce competition, several railroads made agreements among themselves called pools, whose participants shared traffic and earnings and set common rates. Such agreements, though easily circumvented by unscrupulous members who made secret contracts outside the pool, generally discriminated against small shippers.

These discriminatory practices riled several groups of critics, including farmers, small shippers, retailers, bankers, reform politicians, and even some stockholders. During the 1870s, many of these groups demanded that government regulate railroads, especially their pricing practices. By 1880, fourteen states had established commissions or other agencies to limit freight and storage rates charged by state-chartered lines. Railroads bitterly fought these laws, arguing that a higher natural law of private property superseded public authority. This entrenched American belief in the freedom to acquire and use property without government restraint prevented the ultimate step–public ownership of railroads–but did not halt regulation. In 1877 the Supreme Court upheld the principle of railroad regulation in *Munn* v. *Illinois,* saying, "When private property is affected with a public interest it ceases to be *juris privati* only . . . and must submit to be controlled by the public for the common good."

Government regulation of railroads

Although the principle of regulation had won acceptance, dissatisfaction with state measures grew. Critics charged that state regulatory commissions were either too weak or too subservient to railroad interests. Moreover, state commissioners had little control over interstate lines and thus could not affect the largest, most powerful railroads. The Supreme Court affirmed this limited authority in 1886 by declaring in the *Wabash* case that only Congress and not the states could regulate rates on interstate commerce. Consequently, reformers called for stronger laws at the federal level.

Congress responded in 1887 by passing the Interstate Commerce Act. The act prohibited pools, rebates, and long-haul–short-haul rate discriminations; and one of its clauses directed that "all charges . . . shall be reasonable and fair." The law also created the Interstate Commerce Commission (ICC) and gave it power to investigate railroads; to issue "cease-and-desist" orders against illegal practices; and to seek court assistance to enforce compliance with the law.

The Interstate Commerce Act resulted from a political compromise between various supporters of regulation and various defenders of laissez faire. Written to satisfy as many groups as possible, the act was inherently ambivalent. Its basic provisions quieted the cries of protest from farmers and other interests opposed to railroads' monopolistic practices. It affirmed the principle of regulation, forbade discriminatory practices, and gave the ICC power to investigate on its own initiative as well as in response to specific complaints. But the provisions for its enforcement were blurry and left railroads much room for evasion. The ICC could issue cease-and-desist orders, but only the courts could force obedience. In a series of court cases, federal judges chipped away at ICC powers by asserting a right to review ICC orders and by interpreting the Interstate Commerce Act very narrowly. In the *Maximum Freight Rate* case in 1897, the Supreme Court ruled that the act did not grant the ICC power to set rates, and in the *Alabama Midlands* case the same year, the Court shattered prohibitions against long-haul–short-haul discriminations. Between 1887 and 1897, the judiciary overruled 90 percent of ICC rate orders; between 1887 and 1905, the Supreme Court decided against the ICC in fifteen of sixteen cases.

In spite of such setbacks, the era of railroad reform opened new paths for future generations. The right of the federal government to regulate railroads as a public enterprise did receive court support. Regulation at the state level continued, especially with regard to safety and intrastate rates. Strong criticism of railroads forced their executives to become more responsive to public opinion. Finally, establishment of the ICC gave further impetus to the movement to eliminate favoritism in all aspects of society and the economy. Forces of change had begun to gather momentum, but Americans still had to decide whether they desired free competition or cooperation under government regulation.

The Indians' last stand

Railroad expansion not only bound the nation together economically, it had massive impact on previously undeveloped land. The vast domain between the Missouri and the Pacific–the Great Plains and Far West–became more accessible to settlement. But much of this land was not empty. It was the home of thousands of native American tribespeople, whose ways of life differed profoundly from those of most white people and whose presence represented a stubborn barrier to full exploitation of the land. Indian resistance to white intrusion was noble in intent and tragic in consequence; the natives faced insurmountable odds. The great western tribes were simply overwhelmed by an unstoppable migratory invasion.

Beginning in the 1850s, when large numbers of whites first streamed into the West, the Indians faced serious threats to their cultural survival. The newcomers, hungry for land and profits, could not tolerate the humble, nomadic tribes who recognized no individual ownership of lands. Clashes between natives and whites were inevitable and often violent. In California, Oregon, Utah, and Idaho, white miners swiftly dispersed and destroyed Snake, Ute, and Bannock tribes by breaking up small villages, murdering warriors, and seizing land. In the Southwest, Navaho and Apache tribes fought the invaders savagely in the early 1860s. But by 1873 white settlers aided by federal troops had broken most resistance except for periodic raids by young dissidents.

The basic features–and disgraces–of late-nineteenth-century policy toward Indians began with the subjugation of the Great Plains tribes: Sioux and Crows in the north, Pawnee and Cheyenne in the middle Plains, and Comanches and Kiowa in the south. These tribes led a nomadic existence, usually following the buffalo herds. Their economies and cultures revolved around migration. A restless people who took pleasure in the discipline of moving camp and testing unknown territory, the Plains tribes regarded their relationship with nature as sacred. Black Elk, an Oglala Sioux, explained one version of this mystical unity:

Culture of the Great Plains tribes

> Everything an Indian does is in a circle, and that is because the Power of the World always works in circles, and everything tries to be round. . . . The sky is round, and I have heard that the earth is round like a ball, and so are all the stars. The wind, in its greatest power, whirls. Birds make their nests in circles, for theirs is the same religion as ours. The sun comes forth and goes down again in a circle. The moon does the same, and both are round. Even the seasons form a great circle in their changing, and always come back again to where they were. The life of a man is a circle from childhood to childhood, and so it is in everything where power moves.

Plains Indians observed strict sexual divisions of labor. Among the Sioux, for example, men's areas were hunting, religion, and war. Women had responsibility for child rearing, art, and domestic crafts. This sexual division involved no difference in status. Although men controlled the predatory and spiritual realms, women were respected for their craft skills. Their quilling and painting were the tribes' primary forms of artistic expression.

Upon their first extensive contacts with whites, the natives accepted the federal government's policy of defining territorial boundaries for individual tribes and making a separate treaty with each. This tactic, called "concentration," was really a system of divide-and-conquer. It lasted only until the 1860s, when thousands of whites, accompanied by cattle herds and railroads, moved into the Plains. Treaties made one week dissolved the next as eager settlers, aided by insensitive federal officials and nervous soldiers, pressed Indians to cede more territory. The natives resisted with raids on settlements and attacks on troops.

Concentration and reservation policies

A series of bloody battles and massacres prompted a new federal policy in 1867. A commission appointed to establish peace with the Plains Indians decided that all tribes should be concentrated on two reservations, one in Dakota Territory and the other in Oklahoma Territory. Within these reservations, each tribe would occupy a specific piece of land, and white administrators would help them to shed their old ways in favor of a settled agrarian existence. Land agents and government officials cajoled or bribed tribal chiefs into signing treaties to this effect. Tribespeople, often unaware of the full meaning of such treaties, deferred to their leaders' judgment. By fall 1868, federal officials believed they had solved the Indian problem. "We have now selected and provided reservations for all, off the great road," a military commander wrote. "All who cling to their old hunting grounds are hostile and will remain so until killed off."

But whites soon discovered that 125,000 people could not easily be forced to abandon their centuries-old culture. Between 1869 and 1876, many disaffected families left the reservations and vengeful braves fought attempts by the U.S. Army to subdue them. Proving themselves to be skilled guerrilla fighters, these "nontreaty" Indians eluded much larger white forces and terrorized settlements from Texas to Montana. The natives had ample cause for hostility. They had been tricked and bribed into surrendering their homelands. And even the reservations offered them no protection from white greed: the Indian Bureau of the Interior Department was infested with corrupt agents who lined their pockets while furnishing reservations with moldy flour and spoiled meat.

Agreements with the government meant little, as the Sioux discovered in 1875 when federal officials allowed thousands of miners to invade the Dakota reservation in search of gold. Faced with this latest broken promise—and with the approach of the Northern Pacific Railroad, whose construction threatened their territory—the Sioux rebelled. The revolt, led by Chiefs Rain-in-the-Face, Sitting Bull, and Crazy Horse, peaked June 26, 1876, when 2,500 braves annihilated the troops of the rash General George S. Custer near the Little Big Horn River in southern Montana. But within a few months, shortages of supplies and overwhelming odds led to the collapse of Sioux resistance. By fall 1877, the Sioux war was over and other attempts at resistance had been quelled. General William Tecumseh Sherman had subdued Indian rebels in Texas, Chief Joseph of the Nez Perce had surrendered, and Crazy Horse had been murdered by soldiers while imprisoned in an army fort.

Sioux wars

By means of warfare and reservation policy, the government destroyed tribal unity and the power of chiefs. At the same time, white hunters undermined Plains Indian culture even more radically by destroying the huge buffalo herds that provided natives with almost every essential of life. For centuries Indians had cooked and preserved buffalo meat; fashioned hides into clothing, shoes, and blankets; used sinew for thread and bowstrings; carved tools from bones; and made horns into implements. The bulky beasts were easy targets for rifle-toting whites, who killed indiscriminately for sport or to collect the $1 to $3 offered by eastern tanneries for hides. Railroads hired sharpshooters like Buffalo Bill Cody to kill buffalo en masse because herds impeded traffic and a stampede could derail a train. By the mid-1880s, only a few hundred remained of the estimated 13 million bison that had existed in the 1850s. Even more decisively than government policy, extermination of the buffalo forced Indians to abandon their nomadic way of life.

One major step remained: breaking down tribal organization and converting the natives into docile citizens. A new era began in 1871, when Congress declared that the government would no longer recognize Indian tribes as independent nations capable

A Sioux camp in South Dakota, 1891. The Sioux led a nomadic life, living in harmony with the natural environment; when they packed up and moved on, they left the landscape almost undisturbed. This photograph shows the temporary situation characteristic of their camps. Library of Congress.

Destruction of tribal sovereignty

of making treaties with the United States. This decree meant that, in the eyes of the government, chiefs no longer spoke for their people. Between 1883 and 1885, the government encouraged natives to establish their own court systems, extended federal jurisdiction over Indian reservations, and prohibited mass religious gatherings such as the Sun Dance. These steps removed judicial and sacred powers from chiefs, further splintering tribal organization.

By 1887 reservation land held in common was the only remaining feature of tribal unity. Two white groups were agitating for division of these lands into parcels that would be owned by native families individually. Speculators hoped to buy thousands of acres cheaply from the government or to coax Indians into selling their plots. Meanwhile, humanitarian groups such as the Indian Rights Association argued that natives could best be assimilated by turning them into yeoman farmers who tilled their own land. Helen Hunt Jackson's popular book *A Century of Dishonor* (1881) stirred feelings of guilt among humanitarians with its harsh criticism of past policies toward natives.

Reacting to these pressures, Congress in 1887 passed the Dawes Severalty Act. This bill dissolved community-owned tribal lands and granted individual plots to each native family. To prevent Indians from selling their plots to speculators, the government retained ownership of these lands for twenty-five years. The act also granted citizenship to all who accepted the allotments, and authorized the government to sell unallotted land and to set aside the profits for the education of Indians. The Dawes Act completed what invasion, force, and buffalo slaughter had begun; it left native Americans bereft of their culture and disadvantaged in a white country. Only in the Southwest, where pueblo-dwelling Indians avoided allotments, did natives succeed in retaining their aboriginal ways of life.

In 1890 the government made one last show of force–though such a demonstration was hardly necessary. Active resistance having become less feasible, some Sioux Indians turned to the visionary religion of the Ghost Dance movement as a means of preserving native culture. Inspired by a prophet named Wovoka, reminiscent of Tecumseh's brother the Shawnee Prophet of eighty years earlier, the Ghost Dance promised a day when the land and water would swallow up all whites while the Indians danced as ghosts suspended above the calamity. All implements of white civilization, including guns and whiskey, would be buried, and all Indians united as brothers would return to reclaim the earth. The Ghost Dance expressed this vision in a ritual involving five days of slow dancing and meditation.

Ghost Dance movement

Although the Ghost Dance forswore violence, government agents became alarmed about the possibility of renewed Indian uprisings as Wovoka's vision became more popular. Charging that the cult was anti-Christian, they began arresting ghost dancers (meanwhile leaving alone white Seventh-Day Adventists, who anticipated a messianic age much as did the ghost dancers). Late in 1890, the government sent the Seventh Cavalry, Custer's old regiment, to apprehend some Sioux who were moving north from Pine Ridge, South Dakota, and who were believed to be armed for revolt. During the encounter, at a creek called Wounded Knee, the troops trained their new machine guns on the Indians and massacred two hundred men, women, and children in the snow.

By 1934, 138 million acres of Indian land had dwindled to 48 million acres, half of which was useless for farming or mining. That year federal policy was reversed and tribal land ownership was restored. But this move came too late. Natives had been isolated with only their inner strength and minimal government assistance to enable them to survive the battle for subsistence and the prejudice of white society. The West was won at their expense, and they remained grim casualties of an aggressive age.

The ranching frontier

Railroad construction and Indian removal set the stage for one of the West's most colorful and romantic industries, cattle ranching. Early in the nineteenth century, huge herds of cattle, originally introduced by the Spanish, roamed southern Texas and bred with cattle brought by American settlers. The resulting longhorn breed multiplied and became valuable by the 1860s, when the East's growing population increased demand for food, and railroads made transportation of beef more feasible. By 1870 drovers were herding thousands of Texas cattle northward to railroad connections in Kansas, Missouri, and Wyoming. On these long drives, mounted cowboys supervised the herds, which fed on open grassland along the way. At the northern terminus–usually Abilene, Dodge City, or Cheyenne–the cattle were loaded onto trains and sent eastward to Chicago and St. Louis for slaughter and distribution.

The long drive gave rise to its own romantic lore: rugged cowboys (as many as 25 percent of whom were black) with six-shooters, gaudy clothes, and crude manners; riotous cowtowns with raucous saloons and tough-minded women. But it was not very efficient. In trekking 1,500 miles, cattle lost weight and toughened. Herds traveling through Indian lands and farmers' fields were sometimes shot at and later prohibited from such trespass by state laws. The ranchers' only solution was to eliminate long drives by raising herds nearer to railroad routes.

Ranchers soon discovered that crossing sturdy Texas longhorns with heavier Hereford and Angus breeds produced cattle better able to survive northern winters, and cattle raising spread across the Great Plains. Between 1860 and 1880 the cattle population of Kansas, Nebraska, Colorado, Wyoming, Montana, and Dakota increased from 130,000 to 4.5 million.

Cattle raisers were like timber cutters: they needed vast stretches of land where their herds could graze, and they wanted to incur as little expense as possible to use such land. Thus they often bought a few acres bordering streams and turned their herds loose on adjacent public domain, which no one would want to own because it lacked water access. By this method, called open-range ranching, a cattleman

Open-range ranching

Hundreds of cattle file across the Texas prairie on the long drive, raising clouds of dust as they go. A solitary cowboy oversees the procession. Library of Congress, Erwin E. Smith Collection.

could control thousands of acres by owning only a hundred or so.

Neighboring ranchers usually formed associations and allowed their herds to graze together. Herds were distinguished from each other by burning a special mark, or brand, into the hide of every animal. Each ranch had its own brand—a sort of improvised shorthand for documenting title to movable property. Twice each year, crews of cowboys rounded up the cattle. In the spring they separated out cows and newborn calves and burned on each calf the brand of the cow it was following. In the fall roundup, the cowboys separated out mature animals ready to be driven to market and sold.

Roundups provided easterners with colorful images of western life: bellowing cattle, mounted rope-swinging cowboys, the smell of singed hides and smoky campfires. But the roundup was short-lived because it was too successful. Western boosters—never known for understatement—boasted that ranchers made profits of 40 to 50 percent annually. By the early 1880s, the profitability of beef raising lured scores of investors to the industry. As one publication explained:

> A good sized steer when it is fit for the butcher market will bring from $45.00 to $60.00. The same animal at its birth was worth but $5.00. He has run on the plains and cropped the grass from the public domain for four or five years, and now, with scarcely any expense to its owner, is worth $40.00 more than when he started on his pilgrimage.

National and international demand for beef kept rising, and ranchers and capital flowed into the Plains. Soon cattle began to overrun the range.

Fearing depletion of the prairie and loss of control, ranchers began to fence in their pastures with barbed wire—even though they had no legal title to the land. Fences destroyed the open range and often provoked disputes between competing ranchers, between cattle raisers and sheep raisers, and between ranchers and farmers who claimed use of the same land. In 1885, President Cleveland ordered removal of illegal fences on public lands and Indian reservations. Although enforcement was slow, the order signaled that free use of public domain was ending. Moreover, hundreds of thousands of cattle froze or starved during the two savage winters of 1885–1886 and 1886–1887 because barbed wire prevented them from roaming freely in search of food and shelter. Nevertheless, supplies of cattle surpassed demand, and prices tumbled. By spring 1887, steers that had sold for over $9 per hundred pounds four years earlier brought only $2.40 per hundred. By fall the price dropped to $1.90.

Open-range ranching made beef a staple of the American diet and created a few fortunes, but its extralegal features could not survive the rush of history. By 1890, well-organized businesses were taking over the cattle industry and applying scientific methods of breeding and feeding. The cowboy became just another corporate wage earner, though the myth of his freedom and individualism grew rather than faded. Most cattle ranchers now owned or leased the land they used, although some illegal fencing of public domain continued.

Meanwhile, two new groups were contending with cattle ranchers for supremacy on the Plains. From California and New Mexico, sheepherders moved into land east of the Rockies. Ranchers complained that sheep ruined grassland by eating down to the roots and that cattle refused to graze where sheep had been because the "woolly critters" left a repulsive odor. Armed conflict occasionally erupted between cowboys and sheepherders who resorted to violence rather than settle disputes in court, where the judge would discover that both were using the land illegally. More importantly, the farming frontier advanced into the West. From the Missouri to the Pacific there began an agricultural transformation whose social and political ramifications were to affect the entire nation.

Farming the Plains

In an 1880 article, *Harper's New Monthly Magazine* marveled at the success of Oliver Dalrymple's farm in Dakota Territory's Red River valley. "You are in a sea of wheat," the writer rhapsodized. "The railroad train rolls through an ocean of grain. . . . We encounter a squadron of war chariots . . . doing the work of human hands. . . . There are 25 of them in this one brigade of the grand army of 115, under the marksmanship of this Dakota farmer." Dalrymple's farm exemplified two important achievements of the late nineteenth century: the taming of wide, windswept prairies so that the land would yield crops to benefit humankind; and the transformation of agriculture into big business by means of mechanization, long-distance transportation, and scientific cultivation.

These achievements did not come easily. The climate and landscape of the Plains presented formidable challenges. And overcoming these challenges did not guarantee success or even provide security. Agricultural development of the West turned the United States into the world's breadbasket, but it also scarred the lives of hundreds of thousands of men and women who made that development possible.

Migration to the Plains

Settlement of the Plains and the West involved the greatest migration in American history. Between 1870 and 1900, more acres were settled and put under cultivation than in the previous 250 years. Between 1860 and 1910, the number of farms tripled, from 2 million to over 6 million. During the 1870s alone, Kansas gained 350,000 new settlers; and in the 1880s Nebraska's population increased by 250,000. California and Texas grew 216 and 273 percent respectively between 1870 and 1890. Males accounted for the majority of migrants to new agricultural areas, outnumbering women by about six to five—a ratio above the national average but below that of the mining states.

Most migrants came from one of two places of origin: the eastern states and Europe. In fact, several western states opened immigration bureaus in the East and in Europe to lure settlers westward. Land-grant railroads were especially aggressive, advertising cheap land at $2–8 per acre, arranging credit terms, offering reduced fares, and promising instant success. Railroad agents—often former immigrants—greeted newcomers at eastern ports and traveled to Europe to recruit prospective settlers. In California, fruit and vegetable growers imported Japanese and Mexican laborers to work in the fields and canneries.

Most migrants went west because opportunities there seemed to promise a better life. Between 1870 and 1910 the nation's population rose from 40 million to 92 million, and the total urban population swelled by over 400 percent. As a result, demand for farm

A squadron of farm machines sweeps across a wheat field in Minnesota's Red River valley. Mechanization multiplied production and turned farming into a big business, enabling the United States to become the breadbasket of the world. Photographed in the 1880s. Montana Historical Society, Helena.

products grew rapidly. Meanwhile, scientific advances were enabling farmers to use the soil more efficiently. Agricultural experts developed the technique of dry farming, a system of plowing and harrowing that prevented precious moisture from evaporating. Scientists perfected varieties of "hard" wheat whose seeds could withstand northern winters, and millers invented an efficient process for grinding these tougher new wheat kernels into flour. Railroad expansion made remote farming regions more accessible, and grain-elevator construction eased problems of shipping and storage.

In spite of such developments, life on the Plains was much harder than the advertisements suggested. Migrants often encountered scarcities of essentials they had taken for granted back home. Vast stretches of land contained little lumber for housing and fuel. Pioneer families were forced to build houses of sod and to burn manure for heat. Eventually railroads made lumber and coal more available, but both were costly. Water was as scarce as timber. Few families were lucky or wealthy enough to buy land near a stream that did not dry up in summer and freeze in winter. Most had to haul water long distances or try to collect rainwater. Machinery for drilling wells was scarce until the 1880s, and even then it was very expensive. Thus many wells were dug by hand, the men digging to depths of fifty feet and the women hauling dirt in buckets. Windmills were sometimes used to raise water above ground, but they too were expensive to construct.

Hardships of life on the Plains

Even more formidable than the terrain of the Plains was its climate. The expanse between the Missouri River and the Rocky Mountains was divided climatologically along a line of semiaridity running from northeastern North Dakota to southwestern Kansas and southward through the Oklahoma Panhandle, bisecting Texas. East of this line, annual rainfall averaged about twenty-eight inches, enough for most crops (see map). West of the line, life-giving rain was

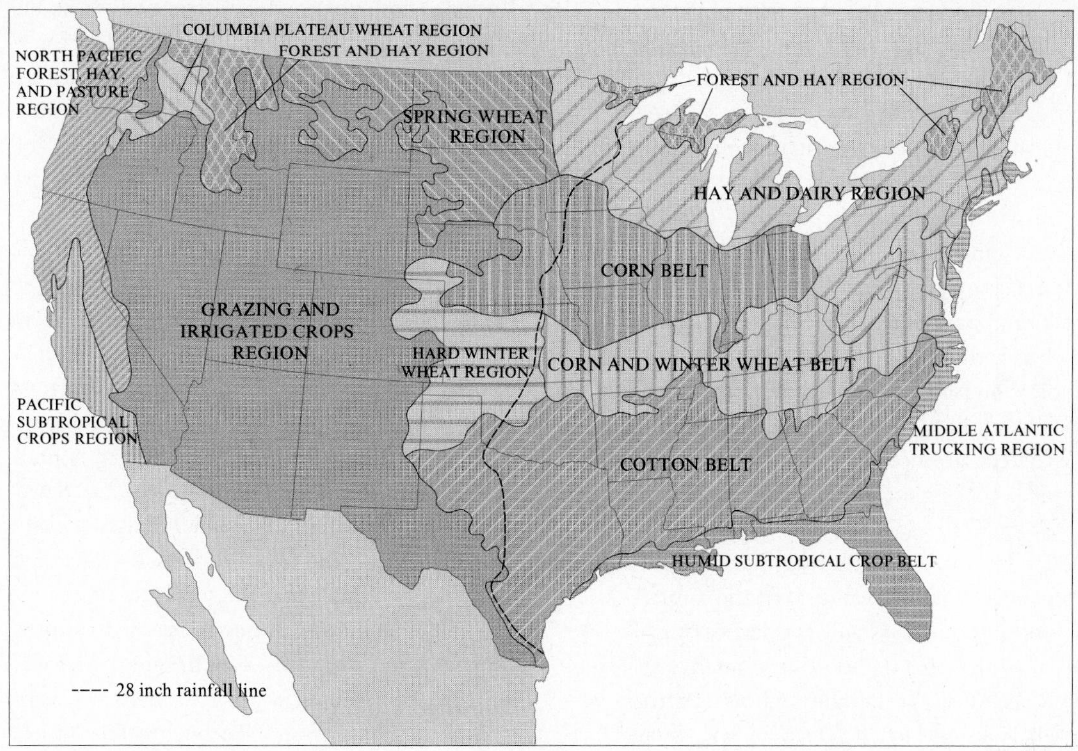

Agricultural regions, 1920. Source: From Charles O. Paullin, *Atlas of the Historical Geography of the United States,* Carnegie Institution of Washington.

never certain; farmers, heartened by adequate water one year, gagged on dust and broke their plows on hardened limestone soil the next.

Weather seldom followed predictable cycles on either side of the line. In summer, weeks of torrid heat and parching winds would suddenly give way to violent storms and flash floods that washed away crops and property. Winter blizzards piled up mountainous snowdrifts that halted all outdoor movement. Severe cold waves and howling winds plunged the temperature below zero. Spring and fall, supposedly temperate seasons, brought their own dangers. In March and April, melting snow swelled streams, and flood waters threatened millions of acres. In the fall, a week without rain could turn dry grasslands into tinder, and the slightest spark could ignite a raging prairie fire.

Even when the climate was better behaved, nature could turn vengeful. Weather that was good for crops was also good for insect breeding. Worms and flying pests ravaged corn and wheat. In the 1870s and 1880s grasshopper plagues literally ate up entire farms. Heralded only by the rising din of buzzing wings, a cloud of insects a mile high and miles long would smother the land and devour everything in sight: plants, seeds, tree bark, and clothes. In his poignant novel *Giants in the Earth,* Ole Rolvaag described what must have been a sickening experience: "The whole place was a weltering turmoil of raging little demons; if one looked for a moment into the wind, one saw nothing but glittering, lightning-like flashes—flashes that came and went in the heat of a cloud made up of innumerable dark-brown clicking bodies." As one farmer lamented, the "hoppers left behind nothing but the mortgage."

Settlers of the Plains also had to contend with social isolation. The European pattern, whereby farmers lived together in a village and traveled each day to their nearby fields, was rare in the American West. Instead, various peculiarities of land disposition compelled rural dwellers to live apart from each other.

Social isolation

Traditionally, Americans divided land into square or rectangular parcels, and few could afford to live in one place and farm somewhere else. The Homestead Act of 1862 and other measures adopted to facilitate western settlement offered free or cheap plots to people who would live on and improve their property. Because most homesteads and other plots acquired by small farmers were rectangular—usually encompassing 160 acres—at most four families could live near each other, but only if they congregated around the same four-corner boundary intersection. In practice, farmers usually lived back from their boundary lines, and at least a half-mile separated farmhouses. Often border land was unoccupied, making neighbors even more distant.

Many observers wrote about the loneliness and monotony of life on the Plains. Men escaped the oppressiveness by working outdoors and taking occasional trips to sell crops or buy supplies. But women were more isolated, confined by domestic chores to the household, where, as one writer remarked, they were "not much better than slaves. It is a weary, monotonous round of cooking and washing and mending and as a result the insane asylum is ⅓d filled with wives of farmers."

The letters that Ed Donnell, a young Nebraska homesteader, wrote to his family reveal how time and circumstances could dull optimism. In fall 1885, Donnell wrote his mother in Missouri, "I like Nebr first rate. . . . I have saw a pretty tuff time a part of the time since I have been out here, but I started out to get a home and I was determined to win or die in the attempt. . . . Have got a good crop of corn, a floor in my house and got it ceiled overhead." Already, though, Donnell was getting lonely and tired. He went on, "There is lots of other bachelors here but I am the only one I know who doesn't have kinfolks living handy. . . . You wanted to know when I was going to get married. Just as quick as I can get money ahead to get a cow. . . . A fellow cant do much good on a new place when he has everything to do both indoors and out." A year and a half later, Donnell's dreams were dissolving, and he was beginning to look for a second chance elsewhere. As he explained to his brother, "The rats eat my sod stable down. . . . I may sell out this summer, land is going up so fast. . . . If I sell I am going west and grow up with the country." By fall, things had worsened, and Donnell wrote his parents, "We have been having wet weather for 3 weeks and is still raining. . . . My health has been so poor this summer and the wind and the sun hurts my head so. I think if I can sell I will . . . move to town for I can get $40 a month working in a grist mill and I would not be exposed to the weather."

Most farm families survived by depending on their inner resolve and by organizing churches and clubs where they could socialize and share experiences a few times a month. And by the early 1900s, two external developments had combined to bring rural settlers into closer contact with modern life (though people in sparsely settled regions beyond the 28-inch rainfall line remained isolated for several more decades). Starting in the 1870s and 1880s, mail-order houses—chiefly Montgomery Ward and Sears Roebuck—expanded and made the products of the industrial society available to almost everyone. Emphasizing personal attention to customers, Ward's and Sears Roebuck were outlets for sociability as well as material goods. Letters from customers to Mr. Ward often reported family news and sought advice on everything from birthday gifts to child care. A man from Washington state wrote, "As you advertise everything for sale that a person wants, I thought I would write you, as I am in need of a wife, and see what you could do for me." Another wrote: "I suppose you wonder why we haven't ordered anything from you since the fall. The cow kicked my arm and broke it and besides my wife was sick, and there was the doctor bill. But now, thank God, that is paid, and we are all well again, and we have a fine new baby boy, and please send plush bonnet number 29d8077. . . ."

Mail order companies and Rural Free Delivery

During the 1890s, scores of rural communities petitioned Congress for extension of the postal service, and in 1898 the government made Rural Free Delivery (RFD) widely available. Now farmers no longer lacked news and information; they could receive letters, newspapers, advertisements, and catalogues at home nearly every day. In 1913 the postal service inaugurated parcel post, which enabled people to receive packages, such as orders from Ward's and Sears, more easily. By 1920, RFD and parcel post had provided rural families access to industrializing society.

In the years following the Civil War, the extension

Western women performed heavy domestic chores with little assistance. This woman is using a commercial tub and washboard—possibly bought from a Sears or Ward's catalogue—to do the family wash. Library of Congress.

of the farming frontier, growing national and international markets for food, and the advent of railroads to ship goods from farm to market brought about an agricultural revolution. But that transformation would not have been possible, nor would the Plains have been conquered, without the expanded use of machinery. When the Civil War drew many men away from farms in the upper Mississippi River valley, the women and male laborers who remained behind began using reapers and other implements more extensively to meet demand for grain and to take advantage of high prices. After the war, continued demand and high prices encouraged farmers to depend more on machines, and inventors perfected better implements for farm use. Seeders, harrows, combines, binders, mowers, headers, cultivators, rotary plows, and other machines were introduced to the Plains and California in the 1870s and 1880s.

Mechanization of agriculture

For centuries the acreage of grain a farmer could plant had been limited by the amount that could be harvested by hand. Machines—first driven by animals, then by steam—increased productivity beyond imagination. Before mechanization, a single farmer could harvest about 7.5 acres of wheat. With an automatic binder that cut and tied bundles of grain, the same farmer could harvest 135 acres. Figures for the 1890s compiled by the U.S. Commissioner of Labor revealed how dramatically machines had reduced the time and cost of farming a single acre of various crops (see table, page 456).

At the same time, Congress and agricultural scientists were making efforts to improve existing crops and develop new ones. The 1862 Morrill Land Grant Act (see page 380) gave each state public lands to sell in order to finance agricultural and industrial colleges. Although the act discriminated against western states by granting 30,000 acres for each senator and representative—New York

Legislative and scientific aid to farmers

Time and Cost of Farming an Acre of Land by Hand and by Machine

	HOURS REQUIRED		LABOR COST	
CROP	HAND	MACHINE	HAND	MACHINE
Wheat	61	3	$3.65	$ .66
Corn	39	15	$3.62	$1.51
Oats	66	7	$3.73	$1.07
Loose hay	21	4	$1.75	$ .42

Source: Ray Allan Billington, *Westward Expansion: A History of the American Frontier,* Second Edition (New York: Macmillan, 1960), p. 697.

thus received about 1 million acres, Kansas only 90,000—it did promote the establishment of educational institutions that aided agricultural development. The Hatch Act of 1887 provided for agricultural experiment stations in every state, further encouraging the advancement of farming technology.

Farming received a great boost from science in the late nineteenth century. American agriculturists adapted hardy new varieties of wheat from Asia and India, alfalfa from Mongolia, corn from North Africa, and rice from the Orient. Californian Luther Burbank developed a wide range of new plants by cross-breeding. And Tuskegee Institute's chemist George Washington Carver created hundreds of new products from peanuts, soybeans, sweet potatoes, and cotton wastes and taught methods of soil improvement and crop diversification. Scientists also developed means of combating corn rot, wheat rust, hog cholera, and hoof-and-mouth disease.

Settlement of the West and the various technological and scientific advances that made it possible altered American agriculture and forced farmers to adjust to a new age. Their adjustments were neither smooth nor painless. The social and economic problems that accompanied agricultural transformation were eventually to shape a climactic chapter in nineteenth-century American history.

The South after Reconstruction

In 1880 four times as many farmers lived in the South as on the Plains. Ravaged by a civil war that had killed a third of all draft animals and destroyed half the region's farm equipment, southern agriculture recovered slowly. Southerners still had millions of acres of rich farmland, but severe obstacles blocked full development. High prices for seed and implements; declining prices for crops; taxes; and most of all, debt trapped many white families in perpetual poverty. Conditions were even worse for blacks, who had to endure brutal racial prejudice along with economic and social hardship. To achieve sectional economic independence, some southern leaders tried to promote industrialization. Their efforts partially succeeded, but by the early 1900s many southern industries were mere subsidiaries of northern firms. Moreover, southern planters, shippers, and manufacturers depended heavily on northern banks for credit to finance their operations. And while they were striving for progress, many southerners nurtured myths about a romantic prewar era of aristocratic grace, conflict-free race relations, and moral purity. These fantasies sustained the South's sense of distinctiveness but warped the national image of southern culture.

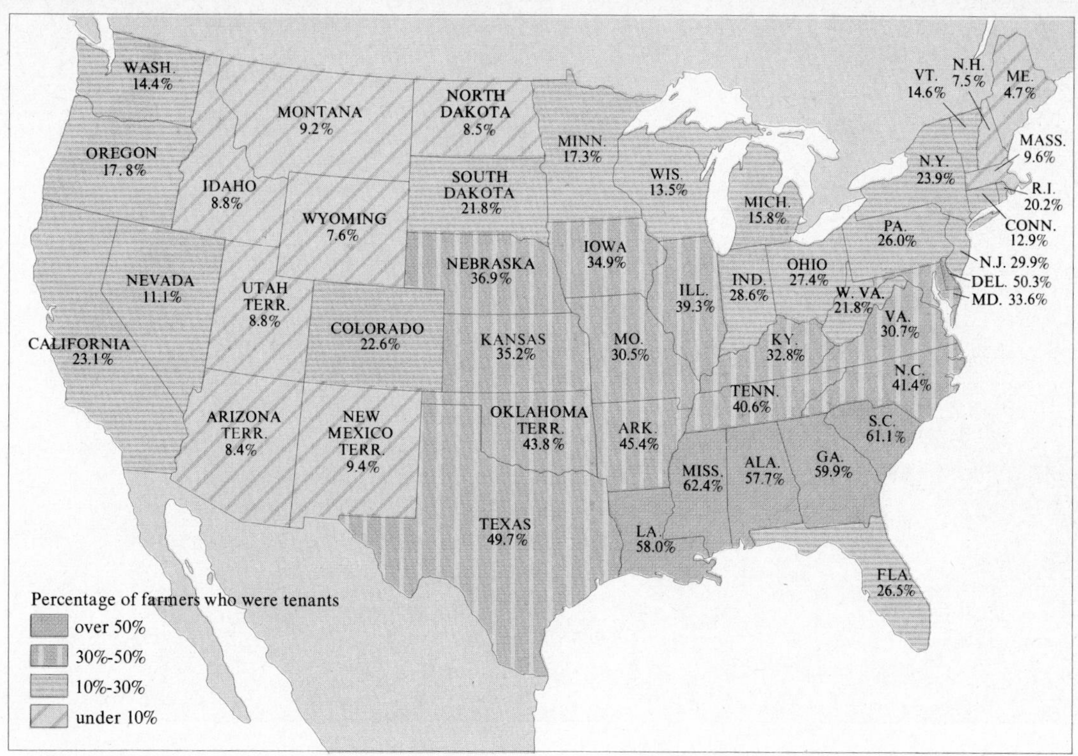

Farm tenancy, 1890

During and after Reconstruction, a significant shift in the nature of agricultural labor swept the South. Between 1860 and 1880, the total number of farms in southern states more than doubled, from 450,000 to 1.1 million, and the size of the average farm decreased from 347 to 156 acres. Despite the proliferation of farms, the number of land owners did not increase. Instead, southern agriculture became dominated by sharecropping and tenant farming (see page 419). Over one-third of the farmers counted in 1880 were sharecroppers and tenants, and the proportion increased to two-thirds by 1920 (see map).

This system entangled millions of southerners in a web of humiliation. At its center was the crop lien, which worked in the following way. Most farmers were too poor ever to have cash on hand. Forced to borrow in order to buy necessities, they could offer as collateral only what they could grow. Thus a farmer in need of supplies would deal with a nearby "furnishing merchant," who would exchange supplies for a certain portion, or lien, of the farmer's forthcoming crop. Often the merchant and the landowner were the same person; profits from stores were used to buy farms or profits from farms were invested in stores. In the fall, after the crop had been harvested and brought to market, the merchant collected his debt. But all too often the farmer's debt exceeded his crop's value, and the merchant often took advantage of the customer's powerlessness by inflating prices to ensure that such debts could not be paid. Thus the farmer still owed the merchant, had received no cash for the crop, and still needed food and supplies. His only choice was to commit the next year's crop to the the merchant and sink deeper into debt.

Crop lien system

The prices charged to credit customers averaged 30 to 40 percent higher than those charged to cash customers. Credit customers also had to pay interest of 33 to 200 percent on the advances they received. Suppose, for example, a farmer needed a 20-cent bag of seed or a 20-cent slab of bacon and had no cash to pay for it. The furnishing merchant would extend credit for the purchase but would also boost the price to 28 cents. At year's end that 28-cent loan would have accumulated interest, raising the farmer's debt to, say, 42 cents–more than double the item's original cost.

In the post-Reconstruction South, black sharecroppers such as these fared little better than under slavery. Tied to crop liens that kept them in perpetual debt, they lived in tiny shacks and struggled against white discrimination. Brown Brothers.

The farmer, having pledged more than his crop's worth against scores of such debts, fell behind in payments and never recovered. If he fell too far behind, he could be evicted. As one writer remarked about the crop-lien system, "when one of these mortgages has been recorded against the Southern farmer, he had usually passed into a state of helpless peonage."

Dependence on northern credit and crop liens hindered agricultural expansion in the South. The constant need to settle debts forced merchants and farmers to rely almost exclusively on sure-money crops, namely cotton and tobacco. But overproduction of these crops plunged prices, making debts even more difficult to settle (see page 419). In 1894, southern farmers planted over twice as many acres of cotton as they did during 1873, but the total 1894 crop was worth less on the market than the 1873 crop. Moreover, reliance on staple crops exhausted the soil and discouraged investment in agricultural machinery. In 1900 the total value of farm implements in the South was half what it had been in 1860, and scientific agriculture, which had been so important to western expansion, had barely affected southern farming. At the turn of the century, then, the South's economy had changed very little since the Civil War. Slavery had disappeared, but cotton culture remained dominant and a new exploitative labor system had emerged.

Black people found that conditions under freedom differed very little from slavery. As in the prewar era, blacks adapted to racial bias by developing and controlling their own social institutions: churches, schools, and family networks. Though abolition of slavery altered their legal status, it did not improve their economic and social opportunities relative to those of whites. In 1880 some 90 percent of all southern blacks depended for a living on farming or personal and domestic service—the same occupations they had had as slaves.

Pushed into sharecropping and burdened with crop liens, blacks also had to contend with new forms of social and political oppression. With slavery dead, white supremacists had to fashion new means of keeping blacks in a position of inferiority. Southern leaders, embittered by northern interference in race relations during Reconstruction and anxious to reassert their authority after the withdrawal of federal troops (see page 431), instituted racist measures in all realms of life. Foremost among these measures were political disfranchisement, segregation laws, and violence.

In the aftermath of the 1877 compromise, southern politicians steadily overlooked their own promises to protect civil rights guaranteed by the Thirteenth, Fourteenth, and Fifteenth Amendments. Fearful that some political faction might manipulate black voters for its own gain, white leaders decided that disfranchisement was the best way to neutralize the so-called Negro vote. Beginning with Georgia in 1877, southern states levied taxes of $1 to $2 on all citizens wishing to vote. Though seemingly trivial, these poll taxes were prohibitive to most black voters, many of whom were so deeply in debt to furnishing merchants and landlords that they never had cash for any purpose. Other schemes disfranchised black voters who could not read. For example, voters might be required to deposit ballots for different candidates in different ballot boxes. In order to do so correctly, voters had to be able to read instructions; otherwise, their votes were invalidated.

Disfranchisement of blacks

Dissatisfied with these measures and fearful that northern Republicans might enact federal supervision of elections, southern states in the 1890s took more direct steps to prevent blacks from voting. The Fifteenth Amendment prohibited states from denying the franchise to people "on account of race, color, or previous condition of servitude." But state legislators soon found ways to exclude black voters without ever mentioning conditions specified by the amendment (see page 414). In 1890, Mississippi led the way by requiring all voters to prove that they could read and interpret the Constitution. White registration officials applied much stiffer standards to blacks than whites, even to the extent of declaring black college graduates ineligible on grounds of illiteracy. In 1898 Louisiana enacted the first grandfather clause, and other southern states soon followed suit. All these measures proved effective. In Louisiana, for example, there were 130,334 registered black voters in 1896; eight years later there were 1,342. By the early 1900s, blacks had effectively lost their political rights in every southern state except Tennessee.

Racial discrimination also stiffened in social affairs, where it affected blacks of all ages and both sexes, not just males of voting age. A widespread informal system of separation had governed race relations in the antebellum South. After the Civil War, this system was codified in law. In a series of cases during the 1870s, the Supreme Court opened the door to discrimination by ruling that the Fourteenth Amendment protected citizens' rights only against infringement by state governments. The federal government, according to the Court, had no control over infringement by individuals or organizations. If blacks wanted protection under the law, the Court said, they must seek it from the states, which under the Tenth Amendment retained all powers not specifically assigned to Congress.

Spread of Jim Crow laws

The climax to these rulings came in 1883, when in the *Civil Rights Cases* the Court struck down the 1875 Civil Rights Act, which had prohibited segregation in public facilities such as streetcars, hotels, theaters, and parks. Again the Court declared that the federal government could not regulate the behavior of private individuals in matters of race relations. Subsequent lower-court cases in the 1880s established the principle that blacks could be restricted to "separate-but-equal" facilities. The Supreme Court upheld the separate-but-equal doctrine in *Plessy* v. *Ferguson* (1896), and officially applied it to schools in *Cummins* v. *County Board of Education* (1899).

Thereafter, segregation laws—known as Jim Crow laws—spread rapidly. Between 1890 and 1920, discriminatory legislation piled up throughout the South, confronting black people with countless daily reminders of their inferior status. State laws and local ordinances restricted blacks to the rear of streetcars, to separate drinking and toilet facilities, and to separate sections of hospitals, asylums, and cemeteries. A Birmingham, Alabama, ordinance required that the races be "distinctly separated . . . by well defined physical barriers" in "any room, hall, theatre, picture house, auditorium, yard, court, ball park, or other indoor or outdoor place." Local laws defined certain districts or blocks as all-black or all-white. Mobile, Alabama, passed a curfew requiring blacks to be off the streets by 10 P.M. A New Orleans law confined black and white prostitutes to separate districts, and Atlanta required separate Bibles for black witnesses swearing before court.

Whites reinforced disfranchisement and segregation with violence. Between 1880 and 1918, over 2,400 blacks were lynched in the South, compared to 100 in the North. Race riots—some of them particularly bloody—became more frequent in the South. In 1898 white mobs in Wilmington, North Carolina, attacked the black community, killing at least eleven people and injuring scores of others. In 1906 a riot in Atlanta left ten blacks and two whites dead. Outnumbered and outgunned, blacks vented their frustration in the highest places. After the Wilmington riot, a black woman wrote to President McKinley, "Will you for God sake in your next message to Congress give us some relief? . . . Today we are mourners in a strange land with no protection near. . . . The laws of our state is no good for the Negro anyhow." For her and thousands of other black southerners, race relations had improved only nominally since before the Civil War.

Industrialization of the South

In industry, breezes of change were being stimulated by new manufacturing initiatives, but there too a distinctively southern quality prevailed. Two of the South's leading industries in the late nineteenth century relied on the traditional staple crops, cotton and tobacco. In the 1870s, textile mills began to sprout up in the Cotton Belt states. Powered by the region's abundant rivers and streams, manned cheaply by poor whites eager to escape crop liens, and fostered by low taxes, such mills grew rapidly. By 1900 the South had four hundred mills with a total of over 4 million spindles, and twenty years later the region was clearly replacing New England in textile manufacturing supremacy. Proximity to raw materials and cheap labor also aided the tobacco industry, and the invention in 1880 of a cigarette-making machine immensely enhanced the marketability of tobacco.

Cigarettes and other tobacco products were manufactured in cities by black and white workers; textile mills were concentrated in small towns, and developed their own exploitative labor system. Financed mostly by local investors, mills employed women and children from nearby poor white families and paid them 50 cents a day for twelve or more hours of work. Such wages were barely half what northern workers received. Many companies built squalid villages around their mills and controlled all housing, stores, schools, and churches. Criticism of the company was forbidden, and attempts at union organization were squelched. Mill families soon found that factory jobs changed their status very little. The company store simply replaced the furnishing merchant, and the mill owner replaced the landlord.

Several other industries were launched in the South, but mainly under the sponsorship of northern or European capitalists. Between 1890 and 1900, for example, northern lumber syndicates moved into the pine forests of the Gulf states, boosting production by 500 percent. During the 1880s, northern investors developed southern iron and steel production, much of which centered in the boom city of Birmingham. Coal mining and railroad construction also expanded rapidly, but New York and London financiers dominated the boards of directors of most companies.

Regardless of outside influence, industrialization prompted southern boosters to herald the emergence of a New South ready to compete economically with other sections. Henry Grady, editor of the Atlanta *Constitution* and the most articulate voice of southern progress, proclaimed, "We have sowed towns and cities in the place of theories, and put business in place of politics. We have challenged your spinners in Massachusetts and your iron-makers in Pennsylvania. . . . We have fallen in love with work." Yet in 1900 the South remained as rural as it had been in 1860. Staple-crop agriculture supported its economy, and white supremacy permeated its social and political relations. Furthermore, the South attracted few immigrants because of its relative lack of industrial jobs, and thus enjoyed little of their energizing influence. A New South would emerge, but not until after a world war and a massive black exodus had jostled old habits and attitudes. Until then, southern society continued to grasp at ways to escape its dependent economic status while holding on to its old racial order.

Stirrings of agrarian unrest

The inequities of the southern agricultural system gave rise to the first rumblings of a mass democratic movement that was to shake American society in the late nineteenth century. The agrarian revolt—a complex mixture of strident rhetoric, nostalgic dreams, and hard-headed egalitarianism—began when farmers' alliances formed in Texas in the late 1870s, then spread across the Cotton Belt and the Plains in the 1880s. The movement caught on chiefly in areas where farm tenancy, crop liens, furnishing merchants, railroads, banks, weather, and insects threatened the ambitions of hopeful farmers. Once under way, it inspired visions of a truly cooperative, democratic society.

Agricultural expansion in the West and South exposed millions of people to the hardships of rural life. Uncertainties might have been more bearable if the rewards had been more promising, but such was not the case. As farmers put more land under cultivation, as mechanization boosted productivity, and as foreign competition increased, supplies exceeded national and worldwide demand for agricultural products. Consequently, prices for staple crops dropped steadily between the end of the Civil War and 1900. A bushel of wheat that sold for $1.45 in 1866 brought only $.80 in the mid-1880s and $.49 by the mid-1890s. Meanwhile transportation, storage, and commission fees rose. Costly seed, fertilizer, manufactured goods, taxes, and mortgage interest combined with social isolation to trap many farm families in disadvantageous and sometimes desperate circumstances. In order to buy necessities and pay bills, farmers had to produce more. But the spiral only wound more tightly, since the more farmers produced, the lower prices dropped.

Even before the full impact of these developments was felt, farmers had begun to organize to relieve their mounting distress. With aid from government officials, particularly Oliver H. Kelley of the Department of Agriculture, farmers founded a network of local organizations called Granges in almost every state during the late 1860s and early 1870s. By 1875 the Grange had nearly twenty thousand local branches and over 1 million members. Strongest in the Midwest and South, Granges served chiefly as social organizations, sponsoring meetings and educational events to help relieve the loneliness of farm life. Family-oriented and open to all, local Granges made explicit provisions for women's participation.

Grange movement

As membership flourished, Granges moved beyond social functions into economic and political action. At its 1874 national convention, the Grange proposed to avoid high retail prices by forming local cooperatives to buy equipment and supplies directly from manufacturers. Granges also encouraged the formation of sales cooperatives, whereby farmers would pool their grain and dairy products and then divide the profits. In a few instances, Grangers operated implements factories and insurance companies. Most such enterprises failed, however, because farmers lacked cash for cooperative buying and because ruthless competition from large manufacturers and dealers undercut them. In politics, Grangers used their numbers to some advantage, electing sympathetic legislators and pressing for laws to regulate transportation and storage rates.

Granges nevertheless declined in the late 1870s because their essentially conservative tactics did not meet members' needs. The requirement that cooperatives run on a cash-only basis excluded large numbers of farmers who never had any cash. Efforts to regulate business and transportation withered when corporations and railroads won court support against "Granger laws." Politically, Granges disavowed third parties but could not overcome the power of business interests within the established parties. Finally, the Grange's promotion of thrift and hard work was of little value to families already overburdened with both virtues. Thus, after a brief assertion of influence, the Grange reverted to an organization of farmers' social clubs. Its short-lived agrarian campaign served, however, as a precedent for future action.

Rural activism then shifted to the Farmers' Alliances, two networks of organizations—one in the Plains and one in the South—that by 1890 constituted a genuine mass movement. The first alliances sprang up in Texas, where hard-pressed farmers rallied against crop liens, furnishing merchants, and railroads in particular, and against money power in general. Adopting an effective system of traveling lecturers to recruit members, alliance leaders extended the movement to other southern states, and by 1889 the Southern Alliance boasted over 3 million members. This number included the powerful Colored Farmers' National Alliance, which claimed over 1 million black members. A similar movement flourished in the Plains, where by the late 1880s 2 million members were organized in Kansas, Nebraska, and the Dakotas.

Farmers' Alliances

Motivated by outrage, alliance members pushed the Grange concept of cooperation to new limits by

This engraving of a Grange meeting in Winchester, Illinois, illustrates the communal nature of the Grange; note the many women in the audience. The sign held at the center of the picture reads "President $50,000 a year / Congressmen 7,000 / Farmers 75 cts a week." From *Frank Leslie's Illustrated Newspaper*, August 30, 1873. Library of Congress.

sponsoring organizational rallies, mass educational meetings, and cooperative buying and selling agreements. "I hold," asserted Charles W. Macune, the astute alliance leader from Texas, "that cooperation . . . will be the means by which the mortgage-burdened farmers can assert their freedom from the tyranny of organized capital and retain the reward . . . which they so richly deserve and which they are now so unjustly denied." Seeing themselves as laborers battling capitalists in a new age rather than as traditional Jeffersonian yeomen, some alliance members advocated unity with the Knights of Labor and other workers' groups.

Beyond urging democratic cooperation, the alliance movement proposed a scheme to alleviate the most serious rural problems: lack of cash and credit. The subtreasury plan, adapted by Macune from French and Russian precedents, called for the federal government to construct warehouses in every major agricultural county. At harvest time, farmers could store their crops in these subtreasuries while awaiting higher prices, and the government would loan farmers treasury notes amounting to 80 percent of the market price the stored crops would bring. Farmers could use these subtreasury notes as legal tender to pay debts and make purchases. Once the stored crops were sold, farmers would pay back the loans plus small interest and storage fees.

Subtreasury plan

The subtreasury scheme was meant to replace the crop-lien system and to give farmers greater control over their financial affairs. No longer would merchants be able to take advantage of farmers at harvest time, when market gluts depressed prices. No longer would farmers have to mortgage crops (through crop liens) at high interest. And no longer would they lack cash to buy supplies. Moreover, by issuing subtreasury notes, the government would be injecting more money into the economy and encouraging the kind of inflation agrarian reformers desired: inflation that would raise crop prices without raising the costs of supplies and rents. If government subsidized business, reasoned alliance members, why should it not aid agriculture and help farmers earn a decent living too?

Implementation of their plans and programs confronted alliance members with questions of political participation. Could farmers work within the two established parties, or should they form a third party directly responsive to their interests? If all the various alliance groups, North and South, had been able to unite under one banner, they would have made for a formidable political force. But attempts at merger were thwarted by sectional differences and personality clashes. A meeting in St. Louis in 1889 failed to unify major farm groups; white southerners, fearing reprisals from landowners and objecting to the participation of blacks, rejected proposals that would have ended secrecy in alliance activities and white-only membership rules. Northerners too shied away from amalgamation, fearing they would lose independence in a large organization that would probably be dominated by more experienced southern leaders. Differences on issues also prevented unity. Northern farmers, who were mostly Republicans, wanted protective tariffs to keep out foreign grain; white southerners, mostly Democrats, wanted low tariffs. Nevertheless, both alliances favored government control of transportation and communications, liberal credit policies, equitable taxation, prohibition of alien land ownership, and currency reform.

Growing membership and rising confidence drew alliances more deeply into politics. By 1890, farmers had elected a number of officeholders sympathetic to their programs—especially in the South, where alliance members controlled four governorships, eight state legislatures, forty-four seats in the U.S. House of Representatives, and three seats in the U.S. Senate. In the Midwest, alliance candidates often ran on independent third-party tickets, and achieved some success in Kansas, Nebraska, and the Dakotas. These candidates' campaigns included spirited rallies and parades that resounded with songs and orations; their banners proclaimed "We Are All Mortgaged But Our Votes." During the summer of 1890, the Kansas Alliance held a "convention of the people" and nominated candidates who swept the fall elections. The formation of this People's party, whose members were called Populists, gave a name to the movement that grew out of alliance political activism.

Rise of Populism

The 1890 election results energized new efforts to consolidate all alliance groups into a single Populist party. A May 1891 meeting of northern and southern alliances in Cincinnati fizzled when southerners chose to remain Democrats rather than risk joining a third party. But by early 1892, southern alliance members were ready for independent action. Meeting with their northern counterparts in St. Louis, they issued a call for a People's party convention in Omaha on July 4, to draft a national platform and nominate a presidential candidate.

The new party's platform, ratified by the 1,300 delegates who gathered in Omaha, was one of the most comprehensive reform documents in American history. Declaring in its preamble that "wealth belongs to him that creates it," the Omaha platform presented a host of proposals generated by rural unrest. Most of its planks addressed three central issues: transportation, land, and money. Frustrated with weak state and federal regulation of transportation, the Populists demanded government ownership of railroad and telegraph lines. They called on the federal government to reclaim all land owned for speculative purposes by railroads and aliens. The monetary plank called for a flexible currency system based on free and unlimited coinage of silver that would increase the money supply and enable farmers to pay their debts more easily (see Chapter 20). Other planks advocated a graduated income tax, postal savings banks, and such reforms as the direct election of U.S. senators and shorter hours for workers. As its presidential candidate, the party nominated James B. Weaver of Iowa, a former Union general and greenback supporter.

The Populist campaign featured a number of colorful personalities whose vivid rhetoric had been enlivening local politics for several years. The Kansas plains rumbled with the speeches of Sockless Jerry Simpson, an unschooled but canny rural reformer; Mary Lease, a fiery orator who urged farmers to "raise

Important events

1859–60	Gold rushes in Nevada, Colorado, and Idaho
1862–64	Gold rushes in Arizona and Montana
1862	Homestead Act Morrill Land Grant Act
1865–67	War with western Sioux
1869	First transcontinental railroad, the Union Pacific, completed
1873	Major silver discovery of Comstock Lode (Nevada)
1874	Barbed-wire fence patented
1875–76	Indian war in Black Hills
1876	Gold rush in Black Hills
1877	Nez Perce Indian uprising
1878	Timber and Stone Act
1879	Silver discovery at Tombstone, Arizona
1881	Helen Hunt Jackson, *A Century of Dishonor*
1882–83	Transcontinental routes of Santa Fe, Southern Pacific, and Northern Pacific completed
1883	*Civil Rights Cases*
1885–86	Disastrous winters in Plains states
1887	Dawes Severalty Act Interstate Commerce Act Farm prices collapse
1889–90	Ghost Dance and Battle of Wounded Knee
1890–98	Disfranchisement of blacks in South
1892	Populist convention in Omaha
1893	Great Northern Railroad completed
1896	*Plessy* v. *Ferguson*
1898	Wilmington (North Carolina) race riot Louisiana enacts first grandfather clause, restricting voting rights of blacks
1899	*Cummins* v. *County Board of Education*

less corn and more hell"; and William Peffer, an influential editor whose Methuselah-style beard made him the butt of opponents' political cartoons. The South produced equally forceful but somewhat less flamboyant leaders, such as Charles W. Macune of Texas, Thomas Watson of Georgia, and Leonidas Polk of North Carolina. And there was Minnesota's Ignatius Donnelly, a pseudoscientist and writer of apocalyptic novels who became the chief organizer and ideologue of the northern Plains. Finally, the campaign had its opportunists, like James Hogg of Texas and Pitchfork Ben Tillman of South Carolina, who were not genuine Populists but used the rising agrarian fervor for their own political ambitions.

Although Weaver received only 8 percent of the total popular vote in 1892, Populism had become a national force. Not since 1856 had a third party won so many votes in its first national effort. The party's central dilemma—whether to stand by its ideals at all costs or compromise those ideals in order to gain power—still loomed ahead. Over the next four years, Populist unity would crumble over the issues of silver coinage and whether or not to merge with a major party (see Chapter 20). But in the early 1890s, rural dwellers in the southern and Plains states still foresaw a promising future. The alliance movement had kindled an emotional faith. Amid hardship and desperation, millions of people had begun to believe that they could overcome corporate power with a cooperative democracy in which government would act to ensure equal opportunity. A banner hanging above the stage at the Omaha convention summed up the movement's spirit: "We do not ask for sympathy or pity. We ask for justice."

Suggestions for further reading

The western frontier

Ray A. Billington, *Westward Expansion* (1967); Frederick Merk, *History of the Westward Movement* (1978); J. Stanley Clark, *The Oil Century: From the Drake Well to the Conservative Era* (1958); Odie B. Faulk, *Tombstone: Myth and Reality* (1972); William H. Goetzmann, *Exploration and Empire* (1966); William S. Greever, *Bonanza West: Western Mining Rushes* (1963); Robert V. Hine, *The American West* (1973); Julie Roy Jeffrey, *Frontier Women* (1979); Rodman W. Paul, *Mining Frontiers of the Far West* (1963); Rodman W. Paul, *The Frontier and the American West* (1971); Henry Nash Smith, *Virgin Land: The American West as Symbol and Myth* (1950); Roberta B. Sollid, *Calamity Jane* (1958); L. Steckmesser, *The Western Hero in History and Legend* (1965).

Railroads

Alfred D. Chandler, ed., *Railroads: The Nation's First Big Business* (1965); Robert W. Fogel, *Railroads and Economic Growth* (1964); Edward C. Kirkland, *Men, Cities, and Transportation* (1948); Ari Hoogenboom and Olive Hoogenboom, *A History of the ICC* (1970); Gabriel Kolko, *Railroads and Regulation* (1965); Albro Martin, "The Troubled Subject of Railroad Regulation in the Gilded Age," *Journal of American History,* 61 (1974), 339–371; George H. Miller, *Railroads and the Granger Laws* (1971); Gerald D. Nash, "The Interstate Commerce Act of 1887," *Pennsylvania History,* 24 (1957), 181–190; George R. Taylor and Irene Neu, *The American Railroad Network* (1956); O. O. Winther, *The Transportation Frontier* (1964).

Indians and ranching

Ralph K. Andrist, *The Long Death: The Last Days of the Plains Indians* (1964); Lewis Atherton, *The Cattle Kings* (1961); Joe B. Frantz and Julian Choate, Jr., *The American Cowboy* (1955); Ernest S. Osgood, *The Day of the Cattleman* (1929); Francis Paul Prucha, *American Indian Policy in Crisis* (1976); Robert M. Utley, *Frontier Regulars: The United States Army and the Indian* (1973); Wilcomb E. Washburn, *Red Man's Land/White Man's Law* (1971).

Settlement of the Plains

Allan G. Bogue, *From Prairie to Corn Belt* (1963); Everett Dick, *The Sod-House Frontier* (1937); Gilbert C. Fite, *The Farmer's Frontier* (1966); Fred A. Shannon, *The Farmer's Last Frontier* (1963); Walter Prescott Webb, *The Great Plains* (1931).

The new South

Thomas D. Clark and Albert D. Kirwan, *The South Since Appomattox* (1967); Vincent P. DeSantis, *Republicans Face the Southern Question, 1877–1897* (1959); Herbert J. Doherty, Jr., "Voices of Protest from the New South, 1875–1910," *Mississippi Valley Historical Review,* 42 (1955), 45–66; Paul Gaston, *The New South Creed* (1970); Dewey Grantham, Jr., *The Democratic South* (1963); Sheldon Hackney, *Populism to Progressivism in Alabama* (1969); Stanley P. Hirshson, *Farewell to the Bloody Shirt: Northern Republicans and the Southern Negro* (1962); J. Morgan Kousser, *The Shaping of Southern Politics* (1974); Melton A. McLaurin, *Paternalism and Protest: Southern Cotton Mill Workers and Organized Labor* (1971); Howard N. Rabinowitz, "From Exclusion to Segregation: Southern Race Relations, 1865–1890," *Journal of American History,* 63 (1976), 325–350; Theodore Saloutos, *Farmer Movements in the South, 1865–1933* (1960); C. Vann Woodward, *Origins of the New South* (1951); C. Vann Woodward, *The Strange Career of Jim Crow* (1966).

Farm protest

William D. Barns, "Oliver H. Kelley and the Grange," *Agricultural History,* 41 (1967), 229–242; Gerald Gaither, *Blacks and the Populist Revolt* (1977); Lawrence Goodwyn, *Democratic Promise; The Populist Movement in America* (1976); Earl W. Hayter, *The Troubled Farmer* (1968); John D. Hicks, *The Populist Revolt* (1931); Norman Pollack, *The Populist Response to Industrial America* (1962); Fred A. Shannon, *American Farmers' Movements* (1957); Paul Studenski and Herman E. Krouss, *Financial History of the United States* (1952). See Chapter 20 for other works on farm protest and populism.

17 THE MACHINE AGE, 1877–1920

Conrad Carl tried to appear calm, but he was understandably nervous. It was spring 1882, and Carl, who for nearly thirty years had been a tailor in New York City, was appearing before a group of U.S. senators in Washington, D.C. The Committee on Education and Labor was conducting an investigation into the causes of recent labor unrest, and Senator James L. Pugh, a former Confederate congressman from Alabama, was asking Carl to explain changing work conditions in the tailoring business.

Admitting that his testimony would probably cost him his job, Carl nevertheless answered candidly. When he first began tailoring, Carl explained, he and his wife and children had pieced together garments by hand. The pace of their work was relaxed, yet he was able to save a few dollars each year. Then, said Carl, "in 1854 or 1855, . . . the sewing machine was invented and introduced, and it stitched very nicely, nicer than the tailor could do; and the bosses said: 'We want you to use the sewing machine; you have to buy one.' "

Carl and his fellow tailors used their meager savings to buy machines, hoping they could earn more by producing more. But their employers thought differently; they cut wages instead of raising them. The tailors "found that we could earn no more than we could without the machine; but the money for the machine was gone now, and we found that the machine was only for the profit of the bosses; that they got their work quicker, and it was done nicer." Moreover, Carl, now old and discouraged, had seen that mechanization had other troubling and disappointing effects on workers and those around them. "The machine," he said, "makes too much noise in the place, and the neighbors want to sleep, and we have to stop sewing earlier, so we have to work faster. We work now in excitement–in a hurry. It is hunting; it is not work at all; it is a hunt."

Conrad Carl's testimony to the Senate committee was one worker's view of the industrialization that was relentlessly overtaking American society. The forces prevailing in the new order were both inspiring and ominous. The factory and the machine broke down manufacturing into minute, routinized tasks and organized work according to the dictates of the clock. The city–long the vanguard of commercial growth–now furnished labor, capital, and consumers for industrial transformation. The railroad linked markets and hastened delivery of goods and raw materials. And the large corporation amassed frightening power in the quest for productivity and profits. All these influences profoundly changed the structure of society, relationships among its constituent groups, and the rhythms of work and everyday life.

Industrialization is a process whose complexity defies precise definition. It is thus best understood by considering its predominant characteristics, which in America were:

1. production by machine rather than by hand
2. involvement of an increasing proportion of the work force in manufacturing
3. production concentrated in large, intricately organized factories
4. accelerated technological innovation, emphasizing new inventions and applied science
5. expanded markets, no longer merely local and regional in scope
6. growth of a nationwide transportation network based on the railroad, and an accompanying communications network based on the telegraph and telephone
7. increased capital accumulation for investment in expansion of production
8. growth of large enterprises and specialization in all forms of economic activity
9. rapid population increase
10. steady increase in the size and predominance of cities

A few numbers will help to illustrate these patterns. In 1860 about a quarter of the American labor force worked in industry and transportation; over half did so in 1920. The number of people gainfully employed rose from 17.4 million in 1880 to 41.6 million in 1920. Total miles of railroad track grew from 31,000 in 1860 to 193,000 in 1900. In 1870 Western Union handled over 9 million telegraph messages on 112,000 miles of wire; by 1900 it processed over 63 million messages on 933,000 miles of wire. And the value of exports increased twelvefold between 1879 and 1920. By the twentieth century, the United States was not only the world's largest producer of raw materials and food, but the most productive industrial nation as well.

Accelerated migration off farms and mass immigration from abroad swelled the industrial work force;

but machines, more than people, boosted American productivity. Only by using more machines could manufacturers lower production costs and significantly raise each worker's output. Mechanization relied on the use of standardized parts and made for more specialization on factory assembly lines.

A spirit of nationalism infected American industrialization. Many industrialists believed (or said they believed) that productivity was the key to national welfare. Thus John D. Rockefeller linked his business activities to a nationalistic mission, explaining, "I wanted to participate in the work of making our country great. I had an ambition to build." Yet the accomplishments of industry involved wanton waste and exploitation of the nation's resources–the "great barbecue," where hungry entrepreneurs drooled over the temptations of wealth. The vigor and creativity that marked the half-century between the end of the Civil War and the beginning of the First World War were clearly both constructive and destructive.

These trends weighed most heavily on the industrial work force. Economic growth furnished jobs and income to millions of families who had left American farms and European villages in search of a better existence. But industry's emphasis on productivity and profitability often kept wages at or below subsistence levels and harnessed workers to monotonous routines. Fearful that American industrialism might create a class of helpless proletarians, laborers fought to retain independent work habits and to be paid a living wage. Although the period was not a triumphant one for labor, it did contain a strong undercurrent of worker activism in reforms, cooperatives, and unions in an effort to reconcile new economic realities with the desire to live in comfort and dignity.

Thomas Alva Edison (1847–1931) posing in his Menlo Park laboratory. Edison developed countless inventions, including the incandescent light bulb, the phonograph, and the Kinetoscope, an early form of animation. He was a skilled publicist, capable of organizing and selling his revolutionary ideas. National Park Service.

Technology and the quest for wealth

In 1876, Thomas A. Edison and his associates moved into a long wooden shed in Menlo Park, New Jersey, where Edison intended to turn out "a minor invention every ten days and a big thing every six months or so." Here was the brash American spirit adapting itself to a new age. If Americans wanted new products, they could not wait for discoveries; they had to organize and work purposefully to bring about progress. Edison envisioned his Menlo Park laboratory as an invention factory, a place where creative people would pool their ideas and skills to fashion marketable products. Such efforts were part of a process that went hand in hand with American industrialization at the end of the nineteenth century.

The years between 1865 and 1900 were an age of invention. Many important devices–notably the steam

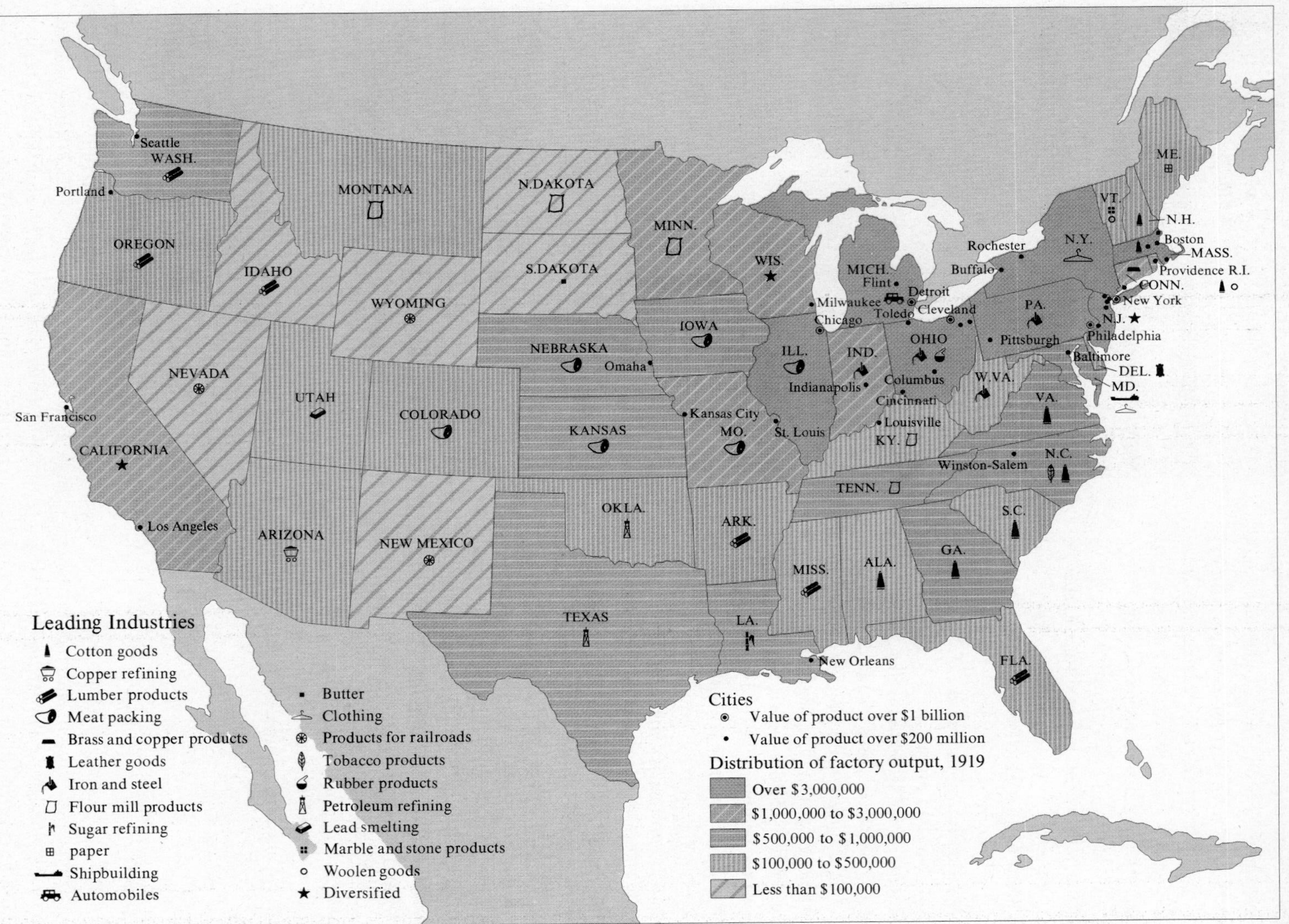

Industrial production, 1919. Source: © American Heritage Publishing Co., Inc. *American Heritage Pictorial Atlas of United States History;* data from U.S. Bureau of the Census, *Fourteenth Census of the United States, 1920.* Vol. IX: *Manufacturing* (Washington: U.S. Government Printing Office, 1921).

engine, the dynamo (generator), and the sewing machine—that had existed since the early nineteenth century were adapted to the needs of industry and agriculture from the 1860s onward (see map). Moreover, late-nineteenth-century inventions and refinements in electricity, internal combustion, and industrial chemistry laid the technical foundations for twentieth-century industrial development. The patent system, created by the Constitution to "promote the Progress of science and useful Arts," testified to an outburst of American inventiveness. Between 1790 and 1860 the U.S. Patent Office had granted a total of 36,000 patents. In 1897 alone, however, it granted 22,000 patents, and in the seventy years after 1860 it granted 1.5 million.

Birth of the electrical industry

Over the past hundred years, nothing has changed daily life more than electricity. As former Harvard president Charles W. Eliot once put it, electricity is "carrier of light and power; devourer of time and space; bearer of human speech over land and sea; greatest servant of man." Americans pioneered in the electrical industry, and Edison, Bell, and Westinghouse are enshrined in the nation's gallery of heroes.

Edison came close to fulfilling the goal he set for his work at Menlo Park. He patented over a thousand inventions, many of which used electrical power to transmit light, sound, and images. Perhaps the biggest of his "big-thing" projects began in 1878 when he formed the Edison Electric Light Company and embarked on a search for a cheap, efficient means of indoor lighting. In urban industrial America, the traditional gas, candle, and oil lamps had become impractical for lighting streets and large buildings. So Edison turned to light made by an electric current flowing between two carbon rods. His major contribution was perfection of an incandescent bulb, which used a filament in a vacuum. At the same time he worked out a *system* of power production and distribution—an improved dynamo and a parallel circuit of wires—that would provide cheap, convenient lighting to a large number of customers. Aware that he had to make his ideas marketable, Edison acted as his own publicist. During the 1880 Christmas season he illuminated Menlo Park with forty incandescent bulbs, and in 1882 he built a power plant that would light eighty-five buildings in New York's Wall Street financial district. When this Pearl Street Station began service with great fanfare, a New York *Times* reporter marveled that working in his office at night "seemed almost like writing in daylight." The next year, New Yorkers celebrated Edison's achievement by staging a ballet complete with an electrically lighted model of the Brooklyn Bridge and ballerinas whose costumes were wired so they glowed.

Edison's system had a major limitation: it used direct current at low voltage, and could thus send electric power only a mile or two. George Westinghouse, an inventor from Schenectady, New York, who at age twenty-three had become famous for devising an air brake, solved the problem. Westinghouse used alternating current and transformers to reduce high-voltage power to lower voltage levels, thus making transmission over long distances cheaper.

Once Edison and Westinghouse had made their technological breakthroughs, others helped them distribute their inventions to a wide market. Samuel Insull, Edison's private secretary, who later amassed a huge electric-utility empire, deftly attracted investments and organized Edison power plants across the country. In the late 1880s and early 1890s, financiers Henry Villard and J. P. Morgan consolidated patents in electric lighting and merged equipment-manufacturing companies into the General Electric Company. Equally important, General Electric and Westinghouse Electric established research laboratories that paid practical-minded scientists to find new uses for electricity. Under talented scientist and organizer Willis M. Whitney, the General Electric lab pioneered in myriad developments ranging from vacuum tubes for radios through tungsten filaments for light bulbs to atomic theory. A successful entrepreneur, according to Whitney, could never rely on prevailing technology. "Our research laboratory," he declared, "was a development of the idea that large industrial organizations have both an opportunity and a responsibility for their own life insurance. New discovery can provide it."

But research laboratories did not eliminate individual dreamers. One such optimist was Henry Ford, who in the 1890s worked as an electrical engineer in Detroit's Edison Company and in his spare time experimented with a gasoline-burning internal combustion engine to power a vehicle. George Selden, a Rochester, New York, lawyer, had been tinkering

One day's output at the Ford factory in Highland Park, Michigan, 1913. Bodies were added to the chassis at a later stage of production. Brown Brothers.

with internal combustion engines since the 1870s. But Ford's vision and organizational genius spawned a massive industry.

Like Edison, Ford had a scheme as well as an invention. In 1909 he declared, "I am going to democratize the automobile. When I'm through everybody will be able to afford one, and about everyone will have one." The way to do so, according to Ford, was to produce millions of identical cars in exactly the same fashion. The key was mass production, and the watchword was *flow.* Copying the meatpacking system whereby an animal carcass moving on an overhead trolley was carved up in a series of simple operations, Ford set up assembly lines that drastically reduced the time and cost of producing cars. Instead of a single worker being responsible for making and assembling the entire automobile, production was broken down so that each worker had responsibility for only one task, constantly repeated, and there was a continuous flow of these tasks from raw materials to finished product. When the Ford Motor Company began operation in 1903, there were only 8,000 autos on the streets of Detroit. In 1910, the first year the famous Model T was marketed, Ford sold 10,000 cars. By 1914, the year after the first moving assembly line was inaugurated, 248,000 Fords were sold. Many of them cost as little as $490 apiece, only about one-fourth of what they would have cost a decade earlier.

Mass production of the automobile

Even this price was beyond the means of many workers, who earned at best $2 a day. In 1914, however, Ford tried to set an example and boost buying power by paying workers $5 a day. "This is neither charity nor wages," he explained, "but profit sharing and efficiency engineering." Moreover, rising automobile production made for more jobs, higher earnings, and higher profits in such related industries as paint, rubber, and glass. The petroleum industry too was revolutionized, its products now being used more for propulsion than for illumination or lubrication. The value of automobiles manufactured, only $6 million in 1900, had ballooned to $420 million by 1914. The Model T was indeed replacing the family horse.

In tinkerers' shops and research laboratories, Americans were adapting theoretical scientific discoveries to practical production. Their skill was especially striking in engineering and chemistry. American producers successfully applied metallurgical and chemical techniques to simplify the processes of making tin plate, pig iron, and steel. In the 1880s and 1890s, pasteurization and new understanding of enzyme reactions transformed the brewing industry and enabled new companies to distribute fresh beer more widely. Explosives were utilized in mining and construction. And a fledgling industrial-chemicals industry, led by E. I. du Pont de Nemours & Company, created products that surpassed people's dreams.

Advances in the chemical industry

The du Ponts did for the chemical industry what Edison and Ford had done for the electrical and automobile industries. The du Pont family had been manufacturing gunpowder and other explosives in America since the early 1800s. In 1902 three du Pont cousins, Alfred, Coleman, and Pierre, took over the family company and began to broaden production. Although early projects involved the development of safer, more sophisticated explosives, longer-range outcomes resulted from the accompanying discovery of synthetic materials. The du Pont laboratories, branching out from explosives research in 1911, began to adapt the flammable substance cellulose to the eventual production of such materials as photographic film, rubber, lacquer, and textile fibers. The company also pioneered in systematic organization, devising efficient methods of executive management, accounting, and earnings investment.

A host of other machines and processes helped to alter the nation's economy and everyday life between 1865 and 1900. The telephone and typewriter revolutionized communications, making face-to-face conversations less important and facilitating business correspondence and record-keeping. Sewing machines made mass-produced clothing available to almost everyone. Refrigeration changed American dietary habits by making it easier to preserve meat, fruit, vegetables, and dairy products. Streetcars, elevated railroads, and subways extended city limits and enabled people to live farther from their workplaces. Cash registers and adding machines revamped accounting and created new clerical jobs.

All these developments and more thrust the United States into the vanguard of industrial nations. Other effects, however, were less positive. Industrial expansion created countless new jobs, but because most machines and inventions were labor-saving, fewer workers could produce more in less time—as Conrad Carl knew all too well. Mechanization not only destroyed time-honored crafts but subordinated men and women to rigid schedules and repetitive routines. On another level, the scramble for patents resulted in as much waste as technological advancement. Entrepreneurs spent huge sums hoping to profit from inventing something slightly different from what already existed, or purchased patents on the remote chance they might be profitable. Companies like Bell Telephone and individuals like George Selden clogged the courts with suits alleging patent infringement. To minimize uncertainty, manufacturers pooled existing patents and tried to monopolize new discoveries by confining research to their own labs. As in farming and mining, bigness and consolidation were engulfing the individual.

The triumph of industrialism

When railroad tycoon Cornelius Vanderbilt died in 1877, he left a fortune worth $90 million. By the time his son William died just eight years later, the inheritance had doubled. The growth of the Vanderbilt fortune testifies not only to the explosion of fantastic personal wealth for a privileged few in the late nineteenth century but also to the accelerated pace of economic activity that created such wealth. Across the nation, production reached levels that would have been unimaginable before the Civil War, and lust for profit permeated the national spirit. As Henry George, a critic of this mentality, wrote in 1879, "Get money—honestly if you can, but at any rate get money! This is the lesson that society is daily and hourly dinning into the ears of its members."

In the industrial sector, profits resulted from higher production at lower costs. As railroads and technological innovations made large-scale production more economical, sizable factories began to replace small ones. Between 1850 and 1900 the average amount of capital invested in a manufacturing firm increased from $700,000 to $1.9 million. Only large factories could afford to buy new machines and operate them at full capacity. And large factories could best take advantage of discount rates for shipping products in bulk and for buying raw materials in quantity. Economists call such advantages *economies of scale.*

Machines and large factories made such efficiencies possible, but profitability was as much a matter of organization as of mechanics. In other words, running a

New emphasis on efficiency

successful factory depended on how production was *arranged* as well as on the machines that were used. Thus by the 1890s, engineers and managers were working intently to increase output economically and efficiently, putting the primary emphasis on time.

A laborer poses by a huge ore breaker at the Utah Copper Company, around 1900. As machines became larger and more efficient, workers' skills became less important. State Historical Society of Wisconsin.

Of the many people who espoused systems of efficient production, the most influential was Frederick W. Taylor. As a foreman and engineer for the Midvale Steel Company in the 1880s, Taylor observed that the company–in fact, all companies–would always have fixed costs of taxes, insurance, interest on loans, and depreciation of buildings and equipment. He concluded that the only way to lessen the impact of fixed costs and thus increase profits was to base production on scientific studies of "how quickly the various kinds of work . . . ought to be done." The "ought" was crucial because it signified the goal of producing more for a lower cost per unit–meaning reducing labor costs by eliminating unnecessary workers. The "how quickly" meant that time and money were equivalent.

In 1898 Taylor took his stopwatch to the Bethlehem Steel Company, where he undertook a five-month study to illustrate how his principles of scientific management worked. His experiments, he explained, involved identifying the "elementary operations of motions" used by specific workers, eliminating "all useless movements," selecting better tools, and devising "a series of motions which can be made quickest and best." Applying the technique to the shovelling of ore, Taylor eventually designed fifteen kinds of shovels for different tasks and prescribed the proper motions for using each shovel. As a result he reduced a crew of 600 men to 140 and cut company costs in half. The remaining shovelers received higher wages.

Taylor's writings helped to make time studies and scientific management a national obsession. They heightened the emphasis on large-scale production and economies of scale while minimizing the importance of factory workers relative to clerks and planners. Workers' skills became less valued, and managers increasingly controlled the pace and scale of output. Time rather than quality became the measure of acceptable work, and science rather than tradition determined the right ways of doing things. As integral features of the assembly line, where work was divided up into specific time-determined tasks, employees had become another kind of interchangeable part.

By the late 1880s, large manufacturers were adding new marketing techniques to their technological and organizational innovations. Meat processor Gustavus Swift built branch slaughterhouses and refrigerated warehouses and railroad cars in order to enlarge the market for fresh meat. James B. Duke, who organized the American Tobacco Company and made cigarettes a big business, saturated communities with billboards and free samples and offered premium gifts to retailers for selling more cigarettes. In 1889 alone, he spent $800,000 on promotion–twice his net earnings. Companies like International Harvester and Singer Sewing Machine set up systems for servicing their products and introduced financing schemes to permit customers to buy the machines more easily. In many instances marketing innovations enabled producers to sell directly to retailers, squeezing out wholesalers and eliminating the excess costs wholesaling entailed. Mail-order firms, large department stores, and chain stores pushed direct sales to new limits and in the process invented new methods of retailing. As one Woolworth store advertised, "Larger purchases . . . direct from manufacturers explain the high values we offer."

New marketing techniques

The corporate consolidation movement

Neither the wonders of industrial production nor the buoyant language of market promotion could mask unsettling factors in the American economy. Competition and the resulting race for higher productivity and new markets had costs as well as benefits. New technology demanded that factories operate at near-capacity in order to produce goods most economically. But the more manufacturers produced, the more they had to sell. And in order to sell more, they had to reduce prices. In order to profit more, they expanded production further and often reduced wages. In order to expand, they had to borrow money. In order to repay the money, they had to produce and sell even more. This circular process strangled small firms that could not keep pace and thrust workers into conditions of constant uncertainty. The same pressures and consequences affected trade, banking, and transportation as well as manufacturing.

Such conditions encouraged rapid growth–but optimism could dissolve at the hint that debtors were unable to meet their obligations. In the final third of the nineteenth century, financial panics afflicted the economy at least once a decade, depressing prices and putting workers out of jobs. The depressions that began in 1873, 1884, and 1893 each hovered over the nation for several years. Business leaders failed to agree on what caused the declines. Some blamed overproduction; others pointed to underconsumption; still others attributed downturns to lax credit and investment practices. Whatever the reasons–and there were usually several–businessmen began seeking ways to combat the uncertainty of the business cycle. In those years of boom and bust, many turned to more centralized and cooperative forms of economic power, notably corporations, pools, trusts, and holding companies. These new devices of control in turn altered traditional American beliefs in individual effort.

Industrialists, unlike laborers, never questioned the capitalist system or lost faith in entrepreneurial leadership. Instead, they built on the corporate base that had supported American economic growth since the early 1800s. The corporation had been given a special American flavor by general incorporation laws passed by the states to encourage commerce and industry (see page 242). Under such laws as they developed in the middle of the nineteenth century, almost anyone could start a company and raise money by selling stock to investors, who could share in the profits without being held liable for company debts. State laws and corporation bylaws placed company administration in the hands of managers. Stockholders could share in profits yet avoid most losses because of their

The consolidation movement enabled trusts like Standard Oil to grow while competitors withered and died. Thus this 1905 cartoon, based on a comment by John D. Rockefeller, Jr.: "The American Beauty rose can be produced in all its splendor only by sacrificing the early buds that grow up around it." Culver.

limited liability. Corporations proved to be the best instruments for raising the capital needed for industrial expansion, and by 1900 they were responsible for two-thirds of all goods manufactured in the United States. Moreover, in the 1880s and 1890s corporations received broad judicial protection when the Supreme Court ruled that they, like individuals, were covered by the Fourteenth Amendment. In other words, states could not deny corporations the equal protection of the laws and could not deprive them of rights or property without due process of law.

As economic disorder and the urge for profits mounted, corporation managers began to seek stability in new and larger forms of economic concentration. Between the late 1880s and early 1900s, an epidemic of consolidation swept the United States, eventually resulting in the massive conglomerates that have dominated the American economy in the twentieth century. At first, however, such efforts were tentative and informal, consisting mainly of cooperative agreements among firms that made the same product or offered the same service. Through these arrangements, called *pools,* competing companies tried to control the market by agreeing how much each should produce and what prices should be charged. Used by railroads (to divide up traffic), steel producers, and whiskey distillers, pools depended on their members' honesty. Such "gentlemen's agreements" worked during good times when there was enough business for all; but during slow periods, the desire for profits often tempted pool members to evade their commitments by secretly reducing prices or selling more than the agreed quota. There was no mechanism to enforce pooling arrangements; because pools were extralegal and did not fall under the jurisdiction of any court, pool members could not sue each other for broken promises. The Interstate Commerce Act of 1887 outlawed pools, but by then their usefulness was already fading.

Methods of consolidation

John D. Rockefeller disliked pools, calling them "ropes of sand." In 1879 one of his lawyers, Samuel Dodd, devised a means to overcome the limitations of pools and still control the market. Dodd adapted an old device called a *trust* whereby companies could turn over control of their stock to a board of trustees, which then supervised all operations. This device allowed Rockefeller to integrate the management of his original Standard Oil Company of Ohio with that of all the other companies he had gobbled up, thus strengthening his grip on the highly profitable petroleum industry. Then in 1888 New Jersey adopted new incorporation laws allowing corporations chartered there to own property in other states and to own stock in other corporations. This liberalization led to the creation of the *holding company,* which controlled a partial or complete interest in other companies. Holding companies could in turn merge their constituent companies' assets (physical plant, equipment, inventory, cash, and the like) as well as their management. Thus Rockefeller incorporated Standard Oil of New Jersey, merging the assets of forty constituent companies. By 1898, Standard Oil refined 83.7 percent of all the oil produced in the nation, controlled most pipelines, and had moved into natural-gas production and ownership of oil-producing properties.

Standard Oil's expansion into activities besides oil refining exemplified a new form of integration that accompanied the rise of trusts. In an effort to control the market, many companies took over several levels of production and distribution, including control of raw materials and transportation as well as manufacturing. The prime example of this *vertical integration* was Gustavus Swift's meat-processing operation. During the 1880s, Swift boldly invested in livestock, slaughterhouses, refrigerator cars, and a marketing organization of butchers so as to assure sale of his beef without unexpected inconvenience. The device of the holding company aided this kind of consolidation, which fused a broad range of business activities into one entity under unified management.

Originally designed as an arrangement whereby responsible individuals would manage the financial affairs of people unwilling or unable to handle them alone, the trust became the answer to industry's search for order. Between 1889 and 1903, some three hundred combinations were formed, most of them trusts and holding companies. By far the most spectacular was the U.S. Steel Corporation, financed by J. P. Morgan. This new enterprise, made up of iron-ore properties, freight carriers, wire mills, plate and tubing companies, and other firms, was capitalized at over $1.4 billion. Other mammoth combinations included the Amalgamated Copper Company, the American Sugar Refining Company, the American Tobacco Company, the U.S. Leather Company, and the U.S. Rubber Company, each worth over $50 million.

The merger movement was promoted by a new species of businessmen, whose vocation was financial organizing rather than producing a particular good or service. These consummate opportunists sought out candidates for combination, formed centralized corporations, and then persuaded producers to sell their firms to the new company. These businessmen usually raised money by selling stock and borrowing from banks. Unwedded to any one industry, their attention ranged widely. Thus W. H. Moore organized the American Tin Plate Company, the Diamond Match Company, and the National Biscuit Company. C. R. Flint helped create the National Starch Company and the U.S. Rubber Company, and tried but failed to amalgamate the electric light and power industry. Elbert H. Gary aided consolidation of the barbed-wire industry and the organization of U.S. Steel. And shrewd investment bankers like J. P. Morgan and Jacob Schiff piloted the merger movement, inspiring awe with their financial power and organizational skills.

The growth of corporations in the late nineteenth century turned stock exchanges into pulsating centers of activity where investors bought and sold stocks and bonds feverishly. By the end of 1886, trading on the New York Stock Exchange had reached 1 million shares a day. By 1914 the number of industrial stocks traded had reached 511, compared to 145 in 1869. This investing mania could not have occurred without growth in the capital available for such purposes. Between 1870 and 1900 foreign investment in American companies rose from $1.5 billion to $3.5 billion. More important, personal savings and institutional investment mushroomed: the assets of savings banks, concentrated in the Northeast and on the West Coast, rose by $900 million between 1875 and 1897, to a total of $2.2 billion. State regulations were gradually loosened to enable banks to invest in railroads and industrial enterprises. Commercial banks, insurance companies, and corporations also invested heavily. As one journal proclaimed, "Nearly the whole country (including the typical widow and orphan) is interested in the stock market." Though this statement was a gross exaggeration, it reflected what optimistic industrial capitalists wanted to believe.

The gospel of wealth

To corporate investors, growth was not only desirable; it was necessary. Profits depended on it, and profits meant everything. Pursuit of wealth had become a struggle for life. As Milton H. Smith of the Louisville and Nashville Railroad put it, "Society, as created, was for the purpose of one man's getting what the other fellow has, if he can, and keep out of the penitentiary." Such sentiments summed up the self-interest at the bottom of laissez-faire philosophy.

But the merger movement that resulted in trusts and holding companies upset this philosophical underpinning. J. P. Morgan, whose steely eyes, full mustache, and bulky frame made him a commanding figure among American capitalists, heralded the new order when he told a meeting of railroad directors, "The purpose of this meeting is to cause the members of this association to no longer take the law into their own hands . . . as has been too much the practice heretofore. This is not elsewhere customary in civilized communities, and no good reason exists why such a practice should continue among railroads." Business leaders turned to consolidation under the new corporate forms both to promote growth and to cut down wasteful competition. The monopolistic companies that resulted, however, found it necessary to justify their size and power to a public raised on the ideology of open competition.

Apologists for business thus eagerly embraced the doctrine of Social Darwinism, which seemed to justify aggression in human society. Developed by English philosopher Herbert Spencer and preached in the United States by Yale professor William Graham Sumner, Social Darwinism loosely adapted Charles Darwin's theory of the origin of species to the traditional principles of laissez faire. Human society had evolved naturally, the Social Darwinists reasoned, and any interference with existing institutions would only hamper progress and aid the weak. In a free society operating according to the principle of survival of the fittest, power would flow naturally to the most capable. Property holding and acquisition were therefore sacred rights, and wealth was a mark of well-deserved power and responsibility. Civilization depended on this system, explained Sumner. "If we do not like the survival of the fittest," he wrote, "we have only one possible alternative, and that is survival of the unfittest." Clergymen, journalists, and popular writers also proclaimed the doctrine of Social Darwinism, assuring the public that progress would result only from natural evolution.

Social Darwinism

This philosophy required that people be left free to accumulate and dispose of wealth. In fact, however, the new corporate forms, with their domination of production and finance, prevented most individuals who did not already have wealth from acquiring it. In response to this inconsistency, extensions of Social Darwinist theory gave rise to various forms of paternalism–providing for the needs of those less fortunate or less capable–on the part of the elite. Thus captains of industry strongly believed that their wealth carried moral responsibilities. John D. Rockefeller once stated, "I believe it is my duty to make money and still more money and to use the money I make for the good of my fellow man according to the dictates of my conscience." This belief implied a right to define what was good and necessary for society, and especially for workers. It meant that the wealthy could and should endow churches, hospitals, and schools, since such gifts promoted progress by raising the "moral culture" of all classes. But it also meant that government should not force the rich, through taxation or regulation, to become more humanitarian. The moral stewardship of paternalism allowed the wealthy freedom to define how their money should be spent for the social good, but denied self-determination to the vast majority of the population.

The new urge for efficiency also bolstered paternalistic impulses by glorifying systematic organization. Under scientific management, professional experts determined schedules, production quotas, techniques, and tools. Their rigid secular principles acquired almost religious certitude: there was only one true way to economic efficiency. Once business leaders had accepted these principles for their own companies, they were only a short step from applying them to the rest of society. Scientific management could, it appeared, apply to politics and personal affairs just as easily as it did to factories.

Paradoxically, business executives who exalted individual initiative and independence also pressed for government assistance. They denounced any measures that might aid unions or regulate factory conditions; such legislation, they said, thwarted natural economic laws. At the same time, though, they lobbied forcefully for subsidies, bounties, loans, and tax relief that would encourage business growth. Tariffs were by far the largest form of government assistance to industry. By putting high import duties on competing goods from abroad, such as kerosene, steel rails, worsted wools, and tin plate, Congress enabled American producers to keep the prices of their goods relatively high. Industrialists argued that tariff protection encouraged the development of new products and the founding of new enterprises. But tariffs also forced consumers to pay, in the form of artificially high prices, for industrialists' investments.

Government assistance to business

Railroads and industrial firms also manipulated state and local governments to their own advantage. As reformer Henry Demarest Lloyd remarked in 1881, Standard Oil "has done everything with the Pennsylvania legislature except refine it." In the South, railroads and mining companies often leased prisoners to work as laborers. Such companies paid the states about 10 cents per prisoner for a day's work, in preference to paying a free laborer $1 a day. Although business executives believed that natural law would lead directly to economic progress, they were not above enlisting help to ensure that natural law would work profitably for them.

Whatever their inconsistencies, business leaders took great pride in the achievements of their era. Many accepted credit for the meteoric rise of the American standard of living–national wealth rose 550 percent between 1860 and 1900, and per capita income increased 150 percent–and they scoffed at charges that only the wealthy were benefiting from this golden age. Carroll D. Wright, a pioneering social statistician, denied that the rich were getting richer and the poor poorer. "To the investigator," he testified, "the phrase should be, The rich are growing richer; many more people than formerly are growing rich; and the poor are better off." Moralists like E. L. Godkin, editor of the *Nation,* complained that "wealth is a purveyor of meat, drink, clothing, and ornamentation which ... 'makes hay' of all noble standards of individual and social conduct." But Burlington Railroad president Charles E. Perkins spoke for the majority:

> Have not great merchants, great manufacturers, great inventors, done more for the world than preachers and philanthropists? ... History and experience demonstrates that as wealth has accumulated and things have cheapened, men have improved ... in their habits of thought, their sympathy for others, their ideas of justice as well as of mercy. ... Material progress must come first and ... upon it is founded all other progress.

The trouble with this materialistic philosophy was that it rested on a shaky foundation. Believers first justified it by invoking natural economic law and the survival of the fittest. But mounting criticism forced them into the illogical position of defending such principles by emphasizing how fragile they were. Thus, they warned, any interference in the business system by labor unions or by government–in the form of regulation, taxation, or support for the underprivileged–would upset everything and stall or even reverse progress. Government interference in the form of tariffs and other aid was quite another matter.

Dissenting voices

Writers who attacked trusts rarely challenged this reasoning; instead, they based their arguments on the traditional American beliefs in decentralization and opportunity. In doing so, they argued within the same framework of values as did corporate leaders who defended the new economic system. While defenders insisted that trusts were the natural and efficient outcome of economic development, critics charged that trusts were unnatural because they were created by greed, and inefficient because they stifled opportunity. Underlying such charges was a deep-seated fear of monopoly. As Charles Francis Adams, a member of the family that produced two presidents, put it, "In the minds of the great majority, and not without reason, the idea of any industrial combination is closely connected with that of monopoly, and monopoly with extortion." Those who feared monopoly believed that large corporations could exploit consumers by fixing prices, demean workers by cutting wages, destroy opportunity by eliminating small businesses, and threaten democracy by corrupting politicians–all of which was not only unnatural but immoral. To critics of trusts, ethics eclipsed economics.

Characteristically, intellectuals believed there was a better way to achieve progress. By the mid-1880s, a number of young professors, troubled by the growing size of industrial and financial organizations, began to challenge Social Darwinism and laissez faire. Some, like pioneering sociologist Lester Ward, attacked the application of evolutionary theory to social and economic relations. In *Dynamic Sociology* (1883), Ward argued that human control of nature, not natural law, accounted for the advance of civilization. To Ward, a system that guaranteed survival only to the fittest was wasteful and brutal; instead, he reasoned, unified and cooperative activity, fostered by planning and government intervention, was the most progressive means to unity and happiness. Economists Richard Ely, John R. Commons, and Edward Bemis agreed that natural forces should be harnessed for the public good. In 1885 they and others of like mind formed the American Economic Association and denounced the laissez-faire system for its "unsound morals." They preferred the positive assistance of the state, which was, Ely declared, "an educational and ethical agency whose positive aid is an indispensable condition of human progress."

While academics were recommending intervention in and adjustments of the natural economic order, others were proposing more utopian schemes for combating monopolies. Reformer Henry George, whose early life of poverty as a printer and writer had sensitized him to the exploitative power of large enterprises, declared that inequality stemmed from the ability of a few to profit from rising land values. Land values rose, George argued, without effort on the part of owners merely because a growing population increased the demand for living and working space, especially in cities. To restore equality, George proposed to tax the "unearned increment"–the rise in land values caused by increased market demand rather than by owners' improvements–and to eliminate all other taxes. By confiscating undue profits, George insisted, this single tax would end monopolistic tendencies and ensure social progress. George's scheme, argued forcefully in his book *Progress and Poverty* (1879), had great popular appeal over the next quarter-century and almost won him the mayoralty of New York in 1886.

Utopian economic schemes

Unlike George, who approved of private ownership, novelist Edward Bellamy envisioned a socialist state in which government would own and oversee the means of production and distribution and would unite all people under moral laws. Bellamy outlined his vision in the utopian *Looking Backward, 2000–1887,* published in 1888. The novel, which sold over 1 million copies within a few years, warned that catastrophe would result from the extremes of wealth and poverty that characterized American society. The remedy, said Bellamy, was a fully nationalized state free of the greed of bankers, industrialists, lawyers, and politicians. A "principle of fraternal cooperation" would replace vicious competition and wasteful monopoly, and a classless society living under the Golden Rule would erase inequality and corruption. Bellamy's system, which he called Nationalism, rested on his belief that all people are interested in "breaking the meshes which entangle us, and struggling upward to a higher, nobler plane of existence." His ideas sparked the formation of Nationalist clubs and publications all over the country, and vitalized popular appeals for civil service reform, social welfare measures, and government ownership of railroads and utilities.

Journalist and reformer Henry Demarest Lloyd arrived at a similar conclusion by a different route. His *Wealth Against Commonwealth* (1894) was a quasi-scholarly indictment of the ways Standard Oil had achieved monopolistic supremacy. Using his evidence loosely, Lloyd portrayed John D. Rockefeller as a ruthless ogre who trampled widows and invalids as well as competing oil refiners in his rush for profits. Lloyd warned that such unbridled aggression and resulting monopolistic power would lead only to public enslavement. As an alternative, he offered a cooperative commonwealth similar to Bellamy's. Government ownership and operation of the means of production, Lloyd exclaimed, would create a society in which "the organization of processes have become so far developed that the profit-hunting Captains of Industry may be replaced by the public-serving Captains of Industry. . . . We are to have a private life of new beauty. . . . We are to be commoners, travelers to Altruria."

While George, Bellamy, Lloyd, and others grappled with ways to meet what they believed to be a moral crisis of civilization, public clamor against monopolies and trusts began to prod legislators into action. Before 1900, very few people advocated the kind of government ownership Bellamy and Lloyd envisioned, but several state governments did take steps to prohibit monopolies and regulate big business. By the end of the century, fifteen states had constitutional provisions outlawing trusts, and twenty-seven had laws forbidding pools. Most of these were states in the agricultural South and West, responding to antimonopolistic pressure exerted by various farm organizations. Such laws, along with those regulating railroads, established precedents for government intervention. But problems of definition and enforcement mounted. State attorneys general lacked the staff and judicial support for a concerted attack on big business, and corporations always found ways to evade restrictions. Consequently, the need for national legislation only became more pressing.

Antitrust legislation

Throughout the 1880s both major parties moved

gingerly toward such legislation, and in 1890 Congress passed the Sherman Anti-Trust Act. The act was a result more of politics than of economics. Introduced by Senator John Sherman of Ohio and rewritten by eastern conservatives in the Senate, the law made illegal "every contract, combination in the form of trust or otherwise, or conspiracy in the restraint of trade." People found guilty of violating the law faced fines and jail terms, and those injured by illegal combinations could sue for triple damages. However, the law was vague–purposely so, some have said, because that was the only way it could have been passed. It did not define clearly what a restraint of trade was. Moreover, it entrusted interpretation of its provisions to the courts, which at that time were strong allies of business. As one corporate lawyer scoffed, "Legislators madly dashed to the work, threw ink upon paper, and called it a statute and legislation, and they asked the courts to enforce it–enforce a statute based upon doubt and guess and speculation and against the natural laws of trade and business."

The Sherman Anti-Trust Act was intended to encourage free competition by prohibiting unreasonable restraints of trade, but judges–particularly the Supreme Court–made it difficult to distinguish between reasonable and unreasonable. When in 1895 the government prosecuted the so-called Sugar Trust for owning 98 percent of the nation's sugar-refining capacity, eight of the nine Supreme Court judges ruled that control of manufacturing did not necessarily mean control of trade (*U.S.* v. *E. C. Knight Co.*). According to the Court, the Constitution empowered Congress to control interstate commerce, but manufacturing, which in the case of sugar took place entirely within the state of Pennsylvania, did not fall under congressional control. The Sugar Trust, said one justice, was attempting to increase its profits from refining, but was not trying to restrain trade.

This interpretation left the antitrust act with only token power to combat industrial bigness. The law, passed to soothe public clamor, found little support among public officials, even those entrusted with enforcing it. Thus Attorney General Richard Olney was prompted to remark, "You will have observed that the Govt has been defeated in the Supreme Court on the trust question. I always supposed it would be & have taken the responsibility of not prosecuting under a law I believed to be no good." Between 1890 and 1900 the federal government prosecuted only eighteen cases under the act. The most successful of these were aimed at railroads directly involved in interstate commerce. Ironically, the Sherman Act did serve government officials as a tool for breaking up labor unions: courts that did not consider monopolistic production a restraint of trade willingly applied antitrust provisions to union strikes that affected trade.

The antimonopoly spirit did not die–in fact, "trustbusting" accelerated between 1900 and the First World War. But the problems of enforcing the Sherman Act reflected the uneven distribution of power among American interest groups. Corporate enterprises had been the first to consolidate and work on behalf of their own self-interest, and they controlled great resources of economic and political power. Other groups–farmers, laborers, intellectuals, humanitarians–had numbers and ideas but lacked power. Almost all members of these groups desired the material gains that technology and large-scale production and organization were providing, but they increasingly feared that business was acquiring too much influence. How to rebalance society became the pressing dilemma of industrialism.

The changing status of labor

By 1880, when almost 5 million Americans worked in manufacturing, construction, and transportation, the status of labor had shifted dramatically from what it had been a generation earlier when there were only 1.5 million workers in these industries (see figure). Most workers could no longer accurately be termed producers–as craftsmen and farmers had traditionally considered themselves. The enlarged working class now consisted mainly of employees–people who worked only when someone else hired them, not when or how they pleased. Whereas producers were paid by consumers according to the quality of what they produced, employees were increasingly paid wages based on time spent on the job.

As mass production subdivided manufacturing into minute tasks, workers spent their time repeating

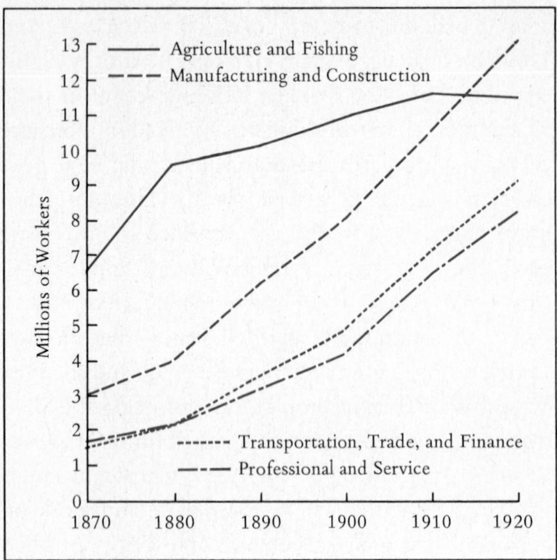

Growth of the Labor Force, 1870–1920. Source: *The Statistical History of the United States, from Colonial Times to the Present* (Washington, D.C.: Government Printing Office), p. 74.

one specialized operation. One investigator who looked into the effects of specialization on a typical laborer found that

> he became a mere machine. . . . Take the proposition of a man operating a machine to nail on 40 to 60 cases of heels in a day. That is 2,400 pairs, 4,800 shoes in a day. One not accustomed to it would wonder how a man could pick up and lay down 4,800 shoes in a day, to say nothing of putting them . . . into a machine. . . . That is the driving method of the manufacture of shoes under these minute subdivisions.

No longer was it up to the worker to decide when to begin and end the work day, when to rest, and what tools and techniques to use. Especially as assembly-line production spread, employees lost their sense of individualism. As a Massachusetts factory worker complained in 1879, "During working hours the men are not allowed to speak to each other, though working close together, on pain of instant discharge. Men are hired to watch and patrol the shop." And workers were now surrounded by others who, just like themselves, worked at the same rate for the same pay, regardless of the quality of their work.

The men and women affected by these changes did not accept them passively. Workers reacted to industrialization by struggling to retain their independence and self-respect in the face of employers' ever-increasing power. As new groups of people encountered the industrial system, they resisted in various ways. Artisans such as cigar makers, glass workers, and coopers, caught in the transition from hand labor to machine production, fought to preserve the pace and quality of their efforts and held on to such customs as appointing a fellow worker to read aloud while they worked. When immigrants went to work in factories, they often succeeded in getting their relatives and friends hired, thus maintaining the on-the-job family and village ties they had always known. Off the job, workers continued to get together for traditional leisure-time activities like social drinking and holiday celebrations.

Employers in turn took steps to limit workers' independence, which they thought threatened efficiency and productivity. In order to make workers docile (like machines), they supported temperance and moral reform societies, dedicated to combating supposed drinking and debauchery on and off the job. They established piece rates, paying workers only for the number of items they produced, to encourage maximum use of new machines. And they lowered wages, forcing people to work harder and longer just to maintain the same income.

As machines and assembly-line production reduced the need for skilled workers, employers cut wage costs further by hiring more women and children. In 1870

Employment of women and children

there were 354,000 women employed in manufacturing (11 percent of all manufacturing laborers); in 1900 there were 1.2 million women (20 percent of all manufacturing laborers), including 45 railroad engineers and stokers, 185 blacksmiths, and 408 machinists. But most female industrial workers were employed in low-paying, menial jobs in textile mills, laundries, and candy factories, where they earned as little as $1.56 for seventy hours of labor. For similar work, men received $7 to $9. Like men, women were exposed to physical danger on the job. As one female garment worker testified, "The machines go like mad all day, because the faster you work the more money you get. Sometimes in my haste I get my finger caught and the needle goes right through it. It goes so quick though, that it does not hurt much. I bind the finger up with a piece of

Even as work became more routinized, workers held onto traditional customs. In this photograph a cigar maker reads the newspaper to his fellow workers, according to tradition. International Museum of Photography, George Eastman House.

cotton and go on working. We all have accidents like that."

Although most working children toiled on their parents' farms, the number in nonagricultural occupations tripled between 1870 and 1900. In 1900, 13 percent of all textile workers were below age sixteen. In other industries too, mechanization created a number of light unskilled tasks (such as running errands and helping machine operators) that children could handle at a fraction of adult wages. Many parents lied about their children's ages to help them get jobs to supplement the family income. By 1900, child labor laws and further automation had reduced the total number of children working in manufacturing, but many more still held jobs in street trades–shining shoes and peddling newspapers–and as clerks and helpers in stores.

While working conditions loomed as the major issue laborers had to face, the problem of wages was often the immediate catalyst of worker unrest. Many employers believed in the "iron law of wages," which dictated that employees be paid according to the conditions of supply and demand. Ideally, this principle meant that workers would receive the highest possible wages that would not drive the employer out of business. But in reality it meant that employers did not have to raise wages–and could even lower them–as long as there were people who would accept low pay. Employers justified the system with references to old-fashioned individual freedom: if a worker did not like the wages being paid, he or she was free to quit and find a job elsewhere. Wage earners saw things differently. They believed the wage system trapped and exploited them. As one Massachusetts worker testified in 1879, "The market is glutted, and we have seasons of dullness; advantage is taken of men's wants, and the pay is cut down; our tasks are increased, and if we remonstrate, we are told our places can be filled. I work harder now than when my pay was twice as high."

Textile mills and other factories employed thousands of children like Addie Laird, a twelve-year-old spinner in a cotton factory in North Pownal, Vermont. Reformers tried to prevent the exploitation of child labor, but many families could not do without their children's meager wages. Photographed in 1910 by Lewis Hine. National Archives.

Moreover, even a steadily employed status was uncertain. Repetitive tasks using high-speed machinery dulled workers' concentration, and the slightest mistake could cause a serious injury. Industrial accidents rose steadily before 1920, killing or maiming hundreds of thousands of people each year. Even as late as 1913, after factory owners had installed some safety devices, some 25,000 people died in industrial mishaps, and close to 1 million were injured. And each year several sensational disasters, such as explosions, mine cave-ins, and fires, aroused public clamor for better safety regulations. The most notorious of these tragedies was the fire at New York City's Triangle Shirtwaist Company in 1911, which killed 146 workers, most of them women. Equally tragic, however, were the countless accidents that resulted in mangled limbs, infected cuts, and chronic illness and death. A railroad coupler described his own accident in 1888:

Working conditions

> It was four or five months before I "got it." I was making a coupling one afternoon. . . . Just before the two cars were come together, the one behind me left the track. . . . Hearing the racket, I sprang to one side, but my toe caught the top of the rail. I was pinned between the corners of the cars as they came together. I heard my ribs cave in like an old box smashed with an ax.

Such accidents occurred with alarming frequency. In the railroad industry alone between 1900 and 1917, 72,000 workers were killed and nearly 2 million injured on trains and tracks; another 158,000 deaths and 237,000 injuries occurred in repair shops and roundhouses.

Families stricken by such accidents suffered acutely, because disability insurance and pensions were almost nonexistent. Nineteenth-century laissez-faire attitudes prevented protective legislation for workers, and employers would not take responsibility for employees' well-being. As one railroad manager told his workers, "The regular compensation of employees covers all risk or liability to accident. If an employee is disabled by sickness or any other cause, the right to claim compensation is not recognized." The only recourse for a stricken family was to sue and prove in court that the killed or injured worker did not realize the risks involved in the job and had not caused the accident. Needless to say, very few judges would accept such an argument, and few families could afford a lawyer to pursue a disability case.

Reformers in several states passed laws to ease working conditions, but the Supreme Court limited their impact by making narrow interpretations of what jobs were dangerous and which workers needed protection. Initially, in *Holden* v. *Hardy* (1896), the Court decided to uphold a law regulating the working hours of miners because their work was so dan-

Strikebreaking train operators being dragged from their work in Pittsburgh during the 1877 railroad strikes. Strikers did extensive damage to railroad cars and equipment throughout the country. Library of Congress.

gerous that overly long hours would increase the threat of injury. In *Lochner* v. *New York* (1905), however, the Court struck down a law limiting bakery workers to a sixty-hour week and a ten-hour day. In response to the argument that the state had authority to protect workers' health and safety, the Court ruled that baking was not a dangerous enough occupation for the legislature to restrict the right of workers to sell their labor freely. According to the Court, interference with the right of individuals to make contracts for their labor would violate the Fourteenth Amendment's guarantee that no state could "deprive any person of life, liberty, or property without due process of law." Then, in *Muller* v. *Oregon* (1908), the Court resorted to a different rationale to uphold a law limiting working hours for women to ten a day. In this case, heralded by liberals as a progressive decision, the Court set aside its *Lochner* argument. Labor legislation for women was necessary, the Court asserted, because a woman's health "becomes an object of public interest and care in order to preserve the strength and vigor of the race."

Throughout the nineteenth century, tensions rose and fell as different groups of men and women confronted mechanization, government neglect, and wage scales that did not keep pace with the rising cost of living. Adjustments were made in different ways as different groups–rural migrants, foreign immigrants, women, and children–entered the industrial labor force. Some people bent to the demands of the factory, the machine, and the time clock. Some tried to blend old ways of working into the new system. Some never adjusted and wandered from place to place, from job to job. Others, however, turned to organized resistance.

Worker protest

In many ways, the year 1877 was a historical watershed. In July of that year, a series of strikes broke out among railroad workers who were protesting wage cuts. Violence spread across Pennsylvania and Ohio all the way to Chicago and St. Louis. Strikers derailed trains and burned rail yards. Militia companies organized by employers broke up picket lines and fired into threatening crowds. In several areas, factory workers, wives, and even local merchants aided the striking workers, while railroads enlisted strikebreakers to replace union men. The worst violence occurred in Pittsburgh, where on July 21 troops bayoneted and then fired on a crowd of demonstrators, killing ten and wounding many more. Infuriated, the crowd drove the soldiers into a railroad roundhouse and set fire to the company's property, destroying 39 buildings, 104 engines, and 1,245 freight and passenger cars. The next day, the troops shot their way out of the roundhouse and killed twenty more citizens before fleeing the city.

After more than a month of unprecedented carnage that reached from West Virginia and Maryland to Illinois, Texas, and California, President Rutherford B. Hayes sent federal troops to restore order and end the strikes. His action marked the first significant use of troops to quell labor unrest. Thereafter, use of federal and state troops became a normal method of suppressing strikes, and nervous employers frequently hired armed guards to protect strikebreakers.

The immediate cause of these strikes was the squeeze of depression. In the economic slump that followed the Panic of 1873, railroad managers had cut wages, increased workloads, and laid off workers, especially those who had protested by joining a union. Such actions drove workers to strike and riot. Laborers in other industries who suffered the same conditions sympathized with the strikers, as did many other members of their communities. A Pittsburgh militiaman, ordered out to break the 1877 strike by his fellow townsmen, remembered, "I talked to all the strikers I could get my hands on, and I could find but one spirit and one purpose among them—that they were justified in resorting to any means to break down the power of the corporations."

The union movement

Anxiety over their loss of independence drove some workers to unionize in protection of their interests. The union movement had precedents but few successful ones. Craft unions, composed of skilled workers in a particular trade, dated from the early nineteenth century, but their emphasis on exclusive membership left them without broad power. The National Labor Union, which flourished briefly after its founding in 1866, grew to 650,000 members but died during the depression of the 1870s. The only broad-based labor organization to survive that depression was the Knights of Labor. Founded in 1860 by Philadelphia garment cutters, the Knights opened their doors to other workers during the 1870s. In 1879, when the organization still had fewer than 10,000 members, it dropped its secret activities and elected Terrence V. Powderly, a Catholic machinist, as grand master. Under Powderly's guidance, Knights membership mushroomed, peaking at 730,000 in mid-1886.

Arising at a time when the industrial system was not yet firmly established, the Knights of Labor tried to escape from the bleak future that industrialism portended by building an alliance among all workers. Thus the organization recruited women and blacks as well as immigrants and unskilled and semi-skilled workers, who were excluded from craft unions. Like the farmers' alliances, with which they felt kinship, the Knights believed that all workers could stand together against the forces of monopoly—corporations, banks, railroads, and lawyers—to create a more harmonious society. The goal, argued Powderly, was to "eventually make every man his own master—every man his own employer. . . . There is no good reason why labor cannot, through cooperation, own and operate mines, factories, and railroads."

Knights of Labor

Technological and economic changes were making it impossible for each worker to be his or her own employer. But like many farmers, the Knights saw producer and consumer cooperatives as preferable alternatives to the forces of greed that surrounded them. They agreed with Edward Bellamy that a society in which all groups lived cooperatively was possible. This view was the source of the organization's strength and of its weakness. The Knights attracted hundreds of thousands of members, especially after mid-1885 when they forced Jay Gould, the hated railroad baron, to yield to labor demands on his railroad system. But the cooperative idea, while attractive in the abstract, did not give laborers much bargaining power with employers. It was simply too vague a concept, and employers held most of the economic leverage. Strikes were a means of seeking immediate goals, but Powderly and other leaders were uncertain:

would strikes, which could become violent, help or hinder the long-range goal of peace and cooperation? As strikes began to fail in 1886, as Powderly began to denounce radicalism and violence, and as the more militant craft unions broke away, Knights membership dwindled. The union survived only in a few small towns, where a brief and vain attempt was made to unite with the Populists in the 1890s. The special interests of craft unions overcame the Knights' general appeal, and dreams of the unity of labor faded.

As the depression of the 1870s subsided and better conditions returned in the early 1880s, a number of labor groups, including the Knights of Labor, began to campaign for an eight-hour work day. This effort on the part of workers to regain control of their work gathered most momentum in Chicago, where radical anarchists as well as various craft unions—perhaps as many as 100,000 workers in all—agitated for the cause. On May 1, 1886, the workers' deadline for achieving their goal, city police were mobilized to prevent possible disorder, especially among striking workers at the huge McCormick reaper factory. The day passed calmly, but two days later police stormed an area near the McCormick plant and broke up a battle between striking unionists and nonunion workers hired as strikebreakers. The police shot and killed two unionists and wounded several others. The next evening, labor groups organized a rally at Haymarket Square, near downtown Chicago, to protest police brutality. As a company of police officers approached the meeting, a bomb exploded near their front ranks, killing seven and injuring sixty-seven. Mass arrests of anarchists and unionists followed. Eventually eight men, all anarchists, were tried and convicted of the bombing, though there was no evidence of their guilt. Four were executed and one committed suicide in prison. The remaining three were pardoned in 1893 by Illinois governor John P. Altgeld, who believed they had been victims of the "malicious ferocity" of the courts.

Haymarket riot

The Haymarket bombing drew public attention to labor campaigns for better conditions but also revived the long-standing American fear of radicalism. The fact that strikes had erupted all over the country in 1886, not just in Chicago, and that anarchists and socialists, many of them foreign-born, had participated in some of the agitation, created a sense of crisis, a feeling that forces of law and order had to act swiftly to prevent social turmoil. To protect their city, private Chicago donors helped to establish Fort Sheridan and the Great Lakes Naval Training Station. Elsewhere police forces and armories were strengthened. And employer associations multiplied. These associations of manufacturers in the same industry often arose during or after a strike, and worked thereafter to counter labor militancy by agreeing to resist strikes and by purchasing strike insurance.

A group of female delegates to the 1886 Knights of Labor convention. The Knights were one of the few labor organizations that actively recruited women. Note that motherhood and union activity could coexist. Library of Congress.

The newly formed American Federation of Labor was the major workers' organization to emerge after the 1886 upheavals. A combination of national craft unions, the AFL initially had about 140,000 members, most of whom were skilled native workers. As a federation, it allowed member unions independence in their own areas of interest, but tried to develop a general policy that would suit the self-interest of all members. Led by Samuel Gompers, the pragmatic and opportunistic head of the Cigar Makers' Union, AFL unions avoided the idealistic rhetoric of worker solidarity to press for specific goals, such as higher wages, shorter hours, and

American Federation of Labor

The Haymarket riot, Chicago, 1886. A bomb explodes among a police brigade trying to break up the labor demonstration. In retaliation, police fired into the crowd of strikers, killing seven men. The caption for the drawing, which appeared in *Harper's Weekly,* falsely identified the incident as an "anarchist riot." Library of Congress.

the right to bargain collectively. As Gompers's associate Adolph Strasser explained, "We have no ultimate ends. We are going from day to day. We are fighting only for immediate objects–objects that can be realized in a few years." Thus the AFL, in contrast to the Knights of Labor, accepted industrialism and worked to achieve better conditions within the wage-and-hours system.

Under Gompers the AFL grew to over 1 million members by 1901 and 2.5 million by 1917, when it included 111 national unions and 27,000 local unions. The national organization required all constituent unions to hire organizers to expand membership, and it collected dues for a fund to aid members on strike. The AFL generally refrained from political activity, though it occasionally supported prolabor candidates and party prolabor platforms.

The AFL and the labor movement in general staggered in the early 1890s, when once again labor violence evoked public fears. In July 1892, Henry C. Frick, the stubborn president of the Carnegie Steel Company, closed the company plant in Homestead, Pennsylvania, when the AFL-affiliated Amalgamated Association of Iron and Steelworkers refused to accept pay cuts and went on strike. Shortly thereafter, angry workers attacked and routed three hundred Pinkerton guards hired by Frick to protect the plant. State militia then moved in to protect the factory, and after five months the strikers gave in. By then public opinion had turned against the strike because of an attempt by a young anarchist—who was not a striker—to assassinate Frick.

In 1894, workers at the Pullman Palace Car Company walked out in protest over exploitative policies at the company town near Chicago. The paternalistic company head George Pullman tried to do everything for the twelve thousand residents of his so-called model town. His company owned and controlled the land and all buildings, the school, the bank, and the water and gas systems. It paid workers' wages, fixed their rents, determined what prices they would pay for the necessities of life, and employed spies to report on disgruntled workers. One laborer grumbled, "We are born in a Pullman house, fed from the Pullman shop, taught in the Pullman school, catechized in the Pullman church, and when we die we shall be buried in the Pullman cemetery and go to the Pullman hell."

Pullman strike

One thing Pullman would not do was negotiate with workers. When the depression that began in 1893 threatened his business, Pullman managed to maintain profits and pay dividends to stockholders by cutting wages 25–40 percent but holding firm on rents and prices in the model town. Workers, squeezed into debt and deprivation, sent a committee to Pullman in May 1894 to protest his policies. Pullman reacted by firing three of the committee. The enraged workers, most of whom had joined the American Railway Union, called a strike. Pullman retaliated by shutting down the plant. When the American Railway Union, led by the charismatic young organizer Eugene V. Debs, voted to aid the strikers by boycotting all Pullman cars, Pullman stood firm and rejected arbitration. The railroad owners' association then enlisted the aid of U.S. Attorney General Richard Olney, who obtained a court injunction to prevent the union from "obstructing the railways and holding up the mails." In response to further worker obstinacy, President Grover Cleveland sent federal troops to Chicago, supposedly to protect the mails but in reality to crush the strike. Within a month the strike was over, and Debs was jailed for six months for contempt of court in defying the injunction. The Supreme Court upheld Debs's sentence on the grounds that the federal government had the power to remove obstacles to interstate commerce.

After the turn of the century, a number of battles occurred between workers and employers in the mining industry. The fledgling United Mine Workers led several strikes in the coal fields of Pennsylvania, Colorado, and West Virginia between 1902 and 1922. Out of the western mining struggles emerged the Industrial Workers of the World (IWW), a radical labor organization that fused the Knights of Labor vision of worker solidarity with the tactics of strikes and sabotage. Using the rhetoric of class conflict—"The final aim is revolution," according to an IWW organizer—the IWW attracted far greater attention than its small membership warranted, and its activities frequently became the subject of debates on labor reform during the Progressive era (see Chapter 21).

It must be emphasized that during the half-century following the Civil War, only a small fraction of American workers belonged to unions. In 1900 only about 1 million out of a total of 27.6 million workers were unionized. In 1920, total union membership had grown to 5 million—still only 13 percent of the work force. The union movement was strong among workers in the building trades, transportation, communications, and to a lesser extent manufacturing. But organizers took no interest in large segments of the industrial labor force and intentionally excluded others. Many unions, such as those of the AFL, were openly hostile toward women. Since the early years of industrialization in America, female workers had organized their own unions; some, such as the Collar Laundry Union of Troy, New York, organized in the 1860s, had been successful in carrying out strikes and achieving higher wages. The first broad-based women's union was the Women's Trade Union League (WTUL), founded in 1903 and patterned after a similar union in England. The WTUL worked for protective legislation for women workers, sponsored educational activities, and joined the cause for women's suffrage. Although the WTUL had some forceful working-class leaders—notably Agnes Nestor, a glove maker, Rose Schneiderman, a cap maker, and Mary Anderson, a shoe worker—it was dominated by middle-class women who had humane but generally nonmilitant purposes in helping working women. Then in the early 1920s, the WTUL fought a constitutional amendment guaranteeing equal rights to

Women, immigrants, and blacks in the labor movement

Important events

1873–78	Depression
1877	Widespread railroad strikes
1879	Henry George, *Progress and Poverty* Edison perfects the incandescent light bulb
1882	Formation of Standard Oil trust
1884–85	Depression
1886	Haymarket riot American Federation of Labor founded
1888	Edward Bellamy, *Looking Backward*
1890	Sherman Anti-Trust Act
1892	Homestead Steel strike
1893–97	Depression
1894	Pullman strike Henry Demarest Lloyd, *Wealth Against Commonwealth*
1901	United States Steel Corporation founded
1902	Reorganization of E. I. du Pont de Nemours and Company
1903	Ford Motor Company founded
1910	Ford Model T first marketed
1913	First moving assembly line begins operation at Ford

women, arguing that women needed protection from exploitation more than they needed equality. Such reasoning fit the assertion of males who argued that women belonged in their own sphere at home, out of the work force and out of unions. Because the WTUL backed away from active union organization, it lost the support of working class women, and by 1930 it had virtually dissolved.

Organized labor also excluded most immigrant and black workers. Some trade unions welcomed skilled immigrants—in fact, foreign-born craftsmen were prominent leaders of several unions—but only the Knights of Labor and the IWW had firm policies of accepting immigrants and blacks. A few AFL unions included blacks, but exclusion policies kept out the vast majority. Resentments already fueled by long-held prejudices increased when blacks and immigrants worked as strikebreakers. It is likely that few strikebreakers understood the full effects of such employment when they were recruited to fill the jobs of striking workers; but even for those who did, the lure of employment was too great to resist.

The millions of men, women, and children who were not unionized tried in their own ways to cope with the pressures of the new machine age. Increasing numbers of workers, both native-born and immigrants, turned to fraternal societies. These organizations, which for small monthly or yearly contributions provided members with life insurance, sickness benefits, and funeral expenses, became increasingly widespread by the early twentieth century. For many workers, issues of wages and hours were meaningless; obtaining and holding a job was the first priority. Job instability and the seasonal nature of work seriously hindered organizing efforts. Few companies employed a full work force all year round; most employers hired during peak seasons and laid off workers during slack periods. Thus employment rates often fluctuated wildly. The 1880 census showed that in some communities 30 percent or more of adult males had been unemployed at some time during the previous year.

For most American workers, then, the machine age had dubious results. Industrial wages rose between 1877 and 1914, boosting purchasing power and enabling the creation of a mass market for standardized goods (see Chapter 19). Yet in 1900 most employees worked sixty hours a week at wages that averaged 20 cents an hour for skilled work and 10 cents an hour for unskilled work. Factory workers fortunate enough to hold a job all year could expect annual incomes of only \$400 to \$500. Moreover, as wages rose, living costs increased even faster. The industrial transformation had thrust the United States into international leadership in economic capability. But in factories as well as on farms, some people were beginning to question whether a system based on ever-greater profits was the best way for Americans to create a world of peace and prosperity.

Suggestions for further reading

General

Daniel J. Boorstin, *The Americans: The Democratic Experience* (1973); Thomas C. Cochran and William Miller, *The Age of Enterprise* (1942); Carl N. Degler, *The Age of the Economic Revolution* (1977); Sigmund Diamond, ed., *The Nation Transformed* (1963); John A. Garraty, *The New Commonwealth, 1877–1890* (1968); Ray Ginger, *The Age of Excess* (1965); Samuel P. Hays, *The Response to Industrialism* (1975).

Technology and invention

Robert W. Bruce, *Bell: Alexander Graham Bell and the Conquest of Solitude* (1973); Roger Burlingame, *Henry Ford* (1957); George H. Daniels, *Science and Society in America* (1971); Sigfried Giedion, *Mechanization Takes Command* (1948); Frank E. Hill, *Ford: The Times, the Man, the Company* (1954); Matthew Josephson, *Edison* (1959); Leo Marx, *The Machine in the Garden: Technology and the Pastoral Ideal* (1964); Elting E. Morison, *Men, Machines, and Modern Times* (1966); Allan Nevins and Frank E. Hill, *Ford,* 3 vols. (1954–1962); Nathan Rosenberg, *Technology and American Economic Growth* (1972); Harold I. Sharlin, *The Making of the Electrical Age* (1963); Peter Temin, *Steel in Nineteenth Century America* (1964); Frederick A. White, *American Industrial Research Laboratories* (1961).

Industrialism, industrialists, and corporate growth

W. Elliot Brownless, *Dynamics of Ascent: A History of the American Economy,* 2nd ed. (1979); Stuart Bruchey, *Growth of the Modern Economy* (1973); Alfred D. Chandler, *Pierre S. du Pont and the Making of the Modern Corporation* (1971); Alfred D. Chandler, *Strategy and Structure: Chapters in the History of American Industrial Enterprise* (1966); Alfred D. Chandler, *The Visible Hand: The Managerial Revolution in American Business* (1977); Thomas C. Cochrane, *Business in American Life* (1972); Francis L. Eames, *The New York Stock Exchange* (1968); Rendigs Fels, *American Business Cycles, 1865–1897* (1959); Samuel Haber, *Efficiency and Uplift: Scientific Management in the Progressive Era* (1964); Robert Higgs, *The Transformation of the American Economy, 1865–1914* (1971); Matthew Josephson, *The Robber Barons* (1934); Edward C. Kirkland, *Industry Comes of Age* (1961); Harold C. Livesay, *Andrew Carnegie and the Rise of Big Business* (1975); David F. Hawkes, *John D.: The Founding Father of the Rockefellers* (1980); Allan Nevins, *Study in Power: John D. Rockefeller,* 2 vols. (1953); Glen Porter, *The Rise of Big Business* (1973); Joseph Wall, *Andrew Carnegie* (1970).

Attitudes toward industrialism

Edward Bellamy, *Looking Backward* (1888); Sidney Fine, *Laissez Faire and the General Welfare State* (1956); Louis Galambos and Barbara Barron Spence, *The Public Image of Big Business in America* (1975); Henry George, *Progress and Poverty* (1880); Richard Hofstadter, *Social Darwinism in American Thought,* rev. ed. (1955); Henry Demarest Lloyd, *Wealth Against Commonwealth* (1894); Robert McCloskey, *American Conservatism in the Age of Enterprise* (1951).

Work and labor organization

Robert V. Bruce, *1877: Year of Violence* (1959); Stanley Buder, *Pullman* (1967); Henry David, *The Haymarket Affair* (1936); Alan Dawley, *Class and Community* (1977); Melvyn Dubofsky, *Industrialism and the American Worker* (1975); Melvyn Dubofsky, *We Shall Be All: A History of the Industrial Workers of the World* (1969); Philip S. Foner, *The Great Labor Uprising of 1877* (1977); Herbert G. Gutman, *Work, Culture and Society in Industrializing America* (1976); Stuart Bruce Kaufman, *Samuel Gompers and the Origins of the American Federation of Labor* (1973); Susan Estabrook Kennedy, *If All We Did Was To Weep At Home: A History of White Working Class Women in America* (1979); Leon Litwack, ed., *The American Labor Movement* (1962); Harold Livesay, *Samuel Gompers and Organized Labor in America* (1978); Milton Meltzer, *Bread and Roses: The Struggle of American Labor, 1865–1915* (1967); David Montgomery, *Workers' Control in America: Studies in the History of Work, Technology, and Labor Struggles* (1979); Joseph G. Rayback, *A History of American Labor* (1959); Philip Taft, *The A. F. of L. in the Time of Gompers,* 2 vols. (1957–1959); Philip Taft, *Organized Labor in America* (1964); Daniel J. Walkowitz, *Worker City, Company Town* (1978); Barbara Mayer Wertheimer, *We Were There: The Story of Working Women in America* (1977); Leon J. Wolff, *Lockout: The Story of the Homestead Strike of 1892* (1965); Irwin Yellowitz, *Industrialization and the American Labor Movement* (1977).

Like other Americans of his day, popular writer James W. Buell found city life both fascinating and bewildering. "The first visit to New York," Buell wrote in *The Mysteries and Miseries of America's Great Cities* (1883),

> is always productive of a singular sensation . . . that you are as much out of your sphere as though some mighty occult force has suddenly transported you to a strange planet, the inhabitants of which were rushing about in their efforts to destroy themselves and every world in the infinite firmament.

The sights, sounds, and smells of the city were enough to daze any visitor. Clanging trolleys, smoky air, crowded streets, a jumble of languages, canyon walls of masonry–all these sensations and more contrasted starkly with the slow, quiet pace of village and farm. During the nineteenth century the United States became the most rapidly urbanizing nation in the western world. And its cities were places both of misery and of opportunity.

By the middle third of the nineteenth century, the nation's urban population–those living in places with eight thousand or more people–had begun to grow much faster than its rural population (see pages 227–229). But not until the 1880s did the United States begin to become a truly urban nation. By 1920 the major milestone of urbanization had been passed: that year's census showed that, for the first time, a majority of Americans (51.4 percent) lived in cities. This new fact of national life was fully as significant as the disappearance of the frontier in 1890. The era of the yeoman farmer was fading.

The city became a dominant force in American life by serving as a marketplace, which brought together the people, resources, and ideas that were in turn responsible for many of the changes American society was experiencing. By 1900 every section of the country had powerful urban centers, and a network of small, medium, and large cities spanned the entire continent. Only such industrializing states as Rhode Island and Massachusetts had been highly urbanized early in the nineteenth century, but other states' urban populations grew rapidly after the Civil War. By 1890 cities housed at least 40 percent of the populations of California, Colorado, Illinois, Ohio, and Maryland, as well as seven states in the Northeast. Even in the traditionally rural South, at least one out of every four people was a city dweller by 1920.

American cities attracted both exuberant admirers and sneering detractors. Some people reveled in the social and economic opportunities cities offered. As one editor wrote, it was "better [to] be the 1/1,000,000,000 of New York than the 1/1 of Aroostook County." Others found the crudeness of cities disquieting. "Having seen it," Rudyard Kipling wrote of Chicago, "I urgently desire never to see it again." But whatever people's personal impressions, the city had become basic to American life. To a large extent, modern American society has been shaped by the ways people built their cities and adjusted to the new urban environment.

The birth of the modern city

In March 1912, a party of street-railway officials boarded a private trolley car in downtown Boston. Traveling west to Worcester and Springfield in Massachusetts, then south to Hartford, New Britain, New Haven, Bridgeport, and Stamford in Connecticut, the car carried its passengers from one set of tracks to another. The journey ended when the car rolled into New York City, having made the entire trip on a continuous route of streetcar–not railroad–tracks. With enough patience and enough nickels for $2.40 in fares and transfers, anyone could have made the same trip. The possibility of such a journey illustrates the extraordinary connection between mass transit and urban growth that occurred at the end of the nineteenth century.

New shape of the city

By that time, the modern American city was reaching maturity. The compact city of the early nineteenth century–where residences were mixed in among shops, factories, and warehouses–had burst open. From Boston to San Francisco, developed areas sprawled outward several miles from the original central core. No longer did walking distance determine a city's size, and no longer did different social groups live physically close together–poor near rich, immigrant near native, black near white. Instead, cities

Sometimes the extension of mass transit preceded residential development. This trolley line in Oak Park, Illinois, a suburb of Chicago, was built in anticipation of the housing construction that eventually filled the lots on either side of the tracks. Photographed in 1903. Oak Park Public Library.

were divided into distinct districts: working-class neighborhoods, black ghettos, a ring of suburbs, business districts. Two forces were responsible for this new arrangement. One was centrifugal, propelling people and enterprises outward from the confines of the old walking city. The other was centripetal, drawing human and economic resources inward. Mass transportation powered the centrifugal force; economic change, the centripetal.

Mass transportation enabled people to move faster and farther. Before the 1870s, horse- and mule-drawn vehicles had been the major means of mass transport. But they were inefficient. They could carry relatively few riders, and purchasing, feeding, and cleaning up after the animals was costly. In 1880, for example, the 150,000 horses in New York City and Brooklyn produced between 1,000 and 1,500 tons of manure daily, about 1.5 pounds per human inhabitant. Though of a different nature than it is today, pollution was a fact of urban life in the nineteenth century too.

Once the technology was developed for doing so, entrepreneurs began to seek better ways to transport people. Steam-powered commuter railroads had appeared in a few cities during the 1850s and 1860s, but not until the late 1870s did inventors begin to mechanize municipal mass transit. The first power-driven devices were cable cars—carriages that traveled over tracks by clamping onto a moving underground wire. Cheaper than horse cars, cable cars could also haul passengers up and down steep hills. In the 1880s cable-car lines were constructed in Chicago, San Francisco, and many other cities.

Mechanization of mass transportation

By the 1890s, however, electric-powered streetcars were replacing the early forms of mass transit. Designed almost simultaneously by Charles J. Van Doeple in Montgomery, Alabama, and Frank Sprague in Richmond, Virginia, electric trolleys spread quickly to nearly every large city. Between 1890 and 1902, total mileage of electrified track in American cities grew

Outward urban sprawl created pleasant neighborhoods for families who could afford to flee the crowds, noise, crime, and pollution of the central city. Thus middle-class suburbs like this one in Toledo, Ohio, with their large detached houses, grassy yards, and tree-lined streets, became common in the late nineteenth and early twentieth centuries. Photographed in 1899. Library of Congress.

from 1,300 to 22,000 miles. Meanwhile horse-railway track shrank from 5,700 to 250 miles. "The long-haired mule shall no longer adorn our streets," mused one observer.

In a few cities, transit companies raised part of their track onto stilts, enabling vehicles to travel through jammed downtown districts without interference from other traffic. And in Boston, New York, and Philadelphia, mass transit companies dug underground passages for their cars, again to avoid tie-ups and delays. These elevated railroads and subways were, however, extremely expensive to construct. They thus appeared only in the few cities where companies could amass enough capital to build them and where there were enough riders to make for high profits.

Mass transportation lines launched millions of urban dwellers into outlying neighborhoods and created a commuting public. Now those who could afford the fare—usually five cents a ride—could live outside the crowded, dirty central city and still return there for work, shopping, and entertainment. Working-class families, whose incomes rarely topped a dollar a day, found even the nickel fare too high and could not take advantage of the streetcars. But for the growing middle class, a home in a quiet, tree-lined neighborhood became a real possibility. Real estate development boomed around the periphery of scores of cities. Between 1890 and 1920, for example, developers in the Chicago area opened 800,000 new lots—enough to house at least three times the city's population in 1890. A home several miles from downtown

Beginnings of urban sprawl

was inconvenient, but the benefits seemed to outweigh the costs. As one suburbanite wrote in 1902, "It may be a little more difficult for us to attend the opera, but the robin in my elm tree struck a higher note and a sweeter one yesterday than any *prima donna* ever reached."

Urban sprawl was essentially unplanned. Eager to capitalize on new commuting possibilities, thousands of small investors who bought residential land in anticipation of settlement paid little attention to the need for parks, traffic control, and public services. Moreover, construction of mass transit lines was guided by the profit motive and thus served the urban public unevenly. Streetcar lines serviced mainly those neighborhoods that promised the most riders—whose fares, in other words, would provide dividends for stockholders.

Streetcars, elevateds, and subways altered commercial as well as residential patterns. As consumers moved outward along mass transit lines, businesses followed. Secondary business centers sprouted at trolley line intersections and elevated-railway stations. Branches of downtown department stores and banks joined groceries, theaters, drug stores, taverns, and specialty shops to create neighborhood shopping centers, the forerunners of today's shopping malls. Meanwhile, the urban core became the work zone, where offices, stores, warehouses, and factories hulked over streets clogged with traffic. Districts like Chicago's Loop and New York's lower Manhattan concentrated together practically every kind of business and cultural institution.

Cities also became the main arenas for industrial growth, generating and attracting concentrations of economic power. As centers of resources, labor, transportation, and communications, cities provided everything factories needed. Capital accumulated by the early commercial enterprises of cities—attracting and distributing raw materials and finished goods—fed industrial investment once mass production became possible. And urban populations furnished consumers for myriad new products. Thus urban growth and industrialization wound together in a mutually productive spiral. The further industrialization advanced, the more opportunities it created for work and investment in cities. Increased opportunity drew more people to cities; as workers and as consumers, they in turn fueled further industrialization. By the end of the nineteenth century, urban firms were producing nine-tenths of America's industrial output.

Urban-industrial development

Although most cities contained a wide variety of industrial activities, specialization in a single kind of production became common. Some cities used large numbers of immigrant workers in the mass production of clothing. The shoe industry became prominent in Philadelphia and Lynn, ready-made garments in New York City, and textiles in several New England cities. Other cities processed products from surrounding agricultural regions: flour in Minneapolis, cottonseed oil in Memphis, beer in Milwaukee. Still others processed natural resources: gold and copper in Denver, fish and lumber in Seattle, coal and iron in Pittsburgh and Birmingham, oil in Houston and Los Angeles. These and countless other activities increased the magnetic attraction of cities and broadened urban opportunities.

Urban growth and industrial development transformed the national economy and freed the United States from dependence on European capital and manufactured goods. Imports and foreign investments still flowed into the country. But by the second decade of the twentieth century, cities and their factories, stores, and banks were converting the United States from a debtor agricultural nation into a major industrial and financial power.

Peopling the cities

Economist Edmund J. James had good reason to assert in 1899 that the era he was living in was "not only the age of cities but the age of great cities." Between 1870 and 1920, the total number of people living in American cities exploded from 9.9 million to 54.3 million. During the same period, the number of cities with populations over 100,000 grew from fifteen to sixty-eight, and the number with more than 500,000 people swelled from two to twelve (see maps, pages 498–499). These figures are dramatic enough by themselves, but they also summarize millions of stories of hope and frustration, adjustment and confusion, success and failure.

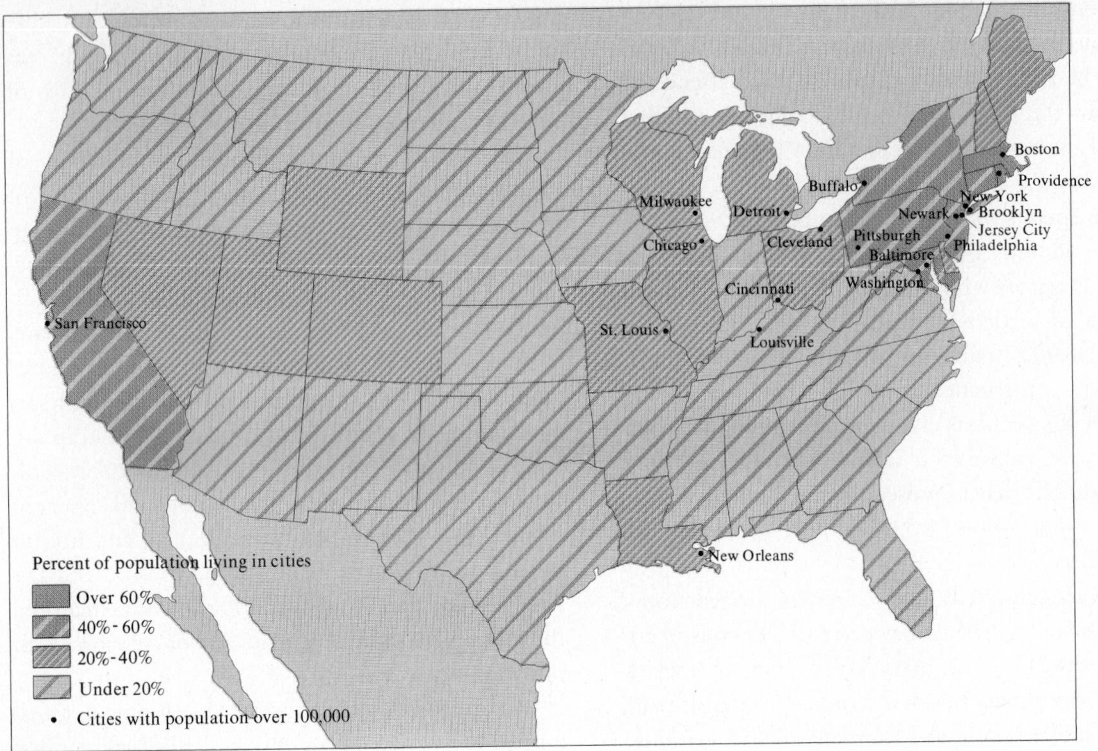

Urbanization, 1880

The population of any given place can grow in three ways: by the extension of its borders to include nearby land and people; by natural increase—an excess of births over deaths; and by migration—an excess of in-migrants over out-migrants. From the end of the Civil War until the early 1900s, many cities annexed nearby suburbs and other areas, thereby increasing their populations. Everywhere the thirst for expansion was insatiable. The most notable consolidation occurred in 1898 when New York City, which had previously consisted only of Manhattan, merged with four surrounding boroughs and grew overnight from 1.5 million to over 3 million people. As one observer remarked, "Those who locate near the city limits are bound to know that the time may come when [the city] will extend the limits and take them in." More important, annexation added land where new city dwellers could live. Cities like Chicago, Minneapolis, and Cincinnati incorporated hundreds of undeveloped square miles into their borders in the 1880s, only to see them fill up in succeeding decades. Although annexation did increase urban populations, its major effect was to enlarge the physical size of cities.

How cities grew

As death rates declined in the late nineteenth century, the populations of most cities increased naturally. But urban birth rates also fell steadily throughout the nineteenth century. As a result, natural increase did not account for very much of any city's population growth—usually no more than 20 percent over a decade.

Migration and immigration made by far the greatest contribution to urban population growth. In fact, migration to cities nearly matched the migration to the West that was occurring at the same time. Each year millions of people were on the move, many of them lured by the cities' promise of opportunity. Urban newcomers arrived from two major sources: the American countryside and Europe. Asia, Canada, and Latin America also supplied immigrants, but in much smaller numbers.

In all sections of the country, a variety of factors dashed farmers' hopes and drove farm families off the land and toward the cities. The rural populations of Vermont, New York, Ohio, Illinois, and other states

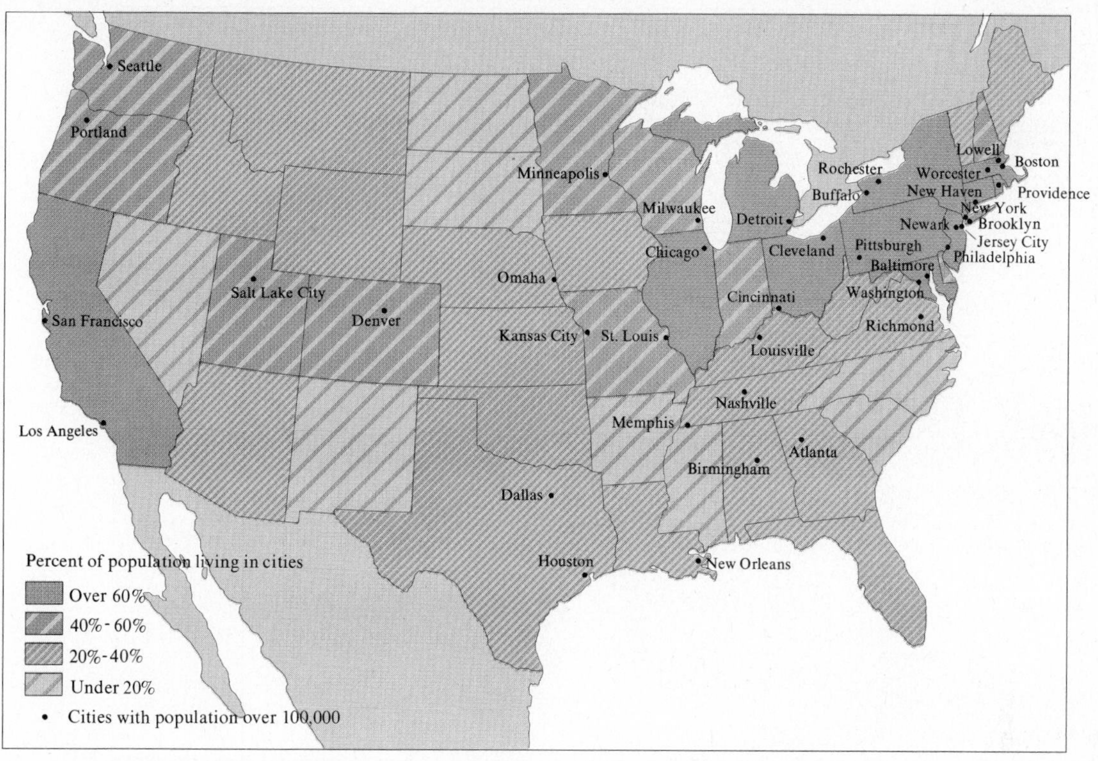

Urbanization, 1920

Major waves of migration and immigration

declined during the 1880s as their urban populations mushroomed. Growth occurred not only in New York, Cleveland, Detroit, and Chicago, but also in scores of secondary cities like Toledo, Indianapolis, Grand Rapids, Peoria, Salt Lake City, Birmingham, and San Diego. The thrill and bustle of city life beckoned especially to young people. A character in George Fitch's play *The City* voiced the dreams of many youths when she exclaimed, "Who wants to smell new-mown hay, if he can breathe in gasoline on Fifth Avenue instead! Think of the theaters! the crowds! *Think* of being able to go out on the street and *see some one you didn't know by sight!*"

An even larger group of newcomers consisted of immigrants who had fled European farms and villages to American shores. Many did not intend to stay. They hoped instead to make enough money to return home and live in greater comfort and security. For every hundred foreigners who entered the country, around thirty left. Still, most of the 26 million European immigrants who arrived between 1870 and 1920 stayed, and the great majority settled in cities, where they helped to shape modern American culture. "America appealed to me very much," one immigrant remembered. "The whole country seemed to be at the roof of the world."

The influx of immigrants came in two waves. The first began in the 1840s and crested in the 1880s, and the second climaxed between 1900 and 1910. The first wave consisted mainly of Protestants and Catholics from Germany, Scandinavia, Ireland, and England, most of whom entered through eastern ports. At the same time a small number of Chinese and Mexicans arrived in the West and Southwest. The second wave contained mainly Catholics and Jews from eastern and southern Europe, plus smaller contingents from Canada and Mexico (see maps, page 500). Although immigrants from northern and western Europe continued to arrive after 1890, the numerical shift between the two waves was dramatic. In 1882, for example, 87 percent of that year's 648,000 immigrants came from northern or western Europe; some 251,000 were Germans. In 1907, however, 81 percent of the 1.2 million immigrants came from southern or eastern Europe,

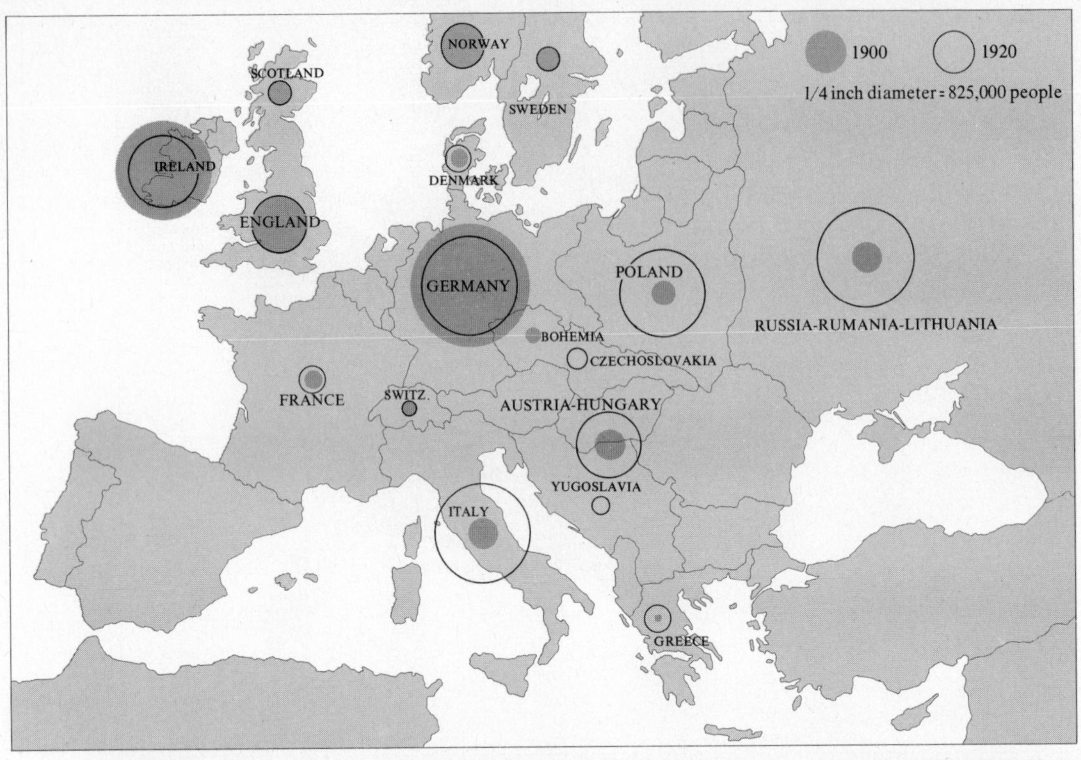

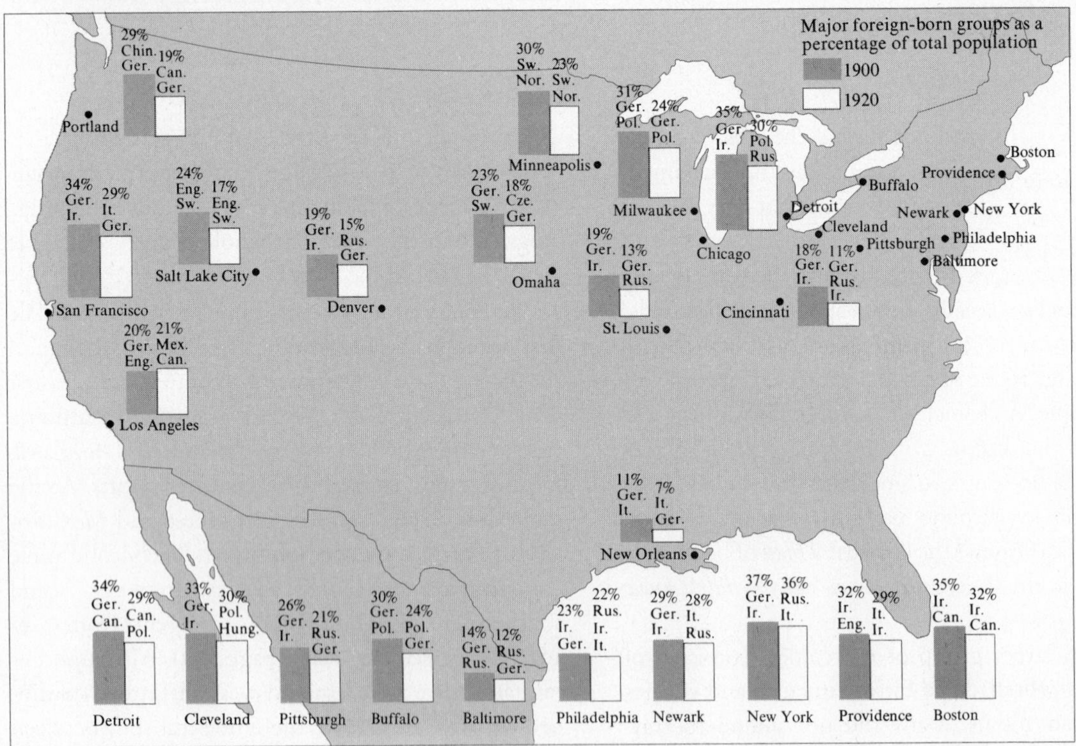

Sources of foreign-born population, 1900 and 1920

Foreign-Born Population of the United States, 1870–1930, in Thousands

PLACE OF BIRTH	1870	1880	1890	1900	1910	1920	1930
England, Scotland, and Wales	770.2	917.6	1,251.4	1,167.6	1,221.3	1,135.5	1,224.1
Ireland	1,855.8	1,854.6	1,871.5	1,615.5	1,352.3	1,037.2	923.6
Other Northern Europe	498.4	723.0	1,257.8	1,419.6	1,665.5	1,657.4	1,580.3
Germany	1,690.5	1,966.7	2,784.9	2,663.4	2,311.2	1,686.1	1,608.8
Eastern Europe	93.9	221.0	635.7	1,473.2	3,702.8	4,448.7	4,289.0
Southern Europe	25.9	58.3	206.6	530.2	1,525.9	1,911.2	2,106.3
Canada	493.5	717.2	980.9	1,179.9	1,204.6	1,224.9	1,286.4
Other American	57.9	89.5	107.3	137.5	284.6	602.1	815.8
Other Foreign	81.0	132.2	153.3	154.4	247.7	317.5	369.8
Total Foreign-born	5,667.2	6,679.9	9,249.6	10,341.3	13,515.9	13,920.7	14,204.1

Percentages of Total Population

PLACE OF BIRTH	1870	1880	1890	1900	1910	1920	1930
England, Scotland, and Wales	13.6	13.7	13.5	11.3	9.1	8.2	8.6
Ireland	32.7	27.8	20.2	15.6	10.0	7.5	6.5
Other Northern Europe	8.8	10.8	13.6	13.7	12.3	11.9	11.1
Germany	29.8	29.4	30.1	25.8	17.1	12.1	11.3
Eastern Europe	1.7	3.3	6.9	14.2	27.4	32.0	30.2
Southern Europe	0.5	0.9	2.2	5.1	11.3	13.7	14.8
Canada	8.7	10.7	10.6	11.4	8.9	8.1	9.1
Other American	1.0	1.3	1.2	1.3	2.1	4.3	5.7
Other Foreign	1.4	2.0	1.7	1.5	1.8	2.3	2.6

including 286,000 Italians and 259,000 Russians. Together, the two waves of immigration helped swell the number of foreign-born people in the United States from 5.7 million in 1870 to 14 million in 1920 (see table).

The differences between the two waves of immigrants were in many ways more imagined than real. Many natives feared that the strange customs, non-Protestant religions, illiteracy, and poverty of the "new" immigrants made them less desirable and assimilable than the "old" immigrants, whose languages and beliefs seemed less alien. This view received sober support from authorities like future president Woodrow Wilson, who wrote in his popular *History of the American People* (1902), "The immigrant newcomers of recent years are men of the lowest class from the South of Italy, and men of the meaner sort out of Hungary and Poland, men out of the ranks

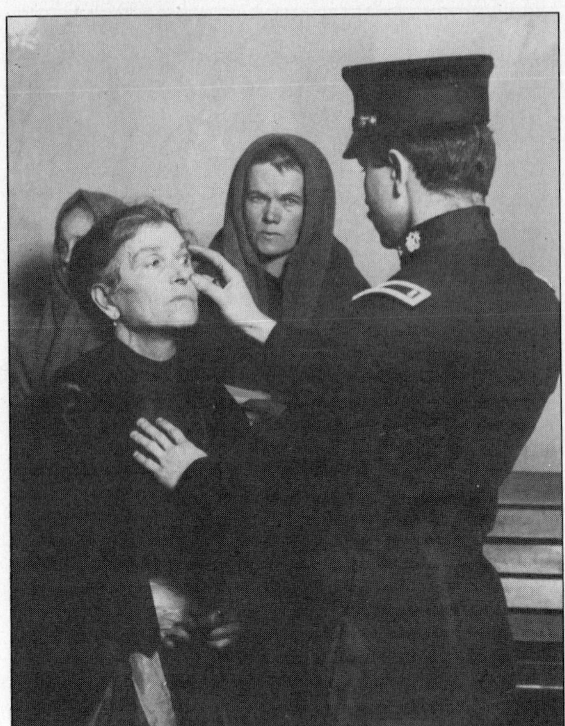

An immigrant woman undergoing a health examination at Ellis Island in New York Harbor. The Keystone-Mast Collection, University of California, Riverside.

where there was neither skill nor energy, nor any initiative or quick intelligence."

In reality, however, the old and new immigrants resembled each other more closely than many Americans wished to believe. The majority of both groups were young–some 60 to 80 percent of all immigrants were between fifteen and forty-four–and male: about 60 percent were men. The majority of both groups settled in cities, though a somewhat greater proportion of the new immigrants did so–78.6 percent to 68.3 percent. Most lived initially in the old districts of the central city vacated by residents who had moved to newly developed outlying neighborhoods.

Perhaps most important, all immigrants brought with them memories of their homelands and adjusted to American life in light of those memories. In new surroundings where the language was a struggle, the workday followed the clock rather than the sun, and housing and employment were often uncertain, immigrants anchored their lives on what they knew best: their culture. Many immigrant neighborhoods were made up of enclaves of Irish immigrants from the same county, Italians from the same province, and Russian Jews from the same *shtetl* (village). In these transplanted communities, Old World customs persisted. People practiced their religions as they always had, held traditional feasts and pageants, married within their group, and pursued old feuds with people from rival villages and provinces. As in eastern Europe, Jewish men grew long sidelocks, women wore wigs, and children were sent to afternoon religious training. Italians transplanted the system whereby a boss, or *padrone,* found jobs for unskilled workers by acting as a broker between an employer and a labor gang. Though the *padrone* profited excessively from this arrangement and often abused his power, he performed an important function. As one immigrant testified, "Signorino, we are ignorant and do not know English. Our boss brought us here, knows where to find work, makes contracts with companies. What should we do without him?"

Immigrant cultures

Yet the very diversity of American cities forced most immigrants to modify their attitudes and habits. Few newcomers could avoid contact with people different from themselves, and few could prevent such contacts from altering their traditional ways of life. Although many foreigners identified themselves by their village or region of birth, native-born Americans categorized immigrants by nationality–a tendency that resulted both from innocent classification and from vicious stereotyping. Thus people from County Cork and County Limerick were lumped together as Irish or "drunken micks"; those from Schleswig and Wurttemberg became Germans or "fat krauts"; and those from Calabria and Campobasso became Italians or "dumb dagoes." Mutual benefit and fraternal societies that aided the sick and paid burial expenses continued to be organized along village and provincial lines. But other immigrant institutions, such as newspapers and churches, found they had to appeal more broadly to the entire nationality group in order to survive.

Still other forces chipped away at old loyalties. Although many immigrants struggled to maintain their native languages and to pass them down to younger generations, English was taught in the schools and needed on the job; it soon penetrated nearly every community. Because the goods available in America

An immigrant family at home in their tenement. Though immigrant families were often large and their living conditions difficult, the newcomers displayed resilience and persistence in adapting to a strange environment. The people shown here were poor but proud, with a sense of integrity that shows in their faces. Bettmann Archive.

often differed from those of the homeland, immigrants were forced to adjust their life styles to resemble those of other Americans. Foreigners did not automatically adopt American habits: they continued to cook ethnic meals using American foods and fashioned American fabrics in European styles. Still, convenience and availability influenced their material culture. Thousands of immigrant families bought the American ready-made clothing and mass-produced furniture that were commonplace in the larger society.

The influx of so many immigrants between 1870 and 1920 transformed the United States from a basically Protestant nation into a society of Protestants, Catholics, and Jews. Newcomers from Italy, Hungary, and what would become Czechoslovakia, Yugoslavia, and Poland joined the Irish and Germans to boost the proportion of Catholics in several large cities. In places like Buffalo, Cleveland, Chicago, and Milwaukee, Catholic immigrants and their offspring approached a majority of the population. German and eastern European immigrants gave New York one of the largest Jewish populations in the world.

Partly in response to Protestant-based charges that they could not retain Old World religious beliefs and still assimilate into American society, many Catholics and Jews tried to accommodate their faiths to the new environment. A number of Catholic clerical leaders and Jewish rabbis–usually from older, more established immigrant groups–supported liberalizing trends such as the use of English in services, the phasing-out of Old World rituals such as saints' feasts, and a preference for public over parochial schooling. As long as new immigrants continued to arrive, however, these tendencies met stiff opposition. The newcomers usually sought to retain their traditional religious practices, whether the folk Catholicism of southern Italy or the orthodox Judaism of eastern Europe; they recoiled from attempted reforms. Thus Catholic immigrants continued to press for ethnically separate parishes in spite of church attempts to make American Catholicism more uniform. Bishops often had to accede to strong pressure for Polish rather than German-born priests to serve predominantly Polish congregations, for French-Canadian rather than Irish priests to serve predominantly French-Canadian congregations. Eastern European Jews hostile to Reform Judaism (see page 315) established the Conservative branch of their faith, which retained more traditional ritual though it did abolish the segregation of women in synagogues and eased English prayers into the service.

In the 1880s, another group of migrants began to move into American cities. Thousands of rural blacks moved northward and westward, fleeing crop liens, violence, and political oppression and seeking better employment. Although their numbers would grow much larger after 1915, thirty-two cities contained ten thousand or more blacks by 1900, and 79 percent of all blacks outside the South lived in cities. Black migrants resembled foreign immigrants in their peasant backgrounds and economic motivations, but they differed in several important ways. Because very few factories would employ blacks, most black workers found jobs in the service sector–cleaning, cooking, carting–rather than the industrial trades. Also, because the majority of jobs in domestic and personal service were traditionally female jobs, black women outnumbered black men in most cities. In places like New York, Baltimore, and New Orleans, there were five black women for every four black men.

Black migration to the cities

Together the three major migrant groups that peopled American cities–native whites, foreigners, and native blacks–sowed the seeds of modern American culture, to which each group made important contributions. Just as the cities had grown up because they centralized the varied economic functions of commerce, finance, and production, so too they nurtured rich cultural variety: American folk music and literature, Italian cuisine, Irish comedy, Yiddish theater, Afro-American jazz and dance, and much more. Like their predecessors, newcomers in the late nineteenth century changed their environment as much as they were changed by it.

Straining to meet urban needs

The migration patterns and economic and technological changes of the late nineteenth century segmented urban society into racial, ethnic, and class divisions. Outward residential sprawl separated the most advantaged classes from the least advantaged, most of whom were newcomers. Lacking resources and unfamiliar with urban ways, immigrants and native migrants jammed inner-city districts, where they were known less for their contributions than for the problems they bred. Late-nineteenth-century American cities seemed to harbor all the evils that plagued the modern world: crowding, disease, crime, poverty, decay, and other unpleasant conditions that result when large numbers of people are jammed tightly together. These problems were compounded by rapid growth and by the fact that neither government nor the marketplace were willing or equipped to handle them. City dwellers generally adjusted as best they could until technology, science, private enterprise, or public authority could alleviate their problems. Some urban ills still await solution.

One of the most persistent shortcomings of American cities has been their failure to provide adequate housing to all who need it. This failure has deep roots in nineteenth-century urban development. The low-paying jobs of most working-class household heads restricted the type of housing they could obtain for their families. As they had done in Europe and in American rural areas, urban newcomers usually rented

Housing problems

The Lower East Side of New York City, home of thousands of Russian Jews and other immigrants, was one of the most famous ethnic districts in the nation. Inside the tenements people were jammed together in alarming squalor. But the streets were always alive with peddlers and pedestrians, giving the area a rich cultural fabric. Photographed in the first decade of the twentieth century. Library of Congress.

their living quarters. Few could afford to buy or build a house. As cities grew, landlords took advantage of shortages in low-cost rental housing by splitting up existing buildings to house more people, constructing multiple-unit tenements, and hiking rents. Low-income families adjusted to high housing costs and short supply by sharing space and expenses. Thus it became common in many big cities for a one-family apartment to be occupied by two or three families or by one family plus a number of paying boarders.

The result was unprecedented crowding. In 1893, there were 702 people per acre in the heart of New York City's immigrant-packed lower East Side, one of the highest population densities in the world. Low-rent districts had distinctive physical appearances: block after block of six- to eight-story barracks-like buildings in New York; dilapidated row houses in Baltimore and Philadelphia; converted slave quarters in Charleston and New Orleans; and crumbling two- and three-story frame houses in Boston, Chicago, and St. Louis. Everywhere the crowding was acute.

Inside many buildings, living conditions were intolerable. The largest rooms were barely ten feet wide, and interior rooms either had no windows at all or opened onto narrow shafts that bred vermin and rotten odors. "You see," said an immigrant housekeeper describing one such shaft, "it's damp down there, and the families, they throw out garbage and dirty papers and the insides of chickens, and other unmentionable filth. . . . I just vomited when I first cleaned up the air

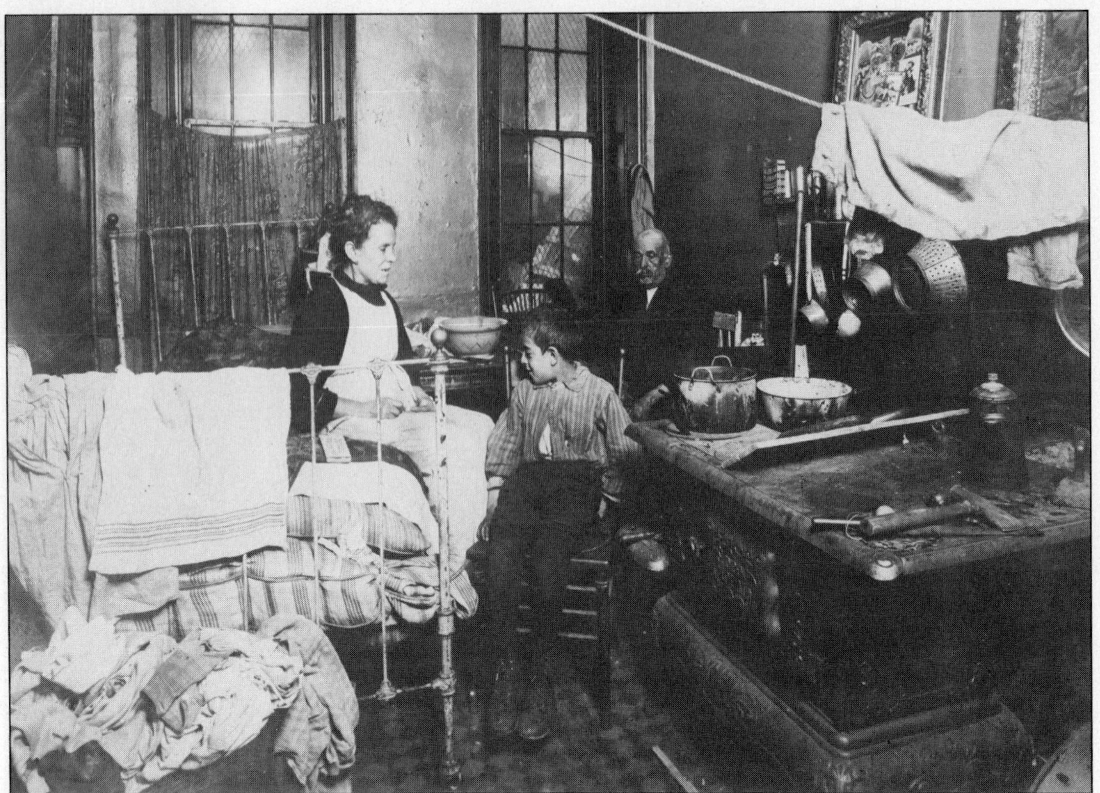

A tiny tenement room often had to serve as sleeping quarters, living space, storage space, kitchen, and washroom all at once. This family, too poor to afford more space, had to improvise, using the stove both for cooking and heat and the mattresses both for sitting and sleeping. Note the clothes stored on the floor, the wash basin resting beside the bed, and the laundry hanging on an overhead line. Photographed by Lewis Hine. Library of Congress.

shaft." Few buildings had indoor plumbing, and the only source of heat was coal-burning stoves. The crush of people and lack of privacy in such quarters offended middle-class sensibilities. As a dismayed New York *Times* reporter wrote, "young girls are found sleeping on the floor in rooms where are crowded men, women, youths, and children. Delicacy is never known, purity is lost before its meaning is understood."

In several places acute housing problems aroused concerned citizens to mount reform campaigns. New York State took the lead in 1867, 1879, and 1901 by legislating light, ventilation, and safety codes for new tenement buildings. These and similar laws in other states could not remedy the ills of existing buildings, but they did impose government regulation on landlords' property rights. A few housing reformers, such as Jacob Riis and Lawrence Veiller, advocated housing low-income families in model tenements, with more spacious, airier rooms and better facilities. Model tenements, however, required landlords and investors to accept lower profits—a sacrifice few were willing to make. Neither humanitarian reformers nor public officials would consider government support of better housing, fearing such a step would undermine private enterprise. Still, the various codes and commissions that resulted from reform campaigns did strengthen the power of local government to regulate housing construction.

Although housing reforms had only limited success, scientific and technological advances enabled city dwellers and the nation in general to live in greater comfort and safety. By the 1880s and 1890s, most doctors had accepted the germ theory of disease. As a result, cities established more efficient systems of water purification and sewage disposal. Although disease and death rates remained higher in the city than the countryside, and tuberculosis and other respiratory ills continued to plague inner-city districts, public-health regulations reduced death rates and helped to control such dread diseases as cholera, typhoid fever, and diphtheria. Street paving, modernized firefighting equipment, and electric streetlighting spread rapidly across urban America. Steel-frame construction, which supported a building by a metal skeleton rather than masonry walls, made possible the construction of skyscrapers—and thus more efficient use of scarce, costly urban land. Electric elevators and improved steam-heating systems serviced these increasingly tall buildings. Streetcars and subways hastened the pace of urban travel, and steel-cable suspension bridges, developed by John A. Roebling and epitomized by the great Brooklyn Bridge (completed in 1883), linked metropolitan sections more closely.

But none of these improvements lightened the burden of poverty borne by large numbers of city dwellers. The urban economy, though generally expanding, advanced erratically. Employment opportunities, especially for unskilled workers in manufacturing and construction, rose and fell with business cycles and changing seasons. Often, to make ends meet, more than one member of a working-class family had to work. But the wages other family members could earn were minuscule. Thus an ever-increasing number of urban families lived on the margins of survival, where any kind of unlucky occurrence could plunge them into destitution.

Urban poverty

In 1904, social worker Robert Hunter published *Poverty,* a study that bared the contrast between the myth of equality and the grim realities of life. Though his data were extreme because of the vicissitudes of urban life, they showed evidence of tragic conditions throughout the United States, not just in cities. "There are," he wrote,

> probably in fairly prosperous years no less than 10,000,000 persons in poverty [out of a total population of about 80,000,000]; that is to say, underfed, underclothed, and poorly housed. Of these about 4,000,000 persons are public paupers. Over 2,000,000 working-men are unemployed from four to six months in the year. About 500,000 male immigrants arrive yearly and seek work in the very districts where unemployment is greatest. Nearly half of the families in the country are propertyless. Over 1,700,000 little children are forced to become wage-earners when they should still be in school. About 500,000 women find it necessary to work, and about 2,000,000 are employed in factories, mills, etc. Probably no less than 1,000,000 workers are injured or killed each year while doing their work, and about 10,000,000 of the persons now living will . . . die of . . . tuberculosis.

Since colonial days, Americans have never agreed on how much responsibility the general public should assume for poor relief. In the late nineteenth and early twentieth centuries, many people held to the traditional beliefs that anyone could escape poverty through hard work and clean living and that poverty was inevitable only because some people were weaker than others. Such reasoning, fed by Social Darwinism, bred fears that assistance to poor people would encourage paupers to depend on public relief rather than self-reliance. As the numbers of poverty cases increased, this attitude hardened, and many city governments discontinued direct grants of food, fuel, and clothing to needy families. Instead, cities either provided relief in return for work on public projects or sent special cases to state-run institutions such as almshouses, orphanages, and homes for the blind, deaf, mentally ill, and physically handicapped.

Private philanthropic agencies also concerned themselves with helping only the "worthy poor," but their efforts to organize relief more efficiently did foster some change in attitude. Between 1877 and 1892, philanthropists in ninety-two cities formed Charity Organization Societies, an attempt to put social welfare on a more scientific and systematic basis by merging disparate charity groups into a single coordinated unit. Believing poverty to be the result of personal defects such as alcoholism and laziness, members of these organizations spent most of their time visiting poor families and encouraging them to be thriftier and more virtuous.

Yet close observation of the poor caused some social welfare workers to conclude that people's environments, rather than their personal defects, caused poverty. That is, they came to believe that the ills of poverty could be cured by improving housing, sanitation, and job opportunities rather than by admonishing the poor to be more moral. This new attitude, which had been gaining ground since the mid-nineteenth century, fueled drives for building codes, factory regulations, and public-health measures. The environmental interpretation of poverty also motivated investigations of slum conditions and the establishment of settlement houses to improve life in inner-city neighborhoods. Nevertheless, most middle- and upper-class Americans remained wedded to the belief that in a society of abundance only the unfit were poor, and that relief of poverty should be tolerated but never encouraged. As one charity worker urged, relief "should be surrounded by circumstances that shall . . . repel every one . . . from accepting it."

Even more than crowding and pauperism, crime and disorder alarmed Americans and nurtured fears that urban growth, especially the growth of slums, was corrupting the nation. Though the causes of criminal behavior are unclear, there has always been a close correlation between high crime rates and areas of high poverty, overcrowding, and transiency. The more cities grew, it seemed, the more they shook with violence. In Chicago, for example, the annual number of murders increased from 1,266 (or 25 per million people) in 1881 to 7,840 (or 107 per million) in 1898. Pickpockets, swindlers, sneak thieves, and holdup men roamed every city. Native whites were quick to blame immigrants and blacks for the so-called crime waves that swept the nation. Indeed, the names and origins of some of the most notorious criminals seemed to support such accusations.

Crime and violence

Yet it is possible that as a greater proportion of the population concentrated in cities, crime merely became more conspicuous and sensational rather than more prevalent. To be sure, urban wealth and the mingling of different kinds of people provided new opportunities for lawless behavior, such as organized thievery, petty larceny, vice, and violent grudge-settling. But how do such activities compare to the lawlessness and brutality of backwoods mining camps and southern plantations? Moreover, in spite of distress over Irish bank-robbery gangs, German pickpockets, and Italian Black Hand murderers, there is little evidence that more immigrants than natives populated the rogues' gallery. One investigation of jails in 1900 concluded that "we have ourselves evolved as cruel and cunning criminals as any that Europe may have foisted upon us."

Whatever the extent of criminality, city life in the late nineteenth and early twentieth centuries certainly supported the thesis that there is a tradition of violence in the United States. Cities served as arenas for many of the era's worst riots. As laborers and employers tried to adjust to the uncertainties of industrialization, violence became, in the words of one observer, "a sort of natural and inevitable concomitant." And urban ethnic and racial minorities were often victims of the violent bigotry that was the underside of the American myth of equality. The cityward movement of black people roused white fears, and as the twentieth century dawned, a series of race riots spread across the nation: Wilmington, North Carolina, 1898; Atlanta, Georgia, 1906; Springfield, Illinois, 1908. In the cities of the Southwest and Pacific Coast, Chinese and Mexican immigrants often felt the vicious sting of native intolerance. And in addition to the most violent outbreaks, thousands of minor disruptive events made cities scenes of constant turbulence. In Providence, Rhode Island, in 1914, for example, a band of Italian immigrants protested a pasta dealer's decision to raise prices by breaking into his shop, scattering his macaroni onto the street, and battling the police who tried to restore order. In several cities, Jewish women protesting high prices at kosher meat markets had to be restrained by police.

Since early in the nineteenth century, city dwellers had increasingly depended on the police to protect life and property. But by the early 1900s law enforcement had become a complicated and controversial issue, because different groups had different interpretations of the law and how it should be enforced. Nearly everywhere, the police had three major functions: preventing and investigating crime, preserving order, and aiding people in trouble. The third function was and is the least controversial, least publicized, but most common. It included such deeds as searching for a lost child, rescuing someone from danger, and providing directions.

The first and second have always been more controversial, because they have raised questions about

The burgeoning cities required large professional police forces to keep order and protect life and property. Station houses like this one became important neighborhood outposts, and the police department an avenue of upward mobility for immigrants. Library of Congress.

how equally police power is applied. Disadvantaged groups—usually ethnic and racial minorities—could not escape arrest as easily as those with economic or political influence. Individual police officers and station-house captains could apply the law less harshly to members of their own ethnic group (police work was a route of mobility for several immigrant groups) or to people who bought exemptions in the form of bribes or payoffs. Moreover, political and business leaders often enlisted the government's police power to break up strikes and demonstrations, but not to end or alleviate the exploitative conditions that caused such unrest among workers.

As the public's chief law-enforcement agency, the police were often caught between conflicting pressures for swift and severe action on the one hand and leniency on the other. For example, religious, business, and humanitarian leaders clamored for police crackdowns on drinking, gambling, and prostitution; but other people—including some from the complaining groups—privately supported loose law enforcement so they could indulge in these so-called customer crimes. As American society became more diversified, especially in the cities, and as different groups asserted different interests, achieving a balance between the idealistic intentions of criminal law and people's desire for individual freedom became increasingly difficult. It has remained so to this day.

Solving the mounting problems of city life seemed to many Americans to demand greater government action. Thus city governments passed more laws and ordinances that regulated housing, provided poverty relief, and expanded police power. Yet public responsibility always ended at the boundaries of private property. Constrained by laissez faire, local governments could do little to provide a better life for many of their citizens. Eventually some advances in housing construction, sanitation, and medical care did reach slum dwellers. But for most people, the only hope was to look to the next generation or to move elsewhere.

Promises of mobility

In the half-century between the Civil War and the First World War, Baptist minister Russell Conwell delivered the same sermon more than six thousand times to untold millions across the United States. Titled "Acres of Diamonds," his immensely popular lecture affirmed the widespread belief that any American could achieve success. People did not have to look very far for riches, Conwell preached; acres of diamonds lay at everyone's feet. Night after night, Conwell would declare to his audience, "the opportunity to get rich, to attain unto great wealth, is here . . . within the reach of almost every man and woman who hears me speak tonight . . . I say you ought to get rich, and it is your duty to get rich . . . If you can honestly attain unto riches it is your Christian and Godly duty to do so." Success, then, was not only possible; it was a religious obligation. But how possible was it for people actually to improve their lot and fulfill that duty?

Basically, there were three ways a person could get ahead: occupational advancement (and the higher income that accompanied it); acquisition of property (and the potential for greater wealth it represented); and migration to an area of better conditions and greater opportunity. In the period between 1877 and 1920, these options were open chiefly to white men. Although many women worked, owned property, and migrated, their social standing was usually defined by the men in their lives—their husbands, fathers, or other kin. Many women did improve their economic status by marrying men with wealth or potential, but other avenues were mostly closed. Women had access to far fewer occupational opportunities; they usually obtained what property they had through inheritance; and those who migrated usually accompanied their families. Men and women who were Afro-American, American Indian, Mexican-American, or members of other racial minorities had even fewer opportunities for success. Pinned to the bottom of society by prejudice, these groups were expected to accept their inherited station.

To a large number of Americans, however, the extensive urban and industrial expansion of the late nineteenth century should have offered broad opportunity for occupational mobility. Thousands of small businesses were needed to supply goods and services to burgeoning urban populations. As corporations grew larger and centralized their operations, they required a variety of managerial and clerical personnel. Although large loans were sometimes hard to obtain, a person could open a saloon or a small store for only $200 or $300. And rudimentary knowledge of accounting or typing could qualify one for a number of white-collar jobs that sometimes paid better than manual labor. Thus nonmanual work and the higher social status that accompanied it were altogether possible.

Occupational mobility

Such advancement occurred often. To be sure, only a very few traveled the rags-to-riches path that men like Andrew Carnegie and Henry Ford had discovered. Studies of the era's wealthiest businessmen have shown that the vast majority started their careers with distinct advantages: American birth, Protestant religion, better-than-average education, and relatively affluent parents. Yet considerable movement occurred along the path from rags to moderate success as men climbed from manual to nonmanual jobs or saw their children do so. Thus personal successes like that of Meyer Grossman, a Russian immigrant to Omaha, Nebraska, who worked as a teamster before saving enough to open a successful furniture store, were relatively common.

Rates of occupational mobility in late nineteenth- and early twentieth-century American communities were slow but steady. In new, fast-growing cities such as Atlanta, Los Angeles, and Omaha, approximately one in five manual workers rose to white-collar or owner's positions within ten years—provided they stayed in the city that long. In older northeastern cities like Boston and Newburyport, upward mobility averaged closer to one in six in ten years. Some people slipped from a higher to a lower rung of the occupational ladder, but rates of upward movement were almost always double the downward rates. Although patterns were far from consistent, immigrants generally experienced lower rates of upward mobility and higher rates of downward mobility than natives did. Still, regardless of birthplace, the chances for a white male to rise occupationally over the course of his career or to have a higher-status job than his father had were relatively good.

It must be remembered, however, that what con-

Sitting at a desk all day, without exercise or fresh air, could be stifling. To keep employees from becoming too sedentary, some companies encouraged occasional exercise sessions, like this one at the National Cash Register Company. National Cash Register Company.

stitutes a better job depends on the individual's own definition of improvement and desires. Many an immigrant artisan, such as a German carpenter or an Italian shoemaker, would have considered an accountant's job demeaning and unproductive. People with long traditions of pride in manual labor neither wanted nonmanual jobs nor encouraged their children to seek them. As one Italian tailor explained, "I learned the tailoring business in the old country. Over here, in America, I never have trouble finding a job because I know my business from the other side [Italy]. . . . I want that my oldest boy learn my trade because I tell him that you could always make at least enough for the family."

Moreover, movement into business ownership entailed risks. Rates of failure were high among shopkeepers, saloon owners, and the like because business was so uncertain. Thus many manual workers sought security rather than mobility, preferring a steady wage to the risks of ownership. A Sicilian who lived in Bridgeport, Connecticut, observed that "the people that come here they afraid to get in business because they don't know how that business goes. In Italy these people don't know much about these things because most of them work on farms or in [their] trade."

In addition to or instead of advancing occupationally, a person could achieve social mobility by acquiring property. But property was not easy to acquire in turn-of-the-century America. Banks and savings institutions were far stricter in their lending practices than they would become after the 1930s, when the federal government began to bolster real-estate financing. Mortgage loans carried high interest rates and short repayment periods. Thus renting, even

Acquisition of property

of single-family houses, was common, especially in big cities. Nevertheless, a general rise in wage rates enabled many families to build savings accounts, which could be used as down payments on property. Among working-class families who stayed in Newburyport for as long as ten years, a third to a half managed to accumulate some property; two-thirds did so within twenty years. Some, including large numbers of immigrants, accumulated the cash to finance property by sending their children into the labor market instead of to school. In 1900, 36.3 percent of urban American families owned their homes. That figure may not seem large; yet it was higher than the ownership rates of comparable societies. The 1900 federal census noted that the United States had the highest rate of home ownership among all Western nations except Denmark, Norway, and Sweden.

Residential mobility

Finally, each year millions of families tried to improve their living conditions by packing up and moving elsewhere. As early as 1847, a foreign visitor, amazed by American transiency, wrote, "If God were suddenly to call the world to judgment He would surprise two-thirds of the American population on the road like ants." And Americans have always followed the maxim that movement means improvement. This urge to move affected every region, every city. From Boston to San Francisco, from Minneapolis to San Antonio, no more than half the families residing in a city at any point in time could be found there ten years later. Population turnover was consistently high from 1850 until well into the twentieth century.

Some evidence shows that many people who left one place for another, particularly unskilled workers, did not improve their status; they simply floated from one low-paying job to another. Others, however, did find greener pastures. Studies of turn-of-the-century Boston, Omaha, Atlanta, and other cities have revealed that most of the men who rose occupationally had migrated from somewhere else. Thus while cities frustrated the hopes of some, they offered opportunities to others.

In addition to population movement between cities, extraordinary numbers of people moved from one residence to another within the same city. In contemporary American communities, one in every five families moves in any given year. A hundred years ago, the proportion was closer to one in four, or even one in three. In Omaha between 1880 and 1920, for example, nearly 60 percent of those families who remained in the city for as long as fourteen years had lived at three or more addresses during that span of time. Population turnover affected almost every neighborhood, every ethnic and occupational group.

Rapid residential flux undermined the stability of even the most homogeneous neighborhoods. Rarely did a single nationality comprise a clean-cut majority in any large area, even when that area was known as Little Italy, Jewtown, Over-the-Rhine, or Greektown. Even in as heavily ethnic a city as Chicago, a survey of one district found an amazing kaleidoscope of immigrants packed tightly together:

Ethnic neighborhoods and ghettos

> Between Halsted Street and the river live about ten thousand Italians, Neapolitans, Sicilians, and Calabrians. . . . To the South on Twelfth Street are many Germans, and the side streets are given over almost entirely to Polish and Prussian Jews. Further south, three Jewish colonies merge into a huge Bohemian colony. . . . To the north-west are many Canadians . . . and to the north are many Irish.

Moreover, the families inhabiting a certain neighborhood at one point in time were not likely to be living there five or ten years later. Residential change dispersed immigrants from their original areas of settlement into many different neighborhoods. In New York, Boston, and other eastern ports, ethnically homogeneous districts did exist, and people tended to change residences within those districts rather than move away from them. Elsewhere, however, most immigrant families lived dispersed in ethnically mixed neighborhoods rather than in ghettos.

In most places an area's institutions and enterprises, more than the people who actually lived there, identified it as an ethnic neighborhood. A certain part of town, familiar and accessible to a particular group, became the location of its churches, clubs, bakeries, meat markets, and other establishments. Often many members of the group lived nearby, while others lived farther away but could travel there on streetcars or on foot. Thus some of the secondary business centers that formed at the intersections of mass transit routes became locations of ethnic business and social activity. A Bohemian Town, for example, received its nickname because it was the location of Swoboda's Bakery, Cermak's Drug Store, Cecha's Jewelry, Knezacek's Meats, St. Wenceslaus Church, and the Bohemian Benevolent Association. Such institutions gave a district an ethnic identity even though the surrounding neighborhoods were mixed and unstable.

The true meaning of the term *ghetto* as a place of enforced residence from which escape is difficult applied to only one major urban group in this era, black Americans. Prejudice and discrimination not only trapped blacks at the bottom of the occupational ladder but operated in housing markets to limit their residential opportunities. Whites organized protective associations that pledged not to sell homes in white neighborhoods to blacks, and occasionally used violence to scare away black families who did move in. Such efforts seldom worked. Whites who lived on the edges of black neighborhoods often fled, leaving their homes and apartments to be sold and rented to black occupants. Whether in Boston, Birmingham, Omaha, or Los Angeles, totally black residential districts expanded while native white and ethnic neighborhoods dissolved. By 1920 ten Chicago census tracts were over 75 percent black. In Detroit, Cleveland, Los Angeles, and Washington, D.C., two-thirds or more of the total black population lived in only two or three wards. Within these districts, blacks nurtured distinct cultural institutions that helped them to adjust to urban life: storefront churches, business and educational organizations, social clubs, saloons, and other entertainment centers. But the ghettos also bred frustration and escapism, the result of stunted opportunity and racial bigotry. Color, more than any other factor, made the urban experiences of blacks different from those of whites.

All groups, however, including blacks, could and did move—if not from one part of the city to another, then from one city to another. Americans were always seeking greener pastures, and the hope that things might be better somewhere else acted as a kind of safety valve, relieving some of the tensions and frustrations that simmered inside the city. At times these tensions and frustrations erupted into violence; more often, people simply left to seek a better life elsewhere. A railroad ticket from one city to another cost only a few dollars; often there was little to lose by moving.

Moreover, the possibilities for upward mobility, however limited, seemed to temper people's dissatisfaction. Although the gap between the very rich and the very poor widened, the expanding economies of American cities created more room in the middle of the socioeconomic scale. Few could hope to become another Rockefeller, but many could become respectable merchants, shopkeepers, foremen, clerks, or agents. And if advancement was not possible in one generation, it could be possible in the next. Finally, even if migration, occupational mobility, and property acquisition offered little hope of improvement or relief, there was still one sphere to which city dwellers could turn: politics.

The rise of urban boss politics

Andrew D. White was dismayed and disgusted. "We . . . are putting ourselves on a basis which has always failed," wrote the American educator and diplomat in 1890. He could not accept "the idea that a city is a political body, and therefore that it is to be ruled . . . by a city proletarian mob . . . and . . . that men who carry their ward can control the city." Such an arrangement, White concluded, made American city government "the worst in Christendom." But others characterized the same situation much differently. Referring to Israel Durham of Philadelphia, the very kind of politician whom White despised, one journalist wrote, "Everybody likes him, hundreds love him, and almost everybody calls him 'Iz.' " What was it that provoked such impassioned differences of opinion? It was the urban political machine, one of the most remarkable and notorious of American institutions.

The sudden growth and mounting rivalry among social and economic interest groups that occurred in the late nineteenth century mired cities in a governmental swamp. From suburbs to slums, burgeoning populations, business expansion, and technological change created urgent needs for water, sewers, police and fire protection, schools, parks, and many other services. Such needs simply strained government institutions beyond their capacities. Furthermore, city governments approached these needs in a disorganized fashion. Legislative and administrative functions were typically dispersed among a mayor, a city council, and independent boards that administered health regulations, public works, poverty relief, and other matters. Philadelphia at one time had thirty different boards plus a mayor and a council to tend to the city's needs. And state governments often imposed their will on city administrations, appointing board members and limiting local prerogatives to levy taxes and sell bonds to raise revenue.

Power thrives on confusion and out of this governmental chaos arose the political machine. Unlike political parties, which ideally exist for higher purposes than merely electing their candidates to office, machines were organizations whose main goal was getting and keeping political power. In order to achieve that goal, a machine had to win popular support. Machine politicians routinely used bribery and graft to further their ends. But they could not have succeeded if they had not provided relief, security, and municipal services to large numbers of people. By doing so, machine politicians alleviated many urban problems and accomplished things that other agencies had been unable or unwilling to attempt.

Political machines

Machines were also beneficiaries of the new urban conditions. As cities grew larger and economically more complex, business leaders either vied to use government to advance their own interests or withdrew from local affairs to pursue their interests in interurban or interregional economic organizations. At the same time, hordes of newcomers, often unskilled and foreign-born, crowded into the cities. Enfranchised by liberal voting qualifications, the men of these groups became a substantial political force.

These circumstances bred a new kind of leader: the political boss. Conflicting interest groups needed brokers who could bypass governmental stalemates, and urban newcomers had needs that required government attention. Bosses and machines did just that; they established power bases among new urban voters and used politics to solve urban problems. Machines made politics a full-time profession. According to George Washington Plunkett, a small-time boss in New York City who published his memoirs in 1905, "As a rule [the boss] has no business or occupation other than politics. He plays politics every day and night in the year and his headquarters bears the inscription, 'Never closed.' "

Bosses and machines were rarely as dictatorial or corrupt as their critics charged. To be sure, fraud, bribery, and thievery tainted the system. Bosses such as Philadelphia's "Duke" Vare, Kansas City's Tom Pendergast, and New York's Richard Croker lived like kings, though their official incomes were slim. But from the 1880s onward, most machines evolved into highly organized political structures that wedded accomplishments for the city with personal gain for politicians.

The system rested on a popular base and was held together by loyalty and service. City machines were coalitions of smaller machines that derived their power directly from the neighborhoods, particularly inner-city neighborhoods inhabited by the native and immigrant working classes. In return for votes, bosses and their henchmen provided jobs, built parks and bathhouses, distributed food to the needy, and helped when someone ran afoul of the law. Such personalized service cultivated mass attachment to the boss; never before had government or public leaders assumed such responsibility for people in need.

Moreover, bosses were genuinely public people. They attended weddings and wakes, joined clubs, and held open house in local saloons where neighborhood people could contact them personally. Each boss had his own style. Pittsburgh's Christopher Magee gave his city a zoo and a maternity hospital. Brooklyn's Hugh McLaughlin provided free burial services. Boston's James Michael Curley would approach a haggard old woman and tell her that "a woman should have three attributes. She should have beauty, intelligence, and money." Then he would press a silver dollar into her hand, adding, "Now you have all three."

Techniques of bossism

In order to finance their largesse and support their system, bosses exchanged favors for votes or money. Their power over local government enabled machines to control the letting of contracts, the granting of utility or streetcar franchises, and the distribution of city jobs. Recipients of city business and jobs were expected to repay the machine with a portion of their dent Grover Cleveland, who became mayor of Buffalo in 1881, were to reduce city budgets, make employees work longer, and cut taxes.

As a means of introducing sound business principles to government, civic reformers supported a number of structural changes, such as city-manager and commission forms of government and nonpartisan, citywide election of officials. Each of these reforms was aimed at removing politics from government and placing local decision making in the hands of experienced experts. Armed with such strategies, reformers believed they could centralize administration under their control and thereby undermine bosses' ward and neighborhood power bases. They rarely realized, however, that bosses succeeded because they used government to meet people's needs. Reformers only noticed the waste and corruption that machines bred.

Structural reforms in government

A few reformers did move beyond structural changes to a genuine concern for social problems. Hazen S. Pingree, mayor of Detroit from 1889 to 1896; Samuel "Golden Rule" Jones, mayor of Toledo from 1897 to 1904; and Thomas L. Johnson, mayor of Cleveland from 1901 to 1909, worked to provide jobs for poor people, to reduce charges by transit and utilities companies, and to establish greater governmental responsibility for the welfare of all citizens. Some supported public ownership of gas, electric, and telephone companies–a quasi-socialistic reform that alienated their business allies. But Pingree, Jones, and Johnson were exceptions. Most civic reformers were narrow of vision. Although they achieved temporary success, they could not match the bosses' political savvy and soon found themselves out of power.

Nevertheless, the seeds of social reform were beginning to sprout outside of politics. Convinced that laissez-faire ideology could no longer work in a complex urban-industrial world, a number of men and women–mostly young and middle-class–embarked on campaigns for social betterment. Driven by an urge to identify and address urban problems, these people thought they could control and solve those problems. Their attempts laid the foundation for the progressive reforms that would become a national movement in the early twentieth century (see Chapter 21).

Social reform

Political bosses won friends and courted votes through their benevolence. Timothy D. "Big Tim" Sullivan sponsored this huge free barbecue for constituents in a New York City neighborhood. Brown Brothers.

profits or salaries and to cast supporting votes on election day. Bosses called this process gratitude; critics called it graft. Machines constructed public buildings, sewer systems, mass transit lines, and more that otherwise might not have been built; but bribes and kickbacks made such projects costly to taxpayers. Moreover, machines dispensed favors to illegal businesses as well as legitimate ones. Payoffs from gambling, prostitution, and illegal liquor traffic were important sources of machine revenue.

Between 1880 and 1920, nearly every major city experienced some kind of bossism. Hierarchical machine organization, whereby a city boss presided over neighborhood bosses, was most highly developed in New York City. There, after the downfall of Boss William M. Tweed in the early 1870s, "Honest John" Kelly took over Tweed's Tammany Hall organization and molded it into a tight structure by combining Tammany more thoroughly with the Democratic party. In the late 1880s, Richard Croker assumed control of Tammany Hall and completed Kelly's efforts by making neighborhood bosses more dependent on the city boss for jobs and money and by allying with wealthy businessmen. By contrast, the machine system in Chicago was decentralized, with several ward bosses exercising independent power and cultivating their own special interests.

Medium-sized cities generally had a single boss who used the inner-city districts as his power base. Omaha's Tom Dennison, Cincinnati's George Cox, and Kansas City's Jim Pendergast (Tom's brother) were all downtown saloon keepers who became powerful political brokers. In the South, bosses such as New Orleans' Martin Behrman and Memphis's Edward H. Crump drew strength from the region's well-established Democratic party. Some northern cities, notably Cincinnati, Pittsburgh, and Philadelphia, had Republican machines and bosses. A few bosses, such as San Francisco's Abe Ruef and Minneapolis's "Doc" Ames, were well educated. But many, including St. Louis's Ed Butler and New York's "Big Tim" Sullivan, never finished grammar school and received their most influential training in the city streets and tenements.

Bosses held onto their power because they knew people's needs firsthand and because they tended to the problems of everyday life. Martin Lomasney, boss of Boston's South End, explained, "There's got to be in every ward somebody that any bloke can come to—no matter what he's done—and get help. Help, you understand, none of your law and justice, but help." In an era when unemployment insurance and welfare were virtually unknown, machine politicians believed government existed to aid people in need and to provide services.

The boss system, however, was neither innocent nor fair. Jobs, Christmas turkeys, and funeral money were accompanied by bribery, thievery, and extortion. Moreover, bosses never distributed favors equitably. New immigrant groups such as Italians and Poles, and racial minorities like blacks and Latinos, received only token recognition, if any, from machines. Nevertheless, in an age of economic individualism, bosses were no more guilty of self-interest and discrimination than the respectable businessmen who exploited workers, spoiled the landscape, and manipulated government in pursuit of profits. Sometimes humane and sometimes criminal, bosses were brokers between various sectors of urban society and an uncertain world.

Civic reform

Machine politics between 1877 and 1920 brought some order to city government, met some of the needs of immigrants and other inner-city residents, and lined the pockets of some leaders and their busi-

Settlement houses were especially successful in their efforts on behalf of the women and children of inner-city neighborhoods. This day nursery, photographed in 1907, was typical of settlement-house services. The Keystone-Mast Collection, University of California, Riverside.

> to the lowest mark, and . . . it made odious the very name of the slum. . . . When today we have to fight for the things that make for the city's good . . . we fight no longer for but with the people. And this is the settlement's doing.

The National Consumers League provided another reform outlet for educated upper- and middle-class women. Founded by Josephine Shaw, a socially prominent Massachusetts widow, the Consumers League initially worked to improve the wages and working conditions of young women who worked in department stores. After Florence Kelley became the league's general secretary, the organization expanded its activities to include protection of child laborers and amelioration of potential health hazards. For example, local branches supported such consumer-protection measures as the licensing of food vendors and the inspection of dairies to ensure the sale of uncontaminated food and milk.

While settlement-house workers tried to revive neighborhoods, other reformers tried to beautify whole cities. Inspired by the World's Columbian Exposition of 1893, a dazzling world's fair held in the specially built White City on Chicago's South Side, architects and city planners worked to redesign the urban landscape. Led by architect Daniel Burn-

Beautification campaigns

ham, the City Beautiful movement undertook to build new civic centers, parks and boulevards, and transportation systems that would make cities more attractive as well as economically efficient. "Make no little plans," Burnham urged city officials. "Make big plans; aim high in hope and work." This attitude spawned beautifying projects in Chicago, San Francisco, and Washington, D.C., in the first decade of the twentieth century. Yet most big plans turned out to be only big dreams. Neither the public nor the private sector could muster enough money to undertake major projects, and planners disagreed with each other and with social reformers over whether or not beautification would really solve urban problems.

Whether they concentrated on changing government, social services, or city design, urban reformers wanted to save cities, not abolish them. The men and women of the various reform movements believed that they could improve urban life by restoring feelings of service and cooperation among all citizens. They often failed to realize, however, that cities were places of great diversity and that different people had different views of what reform actually meant. Distributing city jobs on the basis of civil service exams rather than political patronage meant progress to governmental reformers, but to working-class men it signified reduced employment opportunities. Moral reformers pushed for prohibition of the sale of alcoholic beverages to prevent working-class breadwinners from wasting their wages and ruining their health, but European immigrants saw such crusades as interference in their long held wine- and beer-drinking customs. Planners saw new civic buildings and transportation systems as modern necessities, but such structures often replaced low-cost housing units and displaced the poor. Thus the results of early urban reform were mixed; the American reform tradition merged idealism with naivete and insensitivity.

The legacy of urbanism

Much of what American society has become today originated in the urbanization of the late nineteenth century. American cities may have been less orderly and beautiful than European cities, but they hummed with energy and excitement. When old-fashioned native inventiveness met the traditions of European, African, and Asian cultures, a new kind of society emerged. This new society seldom functioned smoothly; in fact, there really was no coherent urban community, only a collection of subcommunities. Yet its jumble of social classes, ethnic and racial groups, political organizations, and other components left important legacies.

Martin Lomasney, the Boston ward boss, once observed that "one of the strongest human cravings is to be left alone and the uplifter is never liked." By the early 1900s, American cities had become so diverse socially that immigrant groups were straining to protect their cultures in a changing, bewildering world. Fearful and puzzled native-born Americans tried a host of ways to Americanize and uplift immigrants, but the newcomers stubbornly clung to their religious rituals, languages, family and social organizations, and drinking habits. Optimists had envisioned the American nation as a melting pot where various nationalities would blend into a new, unified people. Instead, many ethnic groups proved to be unmeltable, and nonwhite racial minorities got burned on the bottom of the pot.

Cultural pluralism

As a result of immigration and urbanization, the United States became a culturally pluralistic society—not a melting pot but a salad bowl. As one immigrant priest told a social worker, "There is no such thing as an American." He meant the same thing literary critic Randolph Bourne meant when he dubbed the United States "a cosmopolitan federation of national colonies." This kind of reasoning produced hyphenated identifications: people considered themselves Irish-American, Italo-American, Polish-American, and the like.

Pluralism and its attendant interest-group loyalties made politics an important institution. If America was not a melting pot, then different groups were competing with each other for power, wealth, and status. When lack of skills, education, capital, and influence closed off paths to success, immigrants turned to politics to protect their interests and to open up new opportunities. American cities became arenas in which different groups formed coalitions to achieve their goals. But such coalitions were fragile, and their membership shifted according to the issue in question.

In general, groups that opposed the interference of government in matters of personal liberty identified with the Democratic party, while those that believed government could be an agent of moral reform identified with the Republican party. The former included immigrant Catholics and Jews, who believed that God and faith should guide their behavior through ritual and sacraments. The latter consisted mostly of native and immigrant Protestants, who believed that salvation could best be achieved by purging the world of evil and that legislation might be necessary to protect people from sin.

Cultural-political alignments

Adherents of these two cultural traditions battled over how much control government should exercise over people's lives. The most provocative issue was use of leisure time and celebration of Sunday, the Lord's day. In the Puritan tradition, natives supported blue laws (see page 290) designed to prevent the desecration of the Sabbath by prohibiting various commercial and recreational activities. European immigrants, accustomed to feasting and playing after church, fought Sunday closings of saloons and other restrictions on the only day they had free for fun and relaxation. Thus in 1913, when the New York General Assembly proposed a law granting cities authority to end restrictions on Sunday baseball games and liquor sales, both sides argued vehemently. One rural Republican charged that such a measure amounted to "amending Moses' law," and a New York City Democrat of Irish lineage retorted that "Moses was an organization Democrat" who wrote the commandment "Don't covet your neighbor's rights." At about the same time, the Illinois and Ohio legislatures were split over whether or not to legalize boxing, which small-town Republicans opposed and urban Democrats favored. Similar splits developed elsewhere over public versus parochial schools and prohibition versus the free availability of liquor.

Such conflicts, plus the ever-growing diversity of the American population, animated the dialogue between bosses and reformers and illustrate why local and state politics were so heated in the late nineteenth and early twentieth centuries. Some people carried polarization to its extreme and tried to suppress everything new and allegedly un-American. In several communities during the 1890s, the American Protective Association achieved considerable influence by attacking "the diabolical works of the Catholic Church" and demanding an end to immigration. Some of this sentiment influenced national legislation. In 1882, Congress bowed to pressure from West Coast nativists and prohibited Chinese immigration for ten years. In 1902 a new law excluded the Chinese permanently. And periodic attempts were made to prevent foreign-born citizens from voting by imposing literacy tests on them.

Such efforts generally failed, though, because too many people had a stake in the country's cultural diversity. By 1920, immigrants and their offspring outnumbered natives in many cities, and the national economy depended on the new workers and consumers. Even though a slight majority (about 51 percent) of the nation's population was still descended from people who arrived before the Revolution, the newcomers had been able to influence the course of American history. They had transformed the United States into an urban nation; they had given American culture its rich and varied texture; and they had laid the foundations for the political liberalism and sensitivity to individual liberty that would characterize American politics and society in the future.

Suggestions for further reading

Urban growth

Howard P. Chudacoff, *The Evolution of American Urban Society*, rev. ed. (1981); Blake McKelvey, *The Urbanization of America* (1963); Arthur M. Schlesinger, *The Rise of the City* (1933); George R. Taylor, "The Beginnings of Mass Transportation in Urban America," *Smithsonian Journal of History*, 1 (1966), 35–50; Sam Bass Warner, Jr., *Streetcar Suburbs* (1962); Sam Bass Warner, Jr., *The Urban Wilderness* (1972).

Immigration, ethnicity, and religion

Aaron I. Abell, *American Catholicism and Social Action* (1960); Aaron I. Abell, *The Urban Impact on American Protestantism* (1943); Josef J. Barton, *Peasants and Strangers: Italians, Rumanians, and Slovaks in an American City* (1975); John Bodnar, *Immigration and Industrialization* (1977); John W. Briggs, *An Italian Passage* (1978); Kathleen Neils Conzen, "Immigrants, Immigrant Neighborhoods, and Ethnic Identity," *Journal of American History*, 66 (1979),

603–615; Robert D. Cross, *The Church and the City* (1967); Leonard Dinnerstein and David Reimers, *Ethnic Americans* (1975); John B. Duff, *The Irish in the United States* (1971); Nathan Glazer and Daniel P. Moynihan, *Beyond the Melting Pot,* rev. ed. (1970); Milton Gordon, *Assimilation in American Life* (1964); Victor Greene, *For God and Country: The Rise of Polish and Lithuanian Ethnic Consciousness in America* (1975); Oscar Handlin, *The Uprooted,* 2nd ed. (1973); Marcus Lee Hansen, *The Immigrant in American History* (1940); John Higham, *Strangers in the Land: Patterns of American Nativism* (1955); Francis L. K. Hsu, *The Challenge of the American Dream: The Chinese in the United States* (1971); Maldwyn A. Jones, *American Immigration* (1960); Edward R. Kantowicz, *Polish-American Politics in Chicago* (1975); Matt S. Maier and Feliciano Rivera, *The Chicanos: A History of Mexican Americans* (1972); Henry F. May, *Protestant Churches and Industrial America* (1949); Humbert S. Nelli, *The Italians of Chicago* (1970); Moses Rischin, *The Promised City: New York's Jews* (1962); Barbara Solomon, *Ancestors and Immigrants* (1965); David Ward, *Cities and Immigrants* (1971); Thomas Wheeler, ed., *The Immigrant Experience* (1972).

Urban needs and services

Robert H. Bremner, *From the Depths: The Discovery of Poverty* (1956); James H. Cassedy, *Charles V. Chapin and the Public Health Movement* (1962); Marvin Lazerson, *Origins of the Urban School* (1971); Thomas L. Philpott, *The Slum and the Ghetto* (1978); James F. Richardson, *The New York Police* (1970); Barbara Gutmann Rosencrantz, *Public Health and the State* (1972); Mel Scott, *American City Planning Since 1890* (1969); Selwyn K. Troen, *The Public and the Schools* (1975); Christopher Tunnard and Henry Hope Reed, *American Skyline* (1955); David B. Tyack, *The One Best System: A History of American Urban Education* (1974).

Mobility and race relations

Howard P. Chudacoff, *Mobile Americans* (1972); Clyde Griffen and Sally Griffen, *Natives and Newcomers* (1977); David M. Katzman, *Before the Ghetto* (1973); Thomas Kessner, *The Golden Door* (1977); Kenneth L. Kusmer, *A Ghetto Takes Shape* (1976); Gilbert Osofsky, *Harlem: The Making of a Ghetto* (1966); Howard N. Rabinowitz, *Race Relations in the Urban South* (1978); Allan H. Spear, *Black Chicago* (1967); Stephan Thernstrom, *The Other Bostonians: Poverty and Progress in the American Metropolis* (1973).

Boss politics

John M. Allswang, *Bosses, Machines and Urban Voters* (1977); Blaine Brownell and Warren E. Stickle, eds., *Bosses and Reformers* (1973); Alexander B. Callow, Jr., ed., *The City Boss in America* (1976); Lyle Dorsett, *The Pendergast Machine* (1968); Zane L. Miller, *Boss Cox's Cincinnati* (1968); Bruce M. Stave, ed., *Urban Bosses, Machines, and Progressive Reformers* (1972).

Urban reform

John D. Buenker, *Urban Liberalism and Progressive Reform* (1973); James B. Crooks, *Politics and Progress* (1968); Allen F. Davis, *American Heroine: The Life and Legend of Jane Addams* (1973); Allen F. Davis, *Spearheads for Reform* (1967); Michael Ebner and Eugene Tobin, eds., *The Age of Urban Reform* (1977); Melvin Holli, *Reform in Detroit* (1969); C. H. Hopkins, *The Rise of the Social Gospel in American Protestantism* (1940); Roy M. Lubove, *The Progressive and the Slums* (1962); Martin J. Schiesl, *The Politics of Efficiency: Municipal Administration and Reform in America* (1977); John G. Sproat *The Best Men: Liberal Reformers in the Gilded Age* (1968).

50
25
35¢
10¢

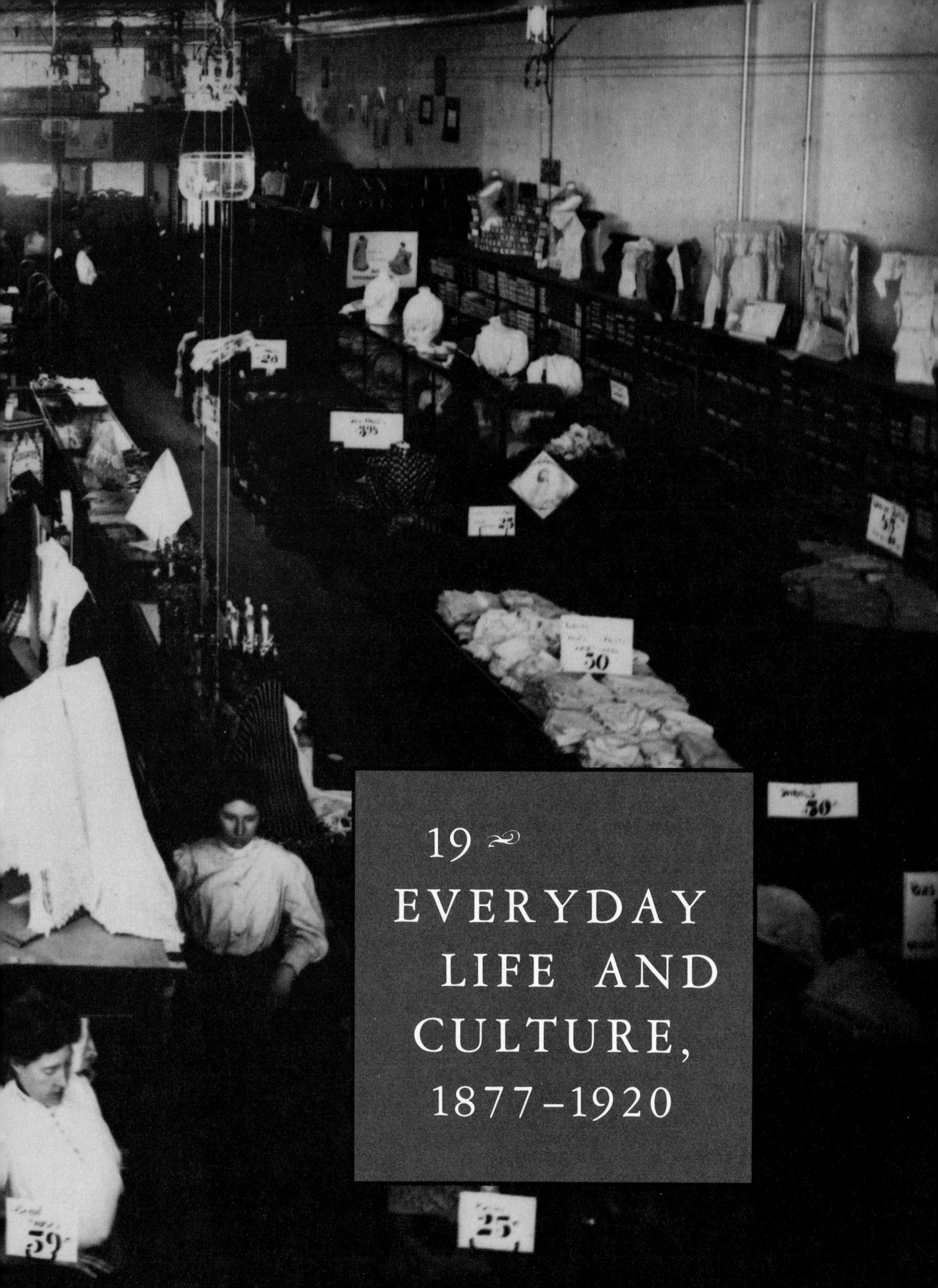

19 ~ EVERYDAY LIFE AND CULTURE, 1877–1920

In 1880 F. W. Woolworth, hesitating because he was not sure he could sell such articles, ordered $25 worth of Christmas ornaments for his newly opened Five and Ten Cent Store in Lancaster, Pennsylvania. His doubts quickly vanished; customers bought every ornament in stock, convincing him that the holiday season offered extraordinary opportunities for sales. By the early 1900s, Woolworth's orders for ornaments alone totaled hundreds of thousands of dollars, and sales of Christmas gifts had skyrocketed. December had become the most profitable month of the year for his expanding chain of stores. The Christmas season, Woolworth advised his store managers in 1891, "is our harvest time. Make it pay." In distinctly American fashion, Christmas had become a shopping holiday as much as a religious one—a Festival of Consumption whose transformation aptly symbolized the changing character of American society.

During the half-century between the end of Reconstruction and the end of the First World War, the United States began to shift its focus from production to consumption. The nation's farms and industries were producing so much that Americans could afford to reorient their attitudes toward material wants. What had once been accessible only to a few suddenly became available to many; what had formerly been dreams became necessities. No trend affected everyday life more decisively than this one. And as Americans tried to adapt to the new values of consumption and its attendant conflicts, they raised questions about themselves that have not been resolved to this day.

Most Americans at the end of the nineteenth century were still relatively isolated. In 1880, seven out of every ten people lived on farms and in towns with fewer than 2,500 inhabitants. Life in such places was shaped by the dictates of nature and the traditional institutions of family and church. In the fields and in the household, people literally worked from sunup to sundown—though they could usually control their own work pace and the number of breaks they took. Animals, particularly livestock, required constant attention. Most foods and clothes were made in the home or nearby. Houses were heated by wood- or coal-burning stoves and lit by oil lamps; most had no bathroom, only basins and tubs indoors and privies or outhouses in the back yard. People burned what little trash they had, fed their garbage to animals, and poured waste water outside. Besides church, people mingled at the general store or pharmacy, and at such special occasions as fairs, circuses, political rallies, and evangelical revivals. Fatigue and pitch-darkness restricted nighttime activities; street lights were rare. People normally went to bed at nine or ten P.M. and rose at four or five A.M.

But such scenes were changing rapidly. In 1880 there were only twenty cities with populations over 100,000; by 1920 there were sixty-eight. In these cities there developed a new kind of neighborhood society in which street corners, saloons, shops, and commercial amusements replaced the village church and general store. People tended to spend more time with their peers—members of the same age group—and less with their families. Moreover, the rapid spread of intercity transportation and of postal, telephone, and electrical service drew even isolated communities into the orbit of consumerism. American inventiveness combined with technology, mass production, and mass marketing to produce and make available myriad goods that had not previously existed or had been the exclusive property of the wealthy. This new material well-being, brought about by the advent of such products as ready-made clothes, home appliances, and automobiles, had a dual effect. It enabled Americans of differing status to join communities of consumers—communities defined not by place or class but by common possession. But it also accentuated the differences between those who could afford such goods and services and those who could not.

Standards of living

If the affluence of a society can be measured by how quickly it converts luxuries into commonplace articles of everyday life, the United States was indeed becoming affluent in the years between 1880 and 1920. In 1880, for example, almost no one smoked cigarettes. (That year a young Virginian named James Bonsack invented a cigarette-making machine.) Only wealthy women could afford silk stockings, and only residents of Florida, Texas, and California could enjoy the luxury of fresh oranges. The sweets people ate were made at home, and few people ever bought soap. But by 1899, manufactured and perishable products were be-

A middle-class girl poses with her newly acquired Christmas gifts. New mass-production and marketing techniques, developed in the late nineteenth century, made such materialism possible. Library of Congress.

coming increasingly common. That year Americans bought 2 billion cigarettes (an average of 27 per person) and 151,000 pairs of silk stockings, consumed oranges at the rate of 100 crates for every 1,000 people, and spent an average of $1.08 per person on store-bought candy and pastries and $.63 on soap. By 1921 the transformation was even more advanced. Americans smoked 43 billion cigarettes that year (403 per person), ate 248 crates of oranges per 1,000 people, bought 217 million pairs of silk stockings, and spent $1.66 per person on confectionery goods and $1.40 on soap. How did Americans afford these goods? How did changes in standards of living come about?

Personal income

What people can afford depends largely but not entirely on their resources and incomes. Data for the period from 1880 to 1920 are scattered, but there is no doubt that incomes rose. As always, the rich got richer. The rapidly expanding economy spawned massive fortunes and created a new industrial elite. In "The Coming Billionaire," an article published in *Forum* magazine in 1891, Thomas G. Shearman estimated that there were already 120 American men worth at least $10 million. By 1920, when income-tax figures made possible the first accurate tabulations of income distribution, the richest 5 percent of the population

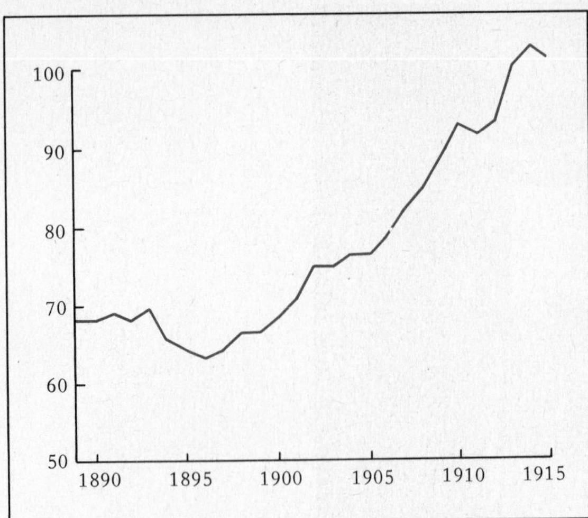

Cost of Living Index, 1889–1915

was receiving almost a fourth of all income in the country. Returns on investments were even more remarkable; the same top 5 percent was receiving almost half of all interest payments and 85 percent of all stock and bond dividends.

But incomes also rose among the middle classes. For example, the average pay for clerical workers rose from $848 a year in 1890 to $1,156 in 1910, an increase of 36 percent. Salaries for postal clerks and carriers climbed by 20 percent, from $878 in 1890 to $1,049 in 1910. After the turn of the century, employees of the federal executive branch were averaging $1,072 a year, and college professors $1,100–not handsome sums, but much more than manual workers received. With these incomes, the middle class could afford relatively comfortable housing. A six to seven room house cost around $3,000 to buy or build and $15 to $20 per month to rent.

Significantly, average salaries for public school teachers almost doubled between 1890 and 1910. But their extreme meagerness–$256 in 1890, $492 in 1910–reflected continued exploitation of women, who made up the majority of the profession. School teachers were middle class in education and employment, working class in income level.

Wages for industrial workers increased as well, though they varied widely and income figures were deceiving. On the average, the annual wages of industrial workers rose from $486 in 1890 to $558 in 1910. But hourly rates show how wages varied within this class. In 1892 a soft-coal miner received 18 cents an hour, an iron worker about 17 cents. In industries with large female work forces, however, wages were measurably lower: in 1892 shoe workers got 14 cents an hour, paper workers 12 cents. By 1910, wages had risen in all these industries. Coal miners received 21 cents an hour; iron workers, 23 cents; shoe workers, 19 cents; and paper workers, 17 cents. Pay for farm laborers followed the same trend, rising from an annual average of $233 in 1890 to $336 in 1910. (Farm wages were low partly because farm laborers generally received room and board along with their pay.) Regional variations were wide in almost all industries. Wages tended to be much lower in the South than in the Northeast, and generally higher in the Midwest and West, especially in fast-growing cities where demand for workers was high. Except in a few skilled trades, immigrants and blacks received lower pay than native whites for the same work.

Income figures, however, ignore a vital aspect of living standards. Wage increases mean little if living costs rise as fast or faster than incomes. In fact, this is what happened in the United States around the turn of the century. According to one economic index, the weekly cost of living for a typical wage earner's family of four rose over 47 percent between 1889 and 1913 (see figure). For example, a quantity of food and other items that may have cost $6.78 in 1889 increased, after a slight dip in the mid-1890s, to $10.00 by 1913. Specifically, a dozen eggs that cost 21 cents in 1890 rose to 34 cents by 1910, a climb of 60 percent. During the same period, the price of a pound of bacon doubled, from 12.5 cents to 25.5 cents. Very rarely did the income for a particular occupation rise at the same rate as the cost of living. Thus, particularly for the working class, it was becoming harder, not easier, to pay for life's necessities.

Cost of living

How then could Americans afford the new goods and services that the industrial age offered? Obviously, many could not. The daughter of a textile worker, recalling her school days at the turn of the century, described how "some of the kids would bring bars of chocolate, others an orange . . . I suppose they were richer than a family like ours. My father used to buy a bag of candy and a bag of peanuts every payday. . . . And that's all we'd have until the next payday. If we asked for something my mother would say, 'Well,

Young women take a typing exam to qualify for civil service jobs. The increasing paperwork in business and government and the invention of the typewriter, which facilitated record-keeping and correspondence, enabled thousands of women to obtain secretarial jobs. Chicago Historical Society.

we're too poor. We can't afford to buy that.' " Another woman explained how her family coped with high prices and low wages: "My mother made our clothes. People then wore old clothes. My mother would rip them out and make them over."

Still, a working-class family could raise its income and partake at least partially in consumer society by sending children and women into the labor market. Thus in a household where the father made $600 a year, the wages of other family members might lift the total income to $800 or $900. The more children a family had, especially among immigrants, the greater the possibilities for additional income. Between 1890 and 1900, the number of working men and women aged fourteen to nineteen grew by over 36 percent (from 3 million to 4.1 million), and the number of adult women who worked rose by 45 percent. (Meanwhile, total population increased by just 25 percent.) Though the number of working children under age fourteen is impossible to determine because much of such work was part-time and/or illegal, it seems certain that the incidence of child labor increased considerably. In 1900, an estimated 3 million children–17 percent of those between the ages of five and fifteen–were working full- or almost full-time. Many families also rented household space to boarders and lodgers, a practice that could yield up to $200 or $300 a year. These means of increasing family income enabled people to spend more and save more. Between 1889 and 1901, for example, working-class families markedly increased their expenditures for such items as life insurance, amusements, alcoholic beverages, and union dues. Thus workers were able to improve their living standards, but not without sacrifices in their family and home life.

Expansion of the labor force

Between 1890 and 1920, the American labor force almost doubled, from 21 million workers to 40 million. (Total population in those years grew by just 77 percent.) But these figures are somewhat misleading: in general, they represent a change in the nature of work rather than an increase in the number of available jobs relative to the number of people who could work. In the rural society that the United States was in the nineteenth century, women and children worked at tasks that were important to the family's daily existence–cooking, cleaning, planting, and harvesting. Their jobs were often hard to define, and they seldom appeared in employment figures because they earned no wages. But as the nation industrialized and the agricultural sector's share of the national income and population declined, waged and salaried employment became more common. (The total number of people in farm jobs rose by only 5 percent between 1890 and 1910, and actually fell between 1910 and 1920.) Jobs in industry and commerce were both easier to define and easier to count. It is probable, then, that the proportion of Americans who were working was not increasing markedly–most Americans, male and female, had always worked. What was new was the increase in paid employment, which also made purchases of consumer goods and services more affordable.

Female employment

The entrance of more women into the labor force marked the acceleration of an important trend. Farm women had always worked, and large numbers of women in northern towns and cities had entered factory work during the nineteenth century. Furthermore, women had traditionally worked in domestic service (cooking, cleaning, laundering) and as shopkeepers. What was new in the late nineteenth century was the increased number of southern women who worked for wages. By the 1890s, southern women, most of them white (large numbers of black women were already employed as domestics) were flocking to jobs not only in the rapidly multiplying textile mills but also in binderies, paper factories, and cigarette factories. In addition, thousands of women nationwide were being hired for new white-collar jobs as clerks, stenographers, salespersons, and the like–jobs created by the growth of retail establishments and corporate record keeping.

Most female workers were young, unmarried, and poorly paid. They usually lived with their parents or in rooming houses. Saleswomen earned only $6 or $7 a week; factory workers often received even less. Some married women worked in factories or offices, but more earned money at home. Censuses and other surveys often missed the large numbers of mothers who took in laundry, strung beads and linked chains for costume jewelry, made artificial flowers, or did mending and tailoring. Such jobs enabled women to tend to their household tasks and earn money as well, either to supplement the family income or to satisfy their own needs. As one married woman remarked, "I like to have my own money. I like the work and would rather have $50 earned myself than $100 saved out of my husband's pay."

Life expectancy

Medical and technological developments eased some of life's struggles, and their impact on living standards increased after 1900. Advances in medicine and better living conditions sharply reduced death rates and extended the life span. Between 1900 and 1920, for example, life expectancy rose from 51 to 56.5 years for women, and from 48 to 54 for men. In 1900, there were 1,755 deaths per 100,000 people; by 1921 the death rate had dropped by one-third to 1,164. During the same period there were spectacular declines in the death rates from diseases such as typhoid, diphtheria, influenza (except for a harsh epidemic in 1918 and 1919), tuberculosis, and intestinal ailments–diseases that had been the scourge of earlier generations. There were, however, significant increases in deaths from cancer, diabetes, and heart disease. Americans also found new ways to kill themselves: although the suicide rate remained about the same, homicides and automobile deaths soared between 1900 and 1920.

Not only were amenities and luxuries more readily available in the early 1900s than they had been a half-century earlier, but the means to upward mobility seemed more accessible as well. The spread of public education–particularly the increased number of high schools–helped equip young people to achieve a higher standard of living than their parents. Between 1890 and 1922 the number of students enrolled in public high schools grew ten times, from 203,000 to 2.3 million. And more than ever before, education was becoming the key to success. The creation of new white-collar occupations in the growing service industries helped to stem the downward mobility that had resulted when mechanization pushed skilled workers out of their crafts. Yet the United States was not a meritocracy–a society in which the most able individuals rise to the top. The inequality that had pervaded nineteenth-century society remained. A caste system still prevailed: race and sex, more than any other factors, determined one's status. Religion and ethnicity influenced social relations even more, perhaps, than in the early nineteenth century before the nation's cultural mosaic had been completed.

Moreover, the new material abundance and consumerism of the twentieth century seemed to make places, things, and experiences too similar. Some people mourned for the more individualistic, self-reliant (and partly mythical) past, when Americans had had to pay more attention to summer heat and winter cold, when they had had to make things for themselves. Critics charged that the new society was creating products and demands that were unnecessary and even harmful. But it was too late to turn back. Americans had set their course toward a future that promised prosperity and comfort.

The quest for convenience

One of the most representative agents of the revolution in American life styles at the end of the nineteenth century was the toilet. The chain-pull, wash-down water closet, invented in England around 1870, was adopted in the United States in the 1880s. Shortly after 1900 the flush toilet was developed; thanks to mass production of enamel-coated fixtures, it soon became common in American homes and buildings.

The indoor toilet, suddenly cheaper and easier to install, brought about a shift in habits and attitudes. In the past, people had believed there was no danger in disposing of human waste on or below the ground; only luxury hotels and estates had private bathrooms. By the 1880s, however, acceptance of the germ theory of disease had raised fears about human pollution as a source of infection and water contamination. Much more rapidly than Europeans did, Americans combined a desire for cleanliness with an urge for convenience, and water closets became widely available and widely used, especially in middle-class urban households. Bodily functions took on a more unpleasant image, and the home bathroom became a place of utmost privacy. Also, the toilet plus the private bathtub gave Americans new ways to use–and waste–water. This process can be seen as part of a broader change that accompanied industrialization and mass production: the democratization of convenience.

The tin can also altered life styles. Before the mid-nineteenth century, Americans ate most foods only in season. Drying, smoking, and salting could preserve meat for a short time, but the supply of fresh meat, like that of fresh milk, depended on ready accessibility; there was no way to prevent spoilage. But around 1810, a French inventor developed the cooking-and-sealing process of canning. And in the 1850s, an American named Gail Borden developed a means of condensing and preserving milk. Canned goods and condensed milk became more common during and after the Civil War, but their availability was limited because cans had to be made by hand. By 1880, however, inventors had fashioned stamping and soldering machines that could mass-produce cans from tin plate. Suddenly all kinds of foods could be preserved and bought at all times of the year. Americans had acquired still another means of overcoming nature–and littering the landscape.

Processed and preserved foods

Other trends and inventions helped make it possible for Americans of all classes to vary their daily diets. Growing urban populations created the demand that encouraged fruit and vegetable farmers to raise more produce. Railroads and especially refrigerator cars enabled growers and meat packers to ship perishables greater distances and to preserve them for longer periods. Thus by the 1890s, northern city dwellers could enjoy southern and western strawberries, grapes, and tomatoes, previously available for a month at most, up to six months of the year. In addition, increased use of iceboxes enabled families to store perishables. An easy means of producing ice commercially had been invented in the 1870s, and by 1900 the nation had more than two thousand commercial ice plants, most of which made home deliveries. The icebox became a fixture in the up-to-date middle-class home, and remained so until the mechanized refrigerator replaced it in the 1920s and 1930s.

A peach-canning factory in Visalia, California. Canners used a special cooking and sealing process to preserve food, an advance that permitted year-round distribution of fruits and vegetables to all parts of the country. Keystone-Mast Collection, University of California, Riverside.

Even the working class had a more diversified diet. The lowest-income people still ate what their counterparts in previous eras had eaten: the cheapest foods, heavy with starches and carbohydrates. Southern textile workers, for example, ate corn mush and fatback almost every day. But many families could take advantage of previously unavailable meats, fruits, and vegetables to achieve more varied fare. The family of a steelworker ate these typical meals in 1910:

Monday
Breakfast: oatmeal, milk, eggs, bacon, bread, butter, jelly, coffee
Dinner: soup, bread, fruit.
Supper: meat, beans, potatoes, fruit, beets, pickles

Tuesday
Breakfast: chocolate, eggs, bread, butter, jelly
Dinner: spinach, potatoes, pickles, warmed-over meat, bread, butter
Supper: milk, sweet potatoes, carrots, beans, tomatoes, tea, bread, butter, fruit

Meals like these included few salads or green vegetables; they provided the high-calorie diet necessary for men and women who toiled long hours at hard, hot jobs. Such a diet cost a working-class family of five or six people slightly over $5 a week, or about $260 a year. Workers did have to spend a high percentage of their income—almost half the main breadwinner's yearly wages—on food. But they never experienced the severe malnutrition that plagued other developing nations.

Just as tin cans and iceboxes made many foods widely available, the sewing machine brought about a revolution in clothing. In the eighteenth century, almost all the clothes Americans wore were made at home. In keeping with the proverb "clothes make the man," a person's social status was signaled largely by what he or she wore. Then in the 1830s the sewing machine (invented in Europe but developed by Americans Elias Howe, Jr., and Isaac M. Singer) came into use for clothing and shoe manufacture. Demand for uniforms during the Civil War boosted the ready-made clothing business, and by 1890 annual retail sales of mass-produced garments had reached $1.5 billion. Mass production enabled clothing manufacturers to turn out good-quality garments at relatively low cost and to develop standard sizes to fit different body shapes. By the turn of the century, only the poorest families could not buy ready-made or "ready-to-wear" clothes, and tailors and seamstresses, once the originators of fashion, had largely been relegated to repair work.

Ready-made clothing

The clothing revolution had a socially leveling effect. The availability of inexpensive, sturdy garments and shoes lessened social distinctions in dress. Rich and poor alike bought their clothes "off the rack." As one merchant crowed, "We have provided not alone abundant clothing at a moderate cost for all classes of citizens, but we have given them at the same time the style and character in dress that is essential to the self-respect of a free democratic people." Thus the ready-made garments that were produced by tens of thousands of immigrants huddled over sewing machines in lofts and tenement rooms had the unforeseen effect of transforming those foreign-born laborers into Americans. (When the hero of Abraham Cahan's novel *The Rise of David Levinsky* arrives in New York in 1885, a benefactor buys him a new wardrobe from a variety of

In just a few decades American fashions changed dramatically. Dark, heavy fabrics (left) gave way to lighter, more colorful clothing (right, worn by Governor of New York Al Smith and his wife). Keystone-Mast Collection, University of California, Riverside.

stores. Afterward, his sponsor looks over the new wardrobe and remarks, "Now you won't look green. . . . That will make you look American.")

By 1900 mass-produced clothing had also enabled a large segment of the population to become concerned with style. Restrictive Victorian fashions still dominated women's clothing, but some of the most burdensome features were beginning to be abandoned. After 1900, women's dress design placed greater emphasis on comfort. Designers used less fabric; by the 1920s a dress required three yards of material instead of ten. Long sleeves and skirt hemlines receded, and high-boned collars disappeared. Petite was still the ideal, however: the most desirable waist measurement was 18 to 20 inches. (Corsets, were big sellers at 79 cents apiece, and reformers complained that women often tried to squeeze into dresses, gloves, and shoes that were a size too small.) Colors emphasized female modesty. An article in the *Ladies' Home Journal* in 1899 took note of both fashion and changing female employment patterns when it advised:

> If tempted to give a gown for office wear, let it be one of black, brown, or gray cravenetted serge. Of the three colors, black is to be preferred, on account of the unwritten law governing the style of dress adopted by the majority of self-supporting women.

At the turn of the century, long hair tied at the back of the neck was the most popular style. But by the First World War, when many women worked in hospitals and factories, shorter, more manageable styles had become more acceptable.

Men's clothes too became lighter-weight and more stylish. Before 1900, among the middle and more affluent working classes, a man would have had no more than two suits, one for Sundays and special occasions and one for everyday wear. No distinction was made between summer and winter suits. After 1900, however, manufacturers began to produce garments from fabrics of different weights. Soft felt hats began to replace derbies. (After 1915, the Sears catalogue no longer advertised derbies.) Soft collars and cuffs replaced stiff ones, and plain dark-blue serge gave way to softer shades and more intricate weaves. Workingmen's clothes did not change markedly: laborers still needed the most durable, least expensive overalls, shirts, and shoes. But for those of even modest means, fashion was no longer a badge of class. It too had become a feature of mass consumerism.

Department and chain stores

Department stores and chain stores helped both to create and to serve this new world of consumerism. The great boom in department-store growth occurred between 1865 and 1900, when companies like Macy's, Wanamaker's, Jordan Marsh, and Marshall Field became fixtures of metropolitan America. With their open displays of clothing, housewares, and furniture—all available in large quantities to anyone who had the purchase price—department stores effected a merchandising revolution. Not only did they offer wide variety; they added home deliveries, liberal exchange policies, and charge accounts. The Great Atlantic Tea Company, founded in 1859, was to become the first chain-store system. Renamed the Great Atlantic and Pacific Tea Company in 1869 and known more familiarly as A&P, the firm's stores sold groceries on a cash-and-carry basis. By buying in volume, the chain could sell to the public at low prices. By 1912 there were almost five hundred A&P stores, and more were being built in communities of all sizes across the nation. Other chains, such as Woolworth's, grew rapidly during the same period.

Though the greatest expansion of chain stores did not occur until after 1920, large-volume, broad-variety food and department stores had changed the nature of shopping long before then. They offered the personal convenience (like credit and deliveries) formerly available only at neighborhood specialty shops that catered to the wealthy, and they provided such services in attractive, sometimes ornate settings. Not only could anyone buy the goods for sale, but anyone who wanted to could enter and just look. And no longer were clothes, furniture, and even some foods stocked merely to meet a demand. Now they were displayed in large quantities, to entice shoppers who had no need or intention of buying them. Shopping and consuming had become an American pastime.

Family life

Though the overwhelming majority of Americans continued to live their lives within a family, this most basic of social institutions underwent considerable strain during the industrial era. As American society became more affluent and complex, it generated new institutions—schools, social clubs, political organizations, and others—that competed with the family to provide nurture, education, companionship, and security. Many popular and scholarly writers, alarmed by the new trend, warned that rising divorce rates, the growing separation between home and work, the entrance of large numbers of women into the work force, and loss of parental control over children spelled peril for home and family. In 1913, for example, one reformer lamented that there had been "so many changes in the conditions of life and point of view in the last twenty years that the parent of today is absolutely unfitted to decide the problems of life for the young man and woman of today." Yet the family retained its fundamental usefulness as a cushion in a hard, uncertain world.

Family and household structures

Throughout modern Western history, most people have lived in two overlapping kinds of basic units: the household and the family. A *household* is a residential unit, a group of related and/or unrelated people who live in the same abode. A *family* is a group of people related by kinship, some of whom typically live together. The distinction between household and family is important in describing how Americans lived in the late nineteenth and early twentieth centuries, since the two institutions followed different patterns.

At the most elementary level, Americans between 1877 and 1920 grouped themselves in traditional ways. As in the past, the vast majority (75 to 80 percent) of American households consisted of *nuclear families*—usually a married couple with or without children and including no other relatives. About 15 to 20 percent of households consisted of *extended families,* which might include grandparents, grandchildren, aunts and uncles, in-laws, cousins, or combinations of such relatives. About 5 percent of the population lived alone. Despite slight variations from

A late-nineteenth-century family picnic. Though the extended family of parents, children, grandparents, aunts, and uncles did not often live together, kinship and the support relatives gave each other were an important part of everyday life. The Schlesinger Library, Radcliffe College.

one ethnic, racial, or socioeconomic group to another, the prevailing pattern held relatively constant among all groups.

Several factors explain this pattern. Because the United States was a nation of immigrants, who tended to be young, the country had a very young population. In 1880 the median age was under twenty-one, and by 1920 it was still only twenty-five. (Presently it is 30.) Moreover, fewer people than now lived to old age. In 1900 the death rate among people aged forty-five to sixty-four was over twice what it is today. As a result, there were relatively few old people: in 1900 only 4 percent of the population was sixty-five or older, compared to almost 12 percent today. Thus few families could form extended three-generation households. Fewer children than today knew their grandparents, and the experience of being a grandparent was rarer. Upward social mobility and migration separated many families, and the ideal of a home of one's own encouraged nuclear household organization.

The relative size of nuclear families did change over time, however. In the nineteenth century almost the entire Western world experienced a decline in fertility. In the United States the decline began early in the century and accelerated toward the end of the century.

Birth rates

In 1880 the birth rate was 39.9 live births per 1,000 people; by 1900 it had dropped to 32.3, by 1920 to 27.7. The reasons for this decline remain unclear. The pattern seems to have been that women in the settled eastern areas of the country were ending childbearing at an earlier age—thus limiting the span during which they bore children—than were women in western areas. Possibly the greater availability of arable land in the West encouraged larger families; differences in a child's productivity may also have had an effect. On the farms, where children could work at home or in the fields at an early age, a new child contributed a new set of hands to the family work force. But in the wage-based eastern economy, children could not contribute significantly to the family income for many years; a new child therefore represented another mouth to feed. Throughout the nation, as diet and medical care improved, infant mortality fell, and families did not have to have many children just to ensure that some would survive. It also appears that decisions to limit family size–by abstaining from sex during the wife's fertile period, or by means of other forms of contraception and abortion–resulted from people's growing consciousness that they could improve the quality of life for themselves and their children if their families were smaller than their ancestors' families. Demographers and historians, however, have not been able to validate these speculations with solid evidence.

Though fertility rates among blacks, immigrants, and rural dwellers were consistently higher than those of white native urban dwellers, the birth rates of all groups fell dramatically. As a result, families with six or eight children became less common; three or four children became more common. Thus the nuclear family tended to reach its maximum size and then to empty faster than in earlier eras.

In spite of the predominance of the nuclear family, the household typically expanded and contracted drastically over the lifetime of a given family. First, the size of the family fluctuated as children were born and later left home. Though there were many variations, both male and female children, especially in working-class families, often left home before they were twenty years old, usually to work. Second, the process of leaving home made for huge numbers of young people–and some older people–who lived as boarders and lodgers, especially in cities. Middle- and working-class families commonly took in boarders to help pay the rent or to occupy unused rooms vacated by grown children. Immigrants often lodged newly arrived relatives and fellow villagers until they could establish themselves. Some historians have estimated that there was a 50-percent chance that a city dweller at the end of the nineteenth century would live as a boarder or take in boarders at some time during his or her life.

Boarding

The practice of boarding stirred middle-class concern about health and morality. In 1912, housing reformer Lawrence Veiller charged that "room overcrowding as we know it in America is entirely wrapped up with the lodger evil." And the U.S. Bureau of Labor lamented in 1910 that

> the close quarters often destroy all privacy, and the lodger or boarder becomes practically a member of the family. . . . While such conditions, through custom and long usage, lose the startling effect that they would have to one unused to them, they cannot help but blunt a girl's sense of proper relations with the opposite sex and foster standards which are not acceptable in this country.

Yet for those who experienced it, boarding was a highly useful practice. As one immigrant woman recalled:

> We had four boarders and I had to cook for them. When I first came here I didn't want to do this because everybody want to have their own house. Well, I change my mind because everybody was doing this thing. That time some of the people that came from the other side didn't have no place to stay and we took some of the people in the house that we knew. . . . This is the way that everybody used to do it that time.

Boarding was a transitional stage for immigrants and young people who had left home, providing them with a quasi-family environment until they set up their own households. And it gave the household flexibility, bringing in extra income to meet household needs.

Some households also included extended family members who lived as quasi-boarders. Especially in communities where economic hardship or rapid growth made housing expensive or scarce, newlyweds tended to live with the husband's or wife's parents until they could afford a place of their own. Often a family would take in a widowed parent or unmarried sister or brother who would otherwise have had to live alone. For immigrants and migrants, the family served as a refuge in a strange new place. Having moved from the Old World to the New or from one region to another, they sought out relatives who had preceded them. A Russian Jewish woman prepared for emigration to the United States by writing to relatives in New York. "When I came off the ship," she recalled, "an uncle of mine was supposed to pick me up.

. . . But I didn't live with this uncle because I had my mother's sister so I stayed with her."

Kinship, then, had important functions, especially for immigrants and others in need. At a time when welfare and service agencies were rare the family continued to be the institution to which people could turn. Even when relatives did not live together, they often lived nearby and could help each other out with child care, meals, shopping, advice, consolation, and the like. Family members also obtained jobs for each other. Factory foremen usually had responsibility for hiring, and they often recruited new workers recommended by their employees. According to one new arrival, "After two days my brother took me to the shop he was working in and his boss saw me and he gave me the job." A woman who worked in an optical factory recalled, "My uncle was foreman there. . . . That was my first job. I worked there with my mother. . . . My sister worked there a while too."

Kinship obligations

The obligations of kinship, however, were not always welcome or even helpful. Immigrant families often put pressure on last-born children to stay at home and care for aging parents, a practice that stifled those children's opportunities for education, marriage, and economic independence. As an aging Italian-American father confessed, "One of our daughters is an old maid [and] causes plenty of troubles. . . . It may be my fault because I always wished her to remain at home and not to marry for she was of great financial help." Tensions also developed when one relative felt another was not helping out enough. One woman, for example, complained that her brother-in-law "resented the fact that I saved my money in a bank instead of handing it over to him." Nevertheless, kinship, for better or worse, provided people a means of coping with the stresses of urban industrial society. Social and economic change did not dissolve family ties.

While the family remained resilient and adaptable, subtle but momentous changes began to occur in individual life patterns. Before the twentieth century, the stages of life were less distinct than they are today, and generations blended into each other with relatively little separation. Childhood, for instance, was regarded as a period during which young people prepared for adulthood by assuming gradually more adult roles and responsibilities. The subcultures of childhood—toddlers, school children, adolescents, and the like—were not nearly as clear-cut as they are today. Because relatively few people lived past sixty-five or left work voluntarily, retirement and homes for the elderly were rare, and old age was not singled out as a distinct stage of life either. Married couples had relatively large numbers of children born over a longer time span than is characteristic among twentieth-century couples, so active parenthood occupied most of their adult lives. And because older children often cared for their younger sisters and brothers, they may have begun parenting even before reaching adulthood.

Stages of life

By the turn of the century, demographic and social changes had altered these patterns. Decreasing fertility rates reduced the period of parental responsibility, so more middle-aged couples experienced an "empty-nest" stage when all their children had grown up and left home. Longer life expectancy and a growing tendency on the part of employers, especially in manufacturing, to force the retirement of aged workers further isolated the old from the young. At the same time, work became more specialized and education more formalized—especially after the passage of compulsory-school-attendance laws. Childhood and adolescence therefore became more distinct from adulthood. As a result of these and other trends (including the lower fertility rate, which gave people fewer sisters and brothers to relate to), Americans began to become more age- and peer-conscious. Peoples' roles in school, in the family, on the job, and even in the community came to be defined by age as much as by any other characteristic.

At the turn of the century, family life and its functions were both changing and holding firm. New institutions were assuming tasks formerly performed by the family. Schools were making education more of a community responsibility. Employment agencies, personnel offices, labor unions, and legislatures were beginning to take responsibility for employee recruitment and job security. And age-based peer groups were exerting greater influence over peoples' values and activities. In addition, migration and a soaring divorce rate seemed to be splitting families apart: 19,633 divorces were granted in the United States in 1880; by 1920, that number had grown to 167,105. Yet in the face of these changes, the family remained a resilient institution. Households and families adjusted, sometimes from one year to the next, by expanding and contracting to meet temporary needs. And kinship remained a dependable though not always appreciated institution. In the early 1900s, popular and scholarly writers were predicting the decline of the family just as they are today. But for the majority of people, family life was vital. "As I grew up, living conditions were a bit crowded," one woman reminisced, "but no one minded because we were a family [and we were] thankful we all lived together."

The birth of mass culture

Before the end of the nineteenth century, what people consumed, talked about, and did with their spare time were individual matters, often dictated by subsistence needs. Social institutions were local, and contacts with the broader world were limited. But the revolutions in transportation, industrialization, and urbanization upset these traditional patterns. Technological and industrial changes created a variety of new standardized goods and services, as well as a more developed money economy. Urbanization expanded the nation's cultural centers. The commonest form of nonwork mass activity was still church attendance, but the industrial age was fostering new recreations that increasingly filled people's spare time. The explosive development of leisure-time pursuits that occurred between 1877 and 1920 eventually gave rise to a genuine mass culture.

For a nation nurtured on a frontier tradition of hard work and distaste for wasted time, the leisure-time revolution of the late nineteenth century marked a dramatic shift. American inventors and tinkerers had always tried to create labor-saving devices, but not until the late nineteenth century did the effects of technological development become truly time-saving. Mechanization and assembly-line production helped to reduce the average work week for manufacturing workers from sixty-six hours in 1860 to sixty in 1890 and fifty-one in 1920. These reductions not only meant shorter workdays but also freer weekends. Middle-class white-collar workers in the cities spent eight to ten hours a day on the job, and often worked only half a day or not at all on weekends. Even on farms, mechanization helped to expand free time. Americans began to have time for a variety of diversions, and for the first time a substantial segment of the economy began providing for—and profiting from—leisure. By the early 1900s, many Americans were enmeshed in the business of play.

Increase in leisure time

After the Civil War, amusement became an organized activity like production and consumption. The vanguard of this trend was sports. Formerly a fashionable indulgence of the genteel class, organized sports quickly became the most popular pastime of all classes, attracting huge numbers of participants and spectators of both sexes. Even those who could not play or watch became involved by reading about sports in the newspapers.

The first and most popular organized sport was baseball. Having evolved out of older bat, ball, and base-circling games, baseball was formalized in 1845 when a group of business and professional men in New York organized the Knickerbocker Club and codified the rules of the game. By 1860 there were at least fifty baseball clubs, and pick-up games were played on vacant city lots and open rural fields across the nation. In 1869 a professional club, the Cincinnati Red Stockings, went on a national tour, and several other clubs quickly followed suit. The National League of Professional Baseball Clubs, founded in 1876, gave the sport a more stable, businesslike structure. By the 1880s, professional baseball was a big business: in 1887, for example, over 51,000 people paid to watch a championship series between St. Louis and Detroit. In 1903, the National League and competing American League (formed in 1901) began a World Series between their championship teams (the Boston Red Socks beat the Pittsburgh Pirates in that first series), further entrenching baseball as the national pastime.

Baseball

Baseball appealed mostly to men. But croquet, which also swept the nation after the Civil War, attracted both sexes. As one playing manual observed, "Hitherto, while men and boys have had their healthful means of recreation in the open air, the women and girls have been restricted to the less exhilarating sports of indoor life." Across the country, middle- and upper-class people held croquet parties

Croquet and cycling

Opening day at the first World Series, Boston, 1903. This match between Pittsburgh (National League) and Boston (American League) evidenced the growing popularity of professional baseball, as increasing numbers of Americans found the time and money to support spectator sports. Northeastern University, World Series Room.

and even rigged wickets with candles for night games. In an era when the removal of work from the home had begun separating men and women, croquet provided an opportunity for social contact between the sexes. Polite deportment was emphasized: "Grace in holding and using the mallet, easy and pleasing attitudes in playing, promptness in taking your turn, and gentlemanly and ladylike manners generally throughout the game are [important] points," noted one instructor.

Bicycling achieved a popularity rivaling that of baseball–especially after 1899, when the cumbersome velocipede, with its huge front wheel and tall seat, gave way to the safety bicycle with pneumatic tires and wheels of identical size. By 1893 Americans owned over 1 million bicycles, and cycling clubs such as the League of American Wheelmen were pressing state and local governments to build more paved roads. One journal boasted that cycling cured dyspepsia, headaches, insomnia, and sciatica, and gave "a vigorous tone to the whole system." Like croquet, bicycling brought men and women together. Moreover, the bicycle played an influential role in freeing women from the constraints of Victorian fashions. In order to ride bikes, even the dropped-frame female models, women had to wear divided skirts and simple undergarments. Gradually the freer styles of cycling costumes began to influence everyday fashions. Finally, coed riding, especially on the bicycle-built-for-two, provided for the combination of courtship with exercise. As the 1900 census declared, "Few articles . . . have created so great a revolution in social conditions as the bicycle."

Tennis and golf won enthusiasts of both sexes in the late nineteenth century, but remained pastimes of the wealthy. Both were played mostly at private clubs and lacked baseball's team competition and cycling's informality. American football also began as a sport for people of high social rank. At first mainly an intercollegiate sport, football attracted mostly players and spectators wealthy enough to have access to higher education. By the end of the century, however, football was attracting a broader class of supporters. The 1893 Princeton-Yale game was attended by fifty thousand spectators—a number suggesting that the fans were drawn from several social classes—and informal football games were being played in the yards and playgrounds of many communities.

Football

At the same time, college football was becoming a national scandal because of its violence and the use of "tramp athletes," nonstudents whom colleges hired to play on their teams. Critics charged that football mirrored the worst features of American society. An editor of the *Nation* complained in 1890 that "the spirit of the American youth, as of the American man, is to win, to 'get there,' by fair means or foul; and the lack of moral scruple which pervades the struggles of the business world meets with temptations equally irresistible in the miniature contests of the football field." A Yale football player was reported to have visited a slaughterhouse before a game and soaked his jersey in blood to make himself appear more ferocious. The scandals climaxed in 1905, when 18 football players were killed and over 150 seriously injured. President Theodore Roosevelt, a strong advocate of athletics, convened a White House conference to discuss ways of eliminating brutality and foul play. The conference founded the Intercollegiate Athletic Association (renamed the National College Athletic Association in 1910) to police college sports. In 1906 the association altered the rules of football to make it less violent and more open. The new rules extended the distance to be gained by the first down from 5 to 10 yards, legalized the forward pass, and tightened player eligibility requirements.

In a society that considered females biologically and emotionally weaker than males, women were mostly confined to the more genteel sports: croquet, archery, riding, and bicycling. Yet, as more women attended college, they began to pursue more forms of physical activity. Believing that in order to succeed intellectually they needed to be active and healthy, college women participated in a variety of sports, ranging from rowing to track to baseball and swimming. Eventually basketball became the most popular sport among college women. Invented in 1891 as a winter sport for men, basketball was given women's rules (that limited dribbling and running and encouraged passing) by Senda Berenson of Smith College in the 1890s, and intercollegiate games became common across the country.

The rise of American show business paralleled the rise of sports, and similarly became a mode of leisure created by and for the common people. Circuses—traveling shows of acrobats, equestrian acts, and animals—had existed since the 1820s and 1830s. But after the Civil War, railroads enabled circuses to reach more of the country, and the popularity of the big show increased enormously. Meanwhile circuses became impressive feats of organization. Their mobility required skillful planning of schedules, transportation, and promotion. And the swift construction and dismantling of the huge tent city required by two- and three-ring circuses with side shows, menageries, and private quarters was done with factory-like precision.

Circuses

Circuses offered two main attractions: so-called freaks of nature, both human and animal, and the temptation and conquest of death. Both reinforced popular confidence in human mastery of the environment, while exposing audiences to nature's thrilling mysteries and perils. More important, however, was the sheer astonishment aroused by the trapeze artists, lion tamers, high-wire artists (sometimes on bicycles), acrobats, and clowns. Writer Hamlin Garland captured the circus's effect on a thousand towns and villages:

> From the time the "advance man" flung his highly colored posters over the fence till the coming of the glorious day, we thought of little else. . . . It was our brief season of imaginative life. In one day—in a part of one day—we gained a thousand new conceptions of the world and of human nature. It was the embodiment of all that was skillful and beautiful in human action. . . . It gave us something to talk about.

Several branches of American show business matured with the growth of cities. Popular drama, musical comedy, and vaudeville all gave Americans a chance to escape from the ambiguities and harsh realities of urban-industrial life into melodrama, nostalgia, adventure, and comedy. The plots were simple, the heroes and villains instantly recognizable. And for urbanized people increasingly distant from the frontier, popular plays brought to life the mythical Wild West and Old South through the stories of Davy Crockett, Buffalo Bill, and Civil War romances. Virtue, honor, and justice always triumphed in melodramas such as *Uncle Tom's Cabin, The Old Homestead,* and *The Wild West,* reinforcing the popular belief that even in an uncertain and disillusioning world, goodness would nevertheless prevail.

Popular drama and musical comedy

Musical comedies bolstered national optimism with song, humor, and dance. American musical comedy grew out of the lavishly costumed extravaganzas and comic operettas popular in Europe. By introducing American themes (often involving ethnic groups), folksy humor, and catchy tunes and dances, these shows launched the nation's most popular songs and entertainers. George M. Cohan, born into an Irish family of vaudeville entertainers, became the master of the American musical comedy after the turn of the century. Drawing on urbanism, patriotism, and traditional values in songs like "Yankee Doodle Boy" and "You're a Grand Old Flag," Cohan helped to reinforce a sense of moral superiority (a feeling that aided the nation during the First World War but failed it afterward). Comic opera too became a fad, and the talented, beautiful, dignified Lillian Russell its most admired performer. The first American comic operas were weak imitations of European musicals, such as those by Gilbert and Sullivan. But by the early 1900s, composers like Victor Herbert were writing for American audiences. Shortly thereafter Jerome Kern began to write more sophisticated musicals, and American musical comedy came into its own.

The French term *vaudeville* first referred to light drama with musical interludes, but in the United States vaudeville became a unique form of entertainment with no European roots. Originally staged by saloonkeepers to attract customers, vaudeville variety shows were developed by skilled promoters who used the term to lend respectability to a once-disreputable entertainment. Vaudeville was probably the most popular entertainment in early twentieth-century America because its variety made it attractive to mass audiences. Shows included magic and animal acts, juggling, stunts, comedy (especially ethnic humor), and song and dance. Around 1900, the number of vaudeville theaters and troupes skyrocketed. Fostered by sharp promoters who did for entertainment what Edison and Ford did for technology, vaudeville quickly became big business. The most famous promoter, Florenz Ziegfeld, brilliantly packaged popular entertainment in a stylish format–the Ziegfeld Follies–and gave the nation a new model of femininity, the Ziegfeld Girl, whose graceful dancing and alluring costumes were meant to suggest a haunting sensuality.

Vaudeville

Show business provided new economic opportunities for women, blacks, and immigrants, but also indulged in stereotyping and exploitation. Lillian Russell, vaudeville singer and comedienne Fanny Brice, and burlesque queen Eva Tanguay attracted intensely loyal fans, commanded handsome fees, and won respect for their genuine talents. In contrast to the demure Victorian female, they conveyed pluck and creativity. There was something both shocking and refreshingly confident about Eva Tanguay when she sang earthy songs like "I Want Someone to Go Wild with Me," "It's All Been Done Before But Not the Way I Do It," and her theme song "I Don't Care." But lesser female performers were often exploited by male promoters and theater owners, many of whom wanted only to titillate the public with the sight of scantily clad women.

Before the 1890s, the only form of entertainment open to black performers was the minstrel show. By century's end, however, minstrel shows had given way to more sophisticated Negro musicals, and blacks had begun to break into vaudeville. As stage sets shifted from the plantation to the city, the music shifted from folk tunes to ragtime, which attracted white audiences as well as black. Pandering to the prejudice of white audiences, composers and performers of both races ridiculed blacks. The popularity of songs like "He's Just a Little Nigger, But He's Mine All Mine," and "You May Be a Hawaiian on Old Broadway, But You're Just Another Nigger to Me" is evidence that blacks on the stage suffered in the same way they did elsewhere in society. Even Burt Williams, a highly paid black comedian and dancer who was one of the era's most talented

Black musicals and ethnic humor

A newsstand beneath an elevated railway station displays a large variety of popular magazines and newspapers. By the early 1900s these publications were read by millions daily—for their advertisements as well as for their news and sports. Ford Archives.

Just as advertising became news, news often became a form of advertising, or at least of publicity. Canny publishers made people crave news just as they craved amusements and consumer goods. City life and the increase in leisure time seemed to nurture a fascination with the sensational, and from the 1880s onward popular newspapers increasingly whetted and catered to that desire.

Popular journalism

Joseph Pulitzer, a Hungarian immigrant who bought the New York *World* in 1883, pioneered the development of journalism as a branch of mass culture. Believing that newspapers should be "dedicated to the cause of the people rather than to that of the purse potentates," Pulitzer filled the *World* with stories of disasters, crimes, and scandals. Sensational headlines, set in large bold type like that of advertisements, screamed from every page. Pulitzer's journalists not only reported the news but sought it out—and sometimes even created it. *World* reporter Nellie Bly (whose real name was Elizabeth Cochrane) faked her way into an insane asylum and wrote a sensational exposé of the sordid conditions she found. Other reporters staged similar stunts and sought out heart-rending human-interest stories. Pulitzer also popularized the comics, and the yellow ink they were printed in lent his new emphasis on the sensational and lurid the nickname "yellow journalism."

Pulitzer's strategy was immensely successful. In one year he increased the *World*'s daily circulation from 20,000 to 100,000, and by the late 1890s it had reached 1 million. Soon other publishers, such as William Randolph Hearst (who bought the New York *Journal* in 1895 and started an empire of mass-circulation newspapers), adopted Pulitzer's techniques. Yellow journalism became a nationwide phenomenon, enhancing interest in bizarre aspects of the human condition and kindling sentiments for reform.

Pulitzer and his rivals fanned popular interest even further by emphasizing sports and women's news. Newspapers had always reported on sporting events, but the yellow-journalism papers gave such stories far greater prominence by printing separate, expanded sports sections. Such sections did more than anything else to promote sports as a leisure-time attraction. Sports news became a new addiction, recreating much of a particular game's excitement and suspense through narrative and statistics. Baseball, with its proliferating amateur and professional leagues, heated rivalries between city- and group-sponsored teams, and extended season moving suspensefully toward a climactic championship, proved especially suited to the new journalism. But other sports, such as horse racing, bicycle racing, boxing, basketball, and football, were also staples of the sports section. And at the same time they expanded sports news, mostly for male readers, newspapers were adding more women's news. A special section devoted to household tips, advice and fashion, decorum, and social and women's-club news captured the interest of female readers. Like crime and disaster stories, sports and women's sections helped to make the news a mass commodity.

By the early twentieth century, the communications media, like the mass consumption of goods, were drawing the country together. Alongside newspapers, mass-circulation magazines were overshadowing the expensive elitist journals of earlier eras. Publications like *McClure's,* the *Saturday Evening Post, Everybody's,* and *Ladies' Home Journal* offered human-interest stories, muckraking exposés (see pages 576–577), titillating fiction, and eye-catching advertisements to a growing mass market. And the total number of books published more than quadrupled between 1880 and 1917. This rising popular consumption of news and books was accompanied–and fueled–by a growing literacy rate. Between 1870 and 1920, the proportion of Americans aged ten or over who could not read or write dropped from 20 percent to 6 percent.

Other forms of communication were also expanding. In 1891 there were only 0.3 telephones per 100 people in this country; by 1901 the number had grown to 2.1, and by 1921 it had swelled to 12.6. In 1900 Americans sent 79.7 million telegrams and used 4 billion postage stamps; in 1917 they sent 155.3 million telegrams, and in 1922 they used 14.3 billion stamps. Little wonder, then, that the term *community* took on new dimensions, as people used the media, the mail, and the telephone to extend their horizons far beyond their place of residence. More than ever before, people in different parts of the country knew about and discussed the same staples of mass culture, whether it was a sensational murder, a sex scandal, or the fortunes of a particular entertainer or athlete. America was becoming a mass society.

The public sentiment

The same society that celebrated the machine and all its benefits also idolized Tarzan the Ape Man. American culture has long focused one eye on an increasingly complex technological future while casting the other longingly back at a sentimentalized, simpler past. The two dispositions shared the popular mind with particular vividness between 1877 and 1920. When modern wonders like telephones, high-speed printing presses, phonographs, cameras, and projectors made information and entertainment more accessible, people demanded diversions that reaffirmed the traditional values of optimism, individualism, and freedom. Thus in 1914, just when they were beginning to fully appreciate automobiles, movies, and electricity, Americans made Edgar Rice Burroughs's *Tarzan of the Apes* a best seller.

Popular fiction writers in tune with the times concentrated on the sensational. Such efforts were not exactly new; since the 1840s, low-priced, paperbound adventure novels known as shilling shockers had circulated widely among the literate public. After the Civil War such books, now called dime novels, became the most

Dime novels

widely read variety of American literature, especially among youths. As one man recalled, "I read them at every chance; so did every normal boy of my acquaintance. . . . We swapped them on the basis of two old volumes for every new one; we maintained a clandestine circulating library system which had its branch offices in every stableloft in our part of town." The principal publisher of dime novels was Erastus Beadle, whose firm Beadle and Adams issued over thirteen hundred titles in the three decades before it went out of business in 1897. Popular magazines like *Tip Top Weekly,* which serialized adventure stories, attracted hundreds of thousands of readers.

Dime novels and similar popular literature offered three types of stories to young readers. The first evoked the Wild West for a population that was seeing the frontier fade into the past. Intertwining fact and fiction with typically American abandon, writers like Zane Grey wove adventure stories around famous folk heroes like Buffalo Bill Cody, The Lone Ranger, and Wild Bill Hickok. During the 1880s, however, many authors, recognizing the lure and growing impact of city life, began to give their tales urban settings and themes. Detective thrillers became the leading type of popular urban fiction, and hard-nosed, wily characters like Old Cap Collins and Nick Carter captivated readers of various ages. Just before the end of the century, science fiction and superheroes came to the fore. Elaborating on the marvels of new scientific discoveries, such works as the Tom Swift series described space ships, gravity nullifiers, and other inventions that surpassed even Edison's imagination.

One popular writer, Horatio Alger, moved beyond the fantasies of dime novels and offered his readers a formula for contending with new social and economic forces. A failed Unitarian clergyman, Alger began writing boys' stories in the 1860s, producing some 130 titles over the next three decades. Each of his books tells the success story of an adolescent boy facing the problem of finding a place in an urban industrial world. As Alger's titles attest, each emphasizes the virtues of self-reliance and hard work: *Work and Win, Do and Dare, Struggling Upward, Rise from the Ranks.* "Have you got grit?" an employer asks the hero of *Strive and Succeed.* "Do you generally succeed in what you undertake? Grit weighs heavily in this world."

Moral messages of popular fiction

Alger's heroes begin their lives in poverty, and call on ambition, honesty, courage, thrift, and luck to overcome some obstacle and achieve success. But his message was more than an exhortation to morality and frugality. The moral of Alger's stories was that success came to those who were not only virtuous but alert enough to capitalize on a lucky break. Thus Ragged Dick, the hero of Alger's first novel, is clean, honest, and polite, but his opportunity to escape poverty arrives when he rescues the drowning child of a banker. The hero of *Bound to Rise* ministers to a lonely old man who repays him with a bundle of real estate deeds. Thus while the main theme was overcoming poverty, the model to strive for was the kind, generous millionaire. Alger believed in a cause-and-effect relationship between virtue and wealth.

Just before Alger's death in 1899, one of America's most popular superheroes, Frank Merriwell, was created by Gilbert Patten (the pen name of Burt Standish), a writer of hack fiction since his teens. Frank Merriwell's adventures had a common theme that accorded with the way many Americans liked to think of themselves and their nation: he attempted and accomplished the impossible. Merriwell's name symbolized American virtues: according to Patten, "I took the three qualities I most wanted him to represent–frank and merry in nature, well in body and mind–and made the name Frank Merriwell." In a series of adventures, first at Farndale Academy, later at Yale and as a world traveler, Merriwell provided youthful readers one of the first character models in popular fiction. Whether performing amazing athletic feats or daring rescues, he was a picture of refinement and valor who taught by example, not by preaching. In one story, Frank knocks down a thug hired to break his arm before a big game. Graciously, Frank helps him to his feet and befriends him. The thug exclaims, "Gee, I don't know w'y it is, but jes' bein' wid youse makes me want ter do de square t'ing."

Patten's success was phenomenal. He began writing the Merriwell series for *Tip Top Weekly* in 1896 and continued for 896 consecutive issues until 1915, by which time the magazine's circulation had reached 125,000. The serials were also published as paperback novels with titles such as *Frank Merriwell's Trip West, Frank Merriwell at Yale, Frank Merriwell's Air Voyage,* and *Frank Merriwell on Wall Street.* Patten eventually wrote 208 such novels, all stressing youthful ideals.

Work and Leisure at the Turn of the Century, 1885–1910

Bicycles and tricycles (considered appropriate for women in skirts) were popular inventions of the late nineteenth century. Manufacturers promoted them as a pleasant and healthful means of spending one's leisure hours. The emphasis on the value of exercise was significant. It revealed that growing numbers of men were no longer working at physically demanding tasks. It also marked the beginning of the end of the Victorian notion that women were too fragile for physical exertion. The New-York Historical Society.

Hester Street, on New York's Lower East Side, was the shopping center for a large immigrant community. There immigrant families purchased food and clothing, socialized, and escaped the confines of their often dingy and crowded apartments. Even if families had little money to spend on anything but the necessities of life, they could watch salesmen demonstrate various wares and dream of the day when they would be able to afford a luxury or two. The Brooklyn Museum, Dick S. Ramsay Fund.

As time passed, work and leisure became more and more distinct. Americans began to spend the wages they had earned in factories and offices on separate leisure-time activities. One popular entertainment was theater. *Blue Jeans,* the melodrama advertised at right, drew its title from a well-known nineteenth-century consumer good, denim trousers. Culver Pictures, Inc.

By the late nineteenth century many young men had entered sales or service jobs, and the chief work of many well-to-do women had become shopping. The advertisement for a millinery store at left shows both trends clearly. The female shoppers select fancy goods for hats while the all-male sales force waits on them. The formal, orderly, idealized middle-class scene presents a sharp contrast to the scene on Hester Street. The New-York Historical Society.

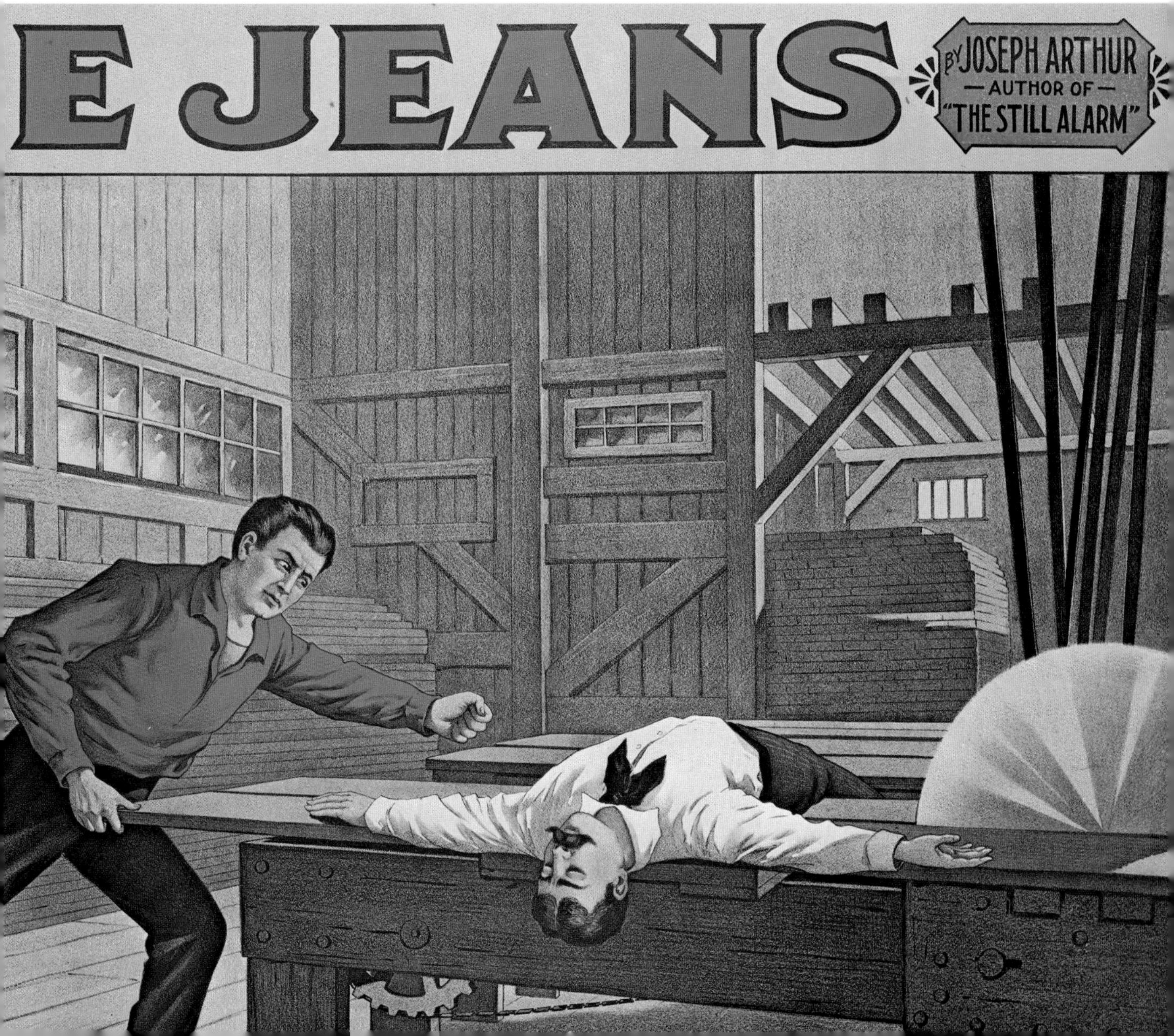

Bowling, another new commercial entertainment, drew thousands of participants and spectators, especially to tournaments like the one shown at left. The New-York Historical Society.

By the early twentieth century, stress on physical fitness had caused changes in dress and behavior for both sexes. Nineteenth-century women, governed by strict rules of modesty and fashion, had worn floor-length gowns with long sleeves even on beaches. The young bathers shown below, painted in 1908, wore shockingly brief clothing in comparison. Compare the clothing in the bicycle poster, painted in 1885. Collection Walker Art Center, Minneapolis, Gift of the T. B. Walker Foundation.

Young women found similar escape and inspiration in sentimental tales about growing up and about animals. One of the most widely read was Louisa May Alcott's *Little Women,* published in two parts in 1868 and 1869. This novel, which eventually sold over 2 million copies, recreated the domestic delights and moral trials of four girls based on Alcott and her sisters. A generation later, Gene Stratton-Porter's romantic novels about animals, like *Freckles* (1904) and *Laddie* (1913), became the best sellers of her day. Others in the same vein were Margaret Sidney's *Five Little Peppers* (1880), Anna Sewell's *Black Beauty* (1890), Kate Douglas Wiggins's *Rebecca of Sunnybrook Farm* (1903), and Lucy M. Montgomery's *Anne of Green Gables* (1908).

Popular literature for adults also oozed with escapism and sentimentality. The best-selling titles of the late nineteenth century included Marie Corelli's *Thelma* (1887) and Charles Majors's *When Knighthood Was in Flower* (1898)–both romances about mythical places of chivalry and honor–and *Ben Hur* (1880), General Lew Wallace's powerful religious melodrama set in the Roman Empire. Not since *Uncle Tom's Cabin* had a book captured as much attention as *Ben Hur,* which sold 2 million copies by 1933. Its publication heralded a rage for historical fiction that began in the 1890s and has continued to this day. Self-help and inspiration, both perennial themes in American popular literature, also blossomed. The style pioneered by *Poor Richard's Almanac,* McGuffey's readers, and Horatio Alger's novels was developed in such works as Samuel Smiles's four best sellers *Self-Help* (1860), *Character* (1871), *Thrift* (1875), and *Duty* (1880); Andrew Carnegie's *Gospel of Wealth* (1901); and Russell Conwell's published sermon "Acres of Diamonds" (see page 510).

Frank Merriwell, the fictional hero of hundreds of sports and adventure stories, became a popular character model for young men. The caption for this illustration reads, " 'I will give you five hundred dollars,' said Cutter, 'to show me how to throw the double shoot.' " Published in *Tip Top Weekly* and in paperback between 1896 and 1915, the Merriwell stories represented only a small fraction of the popular literature available to readers of all ages. Culver.

While some popular writers focused on escapism, other writers were trying to introduce realism into romance. During the 1870s and 1880s, a number of "local-color" writers began producing works that depicted the people and environment of a particular region more realistically. This movement was largely centered in the South, whose writers felt compelled to rebuild the region's national image. Works by Joel Chandler Harris, who created the popular Uncle Remus stories; Mary Noailles Murfree, who located her tales in Appalachia; and George Washington Cable, who captured the aura of exotic New Orleans, all reproduced authentic characters and dialects. The realist movement permeated other regions as well. The regional writers of the Far West and Midwest, who actually preceded the southern local colorists, included Bret Harte, who spun tales about the California mining experience; Edward Eggleston, who recreated the life of his native southern Indiana; and Constance Fenimore Woolson, who wrote about the lumbering and fur-trading districts of the Great Lakes. Each of these writers used authentic manners, customs, and ways of speech to depict a romantic, rustic past.

Local colorists

One local colorist moved beyond romance and adventure, and in doing so won recognition from intellectuals as well as the masses. Mark Twain (the pen name of Samuel Clemens) was a regional writer by reputation. Twain was a westerner who had grown up in Hannibal, Missouri, worked as a river pilot on the Mississippi, and traveled through the mining towns of the Far West. Though he wrote several works about Europe, such as *Innocents Abroad* (1869) and *A Connecticut Yankee at King Arthur's Court* (1889), he was best known for his books about the American West: *Tom Sawyer* (1876), *Life on the Mississippi* (1883), and *Huckleberry Finn* (1884). These antisentimental novels were realistic portrayals of western life and of human weakness. Twain was sensitive to both the comic and the tragic sides of life, and his writing reflected the dynamic energy and materialism of his era. He once wrote that "my books are mainly autobiographies," and his most famous character, Huck Finn, who has thrilled schoolchildren and occupied the minds of American literature students for a century, seemed to represent the daring, hypocrisy, and amiability of both Twain and his nation.

Literary classics

A number of Twain's contemporaries shunned the falseness of escape writing and focused instead on the moral tests life holds. Realists like William Dean Howells and Henry James wrote chiefly about upper-class Americans (James usually wrote about Americans in Europe), but other realists examined the lives of more ordinary Americans and in so doing opened new literary vistas. These writers, sometimes called naturalists, often viewed life in terms of the survival of the fittest; they portrayed ruthless struggles for life and power in frank detail. Among the naturalists were Stephen Crane, whose *Maggie: A Girl of the Streets* (1893) shocked readers with its candid description of slum life and sexual immorality; Hamlin Garland, whose *Main Traveled Roads* (1891) portrayed a side of rural America that local colorists avoided; Frank Norris, whose *McTeague* (1899) graphically depicted the brutality of human greed; Jack London, whose stories of the West and Northwest portrayed both humans and animals as violent; and Theodore Dreiser, whose *Sister Carrie* (1900) showed that people do not always suffer for their wrongdoings.

The escapism of popular fiction and the realism of serious fiction, though seemingly at odds, offered similar commentaries on the American society of the early twentieth century. It was no coincidence that Frank Merriwell replaced Horatio Alger's heroes in popular fiction around 1900: by then Americans knew that it took more than honesty, energy, and a timely rescue to become rich. Numberless little-noticed revolutions had transformed the world that Alger and others had known. The obstacles to success were not simple, and making one's way in the world required technological skills, organizational know-how, and a lot of capital. More sophisticated and more familiar with the possibilities of a consumption-oriented society, readers craved more from their heroes, such as prowess in the new mass cult of sports (Merriwell), conquest of science (Tom Swift), or abilities to commune with nature (Gene Stratton-Porter's characters).

Meanwhile serious authors, striving to recreate realistically what they saw around them, examined the dark side of progress. Whereas virtue still triumphed in popular and juvenile literature, naturalist writers saw that the new demands the industrial age placed on individuals threatened the traditional American values of family, nature, frugality, and moral restraint. The challenges of adjusting to a growing emphasis on consumption would become a major theme of twentieth-century American history.

Suggestions for further reading

Living standards and new conveniences

Daniel J. Boorstin, *The Americans: The Democratic Experience* (1973); James H. Collins, *The Story of Canned Foods* (1924); Richard O. Cummings, *The American and His Food* (1940); Boris Emmet and J. E. Jeuck, *Catalogues and Counters: History of Sears, Roebuck and Company* (1950); *Historical Statistics of the United States,* 2 vols., (1976); Godfrey M. Lebhar, *Chain Stores in America* (1962); Clarence D. Long, *Wages and Earnings in the United States, 1860–1890* (1960); H. Pasadermadjian, *The Department Store* (1954); Lawrence Wright, *Clean and Decent* (1960).

Family and individual life cycles

W. Andrew Achenbaum, *Old Age in the New Land* (1979); Howard P. Chudacoff, "The Life Course of Women, 1865–1915," *Journal of Family History,* 5 (1980), 274–292;

Howard P. Chudacoff and Tamara K. Hareven, "From Empty Nest to Family Dissolution," *Journal of Family History,* 4 (1979), 69–83; Carl N. Degler, *At Odds: Women and the Family in America* (1980); Michael Gordon, ed., *The American Family in Social-Historical Perspective,* 2nd ed. (1978); Tamara K. Hareven, ed., *Anonymous Americans* (1971); Tamara K. Hareven, ed., *Transitions: The Family and Life Course in Historical Perspective* (1978); Tamara K. Hareven and Maris Vinovskis, eds., *Family and Population in Nineteenth Century America* (1978); Joseph Kett, *Rites of Passage: Adolescence in America* (1979); John Modell and Tamara K. Hareven, "Urbanization and the Malleable Household: An Examination of Boarding and Lodging in American Families," *Journal of Marriage and the Family,* 35 (1973), 299–314; David J. Pivar, *Purity Crusade: Sexual Morality and Social Control, 1868–1900* (1973); Dorothy Ross, *G. Stanley Hall: The Psychologist as Prophet* (1972); Richard Sennett, *Families Against the City* (1970); Robert V. Wells, "Demographic Change and the Life Cycle of American Families," *Journal of Interdisciplinary History,* 2 (1971), 273–282; Virginia Yans-McLaughlin, *Family and Community: Italian Immigrants in Buffalo* (1977).

Mass entertainment and leisure

Gunther Barth, *City People* (1980); John R. Betts, *America's Sporting Heritage* (1974); Allison Danzig, *History of American Football* (1956); John E. DiMeglio, *Vaudeville U.S.A.* (1973); Foster R. Dulles, *America Learns to Play* (1966); Roland Gelatt, *The Fabulous Phonograph* (1965); John F. Kasson, *Amusing the Million: Coney Island at the Turn of the Century* (1978); Arthur Knight, *The Liveliest Art* (1957); John A. Lucas and Ronald Smith, *Saga of American Sport* (1978); Joseph A. Musselman, *Music in the Cultured Generation: A Social History of Music in America, 1870–1900* (1971); Beaumont Newhall, *The History of Photography,* rev. ed. (1964); Harold Seymour, *Baseball,* 2 vols. (1960–1971); Robert Sklar, *Movie-Made America* (1976); Dale A. Somers, *The Rise of Sports in New Orleans* (1972); Sigmund Spaeth, *History of Popular Music* (1948); Robert C. Toll, *On With the Show: The First Century of Show Business in America* (1976); David Q. Voigt, *American Baseball,* 2 vols. (1966–1970).

Advertising and journalism

George Juergens, *Joseph Pulitzer and the New York World* (1966); Frank L. Mott, *American Journalism,* 3rd ed. (1962); Frank L. Mott, *A History of American Magazines,* 5 vols. (1930–1968); Frank Presbrey, *The History and Development of Advertising* (1929); W. A. Swanberg, *Citizen Hearst* (1961); Bernard A. Weisberger, *The American Newspaperman* (1961); James P. Wood, *The Story of Advertising* (1958).

Popular literature

Katharine Anthony, *Louisa May Alcott* (1938); John G. Cawelti, *Apostles of Success in America* (1965); John L. Cutler, *Patten and His Merriwell Saga* (1934); Theodore P. Greene, *America's Heroes: The Changing Models of Success in American Magazines* (1970); Frank L. Mott, *Golden Multitudes: The Story of Best Sellers in the United States* (1947); Edmund L. Pearson, *Dime Novels* (1929); Moses Rischin, ed., *The American Gospel of Success* (1965); Henry Nash Smith, *Mark Twain* (1962); John W. Tebbel, *From Rags to Riches: Horatio Alger, Jr. and the American Dream* (1963); Dixon Wector, *Sam Clemens of Hannibal* (1952); Irvin G. Wyllie, *The Self-Made Man in America* (1954).

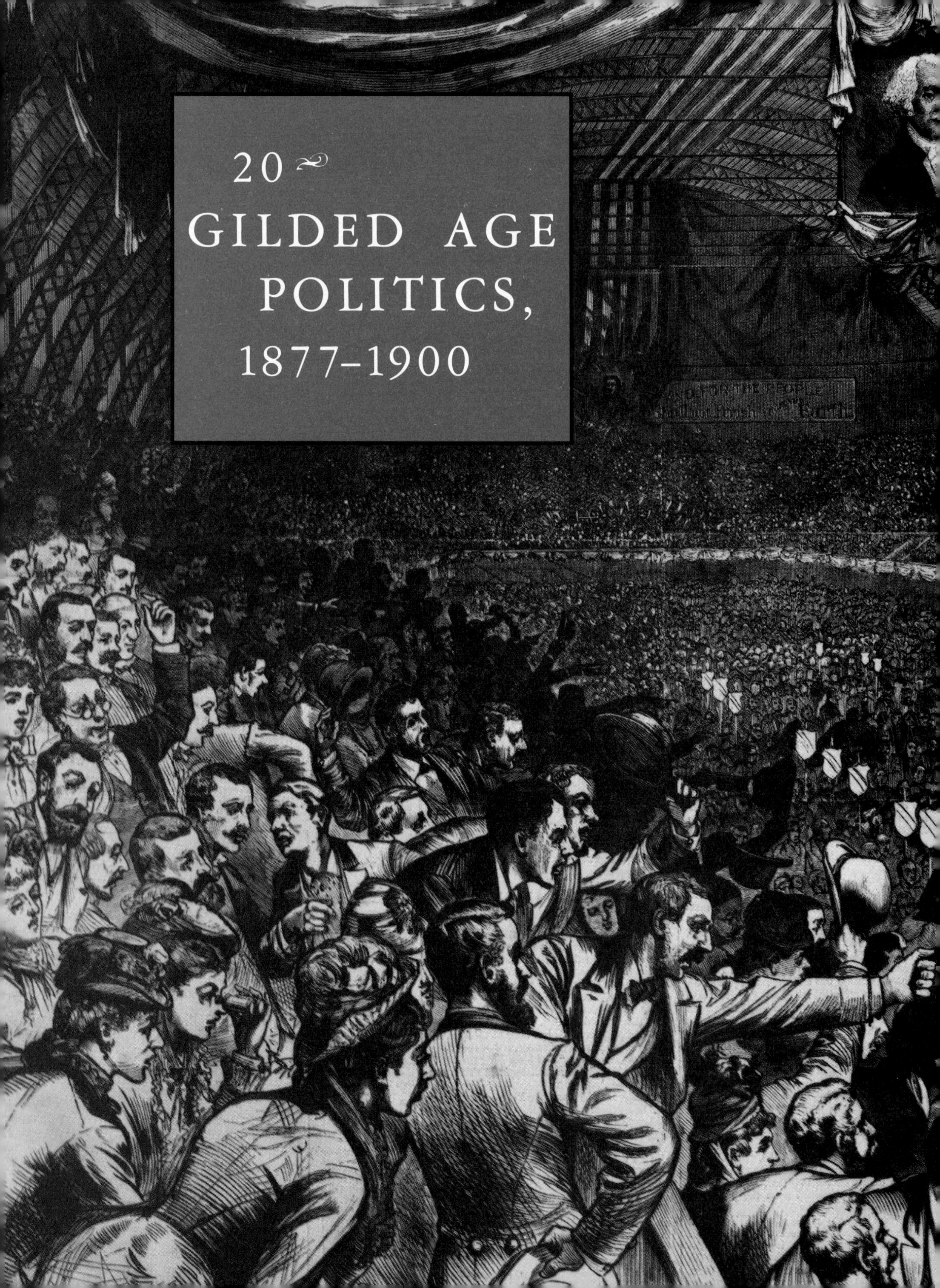

20 GILDED AGE POLITICS, 1877–1900

Esther Morris's craggy face must have cracked a satisfied grin as she thought about what was happening on July 23, 1890. On that day, a day celebrating Wyoming's newly won statehood, Mrs. Morris had the honor of presenting a commemorative flag to the governor. Six feet tall and toughened by life on the frontier, Esther Morris had migrated with her husband and children to Wyoming Territory in 1869. There she had played a chief role in convincing the territorial legislature to legalize full voting rights for women. When Wyoming applied for statehood twenty years later, its constitution retained the women's suffrage provision, the first state constitution to do so.

Congress had hesitated when this document was presented. Could it admit to the Union a state that allowed women to vote? Debate was heated, even provoking some southerners, who ordinarily stood for states' rights to argue that states could not decide individually whether women should vote. When it appeared that statehood would not be granted, territorial delegate Joseph Carey telegraphed the Wyoming legislature that it might have to drop the suffrage provision. The legislature reportedly replied, "We will remain out of the Union a hundred years rather than come in without the women." In a close vote, the House and later the Senate voted to admit Wyoming with female suffrage intact, giving Esther Morris and thousands of other women cause for satisfaction.

Wyoming women thus entered the American political process, but they were exceptions. In 1900 the majority of Americans–including women in all other states, black men and women in many southern states, Indians, and unnaturalized immigrants–still could not vote. Moreover, the political process suffered from more than exclusivity. Corruption and the greed of privileged interests tugged at the fabric of democracy, and the venality of the era prompted novelists Mark Twain and Charles Dudley Warner to dub it the Gilded Age.

Politics, more than any other sphere, seemed to express the prevailing mood. Officeholders used their positions to amass personal fortunes and dispense patronage appointments to their supporters. Political parties vied more over the spoils of office than the affairs of the nation. Congress, split by powerful partisan and regional rivalries, did grapple with important issues, such as the tariff, the currency, and civil service, and passed some legislation initiating needed reforms. But most congressional accomplishments were either weak compromises or favors to special interests. Meanwhile the presidency was filled by a series of honest, respectable men who seldom took legislative initiatives; and when they did, they often found themselves beaten back by opposing forces in Congress.

The system faltered in the 1890s when a deep economic depression overspread the nation, exposing the gap between those with political influence and those who were excluded and aggravating conflicts between opposing interest groups: farmers versus businessmen; debtors versus creditors; employees versus employers. In the midst of the depression, a presidential campaign stirred Americans as they had not been stirred for a generation. Two candidates, William Jennings Bryan and William McKinley, and three parties, Democrats, Populists, and Republicans, compressed all the symbols of the era into a single election. The nation emerged from the turmoil of the 1890s with new political alignments, just as it had developed new economic configurations. These new alignments prepared the way for the new century, and for a new era of reform in which causes like that of Esther Morris would receive greater attention.

Cynical parties and emotional issues

Lord James Bryce, a British historian and diplomat who wrote a classic study called *The American Commonwealth* (1888), penned a disparaging analysis of American political parties in the Gilded Age that critics adopted for the next seventy-five years. Referring to Democrats and Republicans, Bryce observed that "neither party has any principles, any distinctive tenets. Both have traditions. Both claim to have tendencies. Both have certainly war cries, organizations, interests enlisted in their support. But these interests are in the main the interests of getting or keeping the patronage of the government." The two parties, he continued, "were like two bottles. Each bore a label denoting the kind of liquor it contained, but each was empty." The historian Henry Adams, grandson and great-grandson of presidents, agreed, noting that the

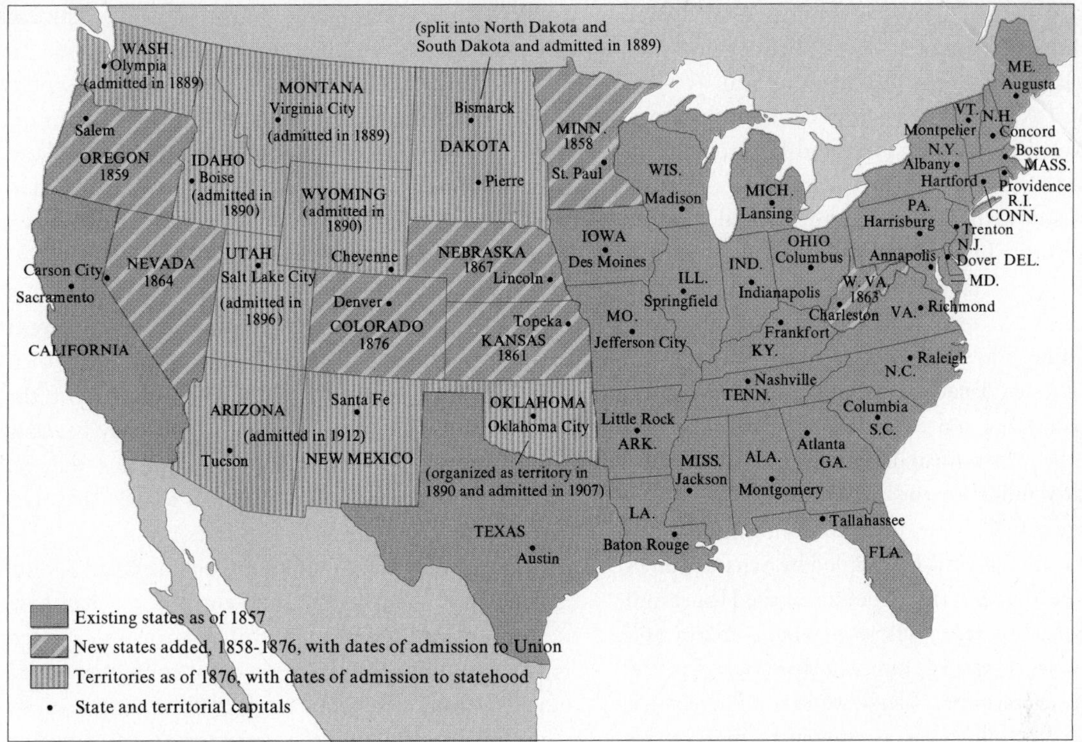

The United States, 1876–1912

period between 1870 and 1895 "was poor in purpose and barren in results." But were the two major parties really so lacking in distinctive tendencies and so alike in interests? Was the period so barren politically that government could accomplish very little?

From the voters' perspective, politics appeared anything but barren. At no other time in the nation's history was public interest in elections higher. Except in the South, where blacks endured growing voting restrictions, 80 to 90 percent of eligible voters cast ballots in local and national elections. (Fewer than 50 percent typically do so today.) Politics was the prime form of mass entertainment, outdistancing even baseball, vaudeville, and circuses. Though only men could vote, campaigns were absorbing community events that excited women and children as well. Voting was only the last stage in a process that included rallies, parades, picnics, and speeches, all of which were as much public amusement as civic responsibility. As one observer remarked, "What the theatre is to the French, or the bull fight . . . to the Spanish . . . [election campaigns] and the ballot box are to *our* people."

Voter participation

Politics was a personal as well as a community activity. In an era before advertising, polls, and the mass media influenced political choices, people formed strong loyalties to individual politicians, loyalties that often overlooked crassness and corruption.

Allegiances to parties and to individual politicians were usually so evenly distributed that no major faction or party gained lasting supremacy. Between 1877 and 1897, Republicans held the presidency for twelve years, Democrats for eight. The same party controlled the presidency and both houses of Congress for only three two-year spans: the Republicans twice, the Democrats once. Throughout the 1880s and early 1890s elections were extremely close, especially on the national level. The balance persisted despite the admission of six territories to statehood during this period (see map).

Government appeared to accomplish little in the Gilded Age because little was expected of it. Most Americans wanted an impartial government that did not interfere in social and economic matters. Also, struggles between and within parties stymied passage of effective, lasting legislation. Because the president was rarely of the same party as the majority of Congress, the two branches often blocked rather than supported each other's efforts to achieve reform.

In some ways, the major parties did look the same. Both were led by wealthy men, and both contained large numbers of farmers and wage earners as well as merchants and manufacturers. And internal quarrels split each party. In the Republican party, factional feuds and personal rivalries took precedence over national concerns. On one side stood the Stalwarts, led by New York's pompous Senator Roscoe Conkling. A physical-fitness devotee and former boxer who once was dubbed "the finest torso in public life," Conkling sought party influence and government jobs for his supporters over all other political concerns. On the other side were the Half-Breeds, led by Senator James G. Blaine of Maine, former Speaker of the House and twice secretary of state, whose magnetic charm and thrilling oratory earned him consideration for the presidency several times. Blaine wanted influence just as much as Conkling, but attempted to disguise his greed and sought the support of independents. On the sidelines were the more idealistic liberals, or Mugwumps, who, like Senator Carl Schurz of Missouri, disliked the political roguishness that perverted their party and believed that only righteous, dedicated men like themselves should govern. Meanwhile Democrats tended to subdivide into white-supremacy southerners, immigrant-stock urban machine members, and business interests favoring low tariffs. Like Republicans, Democrats eagerly pursued the spoils of office.

Party factions

Yet the two parties and the voters differed substantively over long-standing political and economic issues, such as sectional rivalry, tariffs, and the currency. Long after Reconstruction ended, Americans were haunted by the sectional conflict and political disruptions that had followed the Civil War. Republicans capitalized on the war by "waving the bloody shirt" whenever they faced a Democratic challenge. As one Republican orator harangued in 1876, "Every man that tried to destroy this nation was a Democrat. . . . Soldiers, every scar you have on your heroic bodies was given you by a Democrat." In the South voters also waved the bloody shirt, calling all Republicans traitors. The use of such emotional appeals persisted well into the 1880s.

Sectional conflict

Politicians were not the only ones who attempted to profit by keeping the memory of the war alive. In the 1880s and 1890s, the Grand Army of the Republic, an organization of Union army veterans numbering over 400,000, allied itself with the Republican party and pressured Congress into legislating generous pensions for former soldiers and their widows. The bullying tactics of veterans' lobbyists angered some legislators, but few could resist the demands of this huge interest group. "The pension agents who sit around this Capitol," griped one senator, "issue their circulars and decrees . . . and the Senators of the United States, great and mighty as they may be, bow to the behests . . . and vote the money that they require, and they are afraid not to do it for fear that they would lose political status at home."

Certainly many pensions were well deserved. Union soldiers had been poorly paid, and the war had widowed thousands of women. But for many other veterans, the emotional wake of the great conflict provided an opportunity to profit at the public's expense. By the end of the century the government was spending $157 million annually for soldiers' pensions, one of the largest welfare commitments the federal government has ever made. No Confederate veterans ever received any of the largesse, though several southern states did fund small pensions and built old-age homes for ex-soldiers.

Few politicians could afford to oppose Civil War pensions, but a number of reformers mustered their energies in an attempt to dismantle the spoils system. The practice of awarding government jobs to party workers, regardless of their qualifications, had taken root in the antebellum years and blossomed after the Civil War in the federal government as well as the machine-ruled cities. As federal building construction, the postal service, the diplomatic corps, and other government activities expanded, so did the number of jobs on the public payroll. Between 1865 and 1891 the number of federal government positions tripled, from 53,000 to 166,000. Elected officials scrambled to control the new appointments as a means of cementing support for themselves and their parties. In return for the relatively short hours and high pay of government jobs, appointees pledged their votes and a portion of their earnings.

Civil service reform

A system so susceptible to corruption ruffled a

Before the Pendleton Act of 1883, many government positions were filled by patronage: hat in hand, job seekers beseeched the president to find a place for them. Here a member of Congress presents constituents for office in return for their past political support. Library of Congress.

growing number of independents, who began advocating appointments and promotions based on merit rather than connections. The movement gained momentum during the 1870s, when scandals in the Grant administration bared the defects of the spoils system. It reached full flower in 1881 with the formation of the National Civil Service Reform League, an organization of wealthy lawyers, writers, ministers, and professors led by George W. Curtis, editor of *Harper's Weekly,* and E. L. Godkin, editor of the *Nation.* The same year, Charles Guiteau, a frustrated and demented job-seeker, assassinated President James Garfield, and the murder hastened the drive for civil service reform. Late in 1882 Congress passed the Pendleton Civil Service Act, and President Chester Arthur signed it early in 1883.

The law created the Civil Service Commission, which would supervise competitive examinations for government positions. Significantly, however, the act gave the commission jurisdiction over only about 10 percent of federal jobs–although the president could expand the list. The remaining jobs were subject to the old spoils system. Also, the examinations were to apply only to new applicants, not to incumbents. These limitations explain why Republicans–then the majority in Congress–strongly supported the Pendleton Act, while most Democrats opposed it. As one Democratic senator complained, it was simply "a bill to perpetuate in office the Republicans who now control the patronage of the Government." Nevertheless the law, and especially one provision outlawing political contributions by officeholders, signaled a change.

Successive presidents expanded the number of classified jobs—though they did so more to protect their appointees against replacement than to support the principle of the merit system.

Civil service reform has often been considered one of the major accomplishments of the Gilded Age; yet its actual impact can be debated. Certainly the system of hiring government workers needed improvement. Under the spoils system, clerical jobs were given to people who could neither read nor write, and because the diplomatic corps contained so many untrained officers (many of whom could not speak the language of the country to which they were sent), the American foreign service was one of the most incompetent in the field. But civil service reformers were by no means egalitarians who wanted to give all qualified Americans a chance to participate in government. They were conservatives who wanted to restore an era when public servants were chosen from among men whose birth, wealth, and education supposedly fitted them for leadership. Moreover, the spoils system did serve a useful function: it financed the two major political parties, in an era when no other form of support existed. And it was an open and accepted system of party support, far less sinister than the system of secret contributions from large corporations that replaced it. Finally, no one has ever proven that the quality of government service improved under civil service. The entrenched government bureaucracy that resulted is still a problem today.

Tariff policy

In the 1880s tariffs and money, not government jobs, attracted the most attention in Congress. Through the mid-nineteenth century Congress had raised most tariff rates to protect American manufactured goods and some agricultural products from European competition. By the 1880s there were separate tariffs on over four thousand items, and the resulting revenues were making for an embarrassing surplus in the federal treasury. Though a few economics professors and some farmers argued for free trade, most Americans still believed high tariffs were necessary to preserve the prosperity of industrialists and the jobs of wage earners.

The Republican party, claiming responsibility for economic growth, made protective tariffs a core feature of its policies. Democrats and other critics complained that tariffs made prices artificially high, benefiting those interests, such as woolen manufacturers, whose products were protected while hurting farmers whose crops were not protected and consumers who had to buy manufactured goods. Although Democrats generally saw a need for some protection of American goods and raw materials, they favored lower tariff rates to encourage foreign trade and to reduce the treasury surplus.

The problem for politicians who wanted to reduce tariff rates was how to enact cuts without angering producers and manufacturers of protected goods. The McKinley Tariff of 1890, passed after Republican electoral victories in 1888, reflected this dilemma. To please one faction, the act placed raw materials such as sugar, coffee, and tea on the free list. It also raised the rates on some manufactured goods, such as woolens, so high as to ensure that little would be imported—thereby contributing to a reduction of revenue because few duties would be collected. At the same time the act sought to soothe some farmers by placing duties on agricultural products, presumably to protect American farm goods from foreign competition. Finally, due to the influence of Secretary of State James G. Blaine, the McKinley Tariff included a reciprocity clause. Designed to encourage new foreign trade and to discourage foreign retaliation against high American duties, reciprocity gave the president authority to remove items from the free list if their countries of origin placed unreasonable tariffs on American goods.

Privileged interests continued to dominate tariff policy in the 1890s. When in 1894 House Democrats supported by President Grover Cleveland passed a bill to reduce tariff rates, Senate Republicans, aided by southern Democrats eager to protect their region's infant industries, added some six hundred amendments restoring most cuts. In 1897 a new tariff bill, the Dingley Act, raised rates even further, though it greatly expanded reciprocity provisions.

Monetary policy

The currency controversy was even more tangled than the tariff issue. In brief, it involved opposing reactions to the fall in prices caused by increased industrial and agricultural production after the Civil War. Farmers, most of whom were debtors, suffered particularly severely because they had to pay fixed mortgage and interest payments even while their incomes declined because prices for their crops were dropping. Correctly perceiving that an insufficient money supply had made their debts more expensive relative to other prices, farmers favored schemes like the coinage of silver to increase the amount of currency in circulation. Creditors, on the other hand, believed that overproduction had caused the price decline. They thus favored a more stable, tightly controlled money supply backed only by gold as a means of maintaining the confidence of native and foreign investors in the American economy.

But the issue involved more than economics. Even more than the tariff, the quantity and quality of money symbolized a whole series of conflicts–social, regional, and emotional. The question was not a partisan one; there were Republicans and Democrats on both sides. But the creditor-versus-debtor conflict translated easily into haves versus have-nots. It also involved a sectional cleavage, the western silver-mining areas and agricultural regions of the South and West against the more conservative industrial Northeast. Finally, the issue had moral, almost religious, overtones. Gold, the traditional basis of money, was a durable yet malleable metal. Those qualities plus its beauty and rarity gave it a magical potency; for centuries people had considered gold a God-given symbol of value. But others considered the gold standard for currency too limiting for the machine age; prosperity, they felt, demanded new attitudes. As the financier Jay Gould once sneered, "Why should this Grand and Glorious country be stunted and dwarfed . . . by these miserable 'hard coin' theorists, the musty theories of a bygone age?"

By the late 1870s, the currency controversy had become a matter of gold versus silver. Up to that time the government had coined both silver and gold dollars; a silver dollar weighed sixteen times more than a gold dollar, meaning that gold was officially worth sixteen times as much as silver. But gold discoveries since 1849 had increased the supply, lowering gold's market price relative to that of silver. Thus producers of silver, which was now worth more than one-sixteenth the value of gold, preferred to sell their metal on the open market rather than to the government. As a result, silver dollars disappeared from circulation–owners hoarded them rather than spend them–and in 1873 Congress officially stopped coining silver dollars. At about the same time, European nations also stopped buying silver. Thus the United States and many of its trading partners adopted the gold standard, meaning that their currency was backed chiefly by gold.

Within a few years, however, new mines in the American West began to flood the market with silver, and its price dropped. Gold was now worth more than sixteen times what silver was worth. It became profitable to spend silver dollars–and would have been worthwhile to sell silver to the government in return for gold, but the government was no longer buying it. Debtors, who were suffering from the depression of the mid-1870s in addition to falling prices, and who saw silver as a means of expanding the currency supply, now joined with silver producers to denounce the "Crime of '73" and to press for resumption of coinage at the old sixteen-to-one ratio.

Congress, split into silver and gold factions, tried to neutralize the issue with compromise legislation: the Bland-Allison Act of 1878, which required the treasury to buy $2 to $4 million worth of silver each month; and the Sherman Silver Purchase Act of 1890, which fixed the monthly purchase of silver in weight (4.5 million ounces) rather than in dollars. But neither act satisfied the different interest groups. Renewed prosperity in 1879, fueled by increased foreign trade and a resulting favorable balance of trade with Europe, caused crop prices to rise and gold to flow in from overseas, temporarily calming the silverite fervor. The Sherman Act, passed partially in response to an economic decline in the mid-1880s, failed to expand the money supply: as the price of silver dropped, the government, now required only to buy a certain weight of silver, could spend less to purchase the stipulated number of ounces. Thus the money supply was not increased as substantially as some had hoped. Not until after a depression in the 1890s and an emotion-filled presidential election would the money issue subside.

Women's suffrage

While debates over tariffs and money raged, Congress and state legislatures began to face the issue of women's suffrage more squarely than ever before. After the Civil War, several events mobilized women to pursue the vote. Late in 1869 a Missouri couple, Francis and Virginia Minor, drew up a resolution stating that the Constitution and its amendments had already given women the right to vote. According to the Minors' theory, the Constitution granted citizenship to "all persons born or naturalized in the

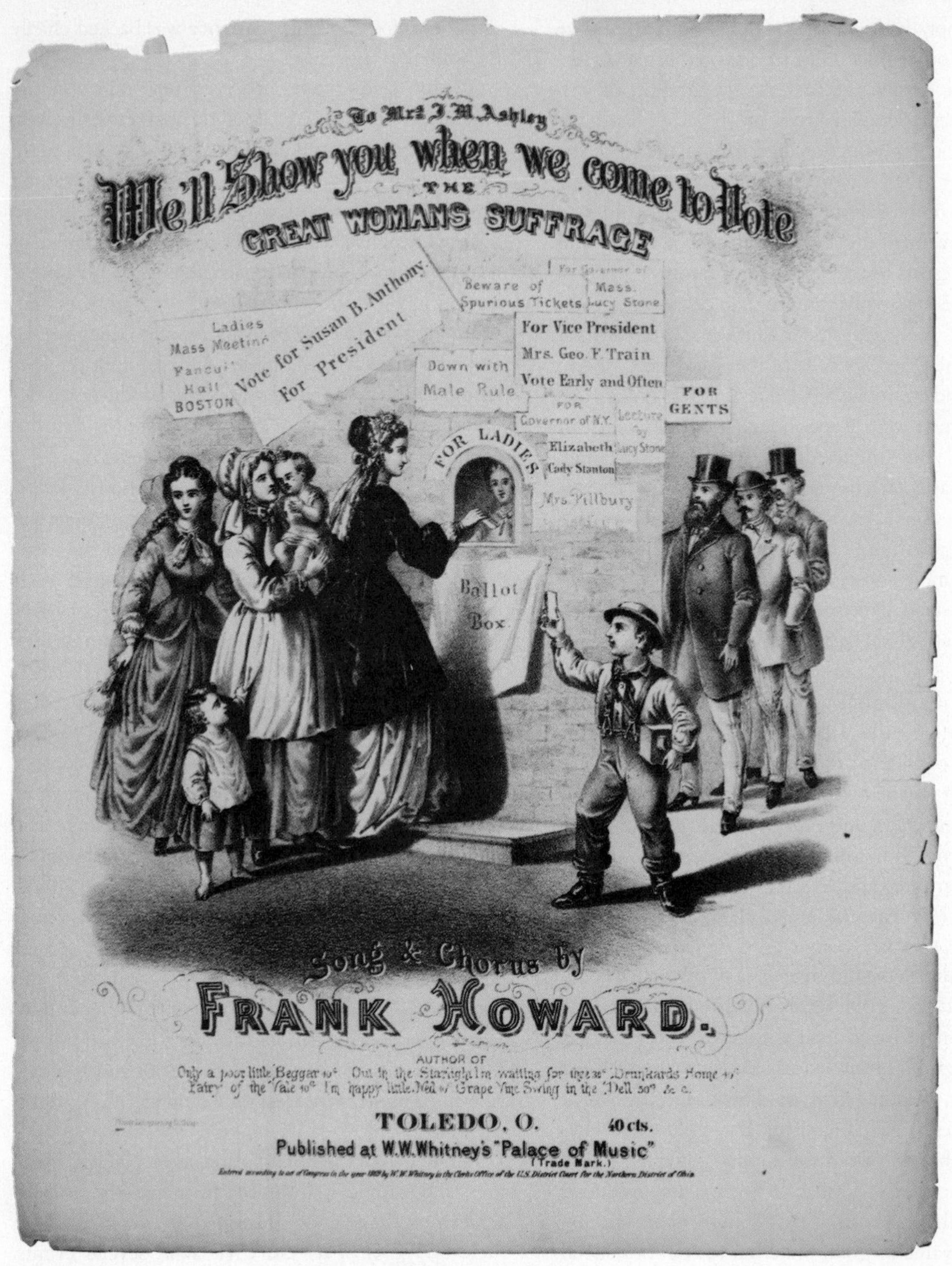

Sheet music for a late-nineteenth-century song about women's suffrage. Women increased their agitation for the vote until in 1878 a constitutional amendment granting them suffrage was introduced in Congress. The Senate killed the measure that year, but women's groups like the National Woman Suffrage Association continued to fight for the cause. American Antiquarian Society.

United States," and no state could abridge the "privileges or immunities" of any citizen, including his–or her–right to vote. Eventually the Minors, with support from the National Woman Suffrage Association (NWSA), sued a St. Louis registrar who had refused to permit Mrs. Minor to vote. After a series of adverse decisions in lower courts, the case went to the Supreme Court in 1874. The majority opinion written by Chief Justice Morrison R. Waite upheld the lower courts, declaring that suffrage did not automatically accompany citizenship and that states could legally withhold voting rights from certain classes of citizens, such as criminals, the insane–and women.

The Minor decision did not deter the cause of women's suffrage or the NWSA. Early in 1878 Susan B. Anthony, the indomitable fighter for human rights, convinced her friend Senator A. A. Sargent of California, a strong supporter of women's suffrage, to introduce in Congress a constitutional amendment stating that "the right of citizens of the United States to vote shall not be denied or abridged by the United States or by any state on account of sex." (The Women's Suffrage Amendment finally passed forty-two years later was identical to this "Anthony Amendment.") In 1878, the bill was killed by a Senate committee, but supporters reintroduced it several times over the next eighteen years. On the few occasions when the bill reached the Senate floor, it was voted down by senators who expressed their fears that suffrage would interfere with women's family responsibilities and ruin female virtue.

While the NWSA and others fought for the vote on the national level, the American Woman Suffrage Association worked for constitutional amendments at the state level. Between 1870 and 1910, there were seventeen referenda in eleven states (all but three of which were west of the Mississippi River) to legalize women's suffrage. These attempts almost always failed because the women involved, aided by a few male supporters, lacked the funds and personnel to conduct sustained campaigns. Yet the suffrage movement survived. Efforts at the state level attracted attention from newly formed women's clubs and trained a corps of female leaders in organizing and public speaking. Moreover, women did attain partial victories: by 1890 nineteen states allowed women to vote on school issues, and three granted suffrage on tax and bond issues. By the time Wyoming was admitted to the Union in 1890 in spite of its women's suffrage provision, the groundwork was well laid for the next generation's battle for national voting rights.

Thus legislative leaders did address some of the basic issues of the day, but they failed to agree on clear solutions. Congressmen and their constituents were so divided among factions and interest groups that the only passable legislation was the kind, like the Pendleton Act, that was ideal to no one but acceptable to most. And while complex problems like the tariff demanded careful study, most politicians preferred to devote their energies to party and factional concerns–to say nothing of their own re-election. As a result, Congress, and particularly the Senate, became an oratorical battleground for party and intraparty rivalry. Between late 1879 and early 1881, for example, the prevailing question within the legislative and executive branches of the federal government was not the nation's economic or social condition, but which member of which Republican faction would be appointed to the patronage-rich post of Collector of the Port of New York. Politics has always been the art of compromise, but in the two decades after Reconstruction, compromise became equated with the postponement of major decisions.

The decline of the presidency

Woodrow Wilson once said that a good president should be chief adminstrator, chief of legislation, and chief of the party. In the years between 1877 and 1900, American presidents seldom fulfilled any of these functions. Their administrations contrasted sharply with those of more headstrong predecessors like Jackson and Lincoln. Proper, honorable, and honest, Presidents Hayes, Garfield, Arthur, Cleveland, Harrison, and McKinley won public respect but seldom provoked strong positive or negative emotions. Like other politicians, they used symbols. Hayes served lemonade at the White House to emphasize that, unlike his predecessor Grant, he was no hard drinker. McKinley put aside his cigar in public so photographers would not catch him setting a bad example for youth. But none of the era's six presidents was an inspiring personality, nor could any of them dominate the factional chieftains of their parties.

Thus for the quarter-century following Reconstruction the presidency was on the defensive, and the nation experienced what Wilson described as "congressional government," with Congress determining most policy initiatives. Until the 1890s no serious crisis threatened the nation, so no president was in a position to assume emergency powers. The nature of domestic issues coupled with the generally nonassertive personalities of the presidents created an atmosphere in which the presidency had little independence. The nation's growing involvement in foreign affairs and the wars and treaties accompanying that involvement did give Presidents Cleveland and McKinley a few opportunities for initiative, but they too had to bow to the pressures of Congress. Cleveland initiated a few pieces of legislation and used the veto to fight some congressional abuses, but he had no intention of expanding his presidential prerogatives. "I shall keep right on doing executive work," he once stated. "I did not come here to legislate." The restoration of presidential activism would have to await a new century and the administration of Theodore Roosevelt.

Hayes, Garfield, and Arthur

Rutherford B. Hayes (1877 to 1881) personified the belief that the president was a caretaker elected to execute what Congress initiated. Honest, prudent, and a model of self-control, Hayes had been a Union general and an Ohio congressman and governor before his disputed election to the presidency. Once in office, he avoided such controversial issues as the tariff and sectional rivalry. He did, however, take a conservative position on currency, and ordered out troops to aid local militia during the 1877 railroad strikes. Hayes also pleased civil service advocates by appointing reformer Carl Schurz to the cabinet and battling New York's patronage king, Senator Roscoe Conkling. (He fired Conkling's protégé, Chester Arthur, from the post of New York Customs House Collector.) But Hayes also demanded that his own appointees contribute to Republican coffers for the 1878 elections. He was not a beloved leader. As one reformer wrote, "I have little or no patience with Mr. Hayes. He is a victim of . . . good intentions and his contributions to the pavement of the road to the infernal regions are vast and nefarious."

When Hayes refused to run for re-election in 1880, Republican factions battled over whom to nominate, then compromised by selecting another Ohio congressman and Civil War hero, James A. Garfield. A husky, serious, and cautious man, Garfield defeated the Democrats' Winfield Scott Hancock, also a Civil War hero, by just 40,000 votes out of over 9 million. By carrying the pivotal states of New York and Indiana, however, Garfield won in the electoral college by a comfortable margin, 214 to 155. Garfield spent most of his brief presidency trying to secure an independent position among party potentates like Blaine and Conkling. He appeared to have no relish for his responsibilities, and especially disliked dealing with the hordes of office seekers. "Once or twice," he complained, "I felt like crying out in the agony of my soul against the greed for office and its consumption of my time." He did please civil service reformers by refusing to satisfy Conkling's demands, but Garfield's opportunity to make lasting contributions ended in July 1881 when the crazed Charles Guiteau shot him in a Washington railroad station. Not seriously wounded at first, Garfield lingered for seventy-nine days while doctors tried unsuccessfully to remove a bullet lodged in his back. His condition steadily deteriorated, and he finally succumbed to infection, dying September 19.

Garfield's vice president and successor was New York politician Chester A. Arthur, the spoilsman Hayes had fired in 1878. Arthur had been nominated for vice president only to help the Republicans carry New York state; his elevation to the presidency made reformers shudder. Yet he became a dignified and temperate executive. Arthur lent some support to civil service reform and signed the Pendleton Act. He urged Congress to modify outdated tariff rates, and spoke in favor of federal regulation of railroads. Using the veto as a means to influence Congress, Arthur killed a number of bills that excessively benefited privileged interests. But like his two predecessors, Arthur had no taste for his office. Suffering from illness, he made little effort to run in 1884.

The 1884 presidential campaign magnified the political banalities of the era. The Republicans nominated James G. Blaine, whose impressive leadership skills and political popularity were offset by his unsa-

Grover Cleveland made it known that he would not tolerate wasted time and money. Here his no-nonsense attitude startles a group of hangers-on bearing petitions and grievances. A civil service reform bill sits on Cleveland's desk. Library of Congress.

vory methods of enriching himself. (Blaine frequently used his influence to obtain favorable financial deals for railroads, and was in turn paid handsomely.) The Democrats named New York's Governor Grover Cleveland, a rotund and righteous bachelor whose respectable reputation was tainted by his having once fathered an illegitimate son–a fact he admitted openly during the campaign. Both parties focused on the sordid side of the opposition, and disapproval of Blaine was so strong that a number of Mugwumps deserted the Republican party for Cleveland. On election day Cleveland beat Blaine by only 23,000 popular votes; his tiny margin of 1,149 votes in New York gave him that state's 36 electoral votes, enough to squeeze a 219–182 victory in the electoral college. Cleveland may have won New York solely because in the last week of the campaign a local Protestant minister publicly equated Democrats with "rum, Romanism, and rebellion" (drinking, Catholicism, and the Civil War). Catholics and others took this as a vicious attack on their beliefs. The Democrats eagerly publicized the slur among New York's numerous Irish-Catholic population, urging voters to protest by turning out for Cleveland.

Cleveland and Harrison

Cleveland, the first Democratic president since Buchanan, complained like his Republican predecessors of the "cursed constant grind" of his office and the "want of rest." He did, however, exercise more vigorous leadership. Cleveland used the veto extensively against outrageous pension bills, and he extended the scope of civil service. But his most forceful action was his unsuccessful campaign for tariff reform. Worried about the growing treasury surplus, Cleveland urged Congress to cut duties on most raw materials and manufactured goods. When advisers warned him that his stand might weaken his chances for re-election, the president retorted, "What is the use of being elected or re-elected, unless you stand for something?" Cleveland's firmness did not prevail, though. The Mills tariff bill of 1888, passed by the House in response to Cleveland's wishes, would have reduced some rates. But it was killed by the Senate. Although the Democrats renominated Cleveland for the presidency in 1888, they selected a protectionist as his running mate, and protectionists in the party were soon able to convince Cleveland to temper his attacks on high tariffs.

Republicans in 1888 nominated Benjamin Harrison, an intelligent but chilly former senator from Indiana and grandson of President William Henry Harrison. The campaign was less savage than the 1884 campaign had been, but it was far from clean. Some shrewd Republicans manipulated the British minister in Washington into stating that Cleveland's re-election would be good for England. Irish Democrats took offense as intended, and Cleveland's campaign was weakened. Perhaps more helpful to Harrison was the pervasive bribery and multiple voting that helped him to win Indiana by just 2,300 votes and New York by only 14,000. (Democrats also indulged in bribery and vote fraud, but the Republicans were more successful at it.) These crucial states assured Harrison's victory; though Cleveland outpolled Harrison by 90,000 popular votes, Harrison carried the electoral vote by 233 to 168. After the election, Harrison told Matt Quay, the Republican national chairman, "Providence has given us the victory." Quay later quipped to a friend, "Think of the man. He ought to know that Providence hadn't a damned thing to do with it. . . . [He] would never learn how close a number of men were compelled to approach the gates of the penitentiary to make him president."

Harrison was the first president since 1875 whose party controlled both houses of Congress, but he did little to take advantage of this circumstance by asserting himself as a party or legislative leader. Several aspects of his administration were similarly contradictory. Harrison was a fiscal conservative, but under his administration Congress passed the first peacetime budget to exceed $1 billion. At Harrison's urging the House passed a "force bill" to protect blacks' civil rights by allowing federal courts to investigate irregularities in voter registration and jury selection; but Republican senators filibustered and then tabled the bill, causing the president to abandon the cause. And though Harrison supported a boost in protective tariff rates and reciprocity agreements to aid business, he agreed to the Sherman Anti-Trust Act and the Sherman Silver Purchase Act (1890), both of which were considered damaging to business. Harrison professed support for civil service and appointed Theodore Roosevelt a civil service commissioner, but the president's lackluster character prompted the reform-minded and impatient Roosevelt to call him a "cold-blooded, narrow minded, prejudiced, obstinate, timid old psalm singing Indianapolis politician."

Cleveland and Harrison ran against each other again in 1892. This time Cleveland attracted heavy contributions from business and beat Harrison by 380,000 popular votes (3 percent of the total) and by 277 to 145 electoral votes. The victory was less decisive than it might have been, however, because of James B. Weaver's third-party challenge (see page 463). The Populist candidate garnered over 1 million votes, winning majorities in four states and 22 electoral votes. The forces of equilibrium were weakening.

In office once more, Cleveland took bolder steps to meet the problems of currency, tariffs, and labor unrest. But his actions reflected a narrow orientation to the interests of business and bespoke political weakness. In order to protect the nation's gold reserve, which was shrinking during the Panic of 1893, Cleveland enlisted aid from bankers, who bailed out the nation on terms highly favorable to themselves. During the election campaign Cleveland promised sweeping tariff reform, but he made little effort to line up support for such reform in the Senate, where protectionists undercut all efforts to reduce rates. And when 120,000 boycotting railroad workers paralyzed western trade in the 1894 Pullman strike (see page 489), Cleveland bowed to the requests for federal troops from railroad managers and Attorney General Richard Olney. Throughout Cleveland's second term, events—particularly the economic downturn and the Populist ferment—seemed too much for the president. Cleveland's party abandoned him in 1896.

The depression of the 1890s

Early in 1893, shortly before Grover Cleveland assumed the presidency for the second time, a seemingly minor but ominous economic event occurred: the Philadelphia and Reading Railroad, once a thriving and profitable line, went into bankruptcy. Like other railroads, the Philadelphia and Reading had borrowed heavily to lay more tracks and make costly improvements, such as new stations and bridges. But overexpansion cut into revenues. Profits dwindled, and the company was unable to pay its debts.

The same problem nagged manufacturers. For example, output at the McCormick farm machinery factories was nine times greater in 1893 than it had been in 1879, but revenues had only tripled. To compensate, the company tried to boost profits by automating its plants (another heavy expense) and squeezing more work out of fewer laborers. But this strategy only enlarged the debt and increased unemployment. And it pushed unemployed workers into the same plight as their employers: they could not pay their creditors.

Banks suffered too. As primary lending agents, their problems compounded when customers defaulted. The failure of the National Cordage Company in May 1893 set off a chain reaction of business and bank closings. During the first four months of 1893, 28 banks failed. By May the number had grown to 54, and in June it reached 128. In 1894 one adviser warned President Cleveland, "We are on the eve of a very dark night." He was right; between 1893 and 1897, the nation suffered the worst economic depression it had yet experienced.

Falling prices and mounting unemployment arrived in the wake of business failures. Although records are sketchy, it appears that about 2.5 million people, or nearly 20 percent of the labor force, were out of work for some time during the depression. Everywhere families had to cut back on expenditures. Falling demand caused the cost of living to drop by 7 percent between 1892 and 1895, but that decline was more than offset by layoffs and wage cuts. Woolen workers who received $2.06 a day in 1892 made only $1.84 in 1894. Many people could not afford basic necessities. New York police estimated that twenty thousand homeless and jobless people roamed the city's streets. Surveying the impact of the depression on his own city of Boston, Henry Adams wrote, "Men died like flies under the strain, and Boston grew suddenly old, haggard, and thin."

As the depression deepened, currency problems reached a critical stage. The Sherman Silver Purchase Act of 1890 had committed the government to buy 4.5 million ounces of silver each month (see page 555). Payment was to be in gold, at the ratio of one ounce of gold for every sixteen ounces of silver. But the western mining boom made silver more plentiful, and its value relative to gold fell accordingly. Thus every month the government exchanged gold, whose worth remained fairly constant, for less valuable silver. Fearful that the dollar, which was based on the treasury's holdings in silver and gold, was losing its value, businessmen at home and abroad began to exchange paper money and securities for gold. As a result, the nation's gold reserves dwindled, falling below $100 million in April 1893.

Currency problems

The $100-million level was psychologically significant. If businessmen believed that the country's gold reserve was disappearing, they would lose confidence in its economic stability and refrain from investing. For example, British capitalists owned some $4 billion in American stocks and bonds. If the dollar were to depreciate too much, they would stop investing in American economic growth. Yet the lower the gold reserve dropped, the more people rushed to redeem their money and securities–to get their gold before it disappeared. The panic spread, causing further bankruptcies and unemployment.

President Cleveland, promising to protect the gold reserves, called a special session of Congress to repeal the Sherman Silver Purchase Act. But though the repeal was passed in October 1893, the run on the treasury continued through 1894. By early 1895 gold reserves had fallen to only $41 million. In desperation, Cleveland accepted an offer of 3.5 million ounces of gold in return for $62 million worth of federal bonds from a banking syndicate led by J. P. Morgan. When the bankers resold the bonds to the public, they profited handsomely at the nation's expense. Cleveland claimed that the gold reserves had been saved, but discontented farmers, workers, silver miners, and even some members of Cleveland's own party saw only humiliation in the president's actions. "When Judas betrayed Christ," charged South Carolina's Senator "Pitchfork Ben" Tillman, "his heart was not blacker than this scoundrel, Cleveland, in betraying the [Democratic party]."

No one knew what was really happening to the president. At about the same time that Cleveland called Congress into special session, doctors discovered a malignant tumor on his palate. The cancer required immediate removal. Fearful that public knowledge of his illness would hasten the run on gold, and intent on preventing Vice President Adlai E. Stevenson, a silver supporter, from gaining influence, Cleveland kept his condition a secret. He announced that he was going sailing with a friend, and doctors removed his cancerous upper left jaw while the yacht sailed up the East River from New York City. Outfitted with a rubber jaw, Cleveland returned to shore five days later and resumed a full schedule, enduring terrible pain to dispel rumors that he was seriously ill. He eventually recovered, but those who knew about his operation believed it had sapped his vitality.

The deal between Cleveland and Morgan had little effect on most peoples' lives. Across the country families were out of money and out of work. After a slight improvement in 1895, the economy plunged again. Farm income, on the decline since 1887, continued to slide. Steel mills and textile factories closed. Local banks that remained open restricted withdrawals and refused to honor checks. In the South depositors had to notify savings banks sixty days in advance to withdraw their money. Immigration in the mid-1890s dropped to almost 200,000 a year less than in the early 1890s. Both economic hardship and reduced immigration depressed housing construction, drying up an important source of jobs. Each night police stations in almost every city became crowded with vagrants who had no place else to stay.

In the final years of the century, new gold discoveries, good harvests, and saner industrial growth brought better times. But, though few Americans realized it, the depression had hastened the crumbling of an old system and the emergence of a new one. The processes of industrial development and technological change had been under way for some time. Since the 1850s, railroads had been at the center of American economic development, opening new markets, boosting steel and coke production, spawning numerous subsidiary industries, and expanding banking and finance. But the organizational features of the new business system—consolidation and a trend toward bigness—were just beginning to solidify when the depression hit.

Emergence of new economic structures

What had happened was that the national economy had reached the point of interdependence, the point at which the fortunes of a business in one part of the country had repercussions elsewhere. By the 1890s railroads were overextended; their reckless investments inevitably crumbled. And when railroads collapsed, they pulled other industries down with them. In the first half of 1893, for example, thirty-two steel companies failed. In all, five hundred banks and sixteen thousand businesses toppled into bankruptcy that same year.

To complicate matters, agriculture too had been languishing for several years. After 1870 commercial farming—growing crops for profit rather than for subsistence—had expanded to the point that American farmers were competing with foreign producers for world markets. Thus American farmers had to contend not only with fluctuating transportation rates and falling crop prices at home (see pages 445 and 461), but also with Canadian and Russian wheat growers, Argentine cattle ranchers, Indian and Egyptian cotton producers, and Australian wool producers. A mounting worldwide supply, and even surplus, of farm products drove down prices further, and American farmers borrowed more in order to produce enough to make ends meet. But the more they produced, the more surplus they created. As a result prices dropped further, forcing them to produce and borrow still more. When farmers fell into debt and lost their purchasing power, their depressed condition in turn affected the economic health of railroads, farm-implements manufacturers, banks, and other businesses. The downward spiral reversed late in 1897, but the depression had left deep scars.

Undercurrents of protest

The depression bared social as well as economic problems in the industrial system. For half a century technological and organizational changes had increasingly widened the gap between employers and employees. By the 1890s workers' protests against exploitation threatened economic and political upheaval. In 1894, when the American economy plunged, there were over thirteen hundred strikes and countless riots. Violence reached an alarming pitch in several places, and radical rhetoric escalated. Contrary to the fears of business leaders, all the protesters were not anarchists or communists from Europe come to sabotage American democracy. The disaffected included thousands of rural, small-town, and urban men and women who wanted a better chance, regardless of how the government was organized. Far from giving birth to radicalism, the uncertainties of the age merely brought to the surface an activist undercurrent that has flowed throughout American history.

The era of protest began with the great railroad strikes of 1877 (see pages 485–486). The vehemence of those strikes and the support they drew from other working-class people aroused fears that the United States would repeat what had happened in France six years earlier, when a popular uprising overturned the government and introduced communist principles. Such anxieties were heightened by another railroad strike in 1880, the Haymarket riot of 1886, a general strike in New Orleans in 1891, and the prolonged strike at the Homestead Steel plant in 1892. In the West, too, miners were becoming embittered; in 1892 violence broke out at a silver mine in Coeur d'Alene, Idaho. Angered by wage cuts and a lockout, strikers seized the mines and battled federal troops sent to subdue them. Such actions convinced business executives that force was the only effective response to the radical wave, apparently fomented by socialists and anarchists.

Socialists had been involved in these and other incidents, but their numbers were small. Most American socialists were immigrant Marxists. Led by Daniel DeLeon, the fiery West-Indian-born lawyer and lecturer who dominated the Socialist Labor Party, they agreed with Karl Marx, the father of communism, that whoever controlled the means of production held the power to determine how well people lived. Marx had written that capitalism increased the output of goods by oppressing labor, divorcing workers from the means of production, and pitting classes against each other. No longer did workers have control over how a product would be made; mechanization and the division of labor had demeaned them. Marx predicted that workers throughout the world would become so discontented they would revolt and seize factories, farms, banks, and transportation lines. The governments resulting from this revolution would end exploitation and erase class differences, paving the way for a new order of social justice. Marx's vision appealed to some workers because it promised them independence and abundance, and to intellectuals because it promised an end to class conflict and crude materialism.

Socialism

American socialism suffered from internal disagreements and lack of strong leadership. DeLeon had an antagonistic personality, and his invective against friends as well as enemies weakened the unity of the Socialist Labor Party. But events in 1894 triggered changes within the movement. That year the government's quashing of the Pullman strike and of the newly formed American Railway Union created a new and inspiring socialist leader. Eugene V. Debs, the railway union's president, had become a socialist while serving a six-month prison term for defying an injunction against the strike. Once released, the bald, forceful Indianan became the leading spokesperson for American socialism, combining visionary Marxism with Jeffersonian and Populist antimonopolism. Though never good at organizing, Debs attracted huge audiences and captivated them with his passion and eloquence. His attacks on the free enterprise system were indignant. "Many of you think you are competing," he would lecture. "Against whom? Against Rockefeller? About as I would if I had a wheelbarrow and competed with the Santa Fe [railroad] from here to Kansas City." Debs's major accomplishments would have to await the two decades after 1900, but in the late 1890s the group soon to be called the Socialist Party of America was already beginning to unite around him.

In 1894, however, it was not the tall, animated Debs but a short, quiet, frustrated businessman from Massillon, Ohio, who captured public attention. His name was Jacob S. Coxey, and like Debs he had a vision. The year before, Coxey had become convinced that, to help debtors, the government should issue paper money unbacked by gold–purposeful inflation, in other words. As the depression spread, Coxey recommended a federal job program financed by an issue of

Coxey's army

Coxey's Army. Jacob Coxey (in the foreground, in front of the flag) leads the procession of unemployed workers that became the first of many to march on the capital seeking government relief. In his hand Coxey carries a "war club of peace." Library of Congress.

$500 million of this "legal tender" paper money to relieve unemployment and revive consumer spending. He planned to publicize his scheme by leading a march from Massillon to Washington, D.C., gathering a "commonweal army" of unemployed workers along the way. Coxey was so enthusiastic about his project that he christened his newborn son Legal Tender and proposed that his eighteen-year-old daughter lead the procession in a red-white-and-blue gown on a white horse.

About two hundred strong, Coxey's army left Massillon on March 24, 1894. As one supporter wrote to "the General," "I am satisfied that this is the turning point in the history of the United States. Indeed I may say the world. The results will be far reaching, and the name of *Coxey* will go thundering down the ages relegating to oblivion that of Washington and Lincoln." Moving eastward across Ohio and into Pennsylvania, the army received food, housing, and recruits from a score of depressed industrial towns and rural villages. Many participants succumbed to boredom or the rigors of the weather and dropped out of the march, but elsewhere in the country similar armies organized and began the trek toward Washington.

Coxey and his troops, including women and children, entered the capital on April 30. The next day (May Day, a date that made the police nervous because of its traditional association with socialist demonstrations), the citizen army of some five hundred people marched to the Capitol, armed with "war clubs of peace." When Coxey and a few others vaulted the wall surrounding the Capitol grounds, a hundred mounted police moved in and routed the crowd. According to one witness, "Women and children were ruthlessly ridden down. A commonwealer who had in some way escaped from the ranks, stood behind a tree and struck a policeman a terrible blow in the back with his war club of peace. The next officer that came up saw the attack and clubbed the commonwealer into insensibility." Coxey tried to speak from the Capitol steps, but the police arrested him for ignoring Keep Off the Grass signs and dragged him away. As the arrests and clubbings continued, Coxey's dreams of a demonstration of 400,000 jobless workers dissolved. Like the strikes, the people's first march on Washington had yielded to police muscle.

Coxey's march was an expression of frustration by people who were seeking relief from the uncertainties of industrialization. Unlike socialists, who believed in altering the whole economic system, the Coxey commonwealers merely wanted more jobs and better working conditions. Today, in an age of strong union contracts, regulation of business, and government-sponsored job relief in times of high unemployment, their goals do not appear radical. Yet the brutal reactions of officials reveal how threatening the dissenters, from Coxey to Debs, must have seemed. Strikes and petitions, including the "petition in boots," clearly could not redress the protesters' grievances, but the ballot box remained a possibility. That is where farmers turned in 1896.

The battle of the standards and the election of 1896

William Jennings Bryan arrived at the Democratic national convention in Chicago in July 1896 as a member of a contested Nebraska delegation. A former congressman whose support for free coinage of silver had annoyed President Cleveland, he was only thirty-six years old, avidly religious, and highly distressed by what the depression had done to midwestern farmers. The convention, as expected, chose to seat Bryan and his colleagues instead of a competing faction that supported the gold standard. Shortly afterward, as a member of the party's resolutions committee, Bryan helped to write a platform calling for free coinage of silver.

When the platform was presented to the full convention, Bryan rose to speak on its behalf. Even in the heat and humidity of the Chicago summer, Bryan's now-famous closing words chilled the delegates:

> Having behind us the producing masses of this nation and the world, supported by the commercial interests, the laboring interests, and the toilers everywhere, we will answer their [the business interests'] demand for a gold standard by saying to them: You shall not press down upon the brow of labor this crown of thorns, you shall not crucify mankind upon a cross of gold.

The speech could not have been more timely; indeed, Bryan planned it to be so. Friends who had been pushing Bryan for the presidential nomination now had no trouble enlisting support. The convention flowed to Bryan, and its zeal forced the newly formed Peoples party–the Populists–to adopt the Nebraskan as its nominee too. The "great campaign" had begun in earnest.

Free silver

Silver was the central symbol and the most emotional issue of the 1890s. Though the currency problem was one of the most complex facing American political leaders, many people saw silver as a simple solution to the nation's ills. To them, free silver meant the end of special privilege for the rich and the return of government to the people. William H. Harvey, author of the immensely popular *Coin's Financial School* (1894), preached that by coining silver "you increase the value of all property by adding to the number of money units in the land. You make it possible for the debtor to pay his debts; business to start anew, and revivify all the industries of the country, which must remain paralyzed so long as silver as well as all other property is measured by a gold standard."

The silver issue was central to the Populist crusade against the "money power." The Populist movement had arisen out of genuine economic, political, and social grievances among farmers in the Plains and the South, where falling agricultural prices, rising debts, social isolation, racist exploitation, and the brutalities of nature drove people into a mass movement of protest (see pages 460–464). In the true evangelical tradition, the Populists saw evil and corruption as all-pervasive, and demanded moral reform that would eliminate greed and restore human compassion in business and government. Populist lectures resembled camp meetings, the orators promising to carry out God's will and revive a lost world of harmony and faith. One observer described the spirit of such gatherings as "a pentecost of politics in which a tongue of flame sat upon every man." Yet Populists could be hardheaded. While some speakers spouted biblical allegory or quoted Jefferson, others urged government ownership of some businesses and strict regulation of others, a graduated income tax to redistribute wealth, direct election of senators, and stabilization of prices.

Growth of the Populist party

In the early 1890s the Populists carried their crusade into local and state elections throughout the West and South. In 1892 their presidential candidate drew more than 1 million votes, and Populist candidates in 1894 made good showings. Nevertheless, the party could claim only a few electoral victories. Like all third parties, the Populists were underfinanced and underorganized. They had strong and colorful candidates, but not enough of them to blanket an area and wrest control from the two major parties. Moreover, many sympathetic voters were reluctant to break old habits and loyalties, and the Populists had trouble luring supporters away from the Republicans and Democrats.

Thus in 1896 Populists faced the choice of joining with sympathetic branches of the major parties or going down to defeat another time. Except in the Rocky Mountain states, where free coinage of silver had strong support, the Republicans were unlikely allies. Although Republican politicians could be as moralistic as the Populists, their anti-inflationist conservatism, support for the gold standard, and big-business mentality stood for everything the Populists opposed. In the North and West, alliance with Democrats was more plausible. In many areas the Democratic party retained vestiges of antimonopoly ideology as well as some sympathy for a looser currency system—although gold Democrats like President Grover Cleveland and Senator David Hill of New York did exert powerful opposition. Populists believed they also had links with traditionally Democratic urban workers, who, they assumed, suffered from the same kind of oppression that stifled farmers. In the South, fusion with Democrats seemed less likely, since there the party was the very power structure against which Populists had revolted in the late 1880s.

Presidential campaign of 1896

The presidential campaign of 1896 brought the nation's political wanderings to a climax. Each party was divided. The Republicans, under the direction of Marcus Alonzo Hanna, a jovial, prosperous, and crafty Ohio industrialist, had the fewest problems. Since early in 1895, Hanna had been maneuvering to win the nomination for Ohio's William McKinley, who was then governor. By the time the party convened in St. Louis in 1896, it was clear that Hanna had corralled enough delegates to succeed. "He has advertised McKinley," quipped Theodore Roosevelt, "as if he were a patent medicine." The Republicans' only trauma occurred when the party adopted a moderate platform supporting gold, rejecting a prosilver stance proposed by Senator Henry M. Teller of Colorado. Teller, who had been among the party's founders forty years earlier, walked out of the convention in tears, taking a small group of silver Republicans with him.

At the Democratic convention, silver delegates paraded through the Chicago Amphitheatre wearing silver badges and waving silver banners. Observing their tumultuous demonstrations, one eastern delegate wrote, "For the first time I can understand the scenes of the French Revolution!" "All the silverites need is a Moses," remarked a New York *World* reporter. They found one in Bryan. It took Bryan five ballots to win the nomination, but finally the magnetism of the Boy Orator proved irresistible. In bowing to the silverite will of southerners and westerners and repudiating Cleveland's policies in its platform, the party became more attractive to discontented farmers. But like the Republicans, it too drove away a dissenting minority wing. A group of gold Democrats withdrew and nominated their own candidate.

Bryan's nomination presented the Populist party with a dilemma. Should Populists join Democrats in support of Bryan, or should they nominate their own candidate and preserve their party's independence? Tom Watson of Georgia, expressing strong southern sentiment against fusion with the Democrats, warned

William Jennings Bryan (1860–1925), the spellbinding orator whose speech on behalf of free silver thrilled thousands of western and southern agrarians in 1896. Library of Congress.

that "the Democratic idea of fusion [is] that we play Jonah while they play whale." But others reasoned that supporting a different candidate would split the anti-McKinley vote and allow the Republicans to win. In the end the convention compromised, first naming Watson as its vice-presidential nominee to preserve party identity (the Democrats had nominated Maine shipping magnate Arthur Sewall for vice president) and then nominating Bryan for the presidency.

The campaign, in the words of journalist William Allen White, "took the form of religious frenzy. . . . Far into the night, the voices rose—women's voices, children's voices, the voices of old men, of youths and of maidens, rose on the ebbing prairie breezes, as the crusaders of the revolution rode home, praising the people's will as though it were God's will and cursing wealth for its iniquity." Republicans countered Bryan's moral evangelism and attacks on privilege (he repeatedly preached that "every great economic question is in reality a great moral question") by predicting chaos if he should win. While the Great Commoner raced around the country giving as many as twenty speeches a day, Mark Hanna invited hundreds of thousands of people to McKinley's home town of Canton, Ohio, where the candidate plied them with appealing speeches on moderation and prosperity. Leaving moralizing to the Democrats, Republican candidates adopted the pragmatic approach of appealing to a wide variety of voters by promising something for everyone and a live-and-let-live philosophy for all. Employers were said to have threatened lower wages and job losses if workers did not vote for McKinley, but such charges were hard to prove.

The election results revealed that the political stand-off had finally ended. McKinley, the symbol of

William McKinley (1843–1901) ran for president in 1896 on a platform that linked business prosperity with national prestige and economic well-being. Library of Congress.

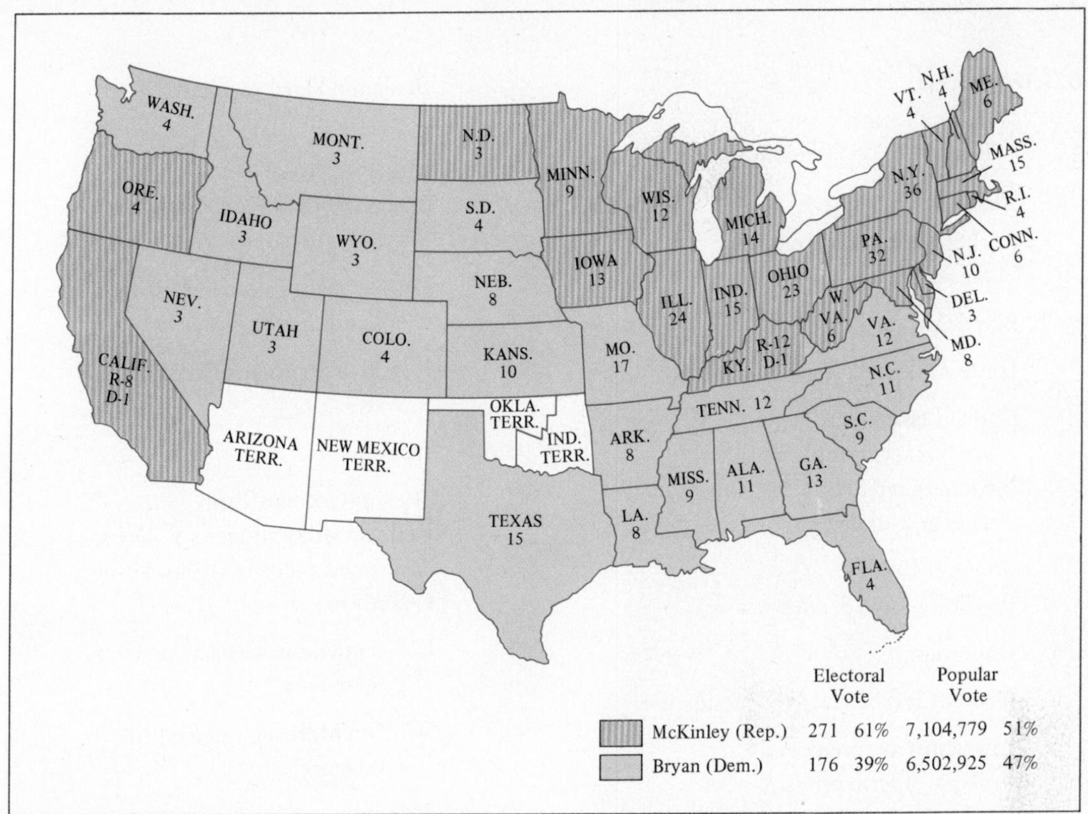

Presidential election, 1896

Republican pragmatism and the new economic order, beat Bryan by over 600,000 popular votes and by 271 to 176 in the electoral college (see map). It was the most one-sided presidential election since 1872. As Henry Adams put it, "For a hundred years, the American people had hesitated, vacillated, swayed forward and back, between two forces, one simply industrial, the other capitalistic, centralizing, and mechanical. . . . The issue came on the single gold standard, and the majority declared itself once and for all, in favor of a capitalistic system with all its necessary machinery."

Election results

The Populists had done all they could to rally the nation. Bryan had tried to offset the huge Republican campaign chest, estimated at between $3.5 and $7 million, by traveling eighteen thousand miles and giving over six hundred speeches, but lean campaign finances and his obsession with the silver issue undermined their cause. Silver especially prevented the Populists from building the urban-rural coalition that would have given them political breadth. Reformer Henry Demarest Lloyd summarized the matter succinctly: "Free silver," he wrote, "is the cow bird of the reform movement. It waited till the nest had been built by the sacrifices and labor of others, and then it laid its eggs in it, pushing out the others which it smashed to the ground." Farmers' demands for an expanded currency lacked broad appeal. Urban workers shied away from the silver issue because they feared the high prices that would result. Labor leaders like Samuel Gompers of the AFL, though partly sympathetic, would not join with Populists because they were unconvinced that farmers were employees, like industrial workers. And socialists like Daniel DeLeon denounced the Populists as "retrograde" because, unlike socialists, they still believed in free enterprise. Thus the Populist cause fizzled in 1896. Although Populists and fusion candidates made a few gains in state and congressional elections, the Bryan-Watson ticket polled only 222,600 votes nationwide.

As president, McKinley promptly signed the Gold Standard Act (1900), which required that all paper

Important events

1873	Coinage of silver dollars ends
1873–78	Depression
1876	Rutherford B. Hayes elected president
1878	Bland-Allison Act
1880	James A. Garfield elected president
1881	Garfield assassinated; Chester A. Arthur assumes the presidency National Civil Service Reform League founded
1883	Mongrel Tariff Pendleton Civil Service Act
1884–85	Depression
1884	Grover Cleveland elected president
1887	Interstate Commerce Act Collapse of farm prices
1888	Mills Tariff passes House, killed in Senate Benjamin Harrison elected president
1890	McKinley Tariff Sherman Silver Purchase Act Sherman Anti-Trust Act
1892	Populist convention in Omaha Cleveland elected president
1893	Repeal of Sherman Silver Purchase Act
1893–97	Depression
1894	Wilson-Gorman Tariff Pullman strike; Eugene V. Debs arrested and turns to socialism Coxey's march
1895	Cleveland deals with bankers to save gold reserve
1896	William McKinley elected president
1897	Dingley Tariff
1900	McKinley re-elected

money be backed by gold. A seasoned politician, personable and attractive, McKinley was best known for his expertise in crafting high protective tariffs; as a congressman from Ohio, he had guided passage of record high rates in 1890. He accordingly supported the Dingley Tariff of 1897, which raised duties even higher—though it did expand reciprocity provisions. During McKinley's presidency domestic tensions subsided: an upward swing of the business cycle and an increased money supply from new gold discoveries in Alaska, Australia, and South Africa helped to restore prosperity. Good times enabled McKinley to beat Bryan again in 1900, using the slogan "The Full Dinner Pail." Freed from the care of the economy, McKinley spent most of his time on foreign affairs. A strong believer in the need to open new markets abroad, he encouraged imperialistic ventures in Latin America and the Pacific (see Chapter 22).

In future elections, political parties would have to be sensitive to the pluralism of American society. They would have to satisfy a broad spectrum of interests rather than march under the banner of moral perfection. The reform spirit would survive, but its success would depend on cooperation, not on the sermons of righteous evangelists. Ironically, by 1920 many of the Populists' reform goals would be achieved, including regulation of railroads, banks, and utilities; shorter working hours; a variant of the subtreasury system; a graduated income tax; direct election of senators; the secret ballot, and more. These reforms would succeed precisely because a number of groups united behind them. Immigration, urbanization, and industrialization had transformed the United States into a pluralistic society where compromise among interest groups had become a political fact of life. The election of 1896 and the end of the Gilded Age equilibrium confirmed that transformation.

Suggestions for further reading

General

Harold U. Faulkner, *Politics, Reform, and Expansion, 1890–1900* (1959); Ray Ginger, *The Age of Excess* (1965); Richard Hofstadter, *The Age of Reform: From Bryan to FDR* (1955); H. Wayne Morgan, *From Hayes to McKinley* (1969); H. Wayne Morgan, ed., *The Gilded Age* (1970); Paul Studenski and Herman E. Krouss, *Financial History of the United States* (1952); Leonard D. White, *The Republican Era* (1958); R. Hal Williams, *Years of Decision: American Politics in the 1890s* (1978).

Parties, leaders, and political issues

James Bryce, *The American Commonwealth,* 2 vols. (1888); P. H. Buck, *The Road to Reunion* (1937); John H. Dobson, *Politics in the Gilded Age* (1972); Eleanor Flexner, *Century of Struggle: The Women's Rights Movement in the United States* (1959); J. Rogers Hollingsworth, *The Whirligig of Politics: The Democracy of Cleveland and Bryan* (1963); Ari A. Hoogenboom, *Outlawing the Spoils: The Civil Service Movement* (1961); Richard J. Jensen, *The Winning of the Midwest* (1971); David M. Jordan, *Roscoe Conkling of New York* (1971); Matthew Josephson, *The Politicos* (1938); Paul Kleppner, *The Cross of Culture* (1970); Robert D. Marcus, *Grand Old Party* (1971); Samuel T. McSeveney, *The Politics of Depression* (1972); Walter T. K. Nugent, *Money and American Society* (1968); Moisei Ostrogorski, *Democracy and the Organization of Political Parties* (1902); A. M. Paul, *Conservative Crisis and the Rule of Law: Attitudes of Bar and Bench, 1887–1895* (1969); David J. Rothman, *Politics and Power: The United States Senate, 1869–1901* (1966); John G. Sproat, *The Best Men: Liberal Reformers in the Gilded Age* (1968); Woodrow Wilson, *Congressional Government* (1886).

The presidency

Kenneth E. Davison, *The Presidency of Rutherford B. Hayes* (1972); Margaret Leech and Harry J. Brown, *The Garfield Orbit* (1978); Horace Samuel Merrill, *Bourbon Leader: Grover Cleveland and the Democratic Party* (1957); H. Wayne Morgan, *William McKinley and His America* (1963); Allan Peskin, *Garfield* (1978); Thomas C. Reeves, *Gentleman Boss: The Life of Chester Alan Arthur* (1975); H. J. Sievers, *Benjamin Harrison,* 3 vols. (1952–1968).

Undercurrents of protest

William M. Dick, *Labor and Socialism in America* (1972); John P. Diggins, *The American Left in the Twentieth Century* (1973); Ray Ginger, *Bending Cross: A Biography of Eugene Victor Debs* (1969); John Laslett, *Labor and the Left* (1970); Donald L. McMurry, *Coxey's Army* (1929); David Shannon, *The Socialist Party of America* (1955).

Populism and the election of 1896

Peter H. Argersinger, *Populism and Politics: William Alfred Peffer and the People's Party* (1974); Karel D. Bicha, "Jerry Simpson: Populist Without Principles," *Journal of American History,* 54 (1967), 291–306; Paolo Coletta, *William Jennings Bryan: Political Evangelist* (1964); Herbert Croly, *Marcus Alonzo Hanna* (1912); Paul W. Glad, *McKinley, Bryan, and the People* (1964); Paul W. Glad, *The Trumpet Soundeth: William Jennings Bryan and His Democracy* (1964); Lawrence Goodwyn, *Democratic Promise: The Populist Movement in America* (1976); Sheldon Hackney, *Populism to Progressivism in Alabama* (1969); John D. Hicks, *The Populist Revolt* (1931); Stanley L. Jones, *The Election of 1896* (1964); Louis W. Koenig, *Bryan* (1971); Walter T. K. Nugent, *The Tolerant Populists* (1963); Norman Pollack, *The Populist Response to Industrial America* (1962); Norman Pollack, ed., *The Populist Mind* (1967); Martin Ridge, *Ignatius Donnelly* (1962); Allan Weinstein, *Prelude to Populism: Origins of the Silver Issue* (1970); Charles Morrow Wilson, *The Commoner: William Jennings Bryan* (1970); C. Vann Woodward, *Tom Watson* (1938). See Chapter 16 for other works on farm protest.

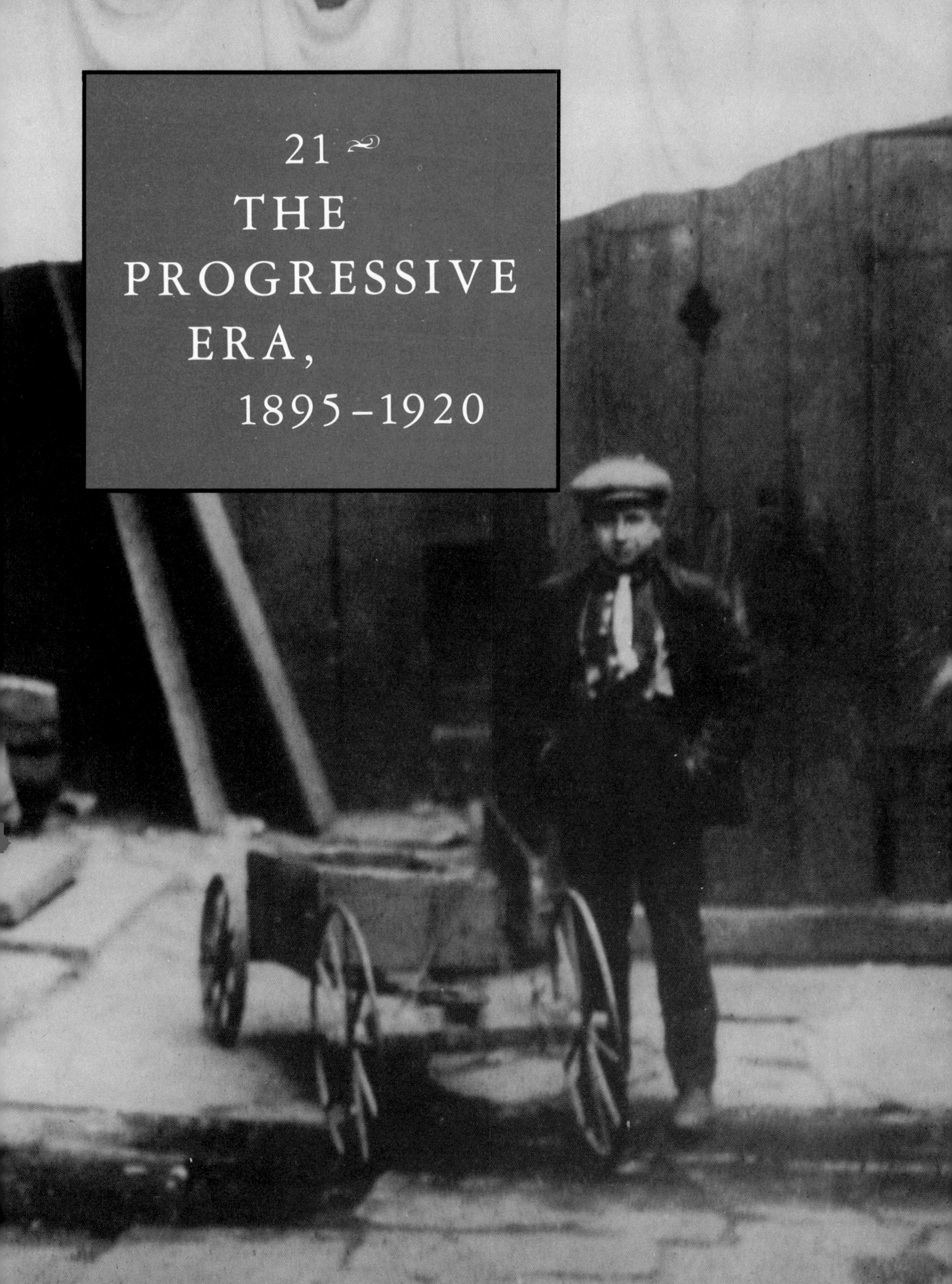

21 THE PROGRESSIVE ERA, 1895–1920

Thomas Edison, of all people, would have known if something was not working properly. He perfected and promoted so many items of modern mass technology—the light bulb, the phonograph, and the motion-picture projector, among others—that he should have had good reason to view his world optimistically. But he did not. With the perceptiveness of the good inventor he was, Edison found American society unsatisfactory and perplexing. Writing to his friend Henry Ford in 1912 about his views on the subject, Edison observed that

> in a lot of respects we Americans are the rawest and crudest of all. Our production, our factory laws, our charities, our relations between capital and labor, our distribution—all wrong, out of gear. We've stumbled along for a while, trying to run a new civilization in old ways, but we've got to start to make this world over.

Americans had always been preoccupied with reforming their society, with "making it over," but between the 1890s and the end of the First World War, an intensified rush of reform swept the country. More and more people who felt as Edison did tried to address the problems of their times directly. Their efforts, inspired by a complicated mixture of calculated self-interest and unselfish benevolence, shaped what can be called the Progressive era.

The decade of the 1890s had been anything but gay. A severe depression, frightening labor violence, political upheaval, and foreign entanglements had shaken the nation. Although many of the promises of technology had been fulfilled, Americans continued to suffer from poverty and disease. In the minds of many, industrialists had become the nation's new monsters, controlling markets, wages, and prices in order to maximize their profits. And the political system seemed corroded by bosses and their henchmen, who used parties to enrich themselves.

From this malaise emerged a broad, complex spirit of reform, so many-sided that it is hard to identify the movement's unifying characteristics. By the 1910s many reformers were calling themselves progressives, and a new political party by that name had formed to embody their principles. Since that time historians have used the term *progressivism* to refer to the reform spirit in general, while anguishing over the movement's meaning and its membership. It is probably most accurate to consider the era between 1895 and 1920 as characterized by a series of movements, each of them aimed in one way or another at renovating or restoring American society, its values, and its institutions.

The urge toward reform had many causes. Industrialization had brought unprecedented productivity, awesome technology, and a cornucopia of new consumer goods. But it had also created unemployment and labor unrest and encouraged wasteful use of natural resources and abuse of corporate power. The rapidly growing network of cities facilitated the amassing and distribution of goods, services, and cultural amenities but also magnified the problems of poverty, disease, crime, and political corruption. Massive influxes of immigrants and the rise of a new class of managers and professionals shook the foundations of the old middle and upper classes. And the debilitating depression that blanketed the nation from 1893 to 1897 brought many leading citizens to realize what working people had known for some time: the central promise of American life was not being kept. Equality of opportunity—whether economic, political, or social—was a myth.

Americans' traditional belief in individualism and economic growth was shaken. People began to doubt that hard work and good character automatically assured success, and that the poor had only themselves to blame for their failure to prosper. Instead, many leaders looked for ways to provide welfare and social justice for everyone. Their thinking challenged entrenched attitudes toward women's role, race relations, public education, scientific thought, family relations, and morality, as well as toward economic and governmental institutions. The reckless pursuit of wealth and the merging of huge corporations came under increasing attack; trustbusting and consumers' rights became important political issues. A new activism infused the presidency, as well as Congress and state and local governments, as elected leaders responded to and inspired demands for reform. More than ever before, Americans looked to their government as an agent that could and should interfere in social and economic relations to protect the common good.

Who were the progressives?

The new middle class that emerged in the closing years of the nineteenth century formed the vanguard of the progressives. This group consisted mainly of young, educated men and women in the professions–law, medicine, social work, religion, teaching, and business–who believed they could use their expertise for the betterment of society. Repelled by inefficiency and immorality in business, government, and human relations, they set out to apply the scientific and rational techniques they had learned in their professions to the problems of the larger society. As the young liberal journalist Walter Lippmann wrote in 1914, "the scientific spirit is the discipline of democracy."

They also had strong faith in progress–hence their name–and in the ability of humankind to create a better world, often using such phrases as "humanity's universal growth" and "the upward spiral of human development." Judge Ben Lindsey of Denver, who spearheaded reform in the treatment of juvenile delinquents, expressed the progressive faith when he wrote, "In the end the people are bound to do the right thing, no matter how much they fail at times." The progressives were confident that if unknowing people were informed about the existence of evil, they would become outraged and demand its eradication.

An energetic organizational impulse moved many Americans, particularly the new generation of professionals and businessmen, to unite to exchange information and work for common goals. Voluntary organizations had been a vital feature of local life since the 1790s, but between about 1895 and 1910 many such organizations became nationwide in scope and membership. They included occupational groups, such as the American Economics Association, American Bar Association, National Association of Manufacturers, and American Public Health Association; interest groups, such as the U.S. Chamber of Commerce, National Consumers League, and National Association for the Advancement of Colored People; and groups concerned with a particular issue, such as the National Municipal League, National Playground Association of America, National Child Labor Committee, National Housing Association, and National Society for the Progress of Industrial Education. Members of these groups hoped both to advance their own interests and to educate others about their goals.

Although a spirit of moral regeneration, political democracy, and antimonopolism lingered from the rural-based populist movement, the prevailing issues of the Progressive era were urban. The progressive quest for social justice, educational and legal reform, and streamlining of government was actually an extension of the urban reform goals of the previous half-century. Indeed, between 1890 and 1920 the proportion of the nation's population living in cities rose from 35 percent to over 51 percent; the number of places with fifty thousand or more people rose from 58 to 144 (see map, page 576). Recognition of the magnitude of such changes, as well as easier communications by mail, telephone, and telegraph, stimulated urban reformers to exchange information and to consolidate their efforts. The formation of the National Municipal League in 1895 and the National Civic Federation in 1900 signaled the beginning of the new reform era. The National Municipal League served as a forum for debate on issues of civic reform, such as bossism versus civil service, revisions of tax laws, nonpartisan elections, and municipal ownership of public utilities. The National Civic Federation broadened discussion of social reforms, such as workers' compensation and arbitration of labor disputes.

In the early stages of the Progressive era, reformers were motivated by personal indignation, if not revulsion, at corruption and injustice. This feeling was shared and expressed by journalists whom Theodore

Muckrakers

Roosevelt dubbed muckrakers (alluding to a character in John Bunyan's *Pilgrim's Progress* who rejected a crown for a muckrake). These writers, unlike journalists who merely reported events, fed the public taste for scandal and sensation by investigating and attacking social, economic, and political wrongs. Their fact-filled articles in *McClure's*, *Hampton's*, and other popular magazines, as well as books, exposed such offenses as the sale of tainted meat, fraudulent insurance schemes, and prostitution. Lincoln Steffens's articles in *McClure's*, later published as *The Shame of the Cities* (1904), ranked among the highlights of muckraker journalism. Steffens hoped his surveys of misrule and unfair privilege would inspire mass indignation and ultimately reform. Other well-known muckraking ef-

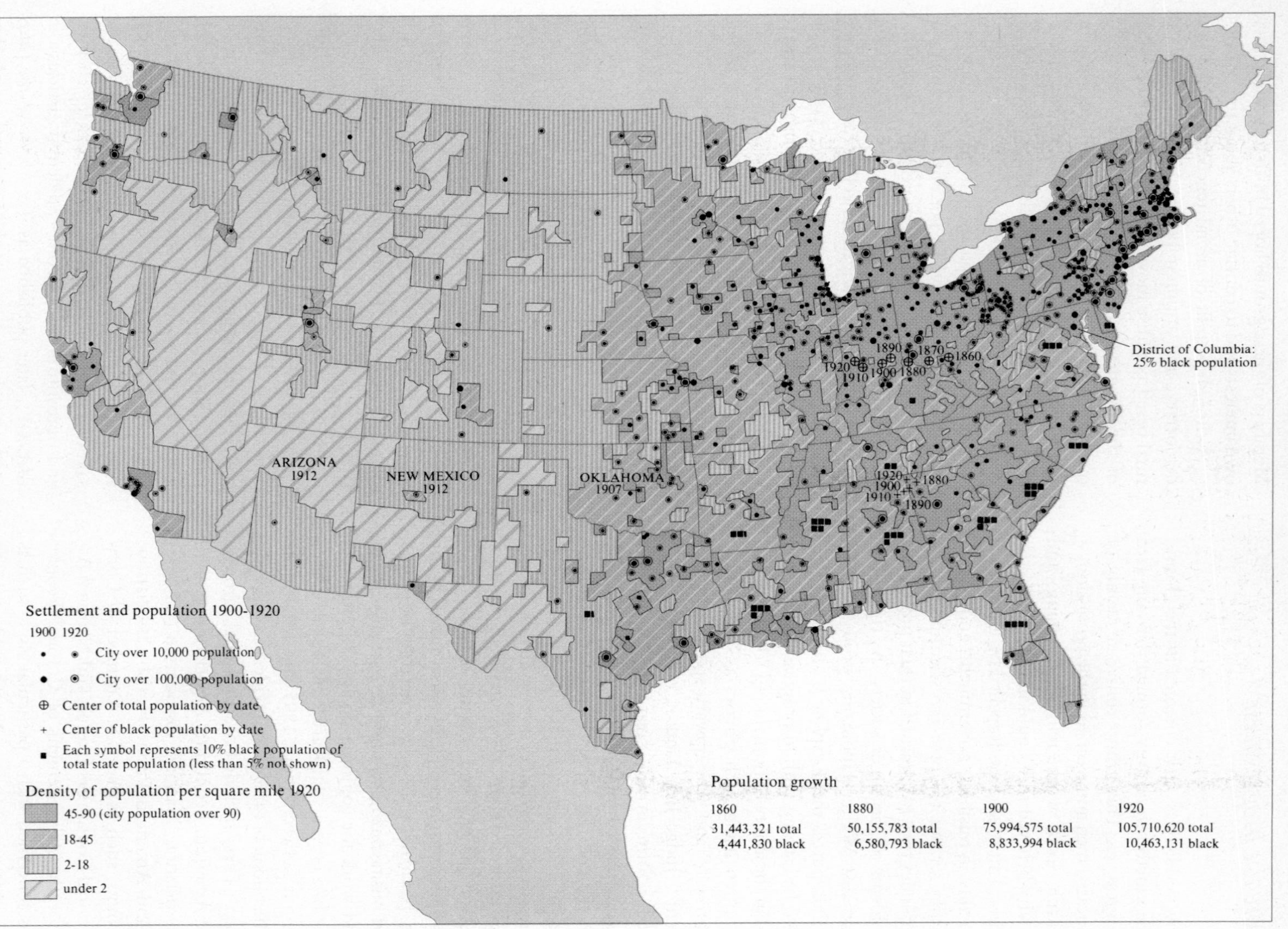

Settlement and population of the United States, 1900–1920. Source: © American Heritage Publishing Co., Inc. *American Heritage Pictorial Atlas of United States History.*

forts included Ida Tarbell's catalogue of abuses by the Standard Oil Company; Upton Sinclair's *The Jungle* (1906) and Charles E. Russell's *Greatest Trust in the World* (1905), both of which attacked the meat-packing industry; Burton J. Hendrick's *Story of Life Insurance* (1907); and David Graham Phillips's *Treason of the Senate* (1906).

Middle-class indignation also revealed itself in opposition to party politics. Reformers had a strong distaste for the bargaining, cronyism, and self-serving they believed permeated boss-ridden parties. They felt, as the journalist William Allen White did, that machines and bosses should "be reduced to mere political scrap iron by the rise of the people." (When reformers referred to "the people," they all too often meant middle-class people like themselves, excluding the native working class, blacks, and immigrants.) To improve government and the political process, these progressives advocated such reforms as nominating candidates through direct primaries instead of party caucuses, and nonpartisan elections to prevent corruption and bribery from entering the elective process. To involve more people in the political process and to make legislators more responsible, they advocated three reform devices: the initiative, which would enable voters to propose new laws on their own; the referendum, which would enable voters to accept or reject a law at the ballot box; and the recall, which would allow voters to remove officials and judges from office before their terms were up. Their goal, like that of the business consolidation movement, was collective efficiency. The government would be reclaimed by replacing the favoritism of the boss system with rational, accountable management chosen by a responsible electorate.

Political reformers

Progressive reformers, then, had an aversion to party politics, not to government. They turned to government for aid in achieving most of their goals, for they had discovered that only government had the leverage they needed. And, after all, if they did not use political power, their opponents would. But political power was only a means toward scientific and bureaucratic ends. Progressive reformers, especially members of the new middle-class professions in which systematic investigation and efficient management were of prime importance, believed with the muckrakers that knowledge was the key to progress. Science and the scientific method—system, planning, control, predictability—were central to their values. Just as corporations were applying scientific management to achieve economic efficiency, progressives would use impersonal decision making and planning to achieve social and political efficiency.

Among social reformers, the urge to serve needy people was sometimes translated into paternalism and intolerance of cultural differences. Efforts to teach immigrants and blacks vocational skills and to control their behavior through prohibition reflected a desire, conscious and unconscious, to keep them in their place and prevent them from challenging white Anglo-Saxon dominance. The line between brother's helper and brother's keeper often blurred, and many poor people came to resent efforts to aid them. Finally, reformers made only feeble attempts, if any, to ensure high employment and decent wages and to fight racism and sexism.

But not all progressive reformers were middle-class professionals. During this era vital elements of what would become modern American liberalism grew out of the working-class urban experience. By the close of the nineteenth century, many urban workers were pressing for government intervention to ensure safety and promote welfare. They wanted improvements in housing and health, safe factories, shorter working hours, workers' compensation, and other reforms. Often these were the very people who supported the political bosses, supposedly the enemies of reform. Workers knew that bosses needed to cultivate support among their constituents, and would cater to their needs. And in fact bossism was not necessarily at odds with humanitarianism. As housing reformer Lawrence Veiller observed, "The mistake that is too often made is in assuming that the boss, because he has an unsavory reputation politically, has ceased to be a human being . . . [and] . . . in assuming that you cannot count upon his help in the particular reform in which you were interested. The direct opposite is usually the case." Indeed, when Tammany Hall boss "Big Tim" Sullivan was asked why he supported a law requiring shorter working hours for women, he explained, "I had seen me sister go out to work when she was only fourteen and I know we ought to help these gals by giving 'em a law which will prevent 'em from being broken down while they're still young."

Working-class reformers

Elizabeth Gurley Flynn (1890–1964) urging on striking workers in North Halden, New Jersey, in 1912. A socialist and a leader of the Industrial Workers of the World, Flynn won prominence through her speaking skills when she was just seventeen. She devoted her life to radical causes. Brown Brothers.

After 1900, voters from inner-city districts populated by migrant and immigrant working-class families elected a number of progressive legislators who had trained in the arena of machine politics. People like New York's Alfred E. Smith and Robert F. Wagner, Massachusetts' David I. Walsh, and Illinois' Edward F. Dunne–all of whom came from immigrant backgrounds–became important reform spokesmen at the state and national levels. They were most successful when they allied with other reformers, particularly those from the middle class, to pass laws aiding labor and social welfare. The chief goal of these legislators was to establish government responsibility for alleviating the hardship that had resulted from urban-industrial growth. They opposed such reforms as prohibition, Sunday closing laws, civil service, and nonpartisan elections, all of which conflicted with their constituents' interests.

Socialists

Some deeply frustrated workers turned to the Socialist party, a faction-ridden mixture of immigrant intellectuals, industrial workers, disaffected populists, and western miners and lumbermen. The Socialist movement mounted its strongest anticapitalist drive between 1900 and the First World War. Some factions made more noise than others. The radical union known as the Industrial Workers of the World–the IWW, or "Wobblies" (see page 489)–organized strife-torn strikes in the western lumber and mining camps, in the steel town of McKees Rocks, Pennsylvania (1907), and in the textile mills of Lawrence, Massachusetts (1912). Led by former miner "Big Bill" Haywood, along with the charismatic seventy-five-year-old Mother Jones and the young radical Elizabeth Gurley Flynn, the IWW reached out to unskilled workers, promising to destroy capitalism and make all workers brothers by enabling them to control their own factories. IWW membership probably never exceeded 150,000, however, and the organization faded during the First World War when federal prosecution–and persecution–sent many of its leaders to jail.

The majority of socialists united behind Eugene V. Debs (see page 563), the tall and personable railroad organizer who drew nearly 100,000 votes in the 1900 presidential election. Though Debs was never able to develop a consistent program beyond his opposition to war and bourgeois materialism, he was a spellbinding spokesman for the radical cause. On his tireless speaking tours, he touched increasing numbers of disenchanted workers and intellectuals. Debs won 400,000 votes in his 1904 campaign for the presidency, and in 1912, at the pinnacle of his and his party's career, he polled over 900,000.

With their stinging attacks on exploitation and unfair privilege, Debs and other socialists like Milwaukee's Victor Berger and New York's Morris Hilquit made attractive overtures to reform-minded people. Some, such as settlement-house worker and child-labor reformer Florence Kelley, identified with the socialist cause. But most progressives avoided radical attacks on free enterprise. Municipal ownership of public utilities was as far as they would go toward changing the system. Indeed, progressives had too much at stake in the capitalist system to overthrow it. Thus even in Wisconsin, where progressivism was most highly developed, progressives would not join with Berger's more radical group. California progressives even formed a temporary alliance with reactionaries to prevent socialists from gaining power in Los Angeles. And few humanitarian reformers objected when in 1918 Debs was jailed for giving an antiwar speech.

The progressive spirit also stirred some elite business leaders. Successful executives like Alexander Cassatt of the Pennsylvania Railroad and William Kent, a Chicago real estate mogul, supported limited government regulation and political reforms as means of protecting their wealth from more radical political elements. Others, like E. A. Filene, founder of Boston's leading department store, and Thomas L. Johnson, a wealthy streetcar magnate, were genuine humanitarians who worked unselfishly for social justice. Business leaders guided organizations like the Municipal Voters League and the U.S. Chamber of Commerce, which supported limited political and economic reform. And women of the elite classes often led reform organizations like the YWCA and Women's Christian Temperance Union.

Business leaders

But it would be a mistake to imagine that the progressive spirit touched all of American society between 1895 and 1920. There were still large numbers of people, heavily represented in Congress, who opposed reform. They disliked government interference in economic affairs–except when it strengthened the tariff–and saw nothing wrong with existing power structures. Outside government, this outlook was represented by big business leaders like J. P. Morgan, John D. Rockefeller, and E. H. Harriman, men who sincerely believed that real progress would result from maintaining the profit incentive. Within government, this ideology was expressed by old-guard Republicans like Senator Nelson W. Aldrich of Rhode Island and House Speaker Joseph Cannon of Illinois. These men had become so accustomed to wielding power that they were contemptuous of democratic reforms. And they had the courts on their side.

With the exception of some minor radical branches of the working-class groups, progressive reformers operated from the center of the ideological spectrum. Moderate, concerned, sometimes contradictory thinkers, they believed on the one hand that the laissez-faire system was obsolete and on the other that radical challenges to the fundamentals of capitalism were dangerous. Like the Jeffersonians, they believed in the conscience and will of the people; like the Hamiltonians, they opted for a strong central government to act in the interest of conscience.

The Progressive era, then, was a complex period of multiple, overlapping, and sometimes conflicting reform movements. The era is best characterized by its challenges to almost every aspect of conventional society: politics, social relationships, ideas, institutions, and morality. The goals of progressive reformers were both idealistic and realistic. As minister-reformer Walter Rauschenbusch wrote, "We shall demand perfection and never expect to get it."

Governmental and legislative reform in the states

What were the responsibilities of government? Answers to this question in the early twentieth century were much different from those of the nineteenth century. Traditionally, theorists had held that a democratic government should be small and unobtrusive, interfering in private affairs only in unique circumstances and withdrawing once balance had been restored. In the late nineteenth century this conception eroded. Corporations, though opposed to government regulation of their activities, nevertheless pursued government aid and protection for their enterprises. Discontented farmers organized to seek government regulation of railroads and other monopolistic businesses. City dwellers, accustomed to the favors furnished by local political machines, came to expect government to act positively on their behalf.

By the turn of the century, professionals and intellectuals were accepting the notion that government could and should exert more power to ensure justice and well-being. They were becoming convinced that a simple, inflexible government was ineffective in a complex industrial age, and that public power was needed to counteract corruption and exploitation. But before reformers could use such power in ways

Robert M. La Follette (1855–1925), one of the most dynamic of progressive politicians. As governor of Wisconsin between 1901 and 1906, La Follette sponsored a program of political reform and business regulation that became known as the Wisconsin Plan. In 1906 he entered the U.S. Senate, where he continued to champion progressive reform. The National Progressive Republican League, which La Follette founded in 1911, became the core of the Progressive party. State Historical Society of Wisconsin.

they believed to be necessary, they would have to recapture government from the evil politicians whose greed had infected the democratic system. Thus an important thrust of progressive activity was the effort to root out corruption in government.

Reformers first attacked this problem in the cities (see pages 516–517). Between 1870 and 1900 opponents of the boss system tried to redirect government through structural reforms such as civil service, nonpartisan elections, and tighter scrutiny of public expenditures. A few reform leaders, like Hazen S. Pingree of Detroit, developed sympathies for broader reforms, such as poverty relief, housing improvement, and prolabor legislation. But most worked chiefly for an efficient–meaning economical–government. After 1900 the momentum for reform brought into being such new institutions as the city manager and city commission forms of government, and stronger regulation or even public ownership of utilities (gas, electricity, telephone, and streetcar companies). Humanitarian mayors like Tom Johnson of Cleveland and Samuel "Golden Rule" Jones of Toledo followed Pingree's lead by paying more attention to social welfare.

Reformers discovered, however, that the city was too small an arena for the kind of political and economic reform they sought. State and federal government offered far more promising opportunities for effecting reform through legislation. Because of their faith in a strong, fair-minded executive, progressives looked to governors and other elected officials to extend and protect the reforms that had been achieved at the local level. The reformers' goals varied from one region or state to another. In the Plains and the Far West, reformers rallied behind railroad regulation and such governmental reforms as the initiative and the referendum. In the South they continued the populist crusade against big business and autocratic politicians. And in the urban-industrial Northeast and Midwest, reformers directed their attention to corrupt political machines and unsafe labor conditions.

The reform movement produced a number of skillful, influential, and often charismatic governors who used executive power to achieve change. Their ranks included Braxton Bragg Comer of Alabama and Hoke Smith of Georgia, who introduced business regulations and other reforms in the South; Albert Cummins of Iowa and Hiram Johnson of California, who battled the railroads that dominated their states; Hazen Pingree of Michigan, who carried his fight against private utilities from the city to the state level; and Woodrow Wilson of New Jersey, whose administrative reforms were copied by other governors. Such men were not always saints, however. Smith supported the disfranchisement of blacks, and Johnson discriminated against Japanese-Americans.

Progressive governors

Probably the most notable progressive governor was Wisconsin's Robert M. La Follette. A self-made small-town lawyer whose short, compact build and thick, bristling hair suited his combative personality, La Follette rose through the ranks of the state Republican party to the governorship in 1900. As governor he initiated a multipronged reform program whose highlights were direct primaries, revision of taxes to prevent corporations from benefiting unfairly over other taxpayers, and regulation of railroad rates. He also created regulatory commissions staffed with experts (including professors from the University of Wisconsin) whose investigations supplied La Follette with facts and figures which he used in fiery speeches to muster public support for his policies. After three terms as governor, La Follette was elected senator and carried his progressive ideals into national politics. "Battling Bob" had a rare ability to take a tempered, scientific approach to reform while still appealing to the people with moving rhetoric. His goal, he once asserted, "was not to 'smash' corporations, but to drive them out of politics, and then to treat them exactly the same as other people are treated."

Not all state leaders were as successful as La Follette. To be sure, the crusade against party politics and corruption did accomplish some permanent changes. By 1916 all but three states had direct primaries, and many states had adopted the initiative, referendum, and recall. And political reformers had achieved a major goal in 1912 when the states ratified the Seventeenth Amendment, which provided for the direct election of U.S. senators (formerly elected by state legislatures). But political reforms did not always bring about the desired results. Party bosses, better organized and more experienced than reformers, were able to control the new primaries as well as elections. The initiative, referendum, and recall often failed because they required sustained campaigns for which few reformers had patience. Moreover, political reformers had little durability; professional politicians moved back into power when enthusiasm for reform waned and reform leaders tired of their crusade.

Progressive legislation

New state laws aimed at bettering social welfare had greater impact than most political reforms, especially in factories. Broadly interpreting their powers to protect the health and safety of their citizens, many states enacted factory inspection laws, and by 1916 nearly two-thirds of the states had insurance for victims of industrial accidents (see map, page 583). A coalition of labor and humanitarian groups supported these laws and even induced some legislatures to grant aid to widows with dependent children. Under pressure from the National Child Labor Committee, nearly every state established a minimum age for employment (varying from twelve to sixteen), and prohibited employers from working children more than eight or ten hours a day. Such laws, however, were hard to enforce. As early as 1900, twenty-eight states, mostly in the North and West (the South was woefully lax in protecting children), had passed some kind of child-labor bill, but such legislation seldom provided for the close inspection of factories that full enforcement required. Moreover, families that needed the income their children brought home encouraged their children to work and lie about their ages. Several groups also joined forces to limit working hours for women. After the Supreme Court upheld Oregon's ten-hour limit in 1908, many more states passed such laws protecting women workers. Finally, the efforts of the American Association for Old Age Security began to succeed in 1914, when Arizona established old-age pensions. Though the law was struck down by the courts, the First World War renewed interest in pensions, and in the 1920s many states drafted laws to provide for needy older people.

These and other social reforms were strongly opposed by people who thought them detrimental to their self-interest or who genuinely believed that government interference in such matters would destroy the free enterprise system. Some business associations bitterly fought consumers' efforts to legislate milk and meat inspections. The National Association of Manufacturers coordinated the battle against regulation of business and working conditions. And legislators friendly to special interests connived to weaken the new laws by failing to fund their enforcement.

Moral reform

Reformers themselves were not always certain about what was progressive, especially in terms of human behavior. The main problem seemed to be whether or not it was possible to create a desirable moral climate through legislation. Some reformers, such as the members of the Social Gospel movement (see page 517), believed that only church-based inspiration and humanitarian work, rather than legislation, could transform society. But other people believed state intervention was necessary to achieve purity, especially in drinking habits and sexual behavior.

Children laboring in the coal mines, a favorite cause of progressive reformers. Workers like these "breaker boys," who removed slag and sorted coal, were often exhausted by their long hours of toil in the dark, dust-filled mines. They had no time for the schooling that might have helped them to escape poverty. Sometimes they met an early death. (Above) Photographed by Lewis Hine. Library of Congress.

The formation of the Anti-Saloon League in 1893 marked a new turn in the long campaign against drunkenness and its effects on society. This organized group of reformers joined with the older Women's Christian Temperance Union (founded in 1873) to publicize the connections between alcoholism and health problems, poverty, unemployment, and family breakups. The result was that a large number of states, counties, towns, and city wards restricted the sale and consumption of liquor (see map). By 1900 almost a quarter of the nation's population lived in communities with such restrictions. But as consumption of alcohol, especially beer, increased after 1900, prohibitionists became convinced that national restrictions were the only solution. By 1917 they had converted to their cause such notables as Supreme Court Justice Louis D. Brandeis and former president William Howard Taft. And in 1918 they induced Congress to pass the Eighteenth Amendment, prohibiting the manufacture, sale, and transportation of intoxicating liquors. (The amendment was ratified in 1919 and implemented in 1920.) Not all prohibitionists were progressive reformers, and by no means all progressives were prohibitionists. Yet the Eighteenth Amendment can be seen as still another outcome of the progressive urge to change society and elevate morality by passing reform legislation.

Public outrage boiled over after 1900 when muckraking journalists began to expose interstate and international rings that kidnapped young women and forced them to become prostitutes, a practice called white slavery. Middle-class moralists, already alarmed by a perceived link between immigration and prostitution in the cities, prodded governments to investigate the problem and recommend corrective legislation. The Chicago Vice Commission, for example,

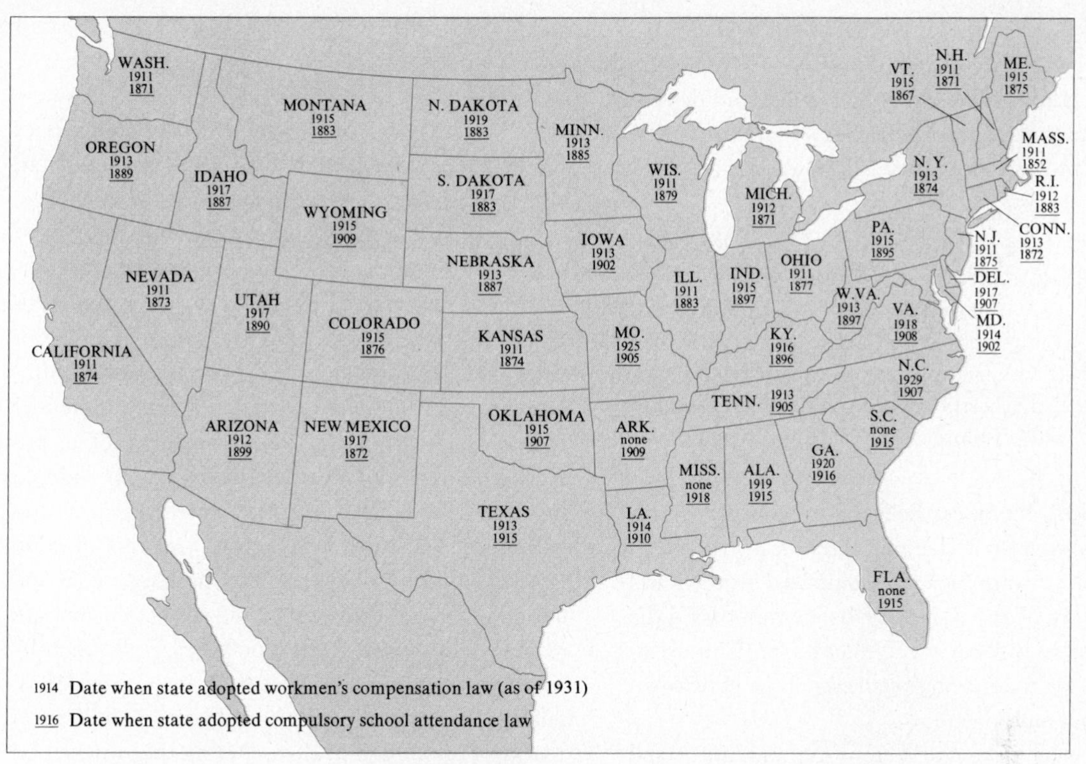

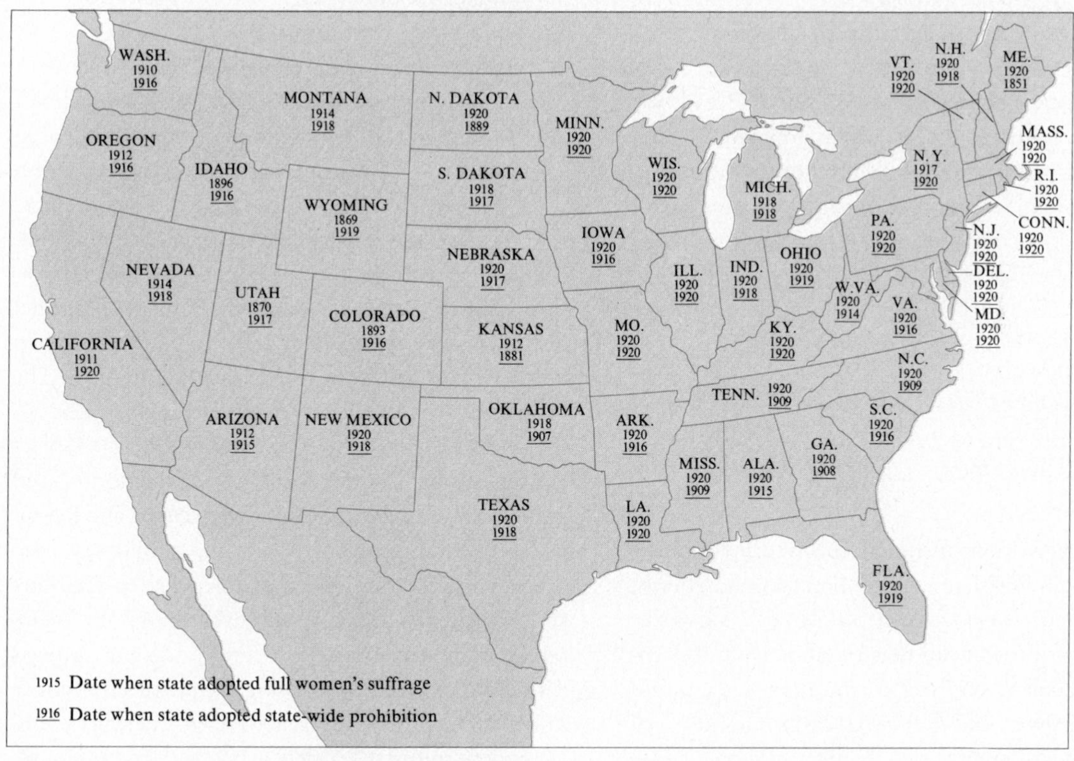

Progressive reform legislation

undertook a "scientific" survey and published its findings, called *The Social Evil in Chicago,* in 1911. The report underscored the poverty, ignorance, and desperation that drove women, especially immigrants and blacks, to prostitution. Above all, however, it asserted that

> it is a man and not a woman problem which we face today–commercialized by men–supported by men–the supply of fresh victims furnished by men. . . . So long as there is lust in the hearts of men [the Social Evil] will seek out some method of expression. Until the hearts of men are changed we can hope for no absolute annihilation of the Social Evil.

Nonetheless, reformers believed they could attack prostitution without changing "the hearts of men." By 1915 nearly every state had outlawed brothels and the soliciting of sex. And in 1910 Congress passed the Mann Act, or White Slave Traffic Act, prohibiting interstate and international transportation of women for immoral purposes.

Like prohibition, the Mann Act did not stand squarely in the middle of progressive reform. Even so, it reflected growing sentiment that state and national governments could do something to stamp out social evils. Reformers believed that the source of evil was not original sin but the social environment. If evil were human-made, then it could be human-destroyed. Thus human intervention, in the form of laws, could help create a heaven on earth.

New ideas in education, law, and the social sciences

While legislation anchored the reform impulse, equally important changes were occurring in schools, courts, and settlement houses during the Progressive era. The new preoccupation with efficiency and scientific management challenged educators, judges, and social scientists to find technical solutions to the problems of modern mass society. Darwin's theory of evolution had upset traditional beliefs; immigration had replaced social uniformity with diverse nationalities; and economic change had shaken old habits of production and consumption. New ways of thinking had to be found, ways that would be meaningful for the new era yet preserve what was best in the past. A new flexibility was needed. Knowledge, as philosopher and educator John Dewey wrote, was "no longer an immobile solid; it has been liquefied. It is actively moving in all the currents of society itself."

Changing patterns of school attendance encouraged these new ways of thinking. As late as the 1870s Americans attended school for an average of only four years, and educators believed their task was to cultivate virtue in children by exposing them to moralistic pieties. For example, *McGuffey's Reader,* used in primary schools throughout the nation, taught children such homilies as "By virtue we secure happiness" and "One deed of shame is succeeded by years of penitence." By 1900, however, the swelling cities and booming factories were providing the tax revenues to make extended mass education possible. Boosted by compulsory attendance laws (see map, page 583), public-school enrollments rose from 6.9 million in 1870 to 17.8 million in 1910. During the same period the number of public high schools grew from five hundred to over ten thousand.

Reformers had long envisioned education as a means of bettering society. As early as 1883, psychologist G. Stanley Hall, whose ideas strongly influenced educational philosopher John Dewey, had noted that the experiences of modern urban schoolchildren were much different from those of their farm-bred parents and grandparents. Thus educational techniques had to adjust in order to prepare children for productive citizenship and self-fulfilling lives. The progressives, with Dewey in the vanguard, took up the cause. According to Dewey, children, not subject matter, should be the focus of school policy, and schools should serve as community centers and instruments of social progress. Above all, said Dewey, education should relate directly to experience. Children should be encouraged to discover things for themselves. Rote memorization and outdated subjects should be replaced by teaching techniques that make knowledge relevant to students' lives and skills useful in modern industrial society.

Progressive education

Progressive education, based on the theories Dewey explored in *The School and Society* (1899) and *Democracy and Education* (1916), was a uniquely

Progressive education. Instead of sitting rigidly at their desks, learning by memorization, these girls are expressing themselves creatively by painting watercolors of flowers. Progressive educators tried to make the students, rather than the subject matter, the center of schooling, stressing personal growth over discipline. Culver.

American phenomenon. Like American economic theory, it emphasized growth. To Dewey, it was personal growth, not mastery of a given body of knowledge, that was the goal of human existence. Because people grew fastest mentally in their youth, and because the family could no longer perform the educational functions it had fulfilled in an agrarian society, schools had to assume responsibility for cultivating intelligence and creativity. From kindergarten (a new development, pioneered by the German educator Friedrich Froebel) through high school, children were supposed to learn through experience. In the Laboratory School that Dewey and his wife Alice directed at the University of Chicago, children were not required to recite lessons as their counterparts had done in the nineteenth century. Instead they examined, built, and discussed things just as they would outside school. As Dewey reasoned,

> there is a certain disorder in any busy workshop; there is not silence, persons are not engaged in maintaining fixed physical postures; their arms are not folded; they are not holding their books thus and so. . . . Our whole conception of school discipline changes when we get this point of view.

Personal growth also became the driving principle behind college education. The purpose of American colleges and universities had traditionally been that of their European counterparts: to train a select few for the professions of law, medicine, teaching, and religion. But in the late nineteenth century, places of higher education multiplied, spurred by public aid and increases in the number of people who could afford tuition. Between 1870 and 1910 the number of colleges and universities grew from 563 to nearly 1,000. By 1910 American institutions had almost as

Colleges and universities

many faculty members (40,000) as there were university students in all of France. As a result, curricula expanded; courses of study broadened as educators sought to make learning meaningful to more students. Harvard University, under President Charles W. Eliot, pioneered in substituting electives for required courses and in experimenting with new teaching techniques.

Much of the expansion in college enrollments, especially in the Midwest and West, was prompted by the Morrill Land Grant Act of 1862 (see pages 380 and 455–456). The new land-grant colleges offered a wide variety of courses that ranged from the classics through natural science to carpentry, farming, and blacksmithing. Many of them considered athletics an important part of a student's growth, and intercollegiate sports became a central feature of student life, as well as a source of school pride and alumni contributions. Southern states, in keeping with the "separate but equal" policy, set up segregated land-grant colleges for blacks. *Separate* was more descriptive of these institutions than *equal,* however; blacks continued to be constrained by inferior educational institutions.

As colleges and universities expanded, so did their enrollment of women. Between 1890 and 1910 the number of females enrolled in institutions of higher learning swelled from 56,000 to 140,000. By the latter date, 106,000 women attended coeducational institutions (many of which were state universities aided by the Morrill Act), while 34,000 attended women's colleges. Women accounted for 40 percent of all college students. Ten years later 283,000 women were attending college, accounting for 47.3 percent of total enrollment. Their numbers alone disproved earlier objections that women were unfit for higher learning because they were mentally and physically inferior to men, but discrimination lingered in admissions and curriculum policies. Most women were encouraged (indeed, they usually sought) to take home economics courses rather than science and mathematics, and most medical schools, including Harvard and Yale, refused to admit women.

At the same time they were developing new ideals and new approaches to knowledge, American colleges–and American schools in general–adopted the prevailing attitude of business: that more is better. Educators justifiably congratulated themselves for drawing more people into schools and for making instruction more meaningful. By 1920, fully 78 percent of all children between ages five and seventeen were enrolled in public elementary and high schools; another 8 percent were in private and parochial schools. These figures represented a huge increase over the attendance rate of 1870. And there were 600,000 college and graduate students in 1920, compared to 52,000 in 1870. Yet few people looked beyond the numbers to assess how well schools were doing their job. The faith that schools could promote equality and justice as well as personal growth and responsible citizenship underwent very little critical analysis.

The law, like education, began to exhibit new emphases on experience and scientific principles. Oliver Wendell Holmes, Jr., associate justice of the Supreme Court between 1902 and 1932, led the attack on the old view of law as universal and unchanging–like the Ten Commandments. "The life of the law," said Holmes, sounding like Dewey, "has not been logic; it has been experience." Holmes's view that law should reflect society's needs challenged the judicial practice of invoking traditional beliefs to obstruct social legislation. Louis D. Brandeis, a brilliant lawyer who joined Holmes on the Supreme Court in 1916, carried Holmes's views one step further by insisting that judges' opinions be based on factual, scientifically gathered information about social realities. In the landmark case *Muller* v. *Oregon* (1908), Brandeis mustered extensive scientific evidence to convince the Supreme Court to uphold Oregon's law limiting women's working hours.

Progressive legal thought

New legal thought, however, met some tough resistance. Judges brought up on laissez-faire economic theory continued to strike down the kind of law progressive lawyers thought necessary for effective reform. Thus in 1905 the Supreme Court overturned a New York law limiting bakers' working hours (*Lochner* v. *New York*) in spite of Holmes's forceful dissent. Holmes claimed that the meaning of liberty "in the Fourteenth Amendment, is perverted when it is held to prevent the natural outcome of a dominant opinion." But the majority argued that the Constitution protected an individual's right to make contracts without government interference, and that this protection thus superseded reform sentiments.

Moreover, even if one agreed that law should reflect society's needs, which part of society should be represented? The United States was a mixed nation, and religion and ethnicity deeply influenced law. In many places a native white Protestant majority required Bible reading in public schools (thereby offending Catholics and Jews), stipulated that business establishments close on Sundays, restricted the religious practices of Mormons and other groups, prohibited interracial marriage, and enforced racial segregation. Though Holmes asserted that laws should be made for "people of fundamentally differing views," Americans have always had difficulty creating and applying such laws.

At about the same time, social science–the study of society and its institutions–experienced changes like those overtaking law and education. In economics, for example, a group of young scholars used statistics to argue that the laws governing economic relationships were not immutable. Instead, they asserted, economic theory should be relevant to prevailing social conditions. Richard T. Ely of Johns Hopkins University and the University of Wisconsin, an early spokesman for the new point of view, argued that opposition to government interference in social and economic affairs had been outmoded by industrialization. Thus, practical solutions to current problems should be derived through "the united efforts of Church, state, and science." A new breed of sociologists led by Lester Ward, Albion Small, and Edward A. Ross agreed, adding that citizens should engage in social (including governmental) planning to cure social ills rather than passively waiting for problems to solve themselves. Meanwhile the so-called progressive historians, Frederick Jackson Turner, Charles A. Beard, and Vernon L. Parrington, were examining the past as a means of identifying current flaws in American society and motivating social change. And political scientists like Woodrow Wilson emphasized the practical over the theoretical, advocating the expansion of government power as a means to ensure justice and progress.

Social science

Motivated by the urge to investigate and apply new social theories, a group of idealistic young men and women set up residences called settlement houses in inner-city slums, where they worked to improve conditions. The earliest settlement houses were founded in New York by Stanton Coit (Neighborhood Guild), Vida Scudder (College Settlement), and Lillian Wald (Henry Street Settlement); in Chicago by Jane Addams and Ellen Gates Starr (Hull House) and Graham R. Taylor (Chicago Commons); and in Boston by Robert A. Woods (Andover House). After 1900 the idea spread to almost every large city and by 1910 there were over four thousand settlements scattered across the country. Well-educated and driven by the desire to help others, settlement workers offered classes, sponsored exhibits and concerts, and undertook surveys of poverty, housing, public health, and other conditions needing reform.

Settlement houses

Though naive and romantic–they sometimes expected working-class immigrants to adopt middle-class values–settlement workers translated many of the new ideas of social science into action. They also marched in the vanguard of such progressive movements as school reform, factory and business regulation, workers' rights, women's suffrage, and governmental reform. Furthermore, settlements gave educated women an opportunity for active service at a time when many professions and business occupations were closed to them. Perhaps most important, settlement-house workers believed they should learn from as well as teach the inner-city residents they wanted to serve. Their first-hand experiences with immigrants and blacks reinforced Jane Addams's theory that settlements were based on "the dependence of classes on each other."

Settlement workers joined with scientists and organizations like the National Consumers League to bring about some of the most far-reaching of progressive reforms: those in the area of public health. After the 1880s, when European scientists discovered that many diseases and infections were caused by bacteria, doctors and social reformers began to press local governments for measures to reduce the threat of disease. By 1900 a number of cities were filtering and chlorinating public water supplies, and enlarged staffs of health inspectors were supervising tighter sanitation regulations. Between 1900 and 1907, expenditures by health departments rose 600 percent in the nation's large cities. The bulk of these funds supported neighborhood clinics and dispensaries that provided health education and medical care to the poor. Progressive women's organizations were particularly successful in sponsoring laws ensuring pure pasteurized milk and regulating the quality of food sold by street vendors.

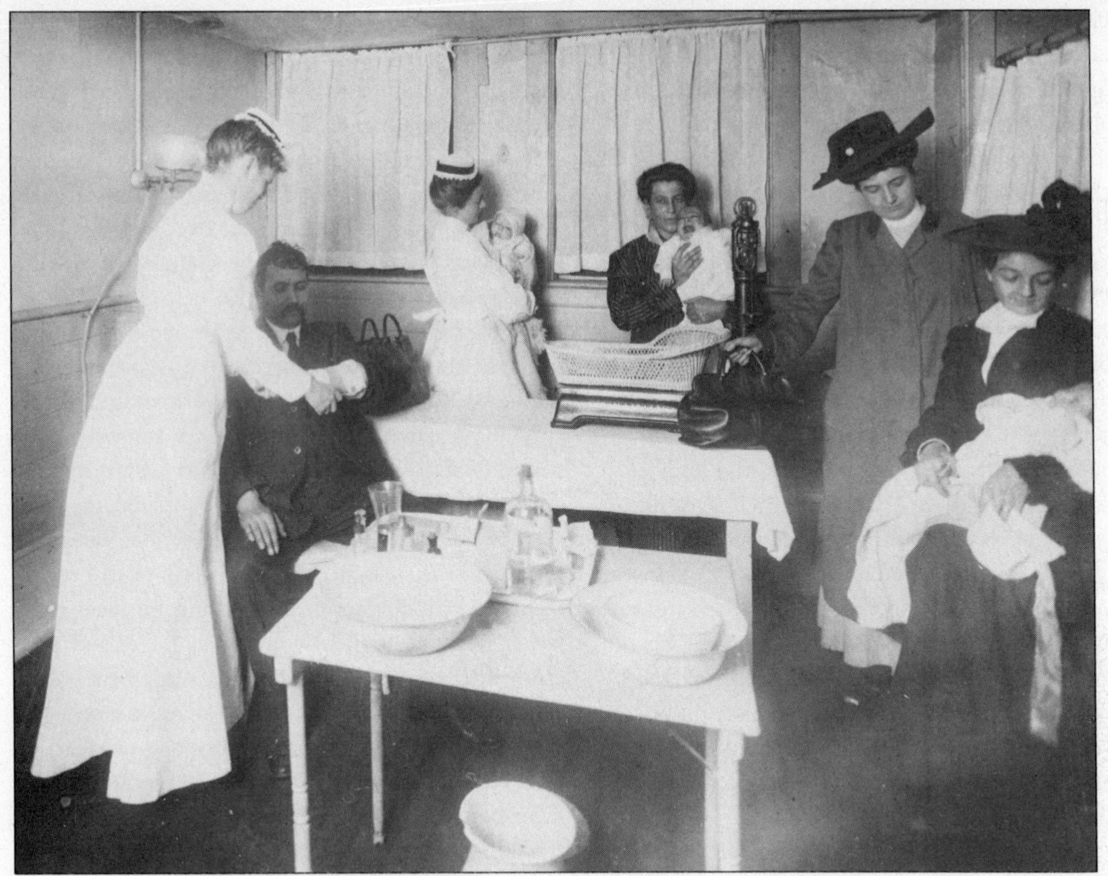

Public health clinics such as this one at Denison House in Dorchester, Boston, were among the most effective projects of progressive reformers. Often sponsored by settlement houses, the clinics ministered to the needs of the inner-city poor, especially mothers caring for infants. Photographed in 1900. The Schlesinger Library, Radcliffe College.

Their efforts helped to generate a movement for consumer awareness that has continued to the present day.

Thus between the end of the nineteenth century and the First World War, a new breed of men and women pressed for institutional change as well as political reform. Largely middle-class in background, trained by new professional standards, confident that new ways of thinking would bring progress, these people helped to broaden the concept of government's role in meeting the needs of a mature industrial society. Inevitably, their questioning attitude toward social relations extended beyond their immediate goals and jostled conventional attitudes toward race and sex.

Challenges to racial and sexual discrimination

W. E. B. Du Bois, the forceful black scholar and teacher, ended an essay in his book *The Souls of Black Folk* (1903) with a call that heralded the twentieth-century civil rights movement: "By every civilized and peaceful method," he wrote, "we must strive for the right which the world accords to men."

By "men" Du Bois meant all human beings, not just one sex. But his statement and its context suggest the dilemma that vexed the two largest groups of underprivileged Americans in the early 1900s: women and nonwhites. Both were trapped in a society dominated by white males. Both suffered from disfranchisement, discrimination, and humiliation. And for centuries both groups had been striving for "the right which the world accords to men"–freedom and equality. The progressive challenge to old ideas and customs gave impetus to blacks' and women's struggles for their rights, but it posed thorny questions as well. Should women and blacks strive to become just like white men, with white men's values and power as well as their rights? Or was there something unique about their racial and sexual identity that should be retained at the risk of sacrificing some gains? Both groups wavered between accepting and rejecting the culture from which they had been excluded.

The problems of blacks in white American society remained regional in scope until well into the twentieth century, though important shifts were beginning to occur. In 1900 only about 900,000, or one in ten blacks, lived in the North (see map, page 576). The rest lived in southern states, where repressive Jim Crow measures had multiplied in the 1880s and 1890s. Southern blacks were not only denied legal and voting rights but were officially segregated in almost all walks of life. They faced constant exclusion and violence. In 1910 only 8,000 out of over 970,000 high-school-age blacks in the entire South were enrolled in high schools. Between 1900 and 1914 over a thousand blacks were lynched by white mobs.

Blacks began to migrate northward in the 1880s, accelerating their rate of departure after 1900. But they found equally pervasive, if more subtle, bigotry in the North. Job and housing discrimination, inferior schools, and segregated neighborhoods characterized northern as well as southern cities. White humanitarians contributed to discrimination by maintaining separate programs and institutions for blacks, rather than integrating them with whites. A half-century after the abolition of slavery, most whites still agreed with the northern historian James Ford Rhodes that blacks were "innately inferior and incapable of citizenship."

Black leaders differed over the issue of how–and whether–to achieve assimilation. In the wake of emancipation, ex-slave Frederick Douglass had urged "ultimate assimilation through self-assertion, and on no other terms." Other blacks who favored isolation from the cruel white society supported migration back to Africa or the establishment of all-black communities in Oklahoma Territory and Kansas. Still others, like T. Thomas Fortune, editor of the New York *Age* and founder of the Afro-American League, advocated militancy. According to one militant, "Our people must die to be saved and in dying must take as many along with them as it is possible to do with the aid of firearms and all other weapons."

Most blacks, however, could neither escape nor conquer white society. They thus had to find other routes to improvement. Self-help, a strategy articulated by educator Booker T. Washington, was one of the most popular alternatives. Born in 1856 to slave parents, Washington worked his way through school and in 1881 founded Tuskegee Institute, a vocational school for blacks. There he developed the philosophy that blacks' hopes for assimilation lay in abandoning self-assertion and at least temporarily accommodating themselves to whites. Rather than fighting for political rights, he said, blacks should work hard, acquire property, and prove they were worthy of their rights. Washington voiced his views in a widely acclaimed speech at the Atlanta Exposition in 1895. "Dignify and glorify common labor," he urged. "Agitation of questions of racial equality is the extremest folly." Envisioning a society where blacks and whites would be separate but share the same goals, Washington observed that "in all things that are purely social we can be as separate as the fingers, yet one as the hand in all matters essential to mutual progress."

Booker T. Washington

Whites, including progressives, welcomed Washington's policy of accommodation because it urged patience and seemed to remind black people to stay in their place. White businessmen, reformers, and politicians chose to regard Washington as representative of all blacks, because he said what they wanted to hear. Yet though Washington endorsed the separate-but-equal policy, he projected a subtle racial pride that would find more direct expression in black nationalism later in the twentieth century, when blacks would take pride in control of their own businesses and schools. Washington never argued that blacks were inferior to whites, he instead argued that their dignity could be enhanced through their self-improvement.

But, to some blacks Washington seemed to favor

Black students practicing woodwork at Hampton Institute, Hampton, Virginia. Like Tuskegee Institute, Hampton offered vocational instruction in the belief that by acquiring skills and working hard, blacks could convince whites they were worthy of equal rights. Library of Congress.

second-class citizenship, which they considered degrading. In 1905 a group of "anti-Bookerites" convened near Niagara Falls and pledged a more militant pursuit of such rights as unrestricted voting, equal access to economic opportunity, integration, and equality before the law. The spokesman for the Niagara movement was W. E. B. Du Bois, a vociferous critic of Washington's policy of accommodation. A New Englander with a Ph.D. from Harvard, Du Bois had the background of a typical progressive. He had studied in Germany, where he learned about both scientific investigation and poetic expression, and he was a professor on the faculty of Atlanta University. Du Bois used scientific methods to compile fact-filled sociological studies of the lives of black ghetto dwellers, and he wrote poetically for the cause of civil rights. In his essays and speeches, Du Bois treated Washington politely, but he could not accept Washington's submission to white domination. "The way for a people to gain their reasonable rights," Du Bois asserted, "is not by voluntarily throwing them away." Blacks needed, instead, to reassert themselves and agitate for what was rightfully theirs.

W. E. B. Du Bois

Du Bois showed that accommodation was an unrealistic strategy, but his own solution may have been just as fanciful. A blunt elitist, Du Bois believed that an intellectual vanguard of cultivated, highly trained blacks, which he called the Talented Tenth, would save the race by setting an example to whites and other blacks. Inevitably, such elitist sentiments had more attraction for middle-class white liberals than for black sharecroppers. Thus when Du Bois and his allies formed the National Association for the Advancement of Colored People (1909), which aimed to use legal redress in the courts to end racial discrimination, the leadership consisted chiefly of white progressives like Jane Addams, John Dewey, and Oswald

Garrison Villard, grandson of abolitionist William Lloyd Garrison. Very few working-class black people belonged. By 1914 the NAACP had fifty branch offices and over 6,000 members, but rarely did its activities touch sharecropping and laboring families.

Whatever strategy they pursued–accommodation or agitation–black Americans faced continued oppression. In fact, those blacks who managed to acquire property and education encountered increased resentment from whites. Race riots like the one in Atlanta in 1906 destroyed middle-class as well as working-class black neighborhoods. And the federal government only aggravated conditions. Under the administration of Woodrow Wilson, segregation within the federal government expanded; southern cabinet members supported racial separation in the rest rooms, restaurants, and offices of government buildings and balked at hiring black workers. Commenting on Wilson's racism in 1913, Booker T. Washington wrote, "I have never seen the colored people so discouraged and so bitter as they are at the present time."

Blacks still sought to fulfill the American dream of success, but many wondered whether membership in a corrupt white society should be part of their quest. Du Bois voiced these doubts poignantly, writing that "one ever feels his twoness–an American, a Negro, two souls, two thoughts, two unreconciled strivings, two warring ideals in one dark body." Somehow blacks would have to reconcile that twoness by combining racial pride with national identity. As Du Bois wrote in 1903, a black

> would not Africanize America, for America has too much to teach the world and Africa. He would not bleach his Negro soul in a flood of white Americanism, for he knows that Negro blood has a message for the world. He simply wishes to make it possible for a man to be both a Negro and an American.

That simple wish would haunt the nation for decades to come.

During this time too, the progressive challenge to social relations stirred women to seek liberation from the traditional confines of hearth and home. But their struggle raised questions of identity that resembled those blacks were facing. What tactics should women use to achieve equality, and what should be their role in society? The writer Henry James summed up the dilemma inherent in such questions when he complained that women who wanted to become just like men were disregarding their own uniqueness. Could women achieve equality with men and at the same time change male-dominated society?

By the early 1900s the trend was definitely toward greater freedom for women. First, more women than ever were taking paid jobs. In 1900 exactly 20 percent of all adult women were in the labor force (among those aged fourteen to twenty-four, the work rate was almost 30 percent). By 1920, though, the percentage of women working was virtually unchanged at 20.5 percent, a major shift had occurred within the ranks of female workers. The most significant trend was in the clerical sector–jobs such as clerks, typists, stenographers, bookkeepers, and the like. In 1880 there were only 38,000 women in these positions, accounting for only 1.9 percent of all employed women. By 1920, however, there were 1.9 million women in clerical jobs, 25.6 percent of all employed women. Meanwhile the proportion of women in domestic service (servants, cooks, laundresses) declined from 40.3 percent in 1890 to 18.2 percent in 1920, though the number in this sector remained about the same (1.3 million to 1.4 million). Growth occurred in the number of female factory workers, from 650,000 in 1890 to 1.8 million in 1920, and of female professionals, from 308,000 to 993,000. But the percentages of all female workers in these categories increased only slightly: factory workers from 20.3 percent to 23.8 percent, and professionals from 9.5 percent to 13.3 percent. Though most women held the lowest-paying, least opportune jobs, and though most working women still saw their domestic role as primary, wage labor gave them some economic independence as well as social contacts that women confined to the home never enjoyed.

Employed women

Second, changing styles of dress and public behavior freed middle-class women from uncomfortable physical and moral restraints. Heavy, tightly-laced clothes became less common after 1900 (see page 531), and women faced less rebuke if they wished to smoke or talk in public about politics or sex. The divorce rate in 1920 was double that of 1890 (in urban areas in 1920 there were 23 divorced women for every 1,000 women who had ever married compared to only

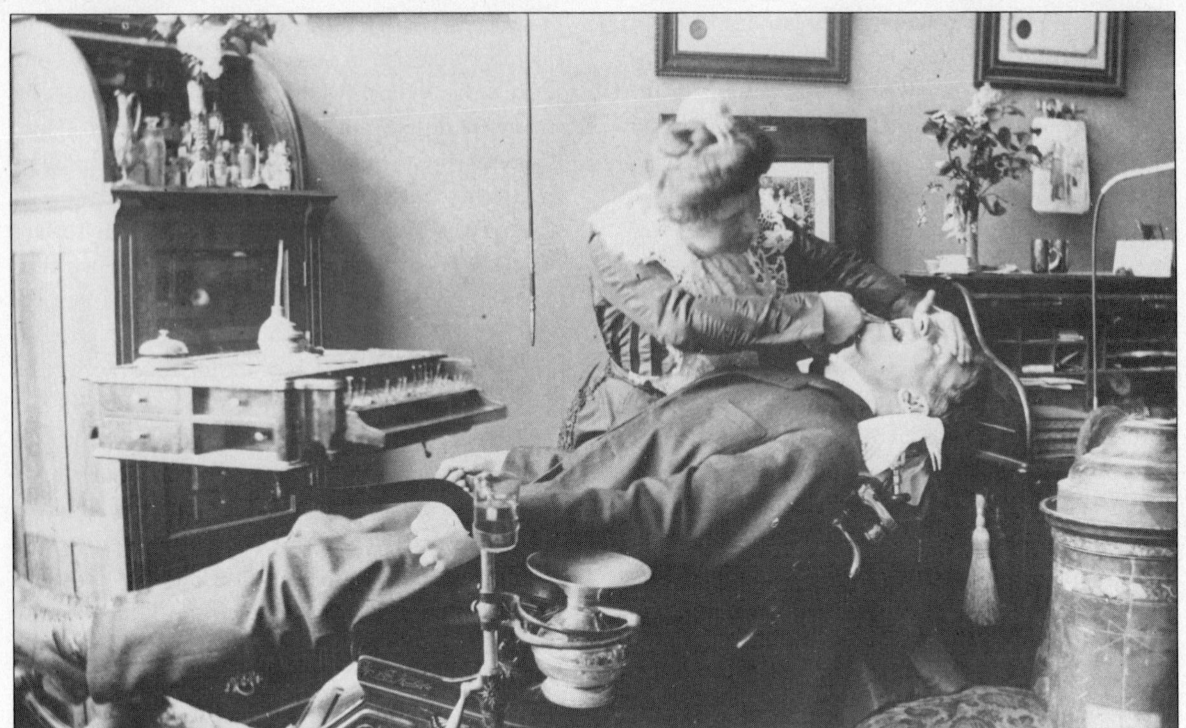

Dr. Olga A. Lentz, one of the first women to enter the male-dominated profession of dental surgery. Asked whether women were suited to dentistry, Lentz replied, "In my opinion they are better fitted than men. . . . The latter use too much force, and often crush a tooth or injure the jaw, in taking one out." Minnesota Historical Society.

11 in 1890), indicating that people were beginning to accept the idea that marriage need not chain together unhappy people. And according to Alfred Kinsey's studies of sexual behavior, published in the 1940s and 1950s, around 1915 more women began experiencing orgasm and premarital sex than in the previous generation.

Despite these breezes of change, however, most women failed to break free from traditional restraints. On the job, they had to defer to male bosses who treated them as inferiors and blocked their path upward. Off the job they were typically expected to carry a heavy load of family responsibilities as well. Single women contributed much of their meager wages to help support their parental families. For single women trapped by domineering parents, the only escape was marriage–and servitude to another man. Finally, the new sexual morality did not break all the old fetters; most women still considered sex a necessary evil, fearing the pain and danger of childbirth and the burden of raising large numbers of children.

Still, the Progressive era did see a number of efforts by and on behalf of women to extend their influence beyond domestic bounds. Some of these efforts derived from radical impulses. Feminist Charlotte Perkins Gilman sounded a clarion call in her book *Women and Economics* (1898), declaring that domesticity and female innocence were obsolete and attacking the male monopoly on economic opportunity. This and Gilman's other writings moved some women, but even more were swept up by the women's club movement, which brought middle-class women together to work for the alleviation of social problems. Consolidated as the Federation of Women's Clubs, which claimed nearly 1 million members by 1910, these groups lobbied forcefully for factory inspection, regulation of child and women's

Charlotte Perkins Gilman

This cartoon supporting women's rights addressed the illogical attitudes of those who believed women should stay out of public affairs. "No man denies that government is public housekeeping," the caption pointed out. Were women allowed to hold office, the artist's reasoning suggested, they could keep public administration—as well as the streets—clean. The Schlesinger Library, Radcliffe College.

labor, housing reform, and pure food and drug laws. At the same time, a number of college-educated and professionally trained women became active in settlement houses and educational reform movements.

A number of such women joined the birth control movement led by Margaret Sanger. As a visiting nurse in New York's East Side immigrant neighborhoods, Sanger distributed information about contraception in hopes of preventing unwanted pregnancies and their tragic consequences among poor women. Her crusade, however, captured the attention of middle-class women, who wanted to limit their own families and to control the growth of immigrant masses. It also aroused the opposition of men and women who saw birth control as a threat to family and morality. In 1914 the latter group caused Sanger to be indicted for sending obscene literature (actually articles on contraception) through the mail, forcing her to flee the country. Sanger persevered and in 1921 formed the American Birth Control League, which enlisted physicians and social workers to convince judges to allow distribution of birth control information. Most states still prohibited the sale of contraceptives, but the issue had entered the realm of public discussion.

Margaret Sanger

Except for a few visionaries like Gilman, the women who participated in reform movements seldom thought about effecting a sexual revolution. Many could not decide which aspects of their identity to cultivate and which to drop. Most women opposed birth control, for example, in the belief that contraception threatened women's status as mothers. Others feared that if women became the equals of men they would lose what they considered the special virtues of the female personality.

Ambivalence about the supposed uniqueness of the feminine character pervaded the suffrage movement,

A group of garment workers gathered at the Women's Trade Union League during the shirtwaist strike in New York, 1909. A favorable settlement of the strike bolstered the strength of the newly organized International Ladies Garment Workers Union. Museum of the City of New York.

which achieved victory in June 1919 when Congress passed the Nineteenth Amendment giving women the vote. The suffrage crusade dated back to the mid-nineteenth century. It had grown out of the abolitionist crusade's insistence that all Americans, regardless of race or sex, were equal and thus deserved the same rights. Confronted by male resistance, however, some women defended female suffrage by arguing that women's special, even superior, traits would humanize politics. Jane Addams, for example, supported the vote for her sex by asking, "If women have in any sense been responsible for the gentler side of life which softens and blurs some of its harsher conditions, may not they have a duty to perform in our American cities?"

Suffragists

Suffragists achieved their first successes at the local level; by 1912 nine states, all of them in the West, allowed women to vote (see map, page 583). After 1900 they pressed increasingly for the vote on the national level. The suffragists' tactics ranged from the moderate but persistent propaganda campaigns of the National American Women Suffrage Association, led by Carrie Chapman Catt, to the active picketing and marching of the National Women's party, led by Alice Paul. All these activities heightened public awareness of the suffragist cause. More decisive, however, was women's participation on the home front during the First World War as factory laborers, medical volunteers, and municipal workers. Their efforts convinced legislators that women could shoulder public responsibilities and gave final impetus to passage of the suffrage amendment.

The suffrage movement often failed to attract working-class women, who had good reason to be wary of middle-class reformers. Naive settlement workers had at first tried to educate working-class women by teaching them such irrelevant skills as how to pour tea from a silver service. Suffragists' pleas for the ballot had little meaning to women who struggled to support themselves on $3 a week. And women's organizations that sought to improve conditions for working women typically took a patronizing attitude that reflected their class bias. "Let us be our sisters' keepers," one organization pledged.

Instead of depending on women of other classes, some working women organized unions to help themselves. The resistance of their male counterparts was immediate and harsh. Of the 8 million female workers in 1910, only 125,000 were members of unions, mostly because unions refused to accept women as members. According to one male union leader, "I believe that woman is not qualified for the conditions of wage labor. . . . The mental and physical makeup of woman is in revolt against wage service. She is competing with the man who is her father or husband or is to become her husband." Yet female employees could fight employers as bitterly as men could. The thousands of New York women shirtwaist workers proved as much in 1909, when they struck for three months and laid the foundation for the powerful International Ladies Garment Workers Union.

Women's labor unions

Some efforts were made to encourage feelings of sisterhood among all classes. Since the early nineteenth century, a number of well-to-do women had recognized that all women had common grievances; that feeling gained some ground in the early 1900s. Thus Alva Belmont, a wealthy supporter of the shirtwaist workers' strike, said in 1909, "It was my interest in women, in women everywhere and every class that drew my attention and sympathies first to the striking shirtwaist girls." This feeling of sisterhood formed the basis of the feminist movement, for as Mrs. Belmont urged, "Women the world over need protection and its is only through the united efforts of women that they will get it."

But women's united efforts failed to create an interest group solid enough or powerful enough to dent political, economic, and social systems run by men. Like blacks, women knew that voting rights would mean little until people's attitudes could be changed. The Progressive era had helped women to clarify the issues that concerned them, but major reforms would await the future. As the feminist Crystal Eastman, echoing Du Bois, observed in the aftermath of the suffrage crusade,

> Men are saying perhaps, "Thank God, this everlasting women's fight is over!" But women, if I know them, are saying, "Now at last we can begin." . . . Now they can say what they are really after, in common with all the rest of the struggling world, is *freedom.*

Theodore Roosevelt and the revival of the presidency

The Progressive era's theme of challenge–to politics, to institutions, to social relations–directed attention to government, especially the federal government, as the ultimate hope of reform. The federal government, however, seemed incapable of assuming such responsibility. Led by lackluster, business-oriented presidents and dominated by two political parties that resembled private clubs more than bodies of impartial statesmen, the government acted mainly for special interests when it acted at all. Then suddenly, in September 1901, the climate changed. The assassination of President William McKinley by an anarchist named Leon Czolgosz vaulted Theodore Roosevelt, the young, vigorous vice president, into the White House.

Political manager Mark Hanna had warned fellow Republicans against nominating Roosevelt for the vice presidency in 1900. "Don't any of you realize," Hanna asked after the nominating convention, "that there's only one life between that madman and the Presidency?" As governor of New York, Roosevelt had become a popular leader by showing sympathy for popular causes and shunning pressure from partisan politicians. So New York Republican bosses rid themselves of their pariah by pushing him into national politics. Little did they realize that they were about to present the nation its most forceful president since Lincoln, a man who would infuse the office with much of its twentieth-century character.

In marked contrast to his predecessors, Theodore Roosevelt lacked the dignified appearance of a president. He stood five-foot-nine but looked shorter. Very nearsighted, he was helpless without his metal-rimmed glasses. He had big, prominent teeth and talked in a high-pitched voice. As a youth he had suffered from asthma. Yet throughout his life he was driven by a near-obsession to overcome his physical limitations and exert what he and his contemporaries called manliness. In his teens he practiced diligently to become an expert marksman and horseman. As a Harvard student he competed on the boxing and wrestling teams. In the 1880s he went to live

Theodore Roosevelt: his early life

on a Dakota ranch, where he roped cattle and brawled with other cowboys.

A descendant of a Dutch aristocratic family, Roosevelt inherited the wealth to indulge in such pursuits. But he also inherited a sense of civic responsibility that he translated into a career in public office. He served three terms in the New York State Assembly, ran for mayor of New York City in 1886 (finishing third), and served on the federal Civil Service Commission, as New York City's police commissioner, and as assistant secretary of the navy. In this series of offices Roosevelt earned a reputation as a combative, politically crafty leader. He also distinguished himself as a historian with his *The Naval War of 1812* (1882) and *The Winning of the West* (1889).

In 1898 Roosevelt thrust himself into the Spanish-American War by organizing a volunteer cavalry brigade, the Rough Riders, to fight in Cuba. His dramatic act excited the public, though it had little impact on the war's outcome. In fact, commentators poked fun at Roosevelt's attempt to inflate his exploits. Mr. Dooley, the fictional Irish saloonkeeper created by humorist and columnist Finley Peter Dunne, parodied Roosevelt's description of the Battle of San Juan Hill this way:

> Ar-rmed on'y with a small thirty-two which I used in th' West to shoot th' fleet prairie dog, I climbed that precipitous ascent in th' face iv th' most gallin' fire I iver knew or heerd iv. . . . The Spanish throops was drawn up in a long line in th' formation known among military men as a long line. I fired at th' man nearest to me an' I knew be th' expression iv his face that th' trusty bullet wint home. . . . Th' bullet sped on its mad flight an' passed through the intire line fin'lly imbeddin' itself in th' abdomen iv th' Ar-rch-bishop iv Santiago eight miles away. This ended th' war.

Nevertheless, Roosevelt returned from the war a folk hero (people called him Teddy, a name he disliked) and was elected governor, then vice president.

As president, Roosevelt became a progressive hero. At heart, though, he was a conservative and an individualist, not a reformer. His impulsive patriotism, admiration for big business, and compulsive dislike of anything he considered effeminate distinguished him from soft-hearted humanitarians. Yet Roosevelt came to conclusions similar to those reached by progressives. His sense of history convinced him that the kind of small government Jefferson had hoped for would not suffice in the modern industrial era. Instead, economic development necessitated a Hamiltonian system of government powerful enough to guide national affairs. Like his supporters, Roosevelt believed in the wisdom and talents of a select few, the "best men" whose superior backgrounds and education qualified them to coordinate public and private enterprise. "A simple and poor society," he observed, "can exist as a democracy on the basis of sheer individualism. But a rich and complex society cannot so exist."

Roosevelt's presidency inaugurated the government regulation of economic affairs that has characterized twentieth-century American history. Roosevelt first turned his attention to big business, where the combination movement had produced giant trusts that controlled almost every sector of the economy.

Roosevelt's policies toward trusts

Though Roosevelt has a reputation as a trust buster, he actually believed in consolidation as the most efficient means to achieve material and technological progress. Rather than return to uncontrolled competition, he preferred to distinguish between good and bad trusts, and to prevent the bad ones from manipulating markets and fixing prices. Thus he instructed the Justice Department to use antitrust laws to prosecute the railroad, meatpacking, and oil trusts, which he believed had unscrupulously exploited the public. Roosevelt's policy triumphed in 1904 when the Supreme Court, convinced by the government's arguments, ordered the dissolution of the Northern Securities Company, the huge railroad combination created by J. P. Morgan and his powerful business allies. (Roosevelt chose, however, not to attack other gigantic trusts, such as U.S. Steel, another of Morgan's creations.)

When the prosecution of Northern Securities began, Morgan reportedly collared Roosevelt and offered, "If we have done anything wrong, send your man to my man and they can fix it up." The president refused. But Roosevelt was more sympathetic to such arrangements than his refusal might suggest. He preferred cooperation between business and government. Rather than prosecute, he urged the Bureau of Corporations (part of the newly created Department of Labor and Commerce) to work with companies to reach

President Theodore Roosevelt (1858–1919) giving a typically rousing political speech at a Flag Day rally. Known for his energetic leadership, Roosevelt revitalized the presidency. Brown Brothers.

joint agreements on mergers and other forms of expansion. Thus through investigation and cooperation the administration exerted pressure on business to regulate itself.

Roosevelt also pushed for regulatory legislation, especially after 1904, when he won a resounding electoral victory by garnering the votes of progressives and businessmen alike. After a year of wrangling with business lobbyists in Congress, he succeeded in 1906 in getting passage of the Hepburn Act, which imposed stricter control over railroads and expanded the powers of the Interstate Commerce Commission. The act gave the ICC more authority to fix railroad rates and outlaw free passes, though it did allow the courts to overturn rate decisions. Progressives like Robert La Follette deplored the fact that Roosevelt had compromised with business representatives like Senator Nelson W. Aldrich of Rhode Island to assure the bill's passage. But Roosevelt's aim was to establish at least the principle of government regulation rather than risk defeat over more idealistic objectives.

Roosevelt showed a similar willingness to compromise on legislation to ensure pure food and drugs. For decades reformers had been urging government regulation of patent medicines and processed meat. The outcry against fraud and adulteration heightened in 1906 with the publication of Upton Sinclair's *The Jungle,* an exposé of Chicago meat-packing plants. Sinclair, a young socialist more interested in freeing workers from oppression than in muckraking, nevertheless shocked public sensibilities by describing scandalous conditions like the following:

Pure food and drug laws

> There was never the least attention paid to what was cut up for sausage; there would come all the way back from Europe old sausage that had been rejected, and that was mouldy and white–it would be dosed with borax and glycerine, and dumped into the hoppers, and made over again for home consumption . . . . There would be meat stored in great piles in rooms; and the water from the leaky roofs would drip over it, and thousands of rats would race about on it. It was too dark in these storage places to see well, but a man could run his hand over these piles of meat and sweep off handfuls of dried dung of rats. These rats were a nui-

sance, and the packers would put poisoned bread out for them; they would die, and then rats, bread, and meat would go into the hoppers together.

On reading Sinclair's novel, Roosevelt ordered an investigation. (Mr. Dooley described his version of what happened when the president read the book: "Tiddy was toying with a light breakfast an' idly turnin' over the pages of the new book. . . . Suddenly he rose from th' table, and cryin': 'I'm pizened,' began throwin' sausages out iv the window . . . since then th' President, like th' rest iv us, has become a viggytarian.") Finding Sinclair's descriptions accurate, he supported legislation that would become the Pure Food and Drug Act and the Meat Inspection Act, both passed in 1906. Like the Hepburn Act, these laws reinforced the principle of government regulation. But as part of the compromise to obtain their passage, the government had to agree to pay for inspections, and meat packers could appeal government decisions in court.

On other issues Roosevelt took stands that both thrilled and frustrated progressives. When, for example, the United Mine Workers struck against coal-mine owners in 1902, the president intervened by using the progressive tactics of investigation and arbitration. The mine workers, led by feisty John Mitchell, wanted higher pay and an eight-hour day, but the owners stubbornly refused to recognize the union or arbitrate the grievances. As winter approached and fuel shortages threatened, Roosevelt mustered public opinion. He warned that he would use federal troops to reopen the mines, thereby forcing both sides to accept arbitration of the dispute by a special commission. The commission decided in favor of higher wages and reduced hours, but also declared that the owners did not have to recognize the union. The decision, according to Roosevelt, created a "square deal" for all. The strike settlement established the federal government as an arbiter in labor disputes affecting the public interest. But it also illustrated Roosevelt's belief that the president or his agents should have a say in which labor demands were legitimate and which were not—just as he could help to guide business regulation. In Roosevelt's mind there were good and bad labor organizations (socialists, for example, were bad), just as there were good and bad business combinations.

On the issue of conservation, Roosevelt displayed the same mix of flamboyant executive action and quiet compromise that he applied to other domestic matters. He built a reputation as a determined conservationist, warning Congress in 1907, "We are prone to think of the resources of this country as inexhaustible; this is not so." A lover of the great outdoors, Roosevelt used presidential power to add almost 150 million acres to the national forests and to preserve vast areas of water and coal from private plunder. He sympathized with professional conservationist Gifford Pinchot, who was the government's chief forester, and in 1908 called forty-four governors and five hundred natural-resource experts to a National Conservation Congress. True to the progressive spirit, Roosevelt wanted a "well-conceived plan" for resource management, a plan for ordered growth rather than mere preservation of nature as it was. But compromises and factors beyond his control weakened his scheme. Timber and mining companies shunned supervision of their wasteful practices, and Congress never authorized enough funds or personnel to enforce federal regulations.

Conservation

Roosevelt also had to compromise his principles in the face of economic crisis. In 1907 a financial panic caused by overspeculation forced some New York banks to close to prevent frightened depositors from withdrawing money. J. P. Morgan helped to stem the panic by persuading other financiers to stop dumping their securities. In return for Morgan's aid, Roosevelt approved a deal allowing U.S. Steel to absorb its competitor, the Tennessee Iron and Coal Company—an act which flouted Roosevelt's trust-busting aims.

During his last year in office, Roosevelt moved further away from the Republican party's traditional alliance with big business. He lashed out at the irresponsible actions of "malefactors of great wealth" and threw his support behind stronger regulation of business and heavier taxation of the rich. Having promised in 1904 that he would not seek re-election, Roosevelt backed his friend Secretary of War William Howard Taft for the nomination in 1908, hoping that Taft would continue to pursue the Roosevelt initiatives. The Democrats nominated William Jennings Bryan for the third time, but the Great Commoner lost again. Aided by Roosevelt, who still had strong popular influence, Taft won by 1.25 million popular votes and a two-to-one margin in the electoral college.

Early in 1909 Roosevelt went to Africa to shoot game (he saw no contradiction between hunting and conservation), leaving Taft to face the political problems his predecessor had managed to postpone. Foremost among them were tariff rates, which had risen to levels that made many articles artificially expensive. Honoring Taft's pledge to cut rates, the House passed a bill sponsored by Representative Sereno E. Payne that provided for numerous downward revisions. As they had in the past, protectionists in the Senate prepared to amend the House bill and revise rates upward. But Senate progressives, led by La Follette, organized a stinging attack on the ways the tariff benefited vested interests. Their campaign forced Taft to try to reach a compromise between the reformers, who claimed they were carrying on Roosevelt's antitrust spirit, and the protectionists who still controlled the Republican party. In the end Senator Aldrich and other protectionists rewrote the bill, restoring many of the cuts, and Taft, who was more reluctant than Roosevelt to interfere in the legislative process, signed it. To many progressives, Taft had failed the test of filling Roosevelt's shoes.

Taft administration

The progressive and conservative wings of the Republican party were rapidly drifting apart. Soon after the tariff controversy a group of insurgents in the House, led by George Norris of Nebraska, challenged Speaker "Uncle Joe" Cannon of Illinois, whose power over committee assignments and scheduling of debate could make or break a piece of legislation. Taft first supported and then abandoned the insurgents, who nevertheless managed to liberalize procedures by enlarging the important rules committee and removing its appointments from Cannon's control. Meanwhile, Taft also angered conservationists by allowing Secretary of the Interior Richard A. Ballinger to remove 1 million acres of forest and mineral land from the reserved list and to fire Gifford Pinchot when he protested a questionable sale of coal lands in Alaska.

In reality Taft was as sympathetic to reform as Roosevelt was. He prosecuted more trusts than Roosevelt; continued to expand the national forest reserves; signed the Mann-Elkins Act of 1910, which bolstered the regulatory powers of the ICC; and supported such labor reforms as the eight-hour day and mine safety legislation. The Sixteenth Amendment, which enabled the establishment of a federal income tax, and the Seventeenth Amendment, which provided for the direct election of U.S. senators, were initiated during Taft's presidency. Like Roosevelt, Taft was forced to compromise with big business, but he lacked Roosevelt's ability to maneuver and to publicize the issues he supported. Roosevelt, who had worked to expand presidential power, had also infused the office with vitality. "I believe in a strong executive," he once asserted. "I believe in power." Taft, on the other hand, believed in the restraint of law. He had been a successful lawyer and judge (he returned to the bench as chief justice of the Supreme Court between 1921 and 1930). His caution and unwillingness to offend disappointed those used to Roosevelt's impetuosity.

Thus in 1910, when Roosevelt returned from Africa boasting over three thousand animal trophies, he found his party torn and tormented. Reformers, angered by Taft's apparent insensitivity to their cause, formed the National Progressive Republican League and rallied behind Robert La Follette for president in 1912–though many hoped Roosevelt would run. Another wing of the party stood loyal to Taft, who had used patronage to build support. Roosevelt, disappointed by Taft's performance (particularly his refusal to back Pinchot), began to speak out and to rekindle public attention. Reviving his rhetoric of 1907 and 1908, he filled his speeches with references to government concern for "the welfare of the people" and for stronger regulation of business. When La Follette became ill early in 1912, Roosevelt threw his hat in the ring for the Republican presidential nomination. La Follette stayed in the race but faded in Roosevelt's shadow.

Taft's supporters controlled the convention and nominated him for a second term, but the Roosevelt forces formed a third party–the Progressive party–and nominated the fifty-three-year-old former president. Meanwhile, the Democrats endured forty-six ballots before selecting as their candidate a relative newcomer, New Jersey's progressive governor Woodrow Wilson. The Socialists, by now an organized and growing party, nominated their perennial candidate Eugene V. Debs. The campaign exposed the voters to the most thorough evaluation of the American political and economic system in nearly a generation.

Woodrow Wilson and the extension of reform

In his acceptance speech before the Progressive party, Theodore Roosevelt had proclaimed, "We stand at Armageddon and we battle for the Lord." But on Inauguration Day 1913, it was Woodrow Wilson who assumed command of the forces of good. "The Nation," he exhorted,

> has been deeply stirred by a solemn passion, stirred by the knowledge of wrong, of ideals lost, of government too often debauched and made an instrument of evil. The feelings with which we face this new age of right and opportunity sweep across our heartstrings like some air out of God's own presence, where justice and mercy are reconciled and the judge and the brother are one.

The election's outcome illustrated the extent to which the electorate had been swept up by the moral fervor of these pronouncements. Wilson won with 42 percent of the popular vote—he was a minority president, though he did capture 435 out of 531 electoral votes (see map). Roosevelt received about 27 percent of the popular vote. Taft finished a poor third, polling 23 percent of the popular vote and only 8 electoral votes. Debs won an impressive 900,000 votes, 6 percent of the total. Thus fully three-quarters of the electorate supported some alternative to the restrained approach to government that Taft represented.

The campaign had featured a sharp debate over the fundamentals of progressive government. On one side stood Roosevelt with a system he called the New Nationalism, a term coined by reform editor Herbert Croly. Roosevelt foresaw a new era of national unity in which governmental authority would balance and coordinate economic activity. He would not destroy big business, which he saw as an efficient way to organize production. Rather, he would establish regulatory commissions, groups of experts who would protect citizens' interests and ensure the wise use of concentrated economic power. Again, Roosevelt was less interested in trustbusting than in supervising corporate enterprise for the general welfare. "The effort at prohibiting all combinations has substantially failed," he claimed. "The way out lies . . . in completely controlling them." Assuring his supporters that he felt fit as a bull moose—a term quickly applied to his new party—Roosevelt glowed with confidence that the New Nationalism would light the nation's future.

The New Nationalism and the New Freedom

Wilson offered a more idealistic scheme in his New Freedom, based on the ideas of the progressive lawyer Louis D. Brandeis. Wilson believed that the concentration of economic power threatened individual liberty, that monopolies had to be broken so that the marketplace could again become open. But he did not want to restore laissez faire. Like Roosevelt, Wilson would enhance governmental authority to protect and regulate. "Freedom today," he declared, "is something more than being let alone. Without the watchful . . . resolute interference of the government, there can be no fair play between individuals and such powerful institutions as the trusts." But Wilson stopped short of the combination of big business and big government inherent in Roosevelt's New Nationalism. In the campaign at least, he spoke in evangelical tones of the need for economic emancipation, the need to "come out of a stifling cellar into the open . . . breathe again and see the free spaces of the heavens."

Roosevelt and Wilson stood closer together than their rhetoric implied. In spite of his faith in experts as regulators, Roosevelt harbored sentiments for individual freedom as strong as Wilson's. And Wilson was not as hostile to concentrated power in business and government as his speeches suggested. Both men strongly supported equality of opportunity, conservation of natural resources, fair wages for workers, and social betterment for all classes. Perhaps more important, both would expand governmental activity through strong personal leadership and bureaucratic reform. Thus, even though he received a minority of the total vote in 1912, Wilson could interpret the results of the election as a popular mandate to subdue powerful trusts and broaden the federal government's concern for social reform.

Though the public had often fondly referred to Roosevelt as Teddy or TR, no one ever called Thomas Woodrow Wilson Tommie or WW. The son of a Presbyterian minister, Wilson was born and raised in the South. His mother, Janet Woodrow, and his first wife, Ellen Axson, were both

Woodrow Wilson: his early career

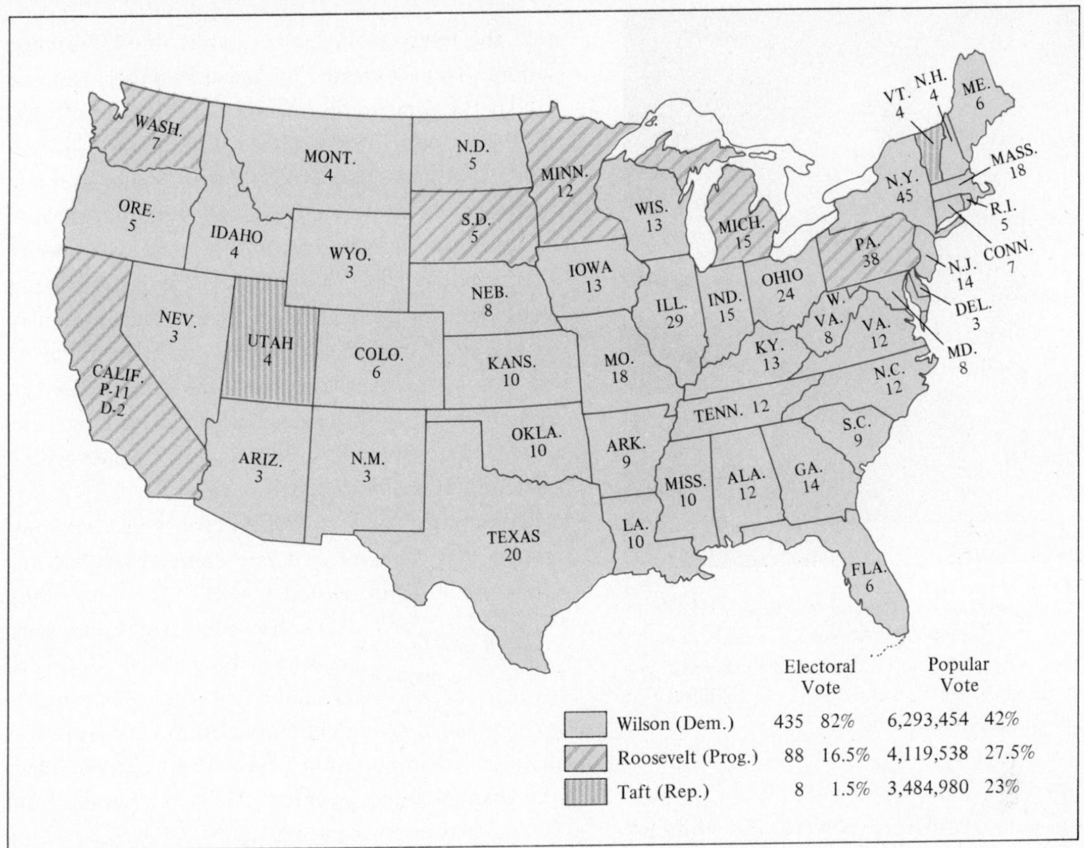

Presidential election, 1912

daughters of Presbyterian ministers. But Wilson chose to become an academic rather than a cleric. He earned a B.A. at Princeton, studied law at Virginia, received a Ph.D. from Johns Hopkins, and became a professor of history, jurisprudence, and political economy. Between 1885 and 1908 he published a number of books on American history and government that established him as a respectable scholar. Wilson's manner and bearing reflected his religious and academic background. Tall, lean, and stiff, he seemed to stare coldly through his pince-nez glasses. He exuded none of Roosevelt's flamboyance, and often spoke self-righteously.

Yet Wilson was an effective and charismatic leader. A superb orator, he could inspire intense loyalty with his eloquent expression of American ideals. He truly believed in progress, liberty, and justice, and he had the ability to present himself as a knowledgeable teacher and statesman. Wilson's convictions had led him early into reform. In 1902 he had become president of Princeton, where he upset tradition with his curricular reforms and battles against what he called the aristocratic elements in the university. In 1910 New Jersey Democrats, eager for respectability, nominated Wilson for the governorship. After winning the election, Wilson repudiated the party bosses and directed passage of a mass of progressive legislation. He was not good at administration, often losing his temper and stubbornly refusing to compromise. But his accomplishments and zealous concern for what was right attracted national attention and won him the Democratic nomination for president in 1912.

As president Wilson found that he had to blend his New Freedom ideals with New Nationalism precepts, and in so doing he set the direction of federal economic policy for much of the twentieth century. The corporate merger movement had proceeded so far that restoration of free competition was impossible. Thus Wilson could only acknowledge economic concentration and try to prevent its abuse by expanding

Looking like a preacher, Woodrow Wilson (1856–1924) delivers a speech at a campaign rally. Wilson's forceful, carefully crafted speeches, which resembled moral lectures more than political pitches, raised citizens' expectations for the fulfillment of his idealistic promises. Brown Brothers.

Expanded regulation of business

the government's regulatory powers. His administration moved toward that end with the passage in 1914 of the Clayton Anti-Trust Act and a measure creating the Federal Trade Commission (FTC). The Clayton Act extended the Sherman Anti-Trust Act of 1890 by outlawing quasi-monopolistic practices such as price discrimination (whereby a company might try to destroy competition by lowering prices in some regions but not others) and interlocking directorates (management of two or more competing companies by the same executives). The FTC, which replaced Roosevelt's Bureau of Corporations, was to investigate corporations and issue cease-and-desist orders against unfair trade practices. Like ICC rulings, accused companies could appeal FTC orders in the courts. Nevertheless, the FTC represented a further step in the protection of consumers.

Wilson pushed federal regulation beyond the confines of corporate behavior and into finance with the Federal Reserve Act of 1913. The law established the nation's first centralized banking system since Andrew Jackson destroyed the Second Bank of the United States. Twelve newly created district banks would hold the reserves of member banks throughout the nation. (The act created many banks rather than one to allay the agrarian fear of a monolithic eastern banking power, which had doomed the bank in Jackson's time.) The district banks would loan money to member banks at a low interest rate, called the *discount rate.* By adjusting this rate (and thus the amount of money a bank could afford to borrow), the district banks would be able to increase or decrease the amount of money in circulation. In other words, depending on the nation's needs, the reserve bank could loosen or tighten credit. Monetary affairs would no longer depend on the supply of gold, and interest rates would be fairer, especially for small borrowers.

Perhaps the only act of Wilson's first administration that re-established free competition was the Underwood Tariff, passed in 1913. For years rising prices had thwarted consumers' desires for the material benefits of the industrial age. Some prices were unnaturally high because government tariffs had discouraged importation of cheap foreign materials and manufactured products. The Underwood Tariff encouraged imports by drastically reducing or eliminating tariff rates. To recover revenues lost due to the reductions, the act levied a graduated income tax on U.S. residents—an option made possible earlier that year when the Sixteenth Amendment was ratified. The income tax was tame by today's standards. Incomes under $4,000 were exempt; thus almost all factory workers and farmers escaped the tax. People and corporations earning $4,000 to $20,000 had to pay a 1-percent tax, and the rate for higher incomes rose gradually to a maximum of 6 percent on earnings over $500,000. Such rates made no holes in the pockets of the rich. But the income tax did become an institutional feature of American life. The tariff had little impact because the outbreak of the First World War in Europe disrupted foreign trade and shifted public opinion toward protectionism (see Chapter 23).

Tariff and tax reform

The European war and the approaching presidential campaign prompted Wilson to support stronger reforms in 1916. Concerned that food shortages might result if farmers could not borrow money to sustain production, the president put aside his views on free competition and backed the Federal Farm Loan Act of 1916. The measure created twelve feder-

Important events

1893	Anti-Saloon League founded
1895	Booker T. Washington's accommodation speech at Atlanta Exposition
1898	Charlotte Perkins Gilman, *Women and Economics*
1899	John Dewey, *The School and Society*
1900	McKinley re-elected
1901	McKinley assassinated; Roosevelt assumes the presidency
1903	Elkins Act Coal strike settled W. E. B. Du Bois, *The Souls of Black Folk*
1904	*Northern Securities* case Theodore Roosevelt elected president Lincoln Steffens, *The Shame of the Cities*
1905	Niagara Falls Convention *Lochner* v. *New York*
1906	Hepburn Act Pure Food and Drug Act Upton Sinclair, *The Jungle*
1907	Economic panic
1908	William Howard Taft elected president *Muller* v. *Oregon*
1909	NAACP founded Payne-Aldrich Tariff
1910	Mann-Elkins Act White Slave Traffic Act Ballinger-Pinchot controversy
1912	Roosevelt runs for president on Progressive (Bull Moose) ticket Woodrow Wilson elected president
1913	Sixteenth and Seventeenth Amendments ratified Underwood Tariff Federal Reserve Act
1914	Federal Trade Commission Act Clayton Anti-Trust Act Margaret Sanger indicted for sending birth control literature through the mail
1916	Wilson re-elected Federal Farm Loan Act Adamson Act
1919	Eighteenth Amendment ratified
1920	Nineteenth Amendment ratified

Aid to farmers and workers

ally supported banks (not to be confused with the Federal Reserve banks) that would lend money at moderate interest rates to farmers who belonged to credit institutions–a watered-down version of something the Populists had agitated for a generation earlier. To stave off railroad strikes that might disrupt transportation at a time of national emergency, Wilson pushed passage of the Adamson Act of 1916, which mandated an eight-hour day and time-and-a-half for overtime for railroad laborers. Finally, Wilson courted the support of social reformers in Roosevelt's camp by backing laws that outlawed child labor and provided workers' compensation for federal employees who suffered from injury or illness.

By emphasizing peace, prosperity, and progressivism, Wilson won a narrow victory in the 1916 presidential election over Republican challenger Charles Evans Hughes, associate justice of the Supreme Court and former progressive governor of New York. Wilson's second term and the subsequent involvement of the nation in the First World War saw a shift away from competition toward interest-group politics and government regulation. During his first term Wilson had been convinced that laws, not regulatory commissions that could easily fall under the influence of the very interests they were meant to regulate, should govern social and economic behavior. But the wartime crisis and the desire for re-election convinced him to adopt different attitudes. The war effort required government coordination of production and cooperation between the public and private sectors. The War Industries Board (see Chapter 23) was one example of such coordination and cooperation. The private businesses that were regulated by the board submitted to its direction on the condition that their own profit motives would be satisfied.

After the war the Wilson administration dropped most cooperative and regulatory measures, including farm price supports, guarantees of collective bargaining, and high taxes. This move away from regulation would stimulate a new era of business ascendancy in the 1920s (see Chapter 24).

The Progressive era in perspective

In 1912 Thomas Edison had cautioned uneasily, "We've got to start to make this world over." But by 1920 not many Americans agreed. A quarter-century of reform, climaxing in the nation's participation in a brutal war, had wrought momentous changes. Government, the economy, and society as they had existed in the nineteenth century were gone forever. Public consciousness of poverty and injustice had been raised to new heights. But for every American who suffered from some form of deprivation, three or four enjoyed material comforts unprecedented in human history. This majority simply could not sustain reform indefinitely. Though the effects of the Progressive era lingered and in some cases expanded after the First World War, a mass consumer society had begun to refocus people's attention from reform to materialism.

The Progressive era was characterized by a welter of confusing and sometimes contradictory goals. Certainly there was no single progressive movement. On the national level, reform programs ranged from Roosevelt's New Nationalism, with its faith in big government as a coordinator of and counterforce to big business, to Wilson's New Freedom, with its promise to dissolve economic concentrations and legislate open competition. At the state and local levels, reformers pursued causes as varied as neighborhood improvement, government reorganization, public ownership of utilities, betterment of working conditions, and moral revival. Although local organizations and national associations coordinated their efforts on particular issues, reformers with different goals often worked at cross-purposes.

The failure of many progressive initiatives testifies to the strength of opposition to reform as well as ambiguities within the reform movements themselves. The courts struck down some key progressive legislation, most notably the federal law prohibiting child labor. In states and cities, adoption of the initiative, referendum, and recall did not encourage greater participation in government; either those mechanisms were seldom used or they became the tools of special interests. On the federal level, new regulatory agencies rarely had the resources for thorough investigations; they had to obtain their information from the companies they were meant to police. Thus government remained under the influence of business and industry, which many people considered quite satisfactory.

Yet in spite of all their weaknesses, the numerous reform movements that characterized the Progressive era did refashion the nation's future. Trustbusting, however faulty, had forced industrialists to become more conscious of public opinion, and reforms initiated by insurgents in Congress had partially diluted the power of dictatorial politicians. Progressive legislation gave government important tools to protect consumers against price-fixing, dangerous products, and other unsavory practices by manufacturers and utilities. The income tax would eventually build government revenues and redistribute wealth. Settlement workers and other social reformers soothed some of the festering sores of urban life. But perhaps most important, progressives challenged old institutions and old ways of thinking. They raised questions about the quality of American life which, though they remained unresolved, made the nation more aware of its principles and promises.

Suggestions for further reading

Progressivism

Richard Abrams, *The Burdens of Progress* (1978); David M. Chalmers, *The Social and Political Ideas of the Muckrakers* (1964); John W. Chambers, *The Tyranny of Change: Amer-*

ica in the Progressive Era (1980); Arthur Ekrich, *Progressivism in America* (1974); Samuel P. Hays, *The Response to Industrialism* (1957); Richard Hofstadter, *The Age of Reform* (1955); William R. Hutchinson, *The Modernist Impulse in American Protestantism* (1976); Gabriel Kolko, *The Triumph of Conservatism* (1963); Henry F. May, *The End of American Innocence* (1959); David W. Noble, *The Progressive Mind,* rev. ed. (1981); William L. O'Neill, *The Progressive Years* (1975); Robert H. Wiebe, *Businessmen and Reform* (1962); Robert H. Wiebe, *The Search for Order* (1968); Harold S. Wilson, *McClure's Magazine and the Muckrakers* (1970); C. Vann Woodward, *Origins of the New South* (1951).

State and local reform

Richard Abrams, *Conservatism in a Progressive Era: Massachusetts Politics, 1900–1912* (1964); Sheldon Hackney, *Populism to Progressivism in Alabama* (1969); Robert S. Maxwell, *La Follette and the Rise of Progressivism in Wisconsin* (1956); George E. Mowry, *The California Progressives* (1951); David P. Thelen, *The New Citizenship: Origins of Progressivism in Wisconsin* (1972); David P. Thelen, *Robert La Follette and the Insurgent Spirit* (1976); James H. Timberlake, *Prohibition and the Progressive Crusade* (1963); Walter I. Trattner, *Crusade for the Children* (1970); Irwin Yellowitz, *Labor and the Progressive Movement in New York State* (1965).

Education, law, and the social sciences

Loren P. Beth, *The Development of the American Constitution, 1877–1917* (1971); Lawrence Cremin, *The Transformation of the School: Progressivism in American Education* (1961); Allen F. Davis, *Spearheads for Reform* (1967); John Dewey, *Democracy and Education* (1916); Martin S. Dworkin, ed., *Dewey on Education* (1959); Mary O. Furner, *Advocacy and Objectivity: A Crisis in the Professionalization of American Social Science* (1975); Thomas L. Haskell, *The Emergence of Professional Social Science* (1977); Samuel J. Konefsky, *The Legacy of Holmes and Brandeis* (1956); David W. Marcell, *Progress and Pragmatism: James, Dewey, Beard, and the American Idea of Progress* (1974); Lawrence Veysey, *The Emergence of the American University* (1970).

Women

Lois Banner, *Women in Modern America* (1974); John C. Burnham, "The Progressive Era Revolution in American Attitudes Toward Sex," *Journal of American History,* 59 (1973), 885–908; Jill Conway, "Women Reformers and American Culture, 1870–1930," *Journal of Social History,* 5 (1971), 164–177; Carl N. Degler, *At Odds: Women and the Family in America* (1980); Eleanor Flexner, *Century of Struggle: The Women's Rights Movement in the United States* (1959); Linda Gordon, *Woman's Body, Woman's Right: A Social History of Birth Control in America* (1976); David Kennedy, *Birth Control in America: The Career of Margaret Sanger* (1970); Aileen Kraditor, *The Ideas of the Women's Suffrage Movement* (1965); Ellen Condliffe Lagemann, *A Generation of Women: Education in the Lives of Progressive Reformers* (1979); William L. O'Neill, *Divorce in the Progressive Era* (1967); William L. O'Neill, *Everyone Was Brave: The Rise and Fall of Feminism in America* (1969); Ross Evans Paulson, *Woman's Suffrage and Prohibition* (1973); Sheila M. Rothman, *Woman's Proper Place* (1978); Leslie Woodcock Tentler, *Wage-Earning Women: Industrial Work and Family Life in the United States, 1900–1930* (1979); Margaret Gibbons Wilson, *The American Woman in Transition* (1979).

Blacks

W. E. B. Du Bois, *The Souls of Black Folk* (1903); George Frederickson, *The Black Image in the White Mind* (1971); Louis R. Harlan, *Booker T. Washington* (1972); Charles F. Kellogg, *NAACP* (1970); James M. McPherson, *The Abolitionist Legacy: From Reconstruction to the NAACP* (1975); August Meier, *Negro Thought in America, 1880–1915* (1963); Elliot M. Rudwick, *W. E. B. Du Bois* (1969); Donald Spivey, *Schooling for the New Slavery: Black Industrial Education* (1978).

National politics

Donald F. Anderson, *William Howard Taft* (1973); John M. Blum, *The Republican Roosevelt,* 2nd ed. (1957); John M. Blum, *Woodrow Wilson and the Politics of Morality* (1956); G. Wallace Chessman, *Theodore Roosevelt and the Politics of Power* (1969); Paolo E. Coletta, *The Presidency of William Howard Taft* (1973); John A. Garraty, *Henry Cabot Lodge* (1953); John Allen Gable, *The Bull Moose Years* (1978); William H. Harbaugh, *The Life and Times of Theodore Roosevelt* (1961); Arthur S. Link, *Wilson,* 5 vols. (1947–1965); Arthur S. Link, *Woodrow Wilson and the Progressive Era* (1954); Edmund Morris, *The Rise of Theodore Roosevelt* (1979); George E. Mowry, *The Era of Theodore Roosevelt* (1958); James Penick, Jr., *Progressive Politics and Conservation: The Ballinger-Pinchot Affair* (1968); Henry Pringle, *Theodore Roosevelt: A Biography,* rev. ed. (1956).

POLICE

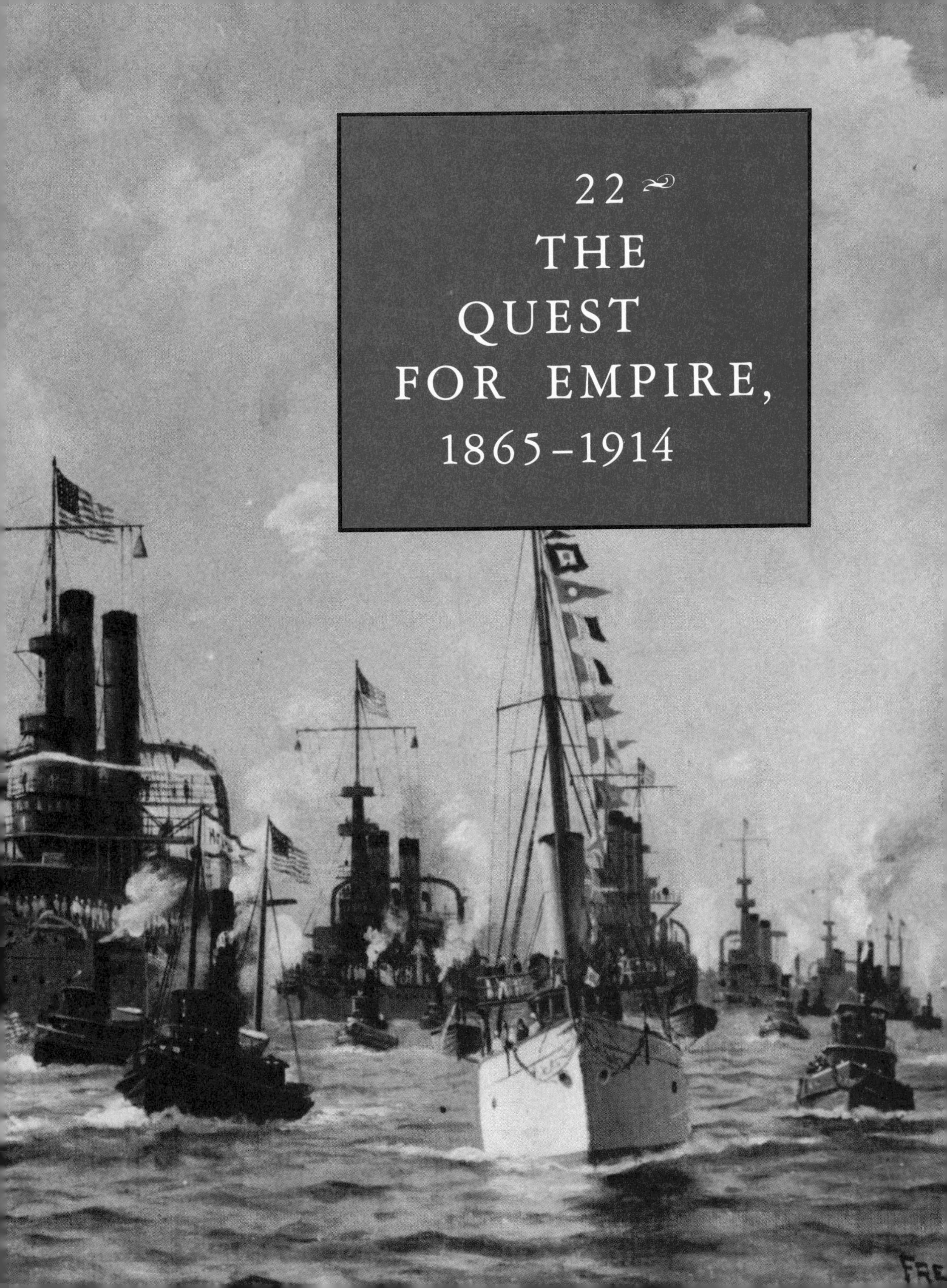

22 THE QUEST FOR EMPIRE, 1865–1914

William H. Seward's travels through scenic Alaska in August 1869 revived his enthusiasm for the huge territory he had, as secretary of state, bought from imperial Russia two years earlier. Its abundant marine treasures–whales, sea otters, seals, salmon–and forests impressed him, as did the opportunities for the fur trade. He remarked effusively on Alaska's rich deposits of iron ore, coal, copper, and gold, unaware of the vast petroleum supplies that would be so eagerly tapped in the twentieth century. At a crowded meeting in Sitka, Seward told the white citizens of that frontier town that they were truly pioneers in an Indian-populated land. But reinforcements were on the way, he assured them, for Alaska was certain to become a prosperous "shipyard for the supply of all nations."

Seward's oratory was exaggerated, but it reflected the optimism so characteristic of nineteenth-century Americans, who saw little but grandeur in the nation's future. The country had long been on an expansionist course. The Russian government, for example, decided to sell Alaska because it did not believe it could hold that part of its empire against the inevitable and traditional American quest for more space, more land, more resources. "In American eyes," the Russian minister to the United States remarked, "this continent is their patrimony. Their destiny is always to expand." Alaska, he regretted, had not "escaped the lust of Americans." The Louisiana Purchase, the annexation of the Floridas, Texas, and Oregon, the Mexican cession of California and other western territories, and the Gadsden Purchase, as well as a bustling foreign trade, provided ample evidence before the Civil War that Americans craved expansion.

But the expansionist road, then and later, was not unchallenged, or consistently traveled. Diplomatic crises, wars, and vigorous national debate always accompanied expansionism. The federal government did not always adequately fund the vehicles of expansion, neglecting the navy until the 1880s and maintaining a foreign service weakened by the political spoils system. Critics slowed expansion with their arguments that it was unnecessary given the undeveloped domain at home. Leaders played politics with foreign policy, complicating the diplomatic process. Still, the quest continued and accelerated in the nineteenth century, reaching fever pitch in the tumultuous decade of the 1890s, when critics' voices were drowned out by shouts for war and foreign territory, and when American power was sufficient to deliver both.

Expansionism revived

The Civil War had temporarily interrupted the country's expansionist course. Once freed from that conflict, however, Americans North and South scouted new frontiers to conquer. Anticipating the passing of the frontier at home, some Americans looked outward to far-flung territories and overseas markets. Seward eyed Cuba, President Grant coveted Santo Domingo, and others envisioned new outposts in the Pacific Ocean as well as the annexation of Canada. Religious leaders contemplated the conversion of "natives" and "savages" to Christianity. Nationalists spoke of exporting America's superior political principles and practices to other peoples. And to ensure the success of these dreams, to protect all these activities, American leaders planned for an enlarged modern navy of the first order. Finley Peter Dunne captured the American mood near the end of the nineteenth century: "We're a gr-reat people,' said Mr. Hennessy, earnestly. 'We ar-re,' said Mr. Dooley. 'We ar-re that. An' th best iv it is, we know we are.' "

Domestic roots of foreign policy

Foreign policy has always sprung from the domestic setting of a nation–its needs, wants, moods, and ideals. The people who guided America's expansionist foreign relations were the same people who kindled the spirit of national growth at home, who championed the transcontinental railroad, forcefully removed native Americans from the avenues of white settlement, extolled the wonders of the machine age, and built America's cities and giant corporations. Most Americans, caught up as they were in making a living or exploiting economic opportunities at home, paid scant attention to external issues or to the intense international rivalry of the post-Civil War era. They usually became alive to foreign policy questions only when war threatened. But America's leaders–in politics, business, labor, agriculture, religion, journalism, education, and the military–were alert to the nation's place in world affairs.

They believed that the United States could prosper far better in a world in which American influence was exerted. They were aware of the interconnections between domestic developments and foreign events.

The expansionism so evident at home after the Civil War was deeply intertwined with foreign policy. The national network of railroads, for example, made it possible for Iowa farmers to transport their crops to seaboard cities and then on to foreign markets. Their livelihood was thus tied to international market conditions, to the outcomes of foreign wars, and to the time-honored American principle of freedom of the seas, which stood as a reminder to other nations that American goods on American ships should be free to cross the oceans, even in time of foreign war. American cities that burgeoned in the late nineteenth century became centers of foreign commerce and cosmopolitan culture. The products of such companies as Standard Oil and International Harvester were shipped to distant markets, and new technology, especially in transportation and communication, was applied to the improved navy required to protect the lucrative commerce. Periodic depressions fostered the belief that the country's surplus production could be sold in foreign markets to restore and sustain economic well-being at home. By promoting economic health, these markets would also contribute to social and political stability. Senator and two-time Secretary of State James G. Blaine put it this way: "With these markets secured new life would be given to our manufactories, the product of the Western farmer would be in demand, the reasons for and inducements to strikers with all their attendant evils would cease."

The tariff too was an issue in both domestic politics and world affairs. Tariff increases designed to protect American industry and agriculture from foreign competition adversely affected those who sold to America, prompting them to enact retaliatory tariffs on American products. In Cuba and Hawaii, American tariff revisions actually induced economic crises, which fed revolutions that ultimately served American interests. The massive influx of immigrants caused diplomatic problems as well as social upheaval at home. Moreover, notions of racial superiority and Jim Crow practices at home influenced American policies toward Asian and Latin American peoples of color, who were considered inferior. And ambitious politicians were tempted to enhance their political reputations by flexing the national muscle in the world arena. The nationalism that permeated domestic growth also lay at the heart of an activist foreign policy, especially as the United States became locked in competition with Great Britain and Germany. In other words, the major domestic questions that preoccupied America from the Civil War to the First World War were closely linked to the nation's diplomacy. The threads of domestic and foreign policy were densely interwoven.

American imperialism

By 1900 the United States had become a world power. Since the Civil War it had acquired Alaska, the Midway Islands, Samoa, the Philippines, Guam, Puerto Rico, Hawaii, and Wake Island. It exercised a protectorate over Cuba and was establishing hegemony–that is, dominance–over much of the Caribbean. The policy of Pan-Americanism and rapprochement with Great Britain had increased the nation's influence in the Western Hempishere. By 1900 the United States had also pledged itself to preserve the Open Door in China. The U.S. Navy was taking its place among the world's foremost fleets. And the nation's export trade amounted to an impressive \$1.5 billion, second only to that of Great Britain. American missionaries, too, were more active abroad than ever before. From 1870 to 1900 the number of Protestant missions established overseas increased 500 percent; in the 1890s American missions in China doubled to one thousand. The *Washington Post,* surveying this catalogue of foreign ventures and the United States victory in the Spanish-American War of 1898, detected "a new appetite, a yearning to show our strength. . . . The taste of empire is in the mouth of the people, even as the taste of blood in the jungle." By no means everybody shared this taste–there were vocal critics of the imperial menu–but the results of expansionism were such that those who did share it ate well.

American expansionism in turn led to imperialism: the imposition of control over other peoples, denying them the freedom to make their own decisions, undermining their sovereign independence. Imperialism took a variety of forms, both formal (annexation, colonialism, or military occupation) and informal (the threat of intervention or economic manipulation).

Sometimes the United States took territories; sometimes it controlled the economic life of others to such an extent that they lost their sovereignty; sometimes American troops intervened, imposed order, and stayed to govern.

With a characteristic mixture of self-interest and idealism, United States leaders believed that imperialism benefited both Americans and those who came under American control. When they intervened in other lands or lectured weaker states, Americans defended their behavior on the grounds that they were extending the blessings of liberty and prosperity to less fortunate people. To critics at home and abroad, however, American paternalism appeared hypocritical. They charged that the use of coercion to compel resistant foreigners to behave and think like Americans violated cherished American principles. For example, to impose on angry Filipinos an American-style political system theoretically based on democratic tenets, American officials censored the press, jailed some dissidents and killed others, and designated candidates for public office. The persistent American belief that other people cannot solve their own problems and that only the American model of government will work produced what historian William Appleman Williams has called "the tragedy of American diplomacy."

Visions of greatness

William H. Seward's career spanned pre-Civil War and post-Civil War expansionism. As senator from New York (1849–1861) and secretary of state (1861–1869) he argued articulately for extension of the American frontier. "There is not in the history of the Roman Empire an ambition for aggrandizement so marked as that which characterized the American people," he once told his Senate colleagues. His own ambition for imperial aggrandizement was very considerable and carefully conceived. He envisioned a large coordinated empire encompassing Canada, the Caribbean, Cuba, Central America, Mexico, Hawaii, Iceland, Greenland, and certain Pacific islands. This empire would be built not by war but by a natural process of gravitation toward the attractive republican United States. Commerce would hurry the process, he thought, noting that it was as merchants that Venice, the Netherlands, and Great Britain had become "masters of the world."

William H. Seward

To ensure the unity of his American empire, Seward appealed for a canal across the Central American isthmus, guessing that Nicaragua was a better site than Panama. He supported the transcontinental railroad as a link to the markets of Asia, and called for telegraph systems to speed communication. To Seward economic expansion at home was essential to expansion abroad, and vice versa. Thus he favored liberal land policies in the West to promote settlement; encouraged immigration (immigrants would provide the labor and talent needed for economic development); and advocated tariffs to protect youthful American factories from foreign competition. Besides the transcontinental railroad, America needed internal improvements–canals, roads, harbors. All these developments, Seward prophesied, would knit the nation together, permitting it to step onto the world stage in grand, united, and independent fashion.

A host of voices echoed Seward's fervent nationalism and quest for expansion and empire. In the aftermath of the bloody Civil War, American leaders tried to heal sectional wounds with soothing patriotic oratory. The 1876 centennial celebration emphasized national unity; Confederate and Union soldiers met to exchange captured flags; patriotic societies like the Daughters of the American Revolution (1890) were organized. Civic pride welled up when American machines earned top marks at world fairs. Notions of American exceptionalism and Manifest Destiny were revived, and predictions of American supremacy in international affairs became commonplace. To the Reverend Josiah Strong, author of the influential book *Our Country* (1885), Americans were a special, God-favored, superior Anglo-Saxon race destined to lead others. "As America goes, so goes the world," he claimed. To Social Darwinists, Americans were a superior people who would surely overcome all competition and thrive. "The rule of the survival of the fittest applies to nations as well as to the animal kingdom," claimed American diplomat John Barrett.

Captain Alfred T. Mahan also believed in American greatness, but assumed that its source was sea power. Since foreign trade was vital to the nation's well-

The call for naval power

being, the nation required an efficient navy to protect its shipping. And the navy in turn required colonies for bases. "Whether they will or no," Mahan wrote, "Americans must now begin to look outward. The growing production of the country demands it." Mahan's widely read book *The Influence of Seapower Upon History* (1890) sat on every good expansionist's shelf. Senator Henry Cabot Lodge of Massachusetts was one politician who read Mahan and enthusiastically endorsed his call for trade, navy, and colonies. An advocate of what he tagged the "large policy," Lodge chided those Americans who shied away from empire. "The tendency of modern times is toward consolidation," wrote Lodge, known popularly as "the scholar in politics" (he held a Ph.D. in history from Harvard). "It is apparent in capital and labor alike, and it is also true of nations. . . . The modern movement is all toward the concentration of people and territory into great nations and large dominions."

People like Seward, Strong, Mahan, and Lodge made the case for expansion and empire that served as the foundation for the imperial outburst of the late 1890s. Their argument seemed all the more urgent in 1893, when Professor Frederick Jackson Turner brought forth his frontier thesis. Turner postulated that an ever-expanding continental frontier had shaped the American character. That "frontier has gone, and with its going has closed the first period of American history." Turner did not explicitly say that a new frontier had to be found overseas. But some thought that was what he meant when he wrote in his famous article "The Significance of the Frontier in American History" that he doubted that "the expansive character of American life has now entirely ceased. Movement has been its dominant fact, and, unless this training has no effect upon a people, the American energy will continually demand a wider field for its exercise."

Articulate spokesmen for a wider field, like Seward and Lodge, belonged to what scholars have variously labeled the foreign-policy elite, the foreign-policy public, or the opinion leaders. Better read and better

Foreign policy elite

traveled than most Americans, more cosmopolitan than provincial in outlook, and politically active, they influenced the making of foreign policy. Unlike domestic policy, foreign policy is seldom shaped by the people. Most Americans simply do not follow international relations or express themselves on its issues. Indeed, studies have demonstrated that no more than 10 to 20 percent of the voting public was alert to world affairs in the late nineteenth century. It was this small group, whom Secretary of State Walter Q. Gresham called "the thoughtful men of the country," whose opinion counted. Increasingly in the late nineteenth century, and especially in the 1890s, they urged an imperialist course. Those members of the political elite who, like President Grover Cleveland, favored economic expansion and United States hegemony in South America, but not the annexation of more territory, gradually lost ground to these chauvinistic pro-empire leaders.

William H. Seward (1801–1872) had a vision of empire matched by few Americans. As secretary of state he added Alaska and Midway Island to the United States domain. Library of Congress.

The imperialists in Washington, D.C, were clannish. They gathered informally to talk about Mahan's ideas, about an isthmian canal, and about the need to sell surpluses abroad. They huddled at Henry Adams's house on H Street or at the nearby home of John Hay, who became secretary of state in 1898. Theodore

Roosevelt, appointed assistant secretary of the navy in 1897, was among them; so was Brooks Adams, Henry's gloomy brother, a publicist for an American presence in China. Lodge, who became a member of the Senate Foreign Relations Committee in 1895, often stopped by, and corporate lawyer Elihu Root, who would later serve in the cabinet, joined in as well. These luminaries kept up the drumbeat for empire, and after their elevation to high office in the 1890s they acquired by force much of the empire that Seward had earlier dreamed would gravitate peacefully to the United States.

Factory, farm, and foreign affairs

Many business people and farmers were part of the foreign-policy public that savored expansion. There were, of course, profits to be made from foreign sales. "It is my dream," cried the governor of Georgia in 1878, to see "in every valley . . . a cotton factory to convert the raw material of the neighborhood into fabrics which shall warm the limbs of Japanese and Chinese." Fear generated foreign trade as well, for the nation's farms and factories produced more than Americans could consume. Foreign commerce, it was believed, could be a safety valve to avert or relieve depression. "The prosperity of our people," reported the secretary of the treasury in the early months of the crippling depression of the 1890s, "depends largely upon their ability to sell their surplus products in foreign markets at remunerative prices."

The tremendous economic growth of the United States after the Civil War stimulated foreign trade, a larger navy to protect this lucrative commerce, a more efficient foreign service, a call for more colonies, and a more activist foreign policy. From the 1860s to 1914, in fact, foreign trade grew faster than the national income. In 1870 United States exports totaled $451 million; in 1880, $853 million; in 1890, $910 million; and in 1900, $1.5 billion. By 1914, at the outbreak of the First World War, American exports had reached $2.5 billion, and European businessmen complained of the "American export invasion." Beginning in the 1870s the United States began to enjoy a long-term favorable balance of trade (exporting more than it imported). Most of America's products went to Europe, but increasing amounts flowed to new markets in Latin America and Asia. Although exports of manufactured items increased, agricultural goods accounted for about three-quarters of the total in 1870 and about two-thirds in 1900. Manufactured goods led export sales for the first time in 1913.

Growth of foreign trade

Breadstuffs, cotton, meat, and dairy products topped the export list in 1900, providing farmers with needed foreign outlets. Over half the annual cotton crop was exported each year. Wisconsin cheesemakers shipped to Britain; the Swift and Armour meat companies exported refrigerated beef to Europe; and wheat farmers proclaimed the Midwest the granary of the world. In fact, the United States was Europe's largest supplier of wheat.

America's ambitious entrepreneurs and large businesses looked to foreign markets, especially in the 1890s when it became clear that the output of industrial products was outdistancing consumption. Rockefeller's Standard Oil sold abroad, notably in Germany, England, Cuba, and Mexico. In the 1870s and 1880s about two-thirds of all American petroleum was exported, and in succeeding decades the figure was about one-half. Fifteen percent of America's iron and steel, 50 percent of its copper, and 16 percent of its agricultural implements were sold abroad by the turn of the century, making many workers in those industries dependent on exports.

So too with machinery. Thomas Edison and Alexander Graham Bell installed England's telephone network. George Westinghouse marketed his air brakes in Europe; Singer exported about 40 percent of its sewing machines; and Cyrus McCormick's "reaper kings" harvested the wheat of Russian fields. Photography baron George Eastman, whose business operated around the globe, remarked that the growth of foreign sales allowed Americans to "distribute our eggs and pad the basket at the same time." At the 1878 World's Fair in Paris, American exhibitors won a higher percentage of awards than any other country. At the Paris fair in 1889 American agricultural machinery was acclaimed, and at Chicago's Columbian Exposition in 1893 American inventive genius—especially in the application of electricity to machines—dazzled foreign visitors.

Foreign economic expansion was also measured in

other ways. Direct American investments abroad reached $3.5 billion by 1914, placing the United States among the top four investor countries. This high ranking convinced some that the financial center of the world was passing from the Thames to the Hudson.

American economic expansion in Latin America was especially impressive, and aroused the nation's diplomatic interest in its neighbors to the South. United States exports to Latin America, which exceeded $50 million in the 1870s, climbed to over $120 million in 1900 and topped $300 million in 1914. Investments by United States citizens in Latin America amounted to a towering $1.26 billion in 1914. In 1899 two of the largest banana importers merged to form the United Fruit Company. Owning much of the land (over 1 million acres in 1913) and the railroad and steamship lines of Central America, United Fruit became a major economic and political force in the region. It developed transportation, cultivated land, and fought to eradicate yellow fever and malaria. As for Mexico, according to historian David Pletcher, it was "truly an economic satellite of the United States" by the early 1900s. Under the dictatorship of Porfirio Díaz (1876 to 1910), American capitalists came to own Mexico's railroads and mines. By the end of his regime, Americans controlled 43 percent of Mexican property and produced more than half that nation's oil.

Economic expansion in Latin America

Economic expansion abroad meant more than pocketbook profits for farmers and businessmen. For nationalists, a vigorous foreign trade was a sign of greatness, a source of pride. Foreign commerce was also a mechanism for exerting political influence. Dunne's Mr. Dooley put it simply: "I tell ye, th' hand that rocks th' scales in th' grocery store is th' hand that rules th' wurruld." Indeed, by the early twentieth century American economic interests were influencing policies on taxes and natural resources in countries like Cuba and Mexico. American interests were responsible for drawing Hawaii into the American imperial net and for spreading American cultural values abroad. Religious missionaries and Singer executives, for example, joined hands in promoting the "civilizing medium" of the sewing machine. "The world is to be Christianized and civilized," declared Josiah Strong. "And what is the process of civilizing but the creating of more and higher wants. Commerce follows the missionary." It is not surprising that many of the recent nationalist revolutions, such as that in Mexico in 1910, were very anti-American.

Singer sewing machines were exported throughout the globe in the late nineteenth century. Here the King of Ou (the Caroline Islands, in the Pacific) operates the Great Civilizer. Though the caption for this company-sponsored photograph read "The Herald of Civilization—Missionary Work of the Singer Manufacturing Company," Singer was interested in more than improving the world's standard of living. The profitable business sold 800,000 sewing machines in 1890, about three-quarters of all the sewing machines sold in the world that year. Courtesy, Robert B. Davies, *Peacefully Working to Conquer the World.*

Transportation, communication, and expansion

Improvements in transportation and communication in the machine age were also significant for American foreign policy: by dramatically reducing the time required to move ships, people, goods, and words, they shrank the globe. And industrial production of awesome armaments and fast steam-powered warships made nations more vulnerable. Drawn closer to one another by technology, nations found that faraway events became more important to their prosperity and security. Technology also served as a major facilitator of their quest for empire.

Impact of the telegraph

The world became a huge communications system. In 1866, through the persevering efforts of Cyrus Field, an underwater transatlantic cable linked European and American telegraph networks. And, backed by J. P. Morgan's capital, James A. Scrymser strung telegraph lines to Latin America, reaching Chile in 1890. Information about markets, diplomatic crises, and war flowed steadily and quickly. Whereas delivery of surface mail from Washington, D.C., to European capitals often took from ten to twenty-one days, the transatlantic cable enabled the State Department to make same-day contact. In a serious squabble with Spain in 1873 over the Cuban-owned gunrunning ship *Virginius*–the Spanish executed some Americans on board–Secretary of State Hamilton Fish made good use of the telegraph system to manage the crisis. The underwater cable also allowed for more efficient naval tactics: Admiral George Dewey received by cable his orders to steam to Manila, where he smashed the Spanish fleet in the opening battle of the Spanish-American War. A few years later an Italian financed with British capital, Guglielmo Marconi, developed wireless telegraphy. Soon the American navy was equipped with wireless sets. When America's battleships–the "Great White Fleet"–sailed around the world in 1907, they used the wireless (see p. 627).

New Navy

Admiral Dewey's flagship, the *Olympia,* belonged to another offshoot of the new technology, the New Navy. Until its modernization, the American navy had been in a sorry state. It had too many wooden ships, some of them rotting. Its shipyards were havens of political patronage; congressional appropriations were frequently wasted. But in 1883 Congress authorized construction of the first steel warships, and a year later the Naval War College was founded at Newport, Rhode Island, to instill more professionalism in the officer corps. American factories went to work to produce steel for hulls, boilers for steam engines, nickel-steel armor plate, high-velocity shells, powerful guns, and precision instruments. American coal and oil fueled the vessels. Andrew Carnegie, displaying none of the pacifism that would later distinguish him as a champion of international peace, exclaimed "there may be millions for us in armor," and signed a highly profitable naval contract.

Gradually, but especially in the 1880s, the navy shifted from sail to steam and from wood to steel–to the delight of Captain Mahan and other naval politicians who popularized the navy's central role in expansion. Businessmen seeking men-of-war escorts for their commercial vessels and scouts for new trade opportunities also cheered the birth of the New Navy. New Navy ships like the *Maine,* the *Oregon,* the *Boston,* and the *Columbia,* thrust the United States into naval prominence. The *Columbia* held the naval record for average sea speed, and the other three figured in the imperialist ventures of the 1890s. Incidentally, many of these steel vessels were named for states and cities in a deliberate campaign to kindle patriotism and local support for naval expansion.

Panama Canal

The relationship between technology, foreign trade, and ships was also apparent in the campaign for an isthmian canal in Central America. Seward vigorously advocated such a canal, and the much-heralded opening of the Suez Canal in Egypt in 1869, as well as the abortive attempt by Ferdinand de Lesseps to duplicate that triumph in Panama, further aroused Americans. "A canal under American control, or no canal," snapped President Rutherford B. Hayes. In 1880, he dispatched two warships to Panamanian waters as a demonstration of his concern. American business organizations petitioned national politicians for a canal, citing better access to Asian and Latin American markets.

But three obstacles stood in the way: the enormous expense of construction, approval by the nation through which the canal would be cut, and the Clayton-Bulwer Treaty with England (1850), which provided for joint control of any canal built in the area. Not until after the Spanish-American War, when that supreme expansionist Theodore Roosevelt became president, did the United States remove the impediments. Roosevelt nudged the British aside in the Hay-Pauncefote Treaty of 1901; urged Panamanian rebels to declare independence from Colombia; sent

The Panama Canal under construction, 1910. To build the locks shown here, workers poured 2.4 million cubic yards of concrete from the huge, T-shaped overhead cranes. A monument to American technological genius, the canal cost over $350 million. Courtesy, Panama Canal Company.

American warships to the isthmus to ensure the rebels' success; signed a treaty (1903) with the infant nation of Panama awarding the United States a canal zone and long-term rights to its control; and lobbied Congress for the substantial funds to dig and fortify a canal.

The completion of the Panama Canal in 1914 marked a major technological achievement. The special bearings and gears used to operate the locks were manufactured by a Wheeling, West Virginia, firm; some fifty Pittsburgh factories and shops made the various bolts and steel girders; and the General Electric Company produced the vital electrical apparatus. People greeted the canal's opening the way people in the 1960s hailed the landing on the moon. But the canal proved very costly in terms of human lives: 5,609 people met their deaths by accident or disease in the process of building the waterway. During the canal's first year of operation, over one thousand merchant ships squeezed through its locks. (Ten years later the annual rate was five thousand, equal to the traffic through the Suez Canal.) The United States fortified the zone with conspicuous sixteen-inch guns, the nation's largest. The guns did not seem out of place, since the same month that the Panama Canal opened its gates–August 1914–the First World War erupted in Europe.

Progress in communication and transportation also facilitated population movement. The oceans became highways. Millions of immigrants could board steamships for cheap and speedy passage to the United States. And Americans could travel abroad for business, pleasure, settlement, diplomatic contact, naval demonstrations, or war. The proliferation of picture

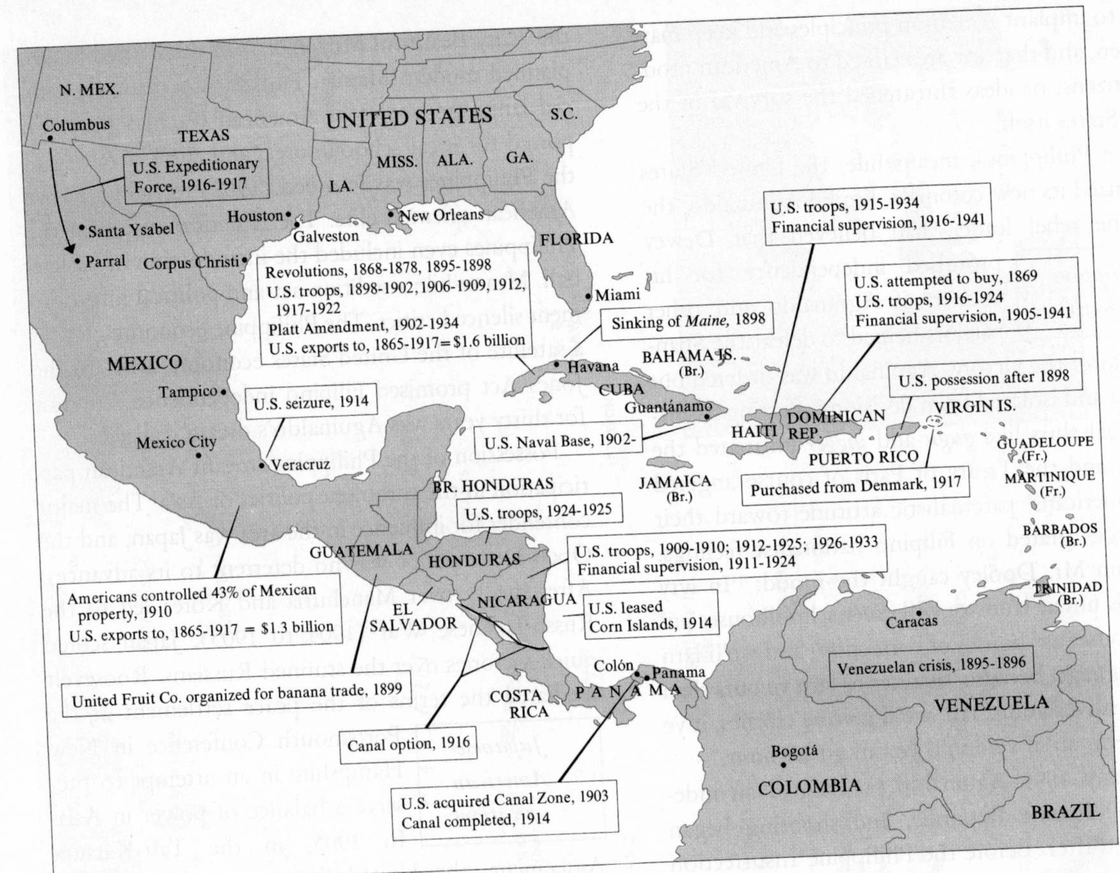

The United States and Latin America

which Japan again pledged the security of American possessions in the Pacific and the United States recognized Japan's interests in Manchuria, Japanese-American relations deteriorated. Japan was alarmed by the new President Taft's ineffective attempt at dollar diplomacy, inducing American bankers to join an international consortium to build a Chinese railway. Dollar diplomacy was an effort to use private funds to serve American diplomatic goals and at the same time to garner profits for American financiers. Realizing neither purpose, Taft's venture seemed only to embolden the Japanese to solidify and extend their holdings in China. When the First World War broke out in Europe, Japan seized the opportunity to grab Shandong and some Pacific islands from the Germans. In 1915 Japan issued its Twenty-One Demands, virtually insisting on hegemony over all China. The Chinese Revolution of 1911 had brought some unity and strength to the Chinese government, but the aggressive Japanese showed little respect for it. Thus parts of China passed into the hands of the Japanese. Americans could only protest feebly.

No such feebleness characterized United States activity in its own backyard of Latin America (see map). Although the Teller Amendment (see page 622) had outlawed annexation, it did not rule out American control of postwar Cuba. American troops remained there until 1902. In Washington, officials prepared the Platt Amendment for inclusion in the new Cuban constitution: a frank avowal of United States hegemony, the Platt Amendment provided that Cuba could not make a treaty with another nation that might impair its independence. In short, all treaties had to be approved by the United States. Furthermore, "Cuba consents that the United States may exercise the right to intervene" to preserve the island's independence and to protect "life, property, and indi-

Platt Amendment

vidual liberty." Cuba was also required to undertake a sanitation program and to lease to the United States a naval base (Guantánamo). These violations of Cuban sovereignty, formalized in 1903, governed Cuban-American relations until 1934. The Cubans, like the Filipinos, resisted their new masters: they marched in the streets against the Platt Amendment, and a revolution in 1906 prompted Roosevelt to send in marines. The marines stayed until 1909, were ordered back for a short time in 1912, and occupied Cuba again from 1917 to 1922. José Marti had warned Cubans from the beginning that the United States posed a threat: "I know the Monster, because I have lived in its lair."

The American presence left an imprint on Cuban life. Americans helped to improve transportation, expand the public school system, found a national army, and improve sugar production. Walter Reed's experiments, based on the theory of Cuban physician Carlos Finlay, proved that the mosquito transmitted yellow fever; American sanitary engineers soon controlled the insect and eradicated the disease from the island. American investments in Cuba grew from $50 million before the revolution to $220 million by 1913, and American exports to the island rose from $26 million in 1900 to $196 million in 1917. But the Cuban nation developed with a colonial mentality, and Cuban nationalists nurtured a resentment that developed into anti-Americanism.

As for the rest of the Caribbean, it became an American lake. "Speak softly and carry a big stick," said Roosevelt. He did wield a big stick, but he seldom curbed his bombastic rhetoric. When the Germans used force in 1902–1903 to try to make the irresponsible Venezuelan government pay its foreign debt, Roosevelt successfully pressed Germany to arbitrate the crisis. And in 1904 the president released his Roosevelt Corollary to the Monroe Doctrine, warning Latin Americans to stabilize their politics and finances to forestall European meddling in their affairs. "Chronic wrongdoing," he lectured, might require "intervention by some civilized nation, and in the Western Hemisphere the adherence of the United States to the Monroe Doctrine may force the United States, however reluctantly, in flagrant cases of such wrongdoing or impotence, to the exercise of an international police power." Roosevelt and his successors were not bluffing. From 1900 to 1917, when the United States entered the First World War, American troops intervened in Cuba, Panama, Nicaragua, the Dominican Republic, Mexico, and Haiti. American officials took control of customs houses to ensure that tariff revenues were properly spent; they renegotiated foreign debts with American banks; they trained national guards and even ran elections.

Roosevelt Corollary

The United States set out to police the Caribbean in the name of order. Whether such order was achieved by the landing of marines, the development of a national guard, a managed electoral process, or a manipulated economy, it was deemed necessary to guarantee United States security and prosperity. After Roosevelt helped to slice off Panama from Colombia in 1903 and initiated the construction of the Panama Canal, Washington would not tolerate disturbances that might threaten the vital waterway. Order was believed essential to American commerce and investment too. Between 1900 and 1917 American exports to Latin America swelled from $132 million to $309 million, and imports from Latin America increased even more. Investments in sugar, tobacco, transportation, and banking also rose impressively. Finally, order seemed imperative to Americans eager to remake Latin American societies in the image of the United States. "When properly directed there is no people not fitted for self-government," Woodrow Wilson remarked. Furthermore, "every nation needs to be drawn into the tutelage of America."

Roosevelt, Taft, and Wilson gave varying expression to this quest for order. The Rough Rider saw world affairs as a constant struggle for international power. The United States, in its own interest, had to lay claim to as much power as possible. The very struggle would ennoble Americans; the result would enrich them. Taft emphasized dollar diplomacy: dollars, not bullets, he predicted, would effect stability and enhance American interests. Wilson was no less a nationalist or pragmatist in desiring to safeguard and expand American prosperity and security. He ordered troops to Haiti, the Dominican Republic, and Mexico, justifying military force by proclaiming it "our peculiar duty" to teach colonial peoples "order and self-control" and "the drill and habit of law and obedience." Wilson became known for his missionary paternalism, his insistence on liberal capitalism and constitutional government. "Wilson was the theologian

President Theodore Roosevelt rode roughshod over all protests in his drive to build the Panama Canal. Note the child sitting next to him–the Panama Republic–nursing on a bottle marked "$10,000,000 for right of way."

of the liberal faith," William A. Williams has written. "He revived and reenergized our propensity to see ourselves as the savior of the universe, and the universe as a slum to be regenerated in the image of the City on the Hill." Whether by means of Roosevelt's big stick, Taft's dollars, or Wilson's sermons–in fact, each president used all three–United States behavior toward its southern neighbors was imperialistic, denying some of them the freedom to make their own choices and thwarting their national sovereignty.

In its relations with Europe, two assumptions controlled American policy before the First World War. One was that the United States should stand outside continental embroilments, and the other was that America's best interests lay in cooperation with Great Britain. The balance of power in Europe was precarious, and seldom did an American president involve the United States directly. At Germany's request, Roosevelt helped to settle a Franco-German clash over Morocco by mediating a settlement at Algeciras, Spain (1906). But the president drew American criticism for entangling the United States in a European problem. Americans endorsed the ultimately futile Hague peace conferences (1899 and 1907) and negotiated various arbitration treaties, but on the whole they stayed outside Europe's embittered arena.

A major offshoot of the German-British rivalry was London's search for American friendship. The makings of the "great rapprochement" had been developing since the late nineteenth century. When the British supported the Americans in the war of 1898, stepped aside in the Hay-Pauncefote Treaty (1901) to permit the building of an

Anglo-American rapprochement

Important events

Year	Event
1861–69	William Seward serves as secretary of state
1866	Transatlantic cable completed France withdraws from Mexico
1867	Acquisition of Alaska and Midway Islands
1870	U.S. exports total $451 million (mostly agricultural goods)
1871	Anglo-American Washington Treaty settles *Alabama* claims
1878	United States monopolizes awards at Paris World's Fair
1883	Advent of New Navy
1884	Naval War College founded
1885	Josiah Strong, *Our Country*
1889	First Pan-American Conference
1890	Alfred T. Mahan, *The Influence of Sea Power Upon History*
1891	Diplomatic crisis with Chile
1893	Severe depression begins Frederick Jackson Turner, "The Significance of the Frontier in American History" Hawaiian revolution begins
1894	Wilson-Gorman Tariff
1895	Crisis over Venezuela Cuban revolution begins Japan defeats China
1896	William McKinley elected president as expansionist
1898	Sinking of the *Maine* Spanish-American War Hawaii and Wake Island annexed Treaty of Paris
1899	Senate passes Treaty of Paris giving the Philippines, Guam, and Puerto Rico to the United States United Fruit Company founded Part of Samoa annexed First Open Door note Outbreak of Filipino Insurrection
1900	Second Open Door note U.S. exports total $1.5 billion McKinley re-elected, defeating anti-imperialist William Jennings Bryan
1901	Theodore Roosevelt becomes president Advent of U.S. domination in the Philippines Hay-Pauncefote Treaty
1903	Panama breaks away from Colombia United States granted canal rights in Panama Platt Amendment
1904	Roosevelt Corollary to the Monroe Doctrine
1905	Taft-Katsura Agreement Portsmouth Conference Roosevelt imposes U.S. financial supervision on Dominican Republic
1906	San Francisco segregates Oriental school children United States invades Cuba
1907	Great White Fleet Gentleman's Agreement with Japan on immigration
1908	Root-Takahira Agreement
1910	Outbreak of the Mexican Revolution
1911	Outbreak of the Chinese Revolution
1912	U.S. troops enter Cuba again U.S. troops occupy Nicaragua (staying until 1925)
1913	Manufactured goods head U.S. export list for the first time
1914	U.S. troops invade Mexico First World War begins Panama Canal opens

American canal, virtually endorsed the Roosevelt Corollary, and withdrew their warships from the Caribbean, Americans warmed toward them. The British overtures paid off in 1917 when the United States threw its arms and men into the First World War on the British side.

From the Civil War to the First World War, expansionism and empire were central to American foreign policy. By 1914 Americans held extensive interests in a world made smaller by modern technology. The outward reach of American policy from Seward to Wilson met opposition from domestic critics, congressional doubters, other nations, and insurgents in subjugated lands, but the trend was never seriously diverted. Ideas of racial supremacy, the belief that the nation needed foreign markets to absorb surplus production so the domestic economy could thrive, a mission to uplift the less fortunate, and emotional appeals to national greatness–all fed the appetite for foreign adventure and commitments. The instruments of expansion and empire were the machines produced by American entrepreneurs and inventors. The underwater cable and wireless, the new steel steamships, the technological achievement of the Panama Canal, the exportation of American products across the globe, and the rifles American soldiers toted into Cuban and Philippine jungles and into the streets of Latin American capitals–all facilitated the imperial odyssey.

Expansion, whether at home or abroad, claimed victims. In 1914 Americans braced themselves for the immediate shock of full-scale war in Europe. In the future, though, their foreign policy would be preoccupied with rebellious challenges to United States hegemony from proud and resentful nationalists victimized by American paternalism. And Americans who sincerely believed that they had been helping others to enjoy a better life would feel betrayed and baffled that their foreign clients could be so ungrateful.

Suggestions for further reading

General

"American Empire, 1898–1903," *Pacific Historical Review,* 48 (1979), entire issue; Robert L. Beisner, *From the Old Diplomacy to the New, 1865–1900* (1975); Charles S. Campbell, *The Transformation of American Foreign Relations, 1865–1900* (1976); Richard D. Challener, *Admirals, Generals, and American Foreign Policy, 1889–1914* (1973); John M. Cooper, Jr., "Progressivism and American Foreign Policy," *Mid America,* 51 (1969), 260–277; John Dobson, *America's Ascent: The United States Becomes a Great Power, 1880–1914* (1978); John A.S. Grenville and George B. Young, *Politics, Strategy, and American Diplomacy* (1967); David Healy, *U.S. Expansionism* (1970); Ronald J. Jensen, *The Alaska Purchase and Russian-American Relations* (1975); George F. Kennan, *American Diplomacy, 1900–1950* (1951); Walter LaFeber, *The New Empire* (1963); William Leuchtenberg, "Progressivism and Imperialism," *Mississippi Valley Historical Review,* 39 (1952), 483–504; H. Wayne Morgan, *America's Road to Empire* (1965); Thomas G. Paterson, ed., *American Imperialism and Anti-Imperialism* (1973); Milton Plesur, *America's Outward Thrust* (1971); Rubin F. Weston, *Racism in United States Imperialism* (1972); William Appleman Williams, *The Tragedy of American Diplomacy,* rev. ed. (1962).

Diplomatic leaders

Howard K. Beale, *Theodore Roosevelt and the Rise of America to World Power* (1956); John M. Blum, *The Republican Roosevelt* (1954); David H. Burton, *Theodore Roosevelt: Confident Imperialist* (1968); William H. Harbaugh, *The Life and Times of Theodore Roosevelt* (1975); Frederick Marks, III, *Velvet on Iron: The Diplomacy of Theodore Roosevelt* (1979); Frank Merli and Theodore A. Wilson, eds., *Makers of American Diplomacy* (1974); Allan Nevins, *Hamilton Fish* (1937); William C. Widenor, *Henry Cabot Lodge and the Search for an American Foreign Policy* (1980).

Economic expansion, technology, and the navy

See the works by Beisner, Campbell, and LaFeber cited above; Paul P. Abrahams, *The Foreign Expansion of American Finance and Its Relationship to the Foreign Economic Policies of the United States, 1907–1921* (1976); Benjamin F. Cooling, *Gray Steel and Blue Water Navy* (1979); James A. Field, Jr., "American Imperialism," *American Historical Review,* 83 (1978), 644–668; Robert B. Davies, *Peacefully Working to Conquer the World: Singer Sewing Machines in Foreign Markets, 1854–1920* (1976); Lloyd A. Gardner, ed., *A Different Frontier* (1966); Kenneth J. Hagan, *American Gunboat Diplomacy and the Old Navy, 1877–1889* (1973); Kenneth J. Hagan, ed., *In Peace and War* (1978); Walter R. Herrick, *The American Naval Revolution* (1966); Peter Karsten, *The Naval Aristocracy* (1972); David M. Pletcher, *Rails, Mines, and Progress: Seven American Promoters in Mexico, 1867–1911* (1958); Howard B. Schonberger, *Transportation to the Seaboard* (1971); Robert Seager, II, *Alfred Thayer Mahan*

(1977); Harold Sprout and Margaret Sprout, *The Rise of American Naval Power, 1776–1918* (1944); Tom Terrill, *The Tariff, Politics, and American Foreign Policy, 1874–1901* (1973); Mira Wilkins, *The Emergence of the Multinational Enterprise* (1970); William Appleman Williams, *The Roots of the Modern American Empire* (1969).

Imperialism and the Spanish-American War

Graham A. Cosmas, *An Army for Empire: The United States Army in the Spanish-American War* (1971); Philip S. Foner, *The Spanish-Cuban-American War and the Birth of American Imperialism* (1972); Willard B. Gatewood, Jr., *"Smoked Yankees" and the Struggle for Empire: Letters from Negro Soldiers, 1898–1902* (1971); Richard Hofstadter, "Cuba, the Philippines, and Manifest Destiny," in *The Paranoid Style in American Politics,* ed. Richard Hofstadter (1967); Walter LaFeber, "That 'Splendid Little War' in Historical Perspective," *Texas Quarterly,* 11 (1968), 89–98; Gerald F. Linderman, *The Mirror of War: American Society and the Spanish-American War* (1974); Ernest R. May, *American Imperialism* (1968); Ernest R. May, *Imperial Democracy* (1961); Julius Pratt, *Expansionists of 1898* (1936); David F. Trask, *The War with Spain in 1898* (1981).

Anti-imperialism and the peace movement

Robert L. Beisner, *Twelve Against Empire* (1968); Peter Brock, *Pacifism in the United States* (1968); Merle E. Curti, *Peace or War* (1936); Charles DeBenedetti, *Peace Reform in American History* (1980); Delber McKee, "Samuel Gompers, the A.F. of L. and Imperialism, 1895–1902," *The Historian,* 2 (1959), 187–199; C. Roland Marchand, *The American Peace Movement and Social Reform, 1898–1918* (1973); David S. Patterson, *Toward a Warless World* (1976); E. Berkeley Tompkins, *Anti-Imperialism in the United States* (1970).

Relations with Latin America

Samuel F. Bemis, *The Latin American Policy of the United States* (1943); David Healy, *The United States in Cuba, 1898–1902* (1963); Walter LaFeber, *The Panama Canal* (1979); Lester D. Langley, *The Cuban Policy of the United States* (1968); Lester D. Langley, *Struggle for the American Mediterranean* (1976); Lester D. Langley, *The United States and the Caribbean, 1900–1970* (1980); David McCullough, *The Path Between the Seas: The Creation of the Panama Canal, 1870–1914* (1977); Allan R. Millett, *The Politics of Intervention: The Military Occupation of Cuba, 1906–1909* (1968); Dana G. Munro, *Intervention and Dollar Diplomacy in the Caribbean, 1900–1921* (1964); Dexter Perkins, *The Monroe Doctrine, 1867–1907* (1937); Ramon Ruiz, *Cuba: The Making of a Revolution* (1968); Karl M. Schmitt, *Mexico and the United States, 1821–1973* (1974).

Asia and the Pacific

Charles S. Campbell, *Special Business Interests and the Open Door Policy* (1951); Warren I. Cohen, *America's Response to China,* 2nd ed. (1980); Raymond A. Esthus, *Theodore Roosevelt and Japan* (1966); Henry F. Graff, ed., *American Imperialism and the Philippine Insurrection* (1969); Akira Iriye, *Across the Pacific* (1967); Akira Iriye, *Pacific Estrangement: Japanese and American Expansion, 1897–1911* (1972); Jerry Israel, *Progressivism and the Open Door* (1971); Paul M. Kennedy, *The Samoan Tangle* (1974); Glenn A. May, *Social Engineering in the Philippines* (1980); Robert McClellan, *The Heathen Chinee: A Study of American Attitudes Toward China, 1890–1905* (1971); Thomas J. McCormick, *China Market* (1967); Charles E. Neu, *The Troubled Encounter* (1975) (on Japan); Julius Pratt, *America's Colonial Experiment* (1950); Daniel B. Schirmer, *Republic or Empire?* (1972) (on the Philippine insurrection); Peter Stanley, *A Nation in the Making: The Philippines and the United States, 1899–1921* (1974); Merze Tate, *The United States and the Hawaiian Kingdom* (1965); Paul A. Varg, *Missionaries, Chinese, and Diplomats* (1958); Paul A. Varg, *The Making of a Myth: The United States and China, 1897–1912* (1968); Leon Wolff, *Little Brown Brother* (1961); Marilyn Blatt Young, *The Rhetoric of Empire* (1968).

Britain

Alexander E. Campbell, *Great Britain and the United States, 1895–1903* (1960); Charles S. Campbell, *From Revolution to Rapprochement: The United States and Great Britain, 1783–1900* (1974); Bradford Perkins, *The Great Rapprochement* (1968).

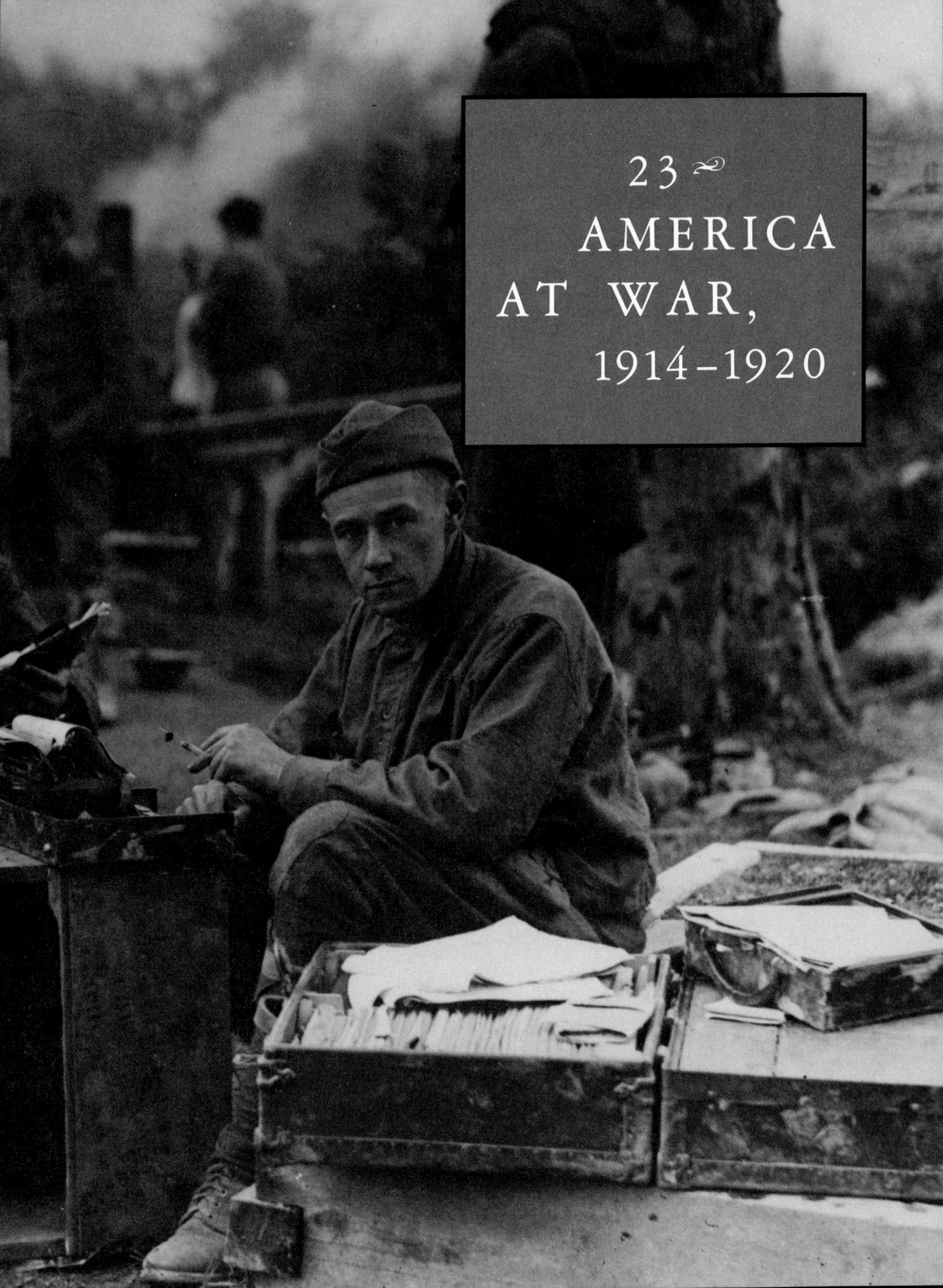

23 AMERICA AT WAR, 1914–1920

She was a Southern woman, born into a Presbyterian minister's family, educated at a small Georgia women's college, and dedicated to making a pleasant home for her husband and daughters. Ellen Axson Wilson was also a painter who had studied at the Art Students' League in New York City, an avid reader of Shakespeare, Milton, and Wordsworth, and a mother who made her children's clothing, nursed them through scarlet fever, and planned the family budget. She watched over her orphaned sisters and brothers, bringing Axson kin into her home for long stays. A well-managed and serene household was a matter of self-conscious pride for her. "A woman's place is to keep one little spot in the world quiet," she said. She was not, in today's sense, an emancipated woman, although she once complained about having to stay home "like the fixtures." Yet she did not confine her activities to the home. She advised decisionmakers and worked for compromise among warring political factions. She advocated improvements in Washington's slums, walking the alleys herself to draw attention to their squalor. "I wonder how anyone who reaches middle age can bear it," she said, in the reformist spirit of the times, "if she cannot feel, on looking back, that whatever mistakes she may have made she has on the whole lived for others and not for herself."

Woodrow Wilson admired her greatly. To him the loving bond that tied them together in twenty-nine years of marriage was central to his own well-being and success. He cherished her loyalty, her intelligence, her selflessness, and her strength in the family. But she had been ill off and on for years. After moving to the White House, fifty-four-year-old Ellen overworked herself. A fall caused injury to her spine, and in the early months of 1914 she contracted Bright's disease. Woodrow Wilson was holding her hand when she died on August 5. "Oh, my God, what am I to do?" he murmured. Seldom have such painful personal and official burdens fallen on a president at the same time. The day before, keeping vigil at her bedside, he had drafted a message offering American mediation to end the bloody war the European nations had just begun. At a time of wrenching bereavement, when the partner who had always helped him in moments of crisis was gone, Woodrow Wilson was called on to make momentous decisions about America's place in the First World War. He found it difficult to concentrate on the affairs of state. "If I hadn't gone into politics," he told Ellen's sister sadly, "she would probably be alive now. The strain of it killed her."

The state of the nation

The Great War in Europe began to consume Wilson's time and energy. Like most Americans, he was shocked by its outbreak; it seemed a return to barbarity, a throwing-off of civilization. Europe, concluded the New York *Times*, "reverted to the condition of savage tribes." Americans had, of course, witnessed and participated in the years of international competition for colonies, the intense quest for markets, the sporadic military encounters, and the buildup in new weaponry. But full-scale war seemed a thing of the past. "The nineteenth-century view of history as progress," historian Henry F. May has written, "received a shattering blow." The battle news was gruesome, with heavy civilian casualties mounting daily. "We were not used to smelling blood from vast human slaughterhouses," recalled William Allen White. Soon after the war began, he remarked "how sad it is that the war is taking the national attention away from justice." Jane Addams agreed that "the spirit of fighting burns away all those impulses . . . which foster the will to justice."

By "justice" White and Addams meant reform. But it was not the war alone that seemed to be sapping progressivism of its vitality. After over a decade of reform, the American people were still sorely divided, and social and economic injustices continued to plague the nation. As they entered 1914, Americans suffered an economic downturn. Labor-capital struggles, such as the Ludlow Massacre in Colorado—in which two women and eleven children were killed when state militia attempted to break a miners' strike—commanded headlines. President Wilson sent federal troops to restore order. Race relations were strained as well, notably by Wilson's decision to segregate federal buildings in Washington, D.C., and by numerous lynchings of blacks (fifty-one in 1914). And nativists angrily protested the fast pace of immi-

Domestic tensions

The Wilson family: from left to right, Margaret, Ellen Axson Wilson, Eleanor, Jessie, and President Woodrow Wilson (1856–1924). After Ellen's death in 1914, the bereaved president married again, in the midst of a debate over American preparedness for the First World War. Library of Congress.

gration: 1.2 million immigrants entered the United States in 1914 alone. Aware of the emotion the European war aroused among ethnic groups in the United States, Wilson appealed for neutrality in thought and action. But German-Americans, Franco-Americans, Italian-Americans, Irish-Americans, and others identified passionately with their warring countries of origin, accentuating ethnic divisions within the United States.

In the fall of 1914, the Democrats were badly beaten in the congressional elections and a conservative political trend seemed under way. Wilson himself contributed to the trend by announcing that the New Freedom had accomplished its reform goals and the nation was entering a "time of healing." Progressivism, it appeared, had spent itself, the weak Clayton Act and Federal Trade Commission being its last achievements. Wilson rejected progressive calls for child labor laws, vigorous antitrust action, and women's suffrage. He began to mend fences with the business community by appointing bankers to the Federal Reserve Board, and people friendly to corporate interests to the Federal Trade Commission. Progressivism, then, was sputtering even before the war intruded.

While Wilson tried to keep America out of the war, to protect American interests as a neutral trader, and—just in case—to prepare the nation militarily, his political fortunes grew worrisome. The Bryan wing of the Democratic party was in revolt, and many progressives no longer looked to Wilson for leadership. Thus political necessity forced him into a turnabout to improve his chances in the election of 1916. Early that year Wilson appointed Louis D. Brandeis to the Supreme Court. Brandeis, an antimonopolist, defender of small business, "people's advocate," and the first Jewish appointee to the high court, was a symbol of progressivism. Wilson also pleased progressives by supporting the Keating-Owen bill to regulate child labor; the Farm Loan Act, which provided capital to farmers who found private banks too conservative in their loan policies; the Adamson Act, which set an eight-hour day for railroad workers; and workers'-compensation legislation. With these political steps, Wilson entered the election of 1916.

The Republicans snubbed Theodore Roosevelt, who wanted the nomination, in favor of Charles Evans Hughes, former reform governor of New York and Supreme Court justice. "The country wasn't in a heroic mood," grumbled Roosevelt. Wilson ran on a platform of peace, progressivism, and preparedness. Bryan jumped on his bandwagon; so did leading progressives. Many were attracted by the Democratic party's campaign slogan: "He Kept Us Out of War." Hughes led a fractured party, and he could not muzzle Roosevelt, whose bellicose speeches suggested that the Republicans would drag Americans into the world war. Wilson received 9.1 million votes to Hughes's 8.5 million, and the president barely won in the electoral college by a 277-to-254 count. The Socialist party, which had earned 902,000 votes four years earlier, dropped to 600,000, largely because Wilson's reforms had attracted some socialists and the ailing Eugene Debs was not the party's standardbearer. But the closeness of the Wilson-Hughes contest provided further evidence that America was deeply divided.

Election of 1916

Within several months, the "peace candidate" Woodrow Wilson led the United States into the First World War on behalf of England and France. The war experience wrought massive changes and accelerated trends already under way in the United States. Wars are emergencies, and during such times the normal way of doing things surrenders to the extraordinary and exaggerated. This period gave rise to increased powers for the presidency, vigorous competition between the executive and legislative branches of government, a temporary halt to immigration, unprecedented centralization and integration of the economy, increased standardization of products by government order, gains for labor followed by numerous strikes, and cooperation between government and business. Indeed, some historians date the "military-industrial complex"—a term coined years later by President Dwight D. Eisenhower—from the First World War.

Although the war experience caused the progressive movement to splinter and fade, especially at the national level, reformers concentrated their efforts on a few issues, such as women's suffrage and prohibition (see pages 582, 594). Tensions between racial and ethnic groups also intensified. Whites who did not like the migration of southern blacks to work in northern defense plants resisted their new neighbors, and race riots revealed once again the depth of racial prejudice. German-Americans were denounced as traitors, and war hawks harassed pacifists. The federal government itself trampled on civil liberties to silence critics of the war and of Wilsonian diplomacy. And, as Communism implanted itself in Soviet Russia, America suffered a postwar Red Scare that did further damage to its reputation as a free and democratic society. In the aftermath of war, groups that sought to consolidate gains made during the war vied with those who sought to restore the prewar status quo. Americans were further unsettled by nagging doubts about rationality, liberalism, and the once-heady premise that new technology—the machine—meant progress; few could argue that the First World War, with all its destructive fury, ranked as a milestone in a journey toward a more humane existence.

The United States emerged from the war a major power in a disrupted and economically hobbled world. Yet Americans who had marched to battle to "save the world for democracy," as Wilson put it, grew disillusioned. They recoiled from the spectacle of the victors squabbling over the spoils, and they chided Wilson for failing to deliver his promised "peace without victory." As in the 1790s, 1840s, and 1890s, Americans engaged in heated national debate about foreign policy and the nation's future course. The president appealed for American membership in a new international organization, the League of Nations, which he touted as a vehicle for reforming world politics. But the Senate killed his diplomatic offspring, fearful that it might entangle Americans once again in Europe's problems, impede the growth of the American empire, and compromise the country's traditional unilateralism in international affairs. On many fronts, then, Americans during the era of the First World War were at war with themselves.

The question of neutrality

In 1914, soon after the Allies (Great Britain, France, Russia, and eventually Japan and Italy) and the Central Powers (Germany, Austria, and eventually Turkey) exchanged declarations of war, President Wilson issued a proclamation of neutrality. He also asked Americans to refrain from taking sides, to "exhibit the fine poise of undisturbed judgment, the dignity of self-control, the efficiency of dispassionate action." The United States, he fervently hoped, would stand as the pre-eminently sane, civilized nation in a deranged international environment.

Wilson's lofty appeal for American neutrality and unity at home collided with three realities. First, ethnic groups in the United States naturally took sides.

Ethnic ties to Europe

Many German-Americans and vehemently anti-British Irish-Americans (Ireland was then trying to break free from British rule) cheered for the Central Powers, as did Swedish-Americans who shared Sweden's long-standing antagonism toward Russia. Americans of British and French ancestry applauded the Allies. Anglo-American traditions and slogans like "Remember Lafayette," as well as the sheer number of Americans with roots in the Allied nations, drew a majority to the Allied cause. To them the war was a matter of democracy against autocracy. Germany's ugly attack on neutral Belgium at the start of the war confirmed in many minds that the "Hun" was the archetype of unbridled militarism, the defiler of innocent women and children. "We definitely have to be neutral," Wilson said privately, "since otherwise our mixed populations would wage war on each other."

Second, America's economic links with the Allies rendered neutrality difficult, if not impossible. England had long been one of the nation's best customers. New war-inspired orders flooded American com-

Economic links with the belligerents

panies and farms, pulling the economy out of its recession. In 1914 American exports to England and France equaled $753 million; in 1916 the figure reached an impressive $2.75 billion. In the same period, however, exports to Germany dropped from $345 million to only $29 million. Much of the American-Allied trade was financed through private American loans, amounting to $2.3 billion during the period of neutrality; in stark contrast, Germany received only $27 million.

The Wilson administration, which at first frowned on the transactions, came to see them as necessary to the economic health of the United States. Without loans to help the Allies pay for American products, one of Wilson's key advisers gloomily told the president, the United States would suffer "restriction of output, industrial depression, idle capital, idle labor, numerous failures, financial demoralization, and general unrest and suffering among the laboring classes." From Germany's perspective, of course, the linkage between the American economy and the Allies signaled an unwelcome and dangerous fact: the United States had become the quite-unneutral Allied arsenal and bank. Americans, however, were caught in a dilemma that further highlighted the difficulty of maintaining pure neutrality: for the United States to cut its economic ties with Britain would constitute an unneutral act in favor of Germany. That is, under international law the British—who controlled the seas—could buy contraband (war-related goods) and non-contraband from neutrals at their own risk. It was Germany's responsibility, not America's, to stop the trade in ways that international law prescribed: an effective blockade of the enemy's territory or the seizure of all goods from belligerent (British) ships and contraband from neutral (American) ships.

The third reason neutrality did not work derived from the pro-Allied sympathies of Wilson administration officials. Shortly after Ellen Wilson's death,

Pro-Allied sympathies

the president received a note from another man who had lost his wife, British Foreign Secretary Edward Grey. Wilson, moved by the thoughtful message, replied that he felt "that we are bound together by common principle and purpose." He was talking about more than shared bereavement. Indeed, for Wilson, a German victory would destroy government by law and "free industry and enterprise." If Germany won the war, he prophesied, "it would change the course of our civilization and make the United States a military nation." Wilson's chief advisers and diplomats—Colonel Edward House, Secretary of State Robert Lansing, and Ambassador to London Walter Hines Page among them—shared these sentiments and were often openly pro-Allied.

Wilson and his administration also believed that Wilsonian principles stood a better chance of international acceptance if Britain, rather than the Central Powers, sat astride the postwar world. Wilsonianism—the name scholars have given to the body of ideas Wilson espoused—consisted of traditional American diplomatic principles, to which Wilson eloquently gave coherence and currency. His ideal world was to be open in every sense of the word: no barriers to commerce, no impediments to democratic politics, no secret diplomatic deals. Empires were to be opened up in keeping with the principle of self-determination. Wilson envisioned free-market, nonexploitative capitalism and political constitutionalism for all nations, to ensure the good society and world peace. His critics complained that Wilson often violated his own tenets in his eagerness to force them upon others.

Wilsonianism

Wilson also articulated the traditional belief in American exceptionalism. America, he believed, had a mission to reform international relations and other societies. American progressivism was to be projected onto the world. "We created this Nation," he intoned, "not to serve ourselves, but to serve mankind." Wilson's missionary zeal blended with a hardheaded pragmatism that bespoke his understanding of the balance of world power and the intertwining of the American economy with the economies of other countries. His inheritance was the expansionism that characterized American foreign policy before the First World War. And he shared with his predecessors the belief that even unsavory methods—such as military intervention—were necessary to protect American interests.

To say that American neutrality was never a real possibility, given ethnic loyalties, economic ties, and Wilsonian preferences, is not to say that Wilson sought to enter the war. He emphatically wanted to keep the United States out of the military conflict, and in fact did so for two and a half years. Time and again, Wilson offered to mediate the crisis; he cautioned both the British and the Germans to limit their war aims; he did not wish for one power to crush the other. The president remarked to Colonel House in early 1917 that "we are the only one of the great white nations that is free from war today, and it would be a crime against civilization for us to go in." But go in the United States did. By the spring of 1917, whatever remained of its tattered neutrality was swept away by the intense winds of American national interest, as defined by Woodrow Wilson.

Americans got caught in the Allied-Central Power crossfire. British naval policy was designed to sever neutral trade with Germany in order to cripple the German economy. The British, "ruling the waves and waiving the rules," declared a loose, ineffective, and hence illegal blockade; outlawed a broad list of contraband (including foodstuffs) which was not supposed to be shipped to Germany by neutrals; mined the North Sea; and harassed neutral shipping by seizing cargoes. American vessels bearing goods for Germany seldom reached their destination. To counter German submarines, the British flouted international law by arming their merchant ships and flying neutral (sometimes American) flags. Wilson frequently protested British violations of neutral rights, pointing out that neutrals had the right to sell and ship noncontraband goods to belligerents without interference. But London often deftly defused American criticism by paying for confiscated cargoes. Sometimes provocative German actions made British behavior seem comparatively mild or inconsequential.

British naval policy

Germany was determined to lift the injurious blockade and to end American-Allied commerce. These ambitious tasks were assigned to the submarine. In February 1915 Berlin announced that it was creating a war zone around the British Isles. All enemy ships in the area would be sunk; neutral vessels were warned to stay out so as not to be attacked by mistake; and passengers from neutral nations like the United States were warned to stay off enemy ships. Serving as his own secretary of state and writing diplomatic messages on his own typewriter, President Wilson stiffly informed Germany that the United States was holding it to "strict accountability" for any losses of American life and property.

Wilson was interpreting existing international law in the strictest sense. That law held that an attacker had to warn a passenger or merchant ship before attacking, so that passengers and crew could disembark into lifeboats for safety. The submarine postdated that rule, but Wilson refused to adjust tradition to this new weapon of war. The Germans thought him un-

Mexico to recover the territories it was forced to give up to its northern neighbor in 1848. Zimmermann hoped, he told other German officials, to *"set new enemies on America's neck*—enemies which give them plenty to take care of over there."

American officials took the message seriously, since at the time Mexican-American relations were extremely tense. The Mexican Revolution, a bloody civil war with strong anti-American overtones, had spilled across the Rio Grande, and the Mexican government was threatening to nationalize American properties. Wilson had twice ordered American troops onto Mexican soil: in 1914 at Vera Cruz, to avenge a petty slight to the American uniform and flag; and again in 1916 in northern Mexico, where General John J. Pershing spent months trying to capture the elusive Pancho Villa after his raid on an American border town. Lansing and Wilson agreed that Zimmermann's telegram constituted "a conspiracy against this country." Wilson knew that war was only a matter of time.

Soon after learning of Zimmermann's ploy, Wilson asked Congress for "armed neutrality" to defend American lives and commerce. Specifically he requested the authority to arm American merchant ships, and more generally the power to "employ any other instrumentalities or methods that may be necessary." In the midst of the debate, Wilson released Zimmermann's telegram to the press; the nation was stunned. Still, antiwar Senators Robert M. La Follette and George Norris, among others, saw the armed-ship bill as a blank check for the president to move the country to war, and filibustered it to death. Wilson, angrily labeling them a "little group of willful men," proceeded to arm America's commercial vessels in spite of them. The decision came too late to prevent the sinking of several American ships. War cries echoed across the nation. The cabinet unanimously urged war. In late March, after a good deal of personal agony and seclusion, Wilson decided to call Congress into special session.

On April 2, 1917, the president stepped before a hushed Congress. His solemn address chided the Germans for "warfare against mankind." Wilson enumerated American grievances: Germany's violation of the principle of freedom of the seas, its disruption of American commerce, its attempt to stir up trouble in Mexico, and its violation of human rights by killing

fair. As they saw it, the slender, frail, and sluggish *unterseebooten* could not surface to warn ships of their imminent destruction: surfacing would deny the U-boats the advantage of surprise. A surfaced submarine was a sitting target for a British deck gun or hand grenade, and British vessels had standing orders to ram U-boats and sink them. Finally, the time required to evacuate passengers usually gave the distressed ship adequate opportunity to radio for help to a British destroyer in nearby waters. Berlin frequently complained to Wilson that he was denying the Germans the one weapon they could use to break the British economic stranglehold, disrupt the Allies' substantial connection with American producers and bankers, and win the war. To all concerned—British, Germans, and Americans—this naval warfare seemed a matter of life and death, a fundamental question of national survival.

From the Lusitania *to war*

Over the next few months the U-boats sank ship after ship. Then the sinking of the *Lusitania* forced the submarine issue for Wilson. The swift, majestic British passenger liner had few rivals for luxurious accommodations. When it left New York City on May 1, 1915, with over twelve hundred passengers, including millionaire Alfred Vanderbilt and other members of the "smart set," it was carrying a cargo of foodstuffs and contraband, including 4.2 million rounds of ammunition for Remington rifles. Before "Lucy's" departure, the newspapers carried an unusual announcement from the German embassy: travelers on British vessels were warned that a war zone existed and that Allied ships in those waters "are liable to destruction." Few passengers paid attention to the notice; few shifted to an American vessel for the transatlantic trip. On May 7, off the Irish coast, U-20 unleased torpedoes at the four-stacked vessel. The *Lusitania* exploded, quickly capsized, and carried 1,198 people to their deaths. One hundred twenty-eight Americans died.

This brutal assault on innocent people angered and saddened Americans. But Wilson and the American people, however great their hatred for Germany, ruled out a military response. Secretary of State William Jennings Bryan advised the president that the tragedy underscored the urgency of his suggestion that Americans not be permitted to travel on belligerent ships and that passenger vessels not be allowed to carry war goods. "Germany has a right to prevent contraband going to the Allies," wrote Bryan, "and a ship carrying contraband should not rely on passengers to protect her from attack—it would be like putting women and children in front of an army." Bryan also urged that simultaneous protest notes be sent to London and Berlin.

Reaction to the sinking of the Lusitania

Wilson moved deliberately. He rejected Bryan's counsel, as well as that of Theodore Roosevelt and others who clamored for war. Instead he sent a note to Berlin insisting on the right of Americans to sail on belligerent ships and demanding that Germany cease its inhumane submarine warfare. "Weasel words" from "the word-lover in the White House," shouted Roosevelt. The Germans were not contrite; they asked Wilson to rethink the relationship between international law and the submarine. Wilson fumed. After a stormy White House meeting marked by Bryan's charge that the Cabinet was pro-Allied, Wilson dispatched a second letter to Germany reiterating the demand that submarines be kept in port. When the president refused to ban American travelers from belligerent ships, Bryan resigned in protest—an uncommon act for secretaries of state, who usually resign quietly. The pro-Allied Robert Lansing was elevated to the top diplomatic post. For some Americans the *Lusitania* disaster became a rallying cry like the Alamo or the *Maine.* Certainly Wilson's attitude toward Germany hardened. To criticism that he was pursuing a double standard favoring the Allies, Wilson responded that the British were taking cargoes and violating property rights, but the Germans were taking lives and violating human rights.

Germany, seeking to avoid war with America, ordered its U-boat commanders to halt attacks on passenger liners. But in mid-August another British vessel, the *Arabic,* was sunk; two American lives were lost. The German ambassador hastened to pledge that never again would an unarmed passenger ship be attacked without warning. But the sinking of the *Arabic* fueled the debate over American passengers on

After the Germans declared unrestricted submarine warfare in February 1917, ships began to go down at an alarming rate. This cartoon, captioned "Without warning," protested the German sinking of the *Laconia* as a brutal attack on innocent Americans. Despite the American flag it flew, however, the *Laconia* was a British liner. Culver.

belligerent vessels. Why not require Americans to sail on American craft? asked critics. From August 1914 to March 1917 only 3 Americans died on an American ship (the American tanker *Gulflight* in May 1915), while about 190 were killed on belligerent ships.

Gore-McLemore resolution

In early 1916 the Gore-McLemore resolution, which would prohibit Americans from traveling on armed merchant vessels or ships carrying contraband, was introduced in Congress. The resolution, it was hoped, would prevent incidents like the *Lusitania* from hurtling the United States into war. But Wilson would tolerate no interference in the presidential making of foreign policy (he had just sent Colonel House to Europe to mediate) and no restrictions on American travel. The resolution, he argued, would destroy the "whole fine fabric of international law." After heavy politicking, the House defeated the resolution 276-to-142 and the Senate followed suit 68-to-14. If America's goal was

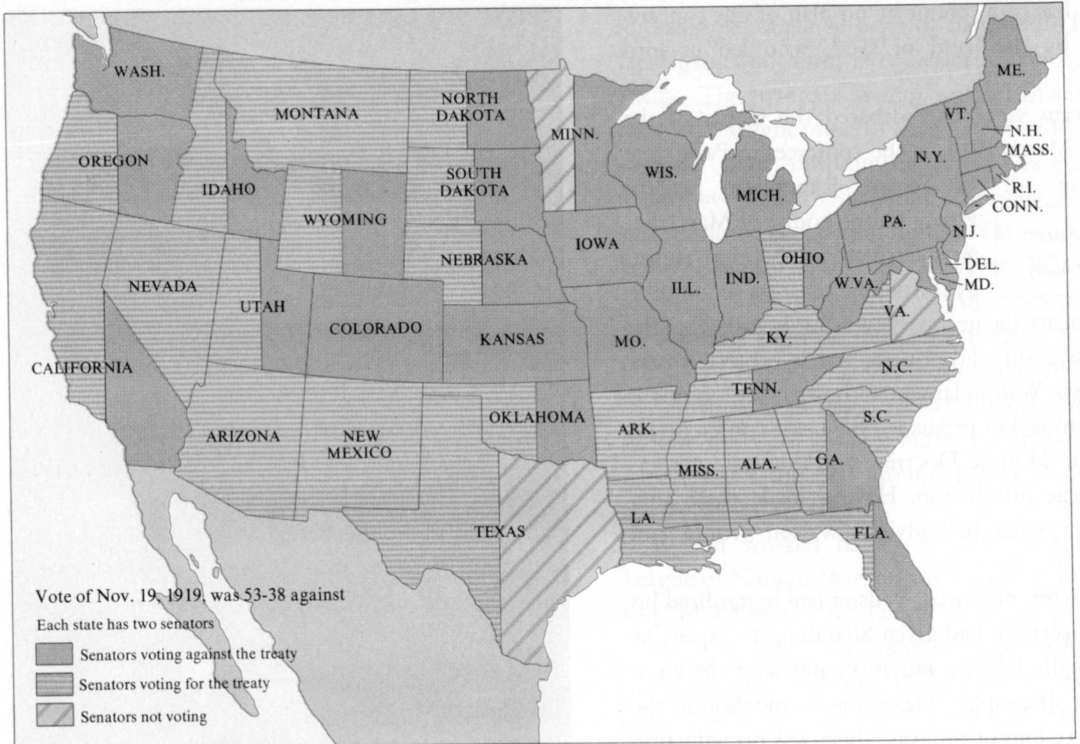

Senate voting on the Treaty of Paris, 1919

language: "I cannot say too often—any man who carries a hyphen about him carries a dagger which he is ready to plunge into the vitals of the Republic." In Colorado, while delivering another passionate speech, the president collapsed. A few days later, in Washington, D.C., he suffered a stroke that paralyzed his left side. Although his mind remained alert, he became grumpy and peevish, fearful of displaying weakness and unable to conduct the heavy business of the presidency. Advised by Secretary of State Lansing and Colonel House to placate senatorial critics so the treaty would have a chance of passing, Wilson refused to "dip [his] colors to dishonorable compromise." Soon Lansing and House were ostracized from the limited presidential circle now controlled by Wilson's second wife. From Senate Democrats he demanded loyalty—a vote against all reservations.

The Senate first tested the treaty's strength in November (see map). In two votes, one on the treaty with reservations and one without, the Senate rejected it. A group of sixteen "Irreconcilables," determined to defeat any treaty, amended or not, voted nay each

Senate rejection of the treaty

time. Again in March 1920, the Senate fell short of the necessary two-thirds vote of approval. Had Wilson permitted Democrats to compromise, to accept the reservations, he could have achieved his fervent goal of American membership in the infant League of Nations. Still he thought there was hope; he vowed to make the 1920 presidential election a referendum on the treaty.

Who or what was responsible for the defeat of the treaty? Wilson's deteriorating health was not an important factor; sick or well, his jaw was set against compromise. Certainly his concessions to a harsh peace at Paris undercut his case in the United States; yet it seems that two-thirds of the Senate were willing to forgive his errors in Versailles if he would accept some reservations. The bitter personal feud between Wilson and Lodge has often been cited as the basic cause of the drama, but this explanation does not explain enough—it does not, for example, explain the determination of the Irreconcilables.

Wilson's obstinate refusal to compromise with his

senatorial foes certainly doomed the treaty. Still, this explanation begs the question: why were Wilson's critics so committed to cripple Article 10, and why was Wilson so dead set against its revision? The answer lies in the fact that at the core of the debate was a fundamental issue of American foreign policy: whether the United States would endorse collective security or pursue its traditional path of unilateralism, as articulated by George Washington in his Farewell Address and by James Monroe in his famous doctrine. Wilson lost because he could not overcome the tenacity of unilateralism, the desire for freedom of choice in international relations and nonalignment. He could not persuade Americans to depart from their past and he could not reform the self-interested behavior of other states. In the end, Woodrow Wilson promised more than he could deliver.

The experience of war

As the war ground to a close in Europe, historian Albert Bushnell Hart glumly observed that the "world is uncouth, dishevelled, possessed of evil spirits, full of woe, wrath, and putridity." He added that "it is easy to see that the United States is a new country." How new? What had changed? America emerged from the war years an unsettled mix of the old and the new. Above all else the war exposed the heterogeneity of the American people and the deep divisions among them: white versus black, nativist versus immigrant, capital versus labor, dry versus wet, men versus women, radical versus progressive or conservative, pacifist versus interventionist, nationalist versus internationalist. Race riots, labor strikes, the Americanization movement, suppression of civil liberties, the Red Scare, the League fight, and male resentment of female workers all underscored the distempers of the times. It is no wonder that after 1920 Americans would seek relief in "normalcy" and escape from what John Dewey called the "cult of irrationality."

During the war the federal government intervened in the economy and influenced people's everyday lives as never before. In the period 1916–1919 annual federal expenditures increased 2,500 percent, and war expenses ballooned to $33.5 billion. The total cost of the war was probably triple that figure, since future generations would have to pay veterans' benefits and interest on loans. Centralization of control in Washington, D.C., and mobilization of the home front also served as a model for the future. Wilson quickly dismantled the emergency machinery at the end of the war. But when the Great Depression struck in the 1930s, memories of the First World War surfaced, suggesting that the government could mobilize the people in another war, this one against economic calamity. The partnership of government and business in managing the wartime economy contributed to the development of a mass society through the standardization of products and the promotion of efficiency.

Costs of the war

The wartime cooperation of government and business also encouraged the growth of trade associations, which numbered about two thousand by 1920. After the war these industrywide groups would continue to lobby to protect their interests and to minimize competition. Wilsonian wartime policies also nourished the continued growth of big business and of oligopoly through the suspension of antitrust legislation. A 1920 Supreme Court decision not to dissolve the giant U.S. Steel Corporation symbolized the persistent trend toward bigness. After a short postwar recession, business power revived to dominate the next decade. American labor, by contrast, entered what one historian has called its lean years.

America's changed place in world affairs also held significance for later generations. By 1920 the United States was the world's leading economic power, producing 40 percent of its coal, 70 percent of its petroleum, and half its pig iron. It rose to first rank in world trade. During the demanding war years, American companies had expanded their overseas operations. Goodyear went into the Dutch East Indies for rubber; tin and copper interests dug new mines in Bolivia and Chile respectively; and Swift and Armour expanded into South America. Preoccupied with the war, competitors like Britain and Germany were outdistanced by American economic expansionists, especially in Latin America. The United States also shifted from a debtor to a creditor nation, becoming the world's leading banker.

Accelerating a twentieth-century trend, Woodrow Wilson centralized decisionmaking in the White

Important events

1914	Wilson orders troops to invade Mexico First World War begins Ellen Axson Wilson dies
1915	Germany declares war zone around British Isles German U-boat sinks *Lusitania* U.S. troops occupy Haiti (staying until 1934) D.W. Griffith, *The Birth of a Nation*
1916	Gore-McLemore resolution defeated Pancho Villa attacks United States; United States invades Mexico *Sussex* torpedoed National Defense Act Revenue Act Woodrow Wilson re-elected president on peace platform United States occupies Dominican Republic (staying until 1924)
1917	Purchase of the Virgin Islands Germany declares unrestricted submarine warfare Zimmermann telegram Russian Revolution United States declares war against Germany Selective Service Act Espionage Act Race riot in East St. Louis, Illinois War Industries Board created War Revenue Act Fuel crisis due to severe winter
1918	Wilson announces Fourteen Points Webb-Pomerene Act Sedition Act Eugene Debs imprisoned for violating Espionage Act American troops fight at Château-Thierry U.S. troops intervene in Russian civil war Allied offensive leads to German defeat Flu epidemic Republicans win congressional elections Armistice
1919	Paris Peace Conference at Versailles Eighteenth Amendment ratified (prohibition) May Day bombings and disturbances Red Summer; Chicago race riot Widespread labor strikes; steel strike U.S. Communist party founded President Wilson suffers a stroke Treaty of Paris rejected by Senate *Schenck* v. *U.S.*
1920	Red Scare and Palmer Raids Nineteenth Amendment ratified (women's suffrage)

House, often writing diplomatic messages himself and serving as his own secretary of state. The disillusionment common to so many Americans after the disappointment of Versailles did not cause the United States to adopt a policy of withdrawal or strict isolationism. But it did feed public sentiment against intervening in European affairs until the Europeans first set their own house in order. The huge debts owed to the United States and the German reparations owed to the Allies meant, of course, that America could not escape from the economic consequences of the peace.

The carnage–10 million people lost their lives in the war–and the use of awesome new weapons like the submarine, poison gas, and the airplane stimulated new appeals for arms control and a revitalized peace movement. At the same time, the military became more professional. The Reserve Officer Training Corps (ROTC) became permanent; the Army War College in Washington, D.C., and the Command and General Staff College at Fort Leavenworth, Kansas, provided upper-echelon training; and the Army Industrial College, founded in 1924, pursued business-military cooperation in the area of logistics and planning. The National Research Council, created in 1916 with governmental and Carnegie and Rockefeller funds, continued after the war as an alliance of scientists and businessmen engaged in research relating to national defense. As before the war, the tendencies toward disarmament on the one hand and preparedness on the other continued to compete.

The international system born in these years was unstable and fragmented. The process of decolonization—a major trend of modern history—was set in motion at this time. Nationalist leaders like Ho Chi Minh of Indochina and Mahatma Gandhi of India, taking to heart the Wilsonian principle of self-determination, vowed to achieve independence for their peoples. Communism became a new and disruptive force in world politics, and the Russians bore a grudge against the Allies, who had futilely tried to thwart their revolution. The several new states in Central and Eastern Europe proved weak, dependent on outsiders for security. The new Germany bitterly resented the harsh peace settlement. Nor was the world economy settled. The war debts and reparations problems would dog international order for years.

The war experience also changed Americans' mood. The war was grimy and ugly, far less glorious than Wilson's lofty rhetoric had it. People recoiled from the photographs of bodies dangling from barbed wire, poison-gas victims, and battleshocked faces. American soldiers were eager to return home. Apparently tired of idealism and cynical about their ability to right wrongs, they craved the latest baseball scores, and stories of the home-run exploits of a new hero, Babe Ruth. Still, for the doughboys the army years were memorable, a turning point in their lives. They shed some of their parochialism, as the title of a popular song hinted: "How 'Ya Gonna Keep 'Em Down on the Farm, After They've Seen Paree?" And they made lasting friendships that would be cemented by membership in the American Legion. A young soldier from Missouri, Harry S Truman of Battery D, would never lose touch with his wartime buddies, and when he became president in 1945 he would bring several of them into the White House as advisers.

Disillusionment with the war

Those progressives who had believed entry into the war would deliver the millennium now marveled at their naiveté. Many lost their enthusiasm for crusades, and many others turned away in disgust from the bickering of the victors. Randolph Bourne commented that progressives felt "like brave passengers who have set out for the Isles of the Blest only to find that the first mate has gone insane and jumped overboard." Some felt betrayed, distraught that the Great War had not proven exceptional. William Allen White angrily wrote to a friend that the Allies "have—those damned vultures—taken the heart out of the peace, taken the joy out of the great enterprise of the war, and have made it a sordid malicious miserable thing like all the other wars in the world."

Woodrow Wilson himself had remarked soon after taking office in 1913, before the Great War, that "there's no chance of progress and reform in an administration in which war plays the principal part." From the vantage point of 1920, looking back on the array of distempers at home and abroad, Wilson would have to agree with his fellow citizens that progress and reform had been dealt substantial blows.

Suggestions for further reading

America in the era of the Great War

John M. Blum, *Woodrow Wilson and the Politics of Morality* (1956); Randolph Bourne, *War and the Intellectuals,* ed. Carl Resek (1964); John W. Chambers, *The Tyranny of Change* (1980); Allen F. Davis, *American Heroine* (1974) (on Jane Addams); Otis L. Graham, Jr., *The Great Campaigns* (1971); Gerd Hardach, *The First World War: 1914–1918* (1977); Ellis W. Hawley, *The Great War and the Search for a Modern Order* (1979); Arthur S. Link, *Wilson,* 5 vols. (1947–1965); Henry F. May, *The End of American Innocence* (1964); Frederic L. Paxton, *American Democracy and the World War,* 3 vols. (1936–1948); Burl Noggle, *Into the Twenties* (1974); Ronald Steel, *Walter Lippmann and the American Century* (1980); Arthur Walworth, *Woodrow Wilson,* 2nd ed. (1969).

Wilsonian foreign policy

Thomas A. Bailey and Paul B. Ryan, *The Lusitania Disaster* (1975); Edward H. Buehrig, ed., *Wilson's Foreign Policy in Perspective* (1957); John M. Cooper, Jr., *The Vanity of Power* (1969); John M. Cooper, Jr., *Walter Hines Page* (1977); Patrick Devlin, *Too Proud to Fight* (1975); Ross Gregory, *The Origins of American Intervention in the First World War* (1971); Ross Gregory, "To Do Good in the World: Woodrow Wilson and America's Mission," in *Makers of American Diplomacy*, eds. Frank Merli and Theodore Wilson (1974); Burton I. Kaufman, *Efficiency and Expansion: Foreign Trade Organization in the Wilson Administration* (1974); N. Gordon Levin, Jr., *Woodrow Wilson and World Politics* (1968); Arthur S. Link, *Woodrow Wilson: Revolution, War, and Peace* (1979); Ernest R. May, *The World War and American Isolation, 1914–1917* (1959); Walter Millis, *Road to War* (1935); Keith L. Nelson and Spencer C. Olin, Jr., *Why War? Ideology, Theory, and History* (1979); Robert E. Osgood, *Ideals and Self-Interest in American Foreign Relations* (1953); Jack J. Roth, ed., *World War I* (1967); Jeffrey J. Safford, *Wilsonian Maritime Diplomacy* (1977); Daniel M. Smith, *The Great Departure* (1965); Barbara Tuchman, *The Zimmermann Telegram* (1958); Arthur Walworth, *America's Moment* (1977); William C. Widenor, *Henry Cabot Lodge and the Search for an American Foreign Policy* (1980); *Wilson's Diplomacy: An International Symposium* (1973).

Preparedness and war

Arthur E. Barbeau and Henri Florette, *The Unknown Soldiers: Black American Troops in World War I* (1974); J. Garry Clifford, *The Citizen Soldiers* (1972); Edward M. Coffman, *The War to End All Wars* (1968); Harvey A. DeWeerd, *President Wilson Fights His War* (1968); Thomas C. Leonard, *Above the Battle: War-Making in America from Appomattox to Versailles* (1978); David Trask, *The United States in the Supreme War Council* (1961); Russell F. Weigley, *The American Way of War* (1973).

The home front

Rodolfo Acuna, *Occupied America: A History of Chicanos*, 2nd ed. (1980); George T. Blakey, *Historians on the Homefront* (1970); Wayne A. Cornelius, *Building the Cactus Curtain: Mexican Migration and U.S. Responses from Wilson to Carter* (1980); Alfred W. Crosby, Jr., *Epidemic and Peace, 1918* (1976); Robert D. Cuff, *The War Industries Board* (1973); Allen F. Davis, "Welfare, Reform, and World War I," *American Quarterly*, 19 (1967), 516–533; Edward R. Ellis, *Echoes of Distant Thunder* (1975); Charles Gilbert, *American Financing of World War I* (1970); Maurine W. Greenwald, *Women, War, and Work* (1980); Frank L. Grubbs, Jr., *The Struggle for Labor Loyalty* (1968); Carol S. Gruber, *Mars and Minerva: World War I and the Uses of the Higher Learning in America* (1975); Robert V. Haynes, *A Night of Violence: The Houston Riot of 1917* (1976); Florette Henri, *Black Migration* (1975); Thomas C. Holt, "Afro-Americans," in *Harvard Encyclopedia of American Ethnic Groups*, ed. Stephen Thernstrom (1980); David M. Kennedy, *Over Here* (1980); Paul A.C. Koistinen, "The 'Industrial-Military Complex' in Historical Perspective: World War I," *Business History Review*, 41 (1967), 378–403; Seward W. Livermore, *Politics Is Adjourned* (1966); Frederick C. Luebke, *Bonds of Loyalty: German-Americans and World War I* (1974); Matt S. Meier and Feliciano Rivera, *The Chicanos* (1972); Mark Reisler, *By the Sweat of Their Brow* (1976) (on Mexican-Americans); Eliot M. Rudwick, *Race Riot at East St. Louis, July 2, 1917* (1964); Jordan A. Schwartz, *The Speculator: Bernard M. Baruch in Washington, 1917–1965* (1981); William M. Tuttle, *Race Riot: Chicago in the Red Summer of 1919* (1970).

Wartime dissent, civil liberties, and the Red Scare

David Brody, *Labor in Crisis: The Steel Strike of 1919* (1965); Charles Chatfield, *For Peace and Justice: Pacifism in America, 1914–1941* (1971); Stanley Coben, *A. Mitchell Palmer* (1963); Charles DeBenedetti, *Origins of the Modern Peace Movement* (1978); Robert L. Friedheim, *The Seattle General Strike* (1965); Sondra Herman, *Eleven Against War* (1969); Donald Johnson, *The Challenge to American Freedoms* (1963); C. Roland Marchand, *The American Peace Movement and Social Reform, 1898–1918* (1973); Paul L. Murphy, *The Meaning of Freedom of Speech* (1972); Paul L. Murphy, *World War I and the Origin of Civil Liberties* (1979); Robert K. Murray, *Red Scare* (1955); H.C. Peterson and Gilbert C. Fite, *Opponents of War, 1917–1918* (1968); William Preston, *Aliens and Dissenters: Federal Suppression of Radicals, 1903–1933* (1966): Francis Russell, *A City in Terror: 1919–The Boston Police Strike* (1975); Harry N. Scheiber, *The Wilson Administration and Civil Liberties, 1917–1921* (1960); David P. Thelan, *Robert M. La Follette and the Insurgent Spirit* (1976); Stephen L. Vaugh, *Holding Fast the Inner Lines: Democracy, Nationalism, and the Committee on Public Information* (1979); James Weinstein, *The Decline of Socialism in America, 1912–1923* (1967).

Hostility toward Bolshevik Russia

Peter G. Filene, *Americans and the Soviet Experiment, 1917–1933* (1967); John L. Gaddis, *Russia, The Soviet Union, and the United States* (1978); Lloyd C. Gardner, ed., *Wilson and Revolution, 1913–1921* (1976); George F. Kennan, *Russia Leaves the War* (1956); George F. Kennan, *The Decision to Intervene* (1958); Christopher Lasch, *The American Liberals and the Russian Revolution* (1962); John Thompson, *Russia, Bolshevism, and the Versailles Peace* (1966); Betty M. Unterberger, ed., *American Intervention in the Russian Civil War* (1969); Betty M. Unterberger, *America's Siberian Expedition, 1918–1920* (1956); William Appleman Williams, *American-Russian Relations, 1781–1947* (1952).

Versailles and the League fight

Thomas A. Bailey, *Woodrow Wilson and the Great Betrayal* (1945); Thomas A. Bailey, *Woodrow Wilson and the Lost Peace* (1944); Inga Floto, *Colonel House in Paris* (1973); Herbert Hoover, *The Ordeal of Woodrow Wilson* (1958); Warren F. Kuehl, *Seeking World Order* (1969); Arno Mayer, *Politics and Diplomacy of Peacemaking* (1967); Charles L. Mee, Jr., *The End of Order* (1980); Keith Nelson, *Victors Divided* (1973); Ralph A. Stone, *The Irreconcilables* (1970).

Aftermath

Stanley Cooperman, *World War I and the American Mind* (1970); Malcolm Cowley, *Exile's Return* (1951); Paul Fussell, *The Great War and Modern Memory* (1975); Stuart I. Rochester, *American Liberal Disillusionment in the Wake of World War I* (1977); Stephen R. Ward, ed., *The War Generation: Veterans of the First World War* (1975).

24 THE NEW ERA OF THE 1920s

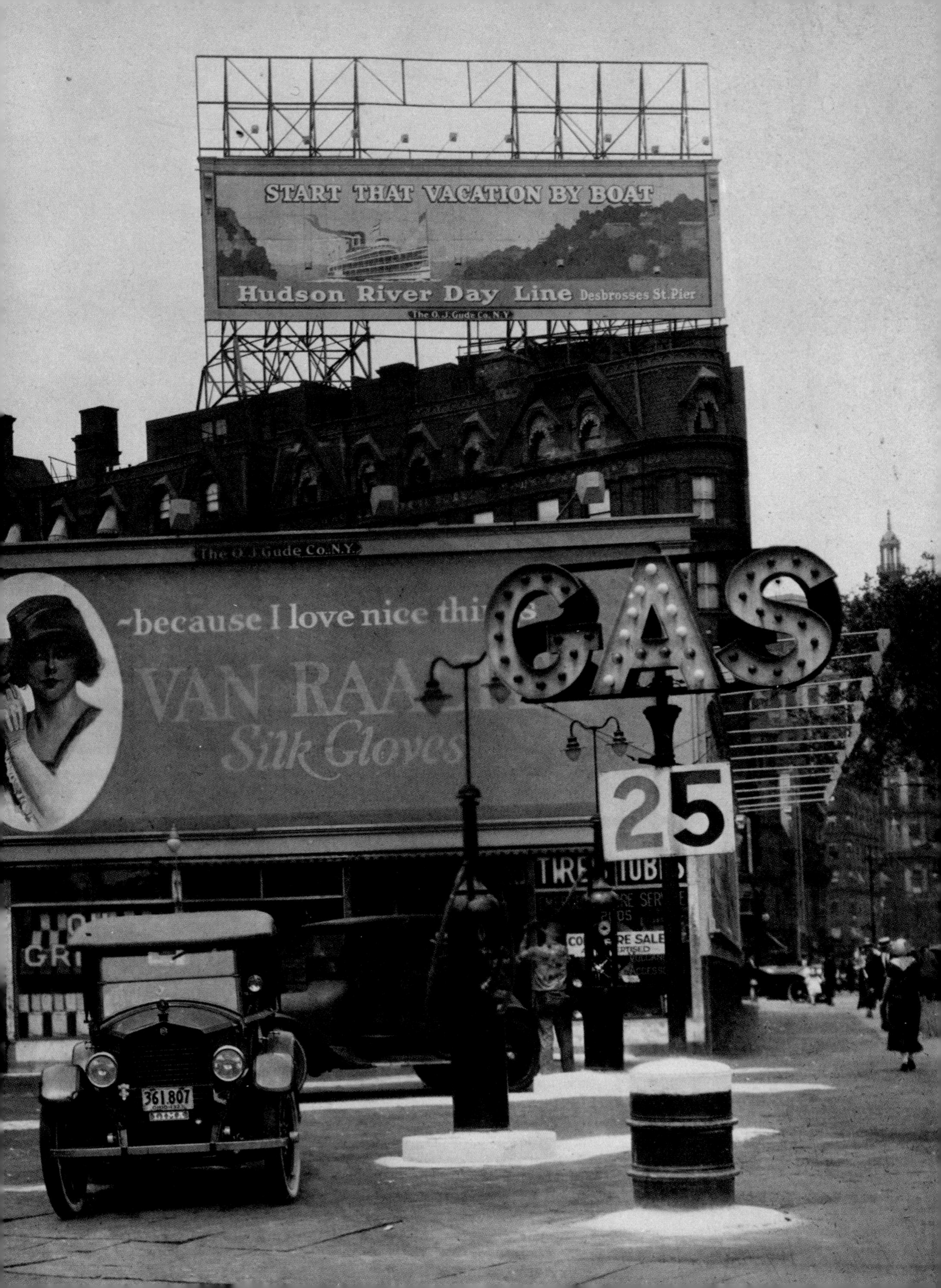
START THAT VACATION BY BOAT
Hudson River Day Line Desbrosses St. Pier
The O. J. Gude Co. N.Y.
The O. J. Gude Co. N.Y.
~because I love nice thi
VAN RAA
Silk Gloves
GAS
25
361 807

At 9:39 P.M. on August 6, 1926, a young American woman trudged out of the rough sea onto the English coast. Nineteen-year-old Gertrude Ederle had left France that morning in an attempt to swim the English Channel, a feat that only five men and no women had ever accomplished. She not only succeeded but swam the treacherous thirty-mile stretch in 14 hours 31 minutes, the fastest time yet recorded.

Already known as a swimming champion–she had won a gold medal at the 1924 Olympics–Ederle now became a champion of women. Her conquest of the Channel, wrote the *Literary Digest*, "would be hailed as a battle won for feminism" and the "unanswerable refutation of the masculine dogma that woman is, in the sense of physical power and efficiency, inferior to man." According to a columnist for the Boston *Globe*, "The Channel has been the means of giving to women new physical dignity."

Yet Americans seemed to appreciate that dignity in narrow ways. Along with adulation, Ederle's feat inspired a profusion of swimsuit ads linking physical fitness to sex appeal. Newspapers and magazines not only heralded her swim but increased their attention to the bathing beauties of the Miss America Pageant, a contest begun in 1922, the year Ederle won her first long-distance race. And whatever her accomplishments, the name of Ederle was never as renowned as those of the era's most admired males: Dempsey, Ruth, Lindbergh, or even Capone.

During the 1920s the flower of consumerism reached full bloom. Spurred by advertising and new forms of credit, Americans eagerly bought automobiles, radios. real estate, and stocks. The majority of the population enjoyed an unparalleled standard of living. The most fundamental and perplexing trend of the 1920s was the effect of the new mass consumer culture on individuals and communities. Changes in work habits, family responsibilities, and health care fostered new uses of time and new attitudes about proper behavior at home and in society.

By the end of the decade, new habits and values had altered American society. Whereas people had once identified with those who believed as they did, they now felt as much, if not more, of a sense of community with fellow consumers of Ford cars, Listerine mouthwash, and Lucky Strike cigarettes. Whereas they had once expressed their individuality in their work and family lives, now more than ever they sought vicarious identification with popular heroes like Gertrude Ederle, Charles Lindbergh, and Jack Dempsey.

The 1920s was not an era of total frivolity. Important reforms occurred at the state and local levels of government, and significant advances were made in science and technology. An outburst of creativity occurred in literature, music, and art. Still, the consumer culture predominated in everyday life, causing Americans to ignore rising debts and other increasingly negative economic signs. Poverty dogged many small farmers, workers in declining industries, and nonwhites living in urban and rural slums.

In many ways the Ederle story illustrates the complexities and ironies of the new era of the 1920s. The decade was a time both of great accomplishments–in economic productivity as well as athletics–and of frivolous commercial stunts, contests, and fads. It was a time of swift social change, of frankness and liberation. But the winds of change also stirred up waves of reaction. The new, more liberal values repelled some groups, such as the Ku Klux Klan, immigration restrictionists, and religious fundamentalists. Such groups reacted by trying to restore a society of simpler values, where people knew their place and deviants were not tolerated. Yet in spite of their efforts, material bounty and increased leisure time in which to enjoy it enticed Americans into a variety of new mass amusements, including games, sports, movies, and fads. In an impersonal world, Americans had turned to mass culture to personalize their lives.

Postwar optimism

Poor Richard's Almanac would have sold poorly in the 1920s. Few Americans of that era had much interest in the virtues of thrift and sobriety that Benjamin Franklin had preached. They saw more attraction in acquisition, speculation, amusement, and salesmanship. Instead of traditional homilies like "waste not, want not," they harkened to the advice of an advertising executive: "Make the public want what you have to sell. Make 'em pant for it." With such an attitude Americans attained the highest standard of living they had yet experienced. Though poverty and social injustice still infected the country, many people shared the belief, as journalist Joseph Wood Krutch put it, that "the future was bright and the present was good fun at least."

The decade did not begin very brightly. Besides political wrangling over membership in the League of Nations and ratification of the Treaty of Paris, race riots, and the Red Scare, the nation suffered a frightening economic decline. For two years after the First World War, consumer spending drove prices up. Then in 1920 people stopped buying, the export trade dropped as wartime orders ended, prices plummeted, and unemployment soared. The collapse hurt farmers the most. Net farm income plunged from a total of nearly $10 billion in 1919 to $4 billion in 1921. Unemployment, which had hovered around 2 percent in 1919, passed 12 percent in 1921. The railroad and mining industries suffered declining profits, and layoffs spread through New England mills as textile companies abandoned outdated factories for the raw materials and cheap labor of the South.

Recovery began in 1922 and continued unevenly until 1929. During this period, industrial output

Postwar economic recovery

nearly doubled. Electric motors were responsible for much of the rise; by 1929 electricity powered 70 percent of American industry, and thousands of steam engines had been relegated to the scrap heap. The new technique of manufacture by assembly line also contributed, adding hundreds of new consumer products to the market. New metal alloys, chemicals, synthetic materials, and preserved foods became commonplace. The expansion of manufacturing and services led to higher profits and wages, which in turn fed demand for more growth. As Americans acquired more money to spend on luxuries such as autos, and as their leisure time expanded, service industries boomed. More people could afford department and specialty stores, restaurants, beauty and barber shops, and movie theaters. This new consumerism was fueled by refined methods of credit, especially the installment or time-payment plan ("a dollar down and a dollar forever," as one critic quipped). Of 3.5 million automobiles sold in 1923, some 80 percent were bought on credit. Poor Richard would have thrown up his hands in disgust.

Behind the prosperity, an economic revolution was coming to a head. First, the consolidation movement that had given birth to trusts and holding companies in the late nineteenth century reached a new stage. Although Progressive-era trustbusting had harnessed big business to some extent, it had not halted oligopoly–the control of a whole industry by a few large firms. By the 1920s many of these companies dominated not only the production but the marketing, distribution, and even financing of a product. Thus in businesses as varied as automobile manufacturing, steel production, meat processing, and railroads, a few sprawling integrated companies predominated. Many oligopolistic firms, like General Electric, General Motors, U.S. Steel, and Western Electric, developed specialized management techniques and sophisticated planning policies to maximize profits and minimize market uncertainties.

The organizational movement that had begun around 1900 also matured in the 1920s. Myriad business and professional associations sprang up to coordinate and protect their members' interests. Retailers and small manufacturers formed trade associations to pool information and attempt market planning. Farm bureaus and cooperative marketing associations promoted scientific agriculture, lobbied for government protection, and tried to stabilize the market. Lawyers, engineers, and social scientists cooperated with business to promote economic growth.

These developments bespoke not only an economically mature nation but an urbanized one. In 1920 for

Climax of urbanization

the first time the federal census revealed that a majority of Americans, 51.4 percent, lived in urban areas (places with 2,500 or more people)–a sign that the city had become the locus of national experience. And indeed, the growth of services and industry both derived from and responded to urbanization. Industries such as steel, oil, and auto production boosted opportunities in cities like Detroit, Pittsburgh, Akron, Birmingham, Houston, and Los Angeles; the service and retail trades accounted for expansion in Atlanta, Kansas City, Minneapolis, and Seattle. The most explosive growth occurred in areas of warm climate–Miami, Tampa, San Diego–where promises of comfort and profit attracted thousands of speculators.

The trend toward urbanization continued during the 1920s, as an estimated 6 million Americans left their farms for nearby or distant cities. Midwestern migrants, particularly young single people, moved to regional centers or to California. A steady stream of poor white and black southerners moved into the burgeoning industrial cities of the South or followed railroad lines north to Chicago, Detroit, Cleveland, and New York. Most foreign immigrants now came from Mexico, which was unaffected by new immigration laws (see page 687). Many Mexicans moved north to work as agricultural laborers in the Southwest, but others flowed into the growing cities of San Antonio, Los Angeles, and Tucson. Like their predecessors, most of the new immigrants to the cities lacked resources and skills. They crowded into low-rent inner-city districts, where their struggle for subsistence compounded urban problems and stirred racist fears.

Blacks accounted for a sizable portion of the migrants fleeing farms. Crushed by tenant farming and lured by new industrial jobs, 1.5 million blacks moved cityward during the 1920s. The black populations of New York, Chicago, Philadelphia, Detroit, Cleveland, and Houston doubled during these years. Forced by necessity and discrimination to seek the cheapest and poorest housing, the newcomers squeezed into ghettos–low-rent districts from which escape was difficult at best. For unlike white migrants, who were free to move away from inner-city districts if and when they could afford to do so, blacks found better housing closed to them. The only way they could expand their housing opportunities was to spill into nearby neighborhoods, a process that sparked resistance and violence. Fears of such expansion prompted white neighborhood associations to adopt restrictive covenants, whereby homeowners pledged not to sell their property to blacks. It was this kind of conflict–over jobs as well as housing–that had kindled race riots in Chicago, Knoxville, Omaha, and Washington, D.C., in 1919.

In response partly to their new urban experiences and partly to race riots and threats, thousands of blacks in northern cities joined movements that glorified black independence. The most influential of these black nationalist groups was the Universal Negro Improvement Association (UNIA), headed by Marcus Garvey, a Jamaican immigrant who believed blacks should separate themselves from a corrupt white society. Proclaiming "I am the equal of any white man," Garvey cultivated race pride through militant mass meetings and parades. He also promoted black capitalism to demonstrate black management skills and promote black values. His newspaper, the *Negro World*, refused to publish ads for hair straighteners and skin-lightening cosmetics, and his Black Star shipping line was intended to help blacks emigrate to Africa.

Marcus Garvey

The UNIA declined in the mid-1920s when the Black Star line went bankrupt (unscrupulous dealers had sold it dilapidated ships) and when the government jailed Garvey for mail fraud and then deported him. Nevertheless, the organization had attracted a huge following (contemporaries estimated it at 500,000; Garvey claimed 6 million) in New York, Chicago, Detroit, and other cities. And Garvey's speeches had served notice that blacks had their own aspirations, which they could and would translate into action.

As urban growth peaked, suburban growth accelerated. Although towns had existed around the edges of urban centers since the nation's earliest years, prosperity and easier transportation–mainly the automobile–made the urban fringe more accessible in the 1920s. Between 1920 and 1930, suburbs of Chicago (such as Oak Park and Evanston), Cleveland (such as Shaker Heights), and Los Angeles (such as Burbank and Inglewood) grew five to ten times as fast as the central cities. Most such suburbs were middle- and upper-class bedroom communities, though they included industrial suburbs like Highland Park (near Detroit) and East Chicago.

Growth of the suburbs

With their own police, fire protection, and water and gas services, many suburbs resisted annexation to core cities. Suburbanites wanted to escape big-city crime, dirt, and taxes, and they fought to preserve local control. "Under local government," one suburban editor reasoned, "we can absolutely control every objectionable thing that may try to enter our limits–but once annexed we are at the mercy of city hall." Particularly in the Northeast and Midwest, the fierce independence of growing suburbs choked off expansion by the central city and divided metropolitan areas in ways that would cause problems for future generations.

The bulging cities and suburbs fostered the development of the new mass culture that gave the decade its character. Most of the consumers who jammed re-

With gloved hand resting on ceremonial sword, Marcus Garvey (1887–1940) joins members of the Universal Negro Improvement Association at a march for equal rights. The UNIA fostered racial pride among millions of blacks in the early 1920s. Black Cross Nurses and the Black Star Steamship Line were just two of its contributions to black society. Brown Brothers

tail establishments, movie houses, and sporting arenas and who embraced fads like crossword puzzles, miniature golf, mahjongg, and marathon dancing were city dwellers. Cities were the places where people flouted law and morality by patronizing speakeasies (illegal saloons), holding petting parties, swearing in public, wearing outlandish clothes, and listening to jazz. They were also the places where women, ethnic and racial minorities, and religious denominations strained hardest to adjust to the new era. And yet Americans could not escape the small-town society of the past. While millions thronged cityward and intellectuals carped that small towns stifled personal growth, other Americans reminisced about the innocence and simplicity of a world gone by. This was the dilemma of a modern nation: how could one anchor oneself in a world of rampant materialism?

Materialism unbound

"One day," Henry Ford recalled, "someone brought to us a slogan which read: 'Buy a Ford and Save the Difference.' I crossed out the 'save' and inserted 'spend'—'Buy a Ford and Spend the Difference.'

It is the wiser thing to do. Society lives by circulation and not by congestion." Ford had a way of making new values sound like old truths. His ardent consumerism was a major theme of the 1920s, to which he contributed materially as well as philosophically. For by 1925 the assembly line at Ford's Highland Park plant was spitting out a motor car for some lucky buyer every ten seconds.

Indeed, between 1919 and 1929 the gross national product–the total value of all goods and services produced in the United States–swelled by 40 percent. Wages and salaries also increased (though not as much) and consumer price indexes generally fell. The result was that real income–the amount of goods and services money could buy–rose. In other words, people had more purchasing power. And they spent as Americans had never spent. In an article in *Survey* magazine in 1928, Eunice Fuller Barnard contrasted selected family expenditures in 1900 with those of 1928:

Expansion of the consumer society

1900	
2 bicycles	$ 70
wringer and washboard	$ 5
brushes and brooms	$ 5
sewing machine (mechanical)	$ 25
Total	$105

1928	
automobile	$700
radio	$ 75
phonograph	$ 50
washing machine	$150
vacuum cleaner	$ 50
sewing machine (electric)	$ 60
other electrical equipment	$ 25
telephone (year)	$ 35
Total	$1,145

Barnard added that certain items, such as education and medical care, had become costlier. Yet she felt the change had been worthwhile. She would rather pay more for a quart of milk knowing it was safer and purer than the "unanalyzed and unclassified" product of a generation earlier. "When some of us bewail the higher cost of living we may be talking about the higher cost of *better* living," Barnard concluded.

The benefits of modern technology were reaching more people than ever before. By 1929 two-thirds of all Americans lived in dwellings that had electricity, compared to one-sixth in 1912. In 1929 one-fourth of all families owned electric vacuum cleaners and one-fifth had electric toasters. Many could afford these and other items such as radios, washing machines, and movie tickets only because more than one family member worked or because the breadwinner took a second job. Nevertheless, new products and services were available to more than just the rich.

Of all the era's technological and economic wonders, the automobile was the vanguard. During the 1920s automobile registrations soared from 8 million to 23 million. Mass production and competition had brought down prices, making cars affordable even to some working-class families. By 1926 a Ford Model T cost under $300 and a Chevrolet sold for $700–at a time when workers in manufacturing earned around $1,300 a year and clerical workers about $2,300. The car had become a source of pride as well as a means of transportation; no sacrifice was too great to obtain one. Thus when an interviewer asked a rural housewife why her family owned a car but not a bathtub, the woman retorted, "Bathtub? You can't go to town in a bathtub."

Effects of the automobile

The motor car altered society as much as the railroad had seventy-five years earlier. Public officials were forced to pay more attention to safety regulations and traffic control. (In 1924 the General Electric Company responded to the needs with the first timed stop-and-go traffic light.) And changes in car design raised moralists' eyebrows. By 1927, five-sixths of all autos were enclosed (in 1919 most had had open tops), making for a privacy that bred fears of "houses of prostitution on wheels." The growing choice of models (there were 108 different automobile manufacturers in 1923) and colors (the old Ford Model T had come only in black; the new Model A came in a variety of colors) allowed automobile owners to express their personal tastes in a growing mass society. But most important, the car had a leveling effect; it was the ultimate symbol of social equality. As one writer observed in 1924, "It is hard to convince Steve Popovich, or Antonio Branca, or plain John Smith that he is being ground into the dust by Capital when at will he may drive the same highways, view the same

The age of electrical home appliances dawned in the 1920s. Here a sales force poses with toaster, vacuum cleaners, and washing machine outside an appliance store in Louisville, Kentucky. University of Louisville Photographic Archive; Caufield and Shook Collection 109089.

scenery, and get as much enjoyment from his trip as the modern Midas."

Americans' newly acquired taste for driving necessitated extensive construction of roads and abundant supplies of fuel. Since the late 1800s farmers and bicyclists had been pressing for improved roads; after the First World War motorists joined the campaign, prompting cities and states to improve local arteries. The important advances came in 1921 when Congress passed the Federal Highway Act, which provided federal aid for state roads; and in 1923 when the Bureau of Public Roads planned a national highway system.

The oil industry, already vast and powerful, shifted its emphasis from products providing illumination and lubrication to products providing propulsion. In 1920 the United States was producing about 65 percent of the world's oil, much of it controlled by the Standard Oil trust. But already Americans were tasting a bitter future, as corporate and government officials warned of fuel shortages and shrinking reserves. Early in 1920 a U.S. Geological Survey report stated that "unless our consumption is checked, we shall by 1925 be dependent on foreign oilfields." In some parts of the country companies limited the amount of gasoline people could buy and doubled the price. But the crisis had a dubious flavor. Just after the shortages and price hikes occurred, the State Department persuaded the British to grant Standard Oil a share in British-controlled Iraqi oilfields. Immediately thereafter, the crisis abated. The incident prompted two British authors to sound a skeptical note in their book *The Oil Trusts and Anglo-American Relations* (1924):

> There is this strange habit peculiar to the American oil industry. . . . Although it doubles its output roughly every ten years, it declares every other year that its peak of production has been passed and that its oilfields are well-nigh exhausted. . . . One

Camping with the auto. The new mobility brought about by the automobile enabled people to travel into the wilderness to enjoy nature—and bring the comforts of home with them. Culver.

cannot doubt that the lugubrious prophecies of American oil men are in some way related to the wish for higher prices.

More than ever, Americans' taste for automobiles and other goods and services was whetted by advertising. By 1929 total advertising expenditures had reached $1.78 billion, nearly as much as was spent on all types of formal education. For many, advertising became the new gospel. In his best-selling *The Man Nobody Knows* (1925), advertising executive Bruce Barton called Jesus "the founder of modern business" because he "picked up twelve men from the bottom ranks of business and forged them into an organization that conquered the world." Barton was not alone. About the same time, a pamphlet titled *Moses, Persuader of Men* declared, "Moses was one of the greatest salesmen and real-estate promoters that ever lived"—demonstrating that advertising could be ecumenical.

Advertising

Although daily newspaper circulation declined during the 1920s, other media assumed vital advertising functions. By 1929 over 10 million families owned radios, which bombarded them almost continuously with advertisements. Station KDKA in Pittsburgh pioneered in commercial radio broadcasting beginning in 1920; by 1922 there were 508 such stations. By 1929 the National Broadcasting Company, which had begun to assemble a network of radio stations three years earlier, was charging advertisers $10,000 to sponsor an hour-long show. Commercial intermissions at movie houses and highway billboards also reminded viewers to buy. Moreover, the products of the new era were designed to sell themselves. Packaging, marketing, and product display became sciences, with the object of creating demand.

Though poor people could not afford many of the new products and services, some of the new trends touched working-class groups, especially those in the cities. Indoor plumbing and electricity became more common in private residences, and canned foods, varied diets, ready-made clothes, and mass-produced shoes became more affordable. With a little cash and credit, almost anyone could purchase an automobile. And even if a family could not afford a radio, a vacuum cleaner, or a vacation in the mountains, there was always hope they would soon be able to. No wonder, then, that spending became a national pastime, and that many people wanted Henry Ford to run for president in 1924.

The business of government, the government of business

In this outburst of materialism, many Americans shed their fear of big business–swayed in part by the testimonials of probusiness propagandists. "Among the nations of the earth today," one writer proclaimed in 1921, "America stands for one idea: *Business* . . . Thru business, properly conceived, managed and conducted, the human race is finally to be redeemed." Government reflected this outlook. As corporations and other organizations became more national in scope, they looked increasingly to the federal government for assistance in integrating the economy. Thus during the 1920s a series of Republican administrations extended Theodore Roosevelt's notion of government-business cooperation–though they often made government a passive coordinator rather than the active director Roosevelt had advocated.

All branches of the federal government supported business interests during these years. In 1921 Congress reduced taxes on corporations and wealthy individuals, and in 1922 it raised tariff rates in the Fordney-McCumber Tariff Act. Presidents Harding, Coolidge, and Hoover appointed strong cabinet officers who pursued policies favorable to business. Regulatory agencies such as the Federal Trade Commission and the Interstate Commerce Commission cooperated with corporations more than they regulated them. And the Supreme Court upheld big business and struck down reform in cases such as *Bailey* v. *Drexel Furniture Company* (1922), which voided restrictions on child labor; and *Adkins* v. *Children's Hospital* (1923), which overturned a minimum wage law for women because it infringed on liberty of contract.

The pursuit of profits and comfort prompted political analysts to lament the death of progressivism. They were partly right; the concern for social and economic justice that had moved the previous generation faded in the 1920s, especially as the image of big business improved. Yet many of the Progressive era's achievements were sustained and consolidated in these years. Although trustbusting fizzled on the federal level, regulatory commissions and other government agencies still monitored business activities and worked to reduce wasteful practices. And in Congress a sizable corps of reformers, led by George Norris of Nebraska and Robert La Follette of Wisconsin, kept progressive causes alive by supporting labor legislation, federal aid to farmers, and continued government operation of a federally constructed hydroelectric dam at Muscle Shoals, Alabama. (Business-oriented politicians wanted to sell or lease the dam and its nitrate plant to private interests.)

Extension of progressive reforms

Most reform, however, occurred at the state and local levels. Following initiatives begun before and during the First World War, thirty-four states instituted or expanded workers' compensation laws in the 1920s. At the same time many states established old-age pensions and other welfare programs. In hundreds of cities and towns, trained social scientists took surveys, gathered data, and drew maps as part of a systematic effort to identify and solve urban problems. Indeed, planning became a common feature of urban government; by 1926 every major city and many smaller ones had planning and zoning commissions that aimed to harness physical growth to the common good. And young men and women continued to work for justice and economic relief as social workers, lawyers, and politicians. Thus during the 1920s the nation's state houses, city halls, and universities trained a new generation of reformers who would eventually influence national affairs during the New Deal government of the 1930s.

Organized labor, which had gained ground during the Progressive era, suffered some setbacks during the 1920s. Public opinion, influenced by prosperity, the new materialism, and probusiness rhetoric, turned against workers who pushed for better wages and disrupted everyday life with strikes. Both the federal government and the Supreme Court frequently stifled union attempts to exercise power during these years.

Early in the decade, for instance, the Justice Department used troops and court injunctions to end strikes by steel, mine, and railroad workers. And Chief Justice William Howard Taft ruled in *Coronado Coal Company* v. *United Mine Workers* (1922) that, contrary to the Clayton Anti-Trust Act of 1912, a striking union could be prosecuted for illegal restraint of trade. Meanwhile, large corporations worked to counteract the appeal of unions by promising workers pensions, profit sharing (which actually amounted to wages withheld for later distribution), and company-sponsored social and sporting events—a policy that became known as *welfare capitalism*. In such a climate, union membership fell from 5.1 million in 1920 to 3.6 million in 1929.

The epitome of the decade's goodwill toward business was President Warren Gamaliel Harding, a Republican elected in 1920 at a time when the populace wanted to avoid national and international crusades. (Woodrow Wilson, ill and out of favor with Democrats, did not win renomination in 1920.) A small-town newspaper publisher and senator from Ohio who enjoyed fellowship with local businessmen, Harding carried his trust of manufacturers and merchants to the White House. Although he appointed several of his cronies to important positions, he selected some capable assistants, notably Secretary of State Charles Evans Hughes, Secretary of Commerce Herbert Hoover, Secretary of the Treasury Andrew Mellon, and Secretary of Agriculture Henry C. Wallace. Mellon, a wealthy industrialist, was particularly active, pushing for tax reductions, centralization and balancing of the federal budget,[1] reduction of the national debt, and higher tariff duties.

Harding administration

Harding's problem was that he had too many friends. His father once reputedly remarked, "Warren, it's a good thing you wasn't born a gal. You'd be in the family way all the time—you can't say no." Harding said yes too often, appointing predatory friends to positions from which they infested government with corruption. Charles Forbes of the Veterans Bureau served time in Leavenworth prison after being convicted of fraud and bribery in connection with government contracts. Thomas W. Miller, alien property custodian, was jailed for accepting bribes. Two other officials, Jess Smith and Charles F. Cramer, committed suicide to escape prosecution. Harding's close friend Attorney General Harry Daugherty was implicated in Smith's scheme of accepting bribes and in other fraudulent acts; he escaped prosecution only by refusing to testify against himself. In the most notorious case of all, a congressional inquiry in 1923 and 1924 revealed that Secretary of the Interior Albert Fall had accepted bribes to lease government property to private oil companies. For his role in the affair, called the Teapot Dome scandal after a Wyoming oil reserve that had been turned over to the Mammouth Oil Company, Fall was fined $100,000 and spent a year in jail. He was the first cabinet officer to be so disgraced.

In June 1923, few Americans knew how corrupt Harding's administration had become. The president, however, had become disillusioned. Amid rumors of mismanagement and crime, he told journalist William Allen White, "My God, this is a hell of a job. I have no trouble with my enemies. . . . But my friends, my God-damned friends . . . they're the ones that keep me walking the floor nights." On a speaking tour of the West that summer, Harding became ill and died in San Francisco on August 2. Though his death preceded the revelation of the Teapot Dome scandal and other charges of corruption, some people later believed that Harding had committed suicide rather than face the brewing storm. Most evidence, however, points to death from natural causes, probably a heart attack. At any rate, Harding was truly mourned. A warm, dignified-looking man who relished a good joke or an evening of poker and drinking, he seemed right for a nation that had just experienced racking upheaval at home and abroad. Only later did people realize, as Harding did, that they had made a mistake.

Harding's successor, Vice President Calvin Coolidge, was far more solemn and certainly less active. In fact, Coolidge usually slept more than half of each day: at least ten hours a night and another two or three in the afternoon. A dour New Englander (Alice Roosevelt Longworth, Theodore's daughter, once quipped that Coolidge looked as if he had been weaned on a pickle), Coolidge had an undistinguished record as Republican governor of Massachusetts. He had first attracted national attention by his firm stand against striking Boston policemen in 1919, a policy that won him the vice-presidential nomination in

[1] Previously Congress had received separate budget requests from each department.

1920. Usually, however, he was content to let events take their course, prompting columnist Walter Lippmann to grumble, "It is a grim, determined, alert inactivity, which keeps Mr. Coolidge occupied constantly."

Coolidge had great respect for private enterprise; he once remarked, "The man who builds a factory builds a temple." Fortunately for him, his administration coincided with extraordinary business prosperity. Aided by Andrew Mellon, whom he retained as secretary of the treasury, and other cabinet officers, he balanced the budget, reduced government debt, lowered income-tax rates (especially for the rich), and began construction of a national highway system. With his generally tightfisted fiscal policies he won business support. Congress took little initiative during these years and assented to most measures recommended by the cabinet and by business associations such as the U.S. Chamber of Commerce. The only disruptions arose over farm policy. Responding to farmers' complaints of falling prices, Congress twice passed bills to establish government-backed price supports for staple crops (the McNary-Haugen bills of 1927 and 1928). But Coolidge vetoed the measure both times.

Coolidge prosperity

"Coolidge prosperity" was the determining issue in the presidential election of 1924. That year both major parties ran candidates who had no quarrel with business supremacy. The Republicans nominated Coolidge with little dissent. At their national convention the Democrats first debated heatedly whether or not to condemn the Ku Klux Klan, finally deciding 543 to 542 against condemnation. Then they endured 103 ballots before breaking a deadlock between southern prohibitionists who favored former Secretary of the Treasury William G. McAdoo and antiprohibition easterners who backed New York's Governor Alfred E. Smith. They finally settled on John W. Davis, a corporation lawyer from New York. Remnants of the progressive movement, along with various farm, labor, and socialist groups, formed a new Progressive party and nominated Robert M. La Follette, the aging reformer from Wisconsin. The new party revived issues unresolved in previous generations: public ownership of utilities; aid to farmers; decreased restraint on organized labor; increased regulation of business.

The election results resembled those of 1912 in reverse: the two probusiness candidates captured most of the votes. Coolidge beat Davis by 15.7 million to 8.4 million popular votes, 382 to 136 electoral votes. Like Taft in 1912, La Follette finished a poor third, receiving a respectable but ineffective 4.8 million popular votes and only 13 electoral votes.

The climate shifted in 1928. This time the Democrats ran Smith; the Republicans, Herbert Hoover (Coolidge declined to run). Both Smith and Hoover were competent men. Hoover had achieved an admirable record as a public administrator, and Smith had supported many social reforms during his governorship. An urbane, gregarious politician of immigrant stock, Smith was the first Roman Catholic to run for president on a major party ticket. As such he had considerable appeal among urban ethnic groups, who were voting in increasing numbers, but he lost the votes of some Protestant southerners and westerners for the same reason. Hoover, who stressed the nation's prosperity, won the popular vote 21 million to 15 million, the electoral vote 444 to 87 (see map, page 680). But Smith's candidacy had important effects on the Democratic party. Smith carried the nation's twelve largest cities, heretofore Republican, and lured millions of foreign-stock voters to the polls for the first time. From 1928 onward the national Democratic party would solidify this urban labor base, which when combined with its traditional strength in the South made the party a formidable new force in national politics.

The new president blended collective effort and individual leadership in a style characteristic of the 1920s. A Quaker from West Branch, Iowa, Hoover was educated at Stanford University. He distinguished himself first as a mining engineer, then as U.S. Food Administrator during the First World War and head of food relief for Europe after the war. But his chief contribution was, as secretary of commerce under Harding and Coolidge, to expand on Theodore Roosevelt's New Nationalism. Recognizing the extent to which large nationwide associations had come to dominate commerce and industry, Hoover mounted a calculated campaign to stimulate cooperation among companies and between business and government. He took every opportunity to make his department a center for the promotion of business, holding conferences, sponsoring studies, and issuing

Hoover administration

Patrons of a speakeasy flout Prohibition in this rare photograph of an illegal saloon. Although a constitutional amendment had outlawed the manufacture and sale of alcoholic beverages, many otherwise respectable and law-abiding citizens willfully broke the law. The Bettmann Archive.

Prohibition Americans became flagrant lawbreakers and supporters of crime. The constitutional amendment and federal law that prohibited the manufacture, sale, and transportation of alcoholic beverages (see pages 581–582) worked well at first. Per-capita consumption of liquor dropped, arrests for drunkenness diminished, and the price of illegal booze rose higher than the average worker could afford. But beyond passing supportive laws, legislators saw little need to enforce Prohibition. In 1922 Congress gave the Prohibition Bureau only three thousand employees and less than $7 million for nationwide enforcement.

Prohibition was partially effective, especially in regions where temperance movements had historically been successful. In fact, some people believe that, had it applied only to hard liquor, not beer or wine, it might have worked more generally. But after about 1925 the noble experiment broke down in the cities, where the desire for personal freedom overwhelmed the weak means of enforcement. The law allowed the manufacture of beer for dilution into near-beer and the sale of alcohol for medicinal and sacramental purposes, but bootleggers cleverly obtained and sold such spirits for other purposes. Smuggling and home manufacture of liquor were rampant. Hundreds of thousands of people made their own wine and bathtub gin, and illegal importation along the country's long borders and shorelines was beyond the reach of the few patrols that attempted to curb it.

Local officials realized it was impractical to devote their scarce resources to strict enforcement of Prohibition. For drinking, like gambling and prostitution, was a business that had willing customers. Police therefore either ignored offenders or took bribes to protect them. Criminal organizations were quick to recognize the possibilities of the situation. The most notorious of such mobs belonged to Al Capone, a burly tough who seized control of illegal liquor and vice organizations in Chicago and parlayed his influence through bribery, intimidation, and violence. With his armed force of gangsters, Capone was able to influence local politics as well as vice operations until 1931, when the federal government convicted and imprisoned him for income-tax evasion.

It is important to recognize that Prohibition and its weak enforcement did not create organized crime. Gangs like Capone's had produced and provided illegal goods and services long before the 1920s. As Capone explained it, "Prohibition is a business. All I do is supply a public demand. I do it in the least harmful way I can." Americans wanted their liquor and their freedom; Capone took advantage of these desires.

Thus during the 1920s Americans were caught between two value systems. On the one hand, the Puritan tradition of hard work, sobriety, and restraint—"waste not, want not"—still prevailed, especially in rural areas where new diversions were unavailable. On the other hand, a liberating age of play beckoned. At no previous time in American history had so many opportunities for recreation presented themselves. Not just mass entertainment such as night clubs, movies, sports, and radio, but personal amusements such as stamp collecting, puzzle working, and playing and listening to music became commonplace. Most of these activities were not illegal or immoral, but many people were increasingly willing to break the law or shun moral tradition if such restrictions interfered with their personal quest for pleasure. As Walter Lippmann wrote in 1931, "The high level of lawlessness is maintained by the fact that Americans desire to do so many things which they also desire to prohibit."

Cultural currents

This tension between value systems pulled artists and intellectuals in new directions. Rejection of old beliefs, particularly in sexual restraint and white Anglo-Saxon superiority, energized an experimental movement in literature, art, and music. Fear that materialism and conformity were being fostered by mass society gave this movement a bitterly critical tinge. Yet critics seldom voiced a radical message; they had no urge to destroy modern society, only to protect the individual from dehumanizing forces.

Literature of alienation

Many of the era's leading literary figures, finding the vulgar materialism of the time hostile to their art, succumbed to disillusionment and became known as the Lost Generation. A number of them, including the novelist Ernest Hemingway and the poets Ezra Pound and T. S. Eliot, moved to Europe. Others, such as the novelists William Faulkner and Sinclair Lewis, remained, but assailed what they saw happening around them. Although the main goals of their writing were innovative forms of expression and the realistic portrayal of emotions, these writers also produced biting social commentary.

The dominant themes of their social criticism were middle- and upper-class materialism and the impersonality of modern society. F. Scott Fitzgerald's *This Side of Paradise* (1920) and *The Great Gatsby* (1925); Lewis's *Babbitt* (1922), *Arrowsmith* (1925), and *Elmer Gantry* (1927); and Eugene O'Neill's plays exposed Americans' overemphasis on money. The powerful antiwar sentiments of John Dos Passos's *Three Soldiers* (1921) and Hemingway's *A Farewell to Arms* (1929) were skillfully interwoven with passionate critiques of the impersonality of modern relationships.

Perhaps the most trenchant social criticism flowed from the pen of H. L. Mencken. A Baltimore newspaperman and founder of the *American Mercury*, Mencken jabbed at prevailing customs and beliefs with stinging cynicism. No group, no individual was too sacred to escape his satire. He jeered at the inane quest for status of the middle-class "booboisie," labeled Woodrow Wilson a "self-bamboozled presbyterian," and scorned political reformers as "saccharine liberals" and "jitney messiahs." A man with a unique flair for language, Mencken could not stomach its misuse. He once charged that President Harding

> writes the worst English I have ever encountered. It reminds me of a string of wet sponges; it reminds me of tattered wash on the line, it reminds me of stale bean soup, of college yells, of dogs barking idiotically through endless nights. . . . It drags itself out of the dark abyss . . . of pish and crawls insanely up to the topmost pinnacle of posh.

A spiritual discontent quite different from that of white writers energized the work of a new generation of young black artists. Largely middle-class and well-educated, these writers represented W. E. B. Du Bois's "Talented Tenth" in background, but their outlook seemed closer to Booker T. Washington's racial self-help (see pages 589–591). They rejected the amalgamation of black and white cultures, exalting the militantly assertive "New Negro," proud of his African heritage. Most of them lived in Harlem, the black neighborhood in upper Manhattan. In this "Negro Mecca" black intellectuals and artists celebrated the development of a modern black culture in what became known as the Harlem Renaissance.

Harlem Renaissance

Harlem in the 1920s fostered an extraordinary number of gifted writers, among them Langston Hughes, who wrote forceful and sometimes humorous poems, stories, and essays; Countee Cullen, a poet with moving lyrical skills; and Claude McKay, whose militant verses sounded a clarion call for rebellion against bigotry. Jean Toomer's novels and poems portrayed black life with passionate realism, and Alain Locke's essays gave early direction to the artistic renaissance. Much of this group's writing addressed issues of identity. For though black intellectuals took pride in African culture, they also realized that black Americans had to assert themselves and come to terms with

Kid Ory's Original Creole Jazz Band. Trombonist Edward "Kid" Ory organized his first band in his native Louisiana, then moved to Los Angeles and Chicago, where he performed New Orleans-style jazz with such noted musicians as King Oliver and Louis Armstrong. Jazz, originated and developed by black artists, became America's most distinctive art form. Schomburg Collection, New York Public Library.

themselves as Americans. Thus Locke urged that the New Negro should "lay aside the status of beneficiary and ward for that of a collaborator and participant in American civilization." Simultaneously, Hughes wrote, "We younger Negro artists who create now intend to express our individual dark-skinned selves without fear or shame. If white people are pleased we are glad. If they are not, it doesn't matter. We know we are beautiful."

Although black authors did not reach many people (Jean Toomer's stirring novel *Cane* sold only five hundred copies when it was first published), black musicians had considerable influence. The Jazz Age, as the decade is sometimes called, owed its name to the music that grew out of black urban culture. Evolving from African and black American folk music, early jazz communicated unrestrained freedom that black people seldom knew in their daily lives. With its emotional rhythms and its emphasis on improvisation, jazz blurred the distinction between composer and performer and created a new intimacy between performer and audience.

Jazz

As blacks moved north from the Mississippi Delta to St. Louis, Kansas City, Chicago, New York, and other cities, they brought jazz with them. By the 1920s dance halls and bars patronized by whites as well as blacks featured jazz, sometimes popularized by white musicians such as Paul Whiteman and Bix Biederbecke. Gifted black performers like trumpeter Louis Armstrong, trombonist Kid Ory, and singer Bessie Smith enjoyed widespread popularity. Phonograph records and radio, better suited than sheet music to the spontaneity of jazz, helped to popularize it. In fact, jazz boosted the growth of the recording industry immensely, and music recorded by black artists and bought by millions of black purchasers (sometimes called race records) gave black Americans a distinctive place in the new consumer culture. More important, jazz endowed America with its most distinctive art form.

In many ways the 1920s were the most creative years the nation had yet experienced. Influenced by jazz and by experimental writing, painters such as Georgia O'Keeffe and John Marin drew on European techniques in an effort to forge a distinctively American style of painting. And although European composers and performers still dominated classical music, Americans such as Henry Cowell, who pioneered electronic music, and the Russian-born Aaron Copland, who built exciting orchestral and vocal works around native folk motifs, began careers that later won wide acclaim. George Gershwin gave popular music increased respectability by blending jazz, classical, and folk musical forms in his serious compositions (*Rhapsody in Blue* and *Concerto in F*), musical dramas (*Porgy and Bess*), and numerous hit tunes. In architecture the skyscraper boom drew worldwide attention, and Frank Lloyd Wright's "prairie style" houses, churches, and schools reflected the magnificence of the American landscape. At the beginning of the decade, essayist Harold Stearns had complained that "the most . . . pathetic fact in the social life of America today is emotional and aesthetic starvation." By 1929 such a contention was hard to support.

Underlying weaknesses

Even in the best of times, running a business was a risky venture. In 1926, perhaps the most prosperous year of the decade, there were 21,883 recorded commercial failures in the United States, 500 more than in 1925 and almost 13,000 more than in 1920. By 1927 the number had increased to 23,146. These figures masked the sad stories of ordinary people whose dreams collapsed with their businesses. An article in the *Saturday Evening Post* poignantly portrayed the aftermath of such failure:

> The business is sold and absorbed by another concern, the residence is occupied by another owner or tenant, the family is soon forgotten even in the social circles where it once moved. Those who were once friends and acquaintances are occupied with their own affairs, new families with plenty of money come to town to attract attention and the ocean of life closes over the wreck with hardly a ripple.

These business failures were but one indication of a softening of the economy in the late twenties. In 1925 and 1926 signs of unhealthiness appeared in the auto and construction industries. After 1926, production and employment in the huge coal-mining industry fell. Labor troubles and declining profits continued to weaken the textile industry. And more than ever, farmers were beset by mounting expenses and slumping returns on their crops. Then in early 1928 construction dipped again and industrial production slowed, triggering a recession that drove unemployment rates to the highest level since 1919.

Several broader problems, less apparent at the time, plagued the nation. First, the scope and complexity of the economy had expanded so greatly after 1900 that market conditions could no longer be stabilized by a few powerful bankers acting in concert. Moreover, bankers continued to allow the amount of money they loaned to exceed the amount they held on deposit, without insurance against loss.

The United States had also become increasingly involved in the international economy as a result of the First World War. To fund their war effort western European countries had piled up huge debts to the United States. But repayment was difficult, because high tariffs kept European merchants out of the American market, slowing European economic recovery. England and France had counted on war reparations from Germany, but when the Germans proved unable to pay the huge sums, the Allies were forced to borrow even more from the United States. By 1929

Important events

1919	Eighteenth Amendment ratified
1920	Nineteenth Amendment ratified Warren G. Harding elected president First commercial radio broadcast
1920–21	Postwar deflation and depression
1921	Federal Highway Act Immigration quotas established Sacco and Vanzetti convicted
1922	Fordney-McCumber Tariff Economic recovery
1923	Harding dies; Coolidge assumes the presidency Peak of Ku Klux Klan activity
1923–24	Exposure of Harding administration scandals
1924	National Origins Act Coolidge elected president; La Follette's third-party movement
1925	Scopes trial
1926	Rudolph Valentino dies
1927	First McNary-Haugen bill vetoed Sacco and Vanzetti executed Charles A. Lindbergh's transatlantic flight Babe Ruth hits sixty home runs *The Jazz Singer*, the first feature movie with sound
1928	Stock market soars Herbert Hoover elected president
1929	Stock market crash

foreign trade and international credit had become so shaky that the slightest financial setback in one country could send tremors through the entire western world.

Finally, a frantic but fragile optimism infected a large segment of the American public. Corporate and private debt ballooned by 66 percent between 1919 and 1929 as more and more people borrowed to feed their acquisitive appetites. Speculation was rampant: people bought and sold frantically in hopes of grabbing quick profits. Occasionally these speculative bubbles burst. The most notable disaster occurred in 1926, when overinvestment and a destructive hurricane halted the mad rush to buy Florida real estate, leaving thousands of people with mortgages on worthless swampland.

Speculation in land and stocks

The stock market vividly reflected this speculative frenzy. Rising corporate profits and dividends drove up stock prices faster and faster after 1924, especially from 1927 through summer 1929. By late 1928 one share of RCA cost $400, the equivalent of several months' income for many people. Unable to pay in full for the stocks they bought, investors borrowed from 50 to 90 percent of the purchase price from brokers who had in turn borrowed from banks and other institutions at increasing rates of interest. By 1929 these loans totaled $6 billion, up from an already staggering $3.5 billion in 1927. The weight of such credit was crushing. The system could stand only as long as stock prices continued to rise; any prolonged fall in prices would cause disaster.

A few people were nervous about the economic outlook. Early in 1928 a banker observed,

> Stocks look dangerously high to me. This bull market has been going on for a long time and although prices have slipped a bit recently, they might easily slip a good deal more. Business is none too good. Of course if you buy the right stock you'll probably be all right in the long run and you may even make a profit. But if I were you I'd wait awhile and see what happens.

Little did the banker know how sound his advice was. For in the next two years the era of expansion and frivolity would end, and the economy would have to be rebuilt from the bottom up.

Suggestions for further reading

Overviews of the 1920s

Frederick Lewis Allen, *Only Yesterday* (1931); John Braeman *et al.*, eds., *Change and Continuity in Twentieth Century America: The 1920s* (1968); Paul A. Carter, *Another Part of the Twenties* (1977); William E. Leuchtenburg, *The Perils of Prosperity* (1958); Robert Lynd and Helen Lynd, *Middletown* (1929); George Soule, *Prosperity Decade* (1947).

Economics and labor

Irving L. Bernstein, *A History of the American Worker, 1920–1933* (1960); Alfred D. Chandler, *Strategy and Structure* (1962); James J. Flink, *The Car Culture* (1975); Jim Potter, *The American Economy Between the Wars* (1974); J. W. Prothro, *The Dollar Decade* (1954); John Rae, *The Road and the Car in American Life* (1971); Leslie Woodcock Tentler, *Wage-Earning Women: Industrial Work and Family Life in the United States, 1900–1930* (1979); Robert Zenger, *Republicans and Labor, 1919–1929* (1969).

Politics and law

David Burner, *Herbert Hoover* (1979); David Burner, *The Politics of Provincialism* (1968); Jerome Clubb and Howard Allen, "The Cities and the Election of 1928," *American Historical Review*, 74 (1969), 1205–1220; Oscar Handlin, *Al Smith and His People* (1958); John D. Hicks, *Republican Ascendancy* (1960); J. Joseph Huthmacher, *Massachusetts People and Politics* (1959); Matthew Josephson and Hannah Josephson, *Al Smith* (1970); Richard Lowitt, *George W. Norris* (1971); Samuel Lubell, *The Future of American Politics* (1952); Donald R. McCoy, *Calvin Coolidge* (1967); Alpheus Mason, *The Supreme Court from Taft to Warren* (1958); R. K. Murray, *The Harding Era* (1969); Andrew Sinclair, *The Available Man* (1965); George Tindall, *The Emergence of the New South* (1967); James Weinstein, *The Decline of Socialism in America, 1912–1925* (1967); Joan Hoff Wilson, *Herbert Hoover: The Forgotten Progressive* (1975).

Social issues

William H. Chafe, *The American Woman: Her Changing Social, Economic, and Political Roles* (1972); David M. Chalmers, *Hooded Americanism: The History of the Ku Klux Klan* (1965); Clarke A. Chambers, *Seedtime for Reform: American Social Service and Social Action, 1918–1933* (1963); E. D. Cronon, *Black Moses: The Story of Marcus Garvey* (1955); David H. Fisher, *Growing Old In America* (1977); Norman F. Furniss, *The Fundamentalist Controversy* (1954); Linda Gordon, *Woman's Body, Woman's Right: A Social History of Birth Control in America* (1976); Joseph R. Gusfield, *Symbolic Crusade* (1963); John Higham, *Strangers in the Land: Patterns of American Nativism* (1955); Kenneth T. Jackson, *The Ku Klux Klan in the City* (1967); Maldwyn A. Jones, *American Immigration* (1960); G. L. Joughin and E. M. Morgan, *The Legacy of Sacco and Vanzetti* (1948); J. Stanley Lemons, *The Woman Citizen: Social Feminism in the 1920s* (1973); William G. McLoughlin, *Modern Revivalism* (1959); Gilbert Osofsky, *Harlem: The Making of a Ghetto* (1965); Andrew Sinclair, *Prohibition: The Era of Excess* (1962); Alan Spear, *Black Chicago* (1967); Theodore Vincent, *Black Power and the Garvey Movement* (1971).

Mass culture

Erik Barbouw, *A Tower of Babel: A History of Broadcasting in the United States to 1933* (1966); Robert Creamer, *Babe* (1974); Kenneth S. Davis, *The Hero, Charles A. Lindbergh* (1959); Arthur Knight, *The Liveliest Art* (1957); Otis Pease, *The Responsibilities of American Advertising* (1958); Randy Roberts, *Jack Dempsey* (1979); Robert Sklar, *Movie-Made America* (1976).

Literature and thought

Robert Crunden, *From Self to Society: Transition in American Thought, 1919–1941* (1972); George H. Douglas, *H. L. Mencken* (1978); Robert Elias, *Entangling Alliances with None: An Essay on the Individual in the American Twenties* (1973); Nathan I. Huggins, *Harlem Renaissance* (1971); Roderick Nash, *The Nervous Generation: American Thought, 1917–1930* (1969); Marvin K. Singleton, *H. L. Mencken and the "American Mercury" Adventure* (1962); Morton G. White, *Social Thought in America: The Revolt Against Formalism* (1937).

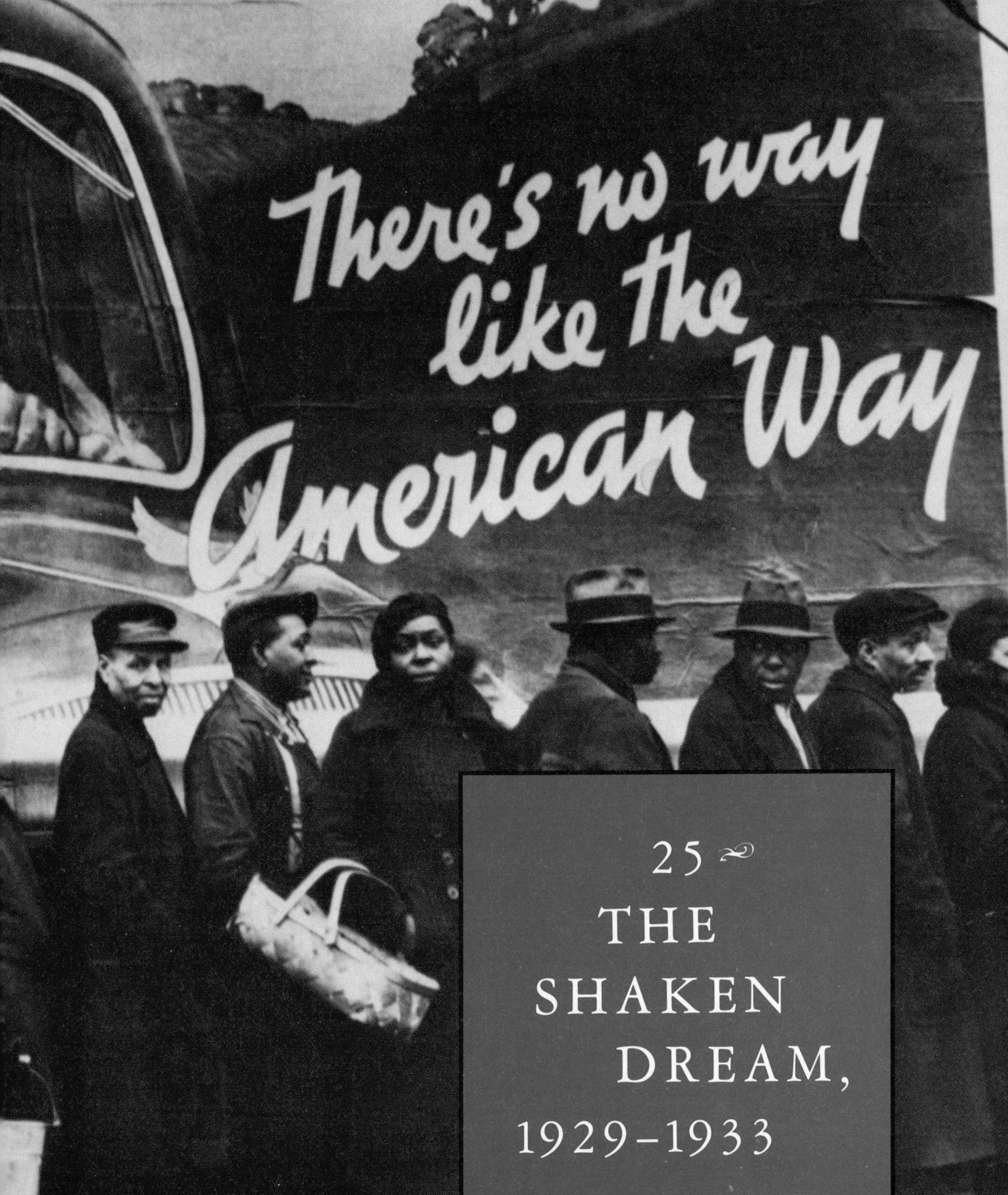

25 THE SHAKEN DREAM, 1929–1933

"Anything wrong wid my work for company?" asked an autoworker of Slavic descent who had just been fired by the Ford Motor Company after fourteen years of employment. No, his work had been good, but cars were not selling. "I haf' no money now . . . lose my home quick, what I do chil'ren, what I do doctor?" When two of his daughters went to work to support the family and their sick mother, he cried, "I ain't man now."

People like John Boris were among the three thousand men and women who gathered on March 7, 1932, for a hunger march to Ford's huge River Rouge plant in Dearborn, just outside Detroit, Michigan. Most of the marchers were former Ford workers like Boris, now unemployed. Dearborn-Detroit authorities nonetheless blamed the march on the Communist party, which had in fact helped to plan the protest and to prepare the list of demands for jobs, food, medical aid, and the right to organize.

At the Dearborn line, the marchers, shivering from the near-zero temperature, were blocked by a phalanx of police. Ordered to disperse because they lacked a parade permit, they refused to retreat. When the police volleyed tear gas, the marchers hurled back rocks and other missiles. The battle then moved toward the number 3 gate of the River Rouge plant, where firefighters hosed down the demonstrators and Ford's stern-faced private police assembled. Suddenly shots rang out, killing two marchers. A policeman shouted, "Get your gats and let them have it," and soon more bullets penetrated the unarmed crowd. By the end of the skirmish, four marchers were dead, more than twenty wounded. Twenty-five police officers had to be treated for wounds from rocks and other objects.

The fundamental source of this trouble was not the Communist party, not the marchers, not the Dearborn police, not Henry Ford himself, but a nationwide disaster called the Great Depression. Detroit was especially hard hit; by fall 1932, 350,000 workers, or about half the city's wage earners, were unemployed. At the River Rouge plant, employment of hourly workers fell from 98,337 to 28,915 during Herbert Hoover's administration (1929–1933). The Ford Hunger March was just one of many desperate cries for relief from the pain of this very human tragedy.

The Great Depression began in 1929 with the stock market crash. Slowly but steadily cascading tremors moved through the economy, and the nation sank from economic downturn to depression. Stunned Americans found it difficult to understand how their mighty economy had failed. Farmers' bins were overflowing, yet everywhere people went hungry. Americans' faith in themselves and in their dream of success had been severely shaken.

The economic catastrophe aggravated old tensions: labor versus capital, white versus black, male versus female. But the nation did not descend into political extremism or violence. Instead, Americans called on their government to help. When President Hoover refused to take strong measures to relieve their hardship, they turned him out of office and elected a new president, Franklin D. Roosevelt. Promising vigorous action and projecting confidence in the nation's ability to reverse the disaster, Roosevelt brought new hope to despairing Americans.

The New Day

There was little sense of impending tragedy in 1928, when 62 percent of Wayne County (Detroit and Dearborn) voters cast their ballots for Republican presidential candidate Herbert Hoover. (In 1932 they would give him only 39 percent.) And in early 1929, when Hoover entered the White House, the byword was optimism. In his inaugural address the president proclaimed a New Day, telling his listeners that the future "is bright with hope." More Americans than ever heard the inaugural address as over a hundred radio stations carried it across the nation.

The new president, known popularly as the Great Engineer, was a proven administrator who promised to bring efficiency to the federal government and harmony to society. He instilled in people confidence that America's economic growth would persist, that the country's problems were manageable. Yet privately Hoover worried that his reputation was being oversold. "They expect the impossible of me and should there arise in the land conditions with which the political machinery is unable to cope, I will be the one to suffer." Hoover's uneasiness also prompted him to sell all his common stock just a few months after taking office because "possible hard times [are] coming."

Hoover's government was a mixture of the old and the new. Sitting in the cabinet, composed largely of businessmen, were six millionaires. Andrew Mellon stayed on as secretary of the treasury. This vastly wealthy man's aluminum monopoly, petroleum and banking interests, and prized art collection marked him as one of the most successful practitioners of the American success story. With his icy and aloof personality and his heartlessness toward human suffering, Mellon contrasted sharply with Hoover, who had earned distinction for his efforts to bring relief to the destitute during the First World War. On the whole, Hoover's appointees to high office were, like Mellon, smug devotees of the existing order, champions of a capitalist utopia. Innovation was not expected from them. In the lower ranks, on the other hand, Hoover brought in the New Patriots, mostly young professionals who agreed with the president that scientific methods could be applied to government to solve its problems. The New Patriots emphasized modernization of operations, collection of data, and rational decision making. In time, Hoover and his experts believed, they could establish a stable social order based on cooperation between government and various civic groups.

Hoover administration

Herbert Hoover (1874–1964), the wealthy mining engineer and businessman who gained a reputation for brilliance and compassion as head of a relief program during the First World War—and lost it when as president he faced the Great Depression. Photographed after Hoover's single term as president. Dr. Erich Salomon, Magnum.

If Hoover and his advisers were optimistic about the future, so were most average Americans. To them American achievements seemed boundless. The new era of the 1920s had given birth to such exciting gadgets as radios and refrigerators; at the movie theaters the new "talkies" amazed viewers with their magical sound. Americans owned no fewer than 23 million automobiles, roughly three-quarters of the world's total. Conquests of new frontiers seemed inevitable, and promoters strove to outdo each other in grandiose displays. As businesspeople in Chicago laid plans for the World's Fair, a huge celebration of material progress, Al Smith and Democratic party Chairman John J. Raskob were organizing a company to build the tallest structure in the world, the Empire State Building. When this monument to the new era was completed, it stood 102 stories high on fashionable Fifth Avenue in New York and had through accidents cost the lives of forty-eight workers. Yet many of its offices were vacant in 1931 when Hoover pushed the button that turned on the building's innumerable lights—sad evidence that dreams could be undermined by economic reality. After walking its marbled hallways, critic Edmund Wilson remarked that it was tragic that the regal building "is advertised now as a triumph in the hour when the planless competitive society, the dehumanized urban community, of which it makes the culmination, is bankrupt."

Business optimism

Still, in the days before the Great Depression sapped the national spirit, reverence for what Hoover called "the American system" ran high. The belief that individuals were responsible for their own condition, that unemployment or poverty suggested personal failing, was widespread. "It is as if we set a race," said Hoover. The individual, seizing the ever-present opportunity, had to demonstrate will power and ambition in the face of competition. The government provided the competitors with an equal start through public education and served as referee to ensure fairness. The winners were the people with the best training, ability, and character.

Prevailing thought also held that changes in the

The photographer Lewis Hine (1874–1940) titled this picture *Icarus,* a reference to the mythological character who died trying to fly on wings made of wax and feathers. This daredevil clings to a cable at the construction site of the Empire State Building, the tallest building in the world when it was completed in 1931. Like Icarus, many a worker fell to his death during the construction of the spectacular landmark. International Museum of Photography, George Eastman House.

business cycle were natural and therefore not to be tampered with. Depressions were to be weathered stoically until the economy inevitably wound its way back to prosperity. As for the government, its job was limited: to ensure equal opportunity and to stimulate the economy through judicious advice and public works projects. "The spread of government," concluded Hoover, "destroys initiative and thus destroys character." He implored people to regulate themselves, to join voluntary associations (such as farm cooperatives and private charities) to right wrongs, but not to expect the federal government to bail them out of their difficulties.

Much of this thinking was, of course, shallow, self-serving, or utopian. Businesspeople had often tinkered with the system out of self-interest. Government had long played favorites or neglected to blow the referee's whistle. Equal opportunity was denied to Americans who were nonwhite or female; educational programs were segregated and unequal. Finally, income and wealth were maldistributed. In 1929 experts estimated that about 60 percent of America's families lived on or below subsistence level ($2,000 a year), despite a 29 percent increase in the number of employed married women over the decade. Nor did workers enjoy fringe benefits such as medical insurance and paid vacations. The Federal Trade Commission reported that 1 percent of the American people owned 59 percent of the country's wealth; 87 percent owned only 10 percent. Over 21 million families had no savings whatsoever. Hoover himself knew that not all was well. "The only trouble with capitalism is capitalists," he complained. "They're too damned greedy." Hoover's ideal capitalist was one who tempered his self-interest to advance the general welfare, who cooperated with others to build a progressive, nonexploitative society. He later admitted that most businesspeople did not approach this ideal.

Distribution of wealth

In the business community, a few firms dominated each industry, squeezing out smaller companies. In 1929 the top two hundred nonfinancial corporations controlled 49 percent of corporate wealth. Using the holding company as a consolidating device, some businesspeople constructed overextended empires. Samuel Insull of Chicago built a utilities network that produced one-eighth of America's electrical power and operated in thirty-nine states. In steel, automobiles, and oil, giant corporations ruled. Even circuses had been consolidated, by John Ringling.

If businesses were well-organized, American workers and farmers were not. Although farmers who owned property had a political voice in the farm bloc and the American Farm Bureau Federation, at least one-third of the nation's farmers were tenants or sharecroppers—dependent, propertyless, unorganized. Nor were unions for everyone. By 1929 only 10 percent of the nonagricultural work force of 30 million was unionized; during the 1920s the membership of the American Federation of Labor had actually decreased by half. Lower wages for women and minorities, the stretch-out (more work for the same pay), harassment of unions, safety hazards, and automation all plagued workers. In Waterbury, Connecticut, clock makers risked death from radium poisoning. In Hartford and New Haven in 1929, the installation of more efficient machinery threw 1,190 rubber workers out of their jobs. And 35,000 orchestra musicians were unemployed in mid-1929 because "machine music" had been installed in the nation's theaters.

Labor disputes in the South bespoke discontent. In Elizabethton, Tennessee, where 40 percent of the rayon mill workers were young women working for 16 to 18 cents an hour, fifty-six hours a week, laborers struck spontaneously for better wages in March 1929. The state militia came in to break the strike, and employees who had joined the United Textile Workers found themselves blacklisted. By 1931, wrote one observer, what remained were a "few hundred unemployed ex-strikers, half-starved and disillusioned, cynical and justly bitter." Just a few months before the strike erupted, Hoover had addressed a large crowd in Elizabethton, extolling the progress of southern industry and its "great reserve of labor."

Elizabethton textile strike

On the eve of the Great Depression, then, America seemed tangled in contradictions: optimism and pessimism; prosperity and hardship; individualism and mass culture; competition and cooperation; progress and deterioration; opportunity and inequality; strength and weakness. But the shortcomings of American life received far less attention than the dramatic accomplishments of the New Era. Then came the Great Depression to deflate the boom mentality, expose infirmities, prompt reanalysis, and redefine the role of the federal government.

The great crash and the Great Depression

The gloom and economic woe that people in mining towns, textile mills, and agricultural communities suffered at the end of the 1920s hardly penetrated the elegant offices of Wall Street. There, all seemed magical; glamour stocks such as General Electric, International Harvester, and Radio Corporation of America soared in value. The bull market attracted millions of buyers, many of whom joined the speculative binge by buying their shares on margin (paying only a portion of the cost in cash and borrowing the rest) or investing their savings. By October 1929 brokers' loans

Reginald Marsh's sketch captured the more-than-usually hectic, noisy, and intense activity of the New York Stock Exchange on the day of the Great Crash. Library of Congress.

to stock purchasers amounted to a staggering $8.5 billion. John J. Raskob, a member of General Motors' board of directors as well as chairman of the Democratic party, was so enthusiastic about the boom that he proclaimed that "anyone not only can be rich, but ought to be rich" by speculating in the stock market.

The get-rich-quick mentality was jolted in September and early October when stock prices dropped. Analysts attributed the dip to "shaking out the lunatic fringe." But on October 24, Black Thursday, a record number of shares was traded; many stocks sold at low prices, and some could find no takers. Stunned crowds gathered outside the frantic New York Stock Exchange, buzzing about the apparent seriousness of the decline. At noon, banking leaders met at the headquarters of J. P. Morgan and Company to halt the skid and restore confidence. They put up $20 million, told everybody about it, and ceremoniously began by buying ten thousand shares of United States Steel. The mood changed and some stocks rallied. The bankers, it seemed, had preserved the dream of success.

Black Thursday

But the nation gradually succumbed to panic. News of Black Thursday spread across the country, and trouble ("sell!") ricocheted back to New York via telephone. Another bolt struck on Black Tuesday (October 29) when stock prices plunged again. The market settled into a grim pattern of declines and weak rallies. Hoover, who had never approved of what he called the "fever of speculation," assured Americans that the economy was sound. He shared the popular assumption that the stock market's ills could be quarantined from the general economy, which was considered basically healthy. Businesspeople, schooled in the credo of progress, comforted themselves with the thought that the stock market would soon right itself. Although their boosterism seems terribly misguided or deceptive today, it was sincerely, if blindly, believed. Anyway, said the secretary of labor, "one doesn't improve the condition of a sick man by constantly telling him how ill he is."

The crash ultimately helped to unleash a devastating depression that drained the nation and its people of their vitality and self-assurance. The economic downturn did not come suddenly; it was more like a leak in a punctured tire than a blowout. Of the several interrelated causes of the Great Depression, one of the most important was the increasing weakness of the economy throughout the 1920s. Had the economy of the new era been strong, it would have stood a better chance of weathering the crash on Wall Street. In fact, some historians suggest that the stock market collapse merely moved an ongoing recession into depression. Throughout the 1920s the agricultural sector was plagued with overproduction, declining prices for farm products, mounting debts, bankruptcies, and small bank failures. Some industries, like coal, railroads, and textiles, were in distress long before 1929, and two mainstays of economic growth, autos and construction, also declined early. What all these weaknesses meant by 1929 was that major sectors of the economy were not expanding; businesspeople were not investing funds to build new plants, hire more workers, and produce more goods. Indeed, the opposite was true: unsold inventories were stacking up in warehouses, investments were shrinking, laborers were being sent home, and consumer purchases were dropping off.

The depression derived, secondly, from pell-mell, largely unregulated speculation on the stock market. Corporations and banks invested large sums in stocks; some speculated in their own issues. Brokers sold stocks to buyers who put up little cash, borrowed in order to purchase, and then used the stocks they bought as collateral for their loans. When the stocks came tumbling down, so did brokers, bankers, and companies. Brokers called up buyers to ask for more cash. Some buyers drained their savings from banks, but when others could not come up with the money, the brokers sold the stock for the little it would command. Bankers, meanwhile, were calling up brokers and other speculators, searching for cash. The domino effect was crushing, and the whole economic system tottered as obligations went unmet. From 1930 to 1933 stock-market losses climbed to $85 billion. A new byword circulated: "Trust God, not stocks."

Third, both the onset and the severity of the depression can be attributed to underconsumption. That is, production (supply) had outstripped consumption (demand). Wages and mass purchasing power had lagged behind the industrial surge of the 1920s; the workers who produced the new consumer products ultimately could not afford to buy them. Why did purchasing decline? Laborers and farmers constituted the great majority of consumers. Yet, as we have seen, farmers suffered economic distress and had to trim their purchases. And as industries like coal, autos, and construction declined, they laid off men and women who then lacked the money to sustain buying. Other laborers lost their jobs because machines displaced them. There was, in short, a sizable nonconsuming group.

Underconsumption

Another important aspect of underconsumption was the unequal distribution of income. In the twenties the rich got much richer while others made only modest gains. Average per-capita disposable income (income after taxes) rose about 9 percent from 1920 to 1929, but the income of the wealthiest 1 percent rose 75 percent. By 1929 the top 10 percent received about 40 percent of the nation's disposable income. Income and wealth, in other words, were concentrated at the top of America's economic ladder. Why did this uneven distribution contribute to underconsumption and depression? Because much of the accumulating income was put into luxuries, savings, investments, and stock-market speculation instead of being spent on consumer goods. Put another way, more money in the hands of workers and farmers and less money building up in the vaults of the wealthy would probably have meant more consumption and hence more stable economic growth.

Fourth, the American business system was shaky, for a few large corporations in each industry–oligopolies–unbalanced it. The old cliché "The bigger they are, the harder they fall" was literally true. Not only did these companies speculate dangerously on the stock market; they built pyramid-like businesses based on shady, if legal, manipulation of assets through holding companies. If one part of the edifice collapsed, the entire structure crumbled. Such was the case with Samuel Insull's mighty electrical empire, wherein one company held the stock of another company, which held the stock of another company, and so on. Sometimes Insull's various companies bought stock from one another, each showing an artificially high profit from the transactions. Even Insull admitted that he was not sure how it all worked; his sixty-five chairmanships, eighty-five directorships, and seven presidencies confused him as much as anybody else. When his vast interlocking network collapsed in 1932, he fled to Europe to escape arrest for fraud. Found in Turkey, he returned to the United States, hired advertising agencies to improve his public image, and in 1934 was acquitted.

A fifth explanation for the deepening effects of the economic crisis is international in scope. As the world's leading creditor and trader, the United States was deeply involved with the world economy. Billions of dollars in loans had flowed to Europe during the First World War and then during postwar reconstruction. Yet in the late 1920s American investors were beginning to keep their money at home, to invest it in the more exciting and lucrative stock market. Europeans, unable to borrow more funds and unable to sell their goods easily in the American market because of high tariffs, began to buy less from America and to default on their debts. Pinched at home, they raised their own tariffs, further crippling international commerce, and withdrew their investments from America. It was Hoover's view that "the European disease had contaminated the United States." He would have been more accurate had he said that the European and American illnesses were mutually infectious.

International economic troubles

Finally, government policies and practices contributed to the crash and depression. The federal government failed to regulate the wild speculation, contenting itself with occasional scoldings of bankers and businesspeople. It neither checked corporate power nor raised income taxes to encourage a more equitable distribution of income. Indeed, it lowered taxes, thus promoting the uneven distribution. And the Federal Reserve Board pursued easy-credit policies, charging low discount rates, or interest rates, on its loans to member banks, even though it knew the easy money was paying for the speculative binge. The "Fed" blundered again after the crash, in 1931. This time the board drastically raised the rate, tightening the money market at a time when just the opposite was needed: loosening to spur borrowing and spending.

Today, in an era of computerized data, daily economic forecasts, special presidential advisers, and the watchdog Council of Economic Advisers (see page 844), it is difficult to recall that in 1929 the state of economic analysis and statistics-gathering was comparatively primitive. The several explanations for the onset of depression were not easily grasped in 1929, especially while people were absorbed in a headlong rush to make as much money as possible as fast as possible. And the conventional wisdom, based on the experience of previous depressions, was that little could be done to correct economic problems. So in 1929 people waited for the deflation to bottom out.

Despairing Americans

As the economy limped into the 1930s, statistics began to tell the story of a national tragedy. Between 1929 and 1933 a hundred thousand businesses failed; corporate profits fell from $10 billion to $1 billion; and the gross national product was cut in half. But what happened to America's banks–and savings–illustrates especially well the cascading nature of the Great Depression. Banks tied into the stock market or foreign investments were badly weakened; some failed. When nervous Americans made runs on banks to salvage their threatened savings, a powerful momentum–panic–took command. In 1929, 659 banks folded; in 1930 the number of failures climbed to 1,350. The next year proved worse, 2,293 banks shutting their doors, and another 1,453 ceased to do business in 1932. By 1933 9 million savings accounts had been lost, amounting to $2.5 billion in losses for stockholders and depositors. Americans who believed that saving was a virtue, a path to material fulfillment, found themselves standing in breadlines with confirmed hobos who had long before rejected the philosophy of success. And hundreds of thousands of schoolchildren who had been encouraged to practice thrift through savings projects discovered that their deposits had disappeared with the banks.

The impact of the depression on individual Americans was not sudden, but gradual. Although most people remained employed, day after day thousands of men and women received severance slips. At the beginning of 1930 the number of jobless had reached at least 4 million; by November it had jumped to 6 million. When President Hoover left office in 1933, about one-fourth of the labor force was idle–13 million workers–and millions more were underemployed, working only part-time. Hoover asked businesspeople not to cut wages. Hourly wages did hold steady for a while, but weekly earnings began to drop off as hours were trimmed back. Then hourly wages were reduced in industry after industry. Overall, labor income dropped by 40 percent during Hoover's presidency. Half the workers in Cleveland went off payrolls; in Lowell, Massachusetts, two-thirds of the labor force was unemployed.

Blacks, women, and the unskilled lost their jobs first; whites and managerial personnel were let go last.

Men wait somberly outside a state unemployment office in San Francisco. Photographed by Dorothea Lange, whose pictorial record of the depression era became an artistic and journalistic classic. Franklin D. Roosevelt Library.

Discriminatory practices based on race and gender were accentuated. Whites displaced many blacks as servants, and Atlanta fired its black sanitation workers to replace them with whites. In the Southwest, signs went up: "No Niggers, Mexicans, or Dogs Allowed."

Female unemployment

Just as blacks and other racial minorities suffered more than whites during the depression, so too women suffered more than men, at least in the labor market. The popular assumption was that women were supposed to be wives and mothers and men breadwinners. Conventional thinking also had it that women who worked were doing so for pinmoney to buy frivolous things. The evidence was, however, that many of the 10 million women who worked (about 22 percent of all workers in 1930) were self-supporting or were keeping their families from slipping into poverty. In fact, because of the depression married women entered the labor force in greater numbers only to encounter growing discrimination on the grounds that they were displacing male heads of households. As one Chicago civic group declared, women "are holding jobs that rightfully belong to the God-intended providers of the household." Some states passed laws forbidding the hiring of married women for civil service positions. Of the 1,500 city school systems surveyed by the National Education Association in 1930 and 1931, 77 percent refused to hire married women as teachers and 63 percent fired female teachers who married while employed.

How could a nation of such abundance and high production, with its factories intact and its workers eager to work, find itself saddled with such utter hardship and human disaster? men and women asked

These makeshift shacks sprang up along New York's East River, between Ninth and Tenth streets, to house the homeless of the depression. "Hooverville" was the disparaging name given to these communities of the unemployed throughout the nation. Culver.

themselves. It was difficult for Americans raised on the philosophy of hard work and self-help to understand the contradiction of poverty amidst plenty. "Why," asked one man, "must they wear shabby clothes? Because we have too much cotton, too much wool, too many mills, and too many hands." Humorist Will Rogers quipped, "We are the first nation in the history of the world to go to the poorhouse in an automobile."

Actually people were putting their cars up on blocks, using other means to search for work in an economic system in which jobs were disappearing daily. In Detroit auto workers roamed from plant to plant, only to discover padlocked gates. "A worker's got no right to have kids any more," cried one. Western apple growers sent their surplus to the cities, where a new class of street-corner entrepreneurs peddled the fruit at five cents each. A reporter portrayed a New York City unemployment office: "The room is almost silent. A slight, despairing hum from the job seekers. Patient, stretched on the rack of a social system that compels this degradation, they stand quite mute. The suspense is painful." A Minneapolis woman described her futile daily vigil at the city unemployment department: "So we sit in this room like cattle waiting for a nonexistent job, willing to work to the farthest atom of energy, unable to work, unable to get food and lodging, unable to bear children. Here we must sit in this shame looking at the floor, worse than beasts at a slaughter."

People's diets deteriorated, malnutrition became common, and the undernourished fell victim more easily to disease. Some people quietly lined up at Red Cross and Salvation Army soup kitchens or queued in breadlines. Others ate only potatoes, crackers, or dandelions, stole dog biscuits from the local dog pound, or scratched through garbage cans for bits of food. Milk consumption decreased to such an extent that Kentucky miners called it medicine and pregnant

Deterioration of public health

women went without essential foods like eggs and vegetables. Because of inadequate diets doctors witnessed an increase in tuberculosis, typhoid, dysentery, and heart and stomach disorders. Lillian Wald of the Henry Street Settlement House in New York City saw semistarved parents trembling uncontrollably: what food they had they had given to their children. In that city in 1932, hospitals reported 95 deaths from starvation. The nation's suicide rate also climbed, though the overall death rate continued its long-term trend downward.

Millions of Americans were not only hungry and ill; they were cold. Unable to afford fuel, some huddled in unheated tenements and shacks. Families doubled up in crowded apartments, but some who were unable to pay the rent were evicted, furniture and all. Urban jungles sprouted up, constructed from packing boxes and other debris usually carted away as junk. Several hundred women took to sleeping in Chicago's Lincoln and Grant parks; in Oakland, California, hundreds of people lived in the leftover concrete waste ducts of Sewer-Pipe City.

In the countryside, hobbled long before the depression struck, economic hardship deepened. Between 1929 and 1933 farm income was cut in half. Though farm prices dropped 60 percent, production decreased only 6 percent as individual farmers struggled to make up for lower prices by producing more, thereby creating an excess. And the surplus that so depressed agricultural prices could not be exported, since foreign demand had shrunk. Drought, foreclosure, clouds of hungry grasshoppers, and bank failures further plagued the American farmer. A Missouri man who could not pay his taxes or his mortgage, nor afford to truck his corn and barley to market, appealed for help: "I have no horses, no car am 73 yrs old, born on this farm but don't seem like I can hold it much longer." On southern cotton plantations, black sharecroppers barely subsisted on an income of less than $300 a year; whites fared little better with $400. Destitute on reservations, Indians received flour from the Red Cross and surplus clothing from the Department of War. When the federal government increased the Indian Bureau's budget by millions, much of the money went to raise the salaries of white employees and to hire more bureaucrats. The sad reality was that Indians received considerable supervision but inadequate supplies.

Plight of the farmers

Going West–1933, painted by Robinson Boardman. This stark rendering of anxious migrants searching for work and a happier life is typical of depression-era art. National Museum of American Art, Smithsonian Institution, Washington, D.C.

Some Americans became transients in search of jobs or food. Desperate tenant farmers–husbands, wives, and children–walked the roads of the South. The California Unemployment Commission reported in 1932 that an "army of homeless" had trooped into the state and moved constantly from place to place, forced by one town after another to move on. Hundreds of thousands jumped aboard freight trains–"rode the rods"–or hitchhiked. Some boys and girls wandered on their own, living in hobo jungles usually populated by adults. Congressman Maury Maverick of Texas, who wanted to find out for himself what it was like, was stunned by his hobo tour: "There was promiscuity, filth, degradation. . . . Men and families slept in jails, hot railroad urinals, cellars, dugouts, tumbledown shacks." Routes south were the most popular, for there the weather was less cruel. During these years many Mexicans and Mexican-Americans moved south of the border, sometimes willingly, sometimes deported by immigration officials or threatened or forced out by California officials eager to purge them from the relief rolls. As an inducement, the government offered free one-way train tickets to Mexico. Perhaps as many as a quarter-million Chicanos left, largely from Texas, California, Indiana, and Illinois.

Economic woe and geographical displacement strained marriage and family life. People postponed marriage, and married couples postponed having children. Demographers estimate that 800,000 marriages that would normally have occurred in the years 1930 through 1933 did not occur because of the depression. As family incomes dropped, birth control became more common and the birth rate fell. Divorces also declined, from 206,000 in 1929 to 164,000 in 1932. Couples may not have been able to afford a divorce, or they may have decided they could face hardship better by sticking together. They made other adjustments, too. Maybe they moved to a less expensive house or apartment; maybe they sold the car or sacrificed the telephone; maybe their sons and daughters were denied a college education; maybe they did without new clothes.

Strains on marriage and the family

With less opportunity for outside recreation, family members were forced to spend more time together. This enforced closeness did not cause difficulty for happy, well-integrated, and stable families, but it did create unpleasantness and disorder in families suffering unemployment and crowded living quarters. Out-of-work fathers felt ashamed, resenting their diminished role. "A child who was playing irritated him," recalled the son of an unemployed Waterloo, Iowa, tool-and-die maker. "It wasn't just my own father. They all got shook up." The self-esteem of fathers and husbands was further undermined by a reversal of sex roles. Especially when women took jobs to support the family, the shift in authority from husband to wife was noticeable. Other women made all their children's clothing and canned vegetables and fruits, becoming in essence the family's provider.

Some men and women tried to massage their despair with humor. Even the president asked comedians to tell jokes to lighten people's burdens. Hoover himself bore the brunt of much of the comedy. "What? You say business is better? You mean Hoover died?" Jackrabbits shot by hungry farmers were "Hoover hogs"; makeshift shanty towns in vacant urban lots were "Hoovervilles"; newspapers were "Hoover blankets"; and empty pockets turned inside out were "Hoover flags." Even homerun-hitter Babe Ruth got into the act. When he was negotiating his salary for 1930 ($80,000) with the New York Yankees, the Babe was criticized for asking for more money than the president of the United States made. He is said to have shot back: "What the hell has Hoover got to do with it? Besides, I had a better year than he did." Eddie Cantor drew laughs when he imitated a hotel clerk asking a stockbroker whether he wanted a room for sleeping or jumping. Others joked about two men who had jumped to their deaths hand in hand because they had a joint account.

Although a third of the nation's movie theaters shut down in the early years of the depression, an average of 60 million Americans a year still paid to see Hollywood's latest offerings. Movies were a form of escape from economic troubles. One studio put it this way: "There's a Paramount Picture probably around the corner. See it and you'll be out of yourself, living someone else's life." The "someone elses" included gangsters (played by Edward G. Robinson and James Cagney) whose lives were success stories in a disordered society, and comedians like the horseplaying Marx brothers, who in *Animal Crackers* (1930) and *Duck Soup* (1933) poked fun at convention. Seductive Mae West, who demonstrated that woman could be the hunter as well as the hunted, and whose line "Come up and see me sometime" became a legend, rose to stardom. And the role of the "fallen woman" who offered sex for personal survival (played by Tallulah Bankhead and Marlene Dietrich) became popular. There were also musicals like the popular *Gold Diggers* (1933) and horror films like *Dracula* (1932) and *Frankenstein* (1932). And then there was the giant monster in *King Kong* (1933) who scaled the Empire State Building and smashed his way through New York City. King Kong, wrote historian Robert Sklar, "may have given the audiences precisely the proper combination of fear for the survival of their society and pleasure at seeing someone, if only a doomed gorilla, vent his rage at it."

Movies as an escape from hardship

The tempered protest

Most Americans met the new crisis not with violence, protest, or political extremism, but with bewilderment and an inability to fix the blame. They scorned businesspeople, of course, but often they blamed themselves as well, as the traditional ideology of the self-made man had taught them to do. There were some grocery-store robberies, an increase in homicides, a few nasty strikes and protest marches, and flirtations with radicalism on the left and right, but they were usually scattered, unconnected, and spontaneous. Nothing like the extreme political convulsions that rocked Europe hit the United States, where Americans patiently waited for the presidential election of 1932 to effect political change. The mass of people simply shunned revolt against the system that had long promised them a bright future. Their few protests sought immediate relief—jobs, food, housing—not long-term radical social change. In the words of a popular song:

I don't want your millions, mister,
I don't want your diamond ring.
All I want is the right to live, mister;
Give me back my job again.
I don't want your Rolls-Royce, mister,
I don't want your pleasure yacht.
All I want is food for my babies;
Give me my old job back.[1]

Instead, despair, sullenness, demoralization, and shock cut deeply into the American psyche. When novelist Sherwood Anderson picked up hitchhikers along the road, he found many of them to be apologetic about their plight. A psychiatrist describing unemployed miners wrote, "They hung around street corners and in groups. They gave each other solace. They were loath to go home because they were indicted, as if it were their fault for being jobless. A jobless man was a lazy good-for-nothing. . . . They felt despised, they were ashamed of themselves." This was the stuff not of revolution, but of self-hatred and melancholy. Robert Hutchins, president of the University of Chicago, thought about the reasons for the temperate response to catastrophe: "How could there be a revolt against a system in which everybody believed, including those who were starving to death because of it?"

[1] From "I Don't Want Your Millions Mister" by Jim Garland. © Copyright 1947 by Stormking Music, Inc. All Rights Reserved. Used by permission.

Scattered protests did, however, raise the specter of popular revolt. In Iowa's Cow War of 1931, angry farmers assailed state tuberculin inspectors who condemned diseased cattle but gave farmers little compensation for their losses. Soon the National Guard was escorting veterinarians on their rounds, arresting uncooperative farmers. In Nebraska, Iowa, and Minnesota, farmers protesting low prices put up barricades, stopped trucks, and dumped milk and vegetables on the road. Some of these demonstrations were organized by the Farmers' Holiday Association. Its leader, Milo Reno, argued that the propertied farmer was the backbone of society and the economy; lift up the farmer and the nation would be lifted out of depression, he reasoned. Reno encouraged farmers to take a holiday—to keep their products off the market until they commanded a better price. The Sioux City milk strike in the summer of 1932 was the association's most dramatic effort, but like others it failed to alter significantly the terrible economic position of farmers. The following year a Wisconsin dairy farmers' strike ended unsuccessfully after National Guardsmen tossed tear gas and charged with fixed bayonets into a crowd of rock-throwing farmers.

Farmers' Holiday Association

Like their forebears in Shays' Rebellion (1786), farmers were more effective in slowing foreclosures on farm properties. By harassing sheriffs, judges, and lawyers, they sometimes prevented evictions; and they conspired at auctions to bid very low on foreclosed land and then turned over the property to its relieved former owners. Their protests contributed to the passage of state laws that inhibited foreclosure.

Isolated protests also occurred in cities and in mining regions. In Chicago, Los Angeles, and Philadelphia, the unemployed marched on city halls. Chicago schoolteachers, protesting drastic budget cuts, pulled down the 1933 World's Fair flag and stormed city hall. And Harlan County, Kentucky, miners struck against wage reductions (1931). Mine owners

Striking farmers dump milk from a nonstriker's truck, Milwaukee, 1933. Such wastefulness shocked Americans, who could not understand why the poor went hungry while the nation overproduced. UPI.

responded with strikebreakers, bombs, the National Guard, the closing of relief kitchens, and eviction. "The law," grumbled one woman, "is a gun thug in a big automobile." Though Theodore Dreiser, Lincoln Steffens, and other socially conscious writers traveled to the poor Kentucky county to draw national attention to the struggle, the strike failed nonetheless.

The most spectacular confrontation shook Washington, D.C., in summer 1932. Congress was considering a bill authorizing immediate issuance of bonuses already allotted to First World War veterans, but not due for payment until 1945. To lobby for the bill, fifteen thousand unemployed veterans and their families converged on the tense nation's capital, calling themselves the Bonus Expeditionary Force (BEF). They camped in crude shacks on vacant lots and in empty government buildings. Blacks mingled with whites; Jim Crow was "absent with leave," said Roy Wilkins of the National Association for the Advancement of Colored People.

Bonus Expeditionary Force

Though President Hoover threw his weight against the bonus bill, the House passed it. The showdown came in the Senate, which voted no after much debate. One BEF member shouted: "We were heroes in 1917, but we're bums today." Many of the bonus marchers then left Washington, but several thousand stayed on. Hoover grew impatient, carelessly labeled them "insurrectionists" and Communists, and refused to meet with them.

In July General Douglas MacArthur, assisted by Majors Dwight D. Eisenhower and George S. Patton, met the veterans and their families with cavalry, tanks, and bayonet-bearing soldiers. The BEF hurled back stones and bricks. What followed shocked the nation. Men and women were chased down by horsemen; children were teargassed; shacks were set afire. As smoke wafted above the capital's stately buildings, a United Press correspondent commented on the ugly scene, "So all the misery and suffering had finally come to this–soldiers marching with their guns against American citizens." Although one might argue whether ex-servicemen deserved special legislative favor, there can be no question that the answer to their predicament was not violence but food. Hoover's image as a humanitarian was badly tarnished, even though he thought MacArthur had gone too far in using force. When presidential hopeful Franklin D. Roosevelt heard about the government's violent attack on the Bonus Army, he turned to his friend and adviser Felix Frankfurter and said: "Well, Felix, this will elect me."

With capitalism on its knees, American Communist leaders anticipated large gains for their party, if not a proletarian revolution. Across the nation they organized "unemployed councils" to arouse class consciousness and agitate for jobs and food. In March 1930 they conducted urban demonstrations, some of which ended in violent clashes with local police. And with the slogan "Fight–Don't Starve," they led a hunger march on Washington, D.C., in 1931.

Communist protests

Their tangles with authority publicized the real human tragedy of the depression.

Still, the Communist party made little headway with either workers or farmers–whether in Harlan County, in New York City, in Washington, D.C., in Dearborn, or in Sioux City. And its special efforts to recruit dispossessed blacks also ended in failure. Ordinary Americans, journalist Gerald Johnson commented, "have no more idea of turning communistic than they have of turning Mohammedan." At first some intellectuals, including many who had returned from so-called exile abroad, sympathized with the party, seeing it as a vehicle for social change, economic planning, and antifascism. Theodore Dreiser, Lincoln Steffens, Jack Conroy, John Dos Passos, and Erskine Caldwell, among others, were attracted by the Communists' frank radicalism. But many of these writers became disenchanted with the Communists' rigid discipline and dogma and their knee-jerk attachment to the Soviet Union. The hero of Conroy's *The Disinherited* (1933) grew critical of the party's abstractions: "That's why them soapboxers never get anywheres. Why don't they talk about beans and potatoes, land and bacon instead of 'ideology,' 'agrarian crisis,' and 'rationalization.' " Total party membership in 1930 was only 6,000; by 1932 it remained small at 12,000.

The Socialist party, which argued with both Communists and capitalists, fared little better. More reformist than radical, more evolutionary than revolutionary, the Socialists ran well in municipal elections after the stock market crash but scored few victories. In the 1932 presidential election, Socialist candidate Norman Thomas received 900,000 votes, a mere 2 percent of the total. (Communist candidate William Z. Foster won a negligible 103,000 votes.) Party membership consisted mostly of older Jewish trade-union leaders, Protestant pacifists, students, and teachers; workers and labor unions gave the party little support. In 1930 the membership rolls listed 9,700 persons; by 1932 the figure had grown to only 17,000, fewer than in 1903. Thomas found it "amazing that the workers were so comparatively quiet." Indeed, few despairing Americans looked to leftist parties and doctrines, protest marches, or violence for relief from their misery. They turned instead to institutions of considerable longevity and stability: their local, state, and federal governments.

Hoover holds the line

When daily appeals began being made to the White House for government relief for the jobless, Hoover at first became defensive, if not hostile. "We cannot legislate ourselves out of a world depression; we can and will work ourselves out," he replied. Hoover rejected direct relief–derisively called the dole–because he believed it would undermine character and individualism. "It is a reassuring thought, in the cold weather," critic Edmund Wilson wrote sarcastically, "that the emaciated men in the bread lines, the men and women beggars in the streets, and the children dependent on them, are all having their fibre hardened." Indeed, to a growing number of Americans, Hoover seemed heartless and inflexible at a time when humanitarianism and activity were called for. Rather than deal with the quarter of the work force that was jobless, he emphasized the many who were still on payrolls. The president did not help his public image by brooding and conveying indifference. "This is not a showman's job," he snapped. "You can't make a Teddy Roosevelt out of me." He required reporters to submit questions twenty-four hours in advance and gave press conferences less frequently. And he made the mistake of being photographed on the White House lawn–feeding his dog.

Reliance on private relief

True to his beliefs, the president urged people to help themselves and their neighbors. He applauded private voluntary relief through charitable agencies such as the Community Chest and the Red Cross. Yet when the need was greatest, donations declined. State and urban officials found their treasuries drying up too. Philadelphia, after hiring the unemployed to paint city buildings, exhausted its relief funds by 1931, leaving 57,000 families without assistance. The "demands of suffering humanity," cried the mayor, required federal action. He got no sympathy from Secretary of the Treasury Andrew Mellon, who with a mixture of conventional wisdom and callousness advised the president to "let the slump liquidate itself. Liquidate labor, liquidate stocks, liquidate the farmers, liquidate real estate. . . . It will purge the rottenness out of the system." Will Rogers cast the problem in a different light. "We got more wheat, more corn, more food, more cotton, more money in the banks, more than any nation that ever lived ever had, yet we are starving to death." "It's simply a case," Rogers advised, "of getting it fixed."

Hoover did try to fix the economy. As the depression intensified, his opposition to federal action diminished. He rejected Mellon's insensitive counsel, hesitantly and gradually energizing the White House and federal agencies to take action—more action than the government had taken before. He met with business and labor leaders, winning pledges from them to maintain wages and production and to avoid strikes. He urged state governors to increase their expenditures on public works. And he created the President's Organization on Unemployment Relief (POUR) to generate private contributions for relief of the destitute. Unfortunately, the chairman, president of the American Telephone and Telegraph Company Walter Gifford, seemed a man of limited concern and vision. Asked by a senator to specify the nation's relief requirements, Gifford said he had no precise information. The incredulous senator leaned forward: "Do you know what the relief needs are in the rural districts of the United States?" Gifford answered simply, "No."

If POUR proved ineffective, Hoover's spurring of federal public works projects (including the Boulder, or Hoover, and Grand Coulee dams) did provide some jobs. Help also came from the Federal Farm Board, created before the depression under the Agricultural Marketing Act of 1929. An outcome of Hoover's emphasis on cooperation among individuals, groups, and government, the Farm Board supported agricultural prices by lending money to cooperatives to buy products and keep them off the market. It even created a special corporation for the purpose. But the board soon found itself short of money and its corporation loaded with surplus commodities. And though the federally sponsored and privately funded National Credit Corporation assisted faltering banks, it barely slowed the number of bank failures. To retard the collapse of the international monetary system, Hoover announced a moratorium on the payment of First World War debts and reparations (1931).

The president also reluctantly asked Congress to charter the Reconstruction Finance Corporation (RFC). Created in 1932 and eventually empowered with $2 billion, the RFC was designed to make loans to banks, insurance companies, and railroads and later to state and local governments. The theory behind the RFC was that it would lend money to large entities at the top of the economic system, and benefits would trickle down to people at the bottom through a sort of percolation process. Liberal Republican Representative Fiorello La Guardia of New York labeled the plan a "millionaires' dole." It did not work; banks continued to collapse and small companies to go into bankruptcy.

Reconstruction Finance Corporation

Despite warnings from prominent economists, Hoover also signed the Hawley-Smoot tariff (1930). A congressional compromise serving a variety of special interests, the tariff raised duties by about one-third. Besides wishing to fulfill a Republican party pledge, Hoover argued that the tariff would help farmers and manufacturers by keeping foreign goods off the market. Actually, the tariff further weakened the economy by making it even more difficult for foreign nations to sell their products and thus earn the money to buy American products and pay off their First World War debts.

Like most of his contemporaries, Hoover believed that a balanced budget was sacred, and deficit spending sinful. In 1931 he appealed for a decrease in federal expenditures and an increase in taxes. The following year he supported a sales tax on manufactured goods, which liberal Democrats charged was an attempt to avoid higher income and corporate taxes. The sales tax was defeated, but the Revenue Act of 1932 raised corporate, excise, and personal income taxes. Hoover seemed caught in a contradiction: he urged people to spend to spur recovery, but his tax policies deprived them of spending money. He never did balance the budget nor did he seek repeal of the legal loopholes that permitted the partners of J. P. Morgan and other wealthy Americans to escape paying income taxes in 1931 and 1932.

Although Hoover expanded public works projects and approved loans to some institutions, he vetoed a variety of relief bills presented to him by the Democratic Congress. "Prosperity," he intoned, "cannot be restored by raids upon the public treasury." He also vetoed a multipurpose development project for the Tennessee River, arguing that its cheap electricity would compete with power from private companies. Clinging to his old view-

Hoover restrains federal activity

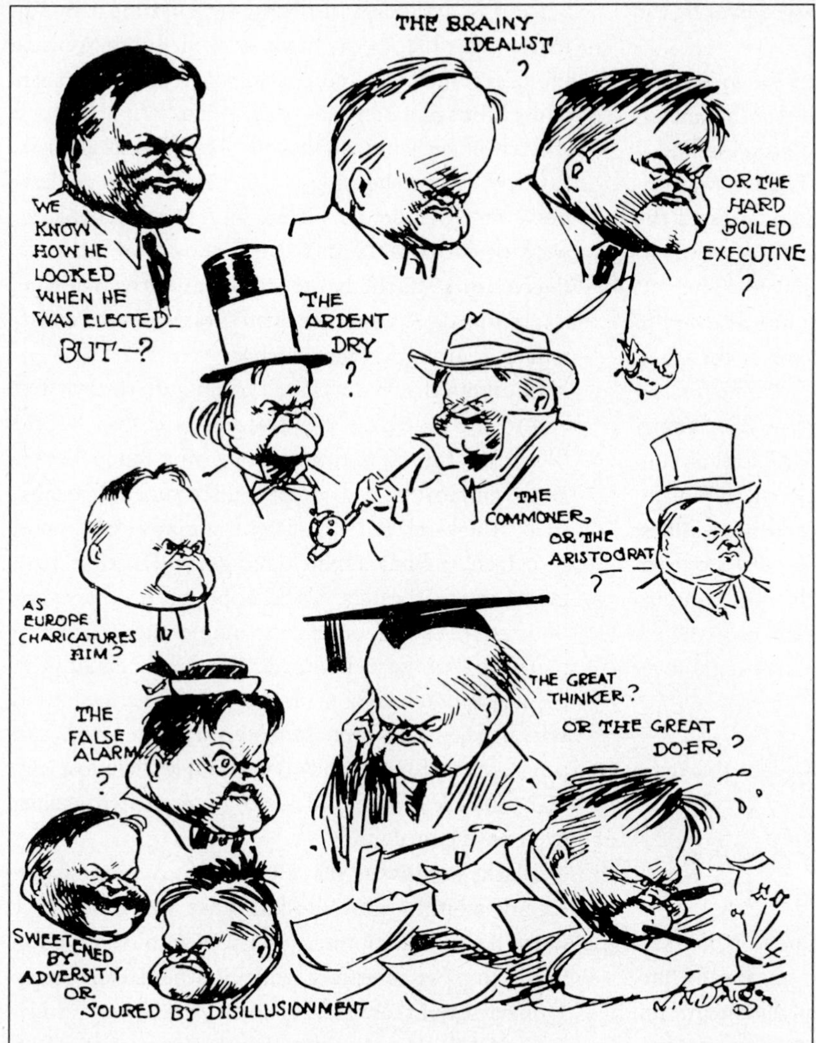

"How will Hoover go down in history?" J. N. "Ding" Darling's cartoon gave only a few of the possibilities and no answers, but demonstrated that Hoover's presidency perplexed many. J. N. "Ding" Darling Foundation, Inc.

points, Hoover stretched government activities as far as he thought he could without violating his cherished principles.

Because Hoover mobilized the resources of the federal government as never before, some historians have depicted him as a bridge to the New Deal of the 1930s. If nothing else, he prepared the way for massive federal activity by giving private enterprise the opportunity to solve the depression—and to fail. They point out, moreover, that Hoover was a progressive trapped by unprecedented events, and that few leaders of the time were sure what to do. But others have argued that Hoover was an ideologue who, when faced with problems of unprecedented magnitude, failed to take bold steps to meet them. Hoover once said that nobody was starving, and in late 1931 he remarked, "Our people have been protected from hunger and cold." Such a statement arose not from heartlessness but from faith in the status quo. Whatever one's interpretation, Hoover's restrained and cautious response to the depression did not mean that he was weak. "Weak Presidents are ignored or brushed aside," historian Albert Romasco has written. "Hoover remained a formidable, effective obstacle to new ideas and innovations until he was blasted away by the presidential election returns."

Hoover's traditionalism was evident too in his handling of prohibition. Despite the Eighteenth Amendment, Americans were producing and drinking liquor with grand illegality and hypocrisy. The law was not and could not be enforced. Yet Hoover resisted the mounting public pressure for repeal. Opponents argued not only that prohibition encouraged crime, but that its repeal would stimulate economic recovery in Milwaukee and St. Louis, increase demand for grain, and revive the nation's old beer, liquor, and pretzel factories. But the president would not, he said, tamper with the Constitution. In his view prohibition contributed to agricultural efficiency, and the liquor industry, having no socially redemptive value, was best left depressed. Instead, Hoover pushed for better enforcement of the Eighteenth Amendment. And during the presidential election campaign of 1932, he stood firm against repeal. As on other issues, Hoover held the line.

The aggravation of racial tensions

While Hoover worried about prohibition, the vast majority of blacks sank deeper into an already precarious mire of fear, political disfranchisement, Jim Crow segregation, and privation. "It was a frightening time," Susie W. Walker of Canton, Mississippi, recalled. "A lot of people didn't know where their next meal was coming from." In 1931, when her daughter was born, "I couldn't even produce breast milk for the baby because we weren't getting enough to eat."

Blacks in the depression

In 1930 about three-quarters of all blacks lived in the South. Most were not permitted to vote; were excluded from juries; could not be treated at the local hospital; were not hired except for the least desirable, most menial jobs; could not enroll at universities; and were denied access to public parks and swimming pools. Blacks living in rural areas (in 1930, 56.9 percent) were propertyless sharecroppers, tenants, or wage hands caught in a cycle of poverty, disease, and illiteracy. The infant mortality rate for blacks in 1930 was double that of whites; pneumonia, tuberculosis, and venereal disease were far more prevalent among black Americans as well. In 1929 black life expectancy was more than ten years lower than white life expectancy (46.7 years versus 57.1). And the specter of the hangman's noose–the unspeakable torture, the crowd shouting for death, the utter lawlessness–was ever before blacks. In 1929 seven blacks were lynched; in 1930, twenty; the following year, twelve. In 1932 the figure was comparatively low at six, but in 1933, when the depression was at its worst, twenty-four blacks were lynched.

Southern blacks continued to migrate to the cities and to the North, as they had since the First World War, but they found conditions not much better. Both employers and unions discriminated against them; the black unemployment rate hovered around 50 percent in Philadelphia, Chicago, and Detroit. And in the movie theaters, blacks appeared on the screen only as yea-saying domestics, jungle natives, plump mammies, or gospel singers. For black Americans, then, the depression made for no dramatic shift in status. They had been stereotyped, segregated, and poor long before 1929. Now, though, they lost menial jobs to whites, and were discriminated against even on the breadlines.

Blacks were aware that Herbert Hoover shared prevailing white racial attitudes; what was more, they knew he was attempting to push them out of the Republican party to attract white Southern Democrats. Hoover sought, as a saying of the time put it, a lily-white GOP. He appointed few blacks to federal office, disbanded the Negro division of the Republican National Committee, rejected appeals for an anti-lynching law, and continued the segregation of the army and federal buildings in the nation's capital. Hoover's philosophy of individualism, opportunity, and fair play was, like the humiliating signs posted across the country, "For Whites Only."

In 1930, the president showed his insensitivity to blacks by nominating Judge John J. Parker of North Carolina to a position on the Supreme Court. Ten years earlier Parker had endorsed the disfranchisement of blacks; the NAACP remembered the speech and protested the nomination. Because Judge Parker had also decided in favor of the yellow-dog contract–a contract in which employees agree not to join a union–and the use of the injunction in labor disputes, the American Federation of Labor joined the protest.

The nine Scottsboro youths in jail in Decatur, Alabama. Seated with attorney Samuel Leibowitz is Haywood Patterson. Brown Brothers.

This combined pressure plus liberal votes in the Senate defeated Parker's nomination, 41 to 39. Unmoved, Hoover stood by his nominee throughout.

Scottsboro trials

Then came Scottsboro, a celebrated civil-liberties case that symbolized the ugliness of race relations in the depression era. One afternoon in March 1931 a freight train pulled into the yard at Paint Rock, near Scottsboro, Alabama. Aboard were some youthful transients traveling free—illegally—in the gondolas and boxcars. When the train stopped, armed sheriff's deputies arrested nine blacks, charging them with roughing up some white hobos and throwing them off the train earlier in the day. When two white women who were removed from the same freight claimed that the blacks had raped them, an angry white mob gathered. Within two weeks eight of the "Scottsboro boys" had been convicted of rape by all-white juries and sentenced to death. The ninth, only twelve years old, was favored by a hung jury. But because court-appointed lawyers had offered little defense for the homeless, illiterate, poorly clad, and sickly youths, the Supreme Court overturned the convictions (1932) on the grounds that the accused had not been granted adequate legal counsel.

New trials opened in 1933, again with all-white juries. This time, however, the Scottsboro Nine were defended by Samuel Leibowitz, a talented attorney

A gloomy Hoover and a buoyant Roosevelt ride to the inauguration in 1933. This magazine cover was never published, apparently because the editors of the *New Yorker* thought it inappropriate after an attempted assassination of the president-elect. Franklin D. Roosevelt Library.

hired by the Communist-sponsored International Labor Defense. To a crowded courtroom, the local prosecutor sneered at Leibowitz, announcing that "Alabama justice cannot be bought and sold with Jew money from New York." Medical evidence showed that the women had not had intercourse on the train. Ruby Bates and Victoria Price had lied, perhaps because they feared arrest as prostitutes. Nevertheless, the first defendant up for retrial, Haywood Patterson, was once again found guilty. Judge James Horton, who had stated that under American law "we know neither black nor white. . . . It is our duty to mete out even-handed justice," was convinced that Patterson was an innocent victim of racial hatred. The courageous Horton overturned the jury's decision.

A new judge was found, a new trial held, and for the third time Patterson was ordered to die. But another Supreme Court ruling intervened, this time because it was evident that in Alabama blacks were systematically excluded from juries. Patterson faced a fourth trial in 1936. Found guilty again, he was given a seventy-five-year jail sentence. Four of the other youths were sentenced to life imprisonment, and the state dropped charges against the remaining four. Not until 1950 were all five out of jail–four by parole and Patterson by escaping from his work gang.

Blacks coped with their white-circumscribed environment and fought back against racism in a variety of ways during the depression. Black Baptist and African Methodist Episcopal churches articulated black concerns; black newspapers like the *Amsterdam News* (in New York), the Chicago *Defender,* and the Pittsburgh *Courier* cultivated racial consciousness. Black Renaissance poets and writers like Langston Hughes promoted civil rights. And Howard University, Tuskegee Institute, and Atlanta University, among others, trained a generation of black leaders. The NAACP, although internally divided, lobbied quietly against a long list of injustices, and A. Philip Randolph's Brotherhood of Sleeping Car Porters defended the rights of black workers. In Cleveland and New York, black doctors protested discriminatory practices at municipal hospitals. In Harlem the militant Harlem Tenants League fought rent increases and evictions, and in some cities black consumers began to boycott white merchants. But America's white leaders made few concessions. Only the Supreme Court, which declared the Texas "white primary" law unconstitutional and attempted to check the legal abuses in the Scottsboro trials, provided a measure of protection for black Americans in the thirties.

Tradition in time of crisis: the election of 1932

Herbert Hoover and the Republican party faced dreary prospects in 1932. The tired and sullen president grumbled at reporters, banks continued to close, and memories of the Bonus March persisted–especially after Hoover distorted the affair by blaming it on the Communists. Hoover kept pointing to international causes for the economic crisis, when Americans were less concerned with abstract explanations than with tomorrow's meal. He grew impatient with critics who held him responsible for the depression. "Is it my fault," he asked a reporter, "that cheap politicians and selfish men over the whole world have refused to see the folly of their policies until it was too late?" His critics replied that as secretary of commerce during the 1920s Hoover shared responsibility for the depression. But what soured public opinion most was that Hoover seemed not to lead at a time when innovative generalship was required, that he refused to budge. "No president," Hoover told a friend, "must ever admit he has been wrong."

In 1932 Republicans who did not want to be associated with a loser ran independent campaigns; Progressive Republicans like Senator George Norris deserted Hoover; W. E. B. Du Bois urged blacks to vote Democratic. The president made few major speeches, rarely left Washington, and when he did venture out was frequently jeered and booed. On the final day of the campaign, when Hoover returned to California to vote, his motorcade was interrupted by stink bombs.

Election of 1932

Franklin D. Roosevelt, on the other hand, enjoyed a different reputation. The smiling, ingratiating governor of New York appealed to the American penchant for optimism. "I figure out that if we can get rid of Old Gloom and put in a feller that can laugh and act human," a cab driver explained, "the Depression will be half over." As governor of New York, Roosevelt had undertaken vigorous relief programs and seen to the establishment of an unemployment commission. In 1932 he outmaneuvered try-again Al Smith and Speaker of the House John Nance Garner to gain the top spot on the Democratic ticket. Breaking with precedent, the fifty-year-old candidate flew to Chicago to accept the nomination in person, calling for a "new deal for the American people."

The two party platforms differed little, but the Democrats were willing to abandon prohibition and to launch federal relief. Roosevelt, playing the political game superbly, promised to help everybody—a Santa Claus campaign, one critic called it. Hoover complained that his opponent was a chameleon on plaid. Indeed, Roosevelt's speeches, pieced together by ghostwriters, seemed contradictory. He would agree with Hoover that the budget had to be balanced, then appeal for costly new programs. When Roosevelt spoke of the forgotten man and declared himself ready to provide direct relief to individuals, Hoover boiled: "This campaign is more than a contest between two men," he said. "It is more than a contest between two parties. It is a contest between two philosophies of government." Roosevelt seemed to agree, explaining his liberalism with a metaphor:

> Say that civilization is a tree which, as it grows, continually produced rot and dead wood. The radical says: "Cut it down." The conservative says: "Don't touch it." The liberal compromises: "Let's prune, so that we lose neither the old trunk nor the new branches." This campaign is waged to teach the country to march upon its appointed course

Important events

1928	Herbert Hoover elected president
1929	Federal Farm Board created Stock market crash
1930	Hawley-Smoot tariff Democratic victories in congressional elections
1931	Scottsboro affair Hoover calls for moratorium on World War I debts and reparations Iowa's Cow War
1932	Reconstruction Finance Corporation established Ford Hunger March in Dearborn, Michigan Sioux City milk strike Bonus March on Washington, D.C. Franklin D. Roosevelt elected president
1933	*King Kong* released

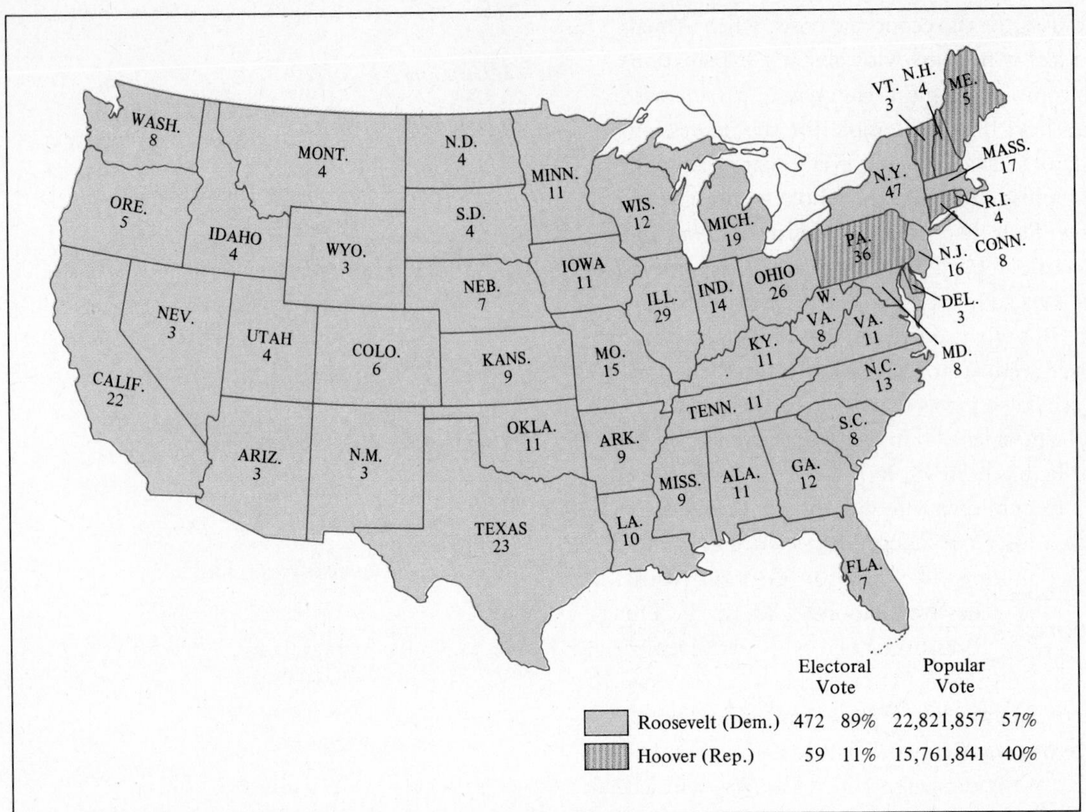

Presidential election, 1932

. . . , avoiding alike the revolution of radicalism and the revolution of conservatism.

More people went to the polls in 1932 than in any election since the First World War. In a crisis-ridden moment Americans quietly, calmly, even routinely followed tradition and peacefully exchanged one government for another. Roosevelt's 22.8 million popular votes far outdistanced Hoover's 15.8 million: 57 percent of the popular vote went to the Democrat, 40 percent to the Republican, and 3 percent to minor party candidates. Hoover won only Vermont, New Hampshire, Maine, Connecticut, Delaware, and Pennsylvania, giving him a paltry 59 electoral votes to Roosevelt's 472 (see map). Cities continued the trend, begun in 1928, of voting Democratic. But although Hoover was in trouble with some black leaders, two-thirds of the black vote remained Republican in 1932. Roosevelt had appealed to southern whites as Hoover had, and he held racial views that differed little from Hoover's.

Democrats also won overwhelming control of the Senate and the House. From November to March, a lame-duck president, a lame-duck Congress (158 of whose members had been defeated) and a hesitant president-elect took little positive action, and the depression continued to cut its debilitating path. Americans wondered what would happen next. Might not radicals make gains? Some thought Roosevelt would reform the American system enough to forestall radical solutions. Others envisioned demagogues, splinter parties, or violence. Hoover feared Roosevelt would implant "collectivism" in the nation, smothering individualism and destroying the American system. But Hoover exaggerated his differences with Roosevelt, who hardly sought the destruction of capitalism. The two parted ways largely on the extent to which the federal government should intervene in economic and social affairs. And the majority of Americans had spoken for more intervention. How strikingly different from their mood four years earlier was their mood on inauguration day 1933.

Suggestions for further reading

Hoover and his administration

David Burner, *Herbert Hoover: A Public Life* (1979); Carl N. Degler, "The Ordeal of Herbert Hoover," *Yale Review,* 52 (1963), 563–583; Martin L. Fausold and George T. Mazuzan, eds., *The Hoover Presidency* (1974); Ellis W. Hawley, *The Great War and the Search for a Modern Order* (1979); Richard Hofstadter, *The American Political Tradition* (1949); Barry D. Karl, "Presidential Planning and Social Science Research: Mr. Hoover's Experts," *Perspectives in American History,* 3 (1969), 347–409; William E. Leuchtenberg, *The Perils of Prosperity, 1914–1932* (1958); James S. Olson, *Herbert Hoover and the Reconstruction Finance Corporation, 1931–1933* (1977); Edgar E. Robinson and Vaughn D. Bornet, *Herbert Hoover* (1975); Albert V. Romasco, *The Poverty of Abundance: Hoover, The Nation, The Depression* (1965); Elliot A. Rosen, *Hoover, Roosevelt, and the Brains Trust: From Depression to New Deal* (1977); Jordan A. Schwarz, *Interregnum of Despair* (1970); Gene Smith, *The Shattered Dream* (1970); Harris G. Warren, *Herbert Hoover and the Great Depression* (1959); William Appleman Williams, *Some Presidents: Wilson to Nixon* (1972); Joan Hoff Wilson, *Herbert Hoover: Forgotten Progressive* (1975).

The Great Depression and its origins

W. Elliot Brownlee, *Dynamics of Ascent,* 2nd ed. (1979); Lester V. Chandler, *America's Greatest Depression, 1929–1941* (1970); Milton Friedman and Anna Schwartz, *The Great Contraction, 1929–1933* (1965); John K. Galbraith, *The Great Crash,* rev. ed. (1972); Robert L. Heilbroner, *The Economic Transformation of America* (1977); Susan Kennedy, *The Banking Crisis of 1933* (1973); Charles Kindleberger, *The World in Depression, 1929–1939* (1973); Broadus Mitchell, *Depression Decade* (1947); Jim Potter, *The American Economy Between the Wars* (1974); Murray N. Rothbard, *America's Great Depression* (1963); George Soule, *Prosperity Decade* (1947); Peter Temin, *Did Monetary Forces Cause the Great Depression?* (1976); Gordon Thomas and Max Morgan-Witts, *The Day the Bubble Burst* (1979).

The American people in hard times

Andrew Bergman, *We're in the Money: Depression America and Its Films* (1971); Irving Bernstein, *The Lean Years: A History of the American Worker, 1920–1933* (1960); Caroline Bird, *The Invisible Scar* (1965); Sidney Fine, *Frank Murphy: The Detroit Years* (1975); John W. Hevener, *Which Side Are You On? The Harlan County Coal Miners, 1931–1939* (1978); David Kennedy, ed., *The American People in the Depression* (1973); Milton Meltzer, *Brother, Can You Spare a Dime?* (1969); Cabel Phillips, *From the Crash to the Blitz, 1929–1939* (1969); Robert Sklar, *Movie-Made America* (1975); Bernard Sternsher, ed., *Hitting Home: The Great Depression in Town and Country* (1970); Studs Terkel, *Hard Times: An Oral History of the Great Depression* (1970); Dixon Wecter, *The Age of the Great Depression, 1929–1941* (1948); Edmund Wilson, *The American Earthquake* (1958).

Protest

Roger Daniels, *The Bonus March* (1971); John P. Diggins, *The American Left in the Twentieth Century* (1973); Donald J. Lisio, *The President and Protest: Hoover, Conspiracy, and the Bonus Riot* (1974); Theodore Saloutos and John D. Hicks, *Twentieth Century Populism: Agricultural Discontent in the Middle West, 1900–1939* (1951); David Shannon, *The Socialist Party of America* (1955); John L. Shover, *Cornbelt Rebellion: The Farmers' Holiday Association* (1965).

Race relations

Dan T. Carter, *Scottsboro,* rev. ed. (1979); John Hope Franklin, *From Slavery to Freedom,* 5th ed. (1980); August Meier and Elliott Rudwick, *From Plantation to Ghetto,* 3rd ed. (1976); Harvard Sitkoff, *A New Deal for Blacks* (1978); Bernard Sternsher, ed., *The Negro in Depression and War* (1969); Raymond Wolters, *Negroes and the Great Depression* (1970); Robert L. Zangrando, *The NAACP Crusade Against Lynching, 1909–1950* (1980).

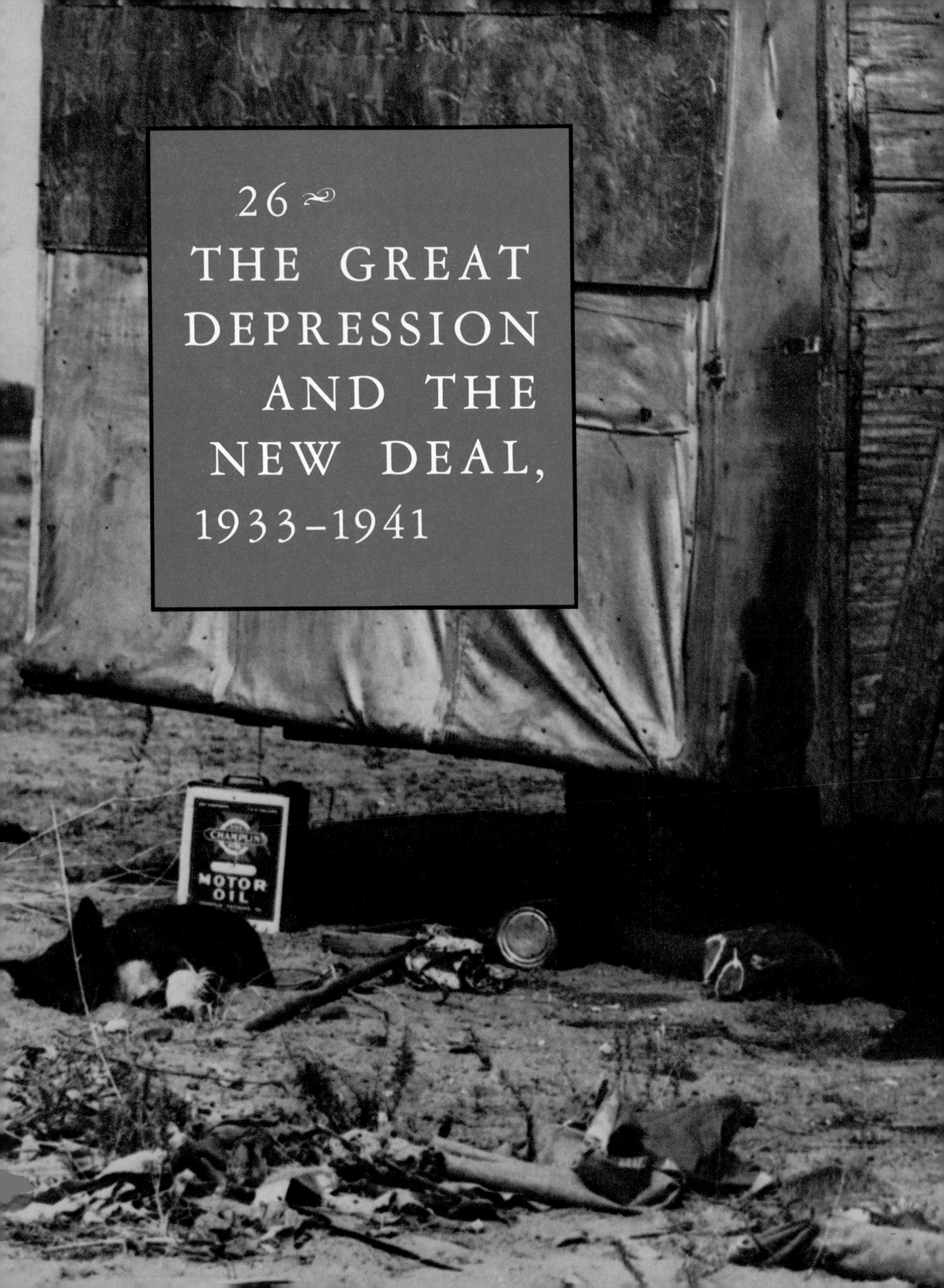

26 THE GREAT DEPRESSION AND THE NEW DEAL, 1933–1941

Franklin D. Roosevelt loved the sea. So in August 1921, when a business associate with a yacht offered a cruise to Roosevelt's summer home on Campobello Island, he happily accepted. Sailing into the frigid waters of the Bay of Fundy between New Brunswick and Nova Scotia, the two encountered rough water, and Roosevelt stood for hours at the helm until the boat was in harbor. Although he was tired, he looked forward to a reunion with his wife Eleanor and their five children.

The next day Roosevelt went fishing and fell overboard. "I never felt anything so cold as that water!" he said later, "so cold it seemed paralyzing." Roosevelt was exhausted, but he did not slacken his pace. The next day there was a forest fire to be fought, followed by another dip in the cold waters. When Roosevelt returned to the house the mail was waiting, and he sat in his wet bathing suit reading letters and newspapers. Finally, he was too tired to stand up.

When Roosevelt awoke the next morning, his left leg seemed cumbersome and ached. He also had a fever. Soon he had no feeling in his left leg, then none in the right. A doctor diagnosed polio. Just two years before, Roosevelt had been the robust assistant secretary of the navy under President Woodrow Wilson. A year before, in 1920, he had been the vice-presidential candidate of the Democratic party. Now he was a cripple, totally paralyzed in both legs.

What should Roosevelt do next? Should he retire from public life, a rich invalid? His answer and his wife's was no. Throughout the 1920s Franklin and Eleanor contended with his new handicap. In the process they both grew as human beings, developing qualities of mind and soul they had not realized they possessed. Rejecting self-pity even though he at times experienced intense pain, Roosevelt worked to rebuild his body. He gained patience. People who had known him before commented that polio had made him a "twice born man," that his "fight against that dread disease had evidently given him new moral and physical strength." As Roosevelt explained it: "If you had spent two years in bed trying to wiggle your big toe, after that anything would seem easy."

For her part, Mrs. Roosevelt learned to do things for herself, such as driving a car; and she began to shape her own career in public life, giving speeches and participating in the activities of the League of Women Voters, the Women's Trade Union League, and the Democratic party. She grew not only independently but in directions different from her husband's interests and activities. Two of her strongest commitments came to be equal opportunity for women and for nonwhites, and she identified especially with the poor and suffering.

In 1933 Franklin D. Roosevelt became president, and the source of strength for a troubled nation. These were the years of the Great Depression. The qualities of character he and Eleanor had discovered and nurtured in the 1920s would prove an invaluable asset in the years to come.

From the first days of his presidency Roosevelt displayed a buoyancy and a willingness to experiment that helped to restore public confidence in the government and the economy. After shoring up the banking system, Roosevelt proposed a succession of laws to aid landowning farmers, blue-collar workers, businesses and local governments facing bankruptcy, the unemployed, the elderly, and even impoverished writers and artists. This sweeping legislation was based on the unorthodox concept of "pump priming," or deficit financing, to spur economic recovery.

Roosevelt's program, which he dubbed the New Deal, inspired opposition from both the left and right. Businesspeople and economic conservatives found it fiscally irresponsible; demagogues and left-wing politicians thought it too conservative. Ultimately it prevailed, however, expanding both the role of the federal government and the popularity of the Democratic party.

During these years the new Congress of Industrial Organizations (CIO) established unions in major industries like autos, steel, and meat packing. Several million workers seized the chance to organize for better wages and working conditions. Nonwhites registered political and economic gains too, though in general they benefited less from the New Deal than whites. Some federal agencies actually worked against blacks; on the other hand, black advisers took posts in the White House, and native Americans discovered that New Dealers respected their culture and tribal rights.

Roosevelt was re-elected in 1936, but soon thereafter his fortunes began to wane. In 1937 the nation sank into a severe economic recession, and Congress rejected Roosevelt's attempt to add sympathetic judges to the federal bench. In 1938 the spate of reform legislation came to an end. But by that time the New Deal had transformed the United States; its legacy is still with us today. Farmers still plant according to federal crop allotments. The elderly and disabled still collect Social Security payments. The Federal Deposit Insurance Corporation still insures bank deposits. And the Securities and Exchange Commission still monitors the stock exchange. One task the New Deal did not accomplish–putting back to work all the people who wanted jobs. That would await the nation's entry into the Second World War.

In November 1930 Franklin D. Roosevelt (1882–1945) read the good news. Re-elected governor of New York by 735,000 votes, he immediately became a leading contender for the 1932 Democratic presidential nomination. Note Roosevelt's leg braces, rarely shown in photographs because of an unwritten agreement by photographers to shoot him from the waist up. UPI.

Roosevelt the man

Franklin D. Roosevelt was born into the upper class of tradition and privilege, the only child of doting parents who heaped on him all sorts of advantages, including tutors and governesses, his own pony and twenty-one-foot sailboat, and numerous trips to Europe. Hyde Park, overlooking the Hudson River about halfway between New York City and the state capital at Albany, was the family home. Roosevelt prepared for college at Groton, an exclusive private school, and was graduated from Harvard in 1903. In fall 1904 he entered the School of Law at Columbia University, and a few months later he announced his engagement to his fifth cousin once-removed, Anna Eleanor Roosevelt, the niece of President Theodore Roosevelt. The next spring they were married.

Franklin D. Roosevelt's early career

For three years Roosevelt practiced law with a firm in New York City, but the work bored him, and he had other ambitions, anyway–political ones. According to one of his fellow lawyers. Roosevelt declared that he planned to run for office as soon as possible, and that his ultimate goal was to be president. He said he might follow the trail blazed by his "Cousin Teddy": first the New York State Assembly, then assistant secretary of the navy, then governor of New York. "Anyone who is governor of New York," Roosevelt concluded, "has a good chance to be President with any luck."

Three years later, in the Democratic sweep of 1910, Roosevelt was elected to the New York State Assembly. An early campaigner for Woodrow Wilson for president, Roosevelt mounted the next rung of his ladder with Wilson's victory in 1912: he accepted Wilson's offer of the post of assistant secretary of the navy. For eight years Roosevelt supervised the navy's purchasing and its relations with labor unions, gaining confidence and shedding much of his smugness. And he learned lessons about the emergence of the United States as a world power and the need for decisive presidential leadership in times of crisis. The value of these lessons would become apparent years later, when he led the nation first in a war against economic depression and then in a world war against Germany, Japan, and Italy.

In 1920 the Democratic party nominated Roosevelt for the vice presidency. Campaigning on the need for the League of Nations and continued domestic reform, he and Governor James M. Cox of Ohio were roundly defeated by Republicans Harding and Coolidge. But Roosevelt suffered his most devastating loss the next year, when he was struck by polio. After deciding to fight his polio rather than succumb to it, Roosevelt practiced law and pursued various business ventures. He also returned to politics, nominating New York's Governor Al Smith for president at both the 1924 and 1928 Democratic conventions and becoming a spokesperson for progressive Democrats.

With Smith's candidacy in 1928 came pressure to run for the governorship of New York. Smith applied much of the pressure himself, realizing that his prospects would be enhanced with Roosevelt's name heading the ticket in New York, the most populous state in the nation. But Roosevelt was apprehensive; he hoped that in a couple of years he might be walking again. Besides, he was only forty-six, with a long political life ahead of him. Smith persevered. "A Governor does not have to be an acrobat," he explained to critics. "We do not elect him for his ability to do a double back-flip."

Roosevelt finally agreed to run, and in November he won by 25,000 votes. Smith not only lost the election, but failed to carry his home state of New York, losing it by 100,000 votes. Right away Roosevelt became an obvious prospect for the 1932 Democratic presidential nomination. "You are," Virginia's Senator Harry Byrd wrote to Roosevelt, "the hope of the Democratic party."

Roosevelt as governor of New York

Roosevelt's governorship coincided with Hoover's presidency, and both coincided with the onset of the Great Depression. But whereas Hoover appeared dour, hardhearted, and unwilling to help the jobless and the poor, Roosevelt seemed just the opposite. He urged unemployment insurance and direct relief payments for the jobless. Under his leadership New York's Temporary Emergency Relief Administration became the first state agency to mobilize on behalf of the poor (1931). Aid to the unemployed, Roosevelt declared, "must be extended by Government, not as a matter of charity, but as a matter of social duty." Modern society, he added, had a "definite obligation to prevent the starvation or dire waste of any of its fellow men and women who try to maintain themselves but cannot."

Roosevelt was also more willing than Hoover to experiment with the economy. He had always been a conservationist; as governor of New York, he advocated creating jobs in publicly funded reforestation, land reclamation, and hydroelectric power projects. He also endorsed and worked for old-age pensions and protective legislation for labor unions. Roosevelt warned people not to dismiss such experimentation "with the word radical. Remember the radical of yesterday is almost [always] the reactionary of today." After he was re-elected in 1930 by a record-setting plurality of 735,000 votes, politicians had to take a serious look at his methods.

Roosevelt's "brains trust"

To prepare a national political platform, Roosevelt surrounded himself with a "brains trust" of lawyers and university professors. Foremost among these advisers were Columbia University professors Rexford G. Tugwell, Raymond Moley, and Adolf A. Berle, Jr. Bigness was unavoidable in the modern American economy, these experts reasoned; thus the cure for the nation's ills was not to go on a rampage of trustbusting, but to place large corporations, monopolies, and oligopolies under effective government control. "We are no longer afraid of bigness," declared Tugwell, speaking in the tradition of Theodore Roosevelt's New Nationalism. "We are resolved to recognize openly that competition in most of its forms is wasteful and costly; that larger combinations in any modern society must prevail. . . . Unrestricted individual competition is the death, not the life, of trade."

Roosevelt and his brains trust agreed that it was essential for the government to take action to restore purchasing power to farmers, blue-collar workers, and the middle classes, and that the way to do so was to cut production. If the demand for a product remained constant and the supply were cut, they reasoned, the price would rise. Producers would make higher profits, and workers would earn more money. This method of combating a depression has been called the economics of scarcity. Unlike Hoover, Roosevelt also advocated immediate and direct relief to the unemployed. Finally, Roosevelt and his advisers rejected Hoover's explanation that the depression was international, not domestic, in origin. They demanded that the federal government engage in centralized economic planning and experimentation to bring about recovery.

The presidential election of 1932 had never been much of a contest (see page 720). But once elected, Roosevelt had to wait until his inauguration on March 4 to act.[1] It was a troubled four months. Almost 13 million unemployed people walked the streets, some of whom participated in hunger riots and job protest marches. Prices for agricultural and manufactured goods continued to plummet, forcing the bankruptcy of countless farms, small businesses, railroads, and even local governments. Industrial production sank to new depths. And while farmers in the Farm Holiday movement poured milk down ditches and threatened to hang foreclosing judges, another kind of holiday was observed in some states: the bank holiday. Throughout the United States, depositors were lining up in front of banks demanding their money. Banks with insufficient funds on hand to pay depositors had to close their doors and declare themselves insolvent. In February, Michigan and Maryland suspended banking operations within their borders, and by March 4, thirty-six other states, including New York, had followed suit. The same month an unemployed bricklayer, Guiseppe Zangara, bought a revolver at a pawnshop in Miami, took it to Bay Front Park, and fired at close range into the car in which Roosevelt was riding (Roosevelt was unharmed). "I do not hate Mr. Roosevelt personally," explained Zangara. "I hate all Presidents . . . and I hate all officials and everybody who is rich."

[1] As a result of that crucial loss of time, the Twentieth Amendment to the Constitution—the Lame Duck Amendment—was ratified. It moved all future inaugurations forward to January 20.

On the afternoon of March 2, 1933, President-elect Roosevelt and his family and friends boarded a train for Washington, D.C., and the inauguration ceremony. Roosevelt was carrying with him rough drafts of two presidential proclamations, one summoning a special session of Congress, the other declaring a national Bank Holiday, suspending banking transactions throughout the nation. It was time for Roosevelt and his administration to go to work, time to produce the New Deal he had promised the American people.

Restoring confidence

"First of all," declared the newly inaugurated president, "let me assert my firm belief that the only thing we have to fear is fear itself—nameless, unreasoning, unjustified terror." In his inaugural address Roosevelt scored his first triumph as president, instilling hope and courage in the rank and file. Roosevelt attacked the nation's bankers, accusing them of having "fled from their high seats in the temple of our civilization." His administration, he said, would take drastic action to "restore that temple to the ancient truths." He invoked "the analogue of war," proclaiming that, as in the First World War, the American people must march forward "as a trained and loyal army willing to sacrifice for the good of a common discipline." And if need be, he asserted, "I shall ask the Congress for the one remaining instrument to meet the crisis—broad Executive power to wage a war against the emergency, as great as the power that would be given to me if we were in fact invaded by a foreign foe."

Congress convened in emergency session on March 9 to begin what observers would call the Hundred

Beginning of the Hundred Days

Days. Roosevelt's initial legislative requests were cautious; portions had even been written by Hoover's advisers. The first measure, the Emergency Banking Relief Bill, was introduced just before 1 P.M. on March 9, passed sight unseen by unanimous House vote, approved 73 to 7 in the Senate, and signed by the president at 8:36 that evening. The act provided for the reopening, under treasury department license, of banks that were solvent and the reorganization and management of those that were not. It also gave the president broad powers over credit, currency, and the buying and selling of gold and silver. But it was a conservative law that left the nation's banking system essentially unchanged, with the same people in charge, and as such was a special disappointment to those who had taken seriously the antibanker rhetoric of Roosevelt's inaugural address. As it was, complained one representative, "The President drove the money-changers out of the Capitol on March 4th—and they were all back on the 9th."

On the next day, March 10, the second bill of the New Deal was introduced in Congress. It too was conservative, and ten days later it became law. Called the Economy Act, its purpose was to balance the federal budget by chopping veterans' benefits and allowances by $400 million and reducing by $100 million the pay of federal employees. Under Roosevelt, the budget balancers had won a battle that could not have been won under Hoover.

On Sunday evening, March 12, the president broadcast the first of his fireside chats, and 60 million

First fireside chat

people heard his comforting voice on their radios. His message: banks were once again safe places for depositors' savings. On Monday morning the banks opened their doors, but instead of queuing up to withdraw their savings, people were waiting outside to deposit their money. "The people trust this administration," a wealthy woman jotted in her diary, "as they distrusted the other." The bank runs were over; people had regained confidence in their political leadership, their banks, even their economic system. "Capitalism," Raymond Moley later wrote, "was saved in eight days."

So far, the New Deal had embraced a drastically deflationary economic policy. Roosevelt next pursued a measure, the Beer-Wine Revenue Bill, that was not only deflationary but would actually take money out of people's pockets. The bill was designed to generate revenues by legalizing the sale of wines and low-alcohol beers and levying a tax on them. (Repeal of prohibition had been proposed by Congress in the Twenty-first Amendment in February 1933; it would be ratified by the states in December 1933.) To many, levying new taxes seemed a strange and backward way to restore purchasing power to people who could not afford to buy what they needed. Roosevelt knew that. "I realize well," he wrote a friend, "that thus far we have actually given more of deflation than of inflation. . . . It is simply inevitable that we must inflate." He added that his "banker friends may be horrified" by the large-scale federal spending that was to come. And beginning in mid-March, Roosevelt did seek congressional authorization to spend.

Launching the New Deal

On March 16, the president sent to Congress the Agricultural Adjustment Bill, his plan to restore farmers' purchasing power. If overproduction was the

Aid to farmers

cause of farmers' problems—falling prices and mounting surpluses—then the government had to encourage farmers to grow less food. Under the domestic allotment plan, as it was called, the government would pay subsidies to farmers to reduce their acreage or plow under crops already in the fields. Farmers would receive payments based on *parity*, a system of regulated prices for corn, cotton, wheat, rice, hogs, and dairy products that would allow them the same purchasing power they had had during the prosperous period of 1909 through 1914. In effect, the government was making up the difference between the actual market value of farm products and the income farmers needed to make a profit. The funds for the subsidies would come from taxes levied on the processors of agricultural commodities.

Roosevelt's farm plan immediately encountered vehement opposition. "The bill before the House," declared an Illinois representative, "is more bolshevistic than any law or regulation existing in Soviet Russia." "We are on our way to Moscow," echoed an-

In February 1933 thousands of Nebraska farmers stormed the steps of the state capitol in Lincoln, demanding economic relief. Just a month before, Edward A. O'Neal, head of the Farm Bureau Federation, had warned a Senate committee: "Unless something is done for the American farmer we will have revolution in the countryside within less than twelve months." UPI.

other. Although the bill was quickly adopted by the House, opposition did not cease, and the Senate became the scene of vigorous debate. How, some people asked, could there be crop surpluses and overproduction when some Americans were hungry and even starving? Underconsumption, they argued, was the result of a maldistribution of wealth and power as well as of goods and services. Some politicians wanted to stimulate inflation by coining silver, printing greenbacks, altering the gold content of the dollar, or taking the nation off the gold standard altogether. Cheap money, they contended, was the farmers' panacea. "For real radicals," concluded Rexford Tugwell, "it [Roosevelt's Agricultural Adjustment Bill] is not enough; for conservatives it is too much; for Jefferson Democrats it is a new control which they distrust. For the economic philosophy [the economics of scarcity] which it represents there are no defenders at all."

On May 12 Congress finally overcame opposition to the domestic allotment plan and passed the Agricultural Adjustment Act (AAA). A month later the Farm Credit Act also became law. By providing short- and medium-term loans to farmers—more than $100 million worth in seven months—the Farm Credit Act enabled many farmers to refinance their mortgages and hang onto their homes and land.

Civilian Conservation Corps (CCC)

Meanwhile, other relief measures became law. On March 21 the president requested massive infusions of relief of three kinds: a job corps called the Civilian Conservation Corps (CCC); direct cash grants to the states to provide relief payments for needy citizens; and public works projects. Ten days later Congress approved the CCC. Within four months 1,300 camps were in operation and 300,000 young men between the ages of eighteen and twenty-five were at work planting trees, clearing camping areas and beaches, and building bridges, dams, reservoirs, fish ponds, and fire towers. More than 2.5 million young men eventually lived and worked in CCC camps. Then on May 12 Congress passed the Federal Emergency Relief Act, which authorized $500 million, half of it in direct grants to the states, the other half to be allocated on the basis of $1

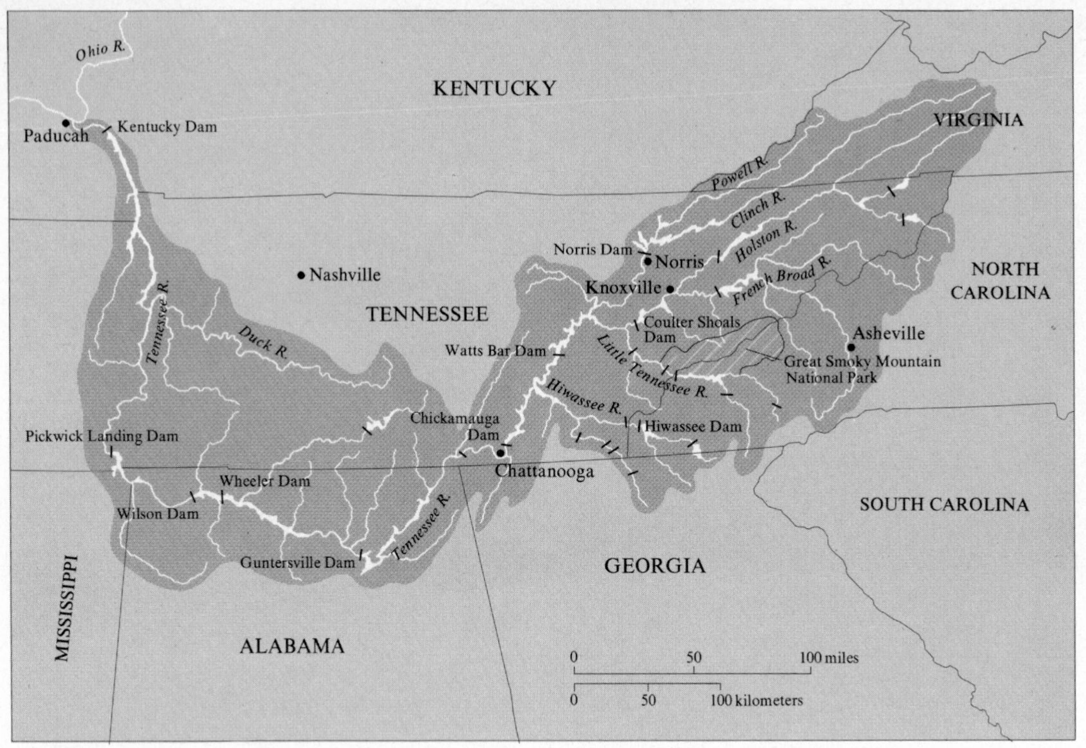

The Tennessee Valley Authority

of federal money for every $3 of state and local money spent on relief.

Roosevelt's proposed plan for public works became Title II of the National Industrial Recovery Act (NIRA). Passed on June 16, it established in the Public Works Administration (PWA) a fund of $3.3 billion to build roads, sewage and water systems, public buildings, and a host of other projects, including ships and naval aircraft. The purpose of the PWA was to prime the economic pump–to stimulate consumer buying power, business enterprise, and ultimately employment by pouring billions of dollars into the economy.

Pump priming was an unorthodox concept in 1933, and Roosevelt resorted to it only as a last-ditch measure. He remained orthodox in his views, anxious to return to a balanced budget at the earliest opportunity. Not until 1936 was the masterwork on pump priming, John Maynard Keynes's *General Theory of Employment, Interest and Money,* published. Roosevelt met with Keynes after the book's publication, but claimed he could not make heads or tails of the British economist's advice to spend massively.

Pump priming was thus a real departure from the fiscal conservatism of the earliest days of the New Deal. But a month earlier Congress had enacted an even bolder program for the depressed Tennessee River valley, which ran through Tennessee, North Carolina, Kentucky, Virginia, Mississippi, Georgia, and Alabama. For years progressives led by Senator George Norris of Nebraska had advocated government operation of the Muscle Shoals electric power and nitrogen facilities on the Tennessee River. But the Tennessee Valley Authority (TVA), as finally established, was a much broader program than the progressive plan. Its dams would not only serve to control floods; they could also generate hydroelectric power, reclaim and reforest land, and prevent soil erosion. Other provisions of the TVA included the production and sale of nitrogen fertilizers to private citizens and of nitrate explosives to the government; the digging of a 650-mile navigation channel from Knoxville to Paducah; and the construction of public-power facilities as a yardstick for determining fair rates for privately produced electric power. The goal of the TVA was nothing less than enhancement of the economic well-being of the entire Tennessee River valley (see map).

If the AAA was the agricultural cornerstone of the New Deal, the National Industrial Recovery Act was the industrial cornerstone. The NIRA, as we have seen, authorized billions of dollars for public works; but it did far more than that. It was a testimony to the New Deal belief in national planning as opposed to an individualistic, intensely competitive laissez-faire economy. A variety of leaders joined in support of the program, including old Bull Moose supporters of Teddy Roosevelt's New Nationalism; big-business advocates of trade associations; union leaders like John L. Lewis of the United Mine Workers; executives who had had experience with planned industrial mobilization in the War Industries Board (WIB) during the First World War, like Bernard Baruch; and long-time proplanning politicians like Senators Robert La Follette, Jr., of Wisconsin and Robert F. Wagner, Sr., of New York. It was essential, they all agreed, for businesses to end cutthroat competition and raise prices by limiting production.

Economic planning under the NIRA

In practice businesses could not cooperate with each other without violating antitrust laws. The only precedent for the industrial self-regulation and business-government cooperation envisioned by New Deal planners was the WIB, which had expired at the end of the First World War. But planners argued that the nation was again engaged in a struggle for survival, this one economic, and that what was again needed was exemption from the antitrust laws. The NIRA granted such exemption through the National Recovery Administration (NRA), whose symbol, the Blue Eagle, was meant to encourage cooperation. Under the law, competing businesses met with government mediators and representatives of workers and consumers to draft codes of fair competition, which limited production, assigned markets, and established prices.

With businesses enjoying new concessions, workers wanted a share of the pie too. Congress guaranteed their right to unionize and to bargain collectively in Section 7(a) of the NIRA, which called for industrywide codes establishing minimum wages and maximum hours.

With the passage of the NIRA, Congress adjourned on June 16, its Hundred Days completed. Roosevelt had delivered fifteen messages to Congress, and fifteen significant laws had been enacted. Those not yet mentioned included the Federal Securities Act, to compel brokers to tell the truth about new securities issues; the National Employment System Act, to match funding of state employment agencies; the Home Owners Refinancing Act, to issue $2 billion in bonds to refinance nonfarm home mortgages; the Banking Act of 1933, to set up the Federal Deposit Insurance Corporation for insuring bank deposits, and divorce investment from commercial banking; and the Emergency Railroad Transportation Act, to encourage financial reorganization of railroads, simplify rate-making, and put railroad holding companies under the supervision of the Interstate Commerce Commission.

End of the Hundred Days

Within a few months the United States had rebounded from shock, hysteria, and near-collapse. "I do not think it is too much to say," noted Rexford Tugwell, "that on March 4 we were confronted with a choice between an orderly revolution . . . and a violent and disorderly overthrow of the whole capitalist structure." In a time of crisis the country had opted for peaceful parliamentary progress. Columnist Walter Lippmann wrote that at the time of the inauguration, the country was a collection of "disorderly panic-stricken mobs and factions. In the hundred days from March to June we became again an organized nation confident of our power to provide for our own security and to control our own destiny."

Throughout the remainder of 1933 and the spring and summer of 1934, more New Deal bills became law. The beneficiaries of many of the new recovery acts were property-owning farmers. In October 1933, for example, the Commodity Credit Corporation was organized under the Agricultural Adjustment Administration. Its purposes were to bolster crop prices by lending money to farmers against their underpriced crops, and to allow farmers to withhold their crops from the market until prices rose. Other laws provided for the compulsory reduction of certain crops (cotton, sugar, tobacco) by licensing and subsidizing cultivators. Still others were designed to prevent farm mortgage foreclosures or to extend credit to farmers.

Nonfarm legislation freed additional hundreds of millions of dollars for unemployment relief and pub-

popular radio stars Ed Wynn and Amos 'n' Andy. For a while he supported the New Deal, calling it "Christ's deal." But he was critical of the AAA's plowing-under of crops and slaughtering of livestock. In late 1934, declaring "these old parties are all but dead," Coughlin organized the National Union for Social Justice and began to criticize the New Deal for having "out-Hoovered Hoover."

Another challenge to the New Deal came from Dr. Francis E. Townsend, who had conceived what he called an Old Age Revolving Pensions plan. Under Townsend's scheme the government would pay monthly pensions of $200 to all citizens over age sixty, on the condition that they spend the money in the same month they received it. Townsend claimed his plan would not only aid the aged but cure the depression by pumping enormous purchasing power into the economy. Though the plan was fiscally impossible, it had a powerful emotional appeal, for it addressed a real need. Many old people suffered extreme deprivation in the 1930s, a time when local relief for the elderly was nonexistent in many places and Social Security had not yet been established. In early 1935 Townsend claimed he had 3.5 million followers.

And then there was Huey Long, the Kingfish, perhaps the most successful demagogue in American history. In 1928 Long was elected governor of Louisiana with the slogan "Every Man a King, But No One Wears a Crown." Highly intelligent, aggressive, and at times brutal, Long sponsored and oversaw projects ranging from hospitals, highways, and bridges to a state university. But more and more he adopted the methods of a dictator, especially after defeating an effort to remove him from office (1929). "I used to try to get things done by saying 'please.' That didn't work," he announced, "and now I'm a dynamiter. I dynamite 'em out of my path."

At first Long supported the New Deal; but he found the Economy Act and the NRA too conservative, and began to believe that Roosevelt had fallen captive to big business and big money. Long countered in 1934 with the Share Our Wealth Society, which advocated the seizure by taxation of all incomes over $1 million and all inheritances over $5 million. With those funds, the government would furnish each family a homestead allowance of $5,000 and an annual income of $2,000, along with free college education, government storage of crops and control of planting, and limitations on working hours. By mid-1935 Long's movement claimed 7 million members, and few doubted that Long aspired to the presidency. Though an assassin's bullet extinguished his amibition in September 1935, the Share Our Wealth movement persisted under a new leader, the vitriolic anti-Semite Gerald L. K. Smith.

Some politicians of the 1930s, like Floyd Olson, governor of Minnesota, declared themselves socialists. Olson sought a third party that would "preach the gospel of government and collective ownership of the means of production and distribution." In neighboring Wisconsin the left-wing Progressive party re-elected Robert La Follette, Jr., to the Senate in 1934, sent seven of the state's ten representatives to Washington, and placed La Follette's brother Philip in the governorship. And the old muckraker Upton Sinclair almost won the Democratic gubernatorial nomination in California in 1934 on the platform End Poverty in California (EPIC).

Left-wing critics of the New Deal

Perhaps the most controversial alternative to the New Deal was the Communist party of the United States of America (CPUSA). In the early days of the depression Communists had organized hunger marches and helped to establish labor unions among auto and electrical workers, seamen, and longshoremen (see pages 712–713). And in 1932 a number of distinguished writers had endorsed the Communist presidential candidate, William Z. Foster. But membership in the CPUSA remained small until 1935, when the party leadership changed its strategy. Proclaiming "Communism is Twentieth Century Americanism," the CPUSA disclaimed any intention of overthrowing the United States government and began to cooperate with left-wing labor unions, student groups, and intellectual organizations.

Russia's response to the Spanish Civil War also encouraged some Americans to join the CPUSA. Of all the nations of Europe, only Russia seemed determined to stem the tide of fascism that had washed over Germany and Italy and in 1936 threatened Spain (see Chapter 27). One convert to the CPUSA, writer and editor Whittaker Chambers, explained that for him Communism offered "what nothing else in the dying world had power to offer at the same intensity—faith and a vision." Still, at its high point for the decade in 1938, the CPUSA had only 55,000 members.

In addition to challenges from the right and the left, the New Deal was threatened by the Supreme Court. In January 1935, in *Panama Refining Co.* v. *Ryan,* the Court struck down part of the NIRA. By granting the president power to prohibit interstate and foreign shipment of oil, the Court ruled, Congress had unconstitutionally delegated legislative power to the executive branch. The decision cast an ominous shadow over other New Deal legislation that granted broad powers to the president to halt the depression; court tests of other provisions of the NIRA and the AAA soon followed. On May 27 the Court unanimously struck down the whole NIRA (*Schechter* v. *U.S.*) on the grounds that it gave excessive legislative power to the White House, and that the commerce clause of the Constitution did not give the federal government authority to regulate intrastate businesses. "America Stunned," screamed headlines in the London *Daily Express,* "Roosevelt's Two Years' Work Killed in Twenty Minutes." Indeed, Roosevelt's industrial recovery program was dead and the Court's narrow interpretation of the commerce clause had jeopardized what was left of the New Deal.

Supreme Court decisions against the New Deal

While the Court's decisions angered New Dealers, they delighted others, including Louis D. Brandeis, the Wilsonian progressive who had served on the Supreme Court since 1916. In the Court's robing room on May 27, Brandeis told one of Roosevelt's lawyers: "This is the end of this business of centralization, and I want you to go back and tell the President that we're not going to let this government centralize everything. It's come to an end." To make their point clear, the Court in January 1936 invalidated the AAA (*U.S.* v. *Butler*), deciding that agriculture was a local problem and thus, under the Tenth Amendment, subject to state, not federal, action.

As Roosevelt looked ahead to the presidential election of 1936, he saw that he was in danger of losing his capacity to lead and to govern. His coalition of all interests was breaking up; radicals and demagogues were offering Americans alternative programs; and the Supreme Court was dismantling the New Deal. In the spring and summer of 1935, Roosevelt took the initiative once more, and the New Deal scored some of its biggest victories. So impressive was the new legislation that historians called it the Second New Deal.

The Second New Deal

The first triumph of the Second New Deal was an innocuous-sounding but momentous law called the Emergency Relief Appropriation Act, which Congress passed and Roosevelt signed in April 1935. The act authorized the president to issue executive orders establishing massive public works programs for the jobless, including the Works Progress Administration (WPA).

Emergency Relief Appropriation Act

Later renamed the Work Projects Administration, the WPA ultimately employed more than 8.5 million people on a total of 1.4 million projects. By the time it was terminated in 1943, the WPA had built over 650,000 miles of highways, streets, and roads, 125,000 public buildings, and 8,000 parks, as well as numerous bridges, airports, and other structures. But WPA did more than lay bricks. Its Federal Theatre Project brought plays, vaudeville shows, and circuses to cities and towns across the country, and WPA artists painted murals in post offices and other public buildings. The Federal Music Project and the WPA Dance Theatre sponsored laboratories for young composers and choreographers. And the Federal Writers' Project hired writers like Conrad Aiken, John Cheever, Claude McKay, John Steinbeck, and Richard Wright to write local guidebooks and regional, ethnic, and folk histories.

Besides the WPA, the Emergency Relief Appropriation Act funded four other relief and public works measures. The Resettlement Administration (RA) resettled destitute families from both rural and urban areas, loaned them money for small farms and equipment, and organized rural homestead communities and suburban greenbelt towns for low-income workers. The Rural Electrification Administration (REA) generated and distributed electricity to isolated rural areas. The National Resources Committee (later known as the National Resources Planning Board) mapped out long-range plans for the use of human and natural resources. And the National Youth Administration (NYA) sponsored work relief programs for people between the ages of sixteen and twenty-five and provided part-time employment for students.

As significant as these achievements were, Roosevelt wanted new legislation, some of it aimed at con-

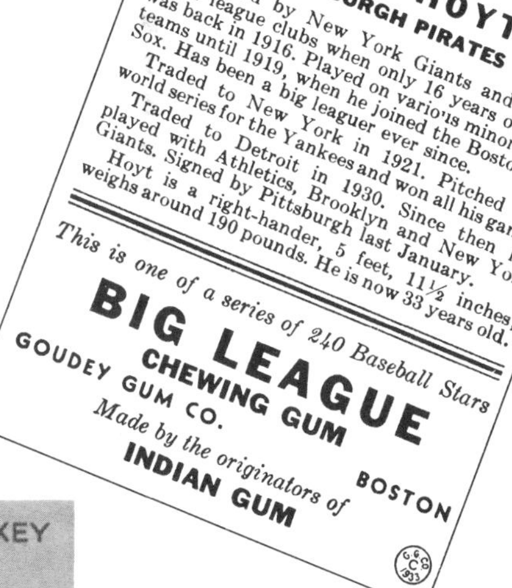

— No. 60 —

WAITE HOYT

PITTSBURGH PIRATES

Was signed by New York Giants and sent to minor league clubs when only 16 years old. This was back in 1916. Played on various minor league teams until 1919, when he joined the Boston Red Sox. Has been a big leaguer ever since.

Traded to New York in 1921. Pitched in 6 world series for the Yankees and won all his games.

Traded to Detroit in 1930. Since then has played with Athletics, Brooklyn and New York Giants. Signed by Pittsburgh last January.

Hoyt is a right-hander, 5 feet, 11½ inches, weighs around 190 pounds. He is now 33 years old.

This is one of a series of 240 Baseball Stars

BIG LEAGUE CHEWING GUM

GOUDEY GUM CO. **BOSTON**

Made by the originators of **INDIAN GUM**

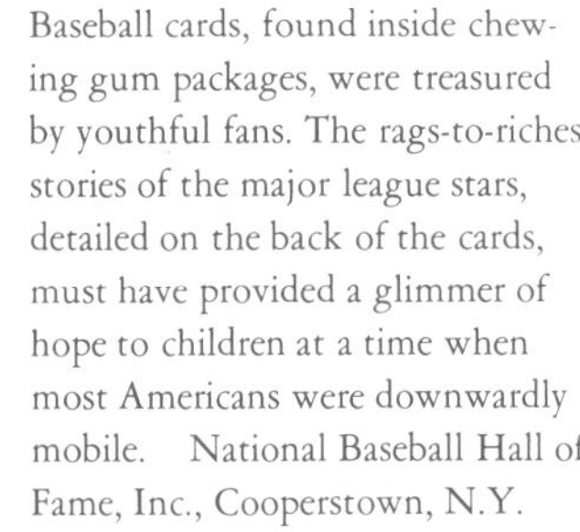

Baseball cards, found inside chewing gum packages, were treasured by youthful fans. The rags-to-riches stories of the major league stars, detailed on the back of the cards, must have provided a glimmer of hope to children at a time when most Americans were downwardly mobile. National Baseball Hall of Fame, Inc., Cooperstown, N.Y.

migrated from farms to cities in the 1920s looked to the government for rent control and food purity laws, regulation of working hours and conditions, and welfare for the unemployed. Before long they too had gravitated to the Democratic party. Graphic proof resides in the big-city voting returns of presidential elections from 1920 to 1936. In 1920 the nation's twelve largest cities gave the Republicans 1.6 million more votes than the Democrats. In 1924 the Republican plurality dropped to 1.25 million, and in 1928 it disappeared. But that was just the beginning of the Democratic groundswell, which in 1932 jumped to 1.9 million and in 1936 to 3.6 million more big-city votes than the Republicans.

By 1936 Roosevelt and the Democrats had forged what observers have called the New Deal coalition. The growing strength of the party in the cities, the suffering wrought by the Great Depression, and the New Deal response to social distress had converged to make Roosevelt the champion of the urban masses. Labor, especially the new unions of the Congress of Industrial Organizations (CIO), was an indispensable member of the coalition (see next section). These unions fused the interests of millions of workers, native and foreign-born, black and white, male and female, skilled and unskilled. And black voters in northern cities, most of whom had been Republicans prior to the 1930s, now cast their lot with the Democratic party (see pages 740–741). Finally, many lifelong Socialists began to vote Democratic. In 1932 Norman Thomas, the Socialist party candidate, had polled 884,000 votes; in 1936 his total slipped to just 187,000. The Democratic party had become the dominant half of the two-party system.

The rise of the CIO

As governor of New York, Franklin Roosevelt had expressed his belief in the right of workers to organize and bargain with their bosses through representatives of their own choosing. Yet he arrived at the White House with no specific program for guaranteeing workers the means to bargain with management. Section 7(a) of the NIRA had not been his idea; when he signed the bill into law he did not appreciate what it meant nor how it could be enforced. Roosevelt had also been a late supporter of the National Labor Relations (Wagner) Act of 1935.

On enactment, Section 7(a) inspired the organization of new unions and the vigorous recruitment of members. "Millions of workers throughout the nation," recalled American Federation of Labor President William Green, "stood up for the first time in their lives to receive their charter of industrial freedom." Organizers for the United Mine Workers (UMW) told coal miners, "President Roosevelt wants you to join the union," and many thousands did. By October 1933 an additional 1.5 million workers had enlisted in unions, bringing total membership to 4 million.

But these gains did not always come easily. Management put up determined resistance in the early and mid-1930s, hiring armed thugs to intimidate workers and break up strikes. Violence surfaced in the steel, automobile, and textile industries and among the dock workers of the West Coast, the lumber workers of the Pacific Northwest, and the teamsters in Minneapolis. Labor confronted yet another obstacle in the AFL craft unions' traditional skepticism and hostility toward industrial unions. Craft unions typically consisted of skilled workers in a particular trade, such as carpentry, plumbing, or typography. Industrial unions, on the other hand, represented all the workers in a given industry, skilled and unskilled. The UMW, the United Brewery Workers, and the International Ladies' Garment Workers Union were all industrial rather than craft unions. Ever since its establishment in 1886, the AFL had been dominated by craft unions. But organizing gains in the 1930s were far more impressive in industrial unions than craft unions, with hundreds of thousands of workers joining unions in such industries as autos, garments, rubber, and steel. What resulted was a struggle for control of the labor movement between craft and industrial union leaders.

Rivalry between craft and industrial unions

Personifying this power struggle were the leaders of the two sides, William Green, leader of the AFL, and John L. Lewis of the UMW. Lewis was probably the most colorful and tenacious labor leader in the nation's history, a fighter with a flair for the dramatic who once said of the mine owners resisting unionization: "They are striking me hip and thigh. . . . right

Strikers in a Fisher Body plant read newspapers as they relax on car seats. The sit-down strike, developed in 1937, proved a powerful weapon in labor-management confrontations. Library of Congress.

merrily shall I return their blows." William Green, on the other hand, was dull. But he was president of the entire AFL, whereas Lewis represented only one of the many unions within the federation. Even as leader of the dynamic industrial union movement, Lewis was still the challenger.

Attempts were made in the mid-1930s to reconcile the craft and industrial union movements, but in late 1935 Lewis resigned as vice president of the AFL. He and other industrial unionists within the AFL formed the Committee for Industrial Organization (CIO). When the AFL's Executive Council demanded that the CIO disband, Lewis replied: "The American Federation of Labor is standing still, with its face toward the dead past." Another effort at reconciliation in 1937 came too late. In 1938 the AFL expelled the CIO unions, and the CIO reorganized itself as the Congress of Industrial Organizations. By that time CIO membership stood at 3.7 million, more than the AFL's 3.4 million.

The CIO, which in the 1930s evolved into a pragmatic bread-and-butter labor organization, had organized millions of workers who had never before had an oppportunity to join unions. Now their dues enabled it to organize even more people. The United Auto Workers (UAW), led by the Reuther brothers, scored a major victory in late 1936. The union, 30,000 strong, demanded recognition from General Motors, Chrysler, and Ford. When GM refused, the UAW launched a new kind of strike: the sit-down. Beginning in the Fisher Body plants in Flint, Michigan, workers refused to leave the plants. To discourage the strikers, GM managers turned off the heat; when that tactic failed, they called the police, who were met by a barrage of missiles–iron bolts and door hinges, coffee mugs, and pop bottles. When the police resorted to tear gas, the strikers turned the plant's water hoses on them, and the police retreated in what the high-spirited strikers called the Battle of the Running Bulls.

Sit-down strikes

The strike lasted for weeks. GM obtained a court order to evacuate the plant, but the strikers continued, risking imprisonment and fines. With the support of their families and neighborhoods, the workers stuck to their rigid discipline. Community women

On Memorial Day 1937, Chicago police used guns, clubs, and tear gas to break up a peaceful picket line at a Republic Steel plant. Ten people were killed and forty wounded in the Memorial Day Massacre. Wide World Photos.

wearing red berets organized an "emergency brigade" to picket and deliver food and supplies to the strikers. In the end the UAW prevailed and GM agreed to recognize the union (1937). Chrysler signed a similar agreement, but Ford held out for four more years, a time of bloody encounters between the UAW and union-busting hoodlums hired by the Ford Service Department.

The sit-down strike spread to other industries and other parts of the country; before long textile, glass, and rubber workers, Woolworth clerks, janitors, dressmakers, and pie bakers were using the technique. Some people condemned the sit-down as a trespass on private property; others endorsed it, including muckraker Upton Sinclair, who wrote that "for 75 years big business has been sitting down on the American people, and now I am delighted to see the process reversed." Soon the new tactic was celebrated in song:

When they tie the can to a union man,
Sit down! Sit down!

When they give him the sack, they'll take him back,
Sit down! Sit down!

When the speed-up comes, just twiddle your thumbs,
Sit down! Sit down!

When the bosses won't talk, don't take a walk,
Sit down! Sit down![2]

In 1937 too the Steel Workers Organizing Committee (SWOC) signed a contract with the nation's largest steelmaker, U.S. Steel, that guaranteed an eight-hour day and a forty-hour week. Other steel companies refused to go along, however. Confrontations between these so-called little steel companies and the SWOC led to violence. On Memorial Day in Chicago, strikers and their families had joined with sympathizers in a peaceful picket line in front of the Republic Steel plant. Suddenly and without provocation the police opened fire. They continued to shoot into the crowd even as people turned away and began to run. A social worker recalled hearing "a dull thud toward the back of . . . my group,

Memorial Day Massacre

[2] Maurice Sugar, quoted in Edward Levinson, *Labor on the March* (New York: Harper and Row, 1938), p. 179.

and as I turned around there was screaming . . . and simultaneously a volley of shots. . . . [The] people that were standing in back of me were all lying on the ground face down. I saw some splotches of blood on some of the fellows' shirts." Of the ten fatalities, none had been shot in the front of the body; of the forty gunshot wounds, only four were frontal.

As senseless as the Memorial Day Massacre was, its occurrence was not surprising. During the 1930s industries had hired private police agents and accumulated large stores of arms and ammunition for use in deterring workers from organizing and joining unions. A Senate committee headed by Robert La Follette, Jr., found that companies had spent millions of dollars in the process. Republic Steel, for example, was the nation's largest single purchaser of tear and sickening gas. Youngstown Sheet and Tube owned 8 machine guns, 369 rifles, 190 shotguns, 450 revolvers, and thousands of rounds of ammunition. The arsenals of these two companies alone, La Follette declared, "would be adequate equipment for a small war." All told, companies had hired almost four thousand private detectives to infiltrate unions, provoke discontent, impede organization, and report on union activities. The agents spied on ninety-three unions, and many actually managed to become union officers.

Through it all, the CIO continued to enroll new members. By the end of 1937 industrial unions had enlisted 600,000 miners, 375,000 steelworkers, 400,000 auto workers, 300,000 textile workers, 250,000 ladies' garment workers, and 100,000 agricultural and packing-house workers. By the end of the decade the CIO had succeeded in organizing most of the nation's mass-production industries.

Mixed progress for nonwhites

For the other cornerstone of the New Deal coalition, black Americans, Franklin D. Roosevelt had become the most appealing president since Abraham Lincoln. Part of the reason was the courageous way he bore his physical disability. Blacks, who suffered from a handicap of their own–racism–knew what courage was. Moreover, Roosevelt seemed a decided improvement over Herbert Hoover, who had nominated a white supremacist to the Supreme Court, favored white Republicans over black in the South, and appeared hardhearted in the face of extreme suffering. Blacks suffered more than whites during the depression, and Roosevelt, in his fireside chats and through his personal magnetism and buoyancy, spoke directly to them. When they saw pictures of black visitors at the White House and read about Roosevelt's Black Cabinet, they were heartened.

Black Cabinet

The Black Cabinet, or black brains trust, was unique in United States history. Occasionally Afro-Americans like Frederick Douglass and Booker T. Washington had advised presidents on patronage. But never before had there been so many black advisers at the White House, and never had they been highly trained professionals. There were black lawyers, journalists, and doctors of philosophy; black experts on housing, labor, and social welfare. William H. Hastie and Robert C. Weaver, both of whom held advanced degrees from Harvard, served in the Department of the Interior. Mary McLeod Bethune, a college president, was director of the Division of Negro Affairs of the National Youth Administration. Eugene Kinckle Jones, executive secretary of the National Urban League, and Lawrence A. Oxley, a professional social worker, served in comparable posts in the Departments of Commerce and Labor. Black social scientists, among them Ralph Bunche, Ira DeA. Reid, Abram L. Harris, and Rayford W. Logan, acted as government consultants.

There were also among the New Dealers some whites who had committed themselves to first-class citizenship for Afro-Americans. Foremost among these people was Eleanor Roosevelt. In 1939, when the acclaimed black contralto Marian Anderson was barred from performing in Washington's Constitution Hall by its owners, the Daughters of the American Revolution, Mrs. Roosevelt arranged for Anderson to sing on Easter Sunday at the Lincoln Memorial. The president himself, however, remained uncommitted to the black civil rights movement. Fearful of alienating southern whites, he never endorsed two key goals of the civil rights struggle: a federal law against lynching and abolition of the poll tax.

Furthermore, some New Deal programs and agencies functioned in ways that were definitely hostile to black Americans, and Roosevelt and Congress shared

Antiblack effects of the New Deal

the blame for their failing. The AAA, rather than benefiting black tenant farmers and sharecroppers, actually forced many of them off the land. The Federal Housing Administration (FHA) refused to guarantee mortgages on houses purchased by blacks in white neighborhoods, and the U.S. Housing Authority financed segregated housing projects. The CCC was racially segregated, as was much of the TVA, which constructed all-white towns, handed out skilled jobs to whites first, and segregated its labor crews. When the NRA agreed to lower wages for blacks, one black newspaper commented, "The Blue Eagle may be for Negroes a predatory bird instead of a feathered messenger of happiness." Finally, waiters, cooks, hospital orderlies, janitors, farm workers, and domestics, many of whom were black, were excluded from Social Security coverage and from the minimum-wage provisions of the Fair Labor Standards Act of 1938. In short, though blacks benefited, they did not get their fair share.

Confronted with the mixed message of the New Deal, many blacks concluded that ultimately they could depend only on themselves and organized self-help and direct-action movements. Black tenant farmers and sharecroppers joined with poor whites to form the Southern Tenant Farmers' Union. In the North blacks boycotted stores in Don't Buy Where You Can't Work campaigns, launched Jobs for Negroes movements, and started tenants' unions to fight high rents. More and more they criticized the NAACP for ignoring the economics of second-class citizenship and for being too middle-class and legalistic in its war on racism. Although the NAACP had scored notable victories in opening up graduate and professional schools to black students, critics charged that these gains benefited only the black bourgeoisie, not the masses who above all needed jobs.

Nowhere was the trend toward direct action more evident than in the March on Washington movement

March on Washington movement

of 1941. In that year billions of federal dollars flowed into American industry as the nation prepared for the possibility of another world war. The government funds generated many thousands of new jobs, but discrimination deprived blacks of their fair share. One executive in the aircraft industry notified black job applicants that "the Negro

In 1938 Eleanor Roosevelt presented the NAACP's Spingarn Medal to the black opera star Marian Anderson. A year later, when the Daughters of the American Revolution refused to let Anderson perform in Washington's Constitution Hall, Roosevelt arranged for her to sing before a much larger crowd at the Lincoln Memorial. Metropolitan Opera Archives.

will be considered only as janitors and in other similar capacities." So in early 1941, A. Philip Randolph, president of the Brotherhood of Sleeping Car Porters, proposed that 50,000 to 100,000 blacks march on the nation's capital to demand equal access to jobs in defense industries.

The idea was a popular one, and by midsummer thousands of blacks were ready to march. Roosevelt and other government officials feared that the march might provoke riots and that Communists might infiltrate the movement. In a mood to compromise, the president announced that if Randolph would cancel the march, he would issue an executive order with "teeth in it" prohibiting discrimination in war industries and in the government. The result was Executive Order No. 8802, issued on June 25, 1941, which established the Fair Employment Practices Committee (FEPC). As August Meier and Elliott Rudwick have

Roosevelt's second term: the unrealized promise

Despite the bold and unprecedented steps of his first term, what Roosevelt faced during his second term was a darkening horizon. The economy faltered again between 1937 and 1939, bringing renewed unemployment and suffering. And Europe drew closer to war, threatening to drag the United States into the conflict (see Chapter 27). In need of support for his foreign and military policies, Roosevelt began to court conservative politicians who had been long-time opponents of his domestic reforms. The eventual result was the demise of the New Deal.

In several instances Roosevelt created his own defeat. The Supreme Court had invalidated much of the work of the First Hundred Days; now Roosevelt feared it would do the same with the fruits of the Second Hundred Days. So in February 1937 the President sent to Congress his Judiciary Reorganization Bill. What the federal judiciary needed, he claimed, was a more enlightened and progressive world view. Indeed, four of the associate justices of the Supreme Court seemed less attuned to the twentieth century than to a nineteenth-century world of natural law and survival of the fittest. Three others were liberals, and two were swing votes: Chief Justice Charles Evans Hughes and Associate Justice Owen J. Roberts. Although the justices had overturned some New Deal legislation on unanimous votes, they had declared other laws unconstitutional by narrow margins of 5 to 4 and 6 to 3.

Roosevelt's court-packing plan

What Roosevelt requested was the authority to appoint a replacement whenever a federal judge failed to retire within six months of reaching age seventy. He wanted the power to name up to fifty additional federal judges, including six to the Supreme Court. Though Roosevelt spoke of understaffed courts and aged and feeble judges, it was obvious that he envisioned using the bill to transform 5-to-4 and 6-to-3 votes against the New Deal into more favorable decisions.

Opposition to Roosevelt's attempt to pack the Court was widespread and vocal. Naturally, Republicans and some conservative Democrats opposed the bill, but liberals resisted as well. In many ways Roosevelt had only himself to blame. Had he made the bill an issue during the 1936 presidential election and won a great victory nevertheless, he could have sent his plan to Congress as the mandate of the people. Instead he had to concede defeat. The bill Roosevelt signed in August made pensions available to retiring judges, but it denied him the power to increase the number of judges.

This episode had an ironic final twist. During the public debate over court packing, the two swing-vote justices, Hughes and Roberts, began to vote in favor of liberal, pro-New Deal rulings. In March 1937, for example, the court upheld a Washington state minimum-wage statute 5 to 4 (*West Coast Hotel* v. *Parrish*). Just a year before, in a case almost indistinguishable from this one, the Court had invalidated a similar New York state law. Then in April the Court upheld the Wagner Act 5 to 4 (*N.L.R.B.* v. *Jones & Laughlin Steel Corp.*), ruling that Congress's power to regulate interstate commerce involved also the power to regulate production of goods for interstate commerce. And in May the Court upheld the Social Security Act 5 to 4. Roosevelt had lost the legislative battle but won the war for a more progressive judicial outlook. Encouraged by the new pensions, judges past the age of seventy did begin to retire, and the president was able to appoint seven new associate justices in the next four years: Hugo Black (1937), Stanley Reed (1938), Felix Frankfurter (1939), William O. Douglas (1939), Frank Murphy (1940), Robert H. Jackson (1941), and James F. Byrnes (1941).

Another New Deal defeat, the renewed economic recession of 1937 through 1939, had no unexpected payoffs. Roosevelt had never abandoned his commitment to the balanced budget. In 1937, confident that most of the problems of the depression had been solved, he began to order drastic cutbacks in government spending. Between January and August 1937 the WPA cut its job rolls in half, from 3 million to 1.5 million people, and the government slashed other relief programs as well. To reduce the inflation rate of 3.6 percent, the Federal Reserve System increased the reserve requirements of member banks. The sudden tightening of credit sent the economy into a tailspin: unemployment soared from 7.7 million in 1937 to 10.4 million the next year.

Recession of 1937–1939

In response to the new recession Roosevelt eventually revived deficit financing, and Congress appropriated billions more for the WPA, the CCC, and other projects and agencies. But even with sudden infusions of relief in 1938, unemployment was still 9.5 million in 1939. Not until the end of that year did the economy return to 1937 levels. Many people wondered whether they had lived through two years of unnecessary recession and hardship. Roosevelt's attempt to return to the balanced budget had revealed that his fiscal ideas were basically orthodox, his commitment to economic pump priming shallow.

Roosevelt's campaign against three conservative southern Democrats in the off-year elections of 1938 revealed his increasing desperation. Senators Walter George of Georgia, "Cotton Ed" Smith of South Carolina, and Millard Tydings of Maryland, all critics of the New Deal, won re-election despite Roosevelt's attempt to purge them from the party. As it turned out, Roosevelt would soon need the support of these conservatives for his programs of military rearmament and preparedness.

In spring 1938, with conflict over events in Europe commanding more and more of the nation's attention, the New Deal came to an end. The last significant laws enacted were a new Agricultural Adjustment Act and the Fair Labor Standards Act, which established minimum wages and maximum hours for many but by no means all workers.

Election of 1940

As the presidential election of 1940 approached, many people wondered whether Roosevelt would run for a third term (no president had ever served more than two terms). Roosevelt himself seemed undecided until May 1940, when Hitler's military advances apparently convinced him to stay on. He confided his decision to no one, however, and even sent a message to the Democratic convention that he did not want to be renominated. But at a timely moment, loudspeakers broadcast the chant "We want Roosevelt!" throughout the convention hall, and delegates began to snake dance up and down the aisles. There is no doubt that Roosevelt wanted the nomination, but he also wanted the appearance of a draft. He was nominated on the first ballot and selected as his running mate Secretary of Agriculture Henry A. Wallace.

The Republican candidate was Wendell Willkie, a utility executive who had been an anti-New Deal Democrat throughout most of the 1930s. As president of the Commonwealth and Southern Corporation, Willkie had battled the Tennessee Valley Authority, condemning it as socialistic, but as a politician he was an unknown. As late as April 1940 he did not have a single delegate to the Republican convention, which was scheduled to open in two months. In May, however, with the Nazi invasion of the Low Countries and France, Willkie's support mounted in the public opinion polls. Other anti-New Deal Democrats joined with eastern Republicans to boost his candidacy, painting him as an internationalist who would halt the Nazi advance before it reached England. This was not the time, his supporters declared, for the traditional isolationism of the Republican party. On the sixth ballot Willkie defeated the early leader at the convention, New York County's District Attorney Thomas E. Dewey. To balance the ticket, Republicans selected an isolationist, Senator Charles McNary of Oregon, as Willkie's running mate.

Willkie campaigned against the New Deal, contending that its meddling in the affairs of business had failed to return the nation to prosperity. He also criticized the government's lack of military preparedness. But Roosevelt pre-empted the defense issue by beefing up military and naval contracts. And as workers streamed into the factories to fill the new orders, unemployment figures tended to drop as well. In his speeches Roosevelt reminded workers that it was his administration that had provided the defense jobs. "You citizens of Seattle who are listening tonight," he pointed out in one radio address, "you have watched the Boeing plant out there grow. . . . You citizens of Southern California can see the great Douglas factories." When Willkie reversed his approach and accused Roosevelt of being a warmonger, the president promised, "Your boys are not going to be sent into any foreign wars."

Willkie never did come up with an effective campaign issue, and when the votes were tallied on election day, Roosevelt had received 27 million votes to Willkie's 22 million. In the electoral college, Roosevelt buried Willkie 449 to 82. Willkie did manage to win the farm and small-town vote in the Midwest, but as in 1936 Roosevelt triumphed in the cities, primarily among working-class, lower-income, and black voters. Although the New Deal was over, Roosevelt was still riding its wave of public approval.

The legacy of the New Deal

Any analysis of the New Deal must begin with Franklin Delano Roosevelt. Assessments of his career varied widely during his presidency. In the 1930s a popularity poll among New York schoolchildren resulted in an easy victory for Roosevelt; God finished a distant second. Other people called Roosevelt a liar, a crook, a madman, a dictator, and a Communist. Most historians have considered him a truly great president, citing his courage, his buoyant self-confidence, his willingness to experiment, and his capacity to inspire the nation during the most somber days of the depression. But those who have criticized him have charged that he was too pragmatic, that he failed to formulate a bold and coherent strategy of economic recovery and political and economic reform.

On this last point, one of Roosevelt's biographers, James MacGregor Burns, has written in Roosevelt's defense: "Everything conspired in 1932 to make Roosevelt a pragmatist, an opportunist, an experimenter." The United States had never faced an economic disaster of the magnitude of the Great Depression; in a time of crisis, Roosevelt had to experiment. "The country needs," Roosevelt once said, "and, unless I mistake its temper, the country demands bold, persistent experimentation." Burns admits that one of the results was that the New Deal lacked coherence. And at times the wary president "failed to exercise creative leadership," playing the fox–devious, crafty, and difficult to pin down–rather than the lion–bold and assertive. Notwithstanding Roosevelt's faults, Burns prefers to see "the lineaments of greatness–courage, joyousness, responsiveness, vitality, faith and, above all, concern for his fellow man."

Though scholars have debated Roosevelt's performance, they all agree that he transformed the presidency. "Only Washington, who made the office, and Jackson, who remade it," Clinton Rossiter wrote in 1956, "did more than Roosevelt to raise it to its present condition of strength, dignity, and independence." Scholars in a later era would charge that Roosevelt laid the foundations of the "imperial presidency" (see Chapter 34). But whether for good or ill, Roosevelt strengthened not only the presidency but the whole federal government. "For the first time for many Americans," William Leuchtenburg has written, "the federal government became an institution that was directly experienced. More than state and local governments, it came to be *the* government." In the past, the federal government had served as a regulator of railroads, corporations, and other businesses; during the New Deal it became a guarantor and stimulator as well. For the first time the government acknowledged a responsibility to bring relief to the jobless and the needy, and for the first time it resorted to deficit spending in order to stimulate the economy.

Strengthening of the presidency

The economy itself remained basically capitalistic under the New Deal. Though the government took on responsibility for the public welfare and the vitality of the economy, the profit motive and private property remained fundamental to the system. And though some redistribution of wealth did result from the New Deal, the wealthy survived as a class. In 1929, for example, the most well-to-do 5 percent of the population received 30 percent of the total family income. By 1941, the same group's share of total income had shrunk, but was still a healthy 24 percent. Most of the income lost by the wealthy ended up in the pockets of the middle and upper-middle classes, not of the poor (see table).

The New Deal brought about limited change in the nation's power structure. Beginning in the 1930s, business interests had to share their political clout with others. Finally the labor movement gained influence in Washington, and farmers got more of what they wanted from Congress and the White House. But there was no real increase in the power of Afro-Americans and other minorities. And if people wanted their voices to be heard, they had to organize in labor unions, trade associations, or other special-interest lobbies.

The New Deal failed in its fundamental purpose: to put people back to work. As late as 1938, over 10 million men and women were still jobless. That year unemployment was 19 percent; over the next two years it fell no lower than 14.6 percent. What plagued the nation throughout the 1930s was underconsumption: people and businesses either could not or would not purchase enough goods to sustain high levels of employment. In 1929, for example, sales of new cars totaled almost $6.5 billion; by

New Deal failure to solve unemployment

Distribution of Total Family Income* Among Various Segments of the Population, 1929–1944 (in percentages)

YEAR	POOREST FIFTH	SECOND POOREST FIFTH	MIDDLE FIFTH	SECOND WEALTHIEST FIFTH	WEALTHIEST FIFTH	WEALTHIEST 5 PERCENT
1929	12.5		13.8	19.3	54.4	30.0
1935–1936	4.1	9.2	14.1	20.9	51.7	26.5
1941	4.1	9.5	15.3	22.3	48.8	24.0
1944	4.9	10.9	16.2	22.2	45.8	20.7

*Monetary and nonmonetary income.

Source: Adapted from U.S. Bureau of the Census, *Historical Statistics of the United States, Colonial Times to 1970,* Bicentennial Edition (Washington: U.S. Government Printing Office, 1975), p. 301.

1933 that figure had dropped to $2.1 billion. Though New Deal pump priming helped to raise auto sales to $5.1 billion in 1936, Roosevelt's attempt to balance the budget reduced the figure to $3.9 billion in 1938. The same thing was true of capital investment in new industrial construction. In 1929 companies had invested $546 million in new buildings, but by 1933 the total had fallen to $128 million. It climbed again to $314 million in 1937, only to plummet in 1938 to $121 million.

Historians have debated whether the New Deal was radical or conservative, revolutionary or evolutionary. Edgar Eugene Robinson, a conservative, has called the New Deal a revolutionary break with the past. According to Robinson, it resulted "in a weakened Constitutional system, in imperiled national security, in diminished national morale, in deteriorated political morality, and in an overburdened economy." William Leuchtenburg, a liberal, has replied that some New Deal ideas had been around for decades before. In his view, the New Deal was "a halfway revolution" that "swelled the ranks of the bourgeoisie but left many Americans–sharecroppers, slum dwellers, most Negroes–outside of the new equilibrium."

Most historians would agree that if the New Deal was a revolution, it was a timid one, with few ideological underpinnings. In the end it was not the New Deal but massive government spending during the Second World War that put people back to work. In 1941, as a result of mobilization for war, unemployment would drop to 9.9 percent, and in 1944, the height of the war, only 1.2 percent of the labor force would be jobless.

Suggestions for further reading

The New Deal

Barton J. Bernstein, "The New Deal: The Conservative Achievements of Liberal Reform," in Barton J. Bernstein, ed., *Towards a New Past: Dissenting Essays in American History* (1968), 263–288; Paul K. Conkin, *FDR and the Origins*

Important events

1932	Franklin D. Roosevelt elected president
1933	13 million Americans unemployed National Bank Holiday Roosevelt's Hundred Days Agricultural Adjustment Act (AAA) Tennessee Valley Authority (TVA) National Industrial Recovery Act (NIRA) Twentieth (Lame Duck) Amendment to the Constitution Twenty-first Amendment repeals the Eighteenth (Prohibition) Amendment
1934	Dr. Francis Townsend's Old Age Revolving Pensions plan established Huey Long's Share Our Wealth Society established Indian Reorganization (Wheeler-Howard) Act Southern Tenant Farmers' Union established Major Democratic victories in congressional elections Father Charles Coughlin's National Union for Social Justice established
1935	Emergency Relief Appropriation Act Works Progress Administration *Schechter* v. *U.S.* invalidates NIRA National Labor Relations Act Social Security Act Huey Long assassinated Committee for Industrial Organization (CIO) established
1936	*U.S.* v. *Butler* invalidates AAA Roosevelt re-elected, defeating Landon Large Democratic majorities elected to both houses of Congress
1937	United Auto Workers' sit-down strikes Roosevelt introduces his "Court-packing" plan *NLRB* v. *Jones & Laughlin* upholds the Wagner Act Memorial Day Massacre Farm Security Administration
1937–39	Business recession
1938	AFL expels the CIO unions CIO reorganized as the Congress of Industrial Organizations (CIO) Fair Labor Standards Act Roosevelt's unsuccessful "purge" of southern Democratic senators 10.4 million Americans unemployed
1939	Marian Anderson's concert at the Lincoln Memorial
1940	Roosevelt re-elected, defeating Willkie
1941	March on Washington Movement Fair Employment Practices Committee (FEPC) established

of the Welfare State (1967); Otis L. Graham, Jr., *Encore for Reform: The Old Progressives and the New Deal* (1967); Ellis W. Hawley, *The New Deal and the Problem of Monopoly* (1966); William E. Leuchtenburg, *Franklin D. Roosevelt and the New Deal* (1963); Arthur M. Schlesinger, Jr., *The Age of Roosevelt*, 3 vols. (1957–1960); William J. Stewart, comp., *The Era of Franklin D. Roosevelt: A Selected Bibliography of Periodical, Essay, and Dissertation Literature, 1945–1971* (1974).

Franklin D. Roosevelt

James MacGregor Burns, *Roosevelt: The Lion and the Fox* (1956); Frank Freidel, *Franklin D. Roosevelt*, 4 vols. (1952–1973); Daniel R. Fusfeld, *The Economic Thought of Franklin D. Roosevelt and the Origins of the New Deal* (1956); Joseph P. Lash, *Eleanor and Franklin* (1971); Edgar Eugene Robinson, *The Roosevelt Leadership* (1955); Rexford G. Tugwell, *The Democratic Roosevelt* (1957).

Memoirs and diaries

John M. Blum, ed., *From the Morgenthau Diaries,* 3 vols. (1959–1967); Harold Ickes, *The Secret Diary of Harold L. Ickes,* 3 vols. (1953–1954); Raymond Moley, *After Seven Years* (1939); Frances Perkins, *The Roosevelt I Knew* (1946); Samuel I. Rosenman, *Working for Roosevelt* (1952).

Voices from the depression

James Agee, *Let Us Now Praise Famous Men* (1941); Ann Banks, ed., *First-Person America* (1980); Federal Writers' Project, *These Are Our Lives* (1939); Studs Terkel, *Hard Times: An Oral History of the Great Depression* (1970); Tom E. Terrill and Jerrold Hirsch, eds., *Such As Us: Southern Voices of the Thirties* (1978).

Alternatives to the New Deal

David H. Bennett, *Demagogues in the Depression* (1969); Abraham Holtzman, *The Townsend Movement* (1963); R. Alan Lawson, *The Failure of Independent Liberalism, 1930–1941* (1971); Donald R. McCoy, *Angry Voices: Left-of-Center Politics in the New Deal Era* (1958); Sheldon Marcus, *Father Coughlin* (1973); James T. Patterson, *Congressional Conservatism and the New Deal* (1967); Charles J. Tull, *Father Coughlin and the New Deal* (1965); Frank A. Warren, *Liberals and Communism: The "Red Decade" Revisited* (1966); Frank A. Warren, *An Alternative Vision: The Socialist Party in the 1930s* (1976); T. Harry Williams, *Huey Long* (1969); George Wolkskill, *The Revolt of the Conservatives: A History of the American Liberty League, 1934–1940* (1962).

Labor

Jerold S. Auerbach, *Labor and Liberty: The La Follette Committee and the New Deal* (1966); Irving Bernstein, *Turbulent Years: A History of the American Worker, 1933–1941* (1969); Melvin Dubofsky and Warren Van Tine, *John L. Lewis: A Biography* (1977); Sidney Fine, *Sit-Down: The General Motors Strike of 1936–1937* (1969); Walter Galenson, *The CIO Challenge to the AFL* (1960); David Milton, *The Politics of U.S. Labor: From the Great Depression to the New Deal* (1980); H. L. Mitchell, *Mean Things Happening in This Land* (1979).

Agriculture

Sidney Baldwin, *Poverty and Politics: The Rise and Decline of the Farm Security Administration* (1967); David E. Conrad, *The Forgotten Farmers: The Story of Sharecroppers in the New Deal* (1965); Richard S. Kirkendall, *Social Scientists and Farm Politics in the Age of Roosevelt* (1966); Walter J. Stein, *California and the Dust Bowl Migration* (1973); Donald Worster, *Dust Bowl: The Southern Plains in the 1930's* (1979).

Nonwhites

John B. Kirby, *Black Americans in the Roosevelt Era: Liberalism and Race* (1980); Harvard Sitkoff, *A New Deal for Blacks* (1978); Raymond Wolters, *Negroes and the Great Depression: The Problem of Economic Recovery* (1970); Donald L. Parman, *The Navajos and the New Deal* (1975); Kenneth Philp, *John Collier's Crusade for Indian Reform, 1920–1954* (1977); Abraham Hoffman, *Unwanted Mexican Americans in the Great Depression: Repatriation Pressures, 1929–1939* (1974); Carey McWilliams, *North from Mexico* (1949); Mark Reisler, *By the Sweat of Their Brow: Mexican Immigrant Labor in the United States, 1900–1940* (1976).

Cultural and intellectual history

Daniel Aaron, *Writers on the Left: Episodes in American Literary Communism* (1961); Andrew Bergman, *We're in the Money: Depression America and Its Films* (1971); Arthur A. Ekirch, Jr., *Ideologies and Utopias* (1971); Richard H. King, *A Southern Renaissance: The Cultural Awakening of the American South, 1930–1955* (1980); Jerre Mangione, *The Dream and the Deal: The Federal Writers' Project, 1935–1943* (1972); Richard H. Pells, *Radical Visions and American Dreams: Culture and Social Thought in the Depression Years* (1973); Warren I. Sussman, "The Thirties," in Stanley Coben and Lorman Ratner, eds., *The Development of an American Culture* (1970), 179–218.

27 DIPLOMACY IN A BROKEN WORLD, 1920–1941

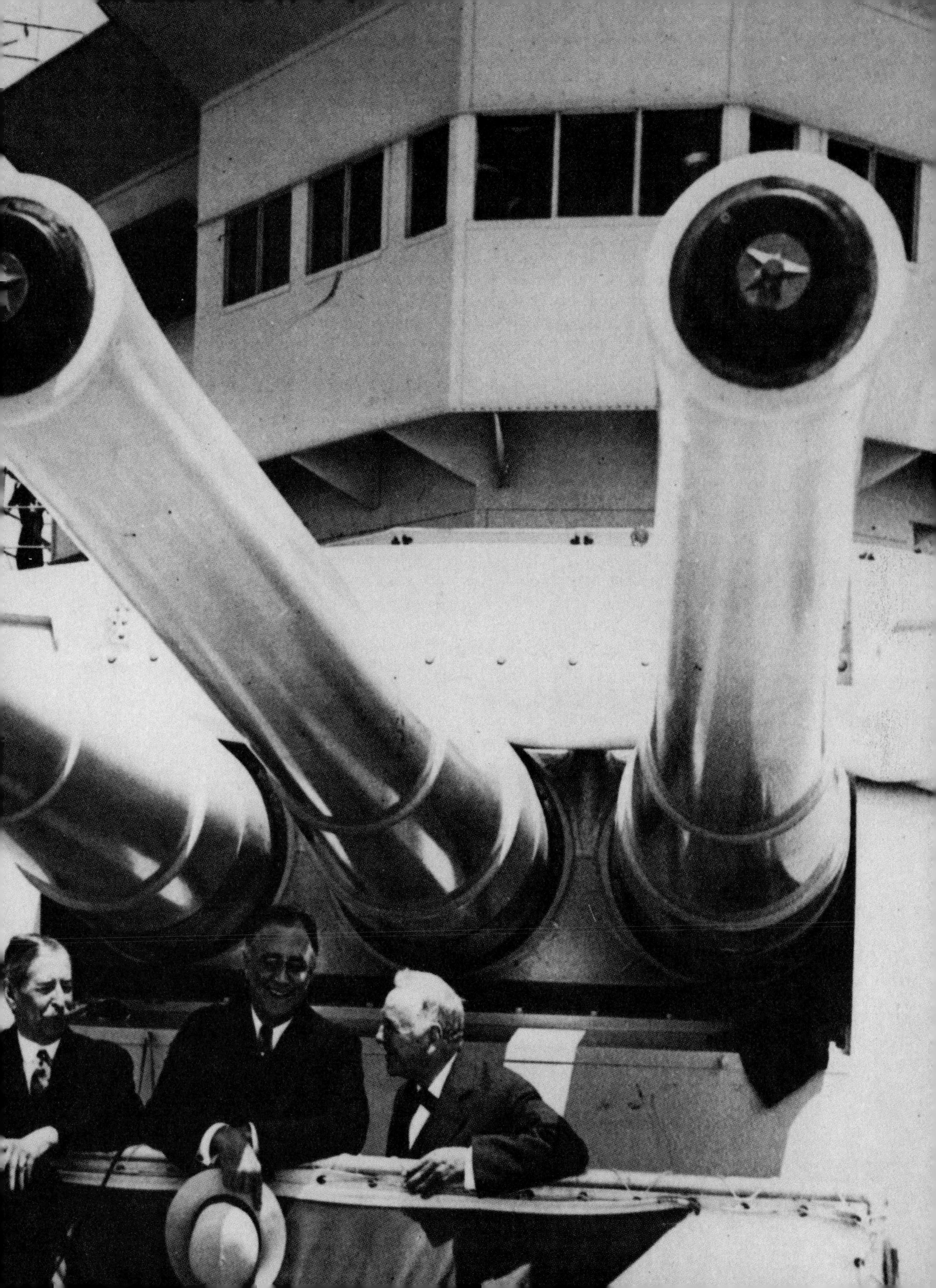

Franklin D. Roosevelt wanted to be like his famous older cousin Theodore. In fact, he set out to ape his cousin's career: both graduated from Harvard, served in the New York State legislature and as governor of that state and assistant secretary of the navy, ran for the vice presidency, and reached the presidency itself. Both were cosmopolitan, well-traveled, full of energy and ambition; both felt an aristocratic obligation to help those less fortunate than themselves. Like his cousin, FDR believed that the United States should have entered the First World War earlier than it did. He never doubted that the United States should exert leadership in the world community, or that military preparedness and a big navy would ensure American security and prosperity.

Like Theodore Roosevelt, FDR was an expansionist and interventionist who had imbibed the arrogant belief that Americans knew what was best for other societies. "Sooner or later . . . the United States must go down there and clean up the Mexican political mess," he remarked in 1914. Later, as assistant secretary of the navy, Roosevelt helped to write the constitution the United States imposed on Haiti. And in 1920 he defended American membership in the League of Nations by boasting that the United States would control the votes of Latin American countries.

FDR's later statements, however, would not have pleased his cousin (who died in 1919). Like most Americans during the interwar period, Roosevelt talked less about preparedness and more about disarmament and the horrors of war. Alert to public criticism of American military intervention in Latin America, he moved toward a Good Neighbor policy and stressed economic rather than military ties. Convinced that nonrecognition of Soviet Russia was counterproductive, he came to favor diplomatic relations with that power. And bewildered like most Americans by the First World War debts-reparations tangle and the havoc of the Great Depression, Roosevelt tried to protect the nation from global economic troubles while preserving and expanding its share in the international marketplace. When Europe and Asia descended into diplomatic crisis and war in the 1930s, Roosevelt declared that the United States should avoid foreign squabbles, and he signed the "isolationist" Neutrality Acts.

Yet in the late 1930s, like many other Americans, Roosevelt changed his mind. Perceiving Germany and Japan as a terrible menace to the national interest, he first appealed for preparedness and then begged the nation to abandon its neutrality in order to aid Britain and France. German victory in Europe, he reasoned, would imperil Western political principles, destroy traditional American economic links, threaten America's sphere of influence in the Western Hemisphere, and place at the pinnacle of European power a fanatical man—Adolf Hitler—whose ambitions and barbarities knew no limits.

At the same time Japan seemed determined to dismember America's friend China, to squelch the principle of the Open Door, and to surround and isolate the American colony of the Philippines. To deter Japanese expansion in the Pacific, Roosevelt cut off supplies of vital American products like oil. But economic warfare only confirmed the Japanese suspicion that the United States was hostile to its empire. Japan's surprise attack on Pearl Harbor finally brought the United States into the Second World War. Americans had wanted peace. But the relentless march of the militarists boded ill for the kind of world Americans thought necessary to their well-being. By 1941 they were convinced that remaining at peace would be more costly than going to war.

Roosevelt and independent internationalism

The man who directed American foreign policy in the vexing depression decade was a believer in personal diplomacy. Roosevelt centralized decision making in the White House, failing on many occasions to inform the Department of State or Secretary Cordell Hull about his thinking. Often he relied on his wit, charm, and knowledge of details to persuade. Using his cigarette holder like a magic wand, this enormously self-confident man spun stories in a happy-go-lucky style that often disarmed his enemies. His penchant for covering over differences sometimes misled or confused people. State Department officers complained that Roosevelt wrote vague and imprecise agreements that invited misinterpretation. "Roosevelt never was much of a stickler for language," Ambassador W. Averell Harriman recalled. Indeed, the president did not always think carefully or thoroughly about international problems, especially early in his long tenure, when he concentrated on the domestic crisis. He shunned complex overviews and abstract theories, preferring to work with the issue at hand "by inspiration," as one of his advisers commented. And he was, as he himself noted, "a good horse trader."

Always the ambitious politician, alert to the temper of the times, Roosevelt both reflected and shaped the public mood in the interwar years. It would be wrong to depict him solely as an opportunistic politician who always did what was expedient; he had his own views, which happened frequently to coincide with popular opinion. And though he seldom strayed from what he thought was public opinion, he did, when he believed it necessary, influence that opinion in his own direction.

Interwar public attitudes on foreign relations have often been characterized as *isolationist.* Historians agree, however, that the term is misleading in its suggestion that the United States cut itself off from international affairs after the First World War. There was isolationist thought: Americans sought to isolate themselves from war, from foreign military intervention, and from entangling commitments that might restrict their freedom of choice. But there was also considerable activity in world affairs—from gunboats on Chinese rivers to negotiations in the financial centers of Europe to manipulation of governments in Latin America. A more useful and accurate description of interwar foreign policy is *independent internationalism.* That is, in the interwar years the United States was active on a global scale but retained its independence of action, its traditional unilateralism. Even had they wanted to, Americans could not have escaped the tumult of international relations; their interests were too far-flung and too vast: colonies, client states, overseas naval bases, investments, trade, missionaries. Franklin D. Roosevelt and his compatriots, then, were isolationists in their adamant desire to avoid war, but independent internationalists in their behavior in foreign affairs.

The desire to avoid war led American leaders to search for nonmilitary means to exercise power. In the aftermath of the First World War, Americans had grown disenchanted with military methods of achieving order and protecting American prosperity and security. "We can never herd the world into the paths of righteousness with the dogs of war," Herbert Hoover said. American diplomats thus put increasing emphasis on conferences, moral lectures and calls for peace, nonrecognition of disapproved regimes, arms control, and economic and financial ties in accord with the principle of the Open Door.

American leaders deemed this last means to power, economic and financial ties, extremely important. In the early 1920s Secretary of State Charles Evans Hughes predicted that "there will be no permanent peace unless economic satisfactions are enjoyed." Like the nation's business leaders, Hughes expected American economic expansion to bring about world stability: out of economic prosperity would spring a world free from political extremes, revolution, aggression, and war. The government thus facilitated business activities abroad through the Webb-Pomerene Act (which excluded from antitrust prosecution those combinations set up for export trade); the Edge Act (which permitted foreign branch banks); and the overseas offices of the Department of Commerce. It also stimulated and monitored foreign loans made by American investors, discouraging those that might be used for military purposes.

Interwar economic expansion

United States economic influence became conspicuous after the First World War. By the late 1920s the United States produced about half the world's industrial goods, ranked first among exporters ($5.4 billion worth of shipments in 1929), and acted as the financial capital of the world (see map, page 754). In the period from 1914 to 1930 private investments abroad grew fivefold, to over $17 billion. To cite some examples, General Electric joined international cartels and invested heavily in Germany; American companies handled a third of the oil sales in France and had begun to exploit Venezuela's rich petroleum resources; the Radio Corporation of America built Poland's radio system. Britain and Germany lost ground to enterprising American businesses in Latin America, where Standard Oil was active in eight nations, the United Fruit Company was a huge landowner, and International Telephone and Telegraph dominated Cuba's communications network.

Many foreigners saw United States expansionism as imperialism. A famous Argentine critic, the writer Manuel Ugarte, asserted that the United States was a

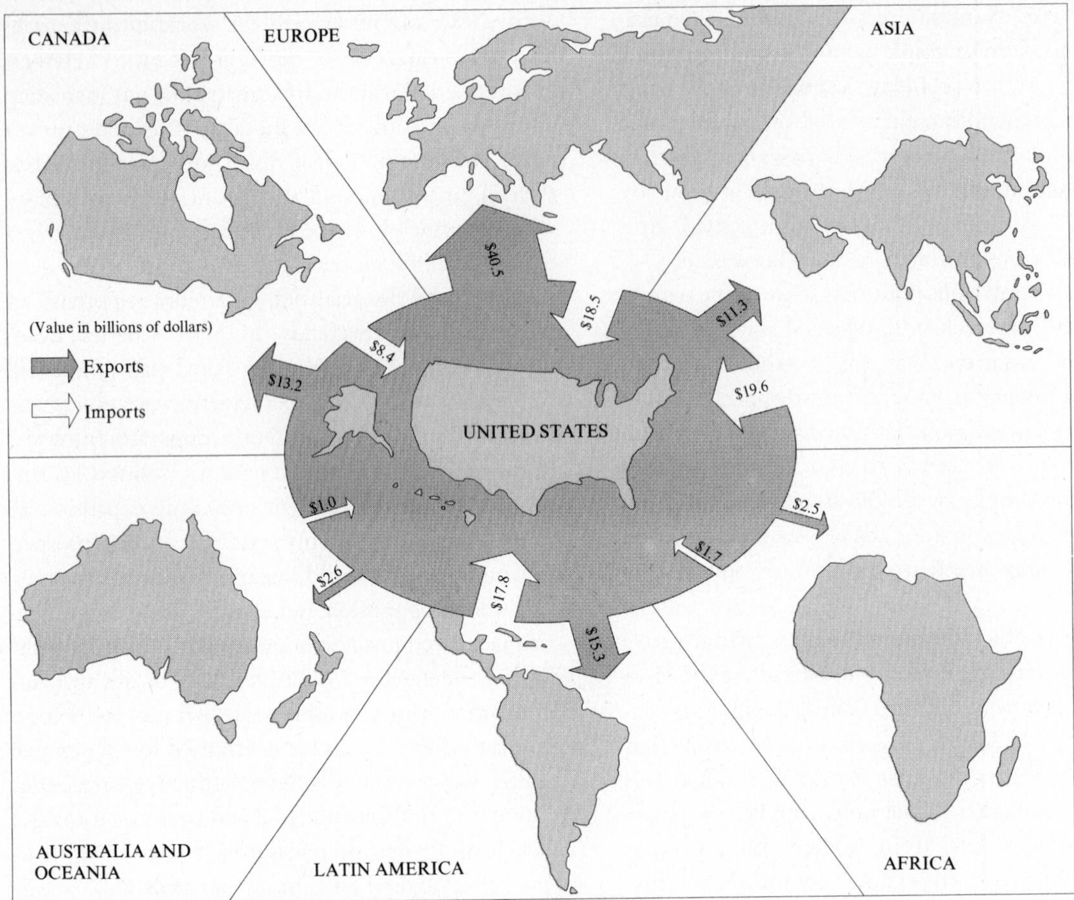

United States foreign trade, 1920–1941

new Rome: it annexed wealth rather than territory, enjoying the "essentials of domination" without the "dead-weight of areas to administrate and multitudes to govern." To such criticisms the American ambassador to Chile replied that "American capital will be the controlling factor in public and private finance in these countries. . . . American civilization, material and cultural, is bound to impress itself upon, and I believe, benefit these peoples. If anti-American critics wish to describe this as our 'imperialism' let them make the most of it."

Negotiating with the Europeans

Not only in Latin America but in Europe many shared the view that the United States was blatantly self-interested. Europe lay in shambles at the end of the war. It is estimated that from 1914 to 1921 there were sixty million casualties in Europe from world war, civil war, massacre, epidemic, and famine. Germany and France each lost 10 percent of its workers. Crops, livestock, factories, trains, forests, bridges—little was spared. Currencies lost value and trading patterns were disrupted. The desperate plight of Europeans drew American sympathies and aid. The American Relief Administration delivered food to needy Europeans, including Russians who were wracked by famine in 1921 and 1922. All told, private charities and official relief programs delivered foodstuffs valued at over half a billion dollars.

But if Americans won praise from Europeans for their humanitarianism, they earned the nickname Uncle Shylock for their handling of war debts and reparations, an issue that dogged international relations for a decade. Twenty-eight nations were tangled in the web of inter-Allied debts which totaled $26.5

First World War debts and reparations

billion, about half of it owed to the United States. Europeans urged Americans to forgive the debts as a magnanimous contribution to the war. During the war, they charged, Europe had bled while America profited. But American leaders insisted on repayment. "They hired the money, didn't they?" Coolidge reportedly said. Other Americans argued that the victorious European nations had gained vast lands and resources through the war; to cancel their debts would be to increase their spoils even more. Senator George Norris, emphasizing domestic priorities, declared that the United States could build highways in "every county seat" if the Europeans would only pay their debts.

The debts question was linked to Germany's $33 billion reparations bill. Hobbled by inflation and economic disorder, Germany had begun to default on its payments. Americans grew worried that German economic troubles would spawn radicalism. To keep Germany afloat, American bankers poured millions of dollars in loans into the floundering nation. A triangular relationship developed: American investors' money flowed to Germany; German reparations payments went to the Allies; the Allies then paid some of their debts to the United States. The American-crafted Dawes Plan of 1924 greased the financial tracks by reducing Germany's annual payments, extending the repayment period, and providing still more loans. And the United States gradually scaled down Allied obligations, cutting the debt by half during the 1920s.

But the triangular arrangement was dependent on continued German borrowing in the United States, and in 1928 and 1929 American lending abroad declined sharply in the face of more lucrative opportunities in the stock market. The American-negotiated Young Plan of 1929, which reduced the total of Germany's reparations, salvaged little as the international economy sputtered and collapsed. That year the British rejected an ingenious offer from Hoover to trade their debt altogether for British Honduras, Bermuda, and Trinidad. By 1931, when Hoover declared a moratorium on payments, the Allies had paid back only $2.6 billion. Wracked by depression, they defaulted on the rest.

In the end, American economic power had proved unable to sustain a healthy world economy. But many nations shared responsibility for the failure. The selfish and vengeful Europeans might have trimmed Germany's huge indemnity. The Germans might have borrowed less from abroad and taxed themselves more. The Bolsheviks might have agreed to pay rather than repudiate Russia's $4 billion indebtedness. And Americans might have tried for a comprehensive, multinational settlement and lower their tariffs, giving Europeans a market in which to earn the money to pay off their debt.

American influence also failed to curb militarism and prevent war. During the 1920s and 1930s peace societies advocated numerous strategies to preserve world order: cooperation with the League of Nations; membership in the World Court; disarmament; arms reduction; curbs on exploitative business ventures; arbitration of international disputes; the outlawing of war; and strict neutrality in times of belligerency. The Fellowship of Reconciliation, the Women's International League for Peace and Freedom, and the National Council for Prevention of War, among others, struggled to remind Americans of the carnage of the First World War and the futility of war as a solution to international problems. Antiwar films like *What Price Glory* (1926) and *Submarine* (1928) emphasized the cruelties of military combat. And in a contest in 1922 the eminent publisher Edward Bok offered a $100,000 prize for the essay that presented the most workable plan for permanent peace. Franklin D. Roosevelt drew up his peace formula, but because his wife Eleanor was one of the judges, it was not included among the more than 22,000 entries. The winner, Charles E. Levermore, secretary of the New York Peace Society, championed immediate entry into the World Court and partial participation in the League of Nations.

At the time the Washington Conference (1921–1922) seemed a substantial step toward arms control.

Washington Conference

There the United States discussed with eight other nations limits on naval armaments. Britain, the United States, and Japan, the three top naval powers, were facing a costly postwar naval arms race, and they welcomed the opportunity to deflect it. As Secretary Hughes argued, the arms competition had to stop because large military expenditures endangered economic rehabilitation. In the Five-Power Treaty the delegates set a ten-year moratorium on the construc-

"Come on in. I'll treat you right. I used to know your daddy." Clarence D. Batchelor's haunting antiwar cartoon recalling the human tragedy of the First World War. The artist won a Pulitzer Prize for his statement. Clarence D. Batchelor, *New York Daily News,* April 25, 1936. Reprinted by permission.

tion of large, or capital, ships, and established a total tonnage ratio of 5:5:3:1.75:1.75 among the five top nations (Britain : United States : Japan : France : Italy). The first three nations actually agreed to dismantle some existing vessels to meet the ratio. To assuage the Japanese, who were vexed over their third-place standing, the United States promised not to build new fortifications in the Philippines.

Several other agreements were reached at the conference. The Nine-Power Treaty reaffirmed the Open Door in China (see page 625). In the Four-Power Treaty, the United States, England, Japan, and France agreed to respect each other's Pacific possessions and to consult in the event of aggression in Asia. In another agreement Japan pledged to pull back from Shandong and Russian Siberia. But although the treaties signed at Washington provided a rare and noble example of mutual disarmament, they did not, critics pointed out, limit submarines, destroyers, or cruisers, and there were no provisions for enforcement of the Open Door declaration. Subsequent conferences in the 1930s produced only angry bickering and meager results, setting back the gains made in Washington.

Kellogg-Briand Pact

Peace advocates next placed their hopes in the Kellogg-Briand Pact of 1928, eventually signed by sixty-two nations. The signatories agreed simply to "condemn recourse to war for the solution of international controversies, and renounce it as an instrument of national policy." The treaty's backers billed it as a first step in a long journey toward international cooperation and the outlawry of war. Though it passed the Senate 85 to 1, many senators thought the document no more than a moral statement, because it lacked provisions for enforcement; Roosevelt dismissed it as unrealistic but harmless. The agreement did in fact prove impotent in the 1930s. But however weak it was, the pact reflected a sincere popular belief that war was barbaric, inhumane, and wasteful; and it served a useful educational purpose in getting people to think about peace and war.

The League of Nations, also looked to as a peacemaker, exhibited a conspicuous feebleness, not only because the United States refused to join, but because members themselves usually chose not to use it to settle disputes. Starting in the mid-1920s, however, American officials did participate discreetly in League meetings on public health, prostitution, drug trafficking, and other such questions. By 1930 American "observers" had sat in on over forty League conferences. And individual jurists like Charles Evans Hughes served on the World Court in Geneva, although the United States also refused to join that institution.

Relations with Russia

Soviet Russia was a special problem in American foreign relations. Following Wilsonian precedent, the Republican administrations of the 1920s refused to recognize the Soviet government, arguing that the Bolsheviks were not meeting their international obligations. The Russians had refused to pay over $600 million owed to Americans for the confiscation of American-owned property and the repudiation of debts incurred before the Bolshevik takeover in 1917.

Beneath a portrait of the Soviet leader Josef Stalin (1879–1953), a Russian-made Model A Ford rolls off the assembly line of the Molotov Auto Plant. In an unusual arrangement for the 1920s, Henry Ford assisted Communist Russia in developing its automobile industry. Sovfoto.

To Americans the Communists were also godless, radical malcontents bent on destroying the American way of life through world revolution. The American Federation of Labor, the American Legion, the Catholic Church, and the New York *Times* all agreed with State Department officers that Moscow should be ostracized. Others, like Senator William Borah, the *New Republic,* and the International Ladies' Garment Workers' Union, although they did not admire the authoritarian Soviet system, urged tolerance of the fledgling government.

Americans gradually increased communication with Russia. In the early 1920s Herbert Hoover, then secretary of commerce, organized a famine relief program for Russia with the mixed motive of humanitarianism and anti-Communism. American food, medicine, and clothing soon reached some 10 million needy Russians. And after the trade ban was lifted in

1920, American businesses began to enter the Soviet marketplace, offering the American technology and machinery sought by V. I. Lenin to reconstruct his scarred nation. International Harvester, General Electric, and Du Pont, among others, signed technical-assistance agreements and trade pacts with Soviet agencies. Henry Ford himself signed a contract in 1929 to build a huge automobile plant using Ford mass-production methods (*Fordizatsia*). By 1930 and 1931 Russia was the largest foreign buyer of American agricultural and industrial equipment.

In the early 1930s, however, trade began to slump. To stimulate business and help the United States pull out of the depression, some businesspeople began to lobby for diplomatic recognition of Russia. "We would recognize the Devil with a false face if he would contract for some pitchforks," quipped Will Rogers. President Roosevelt agreed that a change in policy was necessary, not only to improve trade. Roosevelt believed it foolish not to recognize a major country like Russia; nonrecognition had failed to alter the Soviet system, but closer Russian-American relations might deter the Japanese and stabilize Asia.

After sounding out public opinion, which seemed favorable, and deftly disarming critics of recognition, Roosevelt began negotiations with the Soviet Commissar for Foreign Affairs, Maxim Litvinov. In a classic example of personal, one-on-one diplomacy, Roosevelt hammered out a number of agreements, some of them vague in language: United States recognition of Soviet Russia; future discussion of the debts question; a Soviet promise to forgo propagandistic or subversive activities in the United States; and religious freedom and legal rights for Americans in Russia. The first American ambassador to Soviet Russia enthusiastically opened the American embassy in Moscow in 1934. But within a few years, Soviet-American relations had once again become embittered. Especially upsetting to Americans was Moscow's pact with Nazi Germany in 1939.

Sphere of influence in Latin America

Before the First World War the United States had thrown an imperial net over much of Latin America by means of the Platt Amendment, the Roosevelt Corollary, construction of the Panama Canal, military intervention, and economic domination (see Chapter 22). By the 1920s the supposed benefits of American expansionism—hospitals, schools, roads, telephones, and irrigation systems—were evident in much of Latin America. As one observer put it, America's "imperialistic temper" was "manifested in works of benevolence." A patronizing attitude permeated United States activities in the region. A leading State Department officer told the Foreign Service School that the Latins were incapable of political progress because of their temperament, the tropical climate, and their "low racial quality." They were, however, "very easy people to deal with if properly managed." And managed they were. United States financial advisers supervised government budgets in the Caribbean, and in 1920 American soldiers occupied Cuba, the Dominican Republic, Haiti, Panama, and Nicaragua.

Yet these military expeditions to Latin America were becoming unpopular and counterproductive. Critics like Senator William Borah insisted that South Americans should be granted the right of self-determination. The president was usurping constitutional power, others protested, by ordering troops to Latin America without a congressional declaration of war. Businesspeople feared that nationalists would direct their anti-Yanqui emotion against American *gringos* and their property. And there was the embarrassment of the double standard. Secretary of State Henry L. Stimson outlined the problem in 1932 when he was protesting Japanese incursions in China: "If we landed a single soldier among those South Americans now . . . it would put me absolutely in the wrong in China, where Japan has done all this monstrous work under the guise of protecting her nationals with a landing force."

Good Neighbor policy

Turning away pragmatically from military intervention, then, the United States sought less controversial methods of maintaining its influence in Latin America: Pan-Americanism; support for strong native leaders; the training of national guards; economic penetration; Export-Import Bank loans; and when necessary, political subversion. Although the process began before his presidency, Roosevelt gave it a name in 1933: the Good Neighbor policy. Good Neighborism did not mean that Latin America would escape from the United States sphere of in-

whereby the United States was entitled to the lowest tariff rate set by a nation with which it had a most-favored-nation agreement. For example, if Belgium negotiated an agreement with Germany that reduced the Belgian tariff on German typewriters, American typewriters would receive the same low rate. In 1934 Hull also sponsored the creation of the Export-Import Bank, a government agency that provided loans to foreigners for the purchase of American goods. The bank not only stimulated trade but became a formidable diplomatic weapon, allowing the United States to exact concessions through the approval or denial of loans. Though Hull's ambitious programs brought only mixed results in the short term, they stood as rare examples of internationalism in an era of rampant nationalism.

Meanwhile, as the Great Depression cut a destructive path through the international economy, the peoples of other nations turned to political extremism. In Germany, where 6 million workers were unemployed in the early thirties, Adolf Hitler came to power. Like Benito Mussolini, who had gained control of Italy in 1922, Hitler was a fascist. Fascism (called Nazism, or National Socialism, in Germany) was a collection of ideas and prejudices that included supremacy of the state over the individual; of dictatorship over democracy; of authoritarianism over freedom of speech; and of militarism and war over peace. The Nazis vowed not only to revive German economic and military strength, but to "purify" the German "race" of Jewish influence, for which they blamed Germany's problems. In Japan militarists justified aggression in Asia by arguing that their country was so dependent on foreign trade that it could not survive without foreign economic resources, such as those of Manchuria. Political instability and social unrest also rocked Latin America, where a host of dictators seized governments. Democracies like Britain, France, and the United States seemed paralyzed, preoccupied with their own economic crises and unable or unwilling to halt the momentum toward rearmament and war.

As for the United States, the depression reinforced isolationist, or independent internationalist, thought.

Isolationist sentiment

American memories of the First World War were largely negative: the shelving of reform; civil liberties abuses; unusual federal and presidential power; race riots; inflation; windfalls for business; govern-

fluence. It did mean that the United States would be less blatant in its domination—less willing to defend exploitative business practices, less eager to send in military expeditions, and less wary of consultation with Latin Americans. "Give them a share," FDR recommended. In 1936 he approved a treaty that restored some sovereignty to Panama and increased that nation's income from the canal. Roosevelt's popularity in Latin America grew enormously for this and other such acts.

So did American interests. From 1914 to 1929, direct American investments in Latin America (excluding bonds and securities) jumped from almost $1.3 billion to $3.5 billion. In the same period American exports to the area tripled in value. In country after country Latin Americans felt the repercussions of American economic and political decisions. The price Americans set for Chilean copper determined whether Chile was up or down in the business cycle. American oil executives bribed Venezuelan politicians for tax breaks. In Honduras, where United Fruit and Standard Fruit accounted for most of the nation's revenue, American interests helped to stage a successful coup (1924). And United States influence in Cuba was such that "the American Ambassador was the second most important man in Cuba, sometimes even more important than the [Cuban] President," according to Ambassador to Cuba Earl T. Smith. What was more, American businesses drew substantially greater sums out of Latin America in profits than they put in as investments. Latin American nationalists complained that their resources were being drained away, and that many of their own businesspeople put their profits not into investments at home but into New Orleans and New York banks.

The training of national guards went hand in hand with support of dictators: many Latin American dictators rose to power through the ranks of a U.S.-trained

Training of national guards

national guard. For example, before the United States withdrew its troops from the Dominican Republic in 1924, American personnel created a constabulary. One of its first officers was Rafael Leonidas Trujillo, who became head of the National Army in 1928. Trujillo became president in 1930 through fraud and intimidation, and ruled the Dominican Republic with an iron fist until his assassination in 1961. American loans flowed to him. "He may be an S.O.B.," Roosevelt remarked candidly, "but he is our S.O.B."

In Nicaragua the experience was similar. The United States occupied Nicaragua from 1912 to 1925 and returned in late 1926 during a civil war. The justification for United States involvement was the need to clean up and stabilize Nicaragua's politics. One critic, Senator George Norris, suggested sarcastically that if the United States believed it necessary to dispatch soldiers to ensure free elections, they ought to be sent first to notoriously corrupt Philadelphia and Pittsburgh. Anti-Yanqui resistance, led by the rebel Augusto Sandino, and noisy opposition at home and abroad finally prompted Washington to end the occupation, and in 1933 the U.S. Marines departed. But they left behind a powerful national guard headed by General Anastasio Somoza, who "always played the game fairly with us," according to the top-ranked American military officer there. With American backing, the Somoza family would rule Nicaragua from 1936 to 1979 through corruption, political suppression, and torture, while anti-Americanism simmered among the masses.

The long Marine Corps occupation of black, French-speaking Haiti from 1915 to 1934 had similarly negative results. Even the most charitable historian must point out that American intervention did

Occupation of Haiti

not establish democracy or improve Haitian life. As the prominent critic Samuel Guy Inman put it at the time, American methods inflicted a "punishment more severe than the crime [political instability]." American officials censored the Haitian press; manipulated elections; wrote the constitution; jailed or killed thousands of protesters; managed governmental finances; and created a national guard. Under American supervision, the National City Bank of New York became the owner of the Haitian Banque Nationale and the United States became Haiti's largest trading partner. The American High Commissioner, General John H. Russell of Georgia, actually stated that the Haitian president "has never taken a step without first consulting me."

American black leaders were particularly alert to Haitian issues. Just before his death, Booker T. Washington spoke of the "benevolence" of American intentions and relished the prospect of establishing another Tuskegee Institute in the island nation. But

Senator William E. Borah (1865–1940), an influential isolationist and champion of disarmament, the Kellogg-Briand Pact, nonintervention in Latin America, and the neutrality acts. Few spokesmen matched his passionate oratory or fierce independence. Library of Congress.

The Great Depression and growing isolationism

Secretary of State Cordell Hull liked to say that the character of international relations derived from economic conditions. In the 1930s the effect of economics was particularly apparent as the Great Depression swept through both hemispheres, shattering international order. Hull pointed in 1935 to political extremism, border squabbles, resurgent militarism, increased military expenditures, and new weapons development as products of maimed economies. "We cannot have a peaceful world, we cannot have a prosperous world," he advised, "until we rebuild the international economic structure." Hull was right; the

dence that corporations had bribed foreign politicians to improve arms sales in the 1920s and 1930s, and had lobbied against arms control. And records show that isolationists were correct to suspect American business ties with Nazi Germany and fascist Italy. Twenty-six of the top one hundred American corporations in 1937 had contractual agreements with Germany. And after Italy attacked Ethiopia in 1935, American petroleum, copper, and iron and steel scrap exports to Italy increased substantially, despite Roosevelt's call for a moral embargo on those items. Du Pont, Standard Oil, General Motors, and Union Carbide executives apparently agreed with a Dow Chemical Company officer, who stated, "We do not inquire into the uses of the products. We are interested in selling them." (One exception was the Wall Street firm of Sullivan and Cromwell, which cut lucrative ties with Germany in protest against the persecution of Jews.)

European upheaval and American neutrality

In 1933, resentful of the punitive terms of the Treaty of Paris (1919), Hitler pulled Germany out of the League of Nations, ended reparations payments, and began to rearm. Secretly laying plans for the conquest of neighboring states, he watched admiringly as Mussolini's troops invaded the African nation of Ethiopia in 1935. The next year Hitler ordered his goose-stepping troopers into the Rhineland, an area the Treaty of Paris had declared demilitarized. Germany's timid neighbor France did not resist. "The world belongs to the man with guts!" crowed Hitler.

Soon the aggressors began to join hands. In fall 1936 Italy and Germany formed an alliance called the Rome-Berlin Axis. Shortly thereafter Germany and Japan united against Russia in the Anti-Comintern Pact. To these events Britain and France responded with a policy of appeasement, hoping to curb Hitler's expansionist appetite by permitting him a few nibbles. But the policy eventually proved disastrous; taking advantage of European caution, the German leader continually raised his demands.

In those hair-trigger times, a civil war in Spain turned into an international struggle: from 1936 to 1939 the Loyalist Republicans battled the fascist-backed insurgents of Francisco Franco. Hitler and Mussolini sent military aid to Franco; Russia assisted the Loyalists. France and Britain held to the fiction of a nonintervention pledge that even Italy and Germany had signed. And a few hundred American volunteers known as the Lincoln Battalion joined the fight on the side of the Republicans. When Franco won in 1939, his victory tightened the grip of fascism on the European continent.

Early in 1938 Hitler once again tested the limits of European patience when he sent his soldiers into Austria to annex that nation. In September of the same year he seized the Sudeten region of Czechoslovakia. Appeasement reached its peak that month at the Munich Conference when France and Britain, without consulting the helpless Czechs, agreed to allow Hitler this one last territorial bite. British Prime Minister Neville Chamberlain returned home to proclaim "peace in our time," confident he had quieted the dictator. But in March 1939 Hitler swallowed the rest of Czechoslovakia. Poland was next on his list. Scuttling appeasement, London and Paris announced they would stand by their ally. Undaunted, Germany neutralized Russia by signing the Nazi-Soviet Pact and struck Poland on September 1. Britain and France, dismissed by Hitler as "worms," declared war on Germany two days later. The Second World War had begun.

However much they opposed fascism and disapproved aggression, Americans tried to stay clear of the recurrent crises of the 1930s. Americans resented the fact that some Europeans looked to the United States to do what they themselves refused to do: block Hitler. With each crisis isolationist sentiment rose. In a series of neutrality acts Congress sought to protect the nation by severing the kind of contact that had compromised American neutrality two decades earlier.

Neutrality Acts

The Neutrality Act of 1935 prohibited arms shipments to either side in a war once the president had declared the existence of belligerency. Roosevelt had wanted the authority to name the aggressor and apply an arms embargo against it alone, but Congress was reluctant to leave such matters to the president's discretion. The Neutrality Act of 1936 forbade loans to belligerents. A joint resolution in 1937 declared the

Nazi dictator Adolf Hitler (1889–1945), the maniacal militarist who set out to restore his nation's lost grandeur through annihilation of its enemies. Hitler's seemingly insatiable appetite for conquest convinced many Americans that war was unavoidable. Library of Congress.

United States neutral in the Spanish Civil War; Roosevelt then embargoed arms shipments to both sides. And finally, the Neutrality Act of 1937 introduced the cash-and-carry principle: warring nations wishing to trade with the United States would have to pay cash for their purchases and carry the goods away in their own ships. The act also forbade Americans from traveling on vessels of belligerent nations.

All the while Roosevelt groped for answers to the European disruptions. He abhorred the Nazi regime and fascist Italy; privately he wished for ways to support the British and French against the aggressors. But politician and independent internationalist that he was, he signed the Neutrality Acts and warned against foreign entanglements. In a stirring speech at Chautauqua, New York, in August 1936, Roosevelt made a pitch for the pacifist vote in the upcoming election and declared his commitment to isolationism. "I have seen war. . . . I have seen blood running from the wounded. I have seen men coughing out their gassed lungs. . . . I have seen the agony of mothers and wives. I hate war." He promised that the United States would remain distant from European conflict. During the Czech crisis of 1938 Roosevelt actually endorsed appeasement. The United States, he wrote to Hitler, had "no political involvements in Europe." The results of the Munich Conference, he commented on another occasion, elicited a "universal sense of relief."

But Roosevelt was deeply troubled by the arrogant behavior of the "three bandit nations," Germany, Italy, and Japan. He was disgusted by Nazi persecution of the Jews and by Japanese slaughter of Chinese civilians. Privately he snarled against the refusal of the British and French to collar Hitler in their own backyards. And he worried that the United States was militarily ill-prepared to confront the aggressors.

The United States had not been neglecting its military. Roosevelt's New Deal public works programs included millions for the construction of new ships. In 1935 the president requested the largest peacetime defense budget in American history; three years later, in the wake of Munich, he urgently asked Congress for funds to build up the air force. "Had we had this summer 5,000 planes and the capacity immediately to produce 10,000 per year," he told his chief civilian and military advisers, "Hitler would not have dared to take the stand he did." (Whether Hitler would have been deterred by a militarily superior United States is questionable, given the Führer's view of Americans as a mongrel race incapable of playing an important role in foreign affairs.) The president also began to cast about for ways to encourage the British and French to show more backbone. One result was his agreement in January 1939 to sell bombers to France.

Finally, in his annual message early in 1939, the president lashed out at the international lawbreakers. Soon afterward he urged Congress to repeal the arms embargo and permit the sale of munitions to belligerents on a cash-and-carry basis. Roosevelt saw repeal as an aid to Britain, which dominated the seas. When the Senate Foreign Relations Committee balked, voting down repeal by a 12-to-11 vote, Roosevelt exploded: "I think we ought to introduce a bill for statues of [Senators] Austin, Vandenberg, Lodge and Taft . . . to be erected in Berlin and put the swastika on them." Although he did not yet have the votes to win repeal, he stepped up his public condemnation of the aggressors, warning them that "we, too, have a stake in world affairs." Hitler shot back that the president was a "contemptible . . . creature."

Roosevelt proposes repeal of arms embargo

When Europe fell into the abyss of war in September 1939, Roosevelt declared neutrality. But unlike Woodrow Wilson, he did not ask Americans to be neutral in thought, and he pressed again for repeal of the arms embargo. Senator Arthur Vandenberg, an isolationist from Michigan, roared back that the United States could not be "an arsenal for one belligerent without becoming a target for the other." After much lobbying, debate, and bipartisan consultation, however, Congress revised the neutrality legislation. In November 1939 it lifted the embargo on contraband and approved cash-and-carry exports of arms. Now Roosevelt was ready to aid the Allies–short of war–and to challenge the isolationists more boldly.

A new order in Asia

If United States power was massive in Latin America and limited in Europe, it was minuscule in Asia. Still, there were American interests in that region that required defense in the interwar period: the Philippines and Pacific islands; religious missions; trade and investments; and the Open Door in China. Americans increasingly saw the Japanese as a threat to these interests, and specifically as strong-willed expansionists bent on subjugating China and unhinging the Open Door doctrine of equal trade and investment opportunity. Pearl Buck's best-selling novel *The Good Earth* (1931), made into a widely distributed film six years later, confirmed their opinion with its image of the noble, persevering Chinese peasant. In traditional missionary fashion, Americans came to believe they were China's special friend, its protector and uplifter. "With God's help," Senator Kenneth Wherry proclaimed, "we will lift Shanghai up and up, ever up, until it is just like Kansas City."

The American presence in China aroused serious resistance from the start of the interwar period, first from the Chinese and then from the Japanese. Both

Jiang Jieshi (1887–1976) and his wife Song Meiling were *Time* magazine's Man and Wife of the Year in 1937. Their resistance to Japanese aggression in the 1930s and to Russian advances in the 1940s earned Jiang's regime considerable foreign aid. Reprinted by permission from *Time,* the Weekly Newsmagazine; Copyright Time Inc. 1938.

nations wished to exclude white foreigners from Asia. The highly nationalistic Chinese Revolution of 1911 still rumbled in the 1920s; antiforeign riots increased, visiting damage on American property and harassment and violence on American missionaries, business representatives and sailors. And Chinese nationalists demanded an end to the imperialistic practice of extraterritoriality (the exemption of foreigners accused of crimes from Chinese legal jurisdiction). When nationalist leader Sun Zhongshan (Sun Yat-sen) invited Soviet agent Michael Borodin to help him reorganize the governing Guomindong party, some Americans concluded that the Chinese were going Bolshevik.

In the late 1920s Jiang Jieshi (Chiang Kai-shek) emerged as the pre-eminent leader of this convulsed nation. Jiang ousted Communists from the Guomin-

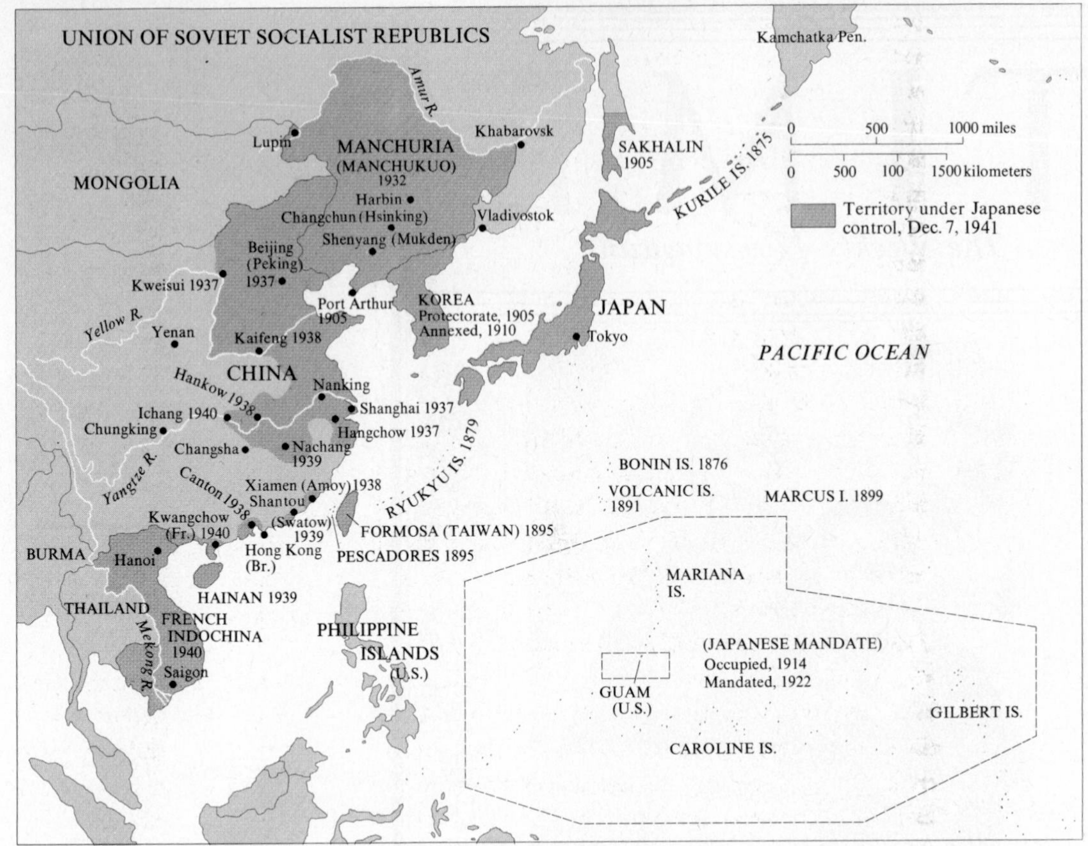

Japanese expansion before Pearl Harbor

Rise of Jiang Jieshi in China

dong, forcing Mao Zedong and his followers to flee to the hills, and sent Borodin back to Russia. Americans applauded his anti-Bolshevik measures and his conversion in 1930 to Christianity. Jiang's new wife, Song Meiling, also won their hearts. The American-educated daughter of a Chinese businessman, Madame Jiang spoke flawless English, dressed in western fashion, and cultivated close social and political ties with prominent Americans. Happier with Jiang than with Sun, United States officials signed a treaty in 1928 restoring control of tariffs to the Chinese. American gunboats and marines remained, however.

The Japanese were suspicious of United States-Chinese ties. In the early twentieth century Japanese-American relations were seldom cordial. Japan intruded more and more into China, driving economic and political stakes into Manchuria, Shandong, and neighboring Korea. Anti-imperialist only in the sense that they wished to oust Western imperialists from Asia, the Japanese were determined to claim Asian territories that produced the raw materials their island nation depended on. When Americans complained of their blatant expansionism, Tokyo reminded Washington of its own sphere of influence in Latin America. The proud Japanese also resented the immigration statute of 1924, which excluded Japanese from entry into the United States. And despite the Washington Conference treaty in 1922, naval competition continued; in fact, American naval officers, betting on a future war with Japan, used that country as the imaginary enemy on the war-game board at the Naval War College. Finally, although the volume of Japanese-American trade was twice that of Chinese-American trade, commercial rivalry strained relations between the two nations. American producers and workers whose profits and jobs were threatened by the importation of inexpensive Japanese goods, especially textiles, organized Buy America campaigns and boycotts.

Relations deteriorated further after the Japanese

Victorious soldiers celebrate in the port of Hankow, China, which fell to the Japanese in October 1938. Paul Dorsey, *Life Magazine* © 1938 Time Inc.

military seized Manchuria in September 1931 (see map). Only nominally a Chinese region, Manchuria was important to the Japanese both as a buffer against the hated Russians and as a vital source of coal, iron, timber, and food. More than half of Japan's foreign investments were in Manchuria; the South Manchurian Railway, which the Chinese had threatened to take over, linked the extensive Japanese holdings. "We are seeking room that will let us breathe," said a Japanese politician, arguing that his tiny, heavily populated nation (65 million people in an area smaller than Texas) needed to expand in order to survive. Though the seizure of Manchuria violated the Nine-Power Treaty and the Kellogg-Briand Pact, the United States did not have the power to compel Japanese withdrawal. The American response therefore went no further than a moral lecture called the Stimson Doctrine (1932): the United States would not recognize any impairment of China's sovereignty or of the Open Door policy, Secretary of State Henry L. Stimson declared.

Japanese seizure of Manchuria

Hardly cowed by timid protests from Western capitals, Japan continued to harry China. In mid-1937 full-scale Sino-Japanese war erupted. The Japanese seized cities and bombed innocent civilians. Senator George Norris, an isolationist who moved further away from his isolationism with each new Japanese thrust, condemned the Japanese as "disgraceful, ignoble, barbarous, and cruel, even beyond the power of language to describe." In an effort to help China, Roosevelt refused to declare the existence of war, thus allowing the Chinese to continue to buy weapons in the United States. In a stirring speech denouncing the aggressors in October 1937, he called for a "quarantine" to curb the "epidemic of world lawlessness."

King George VI of England (1895–1952) and President Franklin D. Roosevelt at a meeting in 1939. The two leaders discussed what the United States would do if Britain went to war against Germany. Roosevelt offered to support the British with naval patrols and asked for bases in the Caribbean and at Bermuda. Franklin D. Roosevelt Library.

People who thought Washington had been too gentle with Japan cheered; confirmed isolationists warned that the president was edging toward war. Actually, Roosevelt had formulated no program to halt the Japanese. When Japanese aircraft sank the American gunboat *Panay*, an escort for Standard Oil Company tankers on the Chang Jiang Zangbo (Yangtze River), in late 1937, Roosevelt demanded an apology but stopped short of retaliation. He was much relieved when Tokyo apologized and offered to pay for damages.

Japan's declaration of a "New Order" in Asia "banged, barred, and bolted" the Open Door, as one American official observed. Alarmed, the Roosevelt administration found small ways to assist China and thwart Japan in 1938 and 1939. Military equipment flowed to the Chinese, as did a $25 million loan. Secretary of State Hull declared a moral embargo against the shipment of airplanes to Japan. The navy, its eye on the Pacific, continued to grow, helped by a billion-dollar congressional appropriation in 1938. And in mid-1939 the United States abrogated the 1911 Japanese-American trade treaty. Yet America continued to ship oil, cotton, and machinery to Japan. The administration hesitated to initiate economic sanctions for fear they would spark an Asian war at a time when the more serious threat was emanating from Berlin. When war broke out in Europe in 1939, Japanese-American relations were stalemated.

On the brink, 1939 to 1941

"What worries me, especially," President Roosevelt told interventionist William Allen White in late 1939, "is that public opinion over here is patting itself on the back every morning and thanking God for the Atlantic Ocean [and the Pacific]." The European war,

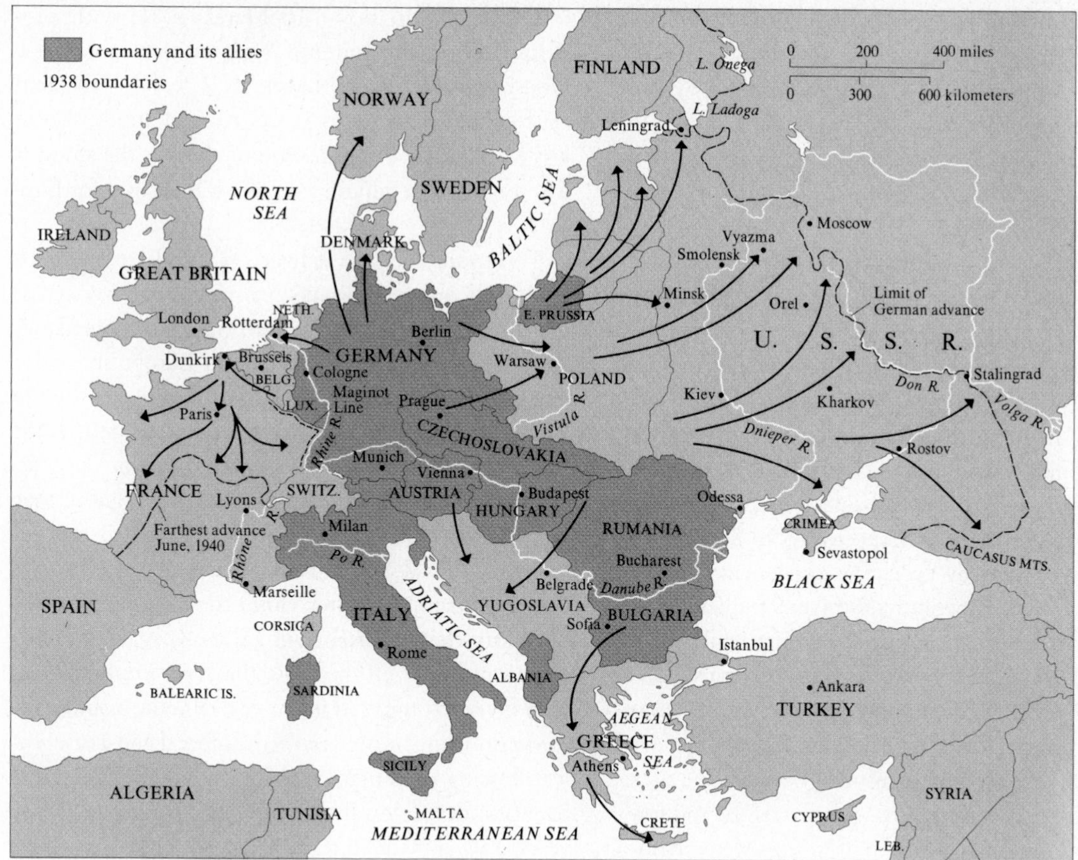

The German advance, 1939–1942

he went on, seriously jeopardized American security, and the American people had better recognize their precarious place in world affairs. Polls showed that Americans strongly favored the Allies, and that most supported aid to Britain and France; but the great majority emphatically wanted the United States to remain at peace. Troubled by this conflicting advice—defeat Hitler, aid the Allies, but stay out of war—the president between 1939 and 1941 "moved two steps forward and one back before he took the giant step forward," as historian Robert A. Divine put it. From neutrality the United States moved to undeclared war and then to war itself.

During those tense months of inching toward belligerency, isolationist sentiment declined. Senator Norris and the *New Republic*, among others, became more interventionist with every new aggression. Alarmed by the swift defeat of one European nation after another, some liberals left the isolationist fold, which became more and more the province of conservatives. Die-hard isolationists organized the America First Committee in fall 1940; interventionists, meanwhile, joined the Century Group or the Committee to Defend America by Aiding the Allies (both formed in mid-1940). Roosevelt, who now called the isolationists "ostriches," even hinted they were pro-Nazi subversives—"conscious disorganizers or unwitting dupes." The White House began to turn over to the Federal Bureau of Investigation letters criticizing Roosevelt's foreign policy.

Decline of isolationism

In September 1939 Poland succumbed to German stormtroopers in just two weeks (see map). In November Soviet Russia marched into Finland, prompting Roosevelt to denounce "this dreadful rape"; by March 1940 Finland had been defeated. The following month Germany invaded Denmark and Norway, a month later the Netherlands and Belgium. "The small countries are smashed up, one by one, like matchwood," sighed the new British Prime Minister

Winston Churchill. In July 1940 France collapsed, frightening Americans even more. Would England be next? After the failure of a peace mission led by his close associate Sumner Welles, Roosevelt told his advisers that though he was "not willing to fire the first shot," he was waiting for some incident to push the United States into war.

In the meantime, assuring people that New Deal reforms would not have to be sacrificed to achieve military preparedness, Roosevelt began to aid the faltering Allies. In May 1940 he ordered the sale of surplus First World War equipment to Britain and France. In July he cultivated bipartisan support for the war by naming Republicans Henry L. Stimson and Frank Knox, ardent backers of aid to the Allies, secretaries of war and the navy respectively. In September he announced that by executive agreement he was trading fifty old American destroyers for leases to eight British bases, including Newfoundland, Bermuda, and Jamaica. Two weeks later he signed into law the Selective Training and Service Act, the first peacetime military draft in American history. The act called for the registration of all men between the ages of twenty-one and thirty-five. Soon over 16 million men had been signed up and draft notices were beginning to be delivered. Ironically, Roosevelt won reelection that fall with promises of peace: "Your boys are not going to be sent into foreign wars." Republican candidate Wendell Willkie, who in the emerging spirit of bipartisanship had refrained from making an issue of foreign policy, snapped: "That hypocritical son of a bitch! This is going to beat me!"

Through the fall Roosevelt spoke of the need for a huge foreign aid program to save England from the Nazis. The United States, he implored, must become the "great arsenal of democracy." He justified his conspicuously pro-Allied stance as a way to keep the United States out of war (by enabling the British to win). In January 1941 the controversial Lend-Lease bill was introduced in Congress. Britain was broke, the president reported. The United States should thus lend military weapons, much as a neighbor lends a garden hose to fight a fire. Roosevelt's analogy did not convince strict isolationist Senator Burton K. Wheeler, who shouted out another comparison: Lend-Lease was "the New Deal's triple A foreign policy; it will plow under every fourth American boy." In March 1941, with pro-British sentiment running high in the nation, the House passed the Lend-Lease Act 317 to 71; the Senate followed suit, 60 to 31. The initial appropriation was $7 billion, but by the end of the war the amount had reached $50 billion, over $31 billion of it for England.

Lend-Lease Act

To ensure the safe delivery of Lend-Lease goods, Roosevelt ordered the navy to patrol halfway across the Atlantic and sent American troops to Greenland. Then a stunning turn of events in Europe spurred a new decision. In June 1941 Hitler struck his erstwhile ally Russia, and news from the quiet western front was soon eclipsed by the vicious warfare in the east. Fearing a German attack on Iceland and arguing that that North Atlantic nation was essential to the defense of the Western Hemisphere, Roosevelt sent American troops one step closer to the Continent. He talked up the importance of aid to Russia; if the Soviets could hold off the more than two hundred German divisions engaged in the east, Britain would gain some breathing time. By November Lend-Lease aid was flowing to appreciative Russians. Churchill, who had thundered loudly against the Communists for years, now applauded the aid: "If Hitler invaded Hell I would make at least a favorable reference to the Devil in the House of Commons," he said.

In August 1941 Churchill and Roosevelt met for four days off Newfoundland. They got along well, trading naval stories, paying deference to one another, and taking pleasure in the fact that Churchill was half American. "It is fun to be in the same decade with you," Roosevelt later wrote to his new friend. At this conference the two leaders wrote the Atlantic Charter, a set of war aims reminiscent of Wilsonianism: collective security, disarmament, self-determination, economic cooperation, and freedom of the seas. Later, on January 1, 1942, twenty-six nations signed the Declaration of the United Nations, pledging themselves to fulfill the charter. According to Churchill, the president told him in Newfoundland that although he could not ask Congress for a declaration of war against Germany, "he would wage war, but not declare it, and that he would become more and more provocative."

Atlantic Charter

In September 1941, there occurred the incident

Roosevelt had been waiting for: the American destroyer *Greer* was fired on (but not hit) by a German submarine. In a special national radio broadcast the president protested the "piracy" and announced a policy he had privately promised to Churchill. American naval vessels would convoy British merchant ships all the way to Iceland and shoot German submarines, the "rattlesnakes of the Atlantic," on sight. Roosevelt practiced deliberate deception in the *Greer* case, for he did not mention that the *Greer* had been tailing the German U-boat for hours, radioing the submarine's location to British airplanes hunting the ship with depth charges. He and his advisers thought it necessary to manipulate public opinion in order to scare Americans into defending Britain.

The United States had in essence entered into an undeclared war with Germany. When in early October a German submarine torpedoed the American destroyer *Kearny* off the coast of Iceland, the president announced that "the shooting has started. And history has recorded who fired the first shot." When later that month the destroyer *Reuben James* went down with the loss of over one hundred American lives, Congress scrapped the cash-and-carry policy and further revised the Neutrality Acts to permit the transport of munitions to England on armed American merchant ships. When would war be declared? tense observers asked themselves.

In retrospect it seems ironic that the Second World War came to the United States via Asia, where Roosevelt so wanted to avoid it in order to concentrate American resources on the defeat of Germany. In September 1940 Americans read the stunning news of the Tripartite Pact, an alliance between Germany, Italy, and Japan. After much debate within the administration, Roosevelt slapped an embargo on shipments of aviation fuel and scrap metal to Japan. Because the president believed the petroleum-thirsty Japanese would consider a cutoff of oil a life-or-death matter, he did not stop the flow of that vital commodity. But after Japanese troops occupied French Indochina in July 1941, Washington froze Japanese assets in the United States, virtually ending trade (including the oil trade) with Japan.

Cut-off of trade with Japan

Tokyo recommended a high-level meeting between President Roosevelt and Prime Minister Prince Konoye, but the United States rejected the idea. American officials insisted that the Japanese first agree to respect China's sovereignty and territorial integrity, and to honor the Open Door policy—in short, to get out of China. Roosevelt also told the Japanese ambassador that his nation would have to withdraw from the Tripartite Pact. Although the American public, according to polls in fall 1941, seemed willing to risk war with Japan to thwart further aggression, Roosevelt was not ready for an Asian war; Europe still claimed first priority. Yet he would not back down in Asia either. Nor would Japan, now eyeing the oil-rich East Indies, abandon its plans for hegemony in Asia—the Greater East Asia Co-Prosperity Sphere.

Roosevelt told his advisers to string out Japanese-American talks to gain time—time to fortify the Philippines, and time to check the fascists in Europe. "Let us do nothing to precipitate a crisis," the president told the cabinet in November 1941. But by breaking the Japanese code ("Operation Magic"), Americans learned that Tokyo had committed itself to war with the United States if the oil embargo was not lifted. In late November the Japanese rejected American proposals that they withdraw from Indochina. On December 1 decoding experts informed the president that Japanese task forces were being ordered into battle. Why not attack first? asked aide Harry Hopkins. No, said Roosevelt, "we would have to wait until it came." Secretary Stimson explained later that the United States let Japan fire the first shot so as "to have the full support of the American people" and "so that there should remain no doubt in anyone's mind as to who were the aggressors." Fearing that they could not win a prolonged war, the Japanese plotted a daring raid on Pearl Harbor in Hawaii. A flotilla of Japanese aircraft carriers crossed three thousand miles of ocean, and on the morning of December 7, planes stamped with the Rising Sun swept down on the unsuspecting American naval base, killing more than 2,400 people, sinking several battleships, and smashing aircraft.

Attack on Pearl Harbor

Though Roosevelt was distressed that the navy, his proud navy, had been caught by surprise, like many Americans he felt relief from the weeks of insufferable tension. But how could Pearl Harbor have happened? Americans asked. Roosevelt did not, as his critics later

Disaster at Pearl Harbor, December 7, 1941. The surprise attack by the Japanese disabled much of America's Pacific fleet. Investigators later complained of negligence in the Navy and War departments, but no courts-martial were initiated. National Archives.

charged, conspire to leave the fleet vulnerable to attack, so the United States could enter the Second World War through the "back door" of Asia. The base was not ready–not on red alert–because a message of warning from Washington had been sent by Western Union telegraph rather than by navy cable and arrived too late. Base commanders were relaxed, thinking Hawaii, so far from Japan, an unlikely target for all-out attack. They expected the assault to come at British Malaya, Thailand, or the Philippines. Mistakes there were, but not conspiracy.

On December 8, referring to the previous day as a "date which will live in infamy," Roosevelt asked Congress for a declaration of war against Japan. A unanimous vote in the Senate and a 388 to 1 vote in the House thrust America into war. (Representative Jeannette Rankin of Montana alone voted no, matching her vote against entry into the First World War.) Three days later Germany and Italy declared war against the United States. Winston Churchill was pleased that America was now fully at war. "Hitler's fate was sealed," he wrote in his memoirs. "Mussolini's fate was sealed. As for the Japanese, they would be ground to powder. . . . I went to bed and slept the sleep of the saved and thankful."

The war was now a global conflict. The old emphasis on independent internationalism, on economic and nonmilitary means to peace, seemed archaic at that

Important events

1919–20	Senate rejects membership in the League of Nations
1921–22	Washington Conference on naval arms control
1922	Bok peace prize Mussolini comes to power in Italy
1924	Dawes Plan for German reparations U.S. occupation of the Dominican Republic ends
1926	American troops occupy Nicaragua (remaining until 1933)
1927	Jiang Jieshi attacks Communists in China
1928	Kellogg-Briand Pact
1929	Stock market crash; onset of the Great Depression Young Plan for German reparations
1930	Hawley-Smoot Tariff
1931	Japan seizes Manchuria Pearl Buck, *The Good Earth*
1932	Stimson Doctrine of nonrecognition
1933	Hitler comes to power in Germany U.S. recognition of Soviet Russia Good Neighbor policy announced United States subverts Cuban revolution
1934	Reciprocal Trade Agreements Act Export-Import Bank founded U.S. occupation of Haiti ends after nineteen years
1935	Italy invades Ethiopia Neutrality Act
1936	United States votes for nonintervention principle at Pan American Conference Outbreak of Spanish Civil War Neutrality Act Roosevelt's antiwar Chautauqua speech
1937	Neutrality Act China Incident Roosevelt's quarantine speech
1938	Mexico nationalizes American-owned oil companies Munich Conference Hitler's persecution of the Jews
1939	Nazi-Soviet pact Germany invades Poland Second World War begins United States repeals arms embargo
1940	Soviets invade Finland Committee to Defend America by Aiding the Allies formed Tripartite Pact Destroyer-bases deal with Great Britain American First Committee formed Selective Service Act
1941	Lend-Lease Act Germany attacks Russia United States freezes Japanese assets, cutting trade Atlantic Charter meeting of Roosevelt and Churchill *Greer* incident Japan attacks Pearl Harbor

stirring moment. And the Great Depression, which had brought on so much of the international havoc—it too faded in memory as the economy geared up for war. The Neutrality Acts that had been designed to insulate the United States from European troubles had been gradually revised and retired under Roosevelt's patient, if oblique and tortured, leadership. The president had wanted to avoid American entry into a second world war, yet he sought also to aid the Allies and thwart Japanese aggression. What he tried to avoid he could not, because he believed that ultimately the United States, deeply involved in international affairs and with economic and strategic interests to protect, had to defend itself overseas. Moreover, the Axis nations loomed as threats to Western civilization itself. And there was the perennial American desire to set things right. As publisher Henry Luce put it in his best-selling book *American Century* (1941), the United States must "exert upon the world the full impact of our influence, for such purposes as we see fit and by such means as we see fit."

As they had so many times before, Americans flocked to the colors. "We are going to win the war, and we are going to win the peace that follows," Roosevelt predicted.

Suggestions for further reading

General

Thomas H. Buckley, *The United States and the Washington Conference, 1921–1922* (1970); James MacGregor Burns, *Roosevelt: The Lion and the Fox* (1956); David H. Culbert, *News for Everyman: Radio and Foreign Affairs in Thirties America* (1976); Robert Dallek, *Franklin D. Roosevelt and American Foreign Policy, 1932–1945* (1979); Robert A. Divine, *Roosevelt and World War II* (1969); L. Ethan Ellis, *Republican Foreign Policy, 1921–1933* (1968); Robert H. Ferrell, *American Diplomacy in the Great Depression* (1957); Elting E. Morison, *Turmoil and Tradition* (1964) (on Henry L. Stimson); Arnold A. Offner, *The Origins of the Second World War* (1975); Julius W. Pratt, *Cordell Hull,* 2 vols. (1964); Raymond Sontag, *A Broken World, 1919–1939* (1971); William Appleman Williams, *The Tragedy of American Diplomacy*, rev. ed. (1962).

Economic foreign policy

Frederick Adams, *Economic Diplomacy* (1976); Derek H. Aldcroft, *From Versailles to Wall Street, 1919–1929* (1977); Herbert Feis, *The Diplomacy of the Dollar, 1919–1932* (1950); Lloyd C. Gardner, *Economic Aspects of New Deal Diplomacy* (1964); Michael J. Hogan, *Informal Entente: The Private Structure of Cooperation in Anglo-American Economic Diplomacy, 1918–1928* (1977); Charles Kindleberger, *The World in Depression* (1973); Carl Parrini, *Heir to Empire* (1969); Mira Wilkins, *The Maturing of Multinational Enterprise* (1974); John Hoff Wilson, *American Business and Foreign Policy, 1920–1933* (1971).

Latin America

Jules R. Benjamin, *The United States and Cuba* (1978); Donald M. Dozer, *Are We Good Neighbors?* (1959); Alton Frye, *Nazi Germany and the American Hemisphere, 1933–1941* (1967); Irwin F. Gellman, *Good Neighbor Diplomacy* (1979); David Green, *The Containment of Latin America* (1971); Stanley Hilton, *Brazil and the Great Powers, 1930–1939* (1975); Lester D. Langley, *The United States and the Caribbean, 1900–1970* (1980); Neil Macaulay, *The Sandino Affair* (1967); Lorenzo Meyer, *Mexico and the United States in the Oil Controversy, 1917–1942* (1977); Robert I. Rotberg, *Haiti* (1971); Ramon Ruiz, *Cuba: The Making of a Revolution* (1968); Karl M. Schmitt, *Mexico and the United States, 1821–1973* (1974); Robert F. Smith, *The United States and Cuba* (1960); Bryce Wood, *The Making of the Good Neighbor Policy* (1961).

Europe, American "isolationism," and war

Thomas A. Bailey and Paul B. Ryan, *Hitler vs. Roosevelt* (1979); Charles A. Beard, *President Roosevelt and the Coming of the War, 1941* (1948); Edward Bennett, *Recognition of Russia* (1970); Mark Chadwin, *The Hawks of World War II* (1968); Charles Chatfield, *For Peace and Justice: Pacifism in America, 1914–1941* (1971); Wayne Cole, *America First* (1953); Wayne Cole, *Charles A. Lindbergh and the Battle Against American Intervention in World War II* (1974); James V. Compton, *The Swastika and the Eagle* (1967); Charles DeBenedetti, *Peace Reform in American History* (1980); Robert A. Divine, *The Illusion of Neutrality* (1962); Robert A. Divine, *The Reluctant Belligerent,* 2nd ed. (1979); Robert H. Ferrell, *Peace in Their Time* (1952); Peter G. Filene, *Americans and the Soviet Experiment, 1917–1933* (1967); Manfred Jonas, *Isolationism in America, 1935–1941* (1966); Warren F. Kimball, *The Most Unsordid Act: Lend-Lease, 1939–1941* (1969); William L. Langer and S. Everett Gleason, *The*

Challenge to Isolation, 1937–1940 (1952); William L. Langer and S. Everett Gleason, *The Undeclared War, 1940–1941* (1953); Joseph P. Lash, *Roosevelt and Churchill, 1939–1941* (1976); Melvin P. Leffler, *The Elusive Quest* (1979); Thomas R. Maddux, *Years of Estrangement: American Relations with the Soviet Union, 1933–1941* (1980); Arnold A. Offner, *American Appeasement* (1969); Bruce Russett, *No Clear and Present Danger* (1972); Theodore A. Wilson, *The First Summit* (1969); John Wiltz, *In Search of Peace: The Senate Munitions Inquiry, 1934–1936* (1963).

China, Japan, and Pearl Harbor

Dorothy Borg and Shumpei Okomoto, eds., *Pearl Harbor as History* (1973); Richard Dean Burns and Edward M. Bennett, eds., *Diplomats in Crisis* (1974); R. J. C. Butow, *Tojo and the Coming of the War* (1961); Warren I. Cohen, *America's Response to China,* 2nd ed. (1980); Roger Dingman, *Power in the Pacific* (1976); Herbert Feis, *The Road to Pearl Harbor* (1950); Waldo H. Heinrichs, Jr., *American Ambassador* (1966) (on Joseph Grew); Akira Iriye, *Across the Pacific* (1967); Akira Iriye, *After Imperialism: The Search for a New Order in the Far East, 1921–1931* (1965); Charles Neu, *The Troubled Encounter: The United States and Japan* (1975); Michael Schaller, *The United States and China in the Twentieth Century* (1979); James C. Thomson, *While China Faced West* (1969).

28 GLOBAL WARS: SECOND, COLD, AND KOREAN, 1941–1953

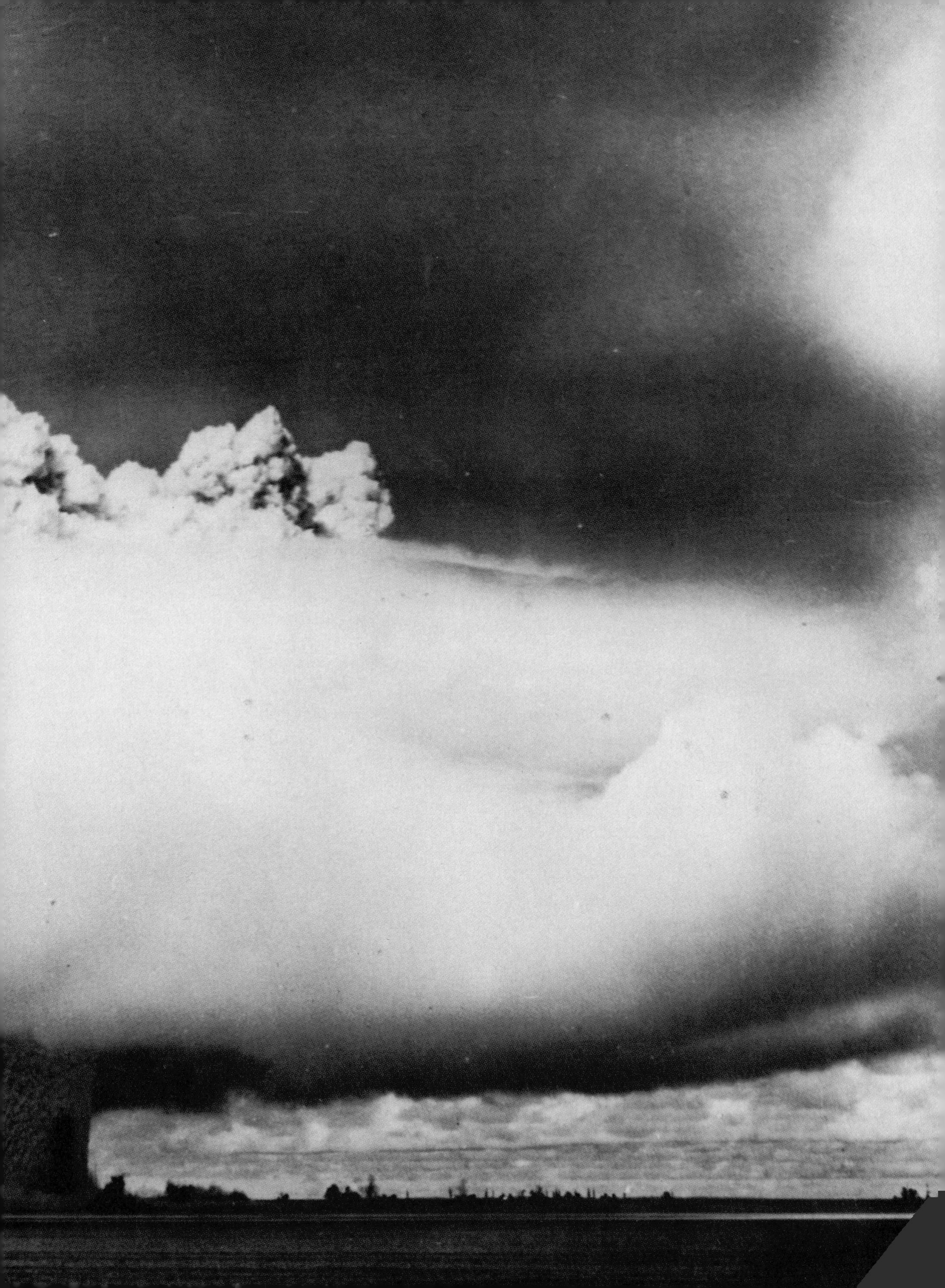

"We are going on a mission to drop a bomb different from any you have ever seen or heard about," Colonel Paul Tibbets informed his crew on the small Pacific island of Tinian. Silent and incredulous, they listened to "Old Bull" describe the strange new weapon, which packed the destructive power of twenty thousand tons of TNT. Resting in the bay of a converted B-29 named the *Enola Gay*, after Tibbets's mother, was "Little Boy"—a ten-thousand-pound uranium bomb on which the airmen had scribbled anti-Japanese graffitti.

After months of training for an unknown assignment, the crew of the 509th Bombardment Group now learned that they were to be responsible for bringing the Manhattan Project to its culmination. This secret atomic project, which had begun in 1942 and had cost about $2 billion, had exploded its first bomb in the desert near Los Alamos, New Mexico, on July 16, 1945.

At 2:45 A.M. on August 6, the *Enola Gay* lumbered down the runway at Tinian. Once airborne, crew members assembled the firing mechanism. "Knock wood," muttered one of them. Several hours later they received a radio message that the weather over Hiroshima was clear. Cruising at over 30,000 feet, they put on welder's goggles and made their run on the unsuspecting city of a quarter-million people.

At 8:15 A.M. the atomic bomb dropped from the aircraft. It exploded in less than a minute, directly on target. A flash of dazzling light shot across the sky. "Everything just turned white in front of me," Tibbets recalled. Then two violent slaps rocked the ship. "My God!" gasped co-pilot Captain Robert Lewis as he watched a huge purplish mushroom cloud boil 40,000 feet into the atmosphere. Dense smoke, swirling fires, and suffocating dust soon engulfed the ground for miles. Much of the city was leveled almost instantly. "Even though we had expected something terrific," Lewis remembered, "what we saw made us feel that we were Buck Rogers twenty-fifth century warriors."

Approximately 130,000 people were killed at Hiroshima; tens of thousands more suffered painful burns and nuclear poisoning. As Hiroshima suffered its unique nightmare, Washington, D.C., celebrated its military and scientific triumph. "This is the greatest thing in history," exclaimed President Harry S Truman on hearing of the successful mission. American planes continued their devastating conventional bombing, and scattered leaflets over Japanese cities warning that they too would be visited with atomic terror unless the Japanese empire surrendered. On August 9 another atomic bomb exploded over Nagasaki, killing at least sixty thousand people. Five days later Emperor Hirohito surrendered his humiliated nation to the Allies. Americans rejoiced that Pearl Harbor had been avenged, and the Second World War was over at last.

Americans had fought for some fifty-seven months to subdue the aggressors. In the Pacific they had driven the fierce and determined Japanese from one island after another before losing patience with conventional warfare and turning to the atom bomb. In Europe, Americans had not become significantly engaged until June 1944, when they joined the massive crossing of the English Channel on D-Day. The huge invasion forced the Germans to retreat back through France to Germany. Battered by merciless bombing raids, leaderless following Adolf Hitler's suicide, and pressed by a Russian advance from the east, the Germans gave up their quest for imperial grandeur. Their surrender came in May 1945, three months before the Japanese capitulation.

Throughout the war the Allies—Britain, Russia, and the United States—were held together by their unanimous goal of defeating Germany. But they squabbled over many issues: when the second, or western front would be opened; how a new international organization would be structured; how Eastern Europe, liberated from the Germans, would be reconstructed; how Germany itself would be governed after defeat. Though Allied leaders met several times at summit conferences to iron out their differences, at the end of the war they seemed more intent on keeping and expanding their own nations' spheres of influence than on building a community of mutual interest. Their difficulties were only a sign of troubles to come.

In the years following the Second World War, the United States, which had emerged from the war the most powerful nation on earth, moved to center stage in international relations. "We are now concerned with the peace of the entire world," General and later Secretary of State George C. Marshall said in 1945.

This new attitude, called globalism, reflected lessons learned during the depression and the war: that events in faraway places seriously affect American prosperity and security; and that the United States must possess the power to thwart threats to its interests. Unfortunately, the new perspective also helped to spawn a new kind of crisis, the postwar Soviet-American diplomatic confrontation called the Cold War. In this new conflict, competitive propaganda, reconstruction programs, alliances, atomic arms development, and spheres of influence condemned the world once again to instability and fear.

Just five years after the Second World War, the Cold War turned hot on the peninsula of Korea. Although the threat of world war did not materialize—the Korean War remained a limited regional conflict—it further spurred American globalism. Throughout the 1950s the United States worked to strengthen its defenses, building up its weaponry, its military alliance systems, and its international intelligence network. And it continued to intervene in the affairs of foreign peoples. With such an arsenal and such an attitude there was no turning back. The United States had become a highly visible, highly committed world power. And participation in the Second World War had begun the process.

Winning the Second World War

"We are now in the midst of a war, not for conquest, not for vengeance, but for a world in which this Nation, and all that this Nation represents, will be safe for our children." President Roosevelt was speaking just two days after the surprise attack on Pearl Harbor. Americans believed with Roosevelt that they were defending their homes and families against aggressive and satanic Nazis and Japanese. Few of them, however, knew much about the principles of the Atlantic Charter (see page 772) or about United States war aims. To most Americans the Second World War was simply a grimy job. Like cartoonist Bill Mauldin's popular GI characters Willy and Joe, who were more interested in tasty food and dry socks than in abstractions, they were eager to get it over with. Americans also seemed wary of lofty rhetoric about the future, remembering how Woodrow Wilson had promised so much and delivered too little during the First World War. The army's Morale Branch, worried that the average American was ignorant or cynical about the reasons for war, hired prominent Hollywood director Frank Capra to produce a series of propaganda films called *Why We Fight.*

In these widely distributed films and in the popular mind, the Allies were heroes, partners in a common effort against evil. Actually, wartime relations between the United States, Great Britain, and the Soviet Union ran hot and cold. Although winning the war claimed top priority, Allied leaders knew that military decisions had political consequences. Should one ally become desperate, for instance, it might sue for a separate peace. And the position of troops at the end of the war might determine the politics of the region they occupied. Thus an undercurrent of suspicion ran beneath the surface of Allied cooperation.

Second front controversy

Roosevelt, British Prime Minister Winston Churchill, and Soviet Premier Josef Stalin differed most over the opening of a second, or western, front. After Germany conquered France in 1940 and moved on to Russia in 1941, the Russians bore the brunt of the war until mid-1944, suffering heavy casualties. Stalin pressed for a British-American landing on the northern coast of Europe to draw German troops away from the eastern front, but Churchill would not agree. The Russians therefore did most of the fighting and dying on land, while the British and Americans concentrated on getting Lend-Lease supplies across the Atlantic and harassing the Germans from the air. When Secretary of State Cordell Hull bemoaned the 200,000 American casualties suffered from 1941 to 1943, the Russians replied, "We lose that many each day before lunch. You haven't got your teeth in the war yet."

Roosevelt was particularly sensitive to the Russian burden and to the suggestion that Americans were shirking their responsibility by avoiding an invasion of Europe. He feared that Russia might be knocked out of the war, leaving Hitler free to send his goose-stepping soldiers into England. In 1942 Roosevelt told the Russians they could expect the Allies to open a second front later that year. The move across the

English Channel, later tagged Operation OVERLORD, was exactly what Stalin sought to take pressure off his wracked country. But Churchill balked. "To postpone that evil day, all his arts, all his eloquence, all his great experience was spent," the prime minister's chief military adviser later wrote. Churchill feared heavy losses in a premature cross-channel invasion; he envisioned British corpses floating on bloody waters, bodies choking the beaches. Though American Generals George C. Marshall and Dwight D. Eisenhower argued for a direct attack on the heart of German power, Churchill held out for a series of small jabs at the enemy's Mediterranean forces. American officials suspected that Churchill's strategy derived from his desire to recover British imperial power in the Mediterranean. And they worried that attacks elsewhere would drain valuable supplies from the mammoth build-up necessary for the cross-channel landing.

Churchill won the debate. Instead of attacking France, the western Allies invaded North Africa in November 1942. Roosevelt had to make an unsavory deal with the pro-Nazi (Vichy) French there to reduce resistance, but deemed it justified in order to get Americans into combat. "We are striking back," the cheered president declared. In the same month the Russians began to blunt the German thrust, pushing Hitler's armies back from Stalingrad. But in early 1943 Stalin was told once again that the second front would be delayed. "Need I speak of the dishearteningly negative expression that this fresh postponement of the second front . . . will produce in the Soviet Union?" he wrote to Roosevelt. He was not mollified by the Allied invasion of Italy in summer 1943. When Italy surrendered in September, it capitulated to American and British officers; Russian officials were not invited to participate. Stalin grumbled that the arrangement smacked of a separate peace and wondered if Roosevelt and Churchill's policy of unconditional surrender for the Axis, announced that January at the Anglo-American conference at Casablanca, had been violated.

With the Grand Alliance badly strained, Roosevelt sought reconciliation through personal diplomacy. The three Allied leaders met in Teheran, Iran, in December 1943. Stalin dismissed Churchill's repetitious justifications for further delaying the second front. Roosevelt had had enough too; with Stalin he rejected Churchill's proposal for another peripheral attack, this time through the Balkans to Vienna. The three finally agreed to launch OVERLORD in early 1944. An appreciative Russia promised to aid the Allies against Japan once Germany was defeated.

D-Day

Like a coiled spring bursting free, the second front opened in the dark morning hours of June 6, 1944: D-Day. Two hundred thousand Allied troops under the command of General Eisenhower scrambled ashore in Normandy, France, in the largest amphibious landing in history. Thousands of ships ferried the gray-faced men within a hundred yards of the sandy beaches. Craft and soldiers became entangled in sharp obstacles and triggered mines, and were pinned down by fire from cliffside pillboxes. Meanwhile, airborne troops dropped behind German lines. Although heavy aerial and naval bombardment and the clandestine work of underground saboteurs had softened up German defenses, the fighting was still fierce. One soldier felt like a "pigeon at a trap shoot." From the White House Roosevelt asked Americans to pray for "our sons, pride of our Nation, [who] this day have set out upon a mighty endeavor, a struggle to preserve our Republic, our religion, and our civilization and to set free a suffering humanity."

After digging in at now-famous places like Utah and Omaha beaches and gaining reinforcements, Allied forces broke through disorderly German lines and gradually ground inland, reaching Paris in August. That same month another force invaded southern France and threw the stunned Germans back. Allied troops soon spread across the countryside, liberating France and Belgium and entering Germany itself in September. With winter came rain, snow, mud and stiffer enemy resistance. In December German panzer divisions counterattacked in Belgium's Ardennes Forest, hoping to push on to Antwerp to halt the flow of Allied supplies through that major Belgian port. Allied forces were surprised; their defenses buckled. But after weeks of heavy fighting in what has come to be called the Battle of the Bulge—because of the noticeable dent in the Allied line—the Allies pushed the enemy back once again. Meanwhile battle-hardened Russian troops streamed through Poland and cut a path to the German capital, Berlin. American forces crossed the Rhine in March 1945 and captured the heavily industrial Ruhr valley. Some units peeled off

D-Day on Omaha Beach, June 6, 1944: army medics administer blood plasma to a survivor of the cross-channel invasion, which opened the second front in Europe. Omaha was strongly defended from high cliffs. Many of the over 25,000 soldiers who jumped into the water from landing craft never made it to shore. U.S. Army, Department of Defense.

to enter Austria and Czechoslovakia, where they met up with Russian soldiers. In bomb-ravaged Berlin, defended largely by teenage boys and old men, Adolf Hitler killed himself in his bunker. On May 8 Germany surrendered.

Allied strategists had devised a "Europe first" formula: knock out Germany first and then concentrate on isolated Japan. Nevertheless the Pacific theater claimed headlines throughout the war, for the American people regarded Japan as the United States' chief enemy. The treacherous Japanese–"monkeys" and "bastards," boomed Admiral William Halsey–had to be repaid for Pearl Harbor. By mid-1942 Japan had seized the Philippines, Guam, Wake, Hong Kong, Singapore, Malaya, and the Dutch East Indies. In the Philippines in 1942 Japanese soldiers forced American prisoners, weak from insufficient rations, to walk sixty-five miles, clubbing, shooting, or starving to death about ten thousand of them. The Bataan Death March hardened even more the American hatred of the Japanese.

In April 1942 Americans began to hit back. They bombed Tokyo, and in May, in the momentous Battle of the Coral Sea, carrier-based U.S. planes halted a

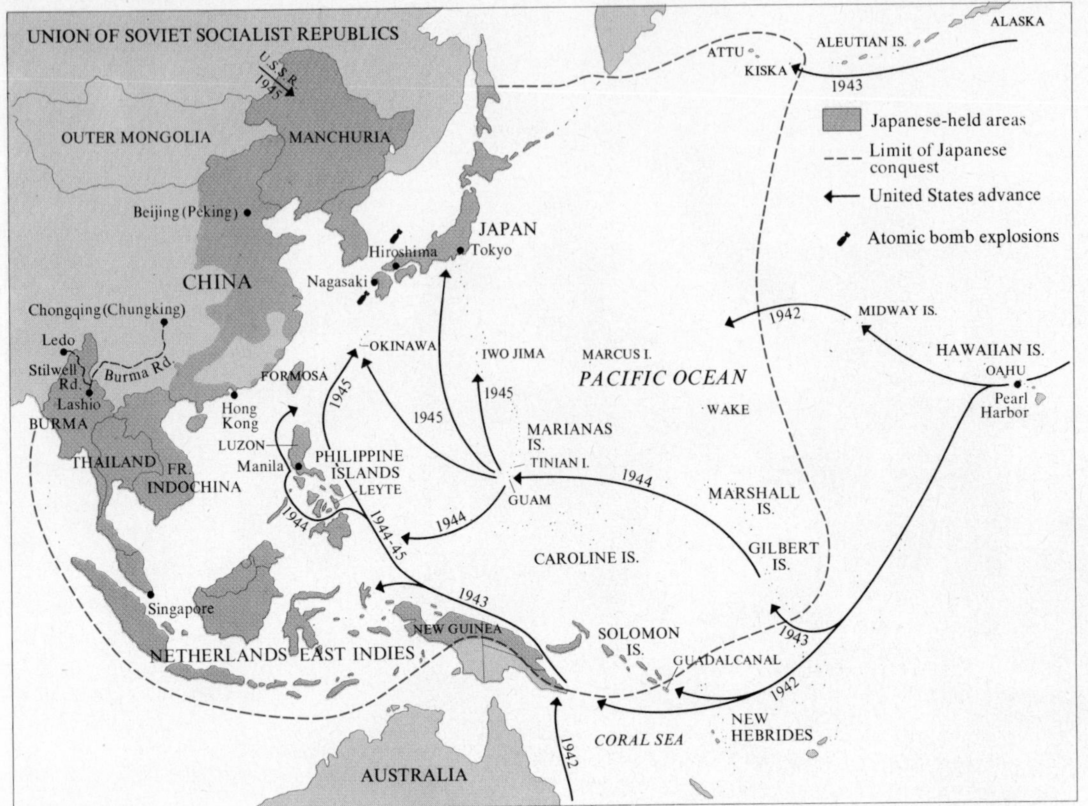

The Pacific war. Source: By permission of the publisher, from *American Foreign Policy: A History* by Paterson et al., p. 474. (Lexington, Mass.: D.C. Heath and Company, 1977).

Japanese advance toward Australia (see map). The next month American forces defeated the Japanese at Midway, sinking four of the enemy's valuable aircraft carriers. The Battle of Midway broke the Japanese momentum and relieved the threat to Hawaii. Thereafter Japan was never able to match American manpower, sea power, air power, or economic power. Still, the war in Asia was heatedly contested until the very end. "There are no breathers in this schedule," exclaimed General H. H. Arnold in the football jargon of the time. "You take on Notre Dame every time you play!"

American offensive in the Pacific

American strategy was to "island-hop" toward Japan itself, skipping the most strongly fortified points whenever possible and taking weaker ones, where Seabee construction battalions would build bases for the next advance. Americans also set out to sink the Japanese merchant marine, in an effort to strand the Japanese armies in their island outposts and to cut off raw materials from the factories of the home island. The first American offensive—at Guadalcanal in the Solomon Islands in summer and fall 1942—gave troops their first taste of jungle warfare: thick vegetation, mosquitoes, scorpions, tropical heat, and rotting gear. From the Solomons the U.S. military pushed relentlessly on, colliding with the entrenched enemy in the Gilberts in the fall of 1942. The Marianas were next, in June 1944. That month too the navy smashed Japanese forces in the Battle of the Philippine Sea. In October General Douglas MacArthur landed at Leyte to reclaim the Philippines for the United States. Then in early 1945 both sides took heavy losses at Iwo Jima and Okinawa. In desperation, Japanese pilots made suicide (*kamikaze*) attacks on American warships, flying their planes directly into the vessels.

Hoping to avoid a humiliating unconditional sur-

The 27,000-ton aircraft carrier U.S.S. *Essex* leads a flotilla of warships through the Pacific, 1943. From these ships American bombers pursued the Japanese from one island to another, toward the home island and defeat. National Archives.

render (and to preserve the emperor's sovereignty), Japanese leaders refused to admit defeat. They hung on while American bombers leveled their cities. In one staggering attack on Tokyo on May 23, 1945, American planes dropped napalm-filled bombs that engulfed the city in a chemically induced firestorm. Eighty-three thousand people died; observers described the ghastly scene as a mass burning.

Impatient for victory, American leaders began to plan for a fall invasion of the Japanese home islands, an expedition that would bring high casualties. But the successful development of an atomic bomb by American scientists provided another route to victory. Shortly after the atomic bombing of Hiroshima and Nagasaki the Japanese surrendered, on the condition that their emperor would remain, at least theoretically, the nation's ruler. Formal ceremonies were held September 2 aboard the battleship *Missouri.* At home in the states, a five-year-old boy heard the news: "This is the best year," he cried. "The war is over. Two wars are over. Everyone is happy. Tin cans are rolling. Everything is confused. And little pieces of paper." And maybe his father would soon be coming home.

Wartime diplomacy

"In our disillusionment after the last war," President Roosevelt noted in 1945, "we gave up the hope of achieving a better peace because we had not the courage to fulfill our responsibilities in an admittedly imperfect world. We must not let that happen again, or we shall follow the same tragic road again—the road to a third world war." Indeed, the lessons of the 1930s weighed heavily on the minds of American diplomats throughout the war. Americans vowed to make a peace that would ensure a postwar world free from depression, totalitarianism, and war. The Atlantic Charter, so reminiscent of Wilson's vision of an open world, was their general guide, tempered and compromised by the interests of the great powers. Thus American goals included the Open Door and lower tariffs; self-determination for liberated peoples; avoidance of the debts-reparations tangle that had plagued Europe after the First World War; expansion of the United States sphere of influence; and management of world affairs by what Roosevelt once called the Four Policemen: Russia, China, Great Britain, and the United States.

Although the major Allies concentrated on defeating the aggressors, their suspicions of one another undermined cooperation. More dogged them than the timing of the second front and the Italian surrender. Eastern European questions proved the most difficult. The Russians sought to fix their boundaries where they had stood before Hitler attacked in 1941. In the case of Poland, this meant that the part of the country the Soviets had invaded and captured in 1939 would become Russian territory. The British and Americans hesitated, preferring to deal with Eastern Europe at the end of the war. But the sustained drive of the Russian armies through the region on the heels of the retreating Germans persuaded Churchill to act. In an October 1944 agreement, he and Stalin struck a bargain: Russia would gain Rumania and Bulgaria as a sphere of influence; Britain would have the upper hand in Greece; and the two would share authority in Yugoslavia and Hungary. The two leaders did not, however, agree on Poland.

Allied disagreement over Eastern Europe

Poland was a special case. In 1943 Moscow had broken off diplomatic relations with the conservative Polish government-in-exile in London. The Poles had asked the International Red Cross to investigate German charges that the Russians had massacred thousands of Polish army officers in the Katyn Forest in 1941. Then an uprising in Warsaw in July 1944 complicated matters still further. Taking advantage of the nearness of Soviet troops, the Warsaw underground rose against the occupying Germans. To the dismay of the world community, Soviet armies stood aside as German troops slaughtered 166,000 people and devastated the city. Stalin explained that military problems prevented the Soviets from helping, but British and American diplomats saw it as Soviet callousness toward the Poles. Finally, in late 1944 and early 1945 the Soviets spawned a pro-Communist government in Lublin. Thus near the end of the war Poland had two competing governments, one in London, recognized by America and Britain, and another in Lublin.

Early in the war the Allies had begun talking about a new international organization. At Teheran in 1943 Roosevelt called for an institution controlled by the Four Policemen. The next year, in an elegant Washington, D.C., mansion called Dumbarton Oaks, American, British, Russian, and Chinese representatives conferred on the details. Since American participation had been endorsed in public opinion polls and congressional resolutions, United States diplomats could proceed with some assurance that their handiwork would not meet the legislative fate of Wilson's League of Nations. The conferees approved a preliminary charter for a United Nations Organization, providing for a supreme Security Council dominated by the great powers and a weak General Assembly (Roosevelt called it "an investigatory body only"). The Security Council would have five permanent members, each with veto power.

Creation of the United Nations Organization

Disagreement surfaced when the United States pushed China forward as a great power entitled to permanent membership on the council: Churchill complained that China was a captive vote on the side of the United States. To mollify him, the United States reluctantly agreed to elevate France to a permanent seat. Russia accepted both France and China, believing that its veto power would protect its national interest against unfriendly decisions. But noting that the United States would have a group of sympathetic votes in the General Assembly among the Latin American states, and that Britain could muster support from members of its Commonwealth, the Soviets asked for a balancing of power. They wanted separate membership in the General Assembly for the sixteen Soviet republics. This issue was not resolved at Dumbarton Oaks, but the meeting proved a success nevertheless. The conferees had achieved 90 percent of their goals, Roosevelt pointed out. "Well, that is what we used to call in the old days a darn good batting average."

The diplomatic batting average on another prob-

The artist and concentration-camp prisoner David Olère titled this wrenching sketch "To Burn Their Sisters and Brothers." The wood that these laborers chopped fueled the crematoria that burned the corpses of executed Jews. At Auschwitz, Poland, twelve thousand people died every day. The Ghetto Fighters House.

lem, Nazi treatment of the Jews, was considerably lower. Even before the war Nazi officials had targeted Jews throughout Europe for persecution. By war's end, about 6 million Jews had been forced into concentration camps and systematically disposed of by firing squads, unspeakable tortures, and gas chambers. Many others who survived the Holocaust could never forget the terror. During the depression the United States and other nations had refused to relax their immigration restrictions to save Jews fleeing persecution. The American Federation of Labor and Senator William Borah, among others, argued that new immigrants would compete with American workers for scarce jobs, and public opinion polls supported their position. The fear of economic competition was, of course, fed by anti-Semitism. Bureaucrats applied the rules so strictly—requiring legal documents fleeing Jews could not possibly provide—that otherwise qualified refugees were kept out of the country. From 1933 to 1945 less than 40 percent of the German-Austrian quota was filled.

Jewish refugees from the Holocaust

Even the tragic voyage of the *St. Louis* did not change government policy. The vessel left Hamburg in mid-1939 with 930 desperate Jewish refugees who lacked proper immigration documents. Denied entry to Havana, the *St. Louis* headed for Miami, where Coast Guard cutters prevented it from docking. Aroused American citizens appealed to Washington, but the ship was forced to return to Europe. Some of those refugees took shelter in countries that were later overrun by Hitler's legions. "The cruise of the *St. Louis*," wrote the New York *Times*, "cries to high heaven of man's inhumanity to man."

As news of the Nazi atrocities filled government files during the war years, American officials futilely attempted to persuade Latin American countries to accept refugees. They also approached the British, who proved unhelpful as well—they would not open Palestine. Some American leaders were themselves lax in their attention to the problem. The State Department officer in charge was Breckinridge Long, a Democratic politician of southern aristocratic background who demonstrated little concern for the Jews. Long actually hindered private citizens' efforts to save victims.

When evidence mounted that Hitler intended to exterminate the Jews, British and American representatives met in Bermuda (1943) but came up with no plans. Secretary Hull made a discouraging report to the president, emphasizing "the unknown cost of moving an undetermined number of persons from an undisclosed place to an unknown destination." Appalled, Secretary of the Treasury Henry Morgenthau, Jr., charged that the State Department's foot-dragging made the United States an accessory to murder. "It takes months and months to grant the visa and then it usually applies to a corpse," he wrote bitterly. Early in 1944, stirred by Morgenthau's well-documented plea, Roosevelt created the War Refugee Board, which set up refugee camps in Europe and saved thousands from death.

But American officials waited too long to act, and they missed a chance to destroy the gas chambers and ovens at the extermination camp at Auschwitz in occupied Poland. They had aerial photographs and diagrams of the camp, but they argued that bombing it would detract from the war effort or prompt the Germans to step up the anti-Jewish terror. In 1944 American planes bombed synthetic oil and rubber plants in the industrial sector of Auschwitz, only five miles from the gas chambers and crematoria. "How could it be," historian David S. Wyman has asked, "that Government officials knew that a place existed where 2,000 helpless human beings could be killed in less than an hour, knew that this occurred over and over again, and yet did not feel driven to search for some way to wipe such a scourge from the earth?"

The Yalta Conference and a flawed peace

With the war in Europe nearing an end, and a host of political questions–including what to do with Germany–yet to be settled, President Roosevelt urged another summit meeting. The three Allied leaders met at Yalta, on the Russian Crimea, in early February 1945. Controversy has surrounded the conference ever since. Roosevelt was obviously ill. "His appearance could change in a couple of hours from looking like a ghost to looking okay," remarked the new Secretary of State Edward Stettinius, Jr. The sixty-two-year-old president suffered from hypertension, heart disease, and hardening of the arteries. His doctors prescribed rest, a reduction in cigarette smoking, and medication, but the president maintained a busy schedule. Critics of the Yalta agreements later charged that Roosevelt was too weak to resist the demands of a guileful Stalin, that he struck a poor bargain. The evidence suggests, however, that Roosevelt was mentally alert and that he managed to sustain his strength during negotiations.

The Yalta meeting has also been criticized because some of its agreements were secret (suggesting the Allies had something to hide) and because it decided the fate of weak nations like Poland and China without their consent. The truth is that some agreements were secret because they contained military information that had to be kept from the still undefeated Japanese and Germans. But the criticism that the Allies paid scant attention to small nations was well-taken. It exposed a general pattern of wartime diplomacy, which was based on the assumption that the most powerful of the Allies would dominate international relations after the war.

Allied goals at Yalta

Each of the Allies entered into the conference with definite goals. Britain sought a place for France in occupied Germany; a curb on Soviet influence in Poland; and protection for the vulnerable British Empire. Russia wanted reparations from Germany, to assist in the massive task of rebuilding at home; possessions in Asia; continued influence in Poland; and a permanently weakened Germany, so that Russia would never again suffer a German attack. The United States lobbied for the United Nations Organization, where it believed it could exercise influence; for a Soviet declaration of war against Japan; for recognition of China as a major power; and for compromise between rival factions in Poland.

Military positions at the time of the conference helped to shape the final agreements. Soviet troops had occupied much of Eastern Europe, including Poland, while the Western Allies were emerging from the Battle of the Bulge. In Asia the Japanese were still zealously resisting the American advance. Millions of Japanese troops in China, Manchuria, Korea, and the home islands seemed ready to die to the last man for the empire. As near as victory was, Britain and the United States still needed the Soviets to win the war.

The unsettled issue of Poland preoccupied the conferees. Stalin repeatedly pointed out that twice in the century German armies had marched through Poland into Russian territory, killing millions. He insisted on a government friendly to Moscow–the Lublin regime–in order to prevent another German onslaught. And he demanded boundaries that would give Poland part of Germany in the west and Russia part of Poland in the east. Churchill boiled over in protest; he wanted the London regime to return to Poland. A compromise was reached under Roosevelt's leadership: a boundary favorable to Russia in the east; postponement of the western boundary issue; and the creation of a "more broadly based" coalition government that would include members of the London government-in-exile. Free elections would be held sometime in the future. The agreement was vague, but given Soviet occupation of Poland, Roosevelt considered it "the best I can do."

As for Germany, the Big Three agreed that it would be divided into four zones, the fourth to go to France. Russia and the United States gave in to Britain on that point; they did not believe that France, which had hardly fought in the war and whose Vichy regime had cooperated with the Germans, deserved such recognition. As for reparations, Russia wanted a precise figure, but Churchill and Roosevelt said they would first have to determine Germany's ability to pay. Without the British, the Americans and Russians agreed that an Allied committee would consider the sum of $20 billion as a basis for discussion in the future, with half the amount to go to the Soviet Union.

Asian issues were debated, and again tradeoffs were devised. Stalin promised to declare war on Japan two or three months after Hitler's defeat. Since the atomic bomb was still on the drawing boards at the time, American military leaders applauded the commitment. The Soviet premier also consented to sign a treaty of friendship and alliance with Jiang Jieshi (Chiang Kai-shek), America's ally in China, rather than with the Communist Mao Zedong. In return the United States agreed to give Russia the southern part of the island of Sakhalin; Lüshun (Port Arthur); and a hand in the operation of Manchurian railroads. To the Russians these concessions amounted to a recovery of rights lost after the Russo-Japanese War in 1905.

Regarding the United Nations Organization, Roosevelt and Churchill gave the Soviets three votes in the General Assembly. The three leaders scheduled the organizing meeting of the United Nations for April 25 in San Francisco (fifty nations launched that body in May). Finally, they restated the Atlantic Charter principles in the Declaration of Liberated Europe, pledging to establish order and to rebuild national economies by democratic methods.

Yalta marked the high point of the Grand Alliance; each of the Allies came away with something, in the tradition of diplomatic give-and-take. But as the great powers jockeyed for influence at the close of the war, neither the spirit nor the letter of Yalta held firm. The crumbling of the alliance became evident at the Potsdam Conference in July and August 1945. Roosevelt had died in April, and Harry S Truman had replaced him. Truman was a novice at international diplomacy, and less patient with the Russians: "I thought he was an S.O.B.," he said of Stalin. Truman departed the conference with the exaggerated notion that the Russians "were planning world conquest." Churchill charged that the Russians were acting unilaterally in Eastern Europe–but he too would soon be gone from the international high councils, defeated at the polls by English voters during the conference.

Potsdam Conference

The Big Three did agree on some general policies for governing Germany. A Control Council made up of the military commanders of the four zones (French, British, American, and Russian) was empowered to oversee "complete disarmament and demilitarization"; the "elimination or control of all German industry that could be used for military production"; and the disbanding of Nazi institutions and laws. The question of reparations continued to divide the victors. In a compromise they decided that each occupying nation should take reparations from its own zone; but they could not agree on a total figure. To resolve other issues, such as peace treaties with Italy, Finland, and Hungary, and territorial questions, the conferees created the Council of Foreign Ministers.

Winston Churchill (1874–1965), Franklin D. Roosevelt, and Josef Stalin (1879–1953), seated left to right, at the Yalta Conference in February 1945. National Archives.

Potsdam left much undone. Truman learned during the conference that scientists had successfully exploded an atomic device in New Mexico, and the knowledge quickly dampened his desire for Russian entry into the war against Japan. There was, in short, little that bound the Allies together as the war drew to a close. Roosevelt's cooperative style was gone; the spirit of Yalta was evaporating; the common enemy, Hitler, was defeated; and America no longer needed Russia in the Pacific theater.

Meanwhile, each of the victors was seeking to preserve and enlarge its sphere of influence. The British claimed authority in Greece and parts of the Middle East; the Russians already dominated much of Eastern Europe; and Americans continued their hegemony in Latin America. The United States also seized several Pacific islands as strategic outposts and laid plans to dominate a defeated Japan. Let the Americans have their Pacific bases, responded Churchill, "but 'Hands off the British Empire' is our maxim." Furthermore, American interests increased their stake in Middle Eastern resources, especially oil, during the war. By 1944 American petroleum companies controlled 42 percent of the proved oil reserves of the Middle East—a nineteenfold increase since 1936. The British resented this intrusion into their traditional sphere, but to American diplomats the United States need for expansion seemed urgent in the disrupted postwar world. In a world shrunk by the advent of the airplane, events everywhere seemed to affect the nation's prosperity and security.

Hitler once said "We may be destroyed, but if we are, we shall drag a world with us—a world in flames." Indeed, *rubble* was the word most commonly invoked to describe the global landscape at the end of the war. Hamburg, Stuttgart, and Dresden had been laid waste; three-quarters of Berlin was in ruins. In England, Coventry and parts of London were bombed out. Across the continent transportation systems had been disrupted and water supplies contaminated. Everywhere ghostlike people wandered about searching desperately for food, and mourning those who

Much of Germany was devastated at war's end. This picture was taken in Pforzheim, West Germany, in 1949. Otto Hagel.

would never come home. Russia had lost 15 to 20 million people; Poland 5.8 million; Germany 4.5 million. In all, about 35 million Europeans died as a result of the war. In Asia untold millions of Chinese and 2 million Japanese died.

Postwar supremacy of the United States

Only one major combatant escaped these grisly statistics: the United States. Its cities were not burned and its fields were not trampled. American deaths from the war—about 400,000—were few compared to the losses of other nations. In fact, Americans came out of the Second World War more powerful than they had gone in. They alone had the atomic bomb. The American air force and navy were the largest anywhere. And though the United States demobilized the major part of its regular army after the war, it still had 2 million men in arms in 1946, 1.6 million in 1949. What is more, only the United States had the capital and economic resources to spur international recovery. America was, gloated Truman, a "giant."

Somehow a new world had to be fashioned out of the ashes of the old. In country after country political affairs were in disarray, as right and left struggled to re-establish a semblance of authority. In Greece leftist rebels battled a British-backed regime; in France Charles De Gaulle argued with socialists and communists; in China civil war wore on. With the European countries in political tumult and economic crisis, their Asian colonies began to break away. For the great powers, there were friends to be won and strategic and economic interests at stake in the outcomes of these contests. And the economic reconstruction of the rubble-strewn nations of Europe and Asia also stimulated competition between the great powers.

But more important, with Japan and Germany eliminated as centers of power, with Britain and France hobbled, Russia and America now began acting as if in a vacuum. The two nations clashed constantly, "like two big dogs chewing on a bone," as Senator J. William Fulbright remarked. This bipolar structure of power would be one of the Second World War's lasting legacies.

Origins of the Cold War

Most Americans agreed with President Truman that the atomic bombing of two Japanese cities had been necessary, to end the war as quickly as possible and to save American lives. Use of the bomb to achieve victory had, in fact, been the primary assumption of the Manhattan Project. At the highest governmental levels and among atomic scientists, alternatives had been discussed: detonate the bomb on an unpopulated Pacific island, with international observers as witnesses; blockade and bomb Japan conventionally; follow up the peace feelers Tokyo had been sending out; encourage a Russian declaration of war. But Truman's aides had rejected these options on the grounds that they would take too long and would not convince the tenacious Japanese they had been beaten. Then too, memories of Pearl Harbor played an undeniable part. "When you have to deal with a beast you have to treat him as a beast," Truman said; and he did not consider his statement a cruel one.

Diplomatic considerations also sped the decision to use the bomb. Leaders envisioned the real and psychological power the bomb would bestow on the United States. It might serve as a deterrent against aggression; it might intimidate Russia into making concessions in Eastern Europe; it might end the war in the Pacific before Russia could claim a role in the management of Asia. "If it explodes, as I think it will," Truman remarked, "I'll certainly have a hammer on those boys" (the Russians).

Atomic diplomacy

The Russians were alert to such thinking. It was hardly a secret that Secretary of State James F. Byrnes (1945–1947) liked to use the implied threat of the bomb during Soviet-American negotiations. At a stormy foreign ministers' conference in London in fall 1945, Soviet Commissar of Foreign Affairs V. M. Molotov asked Byrnes if he had an atomic bomb in his side pocket. Byrnes replied that southerners "carry our artillery in our hip pocket. If you don't cut out all this stalling and let us get down to work, I am going to pull an atomic bomb out of my hip pocket and let you have it." This apparently light moment bore serious meaning: the United States possessed a monopoly on atomic power. Retiring Secretary of War Henry L. Stimson was one among the few who opposed the use of the bomb as a diplomatic lever. As he told the president in September 1945, if Americans continued to have "this weapon rather ostentatiously on our hip, their [the Russians'] suspicions and their distrust of our purposes and motives will increase."

Suspicions and distrust were the stuff of the emerging Soviet-American confrontation, popularly called the Cold War. In an economically devastated world, a world in which colonies were jilting mother countries and leftists were challenging the old guards discredited by the war, Russians and Americans glared at one another, shouted at one another, and supplied client states with the weaponry to fight one another. Each sought leadership in reassembling world order; each sought to build up its own sphere of influence; each was driven by an ideology and a sense of righteousness. "We are in this thing all over the world to the extent that few people realize," Secretary of State Byrnes told the cabinet.

Why were Americans "all over the world"? For one thing, they had determined never to repeat the experience of the 1930s. No more Munichs, no more appeasement, they vowed. And it seemed to Americans in the 1940s that Nazi Germany had merely been replaced by Soviet Russia, that Communism was simply the other side of the totalitarian coin. The popular term "Red fascism" captured this sentiment. In short, the United States intended to use its tremendous power to resist countries like the Soviet Union that seemed bent on subjugating neighboring states and expanding their repressive political systems.

American decision makers also knew that the nation's economic well-being depended on an activist foreign policy. In the postwar years the United States was the largest supplier of goods to world markets: in 1947 its exports amounted to $14 billion. That trade was jeopardized by the postwar economic paralysis of Europe, traditionally America's major customer, and by discriminatory trade practices that violated the Open Door doctrine. "Any serious failure to maintain this flow," declared an assistant secretary of state, "would put millions of American businessmen, farmers, and workers out of business." Indeed, exports constituted about 10 percent of the gross national product; the automobile and machine-tool industries, among others, relied heavily on foreign trade. About 20 percent of American steelworkers owed their jobs to steel exports, and about half of America's wheat was shipped abroad. Surpluses of cotton and tobacco also required foreign outlets. Finally, the United States needed to export in order to pay for imports such as zinc, tin, and manganese. Economic expansionism, so much a part of pre-Cold War history, thus remained a central feature of postwar foreign relations.

New strategic theory also propelled the United States toward an activist, expansionist, globalist diplomacy. "As top dog, America becomes target No. 1," warned Air Force General Carl Spaatz. To be ready for a military challenge in the postwar air age, the nation's defense had to begin far beyond its own borders (see map, page 794). Thus the United States had to acquire overseas air bases. And where would its navy float? "Wherever there is a sea," Navy Secretary James Forrestal declared.

Truman as Cold Warrior

President Truman shared these assumptions. And his personality tended to increase the tension that characterized postwar international relations. Critics said Truman's curt style hampered negotiations. Whereas Roosevelt had been ingratiating, patient, and evasive, reaching for some middle ground, Truman was brash, impatient, and direct. He seldom displayed the appreciation of subtleties so essential to successful diplomacy; for him issues were sketched in black and white, not shades of gray. As a friendly Winston Churchill said of him, Truman "takes no notice of delicate ground, he just plants his foot firmly on it."

Shortly after Roosevelt's death, Truman met Molotov at the White House. The president scolded the commissar sharply, berating Russia for violating the Yalta accords. Molotov denied it. When Truman shot back that the Soviets should honor their agreements, Molotov stormed out of the room. The president was pleased with his "tough method": "I gave it to him straight 'one-two to the jaw.' I let him have it straight." But the Yalta agreements were vague and imprecise, and although Soviet actions in Poland had been heavy-handed, whether they were in violation of the agreements was a matter of interpretation. Unfortunately, this simplistic display of toughness would become a trademark of American Cold War diplomacy.

Provocative Soviet actions

As for the Soviets, they were not easy to get along with either. Dean Acheson, a high-ranking diplomat from 1945 to 1947 and secretary of state from 1949 to 1953, found them rude and abusive. This conservative, mustachioed Phi Beta Kappa graduate of Yale and Harvard Law School could, he said, talk with "everybody who was housebroken." The Russians, he advised, were not: "I think it is a mistake to believe that you can, at any time, sit down with the Russians and solve problems." Indeed, Premier Stalin's blunt *nyets* stung American ears. The Soviets also annoyed Americans by walking out of meetings; delaying talks for long periods while awaiting instructions from Moscow; arguing the same point over and over again; and sometimes changing positions abruptly. The suspicious and secretive Stalin, who was known for "liquidating" his political opponents in the purges of the 1930s, seemed the reincarnation of Hitler. But more than Soviet style bothered Americans. In occupied Eastern Europe Russian officials did not hesitate to suppress non-Communists in conspicuous shows of military might and political manipulation. Americans were outraged.

For their part, the Russians remembered how the West had ostracized them before: "We were always outsiders," complained one Soviet diplomat. Driven

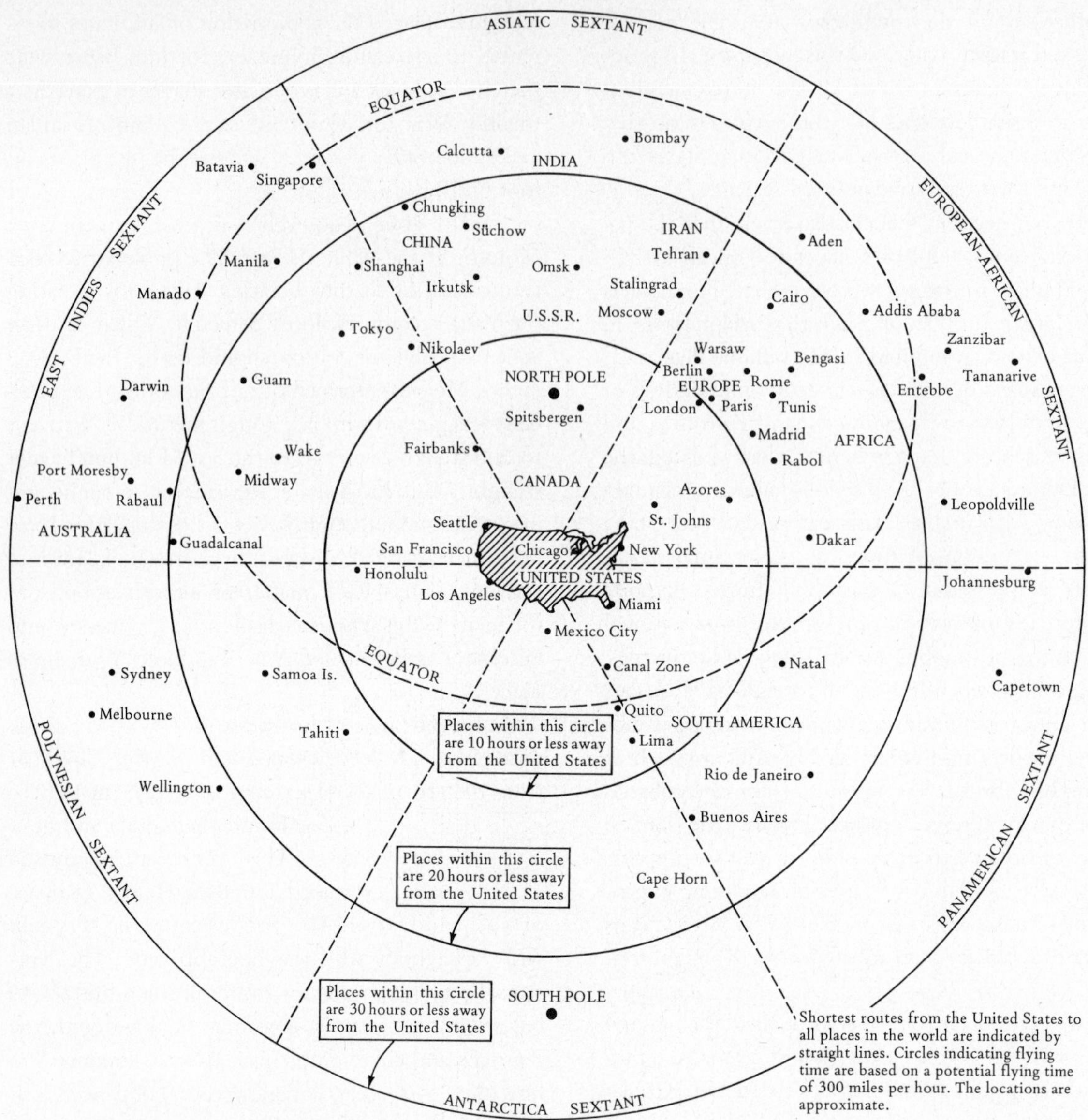

Air-Time Chart of the World. The coming of the airplane changed the way people thought about travel—from ocean or land miles to flying hours. This map by N. L. Engelhardt, Jr., drawn in 1943, was designed to emphasize the shrinking of the globe in the "air age." It demonstrated that not only could Americans move more quickly to all parts of the world, but that foreigners could reach the United States quickly, thus making it more vulnerable to attack from abroad than before. American strategists concluded that the nation's defense required more overseas bases. Source: Adapted from N. L. Engelhardt, Jr.

"Oh, dear, I'd really be enjoying all this if it weren't for Russia." Having emerged from the war as citizens of the wealthiest nation in the world, these comfortable Americans bemoan the existence of Soviet Russia as an obstacle to their complete enjoyment of the postwar era. Drawing by Alan Dunn; © 1947, 1973 The New Yorker Magazine, Inc.

by memories of the past, by fear of a revived Germany, by the huge task of reconstruction, and by Marxist-Leninist doctrine, the Soviets suspected capitalist nations of plotting once again to extinguish the Communist flame. If Americans feared "Communist aggression," Russians feared "capitalist encirclement." In mirror image, each side saw the other as the aggressor, the obstacle to peace.

"After World War II," Senator Fulbright remembered, "we were sold on the idea that Stalin was out to dominate the world." This globalist point of view, common among historians in the 1950s, pitted a generous United States ready to rebuild a peaceful world against a selfish, uncooperative Soviet Union. According to this view, Americans were forced to react defensively against expansionist Russians. But Fulbright came to believe, as have many historians, that Americans exaggerated the Soviet menace. Russia had neither the resources nor, apparently, the intention of dominating the world; it was a regional power in Eastern Europe. Americans perceived the Soviet threat as global largely because they fixed their attention on the utopian Communist aim of world revolution rather than on actual Soviet behavior, limited largely to regions along the Russian border and to bombastic rhetoric.

Revisionist interpretation of the Cold War

According to this *revisionist* point of view, based

partly on secret documents declassified in the 1960s, the United States, flushed with power, took advantage of the postwar power vacuum to expand its overseas interests and shape peace on American terms. When its bold exercise of power aroused a growing number of opponents, in particular the always-suspicious Soviet Union, Americans overreacted. George F. Kennan, one of the chief architects of Cold War policy, later regretted that Americans had created the image of the Soviet Union as "the totally inhuman and malevolent adversary," for their distorted view contributed to the gradual abandonment of diplomacy during the rash of crises that followed the war.

The Cold War and containment in Europe and the Mideast, 1945–1950

The United States and Russia moved from one crisis to another in the aftermath of the war. The first clash came in Poland in 1945, when the Russians refused to admit conservative Poles from London to the Lublin government, as agreed at Yalta. A visit to Stalin by former Roosevelt aide Harry Hopkins in May brought about some broadening of the Lublin regime, but did not change Poland's status as a subservient, Soviet-directed state. The Russians also snuffed out civil liberties in the former Nazi satellite of Rumania. Though they allowed free elections to be held in Hungary and Czechoslovakia, as the Cold War progressed and they came to fear American power more and more, they encouraged Communist coups. First Hungary (1947) and then Czechoslovakia (1948) succumbed to Soviet subversion. Yugoslavia was a unique case: its independent Communist government, led by Josip Broz Tito, successfully broke with Stalin in 1948 after Soviet threats to discipline that nation.

To justify their actions the Soviets complained that the United States was reviving Germany and meddling in Eastern Europe. They cited radio broadcasts that encouraged resistance; clandestine meetings with anti-Soviet groups; repeated calls for elections; and the extension and withholding of loans to gain political influence ("dollar diplomacy"). Russia also charged that the United States was pursuing a double standard in intervening in the affairs of Eastern Europe but expecting Russia to stay out of Latin America and Asia. They pointed to the lack of free elections in Latin American dictatorships. Americans responded that their spheres of influence were far more open, their methods far less repressive than the Russians'. But protest as Washington did, it was unable to roll back Soviet influence in Eastern Europe.

The two adversaries also collided in Iran. By wartime agreement, British, American, and Russian troops occupied Iran. The Russians had some influence in the north, near the Russian-Iranian border, and the British dominated the country's rich oil industry. When American petroleum companies asked the Iranian government for an oil concession, Moscow sniffed a capitalist plot on its border. In March 1946, the date agreed on for troop withdrawal, the Russians stayed on in violation of the wartime treaty. Americans angrily accused the U.S.S.R. of intending to take over Iran. The Russians countered that American military advisers remained in Iran, and that British oil interests ensured Anglo-American political influence in the Teheran government. When the American-dominated United Nations Organization investigated only Soviet actions in Iran, Moscow ordered its delegation to boycott the international body.

Crisis in Iran

In spite of the noisiness of the crisis, Iranian and Soviet diplomats managed to negotiate a settlement in April: Soviet soldiers would depart from Iran in exchange for an oil concession. Americans claimed a Cold War victory, believing their tough words had forced the Soviets to withdraw their troops. In 1947 they turned the tables by persuading the Iranians to go back on their promise of a Russian oil concession. Moscow cried that it had been double-crossed; it had withdrawn its troops from Iran and now Americans were perched on its border.

Soviets and Americans clashed on every front in 1946. They could not agree on the unification of Germany, so they built up their zones independently. Efforts to establish international control of atomic energy failed. The American Baruch Plan, providing for abandonment of the American nuclear monopoly only after the world's fissionable materials had been brought under the control of an international agency, did not satisfy the Soviets. They pointed out that it

A Soviet tank in Gdansk, Poland, April 1945. After driving the Germans from Poland, the Red Army stayed on to ensure the power of the Communist regime in that war-weary nation. Sovfoto.

denied Russia the right to develop its own bomb while the United States continued its supremacy. Even the new World Bank and International Monetary Fund, created at the 1944 Bretton Woods Conference to stabilize trade and finance, became tangled in the Cold War struggle. The Soviets refused to join because the United States so dominated both institutions. In early 1946 Washington unilaterally extended a $3.5 billion loan to Great Britain but turned down a similar Soviet request. Already smarting from an abrupt cutoff of Lend-Lease aid in mid-1945, the Soviets denounced the United States for using its reconstruction dollars to buy friends and punish its enemies.

When in early February 1946 Stalin gave a pre-election speech depicting a world threatened by capitalist acquisitiveness, the American chargé d'affaires in Moscow, George F. Kennan, concluded that Russian fanaticism made even a temporary understanding impossible. Kennan's pessimistic telegram to Washington, which was widely read, fed the growing belief that only toughness would work with the Russians. A few weeks later Winston Churchill made his stirring Iron Curtain speech, warning that Eastern European countries were being cut off from the West by Russia. With the approving Truman sitting on the stage, the former prime minister called for an Anglo-American partnership to resist the Russian menace. Stalin protested that "Russia was not attacking, she was being attacked."

Secretary of Commerce Henry A. Wallace, a critic of Truman's self-conscious get-tough policy, feared the United States was substituting atomic and economic coercion for diplomacy. "'Getting tough,'" he told a Madison Square Garden audience in September 1946, "never brought anything real and lasting–

President Roosevelt, Vice President Harry S Truman (1884–1972), and Secretary of Commerce Henry A. Wallace (1888–1965), left to right, not long before the president's death. Wallace later became a vigorous critic of Truman's get-tough foreign policy and was ousted from the cabinet in September 1946. Library of Congress.

whether for schoolyard bullies or businessmen or world powers. The tougher we get, the tougher the Russians will get." Truman removed Wallace from the cabinet, charging that "the Reds, phonies, and 'parlor pinks' . . . are becoming a national danger. I am afraid they are a sabotage front for Uncle Joe Stalin."

The Cold War escalated further on March 12, 1947, when in response to a request from the British, who could no longer afford to fund their Greek client government, the president addressed a special joint session of Congress. In alarmist language Truman asked for $400 million in aid to Greece and Turkey, both of which were threatened by economic dislocation and Communist political pressure. "It must be the policy of the United States to support free peoples who are resisting attempted subjugation by armed minorities or by outside pressures," Truman declared. It was time to draw the line, to contain the Communist menace. The president's statement quickly became known as the Truman Doctrine. Critics correctly pointed out that there was no evidence that the Soviet Union was involved in the civil war in Greece; that the rebel National Liberation Front had good reason to resent the repressive and corrupt regime supported by the British; and that the resistance movement included non-Communists as well as Communists. Others suggested that aid should be channeled through the United Nations. But Tru-

Truman Doctrine

man's speech had galvanized public support, and after much debate the Senate approved his request 67 to 23. Using American dollars and military advisers, the Greek government defeated the insurgents in 1949.

In July 1947 George F. Kennan, now director of the State Department's policy planning staff, offered another statement of what became known as the containment doctrine. Writing under the name "Mr. X" in the magazine *Foreign Affairs,* this expert on Soviet affairs advocated a "policy of firm containment, designed to confront the Russians with unalterable counterforce at every point where they show signs of encroaching upon the interests of a peaceful and stable world." Such a counterforce, Kennan argued,

Debate over containment

would check Soviet expansion and eventually foster a "mellowing" of Soviet behavior. As to the means with which to implement his advice, Kennan was vague. Together with the Truman Doctrine, Kennan's article became the chief manifesto of Cold War foreign policy.

The highly regarded journalist Walter Lippmann was critical of the containment doctrine. In a series of newspaper articles published in book form as *The Cold War* (1947), Lippmann called containment a "strategic monstrosity" that did not distinguish between areas vital and peripheral to American security. If American leaders thought every place on earth was of strategic importance, he reasoned, the nation's patience and resources would soon be drained. "The policy can be implemented only by recruiting, subsidizing and supporting a heterogeneous array of satellites, clients, dependents and puppets," he warned. Nor did Lippmann share Truman's view that Russia was plotting to take over the world. Truman, he asserted, put too little emphasis on diplomacy.

Lippmann was happier with the Marshall Plan for the reconstruction of Western Europe. In 1946 and 1947 an unusually harsh winter swept over Europe.

Marshall Plan

Coal supplies dwindled; meager food stores were exhausted. European nations, still reeling from the war, lacked the dollars to buy American goods. Especially in France and Italy, leftists and Communists gained in political power. Americans, who had already spent billions of dollars on European relief and recovery by 1947, recalled the troubles of the 1930s: global depression; political extremism; war born of economic discontent. It could not be allowed to happen again. Western Europe, Dean Acheson emphasized, was the "keystone in the arch which supports the kind of a world which we have to have in order to conduct our lives."

On June 5, 1947, Secretary of State George C. Marshall (1947–1949) announced that the United States would finance a massive European Recovery Program. Though Marshall did not exclude Eastern Europe or the Soviet Union, few American leaders believed that Russia would want to join an American project. Congress voted overwhelmingly for the necessary funds—though some budget-conscious conservatives complained that the New Deal was going overseas. Launched in 1948, the Marshall Plan poured $13 billion into Western Europe before it ended in 1952 (see map, page 800). To stimulate business at home, the plan provided that the foreign aid dollars had to be spent in the United States. The recovery program gave way to military assistance in 1951 when it was subsumed under the Mutual Security Administration. By 1952, in fact, 80 percent of American aid to Western Europe was military in nature. From the beginning Russia blasted the Marshall Plan as enslavement of Europe, and went so far as to create a special propaganda agency—the Cominform—to harangue against it. For Eastern Europe the Soviets prepared a feeble imitation, the Molotov Plan.

To strengthen the nation's defenses, Truman worked with Congress to streamline the government's administrative structure under the National Security Act (July 1947). The act created the Department of Defense (replacing the War Department), the National Security Council (NSC) to advise the president, and the Central Intelligence Agency (CIA) to conduct spying and information gathering. By the early 1950s the CIA had expanded its functions to include covert (secret) operations aimed at overthrowing unfriendly foreign leaders and, as a high-ranking American official put it, stirring up economic trouble in "the camp of the enemy" through a "Department of Dirty Tricks." In 1953 the United States Information Agency was created to counter Soviet propaganda.

American officials also reached out to find new foreign friends and build new bases. In 1946, when the United States granted the Philippines independence, it maintained its old military, economic, and political

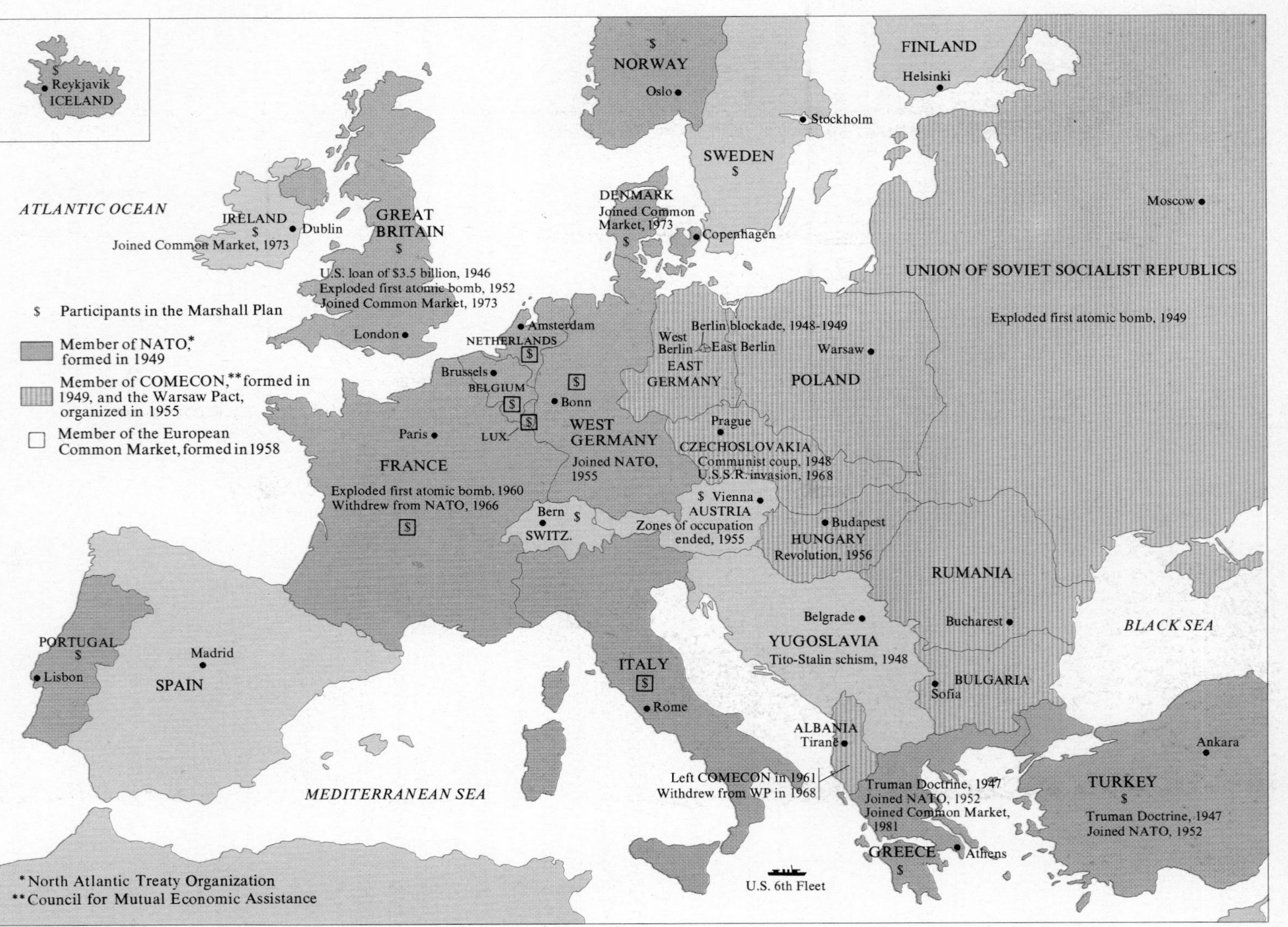

Divided Europe

ties. And in 1947 American diplomats created the Rio Pact—a military alliance with Latin American countries. Under this and other agreements the Truman administration sent several military advisory missions to Latin America, and others to Greece, Turkey, Iran, China, and Saudi Arabia. In 1948 Americans activated an air base in Libya. And in May of that year Truman quickly recognized the new state of Israel, which had been carved out of the British-held territory of Palestine after years of Arab-Jewish dispute. In conjunction with the need for international allies, the president's desire for Jewish-American votes in the upcoming election hurried his decision.

One of the most electric moments in the Cold War came a month later. In June 1948 the Russians cut off Western access to the jointly occupied city of Berlin, located well inside the Soviet zone of Germany. Before the Soviets' bold move, the Americans, French, and British had agreed to fuse their zones into what became known as West Germany. The three allies planned to integrate West Germany, including the three Western sectors of Berlin, into the Western European economy, complete with a reformed German currency. The Soviets, fearing a resurgent Germany tied to the American Cold War camp, may have sparked the Berlin crisis to stimulate negotiations. But if they thought Truman would compromise, they guessed wrong. Instead the president ordered a massive airlift of food, fuel, and other supplies to the isolated city—a plane almost every minute. Finally, in May 1949, their image badly damaged, the Soviets lifted the blockade. They had stimulated the very thing they feared, the creation of the Federal Republic of Germany (West Germany) that month. In retaliation they founded the People's Republic of Germany (East Germany). As for the United States, it claimed another victory for toughness.

On April 4, 1949, believing that a military shield should be added to the economic shield of the Marshall Plan, the United States, Canada, and much of Western Europe founded the North Atlantic Treaty Organization (NATO). The treaty aroused considerable debate at home, for not since 1778 had the United States joined a formal European military alliance. Critics of all political persuasions sprang forth. Senator Robert A. Taft of Ohio—"Mr. Republican"—protested that NATO would provoke an arms race with Russia or cause American soldiers to be stationed in Europe. Others complained that the scheme gave the president power to send troops into combat without a congressional declaration of war, and that it would cost too much, ultimately weakening the nation. Truman responded that NATO would give Europeans the will to resist, the confidence to thwart Communism in their midst. And it would function as a "tripwire," bringing the full military and atomic force of the United States to bear on the Soviet Union if it dared to cross the East-West line. Quietly, administration spokesmen also indicated that NATO was designed to knit Western Europe together, to discourage some nations' tendency toward neutrality. Though the Russians howled that NATO would "kindle the flames of a new war," the Senate ratified the treaty in July, 82 to 13. Truman then asked for a $1.5 billion Mutual Defense Assistance Act, to which Congress also consented, as it did to all Truman's major foreign policy requests.

Creation of NATO

Just before passage of the military aid bill (September 1949), an American aircraft carrying sensitive equipment detected unusually high radioactivity in the atmosphere. It soon became evident that the Soviets had exploded an atomic bomb. "This is now a different world," commented Senator Vandenberg. The American nuclear monopoly was no more, and Western Europe seemed more vulnerable. The Communists were also winning the civil war in China (see pages 803–804) and Moscow was scoring propaganda points by advocating "peaceful coexistence" with the West. American leaders could have responded to this changed state of affairs with diplomatic negotiations. But Secretary of State Dean Acheson announced that there would be no "appeasement"—no seduction by the Soviet "Trojan dove." The United States would instead build "situations of strength" around the world. In early 1950 Truman ordered production of the hydrogen bomb, the "super." And in May Congress finally endorsed funds for technical assistance to developing nations, to draw them into the American sphere of influence (a plan called the Point Four Program, after point 4 of Truman's 1949 inaugural address).

A month before, the National Security Council had delivered to the president a top-secret document

Mao Zedong (1893–1976), founder of the People's Republic of China. His victory over Jiang Jieshi brought the Communists to power in 1949, but until 1979 the United States refused to recognize the government. National Archives.

numbered NSC-68. Predicting continued tension with the Communists and describing a "shrinking world of polarized power," the report appealed for an enlarged military budget to counter the Soviet global design American strategists mistakenly believed existed. Increased taxes and congressional cooperation would be needed, the authors advised; public opinion would have to be mobilized behind huge defense expenditures. Administration officials worried about how to sell this strong prescription to the voters and budget-conscious congressional representatives. "We were sweating over it, and then—with regard to NSC-68—thank God Korea came along," recalled one of Acheson's aides.

NSC-68

The Cold War in Asia, 1945–1951

When the Korean War erupted in mid-1950, it came in the wake of vast changes in Asia. The Second World War accelerated the process of decolonization begun during the First World War. Occupied with defending themselves and then with rebuilding after the war, mother countries were no longer able to resist their colonies' demands for independence. Britain gave up India and what is now Pakistan in 1947, Burma and Ceylon in 1948. And the Dutch reluctantly let go of Indonesia in 1949. The French fought on in Indochina, finally retiring from that outpost in 1954.

The defeat of Japan brought about the division of its empire among the victors. Korea was divided between the United States and the Soviet Union. The Pacific islands (the Marshalls, Marianas, and Carolines) came under American control. Half of Sakhalin went to Russia as agreed at Yalta, and Formosa (Taiwan) was returned to the Chinese. As for Japan itself, the United States monopolized its reconstruction. Though the British and Russians asserted that they too had fought in the Asian theater and deserved a say in the occupation, Ambassador W. Averell Harriman answered that Washington was "very firm on the matter of keeping the power in American hands." Stalin complained that Russia was being treated "like a piece of the furniture" and wondered what the difference was between American domination of Japan and Russian domination of Rumania. But General Douglas MacArthur, who envisioned turning the Pacific Ocean into "an Anglo-Saxon lake," had the last word in Japan. As director of the American occupation, MacArthur wrote a democratic constitution for Japan, revitalized its economy, and destroyed the weapons and warships of the Japanese military.

Reconstruction of Japan

Though United States supremacy in Japan was an established fact, the Russians would not recognize it. Thus, after squabbling with Russia for years over a peace treaty with Japan, the United States finally signed a separate peace in 1951. The treaty restored Japan's sovereignty, ended the occupation, granted the United States a military base at Okinawa, and permitted American troops to be stationed in Japan. Tokyo and Washington also initialed a defense pact. The people who had been called beasts after their surprise attack on Pearl Harbor were now American allies in the Cold War. Along with Germany, Japan was, as Kennan noted, one of "our most important pawns on the chessboard of world politics."

Meanwhile, America's Chinese allies were faltering. The United States was feeding and fueling Jiang Jieshi's Nationalist armies in their battle against Mao Zedong and Zhou Enlai's Communists. Immediately after the Second World War American troops had occupied northern China, flown Nationalist soldiers to Manchuria, and stayed on to advise Generalissimo Jiang's army. From 1945 to 1949 the United States sent China $3 billion in aid, more than it gave most allies. But it soon became evident that Jiang was a weak and unreliable friend. His government was rife with corruption and inefficiency; he was out of touch with the rebellious peasants, whom the Communists enlisted with promises of land redistribution; and he tolerated a grossly unfair tax system. Journalist Theodore White thought the Nationalists combined "some of the worst features of Tammany Hall and the Spanish Inquisition," and Truman privately denounced them as "grafters and crooks." Jiang ignored American advice to root out corruption, halt inflation, and begin land reform. He also worked to disrupt the efforts of the Marshall mission (1945–1947) to negotiate a cease-fire and a coalition government. And he rejected American military advice. "We picked a bad horse," Truman admitted. Still, seeing Jiang as the only viable alternative to Mao, Truman backed him to the end.

American officials were divided on the question of whether Mao was a puppet of the Soviet Union. Some diplomats considered him an Asian Tito–Communist but independent–but most believed he was part of an international Communist movement and would thus give the Soviets a springboard into Asia. In the *White Paper* of 1949–a long government report on America's efforts to contain Communism through aid to Jiang–Secretary Acheson asserted that the "Communist leaders have foresworn their Chinese heritage and have publicly announced their subservience to a foreign power." Thus when the Chinese Communists made secret overtures to begin diplomatic talks in 1945 and again in 1949, American officials rebuffed them. Mao soon decided that he was "leaning to one side" in the Cold War–the Soviet side.

Actually, Americans had overestimated Mao's dependence on the Russians. The Soviet Union gave Mao little support, rejecting his interpretation of Marxism-Leninism and resenting his determination to resist their influence. For its own purposes Russia preferred a weak China under Jiang to a strong China under Mao, an attitude that derived from a long history of Sino-Russian rivalry.

Nonrecognition of the People's Republic of China

In fall 1949, after numerous military setbacks, Jiang fled to the island of Formosa and Mao proclaimed the People's Republic of China. Would the United States extend diplomatic recognition to the new government? Truman hesitated; he tried unsuccessfully to persuade the British to wait. "Are we to refuse to recognize facts, however unpleasant they may be?" asked the British prime minister. "Are we to cut ourselves off from all contact with one-sixth of the inhabitants of the world?" But for several reasons Washington did just that. First, American officials were alarmed by a Sino-Soviet treaty of friendship signed in February 1950. Second, Mao's followers had harassed Americans and seized American-owned property in China. Third, Mao was now openly hostile to the United States, blaming Americans for prolonging the bloody civil war.

But another reason lay behind the policy of nonrecognition. A noisy group of Republican critics called the China lobby, shattering the postwar spirit of bipartisanship, was seeking to blame Jiang's defeat on Truman. Publisher Henry Luce, Senator William Knowland of California, and Congressman Walter Judd of Minnesota won headlines by charging that the United States had "lost" China. Knowland bemoaned the administration's "spirit of defeatism"; Senator Joseph McCarthy of Wisconsin snorted that "egg-sucking liberals" and "queers" had sold China into "atheistic slavery."

Truman and Acheson answered that the United States had never had China to lose, that Jiang was not willing to help himself, and that large-scale military intervention in the Chinese civil war would have been costly and probably interminable. Moreover, major involvement in China would have drained valuable resources from Europe, the primary front in the Cold War. "The United States cannot furnish determination, it cannot furnish the will, and it cannot furnish the loyalty of a people to its government," Acheson insisted, adding, "China lost itself." But the political foes of recognition were formidable, and the United States did not open formal diplomatic relations with the People's Republic of China until 1979—thirty years after Mao's government came to power.

Reaching for some way to offset Jiang's collapse, the National Security Council urged the president to fortify "friendly and independent" states in Asia as a bulwark against Communist expansion. In February 1950 the United States recognized the French puppet regime of Bao Dai in Vietnam, and a few months later decided to extend aid to the beleaguered French there. In April the National Security Council sent the president its alarming report NSC-68. And in May more funds went to Jiang Jieshi in Formosa. It is in this context of globalist thought and action that America's response to war in Korea must be seen.

The Korean War and its global consequences

In the early morning hours of June 25, 1950, thousands of troops under the banner of the Democratic People's Republic of Korea (North Korea) moved across the 38th parallel into the Republic of Korea (South Korea). They "struck like a cobra," recalled General Douglas MacArthur. For years the two Koreas had skirmished along the border the great powers had drawn for them in 1945. Both regimes sought reunification of the divided country, but each on its own terms. Now it appeared that the North Koreans, armed by the Russians, would realize their goal by force, for the South Koreans, armed by the Americans, soon disintegrated. When the news reached Washington, D.C., people recalled Pearl Harbor and braced themselves for a third world war.

For the thirty-third president, it was the 1930s all over again. "Communism was acting in Korea just as Hitler, Mussolini, and the Japanese had acted," Truman recalled. After huddling with his advisers, the president decided to intervene; he ordered MacArthur to send arms to South Korea and to attack North Korean forces from the air. Thinking beyond Korea, he directed the Seventh Fleet to patrol the waters between the Chinese mainland and Jiang's sanctuary, Formosa, thus inserting the United States once again into Chinese politics. Finally, on June 30, Truman ordered American troops into battle. "If Washington only will not hobble me," boasted MacArthur, "I can handle it with one arm tied behind my back." After the Security Council, in the Soviet delegate's absence, voted to assist South Korea, MacArthur became United Nations Commander.

Truman acted decisively for war because he believed, in the Cold War mentality of the time, that the Soviets had masterminded the North Korean attack.

Origins of the Korean War

As an assistant secretary of state put it, the relationship between the Soviet Union and North Korea was "the same as that between Walt Disney and Donald Duck." Though there is little evidence that the Soviets began the Korean War, at the time there was reason to believe that the Soviets were probing for a weak spot in the anti-Communist shield. When American troops withdrew from Korea in mid-1949, the Joint Chiefs of Staff had secretly declared South Korea nonvital to American security. And in a public speech in January 1950, Secretary Acheson had drawn the American defense line in Asia through the Aleutians, Japan, and Okinawa to the Philippines. Although Formosa and Korea were clearly beyond that line, Acheson did say that those areas could expect United Nations (and hence American) assistance in the event of attack. Still, Stalin might have read Acheson's speech as an abandonment of South Korea. Russia may also have been willing to risk war to challenge China for leadership of the Communist world, to disrupt American peace negotiations with its longtime rival Japan, or to extend its sphere of influence in Asia.

But unanswered questions dog the thesis that Russia started the Korean War. The Soviet delegate was absent from the Security Council when it voted to aid South Korea because he was protesting the United Nations' refusal to seat the People's Republic of China. If the Soviets had fomented the war in Korea, it is puzzling that their delegate was not present to

This propaganda poster, published in several languages by the United States Information Service, broadcast the popular view that the Russians were the aggressors in the Korean War—a view scholars have questioned. Wide World.

veto aid to South Korea. Were they caught off guard? And other questions suggest themselves. Why did the Soviets give so little aid to the North Koreans once the war broke out? And why, when they were scoring important propaganda points by advocating peaceful coexistence, would they destroy their gains by igniting a war? It is the opinion of some scholars that the North Koreans began the war, for their own nationalistic reasons. To suggest this is to emphasize the *Korean* rather than international origins of the conflict—to focus on the civil war between the North Korean Communists led by Kim Il-sung and the South Korean government of Syngman Rhee.

In June 1950 such questions were not being asked. Truman and his aides never doubted that Russia was testing their policy of containment; that American prestige was at stake; and that failure to act in Korea would prompt Soviet aggression in Yugoslavia, Iran, or Berlin. And Truman was trapped by his own rhetoric. He had long talked about toughness and the global threat of Communism; to fail to act in Korea would be to invite more harangues from the China lobby. Truman's popularity was in fact declining. The war offered him an opportunity not only to disarm his critics but to fulfill the National Security Council's recommendation to create "friendly and independent" Asian states, perhaps by uniting the two Koreas. In any case, as one headline put it, "Uncle Sam Takes Role as World Cop."

At first the war in "the land that God forgot," as GIs described Korea, went badly for American troops, who accounted for about 90 percent of United Nations forces. Pushed into the tiny Pusan perimeter at the base of South Korea, the Eighth Army weathered

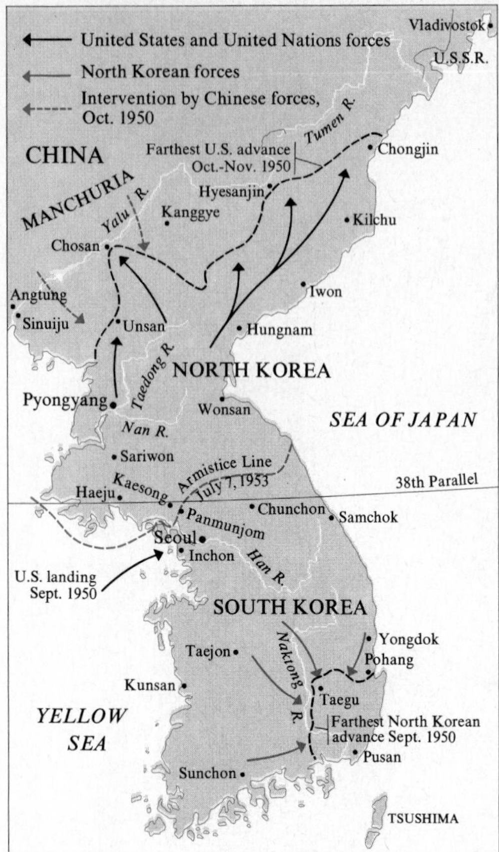

The Korean War, 1950–1953. Source: By permission of the publisher, from *American Foreign Policy: A History* by Paterson et al., p. 378. (Lexington, Mass.: D.C. Heath and Company, 1977).

numerous North Korean assaults. Then on September 15, 1950, MacArthur launched a bold plan: an amphibious landing at Inchon, several hundred miles behind North Korean lines (see map). Soon American soldiers had liberated Seoul, the South Korean capital, and pushed the northern troops back to the 38th parallel. The Inchon triumph, General Maxwell Taylor recalled, had an "intoxicating effect" on American leaders. They redefined their goals, from the containment of North Korea to the reunification of Korea by force. Communism would not only be stopped; it would be rolled back. On September 27 Truman authorized United Nations forces to cross the 38th parallel.

Within several weeks American troops had driven deeply into North Korea. In early November American aircraft began strikes against bridges on the Yalu River, the border between North Korea and the People's Republic of China. The Chinese watched warily, wondering if the Americans who had supported Jiang Jieshi would soon stab at the People's Republic. Mao issued public warnings that China could not permit the continued bombing of its transportation links with Korea or the annihilation of North Korea itself. MacArthur shrugged off the warnings, telling Truman that the Chinese would face the "greatest slaughter" if they entered the war. Officials in Washington agreed. But they were dead wrong. In late October Americans had tangled with some Chinese soldiers, who pulled back quickly after the encounter. Historians have concluded that this was one of many signals to the United States that American advances to the Chinese border should stop, or China would enter the war. A month later an unmoved MacArthur sent his Eighth Army northward in a new offensive. On November 26 tens of thousands of Chinese troops counterattacked, surprising the general's forces and driving them pell-mell southward. Embarrassed, MacArthur demanded that Washington order a massive air attack on China. Truman hesitated, reflecting on the costs and consequences of a wider war. He hinted that he might use the atomic bomb, but he seemed chastened, uneager for an enlarged war with China that might drag on for years.

MacArthur moves against North Korea

By March 1951 the military lines had stabilized around the 38th parallel. Truman contemplated negotiations, and the Soviets stated publicly that they favored a political settlement. But MacArthur had other ideas. The general was making reckless public statements, calling for an attack on China or for Jiang's return to the mainland. Now was the time, he insisted, to smash Communism by destroying its Asian flank. MacArthur also hinted that the president was practicing appeasement. Denouncing the concept of limited war (war without nuclear weapons, confined to one place), he told one congressman: "There is no substitute for victory." On April 10 Truman fired the general for insubordination. MacArthur nevertheless returned home to a tickertape parade, and made a televised address to Congress

Truman fires MacArthur

The Korean War uprooted the civilian population of Korea. Here American infantrymen march to battle while refugees, clutching their belongings, hurry to escape. About half a million Korean civilians were killed during the war. UPI.

that moved many in the audience to tears. One congressman was so spellbound that he murmured, "We saw a great hunk of God in the flesh."

Although Truman's popularity sagged, he withstood calls for his impeachment. The chairman of the Joint Chiefs of Staff, General Omar Bradley, spoke against MacArthur's provocative ideas. Escalation could bring Russia into battle, Bradley pointed out—American bombs had already fallen close to the Siberian port of Vladivostok. And it was unwise to exhaust America's resources in an Asian war that promised no victory when there were allies in Europe to be protected. Indeed, a showdown with Asian Communists, Bradley told a Senate committee, would be "the wrong war, at the wrong place, at the wrong time, and with the wrong enemy." MacArthur soon faded from the public eye; his hints at running for the presidency came to naught.

Armistice talks began in July 1951, but the fighting went on for two more years. Though the new president, Dwight D. Eisenhower, went to Korea personally in December 1952 to fulfill a campaign pledge, his postelection visit brought no settlement. The sticking point in the negotiations was the fate of the prisoners of war (POWs): thousands of North Korean and Chinese captives did not want to return home. In violation of international custom, American officials honored their wishes and refused to ship them back against their will. On July 23, 1953, an armistice was finally signed. The combatants agreed to hand the POW question over to a special panel of neutral nations (which later gave prisoners their choice of staying or leaving). The North Korean-South Korean line was set close to the 38th parallel, the prewar boundary. Thus ended a frustrating war—a limited war that Americans, accustomed to victory, found difficult to accept. The experience was indeed sobering, as was the casualty list of 34,000 Americans dead and 103,000 wounded. Total killed and wounded for all combatants in the Korean War was 1.9 million.

The Korean War had major political consequences. The failure to achieve victory and the public's impatience with a limited war undoubtedly helped to elect Eisenhower. Bipartisanship in foreign policy eroded further, and the powers of the presidency grew as Congress deferred to Truman time and again. Truman had never gone to Congress for a declaration of war, for he believed that as commander-in-chief he had the authority to send troops to Korea. A few dissenters like Senator Robert Taft disagreed, but Truman saw no need to debate the matter. Had he asked for a declaration, he would have had majorities in both houses. But as Dean Acheson later explained, Truman did not wish to invite hearings and "ponderous questions" that might have "muddled up" presidential decisions.

Debate over globalist policy

The Korean War also set off a great national debate. Conservative critics of globalism, like Taft, former ambassador to England Joseph P. Kennedy, and ex-President Herbert Hoover, suggested that America should reduce its overseas commitments and draw its defense line in the Western Hemisphere. If foreign nations were not willing to commit their own resources to defending themselves, the United States had no obligation to help them, they reasoned. But Republican John Foster Dulles countered that "a defense that accepts encirclement quickly decomposes." Truman himself joined the debate with bloated rhetoric exaggerating the Communist threat: "We are fighting in Korea so we won't have to fight in Wichita, or in Chicago, or in New Orleans, or on San Francisco Bay."

The advocates of global defense won the debate. Increased aid flowed to the French for their die-hard stand in Indochina; by 1954, when the French effort finally collapsed, the United States was paying three-quarters of the war's cost. South Korea and Formosa also became major recipients of American foreign aid. And Australia and New Zealand joined the United States in a mutual defense agreement, the Anzus Treaty (1951), which provided that an attack on any of the three countries would be considered an attack on all. Columnist James Reston of the New York *Times* reported from Asia in August 1953 that the "range of American activities in this part of the world is unbelievable." As for the Chinese, who had shed American blood, the American commitment to non-recognition hardened.

The Korean War, Acheson noted happily, removed "the recommendations of NSC-68 from the realm of theory and made them immediate budget issues." Indeed, the military budget shot up to $60 billion in the fiscal year ending in mid-1953, and remained at $35 to $40 billion a year throughout the 1950s. The American military stockpiled scarce raw materials, acquired new bases in Morocco (1951) and Spain (1953), among other places, and increased its supply of nuclear weapons to about 750 by 1951. The army sent six divisions to Europe, and the administration initiated plans to rearm West Germany. In 1952 scientists exploded the first hydrogen bomb on the tiny Pacific atoll of Eniwetok, and the air force christened a new long-range bomber, the B-52. Proponents claimed that the logic of the containment doctrine required this global watch, for if the threat was worldwide, the response had to be worldwide as well. "If you don't pay attention to the periphery," diplomat Dean Rusk warned, "the periphery changes. And the first thing you know the periphery is the center."

But the periphery did not in fact always become the center. Some areas were vital and others were not. Nor did a global watch ensure security. One congressman compared containment to "sending three policemen to surround a building that has 25 exits." And as

Important events

1941	United States enters Second World War
1942	Bataan Death March Allied invasion of North Africa Battles of Coral Sea and Midway halt Japanese advance
1943	Allied invasion of Italy Teheran Conference
1944	War Refugee Board established Cross-channel landing at Normandy Dumbarton Oaks Conference United States retakes Philippines
1945	Yalta Conference Battles of Iwo Jima and Okinawa Roosevelt dies; Harry S Truman assumes presidency United Nations founded at San Francisco Russians install a Communist regime in Poland Germany surrenders Potsdam Conference Atomic bombs devastate Hiroshima and Nagasaki Japan surrenders
1946	American-Russian crisis over Iran American loan granted to Great Britain American loan denied to the Soviet Union Stalin's pre-election speech George F. Kennan's telegram Winston Churchill's iron-curtain speech Paris Peace Conference
1947	Truman Doctrine
1947	Communist takeover in Hungary Kennan appeals for containment doctrine in "Mr. X" article Marshall Plan announced National Security Act Rio Pact
1948	Communist coup in Czechoslovakia Jiang Jieshi suffers defeats in China Organization of American States founded State of Israel founded Tito-Stalin split Berlin blockade and airlift
1949	North Atlantic Treaty Organization founded West Germany formed from three zones Russia explodes an atomic bomb Communist victory in China
1950	United States decides to develop a hydrogen bomb Sino-Soviet treaty NSC-68 Point Four Program launched United States supports French in Indochina Korean War begins U.S. troops cross the 38th parallel Chinese troops enter the Korean War
1951	Armistice talks begin in Korea
1952	Hydrogen bomb exploded Maiden flight of new B-52 bomber Dwight D. Eisenhower elected president
1953	Korean War ends

Walter Lippmann had warned, blind allegiance to the containment doctrine did lead to repeated overseas ventures and alliances with questionable clients and dictators. What was most dangerous, officials assumed wrongly that threats to world peace always sprang from international Communist intrigue. They overlooked the local, non-Communist roots of many rebellions against the status quo, and they underestimated the independence of non-Russian Communists. In the future, Americans would struggle to sustain their simplistic point of view in a revolutionary world where nationalism rather than Communism was the driving force in international affairs—a force that would be subordinated neither to the United States nor to the Soviet Union.

Suggestions for further reading

The Second World War and diplomacy

Stephen A. Ambrose, *The Supreme Commander* (1970); Robert Beitzell, *The Uneasy Alliance* (1972); A. Russell Buchanan, *The United States in World War II,* 2 vols. (1964); James MacGregor Burns, *Roosevelt: The Soldier of Freedom* (1970); Peter Calvocoressi and Guy Wint, *Total War* (1972); Diane S. Clemens, *Yalta* (1970); Robert Dallek, *Franklin D. Roosevelt and American Foreign Policy, 1932–1945* (1979); Robert A. Divine, *Roosevelt and World War II* (1969); Robert A. Divine, *Second Chance: The Triumph of Internationalism in America during World War II* (1967); Henry L. Feingold, *Politics of Rescue* (1970); Herbert Feis, *Churchill, Roosevelt, and Stalin* (1957); Kent R. Greenfield, *American Strategy in World War II* (1963); George C. Herring, *Aid to Russia, 1941–1946* (1973); Stanley Hilton, *Hitler's Secret War in South America, 1939–1945* (1981); Akira Iriye, *Power and Culture: The Japanese-American War, 1941–1945* (1981); Gabriel Kolko, *The Politics of War* (1968); William H. McNeill, *America, Britain, and Russia* (1953); Vojtech Mastny, *Russia's Road to the Cold War* (1979); Samuel Eliot Morison, *Strategy and Compromise* (1958); Samuel Eliot Morison, *The Two-Ocean War* (1963); Arthur D. Morse, *While Six Million Died* (1968); Raymond G. O'Connor, *Diplomacy for Victory* (1971); Gaddis Smith, *Diplomacy during the Second World War, 1941–1945* (1965); John Snell, ed., *The Meaning of Yalta* (1956); Mark Stoler, *The Politics of the Second Front* (1977); Gordon Wright, *The Ordeal of Total War, 1939–1945* (1968).

The atomic bomb

Gar Alperovitz, *Atomic Diplomacy* (1965); Barton J. Bernstein, ed., *The Atomic Bomb* (1976); Robert J. C. Butow, *Japan's Decision to Surrender* (1954); Committee for the Compilation of Materials on Damage Caused by the Atomic Bombs in Hiroshima and Nagasaki, *Hiroshima and Nagasaki* (1981); Herbert Feis, *The Atomic Bomb and the End of World War II* (1966); Gregg Herken, *The Winning Weapon* (1981); Richard G. Hewlett and Oscar E. Anderson, *The New World* (1962); Chalmers M. Roberts, *The Nuclear Years* (1970); Martin J. Sherwin, *A World Destroyed* (1975).

Origins of the Cold War and European policy

Stephen Ambrose, *Rise to Globalism,* 2nd ed. (1980); Barton J. Bernstein, ed., *Politics and Policies of the Truman Administration* (1970); Robert J. Donovan, *Conflict and Crisis* (1977); John L. Gaddis, *The United States and the Origins of the Cold War, 1941–1947* (1972); John Gimbel, *The American Occupation of Germany* (1968); Louis Halle, *The Cold War as History* (1967); Gabriel Kolko and Joyce Kolko, *The Limits of Power* (1972); Bruce Kuklick, *American Policy and the Division of Germany* (1972); Walter LaFeber, *America, Russia, and the Cold War, 1945–1980,* 4th ed. (1980); David McLellan, *Dean Acheson* (1976); Thomas G. Paterson, ed., *Cold War Critics* (1971); Thomas G. Paterson, *On Every Front: The Making of the Cold War* (1979); Thomas G. Paterson, *Soviet-American Confrontation* (1973); Gaddis Smith, *Dean Acheson* (1972); William Taubman, *Stalin's American Policy* (1980); Adam Ulam, *The Rivals* (1971); Daniel Yergen, *Shattered Peace* (1977).

The Truman Doctrine and containment

Thomas H. Etzold and John L. Gaddis, eds., *Containment* (1978); Richard M. Freeland, *The Truman Doctrine and the Origins of McCarthyism* (1972); Charles Gati, ed., *Caging the Bear* (1974); John D. Iatrides, *Revolt in Athens* (1972); George F. Kennan, *Memoirs, 1925–1950* (1967); Bruce R. Kuniholm, *The Origins of the Cold War in the Near East* (1980); Walter Lippmann, *The Cold War* (1947); Thomas G. Paterson, ed., *Containment and the Cold War* (1973); Samuel F. Wells, Jr., "Sounding the Tocsin: NSC-68 and the Soviet Threat," *International Security,* 4 (1979), 116–158; C. Ben Wright, "Mr. 'X' and Containment," *Slavic Review,* 35 (1976), 1–31.

Asia

Dorothy Borg and Waldo Heinrichs, eds., *Uncertain Years* (1980); Warren I. Cohen, *America's Response to China,* 2nd ed. (1980); Herbert Feis, *The China Tangle* (1953); Herbert Feis, *Contest Over Japan* (1967); Akira Iriye, *The Cold War in Asia* (1974); E. J. Kahn, Jr., *The China Hands* (1975); William R. Louis, *Imperialism at Bay: The United States and the Decolonization of the British Empire* (1978); Gary May, *China Scapegoat: The Diplomatic Ordeal of John Carter Vincent* (1979); Charles E. Neu, *The Troubled Encounter: The United States and Japan* (1975); Michael Schaller, *The U.S. Crusade in China, 1938–1945* (1978); Michael Schaller, *The United States and China in the Twentieth Century* (1979); William W. Stueck, Jr., *The Road to Confrontation: American Policy toward China and Korea, 1947–1950* (1981); Christopher Thorne, *Allies of a Kind* (1978); Tang Tsou, *America's Failure in China, 1941–1950* (1963).

The Korean War

Ronald J. Caridi, *The Korean War and American Politics* (1969); Bruce Cummings, *The Origins of the Korean War* (1980); Francis H. Heller, ed., *The Korean War* (1977); Glenn D. Paige, *The Korean Decision* (1968); David Rees, *Korea: The Limited War* (1964); Robert R. Simmons, *The Strained Alliance* (1975); John W. Spanier, *The Truman-MacArthur Controversy and the Korean War* (1959); I. F. Stone, *The Hidden History of the Korean War* (1952); Allen Whiting, *China Crosses the Yalu* (1960).

The wartime emergency spurred the establishment of totally new industries, the best known of which was synthetic rubber. The Japanese, in their conquest of the South Pacific in the weeks following Pearl Harbor, had captured 90 percent of the world's supply of crude rubber. Though the government resorted to conservation measures, including a national speed limit and gasoline rationing to save wear and tear on tires, neither conservation nor recycling could meet wartime needs. So with an investment of $700 million, the government underwrote the creation of a synthetic-rubber industry. By war's end the nation that had been the world's largest importer of rubber had become the world's largest exporter of rubber—all of it synthetic. New industries, of course, introduced new pollutants: smog (first detected in Los Angeles in 1943); artificially made radioactive elements; and petrochemical wastes from such new products as plastics, detergents, and DDT.

To gain the cooperation of business, the WPB and other government agencies met it more than halfway.

Government incentives to business

Whenever possible, Chairman Donald Nelson said, he wanted "to establish a set of rules under which the game could be played the way industry said it had to play it." So the government hired dollar-a-year men from business to staff the wartime bureaus. It offered guaranteed profits in the form of cost-plus-fixed-fee contracts, generous tax writeoffs, and exemption from antitrust prosecution. And it allowed prime contractors to distribute subcontracts as they saw fit, including those involving scarce war-related materials. As a result, some of these corporations functioned like mini-governments. Still other benefits included patent rights on government-funded inventions and purchase options on facilities constructed or operated for the government. Though the rewards were extremely liberal, they made sense for a government—and a nation—that wanted the most possible war goods manufactured in the shortest possible time.

From mid-1940 through September 1944 the government awarded contracts totaling $175 billion, no less than two-thirds of which went to the top one hundred corporations. General Motors received almost $14 billion, or 8 percent of the total; big awards also went to other automobile companies, several aircraft and steel companies, General Electric, AT&T, and Du Pont. The fact is that almost all the industries that benefited from wartime contracts were dominated by big business at the beginning of the war, and the billions of dollars they received in government contracts only accentuated their dominance. Though no one had yet thought to call it the "military-industrial complex," as President Dwight Eisenhower would in 1961, the web of government-business interdependence had begun to be woven.

The other side of the coin was the complete disappearance of half a million small retail, service, and construction firms and the declining significance of the surviving firms. In 1939 firms with fewer than fifty employees had paid 30 percent of all payrolls; by 1943 that figure had dropped to 19 percent. Meanwhile corporations with a thousand or more employees registered gains, from 36 percent in 1939 to 53 percent in 1943.

The big also got bigger in science and higher education. To develop radar and do other research, the Massachusetts Institute of Technology received seventy-five contracts valued at $117 million. The California Institute of Technology came next with forty-eight contracts totaling $83 million, followed by Harvard, Columbia, the University of California, Johns Hopkins, and the University of Chicago. The most spectacular result of a government contract with a university was, of course, the atomic bomb, the facility for the testing of which was run by officials at the University of California at Berkeley. Likewise, the first controlled nuclear chain reaction was set off—under contract—at the Metallurgical Laboratory at the University of Chicago.

Big labor also grew bigger during the war. Union membership ballooned from 8.5 million in 1940 to 14.75 million in 1945, split more or less equally between the American Federation of Labor and the Congress of Industrial Organizations. (Even with this increase, however, only 33 percent of the nonagricultural labor force belonged to labor unions.) In 1942, to minimize labor-management conflict, President Roosevelt created the National War Labor Board (NWLB), sometimes referred to as the Supreme Court for labor disputes. Although the NWLB did not quell all disputes, one of its successes was the maintenance-of-membership formula, which provided that any union member who did not quit within fifteen days of a contract signing would remain

On Christmas Eve 1943, this supply-laden landing ship was on its way to Allied troops in the Pacific. America's total war production in the Second World War was double that of the Axis powers. National Archives.

a member through the life of the contract. Unions were permitted to enroll as many new members as possible, but workers were not required to join a union. Thus the NWLB forged a compromise between the unions' demand for a closed, or union, shop, and management's interest in open shops.

Less successful was the NWLB's Little Steel formula, developed in mid-1942. Denounced by labor as a wage freeze, the formula was an effort to limit wage increases to increases in the cost of living. Union leaders condemned it as subversive of collective bargaining. Workers complained not only that they were prevented from bettering themselves but that only blue-collar workers—not farmers or high-income earners—were held to such a standard. As a result, the production time lost through strikes and other work stoppages tripled in 1943. Machinists in the San Francisco shipyards struck in March, followed by 55,000 rubber workers in April and 28,000 automobile workers in May. "Strikes are spreading at an alarming rate," bemoaned a member of the NWLB, "and unless they

Wartime labor strikes

"Well, it was fun while it lasted." The war, with its government-guaranteed profits, was a boon to big business. In dollar value two-thirds of federal war contracts went to the nation's one hundred largest corporations. Drawing by Alan Dunn; © 1947, 1975 The New Yorker Magazine, Inc.

are checked immediately, the 'no strike-no lockout' agreement will become meaningless." But the worst strikes were yet to come– in the coal fields, where 450,000 soft-coal miners and 80,000 anthracite miners struck. "When the mine workers' children cry for bread," declared John L. Lewis, "they cannot be satisfied with a 'Little Steel formula.'" After three walkouts by miners in two months, the government seized the mines and placed them under the control of the Department of Interior.

Public hostility grew toward organized labor in general and John L. Lewis in particular. To discourage further work stoppages, Congress passed the War Labor Disputes, or Smith-Connally, Act of June 1943. The act conferred on the president the authority to seize and operate any strike-bound plant deemed necessary to the national security, and established a mandatory thirty-day cooling-off period before any new strike could be called. The Smith-Connally Act also gave the NWLB the legal authority to settle labor disputes for the duration of the war. Over the course of the war the NWLB handled close to eighteen thousand disputes, reducing time lost due to strikes to one-third the peacetime level. It did not misuse its power. Though prices rose 31.7 percent during the war, NWLB wage adjustments increased wages by 40.5 percent.

Although the war demanded sacrifices from Americans, it also brought new highs in personal income. It was a bountiful time both for corporations, which doubled their net profits between 1939 and 1943, and for employees, whose wages and salaries rose more than 135 percent from 1940 to 1945. The government did not tax this extra income as heavily as it might have. Despite bold proposals by presidential advisers to prohibit annual incomes of more than $25,000 or to redistribute income through a steeply graduated income tax, President Roosevelt was hesitant to request higher taxes, and Congress was even more hesitant to respond. Instead, the government borrowed approximately 60 percent of the cost of the war, about half of it in the form of war bonds sold to patriotic citizens; the national debt jumped from $49 billion in 1941 to $259 billion in 1945.

Increased mechanization of agriculture

Agriculture also made an impressive contribution to the war effort, not only through hard work but through the introduction of labor-saving machinery to replace the men and women who had gone to the front or migrated to war-production centers. Farming was in the midst of a transition from the family-owned and operated farm to the large-scale, mechanized agribusiness dominated by banks, insurance companies, and farm co-ops. The Second World War accelerated the trend, for wealthy financial institutions were better able than family farmers to pay for expensive new machinery. From 1940 to 1945 the value of American agricultural machinery rose from $3.1 billion to $6.5 billion, and the average acreage per farm jumped from 179 to 195. The use of the new machines and fertilizers boosted farm output per man-hour by 25 percent. At the same time the farm population fell from 30.5 million to 24.4 million. Like business and labor, agriculture was becoming more consolidated in the process of contributing to the war effort.

At the head of the burgeoning national economy stood the federal government, whose size and importance, like that of business and labor, was mushrooming: from 1940 to 1945 the federal bureaucracy expanded from 1.1 million workers to 3.4 million. The executive branch, which included the Office of the Commander-in-Chief and bore the responsibility for directing the war effort, grew the most. Besides raising the armed forces, mobilizing industrial production, pacifying labor and management, and controlling inflation, the executive also had to manage the labor supply. Through the War Manpower Commission (WMC), composed of representatives of various agencies, the government determined where labor was most needed, allocated labor between industry and the armed forces, and recruited new workers.

But the WMC was far from successful in accomplishing its goals, and government operations were becoming more and more complex. The OPA alone (see page 815) succeeded in putting a lid on inflation by issuing a mass of proclamations, orders, and rules that became, in effect, a code of law governing the behavior of landlords, employers, rationing boards, wholesalers, retailers, and consumers. In May 1943, as economic mobilization became increasingly bogged down in red tape, President Roosevelt created the Office of War Mobilization. The OWM's purpose, Roosevelt declared, was to "streamline our activities . . . and keep both our military machine and our essential civilian economy running in team and at high speed." The OWM became, in effect, a court of appeal in disputes between conflicting civilian and military claims.

The military life

Well over 12 million men and women were serving in the U.S. armed forces at the peak of the Second World War in 1945. The army topped the list with 8.3 million, including 100,000 WACS (members of the Women's Army Corps). Though women were prohibited from engaging in combat duty, they worked at a variety of noncombat jobs, not only in the WACS but as WAVES in the navy, as pilots in the WAFS (Women's Auxiliary Ferrying Squadron), and as members of the *Semper Paratus* Always Ready Service (SPARS) and the Women's Reserve of the Marine Corps.

Most troops served overseas for an average of about sixteen months. Some, of course, never returned: total deaths exceeded 405,000; total wounded, 670,000. In terms of human life, the cost of the war was second only to that of the Civil War. Still, compared with losses suffered by other nations, U.S. figures were low. Less than 1 percent of the population was killed or wounded in the war; the Soviet Union lost 8 percent of its population–20 million people.

Those who returned found that their wartime experiences had changed their lives significantly. Practically everyone who served had been a civilian prior to Pearl Harbor, unaccustomed to the almost total lack of freedom in the military. As GIs (from *Government Issue*) they either followed orders or were punished. "Somebody in the army is giving you orders all the time," complained one soldier, "telling you when to do everything, all day long. Freedom! I think that's what I missed most while I was in the army." As a result, many returning veterans were ready to challenge authority. "You're so tied down in the army," explained one GI, "you get so in the habit of taking orders, that when you get back you just kind of go to the opposite extreme."

Many soldiers and sailors, including several million who had never been more than a few miles from their families, became homesick. GIs joked, somewhat bitterly, about having found a home in the army. Letters from family and friends were as essential as food to the troops; many sat around for hours exchanging reminiscences of their hometowns with pals. Others got used to the footloose life and had difficulty settling down again, even after the war. One explained that moving on was "a habit I got into in service. You get the urge to keep going, even if it's only to another town." But if the service encouraged postwar wandering, it also broadened horizons. "Take these kids from the hills," noted one GI, "the service opened their eyes some. . . . And some of these guys from Chicago, why they'd never been outside of Chicago. They talked about fellows 'from the sticks' and they'd never been out in the 'sticks'–they'd never even known what the 'sticks' were."

Broadening of GIs' horizons

Wartime service not only broadened horizons but

Suggestions for further reading

The home front

John Morton Blum, *V Was for Victory: Politics and American Culture during World War II* (1976); Jack Goodman, ed., *While You Were Gone: A Report on Wartime Life in the United States* (1946); Jim F. Heath, "Domestic America during World War II: Research Opportunities for Historians," *Journal of American History*, 58 (1971), 384–414; Richard R. Lingeman, *Don't You Know There's a War On? The American Home Front, 1941–1945* (1970); Francis E. Merrill, *Social Problems on the Home Front: A Study of War-time Influences* (1948); Geoffrey Perrett, *Days of Sadness, Years of Triumph: The American People 1939–1945* (1973); Richard Polenberg, *War and Society: The United States, 1941–1945* (1972).

Economic mobilization for war

John Morton Blum, ed., *From the Morgenthau Diaries: Years of War* (1967); Bureau of the Budget, *The United States at War* (1946); Bruce Catton, *The War Lords of Washington* (1948); George Q. Flynn, *The Mess in Washington: Manpower Mobilization in World War II* (1979); Eliot Janeway, *The Struggle for Survival* (1951); Paul A. C. Koistinen, *The Hammer and the Sword: Labor, the Military, and Industrial Mobilization, 1920–1945* (1979); Donald Nelson, *Arsenal of Democracy* (1946); Smaller War Plants Corporation, *Economic Concentration and World War II* (1946); William M. Tuttle, Jr., "The Birth of an Industry: The Synthetic Rubber 'Mess' in World War II," *Technology and Culture*, 22 (1981), 35–67; Gerald T. White, *Billions for Defense: Government Finance by the Defense Plant Corporation during World War II* (1980).

Farmers, soldiers, and workers

John L. Blackman, Jr., *Presidential Seizure in Labor Disputes* (1967); Melvyn Dubofsky and Warren H. Van Tine, *John L. Lewis: A Biography* (1977); Joel Seidman, *American Labor from Defense to Reconversion* (1953); Samuel A. Stouffer *et al., The American Soldier* (1949); Walter W. Wilcox, *The Farmer in the Second World War* (1947).

State and local history

Lowell J. Carr and James E. Stermer, *Willow Run: A Study of Industrialization and Cultural Inadequacy* (1952); Alan Clive, *State of War: Michigan in World War II* (1979); Philip J. Funigiello, *The Challenge to Urban Liberalism: Federal-City Relations during World War II* (1978); Robert J. Havighurst and H. Gerthon Morgan, *The Social History of a War-Boom Community* (1951).

Civil liberties

Francis Biddle, *In Brief Authority* (1962); Edward S. Corwin, *Total War and the Constitution* (1947); Mulford Sibley and Philip Jacob, *Conscription of Conscience, 1940–1947* (1952); Lawrence Witner, *Rebels Against War: The American Peace Movement* (1969).

Japanese-American internment

Roger Daniels, *Concentration Camps U.S.A.: Japanese Americans and World War II* (1971); Morton Grodzins, *Americans Betrayed: Politics and the Japanese Evacuation* (1949); Bill Hosokawa, *Nisei: The Quiet Americans* (1969); Jacobus tenBroek *et al., Prejudice, War and the Constitution: Causes and Consequences of the Evacuation of the Japanese Americans in World War II* (1954); Michi Weglyn, *Years of Infamy: The Untold Story of America's Concentration Camps* (1976).

Science and education

James Phinney Baxter, *Scientists Against Time* (1946); Richard G. Hewlett and Oscar E. Anderson, Jr., *The New World, 1939–1946* (1962); Isaac Kandel, *The Impact of War upon American Education* (1948); William M. Tuttle, Jr., "Higher Education and the Federal Government: 1940–1945," *The Record*, 71 (1969–1970), 297–312, 485–499.

Politics

James C. Foster, *The Union Politic: The CIO Political Action Committee* (1975); Alonzo J. Hamby, "Sixty Million Jobs and the People's Revolution: The Liberals, the New Deal, and World War II," *The Historian*, 30 (1968), 578–598; Donald R. McCoy, "Republican Opposition in Wartime, 1941–1945," *Mid-America*, 49 (1967), 174–189; John Robert Moore, "The Conservative Coalition in the United States Senate, 1942–1945," *Journal of Southern History*, 33 (1967), 368–376; Roland Young, *Congressional Politics in the Second World War* (1956).

Afro-Americans

A. Russell Buchanan, *Black Americans in World War II* (1977); Richard M. Dalfiume, *Desegregation of the U.S.*

Armed Forces: Fighting on Two Fronts, 1939–1953 (1969); Lee Finkle, *Forum for Protest: The Black Press during World War II* (1975); Harvard Sitkoff, "Racial Militancy and Interracial Violence in the Second World War," *Journal of American History*, 58 (1971), 661–681; Neil A. Wynn, *The Afro-American and the Second World War* (1976).

Women

Karen Anderson, *Wartime Women: Sex Roles, Family Relations, and the Status of Women during World War II* (1980); William H. Chafe, *The American Woman: Her Changing Social, Economic, and Political Roles, 1920–1970* (1972); Chester W. Gregory, *Women in Defense Work during World War II: An Analysis of the Labor Problem and Women's Rights* (1974); Sally Van Wagenen Keil, *Those Wonderful Women in Their Flying Machines: The Unknown Heroes of World War II* (1979); Leila J. Rupp, *Mobilizing Women for War: German and American Propaganda, 1939–1945* (1978).

Colonial Experience (1958); Louis Hartz's *The Liberal Tradition in America* (1955); Richard Hofstadter's *The Age of Reform* (1955); and David Potter's *People of Plenty: Economic Abundance and the American Character* (1954). Historians did not deny the existence of conflict in the American past, but they ascribed it less to societal faults than to psychologically disturbed personalities. Among those people historians identified as maladjusted were abolitionists, feminists, Populists, and progressive reformers. As historian John Higham has noted, "A psychological approach to conflict enables historians to substitute a schism in the soul for a schism in society."

Thus the 1950s were the years of the "silent generation," of mass conformity. College students shunned passionate political convictions, preferring instead to be "cool." Literary critic Irving Howe lamented the shift from alienation to acceptance among intellectuals. And sociologists began to write about organization men and peer-group pressures. "The fifties under Ike," Richard Lingeman of the New York *Times* observed, "represented a sort of national prefrontal lobotomy: tail-finned, we Sunday-drove down the superhighways of life while tensions that later bubbled up in the sixties seethed beneath the placid surface."

Quite clearly, the 1950s did not prepare the nation for the 1960s, which for millions of Americans would become an age not of consensus, but of controversy. But the quiet politics of consensus did serve the interests of middle-class Americans. In the late forties, fifties, and early sixties, the economy boomed, income levels rose, and middle-class couples seized their opportunity to move to the suburbs and start the families they had delayed during the depression and the war. For them, if not for other Americans, the American dream would become a reality.

Suggestions for further reading

The Truman administration

Stephen K. Bailey, *Congress Makes a Law: The Story Behind the Employment Act of 1946* (1950); Barton J. Bernstein, ed., *Politics and Policies of the Truman Administration* (1970); Barton J. Bernstein and Allen J. Matusow, eds., *The Truman Administration: A Documentary History* (1966); Bert Cockran, *Harry Truman and the Crisis Presidency* (1973); Richard O. Davies, *Housing Reform during the Truman Administration* (1966); Robert J. Donovan, *Conflict and Crisis: The Presidency of Harry S Truman, 1945–1948* (1977); Robert H. Ferrell, ed., *Off the Record: The Private Papers of Harry S Truman* (1980); Alonzo L. Hamby, *Beyond the New Deal: Harry S Truman and American Liberalism* (1973); Susan Hartmann, *Truman and the 80th Congress* (1971); R. Alton Lee, *Truman and Taft-Hartley* (1966); Maeva Marcus, *Truman and the Steel Seizure Case: The Limits of Presidential Power* (1977); Allen J. Matusow, *Farm Policies and Politics in the Truman Years* (1967); Harry S Truman, *Memoirs* (1955–1956).

The election of 1948

V. O. Key, *Southern Politics in State and Nation* (1949); Norman D. Markowitz, *The Rise and Fall of the People's Century: Henry A. Wallace and American Liberalism, 1941–1948* (1973); Irwin Ross, *The Loneliest Campaign: The Truman Victory of 1948* (1968); Allen Yarnell, *Democrats and Progressives: The 1948 Presidential Election as a Test of Postwar Liberalism* (1974).

McCarthyism

Daniel Bell, ed., *The Radical Right* (1955); David Caute, *The Great Fear: The Anti-Communist Purge under Truman and Eisenhower* (1978); Robert Griffith, *The Politics of Fear: Joseph R. McCarthy and the Senate* (1970); Robert Griffith and Athan Theoharis, eds., *The Specter: Original Essays on the Cold War and the Origins of McCarthyism* (1974); Earl Latham, *The Communist Controversy in Washington* (1966); Victor Navasky, *Naming Names* (1980); Michael Paul Rogin, *The Intellectuals and McCarthy* (1967); Richard H. Rovere, *Senator Joe McCarthy* (1959); Joseph Starobin, *American Communism in Crisis, 1943–1957* (1972); Athan Theoharis, *Seeds of Repression: Harry S Truman and the Origins of McCarthyism* (1971); Allen Weinstein, *Perjury: The Hiss-Chambers Case* (1978); Allen Yarnell, "Eisenhower and McCarthy: An Appraisal of Presidential Strategy," *Presidential Studies Quarterly,* 10 (1980), 90–98.

The Eisenhower administration

Sherman Adams, *Firsthand Report: The Story of the Eisenhower Administration* (1961); Charles C. Alexander, *Holding the Line: The Eisenhower Era, 1952–1961* (1975); Robert L. Branyan and Lawrence H. Larson, eds., *The Eisenhower Administration, 1953–1961: A Documentary History,* 2 vols. (1971); Dwight D. Eisenhower, *Mandate for Change,*

1953–1956 (1963) and *Waging Peace, 1956–1961* (1965); William Bragg Ewald, Jr., *Eisenhower the President: Crucial Days* (1981); Robert H. Ferrel, ed., *The Eisenhower Diaries* (1981); David A. Frier, *Conflict of Interest in the Eisenhower Administration* (1969); Fred I. Greenstein, "Eisenhower as an Activist President: A Look at New Evidence," *Political Science Quarterly*, 94 (1979–1980), 575–599; Emmet John Hughes, *The Ordeal of Power: A Political Memoir of the Eisenhower Years* (1963); Peter Lyon, *Eisenhower: Portrait of the Hero* (1974); Herbert Parmet, *Eisenhower and the American Crusades* (1972); Gary W. Reichard, *The Reaffirmation of Republicanism: Eisenhower and the Eighty-third Congress* (1975); Elmo Richardson, *The Presidency of Dwight D. Eisenhower* (1979); Mark H. Rose, *Interstate: Express Highway Politics, 1941–1956* (1979).

Civil rights

John W. Anderson, *Eisenhower, Brownell, and the Congress: The Tangled Origins of the Civil Rights Bill of 1956–1957* (1964); Numan V. Bartley, *The Rise of Massive Resistance: Race and Politics in the South during the 1950's* (1969); William C. Berman, *The Politics of Civil Rights in the Truman Administration* (1970); Richard M. Dalfiume, *Desegregation of the U.S. Armed Forces: Fighting on Two Fronts, 1939–1953* (1969); Elizabeth Huckaby, *Crisis at Central High, Little Rock, 1957–58* (1980); Martin Luther King, Jr., *Stride Toward Freedom: The Montgomery Boycott* (1958); Richard Kluger, *Simple Justice: The History of Brown v. Board of Education and Black America's Struggle for Equality* (1975); Donald R. McCoy and Richard T. Ruetten, *Quest and Response: Minority Rights and the Truman Administration* (1973); Harvard Sitkoff, "Harry Truman and the Election of 1948: The Coming of Age of Civil Rights in American Politics," *Journal of Southern History*, 37 (1971), 597–616.

The age of consensus

Daniel Bell, *The End of Ideology: On the Exhaustion of Political Ideas in the Fifties* (1960); Job L. Dittberner, *The End of Ideology and American Social Thought: 1930–1960* (1979); Ronald Lora, *Conservative Minds in America* (1971); George H. Nash, *The Conservative Intellectual Movement in America: Since 1945* (1976); David M. Potter, *People of Plenty: Economic Abundance and the American Character* (1954); David Riesman with Nathan Glazer and Reuel Denney, *The Lonely Crowd* (1950); William H. Whyte, *The Organization Man* (1956).

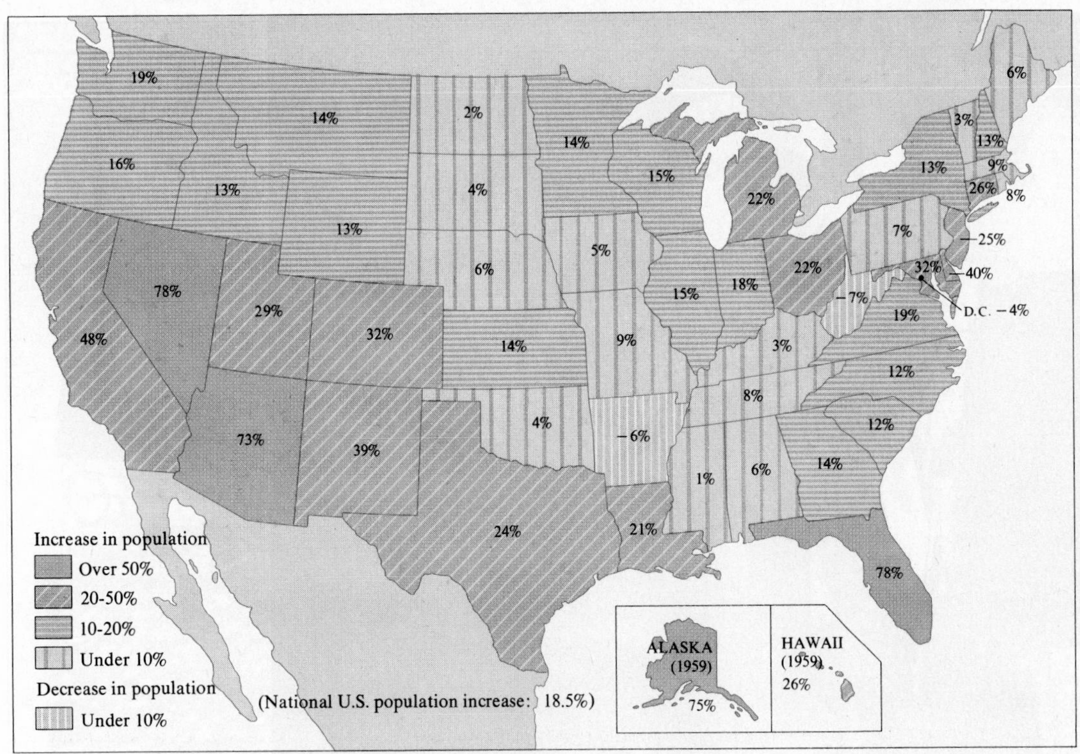

Rise of the "southern rim," 1950–1960

over 38 deaths per 1,000 live births in 1945 to 20 per 1,000 in 1970. At the same time the discovery of wonder drugs such as streptomycin (1945) and aureomycin (1948) reduced deaths from influenza and postsurgical infection. And the Salk polio vaccine, approved for public use in 1955, reduced the number of reported cases of polio 97 percent by 1962. Other diseases, like tuberculosis, whooping cough, and diphtheria, became little more than bad memories.

By no means were all the effects of economic growth beneficial to the average American. In agriculture the movement toward consolidation threatened the survival of the family farm. From 1945 to 1969 the nation's farm population declined from 24.4 million to just over 10 million. The South lost almost a quarter of its farm population in just six years, from 1970 to 1976. As one Iowa farmer lamented, "We lost country life when we moved to tractors." What was more, many of the people who stayed on did so not because they could still make a good living but because they were too old to leave their lifelong homes and follow their children and grandchildren to the cities. Living in relative isolation on limited incomes, the rural aged were among the hidden victims of big business and mechanization.

Many of the people forced off farms in the postwar years ended up in the industrial areas of the South and West, along with young families from the industrial North and East. This mass migration to the Sunbelt had begun during the Second World War, when GIs and their families were ordered to new duty stations and war workers moved to the shipyards and aircraft factories of San Diego and other cities. Soon it encompassed the entire southern rim, the area running from southern California across the Southwest and South all the way to the Carolinas, Georgia, and Florida. Between 1940 and 1950 Houston's population jumped from 385,000 to 596,000. Other Sunbelt cities that boomed shortly after the war were Baton Rouge; Long Beach, California; Miami; Mobile, Alabama; and Phoenix, Arizona.

Growth of the southern rim

The southward and westward migration continued to swell in the 1950s and 1960s (see map). Houston became a center not only of the aerospace industry but of oil and petrochemical production. Tucson, which

Distribution of total personal income* among various segments of the population, 1947–1970 (in percentages)

YEAR	POOREST FIFTH	SECOND POOREST FIFTH	MIDDLE FIFTH	SECOND WEALTHIEST FIFTH	WEALTHIEST FIFTH	WEALTHIEST 5 PERCENT
1947	3.5	10.6	16.7	23.6	45.6	18.7
1950	3.1	10.5	17.3	24.1	45.0	18.2
1960	3.2	10.6	17.6	24.7	44.0	17.0
1970	3.6	10.3	17.2	24.7	44.1	16.9

*Monetary income only.

Source: Adapted from U.S. Bureau of the Census, *Historical Statistics of the Unites States, Colonial Times to 1970,* Bicentennial Edition (Washington: U.S. Government Printing Office, 1975), p. 292.

had been scarcely more than a watering spot on the desert in 1950, grew to a city of 213,000 ten years later. California absorbed no less than one-fifth of the nation's entire population increase in the 1950s—enough, by 1963, to make the Golden State the most populous state in the union.

The economic bases of the southern rim's spectacular growth were easy to identify: big farming, or agribusiness; the aerospace industry; the massive oil industry; land speculation and real estate development; recreation; and, of course, defense spending. Industry was drawn to the southern rim by right-to-work laws, which outlawed the closed union shop, and by low taxes and heating bills.

The millions of people who departed the chilly, drab industrial cities of the North and East for sunnier climes strengthened the political clout of the Sunbelt. In a book published in 1969, Kevin Phillips, a conservative Republican, predicted an emerging Republican majority based on the votes of the South and West. Richard Nixon's triumph in the presidential election of 1968 seemed to support Phillips's thesis. So did the tendency of political parties to nominate Sunbelt candidates for national office. (The nation's four most recently elected presidents have hailed from the Sunbelt—one from Texas, two from California, and one from Georgia. And in 1980 the Census Bureau made it official: for the first time in the nation's history, voters in the South and West accounted for a majority of those eligible to cast ballots.)

The economic boom that made for the political pre-eminence of the Sunbelt also brought increased security for whole classes of Americans. But the headiness of middle-class prosperity tended to camouflage the existence of poverty amidst plenty. The elderly, nonwhites, and divorced, widowed, and deserted women rarely shared in the nation's new affluence. The expanding postwar economy did combine with federal welfare legislation to reduce poverty (see Chapter 33). But even with the reduction in poverty, there was little redistribution of income. The portions of total national income taken home by the rich, the middle classes, and the poor remained about the same from 1947 to 1970 (see table).

The people who did not share in the new affluence were overlooked in part because they were literally

Moving day in a Los Angeles suburb. In that Sunbelt city, as one writer put it, "Almost every day is moving day." J. R. Eyerman, *Life Magazine* © 1953 Time Inc.

not seen: most lived in the inner cities and in rural areas, out of sight of the prosperous middle class. For up-and-coming Americans had moved to suburbia, where poverty was rare.

The growth of suburbs

Closely associated with the affluent society, and especially with the thriving middle class, was the growth of suburban communities. During the first six decades of the twentieth century, cityward migration steadily increased. But in the 1940s a second migration—from the city to the suburbs—began to swell. By 1970 more Americans resided in suburbs than in central cities (see table).

A combination of motives drew people to the suburbs. Many wanted to leave behind the sounds and smells of the city, and to be closer to nature. They wanted homes with yards so that, as one suburbanite put it, "every kid [would have] an opportunity to grow up with grass stains on his pants." Or they wanted the privacy and quiet that detached homes provided, as well as family rooms, extra closets, and utility rooms. Many were also looking for a community of like-minded people, a place where they could have a measure of political influence. Big-city government was dense and impenetrable. In the suburbs citizens could become involved in government and have an impact, particularly on the education their children received. "The American suburb," mused a Pittsburgh building executive in 1960, "is the last outpost of democracy, the only level on which the individual citizen can make his wishes felt, directly and immediately. I think," he went on, "there's something idealistic about the search for a home in the suburbs. Call it a return to the soil. It's something that calls most people sometime in their lives."

Judging from the massive numbers of three- and four-bedroom houses built in the suburbs, there was no question that suburbanites' major concern was their children. "This is a paradise for children," observed a newspaper writer in 1950, referring to the new suburb of which he was a resident. "There are so many babies here," commented one of his neighbors, "you would think everybody would be blasé about them. Still, when a new one is coming, all the neighbors make a fuss over you." This woman and her family had moved to the suburbs just before she was to give birth. "Neighbors I hadn't even met yet just came in and took over," she reported. "They pack your bags, drive you to the hospital if your husband's working, take care of your other baby if you have one." Neighbors even lent the family a carriage, a crib, and a scale.

Such cooperation bespeaks another allure of the suburbs: closeness in age and shared experience. In many suburbs practically all the adults were young parents between the ages of twenty-five and thirty-five, and almost all the children were toddlers. In one suburb of nine thousand homes there were eight thousand children, only about one hundred of whom were old enough for high school; most of the rest were still in playpens. "People could not outdo each other," one resident of this community reported, "because they almost all have the same income. . . . Nobody talks about the [Second World] war much, because they've all been in it. And most of the men

Geographic Distribution of U.S. Population, 1930–1970 (in percentages)

YEAR	CENTRAL CITIES	SUBURBS	RURAL AREAS AND SMALL TOWNS
1930	31.8	18.0	50.2
1940	31.6	19.5	48.9
1950	32.3	23.8	43.9
1960	32.6	30.7	36.7
1970	31.4	37.6	31.0

Source: Adapted from U.S. Bureau of the Census, *Decennial Censuses, 1930–1970* (Washington, U.S. Government Printing Office).

have the same . . . commuting problem—which many have solved by car pools. All this helps to cement neighbors into friends."

Government funding and policies helped these new families to settle in the suburbs. Low-interest GI mortgages and Federal Housing Administration mortgage insurance made the difference for people who would otherwise have been unable to afford a home. Such easy credit combined with postwar prosperity to produce a construction boom. In 1944 there had been only 142,000 housing starts, many of which represented temporary housing for soldiers and war workers. From 1945 to 1946 housing starts climbed from 326,000 to over 1 million, and in 1950 they approached 2 million. Never before had new starts exceeded 1 million; not until the 1980s would they dip below that level.

Housing boom

To produce so much new housing so fast, contractors had to operate on a massive scale. Arthur Levitt and Sons, a firm that built planned communities (Levittowns) in New York, New Jersey, and Pennsylvania, developed the pattern adopted by other companies: using interchangeable materials and designs, Levitt erected rows of nearly identical houses on uniform treeless lots. Pasture lands yielded to whole neighborhoods with astounding rapidity. To supply the new communities, supermarkets, gas stations, shopping centers, and malls—all of them surrounded by vast parking lots—soon dotted the countryside.

Another factor contributing to the growth of suburbs was the rise in automobile production, for in the sprawling new communities a car was a necessity. With the shift to weapons production during the Second World War, auto sales had plummeted from almost 3.8 million in 1941 to about 100 in 1943. But beginning in 1946 sales began to climb; in 1950 they hit 6.7 million. Americans seized the chance to get back on the road again. The number of registered automobiles climbed from 25.8 million in 1945 to 61.7 million in 1960, and total miles traveled jumped from 208 billion in 1943 to 719 billion in 1960.

At the same time highway construction opened up rural lands for the development of suburban communities. In 1947 Congress authorized the construction of a 37,000-mile chain of highways, and in 1956 President Eisenhower signed the Interstate Highway Act, which launched a 42,500-mile nationwide network. Federal funds spent on highways swelled from \$79 million in 1946 to \$429 million in 1950, \$2.9 billion in 1960, and a huge \$4.6 billion in 1970.

Highway construction

Levittown, Long Island, as it appeared in 1958. The first of the postwar suburbs, Levittown offered low-cost mass-produced housing to accommodate veterans and their new families. The Bettmann Archive.

State and local highway expenditures also mushroomed.

By 1976 most of the interstate system had been completed, and some towns along the way had prospered. Route I-70, for example, gave Junction City, Kansas, six new motels, several restaurants, and an economic boost. But the new road also siphoned traffic away from older roads. Small towns along two-lane highways withered as residents left to seek a better living in the city. "They [the towns] didn't dry up and blow away," observed the editor of Junction City's daily newspaper, "but they are much like the towns left off the railroad [lines] 100 years ago."

The spurt in highway construction combined with the mushrooming of suburbia to produce the *megalopolis*, a term first used by urban experts in the early 1960s to refer to the almost uninterrupted metropolitan complex stretching along the northeastern seaboard of the United States. Beginning in Boston and extending 600 miles south through New York, Philadelphia, Baltimore, and Washington, "Boswash" encompassed parts of eleven states and a population of 49 million people, all tied together by interstate highways. Although the suburbs within the megalopolis were politically independent, they were economically dependent on the cities and connecting highways. Other megalopolises that took shape following the Second World War were "Chipitts," a band of heavy industry and dense population stretching from Chicago to Pittsburgh, and "San-San"—San Francisco to San Diego.

The white middle class benefited far more than other Americans from the government-supported housing and highway boom. In 1948 the government cut mortgage subsidies for rental-unit construction and increased subsidies for privately owned single-family houses, a policy that worked against the poorest Americans. Moreover, the FHA refused to guarantee suburban home loans to the poor, nonwhites, Jews, and other "inharmonious racial and ethnic groups." Some federal programs actually worsened conditions for the poor. The National Housing Act of 1949, passed to make available "a decent home and a suitable living environment for every American family," was a failure in several respects. The primary features of the act were "urban redevelopment," or slum clearance; the construction of public housing for low-income people (810,000 units in four years); and FHA mortgages for home buyers. But the program was poorly coordinated, and what resulted from the law was the replacement of slums not with low-income housing but with parking lots, shopping centers, luxury high-rise buildings, highways, and factories. The planned 810,000 housing units for the poor were constructed not in four years but in twenty.

Few people paid much attention to these shortcomings, however. From the late 1940s through much of the 1960s, middle-class suburbanites were busy raising their children.

Ideals of motherhood and the family

In the early twentieth century, Sunday dinner had been an exasperating occasion for the youngest child in a large family, for the youngest was traditionally served last. If the dinner was chicken, the little one often got the back or the neck. "I was the youngest of five children," recalled one young father shortly after the Second World War, "and by the time I was served, all the white meat was gone. . . . I swore to myself that when I grew up I would eat all the white meat I could. So I'm grown up and a father–and my children get first choice!" Times had changed, and so had the ways of the American family.

A good deal of the change was due to the publication in 1946 of Dr. Benjamin Spock's *Baby and Child Care*. The book, which quickly became the bible for new parents, answered many common questions about childrearing. But unlike earlier manuals, *Baby and Child Care* urged mothers to think of their children first and foremost, even at the expense of their own mental and physical health. Dr. Spock's predecessors had advised mothers to consider their own needs as well as their children's. They had recommended early and strict toilet training; "putting away your children at six o'clock" in order to enjoy "the quiet comfort of a still household in the evening"; and ignoring a baby's crying except at feeding time. Now Dr. Spock urged the mother to be constantly available to feed and communicate with her baby, and to remember that "feeding is learning." Spock encouraged the baby's "self-realization," "self-discovery," and "self-motivated behavior." The mother should "watch her child–to see what stage of readiness he is in," and then take a self-scoring achievement test to determine whether "the mother has been encouraging or a bit too bossy in her efforts."

Dr. Spock on childrearing

Though no mother could be all things to her baby, the women who embraced the teachings of Dr. Spock tended to believe they had failed if they were not. Guilt was the inevitable result of the effort to be not only mother but teacher, psychologist, and buddy. The mother of an epileptic son wrote to Dr. Spock: "I try to give him a great deal of affection, although I am a working woman. . . . Sometimes it is so difficult to maintain my control that my hands shake. . . . Does he need the help or do I?" Another mother wrote, "We like to read and listen to music. Maybe we have neglected some aspects of A's development in our own selfishness."

At the same time Philip Wylie, author of the book *Generation of Vipers*, denounced such selfless behavior as Momism. In the guise of sacrificing for her children, Wylie wrote, Mom was pursuing "love of herself." She smothered her children with affection so they would become emotionally dependent on her and would not want to leave home. Other experts agreed. Army psychiatrists blamed recruits' nervous disorders on mothers who, as a psychiatric adviser to the Secretary of War wrote, had "failed in the elementary mother function of weaning [their] offspring emotionally as well as physically."

But women were caught in a double bind, for if they pursued a life outside the home they were accused of being "imitation men" or "neurotic" feminists. Echoing the psychoanalyst Sigmund Freud, critics of working mothers contended that a woman could be happy and fulfilled only through domesticity.

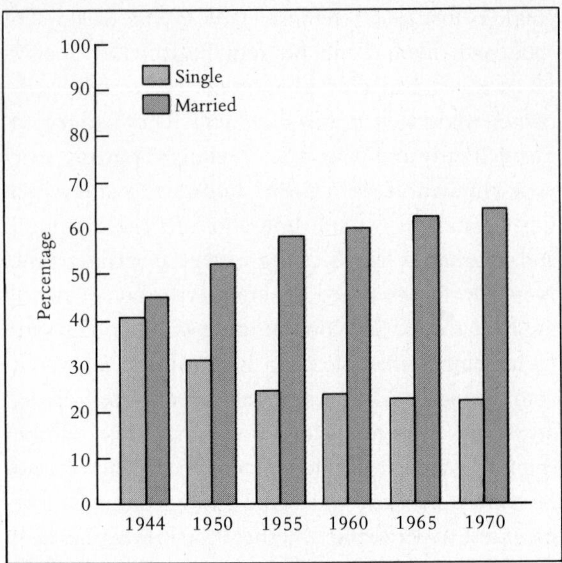

Marital distribution of female labor force, 1944–1970. Source: Adapted from U.S. Bureau of the Census, *Historical Statistics of the United States, Colonial Times to 1970,* Bicentennial Edition (Washington: U.S. Government Printing Office, 1975), p. 133.

"Anatomy is destiny" was their catch phrase; a woman's sex determined her role in life. Reflecting on the contradictory expectations of women, anthropologist Margaret Mead wrote in 1946, "Choose any set of criteria you like, and the answer is the same: women–and men–are confused, uncertain, and discontented with the present definition of women's place in America."

Despite the controversy, women continued the wartime trend toward work outside the home. The female labor force rose from 16.8 million in 1946 to 23.3 million in 1960 and 31.6 million in 1970. These women entered the labor force without the support of an organized women's movement and without challenging sex-role stereotypes. Many of them, of course, were their families' sole source of income; they had to work. Still others took jobs not to challenge notions of male dominance but to earn additional family income, enjoy adult company, or bolster their self-esteem. Despite the cult of motherhood, most of the new entrants to the job market were married, a trend that had begun during the Second World War (see figure). Significantly, most of the new workers were mothers.

For American families, the postwar period was a time of "togetherness." "Ed and His Family Live Together and Love It" was the title of a typical article in a 1954 *McCall's.* "Caring for three lively children makes tremendous demands on Carol. . . . But Ed is a cheerful working partner to her, helps with the children and housework whenever he can, gives everything he has to make his family happy." In return, Ed's wife and children "give him all the love and affection a husband and father could hope for." Carol even took over some household tasks traditionally performed by men: "Paneling that extra room in the cellar used to be the man's job. But Ed and Carol do it together." Despite *McCall's* advocacy of shared tasks, the magazine stopped short of advocating complete equality. "For the sake of every member of the family, the family needs a head. This means Father, not Mother."

Family togetherness

Middle-class American families were preoccupied with education, the key to their children's future financial success. As the baby boom became a grade-school boom, parents rushed to join the Parent-Teacher Association so that they would have a voice in the educational process. They expressed their concern that schools were overcrowded, understaffed, and aimless, or that teachers were using obsolete methods. Educators encouraged their participation. "Just as war is 'too serious a matter to be left to the generals,' so, I think, the teaching of reading is too important to be left to the educators," wrote Dr. Rudolf Flesch in 1955, in his best-selling book *Why Johnny Can't Read.*

Education of the baby boom generation

Two years later when the Russians launched Sputnik, the first earth-orbiting satellite, education became a matter of national security. The Russian success challenged American military and technological superiority, based ultimately on the nation's school system. James B. Conant, Hyman G. Rickover, and other critics argued that what the United States needed to regain its technological leadership was new emphasis on mathematics, foreign languages, and the sciences. In 1958 Congress responded with the National Defense Education Act (NDEA), which funded elementary and high school programs in those disciplines and offered fellowships and loans to college students. Parents were quick to endorse the new programs. After all, public education was the engine of democracy, a guarantee of both upward social mobility and military superiority.

Just as education became intertwined with national security, religion became synonymous with patriotism. As President Eisenhower put it, "recognition of the Supreme Being is the first, the most basic expression of Americanism." For, after all, the United States was locked in mortal combat with an atheistic enemy. In America's Cold War with the godless Soviet Union, ministers, priests, and rabbis became foot-soldiers in the battle for souls. Religious leaders emphasized family togetherness in their appeals for new converts. "The family that prays together stays together," was a famous slogan used during the 1950s. The Bible topped the best-seller lists, and books with religious themes, such as the Reverend Norman Vincent Peale's *The Power of Positive Thinking* (1952), sold in the millions. Meanwhile evangelist Billy Graham exhorted television viewers and stadium audiences throughout the country. From 1945 to 1970 church membership nearly doubled, and money spent on church and charities quintupled.

If Americans were eager to improve their minds and souls, they were not ready to liberate themselves sexually. When Dr. Alfred Kinsey, director of the Institute for Sex Research at Indiana University, published his pioneering book *Sexual Behavior in the Human Male* (1948), the American public was shocked. On the basis of interviews with numerous men, Kinsey estimated that 95 percent of American men had engaged in masturbation, premarital or extramarital intercourse, or homosexual behavior. Princeton's President Harold Dodds denounced the volume as "the work of small boys writing dirty words on fences." Five years later Kinsey caused even more of a disturbance with *Sexual Behavior in the Human Female*, which revealed that 62 percent of women masturbated and 50 percent had intercourse before marriage. Some angry Americans condemned the report as a slanderous attack not only on women, but on motherhood and the family as well. A congressional representative from New York, who tried to bar the report from the mails, charged Kinsey with "hurling the insult of the century against our mothers, wives, daughters and sisters." Sex was nothing new, of course, but its existence was seldom acknowledged in polite conversation or respectable publications—and middle-class Americans wanted it that way.

Socially, the tremendous emphasis on family togetherness tended to isolate the suburban family. Writing in 1957, sociologist David Riesman criticized "the decentralization of leisure in the suburbs . . . as the home itself, rather than the neighborhood, becomes the chief gathering place for the family—either in the 'family room' with its games, its TV, its informality, or outdoors around the barbecue." The floor plan of the ranch-style home, at whose center was the TV set enthroned on a swivel, was ideally suited to the stay-at-home life style. Even when families traveled, they were isolated in the family car.

Critics of suburban life

Riesman was only one of many critics of suburban living and family togetherness. The word *suburbia*, Scott Donaldson wrote in *The Suburban Myth* (1969), had "unpleasant overtones, suggesting nothing so much as some kind of scruffy disease." The titles of magazine articles and books echoed his diagnosis: "Trouble in the Suburbs," "The Crabgrass Roots of Suburbia," *The Split Level Trap*. In Sloan Wilson's novel *The Man in the Gray Flannel Suit* (1955), the main character led a treadmill existence commuting to his white-collar job in the city. And C. Wright Mills, a sociologist, castigated white-collar suburbanites, who "sell not only their time and energy but their personalities as well. They sell . . . their smiles and their kindly gestures." Resentment of this hypocrisy boiled over in David Karp's novel *Leave Me Alone* (1965). Calling his fellow suburbanites "the most dreary collection of slack-jawed yahoos" it had ever been his misfortune to meet, the hero growled: "I don't know what sins against the human spirit and intellect can be excused on the grounds of neighborliness and civic pride, but however many there are, I've gone over my quota tonight. Those of you who aren't cowards are bigots, and those of you who aren't bigots are sheep, and some of you are both."

When all the pluses and minuses were added up, however, most residents of suburbia—male and female, children and adults—seemed to prefer family togetherness to any other life style of which they were aware. Of the college students interviewed by Riesman in the 1950s, the vast majority looked forward to living in the suburbs.

Cowboy star William Boyd ("Hopalong Cassidy") adorned this late-1940s advertisement for a bigger, brighter, clearer TV. Note the elaborate cowboy outfit worn by his young fan. Howard Frank.

Middle-class America at play

The affluence that marked the postwar era was reflected in the materialistic values and pleasures of the period. Having satisfied their basic needs for food, clothing, and shelter, growing numbers of Americans turned their attention to luxury items. "More appliances make mom's work easier," read a typical advertisement. As middle-class families strove to acquire the latest conveniences, shopping became a form of recreation.

Effects of television

Of the new luxuries, television was the most revolutionary in its effects. One man who grew up in the postwar era recalled the purchase of the first family TV set in 1950. "And so the monumental change began in our lives and those of millions of other Americans. More than a year passed before we again visited a movie theater. Money which previously would have been spent for books was saved for the TV payments. Social evenings with friends became fewer and fewer still because we discovered we did not share the same TV program interests." By 1950 television had broken radio's grip on the American public. The number of households with TVs climbed from 8,000 in 1946 to 3.9 million in 1950 and 60.6 million in 1970.

Advertising was the foundation of the television industry, as it had also been for radio. The first TV commercial, made by the Bulova Watch Company in 1941, was a one-minute effort that cost nine dollars. By the end of the decade, American families were spending approximately five hours a day before the television set, and the bargain rates had vanished; annual expenditures for TV advertising totaled $50 million. By 1970 the figure had soared to $3.6 billion. Critics of the television industry have often wondered why American viewers put up with advertising. The answer is that, far from being an unwanted interruption, television advertising was a valuable service to consumers. Keeping up with the Joneses was a major goal of suburbanites, and television advertising provided them visual evidence of just what the Joneses were buying. In the comfort of their living rooms middle-class Americans could study how to elevate their status through the purchase of a particular automobile, cigarette, or electric appliance. Indeed, it was not just commercials but the programs themselves that tantalized viewers with glimpses of the sumptuous life. Situation comedies and dramas were nearly always set in well-furnished suburban homes; the characters dressed in the latest styles and drove the newest cars.

Although attendance at sporting events declined when television was first introduced, overall interest in sports boomed. TV fans watched basketball hero Bob Cousy of the Boston Celtics or baseball stars Mickey Mantle and Willie Mays. Play by play, punch by punch, the feats of America's favorite athletes filled the TV screens.

As television brought the world into their living rooms, Americans began to read newspapers and news magazines a little less carefully, and to listen to radio a lot less frequently (see table). But despite the lure of the tube, book readership went up. One reason for the increased consumption of literature was the mass marketing of the inexpensive paperbound book. Pocket

Changes in Reading, Listening, and Viewing Habits after Purchase of TV Set (in minutes per person)

MEDIUM	BEFORE TV PURCHASE	AFTER TV PURCHASE
Magazines	17	10
Newspapers	39	32
Radio	122	52
Television	12*	173
Total time	190	267

*guest viewing

Source: Thomas E. Coffin, "Television's Impact on Society," *The American Psychologist,* 10 (1955), 633.

Books hit the market in 1939; soon westerns, detective stories, and science fiction filled the newsstands, supermarkets, and drug stores. The comic book, which had become popular in 1939 with the introduction of Superman, became another drug store standard. Reprints of hardcover books and condensed books also did well. Paperback reprint houses published 214 million volumes in 1950 alone, and *Reader's Digest* condensed books, which were introduced in 1950, were selling more than a million apiece by early 1952. Finally, book clubs experienced phenomenal growth: by 1946 there were sixty such clubs with a total membership of 4 million subscribers. All in all, funds spent for books doubled between 1946 and 1960.

One obvious casualty of the stay-at-home suburban culture was the motion picture. While Americans continued to buy paperbacks and comic books in large numbers, many of them stopped visiting movie theaters. After all, why fight traffic to go to a movie when you could watch TV in the comfort of your living room? Why pay a babysitter? From 1946 to 1948 Americans had attended movies at the rate of nearly 90 million a week. By 1950 the figure had dropped to 60 million a week; by 1960, 40 million. Thus the postwar years saw the steady closing of movie theaters—with the notable exception of the drive-in, which appealed to car-bound suburban families.

There was one crucial exception to the downturn in moviegoing. By the late 1950s the first children of the postwar baby boom had become adolescents, and though their parents preferred to stay home and watch television, they themselves flocked to the theaters. No less than 72 percent of moviegoers during the 1950s were under age thirty. Hollywood responded to this youthful new audience with films portraying young people as sensitive and intelligent, adults as boorish and hostile: *The Wild One, Rebel Without a Cause, Blackboard Jungle.* The cult of youth had been born.

Rise of the youth subculture

Soon the music industry was catering to teens with cheap 45 rpm records. Bill Haley, the Everly Brothers, and Buddy Holly thrilled teenagers with a primitive but joyful music called rock-and-roll. Elvis Presley horrified their parents with his suggestive gyrations.

A hula-hoop contest at a New Jersey swim club. A ten-year-old boy won with 3,000 spins. Ralph Morse, *Life Magazine* © 1958 Time Inc.

Before long, Presley's ducktail haircut and leather jacket had become the uniform for rebellious teenage males. Although the roots of the new music lay in black rhythm-and-blues, most white stars did not acknowledge the debt. Presley's hit tune "Hound Dog," for example, had originally been performed by the black singer Big Mama Thornton, but Thornton received little credit for her contribution. The lone black rock-and-roll superstar of the 1950s was Chuck Berry.

While white performers copied black rhythm-and-blues, serious black jazz artists like Charlie Parker and Dizzy Gillespie were experimenting with "bebop." In the 1950s jazz became increasingly fused with classical themes, compositions, and instrumentation. Intellectuals began to study this art form, which had once been looked down on as vulgar.

In the arts Martha Graham was lauded in international dance circles, and Jackson Pollock became the pivotal figure of the abstract expressionist movement, which in the 1950s established New York City as a center of the art world. Rather than work with the traditional painter's easel, Pollock spread his canvas on the floor, where he was free to walk around it, "work from the four sides and literally be *in* the painting." He and other "action painters" worked with sticks, trowels, and knives, and they played with new materials like heavy impasto with "sand, broken glass and other foreign matter added." In the 1960s artists of the Pop Art movement satirized the consumer society, using commercial techniques to depict everyday objects. Andy Warhol painted Campbell soup cans; other artists did blowups of ice-cream sundaes, hamburgers, and comic-strip panels.

Fads

Every era has its fads; the 1950s had 3-D movies (audiences wore special glasses that enhanced the three-dimensional effect of a film) and hula hoops (children spun large hoops around their waists by imitating a hula dancer). And then there were signature items such as Hoppy watches, emblazoned with pictures of cowboy star Hopalong Cassidy. Although such crazes were short-lived, they created multimillion-dollar industries and effectively promoted dozens of movies and TV shows. Other postwar crazes are still with us—Scrabble, Monopoly, canasta, paint-by-number sets, and Barbie dolls, to name just a few. Frisbee-throwing has not only survived but prevailed over similar outdoor games. Many of these toys and games succeeded because they brought the whole family together. Mother, father, and children would gather in the family room for a round of dominoes or outside on the well-trimmed lawn for badminton or croquet.

Some prewar activities flourished in the suburbs, notably golf and bowling. But though middle-class Americans still hunted and fished, they no longer did so at the farm pond or in the woods down the road; they had to travel to get to the country. And travel they did. With more money and leisure time and a much-improved highway system, middle-class families took vacations that had formerly been restricted to the rich. They visited national monuments and parks, went camping, and even ventured abroad.

Needless to say, the consensus society of the 1950s was not conducive to social criticism. The filmgoing public preferred noncontroversial doses of Doris Day and Rock Hudson, Marilyn Monroe, and Dean Martin and Jerry Lewis. Readers bought novels and retreated into the criminal underworld, the wild West, or the science-fiction fantasy worlds of Ray Bradbury and Arthur C. Clarke. Even serious artists tended to ignore the country's social problems. Respected novelists such as Saul Bellow and Bernard Malamud stressed the inner life, and J. D. Salinger's *Catcher in the Rye* (1951) offered only the innocence of childhood and the Zen Buddhist retreat as alternatives to adult hypocrisy.

There were exceptions. Ralph Ellison's *Invisible Man* (1952) gave white Americans a glimpse of the psychic costs to black Americans of exclusion from the white American dream. Two films—*Gentleman's Agreement* (1947) and *Home of the Brave* (1949) examined anti-Semitism and white racism. And in the 1950s, one group of writers repudiated the conventional world of the middle class and the suburbs. Rejecting the same social niceties Kinsey had challenged, the writers of the Beat (for "beatific") Generation flaunted their freewheeling sexuality and consumption of drugs. The Beats produced some memorable prose and poetry, including Allen Ginsberg's long poem *Howl* (1956) and Jack Kerouac's *On the Road* (1957), and they offered American youth an alternative to their parents' materialism and righteous self-congratulation. Though the Beats were mostly ignored during the fifties, millions of young Americans would discover their writings and life style in the late 1960s.

Beat Generation

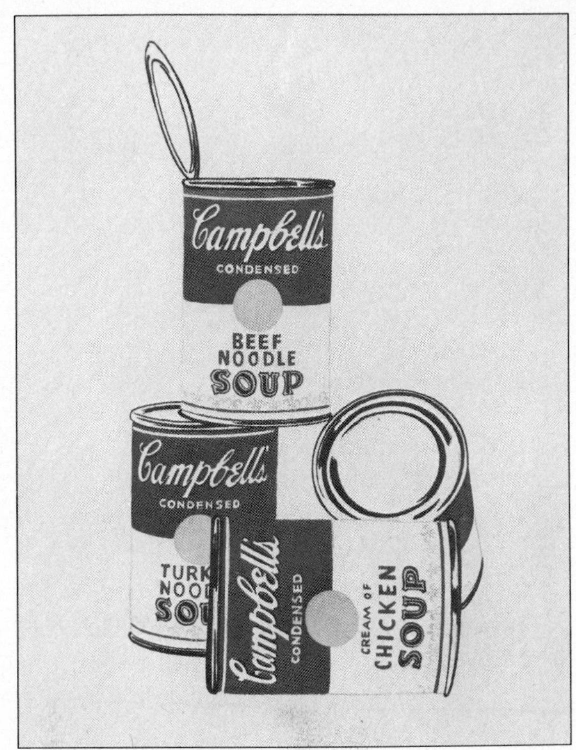

Andy Warhol's *4 Campbell Soup Cans* (1962), a Pop Art satire of the consumer culture. Courtesy Gian Enzo Sperone, Torino, Italy, and Leo Castelli, N.Y.C.

One of the most influential books of postwar years was the best-selling *The Affluent Society* (1958), by economist John Kenneth Galbraith. Galbraith's thesis dovetailed with the middle-class belief that economic growth would bring prosperity to everyone. Some would have more than others, of course, but in time everybody would have enough. "Production has eliminated the more acute tensions associated with [economic] inequality," Galbraith wrote. Not until Chapter 23 did the author mention poverty; when he did, he dismissed it as not "a universal or massive affliction," but "more nearly an afterthought."

Only in the 1960s would middle-class Americans

Important events

1945	Demobilization of 12 million GIs
1946	Beginning of the baby boom Dr. Benjamin Spock, *Baby and Child Care* Over 1 million GIs enroll in colleges 2.1 million autos produced (up from 600 in 1944)
1947	Gross national product ($231.3 billion) begins postwar rise Construction of Levittown, New York, begins 8,000 families own TVs
1948	Postwar rise in women's employment Alfred C. Kinsey, *Sexual Behavior in the Human Male*
1949	National Housing Act
1950	6.7 million autos produced Women's employment reaches 18.4 million
1951	J. D. Salinger, *Catcher in the Rye*
1952	Norman Vincent Peale, *The Power of Positive Thinking* Ralph Ellison, *The Invisible Man*
1953	*The Wild One*, starring Marlon Brando Alfred C. Kinsey, *Sexual Behavior in the Human Female*
1955	Salk polio vaccine approved for use by the government AFL-CIO merger *Rebel Without a Cause*, starring James Dean 7.9 million autos produced
1956	Interstate Highway Act Allen Ginsberg, *Howl*
1957	Peak of baby boom (4.3 million births) Soviet Union launches *Sputnik* Jack Kerouac, *On the Road*
1958	National Defense Education Act
1960	Gross national product reaches $503.7 billion Women's employment reaches 22.5 million
1970	Gross national product reaches $977.1 billion Women's employment reaches 31.2 million Suburbs surpass central cities in population 60.6 million families own TVs

discover that there were millions of poor people living in America: Indians; blacks in urban ghettos and rural shacks; whites in the Appalachian Mountains; tenant farmers and migrant workers; aged men and women; nonunion workers in restaurants, hospitals, laundries, and on garbage crews; and working women, many of whom headed households. Politically and culturally, the 1960s would be vastly different from the consensus years. Ironically, it was to be the products of suburbia–the middle-class children of the baby boom–who would form the vanguard of the assault not only on poverty, but on the whole value system of the American middle class.

Suggestions for further reading

The affluent society

Willard W. Cochrane and Mary E. Ryan, *American Farm Policy, 1948–1973* (1976); Ralph E. Freeman, ed., *Postwar Economic Trends in the United States* (1960); John Kenneth Galbraith, *American Capitalism: The Concept of Countervailing Power* (1952); John Kenneth Galbraith, *The Affluent Society* (1958); Robert Heilbroner, *The Limits of American Capitalism* (1966); A. E. Holmans, *United States Fiscal Policy, 1945–1959* (1961); Ronald L. Mighell, *American Agriculture: Its Structure and Place in the Economy* (1955); John L.

32 AMERICA IN A REVOLUTIONARY WORLD: FOREIGN POLICY SINCE 1953

Shover, *First Majority–Last Minority: The Transforming of Rural Life in America* (1976); Robert Sobel, *The Age of Giant Corporations: A Microeconomic History of American Business, 1914–1970* (1972); Harry M. Trebing, ed., *The Corporation in the American Economy* (1970); Harold G. Vatter, *The U.S. Economy in the 1950's* (1963).

The baby boom

Richard A. Easterlin, *Birth and Fortune: The Impact of Numbers on Personal Welfare* (1980); Landon Y. Jones, *Great Expectations: America & the Baby Boom Generation* (1980); William Petersen, "The New American Family: Causes and Consequences of the Baby Boom," *Commentary*, 21 (1956), 1–6.

Suburbia

William B. Dobriner, *Class in Suburbia* (1963); Philip C. Dolce, ed., *Suburbia: The American Dream and Dilemma* (1976); Scott Donaldson, *The Suburban Myth* (1969); Herbert J. Gans, *The Levittowners* (1967); David Riesman, "The Suburban Dislocation," *Annals of the American Academy*, 314 (1957), 123–146; Robert C. Wood, *Suburbia: Its People and Their Politics* (1959).

Motherhood and family

Elizabeth Bragdon, *Women Today: Their Conflicts, Frustrations and Fulfillments* (1953); William H. Chafe, *The American Woman: Her Changing Social, Economic, and Political Role, 1920–1970* (1972); Carl Degler, *At Odds: Woman and the Family in America from the Revolution to the Present* (1980); Anthony Downs, "The Impact of Housing Policies on Family Life in the United States since World War II," in *The Family*, eds. Alice S. Rossi *et al.* (1978), 163–180; Betty Friedan, *The Feminine Mystique* (1963); Mirra Komarovsky, *Blue-Collar Marriage* (1962); Mirra Komarovsky, *Women in the Modern World: Their Education and Their Dilemmas* (1953); F. Ivan Nye and Lois Wladis Hoffman, eds., *The Employed Mother in America* (1963); Benjamin Spock, *Baby and Child Care* (1946); Nancy Pottisham Weiss, "Mother, the Invention of Necessity: Dr. Spock's *Baby and Child Care*," *American Quarterly*, 29 (1977), 519–546.

Popular culture

John W. Aldridge, *In Search of Heresy: American Literature in an Age of Conformity* (1956); Gregory Battcock, ed., *The New Art* (1966); Ann Charters, *Kerouac* (1973); Andrew Dowdy, *The Films of the Fifties* (1973); Albert Goldman, *Ladies and Gentlemen Lenny Bruce!!* (1971); Maxwell Geismar, *American Moderns: From Rebellion to Conformity* (1958); Charlie Gillett, *The Sound of the City: The Rise of Rock 'N' Roll* (1970); Charles Higham, *Hollywood at Sunset* (1972); Charles Higham and Joel Greenberg, *Hollywood in the Forties* (1968); Richard Kostelanetz, ed., *The New American Arts* (1965); Douglas T. Miller and Marion Novak, *The Fifties: The Way We Really Were* (1977); Bernard Rosenberg and David Manning White, eds., *Mass Culture: The Popular Arts in America* (1957); Robert Sklar, *Movie-Made America* (1975); John Tytell, *Naked Angels: The Lives and Literature of the Beat Generation* (1976); David Manning White, ed., *Pop Culture in America* (1970).

Television

Leo Bogart, *Age of Television* (1958); George Comstock *et al., Television and Human Behavior* (1978); Marshall McLuhan, *Understanding Media* (1964); Marshall McLuhan, *The Medium Is the Massage* (1967); Jerry Mander, *Four Arguments for the Elimination of Television* (1978); Frank Mankiewicz and Joel Swerdlow, *Remote Control: Television and the Manipulation of American Life* (1978); W. Schramm *et al., Television in the Lives of Our Children* (1961).

GO

The insult stung deeply and was not soon forgotten. In August 1955, the ambassador from India, G. L. Mehta, walked into a restaurant at the Houston International Airport, sat down, and waited to order. But Texas law required that whites and blacks be served in separate dining facilities. The dark-skinned diplomat, who had seated himself in a white-only area, was told to move.

From Washington, D.C., Secretary of State John Foster Dulles telegraphed his apologies for this blatant display of racism. And the State Department expressed its regret to New Delhi, fearful that the incident would injure relations with a nation whose allegiance the United States was seeking in the Cold War. Still, words could not erase the damage. "In the minds of Indians," journalist Carl Rowan commented after a visit to India, "the apologies were but the salt of hypocrisy being rubbed with unctuousness into the wound of bigotry."

Such embarrassments were not uncommon in the 1950s. A Mexican consul-general was refused service in a San Antonio café; Burma's minister of education was denied a meal in a Columbus, Ohio, restaurant; and the finance minister of Ghana was turned away from a Howard Johnson's just outside the nation's capital. Secretary Dulles complained that segregationist practices were becoming a "major international hazard," a threat to United States efforts to gain the friendship of new nations in Asia, the Middle East, and Africa. With United Nations committees investigating Jim Crow practices and the world press reporting discrimination against dark-skinned foreign visitors, Americans stood publicly condemned as a people who did not honor the ideal of equality.

Thus when the attorney general appealed to the Supreme Court to strike down segregation in public schools, his introductory remarks took note of the international implications. "It is in the context of the present world struggle between freedom and tyranny that the problem of racial discrimination must be viewed," he warned. The humiliation of dark-skinned diplomats in Washington, D.C., "the window through which the world looks into our house," was damaging to American interests. Racism "furnished grist for the Communist propaganda mills." When the Court finally did order school desegregation in the 1954 *Brown* decision, the Voice of America, a United States propaganda agency, quickly broadcast the good news overseas in thirty-five different languages.

The *Brown* decision came none too soon, for in the 1950s and early 1960s the process of decolonization, accelerated by the Second World War, created a powerful bloc of emerging nations referred to as the Third World. Although Soviet-American competition and its dramatic swings from conciliation to confrontation still absorbed United States leaders, relations with the new Third World became conspicuously troublesome. American presidents from Eisenhower to Reagan have sought ways to gain the new states' allegiance, but their Cold War mentality has tended to frustrate their efforts.

American leaders could have interpreted the angry anti-imperialism, the attacks on foreign-owned properties, the racial, religious, and ethnic tensions, and the political instability and civil war in the Third World as expressions of nationalism, the natural restlessness of new nations, or outcomes of regional disputes. Instead, most American leaders took the globalist perspective, seeing the hoary hand of Moscow behind almost every crisis. American officials also believed that the nationalistic, revolutionary movements of the Third World threatened American economic interests. Thus a combination of Cold War and economic motives led them to resort to coups and military intervention, which only discredited the nation in the eyes of its hoped-for allies. The American intervention in Vietnam, a long, grueling war that proved ruinous for both Vietnam and the United States, revealed the difficulty of American resistance to Third World revolutionary nationalism.

The rise of the Third World

In the 1940s, as a result of changes wrought by the Second World War, a cavalcade of new nations dramatically altered the international community. In the period from 1943 to 1977 no fewer than eighty-four countries cast off their colonial chains. The march to independence was unrelenting: Lebanon (1943), Syria (1944), the Philippines (1946), India (1947), Israel (1948), Indonesia (1949), Libya (1951), Morocco

(1956), Ghana (1957), Guinea (1958). In 1960 alone, eighteen colonies became nations in the accelerating process of decolonization (see map, page 890).

These profound stirrings arose in what is now known as the Third World, those parts of the global community belonging neither to the first world of capitalism—the West—nor the second world of Communism—the East. Often called developing countries, Third World nations are predominantly nonwhite, nonindustrialized, and located in the southern half of the globe. "Our peoples have been the voiceless ones in the world," remarked President Sukarno of Indonesia. Yet by the 1970s Third World nations dominated membership in the United Nations, controlled essential raw materials such as crude oil, and threatened world peace by warring among themselves. And although the Soviet-American confrontation continued to claim center stage in world affairs, Third World nationalist fervor became a conspicuous characteristic of the international system.

With Cold War lines drawn fairly tightly in Europe by the late 1940s (see pages 796–804), Soviet-American rivalry shifted increasingly to the Third World.

Soviet-American rivalry in the Third World

The two giants aggressively courted new allies with foreign aid, technical assistance, goodwill visits, covert (secret) operations, and propaganda. Much was at stake. Third World countries possessed large quantities of strategic raw materials that had once served the needs of the European and Japanese empires and were still avidly sought by industrialized nations. For example, 14 percent of the oil the United States consumed in 1965 was imported, largely from Third World nations. The Third World also attracted foreign investment—in 1959 over a third of America's private foreign investments were in Third World countries. And Third World nations provided markets for American products and technology. Finally, the great powers looked to the new states of the Third World for support in the United Nations and for military and intelligence bases abroad.

But Third World states like India, Ghana, Egypt, and Indonesia did not wish to take sides in the contest between the great powers. To the dismay of both Washington and Moscow, they declared themselves neutral, or nonaligned, in the Cold War. "If we join them," India's highly respected Jawaharlal Nehru cautioned, "we lose our identity." President Eisenhower and Secretary of State Dulles, however, considered neutralism an unacceptable and immoral stance. Nations were supposed to take sides in the life-and-death Cold War; neutralism could only be the first step along the road to Communism. So official thinking went, blinding Americans to the fact that neutralism was a popular policy for new nations struggling to maintain their independence.

If Jim Crow and a negative view of neutralism inhibited United States efforts to strengthen relations with emerging states, so did American hostility toward revolution. Despite its own history, the United States was uncomfortable with significant twentieth-century revolutions—Mexican, Chinese, Russian, Cuban, Vietnamese, and Iranian.

American intolerance of revolution

Although Americans paid lip service to the Spirit of '76, they were intolerant of revolutionary disorder—in part because Third World revolutions were directed against their Cold War allies, but also because such upheavals threatened American investments, markets, and military bases. Indeed, by mid-century the United States had become an established power in world affairs, eager for the stability and order that seemed to ensure its own prosperity and security. During revolutionary crises, therefore, the United States usually threw its support to its European allies or to the conservative propertied classes in the Third World. When forty-three African and Asian states sponsored a United Nations resolution appealing for decolonization (1960), the United States abstained from the vote, signaling that it stood with the white imperialists.

Still another obstacle in America's relations with the rising Third World was the United States' great wealth. Foreigners both envied and resented the "people of plenty," who had so much and wasted so much while poorer peoples went without. American movies offered enticing glimpses of middle-class materialism; American products drew attention at international trade fairs and were coveted items at native marketplaces. And Americans stationed overseas often flaunted their superior standard of living. The popular novel *The Ugly American* (1958) drew attention to the problem by describing the "golden

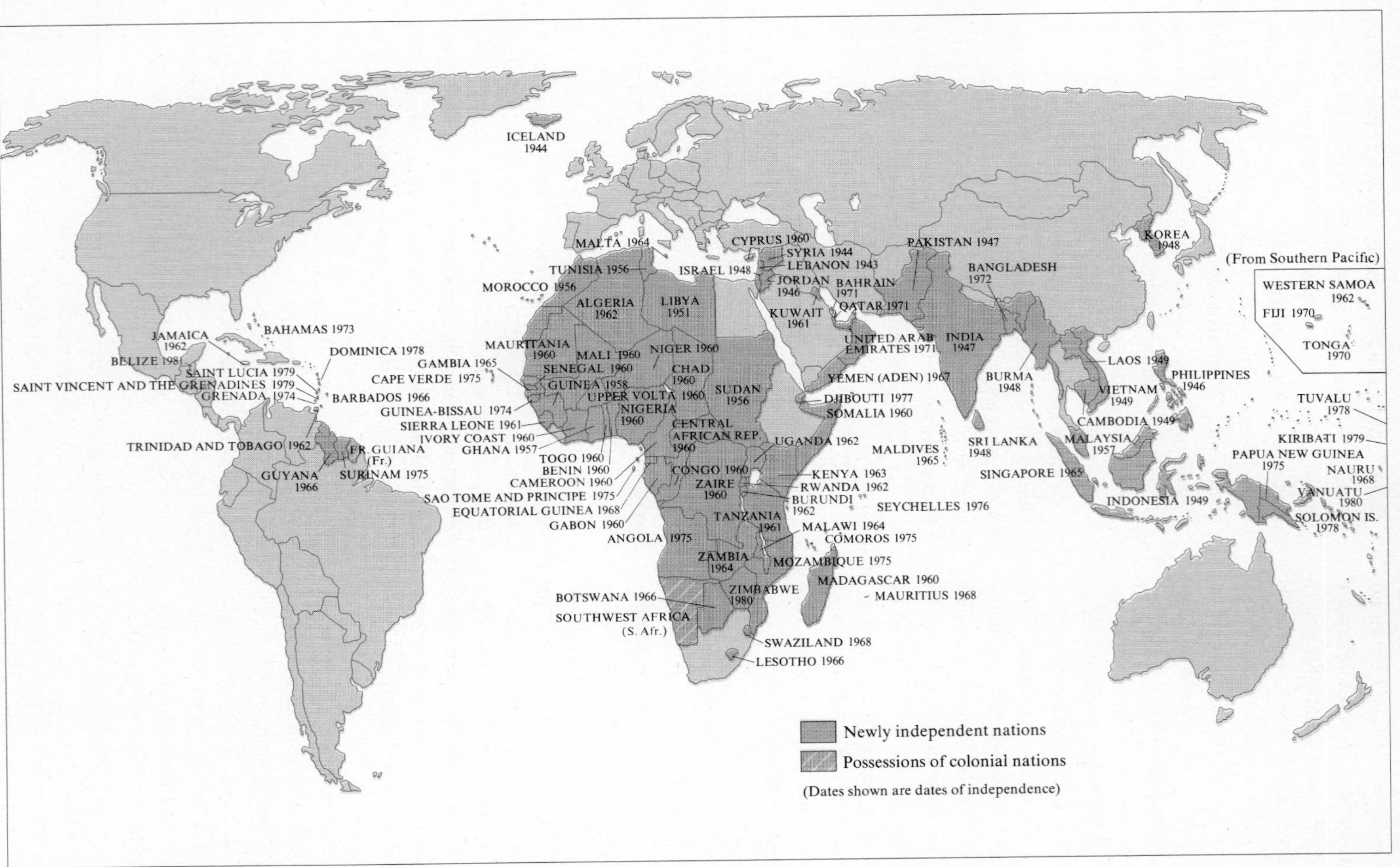

The rise of the Third World: decolonization since 1943

ghettoes" of American diplomats, separated from their poorer surroundings by high compound walls. Finally, many foreign peoples resented the ample profits that giant American corporations extracted from them. For all these reasons, the United States found itself not the model of revolution but the target.

The Soviet Union enjoyed only a slight edge, if any, in the race to win friends in the Third World. It was true that Communist ideology encouraged anticolonialism, and that the Soviet Union was free of association with the long years of Western European imperialism. But though Moscow kept up a heavy drumbeat of propaganda, it could not easily explain away its brutal, sometimes military subjugation of Eastern European countries. The Soviet invasion of Hungary in 1956 earned Russia international condemnation, as did its takeover of Czechoslovakia in 1968. Though Premier Nikita Khrushchev toured India and Burma in the mid-1950s and offered aid to nonaligned Egypt and Indonesia, those nations refused to become Soviet clients. They were not about to replace one imperial master with another, and Russian aid was minuscule compared to American offers. "We will not be subjected–either by West or East," proclaimed Egypt's Gamal Abdel Nasser. Even Communist China, which Americans viewed as part of a Sino-Soviet bloc, drifted away from Soviet influence, much as Yugoslavia had in 1948 under Tito. Ultimately the Soviets, like the Americans, concluded that Third World nations were playing the two superpowers against each other in order to garner larger amounts of aid and armaments.

Taking the globalist perspective developed following the Second World War (see pages 793–796), American officials assumed that Communist agents were stationed throughout the Third World, waiting to exploit economic crisis and human misery. But Americans' suspicions often led them astray. Third World troubles frequently sprouted from native soil, not from Communist plots. Nonetheless, to stem the perceived Communist threat, to curb revolution and civil war, the United States poured money and effort into the Third World. By 1961 over 90 percent of American foreign aid went to the Third World, as well as huge quantities of arms. Agents of the Central Intelligence Agency succeeded in overturning some foreign governments (Iran in 1953, Guatemala in 1954, Chile in 1973) but failed to unseat others (Indonesia in 1958 and Cuba in 1961). The Voice of America and the United States Information Agency advertised American achievements abroad. In some cases the American military took action, as in the invasions of Lebanon in 1958 and the Dominican Republic in 1965.

These many interventions, covert or conspicuous, convinced the Soviets and numerous Third World leaders that the United States was a major menace in world affairs. Some Third World leaders blamed an exploitative United States for persistent hunger and poverty in their countries, although their own decisions sometimes hindered their nations' progress. Underfed India, for example, poured millions of dollars into the production of a nuclear bomb when it might have spent those funds on improving agricultural production. Nonetheless, American interventionism was extensive enough to arouse continued criticism of the United States, and to undermine American efforts to win the Third World to its side in the Cold War.

Eisenhower, Dulles, and Cold War policy

The first American leaders to confront the intertwined questions of the Third World and the Cold War on a large scale were Dwight D. Eisenhower and John Foster Dulles, the architects of 1950s diplomacy. Smiling Ike, with his folksy style, displays of confusion, and apparent preference for the golf course, exasperated Democrats, who charged him with a failure of leadership–"the bland leading the bland." But it was not that simple. As a general in the Second World War, Eisenhower had made tough decisions and negotiated with many of the world's leading officials. He was no novice at hard work or demanding leadership. His appearance of passivity as president may have stemmed from his low-key, hidden-hand style and from his desire to avoid taking public positions until he had had time to consider all the consequences. In 1955 State Department officers unnecessarily urged Eisenhower to avoid discussing a particularly delicate issue at a press conference. "Don't

Secretary of State John Foster Dulles (1888–1959) traveled extensively because he preferred face-to-face negotiations, in which he could use his formidable debating skills. Foreigners often complained that Dulles was too rigid, passing up chances for compromise. The secretary dismissed Soviet peace initiatives as "Trojan doves," for instance. *The Reporter,* 1956. Copyright 1956 by The Reporter Magazine Company, Inc.

worry," replied the president. "I'll just confuse them."

The public image of the bumbling, rambling, aging hero in the White House was all the more convincing in comparison with Eisenhower's secretary of state, the strong-willed John Foster Dulles. Polished, articulate, and experienced, Dulles seemed to have lived his whole life in preparation for the nation's chief diplomatic post. He had traveled internationally, studied at Princeton, and trained in law at George Washington University. At age thirty he had been an adviser to Woodrow Wilson at Versailles. As a senior partner in a prestigious Wall Street law firm Dulles had handled international cases, and as an officer of the Federal Council of Churches he had participated in programs on behalf of international peace. He had advised a Republican presidential candidate (Thomas Dewey) on foreign policy and had helped the Truman administration to organize the United Nations and to negotiate a peace treaty with Japan. When he took office in 1953, then, John Foster Dulles was unmatched in experience.

Secretary of State John Foster Dulles

But this well-qualified secretary of state impressed people as cold, arrogant, stubborn, and preachy. One European newspaper complained that the inflexible Dulles was the "conscience and straitjacket of the free world." Eisenhower thought him "wise," but noted privately that Dulles "seems to have a curious lack of understanding as to how his words and manner may affect another personality." Thus scholars have tended to attribute the strident Cold War rhetoric of the 1950s to Dulles, thinking that he dominated the president. Actually, the Eisenhower-Dulles relationship was mutually cooperative. Eisenhower often directed Dulles personally by telephone and memo, and he participated actively in National Security Council discussions. Because the president agreed with most of Dulles's ideas, he delegated authority to him with confidence.

Dulles was an ambitious man who feared that the right wing of the Republican party would pillory him unless he took a forceful stand against Communist and neutral nations. He well remembered how Senators William Knowland and Joseph McCarthy had tormented Truman's secretary of state, Dean Acheson, claiming that the United States had "lost" China. To avoid a similar fate, Dulles appointed one of McCarthy's henchmen, Scott McLeod, as chief security officer of the State Department. McLeod went about trying to prove what McCarthy had been shouting—that the department was infested with Communists. Making few distinctions between New Dealers and Communists, he and Dulles forced many talented and innocent officers out of the foreign service, including a number of Asian specialists whose valuable expertise was sorely needed. The purge severely weakened the morale of the diplomatic corps, whose members seemed increasingly intimidated and reluctant to offer criticism.

However, McCarthyism cannot explain Eisenhower-Dulles foreign policy. The Communist witch hunt had begun to flag in 1954, the same year Eisenhower beat back an attempt by Senator John Bricker of Ohio to limit presidential power in diplomacy. Bricker, recalling that the Korean War was undeclared and that the Yalta accords of 1945 had never been submitted to the Senate, proposed an amendment to the Constitution providing that executive agreements, like treaties, had to be approved by a two-thirds vote in the Senate. After the defeat of Bricker's challenge, Eisenhower and Dulles had a free hand in foreign policy and enjoyed comfortable legislative margins on key resolutions and programs. Thus the source of American foreign policy in the 1950s was not the McCarthyites, but the Eisenhower-Dulles team.

Eisenhower-Dulles policies

For the most part, Eisenhower and Dulles continued Truman's containment policy, but they introduced some memorable phrases to distinguish their administration from Truman's. Thinking containment too defensive a concept, Dulles invented the concept of *liberation.* (He did not, however, explain precisely how the countries of Eastern Europe could be freed from Soviet control.) *Massive retaliation* was the administration's phrase for the consequences of Soviet aggression: the nuclear obliteration of the Soviet state or its assumed client, the People's Republic of China. The United States' ability to make such a threat was thought to provide *deterrence,* or the prevention of hostile Soviet actions. Although American officials never resorted to the use of nuclear weapons, they did threaten China with massive retaliation in 1953 and again in 1955.

Related to both massive retaliation and deterrence was the so-called New Look of the American military. Eisenhower and Dulles emphasized air power and nuclear weaponry and de-emphasized conventional forces, which they suggested could be supplied by American allies. The president's preference for heavy weapons stemmed in part from his desire to trim the federal budget and reduce taxes while maintaining a strong defense posture. With this huge military arsenal, Eisenhower and Dulles practiced a kind of diplomatic brinkmanship: not backing down in a crisis, even if it meant taking the nation to the brink of war. Adopting a globalist perspective on wrenching changes in the Third World, they conducted a diplomacy best described as holding the line—against Soviet Russia, Communist China, neutralism, Communism, socialism, nationalism, and revolution everywhere. Still, Eisenhower was an uneasy Cold Warrior. He feared nuclear war and frequently offered proposals for disarmament. And he was uncomfortable with the economic cost of militarism. In his celebrated 1953 Chance for Peace speech, the president noted sadly that "every gun that is made, every warship launched, every rocket fired signifies, in the final sense, a theft from those who hunger and are not fed. . . . The cost of one modern heavy bomber is this: a modern brick school in more than 30 cities."

The global watch in the 1950s

After the death of Stalin in 1953, Eisenhower attempted to achieve better relations with the Kremlin. The results of his efforts were mixed. A temporary thaw in the Cold War occurred in 1955 when Russia and the United States agreed to end their ten-year joint occupation of Austria, making it an independent neutral state. The same year Eisenhower and Soviet Premier Nikita Khrushchev journeyed to Geneva for a summit conference, where they "disagreed so nicely," as one reporter put it. Both leaders wanted a united Germany, but each on his own terms. Both sought arms control, but feared inspections would not prevent cheating. Both sought influence in the Third World, and each wanted to weaken the other's sphere of influence.

Meanwhile, the two sides raced to accumulate arms and allies. The United States had superior strength in intercontinental bombers and nuclear weapons, including hydrogen bombs (first tested in 1952). The Soviet Union exploded its own thermonuclear bomb in 1954. In 1955 the United States and its European allies welcomed West Germany into NATO. That year, too, the Southeast Asia Treaty Organization (SEATO) went into effect, bringing Britain, France, Australia, New Zealand, Pakistan, Thailand, and the

Philippines into alliance with the United States against China, considered a Soviet ally. Finally, the United States signed defense treaties with the Nationalist Chinese government on Taiwan and with Turkey, Iraq, Britain, Iran, and Pakistan (the Baghdad Treaty). The goal of these alliances was to surround Communist nations with allies and thus contain them. The Soviets responded with the Warsaw Pact in Eastern Europe.

Khrushchev unwittingly caused new troubles in 1956, when he called for "peaceful coexistence" between capitalists and Communists, denounced Stalin for his crimes against the Russian people, and suggested that Moscow would tolerate different brands of Communism. Soon revolts against Soviet power erupted in Poland and Hungary, testing his new permissiveness. Moscow quickly crushed the rebellions. The Eisenhower administration, which had gone on record as favoring the liberation of Eastern Europe, found itself unable to aid the rebels without igniting a third world war. "Poor fellows, poor fellows," the president remarked. "I think about them all the time. I wish there were some way of helping them." All he could do was to welcome Hungarian immigrants in greater numbers than American quota laws allowed.

Meanwhile, the United States was having its own difficulties. France was resisting American guidance on the defense of Western Europe and shifting its NATO troops to Algeria to put down a colonial rebellion there. As the allies bickered among themselves, the Soviets shocked Americans by propelling the first man-made satellite, Sputnik, into outer space (1957). Just two months earlier, Soviet technicians had fired the first intercontinental ballistic missile (ICBM). Americans now felt vulnerable to attack by air and inferior to the Soviets in rocket technology.

Missile race

Though flights by American U-2 spy planes revealed only minimal deployment of Soviet ICBMs, critics charged that Eisenhower had allowed the United States to fall behind in the missile race. The much-publicized missile gap was a false notion based on misinterpretation of data and inspired in part by political partisanship. "Everyone knows," Air Force General Nathan Twining privately told the president, "we already have a [nuclear] stockpile large enough to completely obliterate the Soviet Union." Nevertheless, Eisenhower ordered a speed-up of the missile program. By the end of 1960 the United States had deployed intermediate-range Thor and Jupiter missiles in Europe; developed long-range (intercontinental) Atlas and Titan missiles; and produced a fleet of Polaris-missile-bearing submarines. As the nation entered the 1960s, it enjoyed overwhelming strategic dominance over the Soviet Union.

While the arms race accelerated, the divided city of Berlin, in East Germany, once again became a Cold War flash point. The Soviets were angry about the placement in West Germany of American bombers capable of carrying nuclear warheads. And they were upset that West Berlin had become an escape route for disaffected East Germans. In 1958 Khrushchev boldly announced that the Soviet Union would recognize East German control of all of Berlin unless East and West began talks on German reunification and rearmament. The Americans, unwilling to give up their hold on West Berlin, sought to strengthen West German ties with NATO. The two sides talked of war; finally Khrushchev backed away from his ultimatum, resolving to take up the issue at future conferences.

Berlin and Germany were on the agenda of a summit meeting planned for Paris in May 1960. But two weeks before the conference an American U-2 spy plane carrying high-powered cameras crashed 1,200 miles inside the Soviet Union. Moscow announced that it had been shot down. At first Washington denied that its planes flew over Soviet territory, but Russian officials blasted that story by displaying the captured pilot, Francis Gary Powers, his aircraft, and the pictures he had been snapping of Soviet military installations. Moscow demanded an apology, Washington refused, and the Russians walked out of the Paris summit.

While West and East sparred over Europe, both kept a wary eye on China. Despite growing evidence of a Sino-Soviet split, American officials continued to think of Communism as a unified world movement. Actually, the Chinese distrusted Russian calls for peaceful coexistence with the United States. To the Chinese, America had a demonstrated record of hostility: aid to Jiang Jieshi (Chiang Kai-shek) until the last days of his regime; continued support for him in exile on Formosa; bloody warfare in Korea; positioning of the Seventh Fleet in the Formosa Straits beginning in 1950; nonrecognition of their People's Republic; and blockage of their membership in the United Nations. To Washington, China was a Soviet ally, an enemy in Korea, a vocal advocate of colonial rebellion, and an international outlaw for the seizure of American property in China (1949). Moreover, Mao Zedong's demand that Formosa become part of the People's Republic threatened an American ally. In essence, the Chinese civil war was still going on, and the United States was still in the middle of it.

In 1954 and 1955 a crisis brought the two nations to the brink of war. Just a few miles off the Chinese coast sat the tiny islands of Quemoy and Matsu. Occupied by sixty thousand of Jiang's troops, they served as bases for commando raids against the People's Republic. In fall 1954 Chinese officials ordered the bombardment of the islands in an attempt to liberate them from Jiang's control. Eisenhower decided to defend the islands. In the "poker game of world politics," Vice President Richard M. Nixon explained, "we should stand ready to call international Communism's bluff on any pot, large or small." So although China had the better legal case, and the small islands were hardly essential to either American or Formosan security, Congress passed the Formosa Resolution (1955), which authorized the president to send American troops to Formosa and its adjoining islands. Two years later the United States installed missiles capable of carrying nuclear warheads on Formosa. Chinese diplomats offered to talk, and in Geneva and Warsaw they held secret meetings with American diplomats. But the two sides came to no agreement, and again in 1958, after continued harassment by Jiang, Chinese guns boomed over Quemoy and Matsu. Eisenhower once again declared he would defend the islands, but he persuaded Jiang to withdraw some of his troops, now 100,000 strong, and signaled to China that the United States did not want a wider war. The crisis passed.

Quemoy and Matsu

If Eisenhower and Dulles believed they had contained the Sino-Soviet threat, they were less sure about challenges in the Third World. In Latin America, where poverty, overpopulation, illiteracy, economic sluggishness, and foreign exploitation fed discontent, anti-American feeling grew. In 1951 the leftist Jacobo Arbenz Guzman was elected president of Guatemala, a poor country whose largest landowner was the American-owned United Fruit Company. To fulfill his promise of land reform, Arbenz expropriated uncultivated land from United Fruit, offering the company some compensation for its loss. But United Fruit dismissed the offer and began an advertising campaign to rally Washington against the so-called Communist threat in Guatemala. The government agreed. Arbenz "thought like a Communist and talked like a Communist, and if not actually one, would do until one came along," said the American ambassador to Guatemala.

Officials cut off aid to Guatemala, and the CIA, under Secretary Dulles's brother Allen, began Operation el Diablo, a secret attempt to subvert the Guatemalan government. When Arbenz learned the CIA was working against him, he turned to Russia, thus confirming American suspicions. The CIA airlifted arms into Guatemala, dropping them at United Fruit facilities, and in June 1954 CIA-supported forces struck from Honduras. American planes bombed Guatemala City, the invaders drove Arbenz from power, and the new pro-American regime returned United Fruit's land.

CIA in Guatemala

Reacting to United States intervention in Guatemala, British Prime Minister Clement Attlee criticized Americans for preaching against Communist aggression while practicing "a plain fact of aggression" themselves. For their part, Latin Americans wondered what had happened to Roosevelt's Good Neighbor Policy. Their growing hostility toward the United States surfaced again in 1958, when hecklers and rock throwers interrupted Vice President Nixon's goodwill trip to South America. The following year university students and some prominent politicians entered the American-managed Panama Canal Zone and planted Panamanian flags there. Scuffles broke out, mobs formed, and riots spread across Panama City. Angry crowds attacked American-owned properties and tore down the embassy's American flag. Scores of people were wounded. In response Eisenhower announced that henceforth both the American and Panamanian flags would fly over the zone—a concession that hardly satisfied Panamanians, who clamored for sovereignty over the zone that had been severed from their nation in 1903.

In the boiling Middle East the Eisenhower administration confronted several challenges to United States influence. American stakes there included the survival

Five leaders of the neutralist, or nonaligned, states, who angered both Americans and Soviets by refusing to take sides in the Cold War. From left to right, Prime Minister Jawaharlal Nehru (1889–1964) of India; President Kwame Nkrumah (1909–1972) of Ghana; President Gamal Abdel Nasser (1918–1970) of Egypt; President Sukarno (1901–1970) of Indonesia; and President Josep Broz Tito (1892–1980) of Yugoslavia. UPI.

of the Jewish state of Israel, carved out of the British mandate of Palestine in 1948, and extensive oil holdings (in the 1950s American companies produced about half the region's petroleum). Oil-rich Iran was a special friend, for the ruling shah had granted American oil companies a 40 percent interest in a new petroleum consortium in return for CIA help in the overthrow of his rival, Mohammed Mossadegh (1953). Mossadegh had attempted the unpardonable sin, nationalization of foreign oil interests.

The major threat to American interests in the Middle East came from Egypt, where the fervent Arab nationalist Gamal Abdel Nasser rose to power determined to push the British out of the Suez Canal Zone and the Israelis out of Palestine. The United States was caught in a double bind. It did not wish to anger the Arabs, for fear of losing its oil holdings. Nor did it wish to lose its ally Israel, which was supported by a vocal Jewish-American lobby. But when Nasser declared neutrality in the Cold War, Dulles lost patience with him. "Do nations which play both sides get better treatment than nations which are stalwart and work with us?" he asked angrily. Eisenhower for his part was not convinced of Nasser's neutrality. "If he was not a Communist," the president wrote later, "he certainly succeeded in making us suspicious of him." Officials decided to withdraw their offer to help finance the Aswan Dam, a project Nasser had dreamed would provide inexpensive electricity and water for

Suez crisis

thirsty Egyptian farmlands. Nasser responded to the decision, which he found "couched in insulting language," by nationalizing the British-owned Suez Canal (1956) and using its $25 million annual profit to finance the dam.

Fearing interruption of the Middle Eastern oil trade, from which Western Europe received 75 percent of its oil, the British and French now conspired with Israel "to knock Nasser off his perch." On October 29, 1956, the Israelis invaded the Suez, joined two days later by Britain and France. Eisenhower fumed that his allies had not consulted him, and that the attack had shifted attention from the Soviet invasion of Hungary. He feared the move might cause Nasser to seek help from the Soviets, inviting the dread enemy into the Middle East. In early November Eisenhower bluntly told London, Paris, and Tel Aviv to pull out, and American officials introduced a resolution in the United Nations condemning their act. The troops withdrew, Egypt paid $81 million for the canal, and the Russians built the Aswan Dam.

In 1957, in an effort to improve the Western position in the Middle East and protect American interests there, the president proclaimed what became known as the Eisenhower Doctrine. The United States would intervene in the Middle East, he said, if any government threatened by a Communist takeover asked for help. Fourteen thousand American troops scrambled ashore in Lebanon the next year to quell an internal political dispute that Washington feared might be exploited by pro-Nasser groups or Communists. American critics protested that the United States was wrongfully acting as the world's policeman.

Kennedy, Cuba, and the quest for Cold War victory

The last days of the Eisenhower administration were not happy ones for the man from Abilene, Kansas. The president lost his key adviser when Secretary Dulles succumbed to cancer in 1959. The anti-American nationalist Fidel Castro emerged victorious in Cuba. And Eisenhower's friendly meeting with Khrushchev at Camp David was followed by such bizarre displays as the premier pounding his shoe on a desk at the United Nations. The next year anti-American riots forced the president to cancel a trip to Japan, and a civil war in the mineral-rich Congo (now Zaire) threatened to become a Cold War contest. Then Vice President Richard M. Nixon lost the presidential election to John F. Kennedy. Kennedy's campaign message: "I think it's time America started moving again."

Although Nixon and Kennedy differed little on foreign policy–as freshman congressional representatives, both had applauded the Truman Doctrine–Kennedy offered Cold War victory instead of stalemate. He promised a bold foreign policy to attract the Third World to the United States side, and he vowed to discipline Russia and China. Kennedy chastised Eisenhower for permitting Communism to make inroads in the Third World. In exaggerated language he warned that "these [are] the days when the tide began to run out for the United States. These were the times when the communist tide began to pour in."

Kennedy as Cold War activist

John F. Kennedy's diplomacy owed much to the past. Remembering the tragedy of appeasement in the 1930s, he concluded that that decade had "taught us a clear lesson: aggressive conduct, if allowed to go unchecked and unchallenged, ultimately leads to war." But just as Nazism had been turned back, Communism would be routed in the 1960s. Kennedy's dynamic style suggested that his administration would mark a new departure in foreign policy. An eloquent speaker, energetic worker, and fierce competitor, Kennedy was an "incandescent man. He was on fire, and he set people around him on fire," said Secretary of State Dean Rusk. As a diplomat, Kennedy was eager to prove his toughness. His administration kept box scores on the missile race, the arms race, the space race, and the race for influence in the Third World. When the young president–he was forty-three when he took office–prepared for his first meeting with Khrushchev, he seemed poised for a contest rather than a talk: "I have to show him that we can be as tough as he is," remarked Kennedy. "I'll have to sit down with him and let him see who he's dealing with."

Kennedy brought with him to Washington a staff of bright, often arrogant people who were determined to score Cold War victories. Journalist Theodore

White called them "action intellectuals." Older and more experienced diplomats and politicians predicted trouble. Undersecretary of State Chester Bowles, for example, complained later that the Kennedy team was "full of belligerence." And Adlai Stevenson told a friend privately that "they've got the damnedest bunch of boy commandos running around down there [in Washington] you ever saw." That there would be no halfway measures was apparent in Kennedy's Inaugural Address: "Let every nation know that we shall pay any price, bear any burden, meet any hardship, support any friend, oppose any foe to assure the survival and the success of liberty." Given these strong words, it is not surprising that there were numerous crises in Kennedy's short tenure as president.

Khrushchev responded to Kennedy's rhetoric with an endorsement of "wars of national liberation" in the Third World. And in late 1961 the Soviet Union ended a moratorium on above-ground nuclear testing by exploding a giant 50-megaton bomb. Khrushchev bragged constantly about Russian ICBMs, raising American anxiety over Soviet capabilities. Intelligence data soon proved the premier's claim a blatant falsehood. But Moscow's actions only strengthened Kennedy in his campaign commitment to a military buildup based on the principle of *flexible response.* Junking Eisenhower's concept of massive retaliation, Kennedy sought ways to meet any kind of warfare, from guerrilla combat in the jungles to a nuclear showdown. In this way, he reasoned, he could contain both the Soviet Union and Third World revolutionary movements. In 1961 the military budget shot up 15 percent, ICBM arsenals swelled further, and plans were laid to increase NATO's nuclear firing power. The government even encouraged citizens to build fallout shelters in their backyards. Though Kennedy could claim credit for the Arms Control and Disarmament Agency and a test-ban treaty with Russia (1963), his real legacy was a huge military expansion that helped to goad the Russians into an accelerated arms race.

Berlin Wall

During this time Berlin continued to claim headlines. The Russians again demanded negotiations to end the Western occupation of Berlin. But Kennedy saw the historic city as "the great testing place of Western courage and will." Instead of negotiating, he asked Congress in 1961 for an additional $3.2 billion for defense and the authority to call up military reservists. The Soviets responded by erecting the Berlin Wall, a concrete-and-barbed-wire barricade designed to halt the exodus of East Germans into West Berlin. An ugly symbol of Soviet repression, the wall inspired protests all over the non-Communist world. In 1963 Kennedy visited the wall and stirred a mass rally of West Berliners with the words "Ich bin ein Berliner" ("I am a Berliner").

But it was over Cuba, a nation whose allegiance the United States had taken for granted since 1898, that Kennedy had his most serious confrontation with the Soviets (see map, p. 900). Cuba became an obsession of American policy makers in 1959, when the bearded, cigar-chomping Fidel Castro emerged from his mountain-based guerrilla camp to oust America's long-time ally Fulgencio Batista. President Eisenhower had made a last-minute attempt to install a friendly military regime there and to deny Castro his hard-fought revolutionary triumph. Incensed, Castro determined to break the influence of American business, which owned 3 million acres of Cuban land, controlled 40 percent of its sugar production and 90 percent of its telephone and electric service, and sold Cuba 70 percent of its imports. Indeed, American investments in the island at the time of Castro's victory totaled about $1 billion. The new president began by confiscating some American-owned property, suspending promised elections, indulging in a barrage of anti-American rhetoric, and signing a trade treaty with Russia (February 1960).

In mid-1960 President Eisenhower grew impatient with Castro and reduced American purchases of Cuban sugar. Castro's response was large-scale seizures of American-owned companies. Soon the Cuban premier began to appeal to Russia for support and to mouth Communist slogans. Historians disagree on whether Castro was always a Communist, or whether Washington's vehement opposition pushed him into Russia's arms. In any case, the Soviet Union gradually came to Cuba's assistance with loans and trade, pleased to be able to spawn discord in the Caribbean. The Monroe Doctrine, Moscow declared, was dead.

During the 1960 presidential campaign Kennedy emphasized the Cuban issue, attacking Eisenhower and Nixon for permitting a "communist satellite" to be set up on "our own doorstep." Unknown to Kennedy, however, Eisenhower had ordered the CIA to

When the ugly Berlin Wall first went up along the border between East and West Berlin, it was hastily constructed of barbed wire. Several years later East German troops added heavy concrete slabs to the barricade, as they are doing here. UPI.

train Cuban exiles for an invasion of their homeland. Just before he left office Eisenhower broke diplomatic relations with Castro and advised Kennedy to advance plans for the invasion. The picture sketched by the CIA appealed to Kennedy: Cuban exiles would land at the Bay of Pigs and secure a beachhead; the Cuban people would rise up against Castro; a Revolutionary Council organized in the United States would enter Havana in triumph. Kennedy was nonetheless uneasy over such a blatant attempt to topple a sovereign government. So that he could publicly deny involvement, he instructed the CIA to refuse air support to the invaders. It is noteworthy that he did not attempt to negotiate with Castro over Cuban-American troubles; nor did he ask Congress for a declaration of war.

Bay of Pigs

The CIA-directed expedition departed from Nicaragua in April 1961. But when the fourteen hundred commandos reached the Cuban shoreline they found Castro's militia waiting for them. The Cuban people did not rise up in sympathy with the invaders, and within two days the invasion collapsed.

Kennedy did not suffer defeat easily. Soon he and his advisers set about finding other means to unseat Castro. "My idea," Attorney General Robert Kennedy said, "is to stir things up on the island with espionage, sabotage, [and] general disorder." The president's brother instructed the CIA to let "no time, money, effort–or manpower–be spared" in a project that came to be known as Operation Mongoose. Government agents moved to disrupt the international sugar market, hamper the island's trade, and oust Cuba from the Organization of American States. They continued to aid anti-Castro groups in Miami and plotted with organized crime leaders to assassinate Castro.

Kennedy's preoccupation with Cuba eventually led to one of the scariest crises of the Cold War, the Cuban missile crisis (1962). Had there been no Bay of Pigs, and no Operation Mongoose, there very likely

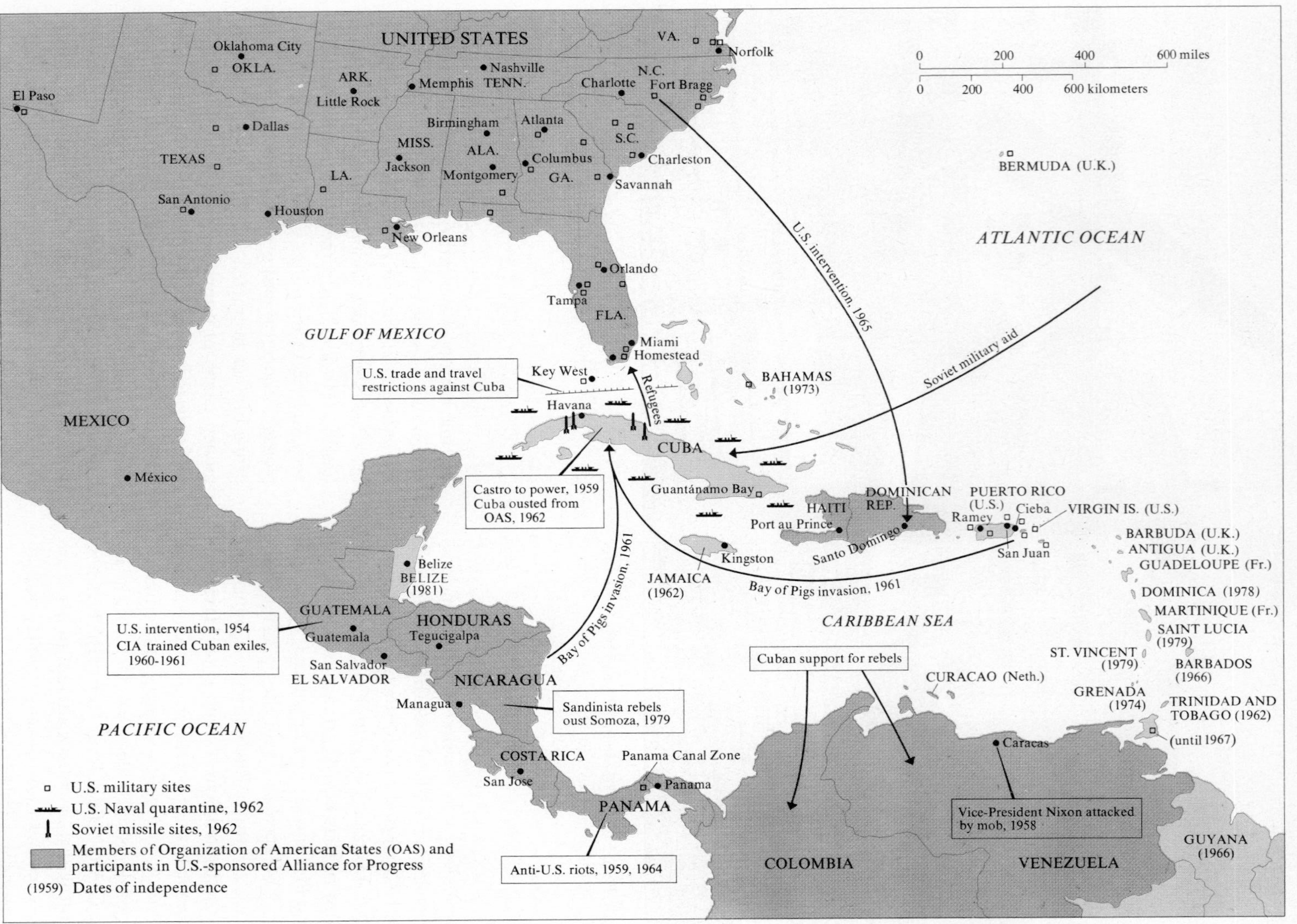

The United States, the Caribbean, and Cuba

In December 1962, in Miami's Orange Bowl, President John F. Kennedy (1917–1963) welcomed home the newly released members of the CIA-sponsored landing force captured by the Cuban militia at the Bay of Pigs. Still determined to unseat Castro, Kennedy received the troops' combat banner, promising, "This flag will be returned to this Brigade in a free Havana." Wide World Photos.

would have been no missile crisis. But for Kennedy, the abortive invasion was a political setback that had to be reversed. For Castro, American hostility represented a real threat to Cuba's independence. And for the Russians, American actions were a challenge to the only pro-Communist regime in Latin America. "We had to think up some way of confronting America with more than words," recalled the Soviet premier. So Castro and Khrushchev devised a daring plan to deter any new American intervention: installation of Soviet missiles and nuclear bombers in Cuba.

Cuban missile crisis

Although the Kennedy administration was aware of a Soviet military buildup on the island, it was not until October 14, 1962, that a U-2 plane photographed nuclear-missile construction sites there. Whether the Soviets had acted to protect Cuba; to improve their own nuclear capability; to trigger negotiations over Berlin; or to force the United States to pull its missiles out of Turkey was not clear. In any case, the president ordered his special advisory executive committee to find a way to remove the missiles from Cuba. One committee member, the venerable Dean Acheson, advised a surprise air strike, likely to kill both Russian technicians and Cubans. But Robert Kennedy scotched that idea; he wanted no Pearl Harbors on his brother's record. The Joint Chiefs of Staff recommended a full-scale military invasion—a Bay of Pigs with American soldiers. But that approach risked a prolonged war with Cuba, a Soviet attack against Berlin, or even nuclear holocaust. Soviet experts Llewellyn Thompson and Charles Bohlen unsuccessfully urged quiet, direct negotiations with Soviet officials. The committee also ruled out private overtures to Castro and an appeal to the United Nations. It was Secretary of Defense Robert S. McNamara who proposed the most acceptable formula: a naval blockade of Cuba, to prevent further military shipments. Halfway between armed warfare and doing nothing, it left the administration free to escalate or negotiate, depending on the Russian response.

Over national television on October 22, Kennedy informed the Soviets of American policy and demanded their retreat. American warships headed for the Caribbean, B-52s loaded with nuclear bombs took to the skies, and American military forces around the globe went on alert. Khrushchev first replied that the missiles would be withdrawn if Washington pledged never to attack Cuba again. Then he demanded the removal of American missiles from Turkey. Kennedy accepted the first condition but rejected the second. (Privately the administration made a loose promise to the Russians to withdraw the missiles from Turkey sometime in the future.) On October 28 Khrushchev accepted the American pledge to respect Cuban sovereignty and promised to dismantle the missiles and return them to the Soviet Union. Americans breathed a collective sigh of relief; this was, said many, Kennedy's finest hour.

But critics then and now have asked whether the crisis was really necessary. Why, they have asked, did the president attempt to solve the crisis with public brinkmanship instead of private negotiations? Television addresses and public confrontations are not the stuff of statesmanship, but of politics—and the congressional elections were just weeks away. They note too that Kennedy passed up an opportunity to protest the presence of the missiles when he met privately with Foreign Minister Andrei Gromyko in the White House on October 18. Finally, critics have claimed that the strategic balance of power was not seriously altered by the placement of Soviet missiles in Cuba. The United States had about 450 missiles capable of reaching Russia, the Soviets only 100 capable of hitting North America.

The Cuban missile crisis humiliated the Soviets. (In the world of diplomacy, it is wise to give the enemy a chance to save face.) Exposed as nuclear inferiors, the Soviets vowed to catch up—and they managed to do so by the late 1960s. The crisis did produce some relaxation in Soviet-American relations. The superpower leaders installed a telephone hot line between the White House and the Kremlin, signed a test-ban treaty, and refrained from further confrontation in Berlin.

Elsewhere in the Third World, Kennedy called for "peaceful revolution" based on the concept of *nation building.* Drawing on the ideas of economist Walt W. Rostow, who joined the administration in Washington, Kennedy determined to build goodwill in Third World countries by helping them through the infant stages of nationhood. One method would be programs aimed at improving agriculture, transportation, and communications. Kennedy thus created the multi-billion-dollar Alliance for Progress in Latin America. And for the same purpose the Peace Corps, founded in 1961, sent dedicated teachers, agricultural specialists, and health workers into developing nations throughout the world. Within three years ten thousand idealistic young men and women had volunteered for service. But the Peace Corps' humanitarian purpose competed with the administration's political needs. Periodic conflicts arose between corps members in the field, who identified with Third World peoples and their desire for neutralism, and headquarters in Washington, where the goal was aligning those peoples with American foreign policy.

Nation building

Besides such special development programs, Kennedy relied on *counterinsurgency:* the training of native police forces by American military and technical advisers. The assumption was that American soldiers—especially the Special Forces units, or Green Berets—would provide a protective shield against insurgents while American civilian personnel worked on economic projects.

Nation building and its methods did not work. Americans naively assumed that they could simply transfer their own institutions and ideas to foreign cultures. Foreigners saw not just the helping hand but unwanted meddling in their affairs. And because monetary aid was usually funneled through a self-interested elite, it often did not reach the very poor. And to people who preferred the relatively quick solutions of a managed economy, the American emphasis on private enterprise seemed inappropriate. "In the end," presidential adviser Arthur M. Schlesinger, Jr., later wrote, counterinsurgency proved "a ghastly illusion. Its primary consequence was to keep alive the American belief in their capacity and right to intervene in foreign lands."

Descent into the longest war: Vietnam

The belief in the right to influence the internal affairs of other countries led to disaster in Southeast Asia. How Vietnam became the site of America's longest war (it lasted a quarter-century, from 1950 to 1975); how the world's most powerful nation spent itself in a futile attempt to subdue a peasant people; how those people suffered enormous losses of life and property and yet persisted, is one of the tragic stories of modern history.

The story begins with the French takeover of Vietnam during the late nineteenth century. For decades the French exploited the colony for its rice, rubber, tin, and tungsten, beating back peasant rebellions against their rule. Not until the Second World War, when the Japanese moved into Indochina, did French authority collapse.

History of imperialism in Vietnam

Seizing their chance, the Viet Minh, an anti-imperialist coalition led by Communists, began guerrilla warfare against the Japanese. Led by the nationalist Ho Chi Minh, they collaborated with American Office of Strategic Services (OSS) agents to harass the Japanese. OSS officers who worked with Ho in Vietnam were impressed by his determination to free his country of outsiders, and by his frequent references to the United States as a revolutionary model. When Ho declared Vietnam's independence in September 1945, his words sounded familiar: "We hold these truths to be self-evident. That all men are created equal." But though Ho wrote to the Truman administration requesting political support and economic assistance for his new government, his letters were never answered. When the Second World War ended, the French returned, and Ho and the Viet Minh took up arms to defend their independence.

The United States did not recognize Vietnamese independence (and in fact attempted to undermine it) for several reasons. First, France was a valued ally in the emerging Cold War. Second, Southeast Asia was important as the world's largest producer of natural rubber, and a rich source of other commodities. Third, the area seemed strategically vital to the defense of Japan and the Philippines. Finally, Ho Chi Minh was a Communist who had lived for a time in Russia. Thus Vietnam became another test in the containment of Communism, the Berlin of Asia. Overlooking the native roots of the revolution and the tenacity of a people fighting on and for their own land, American leaders from Truman through Nixon took a globalist view, interpreting events through a Cold War lens.

In the 1940s Vietnam was a French problem that few Americans watched with keen interest. More dramatic crises in Eastern Europe, Iran, and Western Europe commanded their attention. But when Jiang Jieshi went down to defeat in China, the United States was aroused to action. The Truman administration made two crucial decisions in early 1950. First, it recognized the French puppet government of Bao Dai–a signal that it would not attempt to pressure the French into a negotiated settlement. Thus in Vietnamese eyes the United States became in essence a colonial power, an ally of the hated French. Second, the administration agreed to send ammunition, guns, aircraft, and ultimately military advisers to the French. By 1954 the United States had invested over $2 billion in the war and was bearing 78 percent of its cost.

Despite American aid, the French lost steadily to the Viet Minh. Finally, in 1954 Ho's forces surrounded the French fortress at Dienbienphu. What would the United States do? Could the French be saved? President Eisenhower huddled with his advisers. The Chairman of the Joint Chiefs of Staff urged the president to unleash a massive air strike, using nuclear weapons if necessary. Secretary Dulles recommended that he seek help from Great Britain and Australia. Other advisers suggested sending American troops. But Eisenhower was cautious. If American forces became directly involved in the war–as distinct from merely advising the French–he might not be able to limit the nation's involvement. As one high-level doubter remarked, "One cannot go over Niagara Falls in a barrel only slightly." Army Chief of Staff Matthew Ridgway was also wary. He warned the president that American troops would be fighting in hostile terrain, that air power could not guarantee victory. And American soldiers would have to be moved from elsewhere in Asia and Europe, a shift that might leave other regions vulnerable.

Nevertheless, Eisenhower worried aloud at the prospect of a Communist victory, comparing the weak nations of the world to a row of dominoes, all of which would topple if just one fell. He asked the British to help, but they would make no commitment. At home, members of Congress refused to support military action unless the British went along.

To add to the administration's problems, the French wanted out. They agreed to peace talks at Geneva, where France, the United States, Russia, Britain, China, Laos, and Cambodia joined the two competing Vietnamese regimes of Bao Dai and Ho Chi Minh. It was an unpleasant job for Dulles, who conducted himself, according to one biographer, like a "puritan in a house of ill repute." Dulles could not even bring himself to shake hands with Zhou Enlai, the Chinese representative. When the Geneva accords of 1954 were agreed on, American delegates grumbled about French weakness. Vietnam was temporarily divided at the 17th parallel, with Ho's Democratic Republic confined to the North. National elections would be held in 1956, and the country would thereupon be unified. Neither North nor South was to join a military alliance or permit foreign military bases on its soil.

Geneva Conference

Certain that the Geneva agreements would ultimately mean Communist victory, the United States refused to sign and set about to sabotage them. Soon after the conference a CIA team entered Vietnam and began secret operations against the North, including commando raids across the parallel and the distribution of anti-Communist propaganda. In the South, despite French protests, the United States cultivated the friendship of the anti-French leader Ngo Dinh Diem. A Catholic in a Buddhist nation, Diem had no mass support and many enemies. But with American aid he beat back his opponents, including Bao Dai, and staged a fraudulent election that gave him a remarkable 98 percent of the vote. When Ho called for national elections in keeping with the Geneva agreements, Diem and Eisenhower refused, fearing the charismatic Viet Minh leader would win.

From 1955 to 1961 Diem received more than $1 billion worth of American aid, most of it military. American advisers organized, trained, and supplied the South Vietnamese army. Michigan State University police experts helped to create a national guard. And American agriculturalists worked to improve crops. As American consumer products flowed into a land of peasant villages, Diem's Saigon regime became dependent on the United States for its very existence.

Meanwhile, Diem became bent on dictatorial leadership. He abolished village elections and appointed people beholden to him to public office. He threw thousands of dissenters into jail and shut down newspapers that criticized his corrupt government. In the South non-Communists and Communists alike began to strike back at Diem's irresponsible, self-serving, and repressive government. The Viet Minh embarked on a program of terror, assassinating hundreds of Diem's village officials. The Viet Minh found a receptive audience in the many peasants victimized by Diem's strong-arm tactics. In late 1960 they organized the National Liberation Front, or Viet Cong, which attracted Communists and other anti-Diem groups in the South. The war against imperialism had become a civil war.

Civil war in South Vietnam

In the United States, the newly elected President Kennedy decided to stand firm against the Viet Cong. Kennedy had suffered the humiliations of the Bay of Pigs and the Berlin Wall; he feared further criticism should the United States back down in Asia. But more important, he sought a Cold War victory. So he ordered more military advisers and Special Forces units to South Vietnam, and millions of dollars worth of additional aid. But it all flowed into a rat hole: Diem showed no signs of using the assistance effectively, and his enemies grew in number. Fearing Diem would drag the United States down to defeat, Kennedy pressed him to reform his corrupt government. Meanwhile, Project Beefup was sending more Americans to South Vietnam; by late 1963 16,700 American "advisers" were stationed there. That year 489 Americans were killed, and an American project called the strategic hamlet program actually strengthened resistance to Diem. The program, which aimed to isolate peasants from the Viet Cong by uprooting them, simply backfired. When Diem's troops attacked Buddhists who opposed his religious repression, the country sank further into civil war. Protesting monks poured gasoline over their robes and ignited themselves in the streets of Saigon.

American officials began to think that if Diem could not be reformed, he should be removed. "We could not sit still and be puppets of Diem's anti-Buddhist policies," recalled a high-ranking State Department officer. Moreover, Diem, who knew that American officials were preparing to dump him, was

The Vietnam War, America's longest, not only took a terrible toll in human life but disrupted a peasant society. Here American soldiers search the home of a worried Vietnamese family. About one-quarter of the people of South Vietnam became refugees because of the war. Angry over their forced removal from ancestral lands, many became Viet Cong sympathizers. Philip Jones Griffiths, Magnum Photos.

apparently trying to make peace with the North—"a possible basic incompatibility with U.S. objectives," worried General Maxwell Taylor. Through the CIA, the United States quietly encouraged South Vietnamese generals to stage a coup. With the ill-concealed backing of Ambassador Henry Cabot Lodge, the generals struck in early November 1963. Diem was captured and murdered—only a few weeks before Kennedy himself met death by an assassin's bullet.

With new governments in Saigon and Washington, some analysts thought it an appropriate time for reassessment. The Viet Cong, United Nations General Secretary U Thant, France, and others called for a coalition government in South Vietnam. But the new American president, Lyndon B. Johnson, would have none of it. He declared that America's purpose was victory, for anything less "would only be another name for a Communist take-over."

Johnson and the war without victory

Lyndon B. Johnson was a Texan who liked to say that he lived by the lessons of the Alamo. An old New Dealer, he talked about building Tennessee Valley Authorities around the world. "I want to leave the footprints of America there [in Vietnam]. I want them to say, 'This is what Americans left—schools and hospitals and dams.' " But Johnson's drive to become a global social worker—some commentators called it welfare imperialism—proved a tragic mistake, especially in Vietnam, where America's footprints were those of over 500,000 soldiers, and where bombs and chemical defoliants destroyed instead of built.

Johnson saw the world in simple terms—them against us—and privately disparaged both his allies and his enemies. Vietnam was a "raggedy-ass fourth-rate

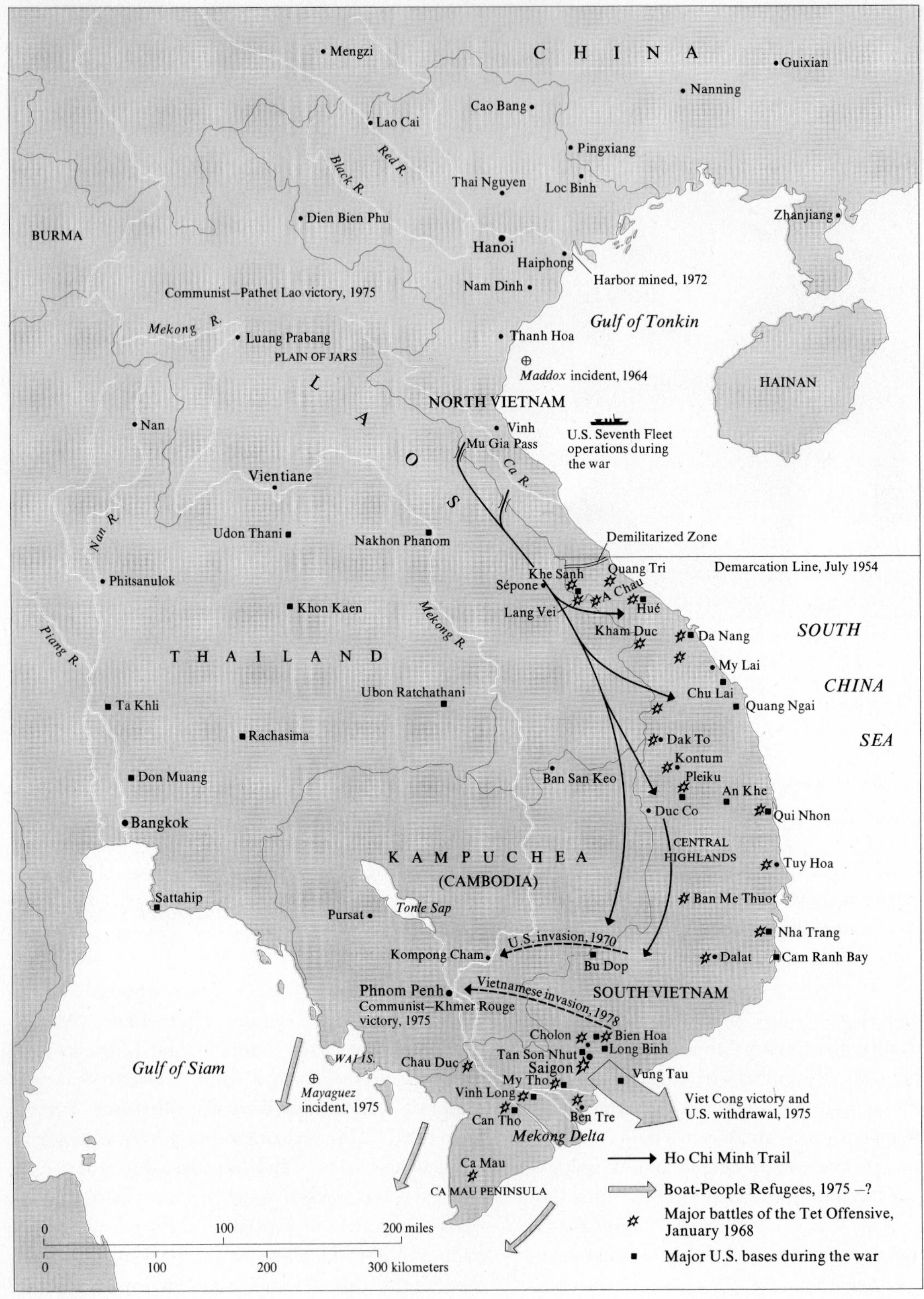

Southeast Asia and the Vietnam War

country," his critics at home "rattlebrains" or "nervous nellies." Johnson sometimes lied or exaggerated, creating what reporters referred to as a credibility gap. His public speeches, larded with trite analogies and delivered in a belabored drawl, led some to suggest that he was unintelligent. They were wrong, for Johnson had a quick mind; his limitation was that he held firmly to fixed ideas about American superiority, the menace of Communism, and the necessity of global intervention. The problem, said Senator J. William Fulbright, chairman of the Foreign Relations Committee, was that both Johnson and the American people suffered from the "arrogance of power."

By early 1964 the Viet Cong controlled nearly half of South Vietnam. Because the new Saigon government was shaky and seemed to be leaning toward neutralism, United States officials cooperated in a second coup. In neighboring Laos, American bombers hit supply routes connecting the Viet Cong with the North Vietnamese, thus widening the scope of the war. Then in August an incident in the Gulf of Tonkin, off the coast of North Vietnam, drew the United States even deeper into the Vietnamese quagmire. While assisting South Vietnamese raiders, the U.S.S. *Maddox* and *C. Turner Joy* were attacked by North Vietnamese boats (see map).

Johnson seized the chance to go on national television and announce retaliatory air strikes above the 17th parallel. He exaggerated the crisis, comparing it to Greece and Turkey in 1947, Berlin in 1948, and Korea in 1950. On August 7 Congress obliged him with the Tonkin Gulf resolution, passed 466–0 in the House and 88–2 in the Senate following brief debate. Only Wayne Morse of Oregon and Ernest Gruening of Alaska dissented from the resolution's sweeping language. The document authorized the president to "take all necessary measures to repel any armed attack against the forces of the United States and to prevent further aggression." Over time the Tonkin Gulf resolution would come to serve as the declaration of war Congress never voted on. Only in 1970 would senators repeal it, realizing too late that they had surrendered their powers in the foreign policy process by giving the president wide latitude to conduct the war as he saw fit.

Tonkin Gulf resolution

Johnson won the presidency in his own right in the fall of 1964, his popularity buoyed by his forceful response to the Tonkin Gulf incident. At his direction the military planned stepped-up bombing of North Vietnam and Laos. Undersecretary of State George Ball urged caution: "Once on the tiger's back we cannot be sure of picking the place to dismount." Nonetheless, when a Viet Cong attack on an American airfield at Pleiku took nine American lives in February 1965, Johnson ordered carrier jets to ravage the North. Soon Operation Rolling Thunder—a sustained bombing program above the 17th parallel—was under way. Before the longest war was over, more bombs would fall on Vietnam than American aircraft had dropped in all of the Second World War. But the North Vietnamese would not give up. They hid in shelters and rebuilt roads and bridges with a perseverance that frustrated and awed American decisionmakers.

The president also sent more troops to the South, arguing that the Americans already stationed there had to be protected. By the end of 1965 184,000 Americans were assigned to Vietnam; in 1966 the figure reached 385,000; in 1969, 542,000. But Ho only increased the flow of arms and men to the rebels in the South; in this seemingly endless war of attrition, each American escalation begot a new Vietnamese escalation. Johnson became skeptical: "When we add divisions, can't the enemy add divisions? If so, where does it end?" Still, he and his aides just could not believe that the Vietnamese rebels could tangle successfully with the greatest power on the face of the earth—at least not for very long.

Americanization of the war

The "Americanization" of the war in Vietnam under Johnson bothered growing numbers of Americans, especially as increased television coverage brought the ugliness of combat into their homes every night. The pictures and stories were not pretty. Innocent civilians were caught in the line of fire; refugees flooded "pacification" camps, only to live there in terror; villages considered friendly to the enemy were burned to the ground. To destroy Viet Cong hiding places, pilots whose motto was "Only You Can Prevent Forests" sprayed chemical defoliants over the landscape. The Viet Cong and North Vietnamese added to the carnage, but American guns, bombs, and chemicals took by far the greatest toll, and the Vietnamese knew it. Indeed, America's search-and-destroy missions were counterproductive; rather than winning the war, they were molding an ever-growing population of anti-American peasants who gave secret aid to the Viet Cong. An American official later admitted, "It was as if we were trying to build a house with a bulldozer and wrecking crane."

Stories of atrocities made their way home too. Most gruesome was the My Lai massacre in March 1968. An American unit, frustrated by its inability to pin down an elusive enemy and eager to revenge the loss of some buddies, shot to death scores of unarmed women and children. Private Paul Meadlo, the father of two children himself, was there. He recalled: "We huddled them up. We made them squat down. . . . I poured about four clips into the group. . . . Somebody told us to switch off to single shot so that we could save ammo. . . . The mothers was hugging their children. . . . Well, we kept right on firing. They was waving their arms and begging. . . . I still dream about it. About the women and children in my sleep. Some days . . . some nights, I can't even sleep."

In early 1966 Senator William Fulbright began to conduct public hearings on whether the national interest was being served by pursuing the war in Asia. What exactly was the threat? senators asked. To the surprise of some, the father of the containment doctrine, George F. Kennan, testified before television cameras that his theory was meant for Europe, not the volatile environment of Southeast Asia. America's European allies grew wary too, watching the United States wasting its resources. Even some GIs became doubters; reports of disobedience, drug use, display of peace symbols, and "fragging" (the murder of an officer by enlisted men, sometimes by means of hand grenades or other explosives) filtered back to Washington. Within the administration, too, disenchantment grew. Secretary of Defense Robert McNamara and Undersecretary of State George Ball resigned, unable to justify further escalation of the war. And in a direct challenge to Johnson's policies, Senator Eugene McCarthy of Minnesota announced his candidacy for the Democratic presidential nomination.

Johnson dug in, snapping at his critics and vowing to continue the battle against Communism. "We are not going to shimmy," he insisted. At times he halted the bombing to encourage Ho Chi Minh to negotiate. Such pauses, however, were often accompanied by increases in American troop strength. And in some cases the United States resumed or accelerated the bombing just when a diplomatic breakthrough seemed imminent—such as in late 1966, when a Polish diplomat's efforts were inexplicably cut short by a resumption of the bombing. Unpersuaded, the North demanded a complete stop to the destruction before sitting down at the conference table. Indeed, American terms were unacceptable to the Communists: nonrecognition of the Viet Cong; withdrawal of northern soldiers from the South; and an end to North Vietnamese aid to the Viet Cong. Assistant Secretary of Defense John McNaughton, another insider who had become a doubter, complained that the United States was seeking "capitulation by a Communist force that is far from beaten."

Then in January 1968, a shocking event forced Johnson to reappraise his position. During Tet, the Vietnamese lunar new year, Viet Cong and North

Tet offensive

Vietnamese forces struck all across South Vietnam, hitting and capturing the provincial capitals. In Saigon raiders actually occupied the American embassy for several hours. American and South Vietnamese units eventually regained much lost ground, inflicting heavy casualties on the enemy. But the destruction of the village of Ben Tre revealed the cost of driving the Viet Cong out. "It became necessary to destroy the town to save it," reported a sober-faced American officer.

The Tet offensive jolted Americans. Hadn't the Viet Cong demonstrated that they could strike when and where they wished? Didn't they have the advantage of fighting on home territory? Why did "their Vietnamese" fight harder than "our Vietnamese"? If all of America's firepower and dollars and half a million troops couldn't defeat the Viet Cong, could anything? Had the American public been lied to? One television reporter asked, "Isn't there something Orwellian about it, that the more we kill, the stronger they get?"

The Tet offensive and its impact on public opinion hit the White House like a thunderclap. The new secretary of defense, Clark Clifford, told Johnson the war could not be won, even if the 206,000 more soldiers requested by the army were sent to Vietnam. The Cold Warrior of Cold Warriors, Dean Acheson, bluntly told a surprised president that the military

In July 1968 a war-weary President Lyndon B. Johnson (1908–1973) pondered what to do next. Just months before, stunned by the Tet offensive, Johnson had decided to drop out of politics and initiate peace talks. Lyndon Baines Johnson Library.

brass did not know what they were talking about. Strained by exhausting sessions with advisers, realizing that further escalation would not bring victory, and faced with serious opposition within his own party, Johnson changed course. In an appearance on national television (March 31) he announced that he had stopped the bombing of most of North Vietnam, asked Hanoi to begin negotiations, and stunned the nation by dropping out of the presidential race. The United States, knowing it could not win, would at least try not to lose.

The wrangling over peace terms was intense and prolonged. As the diplomats talked in Paris, the war ground on. Late in 1968 president-elect Richard M. Nixon met with Johnson and his key advisers to discuss the war. "The travail of the long war was etched on the faces around me," Nixon recalled. "They had no new approaches to recommend to me. I sensed that, despite the disappointment of defeat, they were relieved to be able to turn this morass over to someone else."

Nixon decided to pursue "peace with honor" through "Vietnamization" of the war—building up South Vietnamese forces to replace American troops. And he announced the Nixon Doctrine: that the United States would help those Asian nations that helped themselves. Slowly he began to withdraw American troops from Vietnam, decreasing their number to 139,000 by the end of 1971. But he also increased the bombing in the North, hoping to pound Hanoi into making concessions. Nixon's national security adviser, Henry A. Kissinger, called it jugular diplomacy.

In April 1970 American and South Vietnamese troops invaded Cambodia in search of enemy forces and arms depots. The escalation sparked renewed protest at home. Demonstrations swept college campuses; the Senate forbade the expenditure of funds on the new war. But Nixon and Kissinger were unmoved. They continued to escalate the war, ordering "protective reaction strikes" against the North; the secret bombing of Cambodia; the mining of Haiphong Harbor, near the northern capital, Hanoi; and in December 1972, a massive air strike that demolished every kind of northern structure.

Meanwhile the peace talks seemed to be going nowhere. The South Vietnamese delegate saw defeat coming and purposely stalled the negotiations. But Kissinger was meeting privately with Le Duc Tho, the chief delegate from North Vietnam. Finally the administration, impatient to improve relations with Russia and China, win back the allegiance of its allies, and restore stability at home, made concessions. On January 27, 1973, Kissinger and Le signed a cease-fire agreement. The United States promised to withdraw its remaining troops within sixty days. Other troops would stay in place, and a coalition government that included the Viet Cong would eventually be formed in the South. Pleased that a peace had been made, critics nonetheless noted that the terms of the agreement could have been accepted in 1969, and over twenty thousand American lives spared.

American withdrawal from Vietnam

Leaving behind some advisers, the United States pulled its troops out of Vietnam and reduced its aid program. Both North and South soon violated the cease-fire, and full-scale war erupted once more. As many had predicted, the feeble South Vietnamese government, for so long an American puppet, could not hold out. Just before its surrender, hundreds of American civilians were hastily evacuated by helicopter from the roof of the American embassy in Saigon. In those desperate last moments, crying South Vietnamese surged toward the embassy and the departing aircraft, only to be shoved violently back. On April 29, 1975, South Vietnam collapsed, and shortly after Saigon was renamed Ho Chi Minh City.

The next month a bizarre episode in the Gulf of Siam compounded the tragic American failure in Southeast Asia. The Communist Khmer Rouge had triumphed in Cambodia. That May Cambodian patrol boats seized the American cargo ship *Mayaguez* along with its crew. President Gerald Ford, who had taken over the presidency following Nixon's resignation (see Chapter 34), ordered the U.S. Marines to attack. Patience would have brought the news that the crew members had been released unharmed. Instead, forty Americans died in the needless venture, many of them in a helicopter accident. Nonetheless, Americans applauded the show of force at a time when the United States appeared to be on the retreat.

After twenty-five years, American intervention in Southeast Asia had come to this panicky end. The overall costs of the war were immense. Over 57,000 Americans and hundreds of thousands of Asians died. In monetary terms the war cost the United States more than $150 billion; another $200 billion would be paid in future veterans' benefits. At home the war brought inflation, political schism, attacks on civil liberties, and retrenchment from reform programs (see Chapter 33). The war also had negative consequences internationally: delay in moving toward better relations with the Soviet Union and the People's Republic of China, friction with allies, and the alienation of Third World nations.

Meanwhile, in South Vietnam, Cambodia, and Laos, Communists assumed power and instituted repressive governments. Soon refugees were crowding aboard unsafe vessels in an attempt to escape their battered homelands. Many of these "boat people" immigrated to the United States, where Americans, reluctant to be reminded of their defeat in Asia, received them with mixed feelings. But thoughtful Americans realized that the United States, which had relentlessly bombed, burned, and defoliated once-rich agricultural lands, bore some responsibility for the plight of the hungry Southeast Asian peoples.

This sad conclusion prompted an American ambassador to ask the central question about the American defeat: "how so many with so much could achieve so little for so long against so few"? Rather than seek the answer to that question, most Americans preferred to put the disaster out of their minds. Only the Vietnam veterans seemed unable to forget. In the words of one veteran,

The longest war is over
Or so they say
Again
But I can still hear the gunfire
Every night
From
My bed.

The longest nightmare
Never seems to
Ever
Quite come
To
An end.[1]

Nixon, Kissinger, and détente

For President Richard M. Nixon, Vietnam was a "short-term problem"; for Henry A. Kissinger it was a mere historical "footnote." Both considered the central question of international affairs to be the relationship between the United States and the Soviet Union. Nixon's attitude was not surprising, for as a congressman, senator, and vice president, he had been an ardent cold warrior. As one Soviet official commented, "We very well know with whom we have to deal." Kissinger, a German-born political scientist, had been foreign-policy adviser to Nelson Rockefeller in the 1950s. Nixon appointed him national security adviser, a post he held until 1973, when he became secretary of state.

Ambitious and self-protective, Kissinger isolated or bypassed those who challenged his special ties with the president. He self-consciously developed his public image as "the cowboy leading the caravan alone astride his horse," as he himself put it. As a diplomat Kissinger preferred to exercise his immense powers of persuasion in personal contacts with foreign leaders. Witty, knowledgeable, and deliberate, he was a formidable negotiator. Critics, however, thought he adhered too callously to the principle that the end justifies the means. They cited his willingness to unseat foreign governments through secret operations, as in Chile (see page 913), and to sell massive amounts of arms to dictators like the shah of Iran. Kissinger also had his own staff wiretapped; maintained a policy of secrecy that limited debate; and leaked classified information to the press to generate favorable publicity.

Henry A. Kissinger and détente

Together Nixon and Kissinger pursued a foreign policy designed to promote a global balance of power, or "balance of restraint," and to curb revolution and radicalism in the Third World. The popular word for the new posture toward the Soviets was *détente,* meaning limited cooperation through negotiations, within a general environment of rivalry. But détente was essentially the old policy of containment refurbished. Its purpose was to check Soviet expansion and limit the Soviet arms buildup.

Détente seemed attractive to its architects. The Cold War and limited wars like Vietnam were costing too much. Increased trade with a friendlier Russia might reduce the huge balance-of-payments deficit. But critics, even those who endorsed détente, argued that the Nixon-Kissinger grand strategy promised too much. It presumed, with the arrogance that so often characterized postwar diplomacy, that the United States had the ability to manipulate the world. It assumed that foreign crises could be managed. It saw the world too simply in traditional Cold War terms—friends and enemies. It paid too little attention to nationalism and to many nations' preference for neutralism. And it assumed, wrongly, that troubles abroad could be traced largely to Soviet intrigue. Rather than decreasing the need for intervention, said critics, the new design actually increased it.

Untroubled by such criticisms, Nixon and Kissinger pursued détente with extraordinary energy. To slow the costly arms race, they initiated Strategic Arms Limitations Talks (SALT) with the Soviets. In 1972 the talks produced a SALT treaty that limited antiballistic missile (ABM) systems. ABM systems were defensive systems that made offensive missiles less vulnerable to attack—and hence encouraged the other side to build more missiles to overcome ABM protection. Limiting ABMs was thus a step toward halting a spiraling arms race. A second agreement placed a five-year freeze on the number of offensive nuclear missiles each side could

Strategic Arms Limitations Talks (SALT)

[1] Jan Barry, "The Longest War," from *Winning Hearts & Minds: War Poems by Vietnam Veterans.* Copyright © 1972 by 1st Casualty Press. Reprinted by permission of the author.

The architects of détente, Soviet Communist party boss Leonid Brezhnev (1906–   ) and President Richard M. Nixon (1913–   ), enjoy a light moment after signing the Strategic Arms Limitation Treaty. UPI.

have. At the time of the agreement the Soviets had an advantage in total missiles, but the United States had more warheads per missile. American MIRVs ("multiple independently targeted reentry vehicles") could fire several warheads at different targets in midflight. In short, the United States had a 2-to-1 advantage in deliverable warheads. Since SALT did not restrict MIRVs, the arms race continued.

Evidence of détente arose not only from the SALT process but from the signing of the Quadrapartite Berlin Agreement of 1971. In that document Russia agreed to guarantee Western access to Berlin, thus defusing the potential for crisis that had existed in the city since the 1940s. In other pacts East Germany and West Germany recognized each other and defined rules for border crossings. Yet another sign of détente was a 1972 treaty liberalizing Soviet-American trade and the sale of $1 billion worth of American grain to the Soviets at bargain prices. The huge wheat sales caused shortages at home, stimulating inflation, but farmers applauded Nixon for the bonanza. Nixon and Kissinger also tried to restrain the Soviets indirectly, by making overtures to a Russian enemy. In February 1972 Nixon made a historic trip to the People's Republic of China. The United States had refused to recognize China in 1949; the two nations had battled in the Korean War and tangled over Quemoy and Matsu. But China now considered Russia its chief enemy. The two nations competed for the allegiance of Communists around the world; they shared a long border with a history of military skirmishes that went back for centuries. The Chinese calculated that friendly overtures to the United States might make the Soviets more cautious of them. Nixon reasoned the same way.

Accommodation with the Chinese Communists

Nixon also hoped to open the Chinese market to American products at a time when the American economy was sagging. And he wanted China to sign the Nuclear Non-Proliferation Treaty negotiated in 1968 by the Johnson administration. (France, China, and India had refused to accept the treaty.) So he and

Kissinger visited the Great Wall, ate shark's-fin soup, and traded 150-proof rice-liquor toasts with Mao Zedong and Zhou Enlai. At the end of their trip Nixon and Kissinger issued a communique that said in essence that the United States and China agreed to disagree on a number of issues, and agreed on one: Russia should not be permitted to make gains in Asia. The opening of this Chinese-American dialogue ended one of the Cold War's most troublesome contests. Official diplomatic recognition and exchange of ambassadors was effected in 1979.

Tortuous events in the Middle East, however, revealed how fragile the Nixon-Kissinger grand strategy was. When Nixon took office in 1969 the Middle East was, in the president's words, a "powder keg." In the Six-Day War (1967) Israel had used American weapons to score victories against Egypt and Syria. The Israelis had seized the West Bank and the ancient city of Jerusalem from Jordan, the Golan Heights from Syria, and the Sinai Peninsula from Egypt (see map, page 914). Soviet arms had backed the Arab nations Israel fought. To complicate matters, Palestinian Arabs, many of them expelled from their homeland in 1948 when the nation of Israel was created, had organized the Palestine Liberation Organization (PLO) and pledged to destroy Israel. The PLO made hit-and-run raids on Jewish settlements, hijacked jetliners, and murdered Israeli athletes at the 1972 Olympic Games in Munich.

Arab-Israeli hostilities

On October 6, 1973, Egypt and Syria attacked Israel. In spite of détente, Moscow and Washington were soon locked in confrontation; both superpowers put their armed forces on alert. At the same time, in an attempt to pressure Americans into taking a pro-Arab stance, the powerful Organization of Petroleum Exporting Countries (OPEC) imposed an embargo on shipments of oil to the United States. OPEC also raised prices dramatically.

Faced with an energy crisis at home, the Nixon administration had to find a way to end Middle Eastern hostilities. In October Kissinger arranged a cease-fire; beginning in December he undertook "shuttle diplomacy," flying back and forth repeatedly between Middle Eastern capitals in an exhausting search for a settlement. In March 1974 OPEC lifted the oil embargo. The next year Kissinger persuaded Egypt and Israel to initial a document providing for a United Nations peace-keeping force in the Sinai, and pledging both sides not to use force to resolve their differences. But other problems remained: the homeless Palestinian Arabs; Israeli occupation of Jerusalem and the West Bank; Israel's insistence on building settlements in occupied lands; and Arab threats to destroy the Jewish state. Furthermore, Soviet-American rivalry was still very much alive in the Middle East, especially after the exclusion of the Soviets from the peace negotiations and the defection of Egypt from the Soviet to the American side.

In Latin America, Nixon continued President Johnson's interventionist policies. Johnson had dispatched twenty thousand American troops to the Dominican Republic in 1965, when a leftist government under Juan Bosch seemed likely to supplant the regime of Washington's long-time ally Rafael Trujillo. (Bosch called the affair "a democratic revolution smashed by the leading democracy in the world.") And in a statement dubbed the Johnson Doctrine–that the United States would act to prevent Communists from ascending to office in the Western Hemisphere–the president had reiterated United States power in the region. Thus in 1970, when the people of Chile elected a Marxist president, Salvador Allende, it was all too easy for Nixon to see him as a Communist threat who had to be removed. Nixon suspended foreign aid to Chile, and the CIA began secret operations to disrupt the Chilean economy. Intelligence agents funneled money to newspapers critical of Allende and apparently encouraged military officers to stage a coup. In 1974 a military junta ousted and killed Allende and installed a brutal authoritarian regime in his place. Nixon and Kissinger privately pronounced their policy of "destabilization" successful, while publicly denying their role in the affair.

Intervention in Latin America

In the wake of the crisis, critics observed that the United States seemed no wiser for its experience in Vietnam. Why did the United States continue to meddle in the affairs of other nations? One explanation was that America continued to have an economic interest in them. In the early 1970s American companies like Coca-Cola and IBM earned over half their profits abroad. By the mid-1970s American investments abroad totaled over $133 billion, some of it in danger of expropriation. (Venezuela, for example, na-

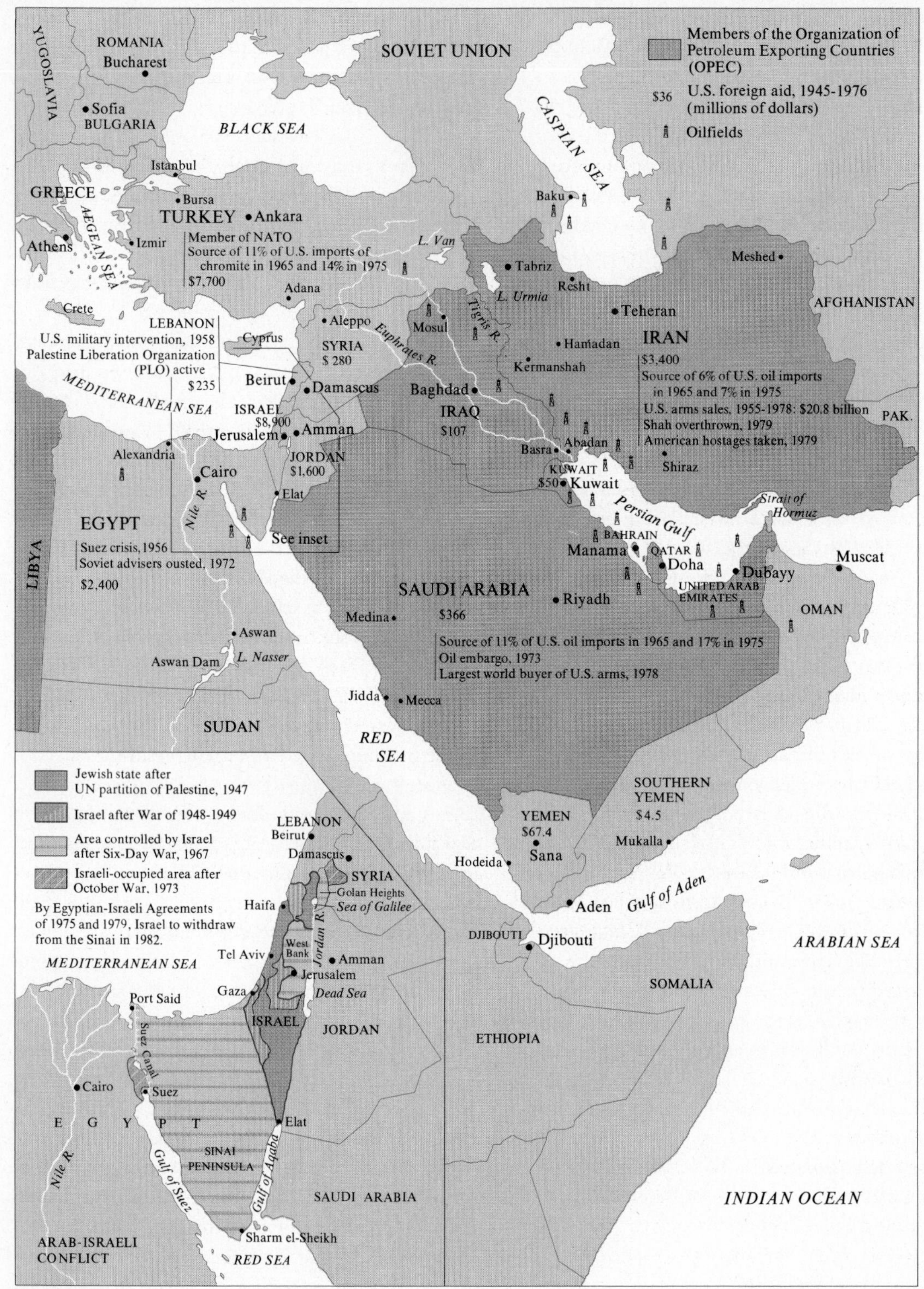

The Middle East

tionalized American oil holdings in 1976.) In Africa alone American investments climbed to nearly $4 billion, $1.5 billion of it in the internationally denounced Republic of South Africa, whose white government practiced *apartheid,* or stringent segregation of the black majority. And United States businesses still depended heavily on imported raw materials like tin, chrome, and manganese. Congressional investigating committees found that multinational corporations like Lockheed Aircraft and Exxon Oil had spent millions of dollars bribing foreign leaders in an effort to promote their own interests.

In this complicated economic environment, the Nixon-Kissinger strategy of a managed world order faltered. Skyrocketing OPEC oil prices fed double-digit inflation in energy-dependent Western nations. The United States ran up huge balance-of-payment deficits to import oil, and the dollar declined in value in foreign money markets. Meanwhile food shortages and famine stalked the poorest nations of the Third World. All these problems threatened world peace, said Kissinger, because economic instability creates political instability.

Like other Americans before him, Kissinger clung to the belief that the United States had the answers to most international problems. In his view the Third World was a mere sideshow to the Soviet-American confrontation; and the United States had to defend its interests there against nationalist challenges. Thus in the mid-1970s about 686,000 American military personnel were stationed abroad; the United States had military links with ninety-two nations; and American arms sales overseas climbed to about $10 billion. These so-called commitments were maintained not only to impress Moscow with American might and will, but to serve as a counterrevolutionary force against nationalist stirrings. As Kissinger put it, America was involved in Africa both to forestall foreign intervention and "to prevent the radicalization" of that continent. Nixon and Kissinger stood, then, in a long line of leaders who counterpoised American power against foreign peoples determined to decide their own fate. Even American allies thought the United States too meddlesome. "Living next to you is in some ways like sleeping with an elephant," said Canadian Prime Minister Pierre Trudeau. "No matter how friendly and even-tempered is the beast, if I can call it that, one is affected by every twitch and grunt."

Carter, Reagan, and continued global tension

When he took office in 1977 President Jimmy Carter vowed to reduce the American military presence overseas, cut back arms sales, and slow the nuclear arms race. He said he would continue détente and speed up the peace process in the Middle East. And he promised to be more understanding of Third World aspirations. Finally, "the soul of our foreign policy," Carter said, would be the championing of individual human rights abroad—the freedom to work, vote, worship, travel, speak out, and get a fair trial. A deeply religious man who wanted to infuse international relations with moral force, Carter intended to replace simple anti-Communism with a foreign policy Americans could be proud of. The president chose as his secretary of state the quiet veteran diplomat Cyrus Vance, who said he had learned from Vietnam that the United States could no longer behave as if it had answers for other peoples' problems.

Carter's human-rights policy

Doubters predicted that the human-rights thrust could not succeed, that it would make the United States into a moral policeman—in short, an interventionist. In fact, in four years Carter managed to free only a few political prisoners. The president also drew criticism for pursuing a double standard: applying the human-rights test to some nations (the Soviet Union, Argentina, and Chile) but not to American allies (the shah's Iran, the Philippines, and South Korea).

From the start Carter's statements were inconsistent, and administration officials squabbled among themselves. One source of the problem was Zbigniew Brzezinski, a Polish-born political scientist who became Carter's national security adviser. The stern-faced Brzezinski was an old-fashioned cold warrior, a critic of détente who tended to view foreign crises in globalist terms—that is, he blamed them on the Soviet Union. One State Department official likened him to a rat terrier constantly nipping at Vance's ankles. More and more Carter listened to Brzezinski; Vance resigned in April 1980, deploring the American drift toward military power as a substitute for diplomacy.

The nuclear-powered attack submarine U.S.S. *Baton Rouge,* launched in 1975. Built at a cost of over $200 million and capable of firing torpedoes or missiles, the vessel was one of several "Los Angeles class" submarines designed to counter Soviet naval strength. Because it did not carry ballistic missiles, the *Baton Rouge* was not prohibited by SALT. Courtesy Newport News Shipbuilding Company.

Despite Carter's goals, détente deteriorated and the Cold War revived during his administration. The president first angered the Soviets by calling on them to respect their citizens' human rights and tolerate dissent. Moscow told him to mind his own business. Then American officials denounced Russia for backing Cuban troops in Africa. And as Sino-American relations improved following the Nixon visit, Soviet leaders worried that the United States was playing its "China card"–building up their rival in order to threaten them.

A thaw came in 1979 when negotiations produced a new treaty, SALT II, that acknowledged Soviet-American nuclear parity. The agreement placed a ceiling of 2,250 delivery vehicles (long-range bombers, ICBMs, and submarine-based missiles) on each side and imposed limits on the number of warheads and the development of new kinds of nuclear weapons. Critics from the right charged that the treaty favored the Soviets; critics from the left protested that it did not go far enough toward quelling the arms race. As if to prove both sides correct, Carter soon announced that the United States would construct an expensive new MX missile system that would shuttle ICBMs back and forth along a vast maze of underground tunnels designed to confuse attackers. The president was gambling that the MX system would win votes for the SALT II treaty from skeptical senators without alarming the Soviets. He alarmed them.

As doubts about Senate ratification of SALT II mounted and Moscow fumed over the MX, events in Afghanistan led to a Soviet-American confrontation. In December 1979 the Red Army bludgeoned its way into the Soviets' southern neighbor to shore up the faltering Communist government, under siege by Moslem rebels. But the rebels persisted, with some aid from the CIA, and analysts predicted that the Soviet Union had sunk into its own Vietnam. Determined to make the U.S.S.R. "pay a concrete price for their aggression," an embittered Carter shelved SALT II, suspended shipments of grain and high-technology equipment to Russia, and launched an international boycott of the 1980 Summer Olympics in Moscow. In the United Nations the United States pressed for a resolution condemning the Soviet Union and was heartened by the positive response of many Third World nations. But all these efforts proved fruitless in that the Soviets refused to withdraw.

The president also announced what was quickly dubbed the Carter Doctrine: the United States would intervene, unilaterally and militarily if necessary, against further Soviet aggression in the petroleum-rich Persian Gulf. Prominent critics spoke out against the declaration. Senator Edward M. Kennedy declared that Americans would rather ration gas than spill the blood of their children for Middle Eastern oil. And George F. Kennan, the father of containment, who like Kennedy was critical of Soviet opportunism, called Carter's reaction exaggerated. It was wrong to assume that the Soviets would attack elsewhere in the Middle East, said Kennan. He faulted Carter for not trying diplomacy first, and for playing all his non-military cards prematurely. "Was this really mature statesmanship on our part?" Kennan asked.

Hostage crisis in Iran

Carter met his toughest test in Iran, where in early 1979 the shah was toppled from his throne by revolutionaries under the leadership of Ayatollah Ruhollah Khomeini, a wrathfully anti-American Moslem cleric. Khomeini remembered that the United States had restored the shah to his throne in 1953 after undermining the democratically elected Mossadegh government, and that the CIA had trained and supplied the shah's ruthless secret police (SAVAK). In November, after the exiled shah was admitted to the United States for medical treatment, mobs stormed the American embassy in Teheran and took American personnel as hostages, demanding the return of the shah for trial, along with his wealth. Although the Iranians eventually released a few of the prisoners, 52 others languished over a year under Iranian guard. Frequently blindfolded or bound, they were subjected to solitary confinement, beatings, and terrifying mock executions. All the while the theocratic Khomeini regime hurled insults at Washington.

Carter would not return the shah to Iran or apologize for past American involvement there. Unable to gain the hostages' freedom through public appeals, foreign emissaries, or United Nations delegations, the president took steps to isolate Iran economically. He froze Iranian assets in the United States and appealed to American allies, largely unsuccessfully, to reduce trade with the Moslem state. In April 1980, frustrated and at low ebb in the public opinion polls, Carter broke diplomatic relations with Iran and ordered a daring rescue mission that miscarried after an equipment failure in the sandy Iranian desert. During the hasty withdrawal two aircraft collided, killing eight American soldiers. The hostages were not freed until January 1981, 444 days after their capture. In the agreement that led to their release, finally reached through the good offices of Algerian diplomats, the United States unfroze Iranian assets and promised not to intervene again in Iran's internal affairs.

Carter brought to fruition Henry Kissinger's efforts to defuse the feud between Egypt and Israel. Through his personal diplomacy, Egyptian President Anwar Sadat and Israeli Prime Minister Menachem Begin met at Camp David in 1979. With the president's help they agreed to a treaty providing for Israel's phased withdrawal from the Sinai Peninsula, which it had occupied since 1967. Other Arab states denounced the agreement for not requiring Israel to relinquish other occupied territories. But the treaty at least ended warfare along one boundary in this troubled area of the world.

Carter also had some success elsewhere in the Third World. His appointment of Andrew Young, a black civil rights activist and congressman, as ambassador to the United Nations earned goodwill among developing nations. Young believed that the United States should stay out of local disputes, even if Communists were involved. Thus when warfare broke out in 1979 between Zaire and Angola, where Cuban troops and Soviet advisers were stationed, Young persuaded the president to stand back until the fighting subsided. Third World leaders were shocked, however, when Young was forced to resign in 1979 after meeting privately with representatives of the outlawed Palestine Liberation Organization.

Carter's achievements in Latin America

In Latin America, Carter concluded two treaties with Panama that provided for gradual return of the Canal Zone to that Central American nation. The treaties, endorsed by the Senate in 1978, aroused heated debate. Former governor of California Ronald Reagan, running hard for the presidency, went so far as to claim that the Canal Zone was sovereign American territory. But others saw that without the treaty the United States might have to fight the Panamanians, who longed for the restoration of territory they believed had been wrongfully severed from their nation. Carter also compromised with nationalist forces in Nicaragua, which had been ruled for decades by the dictatorial Somoza family. When leftist rebels overthrew Somoza in 1979, Carter at first tried to tame their radicalism, but failing, then recognized the revolutionary government. To have resisted it, the president argued, would have been to push Nicaragua into the Cuban or even the Soviet camp.

On November 4, 1979, an Iranian mob seized the American embassy in Teheran and took American personnel prisoner. Demonstrators then challenged President Jimmy Carter to do something about it. The crisis, which had its roots in close United States ties to the repressive government of the fallen shah, lasted more than a year. Wide World Photos.

Playing America's "China card" early in the game, Secretary of State Alexander M. Haig (1924–) journeyed to Beijing in mid-1981 to meet with the Chinese leader Deng Xiaoping. The two agreed Russia was a global bully and promised to cooperate in resisting "Soviet hegemonism." Haig also offered to sell weapons to China. Wide World Photos.

Carter's diplomatic record did not satisfy Americans who wanted superiority in foreign affairs—a reinstatement of the considerable military edge the United States had had in the early years of the Cold War. Critics chided the administration for a post-Vietnam "loss of will." As one Tennessee woman mused: "Growing up, we learned in history that America was the best in everything. We had the respect of the whole world. But where can you go today and be respected for being American?" Her bluntly chauvinistic attitude reflected a broad segment of American public opinion. An Oklahoma couple urged Carter to take up once again Teddy Roosevelt's big stick. "And club the hell out of them if you need to," grumbled the husband. "Our stick is down to a toothpick," his wife protested.

This nostalgia for old-fashioned American militancy found a ringing voice in President Ronald Reagan, elected in 1980 after a campaign charging that the United States was falling behind the Soviets in the arms race and retreating under fire from the Third World. Reagan promised to abandon détente and SALT II, dramatically increase the military budget, and support authoritarian right-wing governments that stood by American foreign policy. About the Vietnam War, Reagan said, "It is time we recognized that ours was, in truth, a noble cause." He named as secretary of state Alexander M. Haig, an overconfident former army general, NATO commander, Kissinger assistant, and aide to Nixon in the last days of Watergate. Haig believed that "there are more important things than peace . . . there are things which we Americans must be willing to fight for."

Reagan and Cold War revival

Important events

1952	Dwight D. Eisenhower elected president
1953	John Foster Dulles appointed secretary of state Josef Stalin dies Korean War ends CIA restores the shah of Iran to power
1954	United States intervenes in Guatemala *Brown* v. *Board of Education of Topeka* Geneva Conference on Indochina Soviet Union explodes a thermonuclear bomb SEATO formed (into effect 1955)
1955	Baghdad Pact formed Warsaw Pact formed
1956	De-Stalinization in Soviet Union Soviet Union invades Hungary Suez crisis
1957	Ghana becomes independent Eisenhower Doctrine Soviet Union launches Sputnik
1958	*The Ugly American* by William J. Lederer and Eugene Burdick U.S. intervenes in Lebanon
1959	Fidel Castro assumes power in Cuba Anti-American riots in Panama
1960	Eighteen colonies become independent nations U-2 incident John F. Kennedy elected president
1961	Peace Corps founded Alliance for Progress Bay of Pigs disaster Berlin crisis American military buildup in Vietnam
1962	Laos peace settlement Cuban missile crisis
1963	Test ban treaty Diem assassinated in Vietnam Kennedy assassinated; Lyndon B. Johnson assumes the presidency
1964	Tonkin Gulf Resolution
1965	U.S. intervenes in the Dominican Republic Operation Rolling Thunder in Vietnam
1965–66	Teach-ins protesting American intervention in Vietnam
1967	Peace rallies across the nation Six-Day War in the Middle East
1968	Tet offensive in Vietnam My Lai massacre Nuclear Non-Proliferation Treaty Soviet invasion of Czechoslovakia Vietnam peace talks open in Paris Richard M. Nixon elected president
1969	Henry A. Kissinger appointed national security affairs adviser Détente policy toward the Soviet Union announced
1970	Invasion of Cambodia Protests on college campuses
1971	*Pentagon Papers* released
1972	Nixon visits China SALT I treaty
1973	Vietnam cease-fire agreement U.S. helps overthrow government of Chile Arab-Israeli War Arab oil embargo
1973–74	Watergate crisis
1974	Nixon resigns the presidency; Gerald R. Ford becomes president

1975	Egyptian-Israeli peace agreement signed South Vietnam falls to Communists *Mayaguez* incident		SALT II nuclear-arms-control treaty signed Soviets invade Afghanistan Carter imposes grain embargo on Soviets and organizes boycott of Moscow Olympic Games
1976	Ford and Kissinger disavow détente in presidential campaign Jimmy Carter elected president	1980	Vance resigns; Edmund Muskie appointed secretary of state Ronald Reagan elected president
1977	Human-rights policy launched Cyrus Vance appointed secretary of state	1981	American hostages in Iran released after 444 days of captivity Alexander Haig appointed secretary of state U.S. becomes more deeply involved in El Salvador Defense budget sharply increased
1978	Panama Canal Treaties		
1979	Egyptian-Israeli peace accord struck at Camp David American embassy officials seized by mob in Teheran, Iran		

Like Haig, Reagan took a globalist view of international relations: "The Soviet Union underlies all the unrest that is going on. If they weren't engaged in this game of dominoes, there wouldn't be any hot spots in the world."

To counter the perceived Soviet threat, the Reagan administration sent military personnel to civil-war-torn El Salvador and Liberia, and negotiated for bases in the Indian Ocean. Reagan and Haig also lectured Moscow in chilling Cold War language, blaming Soviet leaders for fostering international terrorism and for willingness "to commit any crime, to lie, to cheat" to advance worldwide Communist revolution. In a contradictory move early in 1981, however, the president lifted the grain embargo against the Soviet Union—apparently to fulfill a campaign promise to American farmers.

But globalist theories would not stand up for Reagan and Haig in the revolutionary world of the 1980s. American power had declined, but not because Washington stood idly by while the Soviets raced to start fires around the globe. Instead, there was inevitable growth in the power of nations—including allies—recovering from the devastation of the Second World War. There was the rise of the Third World out of the ashes of old colonial empires. And there was growing consumption, and hence a shortage of energy, which made the industrial United States necessarily dependent on other nations. Military expansion could not reverse these trends. "His is a kind of 1952 world," said a former adviser of Reagan. How similar indeed seemed the American outlook of the 1980s to that of the early 1950s. Yet the world had markedly changed.

Suggestions for further reading

General

Stephen Ambrose, *Rise to Globalism,* 2nd ed. (1980); Richard Barnet, *Roots of War* (1973); Robert A. Divine, *Foreign Policy and U.S. Presidential Elections, 1940–1960,* 2 vols. (1974); John L. Gaddis, *Russia, the Soviet Union, and the United States* (1978); Alexander L. George and Richard Smoke, *Deterrence in American Foreign Policy* (1974); Robert C. Johansen, *The National Interest and the Human Interest* (1980); Walter LaFeber, *America, Russia, and the Cold War, 1945–1980,* 4th ed. (1980); James A. Nathan and James K. Oliver, *United States Foreign Policy and World Order,* 2nd ed.

(1981); Kenneth A. Oye et al., *Eagle Entangled* (1979); David M. Potter, *People of Plenty* (1954); Jack Schick, *The Berlin Crisis, 1958–1962* (1974); Ronald Steel, *Walter Lippmann and the American Century* (1980); Adam B. Ulam, *Expansion and Coexistence*, 2nd ed. (1974); Sandy Vogelgesang, *American Dream, Global Nightmare* (1980); William Appleman Williams, *Empire as a Way of Life* (1981); Lawrence Wittner, *Rebels Against War* (1974).

Eisenhower-Dulles diplomacy

Charles Alexander, *Holding the Line* (1975); Blanche W. Cook, *The Declassified Eisenhower* (1981); Robert A. Divine, *Eisenhower and the Cold War* (1981); Louis Gerson, *John Foster Dulles* (1967); Fred I. Greenstein, "Eisenhower as an Activist President," *Political Science Quarterly*, 94 (1979–1980), 575–599; Michael Guhin, *John Foster Dulles* (1972); Townsend Hoopes, *The Devil and John Foster Dulles* (1973); Emmet John Hughes, *The Ordeal of Power* (1963); Herbert S. Parmet, *Eisenhower and the Great Crusades* (1972).

Kennedy and Johnson diplomacy

Graham Allison, *Essence of Decision: Explaining the Cuban Missile Crisis* (1971); Warren I. Cohen, *Dean Rusk* (1980); Herbert Dinerstein, *The Making of a Missile Crisis* (1976); Robert A. Divine, ed., *The Cuban Missile Crisis* (1971); Philip Geyelin, *Lyndon B. Johnson and the World* (1966); David Halberstam, *The Best and the Brightest* (1972); Jim Heath, *Decade of Disillusionment* (1975); Doris Kearns, *Lyndon Johnson and the American Dream* (1976); Thomas G. Paterson, "Bearing the Burden: A Critical Look at JFK's Foreign Policy," *Virginia Quarterly Review*, 54 (1978), 193–212; Walt W. Rostow, *Diffusion of Power* (1972); Arthur M. Schlesinger, Jr., *A Thousand Days* (1965); Arthur M. Schlesinger, Jr., *Robert Kennedy and His Times* (1978); Richard Walton, *Cold War and Counterrevolution* (1972).

The United States and the Third World

Rudolf von Albertini, *Decolonization* (1981); Richard J. Barnet, *Intervention and Revolution*, rev. ed. (1972); Carl N. Degler, "The American Past: An Unsuspected Obstacle in Foreign Affairs," *American Scholar*, 32 (1963), 192–209; John L. S. Girling, *America and the Third World* (1980); Melvin Gurtov, *The United States Against the Third World* (1974); Gabriel Kolko, *The Roots of American Foreign Policy* (1969); Richard B. Morris, *The Emerging Nations and the American Revolution* (1970); Robert A. Packenham, *Liberal America and the Third World* (1973); Ronald Steel, *Pax Americana* (1967); Jennifer S. Whitaker, ed., *Africa and the United States* (1978).

Latin America

Samuel Baily, *The United States and the Development of South America, 1945–1975* (1977); Cole Blasier, *Hovering Giant* (1974); Richard R. Fagen, ed., *Capitalism and the State in U.S.-Latin American Relations* (1979); Walter LaFeber, *The Panama Canal* (1979); Robert H. McBride, ed., *Mexico and the United States* (1981); Ramon Ruiz, *Cuba: The Making of a Revolution* (1968); Peter Wyden, *Bay of Pigs* (1979).

Middle East

Chester L. Cooper, *The Lion's Last Roar: Suez, 1956* (1978); Michael Ledeen and William Lewis, *Debacle: The American Failure in Iran* (1981); George Lenczowski, *The Middle East in World Affairs*, 4th ed. (1980); William B. Quandt, *Decade of Decision: American Policy toward the Arab-Israeli Conflict, 1967–1976* (1977); Barry Rubin, *Paved with Good Intentions: The American Experience and Iran* (1980); Amin Saikel, *The Rise and Fall of the Shah* (1980); Robert W. Stookey, *America and the Arab States* (1975).

Southeast Asia and the Vietnam War

Chester Cooper, *The Lost Crusade* (1970); Frances FitzGerald, *Fire in the Lake* (1972); Leslie H. Gelb and Richard K. Betts, *The Irony of Vietnam: The System Worked* (1979); George C. Herring, *America's Longest War* (1979); George M. Kahin and John W. Lewis, *The United States in Vietnam*, rev. ed. (1969); Anthony Lake, ed., *The Vietnam Legacy* (1976); Guenter Lewy, *America in Vietnam* (1978); Archimedes L. A. Patti, *Why Viet Nam?* (1980); Herbert Y. Schandler, *The Unmaking of a President: Lyndon Johnson and Vietnam* (1977); William Shawcross, *Sideshow: Kissinger, Nixon, and the Destruction of Cambodia* (1979); James C. Thompson, *Rolling Thunder* (1980).

Nixon, Kissinger, and détente

Richard J. Barnet, *The Giants: Russia and America* (1977); Thomas M. Franck and Edward Weisband, *Foreign Policy by Congress* (1979); Charles Gati and Toby T. Gati, *Debate Over Détente* (1977); Lloyd C. Gardner, ed., *The Great Nixon Turnaround* (1973); Stanley Hoffmann, *Primacy or World Order* (1978); Stanley Hoffmann, "The Case of Dr. Kissinger," *New York Review of Books*, 26 (6 December 1979), 14ff.; Bernard Kalb and Marvin Kalb, *Kissinger* (1974); Roger Morris, *Uncertain Greatness: Henry Kissinger and American Foreign Policy* (1977); Fred Warner Neal, ed., *Detente or Debacle* (1979); Edward R. F. Sheehan, *The Arabs, Israelis, and Kissinger* (1976); John G. Stoessinger, *Henry Kissinger* (1976); Tad Szulc, *The Illusion of Peace* (1978); Garry Wills, *Nixon Agonistes* (1970).

Nuclear arms competition

Edgar M. Bottome, *The Balance of Terror* (1971); Robert A. Divine, *Blowing on the Wind* (1978); Jerome H. Kahan, *Security in the Nuclear Age* (1975); Michael Mandelbaum, *The Nuclear Question* (1979); John Newhouse, *Cold Dawn: The Story of SALT* (1973); Samuel B. Payne, Jr., *The Soviet Union and SALT* (1980); George Quester, *Nuclear Diplomacy: The First 25 Years* (1970); George Quester, *The Politics of Nuclear Proliferation* (1973); Chalmers M. Roberts, *The Nuclear Years* (1970); Strobe Talbott, *Endgame: The Inside Story of SALT II* (1979); Thomas W. Wolfe, *The SALT Experience* (1979).

The world economy

Richard J. Barnet, *The Lean Years* (1980); Richard J. Barnet and Ronald Müller, *The Global Reach: The Power of the Multinational Corporations* (1974); Lloyd N. Cutler, *Global Interdependence and the Multinational Firm* (1978); Alfred E. Eckes, *A Search for Solvency: Bretton Woods and the International Monetary System, 1941–1971* (1975); Alfred E. Eckes, *The U.S. and the Global Struggle for Minerals* (1979); Burton I. Kaufman, *The Oil Cartel Case* (1978); Stephen D. Krasner, *Defending the National Interest* (1978); William Paddock and Paul Paddock, *Time of Famines* (1976); Joan E. Spero, *The Politics of International Economic Relations,* 2nd ed. (1981); Mira Wilkins, *The Maturing of Multinational Enterprise* (1974).

The interior of a home in southern Appalachia. In the early 1960s, middle-class whites were shocked to discover that despite economic prosperity, poverty still existed in the United States. Charles Harbutt/Magnum Photos.

education or less, and one-fourth lived in households headed by a single woman. For all these people, there was little cause for hope. The Bureau constructed a budget to show what a poor family of four could afford: one book a year; a new car every twelve to eighteen years; no telephone; a movie once every three weeks; a skirt every five years for the wife; a wool suit every two or three years for the husband.

Naturally, the number of people living in poverty fluctuated with the economy. During the postwar years poverty was most widespread during the recession of 1950, when 36 percent of Americans were classified as poor. With the return of prosperity during the Korean War, the percentage declined to 33; by 1962 it had fallen to about 25 percent. Still, the introduction of automation was creating a class of chronically unemployed unskilled workers. Following the Second World War, unemployment rose steadily from 3.1 percent in 1949 to 5.1 percent in 1958 and over 7 percent in 1961. It was evident too that many people slipped into poverty as a result of divorce, desertion, or a death in the family.

One of the least-known effects of economic hardship on the poor has been physical and emotional illness. A study done in the late 1950s in New Haven, Connecticut, found that the rate of treated psychiatric illness was three times as high for the lowest fifth of income earners as it was for the upper-middle and upper classes. The Cornell University Department of Psychiatry described the "low social economic status individual" as "rigid, suspicious," and having "a fatalistic outlook on life. . . . They are prone to depression, have feelings of futility, lack of belongingness . . . and a lack of trust in others."

In 1962, with the publication of Michael Harrington's *The Other America,* more and more people began to ask whether anyone in the United States should have to suffer so. America's poor, wrote Harrington, were "the strangest poor in the history of mankind": they "exist within the most powerful and rich society the world has ever known. Their misery has continued while the majority of the nation talked of itself as being 'affluent.' " Crowded into the cities or living in rural isolation, the poor had "dropped out of sight and out of mind; they were without their own political voice." With the election of John F. Kennedy, however, these forgotten Americans caught a glimmer of hope.

Walking to their limousine on the way to the inauguration, president-elect John F. Kennedy (1917–1963) and his wife Jacqueline seemed to symbolize youthful energy and idealism. Kennedy's inaugural promise of a New Frontier gave hope to nonwhites and the poor. San Francisco Public Library.

Kennedy and the New Frontier

He was, as Norman Mailer wrote of President John F. Kennedy, "our leading man." The handsome, vigorous new chief executive was young, the first president born in the twentieth century. An intellectual, an eloquent writer, and a patron of the arts, he brought wit and sophistication to the White House.

Kennedy had been born to wealth and politics. His Irish-American grandfather had been mayor of Boston; his millionaire father, Joseph P. Kennedy, served as ambassador to Great Britain. In 1946 the young Kennedy, home from the Second World War a hero, continued the family tradition by campaigning in the Irish-American neighborhoods of South Boston for a seat in the House of Representatives. He won easily.

As a Democratic politician, Kennedy inherited the New Deal commitment to the welfare state. He generally cast liberal votes in line with the prolabor sentiments of his low-income, blue-collar constituents. But on issues of no direct concern to his district—flood control, farm price supports, the Tennessee Valley Authority—he cast his votes with some of the most conservative members of Congress. Kennedy avoided controversial issues like civil rights and the censure of Joseph McCarthy. Though he won a Pulitzer Prize for his book *Profiles in Courage* (1956), a study of politicians who had acted on principle, some critics complained that he himself showed too much profile and not enough courage. Kennedy nevertheless enjoyed an enthusiastic following, especially after his landslide re-election to the Senate in 1958.

Election of 1960

Kennedy's rivals for the 1960 Democratic presidential nomination included Senator Hubert H. Humphrey of Minnesota, the tireless advocate of civil rights and social justice, and Lyndon Baines Johnson of Texas, the powerful majority leader of the Senate. Kennedy defeated his better-known rivals in several key primary elections, and received the party's nod at its convention. Because the Democrats feared losing the South to the Republicans, Kennedy offered Johnson the vice-presidential nomination. The two campaigned for federal aid to education, medical care for the elderly, an end to racial discrimination, and government action to end the recession the country was suffering.

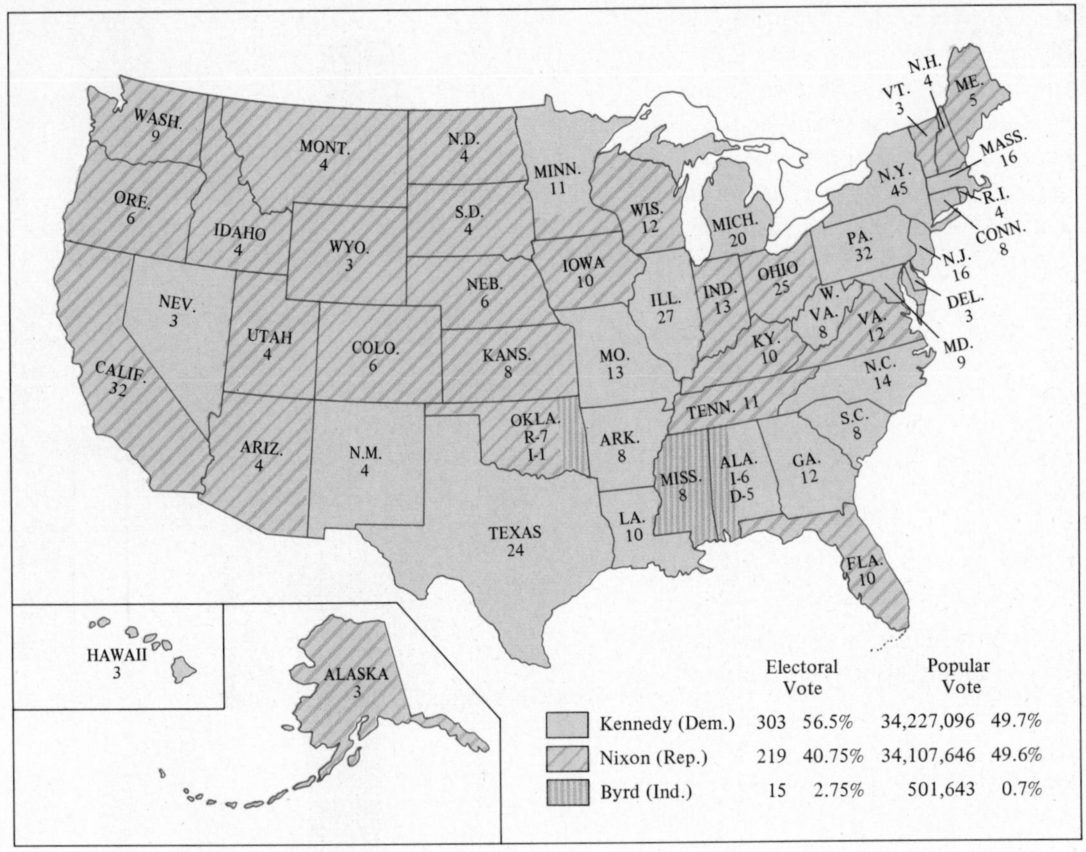

Presidential election, 1960

Kennedy's major liability was his Roman Catholicism. But he addressed the issue head-on, boldly traveling to the Bible belt to do so. Speaking to a group of ministers in Houston, Kennedy expressed his commitment to "an America where the separation of church and state is absolute." Were he elected, Kennedy said, he would take his orders from the American people, not from the Pope. Kennedy scored points with black voters when he responded to an appeal to help the black Baptist minister and civil rights activist Martin Luther King, Jr., gain release from a Georgia county jail. He also promised to sign an executive order forbidding segregation in federally subsidized housing.

Partly in response to these actions, blacks in inner cities turned out in large numbers for Kennedy, providing him with crucial electoral margins in Illinois, Texas, and elsewhere. Kennedy defeated the Republican nominee, Vice President Richard M. Nixon, by a razor-slim margin: 49.7 to 49.6 percent of the popular vote. The electoral college margin, 303 to 219, was actually much closer than the numbers suggest (see map). Nixon would have been the victor with only 9,000 more votes in Illinois and 56,000 more in Texas. But Kennedy's civil rights stand, combined with the economic recession, the U-2 incident, and Kennedy's alarmist charge that the United States was trailing behind the Soviet Union in the missile race (see page 897), spelled Nixon's downfall. Nixon also suffered from an unsavory TV image (he came across as surly and heavy-jowled in televised debates with Kennedy) and a tepid endorsement from outgoing President Eisenhower. Asked to list the significant decisions Nixon had been responsible for as vice president, Eisenhower reportedly replied, "If you give me a week, I might think of one."

In a departure from the Eisenhower administration's staid, conservative image, Kennedy surrounded himself with "the best and the brightest," young men of intellectual verve and impeccable cre-

At the Washington Monument in 1963, the Reverend Martin Luther King, Jr. (1929–1968) moved a crowd of 250,000 with his most famous speech. "I have a dream," King declared fervently, "that my four little children will one day live in a nation where they will not be judged by the color of their skin but by the content of their character." Bob Adelman/Magnum Photos.

"Best and the brightest"

dentials. (On the other hand, Kennedy appointed no women to significant posts.) Secretary of Defense Robert McNamara, forty-four, had been an assistant professor at Harvard at age twenty-four and later the whiz-kid president of the Ford Motor Company. Kennedy's special assistant for national security affairs, McGeorge Bundy, forty-one, had become a dean at Harvard at age thirty-four with only a bachelor's degree. Bundy's top assistant was Walt Rostow, a forty-one-year-old economic historian from MIT who had written a major Cold War study, *The Stages of Economic Growth: A Non-Communist Manifesto.*

Kennedy's program, the New Frontier, was immensely ambitious, promising no less than civil rights for blacks; federal aid to farmers and to education; medical care for all; and the abolition of poverty. But Kennedy promised far more than he could deliver. Long-time members of Congress saw him and his administration as publicity-hungry. Some also feared the president would seek federal aid to parochial schools. The result was the defeat of federal aid to education and of a Kennedy-sponsored boost in the minimum wage. By August 1961, eight months into his first term, it was evident that Kennedy lacked the ability to move Congress.

The new president pursued civil rights with a notable lack of vigor. Not until autumn 1962 did he sign the order forbidding segregation in federally subsidized housing that he had promised blacks during the campaign. Meanwhile he appointed some southern segregationists to the federal bench.

Regardless of lukewarm leadership from the White House, black civil rights activists continued their

Civil Rights movement

struggle through the tactic of nonviolent civil disobedience. Volunteers organized by King's Southern Christian Leadership Conference (SCLC) deliberately violated segregation laws by sitting-in at whites-only lunch counters, libraries, and bus stations throughout the South. When arrested they went to jail as an act of conscience. Freedom Riders with the racially integrated Congress of Racial Equality (CORE) braved attacks by white mobs for daring to desegregate interstate transportation. Meanwhile black students in the South were joining the Student Non-Violent Coordinating Committee (SNCC). More than any other volunteers, it was the SNCC field workers who walked the dusty back roads of Mississippi and Georgia, encouraging blacks to resist segregation and register to vote. The children mostly of southern black maids, laborers, and other low-income workers, SNCC workers understood from experience how racism, powerlessness, and poverty intersected in the lives of Afro-Americans.

As the civil rights movement gained momentum in the early 1960s, President Kennedy gradually made a commitment to first-class citizenship for blacks. In September 1962 he ordered U.S. marshals to protect and assist James Meredith, the first black student to attend the University of Mississippi. Under court order the following spring, federal officials ignored the defiant governor of Alabama, George C. Wallace, and forced the desegregation of the University of Alabama. In June 1963 Kennedy finally requested legislation to outlaw the segregation of public accommodations. When more than 250,000 people, black and white, gathered at the Lincoln Memorial for a March on Washington that August, they did so with the knowledge that President Kennedy was at last on their side.

Meanwhile, television news shows brought civil rights struggles into Americans' homes. The story was sometimes grisly. In 1963 Medgar Evers, director of the NAACP in Mississippi, was murdered in his own driveway. That same year police under the command of Sheriff "Bull" Connor of Birmingham, Alabama, attacked civil rights demonstrators with snarling dogs, firehoses, and cattle prods. And William Moore, a white postman who attempted a one-person freedom march from Baltimore to Mississippi carrying a sandwich board that read "Eat at Joe's, Both Black and White" and "Equal Rights for All," was shot and killed just after entering Alabama.

Then, while Kennedy's public accommodations bill was being held up by a Senate filibuster, two horrifying events helped to convince reluctant politicians that action on civil rights was long overdue. In September white terrorists exploded a bomb during Sunday-morning services at Birmingham's 16th Street Baptist Church. Sunday school was in session, and four black girls were killed. A little more than two months later, on November 22, 1963, John Kennedy was assassinated in Dallas.

Assassination of President Kennedy

Kennedy's murder still baffles many Americans. Was the accused assassin, Lee Harvey Oswald, acting alone or as part of a conspiracy? Was he the only gunman, or were there two? What was Oswald's motive? Whatever the answers, Kennedy's death traumatized the entire nation. In the following days people watched countless TV replays of the stricken president slumping forward in his open-topped limousine. On November 24 they watched numbly as Oswald himself was shot dead by Jack Ruby, a nightclub owner and small-time Mafia figure. The same question was asked: what was Ruby's motive? Some of America's postwar confidence seemed to be riding on the horse-drawn caisson that carried Kennedy's body to the grave. "In retrospect," the British journalist Godfrey Hodgson has written, "people looked back to Friday, November 22, 1963, as the end of a time of hope, the beginning of a time of troubles."

Historians have wondered what John Kennedy would have accomplished had he lived. Although his legislative achievements were meager, he inspired idealism in Americans. When Kennedy said in his inaugural address, "Ask not what your country can do for you. Ask what you can do for your country," tens of thousands of Americans responded by volunteering to spend two years of their lives in the Peace Corps. And the new president created a sense of national purpose through his vigorous support of the space program. Americans beamed when on February 20, 1962, Marine Lieutenant Colonel John Glenn orbited the globe in a space capsule. In his last few months in office, Kennedy had begun to grow as president, making a moving appeal for racial equality and softening his views on the Cold War. And there was the aura of the Kennedys. James Reston of the New York *Times* called Kennedy "a story-book President," handsome, graceful, "with poetry on his tongue and a radiant young woman at his side."

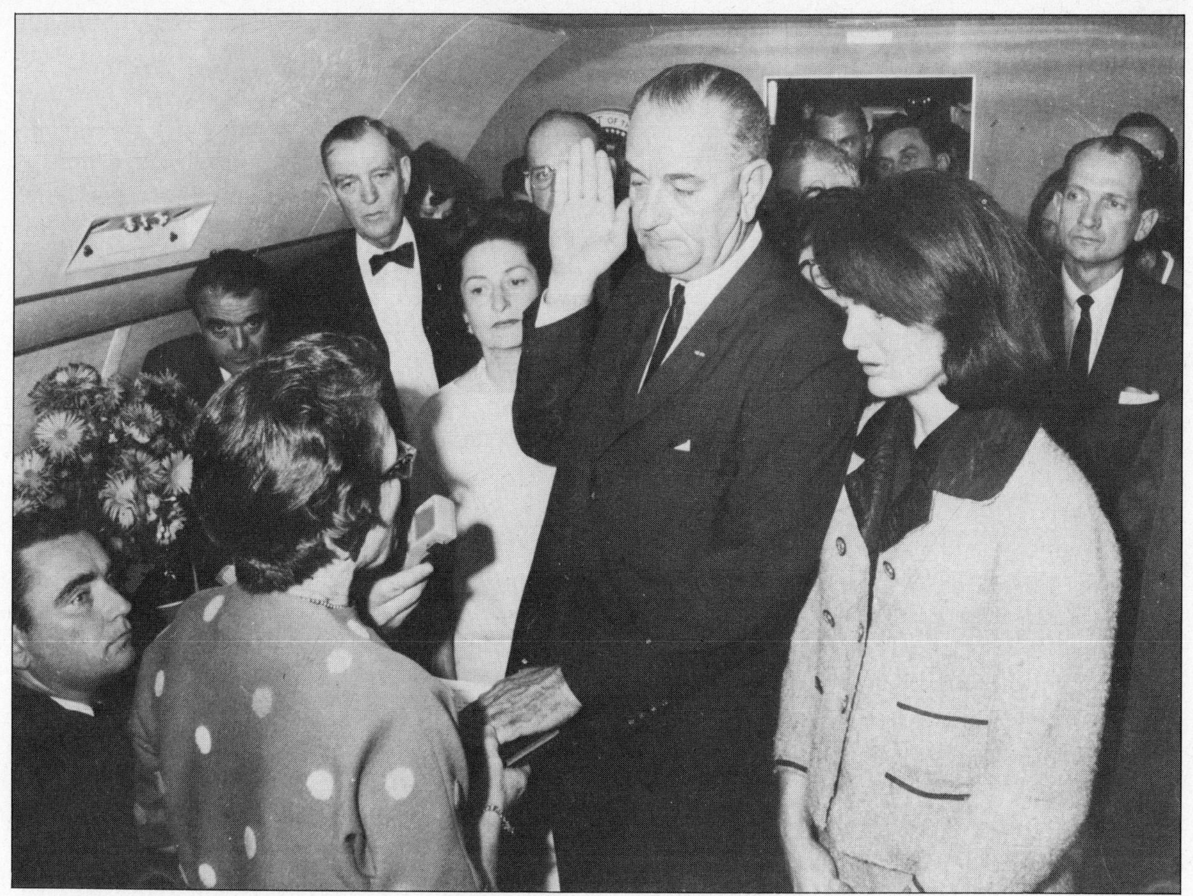

Shortly after the assassination of President Kennedy, Vice President Lyndon B. Johnson (1908–1973) was sworn in as the thirty-sixth president of the United States. The ceremony took place on the presidential plane as it returned to Washington from Dallas. Standing on Johnson's right is his wife, Lady Bird; on his left , a stunned Jacqueline Kennedy. Wide World Photos.

Johnson and the Great Society

The new president, Lyndon Johnson, was a big man physically and a passionate one emotionally. The Senate majority leader from 1954 to 1960, he knew how to manipulate people and power to achieve his ends. "This ponderous . . . Texan knows more about the sources of power in the political world of Washington than any President in this century," wrote columnists Rowland Evans and Robert Novak. "He can be gentle and solicitous as a nurse, but as ruthless and deceptive as a riverboat gambler." In the aftermath of the assassination, Johnson determined to unite the country behind the unfulfilled legislative program of the martyred president. But more than that, he wanted to realize Roosevelt and Truman's unmet goals. He called his new program the Great Society.

Civil Rights Act of 1964

Johnson made civil rights his top legislative priority. "No memorial oration or eulogy," he told a joint session of Congress five days after the assassination, "could more eloquently honor President Kennedy's memory than the earliest passage of the civil rights bill." It was a happy coincidence for the civil rights movement that Johnson, a southerner, had become president. According to Clarence Mitchell, chief lobbyist for the NAACP, Johnson "made a greater contribution to giving a dignified and hopeful status to Negroes in the United States than any other President, including Lincoln, Roosevelt and Kennedy." Within months Johnson had signed into law the Civil Rights Act of 1964, which outlawed not only segregation in public accommodations, but job discrimination against blacks and women. The act authorized the government to withhold funds from public agencies that discriminated on the basis of race, and it gave the attorney general powers to guarantee voting rights and end school segregation.

Johnson also steered through Congress the Economic Opportunity Act of 1964, which allocated almost $1 billion to fight poverty. Forty percent of the money was earmarked for youth training, 30 percent for community action programs, and the remainder for family farms, small businesses, and adult training programs. The act, which became the opening salvo in Johnson's War on Poverty, promised "to eliminate the paradox of poverty in the nation by opening to everyone the opportunity to live in decency and dignity." Finally, Johnson secured the $12 billion tax cut for which Kennedy had labored unsuccessfully.

In the year following Kennedy's death, Johnson sought to govern by consensus, by appealing to the shared values and aspirations of the majority of the nation. Judging by his lopsided victory over his Republican opponent in 1964, Senator Barry Goldwater of Arizona, he succeeded. Johnson garnered 61 percent of the popular vote and the electoral votes of all but six states. Goldwater's narrowness certainly enhanced Johnson's appeal. The Republican candidate alienated voters by urging the abolition of Social Security, the Tennessee Valley Authority, and the postal service, and he impressed them as reckless and provocative when he advocated the use of nuclear weapons in Vietnam. Republican leaders from the liberal eastern wing of the party either refused to support Goldwater or gave him half-hearted endorsements. He seemed to have solid support only in a few states in the Southwest and South.

Election of 1964

Riding on Johnson's coattails, the Democrats won staggering majorities in both the House (295 to 140) and the Senate (68 to 32). Johnson knew that the moment for reform had arrived. "Hurry, boys, hurry," Johnson told his staff just after the election. "Get that legislation up to the Hill and out. Eighteen months from now ol' Landslide Lyndon will be Lame-Duck Lyndon." Congress responded in 1965 and 1966 with the most sweeping reform legislation since 1935. Skillfully guided by Johnson, the liberal Democratic majorities passed a remarkable 69 percent of the president's legislative proposals. The powerful old coalition of southern Democrats and conservative Republicans, which had had its way on 74 percent of House roll-call votes in 1961 and 63 percent in 1963, was victorious on only 25 percent of the votes in 1965.

Three of the bills enacted in 1965 were legislative milestones. The Medicare program insured the elderly against medical and hospital bills. The Elementary and Secondary Education Act became the first general program of federal aid to education. And the Voting Rights Act of 1965 empowered the attorney general to supervise voter registration in areas where fewer than half the minority residents of voting age were registered (see map). When Johnson became president, only one-fourth of the South's black population was registered to vote; when he left office in 1969 the percentage was approaching two-thirds. Other accomplishments included a Teacher Corps to work in impoverished school districts; construction funds for colleges and universities; college scholarships and loans; economic aid to depressed regions; liberalization of immigration laws; expansion of the national parks; and appropriations for the most ambitious federal housing program since 1949.

Perhaps even more ambitious was Johnson's War on Poverty. Because the gross national product had increased from $503 billion to $807 billion between 1961 and 1967, Johnson and his advisers reasoned that the government could expect a "fiscal dividend" of several billion dollars in additional tax revenues. They decided to spend the extra money to wipe out poverty through education and job training programs. As the War on Poverty evolved in 1965 and 1966, it included the Job Corps and Neighborhood Youth Corps, to provide marketable skills, work experience, remedial education, and counseling for young people; the Work-Experience Program for unemployed fathers and mothers; Project Head Start, to prepare low-income preschoolers for grade school; and Upward Bound, for impoverished high school

War on Poverty

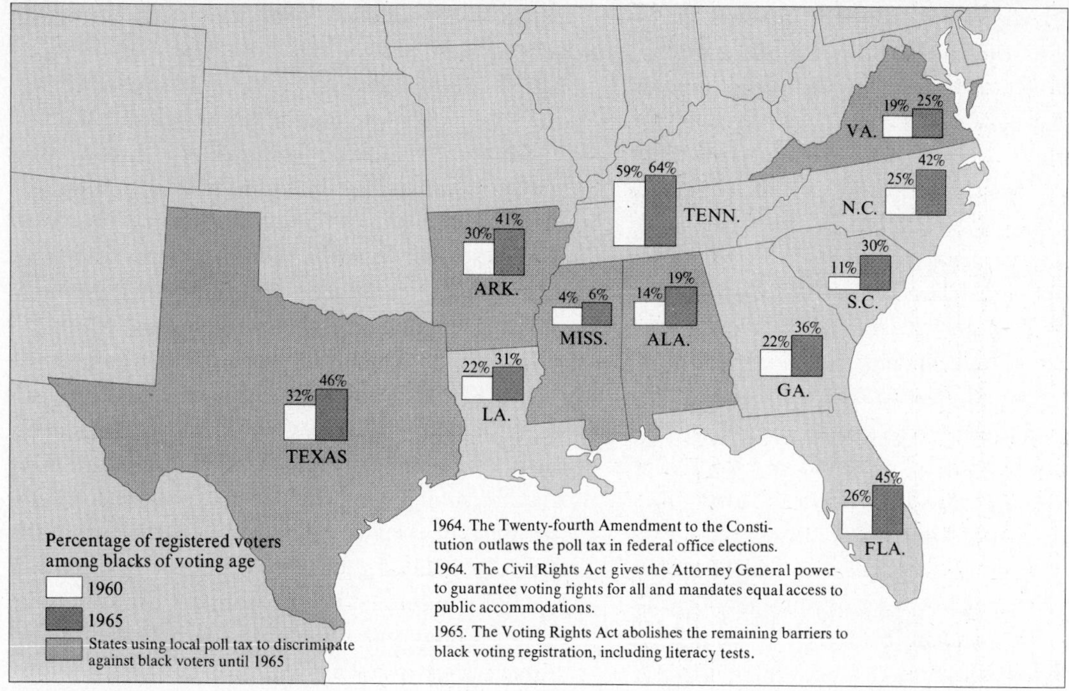

Black voting rights, 1960–1965

students who aspired to a college education. In an innovation that was to arouse the ire of mayors and city councils, these programs encouraged "maximum feasible participation" by the poor in the administration of community action programs. Other antipoverty programs were Legal Services for the Poor; Volunteers in Service to America (VISTA); and the Model Cities program, which directed federal funds toward the upgrading of employment, housing, education, and health in targeted neighborhoods.

In tandem with general economic improvement, the War on Poverty did help to reduce hunger and suffering. The tax cut and fresh infusions of federal funds for defense ended the recession of 1960 and 1961. The social welfare budget soared, and the number of people living in poverty dropped from an estimated 42.5 million in 1962 to 22 million in 1967. Never had Democratic liberals been so confident of their ability to control the swings of the business cycle through Keynesian deficit financing.

Johnson had the good fortune to preside at the same time as a liberal Supreme Court. In 1962, led by Chief Justice Earl Warren, the Court began handing down a series of liberal decisions.

Liberal rulings of the Warren Court

In *Baker* v. *Carr* (1962) and subsequent rulings, the Court declared that the principle of "one person, one vote" must prevail at both state and national levels, thus forcing reapportionment of state legislatures. And it outlawed required Bible readings and prayers in public schools, explaining that such practices placed an "indirect coercive pressure upon religious minorities" (1962).

In 1965 the Court declared that a person did not have to register with the government as a member of a subversive organization, for to do so would violate constitutional safeguards against self-incrimination. It also invalidated substantial portions of the Alien Registration (Smith) Act, which made membership in the Communist party a criminal act. It upheld the Civil Rights Act of 1964 and the Voting Rights Act of 1965, and in *Loving* v. *Virginia* (1967) struck down a state law prohibiting interracial marriage. The Court broadened the interpretation of the Fourteenth Amendment by outlawing segregation in private businesses. And in several rulings that particularly upset conservatives, the Court decreed that books, magazines, and films could not be banned as obscene unless they were "found to be utterly without redeeming social value."

Perhaps most controversial was the Court's transformation of the criminal justice system. Beginning with *Gideon* v. *Wainwright* (1963), the Court ruled that a poor person charged with a felony had the right to a state-appointed lawyer. In *Escobedo* v. *Illinois* (1964), it decreed that the accused had the right to counsel during interrogation, and could remain silent if he or she chose. And in *Miranda* v. *Arizona* (1966), it added that criminal suspects had to be informed by the police not only that they could see a lawyer and remain silent, but that any statements they made could be used against them. Critics denounced the decisions as a victory for criminals, and the John Birch Society, an extreme right-wing organization, began a campaign to impeach Earl Warren.

The period of liberal ascendancy was short-lived. Disillusioned with America's deepening involvement in Vietnam (see Chapter 32), many of Johnson's allies rejected both him and his liberal consensus. At the same time, black civil rights activists scrapped their dream of a racially integrated society and proclaimed the rise of Black Power. Johnson, who had won an overwhelming victory in the election of 1964, less than four years later recognized the depths of his unpopularity and announced that he would not be a candidate for re-election.

Black power and black separatism

Even as the civil rights movement was registering moral and legislative victories, some activists were beginning to grumble that the federal government was not to be trusted. During the Mississippi Summer Project of 1964, hundreds of college-age volunteers from the North had joined SNCC and CORE field workers to establish "freedom schools" for black children. Many of these volunteers believed that the Federal Bureau of Investigation was hostile to the civil rights movement. They alleged that FBI Director J. Edgar Hoover was a racist, and that most FBI agents in the South were native-born white southerners who abhorred the idea of racial equality. They cited incidents in which FBI agents had stood by while nonviolent protesters were attacked by white mobs and police. And they were disturbed by rumors, later proved true, that Hoover had wiretapped and bugged Martin Luther King, Jr.'s home and planted stories in the newspapers about his sexual improprieties. Why, activists asked themselves, had President Johnson allowed Hoover and his agents to remain in office?

Indeed, some FBI informants had not only joined the Ku Klux Klan; they had reportedly become leaders of the terrorist group. One of them had organized the bombing of Birmingham's Sixteenth Street Baptist Church in 1963. Small wonder that during summer 1964 there was an upsurge in racist violence in the South, particularly in Mississippi. White vigilantes bombed and burned two dozen black churches there between June and October, and three civil rights workers were murdered in Philadelphia, Mississippi, by a mob that included sheriff's deputies. Instead of protecting the civil rights workers, southern police, county sheriffs, and state troopers had assaulted and arrested them.

Amid the terror, SNCC volunteers joined with black Mississippians to establish the Mississippi Freedom Democratic Party (MFDP) and sent an opposition delegation to the Democratic national convention. Arguing that the MFDP supported civil rights, while the regular Democratic organization was vehemently segregationist, the MFDP demanded that the convention honor its credentials. But Johnson, fearful of alienating southern whites and more committed to consensus than to civil rights, offered the MFDP only two token at-large seats. The Democratic commitment to racial equality seemed questionable.

The year 1964 also brought the first of the "long hot summers" of race riots in northern cities. In Harlem and Rochester, New York, and in several cities in New Jersey, black anger exploded. A cleaning woman in Harlem expressed the rage she felt. "I clean the white man's dirt all the time," she said with disgust. When the riot began, "something happened to me. I felt like something was crawling in me, like the whole damn world was no good, and the little kids and the big ones and all of us was going to get killed.

Explosion of black anger

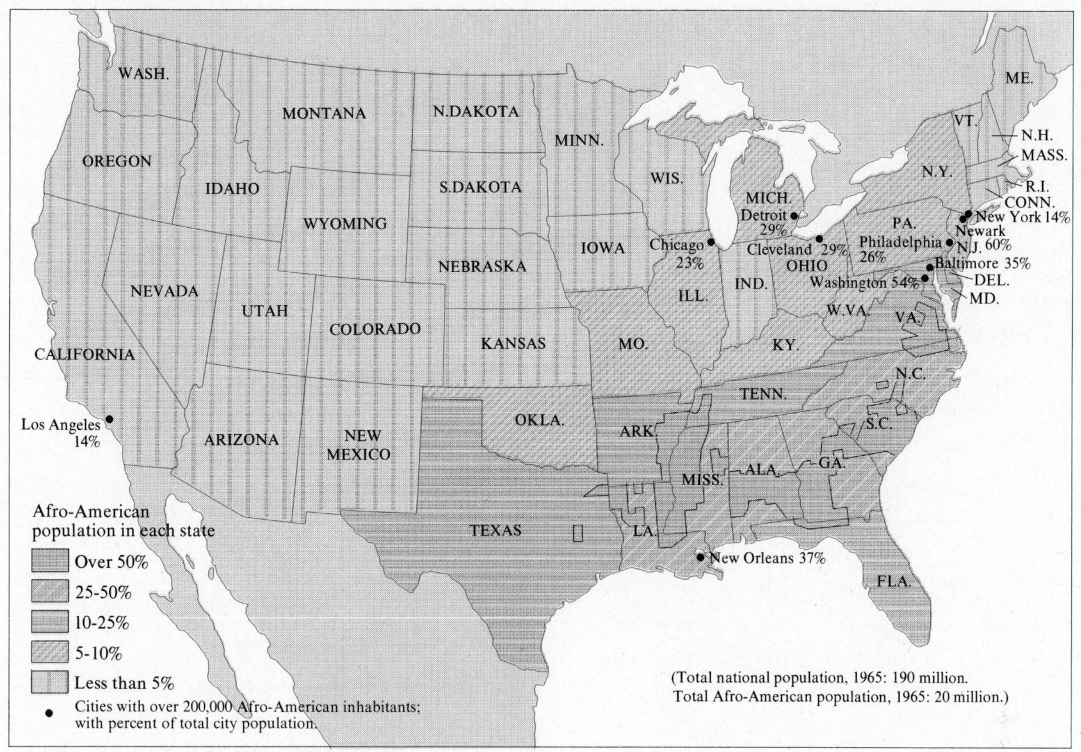

The Afro-American population, 1965. Source: Redrawn by permission of Macmillan Publishing Company, Inc., by Peter Kingsland. Copyright © 1968 by Martin Gilbert.

. . . And I see the cops are white and I was crying. . . . And I took this pop bottle . . . and I threw it down on the cops and I was crying and laughing."

Whites wondered why blacks were venting their frustration in violence at a time when real progress was being made in the civil rights struggle. Part of the reason was that the movement had been largely southern in focus, geared to abolishing Jim Crow and black disfranchisement. In the North public accommodations and the vote had been available to Afro-Americans for decades, but blacks were still living in deep poverty. The black median income was little more than half that of whites: for every dollar the white worker took home in 1964, the black worker earned 54 cents. Black unemployment in the mid-1960s was twice that of whites, and for black males between eighteen and twenty-five it was five times as high. Many black families, particularly those headed solely by women, lived in perpetual poverty. Their number was increasing rapidly, primarily because Aid to Dependent Children (ADC), part of the Social Security Act of 1935, provided payments only if there were no able-bodied man in the household. But the payments were inadequate to pay for a family's rent, utility bills, and household expenses, let alone its food. On the basis of food budgets in 1970, it was estimated that over 60 percent of America's black children were being raised in poverty.

As northern blacks learned of the economic and civil rights gains of the 1960s, they wondered when they would benefit from the Great Society. Unlike southern blacks, northern blacks made up only a small percentage of the population (see map), and they tended to be concentrated in the inner cities. When blacks looked around the ghettos in which they lived, they knew their circumstances were deteriorating. Their neighborhoods were more segregated than ever, for whites had responded to the black migration from the South by fleeing to the suburbs. And as inner-city neighborhoods became all black, so

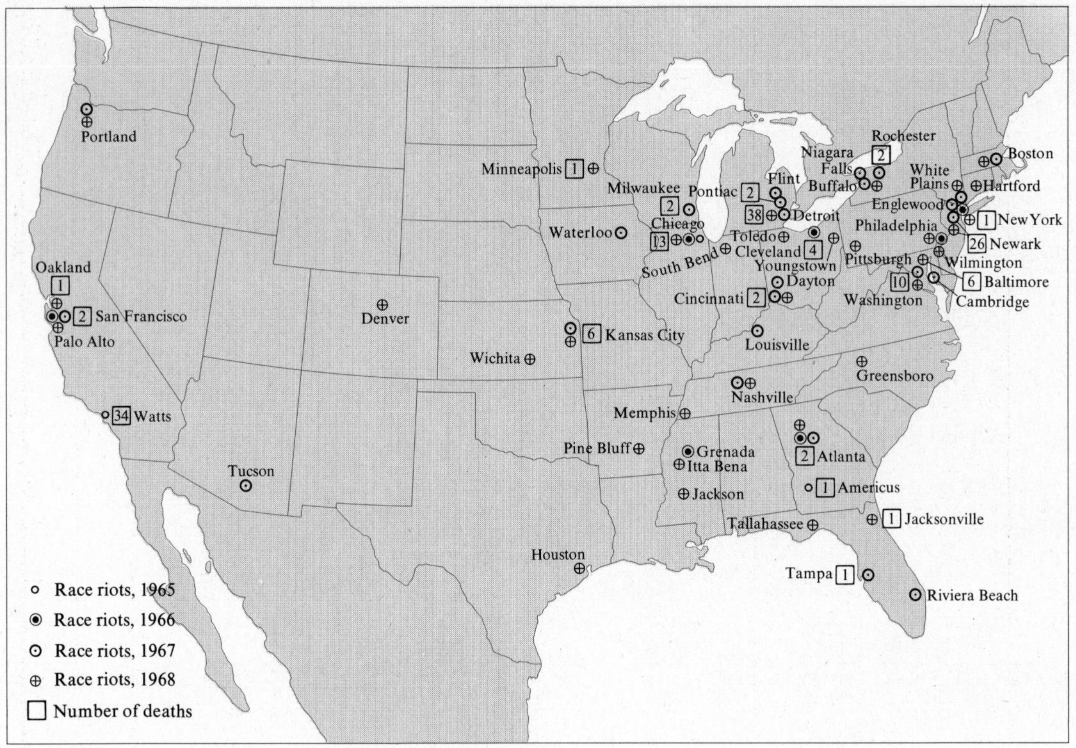

Race riots, 1965–1968

did the neighborhood schools. As one writer commented, "It doesn't cost anything to move a few feet along a hamburger counter to make room for a Negro. But the cost–economic, social, psychological–of abolishing forever a Negro ghetto of half a million souls is only now becoming apparent."

If 1964 was a fiery and violent year, 1965 was even more so. In August blacks gutted the Los Angeles neighborhood of Watts; thirty-four people died (see map). Unlike the race riots of 1919 and 1943, white mobs did not provoke the violence; instead, blacks exploded in anger over their joblessness and lack of opportunity, looting white-owned stores, setting fires, and throwing rocks. "Get Whitey!" they screamed. "Burn, Baby, Burn!" "What white Americans have never fully understood," stated the Kerner Commission in its report several years later, "but what the Negro can never forget–is that white society is deeply implicated in the ghetto. White institutions created it, white institutions maintain it, and white society condones it."

Watts race riot

Other cities exploded in rioting between 1966 and 1968. Besides expressing their rage, rioters increasingly sought the material wealth on display in store windows. "On Twelfth Street," a black resident of Detroit explained during a 1967 riot, "everybody was out, Mama, Papa, the kids, it was like an outing. . . . The rebellion–it was all caused by the [TV] commercials. I mean you saw all those things you'd never be able to get. . . . Men's clothing, furniture, appliances, color TV." The consumer culture had run amuck.

It was obvious that many blacks, especially in the North, had begun to question whether the nonviolent civil rights movement had ever been relevant to their needs. In 1963 Martin Luther King, Jr., had appealed to whites' humanitarian instincts in his famous "I have a dream" speech, delivered before the Washington Monument. But another voice was beginning to be heard, one that urged blacks to seize their freedom "by any means necessary." It was the voice of Malcolm X, a one-time pimp and street hustler who had converted to the Black Muslim religion in prison.

Malcolm X

The Black Muslims, a small sect that espoused separatism from white society, condemned the "white

Malcolm X (1925–1965), the one-time pimp and street hustler who became the leading spokesman not only for the Black Muslims but for many black nationalists and separatists. His autobiography, published after his death, became a classic statement of black pride. Eve Arnold/Magnum Photos.

devil" as the chief source of evil in the world. They attempted to dissociate themselves from white society by repudiating Christianity, their slave surnames, and their allegiance to the United States government. Any nation that permitted mass suffering at home, said Malcolm X, deserved only contempt. Black Muslims exhorted blacks to help themselves by leading sober lives and practicing thrift and industriousness. Unlike Martin Luther King, Jr., they advocated violence in self-defense. By the early 1960s Malcolm X had become their chief spokesperson, and his advice was straightforward. "If someone puts a hand on you, send him to the cemetery."

Malcolm X was murdered in a hail of bullets in February 1965; his assassins were Black Muslims who believed he had become a traitor to their cause. It was true that he had modified some of his ideas just before his death. He had met whites who were not devils, he said, and he had expressed cautious support for the nonviolent civil rights movement. Still, for both blacks and whites Malcolm X symbolized black defiance and self-respect. A powerful figure in life, in death he would become even more of a hero to increasing numbers of black nationalists and proponents of Black Power.

Although Martin Luther King, Jr., continued to be the most admired leader of the civil rights movement, many younger blacks began to question not only his tactic of nonviolence but his dream of racial integration. In 1966 Stokely Carmichael, chairman of SNCC, called on blacks to assert Black Power. According to Carmichael, in order to be truly free from white oppression, blacks had to control their own institutions—businesses, politics, schools. They had to elect black candidates and teach black students in black schools. Soon organizations that had been committed to racial integration and nonviolence began to embrace Black Power. SNCC and CORE purged their white members and repudiated integration, arguing that what black people needed was power, not white friendship.

Black Power

The wellspring of this new militance was black nationalism, the concept that black peoples everywhere in the world shared a unique history and cultural heritage, one that set them apart from whites. Students in colleges and universities pressed for the establishment of black studies programs, and blacks began to call themselves black or Afro-American rather than Negro. More than at any time since the 1920s, Afro-Americans saw themselves as a nation within a nation.

To white America, one of the most fearsome of the new black groups was the Black Panther Party. Armed and wearing leather jackets, Panther leaders Bobby Seale and Huey Newton dedicated themselves to destroying capitalism. What worried white parents was that some of their own children agreed with the Panthers. Denouncing the major political parties, big business and big labor, middle-class affluence and the suburban life style, even the American Dream itself, this vocal minority of the baby-boom generation set out to "change the system."

The New Left and the counterculture

"I'm tired of reading history," a philosophy student at the University of California complained in a letter to a friend in early 1964. "I want to make it." By autumn of that year, Mario Savio would realize his ambition as the leader of the Free Speech Movement (FSM), and Berkeley would become a byword for the campus unrest of the 1960s. The catchwords of the postwar era had been security, consensus, and stability; the 1960s were marked by the rejection of those shopworn values. In the new decade millions of American youths would make what Herbert Marcuse called "the Great Refusal": intensely personal statements of purpose that ran counter to their parents' values and world view.

In many ways the University of California in 1964 was a model university, with a worldwide reputation for excellence. Its chancellor, the economist Clark Kerr, had written a book entitled *The Uses of the University,* in which he likened the university to a big business. But it was just that that bothered some students. Berkeley, a "multiversity" with tens of thousands of students, had become hopelessly impersonal. The students of the baby boom had begun to feel like computer cards lost in a vast bureaucracy. "I am a student," rang one lament of the FSM. "Do not fold, spindle, or mutilate."

Free Speech Movement

After teaching in SNCC's Mississippi Summer Project, Savio and other students had returned to Berkeley with the suspicion that the same power structure that dominated black lives also controlled the bureaucratic machinery of the university. "Last summer I went to Mississippi to join the struggle there for civil rights. This fall I am engaged in another phase of the same struggle, this time in Berkeley. . . . The same rights are at stake in both places," Savio wrote. The struggle began in September 1964, when the university administration banned political recruitment in Sproul Plaza, the gathering place where students spoke on issues, distributed literature, and signed up volunteers for off-campus demonstrations. Savio and other students defied Kerr's ban; the administration responded by suspending them or having them arrested. On October 1 several thousand students surrounded a police car in which one of the militants was being held, immobilizing it for thirty-two hours. Then in December the FSM seized and occupied Sproul Hall, the main administration building. Governor Pat Brown dispatched state police to Berkeley, and over eight hundred people were arrested. Angry students shut down classes in protest. By the end of the decade, the activism born at Berkeley would spread to hundreds of other campuses.

Over two years before the confrontation in Berkeley, another group of students had met in Port Huron, Michigan, to form Students for a Democratic Society (SDS). Like their leaders, Tom Hayden and Al Haber, most SDS members were white college students, the children of middle-class Americans. In their platform, the Port Huron Statement, they acknowledged that they had matured "in complacency." But their comfort had been destroyed by "events too troubling to dismiss": "First, the permeating and victimizing fact of human degradation, symbolized by the Southern struggle against racial bigotry. . . . Second, the enclosing fact of the Cold War, symbolized by the presence of the [hydrogen] Bomb."

Students for a Democratic Society (SDS)

SDS also bemoaned the paradox of poverty amidst plenty, and its statement decried the antidemocratic tendencies of wealthy, powerful corporations. America needed to practice its democratic ideals, not just pay them lip service. "Although mankind desperately needs revolutionary leadership, America rests in national stalemate, its goals ambiguous and tradition-bound instead of informed and clear, its democratic system apathetic and manipulated rather than 'of, by, and for the people.' " SDS sought nothing less than the revitalization of democracy through the return of power to the people.

Inspired by the Free Speech Movement and SDS, a small minority of students joined the New Left. Some were Marxists, others black nationalists, anarchists, or pacifists. Some believed in pursuing social change through negotiation; others were revolutionaries who thought compromise impossible. All were united in their hatred of racism and the war in Vietnam. One of their slogans, "Up Against the Wall," reflected not just their contempt for politicians, generals, corporation executives, college presidents and deans, but their romance with violence. Critics called them arrogant, authoritarian, and even antidemocratic in their scorn for others' opinions, suggesting they did too much shouting and not enough listening. The students of the New Left countered that they had to shout to be heard in the 1960s.

New Left

In the wake of the New Left appeared a phenomenon that observers called the counterculture. Revolutionary figures like Mao Zedong and Che Guevara became campus idols, "Mao caps" a cult uniform and "right on" an all-purpose greeting. Led by Timothy Leary, the LSD prophet, millions of students experimented with marijuana, amphetamines ("speed"), and hallucinogenic drugs.

Countercultural revolution

But it was music more than anything else that reflected the new attitudes. In 1962, the year the founders of SDS gathered at Port Huron, four young musicians from Liverpool, England, recorded "Love Me Do." Long before the Beatles sang "There's gonna be a revolution," it was evident that their music had inspired one. Soon music was the chief vehicle for the countercultural assault on the status quo. Barry McGuire warned of nuclear holocaust in "Eve of Destruction," and Bob Dylan sang of revolutionary answers "blowin' in the wind." Young people cheered Jimi Hendrix, who sang of life in a drug-induced "purple haze"; Janis Joplin, who brought black blues to white Americans; and the Buffalo Springfield, who urged youth to stop and "look what's goin' down." Unlike their 1950s counterparts, the rock superstars of the 1960s enthusiastically acknowledged their roots in black rhythm-and-blues. Joplin, who moved crowds with her version of "Ball and Chain," was quick to give credit to its composer, Big Mama Thornton.

Rock festivals became cultural happenings, the most famous of which was Woodstock (1969), an upstate New York festival that attracted 400,000 people. The huge crowd endured several days of rain and mud together, without shelter and without violence. Some among them began to dream of a peaceful "Woodstock nation" based on love, drugs, and rock music. Beatle John Lennon expressed it best: "All we are saying is give peace a chance."

While some youths sought alternative experiences through drugs and music, others tried to construct alternative ways of life. Among the most conspicuous were the hippies who were drawn to the San Francisco Bay area. In the Haight-Ashbury section of the city, "flower children" created an urban subculture as distinctive as that of any Chinatown or Little Italy. "Hashbury" inspired numerous other communal living experiments. Throughout the country, hitchhikers hit the road in search of communes, America, and themselves.

Woodstock, the upstate New York rock festival that stimulated dreams of a "Woodstock nation." Burk Uzzle/Magnum Photos.

Just as the New Left attracted a minority of students, so the counterculture represented only a small proportion of American youth. But to disconcerted middle-class parents, hippies seemed to be everywhere. Parents carped about long hair, love beads, and patched jeans. They complained that "acid rock" was deafeningly loud, discordant, and even savage. And they feared their children would suffer lifelong damage from drugs. Perhaps most disturbing to parents were the casual sexual mores their children adopted, partly as a result of the availability of birth-control pills. For many young people, living together was no longer equivalent to living in sin. And as attitudes toward premarital sex changed, so did notions about pornography, nudity, homosexuality, sex roles, and familial relationships.

For both cultural and political reasons, the slogan "Make Love, Not War" became popular at mid-decade. With the escalation of the war in Vietnam, the New Left and the counterculture discovered a common cause. Students held teach-ins on the war–open forums for discussion among students, professors, and guest speakers. The first teach-in was held at the University of Michigan in March 1965, shortly after the beginning of Operation Rolling Thunder (see page 907). In May a Berkeley teach-in lasted thirty-six hours and drew some twelve thousand people. State Department officials were dispatched to the teach-ins to defend U.S. policy in Southeast Asia. When they arrived, however, they were met by hecklers and demonstrators.

Antiwar movement

Thousands of young men expressed their opposition to the war by fleeing the draft. By the end of 1972 more than 30,000 draft resisters were living in Canada, an additional 10,000 had fled to Sweden, Mexico, and other countries, and 10,000 more were living under false identities in the United States. During the war half a million men committed draft violations, including an estimated quarter-million who never registered for the draft and another 110,000 who burned their draft cards in protest.

Marches and demonstrations against the war were another popular protest tactic (see map). In April

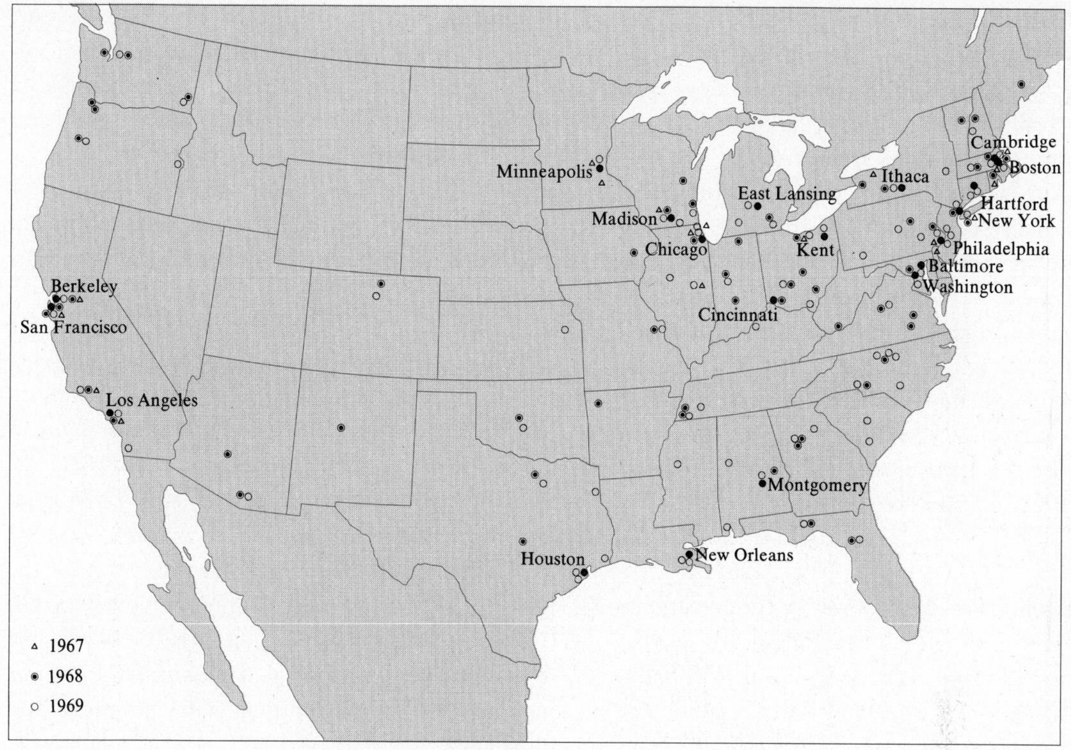

Disturbances on college and university campuses, 1967–1969

1965, 25,000 people marched on the White House, and in October the National Committee to End the War in Vietnam mobilized over 80,000 in demonstrations across the country. During the next two years SDS-led antiwar groups organized marches of several hundred thousand people in New York and San Francisco. And on October 17, 1967, the March on the Pentagon confirmed the fears of government officials that the convergence of student activists, the New Left, and the counterculture threatened the nation's warmaking powers.

By this time growing numbers of Americans, young and old, had quit believing the utterances of their elected leaders. Though President Johnson claimed the United States was fighting in Vietnam for honorable reasons, they wondered how any goal could justify the murder of women and children. As troop levels increased, many recalled ruefully that they had voted for Johnson as the more cautious of the two candidates in 1964. By 1968 almost half a million American soldiers were stationed in Vietnam, and Johnson's credibility had vanished.

1968: a year of protest, violence, and loss

As stormy and violent as the years from 1963 through 1967 had been, many Americans were still trying to downplay the nation's distress in hopes it would go away. "We were in a kind of national sleepwalk," novelist John Hersey wrote, "aware, on a dream level, of black rage; of the undertow of Vietnam . . . of the way Lyndon Johnson's credibility gap was beginning to show." But in 1968 the sleepers awoke to a series of violent quakes.

The first shock hit in late January 1968, when the U.S.S. *Pueblo,* a navy intelligence ship, was captured by the North Koreans near the port of Wonsan. A week later came the Tet offensive (see page 908). For the first time many Americans believed they might lose the war. Then in mid-March came the My Lai massacre, which horrified Americans. Meanwhile, American casualties had been climbing. In a two-week period in May more than eleven hundred U.S. soldiers died, more by far than in any previous two weeks. In fact, more Americans died in the first six months of 1968 than in all of 1967; on July 4, 1968, total American fatalities surpassed thirty thousand.

Controversy over the war deepened. Within the Democratic party, two men rose to challenge Johnson for the 1968 presidential nomination. One of them, the war hawk Governor George C. Wallace of Alabama, exhorted Americans to "stand up for America." The other, Senator Eugene McCarthy of Minnesota, entered the New Hampshire primary solely to contest Johnson's war policies. On March 12 McCarthy won 42 percent of the popular vote and 20 of 24 convention delegates. Yet another Democrat, Senator Robert F. Kennedy of New York, would soon enter the fray.

On March 31, President Johnson went on national television and announced a scaling-down of the bombing in North Vietnam. Then he hurled a political thunderbolt. "I have concluded that I should not permit the Presidency to become involved in the partisan divisions that are developing in this political year," with "America's sons in the field far away . . . with our hopes . . . for peace in the balance every day." Johnson would not be a candidate for re-election.

Assassination of Martin Luther King, Jr.

Less than a week later a white assassin named James Earl Ray shot and killed Martin Luther King, Jr., in Memphis. People still debate whether Ray was a deranged racist acting alone or a pawn in an organized conspiracy. Whatever his motive, his crime aroused instant rage in the nation's ghettos. Blacks rioted in 168 cities and towns, looting and burning white businesses and properties. Thirty-four blacks and five whites died in the violence. Tough talk flared from Maryland's governor Spiro Agnew, who denounced Baltimore's black leaders for not controlling "your people," and from Chicago's Mayor Richard Daley, who ordered police to shoot to kill arsonists. The terror provoked a white backlash against blacks, and hatred mounted on both sides. "When white America killed Dr. King last night, she declared war on us," charged Stokely Carmichael.

Congress responded to King's assassination with its last piece of civil rights legislation, an act outlawing housing discrimination. But it was a lame gesture, largely because Congress refused the government sufficient power to enforce the law. And it did little to placate inner-city blacks, many of whom could not transcend economic barriers to secure a home mortgage.

Student protests multiplied that spring not only in the United States but in Paris, Mexico City, and elsewhere in the world. Between January and June 1968 over two hundred demonstrations rocked colleges and universities across the country. Students protested the involvement of universities in the military-industrial complex. They denounced the spread of urban universities into surrounding poor neighborhoods, the elimination of low-income housing to build gymnasiums, parking garages, and dormitories. In New York students at Columbia University occupied the president's office and other buildings for ten days. On April 30, at the request of Columbia's president, one thousand club-swinging city policemen stormed the occupied buildings, injuring 150 protesters and onlookers.

Most Americans, of course, were not personally threatened by the violence. But nearly all owned TV sets and watched the evening news. And as two scholars wrote in the *Columbia Journalism Review*, it was the nightly news that "made social disorganization a realistic threat to the comfortably-off middle-class urbanites, to suburbanites, to rural residents–to all those, in short, who have seldom faced robbery, mugging, protest marching . . . black power salutes, or perhaps even hostile questions about their values."

Assassination of Robert Kennedy

In April and May Gallup polls reported Robert Kennedy the frontrunning presidential candidate among Democrats. Kennedy had lost to McCarthy in the Oregon primary but won in California that June. While celebrating his victory in Los Angeles's Ambassador Hotel, he decided to take a shortcut through the kitchen to a press conference. Suddenly a young man named Sirhan Sirhan stepped forward with a .22-caliber revolver and fired repeatedly at Kennedy. The assassin, it turned out, was an Arab nationalist who despised Kennedy for his unwavering support of Israel. But the cumulative effect of so many assassinations made some Americans wonder. Whenever a progressive leader rose to prominence, it seemed, he was mowed down. Was it all a coincidence?

Especially heart-stricken were Kennedy's supporters among the poor. During the Poor People's Campaign in summer 1968, thousands of whites and blacks had gone to Washington, D.C., to camp in the tents and shacks of "Resurrection City" and lobby for federal aid to the poor. They adored Kennedy; so did many antiwar liberals and Mexican-Americans. Kennedy had been a warm friend and ally of Cesar Chavez, leader of the United Farm Workers. In 1965, when the UFW struck against growers in Delano, California, Kennedy had visited the strikers to rally support for their *huelga* (strike) and nationwide grape boycott. To Chicanos, blacks, and other poor people, Kennedy was a martyr.

The day after Robert Kennedy's death, President Johnson appointed the Commission on the Causes and Prevention of Violence "to find out why we inflict . . . suffering on ourselves." In late August violence erupted again, at the Democratic national convention in Chicago. The Democrats were divided among Hubert Humphrey, Lyndon Johnson's candidate; peace candidate Eugene McCarthy; and Senator George McGovern of South Dakota, who had inherited some of Kennedy's support. Adding to the dissension were several mule-drawn wagons driven by blacks from the Poor People's Campaign; thousands of antiwar protesters; and the Youth International Party, or Yippies, who had traveled to Chicago for a Festival of Life, which they contrasted pointedly to "Lyndon and Hubert's celebration of death."

Riot at the Democratic national convention

The Chicago police force was still in the psychological grip of Daley's shoot-to-kill directive. Twelve thousand police were assigned to twelve-hour shifts and another twelve thousand army troops and National Guardsmen were on call with rifles, bazookas, and flamethrowers. On Michigan Avenue, in front of the Conrad Hilton Hotel, they attacked, wading into ranks of demonstrators, reporters, and TV camera operators. Throughout the nation viewers watched as club-swinging police beat protesters to the ground. When onlookers rushed to shield the injured, they too were clubbed. Inside the convention hall, Senator Abraham Ribicoff of Connecticut put aside his prepared speech to denounce "those Gestapo tactics in the streets of Chicago."

The Democratic convention nominated Humphrey for president and Senator Edmund Muskie of Maine for vice president. Like Johnson and Kennedy before him, Humphrey was a political descendant of the New Deal, committed to the welfare state and supported by a coalition of northern liberals, big-city bosses, blacks, and union members. First elected to the Senate in 1948, Humphrey was known not just as a passionate champion of civil rights, but as a supporter of the Cold War doctrine of containment that had led to Vietnam. Humphrey's unstinting support of the war angered some of his followers and saddened others, who repudiated him as the candidate of Johnson, Daley, and the war.

The Republicans selected Richard M. Nixon as their presidential nominee. After his defeat by Kennedy in 1960 and his loss in the California gubernatorial race in 1962, Nixon's political career had seemed to be over. But he had spent much of the decade campaigning for fellow Republicans, and had built up a great deal of credit with party regulars and officeholders around the country. In 1968 Nixon cashed in his credits and defeated Governors Nelson Rockefeller of New York and Ronald Reagan of California for the nomination. For his running mate, Nixon chose Governor Spiro Agnew of Maryland.

There was little voter enthusiasm for either Humphrey or Nixon. A Gallup poll taken at the time of the convention revealed that 66 percent of Americans believed the United States should withdraw its troops from Vietnam. Not only independents and McCarthy followers favored an end to hostilities: large majorities of Humphrey and Nixon supporters agreed. Yet, both major candidates endorsed the continuation of the war while negotiations stalled in Paris.

Election of 1968

The candidate with the most appeal for conservatives was George Wallace, the nominee of the American Independent party. Wallace and his supporters argued that the United States should bomb North Vietnam to rubble with thermonuclear weapons. He also appealed to people concerned about law and order, code words for the suppression of protest. If a civil rights protester ever lay down in front of his car, Wallace declared, he would drive over the person.

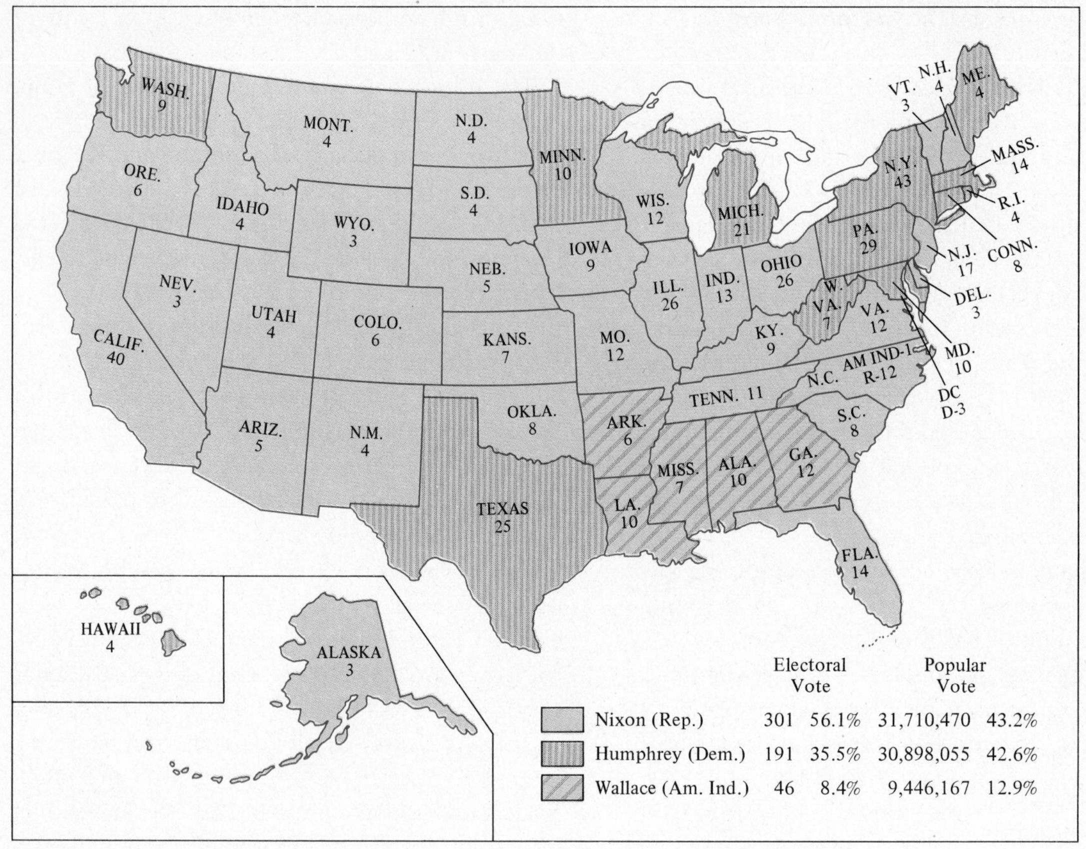

Presidential election, 1968

When the votes were tabulated, Nixon emerged the winner. Just four years after the Goldwater debacle, the Republicans had captured the White House, though by the slimmest of margins. Wallace garnered almost 10 million votes, or 13.5 percent of the total, the best performance by a third party since 1924. His strong showing made Nixon a minority president, elected with only 43 percent of the popular vote (see map).

In late November President Johnson offered the nation his Thanksgiving Proclamation: "Americans, looking back on the tumultuous events of 1968, may be more inclined to ask God's mercy and guidance than to offer Him thanks for His blessings." It had been a stormy year. Soon there would be a new president and a new decade, but Americans doubted whether they could heal the wounds of war, poverty, racism, black rage, youthful disaffection, and the shattered promise of the American Dream.

Nixon and the persistence of chaos

Richard Nixon's presidency was born in chaos. In 1969 a hundred black students armed with rifles and shotguns seized the student union at Cornell University and occupied the building for thirty-six hours. Harvard students took over the president's office before being evicted by police. Bloody confrontations occurred at Berkeley, San Francisco State, Wisconsin, and scores of other colleges and universities. And in October 1969, three hundred Weathermen, members of an SDS splinter group, raced through Chicago's Loop, smashing windows and attacking police officers in an attempt to inspire armed class struggle. A month later half a million people assembled peacefully at the Washington Monument to protest the war. While they appealed to the nation's leaders, President Nixon watched football on TV.

A distraught bystander mourns a slain student at Kent State University, May 1970. Ohio National Guardsmen had fired into a crowd of antiwar protesters, killing four. Kent State University News Service.

The next year was worse. On April 30, 1970, the president appeared on television to announce that the United States had launched an "incursion" into Cambodia. "We will not be defeated," Nixon declared. "If when the chips are down the United States acts like a pitiful helpless giant, the forces of totalitarianism and anarchy will threaten free nations and free institutions throughout the world." Four days later Ohio National Guardsmen fired into a group of protesting students at Kent State University, killing four and wounding eleven. Throughout the country outraged students went on strike, shutting down 250 campuses and pouring into the nation's capital to lobby against the war. Nixon referred contemptuously to the protesters as "these bums, you know, blowing up the campuses."

Killings at Kent State University

On May 8 a group of construction workers angered by the campus protests attacked antiwar demonstrators in the New York financial district, pummeling them to the ground. They then stormed city hall and forced officials to raise the American flag to full staff from half staff, where it had been set in mourning for the slain students. Shortly after, police and state highway patrolmen armed with automatic weapons blasted a women's dormitory at Jackson State, an all-black university in Mississippi, killing two students and wounding nine others. No evidence of student sniping could be found; the police fired no tear gas or warning shots.

If police and soldiers waged official violence in 1970, revolutionaries conducted an unofficial campaign of terror. That year they bombed the New York offices of Mobil Oil, IBM, General Telephone and Electronics, and various banks. In March a radical bomb factory exploded in Greenwich Village, blowing up at least three young revolutionaries. And there were scores of politically motivated skyjackings.

Worst of all, as far as many Americans were concerned, was street crime. "Fortress America: A nation behind locked doors," proclaimed the heading of a *Newsweek* article on crime. Sales of pistols, burglar alarms, and bulletproof vests soared, as did the demand for private guards and special police. Conservatives accused liberals of causing the crime wave by coddling criminals. "You know what a conservative is?" asked Frank Rizzo, the hard-line police-chief-turned-politician who had been elected mayor of Philadelphia. "That's a liberal who got mugged the night before."

Fear of crime

In the tense atmosphere, government officials sometimes overreacted to the disquiet. Governor Nelson Rockefeller of New York did so in September 1971, when more than a thousand inmates of the Attica State Correctional Facility seized thirty-eight guards and took over a cellblock. Rather than give in to the prisoners' demand that he visit Attica to negotiate, Rockefeller ordered state troopers, sheriff's deputies, and guards to storm the prison. Under a pall of tear gas Rockefeller's army regained control of the prison, but at a horrifying cost: thirty-nine dead—twenty-nine inmates and ten hostages.

In the wake of this new wave of riots and violent crime, Nixon became convinced that the nation was descending into anarchy. And he worried, as had Lyndon Johnson before him, that the antiwar movement was Communist-inspired. In June 1970 he ordered the directors of the FBI, the CIA, the National Security Agency, and the Defense Intelligence Agency to formulate a coordinated attack on "internal threats." "Everything is valid," a Nixon aide told the group, "everything is possible." Had it not been for FBI Director J. Edgar Hoover's refusal to cooperate in the illegal plot, the group would have had free rein to open mail, tap telephones, and break into citizens' homes and offices.

The administration also worked to put the Democratic party on the defensive. Vice President Agnew took to the road in September to warn the country of the threats to its internal security and exhort people to vote Republican in the upcoming congressional elections. "Will America be led by a President elected by . . . the American people," he asked, "or will we be intimidated and blackmailed into following the path dictated by a disruptive, radical, and militant minority?" The same month Jeb Stuart Magruder, an assistant to White House chief of staff H. R. Haldeman, defined the theme of the upcoming congressional elections in a memorandum. "The Democrats should be portrayed as being on the fringes: radical liberals who bus children, excuse disorders, tolerate crime, apologize for our wealth, and undercut the President's foreign policy," Magruder wrote. But Republican attempts to discredit the Democrats failed. In the election the Democrats gained twelve seats in the Senate and dropped only two in the House. The Republicans lost eleven state governorships.

Politics of divisiveness

Nixon's fortunes declined further in early 1971. That spring fifteen thousand antiwar activists converged on Washington, dumping trash in the streets and abandoning cars at intersections in an attempt to halt government operations. Over twelve thousand protesters were arrested. And on June 13 the New York *Times* began to publish the Pentagon Papers, a top-secret study of the Vietnam War ordered in 1967 by former Secretary of Defense Robert McNamara. The *Times* had obtained the papers from Daniel Ellsberg, a disillusioned defense analyst with the Rand Corporation, a "think tank" for analyzing national defense policies. Publication of the study revealed that the government had consistently lied to the American people about the war. For instance, in August 1964, when President Johnson announced that North Vietnamese patrol boats had attacked the U.S.S. *Maddox* and *C. Turner Joy*, he did not reveal that the destroyers had been supporting a South Vietnamese raiding party. And the emergency resolution Johnson introduced in Congress as a result of the attack turned out to have been drafted several months before. Some analysts concluded that the attacks themselves might have been a lie, invented to rally public opinion in favor of the war.

Pentagon Papers

In 1971 Nixon also had to contend with inflation, a problem not entirely of his own making. Rather, it was Lyndon Johnson's policy of guns and butter—massive deficit financing to support both the Vietnam War and the Great Society—that had fueled inflation. Not until 1967 had Johnson proposed tax increases to reduce the government deficit and dampen inflation, and not until 1968 had Congress re-

Skyrocketing inflation

sponded with a 10-percent tax surcharge. Johnson had also trimmed federal spending by $6 billion, but the cut was too little too late. Nixon's policies, including a $2.5-billion tax cut in late 1969, only boosted rising prices. By January 1971 the United States was suffering from a 5.3 percent inflation rate and a 6 percent unemployment rate. Soon the word *stagflation* would be coined to describe this coexistence of economic recession (stagnation) and inflation.

That January Nixon shocked both critics and allies by declaring, "I am now a Keynesian." Like his Democratic predecessors, he would try to stimulate the economy through government spending. The budget for fiscal 1971 would have a built-in deficit of $23 billion, just slightly under the all-time high of $25 billion (1968 to 1969). Then in August, in an effort to correct the nation's balance-of-payments deficit, Nixon announced he would devalue the dollar by allowing it to "float" in international money markets. He also requested a tax on imports, the repeal of certain excise taxes, and tax concessions to industry for new capital investments. Finally, to curb inflation, the president froze prices, wages, and dividends for ninety days, then put controls on their increase. Nixon's commitment to the controversial wage and price controls buckled the next year under pressure from businesses and unions. Though some economists, businesspeople, and politicians argued that the controls were bound to fail, others contended that they would have been successful had they been allowed more time to work.

The wage and price controls were just one sign of what surprised observers called Nixon's "great turnabout." Another was his announcement in July 1971 that he would travel to the People's Republic of China, an enemy Nixon had denounced for years. It was clear that the president was preparing for the 1972 presidential election.

The rebirth of feminism

Following the adoption of the Nineteenth Amendment in 1920, the women's rights movement had languished. But in the 1960s feminism was reborn. Just as in the nineteenth century the women's movement had grown out of antislavery, in the twentieth it grew out of the struggle for civil rights. Women discovered they were second-class citizens even in movements dedicated to equal rights. Instead of making policy, they were expected to make the coffee, take the minutes, and sometimes even provide sexual favors. As Stokely Carmichael put it, "the position of women in our movement should be prone."

When women examined their place in society as a whole, they were no more encouraged. In *The Feminine Mystique* (1963), Betty Friedan wrote that the American home had become a "comfortable concentration camp." TV advertisers, magazine writers, beauticians, and psychiatrists had conspired to create the image of a woman "gaily content in a world of bedroom, kitchen, sex, babies and home." For her, nothing could be more rewarding than getting rid of that ring around the collar, having children with cavity-free teeth, and boasting the shiniest kitchen floor on the block. Any woman who was dissatisfied with such a role was considered neurotic. But as Friedan pointed out, the wife-mother who spent her life in a world of children sacrificed her adult frame of reference and sometimes her very identity. Friedan quoted a young mother: "I've tried everything women are supposed to do—hobbies, gardening, pickling, canning, and being very social with my neighbors. . . . I love the kids and Bob and my home. . . . But I'm desperate. I begin to feel that I have no personality. I'm a server of food and putter-on of pants and a bedmaker. . . . But who am I?"

The Feminine Mystique

For the working woman, the outlook was just as bleak. Her problems were sex discrimination in employment, lack of professional opportunities, unequal pay for equal work, the lack of adequate day care for children, and prohibitions against abortion. In 1963 the average woman earned 63 cents for every dollar a man earned. Ten years later the figure had fallen to 57 cents. In practical terms what this gender-based discrimination meant for many women was less food on the table and no new shoes for the kids.

Friedan's book inspired the founding in 1966 of the National Organization for Women (NOW), which battled for "equal rights in partnership with men" in courts and in Congress. Not long after its formation a new generation of radical feminists emerged—once again, the baby boom was making an impact on

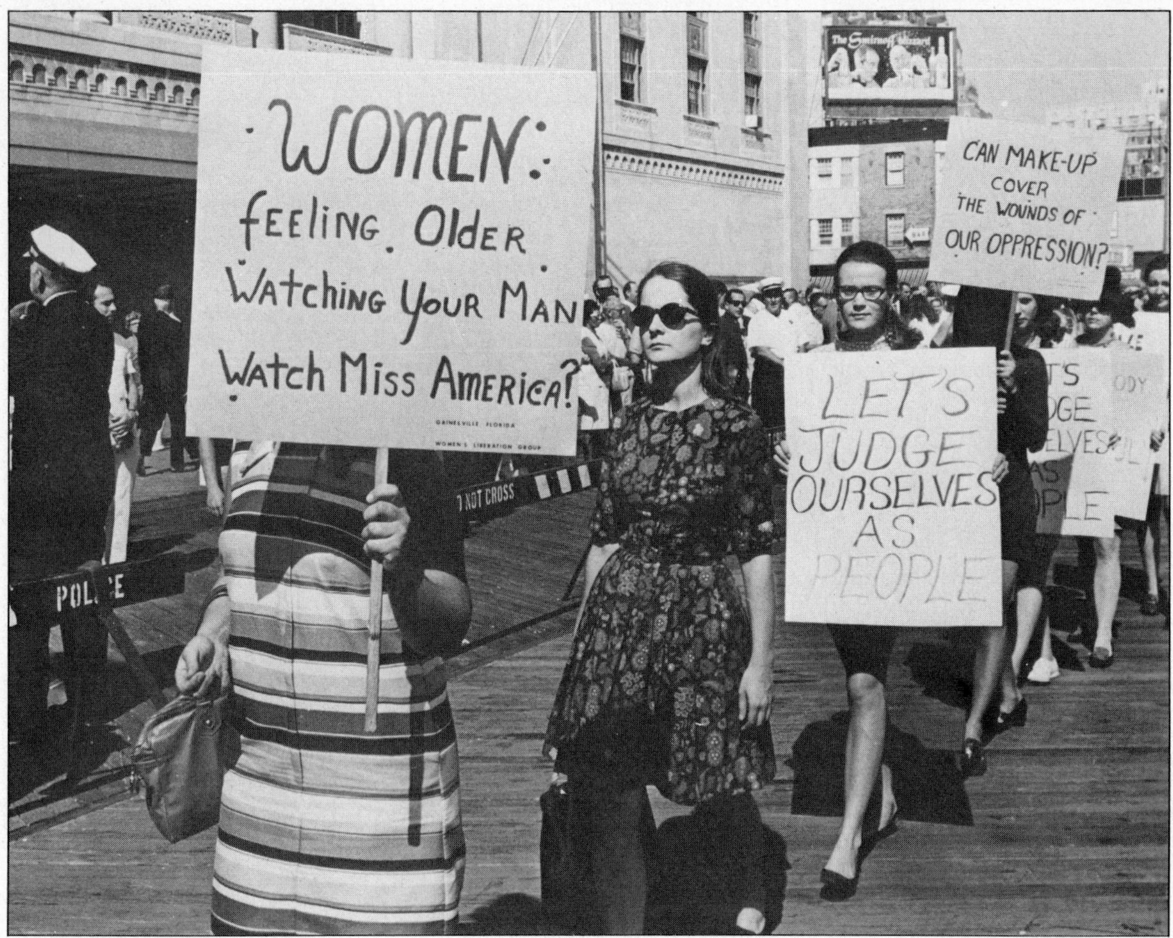

Feminists picketed the Miss America pageant in 1968, condemning the contest for glorifying the "mindless-boob-girlie symbol." UPI.

Radical feminism

American life. Most of these new feminists were white, economically secure, and well educated; many were the daughters of working mothers. Most had been raised in the era of sexual liberation, in which birth-control pills and other contraceptives were taken for granted. The intellectual ferment of their movement produced a new feminist literature: Shulamith Firestone's *The Dialectic of Sex*; Kate Millett's *Sexual Politics*; Robin Morgan's *Sisterhood Is Powerful.* Feminists challenged everything from women's economic, political, and legal inequality to sexual double standards and sex-role stereotypes.

Opposition to feminist goals was widespread and intense. In December 1971 President Nixon vetoed a bill that would have set up a national system of day-care facilities for the children of working mothers. The bill, Nixon asserted, would have committed government to "communal approaches to child-rearing over against the family-centered approach," thus imperiling "the keystone of our civilization," the American family.

Despite such opposition, women made impressive gains in the early 1970s. They entered professional schools in record numbers: from 1969 to 1973, the numbers of women law students almost quadrupled and of women medical students more than doubled. Under Title IX of the Educational Amendments Act of 1972, female college athletes gained the right to the same financial support as male athletes. In the same

Educational and legal advances for women

year Congress approved the Equal Rights Amendment and sent it to the states for ratification. (The Equal Rights Amendment states, "Equality of rights under the law shall not be denied or abridged by the United States or by any State on account of sex.") Two years later the Supreme Court ruled that a woman desiring an abortion had the right to control her own body (*Doe* v. *Bolton* and *Roe* v. *Wade*).

As a result of these victories the women's movement gained new confidence. "If the 1960s belonged to the blacks, the next ten years are ours," remarked one feminist. Friedan added, "There never has been a movement of social change that has affected so many people so quickly. The women's movement is everywhere." But though many new converts would join the movement in the next few years, the antifeminist forces would also grow. By the late 1970s feminism would be threatened with some major defeats.

President Nixon and Vice President Spiro T. Agnew (1918–) celebrate their re-election in 1972. Both resigned in disgrace before completing the second term. Pictorial Parade.

The southern strategy and the election of 1972

Political observers believed that Nixon would have a hard time running for re-election on his first-term record. Having urged Americans to use "cool" words and "lower our voices," he had ordered Vice President Agnew to denounce the press and student protesters. Having espoused unity, he had practiced the politics of polarization. Having campaigned as a fiscal conservative, he had authorized near-record budget deficits. And having promised peace, he had widened the war in Southeast Asia. The president's popularity had dropped from a 61 percent approval rating in January 1970 to 49 percent at the end of 1971.

Democratic legislative victories

Congressional legislative accomplishments had been made more in spite of Nixon than because of him, for the Democrats dominated both houses of Congress during his first term. Eighteen-year-olds gained the vote, social security payments and food-stamp funding were increased, and the Environmental Protection Agency and Occupational Safety and Health Administration were established. Congress responded to the growing environmental movement by passing the Clean Air Act, the Water Quality Improvement Act, and the Resource Recovery Act. (Nixon opposed most of these social welfare, environmental, and voting rights bills.) Finally, Congress voted against funding for the Super Sonic Transport (SST), which Nixon had argued was essential to the nation's economy. (Scientists and environmentalists countered that the gigantic airplane would cause jarring sonic booms and might even destroy the atmosphere.)

One Nixon innovation that bore fruit in 1972 was revenue sharing, a program that returned federal funds to the states to use as they saw fit. Nixon's effort to shift responsibility to state and local governments was known as the New Federalism. A less popular program was the Family Assistance Plan (FAP), under which a family of four would receive a guaranteed income of $1,600 per year plus $860 in food stamps. (Welfare payments fell below that level in twenty states.) The author of *The Other America* called the plan "the most radical idea since the New Deal"; most conservatives denounced it. But a handful of conservatives, among them economist Milton Friedman, supported the FAP, arguing that simple cash payments to the poor would do away with the mammoth welfare bureaucracy. The program did not pass Congress, in part because Democrats considered the benefit payments too low.

In his campaign for re-election, Nixon was less interested in running on his record than in employing a "southern strategy." A product of the Sunbelt himself, Nixon was attuned to the growing political power of that conservative area. Thus he appealed to "the silent majority," the white suburbanites, blue-collar workers, Catholics, and ethnic groups of "middle America." As in the 1970 congressional elections, Nixon equated the Republican party with law and order and the Democratic party with permissiveness, crime, drugs, pornography, the hippie life style, student radicalism, black militancy, feminism, homosexuality, and the dissolution of the family.

Nixon's southern strategy

Actually, Nixon had been pursuing a southern strategy all along. A furor had arisen in February 1970 when the press published a memorandum written by Daniel Moynihan, Nixon's adviser on urban affairs and social welfare. While insisting that blacks should continue to make progress, Moynihan had recommended that "the issue of race could benefit from a period of benign neglect." Moreover, Attorney General John Mitchell had courted southern votes by trying to delay school desegregation in Mississippi and to prevent extension of the 1965 Voting Rights Act. Mitchell sought vigorous prosecution of antiwar activists as well.

The southern strategy had also guided Nixon's nomination of Supreme Court justices. After appointing Warren Burger, a conservative federal judge, to succeed Earl Warren as chief justice, Nixon had selected two southerners to serve as associate justices. One of them, Judge G. Harrold Carswell of Florida, was a segregationist. When the Senate declined to confirm either nominee, Nixon protested angrily, "I understand the bitter feelings of millions of Americans who live in the South." By 1972, however, the president had managed to appoint three more conservatives to the Supreme Court: Justices Harry Blackmun, Lewis F. Powell, and William Rehnquist. Ironically, the new appointees did not always vote as Nixon would have wished. The Court's decisions on abortion, publication of the Pentagon Papers, the death sentence, wiretapping, and busing all ran counter to Nixon's politics.

The Court was at the center of one of the most emotional issues of the 1972 election, busing. In 1971, in *Swann* v. *Charlotte-Mecklenburg,* the justices had upheld a desegregation plan that required a school system in North Carolina to work toward racial integration through massive crosstown busing. The decision caused widespread protest. In March 1972 Governor George C. Wallace of Alabama won the Democratic primary in Florida after taking a strong antibusing stand. Three days later Nixon proposed that Congress pass a busing moratorium, and he appeared on television to denounce busing as a reckless and extreme remedy for segregation. Though Nixon's response to busing was a well-planned part of his southern strategy, it was obvious that his stand appealed to northern whites as well.

Besides Wallace, Democratic candidates for the 1972 presidential nomination included Senators Hubert Humphrey, Edward Kennedy, George McGovern, and Edmund Muskie. After his defeat by Nixon in 1968, Humphrey inspired little enthusiasm. And for many Americans, Kennedy had ceased to be a contender in 1969, when he left the scene of an accident in which a passenger in his car, Mary Jo Kopechne, was killed. Senator Muskie fell victim to a dirty trick, a forged letter published during the New Hampshire primary that accused the senator of laughing at disparaging remarks about Canadian-Americans. When the letter and other slurs brought Muskie to the point of tears in public, he too ceased to be a serious candidate. Governor Wallace was shot by a disturbed young man named Arthur H. Bremer and began a long period of convalescence. After his shooting the right-wing law-and-order vote had no place to turn but to Nixon. In the meantime, Senator McGovern won several primaries and arrived at the Democratic convention with enough votes for the nomination.

Election of 1972

Nixon campaigned for re-election by assuming the elevated role of world statesman: in February 1972 he traveled to China and in May to the Soviet Union.

Important events

1960	John F. Kennedy elected president
1961	Congress of Racial Equality's Freedom Ride
1962	Students for a Democratic Society's Port Huron Statement
1963	Betty Friedan, *The Feminine Mystique*
	March on Washington for Afro-American civil rights
	Birmingham, Alabama, Baptist church bombed
	Kennedy assassinated; Lyndon B. Johnson assumes the presidency
1964	Beatles perform in the United States
	Economic Opportunity Act launches War on Poverty
	Civil Rights Act of 1964
	First of the "long hot summers"
	Free Speech Movement at University of California, Berkeley
	Lyndon Johnson elected president
1965	Malcolm X assassinated
	Civil rights march from Selma to Montgomery, Alabama
	Antiwar demonstrations
	Voting Rights Act of 1965
	Watts race riot
1966	Stokely Carmichael calls for "Black Power"
	National Organization for Women (NOW) established
1967	Race riots in Newark, Detroit, and other cities
	Antiwar March on the Pentagon
1968	U.S.S. *Pueblo* captured by North Korea
	Tet offensive
	My Lai massacre
	Martin Luther King, Jr., murdered
	Race riots in 168 cities and towns
	Student antiwar protests escalate
	Robert F. Kennedy murdered
	Violence at Democratic convention in Chicago
	Richard Nixon elected president
1969	Woodstock festival
	Moratorium Day
1970	U.S. invades Cambodia
	Four students killed at Kent State University
	Two students killed at Jackson State University
1971	Protests in Washington, D.C.; 12,614 people arrested
	Daniel Ellsberg releases Pentagon Papers
	President Nixon announces his New Economic Policy
	Prisoners revolt at New York's Attica State Correctional Facility
1972	Nixon visits China and the Soviet Union
	Equal Rights Amendment (ERA) approved by Congress
	George C. Wallace shot and paralyzed
	Break-in at Watergate
	Revenue-sharing adopted
	Nixon re-elected

Both trips were elaborately staged and televised for maximum political effect. But it was the campaign waged by the Democratic nominee, George McGovern, that handed victory to the Republicans. In the California primary McGovern suggested that the federal government bestow $1,000 on all Americans "from the poorest migrant workers to the Rockefellers." A fiscally irresponsible idea—and a frightening one to the middle classes, who surmised they would have to pay for it—McGovern's pledge provided deadly ammunition to the Republicans in the general elections. When McGovern committed himself to a $30-billion cut in the defense budget, people began to fear he was a neo-isolationist who would reduce the United States to a second-rate power. McGovern's proposals split the Democrats between his supporters—blacks, feminists, antiwar activists, young militants—and old-guard urban bosses, labor and ethnic leaders, and southerners.

Much to Nixon's advantage was the rumor that the Vietnam War was near its end. Troops were being pulled out; by September 1972 the death rate was almost zero. Then in late October, less than two weeks before the election, Henry Kissinger announced a breakthrough in the peace negotiations. "Peace is at hand," he proclaimed. The announcement was deceitful, but it had the desired effect.

Nixon's victory in November was overwhelming. He polled 47 million votes, or 60.7 percent of the votes cast. McGovern garnered only 29 million and won in just one state, Massachusetts. Nixon's southern strategy was supremely successful: he carried all of the Deep South, which had once been solidly Democratic. He also gained a majority of the urban vote, winning over such long-time Democrats as blue-collar workers, Catholics, and ethnics. Only blacks, Jews, and low-income voters stuck with the Democrats. Remarkably, the Democrats retained control of both houses of Congress and won two additional seats in the Senate. Democratic voters were becoming independent, resorting to ticket-splitting when they perceived a Democratic candidate to be unacceptable.

In delivering his second inaugural address in January 1973, Nixon was buoyant. "Let us pledge to make these four years the best four years in America's history, so that on its 200th birthday America will be as young and vital as when it began, and as bright a beacon of hope for all the world." Largely because of Nixon's actions, however, the next four years would be among the most dismal in the nation's history. Nixon's two immediate predecessors had been destroyed in the office: the names Dallas and Vietnam evoked those tragedies. A third name—Watergate—was to signify Richard Nixon's downfall.

Suggestions for further reading

General

Ronald Berman, *America in the Sixties* (1968); Godfrey Hodgson, *America in Our Time* (1976); Peter Joseph, *Good Times: An Oral History of America in the Nineteen Sixties* (1973); William O'Neill, *Coming Apart: An Informal History of America in the 1960s* (1971); Milton Viorst, *Fire in the Streets: America in the 1960s* (1979).

The other Americans

Joseph H. Cash and Herbert T. Hoover, eds., *To Be an Indian: An Oral History* (1971); Harry M. Caudill, *Night Comes to the Cumberland* (1963); J. Wayne Flynt, *Dixie's Forgotten People: The South's Poor Whites* (1979); Leo Grebler *et al.*, *The Mexican-American People* (1970); Michael Harrington, *The Other America: Poverty in the United States* (1962); Susan Estabrook Kennedy, *If All We Did Was to Weep at Home: A History of White Working-Class Women in America* (1979); Oscar Lewis, *La Vida* (1966); Herman P. Miller, *Rich Man, Poor Man* (1971).

The Kennedy administration

Henry Fairlie, *The Kennedy Promise: The Politics of Expectation* (1973); David Halberstam, *The Best and the Brightest* (1972); Jim F. Heath, *Decade of Disillusionment: The Kennedy-Johnson Years* (1975); Arthur M. Schlesinger, Jr., *A Thousand Days: John F. Kennedy in the White House* (1965); Theodore C. Sorenson, *Kennedy* (1965); Theodore H. White, *The Making of the President 1960* (1961).

The Johnson administration

Eric F. Goldman, *The Tragedy of Lyndon Johnson* (1968); Lyndon B. Johnson, *The Vantage Point: Perspectives of the Presidency, 1963–1969* (1971); Doris Kearns, *Lyndon Johnson and the American Dream* (1976); Sar A. Levitan, *The Great Society's Poor Law: A New Approach to Poverty* (1969); Daniel

P. Moynihan, *Maximum Feasible Misunderstanding: Community Action in the War on Poverty* (1970); Hugh Sidey, *A Very Personal Presidency: Lyndon Johnson in the White House* (1968); Theodore H. White, *The Making of the President 1964* (1965).

Civil rights and black power

Carl M. Brauer, *John F. Kennedy and the Second Reconstruction* (1977); Stokely Carmichael and Charles Hamilton, *Black Power* (1967); William H. Chafe, *Civilities and Civil Rights: Greensboro, North Carolina, and the Black Struggle for Freedom* (1980); David J. Garrow, *Protest at Selma: Martin Luther King, Jr., and the Voting Rights Act of 1965* (1978); August Meier and Elliott Rudwick, *CORE: A Study in the Civil Rights Movement, 1942–1968* (1973); David L. Lewis, *King: A Critical Biography* (1970); Benjamin Muse, *The American Negro Revolution: From Nonviolence to Black Power, 1963–1967* (1968); Malcolm X and Alex Haley, *The Autobiography of Malcolm X* (1965); Harris Wofford, *Of Kennedy and Kings: Making Sense of the Sixties* (1980); Howard Zinn, *SNCC: The New Abolitionists* (1964).

The New Left and the counterculture

Morris Dickstein, *Gates of Eden: American Culture in the Sixties* (1977); Kenneth Keniston, *Young Radicals* (1968); Seymour Lipset and Sheldon Wolin, eds., *The Berkeley Student Revolt* (1965); Joyce Maynard, *Looking Back: A Chronicle of Growing Up Old in the Sixties* (1973); Michael Medved and David Wallechinsky, *What Really Happened to the Class of '65* (1976); Philip Norman, *Shout! The Beatles in Their Generation* (1981); James P. O'Brien, "The Development of a New Left in the United States, 1960–1965" (Ph.D. dissertation, University of Wisconsin, 1971); Charles Reich, *The Greening of America* (1970); Theodore Roszak, *The Making of a Counter Culture* (1968); Kirkpatrick Sale, *SDS* (1973); Philip Slater, *The Pursuit of Loneliness,* rev. ed. (1976); Irwin Unger, *The Movement: A History of the New Left, 1959–1972* (1974).

The Nixon administration

Rowland Evans and Robert Novak, *Nixon in the White House: The Frustration of Power* (1971); Daniel P. Moynihan, *The Politics of a Guaranteed Income: The Nixon Administration and the Family Assistance Plan* (1973); Richard M. Nixon, *RN: The Memoirs of Richard Nixon* (1978); Leon E. Panetta and Peter Gall, *Bring Us Together: The Nixon Team and the Civil Rights Retreat* (1971); Kevin Phillips, *The Emerging Republican Majority* (1969); Raymond Price, *With Nixon* (1977); Jonathan Schell, *The Time of Illusion* (1975); Leonard Silk, *Nixonomics* (1972); Theodore H. White, *The Making of the President 1968* (1969); Theodore H. White, *The Making of the President 1972* (1973); Garry Wills, *Nixon Agonistes* (1970).

The rebirth of feminism

William H. Chafe, *The American Woman: Her Changing Social, Economic, and Political Role, 1920–1970* (1972); Sara Evans, *Personal Politics: The Roots of Women's Liberation in the Civil Rights Movement and the New Left* (1978); Shulamith Firestone, *The Dialectic of Sex: The Case for Feminist Revolution* (1970); Betty Friedan, *The Feminine Mystique* (1963); Kate Millett, *Sexual Politics* (1970); Robin Morgan, ed., *Sisterhood is Powerful* (1970); Margaret O'Brien Steinfels, *Who's Minding the Children: The History and Politics of Day Care in America* (1973); Gayle Graham Yates, *What Women Want: The Ideas of the Movement* (1975).

On Inauguration Day President Jimmy Carter (1924–) and his wife Rosalynn caught the public's fancy by walking from the Capitol to the White House. Despite his symbolic beginning, Carter became increasingly isolated both from the American people and from Congress. UPI.

marked degree along the fault line separating the haves and the have-nots." Carter gained almost 90 percent of the black and Mexican-American vote and squeaked to victory by a slim 1.7 million votes out of 80 million. Ford's appeal was strongest among middle- and upper-middle-class voters.

In office, Carter's major accomplishments were in energy, transportation, and conservation policy. To encourage domestic production of oil he instituted phased decontrol of oil prices. To spur development of alternative fuels he created the Synthetic Fuels Corporation. And to moderate the social effects of the energy crisis he called for a windfall-profits tax on excessive profits resulting from decontrol, and grants to the poor and elderly for the purchase of heating fuel. Carter reformed the civil service and created separate Departments of Energy and Education. He deregulated the airline, trucking, and railroad industries and persuaded Congress to ease federal control of banks, which were running short of funds due to the low ceiling on interest rates. His administration established a $1.6 billion "superfund" to clean up abandoned chemical-waste sites. And finally, in what Carter called "the most important decision on conservation matters that the Congress will face in this century," the president placed over 100 million acres of Alaskan land under the federal government's protection as national parks, national forests, and wildlife refuges.

Carter administration

Despite these accomplishments, Jimmy Carter's popularity flagged early. His manner seemed cold and uncommanding, and his singsong voice lacked authority. Indeed, Carter was sorely lacking in leadership. He never established a close working relationship with congressional leaders, nor did he succeed in forging friendly relations with other power bases, such as the AFL-CIO. Elected as an outsider, he remained one throughout his presidency. As one of his former cabinet officers explained, "The Georgians gloried in being outsiders. They never understood . . . that if you are going to govern, then you have to reach out."

Although Carter was an idealist, he seemed unwilling to do battle for his principles. One of his former White House staffers complained that the president was quick "to abandon his litany of seemingly high-minded campaign promises at the first sign of resistance." Other observers doubted that he was ever that committed to the principles he embraced publicly. And although Carter stood for honesty and openness, he seemed to tolerate improper and perhaps illegal behavior among intimates. Bert Lance, director of the Office of Management and Budget, was kept in office long after being accused of conflict of interest and manipulation of bank funds for personal gain. And the president's brother Billy accepted a $220,000 loan from Libya, a government that espoused terrorism and was an avowed enemy of the United States.

Carter's conservative policies alienated Democrats who had grown up in the party's New Deal liberal tradition. His support of deregulation and his opposition to wage and price controls and gasoline rationing ran counter to the liberal Democratic position. Seeing inflation as more of a threat to the nation's health than either recession or unemployment, Carter announced that his top priority would be to cut federal spending, even though doing so would add to the jobless rolls.

But despite his efforts, inflation continued to rise. Liberals grumbled that Carter was a closet Republican, the most conservative Democratic president since Grover Cleveland. In November 1979 Senator Edward Kennedy, fed up with Carter's economic policies, announced that he would contest the president's renomination.

Carter's problems were not entirely of his own making. Not since Eisenhower's eight-year presidency had a president served two full terms; some observers worried that America had invented the "disposable president," to be discarded every four years. And in the wake of Vietnam and Watergate, Congress had put the president in what Nixon's secretary of state, William Rogers, called "a straitjacket of legislation": campaign laws, the impoundment act, and the War Powers Act. Power had clearly shifted from the White House to Capitol Hill. At the same time Congress was filling up with political newcomers, men and women unused to blind obedience to established leadership. Party discipline seemed a thing of the past. The result, stated one of Carter's advisers, was "a shift of authority and responsibility to a body that has trouble speaking with one voice."

Decline of presidential authority

To complicate matters, Capitol Hill was crawling with lobbyists from a multitude of special-interest groups: trade associations, corporations, labor unions, and single-issue groups like the National Rifle Association. Carter complained that the nation had become "fragmented, Balkanized." With party discipline in tatters and each group clamoring for its own program, the president was forced to form what one White House aide called a "roll-your-own majority" for each proposal. The task called for skills Carter did not possess–trading pork-barrel projects for votes, mobilizing public opinion, gladhanding politicians and massaging their egos.

By 1980 the economy was a shambles. Inflation had jumped to 12.4 percent, and buyers around the world had lost confidence in the dollar, causing unprecedented increases in the price of gold. To steady the dollar and curb inflation, the Federal Reserve Board had taken drastic measures in late 1979: it had raised the rates at which it loaned money to banks. As a result auto loans became progressively more difficult to obtain, mortgage interest rates leaped beyond 15 percent, and the prime lending rate (the rate charged to businesses) hit an all-time high of 20 percent.

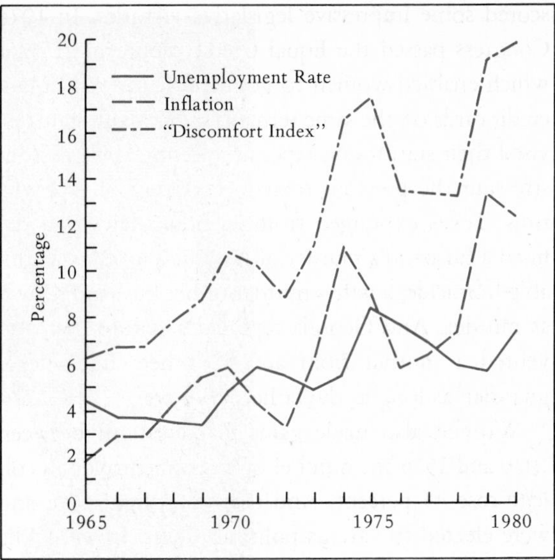

Discomfort index (unemployment plus inflation), 1965–1980. Source: *Economic Report of the President: 1980* (Washington: U.S. Government Printing Office, 1981), pp. 238, 263.

Worse still, by 1980 the nation was in a full-fledged recession, with an unemployment rate of 7.5 percent. For two consecutive quarters it had experienced no growth in the gross national product. And the combined high inflation and high unemployment rates had produced a staggeringly high discomfort index of just under 20 percent (see figure). As Carter assessed his prospects for re-election, he was naturally downcast. In 1976 he had gibed at the incumbent, President Ford, by saying, "Anything you don't like about Washington, I suggest you blame on him." In 1980 Carter was the incumbent, and many Americans blamed him for the problems that plagued the country.

The divided women's movement

In the 1970s, while presidential politics were engaging the energies of party professionals, increasing numbers of women were committing themselves to the struggle for equality with men. Feminists had

President of the United Farm Workers Cesar Chavez (1927–) walks a picket line during a UFW boycott of nonunion produce. Ted Cowell/Black Black Star.

newcomers settled in East Los Angeles, the nation's largest barrio. As David Lizaraga, director of the East Los Angeles Community Union, explained: "If I were in Mexico now, I'd be running across that wire as fast as I could. This is the land of opportunity."

But poverty awaited these new immigrants, as it had previous groups of newcomers. The median family income for Mexican-Americans in 1979 was $11,421, as compared with $16,284 for non-Hispanic families. Nineteen percent of Mexican-Americans lived below the poverty line. Puerto Ricans were worse off, with a median family income of about $8,300, and 30 percent of their number living in poverty. Though the problems with which Hispanics contended were similar to those confronting other nonwhites, they also faced a language barrier. Most inner-city schools were ill-equipped to serve the needs of bilingual students. As a result, only 30 percent of Hispanic high school students graduated, and fewer than 7 percent finished college. Finally, the larger the Hispanic population has become, the more widespread has been the discrimination against them. "Anglos are afraid," said California Assemblyman Richard Alatorre. "They think they will get to be the minorities and we'll be opposing them."

Most Hispanics preferred their family-centered culture to Anglo culture, and for that reason they resisted assimilation. "What we are saying," explained Daniel Villaneuva, a TV executive, "is that we want to be here, but without losing our language and our culture. They are a richness, a treasure that we don't care to lose." A Puerto Rican woman in New York added, "We have been trying to become American for too long, and we are forgetting our roots, culture and the values of our nationality."

Hispanic cultural pride

Instead, like other minorities, Hispanics wanted power—"brown power." Cesar Chavez's United Farm Workers had been the first Hispanic interest group to attract national attention. Another group, the militant Brown Berets, attracted notice for their efforts to provide meals to preschoolers and courses in Chicano studies and consciousness-raising to older students. And throughout the 1970s the Mexican-American political party La Raza Unida was a potent force in the Southwest and East Los Angeles. Still, for a group soon to become the nation's largest minority, Hispanics exercised a disproportionately small share of political power. One reason was that Hispanic America was a tremendously diverse community. Although they shared a language and a religion, Mexican-Americans, Puerto Ricans, Cubans, and other groups differed in countless ways. "We need a Spanish Bobby Kennedy or Martin Luther King," observed Daniel Villanueva. "Right now he's just not there."

During the late 1970s and early 1980s, still other new immigrants joined America's nonwhite population. Between 1970 and 1980 the United States absorbed more than 4 million immigrants and refugees and perhaps twice that number of illegal aliens—more new residents than in any one decade in American history. The boat people and other refugees of the Vietnam War arrived from Indochina, Cuba,

New influx of immigrants

and Haiti; other immigrants came from the Philippines, Korea, Taiwan, India, the Dominican Republic, and Jamaica. In 1980 160,000 boat people poured in from the two islands of Cuba and Haiti alone. Although well-wishers were on hand to greet these people, the history of the nation's treatment of nonwhites, along with the severe recession that began in 1979, did not augur well for them. "Clearly, some people derive great benefit from the present situation," explained Leon Castillo, former commissioner of immigration, in referring to the low wages paid to aliens. The new residents faced a long struggle.

The Me Decade

At the beginning of 1980, the editors of *Time* magazine observed that the 1970s had been "erected upon the smoldering wreckage of the '60s. Now and then, someone's shovel blade would strike an unexploded bomb; mostly the air in the '70s was thick with a sense of aftermath, of public passions spent and consciences bewildered."

The nation had turned apathetic, and perhaps nowhere was this new attitude more evident than among youth. In the 1960s American youths had worked for change in the nation's social, political, and cultural life. But by the mid-1970s the aspirations of young Americans had been transformed. The younger brothers and sisters of the founders of the counterculture had rejected revolutionary idealism. A student at Vassar commented: "We saw it all. We were freshmen in high school when our older brothers and sisters were going off to war or to exile or to revolution. . . . We saw the waste of lives and I think that determined that we would not ruin our own for lost causes." Older Americans took refuge, too, from a lost war, political scandal, and economic distress. As a theologian put it, Americans "have a beleaguered sense in their bones that the old order is dying. Very few want a radical alternative, but few also are working to develop a rationale for the system we've got."

Instead, in the 1970s Americans turned their gaze inward and concentrated on self-expression and personal improvement. As a popular beer commercial proclaimed, "You only go 'round once in life and you've got to grab for all the gusto you can get." That gusto ranged from recreational vehicles to roller skates, disco to punk rock, *The Godfather* to *Star Wars*. Social commentator Tom Wolfe branded the 1970s the Me Decade, a time of diversion and material consumption designed to make Americans' private worlds, in the midst of public confusion, at least tolerable.

Human potential movement

In the self-centered new decade, suggestions for realizing one's full potential were consumed as readily as jogging shoes and health foods. Transactional Analysis (TA), a form of psychotherapy emphasizing interpersonal relationships, was popularized in Eric Berne's *Games People Play* (1969) and Thomas Harris's *I'm OK–You're OK* (1969). Transcendental Meditation (TM), a yogic discipline, drew 350,000 adherents and spawned over two hundred teaching centers. Est (Erhard Seminars Training), a system of encounters meant to enable people to "get in touch with themselves," was grossing $10 million a year in 1975. In addition to these fads, Zen, yoga, the Sufi, Hare Krishna, and other new therapies and exotic religions flourished.

Spiritual revival

As millions of Americans sought to fill spiritual and emotional voids through esoteric movements, millions more were drawn to more traditional beliefs. According to a 1977 survey, about 70 million Americans defined themselves as born-again Christians, and 10 million claimed to have had the experience since 1975. President Jimmy Carter, singers Pat Boone and Johnny Cash, professional football player Roger Staubach, former Black Panther Eldridge Cleaver, and Watergate defendants Jeb Stuart Magruder and Charles Colson all counted themselves among the saved. Religious revivals and evangelical sects were not new, of course, but by the mid-1970s they were a growth industry. In the latter years of the decade evangelicals were grossing $200 million annually in sales of religious books, and the Virginia-based Christian Broadcast Network was earning nearly $60 million from its four stations and 130 affiliates.

Messianic cults

Besides the relatively harmless human potential movements and the traditional religious enthusiasms, a dark undercurrent of cult-like adherence to charismatic leaders ran through the 1970s. In 1973 and 1974, the Reverend Sun Myung Moon, founder of the Unification

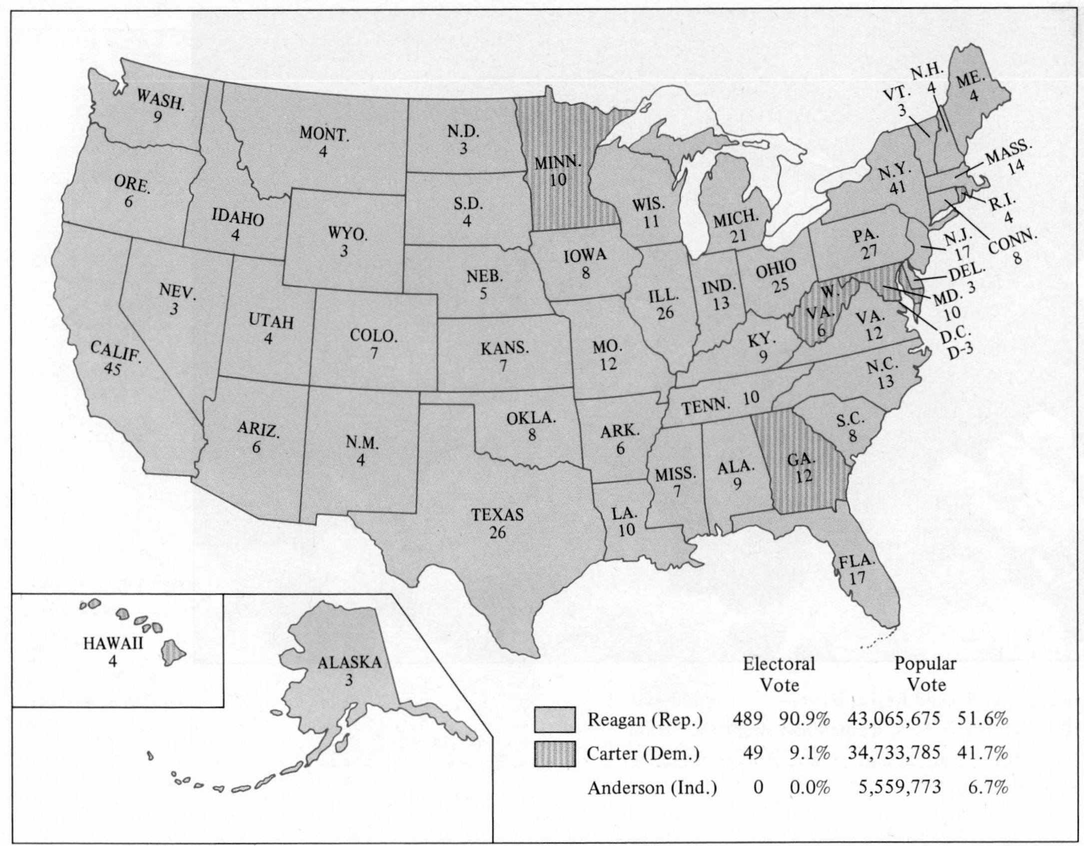

Presidential election, 1980

income taxes and boost the defense budget–a feat John Anderson said could only be done with mirrors. Reagan's stand against abortion and the ERA recommended him to the profamily movement. Indeed, his candidacy united the old right wing with the new. The old right, explained one fund raiser, had never been very interested in social issues. "But when political conservative leaders began to reach out and strike an alliance with social conservatives–the pro-life people, the anti-ERA people, the evangelical and born-again Christians, the people concerned about gay rights, prayer in the schools, sex in the movies or whatever–that's when this whole movement began to come alive. It's happened in a big way just in the last two years, and it's just exploding."

For his part, President Carter had little difficulty beating back the challenge of Senator Edward Kennedy. Kennedy's New Deal liberalism seemed out of place in the 1980s, and memories of Chappaquiddick lingered in voters' minds. The president had more formidable problems. American hostages were still held captive in Iran, and stagflation beset the economy. Carter retreated into the White House, contending that the nation's problems were too serious to allow him time to campaign. His supporters worried about the effect of the independent candidacy of John Anderson, who had bolted the Republican party in the primaries.

As election day approached, some political analysts thought they detected a resurgence of support for Carter. Polls predicted a Reagan victory by 3 to 5 percent, a small margin given the country's problems. But on election day voters gave Reagan and his running mate, George Bush, 51 percent of the vote to 41 percent for Carter and 7 percent for Anderson (see map). Reagan's sweep was nationwide; Carter carried only six states and the District of Columbia. Although the vote was partially an affirmation of Reagan's conservatism, it also signified deep dissatisfaction with Carter.

Important events

1973 Trials of Watergate burglars
Hearings by the Senate Select (Ervin) Committee on Campaign Practices
Acting FBI Director L. Patrick Gray resigns
White House aides John Ehrlichman and H. R. Haldeman resign
Confrontation between the American Indian Movement and the federal government at Wounded Knee, South Dakota
War Powers Act
Arab oil embargo
Vice President Spiro Agnew resigns
Congressman Gerald R. Ford appointed as vice president

1974 Oil price increases by the Organization of Petroleum Exporting Countries (OPEC)
Equal Credit Opportunity Act
Supreme Court orders President Nixon to release the White House tapes
House Judiciary Committee votes to impeach Nixon
Nixon resigns the presidency; Ford becomes president
Nelson Rockefeller appointed as vice president
President Ford pardons Nixon
Ford's WIN (Whip Inflation Now) program

1975 Nuclear accident at Brown's Ferry, Alabama
Antibusing agitation
New York City threatens to default on its debts

1976 Hyde amendment cuts off Medicaid funds for abortions
Jimmy Carter elected president

1977 "Roots" serialized on television
Resurgence of evangelical Christianity

1978 Supreme Court upholds affirmative action (*Bakke* v. *University of California*)
California voters approve Proposition 13
Mass suicides by followers of the Reverend Jim Jones in Guyana
Cleveland defaults on its debts

1979 Nuclear accident at Three Mile Island, Pennsylvania
Moral Majority established by the Reverend Jerry Falwell
Federal Reserve Board tightens the money supply
Iranian militants seize the U.S. embassy in Teheran and hold sixty-six Americans hostage
Russian troops invade Afghanistan

1980 Economic recession
Phased decontrol of oil prices and deregulation of transportation industries
"Boat people" and other refugees arrive in United States
U.S. military mission to rescue the hostages in Iran fails
One hundred million acres of Alaskan land placed in reserve for national parks, forests, and wildlife refuges
Supreme Court rules that the federal government must compensate the Sioux Indian Nation for the Black Hills
Race riots in Miami and Chattanooga
Ronald Reagan elected president
Republicans gain control of U.S. Senate

1981 Fifty-two hostages in Iran released after 444 days

More startling than Reagan's sweep was the capture of eleven Senate seats by Republican candidates, a victory that gave the party a majority in that house. Conservative advertising campaigns had succeeded in defeating most of the targeted liberals, including Senators George McGovern, Frank Church, and Birch Bayh. Republicans also gained thirty-three seats in the House and four state governorships. It seemed clear that Democrats would be running scared in the 1980s.

On January 20, 1981, Ronald Reagan was inaugurated as president. He pledged to work for "an era of national renewal," for "a healthy, vigorous, growing economy that provides equal opportunities for all Americans." On the same day, after 444 days in captivity, fifty-two American hostages boarded an airplane that flew them from Teheran to freedom. Yellow ribbons welcomed the freed Americans, and the nation rejoiced. Seldom had a new administration had a more auspicious beginning.

Reagan's assault on the welfare state

Reagan wasted no time in setting to work. He slashed government spending on social programs, raised the defense budget, and significantly reduced income taxes. He likened himself to Franklin D. Roosevelt; as the president of a nation in severe economic distress, he too would have to take bold action. But unlike Roosevelt's programs, Reagan's executive decisions and legislative proposals drastically shrank the government's functions and responsibilities. In fact, Roosevelt's New Deal programs were among the first to go, along with many of Lyndon Johnson's Great Society programs. "Government is not the solution to our problem," Reagan explained. "Government is the problem." At least for a while, Reagan seemed to have the support of the people in his campaign to return the nation to laissez-faire economics and political conservatism.

Suggestions for further reading

Watergate

Richard Ben-Veniste and George Framption, Jr., *Stonewall: The Real Story of the Watergate Prosecution* (1978); John W. Dean, *Blind Ambition: The White House Years* (1976); Leon Jaworski, *The Right and the Power: The Prosecution of Watergate* (1976); J. Anthony Lukas, *Nightmare: The Underside of the Nixon Years* (1976); John J. Sirica, *To Set the Record Straight: The Break-in, the Tapes, the Conspirators, the Pardon* (1979); Theodore White, *Breach of Faith* (1975); Bob Woodward and Carl Bernstein, *All the President's Men* (1974).

Energy shortages, economic woes

Richard J. Barnet, *The Lean Years: Politics in the Age of Scarcity* (1980); Daniel Bell, *The Coming of the Post-Industrial Society: A Venture in Social Forecasting* (1973); John M. Blair, *The Control of Oil* (1976); Barry Commoner, *The Politics of Energy* (1979); Susan George, *Feeding the Few: Corporate Control of Food* (1978); Robert L. Heilbroner, *An Inquiry into the Human Prospect* (1974); Frances Moore Lappé and Joseph Collins, *Food First: Beyond the Myth of Scarcity* (1977); Harry Mauer, *Not Working: An Oral History of the Unemployed* (1979); James Ridgeway, *Who Owns the Earth* (1980); Robert Stobaugh and Daniel Yergin, eds., *Energy Future: Report of the Energy Project at the Harvard Business School* (1979); Emma Rothschild, *Paradise Lost: The Decline of the Auto-Industrial Age* (1973); Lester C. Thurow, *The Zero-Sum Society: Distribution and the Possibilities for Economic Change* (1980).

The Ford administration

Gerald R. Ford, *A Time to Heal: The Autobiography of Gerald R. Ford* (1979); Jerry Hartmann, *Palace Politics: An Inside Account of the Ford Years* (1980); Clark Mollenhoff, *The Man Who Pardoned Nixon* (1976); Richard Reeves, *A Ford, Not a Lincoln* (1975); Jerald F. terHorst, *Gerald Ford and the Future of the Presidency* (1974).

The Carter administration

Betty Glad, *Jimmy Carter: From Plains to the White House* (1980); Haynes Johnson, *In the Absence of Power: Governing America* (1980); Clark R. Mollenhoff, *The President Who Failed: Carter out of Control* (1980); Robert Shogan, *Promises to Keep: Carter's First 100 Days* (1977); Laurence H. Shoup, *The Carter Presidency & Beyond* (1980); Jules Witcover, *Marathon: The Pursuit of the Presidency, 1972–1976* (1977).

Women's struggles

Susan Brownmiller, *Against Our Will: Men, Women and Rape* (1975); Jo Freeman, *The Politics of Women's Liberation* (1975); Linda Gordon and Allen Hunter, "Sex, Family & the New Right: Anti-feminism as a Political Force," *Radical America,* 11 (1977–1978), 9–18; Kenneth Keniston, *All*

Our Children: The American Family Under Pressure (1977); Juanita Kreps, *Sex in the Marketplace: American Women at Work* (1971); Christopher Lasch, *Haven in a Heartless World: The Family Besieged* (1977); Maggie Scarf, *Unfinished Business: Pressure Points in the Lives of Women* (1980).

Nonwhites in contemporary America

Vine Deloria, *Behind the Trail of Broken Treaties* (1974); Vine Deloria, *Custer Died for Your Sins: An Indian Manifesto* (1969); Dorothy K. Newman *et al., Protest, Politics, and Prosperity: Black Americans and White Institutions, 1940–1974* (1978); Julian A. Samora and Patricia Vandel Simon, *A History of the Mexican-American People* (1977); Carol B. Stack, *All Our Kin: Strategies for Survival in a Black Community* (1975); Ronald B. Taylor, *Chavez and the Farm Workers* (1975); Arnulfo D. Trejo, ed., *The Chicanos: As We See Ourselves* (1979); J. Harris Wilkinson III, *From Brown to Bakke: The Supreme Court and School Integration, 1954–1978* (1979); William Julius Wilson, *The Declining Significance of Race: Blacks and Changing American Institutions* (1978).

The Me Decade

Robert Boettcher and Gordon L. Freedman, *Gifts of Deceit: Sun Myung Moon, Tongsun Park and the Korean Scandal* (1980); Jim Hougan, *Decadence: Radical Nostalgia, Narcissism, and Decline in the Seventies* (1975); Christopher Lasch, *The Culture of Narcissism: American Life in an Age of Diminishing Expectations* (1978); James Reston, Jr., *Our Father Who Art in Hell: The Life and Death of Jim Jones* (1981); Edwin Schur, *The Awareness Trap: Self-Absorption Instead of Social Change* (1976); Gail Sheehy, *Passages: Predictable Crises in Adult Life* (1976); David F. Wells and John D. Woodbridge, *The Evangelicals* (1975); Tom Wolfe, "The 'Me' Decade and the Third Great Awakening," *New York,* 9 (1976), 26–40.

The new conservatism and the election of Ronald Reagan

Bill Boyarsky, *Ronald Reagan: His Life and Rise to the Presidency* (1981); Alan Crawford, *Thunder on the Right: The "New Right" and the Politics of Resentment* (1980); Carol Felsenthal, *The Sweetheart of the Silent Majority: The Biography of Phyllis Schlafly* (1981); Kirkpatrick Sale, *Power Shift: The Rise of the Southern Rim and Its Challenge to the Eastern Establishment* (1975); Hedrick Smith *et al., Reagan the Man, the President* (1981); Peter Steinfels, *The Neoconservatives: The Men Who Are Changing America's Politics* (1979); Doug Wead and Bill Wead, *Reagan in Pursuit of the Presidency* (1980).

APPENDIX

Historical reference books by subject

Encyclopedias, dictionaries, atlases, chronologies, and statistics

GENERAL AND BIOGRAPHICAL

Concise Dictionary of American Biography (1977); *Dictionary of American Biography* (1928–); *Dictionary of American History* (1976); *Encyclopedia of American History* (1981); *Family Encyclopedia of American History* (1975); George H. Gallup, *The Gallup Poll: Public Opinion, 1935–1971* (1972); George H. Gallup, *The Gallup Poll: Public Opinion, 1972–1977* (1978); John A. Garraty, ed., *Encyclopedia of American Biography* (1974); Bernard Grun, *The Timetables of History: A Horizontal Linkage of People and Events* (1975); Stanley Hochman, *Yesterday and Today: A Dictionary of Recent American History* (1979); *International Encyclopedia of the Social Sciences* (1968–); Thomas H. Johnson, *The Oxford Companion to American History* (1966); Richard B. Morris, *Encyclopedia of American History* (1976); *National Cyclopedia of American Biography* (1898–); U.S. Bureau of the Census, *Historical Statistics of the United States: Colonial Times to 1970* (1975); Charles Van Doren, ed., *Webster's American Biographies* (1974).

THE AMERICAN REVOLUTION

Mark M. Boatner, III, *Encyclopedia of the American Revolution* (1974).

ARCHITECTURE

William D. Hunt, Jr., ed., *Encyclopedia of American Architecture* (1980).

ATLASES

John L. Andriot, ed., *Township Atlas of the United States* (1979); Lester J. Cappon, ed., *Atlas of Early American History: The Revolutionary Era, 1760–1790* (1976); Edward W. Fox, *Atlas of American History* (1964); Edwin S. Gaustad, *Historical Atlas of Religion in America* (1976); *International Geographic Encyclopedia and Atlas* (1979); Kenneth T. Jackson and James T. Adams, *Atlas of American History* (1978); Douglas W. Marshall and Howard H. Peckham, *Campaigns of the American Revolution* (1976); *Rand-McNally Atlas of the American Revolution* (1974); U.S. Department of the Interior, Geological Survey, *National Atlas of the United States of America* (1970); U.S. War Department, *The Official Atlas of the Civil War* (1958); U.S. Military Academy, *The West Point Atlas of American Wars, 1689–1953* (1959).

BLACKS

Peter M. Bergman, *The Chronological History of the Negro in America* (1969); W. A. Low and Virgil A. Clift, eds., *Encyclopedia of Black America* (1981); Harry A. Ploski and William Marr, eds., *The Negro Almanac* (1976); Erwin A. Salk, ed., *A Layman's Guide to Negro History* (1967); Mabel M. Smythe, ed., *The Black American Reference Book* (1976); Edgar A. Toppin, *A Biographical History of Blacks in America* (1971).

THE CIVIL WAR

Mark M. Boatner, III, *The Civil War Dictionary* (1959); E. B. Long, *The Civil War Day by Day: An Almanac, 1861–1865* (1971); Jon L. Wakelyn, ed., *Biographical Dictionary of the Confederacy* (1977); Ezra J. Warner and W. Buck Yearns, *Biographical Register of the Confederate Congress* (1975).

CONSTITUTIONAL HISTORY

Congressional Quarterly, *Guide to the Supreme Court* (1979); Leon Friedman and Fred I. Israel, eds., *The Justices of the United States Supreme Court, 1789–1978: Their Lives and Major Opinions* (1980); *Judges of the United States* (1980).

ECONOMIC HISTORY

Glenn Porter, *Encyclopedia of American Economic History* (1980).

EDUCATION

Lee C. Deighton, ed., *The Encyclopedia of Education* (1971); John F. Ohles, ed., *Biographical Dictionary of American Educators* (1978).

ENTERTAINMENT

Tim Brooks and Earle Marsh, *The Complete Directory to Prime Time Network TV Shows, 1946–present* (1979); John Chilton, *Who's Who of Jazz* (1972); John Dunning, *Tune in Yesterday* [radio] (1976); *Notable Names in the American Theater* (1976); *New York Times Encyclopedia of Television* (1977); Andrew Sarris, *The American Cinema: Directors and Directions, 1929–1968* (1968); Evelyn M. Truitt, *Who Was Who on Screen* (1977).

FOREIGN POLICY

Alexander DeConde, ed., *Encyclopedia of American Foreign Policy* (1978); John E. Findling, *Dictionary of American Diplomatic History* (1980); Richard B. Morris and Graham W. Irwin, eds., *Harper Encyclopedia of the Modern World* (1970); Jack E. Vincent, *A Handbook of International Relations* (1969).

IMMIGRATION AND ETHNIC GROUPS

Stephen Thernstrom, ed., *Harvard Encyclopedia of American Ethnic Groups* (1980).

INDIANS

Frederick J. Dockstader, *Great North American Indians: Profiles in Life and Leadership* (1977); Barry Klein, ed., *Reference Encyclopedia of the American Indian* (1978).

LABOR

Gary M. Fink, ed., *Biographical Dictionary of American Labor Leaders* (1974); Gary M. Fink, ed., *Labor Unions* (1977).

POLITICS AND GOVERNMENT

Congressional Quarterly, *Congress and the Nation, 1945–1976* (1965–1977); Congressional Quarterly, *Guide to U.S. Elections* (1975); Roy R. Glashan, comp., *American Governors and Gubernatorial Elections, 1775–1978* (1979); Joseph E. Kallenbach and Jessamine S. Kallenbach, *American State Governors, 1776–1976* (1977); Svend Peterson, *A Statistical History of the American Presidential Elections* (1963); *Political Profiles, Truman Years to . . .* (1978); John W. Raimo, *Biographical Directory of American Colonial and Revolutionary Governors, 1607–1789* (1980); William Safire, *Safire's Political Dictionary* (1978); Richard M. Scammon, ed., *America at the Polls: Handbook of Presidential Election Statistics* (1965); Arthur M. Schlesinger, Jr., and Fred I. Israel, eds., *History of American Presidential Elections, 1789–1968* (1971); Robert Sobel, ed., *Biographical Directory of the United States Executive Branch, 1774–1977 (1977); U.S. Congress, Senate, Biographical Directory of the American Congress, 1774–1971* (1971); Robert Vexler, *The Vice-Presidents and Cabinet Members: Biographies Arranged Chronologically by Administration* (1975).

REGIONS AND STATES

Robert Bain, *et al.*, eds., *Southern Writers: A Biographical Dictionary* (1979); John Clayton, ed., *The Illinois Fact Book and Historical Almanac, 1673–1968* (1970); Howard R. Lamar, ed., *The Reader's Encyclopedia of the American West* (1977); David C. Roller and Robert W. Twyman, eds., *The Encyclopedia of Southern History* (1979); Walter Prescott Webb, H. Bailey Carroll, and Eldon S. Branda, eds. *The Handbook of Texas* (1952, 1976).

RELIGION

Henry Bowden, *Dictionary of American Religious Biography* (1977); J. Gordon Melton, *The Encyclopedia of American Religions* (1978); Arthur C. Piepkorn, *Profiles in Belief: The Religious Bodies of the United States and Canada* (1977–1979).

SCIENCE

Charles C. Gillispie, ed., *Dictionary of Scientific Biography* (1970–); National Academy of Sciences, *Biographical Memoirs* (1877–).

SPORTS

Ralph Hickok, *New Encyclopedia of Sports* (1977); Ralph Hickok, *Who Was Who in American Sports* (1971); Frank G. Menke and Suzanne Treat, *The Encyclopedia of Sports* (1977); Paul Soderberg, *et al., The Big Book of Halls of Fame in the United States and Canada* (1977).

WARS AND THE MILITARY

R. Ernest Dupuy and Trevor N. Dupuy, *The Encyclopedia of Military History* (1977); Robert Goralski, *World War II Almanac, 1931–1945* (1981); Thomas Parrish, ed., *The Simon and Schuster Encyclopedia of World War II* (1978); *Webster's American Military Biographies* (1978).

WOMEN

Edward T. James, Janet W. James, and Paul S. Boyer, eds., *Notable American Women, 1607–1950* (1971); Barbara Sicherman and Carol Hurd Green, eds., *Notable American Women: The Modern Period* (1980).

Declaration of Independence in Congress, July 4, 1776

The unanimous declaration of the thirteen United States of America

When, in the course of human events, it becomes necessary for one people to dissolve the political bonds which have connected them with another, and to assume, among the powers of the earth, the separate and equal station to which the laws of nature and of nature's God entitle them, a decent respect to the opinions of mankind requires that they should declare the causes which impel them to the separation.

We hold these truths to be self-evident: That all men are created equal; that they are endowed by their Creator with certain unalienable rights; that among these are life, liberty, and the pursuit of happiness; that, to secure these rights, governments are instituted among men, deriving their just powers from the consent of the governed; that whenever any form of government becomes destructive of these ends, it is the right of the people to alter or to abolish it, and to institute new government, laying its foundation on such principles, and organizing its powers in such form, as to them shall seem most likely to effect their safety and happiness. Prudence, indeed, will dictate that governments long established should not be changed for light and transient causes; and accordingly all experience hath shown that mankind are more disposed to suffer, while evils are sufferable, than to right themselves by abolishing the forms to which they are accustomed. But when a long train of abuses and usurpations, pursuing invariably the same object, evinces a design to reduce them under absolute despotism, it is their right, it is their duty, to throw off such government, and to provide new guards for their future security. Such has been the patient sufferance of these colonies; and such is now the necessity which constrains them to alter their former systems of government. The history of the present King of Great Britain is a history of repeated injuries and usurpations, all having in direct object the establishment of an absolute tyranny over these states. To prove this, let facts be submitted to a candid world.

He has refused his assent to laws, the most wholesome and necessary for the public good.

He has forbidden his governors to pass laws of immediate and pressing importance, unless suspended in their operation till his assent should be obtained; and, when so suspended, he has utterly neglected to attend to them.

He has refused to pass other laws for the accommodation of large districts of people, unless those people would relinquish the right of representation in the legislature, a right inestimable to them, and formidable to tyrants only.

He has called together legislative bodies at places unusual, uncomfortable, and distant from the depository of their public records, for the sole purpose of fatiguing them into compliance with his measures.

He has dissolved representative houses repeatedly, for opposing, with manly firmness, his invasions on the rights of the people.

He has refused for a long time, after such dissolutions, to cause others to be elected; whereby the legislative powers, incapable of annihilation, have returned to the people at large for their exercise; the state remaining, in the mean time, exposed to all the dangers of invasions from without and convulsions within.

He has endeavored to prevent the population of these states; for that purpose obstructing the laws for naturalization of foreigners; refusing to pass others to encourage their migration hither, and raising the conditions of new appropriations of lands.

He has obstructed the administration of justice, by refusing his assent to laws for establishing judiciary powers.

He has made judges dependent on his will alone, for the tenure of their offices, and the amount and payment of their salaries.

He has erected a multitude of new offices, and sent hither swarms of officers to harass our people and eat out their substance.

He has kept among us, in times of peace, standing armies, without the consent of our legislatures.

He has affected to render the military independent of, and superior to, the civil power.

He has combined with others to subject us to a jurisdiction foreign to our constitution, and unacknowledged by our laws, giving his assent to their acts of pretended legislation:

For quartering large bodies of armed troops among us;

For protecting them, by a mock trial, from punishment for any murders which they should commit on the inhabitants of these states;

For cutting off our trade with all parts of the world;

For imposing taxes on us without our consent;

For depriving us, in many cases, of the benefits of trial by jury;

For transporting us beyond seas, to be tried for pretended offenses;

For abolishing the free system of English laws in a neighboring province, establishing therein an arbitrary government, and enlarging its boundaries, so as to render it at once an example and fit instrument for introducing the same absolute rule into these colonies;

have been created, or the emoluments whereof shall have been increased, during such time; and no person holding any office under the United States shall be a member of either house during his continuance in office.

Section 7 All bills for raising revenue shall originate in the House of Representatives; but the Senate may propose or concur with amendments as on other bills.

Every bill which shall have passed the House of Representatives and the Senate, shall, before it become a law, be presented to the President of the United States; if he approve he shall sign it, but if not he shall return it with objections to that house in which it originated, who shall enter the objections at large on their journal, and proceed to reconsider it. If after such reconsideration two-thirds of that house shall agree to pass the bill, it shall be sent, together with the objections, to the other house, by which it shall likewise be reconsidered, and, if approved by two-thirds of that house, it shall become a law. But in all such cases the votes of both houses shall be determined by yeas and nays, and the names of the persons voting for and against the bill shall be entered on the journal of each house respectively. If any bill shall not be returned by the President within ten days (Sundays excepted) after it shall have been presented to him, the same shall be a law, in like manner as if he had signed it, unless the Congress by their adjournment prevent its return, in which case it shall not be a law.

Every order, resolution, or vote to which the concurrence of the Senate and House of Representatives may be necessary (except on a question of adjournment) shall be presented to the President of the United States; and before the same shall take effect, shall be approved by him, or being disapproved by him, shall be repassed by two-thirds of the Senate and House of Representatives, according to the rules and limitations prescribed in the case of a bill.

Section 8 The Congress shall have power

To lay and collect taxes, duties, imposts, and excises, to pay the debts and provide for the common defense and general welfare of the United States; but all duties, imposts and excises shall be uniform throughout the United States;

To borrow money on the credit of the United States;

To regulate commerce with foreign nations, and among the several States, and with the Indian tribes;

To establish an uniform rule of naturalization, and uniform laws on the subject of bankruptcies throughout the United States;

To coin money, regulate the value thereof, and of foreign coin, and fix the standard of weights and measures;

To provide for the punishment of counterfeiting the securities and current coin of the United States;

To establish post offices and post roads;

To promote the progress of science and useful arts by securing for limited times to authors and inventors the exclusive right to their respective writings and discoveries;

To constitute tribunals inferior to the Supreme Court;

To define and punish piracies and felonies committed on the high seas and offenses against the law of nations;

To declare war, grant letters of marque and reprisal, and make rules concerning captures on land and water;

To raise and support armies, but no appropriation of money to that use shall be for a longer term than two years;

To provide and maintain a navy;

To make rules for the government and regulation of the land and naval forces;

To provide for calling forth the militia to execute the laws of the Union, suppress insurrections, and repel invasions;

To provide for organizing, arming, and disciplining the militia, and for governing such part of them as may be employed in the service of the United States, reserving to the States respectively the appointment of the officers, and the authority of training the militia according to the discipline prescribed by Congress;

To exercise exclusive legislation in all cases whatsoever, over such district (not exceeding ten miles square) as may, by cession of particular States, and the acceptance of Congress, become the seat of government of the United States, and to exercise like authority over all places purchased by the consent of the legislature of the State, in which the same shall be, for erection of forts, magazines, arsenals, dock-yards, and other needful buildings;—and

To make all laws which shall be necessary and proper for carrying into execution the foregoing powers, and all other powers vested by this Constitution in the government of the United States, or in any department or officer thereof.

Section 9 *The migration or importation of such persons as any of the States now existing shall think proper to admit shall not be prohibited by the Congress prior to the year 1808; but a tax or duty may be imposed on such importation, not exceeding $10 for each person.*

The privilege of the writ of habeas corpus shall not be suspended, unless when in cases of rebellion or invasion the public safety may require it.

No bill of attainder or ex post facto law shall be passed.

No capitation, or other direct, tax shall be laid, unless in proportion to the census or enumeration herein before directed to be taken.

No tax or duty shall be laid on articles exported from any State.

No preference shall be given by any regulation of commerce or revenue to the ports of one State over those of another; nor shall vessels bound to, or from, one State, be obliged to enter, clear, or pay duties in another.

No money shall be drawn from the treasury, but in consequence of appropriations made by law; and a regular statement and account of the receipts and expenditures of all public money shall be published from time to time.

No title of nobility shall be granted by the United States: and no person holding any office of profit or trust under them, shall, without the consent of the Congress, accept of any present, emolument, office, or title, of any kind whatever, from any king, prince, or foreign state.

Section 10 No State shall enter into any treaty, alliance, or confederation; grant letters of marque and reprisal; coin money; emit bills of credit; make anything but gold and silver coin a tender in payment of debts; pass any bill of attainder, ex post facto law, or law impairing the obligation of contracts, or grant any title of nobility.

No State shall, without the consent of Congress, lay any imposts or duties on imports or exports, except what may be absolutely necessary for executing its inspection laws: and the net produce of all duties and imposts, laid by any State on imports or exports, shall be for the use of the treasury of the United States; and all such laws shall be subject to the revision and control of the Congress.

No State shall, without the consent of Congress, lay any duty of tonnage, keep troops or ships of war in time of peace, enter into any agreement or compact with another State, or with a foreign power, or engage in war, unless actually invaded, or in such imminent danger as will not admit of delay.

ARTICLE II

Section 1 The executive power shall be vested in a President of the United States of America. He shall hold his office during the term of four years, and, together with the Vice-President, chosen for the same term, be elected as follows:

Each State shall appoint, in such manner as the legislature thereof may direct, a number of electors, equal to the whole number of Senators and Representatives to which the State may be entitled in the Congress; but no Senator or Representative, or person holding an office of trust or profit under the United States, shall be appointed an elector.

The electors shall meet in their respective States, and vote by ballot for two persons, of whom one at least shall not be an inhabitant of the same State with themselves. And they shall make a list of all the persons voted for, and of the number of votes for each; which list they shall sign and certify, and transmit sealed to the seat of government of the United States, directed to the President of the Senate. The President of the Senate shall, in the presence of the Senate and House of Representatives, open all the certificates, and the votes shall then be counted. The person having the greatest number of votes shall be the President, if such number be a majority of the whole number of electors appointed; and if there be more than one who have such majority, and have an equal number of votes, then the House of Representatives shall immediately choose by ballot one of them for President; and if no person have a majority, then from the five highest on the list said house shall in like manner choose the President. But in choosing the President the votes shall be taken by States, the representation from each State having one vote; a quorum for this purpose shall consist of a member or members from two-thirds of the States, and a majority of all the States shall be necessary to a choice. In every case, after the choice of the President, the person having the greatest number of votes of the electors shall be the Vice-President. But if there should remain two or more who have equal votes, the Senate shall choose from them by ballot the Vice-President.

The Congress may determine the time of choosing the electors and the day on which they shall give their votes; which day shall be the same throughout the United States.

No person except a natural-born citizen, *or a citizen of the United States at the time of the adoption of this Constitution,* shall be eligible to the office of President; neither shall any person be eligible to that office who shall not have attained to the age of thirty-five years, and been fourteen years a resident within the United States.

In case of the removal of the President from office or of his death, resignation, or inability to discharge the powers and duties of the said office, the same shall devolve on the Vice-President, and the Congress may by law provide for the case of removal, death, resignation, or inability, both of the President and Vice-President, declaring what officer shall then act as President, and such officer shall act accordingly, until the disability be removed, or a President shall be elected.

The President shall, at stated times, receive for his services a compensation, which shall neither be increased nor diminished during the period for which he shall have been elected, and he shall not receive within that period any other emolument from the United States, or any of them.

Before he enter on the execution of his office, he shall take the following oath or affirmation:—"I do solemnly swear (or affirm) that I will faithfully execute the office of the President of the United States, and will to the best of my ability preserve, protect and defend the Constitution of the United States."

Section 2 The President shall be commander in chief of the army and navy of the United States, and of the militia of the several States, when called into the actual service of the United States; he may require the opinion, in writing, of the principal officer in each of the executive departments, upon any subject relating to the duties of their respective offices, and he shall have power to grant reprieves and pardons for offenses against the United States, except in cases of impeachment.

He shall have power, by and with the advice and consent of the Senate, to make treaties, provided two-thirds of the Senators present concur; and he shall nominate, and by and with the advice and consent of the Senate, shall appoint ambassadors, other public ministers and consuls, judges of the Supreme Court, and all other officers of the United States, whose appointments are not herein otherwise provided for, and which shall be established by law: but Congress may by law vest the appointment of such inferior officers, as they think proper, in the President alone, in the courts of law, or in the heads of departments.

The President shall have power to fill up all vacancies that may happen during the recess of the Senate, by granting commissions which shall expire at the end of their next session.

Section 3 He shall from time to time give to the Congress information of the state of the Union, and recommend to their consideration such measures as he shall judge necessary and expedient; he may, on extraordinary occasions, convene both houses, or either of them, and in case of disagreement between them, with respect to the time of adjournment, he may adjourn them to such time as he shall think proper; he shall receive ambassadors and other public ministers; he shall take care that the laws be faithfully executed, and shall commission all the officers of the United States.

Section 4 The President, Vice-President and all civil officers of the United States shall be removed from office on impeachment for, and on conviction of, treason, bribery, or other high crimes and misdemeanors.

ARTICLE III

Section 1 The judicial power of the United States shall be vested in one Supreme Court, and in such inferior courts as the Congress may from time to time ordain and establish. The judges, both of the Supreme and inferior courts, shall hold their offices during good behavior, and shall, at stated times, receive for their services a compensation which shall not be diminished during their continuance in office.

Section 2 The judicial power shall extend to all cases, in law and equity, arising under this Constitution, the laws of the United States, and treaties made, or which shall be made, under their authority;–to all cases affecting ambassadors, other public ministers and consuls;–to all cases of admiralty and maritime jurisdiction;–to controversies to which the United States shall be a party;–to controversies between two or more States;–*between a State and citizens of another State;*–between citizens of different States;–between citizens of the same State claiming lands under grants of different States, and between a State, or the citizens thereof, and foreign states, citizens or subjects.

In all cases affecting ambassadors, other public ministers and consuls, and those in which a State shall be party, the Supreme Court shall have original jurisdiction. In all the other cases before mentioned, the Supreme Court shall have appellate jurisdiction, both as to law and fact, with such exceptions, and under such regulations, as the Congress shall make.

The trial of all crimes, except in cases of impeachment, shall be by jury; and such trial shall be held in the State where said crimes shall have been committed; but when not committed within any State, the trial shall be at such place or places as the Congress may by law have directed.

Section 3 Treason against the United States shall consist only in levying war against them, or in adhering to their enemies, giving them aid and comfort. No person shall be convicted of treason unless on the testimony of two witnesses to the same overt act, or on confession in open court.

The Congress shall have power to declare the punishment of treason, but no attainder of treason shall work corruption of blood, or forfeiture except during the life of the person attainted.

ARTICLE IV

Section 1 Full faith and credit shall be given in each State to the public acts, records, and judicial proceedings of every other State. And the Congress may by general laws prescribe the manner in which such acts, records, and proceedings shall be proved, and the effect thereof.

Section 2 The citizens of each State shall be entitled to all privileges and immunities of citizens in the several States.

A person charged in any State with treason, felony, or other crime, who shall flee from justice, and be found in another State, shall on demand of the executive authority of the State from which he fled, be delivered up, to be removed to the State having jurisdiction of the crime.

No person held to service or labor in one State, under the laws thereof, escaping into another, shall, in consequence of any law or regulation therein, be discharged from such service or labor, but shall be delivered up on claim of the party to whom such service or labor may be due.

Section 3 New States may be admitted by the Congress into this Union; but no new State shall be formed or erected within the jurisdiction of any other State; nor any State be formed by the junction of two or more States, or parts of States, without the consent of the legislatures of the States concerned as well as of the Congress.

The Congress shall have power to dispose of and make all needful rules and regulations respecting the territory or other property belonging to the United States; and nothing in this Constitution shall be so construed as to prejudice any claims of the United States, or of any particular State.

Section 4 The United States shall guarantee to every State in this Union a republican form of government, and shall protect each of them against invasion; and on application of the legislature, or of the executive (when the legislature cannot be convened), against domestic violence.

ARTICLE V

The Congress, whenever two-thirds of both houses shall deem it necessary, shall propose amendments to this Constitution, or, on the application of the legislatures of two-thirds of the several States, shall call a convention for proposing amendments, which, in either case, shall be valid to all intents and purposes, as part of this Constitution, when ratified by the legislatures of three-fourths of the several States, or by conventions in three-fourths thereof, as the one or the other mode of ratification may be proposed by the Congress; provided *that no amendments which may be made prior to the year one thousand eight hundred and eight shall in any manner affect the first and fourth clauses in the ninth section of the first article;* and that no State, without its consent, shall be deprived of its equal suffrage in the Senate.

ARTICLE VI

All debts contracted and engagements entered into, before the adoption of this Constitution, shall be as valid against the United States under this Constitution, as under the Confederation.

This Constitution, and the laws of the United States which shall be made in pursuance thereof; and all treaties made, or which shall be made, under the authority of the United States, shall be the supreme law of the land; and the judges in every State shall be bound thereby, anything in the Constitution or laws of any State to the contrary notwithstanding.

The Senators and Representatives before mentioned, and the members of the several State legislatures, and all executive and judicial officers, both of the United States and of the several States, shall be bound by oath or affirmation to support this Constitution; but no religious test shall ever be required as a qualification to any office or public trust under the United States.

ARTICLE VII

The ratification of the conventions of nine States shall be sufficient for the establishment of this Constitution between the States so ratifying the same.

Done in Convention by the unanimous consent of the States present, the seventeenth day of September in the year of our Lord one thousand seven hundred and eighty-seven and of the Independence of the United States of America the twelfth. In witness whereof we have hereunto subscribed our names.

GEORGE WASHINGTON
and thirty-seven others

*Amendments to the Constitution**

AMENDMENT I

Congress shall make no law respecting an establishment of religion, or prohibiting the free exercise thereof; or abridging the freedom of speech, or of the press; or the right of the people peaceably to assemble, and to petition the government for a redress of grievances.

AMENDMENT II

A well-regulated militia being necessary to the security of a free State, the right of the people to keep and bear arms shall not be infringed.

AMENDMENT III

No soldier shall, in time of peace, be quartered in any house without the consent of the owner, nor in time of war, but in a manner to be prescribed by law.

AMENDMENT IV

The right of the people to be secure in their persons, houses, papers, and effects, against unreasonable searches and seizures, shall not be violated, and no warrants shall issue but upon probable cause, supported by oath or affirmation, and particularly describing the place to be searched, and the persons or things to be seized.

*The first ten Amendments (the Bill of Rights) were adopted in 1791.

AMENDMENT V

No person shall be held to answer for a capital, or otherwise infamous crime, unless on a presentment or indictment of a grand jury, except in cases arising in the land or naval forces, or in the militia, when in actual service in time of war or public danger; nor shall any person be subject for the same offense to be twice put in jeopardy of life or limb; nor shall be compelled in any criminal case to be a witness against himself, nor be deprived of life, liberty, or property, without due process of law; nor shall private property be taken for public use without just compensation.

AMENDMENT VI

In all criminal prosecutions, the accused shall enjoy the right to a speedy and public trial, by an impartial jury of the State and district wherein the crime shall have been committed, which district shall have been previously ascertained by law, and to be informed of the nature and cause of the accusation; to be confronted with the witnesses against him; to have compulsory process for obtaining witnesses in his favor, and to have the assistance of counsel for his defense.

AMENDMENT VII

In suits at common law, where the value in controversy shall exceed twenty dollars, the right of trial by jury shall be preserved, and no fact tried by a jury shall be otherwise reexamined in any court of the United States, than according to the rules of the common law.

AMENDMENT VIII

Excessive bail shall not be required, nor excessive fines imposed, nor cruel and unusual punishments inflicted.

AMENDMENT IX

The enumeration in the Constitution, of certain rights, shall not be construed to deny or disparage others retained by the people.

AMENDMENT X

The powers not delegated to the United States by the Constitution, nor prohibited by it to the States, are reserved to the States respectively, or to the people.

AMENDMENT XI
[Adopted 1798]

The judicial power of the United States shall not be construed to extend to any suit in law or equity, commenced or prosecuted against one of the United States by citizens of another State, or by citizens or subjects of any foreign state.

AMENDMENT XII
[Adopted 1804]

The electors shall meet in their respective States, and vote by ballot for President and Vice-President, one of whom, at least, shall not be an inhabitant of the same State with themselves; they shall name in their ballots the person voted for as President, and in distinct ballots the person voted for as Vice-President, and they shall make distinct lists of all persons voted for as President, and of all persons voted for as Vice-President, and of the number of votes for each, which lists they shall sign and certify, and transmit sealed to the seat of government of the United States, directed to the President of the Senate;–the President of the Senate shall, in the presence of the Senate and House of Representatives, open all the certificates and the votes shall then be counted;–the person having the greatest number of votes for President shall be the President, if such number be a majority of the whole number of electors appointed; and if no person have such majority, then from the persons having the highest numbers not exceeding three on the list of those voted for as President, the House of Representatives shall choose immediately, by ballot, the President. But in choosing the President, the votes shall be taken by States, the representation from each State having one vote; a quorum for this purpose shall consist of a member or members from two-thirds of the States, and a majority of all the States shall be necessary to a choice. And if the House of Representatives shall not choose a President whenever the right of choice shall devolve upon them, before *the fourth day of March* next following, then the Vice-President shall act as President, as in the case of the death or other constitutional disability of the President.

The person having the greatest number of votes as Vice-President shall be the Vice-President, if such number be a majority of the whole number of electors appointed; and if no person have a majority, then from the two highest numbers on the list the Senate shall choose the Vice-President; a quorum for the purpose shall consist of two-thirds of the whole number of Senators, and a majority of the whole number shall be necessary to a choice. But no person constitutionally ineligible to the office of President shall be eligible to that of Vice-President of the United States.

AMENDMENT XIII
[Adopted 1865]

Section 1 Neither slavery nor involuntary servitude, except as a punishment for crime whereof the party shall have been duly convicted, shall exist within the United States, or any place subject to their jurisdiction.

Section 2 Congress shall have power to enforce this article by appropriate legislation.

AMENDMENT XIV
[Adopted 1868]

Section 1 All persons born or naturalized in the United States, and subject to the jurisdiction thereof, are citizens of the United States and of the State wherein they reside. No State shall make or enforce any law which shall abridge the privileges or immunities of citizens of the United States; nor shall any State deprive any person of life, liberty, or property, without due process of law; nor deny to any person within its jurisdiction the equal protection of the laws.

Section 2 Representatives shall be apportioned among the several States according to their respective numbers, counting the whole number of persons in each State, excluding Indians not taxed. But when the right to vote at any election for the choice of Electors for President and Vice-President of the United States, Representatives in Congress, the executive and judicial officers of a State, or the members of the legislature thereof, is denied to any of the male inhabitants of such State, being twenty-one years of age and citizens of the United States, or in any way abridged, except for participation in rebellion, or other crime, the basis of representation therein shall be reduced in the proportion which the number of such male citizens shall bear to the whole number of male citizens twenty-one years of age in such State.

Section 3 No person shall be a Senator or Representative in Congress, or Elector of President and Vice-President, or hold any office, civil or military, under the United States, or under any State, who, having previously taken an oath, as a member of Congress, or as an officer of the United States, or as a member of any State legislature, or as an executive or judicial officer of any State, to support the Constitution of the United States, shall have engaged in insurrection or rebellion against the same, or given aid or comfort to the enemies thereof. Congress may, by a vote of two-thirds of each house, remove such disability.

Section 4 The validity of the public debt of the United States, authorized by law, including debts incurred for payment of pensions and bounties for services in suppressing insurrection or rebellion, shall not be questioned. But neither the United States nor any State shall assume or pay any debt or obligation incurred in aid of insurrection or rebellion against the United States, or any claim for the loss of emancipation of any slave; but all such debts, obligations, and claims shall be held illegal and void.

Section 5 The Congress shall have power to enforce, by appropriate legislation, the provisions of this article.

AMENDMENT XV
[Adopted 1870]

Section 1 The right of citizens of the United States to vote shall not be denied or abridged by the United States or by any State on account of race, color, or previous condition of servitude.

Section 2 The Congress shall have power to enforce this article by appropriate legislation.

AMENDMENT XVI
[Adopted 1913]

The Congress shall have power to lay and collect taxes on incomes, from whatever source derived, without apportionment among the several States, and without regard to any census or enumeration.

AMENDMENT XVII
[Adopted 1913]

Section 1 The Senate of the United States shall be composed of two Senators from each State, elected by the people thereof, for six years; and each Senator shall have one vote. The electors in each State shall have the qualifications requisite for electors of [voters for] the most numerous branch of the State legislatures.

Section 2 When vacancies happen in the representation of any State in the Senate, the executive authority of such State shall issue writs of election to fill such vacancies: Provided, that the Legislature of any State may empower the executive thereof to make temporary appointments until the people fill the vacancies by election as the Legislature may direct.

Section 3 This amendment shall not be so construed as to affect the election or term of any Senator chosen before it becomes valid as part of the Constitution.

AMENDMENT XVIII
[Adopted 1919; Repealed 1933]

Section 1 After one year from the ratification of this article the manufacture, sale, or transportation of intoxicating liquors within, the importation thereof into, or the exportation thereof from the United States and all territory subject to the jurisdiction thereof, for beverage purposes, is hereby prohibited.

Section 2 The Congress and the several States shall have concurrent power to enforce this article by appropriate legislation.

Section 3 This article shall be inoperative unless it shall have been ratified as an amendment to the Constitution by the legislatures of the several States, as provided by the Constitution, within seven years from the date of the submission thereof to the States by the Congress.

AMENDMENT XIX
[Adopted 1920]

Section 1 The right of citizens of the United States to vote shall not be denied or abridged by the United States or by any State on account of sex.

Section 2 The Congress shall have power to enforce this article by appropriate legislation.

AMENDMENT XX
[Adopted 1933]

Section 1 The terms of the President and Vice-President shall end at noon on the 20th day of January, and the terms of Senators and Representatives at noon on the 3d day of January, of the years in which such terms would have ended if this article had not been ratified; and the terms of their successors shall then begin.

Section 2 The Congress shall assemble at least once in every year, and such meeting shall begin at noon on the 3d day of January, unless they shall by law appoint a different day.

Section 3 If, at the time fixed for the beginning of the term of the President, the President-elect shall have died, the Vice-President-elect shall become President. If a President shall not have been chosen before the time fixed for the beginning of his term, or if the President-elect shall have failed to qualify, then the Vice-President-elect shall act as President until a President shall have qualified; and the Congress may by law provide for the case wherein neither a President-elect nor a Vice-President-elect shall have qualified, declaring who shall then act as President, or the manner in which one who is to act shall be selected, and such persons shall act accordingly until a President or Vice-President shall have qualified.

Section 4 The Congress may by law provide for the case of the death of any of the persons from whom the House of Representatives may choose a President whenever the right of choice shall have devolved upon them, and for the case of the death of any of the persons from whom the Senate may choose a Vice-President whenever the right of choice shall have devolved upon them.

Section 5 Sections 1 and 2 shall take effect on the 15th day of October following the ratification of this article.

Section 6 This article shall be inoperative unless it shall have been ratified as an amendment to the Constitution by the Legislatures of three-fourths of the several States within seven years from the date of its submission.

AMENDMENT XXI
[Adopted 1933]

Section 1 The eighteenth article of amendment to the Constitution of the United States is hereby repealed.

Section 2 The transportation or importation into any State, Territory, or Possession of the United States for delivery or use therein of intoxicating liquors, in violation of the laws thereof, is hereby prohibited.

Section 3 This article shall be inoperative unless it shall have been ratified as an amendment to the Constitution by conventions in the several States, as provided in the Constitution, within seven years from the date of submission thereof to the States by the Congress.

AMENDMENT XXII
[Adopted 1951]

Section 1 No person shall be elected to the office of President more than twice, and no person who has held the office of President, or acted as President, for more than two years of a term to which some other person was elected President shall be elected to the office of President more than once. But this article shall not apply to any person holding the office of President when this article was proposed by the Congress, and shall not prevent any person who may be holding the office of President, or acting as President, during the term within which this article becomes operative from holding the office of President or acting as President during the remainder of such term.

Section 2 This article shall be inoperative unless it shall have been ratified as an amendment to the Constitution by the legislatures of three-fourths of the several States within seven years from the date of its submission to the States by the Congress.

AMENDMENT XXIII
[Adopted 1961]

Section 1 The District constituting the seat of Government of the United States shall appoint in such manner as the Congress may direct:

A number of electors of President and Vice-President equal to the whole number of Senators and Representatives in Congress to which the District would be entitled if it were a State, but in no event more than the least populous State; they shall be in addition to those appointed by the States, but they shall be considered for the purposes of the election of President and Vice-President, to be electors appointed by a State; and they shall meet in the District and perform such duties as provided by the twelfth article of amendment.

Section 2 The Congress shall have the power to enforce this article by appropriate legislation.

AMENDMENT XXIV
[Adopted 1964]

Section 1 The right of citizens of the United States to vote in any primary or other election for President or Vice-President, for electors for President or Vice-President, or for Senator or Representative in Congress, shall not be denied or abridged by the United States or any State by reason of failure to pay any poll tax or other tax.

Section 2 The Congress shall have the power to enforce this article by appropriate legislation.

AMENDMENT XXV
[Adopted 1967]

Section 1 In case of the removal of the President from office or of his death or resignation, the Vice President shall become President.

Section 2 Whenever there is a vacancy in the office of the Vice President, the President shall nominate a Vice President who shall take office upon confirmation by a majority vote of both Houses of Congress.

Section 3 Whenever the President transmits to the President pro tempore of the Senate and the Speaker of the House of Representatives his written declaration that he is unable to discharge the powers and duties of his office, and until he transmits to them a written declaration to the contrary, such powers and duties shall be discharged by the Vice President as Acting President.

Section 4 Whenever the Vice President and a majority of either the principal officers of the executive departments or of such other body as Congress may by law provide, transmit to the President pro tempore of the Senate and the Speaker of the House of Representatives their written declaration that the President is unable to discharge the powers and duties of his office, the Vice President shall immediately assume the powers and duties of the office as Acting President.

Thereafter, when the President transmits to the President pro tempore of the Senate and the Speaker of the House of Representatives his written declaration that no inability exists, he shall resume the powers and duties of his office unless the Vice President and a majority of either the principal officers of the executive department[s] or of such other body as Congress may by law provide, transmit within four days to the President pro tempore of the Senate and the Speaker of the House of Representatives their written declaration that the President is unable to discharge the powers and duties of his office. Thereupon Congress shall decide the issue, assembling within forty-eight hours for that purpose if not in session. If the Congress, within twenty-one days after receipt of the latter written declaration, or, if Congress is not in session, within twenty-one days after Congress is required to assemble, determines by two-thirds vote of both Houses that the President is unable to discharge the powers and duties of his office, the Vice President shall continue to discharge the same as Acting President; otherwise, the President shall resume the powers and duties of his office.

AMENDMENT XXVI
[Adopted 1971]

Section 1 The right of citizens of the United States, who are eighteen years of age or older, to vote shall not be denied or abridged by the United States or by any State on account of age.

Section 2 The Congress shall have power to enforce this article by appropriate legislation.

PROPOSED AMENDMENT
[Sent to the states, 1972]

Section 1 Equality of rights under the law shall not be denied or abridged by the United States or by any State on account of sex.

Section 2 The Congress shall have the power to enforce, by appropriate legislation, the provisions of this article.

Section 3 This amendment shall take effect two years after the date of ratification.

PROPOSED AMENDMENT
[Sent to the states, 1978]

Section 1 For purposes of representation in the Congress, election of the President and Vice President, and article V of this Constitution, the District constituting the seat of government of the United States shall be treated as though it were a State.

Section 2 The exercise of the rights and powers conferred under this article shall be by the people of the District constituting the seat of government, and as shall be provided by the Congress.

Section 3 The twenty-third article of amendment to the Constitution of the United States is hereby repealed.

Section 4 This article shall be inoperative, unless it shall have been ratified as an amendment to the Constitution by the legislatures of three-fourths of the several States within seven years from the date of its submission.

The American people: A statistical profile

Population of the United States

YEAR	NUMBER OF STATES	POPULATION	PERCENT INCREASE	POPULATION PER SQUARE MILE	PERCENT URBAN/ RURAL	PERCENT MALE/ FEMALE	PERCENT WHITE/ NONWHITE
1790	13	3,929,214		4.5	5.1/94.9	NA/NA	80.7/19.3
1800	16	5,308,483	35.1	6.1	6.1/93.9	NA/NA	81.1/18.9
1810	17	7,239,881	36.4	4.3	7.3/92.7	NA/NA	81.0/19.0
1820	23	9,638,453	33.1	5.5	7.2/92.8	50.8/49.2	81.6/18.4
1830	24	12,866,020	33.5	7.4	8.8/91.2	50.8/49.2	81.9/18.1
1840	26	17,069,453	32.7	9.8	10.8/89.2	50.9/49.1	83.2/16.8
1850	31	23,191,876	35.9	7.9	15.3/84.7	51.0/49.0	84.3/15.7
1860	33	31,443,321	35.6	10.6	19.8/80.2	51.2/48.8	85.6/14.4
1870	37	39,818,449	26.6	13.4	25.7/74.3	50.6/49.4	86.2/13.8
1880	38	50,155,783	26.0	16.9	28.2/71.8	50.9/49.1	86.5/13.5
1890	44	62,947,714	25.5	21.2	35.1/64.9	51.2/48.8	87.5/12.5
1900	45	75,994,575	20.7	25.6	39.6/60.4	51.1/48.9	87.9/12.1
1910	46	91,972,266	21.0	31.0	45.6/54.4	51.5/48.5	88.9/11.1
1920	48	105,710,620	14.9	35.6	51.2/48.8	51.0/49.0	89.7/10.3
1930	48	122,775,046	16.1	41.2	56.1/43.9	50.6/49.4	89.8/10.2
1940	48	131,669,275	7.2	44.2	56.5/43.5	50.2/49.8	89.8/10.2
1950	48	150,697,361	14.5	50.7	64.0/36.0	49.7/50.3	89.5/10.5
1960	50	179,323,175	19.0	50.6	69.9/30.1	49.3/50.7	88.6/11.4
1970	50	203,235,298	13.3	57.5	73.5/26.5	48.7/51.3	87.6/12.4
1980	50	226,504,825	11.4	64.0	NA/NA	48.6/51.4	83.2/16.8

NA = Not available.
*1979 figures

IMMIGRATION TOTALS BY DECADE

YEARS	NUMBER	YEARS	NUMBER
1820	8,385	1901–1910	8,795,386
1821–1830	143,439	1911–1920	5,735,811
1831–1840	599,125	1921–1930	4,107,209
1841–1850	1,713,251	1931–1940	528,431
1851–1860	2,598,214	1941–1950	1,035,039
1861–1870	2,314,824	1951–1960	2,515,479
1871–1880	2,812,191	1961–1970	3,321,677
1881–1890	5,246,613	Total	45,162,638
1891–1900	3,687,546		

REGIONAL ORIGINS OF IMMIGRANTS (in percentages)

	EUROPE						
PERIOD	TOTAL EUROPE	NORTH AND WEST[a]	EAST AND CENTRAL[b]	SOUTH AND OTHER[c]	WESTERN HEMISPHERE	ASIA	ALL OTHER
1821–1830	69.2	67.1	–	2.1	8.4	–	22.4
1831–1840	82.8	81.8	–	1.0	5.5	–	11.7
1841–1850	93.3	92.9	0.1	0.3	3.6	–	3.1
1851–1860	94.4	93.6	0.1	0.8	2.9	1.6	1.1
1861–1870	89.2	87.8	0.5	0.9	7.2	2.8	0.8
1871–1880	80.8	73.6	4.5	2.7	14.4	4.4	0.4
1881–1890	90.3	72.0	11.9	6.3	8.1	1.3	0.3
1891–1900	96.5	44.5	32.8	19.1	1.1	1.9	0.5
1901–1910	92.5	21.7	44.5	26.3	4.1	2.8	0.6
1911–1920	76.3	17.4	33.4	25.5	19.9	3.4	0.4
1921–1930	60.3	31.7	14.4	14.3	36.9	2.4	0.4
1931–1940	65.9	38.8	11.0	16.1	30.3	2.8	0.9
1941–1950	60.1	47.5	4.6	7.9	34.3	3.1	2.5
1951–1960	52.8	17.7	24.3	10.8	39.6	6.0	1.6
1961–1970	34.0	11.7	9.4	12.9	51.7	12.7	1.7

[a] Great Britain, Ireland, Norway, Sweden, Denmark, Iceland, Netherlands, Belgium, Luxembourg, Switzerland, France.

[b] Germany (Austria included, 1938–1945), Poland, Czechoslovakia (since 1920), Yugoslavia (since 1920), Hungary (since 1861), Austria (since 1861, except 1938–1945), U.S.S.R. (excludes Asian U.S.S.R. between 1931 and 1963), Latvia, Estonia, Lithuania, Finland, Romania, Bulgaria, Turkey (in Europe).

[c] Italy, Spain, Portugal, Greece, and other European countries not classified elsewhere.

Source: Stephan Thernstrom, ed., *Harvard Encyclopedia of American Ethnic Groups* (1980), p. 480.

Secretary of Housing and Urban Development	Robert C. Weaver Robert C. Wood	1966–1969 1969
Secretary of Transportation	Alan S. Boyd	1967–1969

THE NIXON ADMINISTRATION

President	Richard M. Nixon	1969–1974
Vice President	Spiro T. Agnew Gerald R. Ford	1969–1973 1973–1974
Secretary of State	William P. Rogers Henry A. Kissinger	1969–1973 1973–1974
Secretary of Treasury	David M. Kennedy John B. Connally George P. Shultz William E. Simon	1969–1970 1971–1972 1972–1974 1974
Attorney General	John N. Mitchell Richard G. Kleindienst Elliot L. Richardson William B. Saxbe	1969–1972 1972–1973 1973 1973–1974
Postmaster General	Winton M. Blount	1969–1971
Secretary of Interior	Walter J. Hickel Rogers Morton	1969–1970 1971–1974
Secretary of Agriculture	Clifford M. Hardin Earl L. Butz	1969–1971 1971–1974
Secretary of Commerce	Maurice H. Stans Peter G. Peterson Frederick B. Dent	1969–1972 1972–1973 1973–1974
Secretary of Labor	George P. Shultz James D. Hodgson Peter J. Brennan	1969–1970 1970–1973 1973–1974
Secretary of Defense	Melvin R. Laird Elliot L. Richardson James R. Schlesinger	1969–1973 1973 1973–1974
Secretary of Health, Education, and Welfare	Robert H. Finch Elliot L. Richardson Casper W. Weinberger	1969–1970 1970–1973 1973–1974
Secretary of Housing and Urban Development	George Romney James T. Lynn	1969–1973 1973–1974
Secretary of Transportation	John A. Volpe Claude S. Brinegar	1969–1973 1973–1974

THE FORD ADMINISTRATION

President	Gerald R. Ford	1974–1977
Vice President	Nelson A. Rockefeller	1974–1977
Secretary of State	Henry A. Kissinger	1974–1977
Secretary of Treasury	William E. Simon	1974–1977
Attorney General	William Saxbe Edward Levi	1974–1975 1975–1977
Secretary of Interior	Rogers Morton Stanley K. Hathaway Thomas Kleppe	1974–1975 1975 1975–1977
Secretary of Agriculture	Earl L. Butz John A. Knebel	1974–1976 1976–1977
Secretary of Commerce	Frederick B. Dent Rogers Morton Elliot L. Richardson	1974–1975 1975–1976 1976–1977
Secretary of Labor	Peter J. Brennan John T. Dunlop W. J. Usery	1974–1975 1975–1976 1976–1977
Secretary of Defense	James R. Schlesinger Donald Rumsfeld	1974–1975 1975–1977
Secretary of Health, Education, and Welfare	Casper Weinberger Forrest D. Mathews	1974–1975 1975–1977
Secretary of Housing and Urban Development	James T. Lynn Carla A. Hills	1974–1975 1975–1977
Secretary of Transportation	Claude Brinegar William T. Coleman	1974–1975 1975–1977

THE CARTER ADMINISTRATION

President	Jimmy Carter	1977–1981
Vice President	Walter F. Mondale	1977–1981
Secretary of State	Cyrus R. Vance Edmund Muskie	1977–1980 1980–1981
Secretary of Treasury	W. Michael Blumenthal G. William Miller	1977–1979 1979–1981
Attorney General	Griffin Bell Benjamin R. Civiletti	1977–1979 1979–1981
Secretary of Interior	Cecil D. Andrus	1977–1981
Secretary of Agriculture	Robert Bergland	1977–1981
Secretary of Commerce	Juanita M. Kreps Philip M. Klutznick	1977–1979 1979–1981
Secretary of Labor	F. Ray Marshall	1977–1981
Secretary of Defense	Harold Brown	1977–1981
Secretary of Health, Education, and Welfare	Joseph A. Califano Patricia R. Harris	1977–1979 1979

Secretary of Health and Human Services	Patricia R. Harris	1979–1981
Secretary of Education	Shirley M. Hufstedler	1979–1981
Secretary of Housing and Urban Development	Patricia R. Harris Moon Landrieu	1977–1979 1979–1981
Secretary of Transportation	Brock Adams Neil E. Goldschmidt	1977–1979 1979–1981
Secretary of Energy	James R. Schlesinger Charles W. Duncan	1977–1979 1979–1981

THE REAGAN ADMINISTRATION

President	Ronald Reagan	1981–
Vice President	George Bush	1981–
Secretary of State	Alexander M. Haig	1981–
Secretary of Treasury	Donald Regan	1981–
Attorney General	William Smith	1981–
Secretary of Interior	James Watt	1981–
Secretary of Agriculture	John Block	1981–
Secretary of Commerce	Malcolm Baldrige	1981–
Secretary of Labor	Raymond Donovan	1981–
Secretary of Defense	Casper Weinberger	1981–
Secretary of Health and Human Services	Richard Schweiker	1981–
Secretary of Education	Terrel Bell	1981–
Secretary of Housing and Urban Development	Samuel Pierce	1981–
Secretary of Transportation	Drew Lewis	1981–
Secretary of Energy	James Edwards	1981–

Party Strength in Congress

		HOUSE					SENATE						
PERIOD	CONGRESS	MAJORITY PARTY		MINORITY PARTY		OTHERS	MAJORITY PARTY		MINORITY PARTY		OTHERS	PARTY OF PRESIDENT	
1789–91	1st	Ad	38	Op	26		Ad	17	Op	9		F	Washington
1791–93	2nd	F	37	DR	33		F	16	DR	13		F	Washington
1793–95	3rd	DR	57	F	48		F	17	DR	13		F	Washington
1795–97	4th	F	54	DR	52		F	19	DR	13		F	Washington
1797–99	5th	F	58	DR	48		F	20	DR	12		F	J. Adams
1799–1801	6th	F	64	DR	42		F	19	DR	13		F	J. Adams
1801–03	7th	DR	69	F	36		DR	18	F	13		DR	Jefferson
1803–05	8th	DR	102	F	39		DR	25	F	9		DR	Jefferson
1805–07	9th	DR	116	F	25		DR	27	F	7		DR	Jefferson
1807–09	10th	DR	118	F	24		DR	28	F	6		DR	Jefferson
1809–11	11th	DR	94	F	48		DR	28	F	6		DR	Madison
1811–13	12th	DR	108	F	36		DR	30	F	6		DR	Madison
1813–15	13th	DR	112	F	68		DR	27	F	9		DR	Madison
1815–17	14th	DR	117	F	65		DR	25	F	11		DR	Madison

PERIOD	CONGRESS	HOUSE MAJORITY PARTY		HOUSE MINORITY PARTY		HOUSE OTHERS	SENATE MAJORITY PARTY		SENATE MINORITY PARTY		SENATE OTHERS	PARTY OF PRESIDENT	
1817–19	15th	DR	141	F	42		DR	34	F	10		DR	Monroe
1819–21	16th	DR	156	F	27		DR	35	F	7		DR	Monroe
1821–23	17th	DR	158	F	25		DR	44	F	4		DR	Monroe
1823–25	18th	DR	187	F	26		DR	44	F	4		DR	Monroe
1825–27	19th	Ad	105	J	97		Ad	26	J	20		C	J. Q. Adams
1827–29	20th	J	119	Ad	94		J	28	Ad	20		C	J. Q. Adams
1829–31	21st	D	139	NR	74		D	26	NR	22		D	Jackson
1831–33	22nd	D	141	NR	58	14	D	25	NR	21	2	D	Jackson
1833–35	23rd	D	147	AM	53	60	D	20	NR	20	8	D	Jackson
1835–37	24th	D	145	W	98		D	27	W	25		D	Jackson
1837–39	25th	D	108	W	107	24	D	30	W	18	4	D	Van Buren
1839–41	26th	D	124	W	118		D	28	W	22		D	Van Buren
1841–43	27th	W	133	D	102	6	W	28	D	22	2	W	W. Harrison
												W	Tyler
1843–45	28th	D	142	W	79	1	W	28	D	25	1	W	Tyler
1845–47	29th	D	143	W	77	6	D	31	W	25		D	Polk
1847–49	30th	W	115	D	108	4	D	36	W	21	1	D	Polk
1849–51	31st	D	112	W	109	9	D	35	W	25	2	W	Taylor
												W	Fillmore
1851–53	32nd	D	140	W	88	5	D	35	W	24	3	W	Fillmore
1853–55	33rd	D	159	W	71	4	D	38	W	22	2	D	Pierce
1855–57	34th	R	108	D	83	43	D	40	R	15	5	D	Pierce
1857–59	35th	D	118	R	92	26	D	36	R	20	8	D	Buchanan
1859–61	36th	R	114	D	92	31	D	36	R	26	4	D	Buchanan
1861–63	37th	R	105	D	43	30	R	31	D	10	8	R	Lincoln
1863–65	38th	R	102	D	75	9	R	36	D	9	5	R	Lincoln
1865–67	39th	U	149	D	42		U	42	D	10		R	Lincoln
												R	Johnson
1867–69	40th	R	143	D	49		R	42	D	11		R	Johnson
1869–71	41st	R	149	D	63		R	56	D	11		R	Grant
1871–73	42nd	R	134	D	104	5	R	52	D	17	5	R	Grant
1873–75	43rd	R	194	D	92	14	R	49	D	19	5	R	Grant
1875–77	44th	D	169	R	109	14	R	45	D	29	2	R	Grant
1877–79	45th	D	153	R	140		R	39	D	36	1	R	Hayes
1879–81	46th	D	149	R	130	14	D	42	R	33	1	R	Hayes
1881–83	47th	D	147	R	135	11	R	37	D	37	1	R	Garfield
												R	Arthur
1883–85	48th	D	197	R	118	10	R	38	D	36	2	R	Arthur
1885–87	49th	D	183	R	140	2	R	43	D	34		D	Cleveland
1887–89	50th	D	169	R	152	4	R	39	D	37		D	Cleveland
1889–91	51st	R	166	D	159		R	39	D	37		R	B. Harrison
1891–93	52nd	D	235	R	88	9	R	47	D	39	2	R	B. Harrison
1893–95	53rd	D	218	R	127	11	D	44	R	38	3	D	Cleveland
1895–97	54th	R	244	D	105	7	R	43	D	39	6	D	Cleveland
1897–99	55th	R	204	D	113	40	R	47	D	34	7	R	McKinley
1899–1901	56th	R	185	D	163	9	R	53	D	26	8	R	McKinley
1901–03	57th	R	197	D	151	9	R	55	D	31	4	R	McKinley
												R	T. Roosevelt

PERIOD	CONGRESS	HOUSE					SENATE					PARTY OF PRESIDENT	
		MAJORITY PARTY		MINORITY PARTY		OTHERS	MAJORITY PARTY		MINORITY PARTY		OTHERS		
1903–05	58th	R	208	D	178		R	57	D	33		R	T. Roosevelt
1905–07	59th	R	250	D	136		R	57	D	33		R	T. Roosevelt
1907–09	60th	R	222	D	164		R	61	D	31		R	T. Roosevelt
1909–11	61st	R	219	D	172		R	61	D	32		R	Taft
1911–13	62nd	D	228	R	161	1	R	51	D	41		R	Taft
1913–15	63rd	D	291	R	127	17	D	51	R	44	1	D	Wilson
1915–17	64th	D	230	R	196	9	D	56	R	40		D	Wilson
1917–19	65th	D	216	R	210	6	D	53	R	42		D	Wilson
1919–21	66th	R	240	D	190	3	R	49	D	47		D	Wilson
1921–23	67th	R	301	D	131	1	R	59	D	37		R	Harding
1923–25	68th	R	225	D	205	5	R	51	D	43	2	R	Coolidge
1925–27	69th	R	247	D	183	4	R	56	D	39	1	R	Coolidge
1927–29	70th	R	237	D	195	3	R	49	D	46	1	R	Coolidge
1929–31	71st	R	267	D	167	1	R	56	D	39	1	R	Hoover
1931–33	72nd	D	220	R	214	1	R	48	D	47	1	R	Hoover
1933–35	73rd	D	310	R	117	5	D	60	R	35	1	D	F. Roosevelt
1935–37	74th	D	319	R	103	10	D	69	R	25	2	D	F. Roosevelt
1937–39	75th	D	331	R	89	13	D	76	R	16	4	D	F. Roosevelt
1939–41	76th	D	261	R	164	4	D	69	R	23	4	D	F. Roosevelt
1941–43	77th	D	268	R	162	5	D	66	R	28	2	D	F. Roosevelt
1943–45	78th	D	218	R	208	4	D	58	R	37	1	D	F. Roosevelt
1945–47	79th	D	242	R	190	2	D	56	R	38	1	D	Truman
1947–49	80th	R	245	D	188	1	R	51	D	45		D	Truman
1949–51	81st	D	263	R	171	1	D	54	R	42		D	Truman
1951–53	82nd	D	234	R	199	1	D	49	R	47		D	Truman
1953–55	83rd	R	221	D	211	1	R	48	D	47	1	R	Eisenhower
1955–57	84th	D	232	R	203		D	48	R	47	1	R	Eisenhower
1957–59	85th	D	233	R	200		D	49	R	47		R	Eisenhower
1959–61	86th	D	284	R	153		D	65	R	35		R	Eisenhower
1961–63	87th	D	263	R	174		D	65	R	35		D	Kennedy
1963–65	88th	D	258	R	177		D	67	R	33		D	Kennedy
												D	Johnson
1965–67	89th	D	295	R	140		D	68	R	32		D	Johnson
1967–69	90th	D	247	R	187		D	64	R	36		D	Johnson
1969–71	91st	D	243	R	192		D	57	R	43		R	Nixon
1971–73	92nd	D	254	R	180		D	54	R	44	2	R	Nixon
1973–75	93rd	D	239	R	192	1	D	56	R	42	2	R	Nixon
1975–77	94th	D	291	R	144		D	60	R	37	3	R	Ford
1977–79	95th	D	292	R	143		D	61	R	38	1	D	Carter
1979–81	96th	D	276	R	157		D	58	R	41	1	D	Carter
1981–83	97th	D	243	R	192		R	53	D	46	1	R	Reagan

Ad = Administration; AM = Anti-Masonic; C = Coalition; D = Democratic; DR = Democratic-Republican; F = Federalist; J = Jacksonian; NR = National Republican; Op = Opposition; R = Republican; U = Unionist; W = Whig. Figures are for the beginning of first session of each Congress, except the 93rd, which are for the beginning of the second session.

	TERM OF SERVICE	YEARS OF SERVICE	LIFE SPAN
John Jay	1789–1795	5	1745–1829
John Rutledge	1789–1791	1	1739–1800
William Cushing	1789–1810	20	1732–1810
James Wilson	1789–1798	8	1742–1798
John Blair	1789–1796	6	1732–1800
Robert H. Harrison	1789–1790	–	1745–1790
James Iredell	1790–1799	9	1751–1799
Thomas Johnson	1791–1793	1	1732–1819
William Paterson	1793–1806	13	1745–1806
*John Rutledge**	1795	–	1739–1800
Samuel Chase	1796–1811	15	1741–1811
Oliver Ellsworth	1796–1800	4	1745–1807
Bushrod Washington	1798–1829	31	1762–1829
Alfred Moore	1799–1804	4	1755–1810
John Marshall	1801–1835	34	1755–1835
William Johnson	1804–1834	30	1771–1834
H. Brockholst Livingston	1806–1823	16	1757–1823
Thomas Todd	1807–1826	18	1765–1826
Joseph Story	1811–1845	33	1779–1845
Gabriel Duval	1811–1835	24	1752–1844
Smith Thompson	1823–1843	20	1768–1843
Robert Trimble	1826–1828	2	1777–1828
John McLean	1829–1861	32	1785–1861
Henry Baldwin	1830–1844	14	1780–1844
James M. Wayne	1835–1867	32	1790–1867
Roger B. Taney	1836–1864	28	1777–1864
Philip P. Barbour	1836–1841	4	1783–1841
John Catron	1837–1865	28	1786–1865
John McKinley	1837–1852	15	1780–1852
Peter V. Daniel	1841–1860	19	1784–1860
Samuel Nelson	1845–1872	27	1792–1873
Levi Woodbury	1845–1851	5	1789–1851
Robert C. Grier	1846–1870	23	1794–1870
Benjamin R. Curtis	1851–1857	6	1809–1874
John A. Campbell	1853–1861	8	1811–1889
Nathan Clifford	1858–1881	23	1803–1881
Noah H. Swayne	1862–1881	18	1804–1884
Samuel F. Miller	1862–1890	28	1816–1890
David Davis	1862–1877	14	1815–1886
Stephen J. Field	1863–1897	34	1816–1899
Salmon P. Chase	1864–1873	8	1808–1873
William Strong	1870–1880	10	1808–1895
Joseph P. Bradley	1870–1892	22	1813–1892
Ward Hunt	1873–1882	9	1810–1886
Morrison R. Waite	1874–1888	14	1816–1888
John M. Harlan	1877–1911	34	1833–1911
William B. Woods	1880–1887	7	1824–1887
Stanley Matthews	1881–1889	7	1824–1889
Horace Gray	1882–1902	20	1828–1902
Samuel Blatchford	1882–1893	11	1820–1893
Lucius Q. C. Lamar	1888–1893	5	1825–1893
Melville W. Fuller	1888–1910	21	1833–1910
David J. Brewer	1890–1910	20	1837–1910
Henry B. Brown	1890–1906	16	1836–1913
George Shiras, Jr.	1892–1903	10	1832–1924

	TERM OF SERVICE	YEARS OF SERVICE	LIFE SPAN
Howell E. Jackson	1893–1895	2	1832–1895
Edward D. White	1894–1910	16	1845–1921
Rufus W. Peckham	1895–1909	14	1838–1909
Joseph McKenna	1898–1925	26	1843–1926
Oliver W. Holmes	1902–1932	30	1841–1935
William R. Day	1903–1922	19	1849–1923
William H. Moody	1906–1910	3	1853–1917
Horace H. Lurton	1910–1914	4	1844–1914
Charles E. Hughes	1910–1916	5	1862–1948
Willis Van Devanter	1911–1937	26	1859–1941
Joseph R. Lamar	1911–1916	5	1857–1916
Edward D. White	1910–1921	11	1845–1921
Mahlon Pitney	1912–1922	10	1858–1924
James C. McReynolds	1914–1941	26	1862–1946
Louis D. Brandeis	1916–1939	22	1856–1941
John H. Clarke	1916–1922	6	1857–1945
William H. Taft	1921–1930	8	1857–1930
George Sutherland	1922–1938	15	1862–1942
Pierce Butler	1922–1939	16	1866–1939
Edward T. Sanford	1923–1930	7	1865–1930
Harlan F. Stone	1925–1941	16	1872–1946
Charles E. Hughes	1930–1941	11	1862–1948
Owen J. Roberts	1930–1945	15	1875–1955
Benjamin N. Cardozo	1932–1938	6	1870–1938
Hugo L. Black	1937–1971	34	1886–1971
Stanley F. Reed	1938–1957	19	1884–1980
Felix Frankfurter	1939–1962	23	1882–1965
William O. Douglas	1939–1975	36	1898–1980
Frank Murphy	1940–1949	9	1890–1949
Harlan F. Stone	1941–1946	5	1872–1946
James F. Byrnes	1941–1942	1	1879–1972
Robert H. Jackson	1941–1954	13	1892–1954
Wiley B. Rutledge	1943–1949	6	1894–1949
Harold H. Burton	1945–1958	13	1888–1964
Fred M. Vinson	1946–1953	7	1890–1953
Tom C. Clark	1949–1967	18	1899–1977
Sherman Minton	1949–1956	7	1890–1965
Earl Warren	1953–1969	16	1891–1974
John Marshall Harlan	1955–1971	16	1899–1971
William J. Brennan, Jr.	1956–	–	1906–
Charles E. Whittaker	1957–1962	5	1901–1973
Potter Stewart	1958–1981	23	1915–
Byron R. White	1962–	–	1917–
Arthur J. Goldberg	1962–1965	3	1908–
Abe Fortas	1965–1969	4	1910–
Thurgood Marshall	1967–	–	1908–
Warren C. Burger	1969–	–	1907–
Harry A. Blackmun	1970–	–	1908–
Lewis F. Powell, Jr.	1972–	–	1907–
William H. Rehnquist	1972–	–	1924–
John P. Stevens, III	1975–	–	1920–
Sandra Day O'Connor	1981–	–	1930–

*Appointed and served one term, but not confirmed by the Senate. NOTE: Chief justices are in italics.

INDEX

EFGHIJ-RM-8987654